GATE PREP SERIES

GATE

Graduate Aptitude Test in Engineering

2022

30 Years Chapter-Wise Solved Papers

(1992-2021)

Computer Science & Information Technology

G. K. PUBLICATIONS (P) LTD.

Title : GATE 2022 : Computer Science and Information Technology 30 years Chapter wise Solved Papers (1992-2021)

Language : English

Editor's Name : Vinit Garg

Typeset & Published by :

Career Launcher Infrastructure (P) Ltd.

A-45, Mohan Cooperative Industrial Area, Near Mohan Estate Metro Station, New Delhi - 110044

Marketed by :

G.K. Publications (P) Ltd.

Plot No. 9A, Sector-27A, Mathura Road, Faridabad, Haryana-121003

ISBN : **978-93-90820-64-1**

Printer's Details : Made in India, New Delhi.

GATE
Computer Science & Information Technology

Contents

Solved Papers (Chapter-Wise)

Verbal Ability

Numerical Ability

Engineering Mathematics

Technical Section

GATE

Graduate Aptitude Test in Engineering

IIT Institutes

GATE 2021 will be conducted by
Indian Institute of Technology, Mumbai

Indian Institute of Technology, Kharagpur

GATE 2020 conducted by
Indian Institute of Technology, Delhi

Indian Institute of Technology, Chennai

Indian Institute of Technology, Guwahati

Indian Institute of Technology, Roorkee

Indian Institute of Technology, Kanpur

Preface

The Graduate Aptitude Test in Engineering (GATE) is an online exam conducted by the IITs for admissions to PG courses in IITs, IISc Bangalore, NITs and many state run universities as well as private universities. Also there are more than 37 PSUs that use GATE score for recruitments. A large number of corporates are also using GATE score as a tool to screen students for placements.

GK Publications is well known as the "publisher of choice" to students preparing for GATE and other technical examinations in the country. We published the first set of books in 1994 when GATE exam, both objective and conventional, was conducted in the paper and pencil environment, and used as a check point for entry to post graduate courses in IITs and IISCs. At that time, students had little access to technology and relied mainly on instructor led learning followed by practice with books available for these examinations.

A lot has changed since then!

Today, GATE is conducted in an online only mode with multiple choice and numerical based questions. The score is valid for three years and is used not only for post graduate courses but is also used by major PSUs for recruitment. Today's students have easy access to technology and the concept of a monologue within the classroom has changed to dialogue where students come prepared with concepts and then discuss topics. They learn a lot of things on the go with their mobile devices and practice for mock tests online.

We, as a leading publisher of GATE books, have also embraced change. Today, our books are no more guides and papers only but come with a fully supported mobile app and a web portal. The mobile app provides access to video lectures, short tests and regular updates about the exam. The web portal in additional to what is available on the app provides full length mock tests to mimic the actual exam and help you gauge your level of preparedness. The combination of practice content in print, video lectures, and short and full length tests on mobile and web makes this product a complete courseware for GATE preparation.

This book includes previous years GATE questions along with detailed solution of each question for better understanding. It will help the GATE aspirants to know an idea about the pattern of questions asked in GATE examination.

We also know that improvement is a never ending process and hence we welcome your suggestions and feedback or spelling and technical errors if any. Please write to us at gkp@gkpublications.com

We hope that our small effort will help you prepare well for the examination.

We wish you all the best!

GK Publications Pvt. Ltd.

About GATE

The Graduate Aptitude Test in Engineering (GATE) conducted by IISc and IITs has emerged as one of the bench mark tests for engineering and science aptitude in facilitating admissions for higher education (M.Tech./Ph.D.) in IITs, IISc and various other Institutes/Universities/Laboratories in India. With the standard and high quality of the GATE examination in 27 disciplines of engineering and science, Humanities and Social Sciences subjects, it identifies the candidate's understanding of a subject and aptitude and eligibility for higher studies. During the last few years, GATE score is also being used as one of the criteria for recruitment in Government Organizations such as Cabinet Secretariat, and National/State Public Sector Undertakings in India. Because of the importance of the GATE examination, the number of candidates taking up GATE exams has increased tremendously. GATE exams are conducted by the IITs and IISc as a computer based test having multiple choice questions and numerical answer type questions. The questions are mostly fundamental, concept based and thought provoking. From 2017 onwards GATE Exam is being held in Bangladesh, Ethiopia, Nepal, Singapore, Sri Lanka and United Arab Emirates. An Institute with various nationalities in its campus widens the horizons of an academic environment. A foreign student brings with him/her a great diversity, culture and wisdom to share. Many GATE qualified candidates are paid scholarships/assistantship, especially funded by Ministry of Human Resources Development, Government of India and by other Ministries. Indian Institute of Technology Bombay is the Organizing Institute for GATE 2021.

Why GATE?

Admission to Post Graduate and Doctoral Programmes

Admission to postgraduate programmes with MHRD and some other government scholarships/ assistantships in engineering colleges/institutes is open to those who qualify through GATE. GATE qualified candidates with Bachelor's degree in Engineering/Technology/Architecture or Master's degree in any branch of Science/Mathematics/Statistics/Computer Applications are eligible for admission to Master/Doctoral programmes in Engineering/Technology/Architecture as well as for Doctoral programmes in relevant branches of Science with MHRD or other government scholarships/ assistantships. Candidates with Master's degree in Engineering/Technology/Architecture may seek admission to relevant Ph.D programmes with scholarship/assistantship without appearing in the GATE examination.

Financial Assistance

A valid GATE score is essential for obtaining financial assistance during Master's programs and direct Doctoral programs in Engineering/Technology/Architecture, and Doctoral programs in relevant branches of Science in Institutes supported by the MHRD or other Government agencies. As per the directives of the MHRD, the following procedure is to be adopted for admission to the post-graduate programs (Master's and Doctoral) with MHRD scholarship/assistantship. Depending upon the norms adopted by a specific institute or department of the Institute, a candidate may be admitted directly into a course based on his/her performance in GATE only **or** based on his/her performance in GATE **and** an admission test/interview conducted by the department to which he/she has applied **and/or** the candidate's academic record. If the candidate is to be selected through test/interview for post-graduate programs, a minimum of 70% weightage will be given to the performance in GATE and the remaining 30% weightage will be given to the candidate's performance in test/interview and/or academic record, as per MHRD guidelines. The admitting institutes could however prescribe a minimum passing percentage of marks in the test/interview. Some colleges/institutes specify GATE qualification as the mandatory requirement even for admission without MHRD scholarship/assistantship.

To avail of the financial assistance (scholarship), the candidate must first secure admission to a program in these Institutes, by a procedure that could vary from institute to institute. Qualification in GATE is also a minimum requirement to apply for various fellowships awarded by many Government organizations. Candidates are advised to seek complete details of admission procedures and availability of MHRD scholarship/assistantship from the concerned admitting institution. The criteria for postgraduate admission with scholarship/assistantship could be different for different institutions. The management of the post-graduate scholarship/assistantship is also the responsibility of the admitting institution. Similarly, reservation of seats under different categories is as per the policies and norms prevailing at the admitting institution and Government of India rules. *GATE offices will usually not entertain any enquiry about admission, reservation of seats and / or award of scholarship / assistantship.*

PSU Recruitments

As many as 37 PSUs are using GATE score for recruitment. It is likely that more number of PSUs may start doing so by next year. Below is the list of PSUs:

MDL, BPCL, GAIL, NLC LTD, CEL, Indian Oil, HPCL, NBPC, NECC, BHEL, WBSEDCL, NTPC, ONGC, Oil India, Power Grid, Cabinet Secretariat, Govt. of India, BAARC, NFL, IPR, PSPCL, PSTCL, DRDO, OPGC Ltd., THDC India Ltd., BBNL, RITES, IRCON, GHECL, NHAI, KRIBHCO, Mumbai Railway Vikas Corporation Ltd. (MRVC Ltd.), National Textile Corporation, Coal India Ltd., BNPM, AAI, NALCO, EdCIL India.

Important :

1. Admissions in IITs/IISc or other Institutes for M.Tech./Ph.D. through GATE scores shall be advertised separately by the Institutes and GATE does not take the responsibility of admissions.
2. Cabinet Secretariat has decided to recruit officers for the post of Senior Field Officer (Tele) (From GATE papers of EC, CS, PH), Senior Research Officer (Crypto) (From GATE papers of EC, CS, MA), Senior Research Officer (S&T) (From GATE papers EC, CS, CY, PH, AE, BT) in the Telecommunication Cadre, Cryptographic Cadre and Science & Technology Unit respectively of Cabinet Secretariat. The details of the scheme of recruitment shall be published in National Newspaper/Employment News by the concerned authority.
3. Some PSUs in India have expressed their interest to utilize GATE scores for their recruitment purpose. The Organizations who intend to utilize GATE scores shall make separate advertisement for this purpose in Newspapers etc.

Who Can Appear for GATE?

Eligibility for GATE

Before starting the application process, the candidate must ensure that he/she meets the eligibility criteria of GATE given in Table.

Eligibility Criteria for GATE 2021

Degree/Program	Qualifying Degree/Examination	Description of Eligible Candidates	Expected Year of Completion
B.E. / B.Tech. / B.Pharm.	Bachelor's degree in Engineering / Technology (4 years after 10+2 or 3 years after B.Sc. / Diploma in Engineering / Technology)	Currently in the 3rd year or higher grade or already completed	2022
B. Arch.	Bachelor's degree of Architecture (5- year course) / Naval Architecture (4- year course) / Planning (4- year course)	Currently in the 3rd year or higher grade or already completed	2023 (for 5-year program), 2022 (for 4-year program)
B.Sc. (Research) / B.S.	Bachelor's degree in Science (Post-Diploma/4 years after 10+2)	Currently in the 3rd year or higher grade or already completed	2022
Pharm. D. (after 10+2)	6 years degree program, consisting of internship or residency training, during third year onwards	Currently in the 3rd/4th/5th/6th year or already completed	2024
M.B.B.S.	Degree holders of M.B.B.S. and those who are in the 5th/6th/7th semester or higher semester of such programme.	5th, 6th, 7th or higher semester or already completed	2022
M. Sc. / M.A. / MCA or equivalent	Master's degree in any branch of Arts/Science/Mathematics/Statistics/ Computer Applications or equivalent	Currently in the first year or higher or already Completed	2022
Int. M.E./ M.Tech. (Post-B.Sc.)	Post-B.Sc Integrated Master's degree programs in Engineering/ Technology (4-year program)	Currently in the 1st / 2nd/3rd/4th year or already completed	2024
Int. M.E./ M.Tech. or Dual Degree (after Diploma or 10+2)	Integrated Master's degree program or Dual Degree program in Engineering/Technology (5-year program)	Currently in the 3rd /4th/5th year or alreadycompleted	2023
B.Sc. / B.A. / B.Com.	Bachelor degree in any branch of Science / Arts / Commerce (3 years program)	Currently in the 3rd year or already completed	2021
Int. M.Sc. / Int. B.S. / M.S.	Integrated M.Sc. or 5-year integrated B.S.-M.S. program	Currently in the 3rd year or higher or already completed	2022
Professional Society Examinations (equivalent to B.E. / B.Tech. / B.Arch.)	B.E./B.Tech./B.Arch. equivalent examinations of Professional Societies, recognized by MoE/UPSC/AICTE (e.g. AMIE by Institution of Engineers-India, AMICE by the Institute of Civil Engineers-India and so on)	Completed Section A or equivalent of such professional courses	NA

In case a candidate has passed one of the qualifying examinations as mentioned above in 2020 or earlier, the candidate has to submit the degree certificate / provisional certificate / course completion certificate / professional certificate / membership certificate issued by the society or institute. In case, the candidate is expected to complete one of the qualifying criteria in 2021 or later as mentioned above, he/she has to submit a certificate from Principal or a copy of marks card for section A of AMIE.

Certificate From Principal

Candidates who have to submit a certificate from their college Principal have to obtain one from his/her institution beforehand and upload the same during the online submission of the application form.

Candidates With Backlogs

Candidates, who have appeared in the final semester/year exam in 2021, but with a backlog (arrears/failed subjects) in any of the papers in their qualifying degree should upload a copy of any one of the mark sheets of the final year,

OR

obtain a declaration from their Principal along with the signature and seal beforehand and upload the same during the online submission of the application form.

GATE Structure

Structure of GATE

GATE 2021 will be conducted on 27 subjects (papers). Table below shows the list of papers and paper codes for GATE 2021. A candidate is allowed to appear in ANY ONE or UP TO TWO papers of the GATE examination. However, note that the combination of TWO papers in which a candidate can appear MUST be from the pre-defined list as given in Table. Also note that for a paper running in multiple sessions, a candidate will be mapped to appear for the examination in one of the sessions ONLY.

List of GATE Papers and Corresponding Codes

GATE Paper	Code	GATE Paper	Code
Aerospace Engineering	AE	Instrumentation Engineering	IN
Agricultural Engineering	AG	Mathematics	MA
Architecture and Planning	AR	Mechanical Engineering	ME
Bio-medical Engineering	BM	Mining Engineering	MN
Biotechnology	BT	Metallurgical Engineering	MT
Civil Engineering	CE	Petroleum Engineering	PE
Chemical Engineering	CH	Physics	PH
Computer Science and Information Technology	CS	Production and Industrial Engineering	PI
Chemistry	CY	Statistics	ST
Electronics and Communication Engineering	EC	Textile Engineering and Fibre Science	TF
Electrical Engineering	EE	Engineering Sciences	XE*
Environmental Science & Engineering	ES	Humanities & Social Sciences	XH**
Ecology and Evolution	EY	Life Sciences	XL***
Geology and Geophysics	GG		

Note: *Environmental Science and Engineering (ES) and Humanities and Social Sciences (XH) are two new papers introduced in GATE 2021.*

*XE Paper Sections	Code	**XH Paper Sections	Code	***XL Paper Sections	Code
Engineering Mathematics (Compulsory) (15 marks)	A	Reasoning and Comprehension (Compulsory) (25 marks)	B1	Chemistry (Compulsory) (25 marks)	P
Any TWO optional Sections (2x35 = 70 marks)		Any ONE optional Section (60 marks)		Any TWO optional Sections (2x30 = 60 marks)	
Fluid Mechanics	B	Economics	C1	Biochemistry	Q
Materials Science	C	English	C2	Botany	R
Solid Mechanics	D	Linguistics	C3	Microbiology	S
Thermodynamics	E	Philosophy	C4	Zoology	T
Polymer Science and Engineering	F	Psychology	C5	Food Technology	U
Food Technology	G	Sociology	C6		
Atmospheric and Oceanic Sciences	H				

*XE (Engineering Sciences), **XH (Humanities & Social Sciences), ***XL (Life Sciences), papers are of general nature and will be comprised of Sections listed in the above table

Note: *Each subject/paper is of total 100 marks. General Aptitude (GA) section of 15 marks is common for all papers. Hence remaining 85 marks are for the respective subject/paper code.*

Combination of Two Papers Allowed to Appear in GATE 2021 (subject to availability of infrastructure and schedule)

Code of The First (Primary) Paper	Codes of Papers Allowed as The Second Paper
AE	XE
AG	ES
AR	CE
BM	BT / XL
BT	BM / XL
CE	AR / ES
CH	CY / PE / XE
CS	MA
CY	CH / XL
EC	IN / PH
EE	IN
ES	AG / CE
EY	XL
GG	MN / PE / PH
IN	EC / EE / PH
MA	CS / PH / ST
ME	XE
MN	GG / XE
MT	PH / XE
PE	CH / GG / XE
PH	EC / GG / IN / MA / MT / ST
PI	XE
ST	MA / PH
TF	XE
XE	AE / CH / ME / MN / MT / PE / PI / TF
XH	----
XL	BM / BT / CY / EY

General Aptitude Questions

All the papers will have a few questions that test the General Aptitude (Language and Analytical Skills), apart from the core subject of the paper.

Duration and Examination Type

All the papers of the GATE 2021 examination will be for 3 hours duration and they consist of 65 questions for a total of 100 marks. Since the examination is an ONLINE computer based test (CBT), at the end of the stipulated time (3-hours), the computer screen will automatically close the examination inhibiting any further action.

Candidates will be permitted to occupy their allotted seats 40 minutes before the scheduled start of the examination. Candidates can login and start reading the instructions 20 minutes before the start of examination. The late login time (if any) recorded by the computer system MUST NOT be beyond 30 minutes from the actual starting time of the examination. Under NO circumstances, will a candidate be permitted to login after 30 minutes from the actual examination starting time. Candidates will NOT be permitted to leave the examination hall before the end of the examination.

Pattern of Question Papers

GATE 2021 may contain questions of THREE different types in all the papers:

(i) **Multiple Choice Questions (MCQ)** carrying 1 or 2 marks each, in all the papers and sections. These questions are objective in nature, and each will have choice of four answers, out of which ONLY ONE choice is correct.

Negative Marking for Wrong Answers: For a wrong answer chosen in a MCQ, there will be negative marking. For 1-mark MCQ, 1/3 mark will be deducted for a wrong answer. Likewise, for 2-mark MCQ, 2/3 mark will be deducted for a wrong answer.

(ii) **Multiple Select Questions (MSQ)** carrying 1 or 2 marks each in all the papers and sections. These questions are objective in nature, and each will have choice of four answers, out of which ONE or MORE than ONE choice(s) is / are correct.

Note: There is NO negative marking for a wrong answer in MSQ questions. However, there is NO partial credit for choosing partially correct combinations of choices or any single wrong choice.

(iii) **Numerical Answer Type (NAT)** Questions carrying 1 or 2 marks each in most of the papers and sections. For these questions, the answer is a signed real number, which needs to be entered by the candidate using the virtual numeric keypad on the monitor (keyboard of the computer will be disabled). No choices will be shown for these types of questions. The answer can be a number such as 10 or –10 (an integer only). The answer may be in decimals as well, for example, 10.1 (one decimal) or 10.01 (two decimals) or –10.001 (three decimals). These questions will be mentioned with, up to which decimal places, the candidates need to present the answer. Also, for some NAT type problems an appropriate range will be considered while evaluating these questions so that the candidate is not unduly penalized due to the usual round-off errors. Candidates are advised to do the rounding off at the end of the calculation (not in between steps). Wherever required and possible, it is better to give NAT answer up to a maximum of three decimal places.

Note: *There is NO negative marking for a wrong answer in NAT questions.*
Also, there is NO partial credit in NAT questions.

Marking Scheme – Distribution of Marks and Questions

General Aptitude (GA) Questions

In all papers, GA questions carry a total of 15 marks. The GA section includes 5 questions carrying 1-mark each (sub-total 5 marks) and 5 questions carrying 2-marks each (sub-total 10 marks).

Question Papers other than GG, XE, XH and XL

These papers would contain 25 questions carrying 1-mark each (sub-total 25 marks) and 30 questions carrying 2-marks each (sub-total 60 marks) consisting of some MCQ type questions, while the remaining may be MSQ and / or NAT questions.

GG (Geology and Geophysics) Paper

Apart from the General Aptitude (GA) section, the GG question paper consists of two parts: Part A and Part B. Part A is compulsory for all the candidates. Part B contains two sections: Section 1 (Geology) and Section 2 (Geophysics). Candidates will have to attempt questions in Part A and questions in either Section 1 or Section 2 of Part B. The choice of Section 1 OR Section 2 of Part B has to be made at the time of online registration in GOAPS. At the examination hall, candidate cannot request for change of section.

Part A consists of 25 questions carrying 1-mark each (sub-total 25 marks and some of these will be MSQ and/or numerical answer type questions while remaining questions will be MCQ type). Either section of Part B (Section 1 and Section 2) consists of 30 questions carrying 2-marks each (sub-total 60 marks and some of these will be MSQ and/or numerical answer type questions while remaining questions will be MCQ type).

XE Paper (Engineering Sciences)

A candidate appearing in the XE paper has to answer the following:

- GA – General Aptitude carrying a total of 15 marks.
- Section A – Engineering Mathematics (Compulsory): This section contains 11 questions carrying a total of 15 marks: 7 questions carrying 1-mark each (sub-total 7 marks), and 4 questions carrying 2-marks each (sub-total 8 marks). Some questions will be of numerical answer type while remaining questions will be MCQ type.
- Any two of XE Sections B to H: The choice of two sections from B to H can be made during the examination after viewing the questions. Only TWO optional sections can be answered at a time. A candidate wishing to change midway of the examination to another optional section must first choose to deselect one of the previously chosen optional sections (B to H). Each of the optional sections of the XE paper (Sections B through H) contains 22 questions carrying a total of 35 marks: 9 questions carrying 1-mark each (sub-total 9 marks) and 13 questions carrying 2-marks each (sub-total 26 marks). Some questions will be of MSQ and/or numerical answer type while remaining questions will be MCQ type.

XH Paper (Humanities and Social Sciences)

A candidate appearing in the XH paper has to answer the following:

- **GA - General Aptitude** carrying a total of 15 marks.
- **Section B1 – Reasoning and Comprehension (Compulsory):** This section contains 15 questions carrying a total of 25 marks: 5 questions carrying 1-mark each (sub-total 5 marks) and 10 questions carrying 2-marks each (sub-total 20 marks). Some questions will be of MSQ and/or numerical answer type while remaining questions will be MCQ type.
- **Any ONE of XH Sections C1 to C6:** The ONE choice of section from C1 to C6 has to be made at the time of online registration in GOAPS. At the examination hall, candidate cannot request for change of section. Each of the optional sections of the XH paper (Sections C1 through C6) contains 40 questions carrying a total of 60 marks: 20 questions carrying 1-mark each (sub-total 20 marks) and 20 questions carrying 2-marks each (sub-total 40 marks). Some questions will be of MSQ and/or numerical answer type while remaining questions will be MCQ type.

XL Paper (Life Sciences)

A candidate appearing in the XL paper has to answer the following:

- **GA – General Aptitude** carrying a total of 15 marks.
- **Section P–Chemistry (Compulsory):** This section contains 15 questions carrying a total of 25 marks: 5 questions carrying 1-mark each (sub-total 5 marks) and 10 questions carrying 2-marks each (sub-total 20 marks). Some questions will be of MSQ and/or numerical answer type while remaining questions will be MCQ type.
- **Any two of XL Sections Q to U:** The choice of two sections from Q to U can be made during the examination after viewing the questions. Only TWO optional sections can be answered at a time. A candidate wishing to change midway of the examination to another optional section must first choose to deselect one of the previously chosen optional sections (Q to U). Each of the optional sections of the XL paper (Sections Q through U) contains 20 questions carrying a total of 30 marks: 10 questions carrying 1-mark each (sub-total 10 marks) and 10 questions carrying 2-marks each (sub-total 20 marks). Some questions will be of MSQ and/or numerical answer type while remaining questions will be MCQ type.

GATE Score

After the evaluation of the answers, the actual (raw) marks obtained by a candidate will be considered for computing the GATE Score. For multi-session papers (subjects), raw marks obtained by the candidates in different sessions will be converted to Normalized marks for that particular subject. Thus, raw marks (for single session papers) or normalized marks (for multi-session papers) will be used for computing the GATE Score, based on the qualifying marks.

Calculation of Normalized Marks for Multi-Session Papers

In GATE 2021 examination, some papers may be conducted in multi-sessions. Hence, for these papers, a suitable normalization is applied to take into account any variation in the difficulty levels of the question papers across different sessions. The normalization is done based on the fundamental assumption that "in all multi-session GATE papers, the distribution of abilities of candidates is the same across all the sessions". This assumption is justified since the number of candidates appearing in multi-session papers in GATE 2021 is large and the procedure for allocation of session to candidates is random. Further, it is also ensured that for the same multi-session paper, the number of candidates allotted in each session is of the same order of magnitude.

Based on the above, and considering various normalization methods, the committee arrived at the following formula for calculating the normalized marks for the multi-session papers.

Nsormalization mark of jth candidate in the ith session $\widehat{M_{ij}}$ is given by

$$\widehat{M_{ij}} = \frac{\bar{M}_t^g - M_q^g}{\bar{M}_{ti} - M_{iq}}(M_{ij} - M_{iq}) + M_q^g$$

where

M_{ij} : is the actual marks obtained by the jth candidate in i^{th} session

$\bar{M}_t^g$: is the average marks of the top 0.1% of the candidates considering all sessions

M_q^g : is the sum of mean and standard deviation marks of the candidates in the paper considering all sessions

$\bar{M}_{ti}$: is the average marks of the top 0.1% of the candidates in the ith session

M_{iq} : is the sum of the mean marks and standard deviation of the ith session

Calculation of GATE Score for All Papers

For all papers for which there is only one session, actual marks obtained by the candidates will be used for calculating the GATE 2021 Score. For papers in multi-sessions, normalized marks will be calculated corresponding to the raw marks obtained by a candidate and the GATE 2021 Score will be calculated based on the normalized marks.

The GATE 2021 score will be computed using the formula given below.

$$\text{GATE Score} = S_q + (S_t - S_q)\frac{(M - M_q)}{(\bar{M}_t - M_q)}$$

where

- M : marks obtained by the candidate (actual marks for single session papers and normalized marks for multi-session papers)
- M_q : is the qualifying marks for general category candidate in the paper
- $\bar{M}_t$: is the mean of marks of top 0.1% or top 10 (whichever is larger) of the candidates who appeared in the paper (in case of multi-session papers including all sessions)
- S_q : 350, is the score assigned to M_q
- S_t : 900, is the score assigned to $\bar{M}_t$

In the GATE 2021 the qualifying marks (M_q) for general category student in each subject will be 25 marks (out of 100) or $\mu + \sigma$, whichever is larger. Here μ is the mean and σ is the standard deviation of marks of all the candidates who appeared in the paper.

After the declaration of results, GATE Scorecards can be downloaded by the GATE qualified candidates ONLY.

The GATE 2021 Committee has the authority to decide the qualifying mark/score for each GATE paper. In case of any claim or dispute with respect to GATE 2021 examination or score, the Courts and Tribunals in Mumbai alone will have the exclusive jurisdiction to entertain and settle them.

GATE Syllabus

Section1: Engineering Mathematics

Discrete Mathematics: Propositional and first order logic. Sets, relations, functions, partial orders and lattices. Monoids, Groups. Graphs: connectivity, matching, coloring. Combinatorics: counting, recurrence relations, generating functions.

Linear Algebra: Matrices, determinants, system of linear equations, eigenvalues and eigenvectors, LU decomposition.

Calculus: Limits, continuity and differentiability. Maxima and minima. Mean value theorem. Integration.

Probability and Statistics: Random variables. Uniform, normal, exponential, poisson and binomial distributions. Mean, median, mode and standard deviation. Conditional probability and Bayes theorem.

Computer Science and Information Technology

Section 2: Digital Logic

Boolean algebra. Combinational and sequential circuits. Minimization. Number representations and computer arithmetic (fixed and floating point).

Section 3: Computer Organization and Architecture

Machine instructions and addressing modes. ALU, data path and control unit. Instruction pipelining, pipeline hazards. Memory hierarchy: cache, main memory and secondary storage; I/O interface (interrupt and DMA mode).

Section 4: Programming and Data Structures

Programming in C. Recursion. Arrays, stacks, queues, linked lists, trees, binary search trees, binary heaps, graphs.

Section 5: Algorithms

Searching, sorting, hashing. Asymptotic worst case time and space complexity. Algorithm design techniques: greedy, dynamic programming and divide and conquer. Graph traversals, minimum spanning trees, shortest paths

Section 6: Theory of Computation

Regular expressions and finite automata. Context-free grammars and push-down automata. Regular and contex-free languages, pumping lemma. Turing machines and undecidability.

Section 7: Compiler Design

Lexical analysis, parsing, syntax-directed translation. Runtime environments. Intermediate code generation. Loop optimisation, Data flow analyses: constant propagation, liveness analysis, common subexpression elimination.

Section 8: Operating System

System calls, processes, threads, inter-process communication, concurrency and synchronization. Deadlock. CPU and I/O scheduling. Memory management and virtual memory. File systems.

Section 9: Databases

ER-model Relational model: relational algebra, tuple calculus, SQL. Integrity constraints, normal forms. File organization, indexing (e.g., B and B+ trees). Transactions and concurrency control.

Section 10: Computer Networks

Concept of layering: OSI and TCP/IP Protocol Stacks; Basics of packet, circuit and virtual circuit-switching; Data link layer: framing, error detection, Medium Access Control, Ethernet bridging; Routing protocols: shortest path, flooding, distance vector and link state routing; Fragmentation and IP addressing, IPv4, CIDR notation, Basics of IP support protocols (ARP, DHCP, ICMP), Network Address Translation (NAT); Transport layer: flow control and congestion control, UDP, TCP, sockets; Application layer protocols: DNS, SMTP, HTTP, FTP, Email.

Chapter-Wise Analysis

GATE PAPERS (Computer Science & Information Technology)

Subject	2011	2012	2013	2014	2015	2016	2017	2018	2019	2020	2021
Engineering Mathematics											
1 mark Questions	2	3	5	5	4	5	5	5	7	3	5
2 marks Questions	7	3	2	5	6	4	2	7	4	8	6
Total Marks	**16**	**9**	**9**	**15**	**16**	**13**	**9**	**19**	**15**	**19**	**17**
Theory of Computation											
1 mark Questions	3	4	1	5	1	3	3	1	2	1	2
2 marks Questions	3	1	2	6	3	3	4	2	3	1	3
Total Marks	**9**	**6**	**5**	**17**	**7**	**9**	**11**	**5**	**8**	**3**	**8**
Digital Logic											
1 mark Questions	3	2	3	3	1	2	1	2	4	2	1
2 marks Questions	3	2	1	5	2	1	3	1	2	1	2
Total Marks	**9**	**6**	**5**	**13**	**5**	**4**	**7**	**4**	**8**	**4**	**5**
Computer Organization & Architecture											
1 mark Questions	3	2	1	2	1	1	2	3	1	4	2
2 marks Questions	2	4	7	2	2	3	3	4	1	5	2
Total Marks	**7**	**10**	**15**	**6**	**5**	**7**	**8**	**11**	**3**	**14**	**6**
Programming & Data Structures											
1 mark Questions	4	2	2	0	5	5	4	4	4	3	2
2 marks Questions	7	6	5	2	3	6	7	4	6	3	3
Total Marks	**18**	**14**	**12**	**4**	**11**	**17**	**18**	**12**	**16**	**9**	**8**
Algorithm											
1 mark Questions	1	4	5	1	4	1	1	1	1	2	4
2 marks Questions	0	2	3	2	4	3	2	3	1	2	4
Total Marks	**1**	**8**	**11**	**5**	**12**	**7**	**5**	**7**	**3**	**6**	**12**
Compiler Design											
1 mark Questions	1	1	2	1	2	1	2	2	2	4	2
2 marks Questions	0	3	2	2	1	1	0	2	3	2	3
Total Marks	**1**	**7**	**6**	**5**	**4**	**3**	**2**	**6**	**8**	**8**	**8**
Operating System											
1 mark Questions	3	1	1	0	2	1	2	4	1	2	3
2 marks Questions	2	3	1	2	2	5	2	3	4	4	1
Total Marks	**7**	**7**	**3**	**4**	**6**	**11**	**6**	**10**	**9**	**10**	**5**
Data Bases											
1 mark Questions	0	3	1	3	1	3	2	0	2	2	2
2 marks Questions	3	3	4	2	2	0	2	2	2	3	3
Total Marks	**6**	**9**	**9**	**7**	**5**	**3**	**6**	**4**	**6**	**8**	**8**

Subject	2011	2012	2013	2014	2015	2016	2017	2018	2019	2020	2021
Computer Networks											
1 mark Questions	5	3	4	4	2	2	3	3	1	2	2
2 marks Questions	2	3	2	2	3	4	2	2	4	1	3
Total Marks	**9**	**9**	**8**	**8**	**8**	**10**	**7**	**7**	**9**	**4**	**8**
***Software Engineering**											
1 mark Questions	0	1	0	0	1	1	0	0	0	0	0
2 marks Questions	0	0	0	1	0	1	0	0	0	0	0
Total Marks	**0**	**1**	**0**	**2**	**1**	**3**	**0**	**0**	**0**	**0**	**0**
***Web Technology**											
1 mark Questions	0	1	0	0	0	1	0	0	0	0	0
2 marks Questions	0	0	0	0	0	1	0	0	0	0	0
Total Marks	**0**	**1**	**0**	**0**	**0**	**3**	**0**	**0**	**0**	**0**	**0**
General & Aptitude											
1 mark Questions	5	5	5	5	5	5	5	5	5	5	5
2 marks Questions	5	5	5	5	5	5	5	5	5	5	5
Total Marks	**15**	**15**	**15**	**15**	**15**	**15**	**15**	**15**	**15**	**15**	**15**

**Topics not included in GATE 2017-2020 Syllabus.*

Verbal Ability

1

CHAPTER

English Grammar

MCQ TYPE QUESTIONS

2016

1. Computers were invented for performing only high-end useful computations. However, it is no understatement that they have taken over our world today. The internet, for example, is ubiquitous. Many believe that the internet itself is an unintended consequence of the original invention. With the advent of mobile computing on our phones, a whole new dimension is now enabled. One is left wondering if all these developments are good or, more importantly, required.

   Which of the statement(s) below is/are logically valid and can be inferred from the above paragraph?

   (*i*) The author believes that computers are not good for us.

   (*ii*) Mobile computers and the internet are both intended inventions

   (*a*) (*i*) only (*b*) (*ii*) only

   (*c*) both (*i*) and (*ii*) (*d*) neither (*i*) nor (*ii*)

2. All hill-stations have a lake. Ooty has two lakes. Which of the statement(s) below is/are logically valid and can be inferred from the above sentences?

   (*i*) Ooty is not a hill-station.

   (*ii*) No hill-station can have more than one lake.

   (*a*) (*i*) only (*b*) (*ii*) only

   (*c*) both (*i*) and (*ii*) (*d*) neither (*i*) nor (*ii*)

3. Identify the correct spelling out of the given options :

   (*a*) Managable (*b*) Manageable

   (*c*) Mangaeble (*d*) Managible

4. Choose the statement(s) where the underlined word is used correctly :

   (*i*) A prone is a dried plum.

   (*ii*) He was lying prone on the floor.

   (*iii*) People who eat a lot of fat are prone to heart disease.

   (*a*) (*i*) and (*iii*) only (*b*) (*iii*) only

   (*c*) (*i*) and (*ii*) only (*d*) (*ii*) and (*iii*) only

5. The policeman asked the victim of a theft, "What did you ?"

   (*a*) loose (*b*) lose

   (*c*) loss (*d*) louse

6. In a world filled with uncertainty, he was glad to have many good friends. He had always assisted them in times of need and was confident that they would reciprocate. However, the events of the last week proved him wrong.

   Which of the following inference(s) is/are logically valid and can be inferred from the above passage?

   (*i*) His friends were always asking him to help them.

   (*ii*) He felt that when in need of help, his friends would let him down.

   (*iii*) He was sure that his friends would help him when in need.

   (*iv*) His friends did not help him last week.

   (*a*) (*i*) and (*ii*) (*b*) (*iii*) and (*iv*)

   (*c*) (*iii*) only (*d*) (*iv*) only

7. An apple costs Rs. 10. An onion costs Rs. 8.

   Select the most suitable sentence with respect to grammar and usage.

   (*a*) The price of an apple is greater than an onion.

   (*b*) The price of an apple is more than onion.

   (*c*) The price of an apple is greater than that of an onion.

   (*d*) Apples are more costlier than onions.

8. He <u>turned a deaf ear</u> to my request. What does the underlined phrasal verb mean?

   (*a*) ignored (*b*) appreciated

   (*c*) twisted (*d*) returned

2015

9. Choose the statement where underlined word is used correctly

   (*a*) The minister <u>insured</u> the victims that everything would be all right.

   (*b*) He <u>ensured</u> that the company will not have to bear any loss.

   (*c*) The actor got himself <u>ensured</u> against any accident.

   (*d*) The teacher <u>insured</u> students of good results

10. The following question presents a sentence, part of which is underlined. Beneath the sentence you find four ways of phrasing the underline part. Following the requirements of the standard written English, select the answer that produces the most effective sentence.

Tuberculosis, together with its effects, ranks one of the leading causes of death in India.

(*a*) ranks as one of the leading causes of death
(*b*) rank as one of the leading causes of death
(*c*) has the rank of one of the leading causes of death
(*d*) are one of the leading causes of death

11. Choose the statement where underlined word is used correctly.

(*a*) When the teacher eludes to different authors, he is being elusive
(*b*) When the thief keeps eluding the police, he is being elusive
(*c*) Matters that are difficult to understand, identify or remember are allusive
(*d*) Mirages can be allusive, but a better way to express them is illusory

12. Fill in the blank with the correct idiom/phrase.

That boy from the town was a __________ in the sleepy village.

(*a*) Dog out of herd (*b*) Sheep from the heap
(*c*) Fish out of water (*d*) Bird from the flock

13. Select the appropriate option in place of underlined part of the sentence.

Increased productivity necessary reflects greater efforts made by the employees.

(*a*) Increase in productivity necessary
(*b*) Increase productivity is necessary
(*c*) Increase in productivity necessarily
(*d*) No improvement required

14. Ram and Shyam shared a secret and promised to each other that it would remain between them. Ram expressed himself in one of the following ways as given in the choices below. Identify the correct way as per standard English.

(*a*) It would remain between you and me
(*b*) It would remain between me and you
(*c*) It would remain between you and I
(*d*) It would remain with me

15. What is the adverb for the given word below? Misogynous

(*a*) Misogynousness (*b*) Misogynity
(*c*) Misogynously (*d*) Misogynous

16. In the following sentence certain parts are underlined and marked P, Q and R. One of the parts may contain certain error or may not be acceptable in standard written communication. Select the part containing an error. Choose D as your Answer: if there is no error.

The student corrected all the errors (P) that the instructor marked (Q) on the answer book (R)

(*a*) P (*b*) Q
(*c*) R (*d*) No Error

17. Choose the statement where underlined word is used correctly.

(*a*) The industrialist had a personnel jet.
(*b*) I write my experience in my personnel diary.
(*c*) All personnel are being given the day off.
(*d*) Being religious is a personnel aspect.

18. Out of the following four sentences, select the most suitable sentence with respect to grammer and usage:

(*a*) Since the report lacked needed information, it was of no use to them.
(*b*) The report was useless to them because there were no needed information in it.
(*c*) Since the report did not contain the needed information, it was not real useful to them.
(*d*) Since the report lacked needed information, it would not had been useful to them.

19. Select the alternative meaning of the underlined part of the sentence.

The chain snatchers took to their heels when the police party arrived.

(*a*) took shelter in a thick jungle
(*b*) open indiscriminate fire
(*c*) took to flight
(*d*) unconditionally surrendered

2014

20. Which of the following options is the closest in meaning to the word underlined in the sentence below?

In a democracy, everybody has the freedom to disagree with the government.

(*a*) dissent (*b*) descent
(*c*) decent (*d*) decadent

21. 'Advice' is ________.

(*a*) a verb (*b*) a noun
(*c*) an adjective (*d*) both a verb and a noun

22. Which of the options given below best completes the following sentence?

She will feel much better if she ________.

(*a*) will get some rest

(*b*) gets some rest

(*c*) will be getting some rest

(*d*) is getting some rest

23. While trying to collect (I) an envelope from under the table, (II) Mr. X fell down (III) and was losing consciousness. (IV)

Which one of the above underlined parts of the sentence is NOT appropriate?

(*a*) I (*b*) II

(*c*) III (*d*) IV

24. Which of the following options is the closest in meaning to the phrase underlined in the sentence below?

It is fascinating to see life forms cope with varied environmental conditions.

(*a*) Adopt to (*b*) Adapt to

(*c*) Adept in (*d*) Accept with

25. In a press meet on the recent scam, the minister said, "The buck stops here". What did the minister convey by the statement?

(*a*) He wants all the money

(*b*) He will return the money

(*c*) He will assume final responsibility

(*d*) He will resist all enquiries

2013

26. The professor (I) ordered to (II) the students to go (III) out of the class. (IV)

Which of the above underlined parts of the sentence is grammatically incorrect?

(*a*) I (*b*) II

(*c*) III (*d*) IV

27. Choose the grammatically INCORRECT sentence:

(*a*) He is of Asian origin.

(*b*) They belonged to Africa.

(*c*) She is an European.

(*d*) They migrated from India to Australia.

28. Choose the grammatically CORRECT sentence:

(*a*) Two and two add four.

(*b*) Two and two become four.

(*c*) Two and two are four.

(*d*) Two and two make four.

29. All engineering students (I) should learn mechanics, (II) mathematics and (III) how to do computation. (IV)

Which of the above underlined parts of the sentence is not appropriate?

(*a*) I (*b*) II

(*c*) III (*d*) IV

2012

30. Choose the most appropriate alternative from the options given below to complete the following sentence :

Suresh's dog is the one _____ was hurt in the stampede.

(*a*) that (*b*) which

(*c*) who (*d*) whom

31. Choose the grammatically **INCORRECT** sentence :

(*a*) They gave us the money back less the service charges of Three Hundred rupees.

(*b*) This country's expenditure is not less than that of Bangladesh.

(*c*) The committee initially asked for a funding of Fifty Lakh rupeesr, but later settled for a lesser sum.

(*d*) This country's expenditure on educational reforms is very less.

32. One of the parts (A, B, C, D) in the sentence given below contains an ERROR. Which one of the following is **INCORRECT** ?

I requested that he should be given the driving test today instead of tomorrow.

(*a*) requested that

(*b*) should be given

(*c*) the driving test

(*d*) instead of tomorrow

ANSWERS

MCQ Type Questions

1. (*d*)	**2.** (*d*)	**3.** (*b*)	**4.** (*d*)	**5.** (*b*)	**6.** (*b*)	**7.** (*c*)	**8.** (*a*)	**9.** (*b*)	**10.** (*a*)
11. (*b*)	**12.** (*c*)	**13.** (*c*)	**14.** (*a*)	**15.** (*c*)	**16.** (*b*)	**17.** (*c*)	**18.** (*a*)	**19.** (*c*)	**20.** (*a*)
21. (*b*)	**22.** (*b*)	**23.** (*d*)	**24.** (*b*)	**25.** (*c*)	**26.** (*b*)	**27.** (*c*)	**28.** (*d*)	**29.** (*d*)	**30.** (*a*)
31. (*d*)	**32.** (*b*)								

EXPLANATIONS

MCQ TYPE QUESTIONS

4. 'lying prone' means lie down flat. 'Prone to' means vulnerable to.

5. Lose (verb)

9. *Insured*–the person, group, or organization whose life or property is covered by an insurance policy.
Ensured–to secure or guarantee

11. Elusive: Difficult to answer.

12. From the statement, it appears that boy found it tough to adapt to a very different situation.

16. The is not required in 'Q'.

30. The correct answer is 'that'. In the given sentence 'was hurt in the stampede' determines which dog belongs to Suresh.

■■

2
CHAPTER

Sentence Completion

MCQ TYPE QUESTIONS

2016

1. The man who is now Municipal Commissioner worked as ___________________.

(*a*) the security guard at a university

(*b*) a security guard at the university

(*c*) a security guard at university

(*d*) the security guard at the university

2. Nobody knows how the Indian cricket team is going to cope with the difficult and seamer-friendly wickets in Australia.

Choose the option which is closest in meaning to the underlined phrase in the above sentence.

(*a*) put up with (*b*) put in with

(*c*) put down to (*d*) put up against

3. The chairman requested the aggrieved shareholders to _________ him.

(*a*) bare with (*b*) bore with

(*c*) bear with (*d*) bare

4. The unruly crowd demanded that the accused be ___________ without trial.

(*a*) hanged (*b*) hanging

(*c*) hankering (*d*) hung

5. Which of the following is CORRECT with respect to grammar and usage?

Mount Everest is ____________.

(*a*) the highest peak in the world

(*b*) highest peak in the world

(*c*) one of highest peak in the world

(*d*) one of the highest peak in the world

6. Despite the new medicine's ______________ in treating diabetes, it is not ____________widely.

(*a*) effectiveness --- prescribed

(*b*) availability --- used

(*c*) prescription --- available

(*d*) acceptance --- proscribed

7. The students _____ the teacher on teachers' day for twenty years of dedicated teaching.

(*a*) facilitated (*b*) felicitated

(*c*) fantasized (*d*) facillitated

8. After India's cricket world cup victory in 1985, Shrotria who was playing both tennis and cricket till then, decided to concentrate only on cricket. And the rest is history.

What does the underlined phrase mean in this context?

(*a*) history will rest in peace

(*b*) rest is recorded in history books

(*c*) rest is well known

(*d*) rest is archaic

9. If I were you, I _________ that laptop. It's much too expensive.

(*a*) won't buy (*b*) shan't buy

(*c*) wouldn't buy (*d*) would buy

10. Choose the most appropriate set of words from the options given below to complete the following sentence.

_________ _________ is a will, _________ is a way.

(*a*) Wear, there, their (*b*) Were, their, there

(*c*) Where, there, there (*d*) Where, their, their

2015

11. Choose the most appropriate word from the options given below to complete the following sentence. The official answered _________ that the complaints of the citizen would be looked into.

(*a*) respectably (*b*) respectfully

(*c*) reputably (*d*) respectively

12. Choose the most appropriate word from the options given below to complete the following sentence.

The principal presented the chief guest with a _________, as token of appreciation.

(*a*) momento (*b*) memento

(*c*) momentum (*d*) moment

13. Choose the appropriate word/phrase, out of the four options given below, to complete the following sentence : Frogs ________.

(*a*) Croak (*b*) Roar

(*c*) Hiss (*d*) Patter

14. Extreme focus on syllabus and studying for tests has become such a dominant concern of Indian students that they close their minds to anything ______ to the requirements of the exam

(*a*) related (*b*) extraneous

(*c*) outside (*d*) useful

15. The Tamil version of_____ John Abraham-starrer Madras café _____ cleared by the Censor Board with no cuts last week but the film's distributors _____ no takers among the exhibitors for a release in Tamil Nadu_____ this Friday.

(*a*) Mr., was, found, on (*b*) a, was, found, at

(*c*) the, was, found, on (*d*) a, being, find at

16. Choose the appropriate word/phase, out of the four options given below, to complete the following sentence:

Apparent lifelessness _____ dormant life.

(*a*) harbours (*b*) lead to

(*c*) supports (*d*) affects

17. Choose the correct verb to fill in the blank below :

Let us _____________.

(*a*) Introvert (*b*) Alternate

(*c*) Atheist (*d*) Altruist

18. Choose the most appropriate word from the options given below to complete the following sentence :

If the Athlete had wanted to come first in the race, he ___________ several hours everyday

(*a*) should practice (*b*) should have practiced

(*c*) practiced (*d*) should be practicing

19. Choose the appropriate word/phrase, out of the four options given below, to complete the following sentence:

Dhoni, as well as the other team members of Indian team, _____ present on the occasion.

(*a*) were (*b*) was

(*c*) has (*d*) have

20. We _______ our friend's birthday and we _______ how to make it up to him.

(*a*) completely forgot — don't just known

(*b*) forget completely — don't just know

(*c*) completely forget —just don't know

(*d*) forgot completely —just don't know

21. Which of the following options is the closest in meaning to the sentence below?

She enjoyed herself immensely at the party.

(*a*) She had a terrible time at the party

(*b*) She had a horrible time at the party

(*c*) She had a terrific time at the party

(*d*) She had a terrifying time at the party

22. Didn't you buy _______ when you went shopping?

(*a*) any paper

(*b*) much paper

(*c*) no paper

(*d*) a few paper

2014

23. Choose the most appropriate word from the options given below to complete the following sentence:

A person suffering from Alzheimer's disease _________ short-term memory loss.

(*a*) experienced (*b*) has experienced

(*c*) is experiencing (*d*) experiences

24. Choose the most appropriate word from the options given below to complete the following sentence:

_________ is the key to their happiness; they are satisfied with what they have.

(*a*) Contentment (*b*) Ambition

(*c*) Perseverance (*d*) Hunger

25. Choose the most appropriate word from the options given below to complete the following sentence:

One of his biggest _____ was his ability to forgive.

(*a*) vice (*b*) virtues

(*c*) choices (*d*) strength

26. After the discussion, Tom said to me, 'Please revert!' He expects me to ________.

(*a*) retract (*b*) get back to him

(*c*) move in reverse (*d*) retreat

27. The value of one U.S. Dollar is 65 Indian Rupees today, compared to 60 last year. The Indian Rupee has ________.

(*a*) Depressed (*b*) Depreciated

(*c*) Appreciated (*d*) Stabilized

28. Choose the most appropriate word from the options given below to complete the following sentence:

Communication and interpersonal skills are ________ important in their own ways.

(*a*) each (*b*) both

(*c*) all (*d*) either

29. Choose the most appropriate pair of words from the options given below to complete the following sentence:

She could not _________ the thought of ________ the election to her bitter rival.

(*a*) bear, loosing (*b*) bare, loosing

(*c*) bear, losing (*d*) bare, losing

30. Choose the most appropriate phrase from the options given below to complete the following sentence:

The aircraft ________ take off as soon as its flight plan was filed.

(*a*) is allowed to (*b*) will be allowed to

(*c*) was allowed to (*d*) has been allowed to

31. Choose the most appropriate word from the options given below to complete the following sentence:

Many ancient cultures attributed disease to supernatural causes. However, modern science has largely helped _____ such notions.

(a) impel (b) dispel
(c) propel (d) repel

32. If she __________ how to calibrate the instrument, she ________ done the experiment.

(a) knows, will have
(b) knew, had
(c) had known, could have
(d) should have known, would have

33. Who ______ was coming to see us this evening ?

(a) you said (b) did you say
(c) did you say that (d) had you said

34. Choose the most appropriate word from the options given below to complete the following sentence:

He could not understand the judges awarding her the first prize, because he thought that her performance was quite ___________.

(a) Superb (b) Medium
(c) Mediocre (d) Exhilarating

2013

35. Friendship, no matter how _______ it is, has its limitations.

(a) cordial (b) intimate
(c) secret (d) pleasant

36. Were you a bird, you_____ in the sky.

(a) would fly (b) shall fly
(c) should fly (d) shall have flown

37. Complete the sentence:

Dare __________ mistakes.

(a) commit (b) to commit
(c) committed (d) committing

38. The Headmaster ______ to speak to you.

Which of the following options is incorrect to complete the above sentence?

(a) is wanting (b) wants
(c) want (d) was wanting

2012

39. Choose the most appropriate alternative from the options given below to complete the following sentence :

Despite several _____ the mission succeeded in its attempt to resolve the conflict.

(a) attempts (b) setbacks
(c) meetings (d) delegations

40. Choose the most appropriate alternative from the options given below to complete the following sentence :

If the tired soldier wanted to lie down, he ___ the mattress out on the balcony.

(a) should take (b) shall take
(c) should have taken (d) will have taken

41. Choose the most appropriate word from the options given below to complete the following sentence :

Given the seriousness of the situation that he had to face, his ___ was impressive.

(a) beggary (b) nomenclature
(c) jealousy (d) nonchalance

2011

42. Choose the most appropriate word from the options given below to complete the following sentence:

If you are trying to make a strong impression on your audience, you cannot do so by being understated, tentative or ______ .

(a) hyperbolic (b) restrained
(c) argumentative (d) indifferent

43. Choose the most appropriate word(s) from the options given below to complete the following sentence.

I contemplated______ Singapore for my vacation but decided against it.

(a) to visit (b) having to visit
(c) visiting (d) for a visit

44. Choose the most appropriate word from the options given below to complete the following sentence:

Under ethical guidelines recently adopted by the Indian Medical Association, human genes are to be manipulated only to correct diseases for which_______treatments are unsatisfactory.

(a) similar (b) most
(c) uncommon (d) available

45. Choose the most appropriate word from the options given below to complete the following sentence:

It was her view that the country's problems had been_________by foreign technocrats, so that to invite them to come back would be counter-productive.

(a) identified
(b) ascertained
(c) exacerbated
(d) analysed

2010

46. Choose the most appropriate word from the options given below to complete the following sentence:

If we manage to ________ our natural resources, we would leave a better planet for our children.

(*a*) uphold (*b*) restrain

(*c*) cherish (*d*) conserve

47. Choose the most appropriate word from the options given below to complete the following sentence:

His rather casual remarks on politics ________ his lack of seriousness about the subject.

(*a*) masked (*b*) belied

(*c*) betrayed (*d*) suppressed

ANSWERS

MCQ Type Questions

1. (*b*)	**2.** (*a*)	**3.** (*c*)	**4.** (*a*)	**5.** (*a*)	**6.** (*a*)	**7.** (*b*)	**8.** (*c*)	**9.** (*c*)	**10.** (*c*)
11. (*b*)	**12.** (*b*)	**13.** (*a*)	**14.** (*b*)	**15.** (*c*)	**16.** (*a*)	**17.** (*b*)	**18.** (*b*)	**19.** (*b*)	**20.** (*c*)
21. (*c*)	**22.** (*a*)	**23.** (*d*)	**24.** (*a*)	**25.** (*b*)	**26.** (*b*)	**27.** (*b*)	**28.** (*b*)	**29.** (*c*)	**30.** (*c*)
31. (*b*)	**32.** (*c*)	**33.** (*b*)	**34.** (*c*)	**35.** (*b*)	**36.** (*a*)	**37.** (*b*)	**38.** (*c*)	**39.** (*b*)	**40.** (*a*)
41. (*d*)	**42.** (*b*)	**43.** (*c*)	**44.** (*d*)	**45.** (*c*)	**46.** (*a*)	**47.** (*c*)			

EXPLANATIONS

MCQ TYPE QUESTIONS

2. From the given underlined phrase copewith means put up with.

4. 'hanged' means death by hanging 'hung' is used only with things and not with people.

6. Here 'effectiveness' is noun and 'prescribed' is verb. So these words are apt and befitting with the given word 'medicine'.

12. The principal presented the chief guest with a memento, as token of appreciation.

13. Frogs make 'croak' sound.

14. Extraneous -irrelevant or unrelated to the subject being dealt with.

15. John-Abraham starrer Madras Cafe talks about the movie not the person, so Mr. is ruled out.

'Find no takers' is not the correct phrase. At this Friday is incorrect.

So, option (*c*) is correct.

16. Apparent: looks like; dormant: hidden

Harbour: give shelter; Effect (verb): results in

18. For condition regarding something which already happened, should have practiced is the correct choice.

23. The correct word to fill in the blank is experiences. This is because the sentence is in present tense and the sense is in present indefinite.

24. Contentment is the right word which is appropriate to the meaning of the sentence. Contentment is the sign of true happiness as it gives a sense of fulfillment.

39. The word despite tells us that missión succeeded even though there were problems. Hence the correct answer is Setbacks.

42. Tone of the sentence clearly indicates a word that is similar to understated is needed for the blank. Alternatively, word should be antonym of strong (fail to make strong impression). Therefore, best choice is restrained which means controlled / reserved / timid.

43. Contemplate is a transitive verb and hence is followed by a gerund Hence the correct usage of contemplate is verb + ing form.

44. The context seeks to take a deviation only when existing / present / current / alternative treatments are unsatisfactory. So word for the blank should be a close synonym of existing / present / current / alternative. Available is the closest of all.

45. Clues: foreign technocrats did something negatively to the problems – so it is counter-productive to invite them. All other options are non-negative. Best choice is exacerbated which means aggravated or worsened.

47. Betrayed, **means** 'showed' or revealed.

■■

3 CHAPTER

Synonyms

MCQ TYPE QUESTIONS

2016

1. The Buddha said, "Holding on to anger is like grasping a hot coal with the intent of throwing it at someone else; you are the one who gets burnt." Select the word below which is closest in meaning to the word underlined above.
(a) burning (b) igniting
(c) clutching (d) flinging

2015

2. The word similar in meaning to 'dreary' is
(a) cheerful (b) dreamy
(c) hard (d) dismal

3. Choose the word most similar in meaning to the given word :
Educe
(a) Exert (b) Educate
(c) Extract (d) Extend

4. Choose the most suitable one word substitute for the following expression
Connotation of a road or way
(a) Pertinacious (b) Viaticum
(c) Clandestine (d) Ravenous

5. Choose the word most similar in meaning to the given word:
Awkward
(a) Inept (b) Graceful
(c) Suitable (d) Dreadful

6. A generic term that includes various items of clothing such as a skirt, a pair of trousers and a shirt as
(a) fabric
(b) textile
(c) fibre
(d) apparel

7. Which of the following combinations is incorrect?
(a) Acquiescence – Submission
(b) Wheedle – Roundabout
(c) Flippancy – Lightness
(d) Profligate – Extravagant

2014

8. A student is required to demonstrate a high level of comprehension of the subject, especially in the social sciences.
The word closest in meaning to comprehension is
(a) understanding (b) meaning
(c) concentration (d) stability

9. While receiving the award, the scientist said, "I feel vindicated". Which of the following is closest in meaning to the word 'vindicated'?
(a) punished (b) substantiated
(c) appreciated (d) chastened

10. Choose the word that is opposite in meaning to the word "coherent".
(a) sticky (b) well-connected
(c) rambling (d) friendly

11. Match the columns:

	Column-1		Column-2
1.	eradicate	P.	misrepresent
2.	distort	Q.	soak completely
3.	saturate	R.	use
4.	utilize	S.	destroy utterly

(a) 1 : S, 2 : P, 3 : Q, 4 : R
(b) 1 : P, 2 : Q, 3 : R, 4 : S
(c) 1 : Q, 2 : R, 3 : S, 4 : P
(d) 1 : S, 2 : P, 3 : R, 4 : Q

2013

12. Which of the following options is the closest in meaning to the word given below:
Primeval
(a) Modern (b) Historic
(c) Primitive (d) Antique

13. Which one of the following options is the closest in meaning to the word given below?
Nadir
(a) Highest (b) Lowest
(c) Medium (d) Integration

14. They were requested not to **quarrel** with others. Which one of the following options is the closest in meaning to the word **quarrel**?
(a) make out (b) call out
(c) dig out (d) fall out

2012

15. Which one of the following options is the closest in meaning to the word given below?

Mitigate

(*a*) Diminish (*b*) Divulge

(*c*) Dedicate (*d*) Denote

16. Which one of the following options is the closest in meaning to the word given below ?

Latitude

(*a*) Eligibility (*b*) Freedom

(*c*) Coercion (*d*) Meticulousness

2011

17. Which of the following options is the closest in the meaning to the word below :

Inexplicable

(*a*) Incomprehensible (*b*) Indelible

(*c*) Inextricable (*d*) Infallible

2010

18. Which of the following options is the closest in meaning to the word below:

Circuitous

(*a*) cyclic (*b*) indirect

(*c*) confusing (*d*) crooked

ANSWERS

MCQ Type Questions

1. (*c*)	**2.** (*d*)	**3.** (*c*)	**4.** (*b*)	**5.** (*a*)	**6.** (*d*)	**7.** (*b*)	**8.** (*a*)	**9.** (*b*)	**10.** (*c*)
11. (*a*)	**12.** (*c*)	**13.** (*b*)	**14.** (*b*)	**15.** (*a*)	**16.** (*b*)	**17.** (*a*)	**18.** (*b*)		

EXPLANATIONS

MCQ TYPE QUESTIONS

1. The meaning of underlined word grasping means clutching (or holding something tightly).

2. *dreary* - depressingly dull and bleak or repetitive.

3. The word similar in meaning to Educe is Extract.

13. Given: A word "Nadir"

To find: Closest meaning word to 'Nadir' in the given options.

Analysis: The dictionary meaning of 'Nadir' is 'Lowest' which is potion (*b*)

Source: Google

Given: A sequence 44, 42, 40,......

To find: Maximum sum of the sequence

Analysis: To find the maximum sum, we have to ignore all the negative terms (they will only decrease the sum). Hence, we terminate the sequence at 0.

Now, the sequence is 44, 42,......,2, 0.

This sequence is an Arithmetic progression with common difference –2. Now, the problem reduces to finding the sum of this A.P.

To find the sum of A.P., we have to find the number of terms in A.P.

Let n be the number of terms

a be the first term

l be the last term

d be the common difference.

$n = ?$

$a = 44, \quad l = 0, \quad d = -2$

Now, $l = a + (n-1)d$

15. 'Mitigate' means to make something less harmful, serious, intense etc. Hence correct answer is 'Diminis'

17. Inexplicable means not explicable; that cannot be explained, understood, or accounted for. So the best synonym here is incomprehensible.

18. Circuitous means round about or not direct

So circuitous : indirect.

■■

4

CHAPTER

Antonyms

MCQ TYPE QUESTIONS

2015

1. Which word is not a synonym for the word *vernacular*?
   (*a*) regional
   (*b*) indigeneous
   (*c*) indigent
   (*d*) colloquial

2011

2. Choose the word from the options given below that is most nearly opposite in meaning to the given word:
   Amalgamate
   (*a*) merge
   (*b*) split
   (*c*) collect
   (*d*) separate
3. Choose the word from the options given below that is most nearly **opposite** in meaning to the given word :
   Frequency
   (*a*) periodicity
   (*b*) rarity
   (*c*) gradualness
   (*d*) persistency

ANSWERS

MCQ Type Questions

1. (*c*) **2.** (*b*) **3.** (*b*)

EXPLANATIONS

MCQ TYPE QUESTIONS

1. *Vernacular* - expressed or written in the native language of a place

Indigent - deficient in what is requisite

2. Amalgamate means combine or unite to form one organization or structure. So the best option here is split. Separate on the other hand, although a close synonym, it is too general to be the best antonym in the given question while Merge is the synonym; Collect is not related.

3. Best antonym is rarity which means shortage or scarcity.

■■

5

CHAPTER

Reasoning Ability

MCQ TYPE QUESTIONS

2016

1. Find the odd one in the following group of words.
mock, deride, praise, jeer

(*a*) mock (*b*) deride
(*c*) praise (*d*) jeer

2. Pick the odd one from the following options.

(*a*) CADBE (*b*) JHKIL
(*c*) XVYWZ (*d*) ONPMQ

3. Pick the odd one out in the following :
13, 23, 33, 43, 53

(*a*) 23 (*b*) 33
(*c*) 43 (*d*) 53

4. R2D2 is a robot. R2D2 can repair aeroplanes. No other robot can repair aeroplanes. Which of the following can be logically inferred from the above statements?

(*a*) R2D2 is a robot which can only repair aeroplanes.
(*b*) R2D2 is the only robot which can repair aeroplanes.
(*c*) R2D2 is a robot which can repair only aeroplanes.
(*d*) Only R2D2 is a robot.

5. A poll of students appearing for masters in engineering indicated that 60% of the students believed that mechanical engineering is a profession unsuitable for women. A research study on women with masters or higher degrees in mechanical engineering found that 99% of such women were successful in their professions.
Which of the following can be logically inferred from the above paragraph?

(*a*) Many students have misconceptions regarding various engineering disciplines.
(*b*) Men with advanced degrees in mechanical engineering believe women are well suited to be mechanical engineers.
(*c*) Mechanical engineering is a profession well suited for women with masters or higher degrees in mechanical engineering.
(*d*) The number of women pursuing higher degrees in mechanical engineering is small.

6. Sourya committee had proposed the establishment of Sourya Institutes of Technology (SITs) in line with Indian Institutes of Technology (IITs) to cater to the technological and industrial needs of a developing country.
Which of the following can be logically inferred from the above sentence?
Based on the proposal,

(*i*) In the initial years, SIT students will get degrees from IIT.
(*ii*) SITs will have a distinct national objective.
(*iii*) SIT like institutions can only be established in consulation with IIT.
(*iv*) SITs will serve technological needs of a developing country.

(*a*) (*iii*) and (*iv*) only (*b*) (*i*) and (*iv*) only
(*c*) (*ii*) and (*iv*) only (*d*) (*ii*) and (*iii*) only

7. **Fact :** If it rains, then the field is wet.
Read the following statements:

(*i*) It rains (*ii*) The field is not wet
(*iii*) The field is wet (*iv*) It did not rain

Which one of the options given below is NOT logically possible, based on the given fact?

(*a*) If (*iii*), then (*iv*) (*b*) If (*i*), then (*iii*)
(*c*) If (*i*), then (*ii*) (*d*) If (*ii*), then (*iv*)

8. Students taking an exam are divided into two groups, **P** and **Q** such that each group has the same number of students. The performance of each of the students in a test was evaluated out of 200 marks. It was observed that the mean of group **P** was 105, while that of group **Q** was 85. The standard deviation of group **P** was 25, while that of group **Q** was 5. Assuming that the marks were distributed on a normal distribution, which of the following statements will have the highest probability of being **TRUE**?

(*a*) No student in group **Q** scored less marks than any student in group **P**.
(*b*) No student in group **P** scored less marks than any student in group **Q**.
(*c*) Most students of group **Q** scored marks in a narrower range than students in group **P**.
(*d*) The median of the marks of group **P** is 100.

9. A smart city integrates all modes of transport, uses clean energy and promotes sustainable use of resources. It also uses technology to ensure safety and security of the city, something which critics argue, will lead to a surveillance state.

Which of the following can be logically inferred from the above paragraph?

(*i*) All smart cities encourage the formation of surveillance states.

(*ii*) Surveillance is an integral part of a smart city.

(*iii*) Sustainability and surveillance go hand in hand in a smart city.

(*iv*) There is a perception that smart cities promote surveillance.

(*a*) (*i*) and (*iv*) only (*b*) (*ii*) and (*iii*) only

(*c*) (*iv*) only (*d*) (*i*) only

10. Find the missing sequence in the letter series.

B, FH, LNP, _ _ _ _.

(*a*) SUWY (*b*) TUVW

(*c*) TVXZ (*d*) TWXZ

11. Michael lives 10 km away from where I live. Ahmed lives 5 km away and Susan lives 7 km away from where I live. Arun is farther away than Ahmed but closer than Susan from where I live. From the information provided here, what is one possible distance (in km) at which I live from Arun's place?

(*a*) 3.00 (*b*) 4.99

(*c*) 6.02 (*d*) 7.01

12. Leela is older than her cousin Pavithra. Pavithra's brother Shiva is older than Leela. When Pavithra and Shiva are visiting Leela, all three like to play chess. Pavithra wins more often than Leela does.

Which one of the following statements must be TRUE based on the above?

(*a*) When Shiva plays chess with Leela and Pavithra, he often loses.

(*b*) Leela is the oldest of the three.

(*c*) Shiva is a better chess player than Pavithra.

(*d*) Pavithra is the youngest of the three.

13. Based on the given statements, select the appropriate option with respect to grammar and usage.

Statements :

I. The height of Mr. X is 6 feet.

II. The height of Mr. Y is 5 feet.

(*a*) Mr. X is longer than Mr. Y.

(*b*) Mr. X is more elongated than Mr. Y

(*c*) Mr. X is taller than Mr. Y

(*d*) Mr. X is lengthier than Mr. Y

14. Social science disciplines were in existence in an amorphous form until the colonial period when they were institutionalized. In varying degrees, they were intended to further the colonial interest. In the time of globalization and the economic rise of postcolonial countries like India, conventional ways of knowledge production have become obsolete.

Which of the following can be logically inferred from the above statements?

I. Social science disciplines have become obsolete.

II. Social science disciplines had a pre-colonial origin.

III. Social science disciplines always promote colonialism.

IV. Social science must maintain disciplinary boundaries.

(*a*) II only (*b*) I and III only

(*c*) II and IV only (*d*) III and IV only

15. Two and a quarter hours back, when seen in a mirror, the reflection of a wall clock without number markings seemed to show 1 : 30. What is the actual current time shown by the clock?

(*a*) 8:15 (*b*) 11:15

(*c*) 12:15 (*d*) 12:45

16. M and N start from the same location. M travels 10 km East and then 10 km North-East. N travels 5 km South and then 4 km South-East. What is the shortest distance (in km) between M and N at the end of their travel?

(*a*) 18.60 (*b*) 22.50

(*c*) 20.61 (*d*) 25.00

17. M has a son Q and a daughter R. He has no other children. E is the mother of P and daughter-inlaw of M. How is P related to M?

(*a*) P is the son-in-law of M.

(*b*) P is the grandchild of M.

(*c*) P is the daughter-in-law of M.

(*d*) P is the grandfather of M.

18. The number that least fits this set: (324, 441, 97 and 64) is ________.

(*a*) 324

(*b*) 441

(*c*) 97

(*d*) 64

19. The overwhelming number of people infected with rabies in India has been flagged by the World Health Organization as a source of concern. It is estimated that inoculating 70% of pets and stray dogs against rabies can lead to a significant reduction in the number of people infected with rabies.

Which of the following can be logically inferred from the above sentences ?

(*a*) The number of people in India infected with rabies is high

(*b*) The number of people in other parts of the world who are infected with rabies is low

(*c*) Rabies can be eradicated in India by vaccinating 70% of stray dogs

(d) Stray dogs are the main source of rabies worldwide

20. A flat is shared by four first year undergraduate students. They agreed to allow the oldest of them to enjoy some extra space in the flat. Manu is two months older than Sravan, who is three months younger than Trideep. Pavan is one month older than Sravan. Who should occupy the extra space in the flat ?

(*a*) Manu (*b*) Sravan

(*c*) Trideep (*d*) Pavan

21. Today, we consider Ashoka as a great ruler because of the copious evidence he left behind in the form of stone carved edicts. Historians tend to correlate greatness of a king at his time with the availability of evidence today. Which of the following can be logically inferred from the above sentences?

(*a*) Emperors who do not leave significant sculpted evidence are completely forgotten.

(*b*) Ashoka produced stone carved edicts to ensure that later historians will respect him.

(*c*) Statues of kings are a reminder of their greatness.

(*d*) A king's greatness, as we know him today, is interpreted by historians.

22. Fact 1 : Humans are mammals.

Fact 2 : Some humans are engineers.

Fact 3 : Engineers build houses.

If the above statements are facts, which of the following can be logically inferred ?

I. All mammals build houses.

II. Engineers are mammals.

III. Some humans are not engineers.

(*a*) II only (*b*) III only

(*c*) I, II and III (*d*) I only

2015

23. Mr. Vivek walks 6 meters North-East, then turns and walks 6 meters South- East, both at 60 degrees to East. He further moves 2 meters South and 4 meters West. What is the straight distance in meters between the point he started from and the point he finally reached?

(*a*) $2\sqrt{2}$ (*b*) 2

(*c*) $\sqrt{2}$ (*d*) $1/\sqrt{2}$

24. There are 16 teachers who can teach Thermodynamics (TD), 11 who can teach Electrical Sciences (ES), and 5 who can teach both TD and Engineering Mechanics (EM). There are a total of 40 teachers, 6 cannot teach any of the three subjects, i.e. EM, ES or TD. 6 can teach only ES. 4 can teach all three subjects, i.e. EM, ES and TD. 4 can teach ES and TD. How many can teach both ES and EM but not TD?

(*a*) 1 (*b*) 2

(*c*) 3 (*d*) 4

25. The given question is followed by two statements: select the most appropriate option that solves the question

Capacity of a solution tank A is 70% of the capacity of tank B. How many gallons of solution are in tank A and tank B?

Statements:

I. Tank A is 80% full and tank B is 40% full

II. Tank A if full contains 14,000 gallons of solution

(*a*) Statement I alone is sufficient

(*b*) Statement II alone is sufficient

(*c*) Either statement I or II alone is sufficient

(*d*) Both the statements I and II together are sufficient

26. Operators □, ◇ and → are defined by

$$a \,\square\, b = \frac{a-b}{a+b};\ a \diamond b = \frac{a+b}{a-b};\ a \rightarrow b = ab.$$

Find the value (66□6) → (66◇6)

(*a*) –2 (*b*) –1

(*c*) 1 (*d*) 2

27. Humpty Dumpty sits on a wall every day while having lunch. The wall sometimes breaks. A person sitting on the wall falls if the wall breaks. Which one of the statements below is logically valid and can be inferred from the above sentences?

(*a*) Humpty Dumpty always falls while having lunch

(*b*) Humpty Dumpty does not fall sometimes while having lunch

(*c*) Humpty Dumpty never falls during dinner

(*d*) When Humpty Dumpty does not sit on the wall, the wall does not break

28. If ROAD is written as URDG, then SWAN should be written as :

(a) VXDQ (b) VZDQ
(c) VZDP (d) UXDQ

29. Select the pair that best expresses a relationship similar to that expressed in the pair :

Children : Pediatrician

(a) Adult : Orthopaedist
(b) Females : Gynaecologist
(c) Kidney : Nephrologist
(d) Skin : Dermatologist

30. The head of a newly formed government desires to appoint five of the six selected members P,Q,R,S,T and U to portfolios of Home, Power, Defense, Telecom, and Finance. U does not want any portfolio if S gets one of the five. R wants either Home or Finance or no portfolio. Q says that if S gets either Power or Telecom, then she must get the other one. T insists on a portfolio if P gets one.

Which is the valid distribution of portfolios?

(a) P-Home, Q-Power, R-Defense, S-Telecom, T-Finance
(b) R-Home, S-Power, P-Defense, Q-Telecom, T-Finance
(c) P-Home, Q-Power, T-Defense, S-Telecom, U-Finance
(d) Q-Home, U-Power, T-Defense, R-Telecom, P-Finance

31. Most experts feel that in spite of possessing all the technical skills required to be a batsman of the highest order, he is unlikely to be so due to lack of requisite temperament. He was guilty of throwing away his wicket several times after working hard to lay a strong foundation. His critics pointed out that until he addressed this problem success at the highest level will continue to elude him.

Which of the statement (s) below is/are logically valid and can be inferred from the above passage?

(i) He was already a successful batsman at the highest level
(ii) He has to improve his temperament in order to become a great batsman
(iii) He failed to make many of his good starts count
(iv) Improving his technical skills will guarantee success

(a) (iii) and (iv) (b) (ii) and (iii)
(c) (i), (ii) and (iii) (d) (ii) only

32. Alexander turned his attention towards India, since he had conquered Persia.

Which one of the statements below is logically valid and can inferred from the above sentence?

(a) Alexander would not have turned his attention towards India had he not conquered Persia.
(b) Alexander was not ready to rest on his laurels, and wanted to march to India
(c) Alexander was completely in control of his army and could command it to move towards India
(d) Since Alexander's kingdom extended to Indian borders after the conquest of Persia, he was keen to move further

33. Tanya is older than Enc.
Cliff is older than Tanya.
Eric is older than Cliff.

If the first two statements are true, then the third statement is

(a) True (b) False
(c) Uncertain (d) Data insufficient

34. Given below are two statements followed by two conclusions. Assuming these statements to be true, decide which one logically follows:

Statements:

I. No manager is a leader.
II. All leaders are executive.

Conclusions:

I. No manager is a executive.
II. All executive is a manager.

(a) Only conclusion I follows.
(b) Only conclusion II follows.
(c) Neither conclusion I nor II follows.
(d) Both conclusion I and II follow.

35. Find the missing sequence in the letter series below :

A, CD, GHI, _?___, UVWXY

(a) LMN (b) MNO
(c) MNOP (d) NOPQ

36. Ms. X will be in Bagdogra from 1/5/14 to 20/5/14 and from 22/5/14 to 31/5/14. On the morning of 21/5/14, she will reach Kochi via Mumbai.

Which one of the statements below is logically valid and can be inferred from the above sentences?

(a) Ms. X will be in Kochi for only one day only in May
(b) Ms. X will be in Kochi for only one day in May
(c) Ms. X will be only in Kochi for one day in May
(d) Only Ms. X will be in Kochi for one day in May

37. Given below are two statements followed by two conclusions. Assuming these statements to be true, decide which one logically follows.

Statement:

I. All film stars are playback singers.

II. All film directors are film stars.

Conclusions:

I. All film directors are playback singers.

II. Some film stars are film directors.

(*a*) Only conclusion I follows

(*b*) Only conclusion II follows

(*c*) Neither conclusion I nor II follows

(*d*) Both conclusions I and II follow

38. Lamenting the gradual sidelining of the arts in school curricula, a group of prominent artists wrote to the Chief Minister last year, asking him to allocate more funds to support arts education in schools. However, no such increase has been announced in this year's Budget. The artists expressed their deep anguish at their request not being approved, but many of them remain optimistic about funding in the future.

Which of the statement(*s*) below is/are logically valid and can be inferred from the above statements?

i. The artists expected funding for the arts to increase this year.

ii. The Chief Minister was receptive to the idea of increasing funding for the arts.

iii. The Chief Minister is a prominent artist.

iv. Schools are giving less importance to arts education nowadays.

(*a*) *iii* and *iv* (*b*) *i* and *iv*

(*c*) *i*, *ii* and *iv* (*d*) *i* and *iii*

39. Four branches of a company are located at M, N, O, and P. M is north of N at a distance of 4 km; P is south of O at a distance of 2 km; N is southeast of O by 1 km. What is the distance between M and P in km?

(*a*) 5.34 (*b*) 6.74

(*c*) 28.5 (*d*) 45.49

40. The given statement is followed by some courses of action. Assuming the statement to be true, decide the correct option.

Statement:

There has been a significant drop in the water level in the lakes supplying water to the city.

Course of action:

I. The water supply authority should impose a partial cut in supply to tackle the situation.

II. The government should appeal to all the residents through mass media for minimal use of water.

III. The government should ban the water supply in lower areas.

(*a*) Statements I and II follow.

(*b*) Statements I and III follow.

(*c*) Statements II and III follow.

(*d*) All statements follow.

2014

41. In a group of four children, Som is younger to Riaz. Shiv is elder to Ansu. Ansu is youngest in the group. Which of the following statements is/are required to find the eldest child in the group?

Statements

1. Shiv is younger to Riaz.

2. Shiv is elder to Som.

(*a*) Statement 1 by itself determines the eldest child.

(*b*) Statement 2 by itself determines the eldest child.

(*c*) Statements 1 and 2 are both required to determine the eldest child.

(*d*) Statements 1 and 2 are not sufficient to determine the eldest child.

42. X is 1 km northeast of Y. Y is 1 km southeast of Z. W is 1 km west of Z. P is 1 km south of W. Q is 1 km east of P. What is the distance between X and Q in km?

(*a*) 1 (*b*) $\sqrt{2}$

(*c*) $\sqrt{3}$ (*d*) 2

43. Rajan was not happy that Sajan decided to do the project on his own. On observing his unhappiness, Sajan explained to Rajan that he preferred to work independently.

Which one of the statements below is logically valid and can be inferred from the above sentences?

(*a*) Rajan has decided to work only in a group.

(*b*) Rajan and Sajan were formed into a group against their wishes.

(*c*) Sajan had decided to give in to Rajan's request to work with him.

(*d*) Rajan had believed that Sajan and he would be working together.

44. Find the odd one in the following group: ALRVX, EPVZB, ITZDF, OYEIK

(*a*) ALRVX

(*b*) EPVZB

(*c*) ITZDF

(*d*) OYEIK

45. Anuj, Bhola, Chandan, Dilip, Eswar and Faisal live on different floors in a six-storeyed building (the ground floor is numbered 1, the floor above it 2, and so on). Anuj lives on an even-numbered floor. Bhola does not live on an odd numbered floor. Chandan does not live on any of the floors below Faisal's floor. Dilip does not live on floor number 2. Eswar does not live on a floor immediately above or immediately below Bhola. Faisal lives three floors above Dilip. Which of the following floor-person combinations is correct?

	Anuj	*Bhola*	*Chandan*	*Dilip*	*Eswar*	*Faisal*
(*a*)	6	2	5	1	3	4
(*b*)	2	6	5	1	3	4
(*c*)	4	2	6	3	1	5
(*d*)	2	4	6	1	3	5

46. Find the next term in the sequence: 13M, 17Q, 19S, ________

(*a*) 21W (*b*) 21V

(*c*) 23W (*d*) 23V

47. If 'KCLFTSB' stands for 'best of luck' and 'SHSWDG' stands for 'good wishes', which of the following indicates 'ace the exam'?

(*a*) MCHTX (*b*) MXHTC

(*c*) XMHCT (*d*) XMHTC

48. "India is a country of rich heritage and cultural diversity."

Which one of the following facts best supports the claim made in the above sentence?

(*a*) India is a union of 28 states and 7 union territories.

(*b*) India has a population of over 1.1 billion.

(*c*) India is home to 22 official languages and thousands of dialects.

(*d*) The Indian cricket team draws players from over ten states.

49. In which of the following options will the expression P < M be definitely true?

(*a*) M < R > P > S (*b*) M > S < P < F

(*c*) Q < M < F = P (*d*) P = A < R < M

50. Find the next term in the sequence: 7G, 11K, 13M, ________

(*a*) 15Q

(*b*) 17Q

(*c*) 15P

(*d*) 17P

51. The multi-level hierarchical pie chart shows the population of animals in a reserve forest. The correct conclusions from this information are:

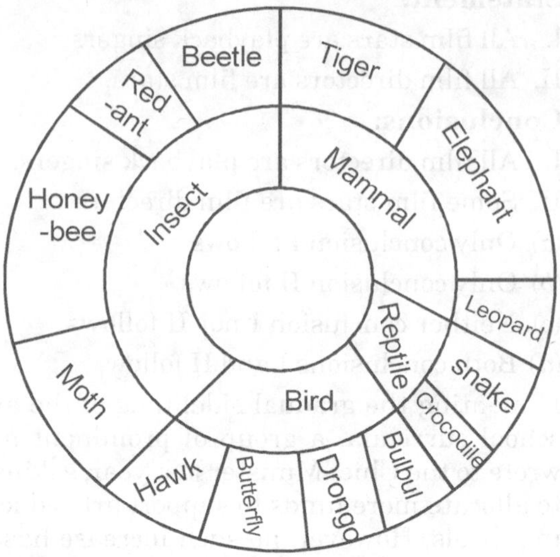

(*i*) Butterflies are birds

(*ii*) There are more tigers in this forest than red ants

(*iii*) All reptiles in this forest are either snakes or crocodiles

(*iv*) Elephants are the largest mammals in this forest

(*a*) (*i*) and (*ii*) only

(*b*) (*i*), (*ii*), (*iii*) and (*iv*)

(*c*) (*i*), (*iii*) and (*iv*) only

(*d*) (*i*), (*ii*) and (*iii*) only

52. Find the odd one in the following group

Q,W,Z,B B,H,K,M W,C,G,J M,S,V,X

(*a*) Q, W, Z, B (*b*) B, H, K, M

(*c*) W, C, G, J (*d*) M, S, V, X

53. Lights of four colors (red, blue, green, yellow) are hung on a ladder. On every step of the ladder there are two lights. If one of the lights is red, the other light on that step will always be blue. If one of the lights on a step is green, the other light on that step will always be yellow. Which of the following statements is not necessarily correct?

(*a*) The number of red lights is equal to the number of blue lights

(*b*) The number of green lights is equal to the number of yellow lights

(*c*) The sum of the red and green lights is equal to the sum of the yellow and blue lights

(*d*) The sum of the red and blue lights is equal to the sum of the green and yellow lights

54. Read the statements:

All women are entrepreneurs.

Some women are doctors.

Which of the following conclusions can be logically inferred from the above statements?

(*a*) All women are doctors

(*b*) All doctors are entrepreneurs

(*c*) All entrepreneurs are women

(*d*) Some entrepreneurs are doctors

55. Find the odd one from the following group:

(*a*) W,E,K,O (*b*) I,Q,W,A

(*c*) F,N,T,X, (*d*) N,V,B,D

56. For submitting tax returns, all resident males with annual income below ₹ 10 lakh should fill up Form P and all resident females with income below ₹ 8 lakh should fill up Form Q. All people with incomes above ₹ 10 lakh should fill up Form R, except non residents with income above ₹ 15 lakhs, who should fill up Form S. All others should fill Form T. An example of a person who should fill Form T is

(*a*) a resident male with annual income ₹ 9 lakh

(*b*) a resident female with annual income ₹ 9 lakh

(*c*) a non-resident male with annual income ₹ 16 lakh

(*d*) a non-resident female with annual income ₹ 16 lakh

57. Which number does not belong in the series below?

2, 5, 10, 17, 26, 37, 50, 64

(*a*) 17 (*b*) 37

(*c*) 64 (*d*) 26

58. A dance programme is scheduled for 10.00 a.m. Some students are participating in the programme and they need to come an hour earlier than the start of the event. These students should be accompanied by a parent. Other students and parents should come in time for the programme. The instruction you think that is appropriate for this is

(*a*) Students should come at 9.00 a.m. and parents should come at 10.00 a.m.

(*b*) Participating students should come at 9.00 a.m. accompanied by a parent, and other parents and students should come by 10.00 a.m.

(*c*) Students who are not participating should come by 10.00 a.m. and they should not bring their parents. Participating students should come at 9.00 a.m.

(*d*) Participating students should come before 9.00 a.m. Parents who accompany them should come at 9.00 a.m. All others should come at 10.00 a.m.

59. The number of people diagnosed with dengue fever (contracted from the bite of a mosquito) in north India is twice the number diagnosed last year. Municipal authorities have concluded that measures to control the mosquito population have failed in this region.

Which one of the following statements, if true, does not contradict this conclusion?

(*a*) A high proportion of the affected population has returned from neighbouring countries where dengue is prevalent

(*b*) More cases of dengue are now reported because of an increase in the Municipal Office's administrative efficiency

(*c*) Many more cases of dengue are being diagnosed this year since the introduction of a new and effective diagnostic test

(*d*) The number of people with malarial fever (also contracted from mosquito bites) has increased this year

60. Geneticists say that they are very close to confirming the genetic roots of psychiatric illnesses such as depression and schizophrenia, and consequently, that doctors will be able to eradicate these diseases through early identification and gene therapy.

On which of the following assumptions does the statement above rely?

(*a*) Strategies are now available for eliminating psychiatric illnesses

(*b*) Certain psychiatric illnesses have a genetic basis

(*c*) All human diseases can be traced back to genes and how they are expressed

(*d*) In the future, genetics will become the only relevant field for identifying psychiatric illnesses

2013

61. Select the pair that best expresses a relationship similar to that expressed in the pair:

Medicine: Health

(*a*) Science : Experiment

(*b*) Wealth : Peace

(*c*) Education : Knowledge

(*d*) Money : Happiness

62. Abhishek is elder to Savar.

Savar is younger to Anshul.

Which of the given conclusions is logically valid and is inferred from the above statements?

(*a*) Abhishek is elder to Anshul

(*b*) Anshul is elder to Abhishek

(*c*) Abhishek and Anshul are of the same age

(*d*) No conclusion follows

63. Complete the sentence:

Universalism is to particularism as diffuseness is to ______

(*a*) specificity
(*b*) neutrality
(*c*) generality
(*d*) adaptation

64. After several defeats in wars, Robert Bruce went in exile and wanted to commit suicide. Just before committing suicide, he came across a spider attempting tirelessly to have its net. Time and again, the spider failed but that did not deter it to retrain from making attempts. Such attempts by the spider made Bruce curious. Thus, Bruce started observing the near-impossible goal of the spider to have the net. Ultimately, the spider succeeded in having its net despite several failures. Such act of the spider encouraged Bruce not to commit suicide. And then, Bruce went back again and won many a battle, and the rest is history.

Which one of the following assertions is best supported by the above information?

(*a*) Failure is the pillar of success.
(*b*) Honesty is the best policy.
(*c*) Life begins and ends with adventures.
(*d*) No adversity justifies giving up hope.

65. Statement: You can always give me a ring whenever you need.

Which one of the following is the best inference from the above statement?

(*a*) Because I have a nice caller tune.
(*b*) Because I have a better telephone facility.
(*c*) Because a friend in need is a friend indeed.
(*d*) Because you need not pay towards the telephone bills when you give me a ring.

66. Statement: There were different streams of freedom movements in colonial India carried out by the moderates, liberals, radicals, socialists, and so on.

Which one of the following is the best inference from the above statement?

(*a*) The emergence of nationalism in colonial India led to our Independence.
(*b*) Nationalism in India emerged in the context of colonialism.
(*c*) Nationalism in India is homogeneous.
(*d*) Nationalism in India is heterogeneous.

67. Select the pair that best expresses a relationship similar to that expressed in the pair :

water : pipe : :

(*a*) cart : road
(*b*) electricity : wire
(*c*) sea : beach
(*d*) music: instrument

68. All professors are researchers

Some scientists are professors

Which of the given conclusions is logically valid and is inferred from the above arguments :

(*a*) All scientists are researchers
(*b*) All professors are scientists
(*c*) Some researchers are scientists
(*d*) No conclusion follows

2012

69. Wanted Temporary, Part-time persons for the post of Field Interviewer to conduct personal interviews to collect and collate economic data. Requirements: High School-pass, must be available for Day, Evening and Saturday work. Transportation paid, expenses reimbursed.

Which one of the following is the best inference from the above advertisement?

(*a*) Gender-discriminatory
(*b*) Xenophobic
(*c*) Not designed to make the post attractive
(*d*) Not gender-discriminatory

70. Given the sequence of terms, AD CG FK JP, the next term is

(*a*) OV (*b*) OW
(*c*) PV (*d*) PW

2011

71. A transporter receives the same number of orders each day. Currently, he has some pending orders (backlog) to be shipped. If he uses 7 trucks, then at the end of the 4th day he can clear all the orders. Alternatively, if he uses only 3 trucks, then all the orders are cleared at the end of the 10th day. What is the minimum number of trucks required so that there will be no pending order at the end of the 5th day?

(*a*) 4
(*b*) 5
(*c*) 6
(*d*) 7

72. Few school curricula include a unit on how to deal with bereavement and grief, and yet all students at some point in their lives suffer from losses through death and parting.

Based on the above passage which topic would not be included in a unit on bereavement?

(*a*) How to write a letter of condolence

(*b*) What emotional stages are passed through in the healing process

(*c*) What the leading causes of death are

(*d*) How to give support to a grieving friend

73. The question below consists of a pair of related words followed by four pairs of words. Select the pair that best expresses the relation in the original pair :

Gladiator : Arena

(*a*) dancer : stage

(*b*) commuter : train

(*c*) teacher : classroom

(*d*) lawyer : courtroom

74. The horse has played a little known but very important role in the field of medicine. Horses were injected with toxins of diseases until their blood built up immunities. Then a serum was made from their blood. Serums to fight with diphtheria and tetanus were developed this way.

It can be inferred from the passage, that horses were

(*a*) given immunity of diseases

(*b*) generally quite immune to diseases

(*c*) given medicines to fight toxins

(*d*) given diphtheria and tetanus serums

2010

75. The question below consists of a pair of related words followed by four pairs of words. Select the pair that best expresses the relation in the original pair.

Unemployed : Worker

(*a*) fallow : land (*b*) unaware : sleeper

(*c*) wit : jester (*d*) renovated : house

76. Hari (H), Gita (G), Irfan (I) and Saira (S) are siblings (i.e. brothers and sisters). All were born on 1st January. The age difference between any two successive siblings (that is born one after another) is less than 3 years. Given the following facts:

I. Hari's age + Gita age > Irfan's age + Saira's age

II. The age difference between Gita and Saira is 1 year. However, Gita is not the oldest and Saira is not the youngest.

III. There are no twins.

In what order were they born (oldest first)?

(*a*) HSIG

(*b*) SGHI

(*c*) IGSH

(*d*) IHSG

77. Modern warfare has changed from large scale clashes of armies to suppression of civilian populations. Chemical agents that do their work silently appear to be suited to such warfare; and regretfully, there exist people in military establishments who think that chemical agents are useful tools for their cause.

Which of the following statements best sums up the meaning of the above passage:

(*a*) Modern warfare has resulted in civil strife

(*b*) Chemical agents are useful in modern warfare

(*c*) Use of chemical agents in warfare would be undesirable

(*d*) People in military establishments like to use chemical agents in war

78. If 137 + 276 = 435 how much is 731 + 672?

(*a*) 534 (*b*) 1403

(*c*) 1623 (*d*) 1513

NUMERICAL TYPE QUESTIONS

2015

1. Fill in the missing value

2014

2. The next term in the series 81, 54, 36, 24,.... is ________

3. Fill in the missing number in the series.

2 3 6 15 ___ 157.5 630

4. What is the next number in the series?

12 35 81 173 357 ____

ANSWERS

MCQ Type Questions

1. (c)	2. (d)	3. (b)	4. (b)	5. (a)	6. (c)	7. (c)	8. (c)	9. (b)	10. (c)
11. (c)	12. (d)	13. (c)	14. (a)	15. (d)	16. (c)	17. (b)	18. (c)	19. (a)	20. (c)
21. (d)	22. (b)	23. (a)	24. (a)	25. (d)	26. (c)	27. (b)	28. (b)	29. (b)	30. (b)
31. (b)	32. (a)	33. (b)	34. (c)	35. (c)	36. (b)	37. (d)	38. (b)	39. (a)	40. (a)
41. (a)	42. (c)	43. (d)	44. (d)	45. (b)	46. (c)	47. (b)	48. (c)	49. (d)	50. (b)
51. (d)	52. (c)	53. (d)	54. (d)	55. (d)	56. (b)	57. (c)	58. (b)	59. (d)	60. (b)
61. (c)	62. (d)	63. (a)	64. (d)	65. (c)	66. (d)	67. (b)	68. (c)	69. (d)	70. (a)
71. (c)	72. (c)	73. (d)	74. (b)	75. (d)	76. (b)	77. (c)	78. (c)		

Numerical Type Questions

1. (3) 2. (16) 3. (45) 4. (725 to 725)

EXPLANATIONS

MCQ TYPE QUESTIONS

1. Given words 'mock, deride and jeer' are synonyms which means mockery. So, the given word praise is odd one.

2. C A D B E, J H K I L

   (+1, +1, +1; +1, +1, +1)

   X V Y W Z, O N P M Q

   (+1, +1, +1; +1, +1, −1)

   So, option (d) is odd one from the given group.

3. The given number 33 is odd one out, because the remaining numbers are prime number.

7. Statements i and ii are not logically possible based on the given fact.

8. Group 'P'

   Mean (μ) = 105

   Standard deviation (σ_1) = 25

   Pr ($\mu - \sigma \le x \le \mu + \sigma$) = 0.6827

   $\therefore$ 68% within one standard deviation

   $$\mu_1 - \sigma_1 = 105 - 25 = 80$$

   $$\mu_1 + \sigma_1 = 105 + 25 = 130$$

   $\therefore$ range = 80 to 130

Distribution of P:

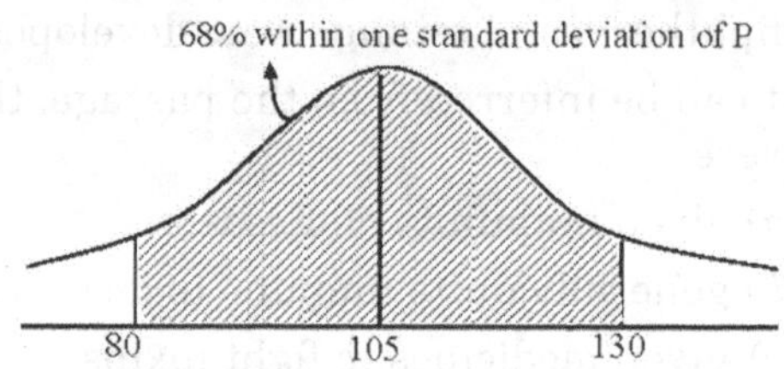

Group 'Q'

Mean (μ_2) = 85

Standard deviation (σ_2) = 5

Pr ($\mu - \sigma \le x \le \mu + \sigma$) = 0.6827

$\therefore$ 68% within one standard deviation

$$\mu_2 - \sigma_2 = 85 - 5 = 80$$

$$\mu_2 + \sigma_2 = 85 + 5 = 90$$

$\therefore$ Range of Q in one standard deviation is 80 to 90

Distribution of 'Q'

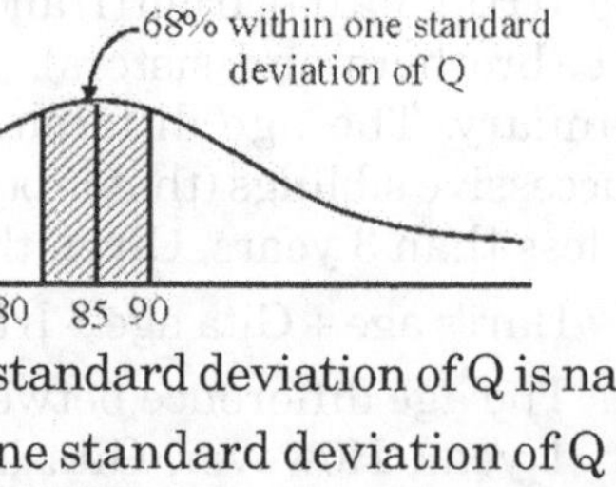

68% within one standard deviation of Q is narrower

$\therefore$ 68% within one standard deviation of Q means most students of group Q.

$\therefore$ Most students of group 'Q' scored marks in a narrower range than students in group 'P'

10. The following letter series is in the order of even letters series

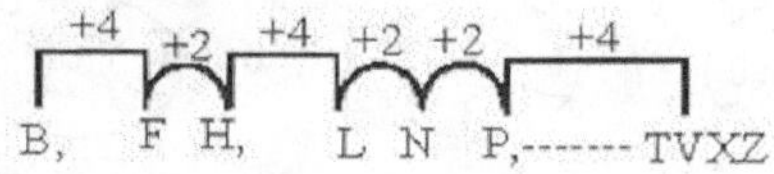

11. From given data, the following diagram can be possible.

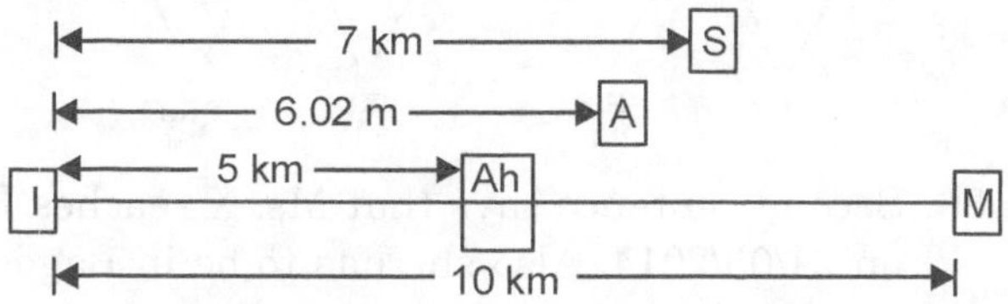

Here S → Susan

A → Arun

Ah → Ahmed

M → Michael

From the above diagram, Arun lives farthest away than Ahmed means more than 5 km but closer than Susan means less than 7 km, from the given alternatives.

So, only option 'c' is possible.

12. From the given question two statements will be followed.

For statment I

Arrange the given data according to their ages

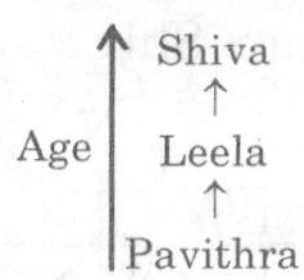

For statement II

Arrange the given data according to their winning

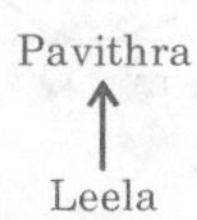

So, from statement I and II, it is clear that only option (*d*) is possible (i.e., statement I).

13.

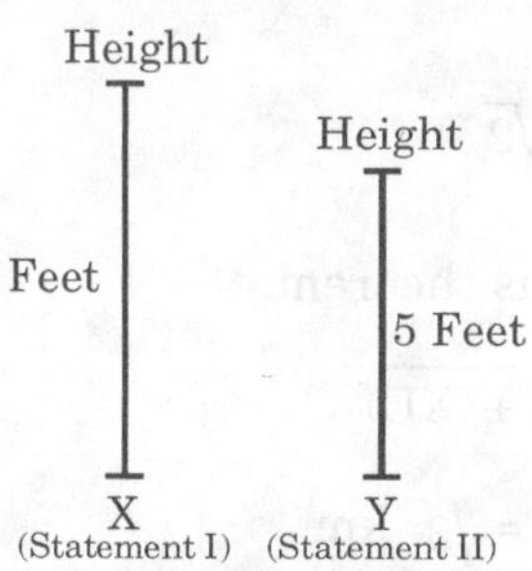

Hence from the given figure Mr. X is taller than Mr. Y by 1 foot.

14. Social science disciplines had a pre-colonial origin.

15.

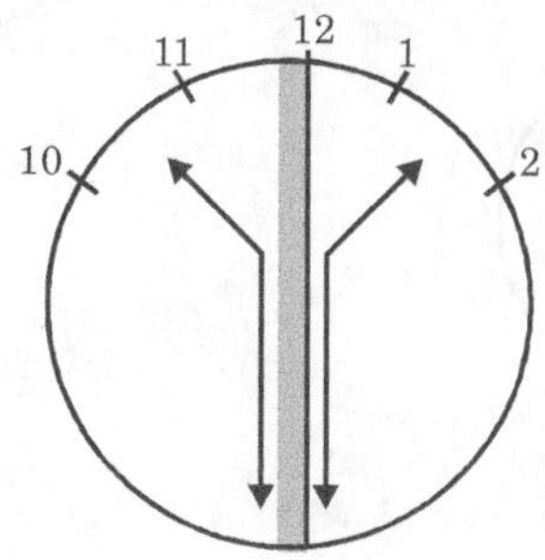

Mirror image of 1 : 20 is 10 : 30

10 : 30 was the time two and quarter hour back so time now will be 12 : 45

16.

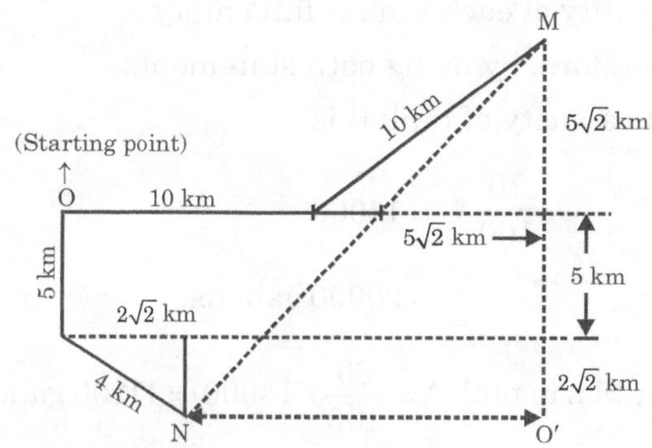

From the given figure

$$MN = \sqrt{(O'M)^2 + (O'N)^2}$$

$$O'M = 5\sqrt{2} + 5 + 2\sqrt{2} = 5 + 7\sqrt{2}$$

$$O'N = 10 + 5\sqrt{2} - 2\sqrt{2} = 10 + 3\sqrt{2}$$

$$MN = \sqrt{(5 + 7\sqrt{2})^2 + (10 + 3\sqrt{2})^2}$$

$$= \sqrt{25 + 98 + 70\sqrt{2} + 100 + 18 + 60\sqrt{2})}$$

$$\approx 20.61 \text{ km}$$

17.

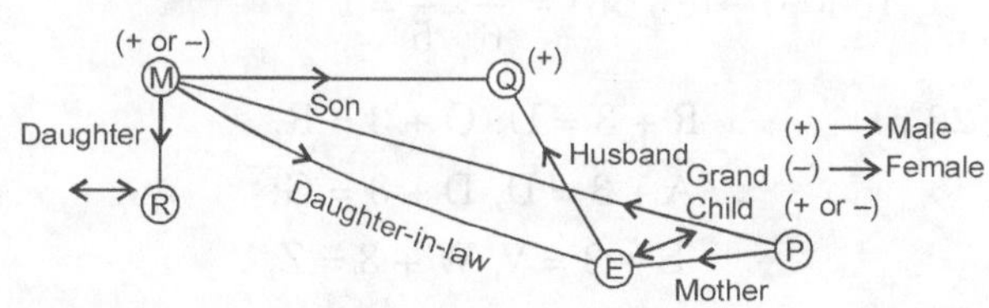

So, from the above relation diagram it is clear that P is the grandchild of M.

20. Manu age = sravan age + 2 months

Manu age = Trideep age – 3 months

Pavan age = Sravan's age + 1 month

From the above statement

Trideep age > Man > Pavan > Sravan

Hence, Trideep can occupy the extra space in the flat.

24.

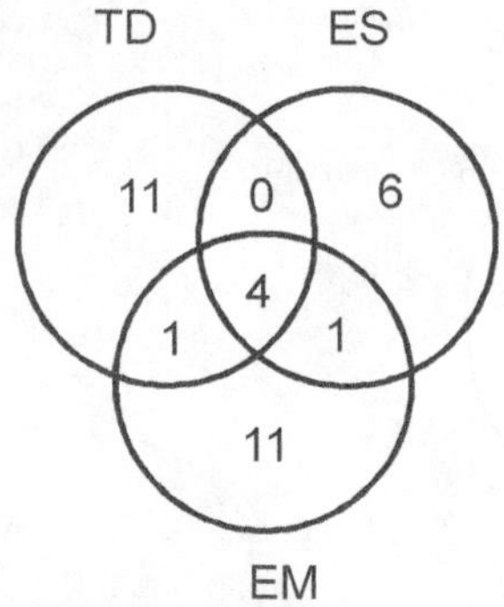

25. Statement-I can be used to solve the question if capacity of both tanks is already known

Statement-II can be used if it is known what quantity of each tank is full/empty.

Therefore, by using both statements

Let capacity of tank B is x

$$\frac{70}{100}x = 14000$$

$$\Rightarrow \quad x = 20000 \text{ gallons}$$

$$\text{Solution in tank A} = \frac{80}{100} \times 14000 = 11200 \text{ gallons}$$

$$\text{Solution in tank B} = \frac{40}{100} \times 20000 = 8000 \text{ gallons}$$

$\therefore$ Total solution = 11200 + 8000 = 19200 gallons

26. $$66 \square 6 = \frac{66-6}{66+6} = \frac{60}{72} = \frac{5}{6}$$

$$66 \diamond 6 = \frac{66+6}{66-6} = \frac{72}{60} = \frac{6}{5}$$

$$(66 \square 6) \rightarrow (66 \diamond 6) = \frac{5}{6} \times \frac{6}{5} = 1$$

28. R + 3 = U, O + 3 = R,
A + 3 = D, D + 3 = G;
S + 3 = V, W + 3 = Z,
A + 3 = D, N + 3 = Q

29. Community of people : Doctor

30. Since U does not want any portfolio, (*c*) and (*d*) are ruled out. R wants Home, or Finance or No portfolio, (*a*) is not valid.

Hence option (*b*) is correct.

34. S + 1: S + 2 :

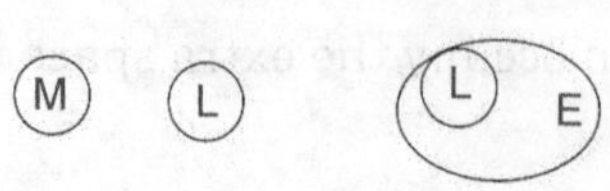

Therefore concluding diagram can be

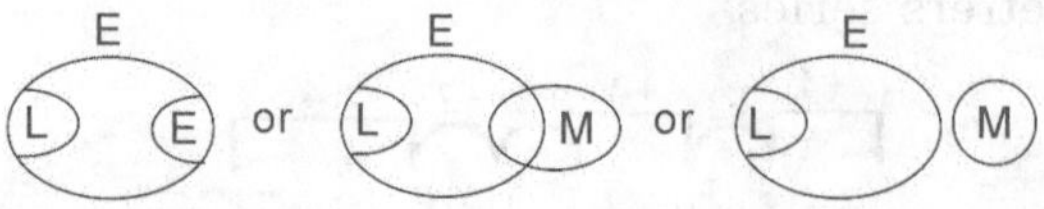

35.

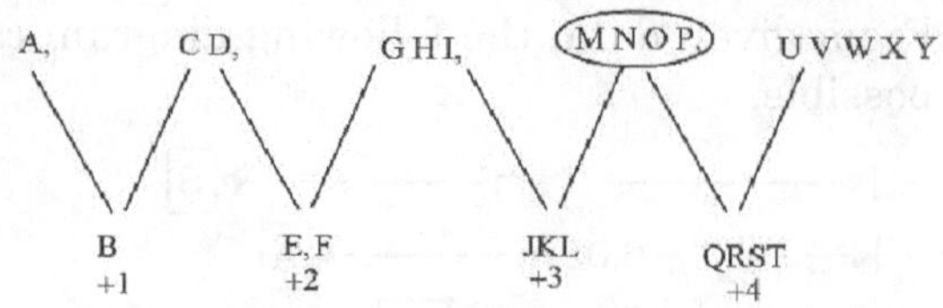

36. Second sentence says that Ms. X reaches Kochi on 21/05/2014. Also she has to be in Bagdogora on 22/05/2014.

$\therefore$ She stays in Kochi for only one day in may.

39.

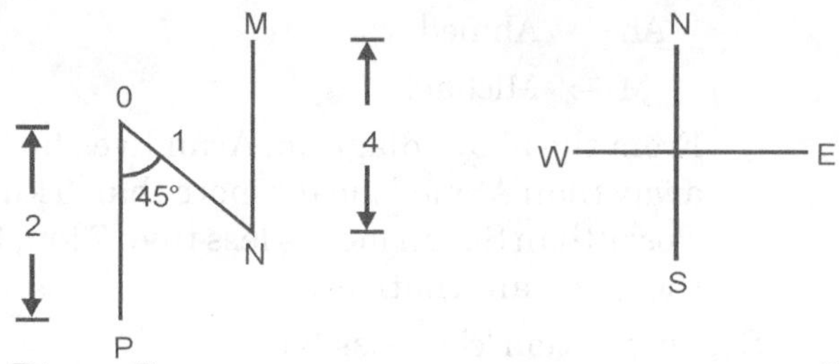

41. Riaz > Som ...(*i*)

Shiv > Ansu ...(*ii*)

Ansu is youngest in the group

$\therefore$ From equations (*i*) and (*ii*)

$\therefore$ Riaz > Som > Shiv > Ansu

42.

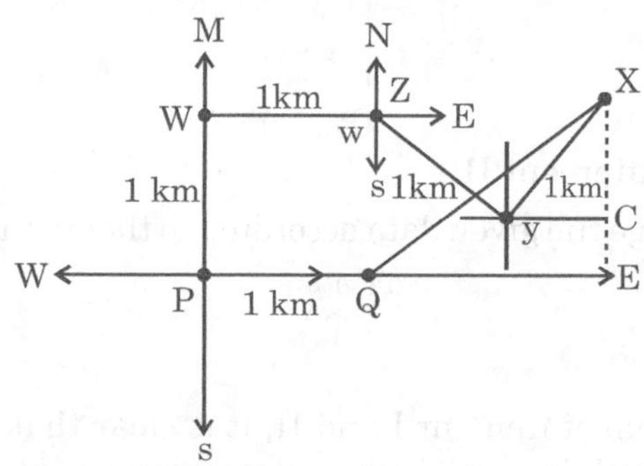

Here XE = 1 km

$$QE = \frac{2}{\sqrt{2}} = \sqrt{2}$$

$\therefore$ using Pythagoras theorem,

$$XQ = \sqrt{(QE)^2 + (XE)^2}$$

$$= \sqrt{2+1} = \sqrt{3} \text{ km}$$

$\therefore$ Statement I itself determines the eldest child which statement 2 is incorrect as Ansu is youngest in the group is not satisfied by statement 2

Hence option (*a*) is correct

44. ALRVX → only one vowel

EPVZB → only one vowel

ITZDF → only one vowel

OYEIK → three vowels

45. (*a*) Anuj: Even numbered floor (2, 4, 6)

(*b*) Bhola: Even numbered floor (2, 4, 6)

(*c*) Chandan lives on the floor above that of Faisal.

(*d*) Dilip: not on 2nd floor.

(*e*) Eswar: does not live immediately above or immediately below Bhola

From the options its clear, that only option (*b*) satisfies condition (*e*).

So, correct Ans is (*b*).

47. KCLFTSB: BST-Best, F-Of, LCK-Luck (Reverse order)

SHSWDG: GD-Good, WSHS-Wishes (Reverse order)

Similarly "ace the Exam'- C-Ace, T-The, XM-Exam

48. Diversity is shown in terms of difference language.

51. It is not mentioned that elephant is the largest animal.

52.

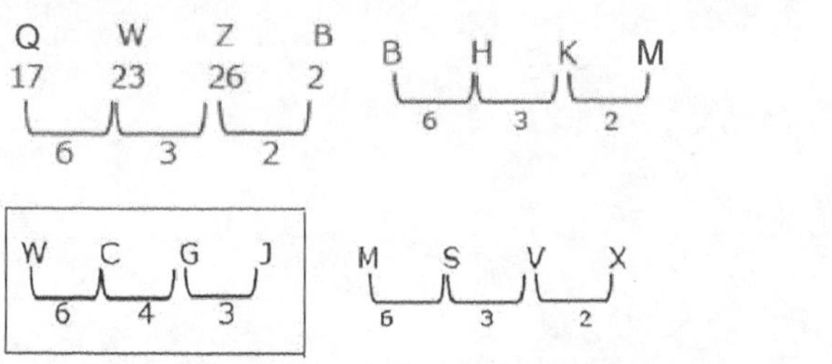

55.

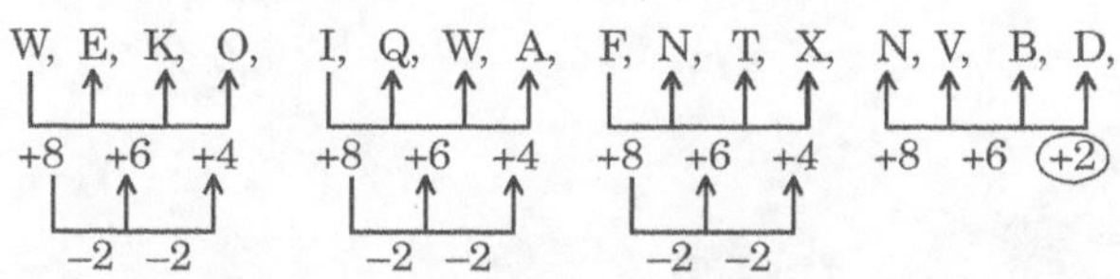

Hence the odd one from the following group is N, V, B, D.

56. By reading the instructions, it is clear that person who fills form T is a resident female with annual income of ₹ 9 Lakh.

59. Among given option, option (*d*) *i.e.* the number of people with malarial fever has increased this year do not contradic the conclusion.

70.

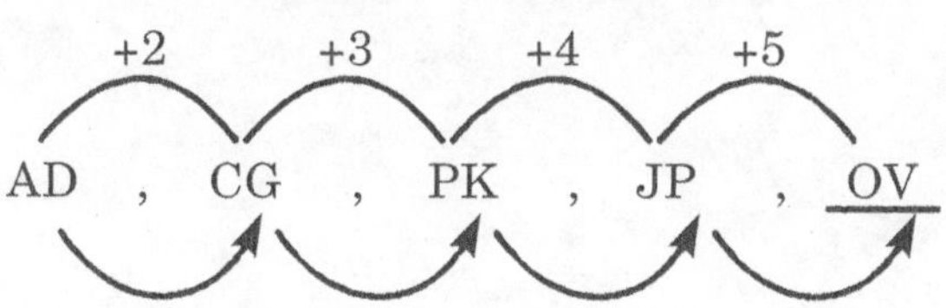

71. Let each truck carry 100 units.

$$2800 = 4n + e$$

where n = normal

$$3000 = 10n + e$$

where e = excess/pending

$$\therefore \quad n = \frac{100}{3}, \quad e = \frac{8000}{3}$$

$$5 \text{ days} \Rightarrow 500\,x = \frac{5100}{3} + \frac{8000}{3}$$

$$\Rightarrow \quad 500x = \frac{8500}{3} = 17$$

$$\Rightarrow \quad x > 5$$

Minimum possible = 6

72. The given passage clearly deals with how to deal with bereavement and grief and so after the tragedy occurs and not about precautions. Therefore, irrespective of the causes of death, a school student rarely gets into details of causes—which is beyond the scope of the context. Rest all are important in dealing with grief.

73. Given relationship is worker: workplace. A gladiator is

(*i*) a person, usually a professional combatant trained to entertain the public by engaging in mortal combat with another person or a wild.

(*ii*) A person engaged in a controversy or debate, especially in public.

74. From the passage it cannot be inferred that horses are given immunity as in option (*a*), since the aim is to develop medicine and in turn immunize humans. Option (*b*) is correct since it is given that horses develop immunity after some time. Refer "until their blood built up immunities". Even option(*c*) is invalid since medicine is not built till immunity is developed in the horses. Option (*d*) is incorrect since specific examples are cited to illustrate and this cannot capture the essence.

76. $H + G > I + S \quad ...(1)$

and $G - S = 1 \quad ...(2)$

G is not oldest, S is not youngest

$\therefore \quad H + 1 > I$

Irfan older than Hari

Gita older than Sarita

From given option SGHI

77. Use of chemical agents in warfare would be undesirable

78. $137 - \overline{001}\ \overline{011}\ \overline{111}$

$+276 - 010\ \ 111\ \ 110$

$\underline{\overline{100}\ \ 011\ \ \overline{101}} = 435$

Octal number system

$\therefore$ $731 - 111\ \ 011\ \ 001$

$672 - 110\ \ 111\ \ 110$

$\underline{\overline{100}}\ \ 010\ \ 011$

Hence 1623

NUMERICAL TYPE QUESTIONS

1. Middle number is the average of number on both sides

$\therefore$ Average of 3 and 3 is $\frac{3+3}{2} = \frac{6}{2} = 3$

2. $81 - 54 = 27;\ 27 \times \frac{2}{3} = 18$

$54 - 36 = 18;\ 18 \times \frac{2}{3} = 12$

$36 - 24 = 12;\ 12 \times \frac{2}{3} = 8$

$\therefore$ $24 - 8 = 16$

3. 2 3 6 15 [45] 157.5 630

1.5 2 2.5 3 3.5 4

$\frac{\text{2nd number}}{\text{1st number}}$ is in increasing order as shown above

4. The given series is

12, 35, 81, 173, 357, ...

The given series follows the following pattern

$12 \times 2 + 11 = 35$

$35 \times 2 + 11 = 81$

$81 \times 2 + 11 = 173$

$173 \times 2 + 11 = 357$

$357 \times 2 + 11 = 725$

Numerical Ability

1 CHAPTER Numbers and Algebra

MCQ TYPE QUESTIONS

2016

1. In a quadratic function, the value of the product of the roots (α, β) is 4. Find the value of

$$\frac{\alpha^n + \beta^n}{\alpha^{-n} + \beta^{-n}}$$

(a) n^4 (b) 4^n

(c) 2^{2n-1} (d) 4^{n-1}

2. Among 150 faculty members in an institute, 55 are connected with each other through Facebook® and 85 are connected through WhatsApp®. 30 faculty members do not have Facebook® or WhatsApp® accounts. The number of faculty members connected only through Facebook® accounts is ________.

(a) 35 (b) 45

(c) 65 (d) 90

3. If $|9y-6| = 3$, then $y^2 - \frac{4y}{3}$ is ________.

(a) 0 (b) $+\frac{1}{3}$

(c) $-\frac{1}{3}$ (d) Undefined

4. If $q^{-a} = \frac{1}{r}$ and $r^{-b} = \frac{1}{s}$ and $s^{-c} = \frac{1}{q}$, the value of abc is .

(a) $(rqs)^{-1}$ (b) 0

(c) 1 (d) r^+q^+s

5. The sum of the digits of a two digit number is 12. If the new number formed by reversing the digits is greater than the original number by 54, find the original number.

(a) 39 (b) 57

(c) 66 (d) 93

6. Two finance companies, P and Q, declared fixed annual rates of interest on the amounts invested with them. The rates of interest offered by these companies may differ from year to year. Year-wise annual rates of interest offered by these companies are shown by the line graph provided below.

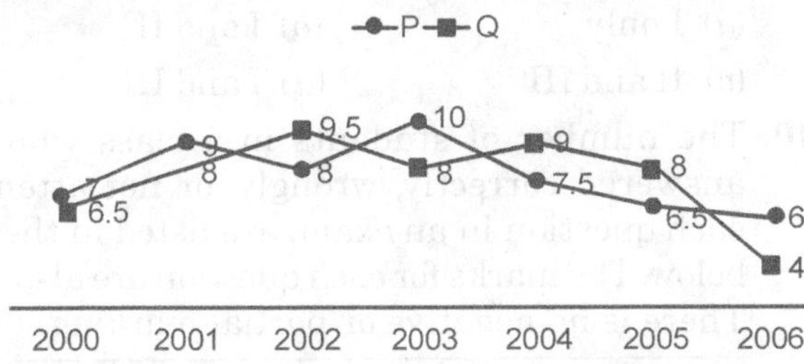

If the amounts invested in the companies, P and Q, in 2006 are in the ratio 8 : 9, then the amounts received after one year as interests from companies P and Q would be in the ratio:

(a) 2 : 3 (b) 3 : 4

(c) 6 : 7 (d) 4 : 3

2015

7. Read the following table giving sales data of five types of batteries for years 2006 to 2012

Year	Type I	Type I	Type I	Type I	Type I
2006	75	144	114	102	108
2007	90	126	102	84	126
2008	96	114	75	105	135
2009	105	90	150	90	75
2010	90	75	135	75	90
2011	105	60	165	45	120
2012	115	85	160	100	145

Out of the following, which type of battery achieved highest growth between the years 2006 and 2012?

(a) Type V (b) Type III

(c) Type II (d) Type I

8. If $a^2 + b^2 + c^2 = 1$, then $ab + bc + ac$ lies in the interval

(a) $\left[1, \frac{2}{3}\right]$

(b) $\left[\frac{-1}{2}, 1\right]$

(c) $\left[-1, \frac{1}{2}\right]$

(d) [2,–4]

9. If the list of letters, P, R, S, T, U is an arithmetic sequence, which of the following are also in arithmetic sequence?

I. 2P, 2R, 2S, 2T, 2U

II. P–3, R–3, S–3, T–3, U–3

III. P^2, R^2, S^2, T^2, U^2

(*a*) I only (*b*) I and II

(*c*) II and III (*d*) I and III

10. The number of students in a class who have answered correctly, wrongly, or not attempted each question in an exam, are listed in the table below. The marks for each question are also listed. There is no negative or partial marking.

Q. No.	Marks	Answered Correctly	Answered Wrongly	Not Attempted
1	2	21	17	6
2	3	15	27	2
3	1	11	29	4
4	2	23	18	3
5	5	31	12	1

What is the average of the marks obtained by the class in the examination?

(*a*) 2.290 (*b*) 2.970

(*c*) 6.795 (*d*) 8.795

2014

11. The monthly rainfall chart on 50 years of rainfall in Agra is shown in the following figure. Which of the following are true? (k percentile is the value such that k percent of the data fall below that value)

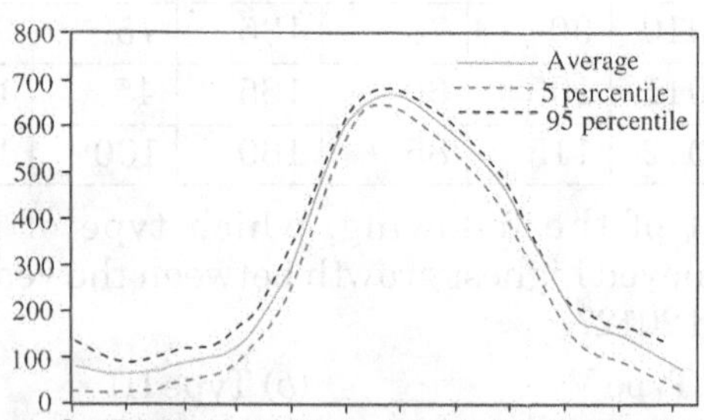

(*i*) On average, it rains more in July than in December

(*ii*) Every year, the amount of rainfall in August is more than that in January

(*iii*) July rainfall can be estimated with better confidence than February rainfall

(*iv*) In August, there is at least 500 mm of rainfall

(*a*) (*i*) and (*ii*)

(*b*) (*i*) and (*iii*)

(*c*) (*ii*) and (*iii*)

(*d*) (*iii*) and (*iv*)

12. The total exports and revenues from the exports of a country are given in the two charts shown below. The pie chart for exports shows the quantity of each item exported as a percentage of the total quantity of exports. The pie chart for the revenues shows the percentage of the total revenue generated through export of each item. The total quantity of exports of all the items is 500 thousand tonnes and the total revenues are 250 crore rupees. Which item among the following has generated the maximum revenue per kg?

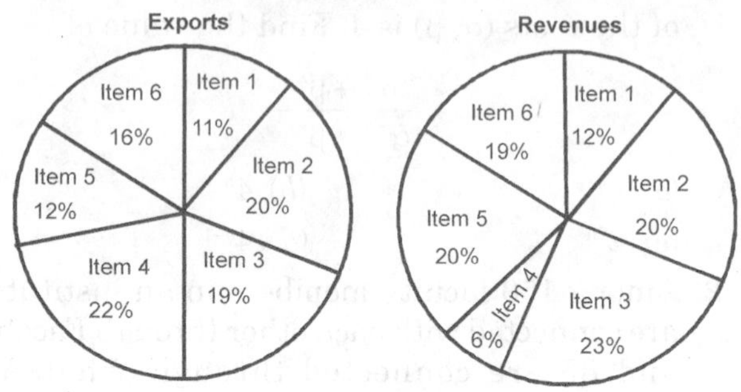

(*a*) Item 2 (*b*) Item 3

(*c*) Item 6 (*d*) Item 5

13. The statistics of runs scored in a series by four batsmen are provided in the following table. Who is the most <u>consistent</u> batsman of these four?

Batsman	Average	Standard deviation
K	31.2	5.21
L	46.0	6.35
M	54.4	6.22
N	17.9	5.90

(*a*) K (*b*) L

(*c*) M (*d*) N

14. The exports and imports (in crores of ₹) of a country from 2000 to 2007 are given in the following bar chart. If the trade deficit is defined as excess of imports over exports, in which year is the trade deficit 1/5th of the exports?

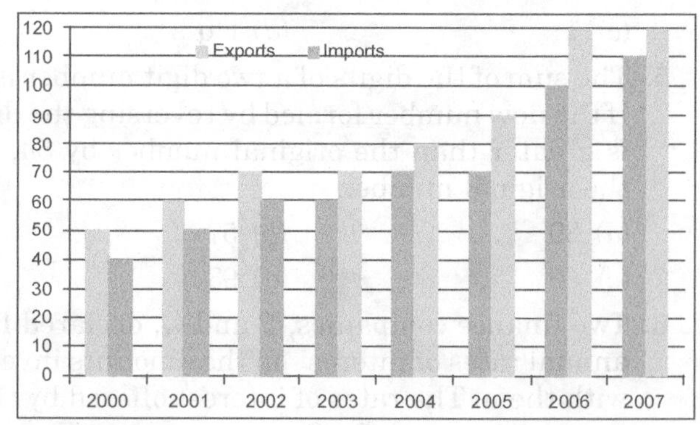

(*a*) 2005

(*b*) 2004

(*c*) 2007

(*d*) 2006

15. The table below has question-wise data on the performance of students in an examination. The marks for each question are also listed. There is no negative or partial marking in the examination.

Q.No.	Marks	Answered Correctly	Answered Wrongly	Not Attempted
1	2	21	17	6
2	3	15	27	2
3	2	23	18	3

What is the average of the marks obtained by the class in the examination?

(*a*) 1.34 (*b*) 1.74

(*c*) 3.02 (*d*) 3.91

16. The ratio of male to female students in a college for five years is plotted in the following line graph. If the number of female students in 2011 and 2012 is equal, what is the ratio of male students in 2012 to male students in 2011?

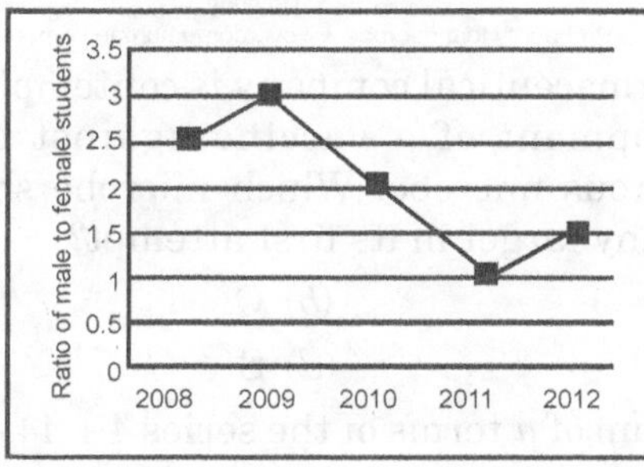

(*a*) 1 : 1 (*b*) 2 : 1

(*c*) 1.5 : 1 (*d*) 2.5 : 1

17. What is the average of all multiples of 10 from 2 to 198?

(*a*) 90 (*b*) 100

(*c*) 110 (*d*) 120

18. The value of $\sqrt{12+\sqrt{12+\sqrt{12+...}}}$ is

(*a*) 3.464 (*b*) 3.932

(*c*) 4.000 (*d*) 4.444

19. If x is real and $|x^2 - 2x + 3| = 11$, then possible values of $|-x^3 + x^2 - x|$ include

(*a*) 2, 4 (*b*) 2, 14

(*c*) 4, 52 (*d*) 14, 52

2013

20. A number is as much greater than 75 as it is smaller than 117. The number is

(*a*) 91

(*b*) 93

(*c*) 89

(*d*) 96

21. Following table provides figures (in rupees) on annual expenditure of a firm for two years - 2010 and 2011.

Category	2010	2011
Raw material	5200	6240
Power & fuel	7000	9450
Salary & wages	9000	12600
Plant & machinery	20000	25000
Advertising	15000	19500
Research & Development	22000	26400

In 2011, which of the following two categories have registered increase by same percentage?

(*a*) Raw material and Salary & wages

(*b*) Salary & wages and Advertising

(*c*) Power & fuel and Advertising

(*d*) Raw material and Research & Development

22. What will be the maximum sum of 44, 42, 40,... ?

(*a*) 502 (*b*) 504

(*c*) 506 (*d*) 500

23. The current erection cost of a structure is ₹ 13,200. If the labour wages per day increase by 1/5 of the current wages and the working hours decrease by 1/24 of the current period, then the new cost of erection in ₹ is

(*a*) 16,500 (*b*) 15,180

(*c*) 11,000 (*d*) 10,120

24. Find the sum of the expression

$$\frac{1}{\sqrt{1}+\sqrt{2}}+\frac{1}{\sqrt{2}+\sqrt{3}}+\frac{1}{\sqrt{3}+\sqrt{4}}+.....+\frac{1}{\sqrt{80}+\sqrt{81}}$$

(*a*) 7 (*b*) 8

(*c*) 9 (*d*) 10

25. In the summer of 2012, in New Delhi, the mean temperature of Monday to Wednesday was 41°C and of Tuesday to Thursday was 43°C. If the temperature on Thursday was 15% higher than that of Monday, then the temperature in °C on Thursday was

(*a*) 40 (*b*) 43

(*c*) 46 (*d*) 49

26. The set of values of p for which the roots of the equation $3x^2 + 2x + p(p - 1) = 0$ are of opposite sign is

(*a*) $(-\infty, 0)$ (*b*) $(0, 1)$

(*c*) $(1, \infty)$ (*d*) $(0, \infty)$

27. Find the sum to n terms of the series 10 + 84 + 734 + ...

(*a*) $\frac{9(9^n+1)}{10}+1$ (*b*) $\frac{9(9^n-1)}{8}+1$

(*c*) $\frac{9(9^n-1)}{8}+n$ (*d*) $\frac{9(9^n-1)}{8}+n^2$

28. If $3 \le X \le 5$ and $8 \le Y \le 11$ then which of the following options is TRUE?

(a) $\frac{3}{5} \le \frac{X}{Y} \le \frac{8}{5}$ (b) $\frac{3}{11} \le \frac{X}{Y} \le \frac{5}{8}$

(c) $\frac{3}{11} \le \frac{X}{Y} \le \frac{8}{5}$ (d) $\frac{3}{5} \le \frac{X}{Y} \le \frac{8}{11}$

29. Following table gives data on tourists from different countries visiting India in the year 2011.

Country	Number of Tourists
USA	2000
England	3500
Germany	1200
Italy	1100
Japan	2400
Australia	2300
France	1000

Which two countries contributed to the one third of the total number of tourists who visited India in 2011?

(a) USA and Japan

(b) USA and Australia

(c) England and France

(d) Japan and Australia

2012

30. If $(1.001)^{1259} = 3.52$ and $(1.001)^{2062} = 7.85$, then $(1.001)^{3321} =$

(a) 2.23 (b) 4.33

(c) 11.37 (d) 27.64

31. Raju has 14 currency notes in his pocket consisting of only ₹ 20 notes and ₹ 10 notes. The total money value of the notes is ₹ 230. The number of ₹ 10 notes that Raju has is

(a) 5 (b) 6

(c) 9 (d) 10

32. The data given in the following table summarizes the monthly budget of an average household.

Category	Amount (Rs.)
Food	4000
Clothing	1200
Rent	2000
Savings	1500
Other expenses	1800

The approximate percentage of the monthly budget **NOT** spent on savings is

(a) 10% (b) 14%

(c) 81% (d) 86%

2011

33. P, Q, R and S are four types of dangerous microbes recently found in a human habitat. The area of each circle with its diameter printed in brackets represents the growth of a single microbe surviving human immunity system within 24 hours of entering the body. The danger to human beings varies proportionately with the toxicity, potency and growth attributed to a microbe shown in the figure below :

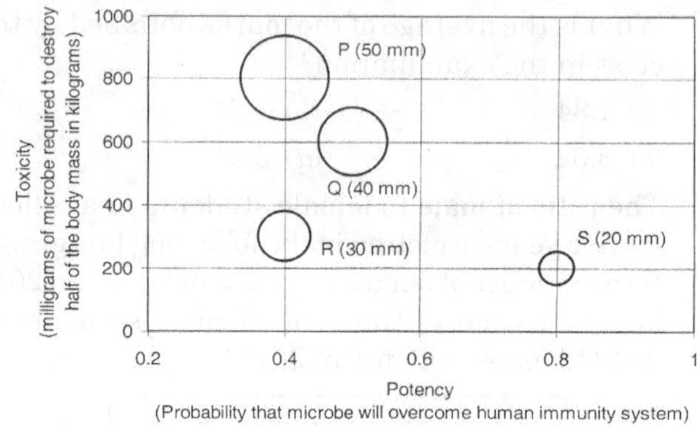

A pharmaceutical company is contemplating the development of a vaccine against the most dangerous microbe. Which microbe should the company target in its first attempt?

(a) P (b) Q

(c) R (d) S

34. The sum of n terms of the series 4 + 44 + 444 + ... is

(a) $(4/81)[10^{n+1} - 9n - 1]$

(b) $(4/81)[10^{n-1} - 9n - 1]$

(c) $(4/81)[10^{n+1} - 9n - 10]$

(d) $(4/81)[10^{n} - 9n - 10]$

35. Given that $f(y) = |y|/y$, and q is any non-zero real number, the value of $|f(q) - f(-q)|$ is

(a) 0 (b) –1

(c) 1 (d) 2

NUMERICAL TYPE QUESTIONS

2016

1. The following graph represents the installed capacity for cement production (in tonnes) and the actual production (in tonnes) of nine cement plants of a cement company. Capacity utilization of a plant is defined as ratio of actual production of cement to installed capacity. A plant with installed capacity of at least 200 tonnes is called a large plant and a plant with lesser capacity is called a small plant. The difference between total production of large plants and small plants, in tonnes is _______.

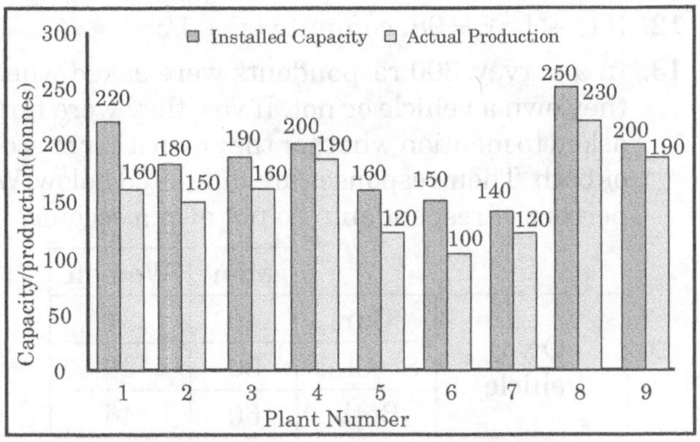

2. The numeral in the units position of

$211^{870} + 146^{127} \times 3^{424}$ is ________.

2015

3. The exports and imports (in crores of Rs.) of a country from the year 2000 to 2007 are given in the following bar chart. In which year is the combined percentage increase in imports and exports the highest ?

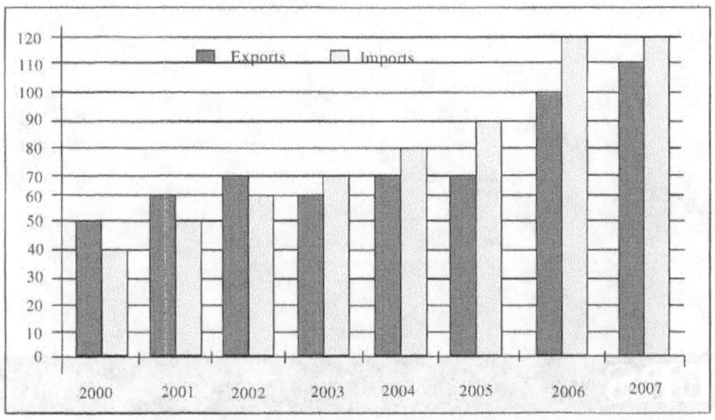

4. The pie chart below has the breakup of the number of students from different departments in an engineering college for the year 2012. The proportion of male to female students in each department is 5 : 4. There are 40 males in Electrical Engineering. What is the difference between numbers of female students in the Civil department and the female students in the Mechanical department?

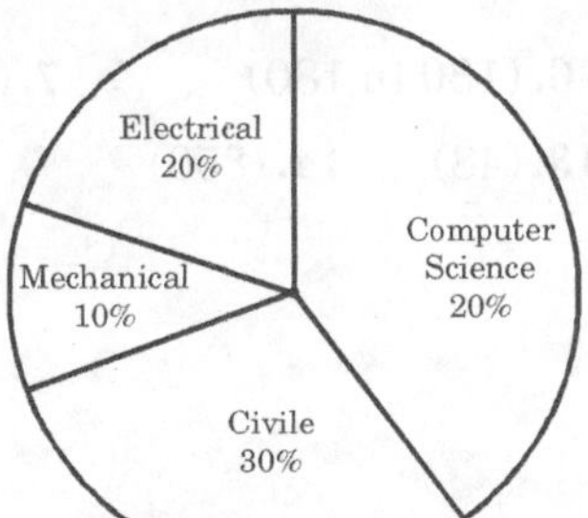

2014

5. A foundry has a fixed daily cost of ₹ 50,000 whenever it operates and variable cost of ₹ 800Q, where Q is the daily production in tonnes. What is the cost of production in ₹ per tonne for a daily production of 100 tonnes?

6. The smallest angle of a triangle is equal to two thirds of the smallest angle of a quadrilateral. The ratio between the angles of the quadrilateral is 3 : 4 : 5 : 6. The largest angle of the triangle is twice its smallest angle. What is the sum, in degrees, of the second largest angle of the triangle and the largest angle of the quadrilateral?

7. In a sequence of 12 consecutive odd numbers, the sum of the first 5 numbers is 425. What is the sum of the last 5 numbers in the sequence?

8. A firm producing air purifiers sold 200 units in 2012. The following pie chart presents the share of raw material, labour, energy, plant & machinery, and transportation costs in the total manufacturing cost of the firm in 2012. The expenditure on labour in 2012 is ₹ 4,50,000. In 2013, the raw material expenses increased by 30% and all other expenses increased by 20%. What is the percentage increase in total cost for the company in 2013?

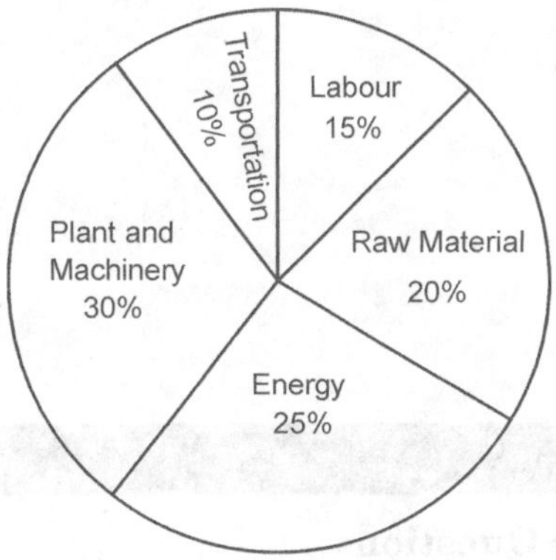

9. A firm producing air purifiers sold 200 units in 2012. The following pie chart presents the share of raw material, labour, energy, plant & machinery, and transportation costs in the total manufacturing cost of the firm in 2012. The expenditure on labour in 2012 is ₹ 4,50,000. In 2013, the raw material expenses increased by 30% and all other expenses increased by 20%. If the company registered a profit of ₹ 10 lakhs in 2012, at what price (in ₹) was each air purifier sold?

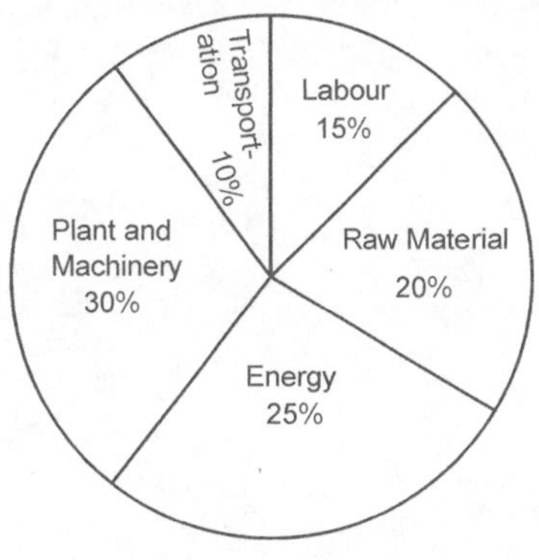

10. The sum of eight consecutive odd numbers is 656. The average of four consecutive even numbers is 87. What is the sum of the smallest odd number and second largest even number?

11. The ratio of male to female students in a college for five years is plotted in the following line graph. If the number of female students doubled in 2009, by what percent did the number of male students increase in 2009?

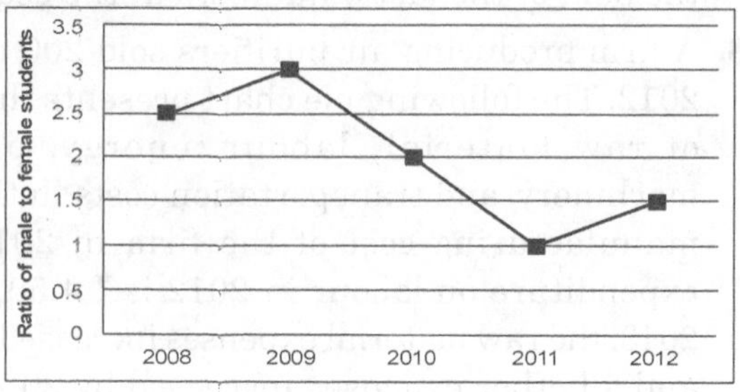

12. If $(z + 1/z)^2 = 98$, compute $(z^2 + 1/z^2)$

13. In a survey, 300 respondents were asked whether they own a vehicle or not. If yes, they were further asked to mention whether they own a car or scooter or both. Their responses are tabulated below. What percent of respondents do not own a scooter?

		Men	Women
Own vehicle	Car	40	34
	Scooter	30	20
	Both	60	46
Do not own vehicle		20	50

14. Round–trip tickets to a tourist destination are eligible for a discount of 10% on the total fare. In addition, groups of 4 or more get a discount of 5% on the total fare. If the one way single person fare is ₹ 100, a group of 5 tourists purchasing round–trip tickets will be charged ₹ ________.

ANSWERS

MCQ Type Questions

1. (*b*) 2. (*a*) 3. (*c*) 4. (*c*) 5. (*a*) 6. (*d*) 7. (*d*) 8. (*b*) 9. (*b*) 10. (*c*)
11. (*b*) 12. (*d*) 13. (*a*) 14. (*d*) 15. (*c*) 16. (*c*) 17. (*b*) 18. (*c*) 19. (*d*) 20. (*d*)
21. (*d*) 22. (*c*) 23. (*a*) 24. (*b*) 25. (*c*) 26. (*b*) 27. (*d*) 28. (*b*) 29. (*c*) 30. (*d*)
31. (*a*) 32. (*d*) 33. (*d*) 34. (*c*) 35. (*d*)

Numerical Type Questions

1. (120) 2. (7) 3. (2006) 4. (32) 5. (1300 to 1300) 6. (180 to 180) 7. (495) 8. (22)
9. (20,000) 10. (163) 11. (140 to 140) 12. (96) 13. (48) 14. (850)

EXPLANATIONS

MCQ TYPE QUESTIONS

1. $\dfrac{\alpha^n+\beta^n}{\alpha^{-n}+\beta^{-n}} = \dfrac{\alpha^n+\beta^n}{\dfrac{1}{\alpha^n}+\dfrac{1}{\beta^n}} = \dfrac{\alpha^n+\beta^n}{\dfrac{\beta^n+\alpha^n}{\alpha^n\times\beta^n}} = \alpha^n\times\beta^n$

$\alpha^n \times \beta^n = (\alpha\times\beta)^n = (4)^n$

So, the value of $\dfrac{\alpha^n+\beta^n}{\alpha^{-n}+\beta^{-n}}$ is 4^n.

2. From question

Total number of faculty members = 150

The number of faculty members having facebook account = (FB) = 55

The number of faculty members having whatsapp = (W) = 85

The number of faculty members do not have face book or Whats App accounts = 30

The number of faculty members having any account = 150 – 30 = 120

The number of faculty members having both the accounts = (FB + W) – 120 = (55 + 85) – 120 = 20

∴ The number of faculty members connected only through Facebook accounts = 55 – 20 = 35

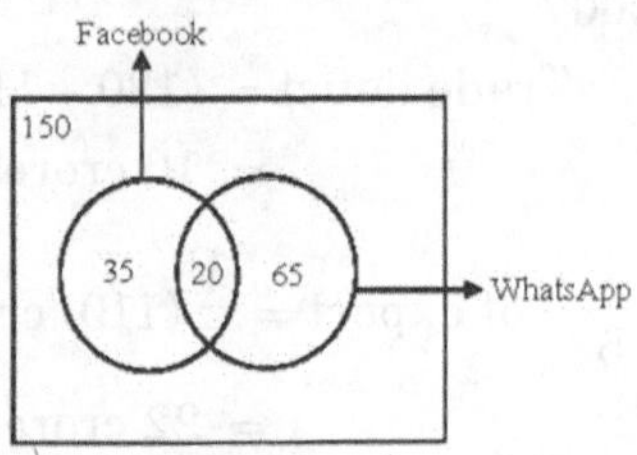

So the number of faculty members connected only through facebook accounts is 35.

3. Given, $|9y-6| = 3$

It has two values either

$(9y-6) = 3$ ...(i)

Or $-(9y-6) = 3$

$9y-6 = -3$ ...(ii)

From equation (i),

$9y = 9$

∴ $y = 1$

Or from equation (ii),

$9y = 3$

∴ $y = \dfrac{1}{3}$

Now $y^2 = \dfrac{4y}{3}$

put $y = 1$,

we get $= 1-\dfrac{4}{3} = -\dfrac{1}{3}$

and also put $y = \dfrac{1}{3}$

we get, $\dfrac{1}{9}-\dfrac{4}{9} = \dfrac{-3}{9} = \dfrac{-1}{3}$

So, the required value is $\dfrac{-1}{3}$.

4. Given $q^{-a} = \dfrac{1}{r}$

$\Rightarrow \dfrac{1}{q^a} = \dfrac{1}{r}$

$\Rightarrow q^a = r$ ...(i)

$r^{-b} = \dfrac{1}{s}$

$\Rightarrow \dfrac{1}{r^b} = \dfrac{1}{s}$

$\Rightarrow s = r^b$ ...(ii)

$s^{-c} = \dfrac{1}{q}$

$\Rightarrow \dfrac{1}{s^c} = \dfrac{1}{q}$

$\Rightarrow s^c = q$ ...(iii)

From equation (i),

$q^a = r$

$(s^c)^a = r$ (from eq. (iii))

$S^{ac} = r$

$S^{ac} = (s)^{\frac{1}{b}}$ (from eq. (ii))

$S^{abc} = S = S^1$

∴ $abc = 1$

So the value of abc is 1

5. Let the two digit number be xy

Now sum of the digit of a two digit number is 12

∴ $x + y = 12$ ...(i)

Now according to question,

$(10y + x) - (10x + y) = 54$

∴ $9y - 9x = 54$

∴ $y - x = 6$ ...(ii)

Now solving equation (i) and (ii) we get,

$x = 3$ and $y = 9$

Hence the original number is 39.

∴ Option (a) is correct.

6. Amount invested by Company P in 2006 = ₹ 8x

and amount invested by Company Q in 2006 = ₹ $9x$

Interest from Company P

$$= \frac{\frac{₹\, 8x \times 6}{100}}{\frac{₹\, 9x \times 4}{100}} = \frac{4}{3}$$

∴ Option (d) is correct.

7. Type-I achieved a growth of 53% in the period which is higher than any other type of battery

10. Total number of students in class = 44

Average of marks,

$$= \frac{(2\times 21)+(3\times 15)+(1\times 11)+(2\times 23)+(5\times 31)}{42}$$

$$= \frac{42+45+11+46+155}{44} = \frac{299}{44} = 6.795$$

∴ Option (c) is correct.

11. In the question the monthly average rainfall chart for 50 years has been given.

Let us check the options.

(i) On average, it rains more in July than in December ⇒ correct.

(ii) Every year, the amount of rainfall in August is more than that in January.

⇒ may not be correct because average rainfall is given in the question.

(iii) July rainfall can be estimated with better confidence than February rainfall.

⇒ From chart it is clear the gap between 5 percentile and 95 percentile from average is higher in February than that in July ⇒ correct.

(iv) In August at least 500 mm rainfall

⇒ May not be correct, because its 50 year average.

So correct option (b) (i) and (iii).

12. Item : 2

$$\frac{\frac{20}{100}\times 250\times 10^7}{\frac{20}{100}\times 500\times 10^3}$$

$0.5\times 10^4 = 5\times 10^3$ $\boxed{1}$ = Item 2

Item : 3

$$\frac{23\times 250\times 10^7}{19\times 500\times 10^3}$$

1.2 = Item 3

Item : 6

$\frac{19}{16} = 1.18 = \text{Item 6}$

Item : 5

$\frac{20}{12} = \frac{5}{3} = 1.6 \Rightarrow \boxed{1.6 = \text{Item 5}}$

14. For 2005,

trade defict = (90 – 70) crores = 20 crores

Now $\frac{1}{5}^{\text{th}}$ of export = $\frac{1}{5}$(70) crores

= 14 crores ≠ 20 crores.

Hence option (a) is wrong.

For 2004,

Trade defict =(80 – 70) crores = 10 crores

Now $\frac{1}{5}^{\text{th}}$ of export = $\frac{1}{5}$(70) crores

= 14 crores ≠ 20 crores.

Hence option (b) is wrong.

For 2007

Trade defict = (120 – 110) crores

= 10 crores

Now $\frac{1}{5}^{\text{th}}$ of export = $\frac{1}{5}$(110) crores

= 22 crores ≠ 10 crores.

Hence option (c) is wrong.

For 2006,

Trade defict = (120 – 100) crores

= 20 crores

Now $\frac{1}{5}^{\text{th}}$ of export = $\frac{1}{5}$(100) crores

= 20 crores = Trade deficts

Hence option (d) is correct.

15. Total question

44 × 2 = 88

44 × 3 = 132

$\frac{144}{132} = \frac{88}{308}$

Total marks obtained = (21×2) + (15×3) + (23×2)

= 133

Total Number of students = 44

$$\text{Average} = \frac{133}{44} = 3.02$$

16. Take number of female students in 2011 = 100

$\therefore$ Number of male in 2011 = 100

No. of female in 2012 = 100

No. of male in 2012 = 150

$$\text{Ratio} = \frac{150}{100}$$

17. All multiples of 10 from 2 to 198

$$= 10, 20, \ldots\ldots\ldots\ldots 190$$

Now
$$a_n = a + (n-1)d$$
$$190 = 10 + (n-1) \times 10$$
$$180 = (n-1) \times 10$$
$$18 = n - 1$$
$$\therefore \quad n = 19$$

Hence total number of multiples are 19.

Now
$$S_n = \frac{n}{2}[2a + (n-1)d]$$
$$= \frac{19}{2}[20 + (18)(10)]$$
$$= \frac{19}{2}[20 + 180] = 1900$$

Now average of all multiples of 10 from 2 to198

$$= \frac{10 + 20 + \ldots + 190}{19}$$
$$\therefore \quad = \frac{1900}{19} = 100$$

18. $\sqrt{12 + \sqrt{12 + \sqrt{12 + \ldots}}}$

For a particular type of question

i.e. $\sqrt{a + \sqrt{a + \sqrt{a + \ldots}}}$ we find a two consecutive number whose product is a. The greater number among the two consecutive number is the answer.

Here $a = 12$

i.e. $12 = 3 \times 4$
↓
greater number

Hence $\sqrt{12 + \sqrt{12 + \sqrt{12 + \ldots}}} = 4$

19. Here it is given that x is real

Now $|x^2 - 2x + 3| = 11$

$\Rightarrow \quad x^2 - 2x + 3 = 11$ or $x^2 - 2x + 3 = -11$

For $x^2 - 2x + 3 = 11 \Rightarrow x^2 - 2x - 8 = 0$

$$b^2 - 4ac = 4 - 4(1)(-8) = 36 > 0$$

Hence roots are real.

and for $x^2 - 2x + 14 = 0$

$$b^2 - 4ac = 4 - 4(1)(14) < 0$$

Hence roots are imaginary

$\therefore$ The value of x is the root of $x^2 - 2x - 8 = 0$

Now
$$x = \frac{+2 \pm \sqrt{4 - 4(1)(-8)}}{2}$$
$$= \frac{2 \pm \sqrt{36}}{2}$$
$$= \frac{2 \pm 6}{2}$$
$$\therefore \quad x = 4, -2.$$

Now for $x = 4$,

$$|-x^3 + x^2 - x| = |-64 + 16 - 4| = 52.$$

and for $x = -2$

$$|-x^3 + x^2 - x| = |+8 + 4 + 2| = 14$$

Hence possible values of $|-x^3 + x^2 - x| = 14, 52$

22.
$$0 = 44 + (n-1)(-2)$$
$$n - 1 = 22$$
$$n = 23$$

Sum
$$= \frac{n}{2}(a + l)$$
$$= \frac{23}{2}(44 + 0)$$
$$= 23 \times 22 = 506$$

Hence (c) is the answer

23. Let 'd' be the # of days required

Let 'h' be the daily working hours.

$\therefore$ dh can be taken as a measure of the total work be done in order to erect the structure.

Now working hours per day $h' = \frac{23}{24}h$

$\therefore$ # of days $\quad d' = \frac{dh}{h'} = \frac{dh}{\left(\frac{23}{24}h\right)} = \frac{24}{23}d$

Let $\quad c$ = daily wages earlier

$$\therefore \quad c = \frac{13{,}200}{d}$$

Now daily wages $c' = \frac{6}{5}c$

$\therefore$ Total new cost $= c' \times d'$

$$= \frac{6}{5} \times \frac{13200}{d} \times \frac{24}{23}d \approx 16{,}500$$

24. Given: The expression

$$S = \frac{1}{\sqrt{1}+\sqrt{2}} + \frac{1}{\sqrt{2}+\sqrt{3}} + ... + \frac{1}{\sqrt{80}+\sqrt{81}}$$

To find: Sum of the expression.

Analysis: Each term of the expression is having irrational denominator. One can also see, that both the elements in the denominator of a term differ by only 1.

This gives an idea that on rationalising the denominator, each denominator will become 1, so the sum will be easier than earlier.

Rationalising the denominator,

$$S = \frac{\sqrt{2}-\sqrt{1}}{(\sqrt{2})^2-(\sqrt{1})^2} + \frac{\sqrt{3}-\sqrt{2}}{(\sqrt{3})^2-(\sqrt{2})^2} + ... + \frac{\sqrt{81}-\sqrt{80}}{(\sqrt{81})^2-(\sqrt{80})^2}$$

$$= \frac{\sqrt{2}-\sqrt{1}}{1} + \frac{\sqrt{3}-\sqrt{2}}{3-2} + ... + \frac{\sqrt{81}-\sqrt{80}}{81-80}$$

$$= \sqrt{2}-\sqrt{1}+\sqrt{3}-\sqrt{2}+....+81-\sqrt{80}$$

Now, one can see that the terms will cancel out.

Each term except $\sqrt{1}$ & $\sqrt{81}$

Occurs twice, once as positive and once a negative. So, after cancelling out, we are left with the following:

$$S = \sqrt{81}-\sqrt{1} = 9 - 1 = 8$$

So, the answer is (*b*).

25. $\frac{\text{Mon + Tues + Wed.}}{3} = 41$

Mon + Tues + Wed. = 123 ...(1)

$\frac{\text{Tues + Wed + Thurs.}}{3} = 43°$

Tue + Wed + Thu. = 129° ...(2)

(2) – (1)

Tues + Wed + Thu – (Mon + Tues. + Wed.)

= 129 – 123 = 6°

Thu. – Mon. = 6° ⇒ $\frac{115x}{100} - x = 6°$

Thus. = Mon × $\frac{115}{100} = \frac{15x}{100} = 6°$

Mon = x $x = 40°$

Thurs = $\frac{115x}{100}$

∴ Thurs = $\frac{115 \times 40}{100} = 46°$

30. Let $1.001 = x$

$x^{1259} = 3.52$, and $x^{2062} = 7.85$

∴ $x^{3321} = x^{1259} . x^{2062}$

= 3.52 × 7.85

= 27.64

31. Let number of ₹ 20 notes be x and ₹ 10 notes be y

∴ $20x + 10y = 230$ ...(1)

and $x + y = 14$ ...(2)

Solving equations (1) and (2), we have

$x = 9$ and $y = 5$

Hence numbers of 10 rupee notes are 5.

32. Total budget = 10,500

Expenditure other than savings = 9000

Hence approximate percentage of monthly budget

$$= \frac{9000}{10500} = 86\%$$

33. By observation of the table, we can say S

	P	Q	R	S
Requirement	800	600	300	200
Potency	0.4	0.5	0.4	0.8

34. Let S = 4 (1 + 11 + 111 + ...)

$$= \frac{4}{9}(9 + 99 + 999 + ...)$$

$$= \frac{4}{9}\{(10-1)+(10^2-1)+(10^3-1)+ .... \}$$

$$= \frac{4}{9}\{(10+10^2+....+10^n)-n\}$$

$$= \frac{4}{9}\left\{10\frac{(10^n-1)}{9}-n\right\}$$

$$= \frac{4}{81}\{10^{n+1}-9n-10\}$$

35. Given : $f(y) = \frac{|y|}{y}$

$$\Rightarrow f(q) = \frac{|q|}{q}$$

$$f(-q) = \frac{|-q|}{-q}$$

$$= \frac{-|q|}{q}$$

$$|f(q) - f(q)| = \frac{|q|}{q} + \frac{|q|}{q}$$

$$= \frac{2|q|}{q} = 2$$

NUMERICAL TYPE QUESTIONS

1. From the given graph large plants which are having installed capacity of at least 200 tonnes are 1, 4, 8 and 9.

So, the total production of large plants

$= 160 + 190 + 230 + 190$

$= 770$

Now the remaining plants with installed capacity is less then 200 tonnes are 2, 3, 5, 6 and 7.

So, total production of small plants

$= 150 + 160 + 120 + 100 + 120$

$= 650$

Then difference $= 770 - 650$

$= 120$

2. Unit digit of $211^{870} + 146^{127} \times 3^{424}$ is $1 + 6 \times 1 = 7$

3. Increase in exports in 2006

$$= \frac{100-70}{70} = 42.8\%$$

Increase in imports in 2006

$$= \frac{120-90}{90} = 33.3\%$$

which is more than any other year.

4. According to question,

There are 40 males in Electrical Engg.

$\therefore$ Total number of females in Electrical Engg.

$= 72 - 40 = 32$

$\therefore$ Total number of students in Electrical Engg. = 72

$\Rightarrow$ 20% = 72

$\therefore$ 30% = Total number of students in Civil Engg.

$\therefore$ Total number of students in Civil Engg.

$$= \frac{30 \times 72}{20} = 36 \times 3 = 108$$

$\therefore$ Number of female students in Civil Engg.

$$= \frac{4 \times 108}{9} = 4 \times 12 = 48$$

Now, total number of students in Mechanical Engg.

$$= \frac{10 \times 72}{20} = 36$$

$\therefore$ Number of female students in Mechanical Engg.

$$= \frac{4 \times 36}{9} = 16$$

$\therefore$ Difference between female students in Civil and Mechanical departments $= 48 - 16 = 32$

5. Fixed cost = ₹ 50,000

Variable cost = ₹ 800Q

Q = daily production in tones

For 100 tonnes of production daily, total cost of production $= 50{,}000 + 800 \times 100 = 130{,}000$

So, cost of production per tonne of daily production

$$= \frac{130{,}000}{100} = ₹\ 1300.$$

6. Let the angles of quadrilateral are $3x$, $4x$, $5x$, $6x$

So, $3x + 4x + 5x + 6x = 360$

$x = 20$

Smallest angle of quadrilateral $= 3 \times 20 = 60°$

Smallest angle of triangle $= \frac{2}{3} \times 60° = 40°$

Largest angle of triangle $= 2 \times 40° = 60°$

Three angles of triangle are 40°, 60°, 80°

Largest angle of quadrilateral is 120°

Sum (2nd largest angle of triangle + largest angle of quadrilateral) = 60° + 120° = 180°.

7. 8th observation is $7 \times 2 = 14$ more than 1st observation

9th observation is 14 more than 2nd observation

10th observation is 14 more than 3rd observation

11th observation is 14 more than 4th observation

12th observation is 14 more than 5th observation

Total $14 \times 5 = 70$

Sum of the first five numbers = 425

Sum of last five numbers = 495

8.

	2012	2013
Transport (10%)	300,000	360,000
Labour (15%)	450,000	540,000
Raw material (20%)	750,000	780,000
Energy (25%)	750,000	900,000
Plant and Machinery (30%)	900,000	1,080,000
Total	**3,000,000**	**3,660,000**

Percentage increase in total cost = 22%

9. Total expenditure $= \frac{15}{100} x = 4{,}50{,}000$

$x = 3 \times 10^6$

Profit = 10 lakhs

So, total selling price = 40,00,000 ...(1)

Total purifies = 200 ...(2)

S.P. of each purifier = (1)/(2) = 20,000

10. Eight consecutive odd number = 656

$a - 6, a - 1, a - 2, a, a + 2, a + 4, a + 6$

$a + 8 = 656$

$a = 81$

Smallest $m = 75$ ...(1)

Average consecutive even numbers

$$\Rightarrow \frac{a-2+a+a+2+a+4}{4} = 87$$

$\Rightarrow a = 86$

Second largest number = 88 ...(2)

Adding equation (1) and (2),

$75 + 88 = 163$

11. Ratio of male to female student in 2008 = 5 : 2

In 2009, let the male student be $5x$ and female student be $2x$

Now if number of female students double in 2009

$\therefore$ Number of female student = $4x$

$\therefore$ Number of male student = $12x$

Gender	2008	2009
Male	$5x$	$12x$
Female	$2x$	$4x$

% of male student increase in 2009

$$= \left[\left(\frac{12x-5x}{5x}\right)\times 100\right]\%$$

$$= \left[\frac{7}{5}\times 100\right]\%$$

$= 140\%$

12. Expanding

$$\left(z+\frac{1}{z}\right)^2 = 98$$

$$\therefore \quad z^2+\frac{1}{z^2}+2(z)\left(\frac{1}{z}\right) = 98$$

$$\therefore \quad z^2+\frac{1}{z^2} = 96$$

13. Total respondents = 300

Now men respondents who do not have scooter

= 40 + 20 = 60

And women respondents who do not have scooter

= 34 + 50 = 84

$\therefore$ Total respondents who do not have scooter

= 60 + 84 = 144

$$\therefore \text{Required percent} = \left(\frac{144}{300}\times 100\right)\% = 48\%$$

14. One way single person fare = ₹ 100

$\therefore$ Two way fare for single person = ₹ 200

$\therefore$ For 5 persons two way fare = ₹ 1000

Now, total discount = (10 + 5)% = 15%

$$\text{Discount amount} = ₹\left[\frac{15}{100}\times 1000\right] = ₹\ 150$$

Amount to be paid = ₹(1000 − 150) = ₹ 850

2 CHAPTER Percentage and Its Applications

MCQ TYPE QUESTIONS

2016

1. In a huge pile of apples and oranges, both ripe and unripe mixed together, 15% are unripe fruits. Of the unripe fruits, 45% are apples. Of the ripe ones, 66% are oranges. If the pile contains a total of 5692000 fruits, how many of them are apples?

(a) 2029198 (b) 2467482
(c) 2789080 (d) 3577422

2. A person moving through a tuberculosis prone zone has a 50% probability of becoming infected. However, only 30% of infected people develop the disease. What percentage of people moving through a tuberculosis prone zone remains infected but does not show symptoms of disease?

(a) 15 (b) 33
(c) 35 (d) 37

3. (x % of y) + (y % of x) is equivalent to ______.

(a) 2 % of xy (b) 2 % of (xy/100)
(c) xy % of 100 (d) 100 % of xy

2014

4. The population of a new city is 5 million and is growing at 20% annually. How many years would it take to double at this growth rate?

(a) 3 – 4 years (b) 4 – 5 years
(c) 5 – 6 years (d) 6 – 7 years

5. One percent of the people of country X are taller than 6 ft. Two percent of the people of country Y are taller than 6 ft. There are thrice as many people in country X as in country Y. Taking both countries together, what is the percentage of people taller than 6 ft?

(a) 3.0 (b) 2.5
(c) 1.5 (d) 1.25

6. Industrial consumption of power doubled from 2000-2001 to 2010-2011. Find the annual rate of increase in percent assuming it to be uniform over the years.

(a) 5.6 (b) 7.2
(c) 10.0 (d) 12.2

7. The Gross Domestic Product (GDP) in Rupees grew at 7% during 2012-2013. For international comparison, the GDP is compared in US Dollars (USD) after conversion based on the market exchange rate. During the period 2012-2013 the exchange rate for the USD increased from ₹ 50/ USD to ₹ 60/ USD. India's GDP in USD during the period 2012-2013

(a) increased by 5% (b) decreased by 13%
(c) decreased by 20% (d) decreased by 11%

2013

8. A firm is selling its product at ₹ 60 per unit. The total cost of production is ₹ 100 and firm is earning total profit of ₹ 500. Later, the total cost increased by 30%. By what percentage the price should be increased to maintained the same profit level.

(a) 5 (b) 10
(c) 15 (d) 30

2012

9. An automobile plant contracted to buy shock absorbers from two suppliers X and Y. X supplies 60% and Y supplies 40% of the shock absorbers. All shock absorbers are subjected to a quality test. The ones that pass the quality test are considered reliable. Of X's shock absorbers, 96% are reliable. Of Y's shock absorbers, 72% are reliable.
The probability that a randomly chosen shock absorber, which is found to be reliable, is made by Y is

(a) 0.288 (b) 0.334
(c) 0.667 (d) 0.720

2011

10. There are two candidates P and Q in an election. During the campaign, 40% of the voters promised to vote for P, and rest for Q. However, on the day of election 15% of the voters went back on their promise to vote for P and instead voted for Q. 25% of the voters went back on their promise to vote for Q and instead voted for P. Suppose, P lost by 2 votes, then what was the total number of voters?

(a) 100 (b) 110
(c) 90 (d) 95

NUMERICAL TYPE QUESTION

2015

1. From a circular sheet of paper of radius 30 cm, a sector of 10% area is removed. If the remaining part is used to make a conical surface, then the ratio of the radius and height of the cone is ____.

ANSWERS

MCQ Type Questions

1. (*a*) **2.** (*c*) **3.** (*a*) **4.** (*a*) **5.** (*d*) **6.** (*b*) **7.** (*d*) **8.** (*a*) **9.** (*b*) **10.** (*a*)

Numerical Type Question

1. (2.06)

EXPLANATIONS

MCQ TYPE QUESTIONS

1. Given,

Total no. of fruits = 5692000

Unripe type of apples = 45% of 15% of 5692000

$$= \frac{45}{100} \times \frac{15}{100} \times 5692000$$

$$= 384210$$

Ripe type of apples $= (100 - 66)\% \times (100 - 15)\% \times 5692000$

$$= \frac{34}{100} \times \frac{85}{100} \times 5692000$$

$$= 1644988$$

$\therefore$ Total no. of apples = 384210 + 1644988 = 2029198

2. The percentage of people moving through a tuberculosis prone zone remains infected but does not show symptoms of disease.

$$= (100 - 30)\% \times 50\% = \frac{70}{100} \times \frac{50}{100} = \frac{35}{100} = 35\%$$

3. (x% of y) + (y% of x)

$$\frac{x}{100} \times y + \frac{y}{100} \times x = \frac{2xy}{100} = 2\% \text{ of } xy$$

$\therefore$ Option (*a*) is correct.

4. $$A = P\left[1 + \frac{r}{100}\right]^t$$

$$10 \text{ million} = 5 \text{ million}\left[1 + \frac{20}{100}\right]^t$$

$$2 = \left[1 + \frac{1}{5}\right]^t$$

$$2 = \left(\frac{6}{5}\right)^t = \log 2 = t \log\left(\frac{6}{5}\right)$$

$$0.301 = t\ 0.0791$$

$$t = \frac{0.301}{0.0791} = 3.8 \text{ years}$$

$\therefore$ Hence around 3–4 years would it take to double the growth rate

5. Let number of people in country y = 100

So, number of people in country x = 300

Total number of people taller than 6ft in both the countries $= 300 \times \frac{1}{100} + 100 \times \frac{2}{100} = 5$

% of people taller than 6ft in both the countries

$$= \frac{5}{400} \times 100 = 1.25\%.$$

7. Per ₹ 100 final value ₹ 107

$\Rightarrow$ per $\frac{100}{50}$ Dollars final value $\frac{107}{60}$

for 100 dollars _____?

$$= \frac{100 \times 50}{100} \times \frac{107}{60} = 89.16$$

Descreased by 11%

9.

	X	Y
Supply	60%	40%
Reliable	96%	72%
Overall	0.576	0.288

$$\therefore \quad P(x) = \frac{0.288}{0.576 + 0.288} = 0.334$$

10.

P	Q
40%	60%
–6%	+6%
+15%	–15%
49%	51%

$\therefore$ 2% = 2 $\Rightarrow$ 100% = 100

NUMERICAL TYPE QUESTION

1. 90% of area of sheet = Cross sectional area of cone

$\Rightarrow 0.9 \times \pi \times 30 \times 30 = \pi \times r_1 \times 30$

($\because$ Slant height of cone (l) = 30)

$\Rightarrow$ 27 cm = r_1

$\therefore$ Height of the cone $= \sqrt{30^2 - 27^2} = 13.08$ cm

Hence ratio of radius and height is 2.06.

3

CHAPTER

Time and Work

MCQ TYPE QUESTIONS

2016

1. P, Q, R and S are working on a project. Q can finish the task in 25 days, working alone for 12 hours a day. R can finish the task in 50 days, working alone for 12 hours per day. Q worked 12 hours a day but took sick leave in the beginning for two days. R worked 18 hours a day on all days. What is the ratio of work done by Q and R after 7 days from the start of the project?

(*a*) 10:11 (*b*) 11:10

(*c*) 20:21 (*d*) 21:20

2. S, M, E and F are working in shifts in a team to finish a project. M works with twice the efficiency of others but for half as many days as E worked. S and M have 6 hour shifts in a day whereas E and F have 12 hours shifts. What is the ratio of contribution of M to contribution of E in the project?

(*a*) 1 : 1 (*b*) 1 : 2

(*c*) 1 : 4 (*d*) 2 : 1

3. It takes 10 s and 15 s, respectively, for two trains travelling at different constant speeds to completely pass a telegraph post. The length of the first train is 120 m and that of the second train is 150 m. The magnitude of the difference in the speeds of the two trains (in m/s) is ______.

(*a*) 2.0 (*b*) 10.0

(*c*) 12.0 (*d*) 22.0

4. The velocity V of a vehicle along a straight line is measured in m/s and plotted as shown with respect to time in seconds. At the end of the 7 seconds, how much will the odometer reading increase by (in m) ?

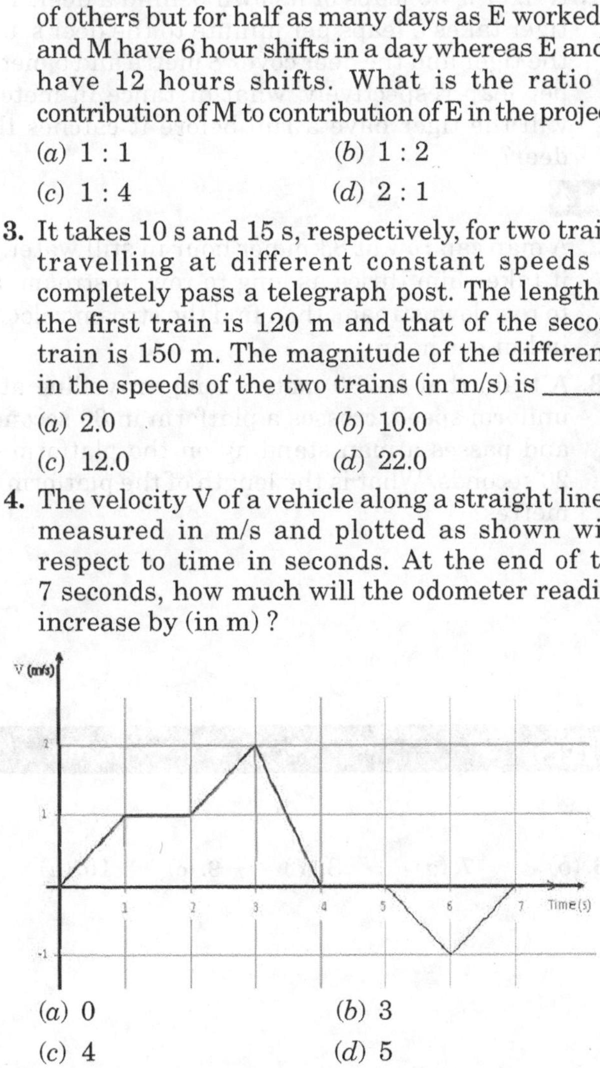

(*a*) 0 (*b*) 3

(*c*) 4 (*d*) 5

5. Ananth takes 6 hours and Bharath takes 4 hours to read a book. Both started reading copies of the book at the same time. After how many hours is the number of pages **to be** read by Ananth, twice that **to be** read by Bharath? Assume Ananth and Bharath read all the pages with constant pace.

(*a*) 1 (*b*) 2

(*c*) 3 (*d*) 4

2015

6. An electric bus has onboard instruments that report the total electricity consumed since the start of the trip as well as the total distance covered. During a single day of operation, the bus travels on stretches M, N, O and P, in that order. The cumulative distances travelled and the corresponding electricity consumption are shown in the table below.

Stretch	Comulative distance(km)	Electricity used (kWh)
M	20	12
N	45	25
O	75	45
P	100	57

The stretch where the electricity consumption per km is minimum is

(*a*) M

(*b*) N

(*c*) O

(*d*) P

2014

7. It takes 30 minutes to empty a half-full tank by draining it at a constant rate. It is decided to simultaneously pump water into the half-full tank while draining it. What is the rate at which water has to be pumped in so that it gets fully filled in 10 minutes?

(*a*) 4 times the draining rate

(*b*) 3 times the draining rate

(*c*) 2.5 times the draining rate

(*d*) 2 times the draining rate

2013

8. A tourist covers half of his journey by train at 60 km/h, half of the remainder by bus at 30 km/h and the rest by cycle at 10 km/h. The average speed of the tourist in km/h during his entire journey is

(*a*) 36 (*b*) 30
(*c*) 24 (*d*) 18

9. A car travels 8 km in the first quarter of an hour, 6 km in the second quarter and 16 km in the third quarter. The average speed of the car in km per hour over the entire journey is

(*a*) 30 (*b*) 36
(*c*) 40 (*d*) 24

2011

10. The fuel consumed by a motorcycle during a journey while traveling at various speeds is indicated in the graph below.

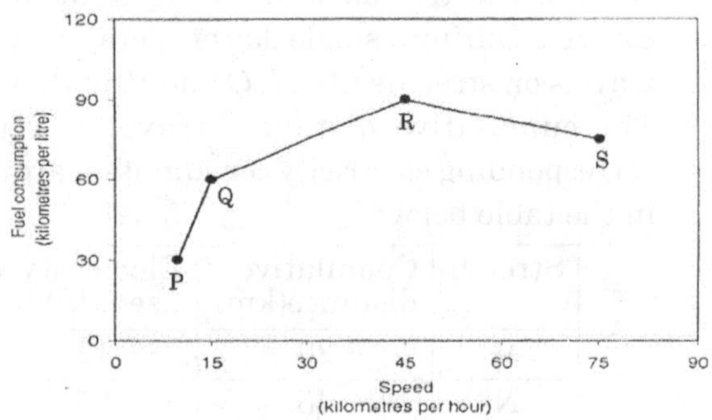

The distances covered during four laps of the journey are listed in the table below

Lap	Distance (kilometers)	Average speed (kilometers per hour)
P	15	15
Q	75	45
R	40	75
S	10	10

From the given data, we can conclude that the fuel consumed per kilometre was least during the lap

(*a*) P
(*b*) Q
(*c*) R
(*d*) S

2010

11. 5 skilled workers can build a wall in 20 days; 8 semi-skilled workers can build a wall in 25 days; 10 unskilled workers can build a wall in 30 days. If a team has 2 skilled, 6 semi-skilled and 5 unskilled workers, how long will it take to build the wall?

(*a*) 20 days
(*b*) 18 days
(*c*) 16 days
(*d*) 15 days

NUMERICAL TYPE QUESTIONS

2015

1. A tiger is 50 leaps of its own behind a deer. The tiger takes 5 leaps per minute to the deer's 4. If the tiger and the deer cover 8 metre and 5 metre per leap respectively, what distance in meters will the tiger have a run before it catches the deer?

2014

2. A man can row at 8 km per hour in still water. If it takes him thrice as long to row upstream, as to row downstream, then find the stream velocity in km per hour.

3. A train that is 280 metres long, travelling at a uniform speed, crosses a platform in 60 seconds and passes a man standing on the platform in 20 seconds. What is the length of the platform in metres?

ANSWERS

MCQ Type Questions

1. (*c*) **2.** (*b*) **3.** (*a*) **4.** (*d*) **5.** (*c*) **6.** (*b*) **7.** (*a*) **8.** (*c*) **9.** (*c*) **10.** (*a*)
11. (*d*)

Numerical Type Questions

1. (800) **2.** (4) **3.** (560 to 560)

EXPLANATIONS

MCQ TYPE QUESTIONS

1. Q can finish 1 day's 1 hour's work

$$= \frac{1}{25 \times 12} = \frac{1}{300}$$

R can finish 1 day's 1 hour's work

$$= \frac{1}{50 \times 12}$$

$$= \frac{1}{600}$$

Now Q working hours

$$= (7 - 2) \times 12$$

$$= 60 \text{ hr}$$

$\therefore$ R working hours = 7 × 18 = 126

After 7 days, the ratio of work done by Q & R is

Q : R

$$\frac{60}{300} : \frac{126}{600}$$

Q : R = 120 : 126

= 20 : 21

2. M is twice as efficient as E but worked for half as many days. So in this case they will do equal work if their shifts had same timings. But M's shift is for 6 hours, while E's shift for 12 hours. Hence, E will do twice the work as M.

Ratio of contribution of M : E in work is 1 : 2.

3. Here the speed of first train $(S_1) = \frac{120}{10} = 12$ m/s

and the speed of second train $(S_2) = \frac{150}{15} = 10$ m/s

$\therefore$ The magnitude of difference in the speeds of two trains $= (S_1 - S_2) = (12 - 10)$ m/s = 2 m/s

4. From the given figure.

The odometer reading increases from starting point to end point.

Odometer reading = Area of the given diagram

Area of the velocity and time graph per second

1st sec $\Rightarrow$ triangle

$$= \frac{1}{2} \times 1 \times 1 = \frac{1}{2}$$

2nd sec $\Rightarrow$ square

$$= 1 \times 1 = 1$$

3rd sec $\Rightarrow$ square + triangle

$$= 1 \times 1 + \frac{1}{2} \times 1 \times 1 = 1\frac{1}{2}$$

4th sec $\Rightarrow$ triangle

$$= \frac{1}{2} \times 1 \times 2 = 1$$

5th sec $\Rightarrow$ straight line

$$= 0$$

6th sec $\Rightarrow$ triangle

$$= \frac{1}{2} \times 1 \times 1 = \frac{1}{2}$$

7th sec $\Rightarrow$ triangle

$$= \frac{1}{2} \times 1 \times 1 = \frac{1}{2}$$

Total Odometer reading at 7 seconds

$$= \left(\frac{1}{2} + 1 + 1\frac{1}{2} + 1 + 0 + \frac{1}{2} + \frac{1}{2}\right) \text{m}$$

$$= 5 \text{ m}$$

So, the odometer reading is increased by 5 m.

6. For $M \Rightarrow \frac{12}{20} = 0.6$

$$N \Rightarrow \frac{25}{45} = 0.55$$

$$O \Rightarrow \frac{45}{75} = 0.6$$

$$P \Rightarrow \frac{57}{100} = 0.57$$

7. $V_{half} = 30(s)$ drawing rate $= s$

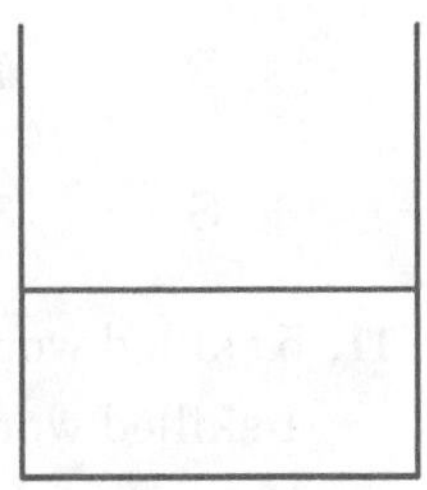

Total volume = 60 S tank

$(s^1)(10) - (s)10 = 30s$

$s^1(s) - s = 3s$

$s1 = 4s$

$s^1 = 4$ drawing rate

8. **Given:** A tourist covers half the journey at 60 km/h, one fourth at 30 km/h and the remaining one fourth at 10 km/h

To find: Avearge speed of the whole journey.

Analysis: One approach to this is to find individual time consumed in each of the three parts and use that value to get total time, and find average speed. So,

Lets assume total length of journey = x km

$\therefore$ First phase at 60 km/h

$$\text{Time } t_1 = \frac{\text{Distance}}{\text{Speed}} = \frac{x}{2}\frac{1}{60} = \frac{x}{120} h$$

Second phase at 30 km/h

$$\text{Distance} = \frac{x}{4}\text{ km}$$

$$\text{Time } t_2 = \frac{x}{4.30} = \frac{x}{120}$$

Third phase at 10 km/h

$$\text{Distance} = \frac{x}{4}\text{ km}$$

$$\text{Time } t_3 = \frac{x}{4.10} = \frac{x}{40}h$$

$$\therefore \quad \text{Total time} = \frac{x}{120}+\frac{x}{120}+\frac{x}{40} = \frac{x}{40}\left(\frac{1}{3}+\frac{1}{3}+1\right)$$

$$= \frac{x}{40}\frac{(1+1+3)}{3} = \frac{5x}{120}$$

$$\therefore \text{Average speed} = \frac{\text{Total Distance}}{\text{Total time}}$$

$$= \frac{x \cdot 120}{5x} = 24 \text{ km}/h$$

Hence, the answer is (c)

9. Average Speed $= \dfrac{\text{Total distance}}{\text{total time taken}}$

$$\text{Total Distance} = \frac{8+6+16}{15+15+15} = \frac{30 \times 60}{45}$$

$= 40$km/h.

10.

	Fuel consumption	Actual
P	60 km/l	$\frac{15}{60} = \frac{1}{4}l$
Q	90 km/l	$\frac{75}{90} = \frac{5}{6}l$
R	75 km/l	$\frac{40}{75} = \frac{8}{15}l$
S	30 km/l	$\frac{10}{30} = \frac{1}{3}l$

11. 5 skilled workers build wall in 20 days

1 skilled worker build wall in 20 × 5 days

Hence in 1 day, part of work done by skilled work

$$= \frac{1}{100}$$

Similarly in 1 day part of work done by semi-skilled workers

$$= \frac{1}{25 \times 8}$$

and in 1 day part of work done by un-skilled worker

$$= \frac{1}{30 \times 10}$$

So part of work done in 1 day by 2 skilled, 6 semi-skilled and 5 unskilled

$$= \frac{2}{100} + \frac{6}{200} + \frac{5}{300} = \frac{1}{15}$$

So work done by given workers in days = 15

NUMERICAL TYPE QUESTIONS

1. Tiger – 1 leap ⇒ 8 meter

Speed = 5 leap/hr = 40m/min

Deer → 1 leap = 5 meter

speed = 4hr = 20m/min

Let at time 't' the tiger catches the deer.

∴ Distance travelled by deer + initial distance between them

50 × 8 ⇒ 400m = distance covered by tiger.

⇒ 40 × t = 400 + 20t

$$\Rightarrow t = \frac{400}{200} = 20 \text{ min}$$

⇒ total distance ⇒ 400 + 20 × t = 800 m

2. Speed of man = 8;

Left distance = d

$$\text{Time taken} = \frac{d}{8}$$

Upstream: Speed of stream = s

⇒ speed upstream = S' = (8 – s)

$$t' = \left(\frac{d}{8-s}\right)$$

Downstream:

$$\text{Given speed downstream} = t'' = \frac{d}{8+s}$$

$$\Rightarrow 3t' = t'' \Rightarrow \frac{3d}{8-s} = \frac{d}{8+s}$$

$$\Rightarrow \quad \frac{3d}{8-s} = \frac{d}{8+s}$$

$$\Rightarrow \quad s = 4 \text{ km/hr}$$

3. Let the length of platform = x.m

and train length = 280 m (given)

According to Question

$$\frac{x+280}{60} = \frac{280}{20}$$

$$\therefore \quad x = 560 \text{ m.}$$

4

CHAPTER

Ratio, Proportion and Mixtures

MCQ TYPE QUESTIONS

2015

1. A cube of side 3 units is formed using a set of smaller cubes of side 1 unit. Find the proportion of the number of faces of the smaller cubes visible to those which are NOT visible.

(*a*) 1 : 4

(*b*) 1 : 3

(*c*) 1 : 2

(*d*) 2 : 3

2011

2. A container originally contains 10 litres of pure spirit. From this container 1 litre of spirit is replaced with 1 litre of water. Subsequently, 1 litre of the mixture is again replaced with 1 litre of water and this process is repeated one more time. How much spirit is now left in the container?

(*a*) 7.58 litres

(*b*) 7.84 litres

(*c*) 7 litres

(*d*) 7.29 litres

ANSWERS

MCQ Type Questions

1. (*c*) **2.** (*d*)

EXPLANATIONS

MCQ TYPE QUESTIONS

1.

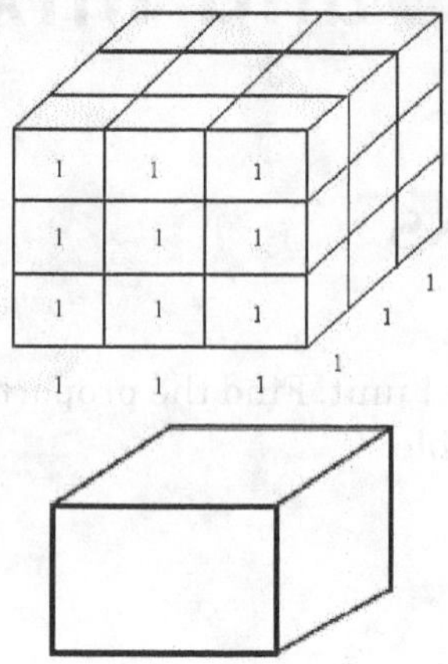

Number of faces per cube = 6

Total number of cubes = 9 × 3 = 27

∴ Total number of faces = 27 × 6 = 162

∴ Total number of non visible faces = 162 – 54 = 108

$$\therefore \frac{\text{Number of visible faces}}{\text{Number of non visible faces}} = \frac{54}{108} = \frac{1}{2}$$

2. $10\left(\frac{10-1}{10}\right)^3 = 10\left(\frac{9}{10}\right)^3 = \frac{729}{1000}$

$$\therefore \frac{729}{1000} \times 1 = 7.29 \text{ litres}$$

5 CHAPTER Permutations and Combinations & Probability

MCQ TYPE QUESTIONS

2016

1. Shaquille O' Neal is a 60% career free throw shooter, meaning that he successfully makes 60 free throws out of 100 attempts on average. What is the probability that he will successfully make exactly 6 free throws in 10 attempts?

(*a*) 0.2508 (*b*) 0.2816

(*c*) 0.2934 (*d*) 0.6000

2015

2. Four cards are randomly selected from a pack of 52 cards. If the first two cards are kings, what is the probability that the third card is a king?

(*a*) 4/52 (*b*) 2/50

(*c*) 1/52 × (1/52) (*d*) 1/52 × (1/52) × (1/50)

3. Five teams have to compete in a league, with every team playing every other team exactly once, before going to the next round. How many matches will have to be held complete the league round of matches?

(*a*) 20 (*b*) 10

(*c*) 8 (*d*) 5

4. Right triangle PQR is to be constructed in the *xy* – plane so that the right angle is at P and line PR is parallel to the-axis. The *x* and *y* coordinates of P, Q, and R are to be integers that satisfy the inequalities: $-4 \le x \le 5$ and $6 \le y \le 16$. How many different triangles could be constructed with these properties?

(*a*) 110 (*b*) 1,100

(*c*) 9,900 (*d*) 10,000

5. A coin is tossed thrice. Let X be the event that head occurs in each of the first two tosses. Let Y be the event that a tail occurs on the third toss. Let Z be the event that two tails occurs in three tosses. Based on the above information, which one of the following statements is TRUE?

(*a*) X and Y are not independent

(*b*) Y and Z are dependent

(*c*) Y and Z are independent

(*d*) X and Z independent

6. Ram and Ramesh appeared in an interview for two vacancies in the same department. The probability of Ram's selection is 1/6 and that of Ramesh is 1/8. What is the probability that only one of them will be selected?

(*a*) $\frac{47}{48}$ (*b*) $\frac{1}{4}$

(*c*) $\frac{13}{48}$ (*d*) $\frac{35}{48}$

7. Given set A = {2, 3, 4, 5} and Set B = {11, 12, 13, 14, 15}, two numbers are randomly selected, one from each set. What is probability that the sum of the two numbers equals 16 ?

(*a*) 0.20 (*b*) 0.25

(*c*) 0.30 (*d*) 0.33

8. The probabilities that a student passes in Mathematics, Physics and Chemistry are *m*, *p* and *c* respectively. Of these subjects, the student has 75% chance of passing in at least one, a 50% chance of passing in at least two and a 40% chance of passing in exactly two. Following relations are drawn in *m*, *p*.*c*:

I. $p + m + c = \frac{27}{20}$ II. $p + m + c = \frac{13}{20}$

III. $(p) \times (m) \times (c) = \frac{1}{10}$

(*a*) Only relation I is true.

(*b*) Only relation II is true.

(*c*) Relations II and III are true.

(*d*) Relations I and III are true.

2014

9. A five digit number is formed using the digits 1,3,5,7 and 9 without repeating any of them. What is the sum of all such possible five digit numbers?

(*a*) 6666660 (*b*) 6666600

(*c*) 6666666 (*d*) 6666606

10. You are given three coins: one has heads on both faces, the second has tails on both faces, and the third has a head on one face and a tail on the other. You choose a coin at random and toss it, and it comes up heads. The probability that the other face is tails is

(*a*) 1/4 (*b*) 1/3

(*c*) 1/2 (*d*) 2/3

2013

11. Out of all the 2-digit integers between 1 and 100, a 2-digit number has to be selected at random. What is the probability that the selected number is not divisible by 7?

(*a*) 13/90 (*b*) 12/90

(*c*) 78/90 (*d*) 77/90

12. What is the chance that a leap year, selected at random, will contain 53 Saturdays?

(*a*) 2/7 (*b*) 3/7

(*c*) 1/7 (*d*) 5/7

13. In a factory, two machines M1 and M2 manufacture 60% and 40% of the autocomponents respectively. Out of the total production, 2% of M1 and 3% of M2 are found to be defective. If a randomly drawn autocomponent from the combined lot is found defective, what is the probability that it was manufactured by M2?

(*a*) 0.35 (*b*) 0.45

(*c*) 0.5 (*d*) 0.4

2012

14. A and B are friends. They decide to meet between 1 PM and 2 PM on a given day. There is a condition that whoever arrives first will not wait for the other for more than 15 minutes. The probability that they will meet on that day is

(*a*) $\frac{1}{4}$ (*b*) $\frac{1}{16}$

(*c*) $\frac{7}{16}$ (*d*) $\frac{9}{16}$

2010

15. Given digits 2, 2, 3, 3, 3, 4, 4, 4, 4 how many distinct 4 digit numbers greater than 3000 can be formed?

(*a*) 50 (*b*) 51

(*c*) 52 (*d*) 54

NUMERICAL TYPE QUESTIONS

2015

1. How many four digit numbers can be formed with the 10 digits 0, 1, 2, ... 9 if no number can start with 0 and if repetitions are not allowed?

2014

2. In any given year, the probability of an earthquake greater than Magnitude 6 occurring in the Garhwal Himalayas is 0.04. The average time between successive occurrences of such earthquakes is _____ years.

3. 10% of the population in a town is HIV^+. A new diagnostic kit for HIV detection is available; this kit correctly identifies HIV^+ individuals 95% of the time, and HIV^- individuals 89% of the time. A particular patient is tested using this kit and is found to be positive. The probability that the individual is actually positive is ______

4. A batch of one hundred bulbs is inspected by testing four randomly chosen bulbs. The batch is rejected if even one of the bulbs is defective. A batch typically has five defective bulbs. The probability that the current batch is accepted is ________

ANSWERS

MCQ Type Questions

1. (*a*) **2.** (*b*) **3.** (*b*) **4.** (*c*) **5.** (*d*) **6.** (*b*) **7.** (*a*) **8.** (*d*) **9.** (*b*) **10.** (*b*)

11. (*d*) **12.** (*a*) **13.** (*c*) **14.** (*c*) **15.** (*b*)

Numerical Type Questions

1. 4536 **2.** (25 to 25) **3.** (0.47 to 0.48) **4.** (0.8145)

EXPLANATIONS

MCQ TYPE QUESTIONS

1. The question clearly explains that shaquille makes 60 free throws out of 100

Hence, Probability of free throw = $\frac{60}{100} = 0.6$

And probability of NOT free throw

$= 1 - 0.6 = 0.4$

So required probability of exactly 6 throws in 10 attempts will be given by

$^{10}C_6\, 0.6^6 \times 0.4^4 = 0.2508$

2. There are 4 kings in a pack of 52 cards.

If 2 cards are selected and both are kings, remaining cards will be 50 out of which 2 will be kings.

3. For a match to be played, we need 2 teams

No. of matches = No. of ways of selections 2 teams out of 5

$= {}^5C_2 = 10$

5. $x = \{HHT, HHH\}$

y depends on x

$z = \{TTH, TTT\}$

$\therefore$ '*d*' is the correct choice.

6. P (Ram) = 1/6; p(Ramesh) = 1/8

p(only at) = p (Ram) × p (not ramesh) + p(Ramesh) × p($n_0 \times R_{am}$)

$= \frac{1}{6} + \frac{7}{8} + \frac{1}{8} \times \frac{5}{6}$

$\Rightarrow \frac{12}{40} = \frac{1}{4}$

7. Here the given sets are

$A = \{2, 3, 4, 5\}$

and $B = \{11, 12, 13, 14, 15\}$

desired outcome = {(2, 14), (3, 13), (4, 12), (5, 11)}

$\therefore \quad n(E) = 4$

and total outcome = 4 × 5 = 20

$\therefore \quad n(s) = 20$

$\therefore$ Probability of an event

$= \frac{n(E)}{n(s)}$

$= \frac{4}{20} = \frac{1}{5} = 0.2$

9. The digit in unit place is selected in 4! Ways

The digit in tens place is selected in 4! Ways

The digit in hundreds place is selected in 4! Ways

The digit in thousands place is selected in 4! Ways

The digit in ten thousands place is selected in 4! Ways

Sum of all values for 1

$4! \times 1 \times (10^0 + 10^1 + 10^2 + 10^3 + 10^4)$

$= 4! \times 11111 \times 1$

Similarly for '3' $4! \times (11111) \times 3$

Similarly for '5' $4! \times (11111) \times 5$

Similarly for '7' $4! \times (11111) \times 7$

Similarly for '9' $4! \times (11111) \times 9$

$\therefore$ sum of all such numbers

$4! \times (11111) \times (1 + 3 + 5 + 7 + 9)$

$= 24 \times (11111) \times 25$

$= 6666600$

10. The probability that the other face is tail is $\frac{1}{3}$.

11. Given: All the 2-digit numbers

To find: Probability of selecting a number at random not divisible by 7

Analysis: Total number of 2-digit numbers

10, 11, ..., 99 → 90 numbers

Unfavourable numbers *i.e.* numbers divisible by

7 : 14, 21, ..., 98

Number of unfavourable numbers = 13

This can be hand counted or we can use the following properties:

Last term = First time + (no. – 1) Diff

98 = 14 + (no. – 1) 7

$\Rightarrow$ no. = 13

$\Rightarrow$ Probability = $\frac{\text{Total} - \text{unfavourable}}{\text{Total}}$

$= \frac{90 - 13}{90} = 77/90$

Hence, the solution is (*d*)

12. at a leap year

52 weeks, and 2 extra day they are (Mon, Tues) (Tues, Wed) (Wed Thu.) (Thus. Fri) (Fri. Sat) (Sat. Sun) (Sun Mond.)

$n(s) = 7$

$n(E) = 2 \quad P(E) = \frac{2}{7}$

14.

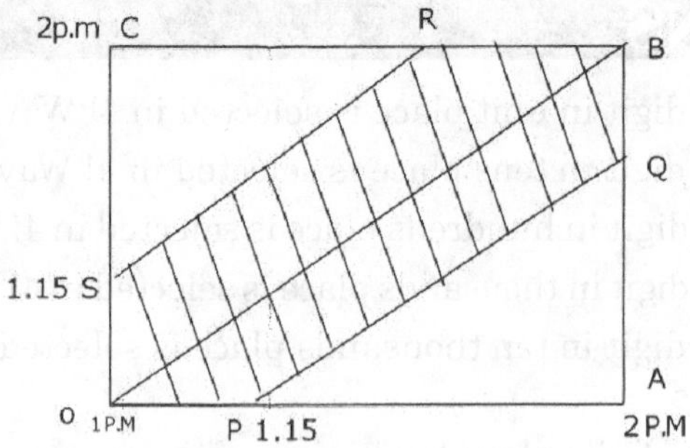

OB is the line when both A and B arrive at same time.

Total sample sapce = 60 × 60 = 3600

Favourable cases = Area of OABC – 2(Area of SRC)

$$= 3600 - 2 \times \left(\frac{1}{2} \times 45 \times 45\right)$$

$$= 1575$$

$$\therefore \text{ Required probability } = \frac{1575}{3600} = \frac{7}{16}$$

15. 2, 2, 3, 3, 4, 4, 4, 4 $\quad x > 3000$

322 — 3, 4	344 — 2, 3, 4
323 — 2, 3, 4	422 — 3, 4
324 — 2, 3, 4	423 — 2, 3, 4
332 — 2, 3, 4	424 — 2, 3, 4
333 — 2, 4	432 — 2, 3, 4
334 — 2, 3, 4	433 — 2, 3, 4
342 — 2, 3, 4	434 — 2, 3, 4
343 — 2, 3, 4	442 — 2, 3, 4
	443 — 2, 3, 4
	444 — 2, 3, 4

NUMERICAL TYPE QUESTIONS

1. In thousands place, 9 digits except 0 can be placed

In hundreds place, 9 digits can be placed (including 0, excluding the one used in thousands place)

In tens place, 8 digits can be placed (excluding the ones used in thousands and hundreds place)

In ones place, 7 digits can be placed (excluding the one used in thousands, hundreds and tens place)

Total number of combinations

$$= 9 \times 9 \times 8 \times 7 = 4536$$

2. Given, in one year, probability of an earthquake > 6 magnitude = 0.04

So, average time between successive earthquakes = 1/0.04 = 25 years

3. Given, 10% of the population is HIV^+, so probability = 0.1 for HIV^+ and 0.9 for HIV^-

The diagnostic kit identifies → 0.95 HIV^+ and 0.89 HIV^- correctly

So, the required probability that the person is actually HIV^+ = 0.95/2 = 0.475

4. Probability for one bulb to be non-defective is

$$\frac{95}{100}$$

∴ Probabilities that none of the bulbs is

defectives $\left(\frac{95}{100}\right)^4 = 0.8145$

6 CHAPTER Miscellaneous

MCQ TYPE QUESTIONS

2016

1. In a 2 × 4 rectangle grid shown below, each cell is a rectangle. How many rectangles can be observed in the grid?

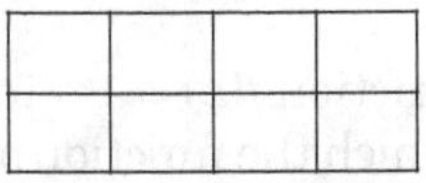

(a) 21 (b) 27

(c) 30 (d) 36

2.

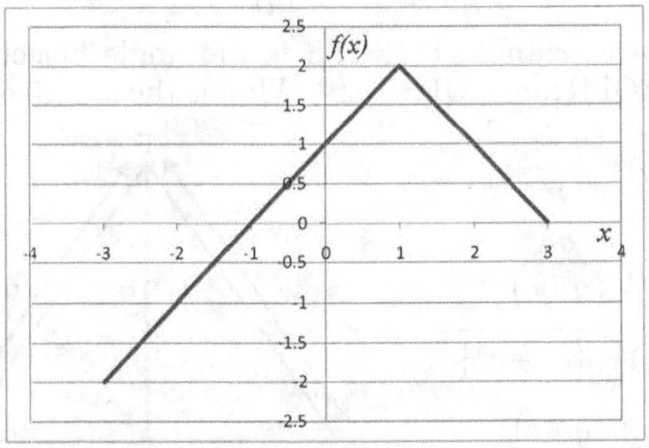

Choose the correct expression for $f(x)$ given in the graph.

(a) $f(x) = 1 - |x - 1|$ (b) $f(x) = 1 + |x - 1|$

(c) $f(x) = 2 - |x - 1|$ (d) $f(x) = 2 + |x - 1|$

3. The volume of a sphere of diameter 1 unit is _______ than the volume of a cube of side 1 unit.

(a) least (b) less

(c) lesser (d) low

4. A window is made up of a square portion and an equilateral triangle portion above it. The base of the triangular portion coincides with the upper side of the square. If the perimeter of the window is 6 m, the area of the window in m² is ________.

(a) 1.43 (b) 2.06

(c) 2.68 (d) 2.88

5. The binary operation □ is defined as $a \square b = ab + (a + b)$, where a and b are any two real numbers. The value of the identity element of this operation, defined as the number x such that $a \square x = a$, for any a, is ______.

(a) 0 (b) 1

(c) 2 (d) 10

6. Which of the following curves represents the function $y = \ln\left(\left|e^{\left[\left|\sin(|x|)\right|\right]}\right|\right)$ for $|x| < 2\pi$?

Here, x represents the abscissa and y represents the ordinate.

(a)

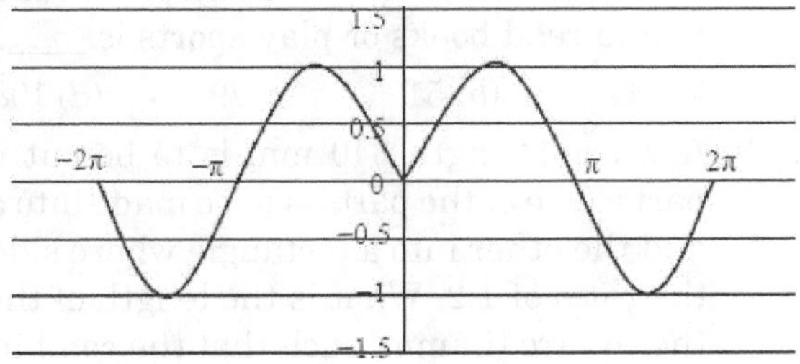

(b)

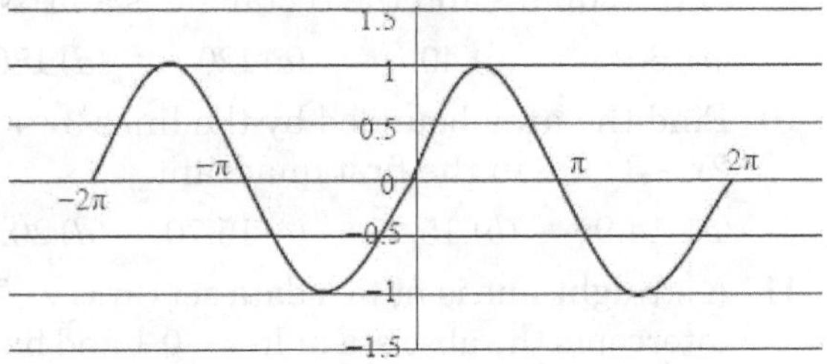

(c)

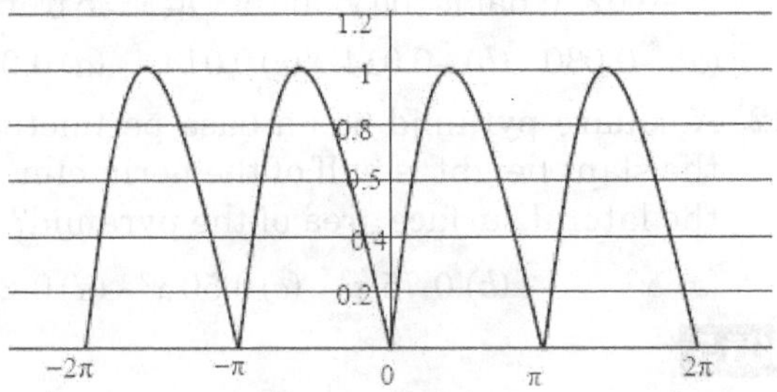

(d)

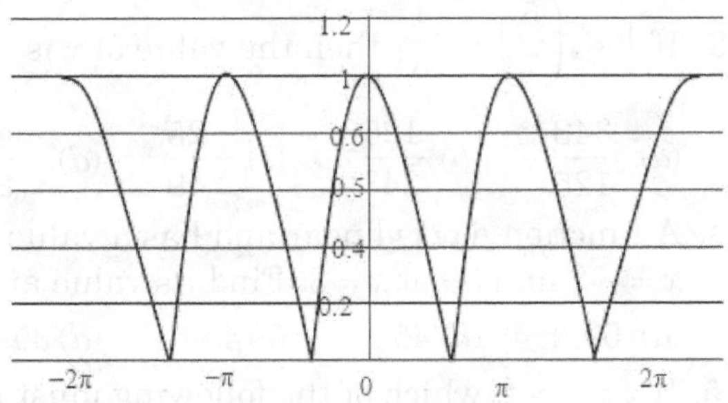

7. Given (9 inches)$^{1/2}$ = (0.25 yards)$^{1/2}$, which one of the following statements is TRUE?

(a) 3 inches = 0.5 yards

(b) 9 inches = 1.5 yards

(c) 9 inches = 0.25 yards

(d) 81 inches = 0.0625 yards

8. The Venn diagram shows the preference of the student population for leisure activities.

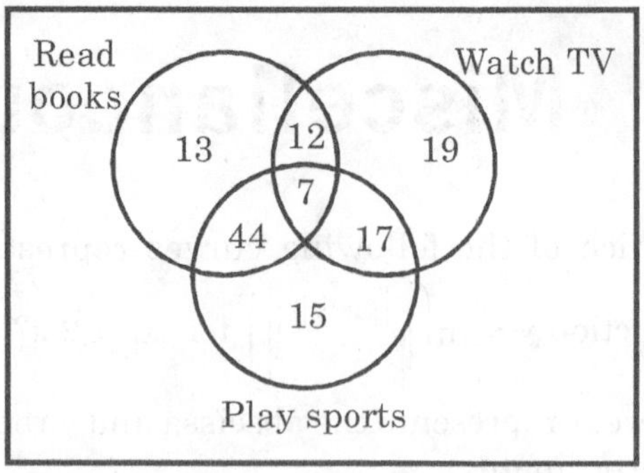

From the data given, the number of students who like to read books or play sports is ____.

(*a*) 44 (*b*) 51 (*c*) 79 (*d*) 108

9. A wire of length 340 mm is to be cut into two parts. One of the parts is to be made into a square and the other into a rectangle where sides are in the ratio of 1:2. What is the length of the side of the square (in mm) such that the combined area of the square and the rectangle is a MINIMUM?

(*a*) 30 (*b*) 40 (*c*) 120 (*d*) 180

10. Find the area bounded by the lines $3x + 2y = 14$, $2x - 3y = 5$ in the first quadrant

(*a*) 14.95 (*b*) 15.25 (*c*) 15.70 (*d*) 20.35

11. A straight line is fit to a data set ($\ln x, y$). This line intercepts the abscissa at $\ln x = 0.1$ and has a slope of -0.02. What is the value of y at $x = 5$ from the fit?

(*a*) –0.030 (*b*) –0.014 (*c*) 0.014 (*d*) 0.030

12. A square pyramid has a base perimeter x, and the slant height is half of the perimeter. What is the lateral surface area of the pyramid?

(*a*) x^2 (*b*) $0.75\, x^2$ (*c*) $0.50\, x^2$ (*d*) $0.25\, x^2$

2015

13. If $\log_x\left(\frac{5}{7}\right) = -\frac{1}{3}$, then the value of x is

(*a*) $\frac{343}{125}$ (*b*) $\frac{125}{343}$ (*c*) $-\frac{25}{49}$ (*d*) $-\frac{49}{25}$

14. A function $f(x)$ is linear and has a value of 29 at $x = -2$ and 39 at $x = 3$. Find its value at $x = 5$.

(*a*) 59 (*b*) 45 (*c*) 43 (*d*) 35

15. If $x > y > 1$, which of the following must be true?

(*i*) $\ln x > \ln y$ (*ii*) $e^x > e^y$

(*iii*) $y^x > x^y$ (*iv*) $\cos x > \cos y$

(*a*) *i* and *ii* (*b*) *i* and *iii*

(*c*) *iii* and *iv* (*d*) *ii* and *iv*

16. $\log \tan 1° + \log \tan 2°$ +-------+ $\log \tan 89°$ is ____.

(*a*) 1 (*b*) $1/\sqrt{2}$ (*c*) 0 (*d*) –1

17. Based on the given statements, select the most appropriate option to solve the given question.

What will be the total weight of 10 poles each of same weight?

Statements:

(I) One fourth of the weight of a pole is 5 kg

(II) The total weight of these poles is 160 kg more than the total weight of two poles.

(*a*) Statement II alone is not sufficient

(*b*) Statement II alone is not sufficient

(*c*) Either I or II alone is sufficient

(*d*) Both statements I and II together are not sufficient.

18. Consider a function $f(x) = 1 - |x|$ on $-1 \le x \le 1$. The value of x at which the function attains a maximum, and the maximum value of function are:

(*a*) 0, –1 (*b*) –1, 0

(*c*) 0, 1 (*d*) –1, 2

19. In a triangle PQR, PS is the angle bisector of ∠QPR and ∠QPS = 60°. What is the length of PS?

(*a*) $\frac{(q+r)}{qr}$

(*b*) $\frac{qr}{(q+r)}$

(*c*) $\sqrt{(q^2+r^2)}$

(*d*) $\frac{(q+r)^2}{qr}$

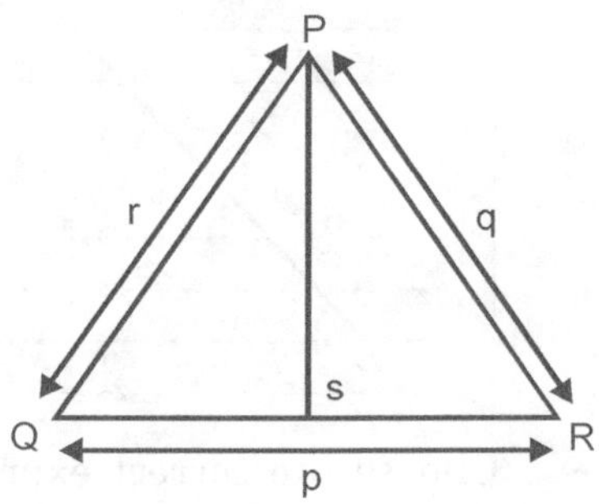

20. Based on the given statements, select the most appropriate option to solve the given question.

If two floors in a certain building are 9 feet apart, how many steps are there in a set of stairs that extends from the first floor to the second floor of the building?

Statements:

I. Each step is ¾ foot high.

II. Each step is 1 foot wide.

(*a*) Statement I alone is sufficient, but statement II alone is not sufficient.

(*b*) Statement II alone is sufficient, but statementI alone is not sufficient.

(*c*) Both statements together are sufficient, but neither statement alone is sufficient.

(*d*) Statement I and II together are not sufficient.

2014

21. If $y = 5x^2 + 3$, then the tangent at $x = 0$, $y = 3$

(*a*) passes through $x = 0$, $y = 0$

(*b*) has a slope of +1

(*c*) is parallel to the x-axis

(*d*) has a slope of –1

22. Let $f(x, y) = x^n y^m = P$. If x is doubled and y is halved, the new value of f is

(a) 2^{n-m} P (b) 2^{m-n} P

(c) $2(n-m)$ P (d) $2(m-n)$ P

23. A regular die has six sides with numbers 1 to 6 marked on its sides. If a very large number of throws show the following frequencies of occurrence: 1 → 0.167; 2 → 0.167; 3 → 0.152; 4 → 0.166; 5 → 0.168; 6 → 0.180. We call this die

(a) irregular (b) biased

(c) Gaussian (d) insufficient

24. Consider the equation : $(7526)_8 - (Y)_8 = (4364)_8$, where $(X)_N$ stands for X to the base N. Find Y.

(a) 1634 (b) 1737 (c) 3142 (d) 3162

25. At what time between 6 *a.m.* and 7 *a.m.* will the minute hand and hour hand of a clock make an angle closest to 60°?

(a) 6 : 22 *a.m.* (b) 6 : 27 *a.m.*

(c) 6 : 38 *a.m.* (d) 6 : 45 *a.m.*

26. The roots of $ax^2 + bx + c = 0$ are real and positive a, b and c are real. Then $ax^2 + b|x| + c = 0$ has

(a) No roots (b) 2 real roots

(c) 3 real roots (d) 4 real roots

2012

27. The cost function for a product in a firm is given by $5q^2$, where q is the amount of production. The firm can sell the product at a market price of ₹ 50 per unit. The number of units to be produced by the firm such that the profit is maximized is

(a) 5 (b) 10 (c) 15 (d) 25

28. Which of the following assertions are **CORRECT ?**

P : Adding 7 to each entry in a list adds 7 to the mean of the list

Q : Adding 7 to each entry in a list adds 7 to the standard deviation of the list

R : Doubling each entry in a list doubles the mean of the list

S : Doubling each entry in a list leaves the standard deviation of the list unchanged

(a) P, Q (b) Q, R (c) P, R (d) R, S

29. A political party orders an arch for the entrance to the ground in which the annual convention is being held. The profile of the arch follows the equation $y = 2x - 0.1x^2$ where y is the height of the arch in meters. The maximum possible height of the arch is

(a) 8 meters (b) 10 meters

(c) 12 meters (d) 14 meters

30. There are eight bags of rice looking alike, seven of which have equal weight and one is slightly heavier. The weighing balance is of unlimited capacity. Using this balance, the minimum number of weighings required to identify the heavier bag is

(a) 2 (b) 3 (c) 4 (d) 8

2011

31. If log (P) = (1/2) Log (Q) = (1/3) Log (R), then which of the following options is TRUE?

(a) $P^2 = Q^3 R^2$ (b) $Q^2 = PR$

(c) $Q^2 = R^3 P$ (d) $R = P^2 Q^2$

32. The variable cost (V) of manufacturing a product varies according to the equation V = 4q, where q is the quanity produced. The fixed cost (F) of production of same product reduces with q according to the equation $F = 100/q$. How many units should be produced to minimize the total cost (V + F)?

(a) 5 (b) 4 (c) 7 (d) 6

33. Three friends R, S and T shared toffee from a bowl. R took 1/3rd of the toffees, but returned four to the bowl. S took 1/4th of what was left but returned three toffees to the bowl. T took half of the remainder but returned two back into the bowl. If the bowl had 17 toffees left, how many toffees were originally there in the bowl?

(a) 38 (b) 31 (c) 48 (d) 41

NUMERICAL TYPE QUESTIONS

2015

1. In the given figure angle Q is a right angle, PS : QS = 3:1, RT : QT = 5:2 and PU : UR = 1:1. If area of triangle QTS is 20 cm², then the area of triangle PQR in cm² is ______.

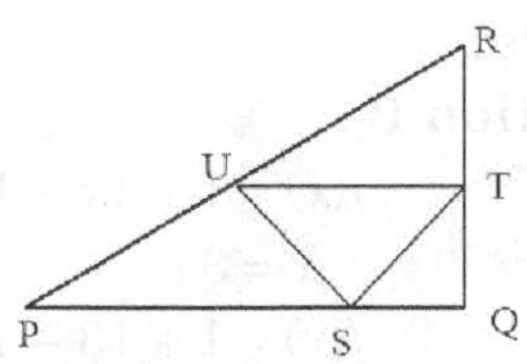

2. If p, q, r, s are distinct integers such that:

$f(p, q, r, s) = \max(p, q, r, s)$

$g(p, q, r, s) = \min(p, q, r, s)$

$h(p, q, r, s)$ = remainder of $(p \times q)/(r \times s)$ if $(p \times q) > (r \times s)$ or remainder of $(r \times s)/(p \times q)$ if $(r \times s) > (p \times q)$

Also a function $fgh(p, q, r, s) = f(p, q, r, s) \times g(p, q, r, s) \times h(p, q, r, s)$

Also the same operations are valid with two variable function of the form $f(p, q)$.

What is the value of fg $(h(2, 5, 7, 3), 4, 6, 8$

2014

3. When a point inside of a tetrahedron (a solid with four triangular surfaces) is connected by straight lines to its corners, how many (new) internal planes are created with these lines? ________.

ANSWERS

MCQ Type Questions

1. (*c*)	**2.** (*c*)	**3.** (*c*)	**4.** (*b*)	**5.** (*a*)	**6.** (*c*)	**7.** (*c*)	**8.** (*d*)	**9.** (*b*)	**10.** (*b*)
11. (*a*)	**12.** (*d*)	**13.** (*a*)	**14.** (*c*)	**15.** (*a*)	**16.** (*c*)	**17.** (*c*)	**18.** (*c*)	**19.** (*b*)	**20.** (*a*)
21. (*c*)	**22.** (*a*)	**23.** (*b*)	**24.** (*c*)	**25.** (*a*)	**26.** (*d*)	**27.** (*a*)	**28.** (*c*)	**29.** (*b*)	**30.** (*a*)
31. (*b*)	**32.** (*a*)	**33.** (*c*)							

Numerical Type Questions

1. 280 **2.** (8) **3.** (6)

EXPLANATIONS

MCQ TYPE QUESTIONS

1. In the given 2×4 rectangle grid, the following type of rectangles are present.

One figured rectangles = 8
Two figured rectangles = 10
Three figured rectangles = 4
Four figured rectangles = 5
Six figured rectangles = 2
Eight figured rectangles = 1

$\therefore$ Total number of rectangles

$$= 8 + 10 + 4 + 5 + 2 + 1 = 30$$

So the number of rectangles observed in the given grid is 30.

2. From the given graph function $f(x)$ must be equals to zero at $x = 3$.

From Option A :

$$f(x) = 1 - |x - 1|$$

at $\quad x = 3$

$$f(x) = 1 - |3 - 1| = 1 - 2 = -1$$

So, it is false

From Option B :

$$f(x) = 1 + |x - 1|$$

at $\quad x = 3$

$$f(x) = 1 + |3 - 1| = 1 + 2 = 3$$

So, it is false

From Option C :

$$f(x) = 2 - |x - 1|$$

at $\quad x = 3$

$$f(x) = 2 - |3 - 1| = 2 - 2 = 0$$

So, it is true.

From Option D :

$$f(x) = 2 + |x - 1|$$

at $\quad x = 3$

$$f(x) = 2 - |3 - 1| = 2 + 2 = 4$$

So, it is false.

Hence the correct expression for $f(x)$ given in the graph is $2 - |x - 1|$.

3. 'Lesser than' is apt because the sentence should be in comparative degree.

4. The possible window will be as follows :

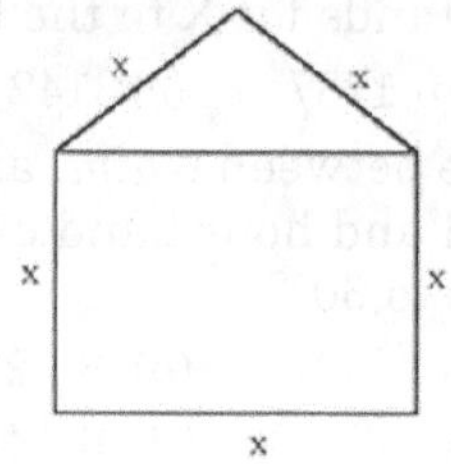

Perimeter of window = $5x$ = 6m

$$x = 1.2 \text{ m}$$

So area of window = Area of triangle + Area of square

$$= \frac{\sqrt{3}}{4}x^2 + x^2$$

$$= \frac{\sqrt{3}}{4}(1.2)^2 + (1.2)^2 = 2.06 \text{ m}^2$$

5. The binary operation is defined

$\Rightarrow a \quad b = ab + (a + b)$

$a \quad x = a$

$\therefore$ From the equation '*b*' is the variable

Option A: $x = 0$

$a \quad o = a \times 0 + (a + 0) = 0 + a = a$

Option B: $x = 1$

$a \quad 1 = a \times 1 + (a + 1) = a + a + 1 = 2a + 1$

Option C: $x = 2$

$a \quad 2 \Rightarrow a \times 2 + (a + 2) = 2a + a + 2 = 3a + 2$

Option D: $x = 10$

$a \quad 10 \Rightarrow a \times 10 + (a + 10) = 10a + a + 10 = 11a + 10$

$\therefore$ Option 'A' only True.

7. $(9 \text{ inches})^{1/2} = (0.25 \text{ yards})^{1/2}$,

Solving we get 9 inch = 0.25 yards

(since 1 inch = 0.028 yard)

8. Given Venn diagram is

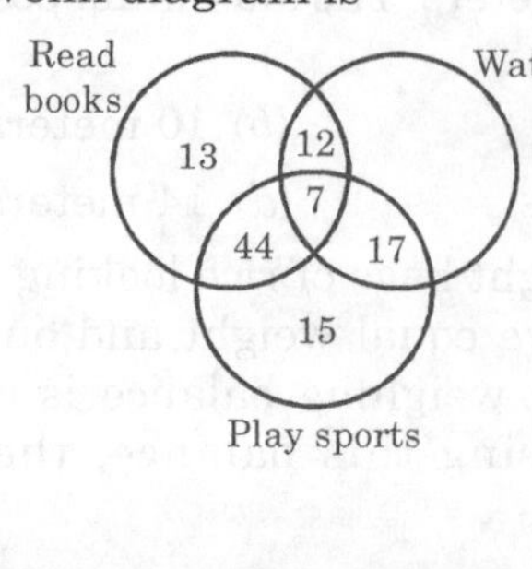

The number of students who like to read books or play sports

$= 13 + 12 + 44 + 7 + 15 + 17 = 108$

10. $A = \left[\frac{14}{3}, 0\right]$

$B = [0, 7]$,

$C = \left[\frac{5}{2}, 0\right]$

$D = \left[0, \frac{-5}{3}\right]$

$E = [4, 1]$,

$F = [0, 1]$

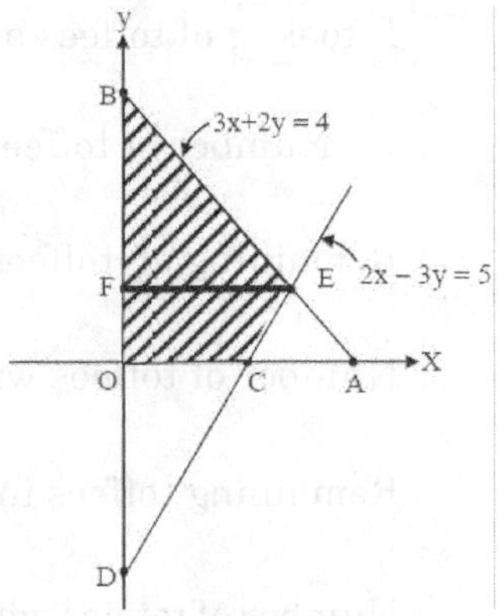

Required area = Area of Δ BFE + Area of quadrilateral FEOC

$= \frac{1}{2} \times 4 \times 6 + \frac{1}{2} \times (4 + 2.5) \times 1$

$= 2 \times 6 + \frac{1}{2} \times 6.5$

$= 12 + 3.25 = 15.25$ sq. units

So, the area bounded by the given lines is 15.25 sq. units.

11. The equation of a straight line is

$y = mx + c$

m = slope = – 0.02

set (log x, y)

Now, the line intercepts the abscissa at

$\log x = 0.1$

So, at abscissa $y = 0$

$\therefore \quad y = mx + c$

$0 = -0.02 \times 0.1 + c$

$\therefore \quad c = 0.002$

$y = mx + c$

$y = -0.02 \times \log x + c$

At $\quad x = 5$

$\therefore \quad y = -0.02 \times \log 5 + 0.002 = -0.030$

So, the value of y is – 0.030.

13. $\frac{5}{7} = x^{-1/3} \Rightarrow \frac{7}{5} = x^{1/3} \Rightarrow \left(\frac{7}{5}\right)^3 = x \Rightarrow x = \frac{343}{125}$

14. $f(x) = 2x + 33 = 2(5) + 33 = 43$

15. For whole numbers, greater the value greater will be its log.

Same logic for power of e.

16. $\log \tan 1° + \log \tan 89° = \log(\tan 1° \times \tan 89°)$

$= \log(\tan 1° \times \cot 1°)$

$= \log 1 = 0$

Using the same logic total sum is '0'.

18. The given function is

$f(x) = 1 - |x|$ on $-1 \le x \le 1$

In order to find maximum and minimum value of function in interval [–1, 1]

At $x = -1$, $\quad f(-1) = 1 - |-1| = 1 - 1 = 0$

At $x = -0.5$, $f(-0.5) = 1 - |-0.5| = 1 - 0.5 = 0.5$

At $x = 0$, $\quad f(0) = 1 - |0| = 1$

At $x = 0.5$, $\quad f(0.5) = 1 - |0.5| = 0.5$

At $x = 1$, $\quad f(1) = 1 - |1| = 1 - 1 = 0$

∴ Hence, maximum value occurs at $x = 0$ and its maximum value is 1.

∴ Option (*c*) is correct.

21. $y = 5x^2 + 3, \frac{dy}{dx} = 10x$

Slope of tangent $= \left(\frac{dy}{dx}\right)_{x=0, y=3} = 10 \times 0 = 0$

Slope = 0

⇒ tangent is parallel to x-axis.

22. $P' = 2^n X^n \left(\frac{1}{2}\right)^m y^m$

$= 2^{n-m} X^n Y^m = 2^{n-m} P$

23. For a very large number of throws, the frequency should be same for unbiased throw. As it not same, then the die is baised.

24. $(7526)_8 - (y)_8 = (4364)_8$

$\Rightarrow y_8 = (7526)_8 - (4364)_8$

$$\begin{array}{cccc} & 4 & (8+2=10) & \\ 7 & \not{5} & 2 & 6 \\ 4 & 3 & 6 & 4 \\ \hline 3 & 1 & 4 & 2 \\ \hline \end{array}$$

When we have base 8, we borrow 8 instead of 10 as done in normal subtraction.

25.

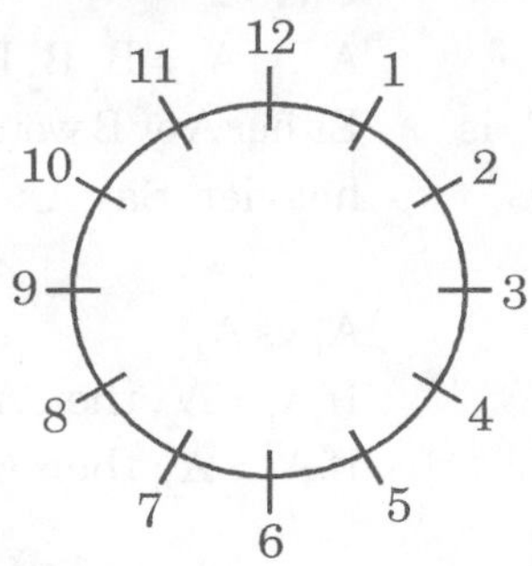

From option

At 6 a.m.

Both hand – 180° aparts,

At 6 : 20 a.m. – both hand apart

⇒ $\quad 180° + 10° - 120° = 70°$

At 6 : 22 a.m. – both hand apart

⇒ $\quad 180° + 12° - 132° = 60°$ (closest)

26. $ax^2 + bx + c = 0$

Roots are real and positive

$\therefore \quad b^2 - 4ac > 0$

By the above condition we get two positive real roots

Now, $ax^2 + b|x| + c = 0$

This can be written as;

$ax^2 + bx + c$

$\Delta = b^2 - 4ac > 0$

Now for $ax^2 - bx + c$

$(-b)^2 - 4ac$

$\Rightarrow \quad b^2 - 4ac$

Again $b^2 - 4ac > 0$

So again we get real roots

Thus we have 4 real roots of $ax^2 + b|x| + c = 0$

27. $P = 50q - 5q^2$

$\frac{dp}{dq} = 50 - 10q; \ \frac{d^2p}{dq^2} < 0$

$\therefore$ p is maximum at $50 - 10q = 0$ or, $q = 5$

Else check with options

28. P and R always holds true

Else consider a sample set {1, 2, 3, 4} and check accordingly

29. $y = 2x - 0.1x^2; \quad \frac{dy}{dx} = 2 - 0.2x; \quad \frac{d^2y}{dx^2} < 0$

$\therefore$ y maximises at $2 - 0.2x = 0$

$\Rightarrow x = 10$

$\therefore y = 20 - 10 = 10$m

30. Let us categorize bags in three groups as

$A_1 A_2 A_3 \quad B_1 B_2 B_3 \quad C_1 C_2$

1st weighing A vs B

Case-1	**Case-2**
$A_1 A_2 A_3 = B_1 B_2 B_3$	$A_1 A_2 A_3 \neq B_1 B_2 B_3$
Then either C_1 or C_2 is heavier	Either A or B would be heavier (Say A > B)
2nd weighing	
C_1 vs C_2	A_1 vs A_2
If $C_1 > C_2$, then C_1	If $A_1 = A_2$, then A_3
If $C_1 < C_2$, then C_2	If $A_1 > A_2$, then A_1
	If $A_1 < A_2$, then A_2

31. $\log P = \frac{1}{2} \log Q$

$= \frac{1}{3} \log(R) = k$

$\therefore \quad P = b^k, Q = b^{2k}, R = b^{3k}$

Hence, $Q^2 = b^{4k} = b^{3k}\, b^k = PR$

32. Checking with all options in formula: (4q+100/q) i.e. (V+F). Option (*a*) gives the minimum cost.

33. Let total number of toffees in bowl be x

R took $\frac{1}{3}$ of toffees and returned 4 to the bowl

$\therefore$ Number of toffees with R = $\frac{1}{3}x - 4$

Remaining of toffees in bowl = $\frac{2}{3}x + 4$

Number of toffees with S = $\frac{1}{4}\left(\frac{2}{3}x + 4\right) - 3$

Remaining toffees in bowl = $\frac{3}{4}\left(\frac{2}{3}x + 4\right) + 4$

Number of toffees with T = $\frac{1}{2}\left(\frac{3}{4}\left(\frac{2}{3}x + 4\right) + 4\right) + 2$

Remaining toffees in bowl

$= \frac{1}{2}\left[\frac{3}{4}\left(\frac{2}{3}x + 4\right) + 4\right] + 2$

Given : $\frac{1}{2}\left[\frac{3}{4}\left(\frac{2}{3}x + 4\right) + 4\right] + 2 = 17$

$\Rightarrow \quad \frac{3}{4}\left(\frac{2}{3}x + 4\right) = 27$

$\Rightarrow \quad x = 48$

NUMERICAL TYPE QUESTIONS

1. Let area of triangle PQR be 'A'

$\frac{SQ}{PQ} = \frac{1}{1+3} = \frac{1}{4}$

$\frac{QT}{QR} = \frac{2}{2+5} = \frac{2}{7}$

$\therefore$ Area of $\Delta QTS = \frac{1}{2} \times SQ \times QT$

$= \frac{1}{2} \times \left(\frac{1}{4}PQ\right) \times \left(\frac{2}{7}QR\right)$

$= \frac{1}{4} \times \frac{2}{7} \times \left(\frac{1}{2} \times PQ \times QR\right)$

$= \frac{1}{14} \times$ Area of ΔPQR

Given 20 cm^2 $= \frac{1}{14} \times A$

$\therefore \quad A = 14 \quad 20 = 280$ cm^2

2. $fg(h(2, 5, 7, 3), 4, 6, 8) = fg(1, 4, 6, 8)$

$= f(1, 4, 6, 8) \times g(1, 4, 6, 8)$

$= 8 \times 1 = 8$

Engineering Mathematics

1 CHAPTER

Linear Algebra

MCQ TYPE QUESTIONS

2016

1. Consider the systems, each consisting of m linear equations in n variables.

(i) If m < n, then all such systems have a solution

(ii) If m > n, then none of these systems has a solution

(iii) If m = n, then there exists a system which has a solution

Which one of the following is **CORRECT**?

(*a*) I, II and III are true (*b*) Only II and III are true

(*c*) Only III is true (*d*) None of them is true

2015

2. Consider the following 2 × 2 matrix A where two elements are unknown and are marked by *a* and *b*. The eigen values of this matrix are –1 and 7. What are the values of *a* and *b* ?

$$A = \begin{pmatrix} 1 & 4 \\ b & a \end{pmatrix}$$

(*a*) *a* = 6, *b* = 4 (*b*) *a* = 4, *b* = 6

(*c*) *a* = 3, *b* = 5 (*d*) *a* = 5, *b* = 3

3. In the matrix $\begin{bmatrix} 1 & -1 & 2 \\ 0 & 1 & 0 \\ 1 & 2 & 1 \end{bmatrix}$, one of the eigen values is 1. The eigenvectors corresponding to the eigen value 1 are

(*a*) $\{\alpha(4,2,1) | \alpha \neq 0, \alpha \in R\}$

(*b*) $\{\alpha(4,2,1) | \alpha \neq 0, \alpha \in R\}$

(*c*) $\{\alpha(\sqrt{2},0,1) | \alpha \neq 0, \alpha \in R\}$

(*d*) $\{\alpha(-\sqrt{2},0,1) | \alpha \neq 0, \alpha \in R\}$

2014

4. Which one of the following statements is TRUE about every *n* × *n* matrix with only real eigenvalues?

(*a*) If the trace of the matrix is positive and the determinant of the matrix is negative, at least one of its eigenvalues is negative.

(*b*) If the trace of the matrix is positive, all its eigenvalues are positive.

(*c*) If the determinant of the matrix is positive, all its eigenvalues are positive.

(*d*) If the product of the trace and determinant of the matrix is positive, all its eigenvalues are positive.

2013

5. Which one of the following does NOT equal $\begin{vmatrix} 1 & x & x^2 \\ 1 & y & y^2 \\ 1 & z & z^2 \end{vmatrix}$?

(*a*) $\begin{vmatrix} 1 & x(x+1) & x+1 \\ 1 & y(y+1) & y+1 \\ 1 & z(z+1) & z+1 \end{vmatrix}$ (*b*) $\begin{vmatrix} 1 & x+1 & x^2+1 \\ 1 & y+1 & y^2+1 \\ 1 & z+1 & z^2+1 \end{vmatrix}$

(*c*) $\begin{vmatrix} 0 & x-y & x^2-y^2 \\ 0 & y-z & y^2-z^2 \\ 1 & z & z^2 \end{vmatrix}$ (*d*) $\begin{vmatrix} 2 & x+y & x^2+y^2 \\ 2 & y+z & y^2+z^2 \\ 1 & z & z^2 \end{vmatrix}$

2012

6. Let A be the 2 × 2 matrix $a_{11} = a_{12} = a_{21} = +1$ and $a_{22} = -1$. Then the eigenvalues of the matrix A^{19} are

(*a*) 1024 and – 1024 (*b*) $1024\sqrt{2}$ and $-1024\sqrt{2}$

(*c*) $4\sqrt{2}$ and $-4\sqrt{2}$ (*d*) $512\sqrt{2}$ and $-512\sqrt{2}$

2011

7. Consider the matrix as given below.

$$\begin{bmatrix} 1 & 2 & 3 \\ 0 & 4 & 7 \\ 0 & 0 & 3 \end{bmatrix}$$

Which one of the following options provides the CORRECT values of the eigenvalues of the matrix?

(*a*) 1, 4, 3 (*b*) 3, 7, 3

(*c*) 7, 3, 2 (*d*) 1, 2, 3

8. Four matrices M_1, M_2, M_3 and M_4 of dimensions *p* × *q*, *q* × *r*, *r* × *s* and *s* × *t* respectively can be multiplied in several ways with different number of total scalar multiplications. For example when multiplied as $((M_1 \times M_2) \times (M_3 \times M_4))$, the total number of scalar multiplications is *pqr* + *rst* + *prt*. When multiplied as $(((M_1 \times M_2) \times M_3) \times M_4)$, the total number of scalar multiplications is *pqr* + *prs* + *pst*.

If *p* = 10, *q* = 100, *r* = 20, *s* = 5, and *t* = 80, then the minimum number of scalar multiplications needed is

(*a*) 248000 (*b*) 44000

(*c*) 19000 (*d*) 25000

2010

9. Consider the following matrix

$$A = \begin{bmatrix} 2 & 3 \\ x & y \end{bmatrix}$$

If the eigenvalues of A are 4 and 8, then

(a) $x = 4, y = 10$ (b) $x = 5, y = 8$

(c) $x = -3, y = 9$ (d) $x = -4, y = 10$

2008

10. The following system of equations

$$x_1 + x_2 + 2x_3 = 1$$
$$x_1 + 2x_2 + 3x_3 = 2$$
$$x_1 + 4x_2 + \alpha x_3 = 4$$

has a unique solution. The only possible value (s) for α is/are

(a) 0

(b) either 0 or 1

(c) one of 0, 1 or – 1

(d) any real number

11. How many of the following matrices have an eigenvalue 1?

$$\begin{bmatrix} 1 & 0 \\ 0 & 0 \end{bmatrix}, \begin{bmatrix} 0 & 1 \\ 0 & 0 \end{bmatrix}, \begin{bmatrix} 1 & -1 \\ 1 & 1 \end{bmatrix} \text{ and } \begin{bmatrix} -1 & 0 \\ 1 & -1 \end{bmatrix}$$

(a) one

(b) two

(c) three

(d) four

2006

12. Consider the polynomial

$p(x) = a_0 + a_1x + a_2x^2 + a_3x^3$, where $a_i \neq 0, i$.

The minimum number of multiplications needed to evaluate p on an input x is

(a) 3

(b) 4

(c) 6

(d) 97

NUMERICAL TYPE QUESTIONS

2016

1. $\lim_{x \to 4} \frac{\sin(x-4)}{x-4} =$ ______.

2. Two eigenvalues of a 3 × 3 real matrix P are $(2+\sqrt{-1})$ and 3. The determinant of P is______.

3. Suppose that the eigenvalues of matrix A are 1, 2, 4. The determinant of $(A^{-1})^T$ is ______.

2015

4. In the LU decomposition of the matrix $\begin{bmatrix} 2 & 2 \\ 4 & 9 \end{bmatrix}$, if the diagonal elements of U are both 1, then the lower diagonal entry l_{22} of L is ______.

5. The larger of the two eigenvalues of the matrix $\begin{bmatrix} 4 & 5 \\ 2 & 1 \end{bmatrix}$ is ______

6. Perform the following operations on the matrix $\begin{bmatrix} 3 & 4 & 45 \\ 7 & 9 & 105 \\ 13 & 2 & 195 \end{bmatrix}$.

i. Add the third row to the second row.

ii. Subtract the third column from the first column.

The determinant of the resultant matrix is _____.

2014

7. Consider the following system of equations :

$$3x + 2y = 1$$
$$4x + 7z = 1$$
$$x + y + z = 3$$
$$x - 2y + 7z = 0$$

The number of solutions for this system is ______.

8. The value of the dot product of the eigenvectors corresponding to any pair of different eigen values of a 4-by-4 symmetric positive definite matrix is ____________.

9. There are 5 bags labelled 1 to 5. All the coins in a given bag have the same weight. Some bags have coins of weight 10 gm, others have coins of weight 11 gm. I pick 1, 2, 4, 8, 16 coins respectively from bags 1 to 5. Their total weight comes out to 323 gm. Then the product of the labels of the bags having 11 gm coins is ___.

10. If the matrix A is such that

$$A = \begin{bmatrix} 2 \\ -4 \\ 7 \end{bmatrix} [1 \quad 9 \quad 5]$$

then the determinant of A is equal to _______.

11. The product of the non-zero eigenvalues of the matrix

$$\begin{vmatrix} 1 & 0 & 0 & 0 & 1 \\ 0 & 1 & 1 & 1 & 0 \\ 0 & 1 & 1 & 1 & 0 \\ 0 & 1 & 1 & 1 & 0 \\ 1 & 0 & 0 & 0 & 1 \end{vmatrix}$$ is _______.

ANSWERS

MCQ Type Questions

1. (*c*) **2.** (*d*) **3.** (*b*) **4.** (*a*) **5.** (*a*) **6.** (*d*) **7.** (*a*) **8.** (*c*) **9.** (*d*) **10.** (*d*)
11. (*a*) **12.** (*b*)

Numerical Type Questions

1. (1) **2.** (15) **3.** (0.125) **4.** 5 **5.** 6 **6.** 0 **7.** 1 **8.** 0 **9.** 12 **10.** 0 to 0
11. 6 to 6

EXPLANATIONS

MCQ TYPE QUESTIONS

1. Statement I

Consider 2 equations in three variables.

$x - y + z = 1$

$-x + y - z = 2$

This system has no solution (inconsistent)

$x = 1$ and $y = 1$

$\therefore$ Statement I is false

Statement II

Consider 3 equations in two variables.

$x + y = 2,$

$x - y = 0,$

$3x + y = 4$

This system has a unique solution

$\therefore$ Statement II is false.

Statement III

Consider a system with 2 equations and two variables

$x + y = 2$ and $x - y = 0.$

The system has a solution $x = 1$ and $y = 1$

$\therefore$ Statement III is true

2. Sum of Eigen value $= 1 + a$

$\therefore\ 6 = 1 + a$

$\therefore\ \boxed{a = 5}$

and product of Eigen value = det (A)

$-7 = a - 4b$

$\therefore\ -7 = 5 - 4b$

$\therefore\ -7 - 5 = -4b$

$\therefore\ \boxed{b = 3}$

$\therefore$ Option (*d*) is correct.

3. X be an eigen vector corresponding to eigen value $\lambda = 1$, then $AX = \lambda X \Rightarrow (A - I)X = 0$

$$\begin{bmatrix} 0 & -1 & 2 \\ 0 & 0 & 0 \\ 1 & 2 & 0 \end{bmatrix}\begin{bmatrix} X \\ Y \\ Z \end{bmatrix} = 0$$

$$\Rightarrow \quad -y + 2z = 0 \text{ and } x + 2y = 0$$

$$\Rightarrow \quad y = 2z \text{ and } \frac{x}{-2} = y$$

$$\therefore \quad \frac{x}{-2} = y = 2z$$

$$\Rightarrow \quad \frac{x}{-4} = \frac{y}{2} = \frac{Z}{1} = \alpha \text{ (say)}$$

$$\Rightarrow \quad X = \begin{pmatrix} -4 \\ 2 \\ 1 \end{pmatrix}\alpha;\ \alpha \neq 0$$

$\therefore$ Eigen vectors are $\{\alpha(-4, 2, 1) | \alpha \neq 0, \alpha \in R|\}$

4. If the trace of the matrix is positive and the determinant of the matrix is negative then atleast one of its eigen values is negative. Since determinant = product of eigen values.

5. Given :

$$\text{A matrix } \begin{vmatrix} 1 & x & x^2 \\ 1 & y & y^2 \\ 1 & z & z^2 \end{vmatrix}$$

To find: Which of the options are not equal to given matrix?

Analysis: Lets try to transform over the given matrix.

$$\begin{vmatrix} 1 & x & x^2 \\ 1 & y & y^2 \\ 1 & z & z^2 \end{vmatrix} \xrightarrow{C_2 \to C_2 + C_1} \begin{vmatrix} 1 & x+1 & x^2 \\ 1 & y+1 & y^2 \\ 1 & z+1 & z^2 \end{vmatrix}$$

$$\text{option } (b): \to \begin{vmatrix} 1 & x+1 & x^2+1 \\ 1 & y+1 & y^2+1 \\ 1 & z+1 & z^2+1 \end{vmatrix} \quad C_3 \to C_3 + C_1$$

$$\begin{vmatrix} 1 & x & x^2 \\ 1 & y & y^2 \\ 1 & z & z^2 \end{vmatrix} \xrightarrow[R_2 \to R_2 + R_3]{R_1 \to R_1 + R_2} \begin{vmatrix} 1 & x+y & x^2+y^2 \\ 1 & y+z & y^2+z^2 \\ 1 & z & z^2 \end{vmatrix}_{: \to \text{option (D)}}$$

$$\begin{vmatrix} 1 & x & x^2 \\ 1 & y & y^2 \\ 1 & z & z^2 \end{vmatrix} \xrightarrow[R_2 \to R_2 - R_3]{R_1 \to R_1 - R_2} \begin{vmatrix} 0 & x-y & x^2-y^2 \\ 0 & y-z & y^2-z^2 \\ 1 & z & z^2 \end{vmatrix}_{\text{option (C)}}$$

We are able to generate option B, C, and D from given matrix.

Hence, option a can be the possible solution, so lets try to operate on option A to see if we can prove it.

$$\begin{vmatrix} . & 0(y+1) & y+1 \\ 1 & z(z+1) & z+1 \end{vmatrix} \rightarrow C_3 \rightarrow C_3 - C_1$$

$$\begin{vmatrix} 1 & x^2 & x \\ 1 & y^2 & y \\ 1 & z^2 & z \end{vmatrix} \xleftarrow{C_2 \to C_2 - C_3} \begin{vmatrix} 1 & x^2+x & x \\ 1 & y^2+y & y \\ 1 & z^2+z & z \end{vmatrix}$$

We know, if we interchange any two columns of a matrix its determinan gets multiplied by '–1'.

Option (*a*) is formed from given matrix by interchanging column 2 and 3

Hence $$\begin{vmatrix} 1 & x & x^2 \\ 1 & y & y^2 \\ 1 & z & z^2 \end{vmatrix} = -\begin{vmatrix} 1 & x(x+1) & x+1 \\ 1 & y(y+1) & y+1 \\ 1 & z(z+1) & z+1 \end{vmatrix}$$

Hence (*a*) is the answer.

6. From the matrix

$$A = \begin{bmatrix} 1 & 1 \\ 1 & -1 \end{bmatrix} A^2 = 2\begin{bmatrix} 1 & 0 \\ 0 & 1 \end{bmatrix} = 2I$$

Where I = 2 × 2 unit matrix

So $A^{19} = (A^2)^9 . A = (2I)^9 A = 2^9 A$

Now, to get Eigen values, we must solve the equation.

$$[\lambda I - A^{19}] = 0$$

$$\begin{vmatrix} \lambda - 2^9 & -2^9 \\ -2^9 & \lambda + 2^9 \end{vmatrix} = 0$$

$\Rightarrow$ $\lambda^2 - 2^{18} - 2^{18} = 0$

$\Rightarrow$ $\lambda = \pm 512\sqrt{2}$

7. Given matrix is upper triangular matrix and its diagonal elements are its eigen values

= 1, 4, 3

8. Multiply as $(M_1 \times (M_2 \times M_3)) \times M_4$

Total number of scalar multiplication is

$= qrs + pqs + pst$

$= 10000 + 5000 + 4000 = 19000$

9. Given : $$A = \begin{bmatrix} 2 & 3 \\ x & y \end{bmatrix}$$

$\therefore$ $[A - \lambda I] = 0$

where, I = unit matrix

$\therefore$ $$\begin{bmatrix} 2-\lambda & 3 \\ x & y-\lambda \end{bmatrix} = 0$$

$\Rightarrow$ $(2 - \lambda)(y - \lambda) - 3x = 0$

Given eign values, $\lambda = 4, 8$

When $\lambda = 4$,

$-2(y - 4) - 3x = 0$

$\Rightarrow$ $3x + 2y = 8$ ...(i)

When $\lambda = 8$,

$-6(y - 8) - 3x = 0$

$\Rightarrow$ $x + 2y = 16$ ...(ii)

Solving equations (i) and (ii), we get

$x = -4, y = 10$

10. For unique solution, $\Delta \neq 0$

$\Delta_1 = \Delta_2 = \Delta_3 = 0$

$$\Delta = \begin{bmatrix} 1 & 1 & 2 \\ 1 & 2 & 3 \\ 1 & 4 & \alpha \end{bmatrix} \neq 0$$

$$\Delta_1 = \begin{bmatrix} 1 & 1 & 2 \\ 2 & 2 & 3 \\ 4 & 4 & \alpha \end{bmatrix} = 0$$

$\Rightarrow$ 0 = 0 (columns same)

so, can't be determined by Δ_1

$$\Delta_2 = \begin{bmatrix} 1 & 1 & 2 \\ 1 & 2 & 3 \\ 1 & 4 & \alpha \end{bmatrix} = \Delta,$$

so, can't be equated to zero

otherwise 0 = 0

$$\Delta_3 = \begin{bmatrix} 1 & 1 & 1 \\ 1 & 2 & 2 \\ 1 & 4 & 4 \end{bmatrix} = 0$$

No α

11. (*i*) $$\begin{bmatrix} 1 & 0 \\ 0 & 0 \end{bmatrix}$$

$\therefore$ $$\begin{bmatrix} 1-\lambda & 0 \\ 0 & -\lambda \end{bmatrix} = 0$$

$\Rightarrow$ $(1-\lambda)(-\lambda) = 0$

Hence eigen values are

$\lambda = 0, 1$

(*ii*) $$\begin{bmatrix} 0 & 1 \\ 0 & 0 \end{bmatrix}$$

$\therefore$ $$\begin{bmatrix} 0-\lambda & 1 \\ 0 & -\lambda \end{bmatrix} = 0$$

$\Rightarrow$ $(-\lambda)(-\lambda) = 0$

Hence eigen values are $\lambda = 0, 0$

(*iii*) $\begin{bmatrix} 1 & -1 \\ 1 & 1 \end{bmatrix}$

$\therefore \quad \begin{bmatrix} 1-\lambda & -1 \\ 1 & 1-\lambda \end{bmatrix} = 0$

$\Rightarrow \quad (1-\lambda)^2 + 1 = 0$

$\lambda^2 - 2\lambda + 2 = 0$

$\Rightarrow \quad \lambda \neq 1$

(*iv*) $\begin{bmatrix} -1 & 0 \\ 1 & -1 \end{bmatrix}$

$\therefore \quad \begin{bmatrix} -1-\lambda & 0 \\ 1 & -1-\lambda \end{bmatrix} = 0$

$\Rightarrow \quad (-1-\lambda)(-1-\lambda) - 1 = 0$

$\Rightarrow \quad (1+\lambda)^2 - 1 = 0$

$\Rightarrow \quad \lambda^2 + 2\lambda + = 0$

Hence eigen values are $\lambda = 0, -2$

12. The expression is $a_0 + a_1x + a_2x^2 + a_3x^3$

The deciding term is the last term which requires most number of multiplications.

For any value of x, the computation of $a_3 \times x \times x \times x$ is essential.

Hence minimum number of multiplications is 3.

NUMERICAL TYPE QUESTIONS

1. $\lim_{x\to 4} \frac{\sin(x-4)}{(x-4)} \quad \left(\frac{0}{0} \text{form}\right)$

Apply L' Hospital Rule :

$\lim_{x\to 4} \left[\frac{\cos(x-4)}{1}\right]$

$\Rightarrow \quad \frac{\cos 0}{1} \Rightarrow 1.$

2. $(2 + i)$ is an eigenvalue

So $(2 - i)$ will be other.

So Determinant will be product of eigenvalues.

So $\quad |A| = (2+i)(2-i) \times 3$

$(2^2 - i^2) \times 3 = 15$

3. Given the eigen values of matrix A is

$\lambda = 1, 2, 4$

$|A| = 1 \times 2 \times 4 = 8$

$\Rightarrow \quad |A^{-1}| = \frac{1}{|A|} = \frac{1}{8}$

$\therefore \quad \left|(A^{-1})^T\right| = |A^{-1}| = \frac{1}{8} = 0.125$

So the determinant of $(A^{-1})^T$ is $\frac{1}{8}$ (i.e. 0.125).

5. The given matrix is

$A = \begin{bmatrix} 4 & 5 \\ 2 & 1 \end{bmatrix}$

Inorder to find eigen values of above matrix

$|A - \lambda I| = 0$

$\therefore \quad \begin{vmatrix} 4-\lambda & 5 \\ 2 & 1-\lambda \end{vmatrix} = 0$

$\therefore \quad (4-\lambda)(1-\lambda) - 10 = 0$

$\therefore \quad 4 - 5\lambda + \lambda^2 - 10 = 0$

$\therefore \quad \lambda^2 - 5\lambda - 6 = 0$

$\therefore \quad \lambda^2 - 6\lambda + 1\lambda - 6 = 0$

$\therefore \quad \lambda(\lambda - 6) + 1(\lambda - 6) = 0$

$\therefore \quad \lambda + 1 = 0$ or λ

$\therefore \quad \lambda = -1$ or $\lambda = 6$

$\therefore$ Larger eigen value of matrix is 6

6. The given matrix is

$A = \begin{bmatrix} 3 & 4 & 45 \\ 7 & 9 & 105 \\ 13 & 2 & 195 \end{bmatrix}$

Now according to question

(*i*) $R_2 \to R_2 + R_3$ (Adding third row to the second row)

$\therefore \quad B = \begin{bmatrix} 3 & 4 & 45 \\ 20 & 11 & 300 \\ 13 & 2 & 195 \end{bmatrix}$

(*ii*) $C_1 \to C_1 - C_3$ (subtracting third column from first column)

$\therefore \quad C = \begin{bmatrix} -42 & 4 & 45 \\ -280 & 11 & 300 \\ -182 & 2 & 195 \end{bmatrix}$

Now $|C| = -42(2145 - 600) - 4(-54600 + 54600) + 45(-560 + 2002)$

$\therefore \quad |C| = -42(1545) - 4(0) + 45(1442)$

$= -64890 + 64890 = 0$

7. $3x + 2y = 1$

$4x + 7z = 1$

$x + y + z = 3$

$x - 2y + 7z = 0$

Augmented matrix is $\begin{bmatrix} 3 & 2 & 0 & 1 \\ 4 & 0 & 7 & 1 \\ 1 & 1 & 1 & 3 \\ 1 & -2 & 7 & 0 \end{bmatrix}$

$R_1 \leftrightarrow R_3 \begin{bmatrix} 1 & 1 & 1 & 3 \\ 4 & 0 & 7 & 1 \\ 3 & 2 & 0 & 1 \\ 1 & -2 & 7 & 0 \end{bmatrix}$

$R_2 \to R_2 - 4R_1\ R_3 \to R_3 - 3R_1, R_4 \to R_4 - R_1$

$$\begin{bmatrix} 1 & 1 & 1 & 3 \\ 0 & -4 & 3 & -11 \\ 0 & -1 & -3 & -8 \\ 0 & -3 & 6 & -3 \end{bmatrix}$$

$$\begin{matrix} R_3 \to 4R_3 - R_2 \\ R_4 \to 4R_4 - 3R_2 \end{matrix} \begin{bmatrix} 1 & 1 & 1 & 3 \\ 0 & -4 & 3 & -11 \\ 0 & 0 & -15 & -21 \\ 0 & 0 & 15 & 21 \end{bmatrix}$$

$$R_4 \to R_4 + R_3 \begin{bmatrix} 1 & 1 & 1 & 3 \\ 0 & -4 & 3 & -11 \\ 0 & 0 & -15 & -21 \\ 0 & 0 & 0 & 0 \end{bmatrix}$$

ρ (A : B) = ρ(A) = 3 = no. of variables

$\therefore$ Unique solution exists

8. The eigen vectors corresponding to distinct eigen values of real symmetric matrix are orthogonal.

9. Let the weight of coins in the respective bags (1 through 5) be a,b,c,d and e-each of which can take one of two values namely 10 or 11 (gm). Now, the given information on total weight can be expressed as the following equation:

$1.a + 2.b + 4.c + 8.d + 16.e = 323$

$\Rightarrow a$ must be odd $\Rightarrow a = 11$

The equation then becomes:

$11 + 2.b + 4.c + 8.d + 16.e = 323$

$\Rightarrow \quad 2.b + 4.c + 8.d + 16.e = 312$

$\Rightarrow \quad b + 2.c + 4.d + 8.e = 156$

$\Rightarrow \quad b$ must be even $\Rightarrow b = 10$

The equation then becomes:

$10 + 2.c + 4.d + 8.e = 156$

$\Rightarrow \quad 2.c + 4.d + 8.e = 146$

$\Rightarrow \quad c + 2.d + 4.e = 73$

$\Rightarrow \quad c$ must be odd $\Rightarrow c = 11$

The equation now becomes:

$11 + 2.d + 4.e = 73$

$\Rightarrow \quad 2.d + 4.e = 62$

$\Rightarrow \quad d + 2.e = 31$

$\Rightarrow \quad e = 11$ and $e = 10$

Therefore, bags labelled 1, 3 and 4 contain 11 gm coins

$\Rightarrow$ Required Product = 1*3*4* = 12.

10. $A = \begin{bmatrix} 2 \\ -4 \\ 7 \end{bmatrix} [1\,9\,5]$

$$A = \begin{bmatrix} 2 & 18 & 10 \\ -4 & -36 & -20 \\ 7 & 63 & 35 \end{bmatrix}$$

$$|A| = 2(-36 \times 35 + 20 \times 63) - 18(-4 \times 35 + 140) + 10(-4 \times 63 + 36 \times 7)$$

$$= 2(-1260 + 1260) - 18(-140 + 140) + 10(-252 + 252) = 0$$

11. $A = \begin{bmatrix} 1 & 0 & 0 & 0 & 1 \\ 0 & 1 & 1 & 1 & 0 \\ 0 & 1 & 1 & 1 & 0 \\ 0 & 1 & 1 & 1 & 0 \\ 1 & 0 & 0 & 0 & 1 \end{bmatrix}$

Let $X = \begin{bmatrix} x_1 \\ x_2 \\ x_3 \\ x_4 \\ x_5 \end{bmatrix}$

$Am = Xm \Rightarrow x_1 + x_5 = m\,x_1 = m\,x_5$

$\Rightarrow x_2 + x_3 + x_4 = m\,x_2 = m\,x_4$

For $m \neq 0$

Say, $x_1 = x_5 = a$

$x_2 = x_3 = x_4 = b$

$\Rightarrow \quad x_1 + x_5 = m\,x_1$

$\Rightarrow \quad 2a = m\,a$

$\Rightarrow \quad m = 2$

$\Rightarrow \quad x_2 + x_3 + x_4 = m\,x_2$

$\therefore \quad 3b = mb$

$\therefore \quad m = 3$

For $m = 0 \Rightarrow$ eigenvalue $m = 0$

$\therefore$ There are 3 distinct eigen value = 0, 2, 3.

Product of non zero eigen value = 2 × 3 = 6.

2 CHAPTER Calculus

MCQ TYPE QUESTIONS

2015

1. $\lim_{x \to \infty} x^{1/x}$ is

(a) ∞ (b) 0

(c) 1 (d) Not defined

2. Let $f(x) = x^{-(1/3)}$ and A denote the area of the region bounded by f(x) and the X-axis, when x varies from – 1 to 1. Which of the following statements is/are TRUE?

I. f is continuous in $[-1, 1]$

II. f is not bounded in $[-1, 1]$

III. A is nonzero and finite

(a) II only (b) III only

(c) II and III only (d) I, II and III

3. The value of $\lim_{x\to\infty}(1+x^2)e^{-x}$ is

(a) 0 (b) $\frac{1}{2}$

(c) 1 (d) ∞

4. In for non-zero x, $af(x)+bf\left(\frac{1}{x}\right)=\frac{1}{x}-25$ where $a \neq b$ then $\int_1^2 f(x)dx$ is

(a) $\frac{1}{a^2-b^2}\left[a(\ln 2-25)+\frac{47b}{2}\right]$

(b) $\frac{1}{a^2-b^2}\left[a(2\ln 2-25)-\frac{47b}{2}\right]$

(c) $\frac{1}{a^2-b^2}\left[a(2\ln 2-25)+\frac{47b}{2}\right]$

(d) $\frac{1}{a^2-b^2}\left[a(\ln 2-25)+\frac{47b}{2}\right]$

2014

5. Let the function

$$f(\theta) = \begin{vmatrix} \sin\theta & \cos\theta & \tan\theta \\ \sin(\pi/6) & \cos(\pi/6) & \tan(\pi/6) \\ \sin(\pi/3) & \cos(\pi/3) & \tan(\pi/3) \end{vmatrix}$$

Where $\theta \in \left[\frac{\pi}{6},\frac{\pi}{3}\right]$ and $f'(\theta)$ denote the derivative of f with respect to θ. Which of the following statements is/are TRUE?

(I) There exists $\theta \in \left(\frac{\pi}{6},\frac{\pi}{3}\right)$ such that $f'(\theta) = 0$

(II) There exists $\theta \in \left(\frac{\pi}{6},\frac{\pi}{3}\right)$ such that $f'(\theta) \neq 0$

(a) I only (b) II only

(c) Both I and II (d) Neither I nor II

6. A function $f(x)$ is continuous the interval [0, 2]. It is known that $f(0) = f(2) = -1$ and $f(1) = 1$. Which one of the following statements must be true?

(a) There exists a y in the interval (0, 1) such that $f(y) = f(y + 1)$

(b) For every y in the interval (0, 1), $f(y) = f(2 - y)$

(c) The maximum value of the function in the interval (0, 2) is 1

(d) There exists a y in the interval (0, 1) such that $f(y) = - f(2 - y)$

7. The value of the integral given below is

$$\int_0^{\pi} x^2 \cos x \, dx$$

(a) -2π (b) π

(c) $-\pi$ (d) 2π

2013

8. Which one of the following functions is continuous at $x = 3$?

(a) $f(x) = \begin{cases} 2, & \text{if } x = 3 \\ x-1, & \text{if } x > 3 \\ \frac{x+3}{3}, & \text{if } x < 3 \end{cases}$

(b) $f(x) = \begin{cases} 4, & \text{if } x = 3 \\ 8-x, & \text{if } x \neq 3 \end{cases}$

(c) $f(x) = \begin{cases} x+3, & \text{if } x \leq 3 \\ x-4, & \text{if } x > 3 \end{cases}$

(d) $f(x) = \frac{1}{x^3-27}$, if $x \neq 3$

2012

9. Consider the function $f(x) = \sin(x)$ in the interval $x \in \left[\frac{\pi}{4}, \frac{7\pi}{4}\right]$. The number and location(s) of the local minima of this function are

(*a*) One, at $\frac{\pi}{2}$

(*b*) One, at $\frac{3\pi}{2}$

(*c*) Two, at $\frac{\pi}{2}$ and $\frac{3\pi}{2}$

(*d*) Two, at $\frac{\pi}{4}$ and $\frac{3\pi}{2}$

2011

10. Given $i = \sqrt{-1}$, what will be the evaluation of the definite integral $\int_0^{\pi/2} \frac{\cos x + i \sin x}{\cos x - i \sin x} dx$?

(*a*) 0

(*b*) 2

(*c*) $-i$

(*d*) i

2010

11. What is the value of $\lim_{n\to\infty}\left(1 - \frac{1}{n}\right)^{2n}$?

(*a*) 0

(*b*) e^{-2}

(*c*) $e^{-1/2}$

(*d*) 1

2009

12. $\int_0^{\pi/4} \left(\frac{1 - \tan x}{1 + \tan x}\right)$ evaluates to

(*a*) 0

(*b*) 1

(*c*) $ln\ 2$

(*d*) $\frac{1}{2}\ ln\ 2$

2008

13. $\lim_{x\to\infty} \frac{x - \sin x}{x + \cos x}$ equals

(*a*) 1 (*b*) -1

(*c*) ∞ (*d*) $-\infty$

14. A point on a curve is said to be an extremum if it is a local minimum or a local maximum. The number of distinct extrema for the curve $3x^4 - 16x^3 + 24x^2 + 37$ is

(*a*) 0 (*b*) 1

(*c*) 2 (*d*) 3

2007

15. Consider the following two statements about the function $f(x) = |x|$

P. $f(x)$ is continuous for all real values of x

Q. $f(x)$ is differentiable for all real values of x

Which of the following is **TRUE?**

(*a*) P is true and Q is false.

(*b*) P is false and Q is true

(*c*) Both P and Q are true

(*d*) Both P and Q are false

NUMERICAL TYPE QUESTIONS

2016

1. A function $f: \mathbb{N}^+ \to \mathbb{N}^+$, defined on the set of positive integers $\mathbb{N}^+$, satisfies the following properties:

$f(n) = f(n/2)$ **if** n is even

$f(n) = f(n + 5)$ **if** n is odd

Let $R = \{i \mid \exists j : f(j) = i\}$ be the set of distinct values that f takes. The maximum possible size of R is ______.

2015

2. $\int_{1/\pi}^{2/\pi} \frac{\cos\left(\frac{1}{x}\right)}{x^2} dx =$ ________.

2014

3. The function $f(x) = x \sin x$ satisfies the following equation. $f''(x) + f(x) + t \cos x = 0$. The value of t is __.

4. If $\int_0^{2\pi} |x \sin x| dx = k\pi$, then the value of k is equal to ______.

ANSWERS

MCQ Type Questions

1. (*c*) **2.** (*c*) **3.** (*c*) **4.** (*a*) **5.** (*c*) **6.** (*a*) **7.** (*a*) **8.** (*a*) **9.** (*d*) **10.** (*d*)

11. (*b*) **12.** (*d*) **13.** (*a*) **14.** (*b*) **15.** (*a*)

Numerical Type Questions

1. (3) **2.** (–1) **3.** (–2) **4.** (4)

EXPLANATIONS

MCQ TYPE QUESTIONS

1. $\lim\limits_{x\to\infty} x^{1/x} = (\infty)^0 = 1$

$\therefore$ Option (*c*) is correct.

4. $af(x) + b.f\left(\frac{1}{x}\right) = \frac{1}{x} - 25$ ...(1)

$\Rightarrow af\left(\frac{1}{x}\right) + b.f(x) = x - 25$ ...(2)

Solving, we get

$$f(x) = \frac{1}{a^2 - b^2}\left[a\left(\frac{1}{x} - 25\right) - b(x - 25)\right]$$

$$\therefore \int_1^2 f(x)dx = \frac{1}{a^2 - b^2}\left[a\{\ln x - 25x\}_1^2 - b\left\{\frac{x^2}{2} - 25x\right\}_1^2\right]$$

$$= \frac{1}{a^2 - b^2}\left[a\{\ln 2 - 25\} - b\left\{\frac{3}{2} - 25\right\}\right]$$

$$= \frac{1}{a^2 - b^2}\left[a\{\ln 2 - 25\} + \frac{47}{2}b\right]$$

5. By Mean value theorem.

6. Define $g(x) = f(x) - f(x + 1)$ in [0,1]. g(0) is negative and g(1) is positive. By intermediate value theorem there is y€(0,1) such that $g(y) = 0$

That is $f(y) = f(y + 1)$.

Thus answer is (*a*)

7. $\int_0^{\pi} x^2 \cos x\, dx = x^2(\sin x) - 2x(-\cos x) + 2(-\sin x)\Big|_0^{\pi}$

$= (\pi^2\sin\pi + 2\pi\cos\pi - 2\sin\pi) - (0 + 0 + 0)$

$= -2\pi$

8. Continuous at $x = 3$?

(*a*) $f(x) = \begin{cases} 2 & \text{if } x = 3 \\ x - 1 & \text{if } x > 3 \\ \dfrac{x+3}{3} & \text{if } x < 3 \end{cases}$

$$\underset{x\to 3-}{\text{Lt}} f(x) = \underset{x\to 3-}{\text{Lt}} \frac{x+3}{3} = 2$$

$$\underset{x\to 3+}{\text{Lt}} f(x) = \underset{x\to 3+}{\text{Lt}}\ x - 1 = 2$$

$$\therefore \underset{x\to 3-}{\text{Lt}} f(x) = f(x)\big|_{x=3} = \underset{x\to 3+}{\text{Lt}} f(x)$$

$\Rightarrow$ This is continuous at $x = 3$

(*b*) $f(x) = \begin{cases} 4 & \text{if } x = 3 \\ 8 - x & \text{if } x \neq 3 \end{cases}$

Option (*b*) is false

$$\underset{x\to 3^-}{\text{Lt}} = \underset{x\to 3^-}{\text{Lt}}\ 8 - x$$

$$= 5 \neq f(x)\big|_{x=3}$$

(*c*) $f(x) = \begin{cases} x + 3 & \text{if } x \leq 3 \\ x - 4 & x > 3 \end{cases}$

$$\underset{x\to 3^+}{\text{Lt}} f(x) = \underset{x\to 3^+}{\text{Lt}}\ x - 4$$

$$f(x)\big|_{x=3} = 3 + 3 = 6 = -1$$

$$\underset{x\to 3^+}{\text{Lt}} f(x) \neq f(x)\big|_{x=3}$$

Option (*c*) is false

(*d*) $f(x) = \dfrac{1}{x^3 - 27}$ if $x \neq 3$

10. $\int_0^{\pi/2} \frac{e^{ix}}{e^{-ix}}\, dx = \int_0^{\pi/2} e^{2ix} dx$

$$= \left(\frac{e^{2ix}}{2i}\right)_0^{\pi/2} = \frac{1}{2i}[e^{i\pi} - 1]$$

$$= \frac{1}{2i}[\cos\pi + i\sin\pi - 1]$$

$$= \frac{1}{2i}[-1 + 0 - 1]$$

$$= \frac{-2}{2i} = \frac{-1}{i} \times \frac{i}{-1} = i$$

11. $\lim_{n\to\infty}\left(1 - \frac{1}{n}\right)^{2n} = \left(\lim_{n\to\infty}\left(1 - \frac{1}{n}\right)^{-n}\right)^2$

$$= (e)^{-2} = e^{-2}$$

$$\left[\text{because } \lim_{n\to\infty}\left(1 - \frac{1}{f(x)}\right)^{-f(x)}\right]$$

12. $\frac{1-\tan x}{1+\tan x}dx = \frac{\cos x - \sin x}{\cos x + \sin x}dx$

Let $\cos x + \sin x = t$

$\Rightarrow (-\sin x + \cos x)\, dx = dt$

$\therefore \quad \left(\frac{1}{t}\right)dt = ln\ t$

$$= \ln(\sin x + \cos x)$$

$$= \ln\left(\sin\frac{\pi}{4} + \cos\frac{\pi}{4}\right)$$

$$= \ln\left(\frac{1}{\sqrt{2}} + \frac{1}{\sqrt{2}}\right) = \frac{1}{2}\ln 2$$

13. $\lim_{x\to\infty}\frac{x - \sin x}{x + \cos x} = \lim_{x\to\infty}\frac{x(1 - \sin x/x)}{x(1 + \cos x/x)}$

$$= \lim_{x\to\infty}\frac{x1 - \sin x/x}{x1 + \cos x/x}$$

$$= \frac{1 - \lim_{x\to\infty}\frac{\sin x}{x}}{1 + \lim_{x\to\infty}\frac{\cos x}{x}} = \frac{1-0}{1+0} = 1$$

14. Given : $y = 3x^4 - 16x^3 + 24x^2 + 37$

For maximum value or minimum

$$\frac{dy}{dx} = 12x^3 - 18x^2 + 43x = 0$$

$\Rightarrow \quad x(x^2 - 4x + 4) = 0$

$\Rightarrow \quad x(x-2)^2 = 0$

$\Rightarrow \quad x = 0, 2, 2$

$$\frac{d^2y}{dx^2} = 36x^2 - 96x + 48$$

At $x = 0$, $\quad \frac{d^2y}{dx^2} = +48$

At $x = 2$, $\quad \frac{d^2y}{dx^2} = 36 \times 4 - 96 \times 2 + 48 = 0$

so only 1 local minima.

either $x = 0$ or complex root

so only value = 0

15. $f(x) = |x|,\ f(x) = \begin{cases} x & x \geq 0 \\ -x & x < 0 \end{cases}$

Graph of $f(x)$ will be

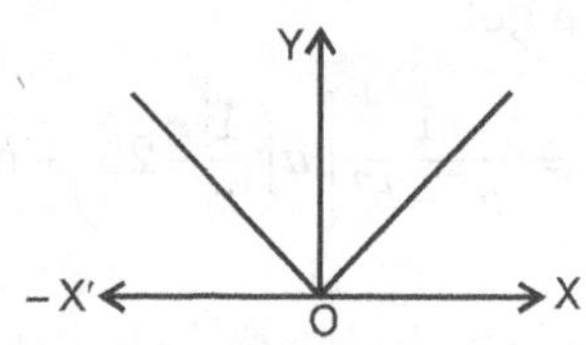

From above graph for $f(x)$, we can easily see that $f(x)$ is continuous for all real values of x.

But $f(x)$ is not differentiable for all real values of x.

For example at $x = 0$,

Left hand derivative $= \lim_{h\to o}\frac{f(O-h) - f(O)}{-h}$

$$= \lim_{h\to o}\frac{-(O-h)}{-h} = -1 = -1$$

Right hand derivative $= \lim_{h\to o}\frac{f(O+h) - (O)}{h}$

$$= \lim_{h\to o}\frac{h}{h} = 1$$

Since, Left hand derivative

$\neq$ Right hand derivative.

Therefore, $f(x)$ is not differentiable at $x = 0$, hence notz differentiable for all real values of x.

NUMERICAL TYPE QUESTIONS

1. Maximum number of distinct values f takes is only 3.

$1^{st} \Rightarrow f(1) = f(2) = f(3) = f(4) = f(8)$

$2^{nd} \Rightarrow f(5) = f(10)$

$3^{rd} \Rightarrow f(6) = f(7) = f(9)$

Remaining all other n values will provide only one of these three values.

3. Given $f''(x) + f(x) + t\cos x = 0$

and
$$f(x) = x\sin x$$
$$f'(x) = x\cos x + \sin x$$
$$f''(x) = x(-\sin x) + \cos x + \cos x$$
$$= 2\cos x - x\sin x$$
$$= 2\cos x - f(x)$$

$\therefore\ 2\cos x - f(x) + f(x) + t\cos x = 0$

$\Rightarrow\quad 2\cos x = -t\cos x$

$\Rightarrow\quad t = -2$

4. $$\int_0^{2\pi} |x\sin x|dx = K\pi$$

$$\Rightarrow \int_0^{\pi} x\sin x\,dx + \int_{\pi}^{2\pi} -(x\sin x)\,dx = K\pi$$

$$\left[\because |\sin x| = -\sin x \quad \pi < x < 2\pi\right]$$

$$\Rightarrow x(-\cos x) - 1(-\sin x)\Big|_0^{\pi} - (-x\cos x + \sin x)\Big|_{\pi}^{2\pi} = K\pi$$

$$\Rightarrow (-\pi\cos\pi + \sin\pi) - 0 - \left[(-2\pi\cos 2\pi + \sin 2\pi) - (-\pi\cos\pi + \sin\pi)\right] = K\pi$$

$$\Rightarrow \pi + 0 - \left[-2\pi + 0 - (\pi + 0)\right] = K\pi$$

$$\Rightarrow 4\pi = K\pi$$

$$\Rightarrow K = 4$$

3 CHAPTER

Probability

MCQ TYPE QUESTIONS

2015

1. In a room there are only two types of people, namely Type 1 and Type 2. Type 1 people always tell the truth and Type 2 people always lie. You given are fair coin to a person in that room, without knowing which type he is from and tell him to loss it and hide the result from you till you ask for it. Upon asking, the person replies the following.

"The result of the toss is head if and only if I am telling the truth."

Which of the following options are correct ?

(a) The result is head

(b) The result is tail

(c) If the person is of Type 2, then the result is tail

(d) If the person is of Type 1, then the result is tail

2013

2. Suppose p is the number of cars per minute passing through a certain road junction between 5 PM and 6 PM, and p has a Poisson distribution with mean 3. What is the probability of observing fewer than 3 cars during any given minute in this interval?

(a) $8/(2e^3)$

(b) $9/(2e^3)$

(c) $17/(2e^3)$

(d) $26/(2e^3)$

2012

3. Suppose a fair six-sided die is rolled once. If the value on the die is 1, 2, or 3, the die is rolled a second time. What is the probability that the sum total of values that turn up is at least 6?

(a) $\frac{10}{21}$ (b) $\frac{5}{12}$

(c) $\frac{2}{3}$ (d) $\frac{1}{6}$

2011

4. If the difference between the expectation of the square of a random variable ($E[X]^2$) and the square of the expectation of the random variable ($(E[X])^2$ is denoted by R, then

(a) $R = 0$

(b) $R < 0$

(c) $R \geq 0$

(d) $R > 0$

5. If two fair coins are flipped and at least one of the outcomes is known to be a head, what is the probability that both outcomes are heads?

(a) $\frac{1}{3}$ (b) $\frac{1}{4}$

(c) $\frac{1}{2}$ (d) $\frac{2}{3}$

6. A deck of 56 cards (each carrying a distinct number from 1 to 5) is shuffled thoroughly. Two coards are then removed one at a time from the deck. What is the probability that the two cards are selected with the number on the first card being one higher than the number on the second card?

(a) $\frac{1}{5}$ (b) $\frac{4}{25}$

(c) $\frac{1}{4}$ (d) $\frac{2}{5}$

7. Consider a finite sequence of random values $X = [x_1, x_2, \ldots x_n]$. Let μ_x be the mean and σ_x be the standard deviation of X. Let another finite sequence Y of equal length be derived from this as $y_i = a^*x_i + b$, where a and b are positive constants. Let μ_y be the mean and σ_y be the standard deviation of this sequence. Which one of the following statements is INCORRECT?

(a) Index position of mode of X in X is the same as the index position of mode of Y in Y.

(b) Index position of median of X in X is the same as the index position of median of Y in Y.

(c) $\mu_y = a\mu_x + b$

(d) $\sigma_y = a\sigma_x + b$

2010

8. Consider a company that assembles computers. The probability of a faulty assembly of any computer is p. The company therefore subjects each computer to a testing process. This testing process gives the correct result for any computer with a probalility of q. What is the probability of a computer being declared faulty?

(a) $pq + (1-p)(1-q)$ (b) $(1-q)p$
(c) $(1-p)q$ (d) pq

9. What is the probability that a divisor of 10^{99} is a multiple of 10^{96}?

(a) 1/625 (b) 4/625
(c) 12/625 (d) 16/625

2009

10. An unbalanced dice (with 6 faces, numbered from 1 to 6) is thrown. The probability that the face value is odd is 90% of the probability that the face value is even. The probability of getting any even numbered face is the same.

If the probability that the face is even given that it is greater than 3 is 0.75, which one of the following options is closest to the probability that the face value exceeds 3 ?

(a) 0.453 (b) 0.468
(c) 0.485 (d) 0.492

2008

11. Aishwarya studies either computer science or mathematics everyday. If she studies computer science on a day, then the probability that she studies mathematics the next day is 0.6. If she studies mathematics on a day, then the probability that she studies computer science the next day is 0.4. Given that Aishwarya studies computer science on Monday, what is the probability that she studies computer science on Wednesday?

(a) 0.24 (b) 0.36
(c) 0.4 (d) 0.6

12. Let X be a random variable following normal distribution with mean + 1 and variance 4. Let Y be another normal variable with mean – 1 and variance unknown. If P (X ≤ –1) = P (P ≥ 2), the standard deviation of Y is

(a) 3 (b) 2
(c) $\sqrt{2}$ (d) 1

2007

13. Suppose we uniformly and randomly select a permutation from the 20! permutations of 1, 2, 3...., 20. What is the probability that 2 appears at an earlier position than any other even number in the selected permutation ?

(a) $\frac{1}{2}$ (b) $\frac{1}{10}$
(c) $\frac{9!}{20!}$ (d) None of these

2006

14. For each element in a set of size $2n$, an unbiased coin is tossed. The $2n$ coin tosses are independent. An element is chosen if the corresponding coin toss were head. The probability that exactly n elements are chosen is

(a) $\frac{\binom{2n}{n}}{4^n}$ (b) $\frac{\binom{2n}{n}}{2^n}$
(c) $\frac{1}{\binom{2n}{n}}$ (d) $\frac{1}{2}$

NUMERICAL TYPE QUESTIONS

2016

1. A probability density function on the interval [a, 1] is given by $1/x^2$ and outside this interval the value of the function is zero. The value of a is ______ .

2. Consider the following experiment.

Step 1. Flip a fair coin twice.

Step 2. If the outcomes are (TAILS, HEADS) then output Y and stop.

Step 3. If the outcomes are either (HEADS, HEADS) or (HEADS, TAILS) , then output N and stop.

Step 4. If the outcomes are (TAILS, TAILS) , then go to Step 1.

The probability that the output of the experiment is Y is (up to two decimal places) ______.

2015

3. Let X and Y denote the sets containing 2 and 20 distinct objects respectively and F denote the set of all possible functions defined from X to Y. let f be randomly chosen from F .The probability of f being one-to-one is ______.

2014

4. Suppose you break a stick of unit length at a point chosen uniformly at random. Then the expected length of the shorter stick is ________.

5. For fair six-sided dice are rolled. The probability that the sum of the results being 22 is $X/_{1296}$. The value of X is ________.

6. The security system at an IT office is composed of 10 computers of which exactly four are working. To check whether the system is functional, the officials inspect four of the computers picked at random (without replacement). The system is deemed functional if at least three of the four computers inspected are working. Let the probability that the system is deemed functional be denoted by p. Then $100\ p$ = ____________.

7. Each of the nine words in the sentence "*The quick brown fox jumps over the lazy dog*" is written on a separate piece of paper. These nine pieces of paper are kept in a box. One of the pieces is drawn at random from the box. The *expected* length of the word drawn is ________. (The answer should be rounded to one decimal place.)

8. The probability that a given positive integer lying between 1 and 100 (both inclusive) is NOT divisible by 2, 3 or 5 is ______ .

9. Let S be a sample space and two mutually exclusive events A and B be such that $A \cup B = S$. If P(.) denotes the probability of the event, the maximum value of P(A)P(B) is __________.

ANSWERS

MCQ Type Questions

1. (*a*) **2.** (*c*) **3.** (*b*) **4.** (*c*) **5.** (*a*) **6.** (*a*) **7.** (*d*) **8.** (*b*) **9.** (*a*) **10.** (*b*)

11. (*c*) **12.** (*a*) **13.** (*d*) **14.**(*a*)

Numerical Type Questions

1. (0.5) **2.** (0.33) **3.** (0.95) **4.** (0.25) **5.** (10) **6.** (11.85 to 11.95) **7.** (3.8 to 3.9)

8. (0.259 to 0.261) **9.** (0.25)

EXPLANATIONS

MCQ TYPE QUESTIONS

2. Given: P # of cars passing every minute

P is a random variable following Poisson's Distribution

$$\therefore \frac{\text{Prob. } (P = K) = \dfrac{\lambda^k e^{-\lambda}}{K!}}{\text{Mean} = E[P] = 1}$$

$\therefore \quad \lambda = 3$

Probability of observing fewer than 3 cars

= Prob. (P = 0) + Prob (P = 1) + Prob (P = 2)

$$= \frac{3^0.e^{-3}}{0!} + \frac{3^1.e^{-3}}{1!} + \frac{3^2.e^{-3}}{2!} = \frac{1}{e^3}\left[1 + 3 + \frac{9}{2}\right] = \boxed{\frac{17}{2e^3}}$$

3.

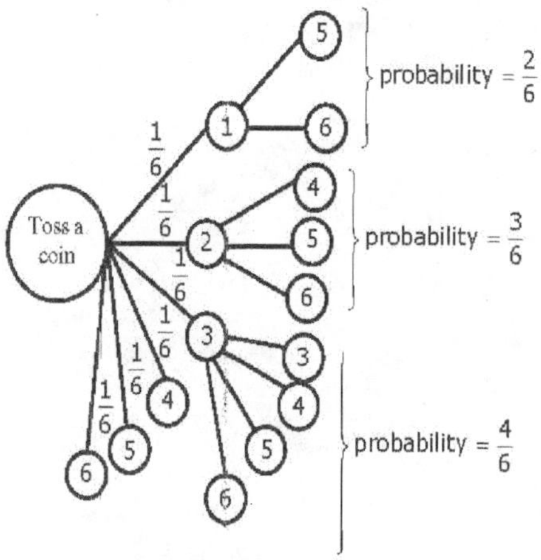

$\therefore$ Required probability

$$= \frac{1}{6} \times \frac{2}{6} + \frac{1}{6} \times \frac{3}{6} + \frac{1}{6} \times \frac{4}{6} + \frac{1}{6} = \frac{15}{36} = \frac{5}{12}$$

5. Sample space = {HH,HT, TH}

Required probability = $\frac{1}{3}$

6. (2, 1), (3, 2), (4, 3), (5, 4)

Required probability = $\frac{4}{5 \times 4} = \frac{4}{20} = \frac{1}{5}$

8. Probability of faulty declared

= (already faulty) × (declared faulty after testing)

Let probability of already faulty = p

Probability that after testing it declares faulty

$= (1 - q)$

$\therefore$ Required probability = $(1 - q)\,p$

9. Total number of divisors of $10^{99} = 2^{99} \times 5^{99} = 2 \times 5$ and that are most direct of 10^{96}

$\equiv (99 + 1)(991 + 1)$

$10^{96} \times 10^3$

$\Rightarrow 10^{96}, 2 \times 10^{96}, 4 \times 10^{96}, 9 \times 10^{96}, 8 \times 10^{96}$

$$\left|\frac{1000}{n}\right| = 0$$

$\Rightarrow 10 \times 10^{96}, 20 \times 10^{96}, 29 \times 10^{96}, 40 \times 10^{96}, 50 \times 10^{96}$

$n = 1$—$100 \quad 125 \times 10^{96}, 250 \times 10^{96}, 500 \times 10^{96}, 100 \times 10^{96}, 100 \times 10^{96}, 200 \times 10^{96}$

= total 16

$\therefore$ Required probability = $\frac{10}{10000} = \frac{1}{625}$

10. Given : P(ODD) = 0.9*P(EVEN) ≠ P(2) = P(4) = P(6) ≠ P(EVEN | Exceeds 3) = 0.75

Now we know

P(ODD) = 1 – P (EVEN)

or 0.9*P (EVEN) = 1 – P (EVEN)

{Given P(ODD) = 0.9*P(EVEN)}

or P(EVEN) = 1/1.9

Because of independent events

P(2) = P(4) = P(6) = P(2 ∪ 4 ∪ 6)/3

= P(EVEN)/3 = 1/(3*1.9)

Now, P(EVEN | Exceeds 3)

= P(EVEN ∩ Exceeds 3)/P(Exceeds 3)

P(Exceeds 3) = P(EVEN ∩ Exceeds 3)/P(EVEN | Exceeds 3)

P(Exceeds 3) = P(4 ∪ 6)/0.75

P(Exceeds 3) = (P(4) + P(6))/0.75

P(Exceeds 3) = (1/3*1.9) + 1/(1.9 * 3))/0.75

P(Exceeds 3) = 0.468

11. Combinations are CMC, CMM, CCC, CCM.

Probability of

CMC = 0.6 × 0.4 = 0.24 —Favourable

CMM = 0.6 × 0.6 = 0.36

CCC = 0.4 × 0.4 = 0.16 —Favourable

CCM = 0.4 × 0.6 = 0.24

Total probability = 1

Favourable = 0.24 + 0.16 = 0.4

$\therefore$ P = 0.4/1

12. Here standard deviation is 3.

13. Number of permutations with '2' in the first position = 19!

Number of permutations with '2' in the second position = 10 × 18!

(fill the first space with any of the 10 odd numbers and the 18 spaces after the 2 with 18 of the remaining numbers in 18! ways)

Number of permutations with '2' in 3rd position = 10 ×´ 9 × 17!

(fill the first 2 places with 2 of the 10 odd numbers and then the remaining 17 places with remaining 17 numbers)and so on until '2' is in 11th place. After that it is not possible to satisfy the given condition, since there are only 10 odd numbers available to fill before the '2'. So the desired number of permu-tations which satisfied the given condition is

19! + 10 × 18! + 10 × 9 × 17! + 10 × 9 × 8 × 16! + ... + 10! × 9!

Now the probability of this happenning is given by

$$\frac{19! + 10 \times 18! + 10 \times 9 \times 17! ... + 10! \times 9!}{20!}$$

Which is clearly not choices (*a*), (*b*) or (*c*)

∴ Answer is (*d*)

14. Required favourable cases

= Number of ways of selecting n elements out of the set of size $2n = \binom{2n}{n}$

Since each toss may result in either Head or Tail (2 possibilities), hence for $2n$ tosses,

total combinations = $2^{2n} = 4^n$

$$\therefore \text{ Required probability} = \frac{\text{Favourable cases}}{\text{Total cases}}$$

$$= \frac{\binom{2n}{n}}{4^n}$$

NUMERICAL TYPE QUESTIONS

1. Total probability = 1

So $$\int_a^1 \frac{1}{x^2} = 1$$

$$\left[-\frac{1}{x}\right]_a^1 = 1$$

$$\frac{1}{a} = 2$$

$$a = \frac{1}{2} = 0.5$$

2. Probability = $\frac{1}{3} = 0.33$.

3. $|x| = 2$

and $|y| = 20$

Total number of function from set x to set y is

$$20^2 = 400$$

and total number of one-one function from set x to set y is

$$^{20}P_2 = \frac{20!}{(20-2)!} = \frac{20!}{18!} \qquad \left(\because {}^nP_r = \frac{n!}{(n-r)!}\right)$$

$$= 20 \times 19 = 380$$

∴ Probabiltiy the F chosen to be one-one function

$$= \frac{380}{400} = \frac{38}{40} = \frac{19}{20} = 0.95$$

4. The smaller sticks, therefore, will range in length from almost 0 meters up to a maximum of 0.5 meters, with each length equally possible. Thus, the average length will be about 0.25 meters, or about a quarter of the stick.

5. 22 occurred in following ways

6 6 6 4 → 4 ways

6 6 5 5 → 6 ways

$$\text{Required probability} = \frac{6+4}{2296} = \frac{10}{2296}$$

⇒ $x = 10$

6. p = P [at least three computers are working]

= P (3 or 4 computers working)

$$= \frac{\left(4_{C_3}\right) \times \left(6_{C_1}\right)}{10_{C_4}} + \frac{4_{C_4}}{10_{C_4}}$$

$$= \frac{5}{42}$$

⇒ 100 p = 11.9.

7. Given words are

THE, QUICK, BROWN, FOX, JUMPS, OVER, THE, LAXY, DOG

LET X be the random variable such that X =length of the word

The Length of the words THE, FOX, THE, DOG is 3

The Length of the words OVER, LAXY is 4

The length of the words QUICK, BROWN, JUMPS, is 5

The corresponding probabilities are given below

x	3	4	5
P(X)	$\frac{4}{9}$	$\frac{2}{9}$	$\frac{3}{9}$

Expected length of the word

$$= \sum xp(x) = 3\left(\frac{4}{9}\right) + 4\left(\frac{2}{9}\right) + 5\left(\frac{3}{9}\right)$$

$= 3.8889$

8. Positive number between 1 to 100 (inclusive) not divisible by 2, 3 or 5 are

{1, 7, 11, 13, 17, 19, 23, 29, 31, 37, 41, 43, 47, 49, 53, 59, 61, 67, 71, 73, 77, 79, 83, 89, 91, 97}

$$P(E) = \frac{26}{100} = 0.26$$

9. Given $A \cup B = S$

$\Rightarrow P(A \cup B) = P(S) = 1$

$\Rightarrow P(A) + P(B) = 1$

($\because$ A & B are mutually exclusive)

$\Rightarrow P(B) = 1 - P(A)$

Maximum value of P(A) P(B) = ?

Maximum value of P (A) [1 – P (A)] = ?

Let P(A) = X

Let $f(x) = x(1 - x) = x - x^2$

for $f(x)$ maximum $\Rightarrow f'(x) = 0$

$\Rightarrow 1 - 2x = 0$

$\Rightarrow x = \frac{1}{2}$

$$f''(x) = -2;\ f''\left(\frac{1}{2}\right) < 0$$

$\therefore$ $f(x)$ has maximum

At $x = \frac{1}{2}$ and maximum value

$$= f\left(\frac{1}{2}\right) = \frac{1}{2}\left(1 - \frac{1}{2}\right) = \frac{1}{2}\cdot\frac{1}{2} = \frac{1}{4} = 0.25$$

■■

4

CHAPTER

Discrete Mathematics

MCQ TYPE QUESTIONS

2016

1. Let a_n be the number of n-bit strings that do NOT contain two consecutive 1s. Which one of the following is the recurrence relation for a_n?

(a) $a_n = a_{n-1} + 2a_{n-2}$

(b) $a_n = a_{n-1} + a_{n-2}$

(c) $a_n = 2a_{n-1} + a_{n-2}$

(d) $a_n = 2a_{n-1} + 2a_{n-2}$

2. A binary relation R on N N is defined as follows: (a,b)R(c,d) if a £ c or b £ d. Consider the following propositions:

P : R is reflexive

Q : R is transitive

Which one of the following statements is TRUE?

(a) Both P and Q are true

(b) P is true and Q is false

(c) P is false and Q is true

(d) Both P and Q are false

3. Which one of the following well-formed formulae in predicate calculus is NOT valid?

(a) $(\forall x p(x) \Rightarrow \forall x q(x)) \Rightarrow (\exists x \neg p(x) \vee \forall x q(x))$

(b) $(\exists x p(x) \vee \exists x q(x)) \Rightarrow \exists x(p(x) \vee q(x))$

(c) $\exists x(p(x) \wedge q(x)) \Rightarrow (\exists x p(x) \wedge \exists x q(x))$

(d) $\forall x(p(x) \vee q(x)) \Rightarrow (\forall x p(x) \vee \forall x q(x))$

4. Consider a set U of 23 different compounds in a Chemistry lab. There is a subset S of U of 9 compounds, each of which reacts with exactly 3 compounds of U. Consider the following statements:

I. Each compound in U\S reacts with an odd number of compounds.

II. At least one compound in U\S reacts with an odd number of compounds.

III. Each compound in U\S reacts with an even number of compounds.

Which one of the above statements is ALWAYS TRUE?

(a) Only I (b) Only II

(c) Only III (d) None

2015

5. Which one of the following is NOT equivalent to $p \leftrightarrow q$?

(a) $(\urcorner p \vee q) \vee (p \vee \urcorner q)$

(b) $(\urcorner p \vee q) \vee (q \rightarrow p)$

(c) $(\urcorner p \wedge q) \vee (p \wedge \urcorner q)$

(d) $(\urcorner p \wedge \urcorner q) \vee (p \wedge q)$

6. Consider the following two statements.

S1 : if a candidate is known to be corrupt, then he will not be elected

S2 : if a candidate is kind, he will be elected

Which one of the following statements follows from S_1 and S_2 per sound interference rules of logic?

(a) If a person is known to corrupt, he is kind

(b) If a person is not known to be corrupt, he is not kind

(c) If a person is kind, he is not known to be corrupt

(d) If a person is not kind, he is not known to be corrupt

7. Which one of the following well formed formulae is tautology ?

(a) $\forall x \exists y R(x, y) \leftrightarrow \exists y \forall x R(x, y)$

(b) $(\forall x[\exists y R(x, y) \rightarrow (x, y)]) \rightarrow \forall x \exists y S(x, y)$

(c) $[(\forall x \exists y (p(x, y) \rightarrow R(x, y))] \rightarrow [\forall x \exists y (\neg P(x, y) V R(x, y)]$

(d) $\forall x \forall y p(x, y) \rightarrow \forall x \forall y p(y, x)$

8. Suppose U is the power set of the set S = {1, 2, 3, 4, 5, 6}. For any T U, let |T| denote the number of element in T and T' denote the complement of T. For any T, R U, let T\R be the set of all elements in T which are not in R. Which one of the following is true ?

(a) $\forall X \in U(|X| = |X'|)$

(b) $\exists X \in U \exists Y \in U(|X| = 5, |Y| = 5 \text{ and } X \cap = Y = \phi)$

(c) $\forall X \in U \forall Y \in U(|X| = 2, |Y| = 3 \text{ and } X/Y = \phi)$

(d) $\forall X \in U \forall Y \in U(X/Y = Y'/X')$

9. For a set A, the power set of A is denoted by 2^A. If A = {5, {6}, {7}}, which of the following options are TRUE ?

I. $\phi \in 2^A$ II. $\phi \subseteq 2^A$

III. $\{5, \{6\}\} \in 2^A$ IV. $\{5\{6\}\} \subseteq 2^A$

(a) I and III only   (b) II and III only

(c) I, II and III only   (d) I, II and IV only

10. If $g(x) = 1 - x$ and $h(x) = \dfrac{x}{x-1}$, then $\dfrac{g(h(x))}{h(g(x))}$ is

(a) $\dfrac{h(x)}{g(x)}$ (b) $\dfrac{-1}{x}$

(c) $\dfrac{g(x)}{h(x)}$ (d) $\dfrac{x}{(1-x)^2}$

11. Suppose L = {p, q, r, s, t} is a lattice represented by the following Hasse diagram :

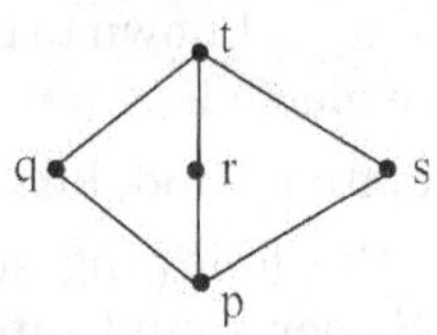

For any $x, y \in L$, not necessarily distinct, $x \vee y$ and $x \wedge y$ are join and meet of x, y respectively. Let $L^3 = \{(x, y, z) : x, y, z \in L\}$ be the set of all ordered triplets of the elements of L. Let p_r be the probability that an element $(x, y, z) \in L^3$ chosen equiprobably satisfies $x \vee (y \wedge z) = (x \vee y) \wedge (x \vee z)$. Then

(a) $p_r = 0$ (b) $p_r = 1$

(c) $0 < p_r \leq \dfrac{1}{5}$ (d) $\dfrac{1}{5} < p_r < 1$

12. Let R be the relation on the set of positive integers such that a aRb if and only if a and b are distinct and have a common divisor other than 1. Which one of the following statements about R is true?

(a) R is symmetric and reflexive but not transitive

(b) R is reflexive but not symmetric and not transitive

(c) R is transitive but not reflexive and not symmetric

(d) R is symmetric but not reflexive and not transitive

13. Let R be a relation on the set of ordered pairs of positive integers such that $((p, q), (r, s)) \in R$ if and only if $p - s = q - r$. Which one of the following is true about R ?

(a) Both reflexive and symmetric

(b) Reflexive but not symmetric

(c) Not reflexive but symmetric

(d) Neither reflexive nor symmetric

2014

14. Consider the statement :

"Not all that glitters is gold"

Predicate *glitters* (x) is true if x glitters and predicate *gold* (x) is true if x is gold. Which one of the following logical formulae represents the above statement?

(a) $\forall x : glitters(x) \Rightarrow \neg gold(x)$

(b) $\forall x : gold(x) \Rightarrow glitters(x)$

(c) $\exists x : gold(x) \wedge \neg glitters(x)$

(d) $\exists x : glitters(x) \wedge \neg gold(x)$

15. Which one of the following propositional logic formulas is TRUE when exactly two of p, q, and r are TRUE?

(a) $((p \leftrightarrow q) \wedge r) \upsilon (p \wedge q \wedge \sim r)$

(b) $(\sim (p \leftrightarrow q) \wedge r) \upsilon (p \wedge q \wedge \sim r)$

(c) $((p \rightarrow q) \wedge r) \upsilon (p \wedge q \wedge \sim r)$

(d) $(\sim (p \leftrightarrow q) \wedge r) \wedge (p \wedge q \wedge \sim r)$

16. Which one of the following Boolean expressions is NOT a tautology?

(a) $((a \rightarrow b) \wedge (b \rightarrow c)) \rightarrow (a \rightarrow c)$

(b) $(a \leftrightarrow c) \rightarrow (\sim b \rightarrow (a \wedge c))$

(c) $(a \wedge b \wedge c) \rightarrow (c \vee a)$

(d) $a \rightarrow (b \rightarrow a)$

17. Consider the following statements:

P: Good mobile phones are not cheap

Q: Cheap mobile phones are not good

L: P implies Q

M: Q implies P

N: P is equivalent to Q

Which one of the following about L, M, and N is CORRECT?

(a) Only L is TRUE.

(b) Only M is TRUE.

(c) Only N is TRUE.

(d) L, M and N are TRUE.

18. The CORRECT formula for the sentence, "not all rainy days are cold" is

(a) $\forall d$ (Rainy (d) $\wedge \sim$ Cold (d))

(b) $\forall d$ ($\sim$ Rainy (d) $\rightarrow$ Cold (d))

(c) $\exists d$($\sim$ Rainy (d) $\rightarrow$ Cold (d))

(d) $\exists d$ (Rainy (d) $\wedge \sim$ Cold (d))

19. Consider the following relation on subsets of the set S of integers between 1 and 2014. For two distinct subsets U and V of S we say U < V if the minimum element in the symmetric difference of the two sets is in U.

Consider the following two statements:

S1 : There is a subset of S that is larger than every other subset

S2 : There is a subset of S that is smaller than every other subset

Which one of the following is CORRECT?

(*a*) Both S1 and S2 are true

(*b*) S1 is true and S2 is false

(*c*) S2 is true and S1 is false

(*d*) Neither S1 nor S2 is ture

20. Let X and Y be finite sets and $f : X \to Y$ be a function. Which one of the following statements is TRUE?

(*a*) For any subsets A and B of X, $|f(A \cup B)| = |f(A)| + |f(B)|$

(*b*) For any subsets A and B of X, $f(A \cap B) = f(A) \cap f(B)$

(*c*) For any subsets A and B of X, $|f(A \cap B)| = \min\{|f(A)|, |f(B)|\}$

(*d*) For any subsets S and T of Y, $f^{-1}(S \cap T) = f^{-1}(S) \cap f^{-1}(T)$

21. Consider the set of all functions $f : \{0,1 \ldots, 2014\} \to \{0,1\ldots, 2014\}$ such that $f(f(i)) = i$, for all $0 \le i \le 2014$. Consider the following statements.

P. For each such function it must be the case the for every i, $f(i) = i$.

Q. For each such function it must be the case that for some i, $f(i) = i$.

R. Each such function must be onto.

Which one of the following is CORRECT?

(*a*) P, Q and R are true

(*b*) Only Q and R are true

(*c*) Only P and Q are true

(*d*) Only R is true

2013

22. What is the logical translation of the following statement?

"None of my friends are perfect."

(*a*) $\exists x\,(F(x) \wedge \neg P(x))$ (*b*) $\exists x\,(\neg F(x) \wedge P(x))$

(*c*) $\exists x(\neg F(x) \wedge \neg P(x))$ (*d*) $\neg \exists x\,(F(x) \wedge P(x))$

23. Which one of the following is NOT logically equivalent to $\neg\exists x\,(\forall y(\alpha) \wedge \forall z\,(\beta))$?

(*a*) $\forall x\,(\exists z\,(\neg\beta) \to \forall y\,(\alpha))$

(*b*) $\forall x\,(\forall z\,(\beta) \to \exists y\,(\neg \alpha))$

(*c*) $\forall x\,(\forall y\,(\alpha) \to \exists z\,(\neg \beta))$

(*d*) $\forall x\,(\exists y\,(\neg \alpha) \to \exists z\,(\neg \beta))$

24. A binary operation $\oplus$ on a set of integers is defined as $x \oplus y = x^2 + y^2$. Which one of the following statements is TRUE about $\oplus$?

(*a*) Commutative but not associative

(*b*) Both commutative and associative

(*c*) Associative but not commutative

(*d*) Neither commutative nor associative.

2012

25. What is the correct translation of the following statement into mathematical logic?

"Some real numbers are rational"

(*a*) $\exists x\,(\text{real}(x) \vee \text{rational}\,(x))$

(*b*) $\forall x\,(\text{real}\,(x) \to \text{rational}\,(x))$

(*c*) $\exists x\,(\text{real}\,(x) \wedge \text{rational}\,(x))$

(*d*) $\exists x\,(\text{rational}\,(x) \to \text{real}\,(x))$

26. How many onto (or surjective) functions are there from an n-element ($n \ge 2$) set to a 2-element set?

(*a*) 2^n (*b*) $2^n - 1$

(*c*) $2^n - 2$ (*d*) $2(2^n - 2)$

2011

27. Which one of the following options is CORRECT given three positive integers x, y and z, and a predicate

$P(x) = \neg\,(x = 1) \wedge \forall y\,(\exists z(x = y^* z) \Rightarrow (y = x) \vee (y = 1))$

(*a*) P(*x*) being true means that *x* is a prime number

(*b*) P(*x*) being true means that *x* is a number other than 1

(*c*) P(*x*) is always true irrespective of the value of *x*

(*d*) P(*x*) being true means that *x* has exactly two factors other than 1 and *x*

2010

28. Suppose the predicate F(*x*, *y*, *t*) is used to represent the statement that person *x* can fool person *y* at time *t*. Which one of the statements below expresses best the meaning of the formula

$\forall x \exists y \exists t\,(\neg F\,(x, y, t))$?

(*a*) Everyone can fool some person at some time

(*b*) No one can fool everyone all the time

(*c*) Everyone cannot fool some person all the time

(*d*) No one can fool some person at some time

29. What is the possible number of reflexive relations on a set of 5 elements?

(*a*) 2^{10} (*b*) 2^{15}

(*c*) 2^{20} (*d*) 2^{25}

30. Consider the set $S = \{1, \omega, \omega^2\}$, where ω and ω^2 are cube roots of unity. If * denotes the multiplication operation, then structure {S, *} forms

(*a*) a group (*b*) a ring

(*c*) an integral domain (*d*) a field

31. Let G = (V, E) be a graph. Define $\xi(G) = \sum_d i_d \times d$, where i_d is number of vertices of degree d in G. If S and T are two different trees with $\xi(S) = \xi(T)$, then

(a) $|S| = 2|T|$ (b) $|S| = |T| - 1$

(c) $|S| = |T|$ (d) $|S| = |T| + 1$

32. In a binary tree with n nodes, every node has an odd number of descendants. Every node is considered to be its own descendant. What is the number of nodes in the tree that have exactly one child?

(a) 0 (b) 1

(c) $(n - 1)/2$ (d) $n - 1$

33. The degree sequence of a simple graph is the sequence of the degrees of the nodes in the graph in decreasing order. Which of the following sequences can not be the degree sequence of any graph?

I. 7, 6, 5, 4, 4, 3, 2, 1 II. 6, 6, 6, 6, 3, 3, 2, 2

III. 7, 6, 6, 4, 4, 3, 2, 2 IV. 8, 7, 7, 6, 4, 2, 1, 1

(a) I and II (b) III and IV

(c) IV only (d) II and IV

2009

34. Which one of the following is the most appropriate logical formula to represent the statement:

" Gold and silver ornaments are precious"

The following notations are used :

$G(x)$: x is a gold ornament.

$S(x)$: x is a silver ornament.

$P(x)$: x is precious.

(a) $\forall x(P(x) \rightarrow (G(x) \wedge S(x)))$

(b) $\forall x((G(x) \wedge S(x)) \rightarrow P(x))$

(c) $\exists x((G(x) \wedge S(x)) \rightarrow P(x))$

(d) $\forall x((G(x) \vee S(x)) \rightarrow P(x))$

35. Consider the following well-formed formulae:

I. $\neg\forall x(P(x))$ II. $\neg\exists x(P(x))$

III. $\neg\exists x(\neg P(x))$ IV. $\exists x(\neg P(x))$

Which of the above are equivalent?

(a) I and III (b) I and IV

(c) II and III (d) II and IV

36. Which one of the following is NOT neccessarily a property of a Group?

(a) Commutativity

(b) Associativity

(c) Existence of inverse for every element

(d) Existence of identity

37. Consider the binary relation

R = {(x, y), (x, z), (z, x), (z, y)} on the set {x, y, z}.

Which one of the following is TRUE ?

(a) R is symmetric but NOT antisymmetric.

(b) R is NOT symmetric but antisymmetric.

(c) R is both symmetric and antisymmetric.

(d) R is neither symmetric nor antisymmetric.

38. For the composition table of a cyclic group shown below

	a	b	c	d
a	a	b	c	d
b	b	a	d	c
c	c	d	b	a
d	d	c	a	b

Which one of the following choices is correct ?

(a) a, b are generators (b) b, c are generators

(c) c, d are generators (d) d, a are generators

39. The binary operation □ is defined as follows:

P	Q	P □ Q
T	T	T
T	F	T
F	T	F
F	F	T

Which one of the following is equivalent to P ∨ Q?

(a) ¬ Q □ ¬ P (b) P □ ¬ Q

(c) ¬ P □ Q (d) ¬ P □ ¬ Q

40. What is the chromatic number of an n-vertex simple connected graph which does not contain any odd length cycle ? Assume $n \geq 2$.

(a) 2 (b) 3

(c) n – 1 (d) n

41. Which one of the following is TRUE for any simple connected undirected graph with more than 2 vertices?

(a) No two vertices have the same degree.

(b) At least two vertices have the same degree.

(c) At least three vertices have the same degree.

(d) All vertices have the same degree.

2008

42. Let fsa and pda be two predicates such that fsa(x) means x is a finite state automaton, and pda(y) means that y is a pushdown automaton. Let equivalent be another predicate such that equivalent (a, b) means a and b are equivalent. Which of the following first order logic statements represents the following

Each finite state automaton has an equivalent pushdown automaton.

(a) $(\forall x\, fsa(x)) \Rightarrow (\exists y\, pda(y) \wedge equivalent(x, y))$

(b) $\sim\forall y\, (\exists x\, fsa(x)) \Rightarrow pda(y) \wedge equivalent(x, y))$

(c) $\forall x\, \exists y\, (fsa(x)) \wedge pda(y) \wedge equivalent(x, y))$

(d) $\forall x\, \exists y\, (fsa(y)) \wedge pda(x) \wedge equivalent(x, y))$

43. P and Q are two propositions. Which of the following logical expressions are equivalent?

I. $P \vee \sim Q$

II. $\sim(\sim P \wedge Q)$

III. $(P \wedge Q) \vee (P \wedge \sim Q) \vee (\sim P \wedge \sim Q)$

IV. $(P \wedge Q) \vee (P \wedge \sim Q) \vee (\sim P \wedge Q)$

(*a*) Only I and II (*b*) Only I, II, and III

(*c*) Only I, II and IV (*d*) All of I, II, III, and IV

44. If P, Q, R are subsets of the universal set U, then $(P \cap Q \cap R) \cup (P^c \cap Q \cap R) \cup Q^c \cup R^c$ is

(*a*) $Q^c \cup R^c$ (*b*) $P \cup Q^c \cup R^c$

(*c*) $P^c \cup Q^c \cup R^c$ (*d*) U

2007

45. Let S be a set of n elements. The number of ordered pairs in the largest and the smallest equivalence relations on S are

(*a*) n and n (*b*) n^2 and n

(*c*) n^2 and 0 (*d*) n and 1

46. Consider the set S = {*a*, *b*, *c*, *d*}.

Consider following 4 partitions $\pi_1, \pi_2, \pi_3, \pi_4$ on S :

$\pi_1 = \{\overline{abcd}\}$, $\pi_2 = \{\overline{ab}, \overline{cd}\}$,

$\pi_3 = \{\overline{abc}, \overline{d}\}$, $\pi_4 = \{\overline{a}, \overline{b}, \overline{c}, \overline{d}\}$.

Let $\prec$ be partial order on the set of partitions $S' = \{\pi_1, \pi_2, \pi_3, \pi_4\}$ defined as follows :

$\pi_i \prec \pi_j$ if and only if π_i refines π_j. The poset digram for $(S', \prec)$ is

(*a*)

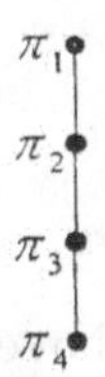

(*b*)

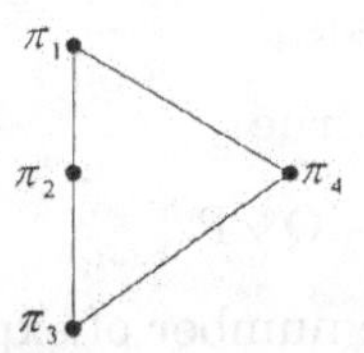

(*c*)

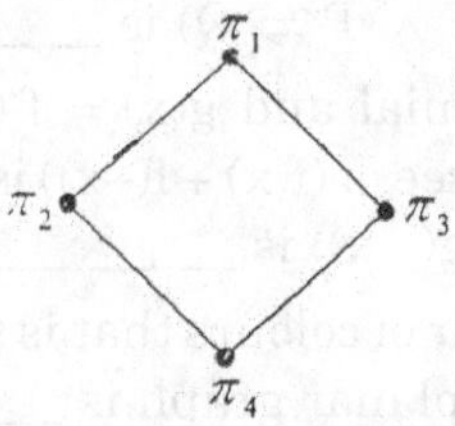

(*d*)

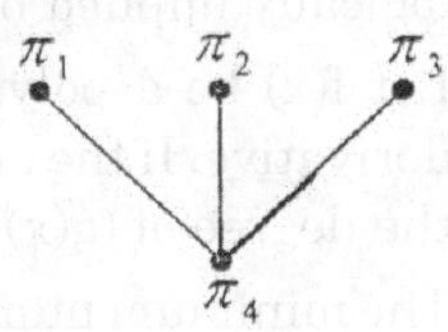

47. Consider set of (column) vectors defined by

$$X = \{x \in R^3 \mid x_1 + x_2 + x_3 = 0$$

where $x^T = [x_1, x_2, x_3]^T\}$.

Which of the following is **TRUE**?

(*a*) $\{[1,-1,0]^T, [1,0,-1]^T\}$ is a basis for the subspace X.

(*b*) $\{[1,-1,0]^T, [1,0,-1]^T\}$ is a linearly independent set, but it does not span X and therefore is not a basis of X

(*c*) X is not a subspace of R^3

(*d*) None of these

48. Let G be the non-planar graph with the minimum possible number of edges. Then G has

(*a*) 9 edges and 5 vertices

(*b*) 9 edges and 6 vertices

(*c*) 10 edges and 5 vertices

(*d*) 10 edges and 6 vertices

49. Consider the DAG with V = {1,2,3,4,5,6}, shown below.

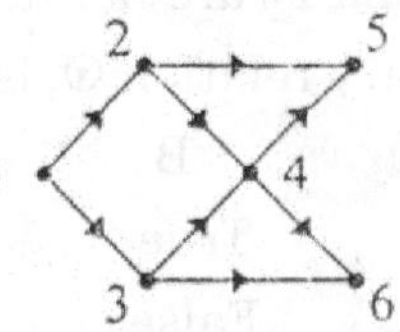

Which of the following is **NOT** a topological ordering?

(*a*) 1 2 3 4 5 6 (*b*) 1 3 2 4 5 6

(*c*) 1 3 2 4 6 5 (*d*) 3 2 4 1 6 5

50. Let *Graph*(x) be a predicate which denotes that x is a graph. Let *Connected*(x) be a predicate which denotes that x is connected. Which of the following first order logic sentences **DOES NOT** represent the statement; *"Not every graph is connected"*?

(*a*) $\neg\forall x$ (Graph(x) $\Rightarrow$ Connected (x))

(*b*) $\exists x$ (Graph(x) $\wedge\neg$ Connected (x))

(*c*) $\neg\forall x$ ($\neg$ Graph(x)) $\vee$ Connected(x))

(*d*) $\forall x$(Graph(x) $\Rightarrow$ $\neg$ Connected(x))

51. Which of the following graphs has an Eulerian circuit?

(*a*) Any k-regular graph where k is an even number

(*b*) A complete graph on 90 vertices

(*c*) The complement of a cycle on 25 vertices

(*d*) None of these

2006

52. Which one of the first order predicate calculus statements given below correctly expresses the following English statement ?

Tigers and lions attack if they are hungry or threatened.

(*a*) $\forall x$ [(tiger (x) $\wedge$ lion (x)) $\to$ {(hungry (x) $\vee$ threatened (x)) $\to$ attacks (x)}]

(*b*) $\forall x$ [(tiger (x) $\vee$ lion (x)) $\to$ {(hungry (x) $\vee$ threatened (x)) $\wedge$ attacks (x)}]

(*c*) $\forall x$ [(tiger (x) $\vee$ lion (x)) $\to$ {(attacks (x) $\to$ (hungry (x) $\vee$ threatened (x))}]

(*d*) $\forall x$ [tiger (x) $\vee$ lion (x)) $\to$ {(hungry (x) $\vee$ threatened (x)) $\to$ attacks (x)}]

53. Consider the following propositional statements

$P_1 : ((A \wedge B) \rightarrow C)) \equiv ((A \rightarrow C) \wedge (B \rightarrow C))$

$P_2 : ((A \vee B) \rightarrow C)) \equiv ((A \rightarrow C) \vee (B \rightarrow C))$

Which one of the following is true ?

(a) P_1 is a tautology, but not P_2

(b) P_2 is a tautology, but not P_1

(c) P_1 and P_2 are both tautologies

(d) Both P_1 and P_2 are not tautologies

54. A logical binary relation ⊙, is defined as follows

A	B	A ⊙ B
True	True	True
True	False	True
False	True	False
False	False	True

Let ~ be the unary negation (NOT) operator, with higher precedence, then ⊙. Which one of the following is equivalent to $A \wedge B$?

(a) (~ A ⊙ B) (b) ~ (A ⊙ ~ B)

(c) ~ (~A ⊙ ~ B) (d) ~ (~ A ⊙ B)

55. Let, X, Y, Z be sets of sizes x, y and z respectively. Let W = X × Y and E be the set of all subsets of W. The number of functions from Z to E is

(a) z (b) $z \times 2^{xy}$

(c) z (d) 2^{xyz}

56. The set {1, 2, 3, 5, 7, 8, 9} under multiplication modulo 10 is not a group. Given below are four plausible reasons. Which one of them is false ?

(a) It is not closed

(b) 2 does not have an inverse

(c) 3 does not have an inverse

(d) 8 does not have an inverse

57. A relation R is defined on ordered pairs of integers as follows

(x, y) R (u, v) if $x < u$ and $y > v$.

Then R is

(a) neither a Partial Order nor an Equivalence Relation

(b) a Partial Order but not a Total Order

(c) a Total Order

(d) an Equivalence Relation

58. Let E, F and G be finite sets.

Let $X = (E \cap F) - (F \cap G)$ and

$Y = (E - (E \cap G)) - (E - F)$.

Which one of the following is true?

(a) $X \subset Y$ (b) $X \supset Y$

(c) $X = Y$ (d) $X - Y \neq \varnothing$ and $Y - X \neq \varnothing$

59. Let S = {1, 2, 3, ..., m} $m > 3$.

Let X_1, ..., X_n be subsets of S each of size 3.

Define a function f from S to the set of natural numbers as, $f(i)$ is the number of sets X_j that contain the element i, i.e. is $f(i) = |\{j \mid i \in X_j\}|$.

Then $\sum_{i=1}^{m} f(i)$ is

(a) $3m$ (b) $3n$

(c) $2m + 1$ (d) $2n + 1$

NUMERICAL TYPE QUESTIONS

2016

1. Let p, q, r, s represent the following propositions.

$p : x \in \{8, 9, 10, 11, 12\}$

$q : x$ is a composite number

$r : x$ is a perfect square

$s : x$ is a prime number

The integer $x \geq 2$ which satisfies $\neg((p \Rightarrow q) \wedge (\neg r \vee \neg s))$ is ______.

2. The coefficient of x^{12} in $(x^3 + x^4 + x^5 + x^6 + ...)^3$ is ______.

3. Consider the recurrence relation $a_1 = 8$, $a_n = 6n^2 + 2n + a_{n-1}$. Let $a_{99} = K \times 10^4$. The value of K is ______.

4. Consider the following expressions:

(i) false (ii) Q

(iii) true (iv) $P \vee Q$

(v) $\neg Q \vee P$

The number of expressions given above that are logically implied by $P \wedge (P \Rightarrow Q)$ is __________.

5. Let f(x) be a polynomial and g(x) = f′(x) be its derivative. If the degree of (f(x) + f(–x)) is 10, then the degree of (g(x) – g(– x)) is __________.

6. The minimum number of colours that is sufficient to vertex-colour any planar graph is __________.

7. The value of the expression 13^{99} (mod 17), in the range 0 to 16, is________

8. Suppose the functions F and G can be computed in 5 and 3 nanoseconds by functional units U_F and U_G, respectively. Given two instances of U_F and two instances of U_G, it is required to implement the computation $F(G(X_i))$ for $1 \leq i \leq 10$. Ignoring all other delays, the minimum time required to complete this computation is ________ nanoseconds.

2015

9. The cardinality of the power set of {0, 1, 2, ..., 10} is ______

10. The number of onto function (surjective function) from set X = {1, 2, 3, 4} to set Y = {a, b, c} is ______.

11. The number of 4 digit numbers having their digits in non-decreasing order (from left to right) constructed by using the digits belonging to the set {1, 2, 3} is _____.

2014

12. The base (or radix) of the number system such that the following equation holds is __________.

$$\frac{312}{20} = 13.1$$

13. Let S denote the set of all functions $f : \{0, 1\}^4 \to \{0, 1\}$. Denote by N the number of functions from S to the set {0,1}. The value of $\log_2 \log_2$ N is______.

14. Let G be a group with 15 elements. Let L be a subgroup of G. It is known that L ≠ G and that the size of L is at least 4. The size of L is ______.

15. If V_1 and V_2 are 4-dimensional subspaces of a 6-dimensional vector space V, then the smallest possible dimension of $V_1 \cap V_2$ is ______.

16. There are two elements x, y in a group (G, *) such that every element in the group can be written as a product of some number of x's and y's in some order. It is known that

$$x * x = y * y = x * y * x * y = y * x * y * x = e$$

where e is the identity element. The maximum number of elements in such a group is ______.

17. A pennant is a sequence of numbers, each number being 1 or 2. An n-pennant is a sequence of numbers with sum equal to n. For example, (1,1,2) is a 4-pennant. The set of all possible 1- pennants is {(1)}, the set of all possible 2-pennants is {(2), (1,1)}and the set of all 3-pennants is {(2,1), (1,1,1), (1,2)}. Note that the pennant (1, 2) is not the same as the pennant (2,1). The number of 10- pennants is __________.

ANSWERS

MCQ Type Questions

1. (b)	2. (a)	3. (d)	4. (b)	5. (c)	6. (c)	7. (c)	8. (d)	9. (c)	10. (a)
11. (d)	12. (d)	13. (c)	14. (d)	15. (b)	16. (b)	17. (d)	18. (d)	19. (a)	20. (d)
21. (b)	22. (d)	23. (a, d)	24. (a)	25. (c)	26. (c)	27. (a)	28. (b)	29. (c)	30. (a)
31. (c)	32. (a)	33. (d)	34. (d)	35. (b)	36. (a)	37. (d)	38. (c)	39. (b)	40. (a)
41. (b)	42. (a)	43. (b)	44. (d)	45. (b)	46. (c)	47. (b)	48. (b)	49. (d)	50. (d)
51. (a)	52. (d)	53. (d)	54. (d)	55. (d)	56. (c)	57. (a)	58. (c)	59. (b)	

Numerical Type Questions

1. (11)	2. (10)	3. (198)	4. (3)	5. (9)	6. (4)	7. (4)	8. (30)	9. (2048)	10. (36)
11. (15)	12. (5)	13. (16)	14. (5)	15. (2)	16. (4)	17. (89)			

EXPLANATIONS

MCQ TYPE QUESTIONS

1. Let n length of string

$$T(n) = a_n$$

10............. or 0.............

T$(n-2)$ T$(n-1)$

$$T(n) = T(n-2) + T(n-1)$$

$$= a_{n-2} + a_{n-1}$$

2. A binary relation R on N × N is defined as (a, b) R(C, d)

Reflexive: (a, a) R(a, a)

Since a ≤ a, and a ≤ a

Transitive: (a, b) R (c, d) and (c, d) R(m, n) then (a, b) R(m, n)

Suppose (a, b) R(c, d)

⇒ a ≤ c and b ≤ d

and (c, d) R(m, n)

⇒ c ≤ m, d ≤ n

Since a ≤ c, and c ≤ m so a ≤ m

b ≤ d and d ≤ n, so b ≤ n

∴ (a, b) R(m, n)

(OR)

P. we have a ≤ a and b ≤ b

⇒ (a, b) R(a, b)

⇒ R is reflexive

∴ P is true

Q. Let (a, b) R(c, d) and (c, d) R (e, f)

⇒ {a ≤ c and b ≤ d} and { c ≤ e and d ≤ f}

⇒ {a ≤ e and b ≤ f}

⇒ (a, b) R (e, f)

⇒ R is transitive

Hence both the statements P and Q are true.

3. (A) The well formed formula is valid, because L.H.S ⇔ R.H.S

(B) The well formed formula is valid, because L.H.S ⇔ R.H.S.

(C)

1.	$\exists_x\{p(x) \wedge q(x)\}$	premise
2.	$p(a) \wedge q(a)$	(1) E.S
3.	p(a)	(2) simplification
4.	q(a)	(2) simplification
5.	$\exists_x p(x)$	(3) E.G
6.	$\exists_x q(x)$	(4) E.G
7.	$\exists_x p(x) \wedge \exists_x q(x)$	(5), (6) conjunction

Proved

(D) Let p(x): x is a musician

and q(x): x is a filmstar

Let U = {Amitabh Bachchan, Arjun Rampal, Akshay Kumar, Ravi Shankar, Bismillah Khan }

Be the universe of discourse.

Here antecedent of the implication is true but consequent is false.

So option (D) is not valid.

4. Let us denote the problem by a non directed graph with 23 vertices (compounds). If two compounds in chemistry lab react with each other, then there exists an edge between the corresponding vertices. In the graph, we have 9 vertices with degree 3 (i.e. odd degree). By sum of degrees of vertices theorem atleast one of the remaining vertices should have odd degree.

6. If the person is kind, he is not known to be corrupt

8. Counter example :

(A) Let X = {1}

⇒ X′ = S – X = {2, 3, 4, 5, 6}

⇒ $|X| = |X'|$

(B) Since $|S| = 6$

and $|X| = 5 = |Y|$

∴ Atleast 4 elements common in X and Y

⇒ X ∩ Y = φ is false

(C) Counter Example :

Let X = {1, 2}

and Y = {2, 3, 4}

then $\frac{X}{Y} = \{1\} = \phi$

(D) $\frac{X}{Y} = X - Y = X \cap Y'$

and $\frac{Y'}{X'} = Y' - X' = Y' \cap (X')'$

$= Y' \cap X = X \cap Y'$

∴ $\frac{X}{Y} = \frac{Y'}{X'}, \forall X, Y \in U$

9. A = {5, {6}, {7}}

Power Set of A, (2^A) = {φ, 5, {6}, {7}, {5, {6}}, {5, {7}}, {{6}, {7}}, {5, {6}, {7}}}

Options I, II and III are satisfied.

∴ Option (*c*) is correct.

10. $g(x) = 1 - x$ and $h(x) = \dfrac{x}{x-1}$

$$\text{Now } g(h(x)) = g\left(\frac{x}{x-1}\right) = 1 - \frac{x}{x-1}$$

$$= \frac{x-1-x}{x-1}$$

$$= \frac{-1}{x-1}$$

$$\text{and } h(g(x)) = h(1-x) = \frac{1-x}{1-x-1} = \frac{1-x}{-x}$$

$$\text{Now } \frac{g(h(x))}{h(g(x))} = \frac{-1}{x-1} \times \frac{(-x)}{1-x} = \frac{-x}{(x-1)^2}$$

Now from option (*a*),

$$\frac{h(x)}{g(x)} = \frac{x}{x-1} \times \frac{1}{1-x}$$

$$= \frac{-x}{(x-1)^2}$$

∴ Option (*a*) is correct.

11. $\frac{1}{5} < P_r < 1$

12. R is not reflexive not transitive

R is symmetric

consider $a = 3, b = 6, c = 8$

The common divisor of 3 & 6 is 3

The common divisor of 6 & 8 is 2

But there is no common divisor of 3 & 8

Hence 3R6, 6R8 but not 3R8

13. Since $p - q \neq q - p$

∴ (p, q) R (p, q)

⇒ R is not reflective

Let (p, q) R (r, s)

then $p - s = q - r$

⇒ $r - q = s - p$

⇒ (r, s) R (p, q)

⇒ R is symmetric

14. It means "It is false that every glitter is gold" or "some glitters are not gold".Then we can say "atleast one glitter object is not gold".

15. P = T*q* = F and *r* = T

Option *a* will become false

Option *c* will become false

Option *d* is always false

16.

a	b	c	$a \leftrightarrow c$	$\sim b$	$a \wedge c$	$\sim b \rightarrow (a \wedge c)$	$(a \leftrightarrow c) \rightarrow (\sim b \rightarrow (a \wedge c))$
F	F	F	T	T	F	T	T
F	F	T	F	T	F	T	F
F	T	F	T	F	F	T	T
F	T	T	F	F	F	T	F
T	F	F	F	T	F	T	F
T	F	T	T	T	T	T	T
T	T	F	F	F	F	F	T
T	T	T	T	F	T	F	T

Hence $(a \leftrightarrow c) \rightarrow (\sim b \rightarrow (a \wedge c))$ is not Tautology.

17. g : mobile is good

c : mobile is cheap

P : Good mobile phones are not cheap

$$\cong g \rightarrow \neg c \cong (\neg g \vee \neg c)$$

$$[\because a \rightarrow b \equiv \neg a \vee b]$$

Q : Cheap mobile phones are not good

$$\cong c \rightarrow \neg g \cong (\neg c \vee \neg g)$$

∴ Both P and Q are equivalent which means P and Q imply each other.

18. Given statement is

$$\sim \forall d[r(d) \rightarrow c(d)]$$

$$\equiv \sim \forall d[\sim r(d) \vee c(d)]$$

$$\equiv \exists d[r(d) \wedge \sim c(d)]$$

Since $p \rightarrow q \equiv \sim p \vee q$ and let $r(d)$ be rainy day, $c(d)$ be cold day).

19. Let U = {1, 2, ... 1008}

V = {1009, ... 2014}

Since subset S_1 will be greater than every other subset *i.e.* V & subset S_2 will be less than every other subset *i.e.* U, So both statements will be true.

20. $f: X \rightarrow Y$ defined by $f(a) = 1, f(b) = 1, f(c) = 2$ where

$X = \{a,b,c\}$ $Y = \{1,2\}$

Let $A = \{a,c\}$, $B = \{b,c\}$ be subsets of X

then $|f(A \cup B)| = 2$; $|f(A)| = 2$; $|f(B)| = 2$

$f(A \cap B) = \{2\}$; $f(A) = \{1,2\}$; $f(B) = \{1,2\}$

$f(A) \cap f(B) = \{1,2\}$

$|f(A \cap B)| = 1$

$\therefore$ Option (a), (b), (c) are not true

Hence, Option (d) is true

21. Let us consider a function (counter example) as

$f(0) = 1$, $f(1) = 0$, $f(2) = 3$, $f(3) = 2, \ldots,$ $f(2012) = 2013$,

$f(2013) = 2012$ and $f(2014) = 2014$

Clearly $f(f(i)) = i$ for $0 \le i \le 2014$

Here $f(i) \ne i$ for every i and $f(i) = i$ for some i

Also f is onto

Hence, only Q and R are true

22. Given : Statement

"None of my friends are perfect"

To find : Logical translation of it.

Analysis : The statement means that of all the friends that I have, none of them are prefect.

Hence, if we look at only friend and if any of them being perfect. We get logical

$$\exists \forall x(F(x) \wedge P(x))$$

This means there is an x who is friend of mine and is also perfect.

Now, we need to negate the statement since none are perfect.

$\therefore$ $\rightarrow \exists x(F(x) \wedge P(x))$

$\rightarrow$ option (D)

In english, this statement is there is no x s.t., F(x) and P(x) is true simultaneously.

24. $x \oplus y = x^2 + y^2$

$y \oplus x = y^2 + x^2$

$= x^2 + y^2$ (Q addition is cumulative)

$= x \oplus y$

$\therefore$ $\oplus$ is cumulative

$(x \oplus y) \oplus z = (x^2 + y^2)^2 + z^2$

$x \oplus (y \oplus z) = 2 \oplus (y^2 + z^2)^2$

$= x^2 + (y^2 + z^2)^2$

Clearly, $(x \oplus y) \oplus z$ 1 $x \oplus (y \oplus z)$

$\therefore$ $\oplus$ is not associative

25. Option A: There exists x which is either real or rational and can be both.

Option B: All real numbers are rational

Option C: There exists a real number which is rational.

Option D: There exists some number which is not rational or which is real.

26. Total number of functions is 2^n, out of which there will be exactly two functions where all elements map to exactly one element, so total number of onto functions is $2^n - 2$

28. Given : F(x, y, t) a predicate

$\forall x \exists y \exists t (\neg F(x, y, t))$

Since $\forall x \exists y \exists t (\neg F(x, y, t))$

$\Rightarrow \forall x \neg (\forall y \forall t (F(x, y, t))$

So, we can say no one can fool everyone all the time.

29. Total number of reflexive relations in set of n elements

$= 2^{n^2-n}$

$= 2^{5^2-5}$ .....(since $n = 5$)

$= 2^{20}$

30. *A group should satisfy following relations :*

(*i*) Closure (*ii*) Inverse

(*iii*) Identity (*iv*) Associative

in $(1, \omega, \omega^2)$

We can say

$1 * \omega = \omega$ all are elements

$\omega * \omega^2 = 1$ of group than

$\omega^2 * 1 = \omega^2$ it is closure

Hence, we think about inverse, then this should satisfy

$a * e = a$

where e is identity element means $\exists e \in G$ have identity element 1

means $1 * \omega = \omega$, $1 * 1 = 1$ identities

$1 * \omega^2 = \omega^2$

Hence it should be inverse

means $a * b = 3$

means b is the inverse element a, b, e 64

here $1 * 1 = 1$, $\omega * \omega^2 = 1$, $\omega^2 * \omega = 1$ } inverse

So, it also hold Associative for this

$a * (b * c) = (a * b) * c$

means $1 * (\omega * \omega^2) = (1 * \omega) * \omega^2$ } Associative

means $(1, \omega, \omega^2)$ is a group.

31. Since $\Sigma\partial(V) = 2e$

$\therefore$ $\xi(s) = \xi(T)$

$\Rightarrow$ $|S| = |T|$

32. Given that a node has odd number of descendants possible only when it is fully binary tree like.

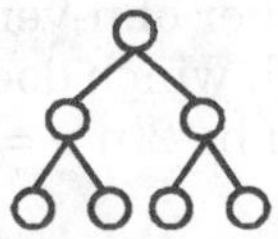

- So in fully binary tree, every node has two child or zero child (zero child when there is one node exactly)
- So, number of nodes in tree that type having exactly one child is zero = e]

33. Havell-Hakimi algorithm can be used to check whether a given degree sequence is a graph or not.

The algorithm is

1. remove top node of the sequence.
2. subtract "1" from as many nodes in remaining sequence as the degree of top node that was removed.
3. rearrange this sequence in non increasing order.
4. check if resulting sequence is a graph.
5. proceed again to step 1.

If the given sequence is not a graph we will see a voilation in step 4, such as presence of negative degrees in the sequence. Otherwise the algorithm will bottom out with a degree sequence consisting of only even no. of 1's and any number of 0's.

Now applying the algorithm to the degree sequence I, II, III and IV, one by one :

I. 7, 6, 5, 4, 3, 2, 1

6, 5, 4, 4, 3, 2, 1	(Step 1)
5, 4, 3, 3, 2, 1, 0	(Step 2)
5, 4, 3, 3, 2, 1, 0	(Step 3)
Sequence is a graph	(Step 4)
4, 3, 3, 2, 1, 0	(Step 1)
3, 2, 2, 1, 0, 0	(Step 2)
3, 2, 2, 1, 0, 0	(Step 3)
Sequence is a graph	(Step 4)
2, 2, 1, 0, 0	(Step 1)
1, 1, 0, 0, 0	(Step 2)
1, 1, 0, 0, 0	(Step 3)

Sequence is a graph

Now, the algorithm ends, since the sequence has only 0's and even number of 1's.

The final sequence corresponds to following valid greah.

Similarly for sequence II.

II. 6, 6, 6, 6, 3, 3, 2, 2

6, 6, 6, 3, 3, 2, 2	(Step 1)
5, 5, 5, 2, 2, 1, 2	(Step 2)
5, 5, 5, 2, 2, 2, 1	(Step 3)
Sequence is a graph	(Step 4)
5, 5, 2, 2, 2, 1	(Step 1)
4, 4, 1, 1, 1, 1	(Step 2)
4, 4, 1, 1, 1, 1	(Step 3)
Sequence is a graph	(Step 4)
4, 1, 1, 1, 1	(Step 1)
3, 0, 0, 0, 1	(Step 2)
3, 1, 0, 0, 0	(Step 3)
Sequence is a graph	(Step 4)
1, 0, 0, 0	(Step 1)
0, – 1, – 1, 0	(Step 2)
0, 0, – 1, – 1	(Step 3)

The sequence is not a graph (Step 4), since negative degrees not possible in a valid graph. So, algorithm ends.

II is cannot be the degree sequence of any graph.

Similarly we can show that III is degree sequence of some graph and IV is not a degree sequence of any grpah.

So, correct answer is choice (d) II and IV.

34. Given : gold and silver ornament are precious.

We use

gold and silver   gold $\vee$ silver

$\forall\ ((G(x) \vee S(x)))$

gold and silver $\rightarrow$ precious

$\forall x((G(x) \vee S(x)) \rightarrow P(x)$

Alternately

"Gold and silver ornaments are precious"

Gold ornaments are alone precious.

Silver ornaments are also alone precious.

Gold and silver ornaments are also precious

$\forall x((G(x) \vee S(x)) \rightarrow P(x))$

35. Universal qualification of P(x) is denoted $\forall x$ P(x). The symbol $\forall$ is called *universal quantifier.*

The existential qualification of predicate P(x) is statement, there exist a value of x for which P(x) is true. The existential qualification of P(x) is denoted by $\exists$(x) P(x). The symbol $\exists$ is called *existential quantitier.*

$\therefore \quad \neg \forall x\, P(x) = \exists x (\neg P(x))$

$\neg$ sign is for not

36. Group is an algebraic system having property of closed under operation, associative, contain identity element and exist inverse of every element.

Alternately

A group (G, *) is a monoid with identity e that the additional property that for every element a ε G there exist an element a' ε G such that $a * a' = a^i \quad a = e$. Thus group is set together with binary operation $*$.

It follows property :

(i) *Associativity :* $(a * b) * c = a * (b * c)$

(ii) *Inverse for every element :*

$a * e = e * a$ for every a ε G

(iii) *Existance of identity :* $a * a' = a' * a$

37. R = {(x, y), (x, z), (z, x), (z, y)}

If (a, b) ∈ R then (b, a) ∉ R to be symmetric but (x, y) ∈ R and (y, x) ∉ R

So, R is NOT Symmetric

If (a, b) ∈ R then (b, a) ∈ R to be Antisymmetric but (x, z) ∈ R and (z, x) ∈R

So, R is NOT Antisymmetric

38.

*	a	b	c	d
a	a	b	c	d
b	b	a	d	c
c	c	d	b	a
d	d	c	a	b

Hence c, d is generator

Alternately

Every element in Cyclic Group can be represented in the power of any generator.

From given table

$a*a = a$

$b*b = a$

$c*c = c^2 = b$

$c^3 = c*c^2 = c*b = d$

$c^4 = c*c^3 = c*d = a$

$d*d = d^2 = b$

$d^3 = d*d^2 = d*b = c$

$d^4 = d*d^3 = d*c = a$

39.

P	Q	P□Q	P∨Q	P□¬Q
T	T	T	T	T
T	F	T	T	T
F	T	F	T	T
F	F	T	F	F

40. Chromatic number of n-vertex simple connected undirected graph which does not contain any odd length cycle will be 2(n > = 2).

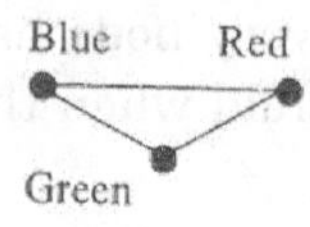

(For n=3 Odd Length Cycle)

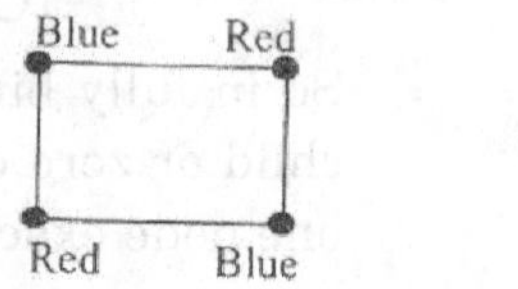

(For n=4 Even Length Cycle)

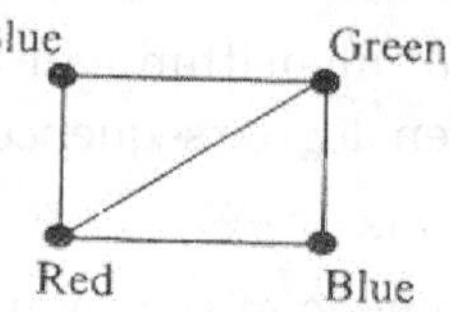

(For n=4 Odd Length Cycle)

41. Atleast 2 vertices have the same degree.

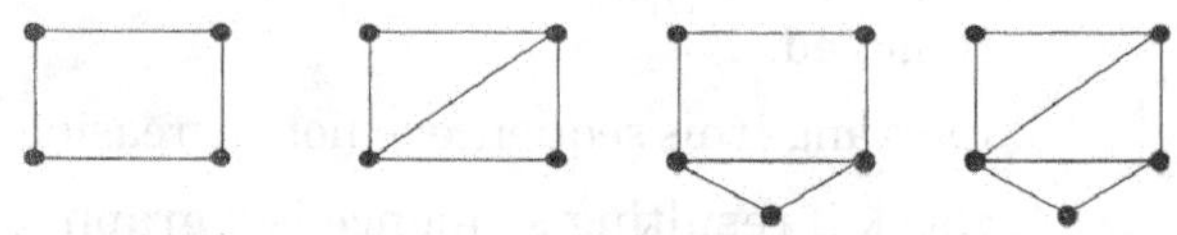

Alternately

For simple corrected graph with more than two vertices at least 2 vertices have the same degree

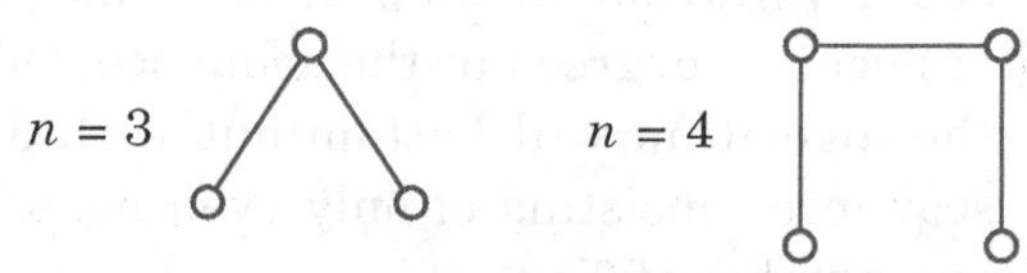

42. "For x which is an fsa, there exists a y which is a pda and which is equivalent to x."

($\forall x$ fsa (x)) $\Rightarrow$ ($\exists y$ pda $(y) \wedge$ equivalent (x, y)) is the logical representation.

43. IT can solved by truth table.

P	Q	P∨ ~Q	(–P∧Q)	P∧Q	P∧–Q	~P∧ ~Q
T	T	T	F	T	F	F
T	F	T	F	F	T	F
F	T	F	T	F	F	F
F	F	T	F	T	F	T

Using above table, we get

P	Q	I	II	III	IV
T	T	T	T	T	T
T	F	T	T	T	T
F	T	F	F	F	F
F	F	T	T	T	T

44.

$P \cap Q \cap R =$ 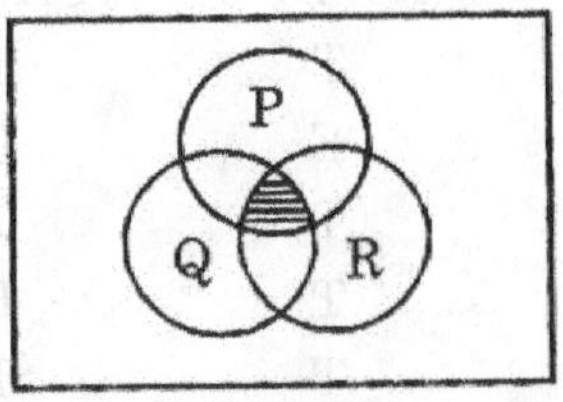

$P^C \cap Q \cap R =$ 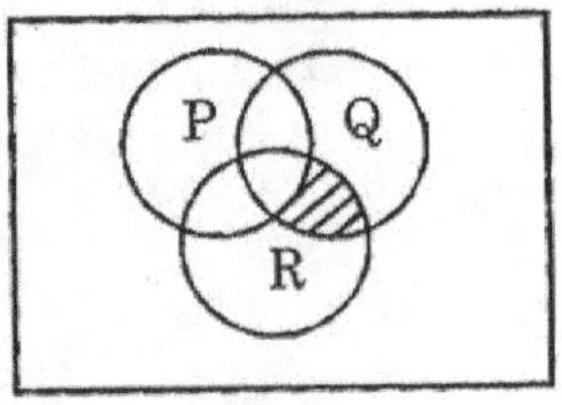

$Q^C =$ 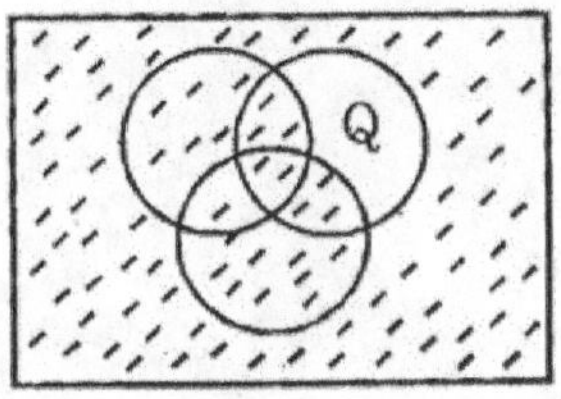

Union of all universal set is

$R^C =$ 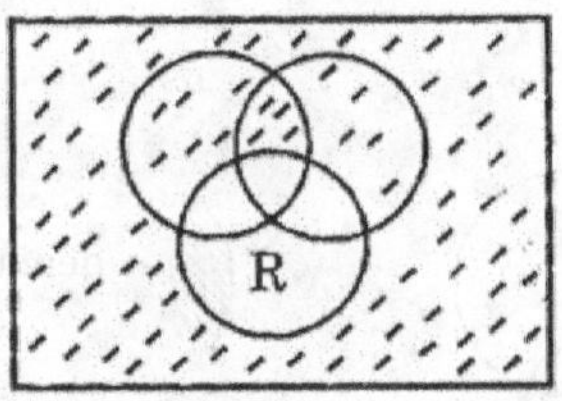

45. Smallest equivalance relation for set of n elements contains n ordered pair and largest equivalance relation contains n^2 ordered pairs.

46.

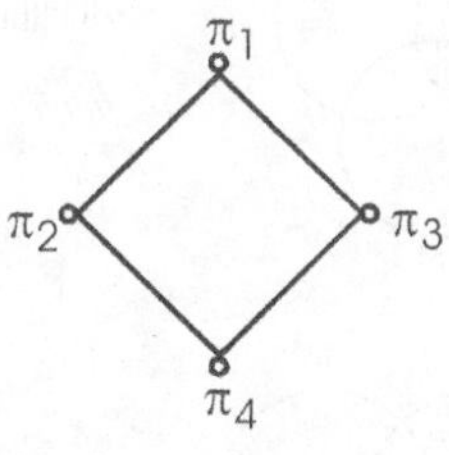

Since, $\pi_i \alpha \pi_j$ only if π_i refines π_j

$$\pi_1 = \{\overline{abcd}\} \text{ refines}$$

$$\pi_2 = \{\overline{ab}, \overline{cd}\}$$

$$\pi_3 = \{\overline{abc}, \overline{d}\}$$

and these both refines

$$\pi_4 = \{\overline{a}, \overline{b}, \overline{c}, \overline{d}\}$$

47.
$$X = \{x \in R^3 \mid x_1 + x_2 + x_3 = 0\}$$

$$X^T = [x_1, x_2, x_3]^T \text{ then}$$

$\{[1, -1, 0]^T, [1, 0, -1]^T\}$ is a linearly independent set because one cannot be obtained from another by scalar multiplication. However $(1, -1, 0)$ and $(1, 0, -1)$ do not span X, since all such combinations (x_1, x_2, x_3) such that $x_1 + x_2 + x_3 = 0$ cannot be exp-ressed as linear combinations of $(1, -1, 0)$ $(1, 0, -1)$.

48. Kurtowsk is 3, 3 ($K_{3,3}$) is non–planer graph with minimum number of edges.

It has 9 edges and 6 vertices.

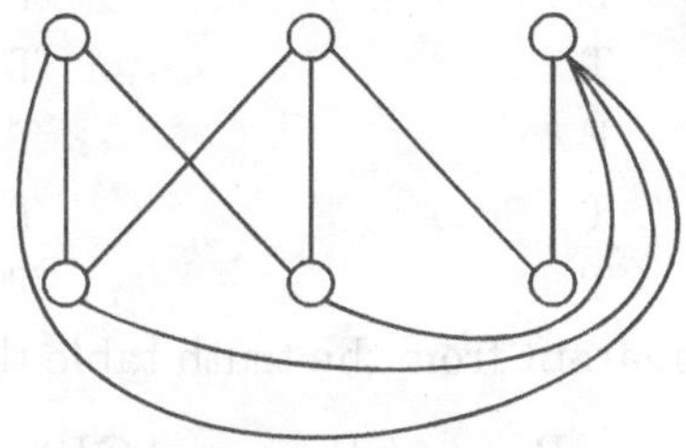

49. Here, INDEG (v) = In degree of verter v.

Since, INDEG (1) = 0

INDEG (2) = 1

INDEG (3) = 1

INDEG (4) = 2

INDEG (5) = 2m

INDEG (6) = 2

Node 1 is with zero indegree, so first node in ordering will always 1. Hence answer (d) is not a topological ordering.

50. $\forall_x$ [Graph (x) $\Rightarrow$ 7 connected (x)] represents "for every x if x is a graph then it is not connected"

51. A k – regular graph is one in which vertex is of degree k. If k is even then, such a graph will have an Eulerian circuit.

52. Given statement can be interpreted as follows :

If x is lion or tiger, if it is hungry or it is threatened, x will attack.

$$P(x) = \text{lion}(x) \vee \text{tiger}(x)$$

$$Q(x) = \text{hungry}(x) \vee \text{threatened}(x)$$

$$R(x) = \text{attacks}(x)$$

$$P(x) \rightarrow (Q(x) \rightarrow R(x))$$

Expanding, $\forall x$ [(lion $(x) \vee$ tiger $(x)) \rightarrow$ {(hungry $(x) \vee$ threatened $(x)) \rightarrow$ attacks (x)}]

53.

A	B	C	A ∨ B	A ∧ B	(A ∨ B) → C	(A ∧ B) →	CA → C	B → C
T	T	T	T	T	T	T	T	T
T	T	F	T	T	F	F	F	F
T	F	T	T	F	T	T	T	T
T	F	F	T	F	F	T	F	T
F	T	T	T	F	T	T	T	T
F	T	F	T	F	F	T	T	F
F	F	T	F	F	T	T	T	T
F	F	F	F	F	T	T	T	T

(A → C) ∧ (B → C)	(A → C) ∨ (B → C)
T	T
F	F
T	T
F	T
T	T
F	T
T	T
T	T

It is apparent from the truth table that P_1 and P_2 are not tautologies.

54.

A	B	A⊙B	~(~A⊙B)	A∧B
T	T	T	~ F = T	T
T	F	T	~ T = F	F
F	T	F	~T = F	F
F	F	T	~T =F	F

55. Number of functions from a set A to a set B where

$$|A| = m$$

and $|B| = n$ is n^m

$$W = X \times Y$$

$$\therefore \quad |W| = xy$$

$$|E| = 2^{xy}$$

$$|Z| = z$$

Hence number of functions from Z to E

$$= (2^{xy})^z = 2^{xyz}$$

56. Binary operation multiplication modulo 10 is defined as follows

$$aob = (a \times b) \% 10$$

The identity element for the given set is 1.

For closure property, $2 \text{ o } 7 = 4 \notin$ set

∴ Set is not closed.

2 and 8 do not have an inverse, 3o7 = 1

∴ 7 is the inverse of 3.

Hence (*c*) is false

57. Reflexive property is an essential condition for Partial order, Total order as well as Equivalence relation.

Given set is not reflexive as $\forall\ x, y \in I$,

(x, y) is not related to (x, y)

58. X and Y sets can be figured out using Venn diagrams.

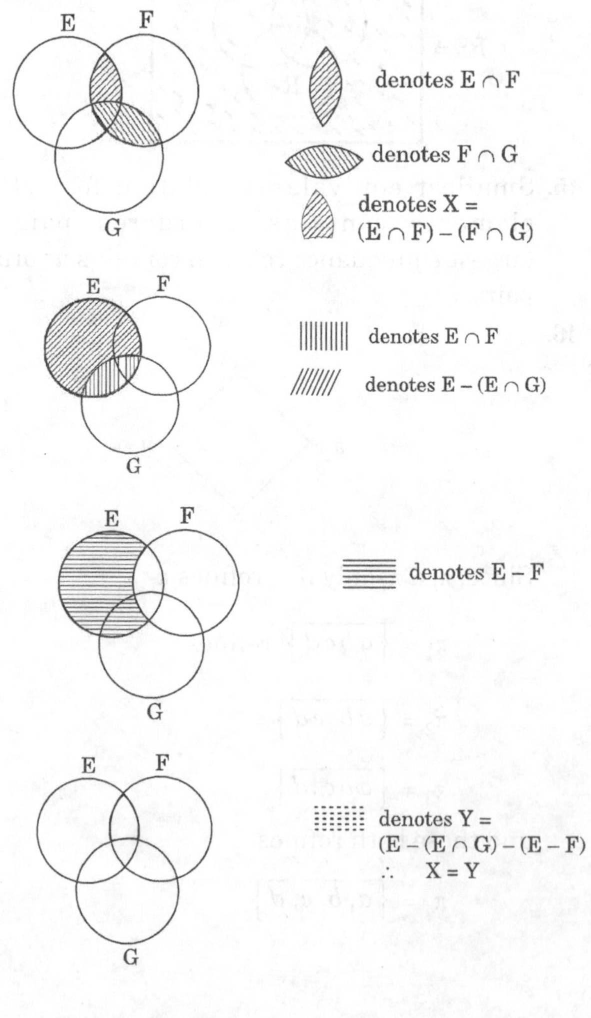

59. Consider an example,

$S = \{1, 2, 3, 4\}$

$m = 4$

$X_1 = \{1, 2, 3\}, X_2 = \{1, 3, 4\}\ n = 2$

$$\sum_{i=1}^{m} f(i) = f(1) + f(2) + f(3) + f(4)$$

$$= 2 + 1 + 2 + 1 = 6 = 3 \times 2 = 3n$$

NUMERICAL TYPE QUESTIONS

1. $p : x \in \{8, 9, 10, 11, 12\}$

$q : x$ is a composite number.

$r : x$ is a perfect square.

$s : x$ is a prime number.

$\{x \geq 2\}$

$\neg((p \Rightarrow q) \wedge (\neg r \vee \neg s))$

$\Rightarrow \neg((\neg p \vee q) \wedge (\neg r \vee \neg s))$

$\Rightarrow ((p' + q) . (r' + s'))'$

$\Rightarrow (p' + q)' + (r' + s')'$

$\Rightarrow pq' + rs$

$\Rightarrow ps + rs$ $\quad q \to$ Composite Number

$\Rightarrow \underbrace{(p + r)s}_{11}$ $\quad q' \to$ Prime Number

So $q' = s$

The prime number from set x is 11

2. $(x^3 + x^4 + x^5 + x^6 \ldots\ldots)^3$

$$\Rightarrow \left(\frac{x}{1-x} - x - x^2\right)^3$$

$$\Rightarrow \left(\frac{x - x(1-x) - x^2(1-x)}{(1-x)}\right)^3$$

$$\Rightarrow \left(\frac{x - x - x^2 + x^2 + x^3}{(1-x)}\right)^3$$

$$\Rightarrow \left(\frac{x^3}{1-x}\right)^3$$

$$\Rightarrow \text{Coefficient of } x^{12} \text{ in } \left(\frac{x^3}{1-x}\right)^3$$

$$\Rightarrow \text{Coefficient of } x^3 \text{ in } \left(\frac{1}{1-x}\right)^3$$

$$\Rightarrow \text{Coefficient of } x^3 \text{ in } (1-x)^{-3}$$

$$f(0) + xf'(0) + \frac{x^2}{2!}f''(0) + \frac{x^3}{3!}f'''(0)$$

$f(x) = (1 - x)^{-3}$

$f'(x) = + 3(1 - x)^{-4}$

$f''(x) = + 12(1 - x)^{-5}$

$f'''(x) = + 60(1 - x)^{-6}$

$$\text{Coefficient of } x^3 \text{ in } (1-x)^{-3} = \frac{60}{3!} = 10$$

3. $a_n = 6n^2 + 2n + a_{n-1}, a_1 = 8.$

$a_2 = 6 \times 2^2 + 2 \times 2 + a_1$

$a_3 = 6 \times 3^2 + 2 \times 3 + a_2$

$= 6 \times 3^2 + 2 \times 3 + 6 \times 2^2 + 2 \times 2 + a_1$

$\vdots$

$a_{99} = 6 \times 99^2 + 2 \times 99 + 6 \times 98^2 + 2 \times 98$

$+ \ldots + 6 \times 2^2 + 2 \times 2 + 8$

$= 6[1^2 + 2^2 + 3^2 + \ldots + 99^2] + 2[1 + 2 + \ldots 99]$

$$= 6.\frac{(99(99+1)(2\times 99+1))}{6} + 2\frac{(99(99+1))}{2}$$

$= 99 \times 100 \times 199 + 99 \times 100$

$= 100 \times 99\ (199 + 1)$

$= 2 \times 99 \times 10^4 = \boxed{198} \times 10^4$

$\Downarrow$ value of K

4. (a) $P \wedge (P \to Q) \Rightarrow Q$

(b) $P \wedge (P \to Q) \Rightarrow P \vee Q$

(c) $P \wedge (P \to Q) \Rightarrow \sim Q \vee P$

So, the number of expression is 3.

5. From the given question

If f(x) is a polynomial of degree 'n'

Then f'(x) is a polynomial of degree (n – 1)

f(x) + f(–x) is a polynomial of degree 10

$\therefore$ g(x) – g(–x) is a polynomial of degree 9

: 10 : SET-2 Afternoon Session

(OR)

If degree of {f(x) + f(x)} = 10, then the largest even exponent of x in f(x) = 10.

Now, the largest odd exponent of x in g(x) = 9

$\therefore$ degree of {g(x) – g(–x)} = 9

6. By 4 – color theorem, Every planar graph is 4 – colorable

7. By Fermat's theorem,

If P is a prime number and P is not a divisor of a, then $a^{P-1} = 1 \pmod P$

Here, 17 is a prime number and 17 is not a divisor of 13.

$\therefore \quad 13^{16} = 1 \pmod P$

$13^{99} = (13)^{96}.(13)^3$

$= (13^{16})^6.2197$

$= 1^6.2197 \pmod{17}$

$\therefore \quad 13^{99} \pmod{17} = 2197 \pmod{17} = 4$

(The remainder obtained by dividing 2197 with 17)

So, the value of the given expression is 4.

8. From the given question

5*G + 3*F = 3*5 + 5*3 = 30 ns

9. Cordinality of power set

{0, 1, 2, ..., 10} = 2^{11} = 2048

11. 1111, 1112, 1113, 1122, 1123, 1133, 1222, 1223, 1233, 1333, 2222, 2223, 2233, 2333, 3333

Total number of 4-digit numbers are 15.

12. Let 'x' be the base or radix of the number system

$$\frac{2\times x^\circ + 1\times x + 3\times x^2}{0\times x^\circ + 2\times x} = 3\times x^\circ + 1\times x + 1\times x^{-1}$$

$$\Rightarrow \quad \frac{2+x+3x^2}{2x} = 3 + x + \frac{1}{x}$$

$$\Rightarrow \quad \frac{3x^2+x+2}{2x} = \frac{3x+x^2+1}{x}$$

$$\Rightarrow \quad 3x^2 + x + 2 = 6x + 2x^2 + 2$$

$$\Rightarrow \quad x^2 - 5x = 0$$

$$\Rightarrow \quad x(x-5) = 0$$

$$\Rightarrow \quad x = 0 \text{ or } x = 5$$

As base or radix of a number system cannot be zero, here $x = 5$

13. The number of functions from A to B where size of A = $|A|$ and size of B = $|B|$ is $|B|^{|A|}$

$\{0,1\}^4 = \{0,1\} X \{0,1\} X \{0,1\} X \{0,1\} = 16$

$|S| = 2^{16}$

$N = 2^{|S|}$

loglog N = log log $2^{|S|}$ = log$|S|$ = log 2^{16} = 16

14. Order of subgroup divides order of group (Lagrange's theorem).

3, 5 and 15 can be the order of subgroup. As subgroup has atleast 4 elements and it is not equal to the given group, order of subgroup can't be 3 and 15. Hence it is 5.

15. Let the basis of 6-dimensional vector space be {e1, e2, e3,e4, e5, e6}. In order for V1 $\cap$ V2 to have smallest possible dimension V1 and V2 could be, say, {e1, e2, e3,e4} and {e3, e4, e5, e6} respectively. The basis of V1 $\cap$ V2 would then be {e3, e4}. => Smallest possible dimension = 2.

16. $x \times x = e \Rightarrow x$ is its own inverse

$y \times y = e \Rightarrow y$ is its own inverse

$(x \times y) \times (x \times y) = e \Rightarrow (x \times y)$ is its own inverse

$(y \times x) \times (y \times x) = e \Rightarrow (y \times x)$ is its own inverse

also $x \times x \times e = e \times e$ can be rewritten as follows

$x \times y \times y \times x = e \times y \times y \times e = e \quad [\because\ y \times y = e]$

$(x \times y) \times (y \times x) = e$ shows that $(x \times y)$ and $(y \times x)$ Are each other's inverse and we already know that $(x \times y)$ and $(y \times x)$ are inverse of its own.

As per (G,*) to be group any element should have only one inverse element (unique)

This process $x \times y = y \times x$ (is one element)

So the elements of such group are 4 which are $\{x, y, e, x \times y\}$

17. No twos : 1 1 1 1 1 1 1 1 1 1 $\Rightarrow$ 1 pennant

Single two : 2 1 1 1 1 1 1 1 1 $\Rightarrow$ 9!/8!1!

= 9 pennants

Two twos : 2 2 1 1 1 1 1 1 $\Rightarrow$ 8!/6!.2! = 28

Three twos : 2 2 2 1 1 1 1 $\Rightarrow$ 7!/3!.4! = 35

Four twos : 2 2 2 2 1 1 $\Rightarrow$ 6!/4!.2! = 15

Five twos : 2 2 2 2 2 $\Rightarrow$ 1

Total = 89 pennants.

Technical Section

CHAPTER 1

Digital Logic

MCQ TYPE QUESTIONS

2016

1. Consider the two cascaded 2-to-1 multiplexers as shown in the figure.

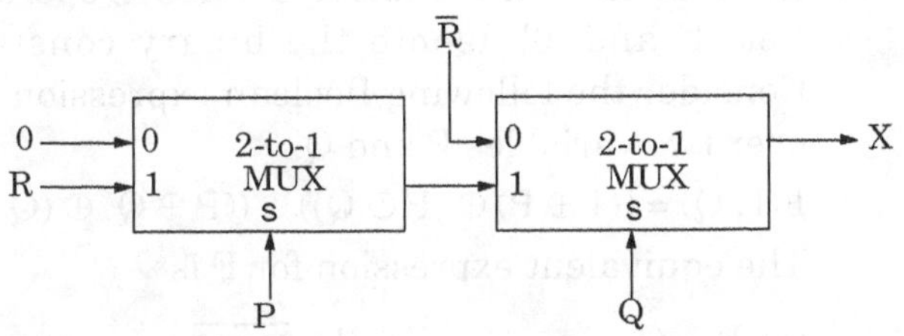

The minimal sum of products form of the output X is

(*a*) $\overline{P}\overline{Q} + PQR$ (*b*) $\overline{P}Q + QR$

(*c*) $PQ + \overline{P}\overline{Q}R$ (*d*) $\overline{Q}R + PQR$

2. Consider a carry lookahead adder for adding two *n*-bit integers, built using gates of fan-in at most two. The time to perform addition using this adder is

(*a*) $\Theta(1)$ (*b*) $\Theta(\log(n))$

(*c*) $\Theta(\sqrt{n})$ (*d*) $\Theta(n)$

3. Let, $x_1 \oplus x_2 \oplus x_3 \oplus x_4 = 0$ where x_1, x_2, x_3, x_4 are Boolean variables, and $\oplus$ is the XOR operator. Which one of the following must always be TRUE?

(*a*) $x_1 x_2 x_3 x_4 = 0$ (*b*) $x_1 x_3 + x_2 = 0$

(*c*) $\overline{x}_1 \oplus \overline{x}_3 = \overline{x}_2 \oplus \overline{x}_4$ (*d*) $x_1 + x_2 + x_3 + x_4 = 0$

2015

4. Consider a 4-bit Johnson counter with an initial value of 0000. The counting sequence of this counter is

(*a*) 0, 1, 3, 7, 15, 14, 12, 8, 0

(*b*) 0, 1, 3, 5, 7, 9, 11, 13, 15, 0

(*c*) 0, 2, 4, 6, 8, 10, 12, 14, 0

(*d*) 0, 8, 12, 14, 15, 7, 3, 1, 0

5. The binary operator ≠ is defined by the following truth table.

p	q	p ≠ q
0	0	0
0	1	1
1	0	1
1	1	0

Which one of the following is true about the binary operator ≠ ?

(*a*) Both commutative and associative

(*b*) Commutative but not associative

(*c*) Not commutative but associative

(*d*) Neither commutative nor associative

6. Consider the operations

$f(X, Y, Z) = X'YZ + XY' + Y'Z'$ and

$g(X, Y, Z) = X'YZ + X'YZ' + XY$.

Which one of the following is correct ?

(*a*) Both {*f*} and {*g*} are functionally complete

(*b*) Only {*f*} is functionally complete

(*c*) Only {*g*} is functionally complete

(*d*) Neither {*f*} nor {*g*} is functionally complete

7. Consider a CSMA/CD network that transmits data at a rate of 100 Mbps (10^8 bits second) over a 1 km(kilometer) cable with no repeaters. If the minimum frame size required for this network is 1250 bytes, what is the signal speed (km/sec) in the cable ?

(*a*) 8000 (*b*) 10000

(*c*) 16000 (*d*) 20000

8. Given the function F = P′ + QR, where F is a function in three Boolean variables P, Q and R and P′ = !P, consider the following statements

(S1)F $= \Sigma(4,5,6)$

(S2)F $= \Sigma(0,1,2,3,7)$

(S3)F $= \Pi(4,5,6)$

(S4)F $= \Pi(0,1,2,37)$

Which of the following is true ?

(*a*) (S1)-False, (S2)-True, (S3)-True, (S4)-False

(*b*) (S1)-True, (S2)-False, (S3)-False, (S4)-True

(*c*) (S1)-False, (S2)-False, (S3)-True, (S4) True

(*d*) (S1)-False-True, (S2) True, (S3)-False, (S4)-False

2014

9. Consider the following Boolean expression for F:

$F(P, Q, R, S) = PQ + \overline{P}QR + \overline{P}Q\overline{R}S$

The minimal sum-of products form of F is

(*a*) PQ + QR + QS (*b*) P + Q + R + S

(*c*) $\overline{P} + \overline{Q} + \overline{R} + \overline{S}$ (*d*) $\overline{P}R + \overline{P}\,\overline{R}S + P$

10. Consider the 4-to-1 multiplexer with two select lines S_1 and S_0 given below.

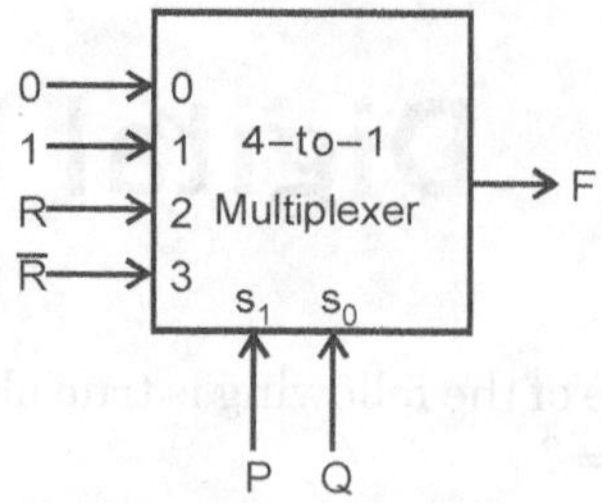

The minimal sum-of-products form of the Boolean expression for the output F of the multiplexer is

(a) $\bar{P}Q + Q\bar{R} + P\bar{Q}R$

(b) $\bar{P}Q + \bar{P}Q\bar{R} + PQ\bar{R} + P\bar{Q}R$

(c) $\bar{P}QR + \bar{P}Q\bar{R} + Q\bar{R} + P\bar{Q}R$

(d) $PQ\bar{R}$

11. The dual of a Boolean function $F(x_1, x_2, ..., x_n, +, \cdot, ')$, written as F^D, is the same expression as that of F with + and · swapped. F is said to be self-dual if $F = F^D$. The number of self-dual functions with n Boolean variables is

(a) 2^n (b) 2^{n-1}

(c) 2^{2^n} (d) $2^{2^{n-1}}$

12. Let $k = 2^n$. A circuit is built by giving the output of an n-bit binary counter as input to an n-to-2^n bit decoder. This circuit is equivalent to a

(a) k-bit binary up counter

(b) k-bit binary down counter

(c) k-bit ring counter

(d) k-bit Johnson counter

13. Consider the following minterm expression for F.

$$F(P,Q,R,S) = \sum 0, 2, 5, 7, 8, 10, 13, 15$$

The minterms 2, 7, 8 and 13 are 'do not care' terms. The minimal sum of-products form for F is

(a) $Q\bar{S} + \bar{Q}S$

(b) $\bar{Q}\bar{S} + QS$

(c) $\bar{Q}R\bar{S} + \bar{Q}R\bar{S} + QR\bar{S} + QRS$

(d) $\bar{P}\bar{Q}\bar{S} + \bar{P}QS + PQS + P\bar{Q}\bar{S}$

14. What is the optimized version of the relation with respect to algebric equation $\pi_{A1}(\pi_{A2}(\sigma_{F1}(\sigma_{F2}(r))))$, where A1, A2 are sets of attributes in r with $A1 \subset A2$ and F1, F2 are Boolean expressions based on the attributes in r?

(a) $\pi_{A1}(\sigma_{(F1 \wedge F2)}(r))$ (b) $\pi_{A1}(\sigma_{(F1 \vee F2)}(r))$

(c) $\pi_{A2}(\sigma_{(F1 \wedge F2)}(r))$ (d) $\pi_{A2}(\sigma_{(F1 \vee F2)}(r))$

15.

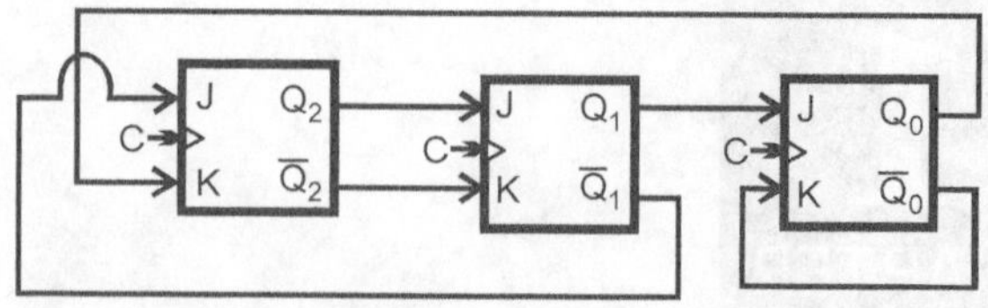

The above synchronous sequential circuit built using JK flip-flops is initialized with $Q_2Q_1Q_0 = 000$. The state sequence for this circuit for the next 3 clock cycles is

(a) 001, 010, 011 (b) 111, 110, 101

(c) 100, 110, 111 (d) 100, 011, 001

16. Let ⊕ denote the Exclusive OR (XOR) operation. Let '1' and '0' denote the binary constants. Consider the following Boolean expression for F over two variables P and Q.

$F(P, Q) = ((1 \oplus P) \oplus (P \oplus Q)) \oplus ((P \oplus Q) \oplus (Q \oplus 0))$

The equivalent expression for F is

(a) $P + Q$ (b) $\overline{P + Q}$

(c) $P \oplus Q$ (d) $\overline{P \oplus Q}$

2013

17. The smallest integer that can be represented by an 8-bit number in 2's complement form is

(a) –256 (b) –128

(c) –127 (d) 0

18. In the following truth table, V = 1 if and only if the input is valid.

Inputs				Outputs		
D_0	D_1	D_2	D_3	X_0	X_1	V
0	0	0	0	x	x	0
1	0	0	0	0	0	1
x	1	0	0	0	1	1
x	x	1	0	1	0	1
x	x	x	1	1	1	1

What function does the truth table represent?

(a) Priority encoder (b) Decoder

(c) Multiplexer (d) Demultiplexer.

19. Which one of the following expressions does NOT represent exclusive NOR of x and y?

(a) $xy + x'y'$ (b) $x \oplus y'$

(c) $x' \oplus y$ (d) $x' \oplus y'$

20. A RAM chip has a capacity of 1024 words of 8 bits each (1K × 8). The number of 2 × 4 decoders with enable line needed to construct a 16K × 16 RAM from 1K × 8 RAM is

(a) 4 (b) 5

(c) 6 (d) 7

2012

21. The decimal value 0.5 in IEEE single precision floating point representation has

(*a*) fraction bits of 000...000 and exponent value of 0

(*b*) fraction bits of 000...000 and exponent value of −1.

(*c*) fraction bits of 100...000 and exponent value of 0

(*d*) no exact representation.

22. The truth table

X	Y	f(X,Y)
0	0	0
0	1	0
1	0	1
1	1	1

represents the Boolean function

(*a*) X (*b*) X + Y

(*c*) X ⊕ Y (*d*) Y

23. Suppose a circular queue of capacity $(n - 1)$ elements is implemented with an array of n elements. Assume that the insertion and deletion operations are carried out using REAR and FRONT as array index variables, respectively. Initially, REAR = FRONT = 0. The conditions to detect *queue full and queue empty* are

(*a*) *full:* (REAR + 1) mod *n* = = FRONT
empty: REAR = = FRONT

(*b*) *full*: (REAR + 1) mod *n* = = FRONT
empty: (FRONT + 1) mod *n* = = REAR

(*c*) *full*: REAR = = FRONT
empty: (REAR + 1) mod *n* = = FRONT

(*d*) *full*: (FRONT + 1) mod *n* = = REAR
empty: REAR = = FRONT

24. What is the minimal form of the Karnaugh map shown below? Assume that X denotes a don't care term.

cd \ ab	00	01	11	10
00	1	X	X	1
01	X			1
11				
10	1			X

(*a*) $\bar{b}\bar{d}$ (*b*) $\bar{b}\bar{d} + \bar{b}\bar{c}$

(*c*) $\bar{b}\bar{d} + a\bar{b}\bar{c}d$ (*d*) $\bar{b}\bar{d} + \bar{b}\bar{c} + \bar{c}\bar{d}$

2011

25. The minimum number of D flip-flops needed design and a mod-258 counter is

(*a*) 9 (*b*) 8

(*c*) 512 (*d*) 258

26. The simplified SOP (Sum of Product) form of the Boolean expression

$(P + \bar{Q} + \bar{R}).(P + \bar{Q} + R).(P + Q + \bar{R})$ is

(*a*) $(\bar{P}.Q + \bar{R})$ (*b*) $(P + \bar{Q}.\bar{R})$

(*c*) $(\bar{P}.Q + R)$ (*d*) $(P.Q + R)$

27. Which one of the following circuits is NOT equivalent to a 2-input XNOR (exclusive NOR) gate?

(*a*)
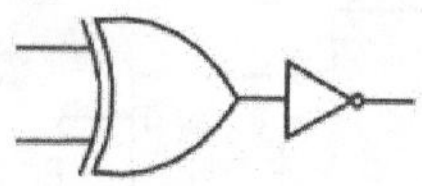
(*b*)
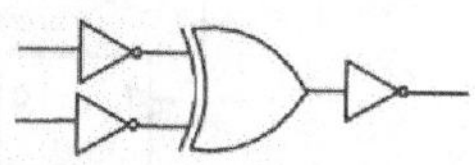

(*c*)
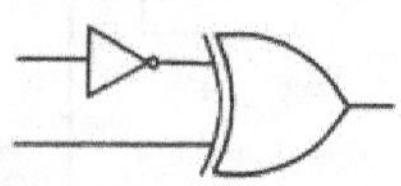
(*d*)
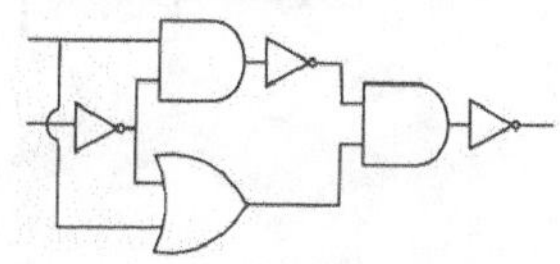

2010

28. The minterm expansion of

$f(P, Q, R) = PQ + Q\bar{R} + P\bar{R}$ is

(*a*) $m_2 + m_4 + m_6 + m_7$

(*b*) $m_0 + m_1 + m_3 + m_5$

(*c*) $m_0 + m_1 + m_6 + m_7$

(*d*) $m_2 + m_3 + m_4 + m_5$

29. P is a 16-bit signed integer. The 2's complement representation of P is $(F87B)_{16}$. The 2's complement representation of 8*P is

(*a*) $(C3D8)_{16}$ (*b*) $(187B)_{16}$

(*c*) $(F878)_{16}$ (*d*) $(987B)_{16}$

30. The Boolean expression for the output f of the multiplexer shown below is

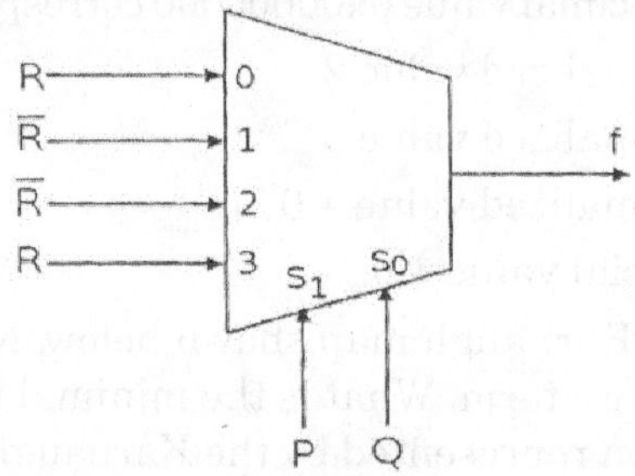

(*a*) $\overline{P \oplus Q \oplus R}$

(*b*) $P \oplus Q \oplus R$

(*c*) $P + Q + R$

(*d*) $\overline{P + Q + R}$

31. What is the boolean expression for the output *f* of the combinational logic circuit of NOR gates given below?

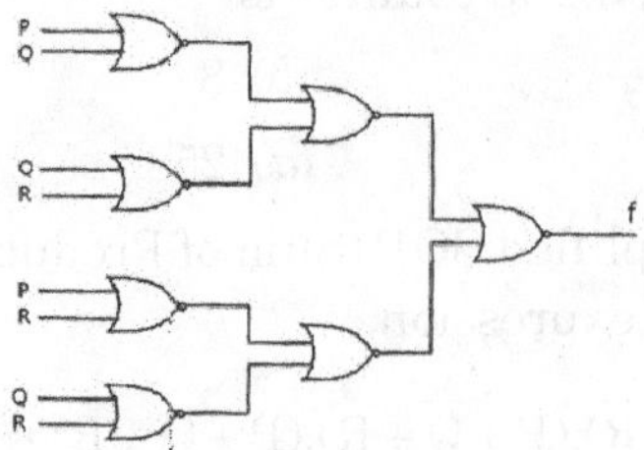

(*a*) $\overline{Q+R}$ (*b*) $\overline{P+Q}$

(*c*) $\overline{P+R}$ (*d*) $\overline{P+Q+R}$

32. In the sequential circuit shown below, if the initial value of the output Q_1Q_0 is 00, what are the next four values of Q_1Q_0?

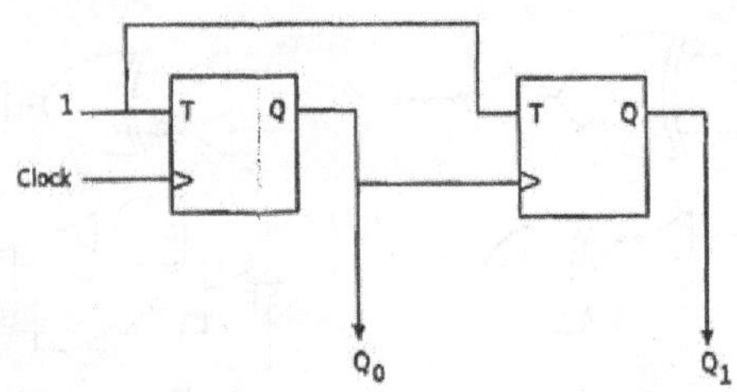

(*a*) 11, 10, 01, 00 (*b*) 10, 11, 01, 00

(*c*) 10, 00, 01, 11 (*d*) 11, 10, 00, 01

2009

33. $(1217)_8$ is equivalent to

(*a*) $(1217)_{16}$ (*b*) $(028F)_{16}$

(*c*) $(2297)_{10}$ (*d*) $(0B17)_{16}$

34. What is the minimum number of gates required to implement the Boolean function (AB + C) if we have to use only 2-input NOR gates ?

(*a*) 2 (*b*) 3

(*c*) 4 (*d*) 5

2008

35. In the IEEE floating point representation the hexadecimal value 0x00000000 corresponds to the

(*a*) normalized value 2^{-127}

(*b*) normalized value 2^{-126}

(*c*) normalized value + 0

(*d*) special value + 0

36. In the Karnaugh map shown below, X denotes a don't care term. What is the minimal form of the function represented by the Karnaugh map?

(*a*) $\overline{b}.\overline{d}+\overline{a}.\overline{d}$

(*b*) $\overline{a}.\overline{b}+\overline{b}.\overline{d}+\overline{a}.b.\overline{d}$

(*c*) $\overline{b}.\overline{d}+\overline{a}.b.\overline{d}$

(*d*) $\overline{a}.\overline{b}+\overline{b}.\overline{d}+\overline{a}.\overline{d}$

cd \ ab	00	01	11	10
00	1	1		1
01	X			
11	X			
10	1	1		X

37. Let r denote number system radix. The only value(s) of r that satisfy the equation $\sqrt{121_r} = 11_r$ is/are

(*a*) decimal 10 (*b*) decimal 11

(*c*) decimal 10 and 11 (*d*) any value > 2

38. Given f_1, f_3 and f in canonical sum of products form (in decimal) for the circuit

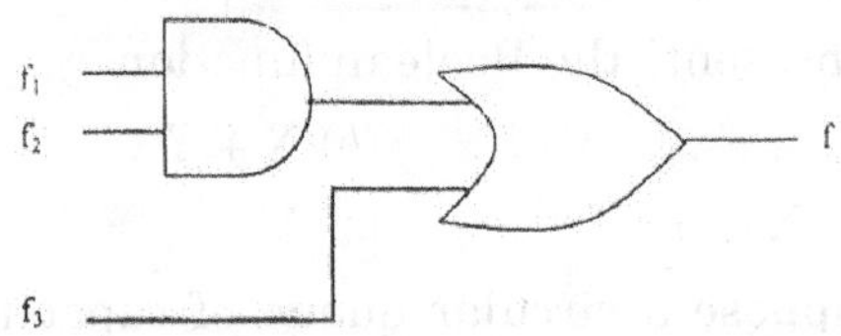

$f_1 = \Sigma m\,(4, 5, 6, 7, 8)$

$f_3 = \Sigma m\,(1, 6, 15)$

$f = \Sigma m\,(1, 6, 8, 15)$

Then f_2 is

(*a*) $\Sigma m\,(4, 6)$ (*b*) $\Sigma m\,(4, 8)$

(*c*) $\Sigma m\,(6, 8)$ (*d*) $\Sigma m\,(4, 6, 8)$

39. If P, Q, R are Boolean variables, then

$$\left(P+\overline{Q}\right)\left(P.\overline{Q}+P.R\right)\left(\overline{P}.\overline{R}+\overline{Q}\right)$$

simplifies to

(*a*) $P.\overline{Q}$ (*b*) $P.\overline{R}$

(*c*) $P.\overline{Q}+R$ (*d*) $P.\overline{R}+Q$

2007

40. What is the maximum number of different Boolean functions involving *n* Boolean variables ?

(*a*) n^2 (*b*) 2^n

(*c*) 2^{2^n} (*d*) 2^{n^2}

41. How many 3-to-8 line decoders with an enable input are needed to construct a 6-to-64 line decoder without using any other logic gates ?

(*a*) 7 (*b*) 8

(*c*) 9 (*d*) 10

42. Consider the following Boolean function of four variables

$$f(w, x, y, z) = \sum(1, 3, 4, 6, 9, 11, 12, 14)$$

The function is

(*a*) independent of one variable

(*b*) independent of two variables

(*c*) independent of three variables

(*d*) dependent on all the variables

43. Let $f(w, x, y, z) = \sum(0,4,5,7,8,9,13,15)$.

Which of the following expressions are **NOT** equivalent to *f*?

(*a*) $x'y'z' + w'xy' + wy'z + xz$

(*b*) $w'y'z' + wx'y' + xz$

(*c*) $w'y'z' + wx'y' + xyz + xy'z$

(*d*) $x'y'z' + wx'y' + w'y$

44. Define the connective * for the Boolean variable *X* and Y as :

$$X^* Y = XY + X'Y'$$

Let $Z = X * Z$.

Consider the following expression P, Q and R.

$$P : X = Y * ZQ : \quad Y = X * Z$$

$$R : X * Y * Z = 1$$

Which of the following is **TURE ?**

(*a*) Only *P* and *Q* are valid

(*b*) Only *Q* and *R* are valid

(*c*) Only *P* and *R* are valid

(*d*) All *P*, *Q*, *R* are valid

45. Suppose only one multiplexer and one inverter are allowed to be used to implement any Boolean function of *n* variables. What is the minimum size of the multiplexer needed?

(*a*) 2^n line to 1 line (*b*) 2^{n+1} line to 1 line

(*c*) 2^{n-1} line to 1 line (*d*) 2^{n-2} line to 1 line

46. In a look-ahead carry generator, the carry generate function G_i and the carry propagate function P_i for inputs, A_i and B_i are given by :

$$P_i = A_i \oplus B_i \text{ and } G_i = A_i B_i$$

The expressions for the sum bit S_i and the carry bit C_{i+1} of the look-ahead carry adder are given by:

$$S_i = P_i \oplus C_i \text{ and } C_{i+1} = G_i + P_i C_i,$$

where C_0 is input carry.

Consider a two-level logic implementation of the look-ahead carry generator. Assume that all P_i and G_i are available for the carry generator circuit and that the AND and OR gates can have any number of inputs. The number of AND gates and OR gates needed to implement the look-ahead carry generator for a 4-bit adder with S_3, S_2, S_1, S_0 and C_4 as its outputs are respectively

(*a*) 6, 3 (*b*) 10, 4

(*c*) 6, 4 (*d*) 10, 5

47. The control signal functions of a 4-bit binary counter are given below (where X is "don't care"):

Clear	Clock	Load	Count	Function
1	X	X	X	Clear to 0
0	X	0	0	No change
0		1	X	Load input
0		0	1	Count next

The counter is connected as follows :

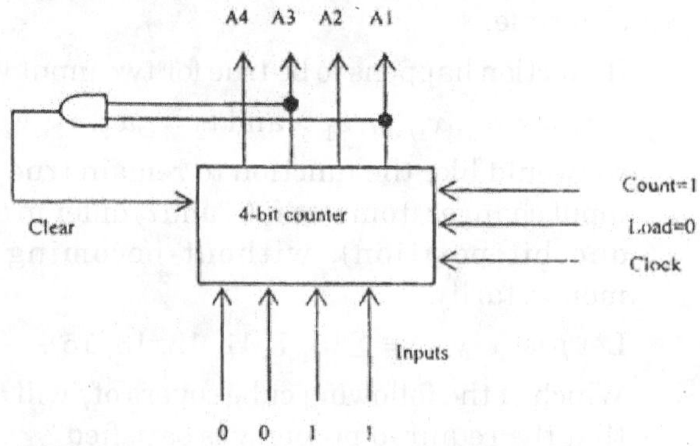

Assume that the counter and gate delays are negligible. If the counter starts at 0, then it cycles through the following sequence

(*a*) 0, 3, 4 (*b*) 0, 3, 4, 5

(*c*) 0, 1, 2, 3, 4 (*d*) 0, 1, 2, 3, 4, 5

2006

48. You are given a free running clock with a duty cycle of 50% and a digital waveform *f* which changes only at the negative edge of the clock. Which one of the following circuits (using clocked D flip-flops) will delay the phase of *f* by 180°?

(*a*)

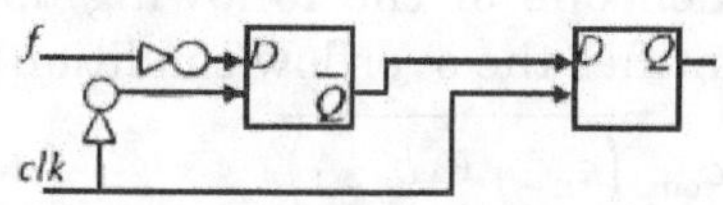

(*b*)

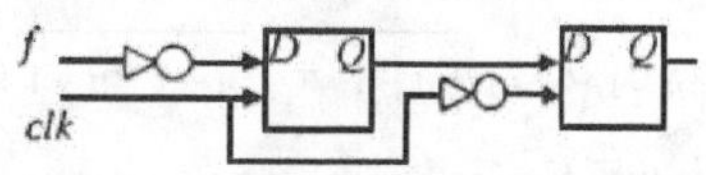

(*c*)

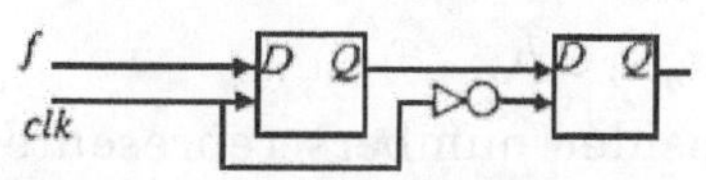

(*d*)

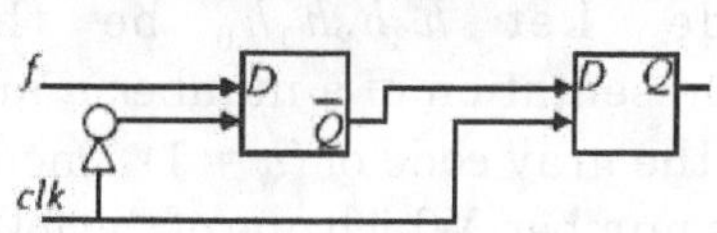

49. Given two three bit numbers $a_2a_1a_0$ and $b_2b_1b_0$ and c, the carry in, the function that represents the carry generate function when these two numbers are added is

(a) $a_2b_2 + a_2a_1b_1 + a_2a_1a_0b_0 + a_2a_0b_1b_0 + a_1b_2b_1 + a_1a_0b_2b_0 + a_0b_2b_1b_0$

(b) $a_2b_2 + a_2b_1b_0 + a_2a_1b_1b_0 + a_1a_0b_2b_1 + a_1a_0b_2 + a_1a_0b_2b_0 + a_2a_0b_1b_0$

(c) $a_2 + b_2 + (a_2 \oplus b_2)(a_1 + b_1 + (a_1 \oplus b_1)(a_0 + b_0))$

(d) $a_2b_2 + \overline{a_2}\, a_1b_1 + \overline{a_2\, a_1}\, a_0b_0 + \overline{a_2}\, a_0\, \overline{b_1}\, b_0 + a_1\, \overline{b_2}\, b_1 + \overline{a_1}\, a_0\, \overline{b_2}\, b_0 + a_0\, \overline{b_2\, b_1}\, b_0$

50. Consider a boolean function $f(w, x, y, z)$. Suppose that exactly one of its inputs is allowed to change at a time.

If function happens to be true for two input vectors $i_1 = < w_1, x_1, y_1, z_1 >$ and $i_2 = < w_2, x_2, y_2, z_2 >$, we would like the function to remain true as the input changes from i_1 to i_2 (i_1 and i_2 differ in exactly one bit position), without becoming false momentarily.

Let $f(w, x, y, z) = \Sigma\,(5, 7, 11, 12, 13, 15)$.

Which of the following cube covers of f will ensure that the required property is satisfied ?

(a) $\overline{w}xz,\ wx\overline{y},\ x\overline{y}z,\ xyz,\ wyz$

(b) $wxy,\ \overline{w}xz,\ wyz$

(c) $wx\overline{yz},\ xz,\ w\overline{x}yz$

(d) $wzy,\ wyz,\ wxz,\ \overline{w}xz,\ x\overline{y}z,\ xyz$

51. We consider the addition of two 2's complement numbers $b_{n-1}\, b_{n-2} \ldots b_0$ and $a_{n-1}\, a_{n-2} \ldots a_0$. A binary adder for adding unsigned binary numbers is used to add the two numbers. The sum is denoted by $c_{n-1}\, c_{n-2} \ldots c_0$ and the carry-out by c_{out}.

Which one of the following options correctly identifies the overflow condition ?

(a) $c_{out}\, \overline{(a_{n-1} \oplus b_{n-1})}$

(b) $a_{n-1}\, b_{n-1}\, \overline{c_{n-1}} + \overline{a_{n-1}\, b_{n-1}}\, c_{n-1}$

(c) $c_{out} \oplus c_{n-1}$

(d) $a_{n-1} \oplus b_{n-1} \oplus c_{n-1}$

52. Consider numbers represented in 4-bit gray code. Let $h_3h_2h_1h_0$ be the gray code representation of a number n and let $g_3\, g_2\, g_1\, g_0$ be the gray code of $(n + 1)$ (modulo 16) value of the number. Which one of the following functions is correct ?

(a) $g_0\,(h_3h_2h_1h_0) = \Sigma\,(1, 2, 3, 6, 10, 13, 14, 15)$

(b) $g_1(h_3h_2h_1h_0) = \Sigma\,(4, 9, 10, 11, 12, 13, 14, 15)$

(c) $g_2\,(h_3\, h_2\, h_1\, h_0) = \Sigma\,(2, 4, 5, 6, 7, 12, 13, 15)$

(d) $g_3\,(h_3h_2h_1h_0) = \Sigma\,(0, 1, 6, 7, 10, 11, 12, 13)$

2005

53. Consider the following circuit.

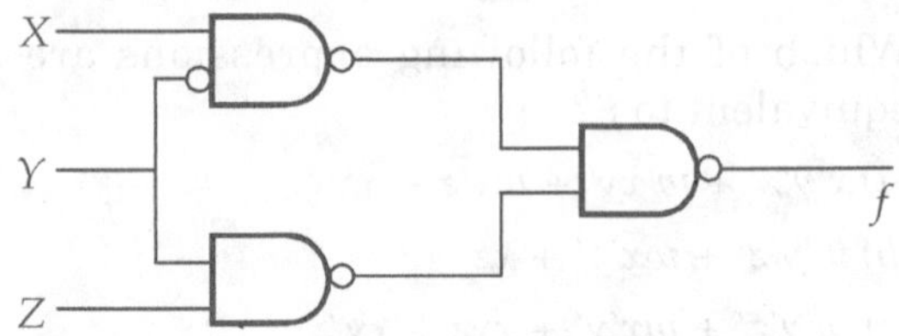

Which one of the following is TRUE?

(a) f is independent of X

(b) f is independent of Y

(c) f is independent of Z

(d) None of X, Y, Z is redundant

54. The range of integers that can be represented by an n bit 2's complement number system is

(a) -2^{n-1} to $(2^{n-1} - 1)$

(b) $-(2^{n-1} - 1)$ to $(2^{n-1} - 1)$

(c) -2^{n-1} to 2^{n-1}

(d) $-(2^{n-1} + 1)$ to $(2^{n-1} - 1)$

55. The hexadecimal representation of 657_8 is

(a) 1AF (b) D78

(c) D71 (d) 32F

56. The switching expression corresponding to $f(A, B, C, D) = \Sigma\,(1, 4, 5, 9, 11, 12)$ is

(a) BC′D′ + A′C′D + AB′D

(b) ABC′ + ACD + B′C′D

(c) ACD′ + A′BC′ + AC′D′

(d) A′BD + ACD′ + BCD′

57. Consider the following circuit involving a positive edge triggered D FF.

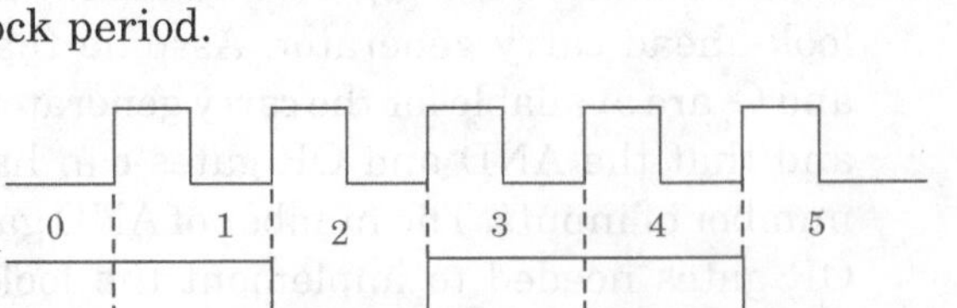

Consider the following timing diagram. Let A_i represent the logic level on the line A in the i-th clock period.

Let A′ represent the complement of A. The correct output sequence on Y over the clock periods 1 through 5 is

(a) $A_0\ A_1\ A_1'\ A_3\ A_4$ (b) $A_0\ A_1\ A_2'\ A_3\ A_4$

(c) $A_1\ A_2\ A_2'\ A_3\ A_4$ (d) $A_1\ A_2'\ A_3\ A_4\ A_5'$

58. The following diagram represents a finite state machine which takes as input a binary number from the least significant bit.

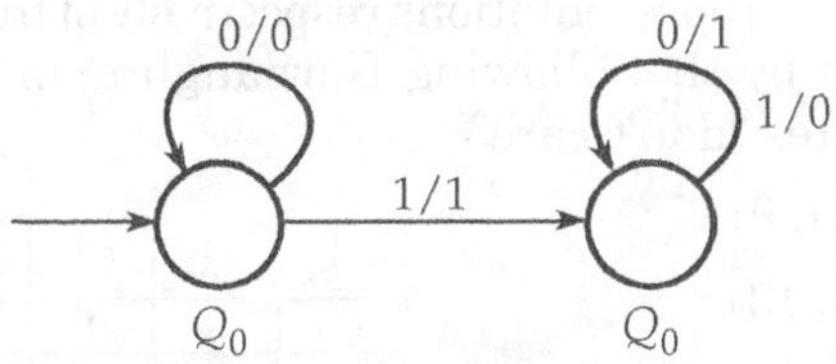

Which one of the following is TRUE?

(a) It computes 1's complement of the input number

(b) It computes 2's complement of the input number

(c) It increments the input number

(d) It decrements the input number

59. Consider the following circuit

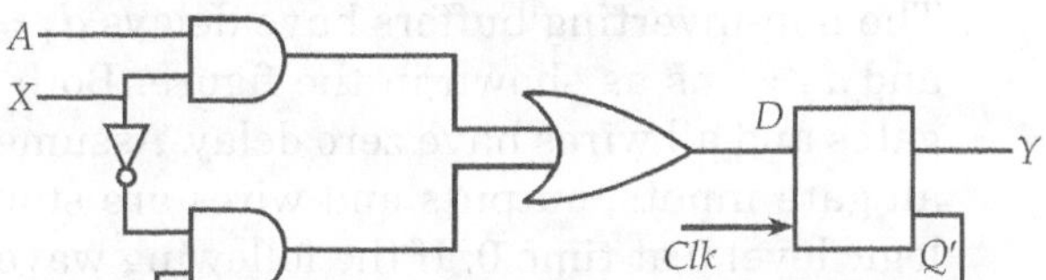

The flip-flops are positive edge triggered D FFs. Each state is designated as a two bit string Q_0Q_1. Let initial state be 00. The state transition sequence is

(a) 00 → 11 → 01 (b) 00 → 11

(c) 00 → 10 → 01 → 11 (d) 00 → 11 → 01 → 10

60. The decimal number 0.239×2^{13} has following hexadecimal representation (without normalization and rounding off)

(a) 0D 24 (b) 0D 4D

(c) 4D 0D (d) 4D 3D

61. The normalized representation for the above format is specified as follows.

The mantissa has an implicit 1 preceding the binary (radix) point. Assume that only 0's are padded in while shifting a field.

The normalized representation of the above number (0.239×2^{13}) is

(a) 0A 20 (b) 11 34

(c) 4D D0 (d) 4A E8

2004

62. Boolean function $x'\,y' + xy + x'\,y$ is equivalent to

(a) $x' + y'$ (b) $x + y$

(c) $x + y'$ (d) $x' + y$

63. In an SR latch made by cross-coupling two NAND gates, if both S and R inputs are set to 0, then it will result in

(a) Q = 0, Q′ = 1 (b) Q = 1, Q′ = 0

(c) Q = 1, Q′ = 1 (d) Indeterminate states

64. If 73_x (in base-x number system) is equal to 54_y (in base-y number system), then possible values of x and y are

(a) 8, 16 (b) 10, 12

(c) 9, 13 (d) 8, 11

65. What is the result of evaluating the following two expressions using three-digit floating point arithmetic with rounding ?

$$(113. + -111.) + 7.51$$

$$113. + (-111. + 7.51)$$

(a) 9.51 and 10.0 respectively

(b) 10.0 and 9.51 respectively

(c) 9.51 and 9.51 respectively

(d) 10.0 and 10.0 respectively

66. A circuit outputs a digit in the form of 4 bits. 0 is represented by 0000, 1 by 0001, ..., 9 by 1001. A combinational circuit is to be designed which takes these 4 bits as input and outputs 1 if the digit ≥ 5, and 0 otherwise. If only AND, OR and NOT gates may be used, what is the minimum number of gates required ?

(a) 2 (b) 3

(c) 4 (d) 5

67. Which are the essential prime implicants of the following Boolean function ?

$$f(a, b, c) = a'\,c + ac' + b'\,c$$

(a) a′ c and ac′ (b) a′c and b′c

(c) a′c only (d) ac′ and bc′

68. Consider the partial implementation of a 2-bits counter using T flip-flops following the sequence 0-2-3-1-0, as shown below.

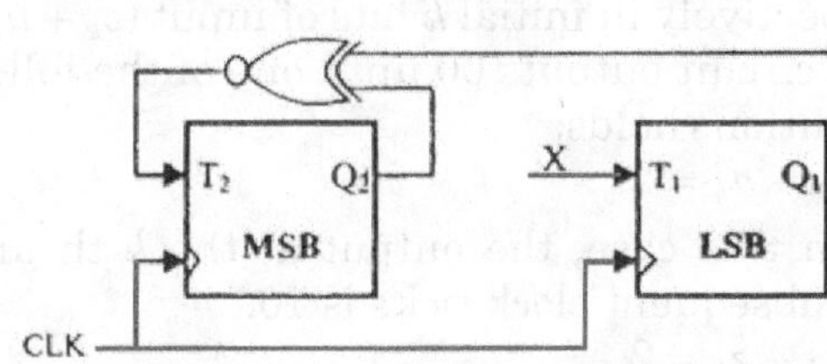

To complete the circuit, the input X should be

(a) Q_2' (b) $Q_2 + Q_1$

(c) $(Q_1 \oplus Q_2)'$ (d) $Q_1 \oplus Q_2$

69. A4-bit carry lookahead adder, which adds two 4-bit numbers, is designed using AND, OR, NOT, NAND, NOR gates only. Assuming that all the inputs are available in both complemented and uncomplemented forms and the delay of each gate is one time unit, what is the overall propagation delay of the adder? Assume that the carry network has been implemented using two-level AND-OR logic.

(*a*) 4 time units (*b*) 6 time units

(*c*) 10 time units (*d*) 12 time units

70. Let A = 1111 1010 and B = 0000 1010 be two 8-bit 2's complement numbers. Their product in 2's complement is

(*a*) 1100 0100 (*b*) 1001 1100

(*c*) 1010 0101 (*d*) 1101 0101

2003

71. Assuming all numbers are in 2's complement representation, which of the following numbers is divisible by 11111011 ?

(*a*) 11100111 (*b*) 11100100

(*c*) 11010111 (*d*) 11011011

72. The following is a scheme for floating point number representation using 16 bits.

Bit position	15	14 . . . 9	8 0
	s	*e*	*m*
	Sign	Exponent	Mantissa

Let *s*, *e*, and *m* be the numbers represented in binary in sign, exponent, and mantissa fields respectively. Then floating point number represented is

$$\begin{cases} (-1)^s \left(1 + m \times 2^{-9}\right) 2^{e-31}, \text{ if exponent} \neq 111111 \\ 0, \text{ otherwise} \end{cases}$$

What is the maximum difference between two successive real numbers representable in this system ?

(*a*) 2^{-40} (*b*) 2^{-9}

(*c*) 2^{22} (*d*) 2^{31}

73. A 1-input, 2-output synchronous sequential circuit behaves as follows :

Let z_k, n_k denote the number of 0's and 1's respectively in initial *k* bits of input ($z_k + n_k = k$). The circuit outputs 00 until one of the following conditions holds.

- $z_k - n_k = 2$.

  In this case, the output at the *k*-th and all subsequent clock ticks is 10.

- $n_k - z_k = 2$.

  In this case, the output at the *k*-th and all subsequent clock ticks is 01.

What is the minimum number of states required in the state transition graph of the above circuit?

(*a*) 5 (*b*) 6

(*c*) 7 (*d*) 8

74. The literal count of a boolean expression is the sum of the number of times each literal appears in the expression. For example, the literal count of ($xy + xz'$) is 4. What are the minimum possible literal counts of the product-of-sum and sum-of-product representations respectively of the function given by the following Karnaugh map ? Here, X denotes "don't care"

xy \ zw	00	01	11	10
00	X	1	0	1
01	0	1	X	0
11	1	X	X	0
10	X	0	0	X

(*a*) (11, 9)

(*b*) (9, 13)

(*c*) (9, 10)

(*d*) (11, 11)

75. Consider the following circuit composed of XOR gates and non-inverting buffers.

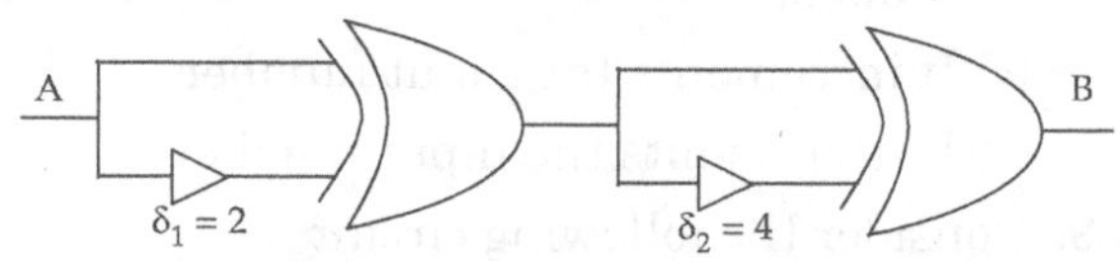

The non-inverting buffers have delays d_1 = 2 ns and d_2 =4 ns as shown in the figure. Both XOR gates and all wires have zero delay. Assume that all gate inputs, outputs and wires are stable at logic level 0 at time 0. If the following waveform is applied at input A, how many transition(*s*) (change of logic levels) occur(*s*) at B during the interval from 0 to 10 ns ?

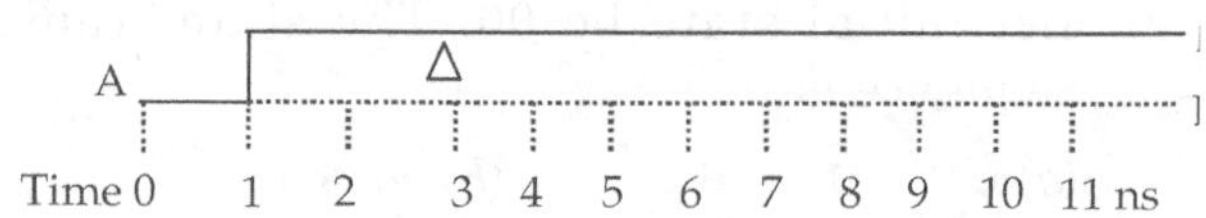

(*a*) 1 (*b*) 2

(*c*) 3 (*d*) 4

2002

76. Minimum sum of product expression for *f*(*w*, *x*, *y*, *z*) shown in Karnaugh-map below is

yz \ wx	00	01	11	10
00	0	1	1	0
01	*x*	0	0	1
11	*x*	0	0	1
10	0	1	1	*x*

(*a*) $xz + y'z$ (*b*) $xz' + zx'$

(*c*) $x'y + zx'$ (*d*) none of these

77. The 2's complement representation of the decimal value – 15 is

(a) 1111 (b) 11111

(c) 111111 (d) 10001

78. Consider the following logic circuit whose inputs are function and output is *f*.

$f_1(dx, y, z)$

$f(dx, y, z)$

$f_2(dx, y, z)$

$f_3(dx, y, z) = ?$

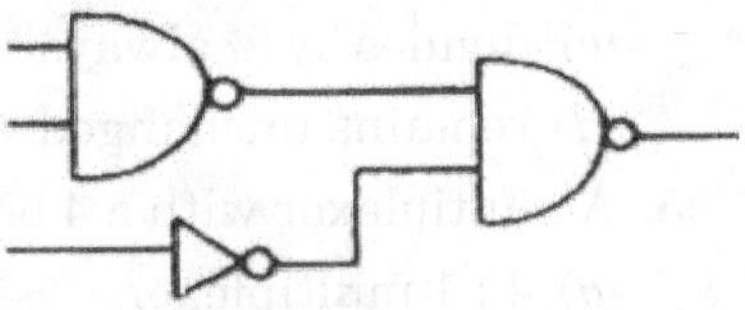

Given that

$f_1(dx, y, z) = \Sigma(d0, 1, 3, 5)$,

$f_2(dx, y, z) = \Sigma(d6, 7)$ and

$f(dx, y, z) = \Sigma(d1, 4, 5)$,

f_3 is

(a) Σ (1, 4, 5), (b) Σ (6, 7)

(c) Σ (0, 1, 3, 5) (d) None of these

2000

79. The number 43 in 2's complement representation is

(a) 01010101 (b) 11010101

(c) 00101011 (d) 10101011

80. The simultaneous equations on the Boolean variables *x*, *y*, *z* and *w*,

$$x + y + z = 1$$

$$xy = 0$$

$$xz + w = 1$$

$$xy + \bar{z}\,\bar{w} = 0$$

have the following solution for *x*, *y*, *z* and *w*, respectively.

(a) 0 1 0 0 (b) 1 1 0 1

(c) 1 0 1 1 (d) 1 0 0 0

81. Which function does NOT implement the Karnaugh map given below ?

wz →	00	01	11	10
xy ↓				
00	0	×	0	0
01	0	×	1	1
11	1	1	1	1
10	0	×	0	0

(a) $(w + x)\,y$

(b) $xy + yw$

(c) $(w + x)(\bar{w} + y)(\bar{x} + y)$

(d) None of these

82. The following arrangement of master-slave flip flops

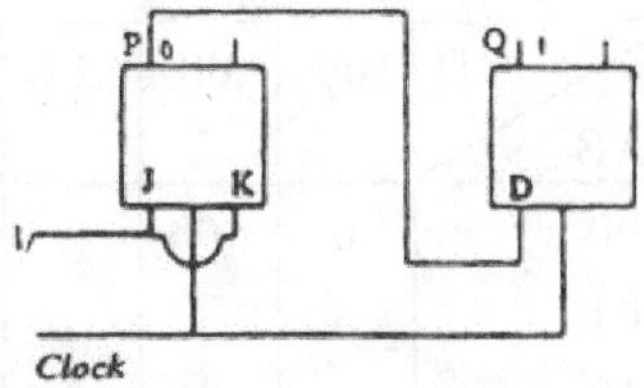

has the initial state of P, Q as 0, 1 (respectively). After three clock cycles the output state P, Q is (respectively),

(a) 1,0 (b) 1,1

(c) 0,0 (d) 0,1

83. Consider the values $A = 2.0 \times 10^{30}$, $B = -2.0 \times 10^{30}$, $C = 1.0$, and the sequence

X : = A + B

Y : = A + C

X : = X + C

Y : = Y + B

executed on a computer where floating point numbers are represented with 32 bits. The values for X and Y will be

(a) X = 1.0, Y = 1.0 (b) X = 1.0, Y = 0.0

(c) X = 0.0, Y = 1.0 (d) X = 0.0, Y = 0.0

84. Design a logic circuit to convert a single digit BCD number to the number modulo six as follows (Do not detect illegal input) :

(a) Write the truth table for all bits. Label the input bits I_1, I_2, ...with I_1 as the least significant bit. Label the output bits R_1, R_2, ...with R_1 as the least significant bit. Use 1 to signify truth.

(b) Draw one circuit for each output bit using, altogether, two two-input AND gates, one two-input. OR gate and two NOT gates.

1999

85. The number of binary relations on a set with *n* elements is

(a) n^2 (b) 2^n

(c) 2^{n^2} (d) None of these

86. The number of binary strings of *n* zeroes and *k* ones that no two ones are adjacent is

(a) ${}^{n-1}C_k$ (b) ${}^{n}C_k$

(c) ${}^{n}C_{k+1}$ (d) None of these

87. Which of the following expressions is not equivalent to $\bar{x}$?

(a) *x* NAND *x* (b) *x* NOR *x*

(c) *x* NAND 1 (d) x NOR 1

88. Which of the following functions implements the Karnaugh map shown below ?

AB \ CD	00	00	11	10
00	0	0	1	0
01	X	X	1	X
11	0	1	1	0
10	0	1	1	0

(*a*) $\overline{A}B + CD$ (*b*) D (C + A)

(*c*) $AD + \overline{A}B$ (*d*) $(C + D)(\overline{C} + D) + (A + B)$

89. Booth's coding in 8 bits for the decimal number – 57 is

(*a*) 0 – 100 + 1000 (*b*) 0 – 100 + 100 – 1

(*c*) 0 – 1 + 100 – 10 + 1 (*d*) 0 0 – 10 + 100 –1

90. Consider the circuit shown below. In a certain steady state, the line Y is at '1'. What are the possible values of A, B, and C in this state ?

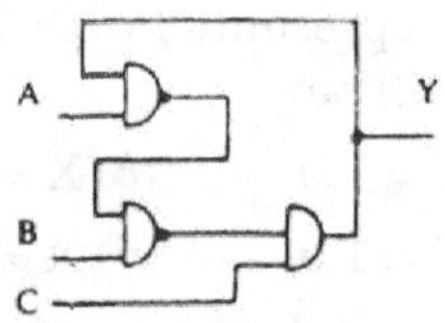

(*a*) A = 0, B = 0, C = 1 (*b*) A = 0, B = 1, C = 1

(*c*) A = 1, B = 0, C = 1 (*d*) A = 1, B = 1, C = 1

91. Which of the following sets of component (s) is/are sufficient to implement any arbitrary boolean function ?

(*a*) XOR gates, NOT gates

(*b*) 2 to 1 multiplexors

(*c*) AND gates, XOR gates

(*d*) Three-input gates that output (*A* . B) + C for the inputs A. B. and C.

92. The number of full and half-adders required to add 16-bit numbers is

(*a*) 8 half-adders, 8 full-adders

(*b*) 1 half-adder, 15 full-adders

(*c*) 16 half-adders, 0 full-adders

(*d*) 4 half-adders, 12 full-adders

93. Zero has two representations in

(*a*) Sign magnitude

(*b*) 1's complement

(*c*) 2's complement

(*d*) none of these

1998

94. What happens when a bit-string is XORed with itself n-times as shown

$[B \oplus (B \oplus (B \oplus (B \ldots\ldots n \text{ times})]$

(*a*) complements when *n* is even

(*b*) complements when *n* is old

(*c*) divides by 2^n always

(*d*) remains unchanged when *n* is even

95. A multiplexor with a 4 bit data select input is a

(*a*) 4 : 1 multiplexor (*b*) 2 : 1 multiplexor

(*c*) 16 : 1 multiplexor (*d*) 8 : 1 multiplexor

96. The threshold level for logic 1 in the TTL family is

(*a*) any voltage above 2.5 V

(*b*) any voltage between 0.8 V and 5.0 V

(*c*) any voltage below 5.0 V

(*d*) any voltage below V_{cc} but above 2.8 V

97. The octal representation of an integer is 3428. If this were to be treated as an eight bit integer is an 8085 based computer, its decimal equivalent is

(*a*) 226 (*b*) – 98

(*c*) 76 (*d*) – 30

98. The function represented by the Karnaugh map given below is

A \ BC	00	01	10	11
0	1	0	0	1
1	1	0	0	1

(*a*) A.B (*b*) AB + BC + CA

(*c*) $\overline{B \oplus C}$ (*d*) A.BC

99. Which of the following operations is commutative but not associative ?

(*a*) AND (*b*) OR

(*c*) NAND (*d*) EXOR

100. (*a*) The implication gate, shown below has two inputs (x and y); the output is 1 except when *x* = 1 and *y* = 0, Realize $f = \overline{x}y + x\overline{y}$ using only four implication gates.

(*b*) Show that the implication gate is functionally complete.

101. (*a*) Solve the following recurrence relation

$X_n = 2x_{n-1} - 1, n > 1$

$x_1 = 2$

(*b*) Consider the grammar

$S \rightarrow Aa \mid b$

$A \rightarrow Ac \mid Sd \mid \in$

Construct an equivalent grammar with no left recursion and with minimum number of production rules.

102. Design a synchronous counter to go through the following states

1, 4, 2, 3, 1, 4, 2, 3, 1, 4 ....

1997

103. Given $\sqrt{224)_r} = 13)_r,$ The value of the radix r is

(*a*) 10 (*b*) 8

(*c*) 5 (*d*) 6

104. Consider the logic circuit shown in the figure. below The functions f_1, f_2 and f (in canonical sum of products form in decimal notation) are :

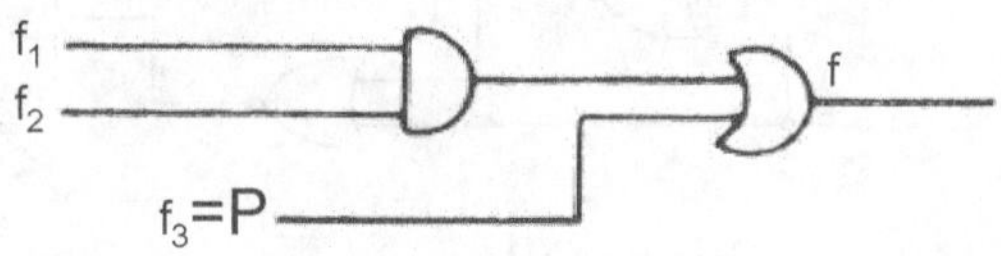

$f_1(w, x, y, z) = \Sigma\ 8, 9, 10$

$f_2(w, x, y, z) = \Sigma\ 7, 8, 12, 13, 14, 15$

$f(w, x, y, z) = \Sigma\ 8, 9$

The function f_3 is

(*a*) Σ 9, 10 (*b*) Σ 9

(*c*) Σ 1, 8, 9 (*d*) Σ 8, 10, 15

1996

105. Which of the following is false ? Read ∧ as AND, ∨ as OR, ~ as NOT, → as one way implication and ↔ as two way implication.

(*a*) $((x \to y) \wedge x) \to y$

(*b*) $((\sim x \to y) \wedge (\sim x \wedge \sim y)) \to x$

(*c*) $(x \to (x \vee \psi))$

(*d*) $((x \vee y) \leftrightarrow (\sim x \to \sim y))$

106. Consider the circuit in given Figure which has a four fit binary number $b_3, b_2\ b_1\ b_0$ as input and a five bit binary number, $d_4\ d_3\ d_2\ d_1\ d_0$ as output. The circuit implements :

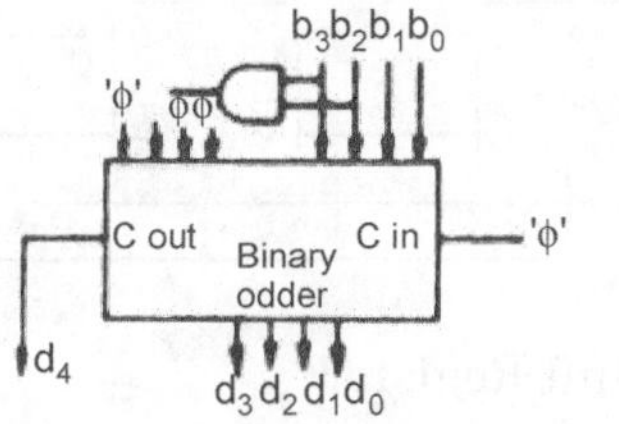

(*a*) Binary of Hex conversion

(*b*) Binary to BCD conversion

(*c*) Binary to grey code conversion

(*d*) Binary to radix-12 conversion

107. Consider the circuit in given Figure *f* implements

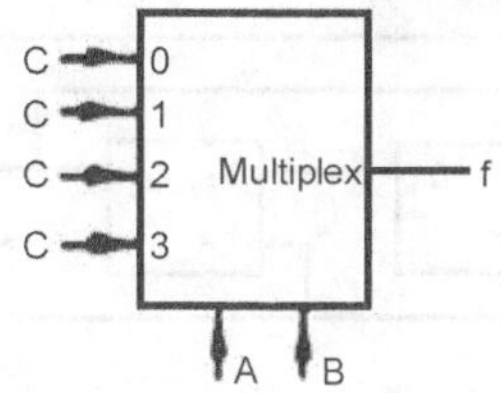

(*a*) $\overline{A}\,\overline{B}C + \overline{A}B\overline{C} + ABC$

(*b*) A + B + C

(*c*) $A \oplus B \oplus C$

(*d*) AB + BC + CA

108. Consider the following state table in given Figure for a sequential machine. The number of states in the minimized machine will be

(*a*) 4

(*b*) 3

(*c*) 2

(*d*) 1

Present state \ x	0	1
A	D0	B1
B	A0	C1
C	A0	B1
D	A1	C1

NEXT STATE OUTPUT

109. What is the equivalent boolean expression in product-of-sums form for the Karnaugh map given in

CD \ AB	00	01	11	20
00		1	1	
01	1			1
11	1			1
10			1	1

(*a*) $B\overline{D} + \overline{B}D$

(*b*) $(B + \overline{C} + D)(\overline{B} + C + \overline{D})$

(*c*) $(B + \overline{D})(\overline{B} + D)$

(*d*) $(B + \overline{D})(\overline{B} + D)$

110. A logic network has two data inputs A and B, and two control inputs C_0 and C_1. It implements the function F according to the following Table.

C_1	C_2	F
0	0	$\overline{A + B}$
0	1	A + B
1	0	$A \oplus B$

Implement the circuit using one 4 to AB Multiplexor, one 2-input Exclusive OR gate, one 2-input AND gate, one 2-input OR gate and one Inverter.

111. Consider the synchronous sequential circuit in Figure

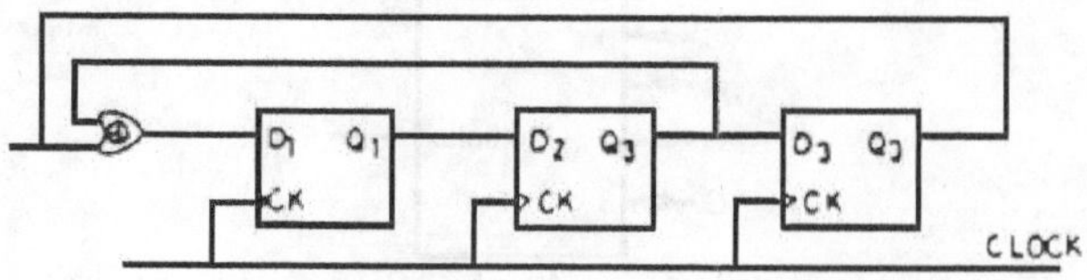

(*a*) Draw a state diagram which is implemented by the circuit. Use the following names for the states corresponding to the values of flip-flops as given below.

Q1	Q2	Q3	State
0	0	0	S_0
0	0	1	S_1
–	–	–	–
–	–	–	–
–	–	–	–
1	1	1	S_7

(*b*) Given that the initial of the circuit is S4, identify the set of states which are not reachable.

1995

112 What values of A, B, C and D satisfy the following simultaneous boolean equations ?

$\overline{A} + AB = 0$, $AB = AC$, $AB + A\overline{C} + CD = \overline{CD}$

(*a*) A = 1, B = 0, C = 0, D = 1

(*b*) A = 1, B = 1, C = 0, D = 0

(*c*) A = 1, B = 0, C = 1, D = 1

(*d*) A = 1, B = 0, C = 0, D = 0

113 The number of 1s in the binary representation of (3* 4096 + 15*256 + 5* 16 + 3) are

(*a*) 8 (*b*) 9

(*c*) 10 (*d*) 12

1994

114 The logic expression for the output of the circuit shown in the figure below is

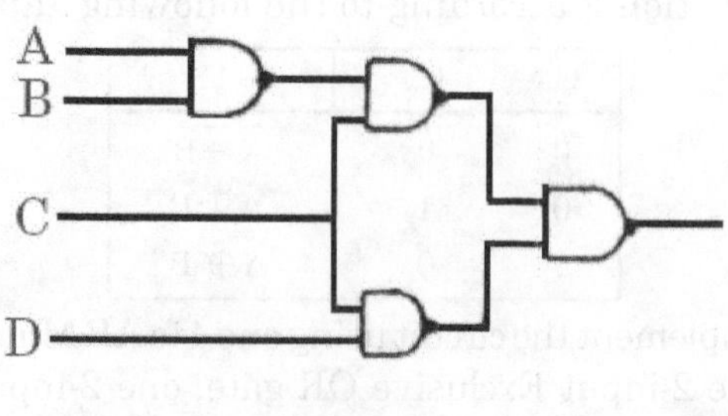

(*a*) $A\overline{C} + B\overline{C} + \overline{C}D$

(*b*) $A\overline{C} + B\overline{C} + \overline{C}D$

(*c*) $ABC = \overline{C}\,\overline{D}$

(*d*) $\overline{A}\,\overline{B} + B\overline{C} + \overline{C}\,\overline{D}$

1993

115. Identify the logic function performed by the circuit shown in Figure

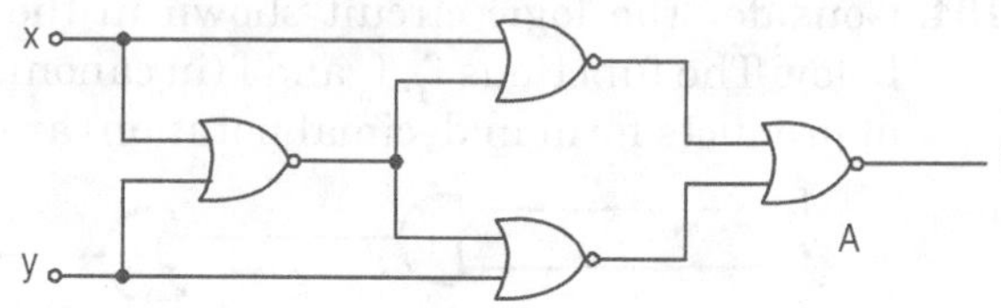

(*a*) exclusive OR

(*b*) exclusive NOR

(*c*) NAND

(*d*) NOR

(*e*) none of these

116. If the state machine described in should have a stable state, the restriction on the inputs is given by :

(*a*) $a.b = 1$

(*b*) $a + b = 1$

(*c*) $\overline{a} + \overline{b} = 0$

(*d*) $\overline{a.b} = 1$

(*e*) $\overline{a + b} = 1$

117. For the initial state of 000, the function performed by the arrangement of the J–K flip-flops in Figur is

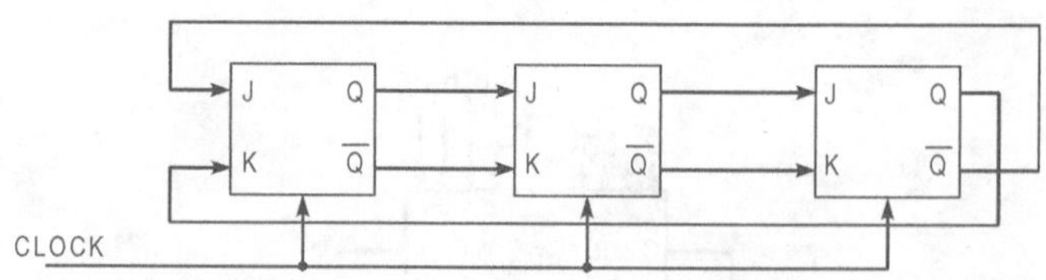

(*a*) Shift Register

(*b*) Mod-3 Counter

(*c*) Mod-6 Counter

(*d*) Mod-2 Counter

(*e*) None of the above

118. Assume that each character code consists of 8 bits. The number of characters that can be transmitted per second through an asynchronous serial line at 2400 baud rate, and with two stop bits, is

(a) 109 (b) 216

(c) 218 (d) 219

(e) 240

119. Convert the following numbers in the given bases into their equivalents in the desired bases.

(a) $110.101)_2 = x)_{10}$ (b) $1118)_{10} = y$)H

120. A ROM is used to store the Truth table for a binary multiplier unit that will multiply two 4-bit numbers. The size of the ROM (number of words number of bits) that is required to accommodate the Truth table is M words N bits Write the values of M and N

121. A certain moving arm disk storage, with one head, has the following specifications.

Number of tracks / recording surface = 200

Disk rotation speed = 2400 rpm

Track storage capacity = 62,500 bits

The average latency of this device is P msec and the data transfer rate is Q bits / sec.

Write the value of P and Q.

1992

122. The operation which is commutative but not associative is

(a) AND (b) OR

(c) EX-OR (c) NAND

123. All digital circuits can be realized using only

(a) Ex-OR gates

(b) Multiplexers

(c) Half adders

(d) OR gates

124. Start and stop bits do not contain an 'information' but are used in serial communication for

(a) Error detection

(b) Error correction

(c) Synchronization

(d) Slowing down the communication

NUMERICAL TYPE QUESTIONS

2016

1. The 16-bit 2's complement representation of an integer is 1111 1111 1111 0101; its decimal representation is ______.

2. We want to design a synchronous counter that counts the sequence 0-1-0-2-0-3 and then repeats. The minimum number of J-K flip-flops required to implement this counter is ________.

3. Consider an eight-bit ripple-carry adder for computing the sum of A and B, where A and B are integers represented in 2's complement form. If the decimal value of A is one, the decimal value of B that leads to the longest latency for the sum to stabilize is______.

4. Let X be the number of distinct 16-bit integers in 2's complement representation. Let Y be the number of distinct 16-bit integers in sign magnitude representation. Then X – Y is __________.

2015

5. The minimum number of JK flip-flops required to construct a synchronous counter with the count sequence (0, 0, 1, 1, 2, 2, 3, 3, 0, 0....) is ________.

6. The number of min-terms after minimizing the following Boolean expression is _______.

$$[D' + AB' + A'C + AC'D + A'C'D]'$$

7. A half adder is implemented with XOR and AND gates. A full adder is implemented with two half adders and one OR gate. The propagation delay of an XOR gate is twice that of an AND/OR gate. The propagation delay of an AND/OR gate is 1.2 microseconds. A 4-bit ripple-carry binary adder is implemented by using four full adders. The total propagation time of this 4-bit binary adder in microseconds is ____________.

8. Suppose X_i for i = 1, 2, 3 are independent and identically distributed random variables whose probability mass functions are $Pr[X_i = 0] = Pr[X_i = 1] = 1/2$ for i =1, 2, 3. Define another random variable $Y = X_1X_2 \oplus X_3$, where $\oplus$ denotes XOR. Then $Pr[Y = 0 | X_3 = 0]$ = _____ .

9. The total number of prime implicates of the function

$f(w, x, y, z) = \Sigma(0, 2, 4, 5, 6, 10)$ is _____ .

10. Consider the equation $(43)_x = (y3)_8$ where x and y are unknown. The number of possible solution is ________

2014

11. Consider the equation $(123)_5 = (x8)_y$ with x and y as unknown. The number of possible solutions is _______ .

1994

12. The number of flip-flops required to construct a binary modulo N counter is ....

13. On the set N of non-negative integers, the binary operation .... is associative and non-commutative.

14. Consider n-bit (including sign bit)2's compliment representation of integer number. The range of integer values, N, that can be represented is .... ≤ N ≤ ....

1992

15. The boolean function in sum of products form where K-map is given below (Fig.1) is ------.

B \ C	0	1
0	1	0
1	A	A

Fig. 1

16. Consider a 3–bit error detection and 1-bit error correction hamming code for 4-bit date. The extra parity bits required would be .... and the 3-bit error detection is possible because the code has a minimum distance of ....

ANSWERS

MCQ Type Questions

1. (d)	2. (b)	3. (c)	4. (d)	5. (a)	6. (b)	7. (d)	8. (a)	9. (a)	10. (a)
11. (d)	12. (c)	13. (b)	14. (a)	15. (c)	16. (d)	17. (b)	18. (a)	19. (d)	20. (a)
21. (b)	22. (a)	23. (a)	24. (b)	25. (a)	26. (b)	27. (d)	28. (a)	29. (a)	30. (b)
31. (a)	32. (a)	33. (b)	34. (d)	35. (d)	36. (a)	37. (d)	38. (c)	39. (a)	40. (c)
41. (b)	42. (b)	43. (d)	44. (d)	45. (c)	46. (c)	47. (d)	48. (b)	49. (a)	50. (a)
51. (c)	52. (b)	53. (a)	54. (a)	55. (a)	56. (a)	57. (a)	58. (b)	59. (d)	60. (d)
61. (d)	62. (d)	63. (d)	64. (d)	65. (a)	66. (c)	67. (a)	68. (d)	69. (a)	70. (a)
71. (a)	72. (c)	73. (c)	74. (a)	75. (c)	76. (b)	77. (d)	78. (a)	79. (c)	80. (c)
81. (d)	82. (a)	83. (b)	84. (*)	85. (c)	86. (a)	87. (d)	88. (b)	89. (b)	90. (a,c,d)
91. (b, c)	92. (b)	93. (a)	94. (d)	95. (c)	96. (d)	97. (b)	98. (c)	99. (c)	100. (*)
101. (*)	102. (*)	103. (c)	104. (b)	105. (d)	106. (d)	107. (d)	108. (b)	109. (c)	110. (*)
111. (*)	112. (a)	113. (c)	114. (b)	115. (b)	116. (b)	117. (c)	118. (c)		

119. (6.625, y = 45E) 120. (M = 256, N = 8) 121. (P = 12.5, Q = $2.5.10^6$)

Numerical Type Questions

1. (–11) 2. (4) 3. (–1) 4. (1) 5. (3) 6. (1) 7. (19.2) 8. (0.75)

9. (3) 10. (5) 11. (3 to 3) 12. (*) 13. (*) 14. (*) 15. ($\overline{B}\overline{C} + \overline{A}\overline{C} + ABC$) 16. (Three, Four)

EXPLANATIONS

MCQ TYPE QUESTIONS

1.

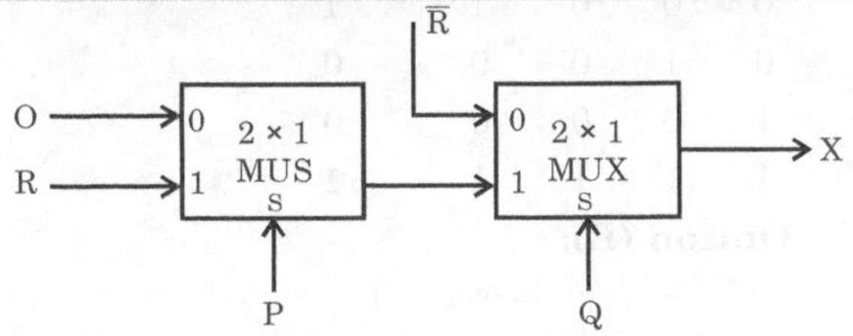

P′ then 0 ⇒ P′ 0 = 0

P then R ⇒ PR

Q′ then R ⇒ Q′R

Q then (0 + PR) ⇒ Q(0 + PR) = QPR.

$$X = Q'R + PQR$$

2. Time to perform addition using this adder is O(log *n*).

4. The counting sequence for given 4-bit Johnson Counter with initial value 0000 is

0, 8, 12, 14, 15, 7, 3, 1, 0

5. The operator ≠ is both cumutative and associative as $p \neq q = q \neq p$ and $p \neq (q \neq r) = (p \neq q) \neq r$

6. Both {*f*} and {*g*} are functionally complete

7. Given L = 1250 Bytes

B = 100 mbps

d = 1 km

V = ?

In CSMA/CD, $L = 2 \times \frac{d}{v} \times B$

$$\Rightarrow \quad V = \frac{2dB}{L}$$

$$= \frac{2 \times 10^3 \times 10^8}{10^4}$$

$$\Rightarrow \quad V = 20{,}000 \text{ km/sec}$$

9. $PQ + \overline{P}QR + \overline{P}Q\overline{R}S$

$= PQ + \overline{P}Q\,(R + \overline{R}S)$

$= PQ + \overline{P}Q\left((R + \overline{R})(R + S)\right)$

$[\because A + BC = (A + B)(A + C)]$

$= PQ + \overline{P}Q(R + S)$

$[\because R + \overline{R} = 1]$

$= Q\left(P + \overline{P}(R + S)\right)$

$= Q\left((P + \overline{P})(P + R + S)\right)$

$[\because A + BC = (A + B)(A + C)]$

$= Q\,(P + R + S)$ $\quad \because [P + \overline{P} = 1]$

$= PQ + QR + QS$

10.

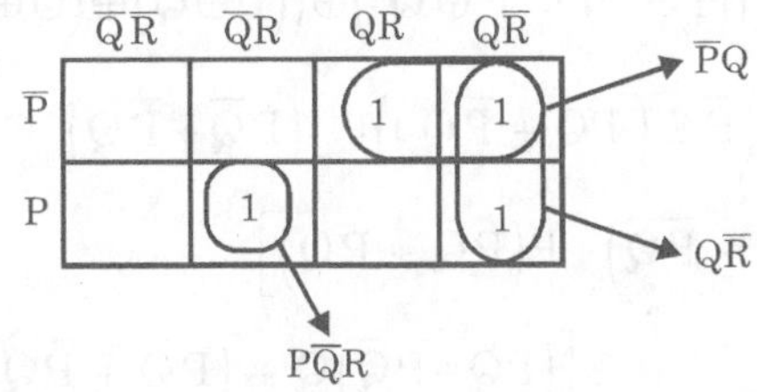

$\overline{P}\overline{Q}.O + \overline{P}Q.1 + P\overline{Q}.R + PQ\overline{R}$

$= \overline{P}Q + P\overline{Q}.R + PQ\overline{R}$

Hence the minimized expression is

$\overline{P}Q + Q\overline{R} + P\overline{Q}R$

11. According to the passage, kaliningrad is a part of Russia despite it not being contiguous with the rest of Russia.

12. Among given option, option (*d*) *i.e.* the number of people with malarial fever has increased this year do not contradic the conclusion.

13.

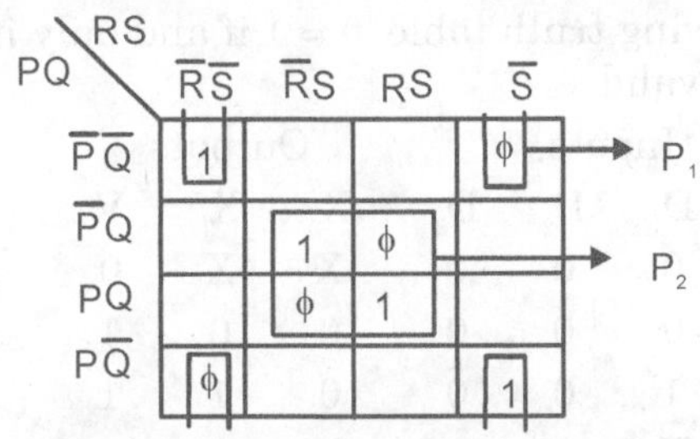

The K-map for the function F is as follows :

$P_1 = \overline{Q}\overline{S}$ and $P_2 = QS$

$\therefore \; F(P, Q, R, S) = P_1 + P_2 = \overline{Q}\overline{S} + QS$

14. π is used to select a subset of attributes and σ_p is used to select subset of tuples matching the predicate P.

$\Pi_{A_1}\left(\Pi_{A_2}\left(\sigma_{F_1}\left(\sigma_{F_2}(r)\right)\right)\right)$

$= \Pi_{A_1}\left(\Pi_{A_2}\left(\sigma(F_1 \wedge F_2)(r)\right)\right)$

and as $A_1 \subset A_2$, so final relation will be displaying values for attributes present in set A.

$\Pi_{A_1}\left(\Pi_{A_2}\left(\sigma(F_1 \wedge F_2)(r)\right)\right) = \Pi_{A_1}\left(\sigma(F_1 \wedge F_2)(r)\right)$

15.

P.S.			FFinputs						N.S.		
Q_2	Q_1	Q_0	J_2	K_2	J_1	K_1	J_0	K_0	Q_2^+	Q_1^+	Q_0^+
			$(\overline{Q}_1)$	(Q_0)	(Q_2)	$(\overline{Q}_2)$	(Q_1)	$(\overline{Q}_0)$			
0	0	0	1	0	0	1	0	1	1	0	0
1	0	0	1	0	1	0	0	1	1	1	0
1	1	0	0	0	1	0	1	1	1	1	1

16. $F(P,Q) = ((1 \oplus P) \oplus (P \oplus Q)) \oplus ((P \oplus Q) \oplus (Q \oplus 0))$

$$= \left(\overline{P} \oplus \left(P\overline{Q} + \overline{P}Q\right)\right) \oplus \left(\left(P\overline{Q} + \overline{P}Q\right) \oplus Q\right)$$

$$= \left[\overline{P}\left(PQ + \overline{P}\,\overline{Q}\right) + P\left(P\overline{Q} + \overline{P}Q\right)\right]$$

$$\oplus \left[\left(PQ + \overline{P}\,\overline{Q}\right)Q + \left(P\overline{Q} + \overline{P}Q\right)\overline{Q}\right]$$

$$= \left(\overline{P}\,\overline{Q} + P\overline{Q}\right) \oplus \left(PQ + P\overline{Q}\right) = \overline{Q} \oplus P$$

$$= PQ + \overline{P}\,\overline{Q} = \overline{P \oplus Q}$$

17. **Option (*a*) :** 256 cannot be represented by 8-bit 2′s complement no.

or 2′S complement representation, the general formula for n-bits is

$(-2^{n-1}$ to $2^{n-1} - 1)$

for $n = 8$, the max negative number is -2^{8-1}

$= -2^7 = -128$

Hence answer is option (*b*).

18. In following truth table, $v = 1$ if and only if the input is valid

Inputs				Outputs		
D_0	D_1	D_2	D_3	X_0	X_1	V
0	0	0	0	X	X	0
1	0	0	0	0	0	1
X	1	0	0	0	1	1
X	X	1	0	1	0	1
X	X	X	1	1	1	1

What function does the truth table represent?

Ans. A

It is a 4 × 2 priority encoder, where highest priority bits (inputs) are to the right and "X" indicates an irrelevant value.

i.e. Any input value there yields the same output since it is superseded by higher-priority input. And the output V indicates if the input is valid.

19. Exclusive NOR of x & y $\overline{x \oplus y}$

Truth table:

x	y	$2 \oplus y$	$\overline{x \oplus y}$
0	0	0	1
0	1	1	0
1	0	1	0
1	1	0	1

Option (A):

x	y	xy	$x'y'$	$xy + x'y'$	Same as $\overline{x \oplus y}$
0	0	0	1	1	
0	1	0	0	0	
1	0	0	0	0	
1	1	1	1	1	

Option (B):

x	y	y'	$x \oplus y'$
0	0	1	1
0	1	0	0
1	0	1	0
1	1	0	1

$\equiv \overline{x \oplus y}$

Option (C):

x	y	x'	$x' \oplus y$
0	0	1	1
0	1	1	0
1	0	0	0
1	1	0	1

$\equiv \overline{x \oplus y}$

Option (D):

x	y	x'	y'	$x' \oplus y'$
0	0	1	1	0
0	1	1	0	1
1	0	0	1	1
1	1	0	0	0

This is not equivalent to $\overline{x \oplus y}$ So, the answer is (*d*)

20. 16 K × 16 RAM

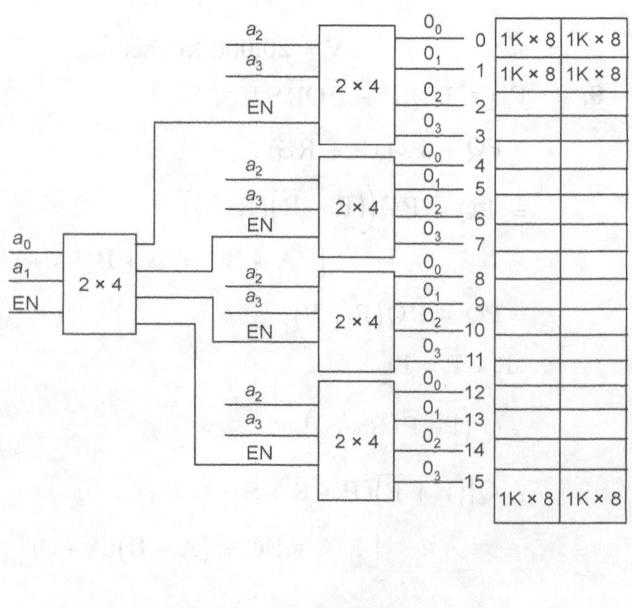

$$16\,k \times 16 = 2^4 + 2^{10} + 2^4 \text{ bit} = 2^{18} \text{ bits}$$
$$1K \times 8 = 2^{10} + 2^3 \text{ bits} = 2^{13} \text{ bits}$$
$$\text{so no of 1K} \times 8 \text{ RAM chips needed} = \frac{2^{18}}{2^{13}} 2^5 = 32$$

21. $(0.5)_{10} = (1.0)_2 \times 2^{-1}$

So, exponent = – 1 and fraction is 000 - - - 000

22. $XY' + XY = X(Y'+Y)$

$= X.1 = X$

23. The ***counter example*** for the condition *full*: REAR = FRONT is Initially when the Queue is empty REAR = FRONT = 0 by which the above *full* condition is satisfied which is false

The ***counter example*** for the condition *full*: (FRONT + 1) mod n = REAR is Initially when the Queue is empty REAR = FRONT = 0 and let n = 3, so after inserting one element REAR = 1 and FRONT = 0, at this point the condition *full* above is satisfied, but still there is place for one more element in Queue, so this condition is also false

The ***counter example*** for the condition *empty* : (REAR + 1)mod n = FRONT is Initially when the Queue is empty REAR = FRONT = 0 and let n = 2, so after inserting one element REAR =1 and FRONT = 0, at this point the condition empty above is satisfied, but the queue of capacity n – 1 is full here

The ***counter example*** for the condition *empty* : (FRONT+l)mod n = REAR is Initially when the Queue is empty REAR = FRONT = 0 and let n = 2, so after inserting one element REAR = 1 and FRONT = 0, at this point the condition *empty* above is satisfied, but the queue of capacity n – 1 is full here

24.

cd \ ab	00	01	11	10
00	1	X	X	1
01	X			1
11				
10	1			X

25. $2^n \geq 258$

$\Rightarrow n = 9$

26.

P \ QR	00	01	11	10
0		1	1	1
1				

$f = (P + \overline{R})(\overline{P} + Q)$
$= P + QR$

Alternate method

$(P + \overline{Q} + \overline{R}).(P + \overline{Q} + R).(P + Q + \overline{R})$

$= \overline{\overline{(P+\overline{Q}+\overline{R}).(P+\overline{Q}+R).(P+Q+\overline{R})}}$

$= \overline{\overline{P}QR + \overline{P}Q\overline{R} + \overline{P}\overline{Q}R}$

$= \overline{\overline{P}Q(R+\overline{R}) + \overline{P}\overline{Q}R}$

$= \overline{\overline{P}Q + \overline{P}\overline{Q}R} = \overline{\overline{P}(Q+\overline{Q}R)}$

$= \overline{\overline{P}(Q+R)}$

$= P + \overline{Q}\,\overline{R}$

27. All options except option '*d*' gives EX-NOR gates

28. Given : $f(P, Q, R) = PQ + Q\overline{R} + P\overline{R}$

By K-map

P \ QR	00	01	11	10
0	m_0	m_1	m_3	m_2 1
1	m_4 1	m_5	m_7 1	m_6 1

($Q\overline{R}$, $P\overline{R}$→, PQ)

These are min terms means sum of products in k-map

Then answer is $\mathbf{PQ + Q\overline{R} + P\overline{R}}$

So answer is $\boldsymbol{m_2 + m_4 + m_6 + m_7}$ because all other answer conflict the requirment.

29. $(F87B)_{16} = \underbrace{1111}_{F}\ \underbrace{1000}_{8}\ \underbrace{0111}_{7}\ \underbrace{1011}_{B}$

But it is 2's complement of P

So for getting original numbers, take 2's complement of $(F87B)_{16}$

It is $\quad P = 0000\ 01111\ 0000101$

$= (1925)_{10}$

Then $\quad P * 8 = 1925 \times 8$

$= 15400$

$(15400)_{10} = 0011110000101000$

Now, 2's complement of this 15400 in binary

$= \underbrace{1100}_{C}\,\underbrace{0011}_{3}\,\underbrace{1101}_{D}\,\underbrace{1000}_{8} = (C3D8)_{16}$

30. Make the table

$P(S_1)$	$Q(S_0)$	Z	
0	0	R	0
0	1	$\bar{R}$	1
1	0	$\bar{R}$	2
1	1	R	3

} as given in figure

Add these all for result because output is the mixing of these signals.

$\therefore\ \bar{P}\bar{Q}R + \bar{P}Q\bar{R} + P\bar{Q}\bar{R} + PQR$

$= \bar{P}(\bar{Q}R + Q\bar{R}) + P(Q\bar{R} + QR)$

$= \bar{P}(Q \oplus R) + P(Q \ominus R) = P \oplus Q \oplus R$

Alternately

P and Q are lines out of which only one will enable at a time.

P	Q	F
0	0	R
0	1	$\bar{R}$
1	0	$\bar{R}$
1	1	R

$\therefore\ P'Q'R + P'QR' + PQ'R' + PQR$

$= P'(Q'R + QR') + P(Q'R' + QR)$

$= P'(Q \oplus R) + P(Q \odot R)$

$= P'(Q \oplus R) + P(Q \oplus R)'$

$= P'Z + PZ'$ ....[take $(Q \oplus R) = Z$]

$= P \oplus Z$

$= P \oplus Q \oplus R$

31. Output

$= \overline{\left(\overline{(P+Q)} + \overline{(Q+R)}\right)} + \overline{\left(\overline{(P+R)} + \overline{(Q+R)}\right)}$

$= \left(\overline{P+Q} + \overline{Q+R}\right)\cdot\left(\overline{(P+R)} + \overline{(Q+R)}\right)$

$\left(\because \left(\overline{A+B}\right) = \bar{A}\,\bar{B}\right)$

$= \left(\bar{P}\bar{Q} + \bar{Q}\bar{R}\right)\left(\bar{P}\bar{R} + \bar{Q}\bar{R}\right)$

$= \bar{P}\bar{Q}\bar{P}\bar{R} + \bar{P}\bar{O}\bar{Q}\bar{R} + \bar{P}\bar{Q}\bar{R}\bar{R} + \bar{Q}\bar{R}\bar{Q}\bar{R}$

$= \bar{P}\bar{Q}\bar{R} + \bar{Q}\bar{P}\bar{R} + \bar{P}\bar{Q}\bar{R} + \bar{Q}\bar{R}$

$= \bar{P}\bar{Q}\bar{R} + \bar{Q}\bar{R}$

$= \bar{Q}\bar{R}(\bar{P}+1)$ .....$\left[\text{since}(\bar{P}+1) = 1\right]$

$= \overline{(Q+R)}$

Alternately

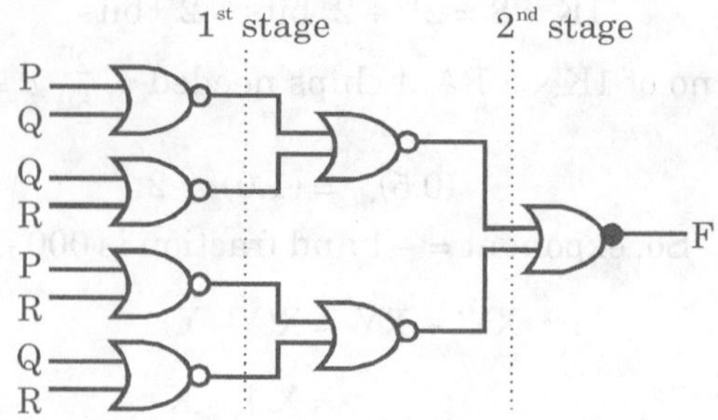

At first stage

- $\overline{(P+Q)}$
- $\overline{(Q+R)}$
- $\overline{(P+R)}$
- $\overline{(Q+R)}$

At second stage

- $\overline{\overline{(P+Q)} + \overline{(Q+R)}}$
- $\overline{\overline{(P+R)} + \overline{(Q+R)}}$

$F = \overline{\overline{\overline{(P+Q)} + \overline{(Q+R)}} + \overline{\overline{(P+R)} + \overline{(Q+R)}}}$

$= \overline{\overline{\overline{(P+Q)} + \overline{(Q+R)}}}\cdot\overline{\overline{\overline{(P+R)} + \overline{(Q+R)}}}$

$= \left(\overline{(P+Q)} + \overline{(Q+R)}\right)\cdot\left(\overline{(P+R)} + \overline{(Q+R)}\right)$

$= \left(P'Q' + Q'R'\right)\cdot\left(P'R' + Q'R'\right)$

$= \underline{P'Q'R' + P'Q'R' + P'Q'R' + P'Q'R'} + Q'R'$

$= P'Q'R' + Q'R' = Q'R'(P' + 1)$

$= Q'R' = \overline{Q+R}$

32. Initially Q_1 Q_0

0 0

Here T flip-flop

If T = 0 the next state is present state

If T = 1 next state is compliment of present

Since T = 1 initially, so outputs is compliment

Next second Q_1 remain 1 since Q_0 become 0 when TIP is 1 (compliment of present), so 2n second clock not present remains in same state.

So sequence is like 11, 10, 01, 00

33. $(1217)_8 = 001\ 010\ 001\ 111$

$0010\ 1000\ 1111 = (028F)_{16}$

Alternately

Given digit in octal 1217.

Convert them in binary $\overline{001}\ \overline{010}\overline{001}\overline{111}$

Now convert binary to hexa

$\underset{2}{\underline{0010}}\ \underset{8}{\underline{1000}}\ \underset{F}{\underline{1111}} = (028F)_{16}$

34. For implementing (AB + C), first we implement AB.

For AND operation 3 NOR GATE required

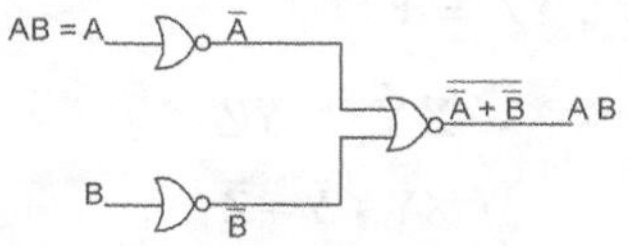

Now for (AB + C)

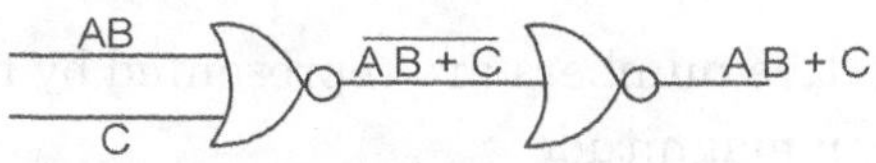

Hence five NOR gates required.

Alternately

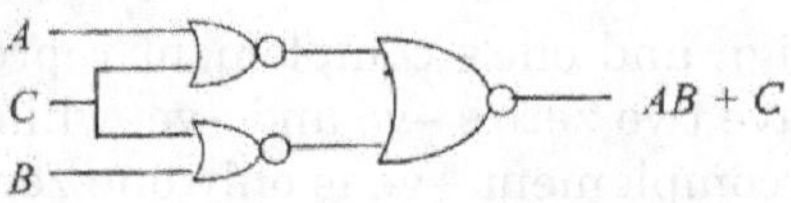

35. Hexadecimal value 0x00000000 in binary

0000 0000 0000 0000 0000 0000 0000 0000 0000 0000

Hence it is normalized to value to.

36. K-Map is

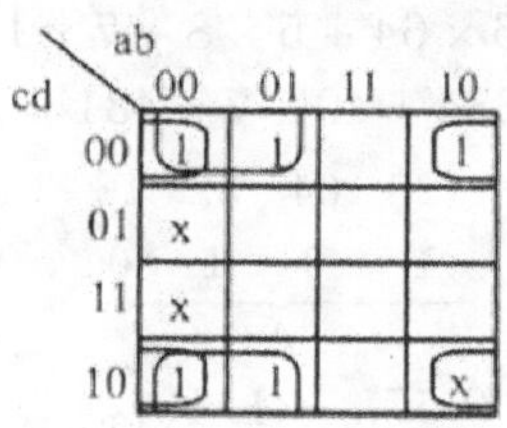

$a'd' + b'd'$

37. $\sqrt{121_r} = (11)_r$

So we till take base r any value that is greater than 2.

38. f_1 and f_2 are connected with and gates, so when $f_2 = \Sigma m(6, 8)$ then f is true for Σm (1, 6, 8, 15)

39. $(P + Q')(PQ' + PR)(P'R' + Q')$

$= (PQ' + PR + PQ' + PRQ')(P'R' + Q')$

$= (PQ' + PR + PRQ')(P'R' + Q')$

$= (PQ' + PR(1 + Q'))(P'R' + Q')$

$= (PQ' + PR)(P'R' + Q')$

$= PQ' + PRQ'$

$= PQ'(1 + R) = PQ'$

40. For n binary variables, we can obtain 2^n distinct minterm or maxterms.

Since function can be either 1 or 0 for each minterm or maxterm, therefore we can form 2^{2^n} function from n variables.

41. Eight 3 – to– 8 line decoders will be needed to construct a 6 – to – 64 line decoder without any other logic gates.

42. Karnaugh map of given function will be as follows:

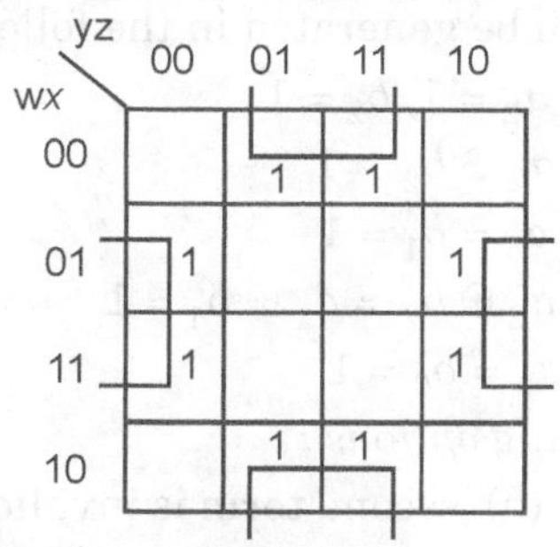

Simplified form of f will be

$$f = x'z + xz'$$

Therefore, it is independent of two variables.

43. Each of the functions P, Q and R includes same minterms which f includes, where S doesn't includes same minterms as f.

$$P = \Sigma(0, 4, 5, 7, 8, 9, 13, 15) = Q = R = f$$

whereas $S = \Sigma(0, 2, 3, 5, 7, 8, 9) \neq f$

44. Truth table for X, Y and Z

X	Y	Z = X * Y	Y * Z	X * Z	X * Y * Z
0	0	1	0	0	1
0	1	0	0	1	1
1	0	0	1	0	1
1	1	1	1	1	1

From above truth table we can say that all P, Q and R are valid.

45. Multiplexes of size 2^{n-1} to 1 will be needed.

46. A 4-bit adder with S_3, S_2, S_1, S_0 and C_4 as its output require 2-1 bit adder and a single one bit adder require 5 AND gates and 2 OR gates in two level logic. Hence required gate are 10 AND gate and 4 OR gates.

47. Counter will start with 0 for Load = 0, Count = 1 and clock it will go to 1, then 2, then 3, then 4 and at last at 5. As soon as it will reach to 5, the clear will become one (1) which will clear the counter to zero.

48. Clock with duty cycle 50%. In choice (*c*), there are two D-Flip Flop if left most is activated or clock value 1 the clock value of right most 1 D flip-flop is 0, so it delay the phase *f* by 180°.

49.

$$\begin{matrix} a_2 & a_1 & a_0 \\ b_2 & b_1 & b_0 \end{matrix}$$

Carry will be generated in the following cases

$$a_2 = 1, b_2 = 1$$

$$a_2 \oplus b_2 = 1$$

and $\quad a_1 = b_1 = 1$

$$a_2 \oplus b_2 = a_1 \oplus b_1 = 1$$

and $\quad a_0 = b_0 = 1$

Considering options :

In option (*b*), second term is invalid

as if $\quad a_2 = 1, b_2 = 0, b_1 = 1, b_0 = 1, c \neq 1$

In option (*c*), a_2 is invalid term

In option (*d*), $a_2\, a_1, b_1$, is invalid as, if

$$a_2 = 0, a_1 = b_1 = 1, b_2 = 0, c^1 \neq = 1$$

Hence only option (*a*) encompasses possibilities.

50.

wx \ yz	00	01	11	10
00	0	0	0	0
01	0	1	1	0
11	1	1	1	0
10	0	0	1	0

The cube covers of (*a*) contain following cells.

$\overline{w}\,xz$	0101, 0111
$wx\,\overline{y}$	1101, 1100
$x\,\overline{y}\,z$	0101,1101
xyz	0111, 1111
wyz	1011,1111

Atleast one member of a pair should satisfy the condition of differing by one bit by at least one member of each of other pairs. This is true regarding the above cubes.

51.

$$B = b_{n-1}\, b_{n-2} \ldots b_0$$

$$A = a_{n-1}\, a_{n-2} \ldots a_0$$

$$S = c_{n-1}\, c_{n-2} \ldots c_0$$

Over flow condition,

$$V = b'_{n-1}\, a'_{n-1}\, c_{n-2} + b_{n-1}\, a_{n-1}\, c'_{n-2}$$

c_{n-1} is c_{out}, so

$$V = c_{out} \oplus c_{n-1}$$

Hence over flow condition is

$$c_{out} \oplus c_{n-1}$$

52. $h_3h_2h_1h_0$ is gray code representation of number n, $g_3g_2g_1g_0$ is gray code representation of $(n+1)$ (modulo 16) $(n+1)$ is 5 bit in decimal it range is 0 to 31.

So, $g_1(h_3h_2h_1h_0) = \Sigma(4, 9, 10, 11, 12, 13, 14, 15)$ is correct function for $(n + 1)$ mod 16.

53.

$$X\overline{\overline{Y}} \,.\, YZ = F$$

$$X\overline{Y} + \overline{YZ}$$

$$X\overline{Y} + \overline{Y} + \overline{Z}$$

$$\overline{Y} + \overline{Z}$$

54. Negative numbers are represented by the forms

1. sign magnitude
2. one's complement
3. two's complement

For sign and one's complement representation, we have two zero's –ve and +ve, while in case of two's complement +ve is only one zero.

This additional code which is waste in top two representation is used to assign one more negative code.

55. Given : $(657)_8$

First we find its decimal.

$$(6 \times 8^2 + 5 \times 8^1 + 7 \times 8^0)$$

$$= 6 \times 64 + 5 \times 8 + 7 \times 1$$

$$= 384 + 40 + 7 = 431$$

256	128 64 32 16	8 4 2 1
0 001	1 0 1 0	1 1 1 1
I	A	F

Hence $\quad (657)_8 = (IAF)_{16}$.

56. Given : $\quad f(A, B, C, D) = \Sigma\,(1, 4, 5, 9, 11, 12)$

$$= \overline{A}\,\overline{C}\,D + B\overline{C}\,\overline{D} + A\overline{B}\,D$$

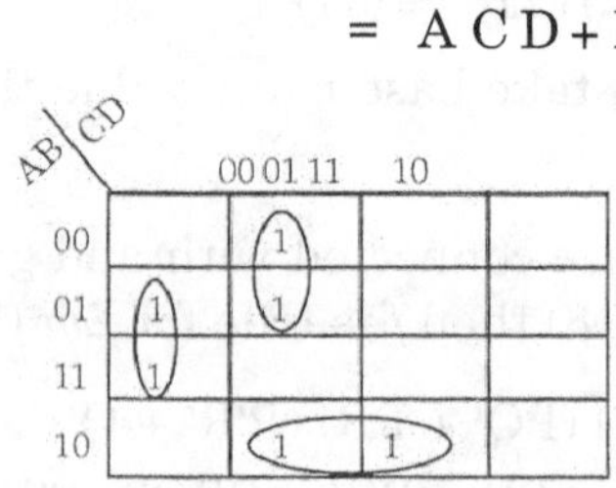

57. $D = A \,.\, X + \overline{X}\,Q$

Consider for first two cases,

$$\overline{X}\,\overline{Q} = 0$$

because X = 1, so $\quad 0.\overline{Q} = 0.$

So, answer depend only on A . X

For first clock pulse '0'

$\Rightarrow \quad D = A_0$

For clock pulse '1'

⇒ output = A_0

⇒ D = again A_1

For clock pulse '2'

⇒ output = A_1

D = $\overline{A_1}$

because A.X = 0 and X = 0

∴ $\overline{X} = 1$

$X\overline{Q} = \overline{Q}$

58. Given : Its input 1 0 1 1 0 → Output 0 1 0 1 0

It follows the concept that whenever we have to find two's complement, take number from the right end (L.S.B) go to left side and print same number as input till first '1' encounter after that complement each number

↓

0 0 1 1 1 0 0

Number which we take are underlined at each step and marks is used to give mark (arrow) of victim one.

↓

0 0 1 1 1 0 0

↓

0 0 1 1 1 0 0

↓

0 0 1 1 1 0 0

↓

0 0 1 0 1 0 0

↓

0 0 0 0 1 0 0

↓

0 1 0 0 1 0 0

↓

1 1 0 0 1 0 0

59.

$D_1 = Q_0 \oplus \overline{Q_1}$

$D_0 = \overline{Q_0}$

Q_0	Q_1	Net state	
0	0	1	1
1	1	0	1
0	1	1	0
1	0	0	0

62.

$$x'y' + xy + x'y$$
$$= x'(y + y') + xy$$
$$= x' + xy$$
$$= (x' + x)(x' + y)$$
$$= x' + y$$

63.

Input		Output
S	R	
0	0	interminate
1	0	1
0	1	0
1	1	? ⟶ indeterminate

64. $(73)_x = (54)_y$

The possible value of x and y is 8 and 11 evaluated by putting the value alternative option.

65. (113. + – 111.) + 7.51

113. + (– 111. + 7.51)

The exponent value is 10.0.

The value evaluated by the expression is 9.51 and 10.0.

66. Output is form of 4 bit and output is 1 when input is greater than 5,

So, output will be 1 in case of

0101 – 5

0110 – 6

0111 – 7

1000 – 8

1001 – 9

This can be implemented with the help of 4 logic gate of type AND OR and NOT.

67. K-map of given function is

c \ ab	00	01	11	10
0			1	1
1	1	1		1

Essential prime implicant of this boolean function is

011, 011 and 110,100

which is a'c and ac' which is *(a)*.

68.

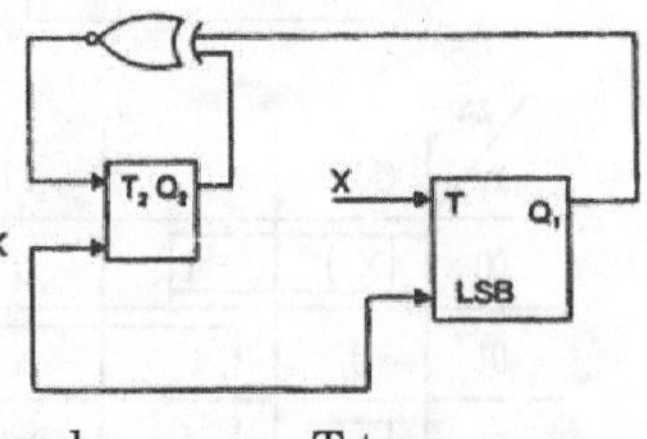

The flip - flop shown are T-type.

To implement this as a 2-bit counter, the input should be input of X - OR of two input Q_1 and Q_2 hence $Q_1 \oplus Q_2$.

69. Adding two 4-bit numbers and delay of each gate is one time limit.

Delay of adder = {4 × delay in one gate}.

= 4 × 1 = 4 time unit

70. A = 11111010

$= -2^7 + 2^6 + 2^5 + 2^4 + 2^3 + 2^1$

$= -6$ (since number. is stored in two's complement format)

B $= 2^3 + 2^1$

$= 8 + 2 = 10$

$\therefore$ AB $= -60$, which is 11000100

71. 2's complement → 00000101 = 5

2's complement of 11100111 is 00011001 = 25

72. 15 14..................9 8...................0

s	e	m
Sign	Exponent	Mantissa

s = signbit

e = exponent $= 2^6 = 0$ to 63

$m = 2^8 = 0$ to 255

Floating point representation is

$(-1)^s (1 + m \times 2^{-9})\, 2^{e-31}$ if the exponent ≠ 111111

$(-1)^s (1 + 2^9\, 2^{-9})\, 2^{e-31} = (-1)^s (1 + 2^0)(2^{e-31})$

If exponent is 111110 or 111101

then $e = 62$

$e_2 = 61$

$\therefore$ Successine difference $= 2^{31}$

73. $z_k = 00.........\ k$

$n_k = 1 + ...\ k$

$z_k + n_k = k$

Number of transition state $= 2^3 - 1 = 7$

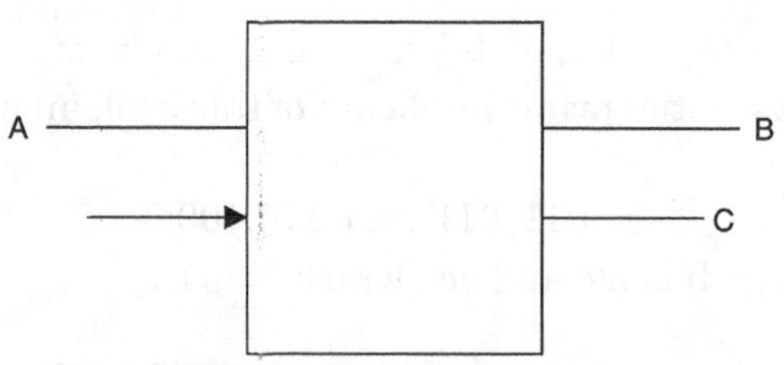

74.

xy \ zw	00	01	11	10
00	X	1	0	1
01	0	1	X	0
11	1	x	X	0
10	X	0	0	X

When we take Sum of Product

literal $= wy + x\overline{z}\overline{w} + x\,\overline{z}\,\overline{y} + \overline{w}\,\overline{x}\,\overline{y}$

Total number of literal count = 9

xy \ zw	00	01	11	10
00	X	1	0	1
01	0	1	X	0
11	1	X	X	0
10	X	0	0	X

When we take Product of Sum

literal= $(z + w + x)(\overline{z} + \overline{w})(\overline{z} + \overline{y})(\overline{x} + y)$

Total number of literal = 11

Minimum possible literal count is (11, 9).

75. Delay $\delta = 2$ ns

$\delta_2 = 4$ ns

At 1 ns, transistion logic 0 to logic 1.

At 2 ns, some transition occur

At 4 ns, some transition occur.

76. For taking minterm (SOP)

$f = xz' = zx'$

yz \ wx	00	01	11	10
00	0	1	1	0
01	x	0	0	1
11	x	0	0	1
10	0	1	1	x

77. Binary number of 15 = 1111

2's complemnt = 0000

$\underline{\quad 1}$

0001

So, we represent decimal value – 15 in 2's complemnt form as → 10001

78.

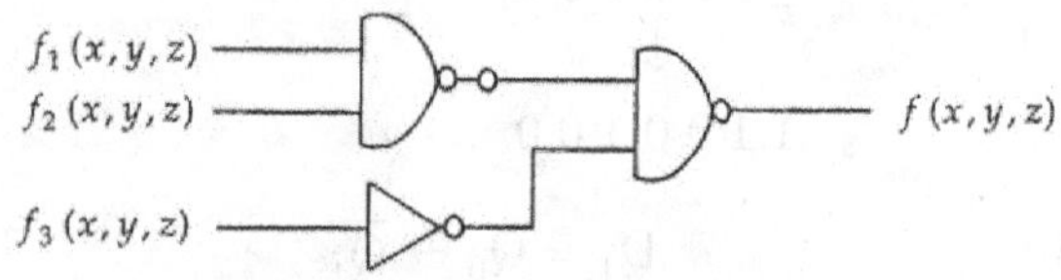

x \ yz	00	01	11	10
0	1			
1	1	1		1

$f_1(x, y, z) = \overline{y}\,\overline{z} + x\,\overline{y} + x\,\overline{z}$

x \ yz	00	01	11	10
0			1	
1			1	

$f_2(x, y, z) = yz$

84. (*a*)

I_4	I_3	I_2	I_1	R_3	R_2	R_1 LSB
Input		LSB		Output		
0	0	0	0	0	0	0
0	0	0	1	0	0	1
0	0	1	0	0	1	0
0	0	1	1	0	1	1
0	1	0	0	1	0	0
0	1	0	1	1	0	1
0	1	1	0	0	0	0
0	1	1	1	0	0	1
1	0	0	0	0	1	0
1	0	0	1	0	1	1

Remember :

(*i*) The input should have 4 bits or output should have 3 bits

(*ii*) You may use 'T' for I and 'F' for zero.

(*iii*) The order R_3 R_2 R_1 is very important as $I_4 I_3 I_2 I_1$

(*b*) INPUTOUTPUT

L.S.B.

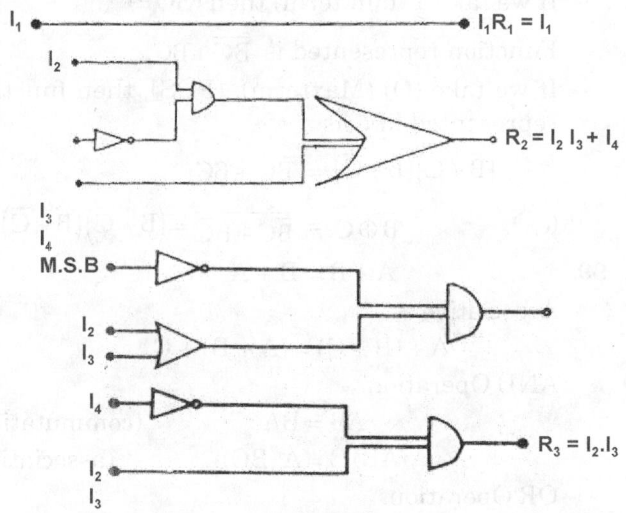

Note : You may draw one combined circuit, the two inputs shown as I_2.

(*a*) A : D A H B: 0 9 H

C : 0 9 H D: 5 1 H

(*b*) A L E : T1 = 1

T2 = T3 = T4 = 0

$\overline{RD}$: T1 = 1

T2 = T3 = 0. T4 = 1

(*c*) The IO/$\overline{M}$ signal and $\overline{RD}$ signal

(*a*) (*i*) 18 H 86 H

(*ii*) D = 00H D = F F H

E = 19H E = 13 H

(*b*) E = | B – C |

D = 00H if B > C

and D = FFH if B < C

(*a*) 3.6 nano seconds

(*b*) 2.96 nano seconds

Equivalent of any of the followings

(*i*) The percentage of unconditional branch instruction is 4%.

(*ii*) The percentage of conditional branch instruction taken is 8%.

(*iii*) The percentage of conditional branch instructions not taken is 8%.

(*a*) ENQUEUE : Push

DEQUEUE : REVERSE, POP, REVERSE

(*b*) (*i*)

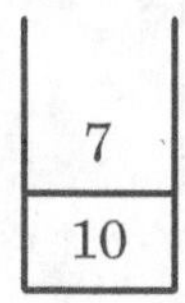

(*ii*)

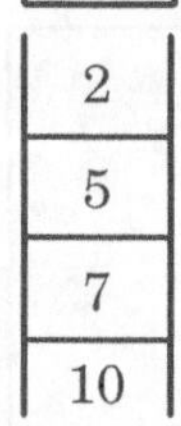

(*iii*)

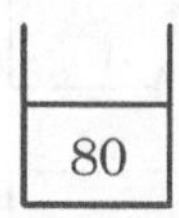

85. The number of ordered pairs of the form (*a*, b) where *a* and *b* belong to the set is n^2 and since each of these pairs may either appear or not appear in any relation, the number of possible relations is 2^{n^2}

86. Place the *n* zeroes in a line. There are *n* + 1 empty places between any two consecutive zeores including before the first zero and after the last zero. So, we can place a one in any of these *n* + 1 locations. So, the number of possible binary strings is $^{n+1}C_k$

87. (*a*) $\overline{x.x} = \bar{x}$ (*b*) $\overline{x+x} = \bar{x}$

(*c*) $\overline{x \cdot 1} = \bar{x}$ (*d*) $\overline{x+1} = 0$

88. Evaluate the Karnaugh map by combining the four 1's in the third column which correspond to the term CD and then the four 1's in the matrix positions (3, 2), (3, 3), (4, 2) and (4, 3) which form a square and correspond to the term AB.

89. 0–100 + 100–1 evaluates to 57 in Booth's coding as below

$(0*2^7) - (1*2^6) + (0*2^5) + (0*2^4) + (1*2^3) + (0*2^2) + (0*2^1) - (1*2^0) = -64 + 8 - 1 = -57$

90. The circuit diagrams for the different choices are shown below

(*a*)

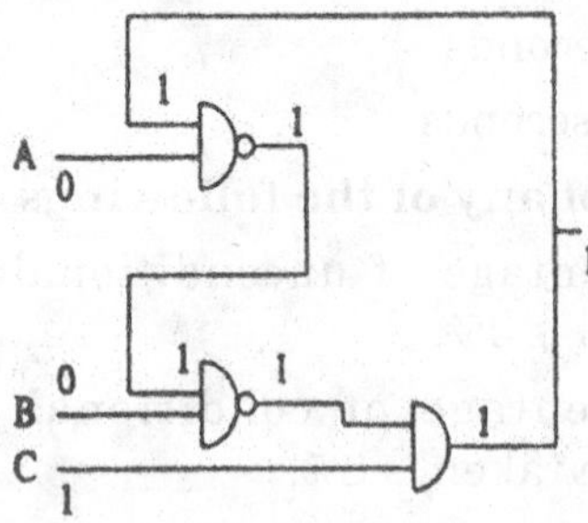

(*b*)

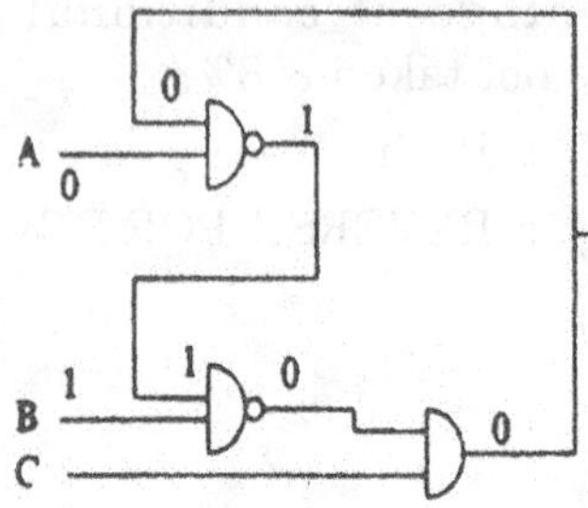

(*c*)

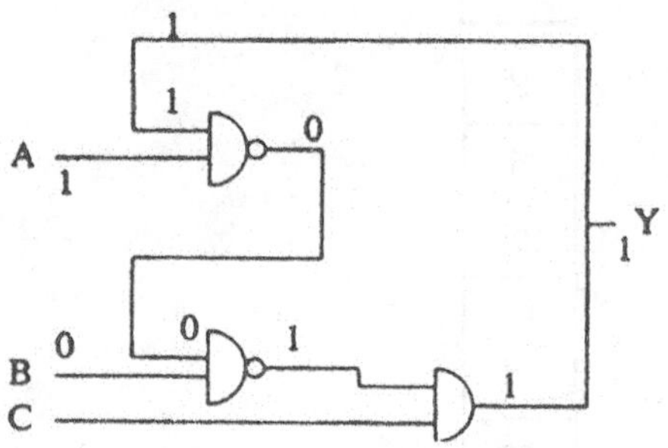

(*d*)

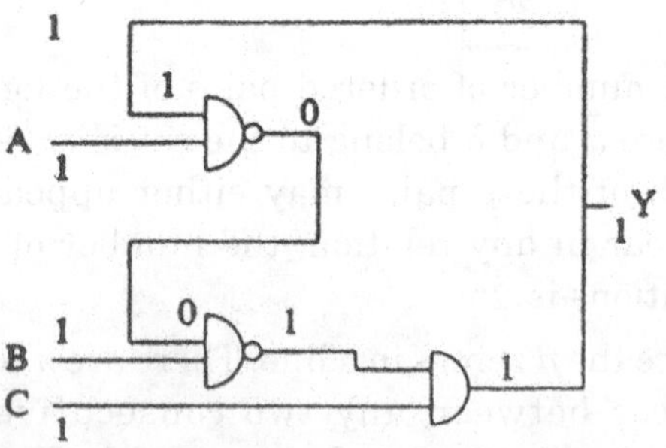

91. The XOR gate can be used to implement NOT by doing A ⊕ 1. Using the AND gate and the NOT realization of XOR, we can get a NAND gate, which is a univeral gate. So, C is right.

The 2 to 1 multiplexer gives the function AX + BX', where X is the selector input. It can be used to implement a NOT by making A = 0 and B = 1, thus we get X'. We can get an AND gate by putting B = 0 and thus getting A.X. Using NOT and AND we can get a NAND, which is a universal gate. So B, is wrong. We also can't implement a NOT gate using A. B. + C. So, D is wrong.

92. The one half-adder can add the least significant bit of the two numbers. Full adders are required to add the remaining 15 bits as they all involve adding carries.

93. Zero can be both positive and negative. So, the sign bit for representation of zero can be 0 and 1.

94. A ⊕ B ⊕ = A.

Take A = B and counting operators.

95. Input line depend on select line

$= 2^n$, where n is select line = 16

Multiplexer is defined

Total input line : output line = 16 : 1

96. Above 2.8 V but less than V_{cc}.

In TTL, $5 - (1.5 + 0.7) = 2.8$ V

97.

	D_7	D_6	D_5	D_4	D_3	D_2	D	D_0	
3428 =	1	1	1	0	0	0	1	0	= –98

98.

A \ BC	00	01	10	110
0	1	0	0	1
1	1	0	0	1

If we take 1 (min term) then (SOP)

Function represented is $\overline{BC} + BC$.

If we take (O) (Maxterm), (POS), then function represented like as

$$(\overline{B} + C)(B + \overline{C}) = \overline{BC} + BC$$

(*c*) $$\overline{B \oplus C} = \overline{\overline{BC} + B\overline{C}} = (B + \overline{C})(\overline{B} + \overline{C})$$

99. $$A + B = B + A$$

Associative

$$A + (B + C) = (A + B) + C$$

AND Operation.

$$AB = BA \quad \text{(commutative)}$$
$$(AB)\,C = A\,(BC) \quad \text{(associative)}$$

OR Operation.

$$A + B = B + A \quad \text{(commutative)}$$
$$(A + B) + C = A + (B + C) \quad \text{(associative)}$$

NAND Operation.

$$\overline{AB} = \overline{BA} \text{ (commutative)}$$
$$(A{\uparrow}B){\uparrow}C \neq A{\uparrow}(B{\uparrow}C)$$
$$\overline{\overline{A \cdot B} \cdot C} \neq \overline{A \cdot \overline{B \cdot C}}$$
$$AB + \overline{C} \neq \overline{A} + BC$$

NOR Operation.

$$\overline{A + B} = \overline{B + A} \quad \text{(commutative)}$$
$$\overline{\overline{A + B} + C} \neq \overline{A + \overline{B + C}} \quad \text{(not associative)}$$

EX-OR Operation.

$$\overline{A \oplus B} = \overline{B \oplus A} \quad \text{(commutative)}$$

$$(A \oplus B) \oplus C \neq A \oplus (B \oplus C) \quad \text{(associative)}$$

100. (*a*)

(*b*)

x	y	
0	0	1
0	1	1
1	0	0
1	1	1

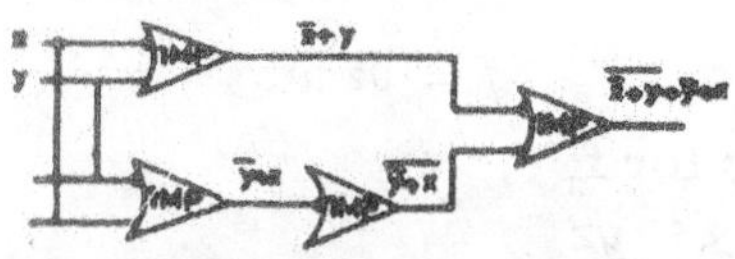

is the truth table for the implication gate and the function $f = x' + y = (x\,y')' = x$ NAND y.

As NAND is functionally complete, 1 MP gate is also functionally complete.

101. (*a*) The given recurrence relation can be put to the form

$$S(k) - 2S(k-1) = -1,\ 5(1) = 2$$

(*i*) The associated homogenous relation, $S(k) - 2S(k-1) = 0$ has characteristic equation

$$a - 2 = 0$$

$$\therefore \quad a = 2$$

The homogeneous solution is $S^{(h)}(k) = b_1 (2)^k$.

(*ii*) Since the R.H.S. is a constant, the particular solution will be a constant, d.

(*iii*) If we substitute $S^{(p)}(k) = d$ into the recurrence relation, we get

$$d - 2d = -1, \text{ or } d = 1$$

$$\therefore \quad S^{(p)}(k) = 1$$

(*iv*) The general solution of the recurrence relation is

$$S(k) = S^{(h)}(k) + S^{(p)}(k)$$

$$= b_1 (2)^k + 1.$$

The initial condition will give one equation to solve in order to determine b_1 ;

$$S(1) = 2$$

$$\Rightarrow \quad b_1 (2)^1 + 1 = 2$$

$$\Rightarrow \quad b_1 = \frac{1}{2}$$

$$S(k) = \frac{1}{2}(2)^k + 1 = 2^{k-1} + 1$$

(*b*) For the left-recursive non-terminal A, where rule is

$$A \rightarrow A\alpha_1 \mid A\alpha_2 \mid \dots \mid A\alpha_n \mid \beta_1 \mid \beta_2 \mid \dots \mid \beta_m$$

where b_1 does not begin with A, replace this rule by the rules

$$A \rightarrow \beta_1 \mid \beta_2 \mid \dots \mid \beta_m \mid \beta_1 A' \mid \dots \mid \beta_m A'$$

$$A' \rightarrow \alpha_1 \mid \alpha_2 \mid \dots \mid \alpha_n \mid \alpha_1 A' \mid \alpha_2 A' \mid \dots \mid \alpha_n A'$$

Applying these rules we have the given grammar

$S \rightarrow Aa$

$S \rightarrow b$

$A \rightarrow Sd \mid SdA' \mid A' \mid E$

$$A' \rightarrow \frac{C}{CA'}$$

102. Synchronous counter to go through the given states 1, 4, 2, 3, 1, 4, 2, 3, 1, 4 ....

Excitation table for the given counter :

A	B	C	J_A	K_A	J_B	K_B	J_C	K_C
0	0	1	1	ϕ	0	ϕ	ϕ	1
1	1	0	ϕ	1	1	ϕ	0	ϕ
0	1	0	0	ϕ	ϕ	0	1	ϕ
0	1	1	0	ϕ	ϕ	1	ϕ	0

The next step is to express the J and K inputs as combinational functions of A, B and C. The information contained in the above table is entered in the K - maps from which we obtain Boolean functions for J_A, J_B, K_B and J_C, K_A and K_C. Knowing these functions we can directly draw the schematic diagram of the counter as shown.

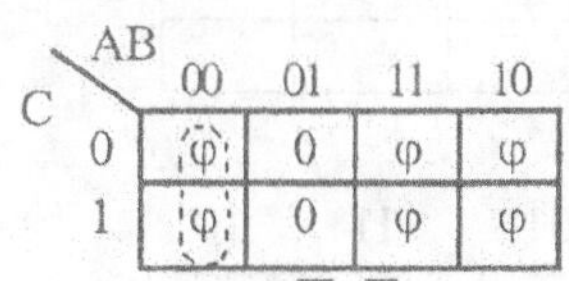

$J_A = \bar{A}\,\bar{B}$

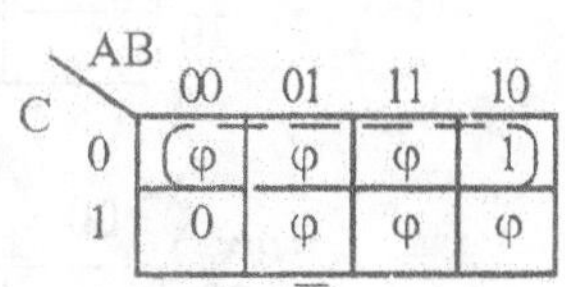

$J_B = \bar{C}$

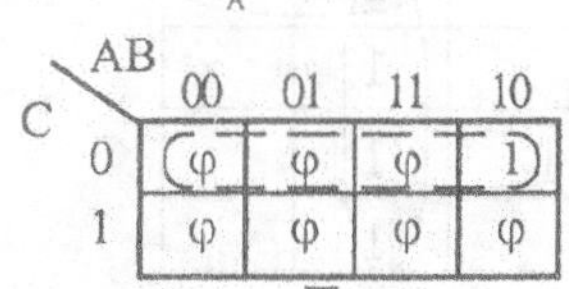

$K_A = \bar{C}$

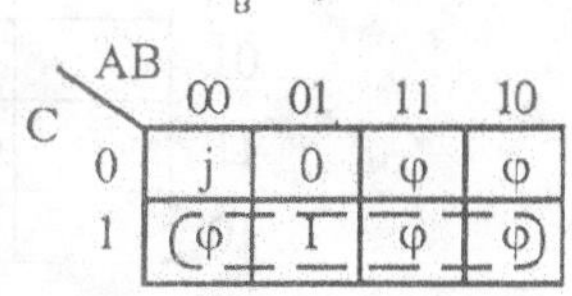

$K_B = C$

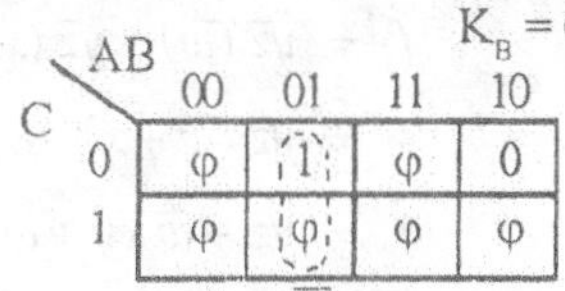

$J_C = \bar{A}\,B$

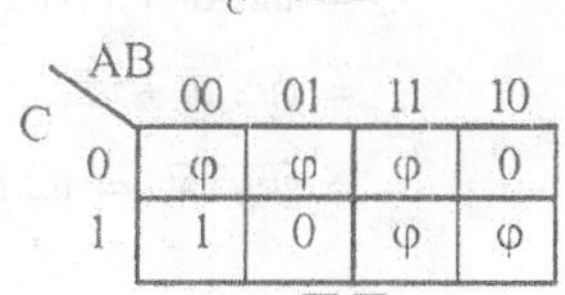

$K_C = \bar{A}\,\bar{B}$

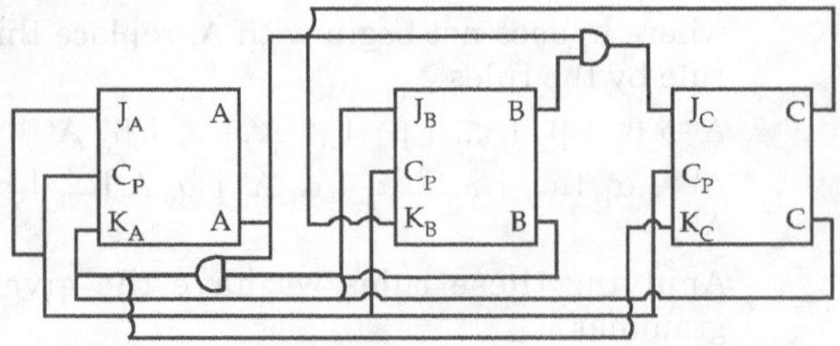

It is assumed that the circuit is initialized to 001 externally in the beginning.

103. $\sqrt{(224)_r} = (13)r$

or $\sqrt{2r^2 + 2r + 4} = r + 3$

or $2r^2 + 2r + 4 = r^{2+9+6r}$

or $^2 - 4r - 5 = 0$

or $(r-5)(r+1) = 0$

or $r = 5$

104. Given $f_1(w, x, y, z) = \Sigma\ 8, 9, 10$

$f_2(w, x, y, z) = \Sigma\ 7, 8, 12, 13, 14, 15$

$f(w, x, y, z) = \Sigma\ 8, 9$

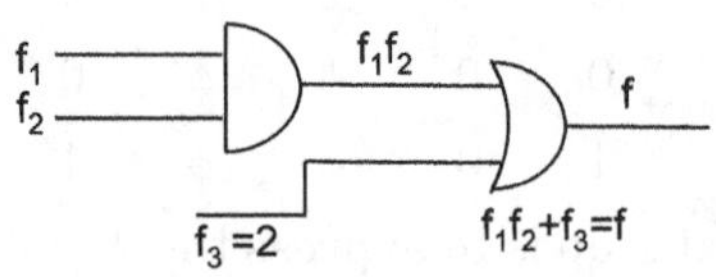

wx \ yz	00	01	11	10
00				1
01				1
11				1
10				

wx \ yx	00	01	11	10
00			1	1
01			1	
11		1	1	
10			1	

$f_1 = y\overline{z}(\overline{w}) + y\overline{z}(x)$

$= y\overline{z}(\overline{w} + x)$

$f_2 = yz + \overline{w}\,\overline{x}y + w \times z$

$f_1f_2 = y\overline{z}(\overline{w} + x)(y2 + \overline{w}\,\overline{x}\,y + w \times z)$

$= (y\overline{z}\,\overline{w} + y\overline{z}x)(y2 + \overline{w}\overline{x}\,y + wxz)$

$= \overline{w}y\overline{z}\,\overline{x} = y\overline{z}\,\overline{w}\,\overline{x}$

wx \ yz	00	01	11	10
00				1
01				1
11				
10				

$f = y\overline{z}\,\overline{w}$

From figure $f = f_1 f_2 + f_3$

$y\overline{z}\,\overline{w} = y\overline{z}\,\overline{w}\,\overline{x} + f_3 = y\overline{z}\,\overline{w}\,\overline{z} + y\overline{z}\,\overline{w}\,x$

$= y\overline{z}\,\overline{w}(x + \overline{x})$

So, $f_3 = y\overline{z}\,\overline{w}\,x$

K map for f_3

wx \ yz	00	01	11	10
00				
01				1
11				
10				

$f_3 = \overline{w}\,x\,y\,\overline{z}$

$f_3 = \Sigma 9$

105. (a) $((x \to y) \wedge x) \to y$

$\Rightarrow (-x \cup y \wedge x) \to y$

$\Rightarrow (y \cup -x \wedge x) \to y$

$\Rightarrow (y \cup \phi) \to y$

which is true.

(b) $((-x \to y) \wedge (-x \wedge y)) \to x$

$\Rightarrow (x \cup y) \wedge (-x \wedge -y) \to x$

$\Rightarrow x \cup (y \wedge \phi) \to x$

$\Rightarrow x \cup \phi \to x$

which is true.

(c) $((x \to (x \vee \phi))$

$\Rightarrow -x \vee (x \vee \phi)$

$\Rightarrow -x \vee x$ which is true.

$\Rightarrow -x \wedge -y \vee x \vee -y) \wedge (x \vee y \vee -x \wedge y)$

$\Rightarrow (-x \wedge -y \vee x) \wedge (x \vee -x \vee y \vee y)$

$\Rightarrow (-x \wedge -y \vee x) \wedge (x \vee -x \vee y)$

$\Rightarrow (\phi \vee -y) \wedge (x \vee y)$

$\Rightarrow \phi$ which is false.

(d) $((x \cup y) \leftrightarrow (-x \to -y))$

$\Rightarrow (x \cup y) \leftrightarrow (x \cup -y)$

$\Rightarrow (-x \vee y) \vee (x \cup -y)) \wedge$

$\Rightarrow ((x \vee y) \vee -(x \cup -y))$

107.

A \ B	0	1
0	C	C
1	C	C

A	B	C
0	0	C
0	1	C
1	0	C
1	1	C

$$F = \overline{A}\,\overline{B}C + \overline{A}BC + A\overline{B}C + ABC$$

$$A \oplus (B\overline{C} + \overline{B}C) = \overline{A}(B\overline{C} + \overline{B}C) + A(\overline{B} + C)(B + \overline{C})$$

$$= \overline{A}B\overline{C} + \overline{A}\,\overline{B}C + A\overline{B}\,\overline{C} + ABC$$

108.

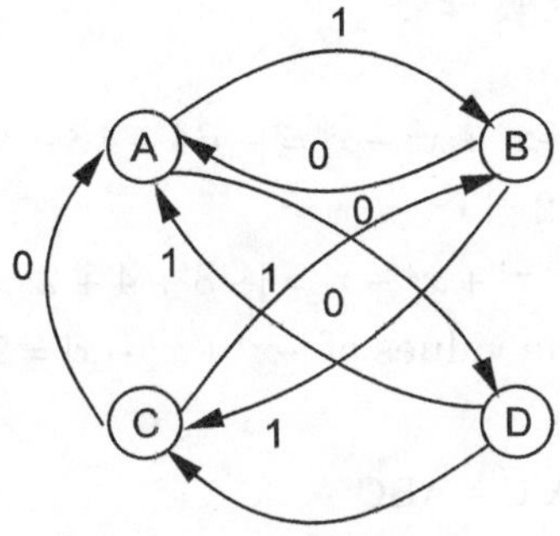

110.

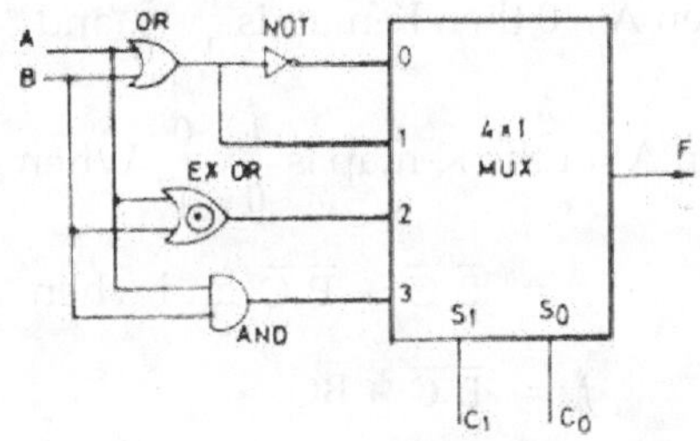

111. (*a*)

(*b*) {S0}

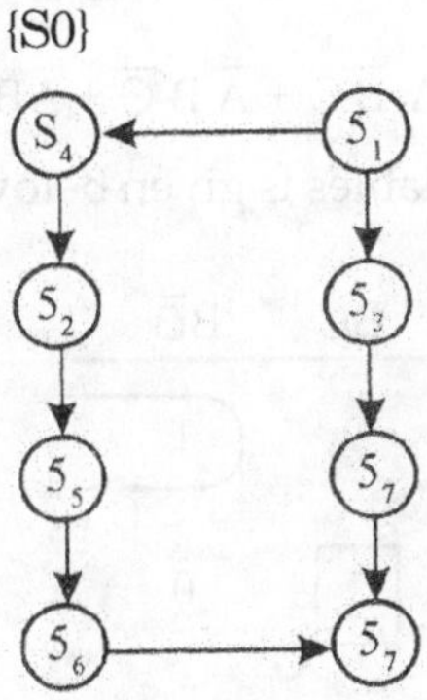

112. Consider second equation, AB = AC

Clearly (*b*) and (*c*) cannot be answer. Since $\overline{C}D = 1$ and $A\overline{C} = 1$ in (*a*). (*a*) satisfies all the three conditions.

113. Consider the given formula

$(3 * 4096 + 15 * 256 + 5 * 16 + 3)$

$= (2 + 1) * 2^{12} + (8 + 4 + 2 + 1) * 2^8 + (4 + 1) * 2^4 + 2^1 + 2^0$

$= (2^1 + 2^0)\,2^{12} + (2^3 + 2^2 + 2^1 + 2^0)\,2^8 + (2^2 + 2^0)\,2^4 + 2^1 + 2^0$

$= 2^{13} + 2^{12} + 2^{11} + 2^{10} + 2^9 + 2^8 + 2^6 + 2^4 + 2^1 + 2^0$

$\downarrow \quad \downarrow \quad \downarrow \quad \downarrow \quad \downarrow \quad \downarrow \quad \downarrow \quad \downarrow \quad \downarrow \quad \downarrow$

$= (1 \quad 1 \quad 1 \quad 1 \quad 1 \quad 1 \quad 01 \quad 01 \quad 001 \quad 1)_2$ has 10 number of 1s.

NUMERICAL TYPE QUESTIONS

1. 1111 1111 1111 0101

-1

1111 1111 1111 0100

⇓

1111 1111 1111 1011

(−11)

3. When all bits in 'B' register is '1', then it gives only the highest delay.

∴ '−1' in 8 bit notation of 2's complement is 1111 1111

4. The number of distinct values

For 2's complement $-(2^{n-1})$ to $+(2^{n-1} - 1)$

For sign magnitude $-(2^{n-1} - 1)$ to $+(2^{n-1} - 1)$

In 2's complement, let n = 2

∴ (-2^{2-1}) to $(2^{2-1} - 1)$

-2 to $+1 \Rightarrow -2, -1, 0, +1$

∴ X = 4

n = 2 in sign magnitude ⇒ −1 to +1

∴ Y = 3

∴ X − Y = 4 − 3 = 1

5. The minimum number of flip-flop required is 3.

6.

AB \ CD	00	01	11	10
00	1	1	1	1
01	1	1	1	1
11	1	1	ⓧ	1
10	1	1	1	1

Ans = 1, ABCD

7. Propagation delay for AND/OR Gate

$= 1 \times 2\ \mu s$

Propagation delay for XOR Gate

$= 2 \times 1.2 = 2.4\ \mu s$

Propagation time for a half adder

$= 1.2 + 2.4 = 3.6\ \mu s$

Propagation time for full adder

$= 2 \times 3.6 + 1.2$

$= 7.2 + 1.2 = 8.4\ \mu s$

Total 4-adders are used in 4-bit binary adder

Hence $8.4 \times 4 =$ **33.6 μs**

8. Given $X_3 = 0$

$\therefore \quad Y = X_1X_2 \oplus X_3 = 0$

gives $\quad X_1X_2 = 0$

$\Rightarrow \quad X_1 = 1,\ X_2 = 0$

or $\quad X_1 = 0, X_2 = 1$

or $\quad X_1 = 0, X_2 = 0$

$$\therefore \quad \Pr\left[Y = 0 | X_3 = 0\right] = \frac{\Pr\left[(Y = 0) \cap (X_3 = 0)\right]}{\Pr(X_3 = 0)}$$

$$= \frac{\Pr[X_1 = 1, X_2 = 0, X_3 = 0] + \Pr[X_1 = 0, X_2 = 1, X_3 = 0] + \Pr[X_1 = 0, X_2 = 0, X_3 = 0]}{\Pr[X_3 = 0]}$$

$$= \frac{\frac{1}{2}\cdot\frac{1}{2}\cdot\frac{1}{2} + \frac{1}{2}\cdot\frac{1}{2}\cdot\frac{1}{2} + \frac{1}{2}\cdot\frac{1}{2}\cdot\frac{1}{2}}{\frac{1}{2}}$$

($\because X_1, X_2, X_3$ are independent)

$$= \frac{3}{4} = 0.75$$

9.

wx \ yz	00	01	11	10
00	*1	0	0	1
01	1	1*	0	1*
11	0	0	0	0
10	0	0	0	1*

There are three groups, and all the containing esential-1, so all are prime implicants as well as essential prime implicants also.

10. $(43)_x = (y3)_8$

$\Rightarrow \quad 3 + 4x = 3 + 8y$

$\Rightarrow \quad 4x = 8y$

$\Rightarrow \quad x = 2y$

$\Rightarrow \quad x \geq 5$

and $\quad y \leq 7$

$\therefore$ 5 solutions are possible which are (14, 7), (12, 6), (10, 5), (8, 4) and (6, 3)

11. Here it is given that x is real

Now $\quad |x^2 - 2x + 3| = 11$

$\Rightarrow \quad x^2 - 2x + 3 = 11$ or $x^2 - 2x + 3 = -11$

For $\quad x^2 - 2x + 3 = 11 \Rightarrow x^2 - 2x - 8 = 0$

$\quad b^2 - 4ac = 4 - 4(1)(-8) = 36 > 0$

Hence roots are real.

and for $\quad x^2 - 2x + 14 = 0$

$\quad b^2 - 4ac = 4 - 4(1)(14) < 0$

Hence roots are imaginary

$\therefore$ The value of x is the root of $x^2 - 2x - 8 = 0$

Now $$x = \frac{+2 \pm \sqrt{4 - 4(1)(-8)}}{2}$$

$$= \frac{2 \pm \sqrt{36}}{2} = \frac{2 \pm 6}{2}$$

$\therefore \quad x = 4, -2.$

Now for $x = 4$,

$$|-x^3 + x^2 - x| = |-64 + 16 - 4| = 52.$$

and for $x = -2$

$$|-x^3 + x^2 - x| = |+8 + 4 + 2| = 14$$

Hence possible values of $|-x^3 + x^2 - x| = 14, 52$

15. $f = \overline{B}\,\overline{C} + \overline{A}\,\overline{C} + ABC$

When A = 0 then K-map is $\begin{matrix} 1 & 0 \\ 1 & 0 \end{matrix}$ and when A = 1 the K-map is $\begin{matrix} 1 & 0 \\ 0 & 1 \end{matrix}$. When A = 0;

$$f = \overline{B}\,\overline{C} + B\,\overline{C} \text{ and when A = 1,}$$

$$f = \overline{B}\,\overline{C} + BC.$$

Hence $\quad f = \overline{B}\,\overline{C} + \overline{A}\,B\,\overline{C} + ABC$

$$= (A + \overline{A})\,\overline{B}\,\overline{C} + \overline{A}B\overline{C} + ABC$$

$$= A\,\overline{B}\,\overline{C} + \overline{A}\,\overline{B}\,\overline{C} + \overline{A}\,B\,\overline{C} + ABC$$

The K-map for three variables is given below :

	$\overline{B}\,\overline{C}$	$\overline{B}C$	BC	$B\overline{C}$
$\overline{A}$	1	0	0	1
A	1	0	1	0

Hence $\quad f = C_1 + C_2 + C_3$

$$= A\,\overline{B}\,\overline{C} + \overline{A}B\overline{C} + ABC$$

$$= \overline{B}\,\overline{C} + \overline{A}\,\overline{C} + ABC$$

16. three, four

2 CHAPTER

Computer Organization and Architecture

MCQ TYPE QUESTIONS

2015

1. A file is organized so that the ordering of data records is the same as or close to the ordering of data entries in some index. Then that index is called

(*a*) Dense (*b*) Sparse
(*c*) Clustered (*d*) Unclustered

2. A positive edge-triggered D flip-flop is connected to a positive edge-triggered JK flip-flop as follows. The Q output of the D flip-flop is connected to both the J and K inputs of the JK flip-flop, while the Q output of the JK flip-flop is connected to the input of the D flip-flop is connected to both the J and K inputs of the JK flip-flop, while the Q output of the JK flip-flop is connected to the input of the D flip-flop. Initially, the output of the D flip-flop is set to logic one and the output of the JK flip-flop is cleared. Which one of the following is the bit sequence (including the initial state) generated at the Q output of the JK flip-flop when the flip-flops are connected to a free running common clock ? Assume that J = K = 1 is the toggle mode and J = K = 0 is the state-holding mode of the JK flip-flop. Both the flip-flops have non-zero propagation delays.

(*a*) 0110110 ..... (*b*) 0100100 .....
(*c*) 011101110 ..... (*d*) 011001100 .....

3. Consider a processor with byte-addressable memory. Assume that all registers, including Program Counter (PC) and Program Status Word (PSW), are of size 2 bytes. A stack in the main memory is implemented from memory location $(0100)_{16}$ and it grows upward. The stack pointer (SP) points to the top element of the stack. The current value of SP is $(016E)_{16}$. The CALL instruction is of two words, the first word is the op-code and the second word is the starting address of the subroutine. (one word = 2bytes). The CALL instruction is implemented as follows:

- Store the current value of PC in the Stack
- Store the value of PSW register in the stack
- Load the starting address of the subroutine in PC

The content of PC just before the fetch of a CALL instruction is $(5FA0)_{16}$. After execution of the CALL instruction, the value of the stack pointer is

(*a*) $(016A)_{16}$ (*b*) $(016C)_{16}$
(*c*) $(0170)_{16}$ (*d*) $(0172)_{16}$

4. Consider a machine with byte addressable main memory of 20^{20} bytes, block size of 16 bytes and a direct mapped cache having 2^{12} cache lines. Let the address of two consecutive bytes in main memory be $(E201F)_{16}$ and $(E2020)_{16}$. What are the tag and cache line address (in hex) for main memory address $(E201F)_{16}$?

(*a*) E, 201 (*b*) F, 201
(*c*) E, E20 (*d*) 2, 01F

5. Consider the following code sequence having five instructions I_1 to I_5. Each of these instructions has the following format.

OP Ri, Rj, Rk

Where operation OP is performed on contents of registers Rj and Rk and the results is stored in register Ri.

I_1 : ADD R1, R2, R_3
I_2 : MUL R7, R1, R3
I_3 : SUB R4, R1, R5
I_4 : ADD R3, R 2, R 4
I_5 : MUL R7,R8, R9

Consider the following three statements.

S1 : There is an anti-dependence between instructions I2 and I5

S2 : There is an anti-dependence between instructions I2 and I4

S3 : Within an instruction pipeline an anti-dependence always creates on or more stalls

Which one of above statements is/are correct ?

(*a*) Only S1 is true
(*b*) Only S2 is true
(*c*) Only S1 and S3 are true
(*d*) Only S2 and S3 are true

2014

6. An access sequence of cache block addresses is of length N and contains n unique block addresses. The number of unique block addresses between two consecutive accesses to the same block address is bounded above by K. What is the miss ratio if the access sequence is passed through a cache of associativity $A \geq k$ exercising least-recently-used replacement policy?
   (*a*) n/N (*b*) 1/N
   (*c*) 1/A (*d*) k/n
7. In designing a computer's cache system, the cache block (or cache line) size is an important parameter. Which one of the following statements is correct in this context?
   (*a*) A smaller block size implies better spatial locality
   (*b*) A smaller block size implies a smaller cache tag and hence lower cache tag overhead
   (*c*) A smaller block size implies a larger cache tag and hence lower cache hit time
   (*d*) A smaller block size incurs a lower cache miss penalty
8. If the associativity of a processor cache is doubled while keeping the capacity and block size unchanged, which one of the following is guaranteed to be NOT affected?
   (*a*) Width of tag comparator
   (*b*) Width of set index decoder
   (*c*) Width of way selection multiplexor
   (*d*) Width of processor to main memory data bus
9. The value of a *float* type variable is represented using the single-precision 32-bit floating point format of IEEE-754 standard that uses 1 bit for sign, 8 bits for biased exponent and 23 bits for mantissa. A *float* type variable X is assigned the decimal value of –14.25. The representation of X in hexadecimal notation is
   (*a*) C1640000H (*b*) 416C0000H
   (*c*) 41640000H (*d*) C16C0000H
10. Consider the following processors (ns stands for nanoseconds).
   Assume that the pipeline registers have zero latency.
   P1: Four-stage pipeline with stage latencies 1 ns, 2 ns, 2 ns, 1 ns.
   P2: Four-stage pipeline with stage latencies 1 ns, 1.5ns, 1.5 ns, 1.5 ns.
   P3: Five-stage pipeline with stage latencies 0.5ns, 1 ns, 1 ns, 0.6 ns, 1 ns.
   P4: Five-stage pipeline with stage latencies 0.5ns, 0.5 ns, 1 ns, 1 ns, 1.1 ns.
   Which processor has the highest peak clock frequency?
   (*a*) P1 (*b*) P2
   (*c*) P3 (*d*) P4
11. A bit-stuffing based framing protocol uses an 8-bit delimiter pattern of 01111110. If the output bit-string after stuffing is 01111100101, then the input bit-string is
   (*a*) 0111110100 (*b*) 0111110101
   (*c*) 0111111101 (*d*) 0111111111

2013

12. In a k-way set associative cache, the cache is divided into v sets, each of which consists of k lines. The lines of a set are placed in sequence one after another. The lines in set s are sequenced before the lines in set $(s + 1)$. The main memory blocks are numbered 0 onwards. The main memory block numbered j must be mapped to any one of the cache lines from
   (*a*) $(j \bmod v) * k$ to $(j \bmod v) * k + (k - 1)$
   (*b*) $(j \bmod v)$ to $(j \bmod v) + (k - 1)$
   (*c*) $(j \bmod k)$ to $(j \bmod k) + (v - 1)$
   (*d*) $(j \bmod k) * v$ to $(j \bmod k) * v + (v - 1)$
13. Consider the following sequence of micro-operations.
   MBR ← PC
   MAR ← X
   PC ← Y
   Memory ← MBR
   Which one of the following is a possible operation performed by this sequence?
   (*a*) Instruction fetch
   (*b*) Operand fetch
   (*c*) Conditional branch
   (*d*) Initiation of interrupt service.
14. Consider a hard disk with 16 recording surfaces (0-15) having 16384 cylinders (0-16383) and each cylinder contains 64 sectors (0-63). Data storage capacity in each sector is 512 bytes. Data are organized cylinder-wise and the addressing format is <cylinder no., surface no., sector no.>. A file of size 42797 KB is stored in the disk and the starting disk location of the file is <1200, 9, 40>. What is the cylinder number of the last sector of the file, if it is stored in a contiguous manner?
   (*a*) 1281 (*b*) 1282
   (*c*) 1283 (*d*) 1284

15. Consider an instruction pipeline with five stages without any branch prediction: Fetch Instruction (FI), Decode Instruction (DI), Fetch Operand (FO), Execute Instruction (EI) and Write Operand (WO). The stage delays for FI, DI, FO, EI and WO are 5 ns, 7 ns, 10 ns, 8 ns and 6 ns, respectively. There are intermediate storage buffers after each stage and the delay of each buffer is 1 ns. A program consisting of 12 instructions I_1, I_2, I_3, ..., I_{12} is executed in this pipelined processor. Instruction I_4 is the only branch instruction and its branch target is I_9. If the branch is taken during the execution of this program, the time (in ns) needed to complete the program is

(*a*) 132 (*b*) 165

(*c*) 176 (*d*) 328

2012

16. Register renaming is done in pipelined processors

(*a*) as an alternative to register allocation at compile time

(*b*) for efficient access to function parameters and local variables

(*c*) to handle certain kinds of hazards

(*d*) as part of address translation

17. The amount of ROM needed to implement a 4 bit multiplier is

(*a*) 64 bits (*b*) 128 bits

(*c*) 1 Kbits (*d*) 2 Kbits

18. A file system with 300 GByte disk uses a file descriptor with 8 direct block addresses, 1 indirect block address and 1 doubly indirect block address. The size of each disk block is 128 Bytes and the size of each disk block address is 8 Bytes. The maximum possible file size in this file system is

(*a*) 3 KBytes

(*b*) 35 KBytes

(*c*) 280 KBytes

(*d*) dependent on the size of the disk

19. Fetch_And_Add (X, *i*) is an atomic Read-Modify-Write instruction that reads the value of memory location X, increments it by the value i, and returns the old value of X. It is used in the pseudocode shown below to implement a busy-wait lock, L is an unsigned integer shared variable initialized to 0. The value of 0 corresponds to lock being available,while any non-zero value corresponds to the lock being not available.

```
AcquireLock (L) {
while (Fetch_And_Add (L, 1))
    L = 1;
}
ReleaseLock (L){
    L = 0;
}
```

This implementation

(*a*) fails as L can overflow

(*b*) fails as L can take on a non-zero value when the lock is actually available

(*c*) works correctly but may starve some processes

(*d*) works correctly without starvation

2011

20. Consider a hypothetical processor with an instruction of type LW R1, 20 (R2), which during execution reads a 32-bit word from memory and stores it in a 32-bit register R1. The effective address of the memory location is obtained by the addition of a constant 20 and the contents of register R2. Which of the following best reflects the addressing mode implemented by this instruction for the operand in memory?

(*a*) Immediate Addressing

(*b*) Register Addressing

(*c*) Register Indirect Scaled Addressing

(*d*) Base Indexed Addressing

21. A computer handles several interrupt sources of which of the following are relevant for this question.

- Interrupt from CPU temperature sensor (raises interrupt if CPU temperature is too high)
- Interrupt from Mouse (raises interrupt if the mouse is moved or a button is pressed)
- Interrupt from Keyboard (raises interrupt when a key is pressed or released)
- Interrupt from Hard Disk (raises interrupt when a disk read is completed)

Which one of these will be handled at the **HIGHEST** priority?

(*a*) Interrupt from Hard Disk

(*b*) Interrupt from Mouse

(*c*) Interrupt from Keyboard

(*d*) Interrupt from CPU temperature sensor

22. An application loads 100 libraries at startup. Loading each library requres exactly one disk access. The seek time of the disk to a random location is given as 10 ms. Rotational speed of disk is 6000 rpm. If all 100 libraries are loaded from random locations on the disk, how long does it take to load all libraries? (The time to transfer data from the disk block once the head has been positioned at the start of the block may be neglected).

(*a*) 0.50 s (*b*) 1.50 s

(*c*) 1.25 s (*d*) 1.00 s

23. An 8 KB direct mapped write-back cache is organized as multiple blocks, each of size 32-bytes.The processor generates 32-bit addresses. The cache controller maintains the tag information for each cache block comprising of the following.

1 Valid bit

1 Modified bit

As many bits as the minimum needed to identify the memory block mapped in the cache?

What is the total size of memory needed at the cache controller to store meta-data (tags) for the cache?

(*a*) 4864 bits (*b*) 6144 bits

(*c*) 6656 bits (*d*) 5376 bits

2010

24. A main memory unit with a capacity of 4 megabytes is built using 1M × 1-bit DRAM chips. Each DRAM chip has 1K rows of cells with 1K cells in each row. The time taken for a single refresh operation is 100 nanoseconds. The time required to perform one refresh operation on all the cells in the memory unit is

(*a*) 100 nanoseconds

(*b*) $100*2^{10}$ nanoseconds

(*c*) $100*2^{20}$ nanoseconds

(*d*) $3200*2^{20}$ nanoseonds

25. A 5-stage pipelined processor has Instruction Fetch (IF), Instruction Decode (ID), Operand Fetch (OF), Perform Operation (PO) and Write Operand (WO) stages. The IF, ID, OF and WO stages take 1 clock cycle each for any instruction. The PO stage takes 1 clock cycle for ADD and SUB instructions, 3 clock cycles for MUL instruction, and 6 clock cycles for DIV instruction respectively. Operand forwarding is used in the pipeline. What is the number of clock cycles needed to execute the following sequence of instructions?

Instruction	**Meaning of instruction**
I_0: MUL R_2, R_0 R_1	$R_2 \leftarrow R_0*R_1$
I_1: DIV R_5, R_3, R_4	$R_5 \leftarrow R_3/R_4$
I_2: ADD R_2, R_5, R_1	$R_2 \leftarrow R_5 + R_2$
I_3: SUB R_5, R_2, R_6	$R_5 \leftarrow R_2 - R_6$

(*a*) 13

(*b*) 15

(*c*) 17

(*d*) 19

26. The progam below uses six temporary variables a, b, c, d, e, f.

```
a = 1
b = 10
c = 20
d = a + b
e = c + d
f = c + e
b = c + e
e = b + f
d = 5 + e
return d + f
```

Assuming that all operations take their operands from registers, what is the minimum number of registers needed to execute this program without spilling?

(*a*) 2 (*b*) 3

(*c*) 5 (*d*) 6

2009

27. How many 32 × 1 RAM chips are needed to provide a memory capacity of 256 k-bytes ?

(*a*) 8

(*b*) 32

(*c*) 64

(*d*) 128

28. A CPU generally handles an interrupt by executing an interrupt service routine

(*a*) as soon as an interrupt is raised.

(*b*) by checking the interrupt register at the end of fetch cycle.

(*c*) by checking the interrupt register after finishing the executing of the current instruction.

(*d*) by checking the interrupt register at fixed time intervals.

29. Consider a 4 stage pipeline processor. The number of cycles needed by the four instructions I_1, I_2, I_3, I_4 in stages S_1, S_2, S_3, S_4 is shown below:

	S_1	S_2	S_3	S_4
I_1	2	1	1	1
I_2	1	3	2	2
I_3	2	1	1	3
I_4	1	2	2	2

What is the number of cycles needed to execute the following loop?

for (i = 1 to 2) {I_1; I_2; I_3; I_4}

(*a*) 16 (*b*) 23
(*c*) 28 (*d*) 30

30. Consider a 4-way set associative cache (initially empty) with total 16 cache blocks. The main memory consists of 256 blocks and the request for memory blocks is in the following order:

0, 255, 1, 4, 3, 8, 133, 159, 216, 129, 63, 8, 48, 32, 73, 92, 155.

Which one of the following memory block will NOT be in cache if LRU replacement policy is used ?

(*a*) 3 (*b*) 8
(*c*) 129 (*d*) 216

2008

31. For a magnetic disk with concentric circular tracks, the seek latency is not linearly proportional to the seek distance due to

(*a*) non-uniform distribution of requests
(*b*) arm starting and stopping inertia
(*c*) higher capacity of tracks on the periphery of the platter
(*d*) use of unfair arm scheduling policies

32. Which of the following is/are true of the auto-increment addressing mode?

I. It is useful in creating self-relocating code
II. If it is included in an Instruction Set Architecture, then an additional ALU is required for effective address calculation
III. The amount of increment depends on the size of the data item accessed

(*a*) I only (*b*) II only
(*c*) III only (*d*) II and III only

33. Which of the following must be true for the RFE (Return from Exception) instruction on a general purpose processor?

I. It must be a trap instruction
II. It must be a privileged instruction
III. An exception cannot be allowed to occur during execution of an RFE instruction

(*a*) I only (*b*) II only
(*c*) I and II only (*d*) I, II and III only

34. For inclusion to hold between two cache levels L1 and L2 in a multi-level cache hierarchy, which of the following are necessary?

I. L1 must be a write-through cache
II. L2 must be a write-through cache
III. The associativity of L2 must be greater than that of L1
IV. The L2 cache must be at least as large as the L1 cache

(*a*) IV only (*b*) I and IV only
(*c*) I, III and IV only (*d*) I, II, III and IV

35. Which of the following are NOT true in a pipelined processor?

I. Bypassing can handle all RAW hazards.
II. Register renaming can eliminate all register carried WAR hazards.
III. Control hazard penalties can be eliminated by dynamic branch prediction.

(*a*) I and II only (*b*) I and III only
(*c*) II and III only (*d*) I, II and III

36. The use of multiple register windows with overlap causes a reduction in the number of memory accesses for

I. function locals and parameters
II. register saves and restores
III. instruction fetches

(*a*) I only (*b*) II only
(*c*) III only (*d*) I, II and III

37. In an instruction execution pipeline, the earliest that the data TLB (Translation Lookaside Buffer) can be accessed is

(*a*) before effective address calculation has started
(*b*) during efective address calculation
(*c*) after effective address calculation has completed
(*d*) after data cache lookup has completed

2007

38. Consider a 4-way set associative cache consisting of 128 lines with a line size of 64 words. The CPU generates a 20-bit address of a word in main memory. The number of bits in the TAG, LINE and WORD fields are respectively

(*a*) 9, 6, 5 (*b*) 7, 7, 6
(*c*) 7, 5, 8 (*d*) 9, 5, 6

39. Consider a disk pack with 16 surfaces, 128 tracks per surface and 256 sectors per track. 512 bytes of data are stored in a bit serial manner in a sector. The capacity of the disk pack and the number of bits required to specify a particular sector in the disk are respectively

(*a*) 256 Mbyte, 19 bits (*b*) 256 Mbyte, 28 bits
(*c*) 512 Mbyte, 20 bits (*d*) 64 Gbyte, 28 bits

40. Consider a pipelined processor with the following four stages :

IF : Instruction Fetch
ID : Instruction Decode and Operand Fetch
EX : Execute
WB : Write Back

The IF, ID and WB stages take one clock cycle each to complete the operation. The number of clock cycles for the EX stage depends on the instruction. The ADD and SUB instructions need 1 clock cycle and the MUL instruction need 3 clock cycles in the EX stage. Operand forwarding is used in the pipelined processor. What is the number of clock cycles taken to complete the following sequence of instructions ?

ADD	R2,	R1,	R0	R2¬R1+R0
MUL	R4,	R3,	R2	R4¬R3*R2
SUB	R6,	R5,	R4	R6¬R5−R4

(*a*) 7 (*b*) 8
(*c*) 10 (*d*) 14

2006

41. A CPU has a cache with block size 64 bytes. The main memory has k banks, each bank being c bytes wide. Consecutive c-byte chunks are mapped on consecutive banks with warp-around. All the k banks can be accessed in parallel, but two accesses to the same bank must be serialized. A cache block access may involve multiple iterations of parallel bank accesses depending on the amount of data obtained by accessing all the k banks in parallel. Each iteration requires decoding the bank numbers to be accessed in parallel and this takes $k/2$ *ns*. The latency of one bank access is 80 *ns*. If $c = 2$ and $k = 24$, then latency of retrieving a cache block starting at address zero from main memory is

(*a*) 92 ns (*b*) 104 ns
(*c*) 172 ns (*d*) 184 ns

42. A CPU has five-stage pipeline and runs at 1 GHz frequency. Instruction fetch happens in the first stage of the pipeline. A conditional branch instruction computes the target address and evaluates the condition in the third stage of the pipeline. The processor stops fetching new instructions following a conditional branch until the branch outcome is known. A program executes 10^9 instructions out of which 20% are conditional branches. If each instruction takes one cycle to complete on average, then total execution time of the program is

(*a*) 1.0 second (*b*) 1.2 seconds
(*c*) 1.4 seconds (*d*) 1.6 seconds

43. Consider a new instruction named branch-on-bit-set (mnemonic bbs). The instruction "bbs reg, pos, label" jumps to label if bit in position pos of register operand reg is one. A register is 32 bits wide and the bits are numbered 0 to 31, bit in position 0 being the least significant. Consider the following emulation of this instruction on a processor that does not have bbs implemented.

temp ← reg and mask
Branch to label if temp is non-zero

The variable temp is a temporary register. For correct emulation, the variable mask must be generated by

(*a*) *mask* ← *0x1 << pos*
(*b*) *mask* ← 0x *ffffffff* >> *pos*
(*c*) *mask* ← *pos*
(*d*) *mask* ← *0xf*

2005

44. Which one of the following is true for a CPU having a single interrupt request line and a single interrrupt grant line?

(*a*) Neither vectored interrupt nor multiple interrupting devices are possible.
(*b*) Vectored interrupts are not possible but multiple interrupting devices are possible.
(*c*) Vectored interrupts and multiple interrupting devices are both possible.
(*d*) Vectored interrupt is possible but multiple interrupting devices are not possible.

45. Normally user programs are prevented from handling I/O directly by I/O instructions in them. For CPUs having explicit I/O instructions, such I/O protection is ensured by having the I/O instructions privileged. In a CPU with memory mapped I/O, there is no explicit I/O instruction. Which one of the following is true for a CPU with memory mapped I/O?

(*a*) I/O protection is ensured by operating system routine (s)
(*b*) I/O protection is ensured by a hardware trap
(*c*) I/O protection is ensured during system configuration
(*d*) I/O protection is not possible

46. What is the swap space in the disk used for?

(*a*) Saving temporary html pages

(*b*) Saving process data

(*c*) Storing the super-block

(*d*) Storing device drivers

47. Increasing the RAM of a computer typically improves performance because

(*a*) Virtual memory increases

(*b*) Larger RAMs are faster

(*c*) Fewer page faults occur

(*d*) Fewer segmentation faults occur

48. Consider a three word machine instruction

ADD A[R0], @ B

The first operand (*d*estination) "A [R0]" uses indexed addressing mode with R0 as the index register. The second operand (source) "@ B" uses indirect addressing mode. A and B are memory addresses residing at the second and the third words, respectively. The first word of the instruction specifies the opcode, the index register designation and the source and destination addressing modes. During execution of ADD instruction, the two operands are added and stored in the destination (first operand).

The number of memory cycles needed during the execution cycle of the instruction is

(*a*) 3 (*b*) 4

(*c*) 5 (*d*) 6

49. Match each of the high level language statements given in List I with the most natural addressing mode given List II.

List I	List II
A. A[1] = B[J];	1. Indirect addressing
B. while [*A++];	2. Indexed addressing
C. int temp = *x;	3. Autoincrement

Codes :

	A	B	C
(*a*)	3	2	1
(*b*)	1	3	2
(*c*)	2	3	1
(*d*)	1	2	3

50. Consider a direct mapped cache of size 32 KB with block size 32 bytes. The CPU generates 32 bit addresses. The number of bits needed for cache indexing and the number of tag bits are respectively

(*a*) 10, 17 (*b*) 10, 22

(*c*) 15, 17 (*d*) 5, 17

51. A 5 stage pipelined CPU has the following sequence of stages:

IF – Instruction fetch from instruction memory,

RD – Instruction decode and register read,

EX – Execute: ALU operation for data and address computation,

MA – Data memory access – for write access, the register read at RD stage is used,

WB – Register write back.

Consider the following sequence of instructions:

I_1 : L R0, 1oc1;R0 <= M[1oc1]

I_2 : A R0, R0 ;R0 <= R0 + R0

I_3 : A R2, R0 ;R2 <= R2 – R0

Let each stage take one clock cycle.

What is the number of clock cycles taken to complete the above sequence of instructions starting from the fetch of I_1 ?

(*a*) 8 (*b*) 10

(*c*) 12 (*d*) 15

52. A device with data transfer rate 10 kB/sec is connected to a CPU. Data is transferred byte-wise. Let the interrupt overhead be 4 msec. The byte transfer time between the device interface register and CPU or memory is negligible. What is the minimum performance gain of operating the device under interrupt mode over operating it under program controlled mode?

(*a*) 15 (*b*) 25

(*c*) 35 (*d*) 45

53. Consider a disk drive with the following specifications:

16 surfaces, 512 tracks/surface, 512 sectors/track, 1 kB/sector, rotation speed 3000 rpm. The disk is operated in cycle stealing mode whereby whenever one byte word is ready it is sent to memory; similarly, for writing, the disk interface reads a 4 byte word from the memory in each DMA cycle. Memory cycle time is 40 nsec. The maximum percentage of time that the CPU gets blocked during DMA operation is

(*a*) 10 (*b*) 25

(*c*) 40 (*d*) 50

Common Data Q. 54 - 55

Consider the following data path of a CPU

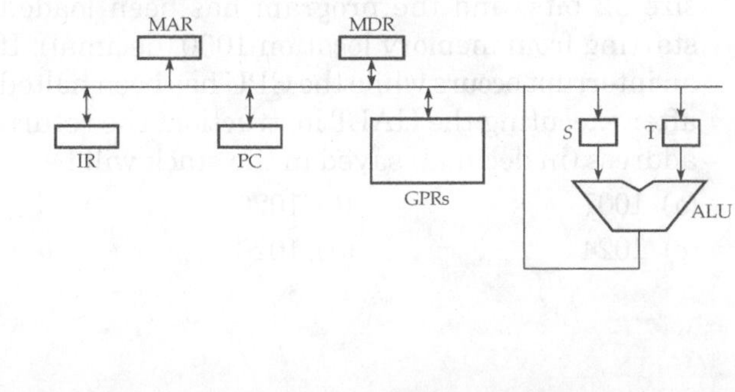

The, ALU, the bus and all the registers in the data path are of identical size. All operations including incrementation of the PC and the GPRs are to be carried out in the ALU. Two clock cycles are needed for memory read operation – the first one for loading address in the MAR and the next one for loading data from the memory bus into the MDR.

54. The instruction "add R0, R1" has the register transfer interpretation R0 < = R0 + R1. The minimum number of clock cycles needed for execution cycle of this instruction is

(*a*) 2 (*b*) 3
(*c*) 4 (*d*) 5

55. The instruction "call Rn, sub" is a two word instruction. Assuming that PC is incremented during the fetch cycle of the first word of the instruction, its register transfer interpretation is

R*n* < = PC + 1;
PC < = M[PC];

The minimum number of CPU clock cycles needed during the execution cycle of this instruction is:

(*a*) 2 (*b*) 3
(*c*) 4 (*d*) 5

2004

56. Consider a multiplexer with X and Y as data inputs and Z as control input. Z=0 selects input X, and Z = 1 selects input Y. What are the connections required to realize the 2-variable Boolean function f = T + R, without using any additional hardware?

(*a*) R to X, 1 to Y, T to Z
(*b*) T to X, R to Y, T to Z
(*c*) T to X, R to Y, 0 to Z
(*d*) R to X, 0 to Y, T to Z

Common Data Q. 57 - 58

Consider the following program segment for a hypothetical CPU having three user registers R1, R2 and R3.

Instruction		Operation	Instruction Size (in words)
MOV	R1,5000	; R1 ¬ Memory[5000]	2
MOV	R2,(R1)	; R2 ¬ Memory[(R1)]	1
ADD	R2, R3	; R2 ¬ R2 + R3	1
MOV	6000, R2	; Memory[6000] ¬ R2	2
HALT		; Machine halts	1

57. Consider that the memory is byte addressable with size 32 bits, and the program has been loaded starting from memory location 1000 (decimal). If an interrupt occurs while the CPU has been halted after executing the HALT instruction, the return address (in decimal) saved in the stack will be

(*a*) 1007 (*b*) 1020
(*c*) 1024 (*d*) 1028

58. Let the clock cycles required for various operations be as follows:

Register to/from memory transfer : 3 clock cycles
ADD with both operands in register: 1 clock cycle
Instruction fetch and decode: 2 clock cycles per word

The total number of clock cycles required to execute the program is

(*a*) 29 (*b*) 24
(*c*) 23 (*d*) 20

59. Consider a small two-way set-associative cache memory, consisting of four blocks. For choosing the block to be replaced, use the least recently used (LRU) scheme. The number of cache misses for the following sequence of block addresses is

8, 12, 0, 12, 8

(*a*) 2 (*b*) 3
(*c*) 4 (*d*) 5

60. The microinstructions stored in the control memory of a processor have a width of 26 bits. Each microinstruction is divided into three fields: a micro-operation field of 13 bits, a next address field (X), and a MUX select field (Y). There are 8 status bits in the inputs of the MUX.

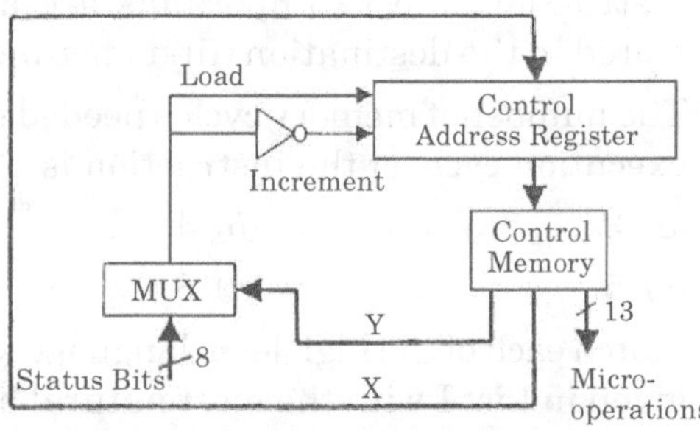

How many bits are there in the X and Y fields, and what is the size of the control memory in number of words ?

(*a*) 10, 3, 1024 (*b*) 8, 5, 256
(*c*) 5, 8, 2048 (*d*) 10, 3, 512

61. A hard disk with a transfer rate of 10 Mbytes/second is constantly transferring data to memory using DMA. The processor runs at 600 MHz, and takes 300 and 900 clock cycles to initiate and complete DMA transfer respectively. If the size of the transfer is 20 Kbytes, what is the percentage of processor time consumed for the transfer operation ?

(*a*) 5.0%
(*b*) 1.0%
(*c*) 0.5%
(*d*) 0.1%

62. A 4-stage pipeline has the stage delays as 150, 120, 160 and 140 nanoseconds respectively. Registers that are used between the stages have a delay of 5 nanoseconds each. Assuming constant clocking rate, the total time taken to process 1000 data items on this pipeline will be

(*a*) 120.4 microseconds

(*b*) 160.5 microseconds

(*c*) 165.5 microseconds

(*d*) 590.0 microseconds

2003

63. For a pipelined CPU with a single ALU, consider the following situations :

I. The $j + 1$–st instruction uses the result of the j-th instruction as an operand

II. The execution of a conditional jump instruction

III. The j -th and j+ 1-st instructions require the ALU at the same time

Which of the above can cause a hazard ?

(*a*) I and II only (*b*) II and III only

(*c*) III only (*d*) All of these

64. Consider an array multiplier for multiplying two n bit numbers. If each gate in the circuit has a unit delay, then total delay of the multiplier is

(*a*) $\Theta(1)$ (*b*) $\Theta(\log n)$

(*c*) $\Theta(n)$ (*d*) $\Theta(n^2)$

65. Consider the ALU shown below.

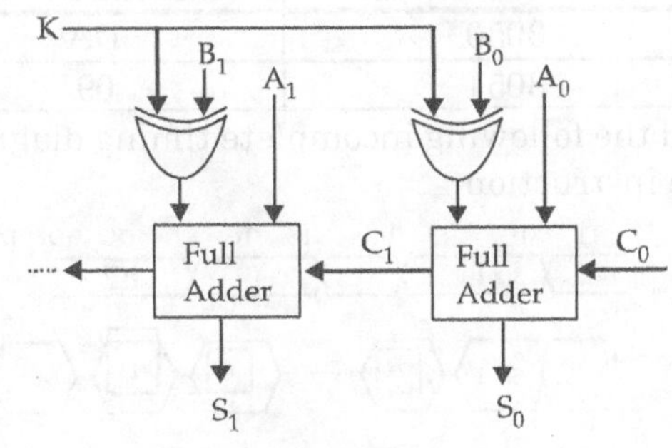

If the operands are in 2's complement representation, which of the following operations can be performed by suitably setting the control lines K and C_0 only (+ and – denote addition and subtraction respectively) ?

(*a*) A + B, and A – B, but not A + 1

(*b*) A + B, and A + 1, but not A – B

(*c*) A + B, but not A – B, or A + 1

(*d*) A + B, and A – B, and A + 1

Common Data Q. 66 - 67

Consider the following assembly language program for a hypothetical prcessor. A, B, and C are 8 bit registers. The meanings of various instructions are shown as comments.

```
    MOV B, # 0    ; b← 0
    MOV C, # 8    ; b← 0
Z : CMP C, # 0    ; compare C with 0
    JZX           ; jump to X if zero flag is set
    SUB C, # 1    ; C ← C – 1
    RRC A, # 1    ; right rotate A through carry
                    by one bit. Thus:
                  ; if the initial values of A and
                    the carry flag are a7...a0 and
                  ; c0 respectively, their values
                    after the execution of this
                  ; instruction will be c0a7...a1
                    and a0 respectively.
    JCY           ; jump to Y if carry flag is set
    JMP Z         ; jump to Z
Y : ADD B, # 1    ; B ← B + 1
    JMP Z         ; jump to Z
X :
```

66. If the initial value of register A is A_0, then value of register B after the program execution will be

(*a*) the number of 0 bits in A_0

(*b*) the number of 1 bits in A_0

(*c*) A_0

(*d*) 8

67. Which of the following instructions when inserted at location X will ensure that the value of register A after program execution is the same as its initial value ?

(*a*) RRC A, #

(*b*) NOP; no operation

(*c*) LRC A, # 1 ; left rotate A through carry flag by one bit

(*d*) ADD A, # 1

2001

68. A CPU has two modes – privileged and non-privileged. In order to change the mode from privileged to non-privileged

(*a*) a hardware interrupt is needed

(*b*) a software interrupt is needed

(*c*) a privileged instruction (which does not generate an interrupt) is needed

(*d*) a non-privileged instruction (which does not generate an interrupt) is needed

69. Consider the following datapath of a simple non-pipelined CPU. The registers A, B, A_1, A_2, MDR, the bus and the ALU are 8-bit wide. SP and MAR are 16-bit registers. The MUX is of size $8 \times (2{:}1)$ and the DEMUX is of size $8 \times (1:2)$. Each memory operation takes 2 CPU clock cycles and uses MAR (Memory Address Register) and MDR (Memory Date Register). SP can be decremented locally.

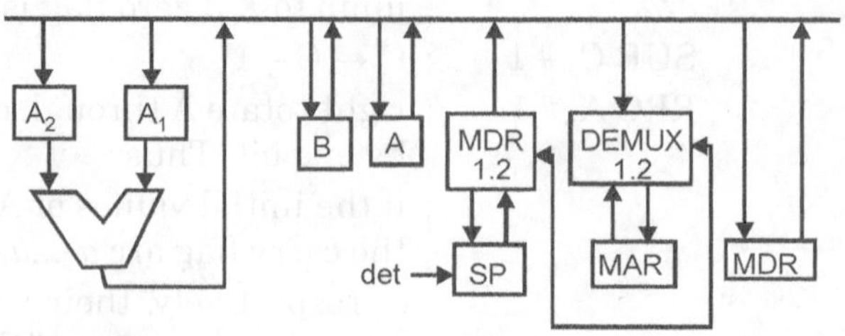

The CPU instruction "push *r*", where = A or B, has the specification

M [SP] ← *r*

SP ← SP – 1

How many CPU clock cycles are needed to execute the "push *r*" instruction ?

(*a*) 2 (*b*) 3

(*c*) 4 (*d*) 5

2000

70. To put the 8085 microprocessor in the wait state

(*a*) lower the HOLD input

(*b*) lower the READY input

(*c*) raise the HOLD input

(*d*) raise the READY input

71. Comparing the time T1 taken for a single instruction on a pipelined CPU with time T2 taken on a non-pipelined but identical CPU, we can say that

(*a*) $T1 \le T2$

(*b*) $T1 \ge T2$

(*c*) $T1 < T2$

(*d*) T1 is T2 plus the time taken for one instruction fetch cycle

72. The 8085 microprocessor responds to the presence of an interrupt

(*a*) as soon as the TRAP pin becomes 'high'

(*b*) by checking the TRAP pin for 'high' status at the end of each instruction fetch

(*c*) by checking the TRAP pin for 'high' status at the end of the execution of each instruction

(*d*) by Checking the TRAP pin for 'high' status at regular intervals

73. The most appropriate matching for the following pairs

X: Indirect addressing 1 : Loops

Y: Immediate addressing 2 : Pointers

Z : Autodecrement addressing 3 : Constants

is

(*a*) X-3, Y-2, Z-1 (*b*) X-1, Y-3, Z-2

(*c*) X-2, Y-3, Z-1 (*d*) X-3, Y-1, Z-2

74. Which of the following need not necessarily be saved on a context switch between processes ?

(*a*) General purpose registers

(*b*) Translation lookaside buffer

(*c*) Program counter

(*d*) All of these

75. A graphics card has on board memory of 1 MB. Which of the following modes can the card not support ?

(*a*) 1600 × 400 resolution with 256 colours on a 17 inch monitor

(*b*) 1600 × 400 resolution with 16 million colours on a 14 inch monitor

(*c*) 800 × 400 resolution with 16 million colours on a 17 inch monitor

(*d*) 800 × 800 resolution with 256 colours on a 14 inch monitor

76. Consider the 8085 instruction IN 09H stored as follows :

Memory Address	Machine Code
3050	DA
3051	09

and the following incomplete timing diagram for the instruction :

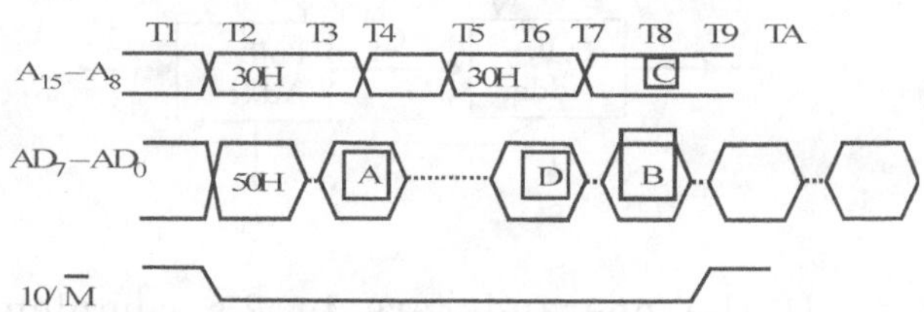

(*a*) Write the contents of the boxes A, B, C and D in hexadecimal in your answer sheet. Do not drawany pictures.

(*b*) Write the state of both ALE and $\overline{RD}$ pins at time units T1, T2, T3, and T4.

(*c*) How do you generate the signal that tells the peripheral to put the data on the bus ? Answer by completing the following statement in your answer book :

By combining signals ....

77. Consider the following 8085 program segment, where registers B and C contain BCD vaules

```
S1:  MVI    A, 99H
     MVI    D, 00H
     SUB    C
     ADD    B
     DAA
S2 : JC     S3
     MOV    E, A
     MVI    A, 99H
     SUB    E
     MOV    E, A
     JZ     S4
     MVI    D, FFH
     JMP    S4
S3 : INC    A
     DAA
     MOV    E, A
S4 : ......
```

(*a*) For the two pairs ($B = 44$, $C = 25$) and ($B = 33$, $C = 46$) at S1,

(*i*) Find the values in register A when control reaches S2.

(*ii*) Find the values in registers D and E when control reaches S4.

(*b*) What, in general, is the value of D and E as a function of B and C when control reaches S4.

78. An instruction pipleline has five stages where each stage takes 2 nanoseconds and all instructions use all five stages. Branch instructions are not overlapped, i.e., the instruction after the branch is not fetched till the branch instruction is completed. Under ideal conditions.

(*a*) Calculate the average instruction execution time assuming that 20% of all instruction executed are branch instructions. Ignore the fact that some branch instructions may be conditional.

(*b*) If a branch instruction is a conditional branch instruction, the branch need not be taken; if the branch is not taken, the following instructions can be overlapped. When 80% of all branch instructions are conditional branch instructions, and 50% of the conditional branch instructions are such that the branch is taken, calculate the average instruction execution time.

1999

79. The maximum gate delay for any output to appear in an array multiplier for multiplying two n bit number is

(*a*) $O(n^2)$ (*b*) $O(n)$

(*c*) $O(\log n)$ (*d*) $O(1)$

80. The main memory of a computer has 2 cm blocks while the cache has 2 c blocks. If the cache uses the set associative mapping scheme with 2 blocks per set, then block k of the main memory maps to the set

(*a*) (k mod m) of the cache

(*b*) (k mod c) of the cache

(*c*) (k mod $2c$) of the cache

(*d*) (k mod 2 cm) of the cache

81. A multi-user, multi-processing operating system cannot be implemented on hardware that does not support

(*a*) Address translation

(*b*) DMA for disk transfer

(*c*) At least two modes of CPU execution (privileged and non-privileged)

(*d*) Demand paging.

82. Arrange the following configurations for CPU in decreasing order of operating speeds:

Hard wired control, vertical micro-programming, horizontal micro-programming.

(*a*) Hard wired control, vertical micro-programming, horizontal micro-programming

(*b*) Hard wired control, horizontal micro-programming, vertical micro-programming

(*c*) Horizontal micro-programming, vertical micro-programming, hard wired control.

(*d*) Vertical micro-programming, horizontal micro-programming, hard wired control.

83. The main difference(s) between a CISC and a RISC processor is/are that a RISC processor typically

(*a*) has fewer instructions

(*b*) has fewer addressing modes

(*c*) has more registers

(*d*) is easier to implement using hard-wired control logic

84. A certain processor supports only the immediate and the direct addressing modes. Which of the following programming language features cannot be implemented on this processor ?

(*a*) Pointers

(*b*) Arrays

(*c*) Records

(*d*) Recursive procedures with local variable

85. An instruction pipeline consists of 4 stages : Fetch (F), Decode operand field (*D*). Execute (E) and Result-Write (W). The 5 instructions in a certain instruction sequence need these stages for the different number of clock cycles as shown by the table below.

Number. of clock cycles needed for

Instruction	F	D	E	W
1	1	2	1	1
2	1	2	2	1
3	2	1	3	2
4	1	3	2	1
5	1	2	1	2

Find the number of clock cycles needed to perform the 5 instructions.

86. Consider the following program fragment in the assembly language of a certain hypothetical processor. The processor has three general purpose registers R1, R2 and R3. The meanings of the instructions are shown by comments (starting with;) after the instructions.

```
X:  CMP R1, 0   ; Compare R1 and 0, set
                  flags appropriately in
                  status register
    JZZ         ; Jump if zero to target Z.
    MOV R2, R1  ; Copy contents of R1 to R2.
    SHR R1      ; Shift right R1 by 1 bit.
    SHL R1      ; Shift left R1 by 1 bit.
    CMP R2, R1  ; Compare R2 and R1 and
                  set flage in status register.
    JZY         ; Jump if zero to target Y.
    INC R3      ; Increment R3 by 1;
Y:  SHR R1      ; Shift right R1 by 1 bit
    JMP X       ; Jump to target X.
Z : ....
```

(*a*) Initially, R1, R2 and R3 contain the values 5, 0 and 0 respectively, what are the final values of R1 and R3 when control reaches Z ?

(*b*) In general, if R1, R2, and R3 initially contain the values n, 0, and 0 respectively. What is the final value of R3 when control reaches Z ?

87. Design a 2K × 8 (2048 locations, each bit wide) memory system mapped at addresses $(1000)_{16}$ to $(17FF)_{16}$ for the 8085 processor using four 1K × 4 memory chips. Each of these chips has the following signal pins :

(*i*) $\overline{CS}$ (*Chip select, data lines are in high impedance state when it is 1*)

(*ii*) $\overline{RD}$ (0 for read operation)

(*iii*) $\overline{WR}$ (0 for write operation)

(*iv*) A_0, A_1, ... A_9 (input address lines. A_0 is the least significant)

(*v*) D_0, D_1, D_2, D_3 (*bi*-directional data lines. D_0 is the least significant)

88. (*a*) A certain processor provides a 'test and set' instruction that is used as follows.

TSET register.flag

This instruction atomically copies flag to register and sets flag to 1. Give pseudocode for implementing the entry and exit code to a critical region using this instruction.

(*b*) Consider the following solution to the producer-consumer problem using a buffer of size 1. Assume that the initial value of count is 0. Also assume that the testing of count and assignment to count are atomic operations.

```
Producer
  Repeat
        Produce an item;
        if count = 1 then sleep;
        Place item in buffer.
        count = 1 :
        wakeup (Consumer);
  Forever
Consumer :
  Repeat
        if count = 0 then sleep :
        Remove item from buffer:
        count = 0:
        wakeup (Producer):
        Consumer item :
  Forever :
```

Show that in this solution it is possible that both the processes are sleeping at the same time.

1998

89. In serial communication employing 8 data bits, a parity bit and 2 stop bits, the minimum band rate required to sustain a transfer rate of 300 characters per second is

(a) 2400 band (b) 19200 band

(c) 4800 band (d) 1200 band

90. Which of the following devices should get higher priority in assigning interrupts ?

(a) Hard disk (b) Printer

(c) Keyboard (d) Floppy disk

91. Which of the following addressing modes permits relocation without any change whatsoever in the code?

(a) Indirect addressing

(b) Indexed addressing

(c) Base register addressing

(d) PC relative addressing

92. Which of the following is true ?

(a) Unless enabled, a CPU will not be able to process interrupts.

(b) Loop instructions cannot be interrupted till they complete.

(c) A processor checks for interrupts before executing a new instruction.

(d) Only level triggered interrupts are possible on microprocessors.

93. Formatting for a floppy disk refers to

(a) arranging the data on the disk in contiguous fashion

(b) writing the directory

(c) erasing the system area

(d) writing identification information on all tracks and sectors

94. The address space of 8086 CPU is

(a) one Megabyte

(b) 256 Kilobytes

(c) 1 K Megabytes

(d) 64 Kilobytes

95. (a) Draw the schematic of an 8085 based system that can be used to measure the width of a pulse. Assume that the pulse is given as a TTL compatible signal by the source which generates it.

(b) Write the 8085 Assembly Language program to measure the width of the pulse. State all your assumptions clearly.

96. Calculate the total time required to read 35 sectors on a 2 sided floppy disk. Assume that each track has 8 sectors and the track to track step time is 8 milliseconds. The first sector to be read is sector 3 on track 10. Assume that the diskette is soft sectored and the controller has a 1 sector buffer. The diskette spins at 300 RPM and initially, the head is on track 10.

97. For a set-associative Cache Organization, the parameters are as follows

t_c — Cache access time

t_m — Main memory access time

l — number of sets

b — block size

$k * b$ — set size

Calculate the hit ratio for a loop executed 100 times where the size of the loop is $n * b$, and $n = k *$ m is a non-zero integer and $1 < m \leq$ l

Give the value of the hit ratio for l = 1

98. (a) Free disk space can be kept track of using a free list or a bit map. Disk addresses require d bits. For a disk with B blocks, F of which are free, state the condition under which the free list uses less space than the bit map.

(b) Consider a disk with C cylinders, t tracks per cylinder, s sectors per track and a sector length sl. A logical file L with fixed record length rl is stored continuously on this disk starting at location (c_L, t_L, s_L), where C_L, t_L and S_L are the cylinder, track and sector numbers, respectively. Derive the formula to calculate the disk address (i.e. cylinder, track and sector) of a logical record n assuming that rl = sl.

1997

99. The concatenation of two lists is to be performed in 0(1) time. Which of the following implementations of a list should be used ?

(a) Singly linked list

(b) Doubly linked list

(c) Circular doubly linked list

(d) Array implementation of list.

100. The conditional expansion facility of macro processors is provided to

(a) test a condition during the execution of the expanded program

(b) to expand certain model statements depending upon the value of a condition during the execution of the expanded program

(c) to implement recursion

(d) to expand certain model statements depending upon the value of a condition during the process of macro expansion.

101. RST 7.5 interrupt in 8085 microprocessor executes service routing from interrupt vector location

(*a*) 0000H (*b*) 0075H
(*c*) 003CH (*d*) 0034H

102. Purpose of a start bit in RS 232 serial communication protocol is

(*a*) to synchronise receiver for receiving every byte
(*b*) to synchronise receiver for receiving a sequence of bytes
(*c*) a parity bit
(*d*) to synchronise receiver for receiving the last byte

103. The correct matching for the following pairs is

(A) DMA I/O (1) High speed RAM
(B) Cache (2) Disk
(C) Interrupt I/O (3) Printer
(D) Condition Code Register (4) ALU

(*a*) A – 4, B – 3, C – 1, D – 2
(*b*) A – 2, B – 1, C – 3, D – 4
(*c*) A – 4, B – 3, C – 2, D – 1
(*d*) A – 2, B – 3, C – 4, D – 1

104. An N-bit carry lookhead adder, where N is a multiple of 4, employs ICs 74181 (4 bit ALU) and 74182 (4 bit carry lookhead generator).

The minimum addition time using the best architecture for this adder is

(*a*) proportional to N
(*b*) proportional to log N
(*c*) a constant
(*d*) none of these

105. The expression (a * b) * c op ...
where 'op' is one of '+', '*' and '↑' (exponentiation) can be evaluated on a CPU with a single register without storing the value of (a * b) if

(*a*) 'op' is '+' or '*'
(*b*) 'op' is '↑' or '*'
(*c*) 'op' is '↑' or '+'
(*d*) not possible to evaluate without storing

106. Contents of A register after the execution of the following 8085 microprocessor program is

MVIA, 55 H
MVI C, 25 H
ADDC
DAA

(*a*) 7AH (*b*) 80H
(*c*) 50H (*d*) 22H

107. A micro instruction is to be designed to specify

(A) none or one of the three microoperations of one kind and
(B) none or upto six microoperations of another kind

The minimum number of bits in the micro-instruction is

(*a*) 9 (*b*) 5
(*c*) 8 (*d*) none of these

108. A D flip-flop is to be connected to an 8085 microprocessor chip as a 1–bit output port with a port address of FF hex. Data bit D_3 should be involved in the data transfer from CPU to the flip-flop. The flip-flop should be cleared on power ON.

(*a*) Using only one NAND gate (fan in of 10), one NOT gate and one D flip-flop, draw the required interface logic circuit (only the relevant signals should be shown)
(*b*) Write a program to generate a squarewave on the output of the flip-flop. ON and OFF periods of the square wave should be 7 bus cycles each

1996

109. An advantage of chained hash table (external hashing) over the open addressing scheme is

(*a*) Worst case complexity of search operations is less
(*b*) Space used is less
(*c*) Deletion is easier
(*d*) None of the above

110. Relative mode of addressing is most relevant to writing

(*a*) coroutines
(*b*) position-independent code
(*c*) shareable code
(*d*) interrupt handlers

111. A ROM is used to store the table for multiplication of two 8-bit unsigned integers. The size of ROM required is

(*a*) 256 × 16
(*b*) 64 K × 8
(*c*) 4K × 16
(*d*) 64 K × 16

112. Number of machine cycles required for RET instruction in 8085 microprocessor is

(*a*) 1 (*b*) 2
(*c*) 3 (*d*) 5

113. For the daisy chain scheme of connecting I/O devices, which of the following statements is true?

(*a*) It gives non-uniform priority to various devices.
(*b*) It gives uniform priority to all devices.
(*c*) It is only useful for connecting slow devices to a processor device.
(*d*) It requires a separate interrupt pin on the processor for each device.

114. A microprogram control unit is required to generate a total of 25 control signals. Assume that during any microinstruction, at most two control signals are active. Minimum number of bits required in the control word to generate the required control signals will be

(*a*) 2 (*b*) 2.5
(*c*) 10 (*d*) 12

115. An 8085 based system has an output port with address 00H. Consider the following assembly language program.

```
ORG     0100H
MVI     A, 00H
LXI     H, 0105H
PCHL
HLT
```

(*a*) What does the program do with respect to the output port ϕϕ H?
(*b*) Show the waveforms at the three least significant bits of the port ϕϕ H.

116. The concurrent programming constructs fork and join are as below

fork < label > which creates a new process executing from the specified label

join < variable > which decrements the specified synchronisation variable (by 1) and terminates the process if the new value is not 0.

Show the precedence graph for S1, S2, S3, S4 and S5 of the concurrent program below.

```
N = 2
M = 2
fork L3
fork L4
S1
L1 : join N
S3
L2 : join M
S5
L3 : S2
goto L1
L4 : S4
goto L2
next :
```

117. A hard disk is connected to a 50 MHz processor through a DMA controller. Assume that the initial set-up of a DMA transfer takes 1000 lock cycles for the processor, and assume that the handling of the interrupt at DMA completion requires 500 clock cycles for the processor. The hard disk has a transfer rate of 2000 kbytes/sec and average block size transferred is 4k bytes. What fraction of the processor time is consumed by the disk, if the disk is actively transferring 100% of the time ?

Level 1 (Cache memory)

Access time = 50 nsec/byte

Size	Hit ratio
8 Kbytes	0.80
16 Kbytes	0.90
64 Kbytes	0.95

Level 1 (Cache memory)

Access time = 200 nsec/byte

Size	Hit ratio
4 Kbytes	0.98
16 Kbytes	0.99
64 Kbytes	0.995

Size	Hit ratio
250 M bytes	1.0

118. A computer system has a three level memory hierarchy, with access time and hit ratios as shown below

Level 1 (Cache memory)

Access time = 50 nsec/byte

Size	Hit ratio
8 M byte	0.80
16 M byte	0.90
64 M byte	0.95

Level 2 (Cache memory)

Access time = 200 nsec/byte

Size	Hit ratio
4 M byte	0.98
16 M byte	0.99
64 M byte	0.995

Level 3

Access time = 5 sec/byte

Size	Hit ratio
260 M byte	1.0

(*a*) What should be the minimum sizes of level 1 and 2 memories to achieve an average access time of less than 100 nsec ?

(*b*) What is the average access time achieved using the chosen sizes of level 1 and level 2 memories ?

1995

Direction choose the correct alternative for each part

119. A single instruction to clear the lower four bits of the accumulator in 8085 assembly language is

(*a*) XRI OFH (*b*) ANI FOH

(*c*) XRI FOH (*d*) ANI OFH

120. Which of the following statements is true ?

(*a*) ROM is a Read / Write memory

(*b*) PC points to the last instruction that was executed

(*c*) Stack works on the principle of LIFO

(*d*) All instructions affect the flags

121. In a vectored interrupt

(*a*) the branch address is assigned to a fixed location in memory

(*b*) the interrupting source supplies the branch information to the processor through an interrupt vector

(*c*) the branch address is obtained from a register in the processor

(*d*) none of these

122. The principle of locality justifies the use of

(*a*) Interrupts (*b*) DMA

(*c*) Polling (*d*) Cache Memory

123. A sequence of two instructions that multiplies the contents of the DE register pair by 2 and stores the result in the HL register pair (in 8085 assembly language) is

(*a*) XCHG and DAD B

(*b*) XTHL and DAD H

(*c*) PCHL and DAD D

(*d*) XCHG and DAD H

124. The capacity of a memory unit is defined by the number of words multiplied by the number of bits/word. How many separate address and data lines are needed for a memory of 4K × 16?

(*a*) 10 address, 16 data lines

(*b*) 11 address, 8 data lines

(*c*) 12 address, 16 data lines

(*d*) 12 address, 12 data lines

125. In a virtual memory system the address space specified by the address lines of the CUP must be .... than the physical memory size and .... than the secondary storage size.

(*a*) smaller, smaller (*b*) smaller, larger

(*c*) larger, smaller (*d*) larger, larger

126. A computer system has a 4K word cache organised in block-set-associative manner with 4 blocks per set, 64 words per block. The number of bits in the SET and WORD fields of the main memory address format is

(*a*) 15, 40 (*b*) 6, 4

(*c*) 7, 2 (*d*) 4, 6

1994

127. Consider the following heap (Figure) in which blank regions are not in use and hatched regions are in use

The sequence of requests for blocks of size 300, 25, 125, 50 can be satisfied if we use

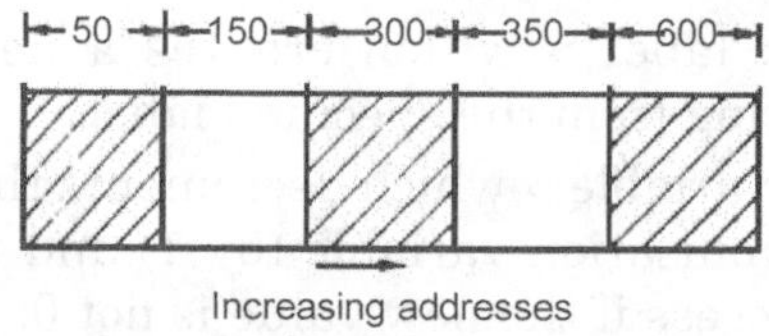

(*a*) either first fit or best fit policy (*any one*)

(*b*) first fit but not best fit policy

(*c*) best fit but first fit policy

(*d*) none of these

128. State True or False with one line explanation

Expanding opcode instruction formats are commonly employed in RISC. (Reduced Instruction Set Computers) machines.

129. Match the following :

(*i*) ECL	(*a*) Unipolar; very high speed difficult to fabricate; good resistance to radiation
(*ii*) Ga As	(*b*) Unipolar; low power; modest speed and packing density

(*iii*) TTL	(*c*) Bipolar; highest speed silicon IC; Low packing density
(*iv*) CMOS	(*d*) Bipolar; modes packing density, inexpensive

NUMERICAL TYPE QUESTIONS

2016

1. A processor can support a maximum memory of 4 GB, where the memory is word-addressable (a word consists of two bytes). The size of the address bus of the processor is at least ________ bits.
2. The size of the data count register of a DMA controller is 16 bits. The processor needs to transfer a file of 29,154 kilobytes from disk to main memory. The memory is byte addressable. The minimum number of times the DMA controller needs to get the control of the system bus from the processor to transfer the file from the disk to main memory is ______.
3. The stage delays in a 4-stage pipeline are 800, 500, 400 and 300 picoseconds. The first stage (with delay 800 picoseconds) is replaced with a functionally equivalent design involving two stages with respective delays 600 and 350 picoseconds. The throughput increase of the pipeline is ______ percent.
4. A processor has 40 distinct instructions and 24 general purpose registers. A 32-bit instruction word has an opcode, two register operands and an immediate operand. The number of bits available for the immediate operand field is__________.
5. Consider a processor with 64 registers and an instruction set of size twelve. Each instruction has five distinct fields, namely, opcode, two source register identifiers, one destination register identifier, and a twelve-bit immediate value. Each instruction must be stored in memory in a byte-aligned fashion. If a program has 100 instructions, the amount of memory (in bytes) consumed by the program text is___________.
6. The width of the physical address on a machine is 40 bits. The width of the tag field in a 512 KB 8-way set associative cache is___________bits.
7. Consider a 3 GHz (gigahertz) processor with a three-stage pipeline and stage latencies τ_1, τ_2, and τ_3 such that $\tau_1 = 3\tau_2/4 = 2\tau_3$. If the longest pipeline stage is split into two pipeline stages of equal latency, the new frequency is________GHz, ignoring delays in the pipeline registers.

2015

8. Consider a system with byte–addressable memory, 32-bit logical addresses, 4 kilobyte page size and page table entries of 4 bytes each. The size of the page table in the system in megabytes is ________.
9. Consider a disk pack with a seek time of 4 milliseconds and rotational speed of 10000 rotations per minute (RPM). It has 60 sectors per track and each sector can store 512 bytes of data. Consider a file stored in the disk. The file contains 2000 sectors. Assume that every sector access necessitates a seek, and the average rotational latency for accessing each sector is half of the time for one complete rotation. The total time (in milliseconds) needed to read the entire file is _______.
10. Consider a non-pipelined processor with a clock rate of 2.5 gigahertz and average cycles per instruction of four. The same processor is upgraded to a pipelined processor with five stages; but due to the internal pipelined delay, the clock speed is reduced to 2 gigahertz. Assume that there are no stalls in the pipeline. The speed up achieved in this pipelined processor is _____.
11. Assume that for a certain processor, a read request takes 50 nanoseconds on a cache miss and 5 nanoseconds on a cache hit. Suppose while running a program, it was observed that 80% of the processors read requests result in a cache hit. The average and access time in nanoseconds is ______.
12. A computer system implements a 40-bit virtual address, page size of 8 kilobytes, and a 128-entry translation look-aside buffer (TLB) organized into 32 sets each having four ways. Assume that the TLB tag does not store any process id. The minimum length of the TLB tag in bits is _______.
13. Consider a typical disk that rotates at 15000 rotations per minute (RPM) and has a transfer rate of 50×10^6 bytes/sec. if the average seek time of the disk is twice the average rotational delay and the controller's transfer time is 10 times the disk transfer time, the average time (in milliseconds) to read or write a 512-byte sector of the disk is __________.
14. A computer system implements 8 kilobyte pages and a +32-bit physical address space. Each page table entry contains a valid bit, a dirty bit, three

permission bits, and the translation. If the maximum size of the page table of a process is 24 megabytes, the length of the virtual address supported by the system is ______ bits.

15. Consider the sequence of machine instruction given below:

MUL R5, R0, R1

DIV R6, R2, R3

ADD R7, R5, R6

SUB R8, R7, R4

In the above sequence, R0 to R8 are general purpose registers. In the instructions shown. The first register stores the result of the operation performed on the second and the third registers.

This sequence of instructions is to be executed in a pipelined instruction processor with the following 4 stages

(1) Instruction Fetch and Decode (IF),

(2) Operand Fetch (OF),

(3) Perform Operation (PO) and

(4) Write back the result (WB).

The IF, OF and WB stages take 1 clock cycle each for any instruction. The PO stage takes 1 clock cycle for ADD or SUB instruction, 3 clock cycles for MUL instruction and 5 clock cycles for DIV instruction. The pipelined processor uses operand forwarding from the PO stage to the OF stage. The number of clock cycles taken for the execution of the above sequence of instructions is ________

2014

16. A machine has a 32-bit architecture, with 1-word long instructions. It has 64 registers, each of which is 32 bits long. It needs to support 45 instructions, which have an immediate operand in addition to two register operands. Assuming that the immediate operand is an unsigned integer, the maximum value of the immediate operand is ________.

17. Suppose a disk has 201 cylinders, numbered from 0 to 200. At some time the disk arm is at cylinder 100, and there is a queue of disk access requests for cylinders 30, 85, 90, 100, 105, 110, 135 and 145. If Shortest-Seek Time First (SSTF) is being used for scheduling the disk access, the request for cylinder 90 is serviced after servicing ________ number of requests.

18. Consider a 6-stage instruction pipeline, where all stages are perfectly balanced. Assume that there is no cycle-time overhead of pipelining. When an application is executing on this 6-stage pipeline, the speedup achieved with respect to non-pipelined execution if 25% of the instructions incur 2 pipeline stall cycles is ________.

19. Consider two processors P_1 and P_2 executing the same instruction set. Assume that under identical conditions, for the same input, a program running on P_2 takes 25% less time but incurs 20% more CPI (clock cycles per instruction) as compared to the program running on P_1. If the clock frequency of P_1 is 1GHz, then the clock frequency of P_2 (in GHz) is ________.

20. A 4-way set-associative cache memory unit with a capacity of 16 KB is built using a block size of 8 words. The word length is 32 bits. The size of the physical address space is 4 GB. The number of bits for the TAG field is ____.

21. A FAT (file allocation table) based file system is being used and the total overhead of each entry in the FAT is 4 bytes in size. Given a 100×10^6 bytes disk on which the file system is stored and data block size is 10^3 bytes, the maximum size of a file that can be stored on this disk in units of 10^6 bytes is ________.

22. Consider a main memory system that consists of 8 memory modules attached to the system bus, which is one word wide. When a write request is made, the bus is occupied for 100 nanoseconds (ns) by the data, address, and control signals. During the same 100 ns, and for 500 ns thereafter, the addressed memory module executes one cycle accepting and storing the data. The (internal) operation of different memory modules may overlap in time, but only one request can be on the bus at any time. The maximum number of stores (of one word each) that can be initiated in 1 millisecond is ________

23. Consider a paging hardware with a TLB. Assume that the entire page table and all the pages are in the physical memory. It takes 10 milliseconds to search the TLB and 80 milliseconds to access the physical memory. If the TLB hit ratio is 0.6, the effective memory access time (in milliseconds) is ________.

24. An instruction pipeline has five stages, namely, instruction fetch (IF), instruction decode and register fetch (ID/RF), instruction execution (EX), memory access (MEM), and register write back (WB) with stage latencies 1 ns, 2.2 ns, 2 ns, 1 and 0.75 ns, respectively (ns stands for nanoseconds). To gain in terms of frequency, the designers have decided to split the ID/RF stage into three stages (ID, RF1, RF2) each of latency 2.2/3 ns. Also, the EX stage is split into two stages (EX1, EX2) each of latency 1 ns. The new design has a total of eight pipeline stages. A program has 20% branch instructions which execute in the EX stage and produce the next instruction pointer at the end of the EX stage in the old design and at the end of the EX2 stage in the new design. The IF stage stalls after fetching a branch instruction until the next instruction pointer is computed. All instructions other than the branch instruction have an average CPI of one in both the designs. The execution times of this program on the old and the new design are P and Q nanoseconds, respectively. The value of P/Q is________.

25. The memoy access time is 1 nanosecond for a read operation with a hit in cache, 5 nanoseconds for a real operation with a miss in cache, 2 nanoseconds for a write operation with a hit in cache and 10 nanoseconds for a write operation with a miss in cache. Execution of a sequence of instructions involves 100 instruction fetch operations, 60 memory operand read operations and 40 memory operand write operations. The cache hit ratio is 0.9. The average memory access time (in nanoseconds) in executing the sequence of instructions is ________.

ANSWERS

MCQ Type Questions

1.(c)	**2.**(a)	**3.**(d)	**4.**(a)	**5.**(b)	**6.**(a)	**7.**(d)	**8.**(d)	**9.**(a)	**10.**(c)
11.(b)	**12.**(b)	**13.**(d)	**14.**(c)	**15.**(c)	**16.**(c)	**17.**(d)	**18.**(b)	**19.**(b)	**20.**(d)
21.(d)	**22.**(b)	**23.**(d)	**24.**(d)	**25.**(b)	**26.**(b)	**27.**(c)	**28.**(c)	**29.**(b)	**30.**(d)
31.(b)	**32.**(c)	**33.**(d)	**34.**(b)	**35.**(a)	**36.**(b)	**37.**(b)	**38.**(b)	**39.**(a)	**40.**(b)
41.(d)	**42.**(b)	**43.**(a)	**44.**(b)	**45.**(a)	**46.**(b)	**47.**(c)	**48.**(c)	**49.**(c)	**50.**(a)
51.(b)	**52.**(b)	**53.**(b)	**54.**(b)	**55.**(b)	**56.**(a)	**57.**(c)	**58.**(b)	**59.**(b)	**60.**(a)
61.(d)	**62.**(b)	**63.**(d)	**64.**(d)	**65.**(d)	**66.**(a)	**67.**(a)	**68.**(b)	**69.**(b)	**70.**(b)
71.(b)	**72.**(c)	**73.**(c)	**74.**(b)	**75.**(b)	**76.**(*)	**77.**(*)	**78.**(*)	**79.**(d)	**80.**(b)
81.(a,b,c)	**82.**(b)	**83.**(a,b,c,d)		**84.**(a,b,c,d)	**85.**(15)	**86.**(*)	**87.**(*)	**88.**(*)	**89.**(c)
90.(c)	**91.**(c)	**92.**(a)	**93.**(d)	**94.**(a)	**95.**(*)	**96.** (944 ms)	**97.** $1-\frac{1}{100b}$	**98.**(*)	**99.**(c)
100.(d)	**101.**(c)	**102.**(a)	**103.**(b)	**104.**(b)	**105.**(a)	**106.**(b)	**107.**(c)	**108.**(*)	**109.**(c)
110.(b)	**111.**(d)	**112.**(c)	**113.**(a)	**114.**(c)	**115.**(*)	**116.**(*)	**117.**(1.5%)	**118.**(*)	**119.**(b)
120.(c)	**121.**(b)	**122.**(d)	**123.**(d)	**124.**(c)	**125.**(c)	**126.**(d)	**127.**(*)	**128.**(False)	

129.(i – c),(ii – a),(iii – d),(iv –b)

Numerical Type Questions

1. (31)	**2.** (456)	**3.**(33.28)	**4.** (16)	**5.** (500)	**6.** (24)	**7.** (4)
8. (4)	**9.** (14020)	**10.** (3.2)	**11.** (14)	**12.** (22)	**13.** (6.1-6.2)	**14.** (36)
15. (13)	**16.** (16383)	**17.** (3)	**18.** (4)	**19.** (1.6)	**20.** (20 to 20)	
21. (99.55 to 99.65)		**22.** (10000 to 10000)		**23.** (122)	**24.** (1.54)	
25. (1.68)						

EXPLANATIONS

MCQ TYPE QUESTIONS

1. Clustered: The ordering of data record is same as or close to the ordering of data entries in same index.
2. 0110110 . . .
4.

4	12	4
TAG	cache block offset	word offset

⇒

E	201	F
TAG	cache block offset	word offset

7. When a cache block size is smaller, it could accommodate more number of blocks, it improves the hit ratio for cache, so the miss penalty for cache will be lowered.
8. When associativity is doubled, then the set offset will be effected, accordingly, the number of bits used for TAG comparator be effected. Width of set index decoder also will be effected when set offset is changed. Width of wag selection multiplexer wil be effected when the block offset is changed. With of processor to main memory data bus is guaranteed to be NOT effected.
9.

S	E	M
1 bit	8 bits	23 bits

$(14.25)_{10} = (1110.01)_2$

$1110.01 \times 2^0 = 1.11001 \times 2^3$

S : 1

E : $(3 + 127)_{10} = (10000010)_2$

M : 11001000 --------

Value stored :

1 1 0 0 0 0 0 1 0 1 1 0 0 1 0 0 0 0 – – –

[C 1 6 4 0 0 0 0]$_H$

10. Clock period (CP) = max stage delay + overhead

So CP_{p1} = Max (1,2,2,1) = 2ns

CP_{p2} = Max (1, 1.5, 1.5, 1.5) = 1.5ns

CP_{p3} = Max (0.5, 1,1,0.6,1) = 1ns

CP_{p4} = Max (0.5,0.5,1,1,1.1) =1.1ns

As frequency $\alpha \dfrac{1}{C.P}$, so least clock period will give the highest peak clock frequency.

So, $f_{p3} = \dfrac{1}{1\text{ns}} = 1$ GHz

11. Given 8 – bit delimiter pattern of 01111110.

Output Bit string after stuffing is 01111100101

⇓

Stuffed Bit

Now, Input String is 0111110101

12. This question can be solved by verifying the options suppose that the cache blocks are arranged as follows:

0	3	6	9	12
1	4	7	10	13
2	5	8	11	14

Here V = 3 and K = 5

then on verifying for any cache block only option(*d*) gives correct answer.

For example: Suppose we need to find for block 9 then

Option (*a*): (9 mod 3) ∗ 5 to (9 mod 3) ∗ 5 + 4 = 0 to 4

Option (*b*): (9 mod 3) to (9 mod 3) + 4 = 0 to 4

Option (*c*): (9 mod 5) to (9 mod 5) + 2 = 4 to 6

Option (*d*): (9 mod 5) ∗ 3 to (9 mod 5) ∗ 3 + 2 = 12 to 14

Now check for option (A), (B) & (C)

Check for block 11

Option (A): (11 mod 3) ∗ 5 to (11 mod 3) ∗ 5 + 4 = 10 to 14

Option (B): (11 mod 3) to (11 mod 3) + 4 2 to 6

Option (C): (11 mod 5) to (11 mod 5) + 2 6 to 8

Clearly option (A) gives correct answer

13. **Given:** A sequence of micro operations

MBR ← PC

MAR ← X

PC ← Y

Memory ← MBR

To find: What these micro operation represents?

Analysis: On converting these operations to normal english

1. First micro operation stores the value of PC into memory Base register (MBR)
2. Second micro operation stores value of X into Memory Address register (MAR)
3. Third micro operation stores value of Y into PC
4. Fourth micro operation stores value of MBR to memory.

So before execution of these instructions PC holds the value of next instruction to be executed. We first stores the value of PC to MBR and then through MBR to memory i.e. we are saving the value of PC in memory and then load PC with a new value. This can be done only in two types of operations conditional branch and interrupt service.

As we are not checking here for any conditions so it is interrupt service.

14. Since starting on disk starts from <1200, 9, 40> so no of sectors left on 9th surface is 24

so, on 9th surface total storage of "12288" B is possible Now, a part from 9th surface, on cylinder no. 1200 only 6 surface is left.

To storage possible on these 6 surface are

$= 6 * 2^6 * 2^9 \rightarrow$ storage on each sector.

$\downarrow$

No. of sectors on each surface

$= 196608$ B

So total on cylinder no. 1200, storage possible

$\Rightarrow 196608 + 12288 = 208896$ B

So Since file size is 42797 kB and out of which 208896 B are stored on cylinder no. 1200. So we are left only with only 43615232 B.

Since in 1 cylinder, Storage Possible is

$$= 2^4 * 2^6 * 2^9 \text{ B} = 524288 \text{ B}$$

$$\text{So we need about} = \frac{43615232}{524288\text{B}}\text{B}$$

$$= 83.189 \text{ more cylinders.}$$

Hence we'll need the **1284th Cylinder** to completely store the file. C_{02} after 1283rd cylinder we will left with data which will need .189

15. Given: Five stage instruction pipeline Delays for FI, DI, FO, EI and wo are 5, 7, 10, 8, 6 ns resp.

To find: Time needed to execute 12 instruction prog.

Analysis: Since the max. time taken by any stage is 10 ns and additional 1 ns is required for delay of buffer. Therefore total time for an instruction to pass from one stage to another is 11ns Now instructions are executed as follows:

$$\xrightarrow[\text{execution with time}]{I_1, I_2, I_3, I_4, I_9, I_{10}, I_{11}, I_{12}}$$

Now when I_4 is in its executioin stage we detect the branch and when I_4 is in WO stage we fetch I_9 so time for execution of instructions from I_1 to I_4 is $= 11 * 5 + (4 - 1) * 11 = 88$ ns.

and time for execution of instructions from I_9 to I_{12} is

$$= 11 * 5 + (4 - 1) * 11 = 88 \text{ ns}$$

But we have 11ns when fetching I_9. i.e. I_9 requires only 44 ns additional instead of 55 ns because time for fetching I_9 can be overlap with WO of I_4

Hence total time is = 88 + 88 – 11 = 165 ns

16. Register renaming is done to eliminate WAR/WAW hazards.

17. For a 4 bit multiplier there are $2^4 \times 2^4 = 2^8$ = 256 combinations.

Output will contain 8 bits.

So the amount of ROM needed is $2^8 \times$ 8bits = 2 Kbits.

18. Each block size = 128 Bytes

Disk block address = 8 Bytes

$$\text{Each disk can contain} = \frac{128}{8} = 16 \text{ addresses}$$

Size due to 8 direct block addresses: 8×128

Size due to 1 indirect block address: 16×128

Size due to 1 doubly indirect block address: $16 \times 16 \times 128$

Size due to 1 doubly indirect block address: $16 \times 16 \times 128$

So, maximum possible file size:

$$= 8 \times 128 + 16 \times 128 + 16 \times 16 \times 128$$
$$= 1024 + 2048 + 32768$$
$$= 35840 \text{ Bytes} = 35\text{k Bytes}$$

19.
```
1. Acquire lock (L) {
2. While (Fetch_And_Add(L, 1))
3.          L = 1.
   }
4. Release Lock(L) {
5.          L = 0;
6.   }
```

Let P and Q be two concurrent processes in the system currently executing as follows

P executes 1,2,3 then Q executes 1 and 2 then P executes 4,5,6 then L=0 now

Q executes 3 by which L will be set to 1 and thereafter no process can set

L to zero, by which all the processes could starve.

20. Here 20 will act as base and content of R_2 will be index

22. 6000 rotations ________ 60 sec

1 rotation ________ 10 ms

∴ Rotational latency = 5 ms

Time for one disk access = 15 ms

Time to load all libraries = 15 × 100

= 1500 ms = 1.5 sec

23.

19 + 2	8	5
↓ TAG	↓ block offset	↓ Byte offset $=2^5$

$$= \frac{2^{13}}{2^5} = 2^8$$

Required answer = 256 × (19 + 2) = 5376 bits

24. Main memory unit has capacity = 4 MB

Number of DRAM chips = $\dfrac{4\,\text{MB}}{1\text{M} \times 1\,\text{bit}} = 32$

1 DRAM chip has 1 K(2^{10}) rows and 1 K(2^{10}) cells

In each row = $32 \times 2^{10} \times 2^{10}$

$= 32 \times 2^{20}$

Time taken in one refresh op^n = 100 ns

Time required to perform one refresh operation on all the cells in MM unit

$= 32 \times 2^{20} \times 100$

$= 3200 \times 2^{20}$ ns

25. Clocks

	1	2	3	4	5	6	7	8	9	10	11	12	13	14	15	16
20	2F	2D	OF	PO	PO	PO	WO									
21		2F	2D	OF	Stall	Stall	PO	P[O	PO	PO	PO	PO	WO			
22			2F	2D	OF	-	-	-	-	-	-	-	PO	WO		
23				2F	2D	OF	-	-	-	-	-	-	-	PO	WO	

So total 15 cycles required.

Alternately

1 2 3 4 5 6 7 8 9 10 11 12 13 14 15

I_0 IF ID OF PO PO PO WO

I_1 IF ID OF .... PO PO PO PO PO PO WO

I_2 IF ID OF ... PO WO

I_3 IF ID OF .... PO WO

So that 15 cycles required.

26. $a = 1$

$b = 10$ Let a is in Accumulator than for b and c we want

$c = 20$ Register than **2 registers** want till now 1 for b and 1 for c

$d = a + b$ Now $d = a + b$ can be stored in Accumulator because we don't want a again

$e = c + d$. Now for ***f*** we wan't **next, one register** because we wan't ***c* & *e*** again

$f = c + e$

$b = c + e$. Now at $b = c + e$ we can store value in register b already, so we don't want another

$e = b + f$. Now at $e = b + f$ we can store it in 0 register of ***b*** because we don't want another

$d = 5 + e$ Now at $d = 5 + e$ we can store it in d because we don't want e again

than we can say only 3 registers we want.

27. Number of chips required $= \dfrac{256 * 1024 * 8}{32 * 1024 * 1} = 64$

28. A CPU generally handles an interrupt by executing ISR by checking the interrupt register after finishing execution of the current instruction.

29.

	1	2	3	4	5	6	7	8	9	10	11	12	13	14	15	16	17	18	19	20	21	22	23
S_1	I_1		I_2	I_3		I_4	I_1		I_2	I_3		I_4											
S_2			I_1	I_2			I_3	I_4		I_1	I_2			I_3	I_4								
S_3				I_1			I_2		I_3	I_4		I_1		I_2		I_3	I_4						
S_4					I_1				I_2		I_3			I_4		I_1	I_2		I_3			I_4	

30.

Set 0	~~0~~ 48
	~~4~~ 32
	8
	~~216~~ 92
Set 1	1
	133
	129
	73
Set 2	
Set 3	~~255~~ 155
	3
	159
	63

31.

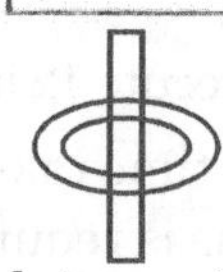

co-centric circular tracks

The seek latency is not linearly proportional to the seak distance due to arm starting and stoping inertia.

32. Auto increment add mode is basically used for incrementing a data. It depends on size of data.

33. For any exception, while executing RFE, no exception is alllowed (no interrupts). It is a priveleged instruction, as soon as exception occurs RFE is called (executed).

34. For inclusion to hole between two cache levels cache hierarchy

L1 must be write through cache.

and L2 cache must be at least as large as L1 cache.

35. In pipelined processor bypassing can handle all RAW hazards and register remaining can eliminate all register carried WAR hazard.

36. The use of multiple windows with overlap causes a reduction in the number of memory accesses for functions local and parameters, register saves and restores and instruction fetches.

37. Translations Lookaside Buffer can be accessed during effective address calculations.

38. For identifying each of 128 lines uniquely,

number of bits required = 7 bits.

Since each line is of size 64 words, so number of bits needed to identify each word uniquely = 6 bits.

Now, since there are 20 bits in address generated by CPU

∴ Bits needed for tag = 20 – (7 + 6) = 7 bits.

39. Size of disk

= Number of surfaces × number of Tracks per surface × number of Sectors per track × capacity of each sector

= 16 × 128 × 256 × 512 bytes

= 256 Mega bytes (MB)

Since, total number of sector in disk

$= 16 \times 128 \times 256 = 512\text{ K} = 2^{19}$ Sector

therefore, it requires 19 bits to specify a particular sector.

40. For each of the three instruction four stages will be there. Since ,it is a pipelined processor, so one instruction may be fetched while other is being decoded or executed or written back action performed in each clock cycle may be represented as

Clock Cycle	ADD	MUL	SUB
1	IF		
2	ID	IF	
3	EX	ID	IF
4	WB	EX	ID
5		EX	
6		EX	
7		WB	EX
8			WB

Only, two instructions cannot be executed simulteneously.

41. The main memory consists of 24 banks, each of 2 bytes. Since parallel accesses to all banks are possible, only two parallel accesses of all banks are needed to traverse the whole data.

For one parallel access,

Total time = Decoding Time + Latency Time

$$= \frac{24}{2} + 80 = 92 \text{ ns}$$

Hence, for 2 such accesses,

time = 2 × 92 = 184 ns

42. For 80% of 10^9 instructions, a single cycle is sufficient as there is no conditional branch. For the rest 20%, an extra cycle will be needed making the number of cycles required to 2.

$$\text{One cycle takes} = \frac{1}{1\text{G}} = 10^{-9} \text{ second}$$

$$\therefore \text{ Total time} = 10^{-9}\left(\frac{80}{100} \times 10^9 \times 1 + \frac{20}{100} \times 10^9 \times 2\right)$$

$$= \frac{4}{5} + \frac{2}{5} = 1.2 \text{ seconds}$$

43. Since only the bit with position *pos* is the deciding factor in jumping to the label, we have to set all other bits to 0 in temp. The mask register required for this purpose just has to have 1 in position *pos*. This can be achieved through *pos* number of left shifts over 1.

44. By Diasy chaing rule.

45. We have two regestion limit and base. So, when we refer memory location which is not in range provided by these two regestor is always cause OS to interface.

46. The swap space is basically used for saving process data. Consider CPU contains two process P_1 and P_2 if P_1 is running on the CPU then P_2 is swap out and all data (Pc for process, content etc) are saved in the disk, when CPU executes process P_2 then all data items of P_1 saved on a risk.

47. As size increase, page frame increase. If we apply any replacement rule which is not cause 'blady anamoly' is always reduce page fault.

48. Here we have to calculate only execution cycle not fetching cycle.

So during fetching cycle we have addresses of 'A' and 'B' (read question carefully).

Now, we have to calculate index addresses by reading value of A → (1)

Then, we have to add R0, we get the address of first source of and we have to read its value →(2)

* Here we have address of B for getting actual value

First, we have to read contents of B → (3)

then value at contents of B → (4)

then we have to write actual answer → (5)

49. Correct matching:

1. A[1] = B[J]	Indexed Addressing Mode
2. While [*A++]	Autoincrement
3. int temp = *x;	Indirect Addressing Mode

50. Here, we have 32 bit virtual address space. 32 kB cache memory hence, we need 15 bit for occuring them (not all for indexing explained next). So 17 used for tag.

But here cache are in block of 32 bytes. So, there actually 1 K (blocks) for a indexing 1 K location, we need 10 bits.

Remainder five are used for selecting byte

17 bit	10	5 bit
⇓	⇓	⇓
for tag	for cache index	for selecting byte within word (32 bytes)

51. Clock Cycles

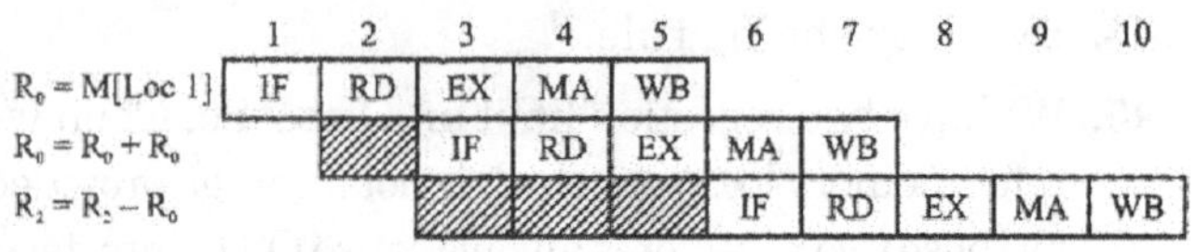

So it requires 10 CPU clock cycles.

52. If overhead of a single byte transfer with interface mode is 4 μ sec, then actual data transfer can be 250000.

Actually transfer take place at the rate → 10000

Now 25 is the minimum performance gain.

53. Round per minute (R.P.M.) = 3000

Round per sec = $\frac{3000}{60} = 50$

In one round data read = 512 * 1kB = 512 KB (Here in round)

We can read one track = $\frac{2^{19}}{4} = 2^{17}$

In one second = $2^{17} * 50$.

Hard disk interrupt = 6553600 C.P.U. (DMA at most)

Each intruption take = 4 *n*sec

So, 6553600 Intrupts takes = 0.262144 s

$\therefore \quad \text{Percentage} = \frac{0.262144}{1} \times 100$

= 26.2144 (approx)

In case, we use 1 kB = 1000, then answer is 25.

54. RTL $R_0 \Rightarrow R_0 + R_1$

Sequence of micro-instruction takes place in following cycles:

I cycle : R_{1out}, S_{in}

II cycle : R_{2out}, T_{in}

III cycle : S_{out}, T_{out}, ALU_{add}, R_{in}

Hence 3 cycles will be required to execute.

55. RTL $R_n = PC + 1$

$P_c = M[Pc]$

Sequence of micro-instrution take place in following cycles:

I cycle : PC_{out}, S_{in}, MAR_{in} (MAR can be loaded with PC_{out})

II cycle : S_{out}, $ALU_{increment}$, $R_{n\ in}$

III cycle : MDR_{out}, PC_{in} (MDR_{out} can be performed once MAR_{in} has been performed)

Hence 3 cycles will be required to execute.

56. This problem can be solved by analysing and eliminating method.

57.

Instruction	Instruction size	Location (Decimal)
MOV R_1, 1000	2	1000 to 1007
MOV R_2, (R1)	1	1008 to 1011
ADD R_2, R_3	1	1012 to 1015
MOV 1005, R_2	2	1016 to 1023
Halt	1	1024 to 1027

If an interrupt occurs the CPU has been halted after executing the HALT instruction the return address 1024 saved in the stack

58.

Operation	Instruction Size	Required Clock cycles
$R_1 \leftarrow$ Memory [500]	2	6 + 2 = 8
$R_2 \leftarrow$ Memory [(R_1)]	1	3 + 2 = 5
$R_2 \leftarrow (R_2 + R_3)$	1	1 = 1
Memory [6000] $\leftarrow R_2$	2	6 + 2 = 8
Machine Halt	1	1 + 1 = 2
		Total = 24

59.

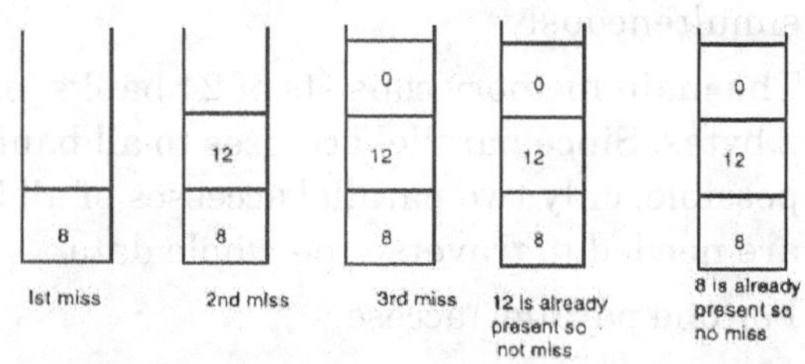

So, total number of miss is (3).

60. Control memory processor has 26 bit microinstruction divided into three field microoperation field is 13.

So, next address field (X) = 10

MAX select field = 3

Size of control = 2^{10} = 1024

61.

$$\text{Data transfer rate} = 10\text{M bytes/sec}$$
$$= 10 \times 2^{10} \text{ k byte/sec}$$
$$\text{Size of transfer} = 20 \text{ k bytes}$$
$$10 \times 2^{10} \times x\% = 20$$
$$10 \times 2^{10} \times \frac{x}{100} = 20 = \frac{20 \times 100}{10 \times 2^{10}} = \frac{200}{1024}$$
$$x = 0.19\%$$
$$x = 0.10\%$$

62. Delay is 5 nanosecond/stage.

Total delay in pipeline = 150 + 120 + 160 + 140 = 570

Delay due to stage delay = 15

Total delay = 585

$$\text{Total time taken} = \frac{1000(\text{data item size})}{585(\text{ns})}$$
$$= 165.5 \text{ microsecond}$$

63. (*i*) j + 1st instruction uses result of the jth instruction as an operand, then read-after-write (RAW) hazard occurs. It is a part of data dependency.

(*ii*) Execution of a conditional jump instruction causes a flushing so conditional dependency occurs.

(*iii*) jth and j + 1st instructions require the ALU at the same time causes write-after-read (WAR) hazard.

64. $1 + 2 + \ldots\ldots\ldots + n = \dfrac{n\,(n+1)}{2} = O\,(n^2)$

65.

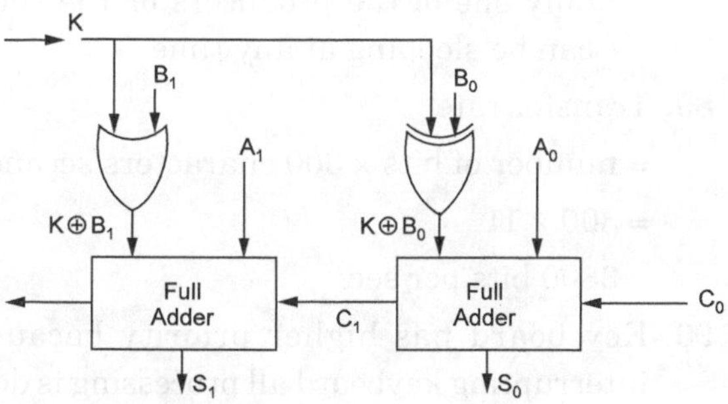

If $k = 1$, $C_0 = 1$

$$S_0 = \overline{B}_0 \oplus A_0 \oplus C_0 = \overline{B}_0 \oplus \overline{A}_0$$
$$= A_0\,\overline{B}_0 + B_0\,\overline{A}_0$$
$$C = \overline{B}_0\,A_0 + \left(\overline{B}_0 \oplus A_0\right) C_0$$
$$= \overline{B}_0\,A_0 + B_0 A_0 + \overline{A}_0\,\overline{B}_0$$
$$= A_0 + \overline{A}_0 \overline{B}_0$$
$$S = A_1 \oplus \overline{B}_1 \oplus C_1$$

If $k = 0$, $C_0 = 1$

$$S_0 = A_0 \oplus \overline{B}_0 \oplus 1 = A_0 \oplus \overline{B}_0 = A_0 B_0 + \overline{A}_0\,\overline{B}_0$$
$$C = A_0 B_0 + (A_0 \oplus B_0) = A_0 + \overline{A}_0 B_0$$

⇒ A+ B and A – B and A + 1

66. $A \leftarrow A_0$

The value of B after execution of the program is number of 0 bits in A_0.

67. After adding the 1 same value will be obtained.

68. Software interrupt that store the old CPU state and brings in a new PSW that belongs to the supervisor mode.

79. The least significant bit will come in constant time as it just requires the multiplication (*b*oolean and operation) of the least significant bits of the multiplicand the multiplier.

80. Since the cache has 2c blocks and there are 2 blocks per set, the cache thus has c sets. So, block *k* of the main memory would map to block (k mod c) of the cache.

81. Address translation is required to give different address spaces to different processes and users.

DMA is required for any disk transfer.

Two modes of execution are required to prevent errant users from harming one another.

Demand paging is not really required for a multi-user, multi processing operating system, though it would help in implementing the same.

82. Hardwired control is the fastest. Since horizontal microprogramming involves lesser number of instructions, it is faster than vertical microprogramming.

83.* RISC has fewer construction that CISC.

- * RISC has fewer addressin modes comparegtion to CISC.
- * RISC has more register. RISC have all poertion done in register.
- * It is hardwired rather than microprogrammed control.
- * Single cycle instruction execution.
- * Fixed length, easily decoded instruction format.

84. Pointers require indirect addressing mode.

Arrays and records required indexing modes.

Recursive procedures with local variables required

85. It will take 15 clock cycles to execute the instructions with pipelining of 4 stages as shown below. We assume that an instruction can be blocked for sometime in case resources are not available.

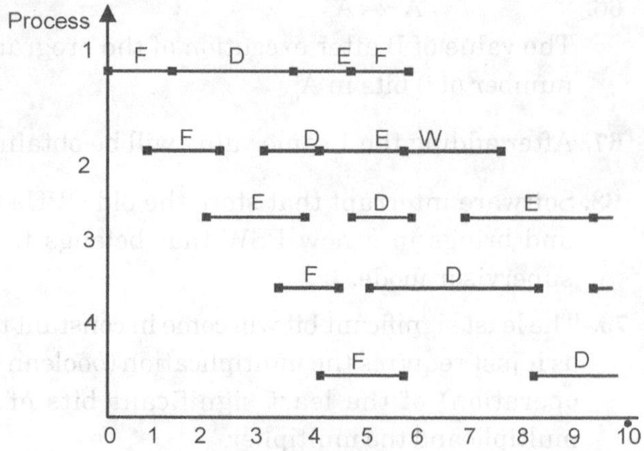

Clock Cycles

86. (*a*) When we do a SHR followed by a SHL on R1, all that is effectively done is to make the last bit of R2 zero. We then compare R2 with R1 to see if the last bit was originally one or zero. If it was one, the counter is incremented. In either case, R1 is shifted right and the whole process is repeated. So, finally the program counts the number of ones in R1—if R3 is initially zero. When R1 is initially 5, and R2 and R3 0, final values are R1 = 0, R3 = 2.

(*b*) In general, the program counts the number of ones in the binary representation of '*n*'.

87. Since we are using four 1 K* 4 memory chips, each chip can store only one nibble at any particular address. So we can store a byte either by storing it in two consecutive nibbles in a chip or we can use two chips, one for storing the higher order nibble and the other for the lower order nibble. The second option is better as it is some sort of interleaving and enables faster memory access (since the entire byte can be made available at once instead for requiring two memory accesses for retrieving two nibbles).

So, we store memory locations 1000 to 13FF in the first two chips, with chip storing the higher order nibble and chip 2 the lower order.

Memory locations 1400 to 17FF are stored in chips 3 and 4, with chip 3 having the higher order nibble. The address lines A_0 to A_9 are used to address the nibble in the chips, and line A10 will be used to select either the first 2 chips or the last 2 chips. The $\overline{RD}$ and $\overline{WR}$ pins in the chips are connected to the corresponding control lines in the bus.

In the case of chips 1 and 3 the data pins will go to the higher order nibble in the data bus, and for chips 2 and 4, they will go to the lower order nibble.

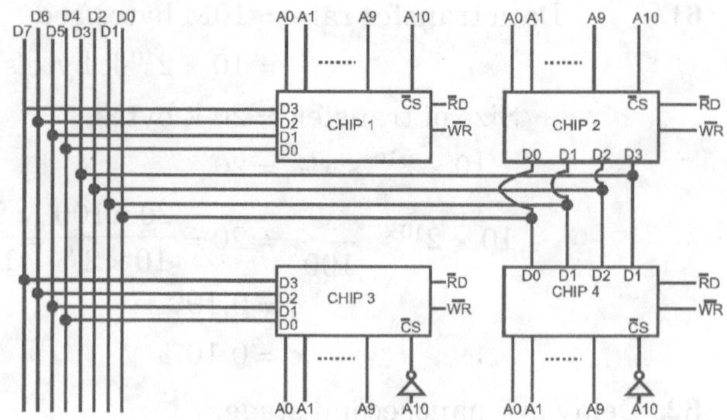

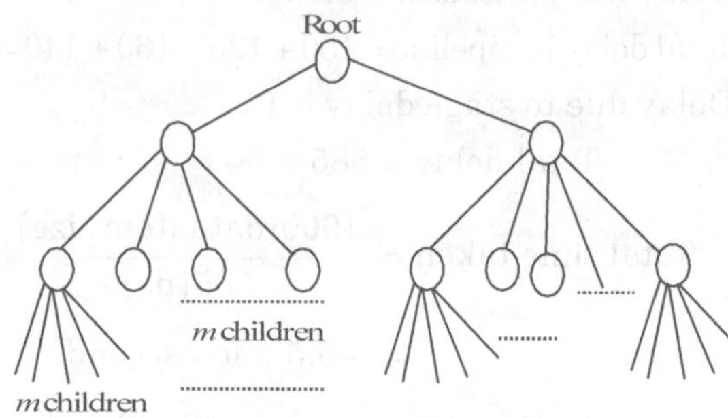

88. (*a*) loop : TEST R1, lock

JNZ loop ; *i.e.* if lock was already true, continue to remain in loop, else exit loop

Critical Section

MOV lock, 1

(*b*) In the given program segment, it is not possible for both processors to be sleeping at the same time. This is because count can take the value either 0 or 1, depending on which only one of the producers or the consumers can be sleeping at any time.

89. Transfer rate

= number of bits × 300 characters/second

= 300 × 11

= 3300 bits per sec.

90. Key board has higher priority because after interrupting keyboard all processing is done after input by keyboard.

91. **Base register addressing.** In this mode, content of a base register is added to the address part of the instruction to obtain the effective address. A base register is assumed to hold a base adress and the address field of the instruction gives a displacement relative to the base address with a base register, the displacement values of instruction do not have to change only the value of the base register requires updating to reflect the begining of a new memory of constant.

92. Unless enabled, a CPU will not be able to process interrupts.

94. Address space of any microprocessor depends on its address line

$= 2^n$, where n is number of address lines.

In the case of 8086 μp address line is 20 bits.

So, its address space $= 2^{20} = 1$ megabyte

96. The time to read one sector

$$= \frac{60}{8 \times 300} = 25 \text{ milliseconds.}$$

To read 35 sectors starting from Track 10, sector 3 we have to read Track 10, side 0, Track 10, side 1, Track 11, side 0, Track 11, side 1, Track 12, Side 0, and the number of sectors read are 8, 8, 8, 8, 5. And Two Track steps are required.

$$\therefore \quad \text{Time} = 25 \times (8 + 8 + 8 + 8 + 5) + 2 \times 8$$

$$= 25 \times (37) + 16$$

$$= 941 \text{ milliseconds.}$$

97. The given Set Associative diagram has been drawn based on the parameters given in the question.

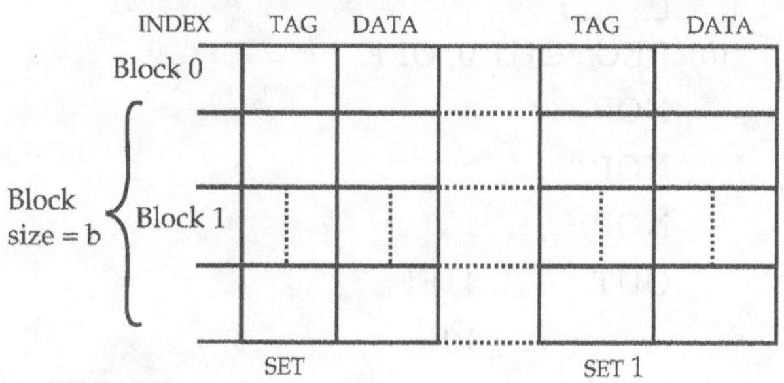

The size of the loop is $n * b$

where $n = k \times m$ and $1 < m \leq 1$.

Means the code in the loop takes m complete sets. For 100 times execution of this loop the total number of references

= Total number of memory locations used from the Set associative memory

$= k \times b \times m \times 100$

Every first reference to a block results in a miss

$\Rightarrow$ total number of misses

= total number of blocks $= k \times m$.

$$\text{Hit ratio} = \frac{\text{Number of hits}}{\text{Total references}}$$

$$= \frac{\text{Total references} - \text{Number of misses}}{\text{Total references}}$$

$$= \frac{k \times b \times m \times 100 - k \times m}{k \times b \times m \times 100} = \left(1 - \frac{1}{100\,b}\right)$$

(*b*) When l = 1.

The hit ratio $\left(1 - \frac{1}{100\,b}\right)$ is independent of l.

Moreover the value of m is chosen to satisfy all the conditions. When l = 1, then m must be 1.

98. (*a*) The number of bits in a Bit Map will be equal to the number of blocks on the disk and the number of bits in a free list will be the product of number of address bits and number of free blocks. i.e. F × D. Obviously the free list will take less space if $D \times F < B$. This is only possible if the value of F is taken such that the number of bits $F \times D < B$. Assuming constant block size and then the number of blocks on the disk will be multiple of 2 say $B = 2^i$.

Obviously, the values of F will be between 0 and $2^{i-3} - 1$

i.e., $0 < F \leq 2^{i-3} - 1$ when $B = 2^i$, $i > 0$ an integer.

(*b*) The second size is same as sector size. So it is required to find the nth sector starting from S_L on track t_L and on cylinder C_L. Assuming the tracks t per cylinder are counted considering the fact that all the platters in the disk have two sides except for the 1st which have one each for the data storage.

Total number of sectors on track = s.

$\Rightarrow$ Total number of sectors per cylinder $= t_s$.

and number of sectors on disk $= Ct_s$.

Let (C_f, T_f, S_f) be the final address of the nth record.

Let $\quad q_0 = n \text{div} (t_s)$, $r_0 = n \bmod (t_s)$.

$C_f = C_L = q_0 + 1$.

Let $\quad q_1 = r_0 \text{ div } s$, $r_1 = r_0 \bmod s$.

$t_f = q_1 - (t - t_L + 1)\,S$

$s_f = r_1 - (s_L + 1)$.

99. **Circular doubly linked list :** Advantage of a two-way list and a circular header list may be combined into a two-way circular header list. The list is circular because the two end nodes point back to the header node.

100. Conditional expansion facility of macro procesors is provided to expand certain model statements depending upon the value of a condition during the process of macro expansion.

101. $7.5 \times 8 = 60$

102. Start bit. Used in RS - 232 for synchronise receiver for receiving every byte.

103. (*a*) DMA I/O → Date is transfer between disk and I/O without involving CPU.

(*b*) Cache → Cache is fastest memory. It is situated between RAM and CPU. In cache, copy of data from main memory is stored in this cache memory for fastest execution.

(*c*) Interrupt → Due to interrupt, I/O is affected, or due to I/O interrupt occur.

(*d*) ALU is a part of condition code register.

104. It depends on log N.

105. Given expression is

$(a * b) *c$ op.

can be evaluated on a CPU with single register without storing the value of $(a * b)$ if '*op*' is '+' or '*'

If *op* is '+', then expression $(a*b)\,c + K$ will execute without storing the value because * precedence is greater than +.

In other case, if *op* is *, the expression $(a * b) * c * K$ is also execution without storing, because processing of any expression is from left to right.

In third case if we take ↑, then the expression $(a * b) * c \uparrow K$, here ( ) precedence is most but ↑ precedence is greater than *, so, first $(a \times b)$ value stored, then calculate $c \uparrow K$, then $(a \times b) * (c \uparrow K)$ be proceed. It violate the condition of CPU. So *op* is '+' or '*'

106. MVI A, 55 H → Load 55 H in Accumulator A

MVIC, 25 H → Load immediate 25 H in register C

ADD C → Add the contents of register C with accumulator.

55 H	0101	0101		
25 H	0010	0101		
7CH	0111	1010	=	7AH

DAA → Decimal Adjust Acumulator

(*a*) If the value of the low order four bits ($D_3 - D_0$) in the accumulator is greater than, or if the AC flag is set, the instruction add 6 (06) to the low order four bits.

(*b*) If the value of the high order four bits ($D_7 - D_4$) in the accumulator greater than, or if the carry flag is set, the instruction adds 6 (60) to the high order four bits.

In 7 CH, lower four bits greater than 9, so add 06 in lower bit

So, 0111	1010	=	7CH
0000	0110	=	06H
1000	0000	=	80H

107. Micro instruction. Each word (i) control memory contains within it a micro instruction. The micro instruction specifies one or more micro operations for the system. A sequence of micro instruction constitutes micro program.

The minimum number of bits = 27

n = number of micro operation

it $n = 3$ (for minimum), so

minimum number of bits = 2^3 = **8**

108. (*a*)

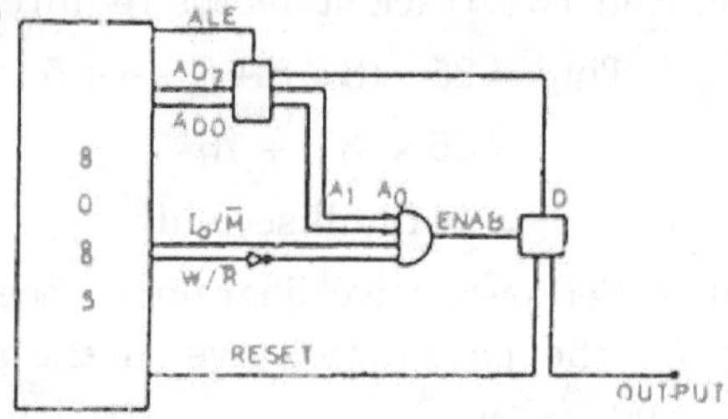

(*b*) BEG : OUT 0, OFF

NOP

NOP

NOP

OUT 4, FF

J BEG

16	60	12
	3	3
	0	

= 3 CH

109. Chained Hash table. In chained hash table, comparison to open addressing scheme is easier in case of deletion.

110. Relative Address Mode. In this mode the content of the program counter added to the address part of the instruction in order to obtain the effective address. The address part of the instruction is usually a signed number (in 2's complement representation) which can be either positive or negative when this number is added to the content of the program counter, the result produces an effective address whose position in memory is relative to the address of next instruction.

111. For ROM total number of address lines and data lines, each are 16.

$$\text{Memory} = 2^{16} = 64K$$

$$\text{ROM size} = 64K \times 16$$

112. RET—Return from subroutine unconditionally.

The program sequence is transferred from the subroutine to the calling program. The two bytes from the top of stack are copied into the program counter and the program execution begins at the new address. The instruction is equivalent to POP program counter.

113. Daisy Chain Scheme. When device A has a cable that plugs into device B has a cable that plugs into device C and device C plugs into a port on the computer, this arrangement is called a Daisy Chain. It usually operates as a bus.

115. (*a*) The program is an infinite loop (of three statements out θθH, INRA and PCHL) and is outputting a sequence of numbers.

ϕ 1, 2 ...., 255, ϕ, 1, ... at port ϕ ϕ H. During each iteration it outputs one number

(*b*) Let three least significant bibs (Isbs) of port ϕϕH be X_0, X_1 and X_2.

The corresponding waveforms are :

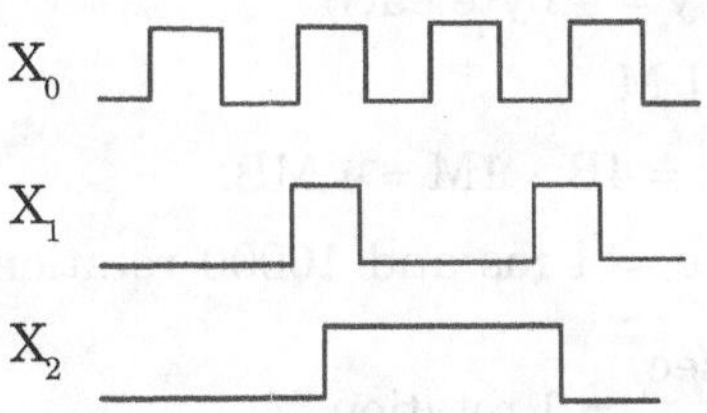

116. Procedure graph for the program is

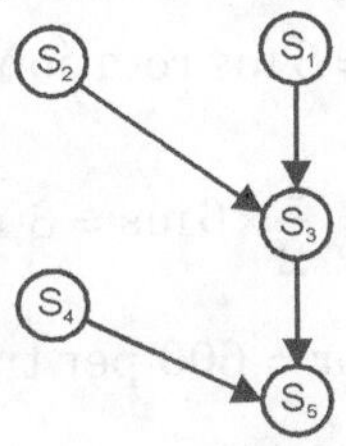

In-degree of S_1, S_2 and $S_4 = 0$

In-degree of S_3, $S_5 = 2$

117. Interval between two DMA transfer

$$= \frac{4 \text{ kBytes}}{2000 \text{ kBytes / sec}}$$

$$= \frac{4 \times 2^{10}}{2000 \times 2^{10}} = 2 \times 10^{-3} \text{ sec.}$$

Number of processor cycles/DMA transfer

= 1000 + 500 = 1500 clock cycles.

Number of processor cycles used for DMA handling/second

$$= \frac{1500}{2 \times 10^{-3}}$$

$$= 750 \times 103 \text{ clocks / second}$$

Fraction of processor time consumed for DMA handlings

$$= \frac{750 \times 10^3}{50 \times 10^6} = 1.5 \times 10^{-2} \text{ or } 1.5\%$$

118. (*a*) Average access time = $\sum_{t=1}^{3} (1\Sigma\eta_{i-1})ti$

From this formula, size of level 1 = 16 kbytes, Size of level 2 = 64 M Bytes

(*b*) Average access time

= 50 + 0.1 × 200 + 0.005 × 5000 = 95 nsec

119. AND immediate with accumulator (ANI). The contents of the accumulator are logically Anded with 8 bit data (operand) and results are placed in accumulator.

120. Stalck works on the principle of last in first out 6-as is (LIFO)

121. The interrupting source supplies the branch information to the processor through an interrupt vector.

122. Cache memory is placed between main memory and CPU.

123. **XCHG :** Exchange H and L with D and E, the contents of register H are exchanged with the contents of register E.

DADH : Add register pair to H and L. Register the 16 bits contents of the specified register pair are added to the contents of the HL register and the sum is saved in the HL register.

124. It is given that the memory is 4K × 16.

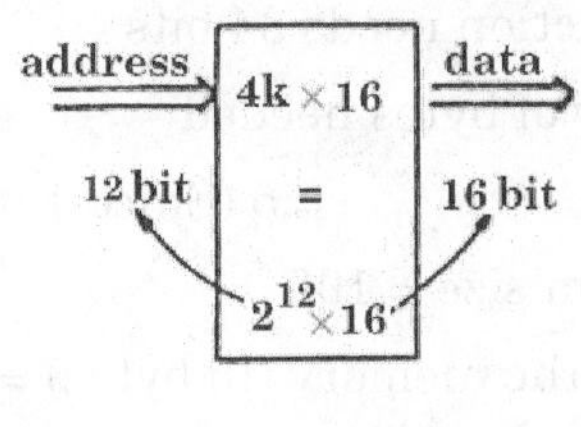

Memory

That is it has 4 words and 16 bits per word.

4K words = 4×2^{10} words = 2^{12} words.

Hence it requires 12 bit address line and 16 bit data line.

125. Virtual memory. Virtual memory is a technique, where program is larger than physical memory that time virtual memory is used for execution for the program.

126. Number of word blocks

$$= \frac{\text{total computer system word}}{\text{64 words per block}}$$

$$= \frac{2^2 \times 2^{10}}{2^6} = 2^6$$

$\therefore$ Number of sets = 2

NUMERICAL TYPE QUESTIONS

1. $\frac{2^{30+2}}{2} = 2^{31}$

So 31 bits required.

2. Data Count Register of DMA controller = 16-bits

Count Value = 2^{16} = 64 KB

Number of controls to transfer = 29154 K

456 times System Bus control is needed.

4. ← 32 bits →

Operation	A_1	A_2	Operand
$\log_2^{40}$	$\log_2^{24}$	$\log_2^{24}$	
6	5	5	xxx

$\therefore$ 32 – 16 = 16

So, the number of bits available for the immediate operand field is 16.

5. According to question

One instruction needs 34 bits

So number of bytes needed

= 5 (Since 1 byte = 8 bits)

$\therefore$ Program size = 100

$\therefore$ Size of the memory (in bytes) = 500

So the amount of memory consumed by the program text is 500 bytes.

6.

cache

Tag	2^{19} Bytes

← 40 bits →

Final Tag

Tag	3	2^{16} Bytes

← 40 bits →

It uses 8 way set associative

$\therefore$ Tag size = 24 bits.

So the width of the tag field is 24 bits.

7. From question

Stage 1 (t_1)	Stage 2 (t_2)	Stage 3 (t_3)
$(3/4)t_2$	$1t_2$	$(3/8)t_2$

Old pipeline Clock frequency is 3GHz if time is t_2.

Stage 1 (t_1)	Stage 21(t_{21})	Stage 22(t_{22})	Stage 3(t_3)
$(3/4)t_2$	$(t_2/2)$	$(t_2/2)$	$(3/8)t_2$

Clock frequency of new pipeline with time

$(3/4)t_2 \rightarrow \frac{4}{3} \times 3$ GHz = 4 GHz

So, the new frequency is 4 GHz.

8. Logical Address = 32 bits

Page size = 4 kilobyte

Page table entry = 4 byte each

No. of pages = 1 M

Page Table size = 4B × 1M = 4 MB.

9. Given seek time = 4 ms and 10000 rotation per minute i.e. $\frac{60\,\text{sec}}{10000}$ = 1 rotation

$\Rightarrow$ 1 rotation = 6 ms rotation latency

$= \frac{1}{2} \times 6\,\text{ms} = 3$ ms

No. of sector = 600 per track,

1 sector = $\frac{6\,\text{ms}}{600}$ = 0.01 ms

2000 sector = 2000 × 0.01 = 20 ms.

Total time required = (2000 × (4 + 3)) + 20

= 14020 ms

10. 3.2

11. Average access time can be calculated as

0.8 × 5 + 0.2 × 50 = 14ns

12. ← 40 bits →

22	5	13
TAG	SET OFFSET	WORD OFFSET

Then TAG bits are 22

13. 15000 rotation in 1 minute

$$1 \text{ rotation} = \frac{1}{15000} \text{ or } \frac{60\,\text{sec}}{1500} = 4 \text{ ms.}$$

$$\text{rotational delay} = \frac{1}{2} \times 4 = 2 \text{ ms}$$

Seek time = 2 × 2 = 4 ms

transfer time = 0.1 ms.

Average time = 4 + 2 + 0.1 = 6.1ms

14. Page size = 8 KB

PAS = 32 bits

$$\text{Number of frames} = \frac{2^{32}}{2^{13}} = 2^{19} \text{ frames}$$

One entry require 24 bits

Page Table size = $n \times e$

$$24 \times 2^{20} \times 3 = n \times 24$$

$$n = 2^{23} \text{ pages}$$

Then length of virtual Address is

23 + 13 = 36 bits

15.

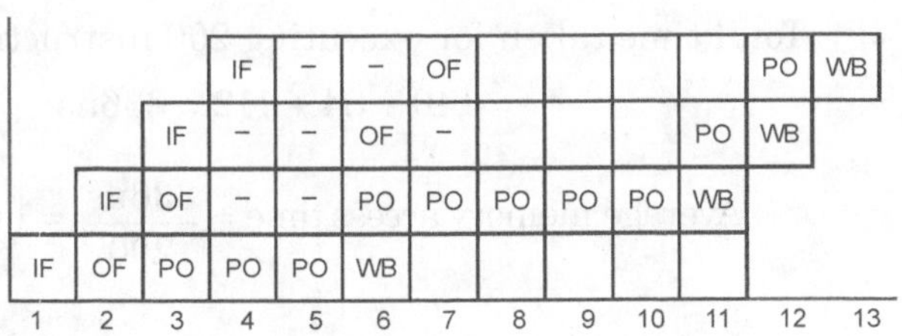

Total clock cycle require = 13

16. 1 Word = 32 bits

Each instruction has 32 bits

To support 45 instructions, opcode must contain 6-bits

Register operand1 requires 6 bits, since the total registers are 64.

Register operand 2 also requires 6 bits

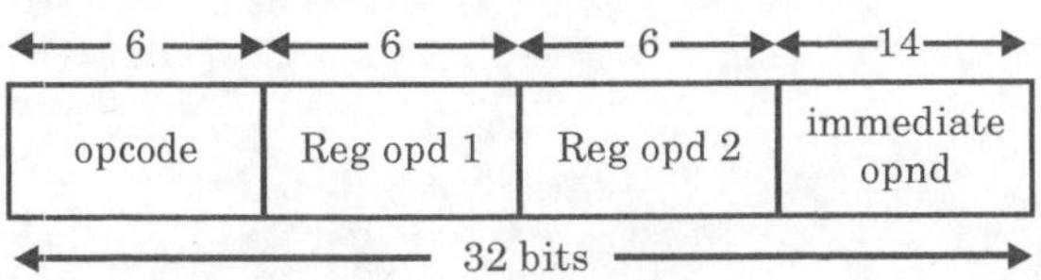

14-bits are left over for immediate Operand Using 14-bits, we can give maximum 16383, Since 2^{14} =16384 from 0 to 16383.

17.

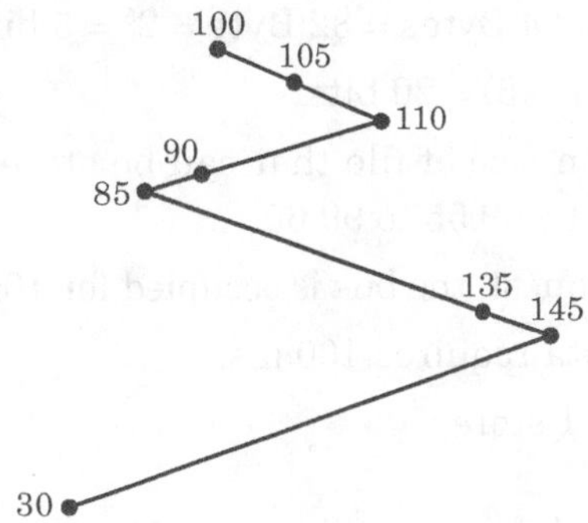

Request for cylinder is served after serving 3 requests (100, 105 and 110)

18. For 6 stages, non-pipelining takes 6 cycles

There were 2 stall cycles for pipelining for 25% of the instructions

$$\text{So pipe line time} = \left(1 + \frac{25}{100} 2\right) = \frac{3}{2} = 1.5$$

$$\text{Speed up} = \frac{\text{Non–pipeline time}}{\text{Pipeline time}} = \frac{6}{1.5} = 4$$

19. $1 \text{ cycle time for } p_1 = \frac{10^9}{1\text{GH}} = 1\text{n.s}$

Assume p_1 takes 5 cycles for a program then p_2 takes 20% more, means, 6 cycles.

p_2 Takes 25% less time, means, if p_1 takes 5 n.s, then p_2 takes 3.75 n.s.

Assume p_2 clock frequency is x GHz.

$$p_2 \text{ taken 6 cycles, so } \frac{6 \times 10^9}{x\,\text{GH}} = 3.75, x = 1.6$$

20. Physical address size = 32 bits

Cache size = 16k bytes = 2^{14} Bytes

block size = 8 words = 8 × 4 Byte = 32 Bytes

(where each word = b Bytes)

$$\text{No. of blocks} = \frac{2^{14}}{2^5} = 2^9$$

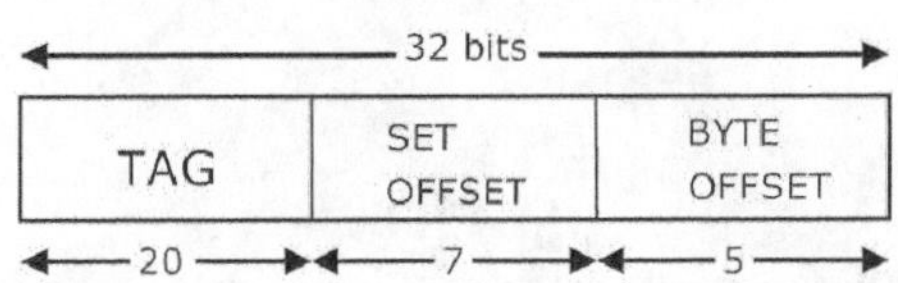

block offset = 9^{bits}

$$\text{No. of sets} = \frac{2^9}{4} = 2^7$$

set offset = 7 bits

Byte offset 8 × 4 Bytes = 32 Byte = 2^5 = 5 bits

TAG = 32 – (7 + 5) = 20 bits.

21. The maximum size of file that can be stored on this disk will be 99.55 to 99.65.

22. Each write request, the bus is occupied for 100 n.s

Storing of data requires 100 n.s.

In 100 n.s. – 1 store

$$\frac{100}{10^6} \text{ n.s.} = 1\text{store}$$

$$1 \text{ m.s.} = \frac{10^6}{100} \text{ stores} = 10000 \text{ stores.}$$

23. $T_{ave} = H_1 \times (T_{TLB} + T_M) + (1 - H_1) \times (T_{TLB} + 2 \times T_M)$

T_{TLB} = time to search in TLB = 10 ms

T_M = time to access physical memory = 30 ms

H_1 = TLB hit ratio = 0.6

$T_{ave} = 0.6 \times (10 + 80) + (1 - 0.6)\ (10 + 2 \times 80)$

$T_{ave} = 0.6 \times 90\text{ms} + 0.4(170)$ ms

$T_{ave} = 54\text{ms} + 68 \text{ ms} = 122\text{ms}$

24.

	No. of stage	Stall cycle	Stall Frequency	Clock period	Average access time
Old design	5	2	20%	2.2ns	P
New design	8	5	20%	1 ns	Q

$$P = \left[80\%(1\text{clock}) + 20\%\left(\underset{\text{Completion}}{1} + \underset{\text{stall clock}}{2}\right)\right] \times T_{c-p}$$

P = (.8 + .6) × 2.2ns = 3.08ns

$$Q = \left[80\%(1\text{clock}) + 20\%\left(\underset{\text{Completion}}{1} + \underset{\text{stall clock}}{5}\right)\right] \times T_{c-p}$$

P =(.8 +.12) × 1ns = 2ns

$$\text{So the value of } \frac{P}{Q} = \frac{3.08\text{ns}}{2 \text{ ns}} = 1.54$$

25. Total instruction

$$= \begin{matrix}\text{100 instruction} \\ \text{fetch operation}\end{matrix} + \begin{matrix}\text{60memory} \\ \text{operand read} \\ \text{operation}\end{matrix} + \begin{matrix}\text{40memory} \\ \text{operand write op}\end{matrix}$$

= 200 instructions (operations)

Time taken for fetching 100 instructions (equivalent to read) = 90 * 1ns + 10*5ns =140ns

Memory operand Read operations

= 90% (60)* 1ns + 10% (60)× 5ns

= 54ns + 30 ns = 84 ms

Memory operand write operation time = 90%(40)* 2ns + 10% (40)*10ns

= 72ns + 40 ns = 112 ns

Total time taken for executing 200 instructions

= 140 + 84 + 112 = 336ns

$$\therefore \text{ Average memory access time} = \frac{336\text{ns}}{200} = 1.68 \text{ ns}$$

■■

3 CHAPTER Data Structures and Algorithms

MCQ TYPE QUESTIONS

2016

1. Consider the following C program.

```
void f(int,short);
void main()
{
    int i = 100;
    short s = 12;
    short *p = &s;
    __________ ;   // call to f ()
}
```

Which one of the following expressions, when placed in the blank above, will NOT result in a type checking error?

(*a*) f(s,*s) (*b*) i = f (i, s)

(*c*) f (i, *s) (*d*) f (i, *p)

2. Let G be a weighted connected undirected graph with distinct positive edge weights. If every edge weight is increased by the same value, then which of the following statements is/are **TRUE**?

P : Minimum spanning tree of G does not change

Q : Shortest path between any pair of vertices does not change

(*a*) P only

(*b*) Q only

(*c*) Neither P nor Q

(*d*) Both P and Q

3. The following function computes the maximum value contained in an integer array p [ ] of size n (n >= 1) .

```
int max (int *p, int n) {
    int a=0, b=n-1;
    while (_______) {
        if (p[a] <= p[b])    { a = a+1; }
        else                 {b = b –1; }
    }
    return p[a];
}
```

The missing loop condition is

(*a*) a ! = n (*b*) b ! = 0

(*c*) b > (a + 1) (*d*) b ! = a

4. What will be the output of the following C program?

```
void count (int n) {
    static int d=1;
    printf (“%d” n) ;
    printf (“%d” d) ;
    d++;
    if (n>l) count (n-1) ;
    printf (“%d” d) ;
}
void main () {
    count (3) ;
}
```

(*a*) 3 1 2 2 1 3 4 4 4 (*b*) 3 1 2 1 1 1 2 2 2

(*c*) 3 1 2 2 1 3 4 (*d*) 3 1 2 1 1 1 2

5. What will be the output of the following pseudo-code when parameters are passed by reference and dynamic scoping is assumed?

```
a=3;
void n (x) {x = x * a; print (x) ;}
void m (y) {a = 1; a = y - a; n (a) ; print (a) ;}
void main () {m (a) ; }
```

(*a*) 6, 2 (*b*) 6, 6

(*c*) 4, 2 (*d*) 4, 4

6. G = (V, E) is an undirected simple graph in which each edge has a distinct weight, and e is a particular edge of G. Which of the following statements about the minimum spanning trees (MSTs) of G is/are **TRUE**?

I. If *e* is the lightest edge of <u>some</u> cycle in G, then every MST of G <u>includes</u> *e*

II. If *e* is the heaviest edge of <u>some</u> cycle in G, then every MST of G <u>excludes</u> *e*

(*a*) I only (*b*) II only

(*c*) both I and II (*d*) neither I nor II

7. B+ Trees are considered BALANCED because

(*a*) the lengths of the paths from the root to all leaf nodes are all equal.

(*b*) the lengths of the paths from the root to all leaf nodes differ from each other by at most 1.

(*c*) the number of children of any two non-leaf sibling nodes differ by at most 1.

(*d*) the number of records in any two leaf nodes differ by at most 1.

8. The following function computes X^Y for positive integers X and Y.

```
int exp(int X, int Y) {
    int res = 1, a = X, b = Y;
while ( b != 0 ){
if ( b%2 == 0) { a = a*a; b = b/2;}
else         { res = res*a; b = b-1;
}
}
return res;
}
```

Which one of the following conditions is TRUE before every iteration of the loop?

(*a*) $X^Y = a^b$

(*b*) $(res * a)^Y = (res * X)^b$

(*c*) $X^Y = res * a^b$

(*d*) $X^Y = (res * a)^b$

9. Consider the following *New-order* strategy for traversing a binary tree:

- Visit the root;
- Visit the right subtree using *New-order;*
- Visit the left subtree using *New-order;*

The New-order traversal of the expression tree corresponding to the reverse polish expression 3 4 ∗ 5 – 2 ^ 6 7 ∗ 1 + – is given by:

(*a*) + – 1 6 7 ∗ 2 ^ 5 – 3 4 ∗

(*b*) – + 1 ∗ 6 7 ^ 2 – 5 ∗ 3 4

(*c*) – + 1 ∗ 7 6 ^ 2 – 5 ∗ 4 3

(*d*) 1 7 6 ∗ + 2 5 4 3 ∗ – ^ –

10. A queue is implemented using an array such that ENQUEUE and DEQUEUE operations are performed efficiently. Which one of the following statements is **CORRECT** (*n* refers to the number of items in the queue) ?

(*a*) Both operations can be performed in O(1) time

(*b*) At most one operation can be performed in O(1) time but the worst case time for the other operation will be $\Omega(n)$

(*c*) The worst case time complexity for both operations will be $\Omega(n)$

(*d*) Worst case time complexity for both operations will be $\Omega(\log n)$

11. The worst case running times of *Insertion sort, Merge sort and Quick sort*, respectively, are:

(*a*) $\Theta(n \log n)$, $\Theta(n \log n)$, and $\Theta(n^2)$

(*b*) $\Theta(n^2)$, $\Theta(n^2)$, and $\Theta(n \log n)$

(*c*) $\Theta(n^2)$, $\Theta(n \log n)$, and $\Theta(n \log n)$

(*d*) $\Theta(n^2)$, $\Theta(n \log n)$, and $\Theta(n^2)$

12. An operator delete (*i*) for a binary heap data structure is to be designed to delete the item in the *i*-th node. Assume that the heap is implemented in an array and *i* refers to the *i*-th index of the array. If the heap tree has depth *d* (number of edges on the path from the root to the farthest leaf) , then what is the time complexity to re-fix the heap efficiently after the removal of the element?

(*a*) O(1)　　(*b*) O(*d*) but not O(1)

(*c*) $O(2^d)$ but not O(*d*)　　(*d*) $O(d2^d)$ but not $O(2^d)$

13. Assume that the algorithms considered here sort the input sequences in ascending order. If the input is already in ascending order, which of the following are TRUE?

I. Quicksort runs in $\Theta(n^2)$ time

II. Bubblesort runs in $\Theta(n^2)$ time

III. Mergesort runs in $\Theta(n)$ time

IV. Insertion sort runs in $\Theta(n)$ time

(*a*) I and II only　　(*b*) I and III only

(*c*) II and IV only　　(*d*) I and IV only

14. The Floyd-Warshall algorithm for all-pair shortest paths computation is based on

(*a*) Greedy paradigm

(*b*) Divide-and-Conquer paradigm.

(*c*) Dynamic Programming paradigm.

(*d*) neither Greedy nor Divide-and-Conquer nor Dynamic Programming paradigm.

15. N items are stored in a sorted doubly linked list. For a delete operation, a pointer is provided to the record to be deleted. For a *decrease-key* operation, a pointer is provided to the record on which the operation is to be performed.

An algorithm performs the following operations on the list in this order: Θ(N) delete, O(logN) insert, O(logN) find, and Θ(N) decrease-key. What is the time complexity of all these operations put together?

(*a*) $O(\log^2 N)$　　(*b*) O(N)

(*c*) $O(N^2)$　　(*d*) $\Theta(N^2 \log N)$

16. In an adjacency list representation of an undirected simple graph G = (V,E), each edge (u, v) has two adjacency list entries: [v] in the adjacency list of u, and [u] in the adjacency list of v. These are called twins of each other. A twin pointer is a pointer from an adjacency list entry to its twin. If |E| = m and |V| = n, and the memory size is not a constraint, what is the time complexity of the most efficient algorithm to set the twin pointer in each entry in each adjacency list?

(*a*) $\Theta(n^2)$ (*b*) $\Theta(n + m)$

(*c*) $\Theta(m^2)$ (*d*) $\Theta(n^4)$

2015

17. The height of a tree is the length of the longest root-to-leaf path in it. The maximum and minimum number of nodes in a binary tree of height 5 are

(*a*) 63 and 6, respectively

(*b*) 64 and 5, respectively

(*c*) 32 and 6, respectively

(*d*) 31 and 5, respectively

18. Which of the following is/are correct inorder traversal sequence(s) of binary search tree(s)?

I. 3, 5, 7, 8, 15, 19, 25

II. 5, 8, 9, 12, 10, 15, 25

III. 2, 7, 10, 8, 14, 16, 20

IV. 4, 6, 7, 9, 18, 20, 25

(*a*) I and IV only

(*b*) II and III only

(*c*) II and IV only

(*d*) II only

19. Consider the following pseudo code, where *x* and *y* are positive integers.

```
begin
    q: = 0
    r : = x
    while r ≥ y do
    being
        r : = r – y
        q : = q + 1
    end
end
```

The post condition that needs to be satisfied after the program terminates is

(*a*) $\{r = qx + y \wedge r < y\}$

(*b*) $\{x = qy + r \wedge r < y\}$

(*c*) $\{y = qx + r \wedge 0 < r < y\}$

(*d*) $\{q + 1 < r - y \wedge y > 0\}$

20. What is the output of the following C code? Assume that the address of *x* is 2000 (in decimal) and an integer requires four bytes of memory ?

```
int main( )
{
    unsigened int x[4] [3] = {(1,2,3),
    {4,5,6}, {7, 8, 9}, {10, 11, 12}};
    printf("%u, %u, %u", x + 3, *(x + 3),
        *(x + 2) + 3);
}
```

(*a*) 2036, 2036, 2036 (*b*) 2012, 4, 2204

(*c*) 2036, 10, 10 (*d*) 2012, 4, 6

21. Consider the following C function.

```
int fun1 (int n)
{
int i, j, k, p, q = 0;
for (i = 1; i < n; ++i)
{
    p = 0;
    for(j = n; j > 1; j = j/2)
    ++p;
    for(k =1; k < p; k = k*2)
    ++q;
}
    return q;
}
```

Which one of the following most closely approximates the return value of the function fun1 ?

(*a*) n^3 (*b*) $n (\log n)^2$

(*c*) $n \log n$ (*d*) $n \log (\log n)$

22. Consider the following function written the C programming language.

```
void foo (char * a) {
    if (*a & & * a ! = ' ')
        putchar (*a);
    }
}
```

The output of the above function on input "ABCD EFGH" is

(*a*) ABCD EFGH (*b*) ABCD

(*c*) HGFE DCBA (*d*) DCBA

23. In a connected graph, a bridge is an edge whose removal disconnects a graph. Which one of the following statements is true?

(*a*) A tree has no bridges

(*b*) A bridge cannot be part of a simple cycle

(*c*) Every edge of a clique with size ≥ 3 is a bridge (A clique is any compete sub graph of a graph)

(*d*) A graph with bridges cannot have a cycle

24. Suppose you are provided with the following function declaration in the C programming language

int partition (int a [ ], int n);

The function treats the first element of a [ ] as a pivot, and rearranges the array so that all elements less than or equal to the pivot is in the left part of the array , and all elements greater than the pivot is in the right part. In addition, it moves the pivot so that the pivot is the last elements of the left part. The return value is the number of elements in the left part.

The following partially given function in the C programming language is used to find the Kth smallest element in an array a [ ] of size n using the partition function We assume k ≤ n.

```
int kth _ smallest (int a [ ], int n, int k)
{
int left _ end partition (a, n);
if (left _ end + 1 == k){
    return a[left _ end];
}
if (left _ end + 1 > k){
    return kth _ smallest (_______);
} else {
return kth_smallest (_______);
}
}
```

The missing argument lists are respectively

(*a*) (a, left _ end,k) and (a + left _ end +1, n – left _ end – 1, k – left _ end – 1)

(*b*) (a, left end,k) and (a, n – left _ end –1, k – left _ end –1)

(*c*) (a + left _ end + 1, n – left end –1, k – left _ end – 1) and (a, left _ end, k)

(*d*) (a, n – left_ end – 1, k – left _ end – 1) and (a, left _ end,k)

25. A graph is self-complementary if it is isomorphic to its complement For all selfcomplementary graphs on *n* vertices, *n* is

(*a*) A multiple of 4

(*b*) Even

(*c*) Odd

(*d*) Congruent to 0 mod 4, or, 1 mod 4

26. The secant method is used to find the root of an equation $f(x) = 0$. It is started from two distinct estimates, x_a and x_b for the root. It is an iterative procedure involving linear interpolation to a root. The iteration stops if $f(x_b)$ is very small and then x_b is the solution. The procedure is given below. Observe that there is an expression which is missing and is marked by? Which is the suitable expression that is to be put in place of ? so that it follows all steps of the secant method?

```
Secant
Initialize : xa, xb, ε, N    // ε = convergence indicator
                             // N=maximum no. of iterations
fb = –f(xb)
i = 0
While (i < N and |fb| > (ε)do
    i = i + 1                // update counter
    x1 = ?                   // missing expression for
    xa = xb                  // intermediate value
                             // rest xa
    xb = xt                  // rest xb
    fb = f(xb)               // function value at new xb
end while
if |fb| > ε then             // loop is terminated with
                                i = N
write "Non-convergence"
else
    Write 'Non-convergence"
Else
Write "return xb"
End if
```

(*a*) $x_b - (f_b - f(x_a))\, f_b/(x_b - x_a)$

(*b*) $x_a - (f_b - f(x_a))\, f_a/(x_b - x_a)$

(*c*) $x_b - (x_b - x_a)\, f_b/(f_b - f(x_a))$

(*d*) $x_a - (x_b - x_a)\, f_a/(f_b - f(x_a))$

27. Consider the following C program segment.

```
#include < stdio.h >
int main ( )
{
    char sl [7] = "1234",*p;
    p sl + 2;
    *p = '0';
    print f("%s",sl)
{
```

What will be printed by the program ?

(*a*) 12 (*b*) 120400

(*c*) 1204 (*d*) 1034

28. The result evaluating the postfix expression 105 + 60 6 / *8 – is

(*a*) 284 (*b*) 213

(*c*) 142 (*d*) 71

29. Consider three software items: Program – X, Control Flow Diagram of Program-Y and Control Flow Diagram of Program – Z as shown below

Program – X :

```
Sumcal(int max int, int value)
{
    int result 0, i = 0;
    if (value < 0)
```

```
        {
            value = – value;
        }
        while((i < value) AND (result
    < = max int))
        {
            i = i + 1;
            result = result + 1;
        }
        if (result < = max int)
        {
            pr int f(result);
        }
        else
        {
            pr int f(" l arg e ");
        }
            pr int f(" end of program") '
    }
```

Control Flow Diagram of Program – Y :

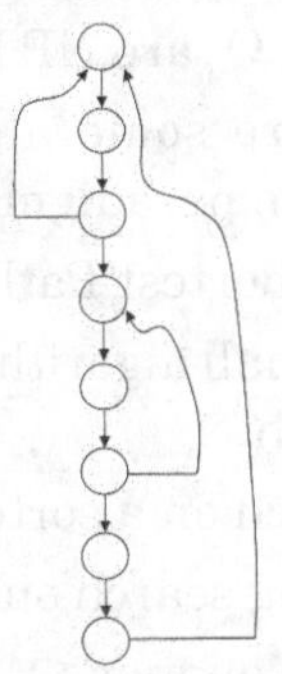

Control Flow Diagram of Program – Z :

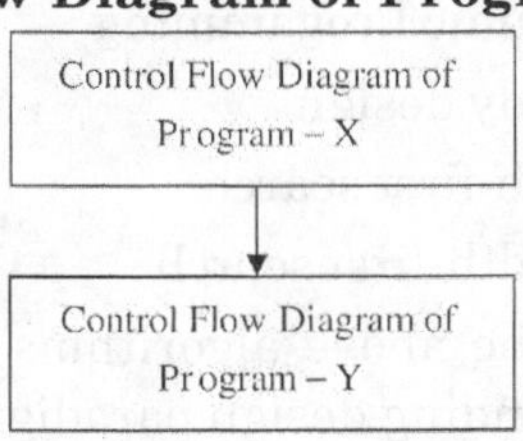

The values of McCabe's Cyclomatic complexity of Program – X, Program-Y, and Program-Z respectively are

(*a*) 4, 4, 7 (*b*) 3, 4, 7

(*c*) 4, 4, 8 (*d*) 4, 3, 8

30. Consider the following recursive C function.

```
Void get (int n)
{
    if (n < 1) return;
    get (n – 1)
    get (n – 3);
    print f("% d", n);
}
```

If get (6) function is being called in main () then how many times will the get () function be invoked before returning to the main ( ) ?

(*a*) 15 (*b*) 25

(*c*) 35 (*d*) 45

31. Consider the following two C code segments. Y and X are one and two dimensional arrays of size n and $n \times n$ respectively, where $2 \le n \le 10$. Assume that in both code segments, elements of Y are initialized to 0 and each element X[i] [j] of array X is initialized to $i + j$. Further assume that when stored in main memory all elements of X are in same memory page frame.

Code Segment 1:

```
//initialize elements of y to 0
//initialize elements X[i][j] of x to i + j
    for (i = 0; i < n; i++)
    Y[i] + = X[0][i];
```

Code Segment 2:

```
//initialize elements of Y to 0
//initialize elements X[i][j] of X to i + j
    for (i = 0; i < n; i++)
    Y[i] + = X[i][0];
```

Which of the following statements is/are correct?

S1 : Final contents of array Y will be same in both code segments

S2 : Elements of array X accessed inside the for loop shown in code segment 1 are contiguous in main memory

S3 : Elements of array X accessed inside the for loop shown in code segment 2 are contiguous in main memory

(*a*) Only S2 is correct

(*b*) Only S3 is correct

(*c*) Only S1 and S2 are correct

(*d*) Only S1 and S3 are correct

32. Match the following :

P : Prim's algorithm for minimum spanning tree

Q : Floyd – Warshal algorithm for all pairs shortest paths

R : Mergesort

S : Hamiltonian circuit

(I) Backtracking

(II) Greedy method

(III) Dynamic programming

(IV) Divide and conquer

(*a*) P-III, Q-II, R-IV, S-I

(*b*) P-I, Q-II, R-IV, S-III

(*c*) P-II, Q-III, R-IV, S-I

(*d*) P-II, Q-I, R-III, S-IV

33. Which one of the following is the recurrence equation for the worst case time complexity of the Quicksort algorithm for sorting n (≥ 2) numbers ? In the recurrence equations given in the options below, c is a constant.

(a) $T(n) = 2T(9n/2) + cn$

(b) $T(n) = T(n - 1) + T(1) + cn$

(c) $T(n) = 2T(n - 1) + cn$

(d) $T(n) = T(n/2) + cn$

34. What are the worst-case complexities of insertion and deletion of a key in a binary search tree ?

(a) $\theta(\log n)$ for both insertion and deletion

(b) $\theta(n)$ for both insertion and deletion

(c) $\theta(n)$ for insertion and $\theta(\log n)$ for deletion

(d) $\theta(\log n)$ for insertion and $\theta(n)$ for deletion

35. Let G = (V, E) be a simple undirected graph, and s be a particular vertex in it called the source. For $x \in V$, let $d(x)$ denote the shortest distance in G from s to x. A breadth first search (BFS) is performed starting at s. Let T be resultant BFS tree. If (u, v) is an edge of G that is not in T, then which one of the following CANNOT be the value of $d(u) - d(v)$?

(a) – 1 (b) 0

(c) 1 (d) 2

36. Consider a max heap, represented by the array : 40, 30, 20, 10, 15, 16, 17, 8, 4.

Array Index	1	2	3	4	5	6	7	8	9
Value	40	30	20	10	15	16	17	8	4

Now consider that a value 35 is inserted into this heap. After insertion, the new heap is

(a) 40, 30, 20, 10, 15, 16, 17, 8, 4, 35

(b) 40, 35, 20, 10, 30, 16, 17, 8, 4, 15

(c) 40, 30, 20, 10, 35, 16, 17, 8, 4, 15

(d) 40, 35, 20, 10, 15, 16, 17, 8, 4, 30

37. An algorithm performs $(\log N)^{1/2}$ find operations, N insert operations, $(\log N)^{1/2}$ delete operations, and $(\log N)^{1/2}$ decreasekey operations on a set of data items with keys drawn form a linearly ordered set. For a delete operation, a pointer is provided to the record that must be deleted. For the decrease-key operation, a pointer is provided to the record that has its key decreased. Which one of the following data structures is the most suited for the algorithm to use, if the goal is to achieve the best asymptotic complexity considering all the operations?

(a) Unsorted array

(b) Min–heap

(c) Sorted array

(d) Sorted doubly linked list

38. An unordered list contain n distinct elements. The number of comparisons to find an element in this list that is neither maximum nor minimum is

(a) $\Theta(n \log n)$ (b) $\Theta(n)$

(c) $\Theta(\log n)$ (d) $\Theta(1)$

39. Consider a complete binary tree where the left and the right subtrees of the root are maxheaps. The lower bound for the number of operations to convert the tree to a heap is

(a) $\Omega(\log n)$ (b) $\Omega(n)$

(c) $\Omega(n \log n)$ (d) $\Omega(n^2)$

40. Consider two decision problems Q_1, Q_2 such that Q1 reduces in polynomial time to 3-SAT and 3 -SAT reduces in polynomial time to Q_2. Then which one of following is consistent with the above statement?

(a) Q_1 is in NP, Q_2 in NP hard

(b) Q_2 is in NP, Q_1 is NP hard

(c) Both Q_1 and Q_2 are in NP

(d) Both Q_1 and Q_2 are NP hard

41. Given below are some algorithms, and some algorithm design paradigms.

1. Dijkstra's Shortest Path
2. Floyd-Warshall algorithm to compute all pair shortest path
3. Binary search on a sorted array
4. Backtracking search on a graph

i. Divide and Conquer

ii. Dynamic Progamming

iii. Greedy design

iv. Depth-first search

v. Breadth-first search

Match the above algorithms on the left to the corresponding design paradigm they follow.

(a) 1 – i, 2 – iii, 3 – i, 4 – v

(b) 1 – iii, 2 – iii, 3 – i, 4 – v

(c) 1 – iii, 2 – ii, 3 – i, 4 – iv

(d) 1 – iii, 2 – ii, 3 – i, 4 – v

42. Which one of the following hash functions on integers will distribute keys most uniformly over 10 buckets numbered 0 to 9 for i ranging from 0 to 2020?

(a) $h(i) = i^2 \bmod 10$

(b) $h(i) = i^3 \bmod 10$

(c) $h(i) = (11 * i) \bmod 10$

(d) $h(i) = (12 * i) \bmod 10$

43. Consider the following array of elements.

< 89, 19, 50, 17, 12, 15, 2,5, 7, 11, 6, 9, 100 >

The minimum number of interchanges needed to convert it into a max-heap is

(a) 4 (b) 5

(c) 2 (d) 3

44. While inserting the elements 71, 65, 84, 69, 67, 83 in an empty binary search tree (BST) in the sequence shown, the element in the lowest level is

(a) 65 (b) 67

(c) 69 (d) 83

45. Consider the equality $\sum_{i=0}^{n} i^3 = X$ and the following choices for X

I. $\theta(n^4)$ II. $\theta(n^5)$

III. $\theta(n^5)$ IV. $\Omega(n^3)$

The equality above remains correct if X is replaced by

(a) only I

(b) Only II

(c) I or III or IV but not II

(d) II or III or IV but not I

46. Let $f(n) = n$ and $g(n) = n^{(1 + \sin n)}$, + where n is a positive integer. Which of the following statement is/are correct?

I. $f(n) = O(g(n))$

II. $f(n) = \Omega(g(n))$

(a) Only I (b) Only II

(c) Both I and II (d) Neither I nor II

47. Assume that a mergesort algorithm in the worst case takes 30 second for an input of size 64. Which of the following most closely approximates the maximum input size of a problem that can be solved in 6 minutes?

(a) 256 (b) 512

(c) 1024 (d) 2048

48. Language L_1 is polynomial time reducible to language L_2. Language L_3 is polynomial time reducible to L_2, which in turn is polynomial time reducible to language L_4. Which of the following is/are true?

I. if $L_4 \in P$, then $L_2 \in P$

II. if $L_1 \in P$ or $L_3 \in P$, then $L_2 \in P$

III. $L_1 \in P$, if and only if $L_3 \in P$

IV. if $L_4 \in P$, then $L_1 \in P$ and $L_3 \in P$

(a) II only (b) III only

(c) I and IV only (d) I only

2014

49. Let G = (V, E) be a directed graph where V is the set of vertices and E the set of edges. Then which one of the following graphs has the same strongly connected components as G?

(a) $G_1 = (V, E_1)$ where $E_1 = \{(u, v) \mid (u, v) \notin E\}$

(b) $G_2 = (V, E_2)$ where $E_2 = \{(u, v) \mid (v, u) \in$ New income $= 1.20 \times E\}$

(c) $G_3 = (V, E_3)$ where $E_3 = \{(u, v) \mid$ there is a path of length ≤ 2 from u to v in E$\}$

(d) $G_4 = (V_4, E)$ where V_4 is the set of vertices in G which are not isolated

50. Consider the following program in C language:

```
# include < stdio.h >
main ( )
{
    int i;
    int * pi = & i;
    scanf ("%d", pi);
    print f ("%d \ n", i + 5);
}
```

Which one of the following statements is TRUE?

(a) Compilation fails.

(b) Execution results in a run-time error.

(c) On execution, the value printed is **5** more than the address of variable **i**.

(d) On execution, the value printed is **5** more than the integer value entered.

51. Consider the following C function in which size is the number of elements in the array E :

```
int MyX(int *E, unsigned int size)
{
    int Y = 0;
    int Z;
    int i, j, k;
    for(i = 0; i < size; i++)
      Y = Y + E[i];
      for (i = 0; i < size; i++)
      for (j = i; j < size; j++)
      {
        Z = 0;
        f   or (k = i; k <= j; k++)
              Z = Z + E[k];
           if (Z > Y)
              Y = Z;
      }
    return Y;
}
```

The value returned by the function MyX is the

(a) maximum possible sum of elements in any sub-array of array E.
(b) maximum element in any sub-array of array E.
(c) sum of the maximum elements in all possible sub-arrays of array E.
(d) the sum of all the elements in the array E.

52. Consider the following pseudo code. What is the total number of multiplications to be performed?

```
D = 2
    for i = 1 to n do
        for j = i to n do
            for k = j + 1 to n do
                D = D * 3
```

(a) Half of the product of the 3 consecutive integers
(b) One-third of the product of the 3 consecutive integers.
(c) One-sixth of the product of the 3 consecutive integers.
(d) None of the above.

53. An ordered n-tuple $(d_1, d_2, \ldots, d_n)$ with $d_1 \geq d_2 \geq \ldots \geq d_n$ is called *graphic* if there exists a simple undirected graph with n vertices having degrees $d_1, d_2, \ldots, d_n$ respectively. Which of the following 6-tuples is NOT graphic?

(a) (1, 1, 1, 1, 1, 1) (b) (2, 2, 2, 2, 2, 2)
(c) (3, 3, 3, 1, 0, 0) (d) (3, 2, 1, 1, 1, 0)

54. Suppose n and p are unsigned int variables in a C program. We wish to set p to $^nC_3$. If n is large, which one of the following statements is most likely to set p correctly?

(a) p = n * (n – 1) * (n – 2) / 6;
(b) p = n * (n – 1) / 2 * (n – 2) / 3;
(c) p = n * (n – 1) / 3 * (n – 2) / 2;
(d) p = n * (n – 1) * (n – 2) / 6.0;

55. Consider the procedure below for the *Producer-Consumer* problem which uses semaphores:

```
semaphore n = 0;
semaphore s = 1;
void producer()
{
   while(true)
   {
    produce();
    semWait(s);
    addToBuffer();
    semSignal(s);
    semSignal(n);
   }
}
void consumer()
{
   while(true)
   {
    semWait(s);
    semWait(n);
    removeFromBuffer();
    semSignal(s);
    consume();
   }
}
```

Which one of the following is TRUE?

(a) The producer will be able to add an item to the buffer, but the consumer can never consume it.
(b) The consumer will remove no more than one item from the buffer.
(c) Deadlock occurs if the consumer succeeds in acquiring semaphore s when the buffer is empty.
(d) The starting value for the semaphore n must be 1 and not 0 for deadlock-free operation.

56. For a C program accessing `X[i][j][k]`, the following intermediate code is generated by a compiler. Assume that the size of an `integer` is 32 bits and the size of a `character` is 8 bits.

```
t0 = i * 1024
t1 = j * 32
t2 = k * 4
t3 = t1 + t0
t4 = t3 + t2
t5 = X[t4]
```

Which one of the following statements about the source code for the C program is CORRECT?

(a) X is declared as "`int X[32][32][8]`".
(b) X is declared as "`int X[4][1024][32]`".
(c) X is declared as "`char X[4][32][8]`".
(d) X is declared as "`char X[32][16][2]`".

57. Suppose a stack implementation supports an instruction REVERSE, which reverses the order of elements on the stack, in addition to the PUSH and POP instructions. Which one of the following statements is TRUE *with respect to this modified stack*?

(a) A queue cannot be implemented using this stack
(b) A queue can be implemented where ENQUEUE takes a single instruction and DEQUEUE takes a sequence of two instructions

(*c*) A queue can be implemented where ENQUEUE takes a sequence of three instructions and DEQUEUE takes a single instruction

(*d*) A queue can be implemented where both ENQUEUE and DEQUEUE take a single instruction each

58. Consider the C function given below.

```
int f(int j)
{
  static int i = 50;
  int k;
  if (i == j)
   {
     printf("something");
     k = f(i);
     return 0;
    }
  else return 0;
}
```

Which one of the following is TRUE?

(*a*) The function returns 0 for all values of j

(*b*) The function prints the string something for all values of j

(*c*) The function returns 0 when j = 50

(*d*) The function will exhaust the runtime stack or run into an infinite loop when j = 50

59. Consider the following combinational function block involving four Boolean variables x, y, a,b where x, a, b are inputs and y is the output.

```
f(x, y, a, b)
{
   if (x is 1) y = a;
   else y = b;
}
```

Which one of the following digital logic blocks is the most suitable for implementing this function?

(*a*) Full adder (*b*) Priority encoder

(*c*) Multiplexor (*d*) Flip-flop

60. Let A be a square matrix size n × n. Consider the following pseudocode. What is the expected output?

```
C = 100;
for i = 1 to n do
for j = 1 to n do
{
  Temp = A[i][j] + C;
   A[i][j] = A[j][i];
   A[j][i] = Temp – C;
}
for i = 1 to n do
for j = 1 to n do
output (A[i][j]);
```

(*a*) The matrix A itself

(*b*) Transpose of the matrix A

(*c*) Adding 100 to the upper diagonal elements and subtracting 100 from lower diagonal elements of A

(*d*) None of these

61. Consider the following rooted tree with the vertex labeled P as the root :

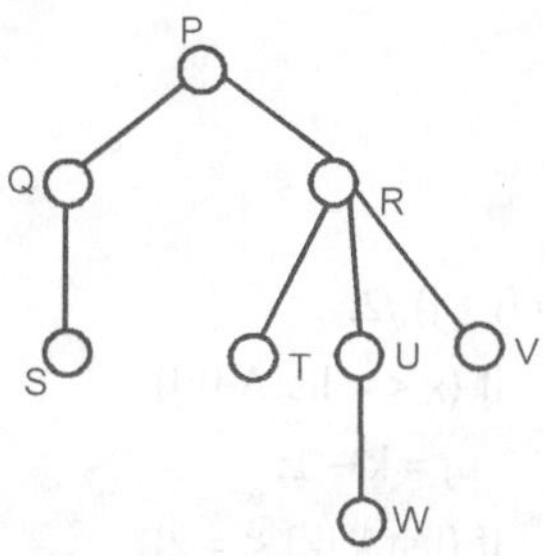

The order in which the nodes are visited during an in-order traversal of the tree is

(*a*) SQPTRWUV

(*b*) SQPTUWRV

(*c*) SQPTWUVR

(*d*) SQPTRUWV

62. Consider the pseudocode given below. The function **Dosomething ( )** takes as argument a pointer to the root of an arbitrary tree represented by the *leftMostChild-rightSibling* representation. Each node of the tree is of type treeNode.

```
typedef struct treeNode* treeptr;
Struct treeNode
{
    Treeptr leftMostchild, rightSibling;
};
Int Dosomething (treeptr tree)
{
   int value =0;
   if (tree ! = NULL) {
      If (tree -> leftMostchild = = NULL)
      value = 1 ;
      else
        value = Dosomething (tree->leftMostchild);
          value = value + Dosometing (tree->rightsibling);
      }
      return (value);
}
```

When the pointer to the root of a tree is passed as the argument to DoSomething, the value returned by the function corresponds to the

(*a*) number of internal nodes in the tree.

(*b*) height of the tree.

(*c*) number of nodes without a right sibling in the tree.

(*d*) number of leaf nodes in the tree.

63. Consider the C function given below. Assume that the array list A contains n (> 0) elements, sorted in ascending order.

```
int ProcessArray (int * listA, int x, int n)
{
    int i, j, k;
    i = 0;
    j = n – 1;
    do {
          k = (i + j) /2;
               if (x < = listA [k])
                    j = k – 1;
               If (listA [k] < = x)
                    i = k + 1;
       } while (i < = j);
          If (listA [k] = = x)
          return (k) ;
          else
          return -1;
}
```

Which one of the following statements about the function ProcessArray is CORRECT?

(*a*) It will run into an infinite loop when x is not in listA.

(*b*) It is an implementation of binary search.

(*c*) It will always find the maximum element in listA.

(*d*) It will return – 1 even when x is present in listA.

64. If G is a forest with n vertices and k connected components, how many edges does G have?

(*a*) $\lfloor n/k \rfloor$ (*b*) $\lceil n/k \rceil$

(*c*) $n - k$ (*d*) $n - k + 1$

65. Let G be a graph with n vertices and m edges. What is the tightest upper bound on the running time of Depth First Search on G, when G is represented as an adjacency matrix?

(*a*) $\Theta(n)$ (*b*) $\Theta(n + m)$

(*c*) $\Theta(n^2)$ (*d*) $\Theta(m^2)$

66. Consider the directed graph given below.

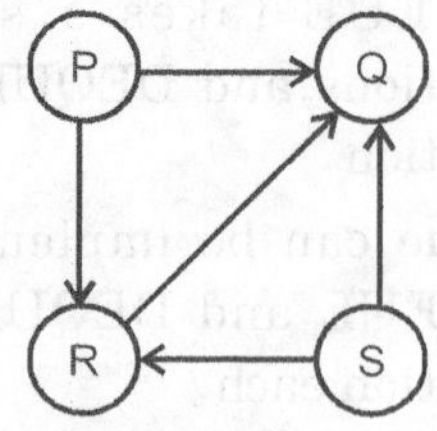

Which one of the following is TRUE?

(*a*) The graph does not have any topological ordering

(*b*) Both PQRS and SRQP are topological orderings

(*c*) Both PSRQ and SPRQ are topological orderings.

(*d*) PSRQ is the only topological ordering.

67. Let P be a quick sort program to sort numbers in ascending order using the first element as the pivot. Let t_1 and t_2 be the number of comparisons made by P for the inputs [1 2 3 4 5] and [4 1 5 3 2] respectively. Which one of the following holds?

(*a*) $t_1 = 5$ (*b*) $t_1 < t_2$

(*c*) $t_1 > t_2$ (*d*) $t_1 = t_2$

68. Suppose a polynomial time algorithm is discovered that correctly computes the largest clique in a given graph. In this scenario, which one of the following represents the correct Venn diagram of the complexity classes P, NP and NP Complete (NPC)?

(*a*)

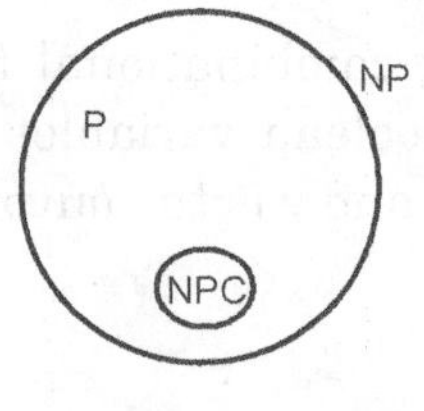

(*b*)

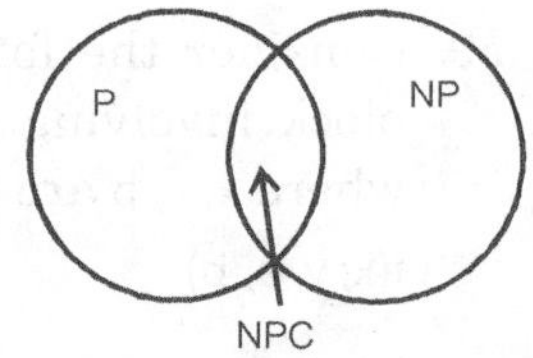

(*c*)

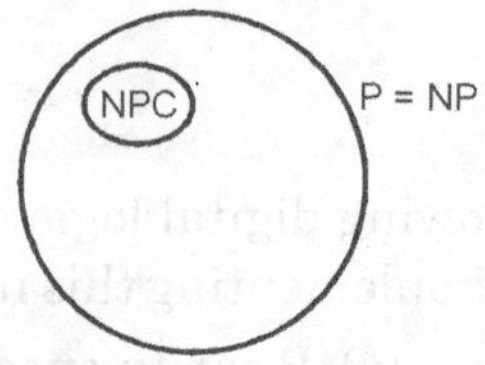

(*d*)

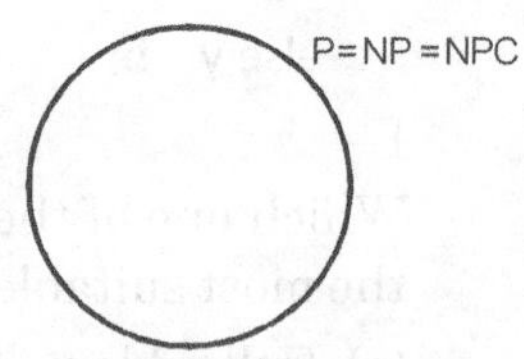

69. A priority queue is implemented as a Max-Heap. Initially, it has 5 elements. The level-order traversal of the heap is: 10, 8, 5, 3, 2. Two new elements 1 and 7 are inserted into the heap in that order. The level-order traversal of the heap after the insertion of the elements is:

(*a*) 10, 8, 7, 3, 2, 1, 5

(*b*) 10, 8, 7, 2, 3, 1, 5

(*c*) 10, 8, 7, 1, 2, 3, 5

(*d*) 10, 8, 7, 5, 3, 2, 1

70. Which one of the following correctly determines the solution of the recurrence relation with T(1) = 1?

$$T(n) = 2T\left(\frac{n}{2}\right) + \log n$$

(a) $\Theta(n)$ (b) $\Theta(n \log n)$
(c) $\Theta(n^2)$ (d) $\Theta(\log n)$

71. Consider the tree arcs of a BFS traversal from a source node W in an unweighted, connected, undirected graph. The tree T formed by the tree arcs is a data structure for computing

(a) the shortest path between every pair of vertices
(b) the shortest path from W to every vertex in the graph
(c) the shortest paths from W to only those nodes that are leaves of T
(d) the longest path in the graph

72. You have an array of n elements. Suppose you implement quick sort by always choosing the central element of the array as the pivot. Then the tightest upper bound for the worst case performance is

(a) $O(n^2)$ (b) $O(n \log n)$
(c) $\Theta(n \log n)$ (d) $O(n^3)$

73. Consider a hash table with 100 slots. Collisions are resolved using chaining. Assuming simple uniform hashing, what is the probability that the first 3 slots are unfilled after the first 3 insertions?

(a) $(97 \times 97 \times 97)/100^3$
(b) $(99 \times 98 \times 97)/100^3$
(c) $(97 \times 96 \times 95)/100^3$
(d) $(97 \times 96 \times 95)/(3! \times 100^3)$

74. Let δ denote the minimum degree of a vertex in a graph. For all planar graphs on n vertices with $\delta \geq 3$, which one of the following is TRUE?

(a) In any planar embedding, the number of faces is at least $\frac{n}{2}+2$
(b) In any planar embedding, the number of faces is less than $\frac{n}{2}+2$
(c) There is a planar embedding in which the number of faces is less than $\frac{n}{2}+2$
(d) There is a planar embedding in which the number of faces is at most $\frac{n}{\delta+1}$

2013

75. Consider an undirected random graph of eight vertices. The probability that there is an edge between a pair of vertices is $\frac{1}{2}$. What is the expected number of unordered cycles of length three?

(a) $\frac{1}{8}$ (b) 1
(c) 7 (d) 8

76. Which of the following statements is/are **TRUE** for undirected graphs?

P : Number of odd degree vertices is even.
Q : Sum of degrees of all vertices is even.

(a) P only
(b) Q only
(c) Both P and Q
(d) Neither P nor Q

77. Consider the following function:

```
int unknown(int n){
    int i, j, k = 0;
for (i = n/2; i < = n; i++)
for (j = 2; 'j< = n; j = j * 2)
    k = k + n/2;
return (k);
}
```

The return value of the function is

(a) $\Theta(n^2)$ (b) $\Theta(n^2 \log n)$
(c) $\Theta(n^3)$ (d) $\Theta(n^3 \log n)$

78. A certain computation generates two arrays a and b such that $a[i] = f(i)$ for $0 \leq i < n$ and $b[i] = g(a[i])$ for $0 \leq i < n$. Suppose this computation is decomposed into two concurrent processes: X and Y such that X computes the array a and Y computes the array b. The processes employ two binary semaphores R and S, both initialized to zero. The array a is shared by the two processes. The structures of the processes are shown below.

Process X:	Process Y:
private i;	private i;
for (i=0; i<n; i++) {	for (i=0; i<n; i++) {
a[i] = f(i);	EntryY(R, S);
ExitX(R, S);	b[i] = g(a[i]);
}	}

Which one of the following represents the CORRECT implementations of Exit X and EntryY?

(a)
```
ExitX(R, S) {
    P(R);
    V(S);
}
EntryY(R, S) {
    P(S);
    V(R);
}
```

(b)
```
ExitX(R, S) {
    V(R);
    V(S);
}
EntryY(R, S) {
    P(R);
    P(S);
}
```

(c)
```
ExitX(R, S) {
    P(S);
    V(R);
}
EntryY(R, S) {
    V(S);
    P(R);
}
```

(d)
```
ExitX(R, S) {
    V(R);
    P(S);
}
EntryY(R, S) {
    V(S);
    P(R);
}
```

79. What is the return value of $f(p, p)$, if the value of p is initialized to 5 before the call? Note that the first parameter is passed by reference, whereas the second parameter is passed by value.

```
int f (int &x, int c) {
    C = C – 1;
        if (c==0) return 1;
    x = x + 1;
        return f(x,c) * x;
}
```

(a) 3024 (b) 6561
(c) 55440 (d) 161051

80. Which one of the following is the tightest upper bound that represents the number of swaps required to sort n numbers using selection sort?

(a) $O(\log n)$ (b) $O(n)$
(c) $O(n \log n)$ (d) $O(n^2)$

81. Which one of the following is the tightest upper bound that represents the time complexity of inserting an object into a binary search tree of n nodes?

(a) $O(1)$ (b) $O(\log n)$
(c) $O(n)$ (d) $O(n \log n)$

82. A scheduling algorithm assigns priority proportional to the waiting time of a process. Every process starts with priority zero (the lowest priority). The scheduler re-evaluates the process priorities every T time units and decides the next process to schedule. Which one of the following is **TRUE** if the processes have no I/O operations and all arrive at time zero?

(a) This algorithm is equivalent to the first-come-first-serve algorithm.
(b) This algorithm is equivalent to the round-robin algorithm.
(c) This algorithm is equivalent to the shortest-job-first algorithm.
(d) This algorithm is equivalent to the shortest-remaining-time-first algorithm.

83. Which of the following statements are TRUE?

1. The problem of determining whether there exists a cycle in an undirected graph is in P.
2. The problem of determining whether there exists a cycle in an undirected graph is in NP.
3. If a problem A is NP-Complete, there exists a non-deterministic polynomial time algorithm to solve A.

(a) 1, 2 and 3 (b) 1 and 2 only
(c) 2 and 3 only (d) 1 and 3 only

84. What is the time complexity of Bellman-Ford single-source shortest path algorithm on a complete graph of n vertices?

(a) $\Theta(n^2)$ (b) $\Theta(n^2 \log n)$
(c) $\Theta(n^3)$ (d) $\Theta(n^3 \log n)$

85. The line graph $L(G)$ of a simple graph G is defined as follows:

- There is exactly one vertex $v(e)$ in $L(G)$ for each edge e in G.
- For any two edges e and e' in G, $L(G)$ has an edge between $v(e)$ and $v(e')$, if and only if e and e' are incident with the same vertex in G.

Which of the following statements is/are **TRUE**?

(P) The line graph of a cycle is a cycle.
(Q) The line graph of a clique is a clique.
(R) The line graph of a planar graph is planar.
(S) The line graph of a tree is a tree.

(a) P only
(b) P and R only
(c) R only
(d) P, Q and S only

86. The number of elements that can be sorted in $\Theta(\log n)$ time using heap sort is

(a) $\Theta(1)$ (b) $\Theta\left(\sqrt{\log n}\right)$
(c) $\Theta\left(\frac{\log n}{\log \log n}\right)$ (d) $\Theta(\log n)$

87. Consider the following operation along with Enqueue and Dequeue operations on queues, where k is a global parameter.

```
MultiDequeue(Q){
        m = k
    while (Q is not empty) and (m > 0) {
            Dequeue(Q)
            m = m - 1
    }
}
```

What is the worst case time complexity of a sequence of n queue operations on an initially empty queue?

(*a*) $\Theta(n)$ (*b*) $\Theta(n+k)$

(*c*) $\Theta(nk)$ (*d*) $\Theta(n^2)$

2012

88. Let G be a simple undirected planar graph on 10 vertices with 15 edges. If G is a connected graph. then the number of bounded faces in any embedding of G on the plane is equal to

(*a*) 3 (*b*) 4

(*c*) 5 (*d*) 6

89. What will be the output of the following C program segment?

```
char inChar = 'A' ;
switch (inChar) {
case 'A' : printf ("Choice A\n");
case 'B' :
case 'C' : print f ("Choice B");
case 'D' :
case 'E' :
default : printf ("No Choice"); }
```

(*a*) No Choice

(*b*) Choice A

(*c*) Choice A, Choice B No Choice

(*d*) Program gives no output as it is erroneous

90. The height of a tree is defined as the number of edges on the longest path in the tree. The function shown in the pseudocode below is invoked as height (root) to compute the height of a binary tree rooted at the tree pointer root.

```
int height (treeptr n)
{ if (n = = NULL) return –1;
    if (n → left = = NULL)
        if (n → right = = NULL) return 0;
        else return [B1] ;           // Box 1
    else { h1 = height (n → left);
        if (n → right = = NULL) return (1 + h1);
        else {h2 = height (n → right);
            return [B2];             // Box 2
        }
    }
}
```

The appropriate expressions for the two boxes B1 and B2 are

(*a*) B1 : (1 + height (n → right)
B2: (1 + max(h1, h2)

(*b*) B1: (height(n → right)), B2: (1 + max(h1, h2))

(*c*) B1: height(n → right), B2: max(h1, h2)

(*d*) B1: (1 + height(n → right)), B2: max(h1, h2)

91. Let G be a complete undirected graph on 6 vertices. If vertices of G are labeled, then the number of distinct cycles of length 4 in G is equal to

(*a*) 15 (*b*) 30

(*c*) 90 (*d*) 360

92. Let G be a weighted graph with edge weights greater than one and G′ be the graph constructed by squaring the weights of edges in G. Let T and T′ be the minimum spanning trees of G and G′, respectively, with total weights t and t′. Which of the following statements is **TRUE**?

(*a*) T′ = T with total weight $t' = t^2$

(*b*) T′ = T with total weight $t' < t^2$

(*c*) T′ ≠ T but total weight $t' = t^2$

(*d*) None of the above

93. Which of the following graphs is isomorphic to

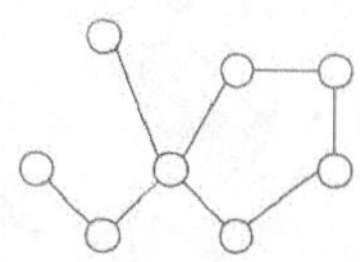

(*a*)

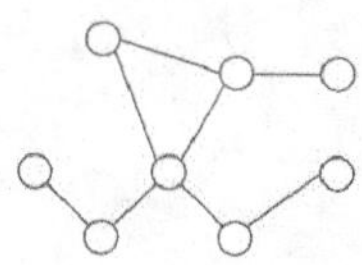

(*b*)

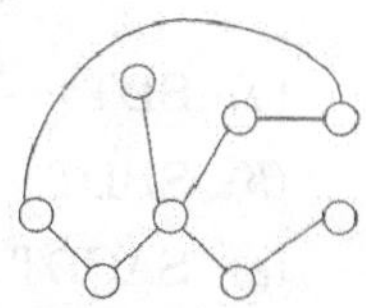

(*c*)

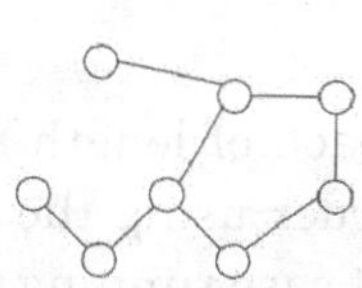

(*d*)

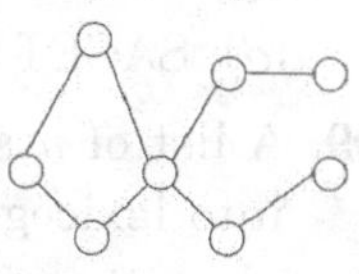

94. Let W(n) and A(n) denote respectively, the worst case and average case running time of an algorithm executed on an input of size n. Which of the following is ALWAYS TRUE?

(*a*) $A(n) = \Omega(W(n))$

(*b*) $A(n) = \Theta(W(n))$

(*c*) $A(n) = O(W(n))$

(*d*) $A(n) = o(W(n))$

95. The recurrence relation capturing the optimal execution time of the *Towers of Hanoi* problem with n discs is

(a) $T(n) = 2T(n-2) + 2$

(b) $T(n) = 2T(n-1) + n$

(c) $T(n) = 2T(n/2) + 1$

(d) $T(n) = 2T(n-1) + 1$

96. The worst case running time to search for an element in a balanced binary search tree with $n2^n$ elements is

(a) $\Theta(n \log n)$ (b) $\Theta(n2^n)$

(c) $\Theta(n)$ (d) $\Theta(\log n)$

97. Assuming $P \neq NP$, which of the following is TRUE?

(a) NP-complete = NP

(b) NP-complete $\cap$ P = $\varnothing$

(c) NP-hard = NP

(d) P = NP-complete

98. Consider the directed graph shown in the figure below. There are multiple shortest paths between vertices S and T. Which one will be reported by Dijkstra's shortest path algorithm? Assume that, in any iteration, the shortest path to a vertex v is updated only when a strictly shorter path to v is discovered.

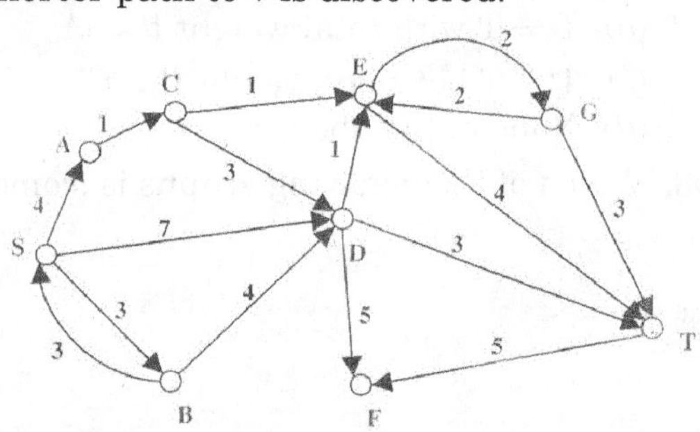

(a) SDT

(b) SBDT

(c) SACDT

(d) SACET

99. A list of n strings, each of length n, is sorted into lexicographic order using the merge-sort alogrithm. The worst case running time of this computation is

(a) $O(n \log n)$

(b) $O(n^2 \log n)$

(c) $O(n^2 + \log n)$

(d) $O(n^2)$

2011

100. A max-heap is heap where the value of each parent is greater than or equal to the value of its children. Which of the following is max-heap?

(a)

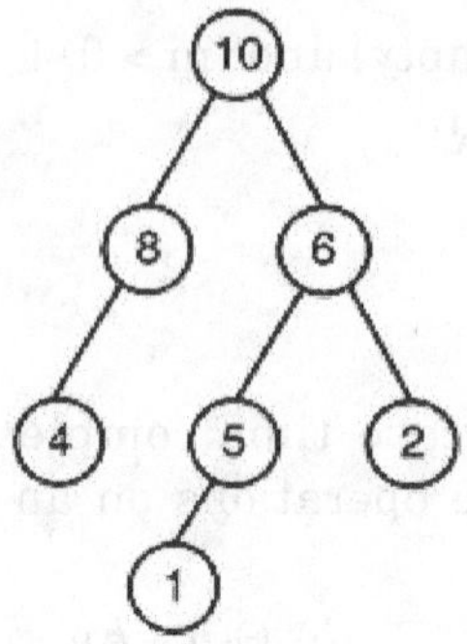

(b)

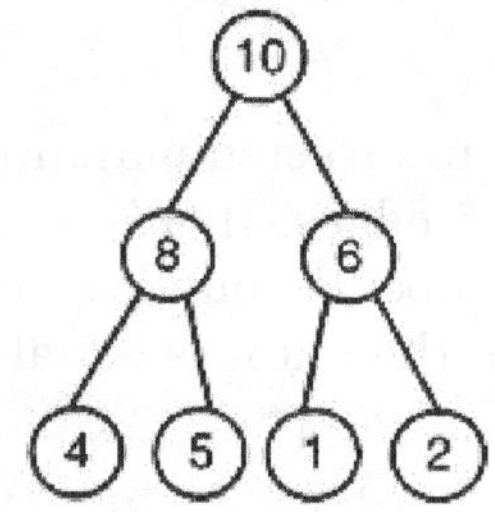

(c)

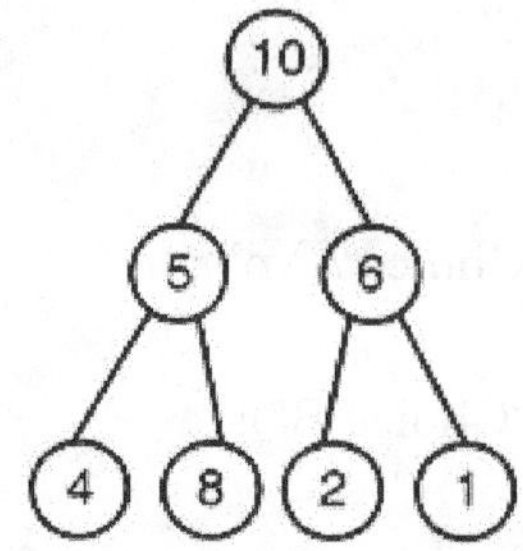

(d)

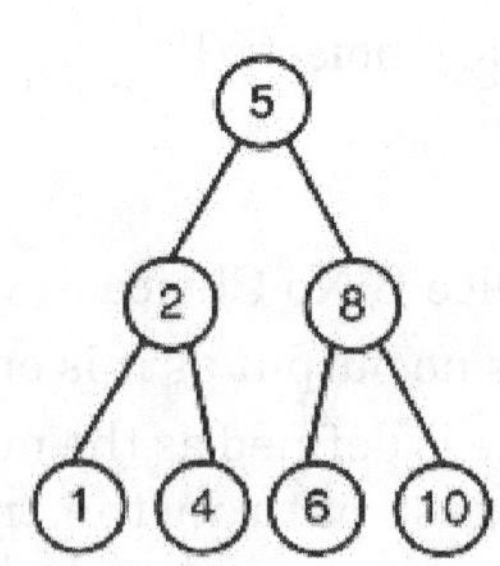

101. What does the following fragment of C program print?

```
Char c [ ] = "GATE2011";
char *p = c ;
printf (:%s", p + p[3] – p[1]);
```

(a) GATE2011 (b) E2011

(c) 2011 (d) 011

102. K4 and Q3 are graphs with the following structures.

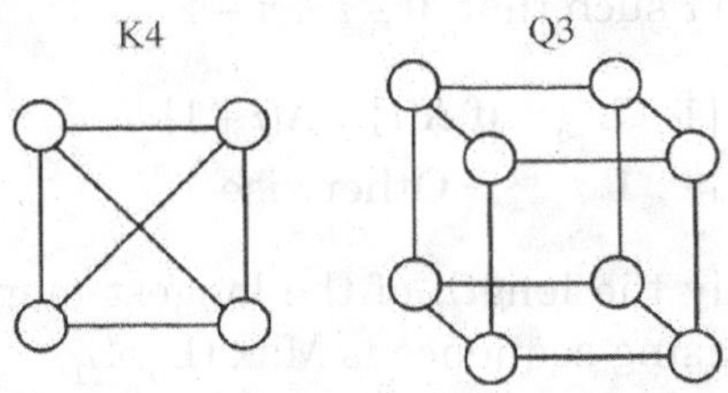

Which one of the following statements is **TRUE** in relation to these graphs?

(*a*) K4 is planar while Q3 is not

(*b*) Both K4 and Q3 are planar

(*c*) Q3 is planar while K3 is not

(*d*) Neither K4 nor Q3 is planar

103. Consider a relational table with a single record for each registered student with the following attributes.

1. *Registration_Num*: Unique registration number of each registered student
2. *UID* : Unique identity number, unique at the national level for each citizen
3. *BankAccount_Num*: Unique account number at the bank. A student can have multiple accounts or joint accounts. This attribute stores the primary account number.
4. *Name* : Name of the student
5. *Hostel_Room*: Room number of the hostel

Which of the following options is **INCORRECT**?

(*a*) *BankAccount _Num* is a candidate key

(*b*) *Registration_Num* can be primary key

(*c*) *UID* is a candidate key if all students are from the same country

(*d*) If S is a superkey such that S ∩ *UID* is NULL then S ∪ *UID* is also a superkey

104. The following is the comment for a C function.

/* This function computes the roots of a quadratic equation

a . *x* ^ 2 + *b* . *x* + *c* = 0. The function stores two real roots in "root 1 and *root2 and returns the status of validity of roots. It handles four different kinds of cases.

(*i*) When coefficient *a* is zero irrespective of discriminant

(*ii*) When discriminant is positive

(*iii*) When discriminant is zero

(*iv*) When discriminant is negative.

Only in case (*ii*) and (*iii*), the stored roots are valid. Otherwise 0 is stored in the roots. The function returns 0 when the roots are valid and –1 otherwise. The function also ensures root 1 > = root 2.

int get_QuadRoots (Float a, float b, float c, float *root1, float *root2);

* /

A software test engineer is assigned the job of doing black box testing. He comes up with the following test cases, many of which are redundant.

Test Case	Input set a	b	c	Expected Output Set root1	root2	Return Value
T1	0.0	0.0	7.0	0.0	0.0	–1
T2	0.0	1.0	3.0	0.0	0.0	–1
T3	1.0	2.0	1.0	– 1.0	–1.0	0
T4	4.0	–12.0	9.0	1.5	1.5	0
T5	1.0	–2.0	– 3.0	3.0	–1.0	0
T6	1.0	1.0	4.0	0.0	0.0	–1

Which one of the following options provide the set of non-redundant tests using equivalence class partitioning approach from input perspective for black box testing?

(*a*) T1, T2, T3, T6

(*b*) T1, T3, T4, T5

(*c*) T2, T4, T5, T6

(*d*) T2, T3, T4, T5

105. Consider evaluating the following expression tree on a machine with load-store architecture in which memory can be accessed only through load and store instructions. The variables *a*, *b*, *c*, *d* and *e* are initially stored in memory. The binary operators used in this expression tree can be evaluated by the machine only when the operands are in registers. The instructions produce result only in a register. If no intermediate results can be stored in memory, what is the minimum number of registers needed to evaluate this expression?

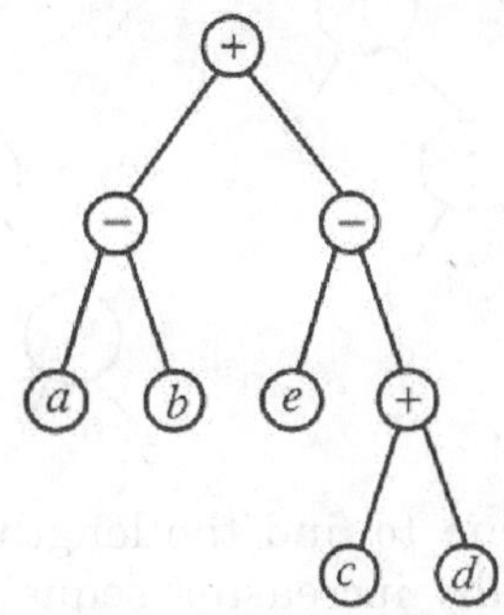

(*a*) 2 (*b*) 9

(*c*) 5 (*d*) 3

106. Consider the following table of arrival time and burst time for three processes P_0, P_1 and P_2.

Process	Arrival time	Burst Time
P_0	0 ms	9 ms
P_1	1 ms	4 ms
P_2	2 ms	9 ms

The pre-emptive shortest job first scheduling algorithm is used. Scheduling is carried out only at arrival or completion of processes. What is the average waiting time for the three processes?

(*a*) 5.0 ms (*b*) 4.33 ms
(*c*) 6.33 ms (*d*) 7.33 ms

107. We are given a set of *n* distinct elements and an unlabeled binary tree with *n* nodes. In how many ways can we populate the tree with the given set so that it becomes a binary search tree?

(*a*) 0 (*b*) 1
(*c*) *n*! (*d*) $\frac{1}{n+1} \cdot {}^{2n}C_n$

108. Consider two binary operators '↑' and '↓' with the precedence of operator ↓ being lower than that of the operator ↑. Operator ↑ is right associative while operator ↓ is left associative. Which one of the following represents the parse tree for expression (7 ↓ 3 ↑ 4 ↑ 3 ↓ 2)?

(*a*)

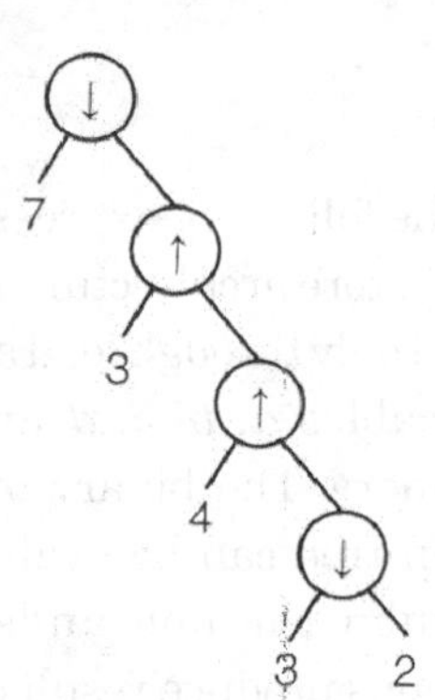

(*b*)

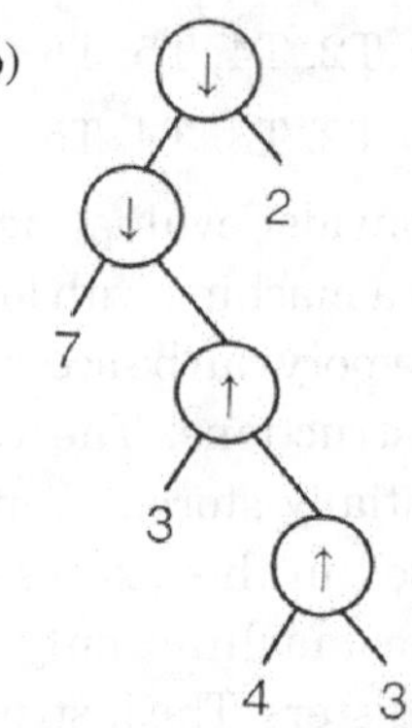

(*c*)

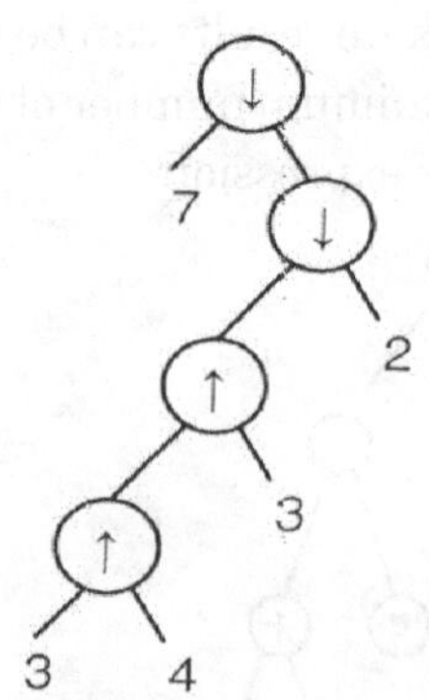

(*d*)

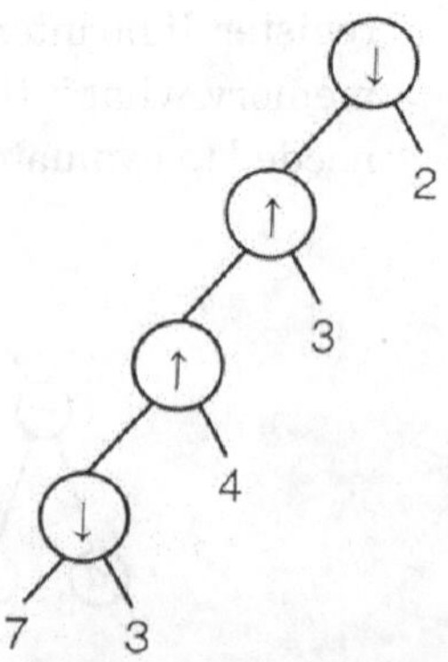

109. An algorithm to find the length of the longest monotonically increasing sequence of numbers in an array A[0 : *n* – 1] is given below.

Let L_i denote the length of the longest monotonically sequence starting at index *i* in the array.

Initialize $L_{n-1} = 1$

for all *i* such that $0 \le i \le n-2$

$$L_i = \begin{cases} 1 + L_{i+1} & \text{if } A[i] < A[i+1] \\ 1 & \text{Otherwise} \end{cases}$$

Finally the length of the longest monotonically increasing sequence is Max $(L_0, L_1, ..., L_{n-1})$.

Which of the following statements is TRUE?

(*a*) The algorithm uses dynamic programming paradigm
(*b*) The algorithm has a linear complexity and uses branch and bound paradigm
(*c*) The algorithm has a non-linear polynomial complexity and uses branch and bound paradigm
(*d*) The algorithm uses divide and conquer paradigm.

2010

110. What does the following program print?

```
# include <stdio. h>
void f (int *p, int *q) {
   p = q;
   *p = 2;
}
int i = 0, j = 1;
int main () {
   f (& i, &j);
   printf ("%d %d/n", i, j);
         return 0;
}
```

(*a*) 2 2 (*b*) 2 1
(*c*) 0 1 (*d*) 0 2

111. What is the appropriate pairing of items in the two columns listing various activities encountered in a software life cycle?

P. Requirements	1. Module Capture Development and Integration
Q. Design	2. Domain Analysis
R. Implementation	3. Structural and Behavioural Modelling
S. Maintenance	4. Performance Tuning

Codes :

	P	Q	R	S
(*a*)	3	2	4	1
(*b*)	2	3	1	4
(*c*)	3	2	1	4
(*d*)	2	3	4	1

112. What is the value printed by the following C program?

```
# include <stdio. h>
int f (int *a, int n)
{
    if (n <=0) return 0;
    else if (*a % 2 == 0) return *a + f (A +1, n – 1);
    else return *a – f (a + 1, n – 1);
}
int main ( )
{
    int a [ ] = {12, 7, 13, 4, 11, 6};
    print f (“%d”, f (a, 6));
    return 0;
}
```

(a) –9

(b) 5

(c) 15

(d) 19

113. The following C function takes a singly-linked list as input argumen.t. It modifies the list by moving the last element to the front of the list and returns the modified list. Some part of the code is left blank.

```
typedef struct node {
          int value;
     struct node *next;
}  Node;
Node *move_to_front (Node *head)
 {
    Node *p, *q;
    if ((head = = NULL) | | (head–>next
= = NULL)) return head;
    q = NULL; p = head;
    while(p–>next != NULL) {
                  q = p;
           p = p–>next ;
    }
    _______________________
    return head;
}
```

Choose the correct alternative to replace the blank line.

(a) q = NULL; p–>next = head; head = p;

(b) q–> next = NULL; head = p; p–>next = head;

(c) head = p; p–>next = q; q–>next = NULL;

(d) q–>next = NULL; p–>next = head; head = p;

114. The following program is to be tested for statement coverage:

```
begin
if (a == b) {S1; exit;}
else if (c == d) {S2;}
   else {S3; exit;}
S4;
end
```

The test cases T1, T2, T3 and T4 given below are expressed in terms of the properties satisfied by the values of variabls a, b, c and d. The exact values are not given.

T1: a, b, c and d are all equal

T2: a, b, c and d are all distinct

T3: $a = b$ and $c\ != d$

T4: $a\ != b$ and $c = d$

Which of the test suites given below ensures coverage of statements S1, S2, S3 and S4?

(a) T1, T2, T3 (b) T2, T4

(c) T3, T4 (d) T1, T2, T4

115. The cyclomatic complexity of each of the modules A and B shown below is 10. What is the cyclomatic complexity of the sequential integration shown on the right hand side?

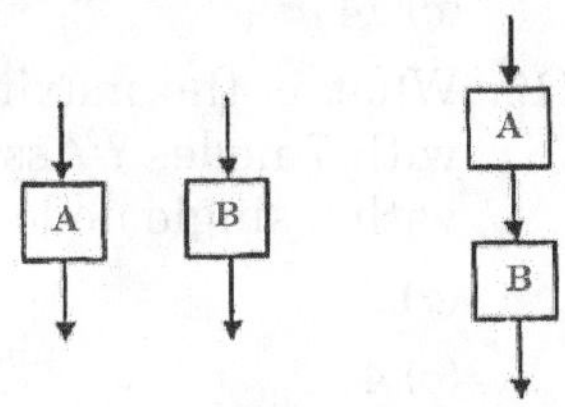

(a) 19

(b) 21

(c) 20

(d) 10

116. Two alternative package A and B are available for processing a database having 10^k records. Package A requires 0.0001 n^2 time units and package B requires 10 $n \log_{10} n$ time units to process n records. What is the smallest value of k for which package B will be preferred over A?

(a) 12 (b) 10

(c) 6 (d) 5

117. The weight of a sequence $a_0, a_1, ..., a_{n-1}$ of real numbers is defined as

$$a_0 + a_1/2 + ... + a_{n-1}/2^{n-1}.$$

A subsequence of a sequence is obtained by deleting some elements from the sequence, keeping the order of the remaining elements the same. Let X denote the maximum possible weight of a subsequence of $a_0, a_1, ..., a_{n-1}$ and Y the maximum possible weight of a subsequence of $a_1, a_2, ..., a_{n-1}$. Then X is equal to

(a) max (Y, a_0 + Y) (b) max (Y, a_0 + Y)

(c) max (Y, a_0 + 2Y) (d) a_0 + Y/2

2009

118. Consider the program below:

```
# include <stdio.h>
int fun (int n, int *f_p) {
int t, f;
if(n <=1){
* f_ p = 1;
return 1;
}
t = fun (n-1, f_p) ;
f = t + * f_p ;
* f_p = t;
return f ;
}
int main ( ) {
int x = 15 ;
printf (" % d/n", fun (5, & x));
return  0;
}
```

The value printed is

(*a*) 6 (*b*) 8

(*c*) 14 (*d*) 15

119. What is the maximum height of any AVL-tree with 7 nodes ? Assume that the height of a tree with a single node is 0.

(*a*) 2 (*b*) 3

(*c*) 4 (*d*) 5

120. What is the number of swaps required to sort *n* elements using selection sort, in the worst case?

(*a*) θ (n) (*b*) θ (n log n)

(*c*) θ (n^2) (*d*) θ (n^2 log n)

121. Which of the following statement (s) is/are correct regarding Bellman-Ford shortest path algorithm?

P. A always finds a negative weighted cycle, if one exists.

Q. Finds whether any negative weighted cycle is reachable from the source.

(*a*) P only (*b*) Q only

(*c*) both P and Q (*d*) neither P nor Q

122. If π_A be a problem that belongs to the class NP. then which one of the following is TRUE ?

(*a*) there is no polynomial time algorithm for π_A.

(*b*) If π_A can be solved deterministically in polynomial time, then P = NP.

(*c*) If π_A is NP - hard , then it is NP - complete.

(*d*) π_A may be undecidable.

123. The running time of an algorithm is represented by the following recurrence relation:

$$T(n) = \begin{cases} n & n \le 3 \\ T\left(\frac{n}{3}\right) + cn & \text{otherwise} \end{cases}$$

Which one of the following represents the time complexity of the algorithm ?

(*a*) θ (*n*) (*b*) θ (*n* log *n*)

(*c*) θ(*n*^{2}) (*d*) θ (*n*^{2} log n)

124. The keys 12, 18, 13, 2, 3, 23, 5 and 15 are inserted into an initially empty hash table of length 10 using open addressing with hash function *h* (*k*) = *k* mode 10 and linear probing. What is the resultant hash table ?

(*a*)

0	
1	
2	2
3	23
4	
5	15
6	
7	
8	18
9	

(*b*)

0	
1	
2	12
3	13
4	
5	5
6	
7	
8	18
9	

(*c*)

0	
1	
2	12
3	13
4	2
5	3
6	23
7	5
8	18
9	15

(*d*)

0	
1	
2	12, 2
3	13, 3,23
4	
5	5, 15
6	
7	
8	18
9	

125. Consider the following graph :

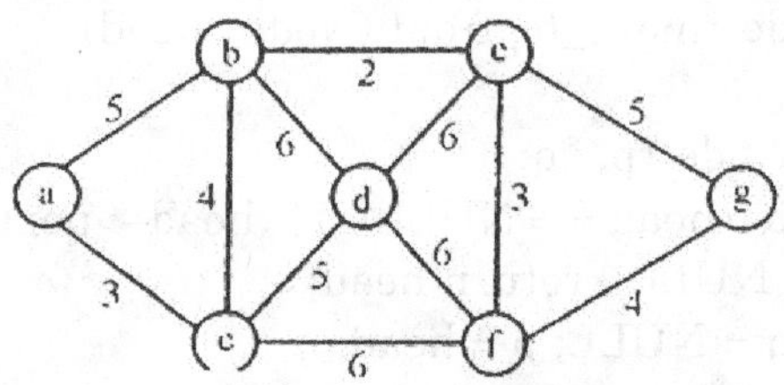

Which one of the following is NOT the sequence of edges added to the minimum spannign tree using Kruskal's algorithm ?

(*a*) (b, e) (e, f) (a, c) (b, c) (f, g) (c, d)

(*b*) (b, e) (e, f) (a, c) (f, g) (b, c) (c, d)

(*c*) (b, e) (a, c) (e, f) (b, c) (f, g) (c, d)

(*d*) (b, e) (e, f) (b, c) (a, c) (f, g) (c, d)

126. In quick sort, for sorting *n* elements, the (n/4)th smallest element is selected as pivot using an O(*n*) time algorithm. What is the worst case time complexity of the quick sort ?

(*a*) θ (*n*) (*b*) θ (*n* log *n*)

(*c*) θ(*n*^{2}) (*d*) θ (*n*^{2} log n)

2008

127. Which combination of the integer variables x, y and z makes the variable a get the value 4 in the following expression?

a = (x > y) ? ((x > z) ? x : z) : ((y > z) ? y : z)

(*a*) x = 3, y = 4, z = 2

(*b*) x = 6, y = 5, z = 3

(*c*) x = 6, y = 3, z = 5

(*d*) x = 5, y = 4, z = 5

128. What is printed by the following C program?

```
int f(int x, int *py, int **ppz)        void main ()
{                                       {
   int y, z;                               int c, *b, **a;
   **ppz + = 1; z = *ppz;                  c = 4; b = &c; a = &b;
   *py + = 2; y = -py;                     printf("%d", f(c,b,a));
   x + = 3;                             }
   return x + y + z;
}
```

(*a*) 18 (*b*) 19

(*c*) 21 (*d*) 22

129. Choose the correct option to fill ?1 and ?2 so that the program below prints an input string in reverse order. Assume that the input string is terminated by a newline character.

```
void reverse (void){
            int c;
    if (?1) reverse ();
            ?2
}
main () {
printf ("Enter Text"); printf ("\n");
reverse (); printf ("\n");
}
```

(*a*) ?1 is (getchar() != '|n'), ?2 is getchar (c);

(*b*) ?1 is (c = getchar ()) != '\n'), ?2 is getchar (c);

(*c*) ?1 is (c != '\n'), ?2 is putchar (c);

(*d*) ?1 is ((c = getchar ()) != '\n'), ?2 is putchar (c) ;

130. The following C function takes a singly-linked list of integers as a parameter and rearranges the elements of the list. The function is called with the list containing the integers 1, 2, 3, 4, 5, 6, 7 in the given order. What will be the contents of the list after the function completes execution?

```
        struct node {
            int value;
     struct node *next;
};
void rearrange (struct node *list) {
struct node *p, *q;
int temp;
if (! list || !list -> next) return;
p = list; q = list -> next;
while (q) {
temp = p -> value; p -> value = q -> value;
q -> value = temp; p = q -> next;
q = p ? p -> next : 0;
}
}
```

(*a*) 1, 2, 3, 4, 5, 6, 7 (*b*) 2, 1, 4, 3, 6, 5, 7

(*c*) 1, 3, 2, 5, 4, 7, 6 (*d*) 2, 3, 4, 5, 6, 7, 1

131. The most efficient algorithm for finding the number of connected components in an undirected graph on n vertices and m edges has time complexity

(*a*) $\Theta(n)$ (*b*) $\Theta(m)$

(*c*) $\Theta(m + n)$ (*d*) $\Theta(mn)$

132. The Breadth First Search algorithm has been implemented using the queue data structure, One possible order of visiting the nodes of the following graph is

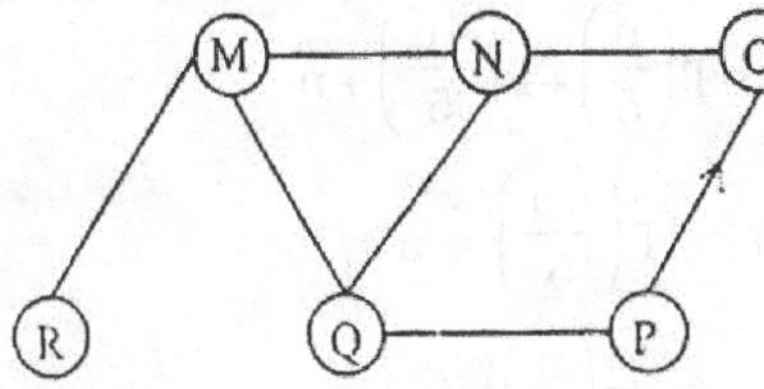

(*a*) MNOPQR (*b*) NQMPOR

(*c*) QMNPRO (*d*) QMNPOR

133. Consider the following functions:

$$f(n) = 2^n$$
$$g(n) = n!$$
$$h(n) = n^{\log n}$$

Which of the following statements about the asymptotic behaviour of f(n), g(n), and h(n) is true?

(*a*) $f(n) = O(g(n))$; $g(n) = O(h(n))$

(*b*) $f(n) = \Omega(g(n))$; $g(n) = O(h(n))$

(*c*) $g(n) = O(f(n))$; $h(n) = O(f(n))$

(*d*) $h(n) = O(f(n))$; $g(n) = \Omega(f(n))$

134. The minimum number of comparisons required to determine if an interger appears more than $\frac{n}{2}$ times in a sorted array of n integers is

(*a*) $\Theta(n)$

(*b*) $\Theta(\log n)$

(*c*) $\Theta(\log^* n)$

(*d*) $\Theta(1)$

135. A B-tree of order 4 is built from scratch by 10 successive insertions. What is the maximum number of node sphitting operations that may take place?

(a) 3 (b) 4
(c) 5 (d) 6

136. G is a graph on n vertices and 2n-2 edges. The edges of G can be partitioned into two edge-disjoint spannint trees.

Which of the following is NOT true for G?

(a) For every subset of k vertices, the induced subgraph has at most 2k-2 edges
(b) The minimum cut in G has at least two edges
(c) There are two edge-disjoint paths between every pair of vertices
(d) There are two vertex-disjoint paths between every pair of vertices

137. Consider the Quicksort algorithm. Suppose there is a procedure for finding a pivot element which splits the list into two sub-lists each of which contatins at least one-fifth of the elements. Let T(n) be the number of comparisons required to sort n elements. Then

(a) $T(n) \le 2T\left(\frac{n}{5}\right) + n$

(b) $T(n) \le T\left(\frac{n}{5}\right) + T\left(\frac{4n}{5}\right) + n$

(c) $T(n) \le 2T\left(\frac{4n}{5}\right) + n$

(d) $T(n) \le 2T\left(\frac{n}{2}\right) + n$

138. The subset-sum problem is defined as follows:

Given a set S of n positive integers and a positive integer W, determine whether there is a subset of S whose elements sum to W.

An algorithm Q solves this problem in O(nW) time. Which of the following statements is false?

(a) Q solves the subset-sum problem in polynomial time when the input is encoded in unary
(b) Q solves the subset-sum problem in polynomial time when the input is encoded in binary
(c) The subset sum problem belongs to the class NP
(d) The subset sum problem is NP-hard

139. Dijkstra's single source shortest path algorithm when run from vertex a in the above graph, computes the correct shortest path distance to

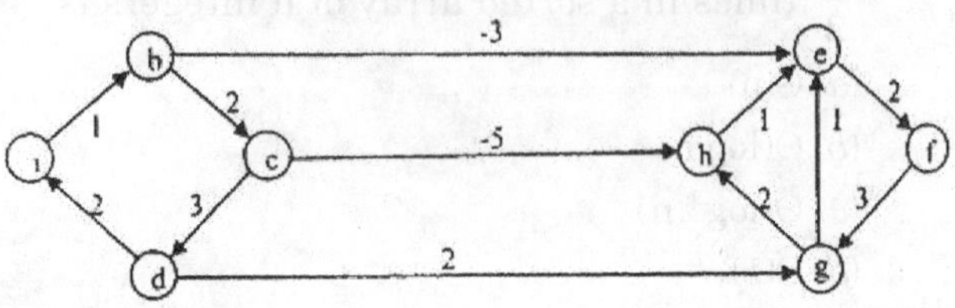

(a) only vertex a
(b) only vertices a, e, f, g, h
(c) only vertices a, b, c, d
(d) all the vertices

140. You are given the postorder traversal, P, of a binary search tree on the n elements 1, 2,....., n. You have to determine the unique binary search tree that has P as its postorder traversal. What is the time complexity of the most efficient algorithm for doing this?

(a) Θ(log n)
(b) Θ(n)
(c) Θ(n log n)
(d) None of the above, as the tree cannot be uniquely determind.

141. We have a binary heap on n elements and wish to insert n more elements (not necessarily one after another) into this heap. The total time required for this is

(a) Θ(log n) (b) Θ(n)
(c) Θ(n log n) (d) $\Theta(n^2)$

2007

142. Consider the following C code segment :

```
int IsPrime(n)
{
        int i,n;
        for(i=2;i < = sqrt(n);i++)
      if (n % i = = 0)
        {printf('Not Prime\n"};
                          return 0;)
          return 1;
}
```

Let T(n) denote the number of times the *for* loop is executed by the program on input *n*. Which of the following is **TRUE** ?

(a) $T(n) = O(\sqrt{n})$ and $T(n) = \Omega(\sqrt{n})$

(b) $T(n) = O(\sqrt{n})$ and $T(n) = \Omega(1)$

(c) $T(n) = O(n)$ and $T(n) = \Omega(\sqrt{n})$

(d) None of these

143. In the following C function, let $n \ge m$.

```
int gcd(n,m)
{
     if(n%m == 0) return m;
     n = n%m;
     return gcd(m,n);
}
```

How many recursive calls are made by this function ?

(a) $\Theta(\log_2 n)$ (b) $\Omega(n)$

(c) $\Theta(\log_2 \log_2 n)$ (d) $\Theta(\sqrt{n})$

144. Consider the following segment of C-code :

```
int J, n;
        j = 1;
  while (j <= n)
        j = j* 2;
```

The number of comparisons made in the execution of the loop for any $n > 0$ is

(a) $\lceil \log_2 n \rceil + 1$ (b) n

(c) $\lceil \log_2 n \rceil$ (d) $\lfloor \log_2 n \rfloor + 1$

145. The following postfix expression with single digit operands is evaluated using a stack

8 2 3 ^ / 2 3 * + 5 1 * –

Note that ^ is the exponentiation operator. The top two elements of the stack after the first * is evaluated are

(a) 6, 1 (b) 5, 7

(c) 3,2 (d) 1,5

146. Consider the following C function :

```
int f(int n)
{static int r = 0;
  if (n < = 0) return 1;
 if (n > 3)
  {r = n;
   return f (n–2) + 2;
  }
   return f(n–1) + r;
}
```

What is the value of f(5) ?

(a) 5 (b) 7

(c) 9 (d) 18

147. Consider the following C program segment where Cell Node represents a node in a binary tree

```
struct CellNode {
struct CellNode * leftchild;
int element;
struct CellNode *rightchild;
};
int GetValue(struct CellNode*ptr){
int value = 0;
if (ptr ! = NULL) {
 if ((ptr->leftChild == NULL) &&
    (ptr->rightChild == NULL))
    value = 1;
 else
    value = value + GetValue (ptr->leftChild)
                 + GetValue
              (ptr->rightChild);
 }
 return(value);
}
```

The value returned by Get Value when a pointer to the root of a binary tree is passed as its argument is

(a) the number of nodes in the tree

(b) the number of internal nodes in the tree

(c) the number of leaf nodes in the tree

(d) the height of the tree

148. The height of a binary tree is the maximum number of edges in any root to leaf path. The maximum number of nodes in a binary tree of height h is

(a) 2^h (b) $2^{h-1}-1$

(c) $2^{h+1}-1$ (d) 2^{h+1}

149. The maximum number of binary trees that can be formed with three unlabeled nodes is

(a) 1 (b) 5

(c) 4 (d) 3

150. Which of the following sorting algorithms has the lowest worst-case complexity ?

(a) Merge sort (b) Bubble sort

(c) Quick sort (d) Selection sort

151. The inorder and preorder traversal of a binary tree are d b e a f c g and a b d e c f g respectively. The postorder traversal of the binary tree is

(a) d e b f g c a

(b) e d b g f c a

(c) e d b f g c a

(d) d e f g b c a

152. Consider a hash table of size seven, with starting index zero, and a hash function $(3x + 4) \bmod 7$. Assuming the hash table is initially empty, which of the following is the contents of the table when the sequence 1, 3, 8, 10 is inserted into the table using closed hashing ? Note that–denotes an empty location in the table.

(a) 8, –, –, –, –, –, 10

(b) 1, 8, 10, –, –, –, 3

(c) 1, –, –, –, –, –, 3

(d) 1, 10, 8, –, –, –, 3

153. In an unweighted, undirected connected graph, the shortest path from a mode S to every other node is computed most efficiently, in terms of *time complexity,* by

(*a*) Dijkstra's algorithm starting from S.

(*b*) Warshall's algorithm

(*c*) performing a DFS starting from S

(*d*) performing a BFS starting from S

154. A complete *n*–ary tree is a tree in which each node has *n* children or no children. Let I be the number of internal nodes and L be the number of leaves in a complete *n*-ary tree. If L = 41, and I = 10, then what is the value of *n?*

(*a*) 3 (*b*) 4

(*c*) 5 (*d*) 6

155. What is the *time complexity* of the following recursive function ?

```
int DoSomething ( int n) {
if   (n <= 2)
       return 1;
else
return (DoSomething (floor  (sqrt(n))) + n);
}
```

(*a*) $\Theta(n^2)$ (*b*) $\Theta(n\log_2 n)$

(*c*) $\Theta(\log_2 n)$ (*d*) $\Theta(\log_2 \log_2 n)$

156. Consider the process of inserting an element into a *Max Heap,* where the *Max Heap* is represented by an *array.* Suppose we perform a binary search on the path from the new leaf to the root to find the position for the newly inserted element, the number of *comparisons* performed is

(*a*) $\Theta(\log_2 n)$ (*b*) $\Theta(n\log_2 n)$

(*c*) Θn (*d*) $\Theta(n\log_2 n)$

157. Let *w* be the minimum weight among all edge weights in an undirected connected graph. Let *e* be a specific edge of weight *w*.

Which of the following is **FALSE** ?

(*a*) There is a minimum spanning tree containing *e*.

(*b*) If *e* is not in a minimum spanning tree *T,* then in the cycle formed by adding *e* to *T,* all edges have the same weight.

(*c*) Every minimum spanning tree has an edge of weight *w*

(*d*) *e* is present in every minimum spanning tree

158. An array of *n* numbers is given, where *n* is an even number. The maximum as well as the minimum of these *n* numbers needs to be determined. Which of the following is **TRUE** about the number of comparisons needed ?

(*a*) At least 2*n* – *c* comparisons, for some constant *c,* are needed.

(*b*) At most 1.5*n* –2 comparisons are needed.

(*c*) At least $n \log_2 n$ comparisons are needed.

(*d*) None of these

2006

159. An implementation of a queue Q, using two stacks S1 and S2, is given below :

```
        void insert (Q, x) {
                push (S1, x);
        }
        void delete (Q) {
            if (stack-empty (S2)) then
                if (stack-empty (S1))
then {
                    print (Q is empty");
                    return;
        }
        else while (! (stack-empty) (S1))) {
                x = pop (S1);
                push (S2, x);
        }
                x = pop (S2);
        }
```

Let n insert and *m(≤ n)* delete operations be performed in an arbitrary order on an empty queue Q. Let *x* and *y* be the number of push and pop operations performed respectively in the process. Which one of the following is true for all *m* and *n* ?

(*a*) $n + m \le x < 2n$ and $2m \le n + m$

(*b*) $n + m \le x < 2n$ and $2m \le y \le 2n$

(*c*) $2m \le x < 2n$ and $2m \le y \le n + m$

(*d*) $2m \le x < 2n$ and $2m \le y \le 2n$

160. Consider the following C-function in which a [*n*] and *b* [*m*] are two sorted integer arrays and c [n + m] be another integer array.

```
void xyz (int a [], int b[], int c []){
    int i, j, k;
    i = j = k = 0;
    while ((i < n) && (j < m))
        if (a[i] < b [j]) c [k ++] = a [i ++ ];
        else c [k ++]  = b [j ++];
    }
```

Which of the following condition (s) hold(s) after the termination of the while loop ?

(*i*) j < m, k = n + j – 1, and a [n – 1] < b [j] if i = n

(*ii*) i < n, k = m + i – 1, and b [m – 1] ≤ a [i] if j = m

(*a*) only (*i*)

(*b*) only (*ii*)

(*c*) either (*i*) or (*ii*) but not both

(*d*) neither (*i*) nor (*ii*)

161. Consider these two functions and two statements S1 and S2 about them.

```
int work 1(int*a, int i, int j)
{
    int x = a[i + 2];
    a[j] = x + 1;
    return a[i + 2] – 3;}
}
```

```
in twork 2(int*a, int i, int j)
{
    int t1 = i + 2;
    int t2 = a[t1];
    a[j] = t2 + 1;
    return t2 – 3;
}
```

S1 : The transformation from work 1 to work 2 is valid, i.e., for any program state and input arguments, work 2 will compute the same output and have the same effect on program state as work 1

S2 : All the transformations applied to work 1 to get work 2 will always improve the performance (i.e. reduce CPU time) of work 2 compared to work 1

(*a*) S1 is false and S2 is false

(*b*) S1 is false and S2 is true

(*c*) S1 is true and S2 is false

(*d*) S1 is true and S2 is true

162. Consider this C code to swap two integers and these five statements :

The code

```
void swap (int * px, int * py) {
    *px = *px – *py;
    * py = *px + *py;
    * px = *py – * px;
}
```

S1 : will generate a compilation error

S2 : may generate a segmentation fault at runtime depending on the arguments passed

S3 : correctly implements the swap procedure for all input pointers referring to integers stored in memory locations accessible to the process

S4 : implements the swap procedure correctly for some but not all valid input pointers

S5 : may add or subtract integers and pointers

(*a*) S1

(*b*) S2 and S3

(*c*) S2 and S4

(*d*) S2 and S5

163. In a binary max heap containing *n* numbers, the smallest element can be found in time

(*a*) $\theta(n)$ (*b*) $\theta(\log n)$

(*c*) $\theta(\log \log n)$ (*d*) $\theta(1)$

164. Consider a weighted complete graph G on the vertex set $\{v_1, v_2, \ldots, v_n\}$ such that the weight of the edge (v_i, v_j) is $2|i - j|$. The weight of a minimum spanning tree of G is

(*a*) $n - 1$ (*b*) $2n - 2$

(*c*) $\binom{n}{2}$ (*d*) n^2

165. To implement Dijkstra's shortest path algorithm on unweighted graphs so that it runs in linear time, then data structure to be used is

(*a*) Queue (*b*) Stack

(*c*) Heap (*d*) B-Tree

166. A scheme for storing binary trees in an array X is as follows. Indexing of X starts at 1 instead of 0. The roots is stored at X [1]. For a node stored at X[*i*], the left child, if any, is stored in X[2*i*] and the right child, if any, in X [2*i* + 1]. To be able to store any binary tree on *n* vertices, the minimum size of X should be

(*a*) $\log_2 n$ (*b*) n

(*c*) $2n + 1$ (*d*) $2^n - 1$

167. Which one of the following in place sorting algorithms needs the minimum number of swaps?

(*a*) Quick sort (*b*) Insertion sort

(*c*) Selection sort (*d*) Heap sort

168. Consider the following C-program fragment in which *i*, *j*, and *n* are integer variables.

for (i = n, j = 0; i > 0; i/ = 2, j + = i);

Let val(*j*) = denote the value stored in the variable *j* after termination of the *for* loop. Which one of the following is true ?

(*a*) val (*j*) = $\theta(\log n)$

(*b*) val (*j*) = $\theta(\sqrt{n})$

(*c*) val (*j*) = $\theta(n)$

(*d*) val (*j*) = $\theta(n \log n)$

169. An element in an array X is called a leader if it is greater than all elements to the right of it in X. The best algorithm to find all leaders in an array

(*a*) solves it in linear time using a left to right pass of the array

(*b*) solves in linear time using a right to left pass of the array

(*c*) solves it using divide and conquer in time $\theta(n \log n)$

(*d*) solves it in time $\theta(n^2)$

170. Consider the following graph :

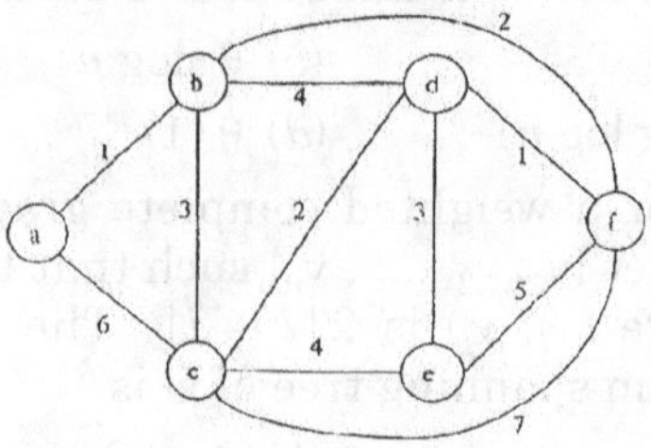

Which one of the following cannot be the sequence of edges added, in that order, to a minimum spanning tree using Kruskal's algorithm ?

(a) (a – b), (d – f), (b – f), (d – c), (d – e)
(b) (a – b), (d – f), (d – c), (b – f), (d – e)
(c) (d – f), (a – b), (d – c), (b – f), (d – e)
(d) (d – f), (a – b), (b – f), (d – e), (d – c)

171. Let T be a depth first search tree in a undirected grpah G. Vertices *u* and *v* are leaves of this tree T. The degrees of both *u* and *v* in G are at least 2. Which one of the following statements is true ?

(a) There must exist a vertex *w* adjacent to both *u* and v in G
(b) There must exist a vertex *w* whose removal disconnects *u* and v in G
(c) There must exist a cycle in G containing *u* and v
(d) There must exist a cycle in G containing *u* and all its neighbours in G

172. A set X can be represented by an array x[n] as follows:

$$x[i] = \begin{cases} 1 & \text{if } i \in X \\ 0 & \text{otherwise} \end{cases}$$

Consider following algorithm in which x, y, and z are boolean arrays of size n :

```
algorithm zzz (x[], y[], z[]){
 int i;
 for (i = 0; i < n; ++ i)
          z[i] = (x [i] ∧ ~ y[i]) ∨ (~ x[i] ∧ y[i])
}
```

The set Z computed by the algorithm is

(a) $(X \cup Y)$ (b) $(X \cap Y)$
(c) $(X - Y) \cap (Y - X)$ (d) $(X - Y) \cup (Y - X)$

173. Consider the following recurrence

$$T(n) = 2T\left(\left\lceil \sqrt{n} \right\rceil\right) + 1,$$

$$T(1) = 1$$

Which one of the following is true ?

(a) $T(n) = \theta(\log \log n)$ (b) $T(n) = \theta(\log n)$
(c) $T(n) = \theta(\sqrt{n})$ (d) $T(n) = \theta(n)$

174. Given two arrays of numbers $a_1, ..., a_n$ and $b_1, ..., b_n$ where each number is 0 or 1, the fastest algorithm to find the largest span (i, j) such that $a_i + a_{i+1} + ... + a_j = b_i + b_{i+1} + ... + b_j$, or report that there is no such span

(a) takes $O(3^n)$ and $\Omega(2^n)$ time if hashing is permitted
(b) takes $O(n^3)$ and $\Omega(n^{2.5})$ time in the key comparison model
(c) takes $\Theta(n)$ time and space
(d) takes $O(\sqrt{n})$ time only if the sum of the $2n$ elements is an even number

175. Consider following code written in a pass-by-reference language like FORTRAN and these statements about the code.

```
Subroutine swap (ix, iy)
          it = ix
L1 :           ix = iy
L2 :           i y = it
    end
    ia = 3
    ib = 8
      call swap (ia, ib + 5)
    print *, ia, ib
    end
```

S1 : The compiler will generate code to allocate a temporary nameless cell, initialize it to 13, and pass the address of the cell to swap

S2 : On execution the code will generate a runtime error on line L1

S3 : On execution the code will generate a runtime error on line L2

S4 : The program will print 13 and 8

S5 : The program will print 13 and –2

Exactly the following set of statement (s) is correct :

(a) S1 and S2 (b) S1 and S4
(c) S3 (d) S1 and S5

2005

176. What does the following C-statement declare?

```
int (*f) (int * ) ;
```

(a) A function that takes an integer pointer as argument and returns an integer
(b) A function that takes an integer as argument and returns an integer pointer
(c) A pointer to a function that takes an integer pointer as argument and returns an integer
(d) A function that takes an integer pointer as argument and returns a function pointer

177. An Abstract Data Type (ADT) is

(*a*) same as an abstract class

(*b*) a data type that cannot be instantiated

(*c*) a data type for which only the operations defined on it can be used, but none else

(*d*) all of these

178. A common property of logic programming languages and functional languages is

(*a*) both are procedural languages

(*b*) both are based on l-calculus

(*c*) both are declarative

(*d*) both use Horn-clauses

179. Which one of the following are essential features of an object-oriented programming language?

(*i*) Abstraction and encapsulation

(*ii*) Strictly-typedness

(*iii*) Type-safe property coupled with sub-type rule

(*iv*) Polymorphism in the presence of inheritance

(*a*) (*i*) and (*ii*) only

(*b*) (*i*) and (*iv*) only

(*c*) (*i*), (*ii*) and (*iv*) only

(*d*) (*i*), (*iii*) and (*iv*) only

180. A program P reads in 500 integers in the range (0, 100) representing the scores of 500 students. It then prints the frequency of each score above 50. What would be the best way for P to store the frequencies?

(*a*) An array of 50 numbers

(*b*) An array of 100 numbers

(*c*) An array of 500 numbers

(*d*) A dynamically allocated array of 550 numbers

181. Consider the following C-program

```
void foo (int n, int sum) {
    int k = 0, j = 0;
    if (n ==0) return;
  k = n % 10; j = n/10;
    sum = sum + k;
     foo (j, sum);
    printf ("% d," k);
  }
    int main () {
 int a = 2048, sum = 0;
     foo (a, sum);
 printf ("% d/n", sum);
 }
```

What does the above program print?

(*a*) 8, 4, 0, 2, 14 (*b*) 8, 4, 0, 2, 0

(*c*) 2, 0, 4, 8, 14 (*d*) 2, 0, 4, 8, 0

182. Consider the following C-program

```
double foo (double) ; /* Line 1 */
      int main () {
    double da, db;
       // input da
     db = foo (da);
 }
  double foo (double a){
     return a;
  }
```

The above code compiled without any error or warning. If Line 1 is deleted, the above code will show

(*a*) no compile warning or error

(*b*) some compiler-warnings not leading to unintended results

(*c*) some compiler-warnings due to type-mismatch eventually leading to unintended results

(*d*) compiler errors

183. Postorder traversal of a given binary search tree, T produces the following sequence of keys

10, 9, 23, 22, 27, 25, 15, 50, 95, 60, 40, 29

Which one of the following sequences of keys can be the result of an inorder traversal of the tree T?

(*a*) 9, 10, 15, 22, 23, 25, 27, 29, 40, 50, 60, 95

(*b*) 9, 10, 15, 22, 40, 50, 60, 95, 23, 25, 27, 29

(*c*) 29, 15, 9, 10, 25, 22, 23, 27, 40, 60, 50, 95

(*d*) 95, 50, 60, 40, 27, 23, 22, 25, 10, 9, 15, 29

2004

184. The goal of structured programming is to

(*a*) have well indented programs

(*b*) be able to infer the flow of control from the compiled code

(*c*) be able to infer the flow of control from the program text

(*d*) avoid the use of GOTO statements

185. Consider the following C function :

```
vaid swap (int a, int b)
 { int temp ;
  temp  = a ;
      a  = b ;
      b  = temp ;
  }
```

In order to exchange the values of two variables x and y.

(*a*) call swap (x, y)

(*b*) call swap (&x, &y)

(*c*) swap (x, y) cannot be used as it does not return any value

(*d*) swap (x, y) cannot be used as the parameters are passed by value

186. A single array A [1..MAXSIZE] is used to implement two stacks. The two stacks grow from opposite ends of the array. Variables top1 and top 2 (top1 < top 2) point to the location of the topmost element in each of the stacks. If the space is to be used efficiently, the condition for "stack full" is

(*a*) (top1 = MAXSIZE/2) and (top2 = MAXSIZE/2+1)

(*b*) top1 + top2 = MAXSIZE

(*c*) (top1 = MAXSIZE/2) or (top2 = MAXSIZE)

(*d*) top1 = top2 – 1

187. The following numbers are inserted into an empty binary search tree in the given order: 10, 1, 3, 5, 15, 12, 16. What is the height of the binary search tree (the height is the maximum distance of a leaf node from the root) ?

(*a*) 2 (*b*) 3

(*c*) 4 (*d*) 6

188. The best data structure to check whether an arithmetic expression has balanced parentheses is a

(*a*) queue (*b*) stack

(*c*) tree (*d*) list

189. Consider the following C function:

```
int f(int n)
{    static int i = 1 ;
  if (n >= 5) return n ;
            n = n+ i ;
                 i ++;
          return f (n) ;
}
```

The value returned by f (1) is

(*a*) 5 (*b*) 6

(*c*) 7 (*d*) 8

190. Consider the following program fragment for reversing the digits in a given integer to obtain a new integer. Let $n = d_1 d_2 \dots d_m$.

```
int n, rev ;
rev = 0 ;
while (n > 0) {
rev = rev * 10 + n % 10 ;
        n = n / 10 ;
}
```

The loop invariant condition at the end of the ith iteration is:

(*a*) $n = d_1 d_2 \dots d_{m-i}$ and $rev = d_m d_{m-1} \dots d_{m-i+1}$

(*b*) $n = d_{m-i+1} \dots d_{m-1} d_m$ or $rev = d_{m-i} \dots d_2 d_1$

(*c*) $n \neq rev$

(*d*) $n = d_1 d_2 \dots d_m$ or $rev = d_m \dots d_2 d_1$

191. Consider the following C program segment:

```
char p [ 20 ] ;
char * s = "string" ;
int length = strlen (s) ;
for (i = 0 ; i < length; i++)
    p[ i ] = s [length – i] ;
printf ("%s", p) ;
```

The output of the program is

(*a*) gnirts (*b*) string

(*c*) gnirt (*d*) no output is printed

192. A circularly linked list is used to represent a Queue. A single variable p is used to access the Queue. To which node should p point such that both the operations enQueue and deQueue can be performed in constant time ?

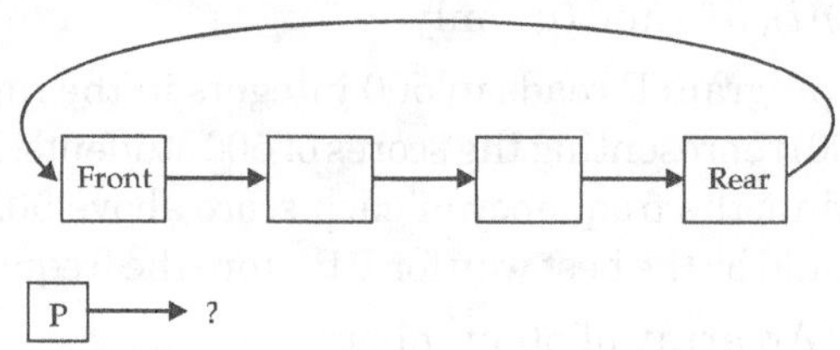

(*a*) rear node

(*b*) front node

(*c*) not possible with a single pointer

(*d*) node next to front

193. The elements 32, 15, 20, 30, 12, 25, 16, are inserted one by one in the given order into a maxHeap. The resultant maxHeap is

(*a*)

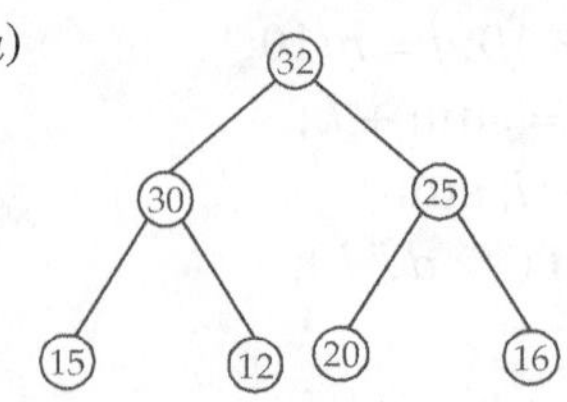

(*b*)

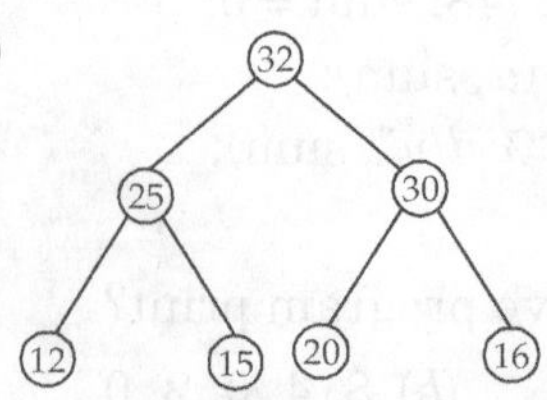

(c)

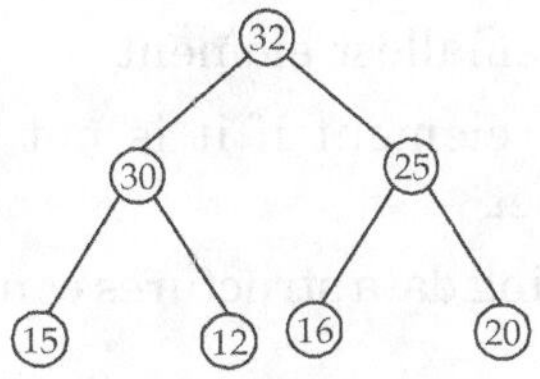

(d)

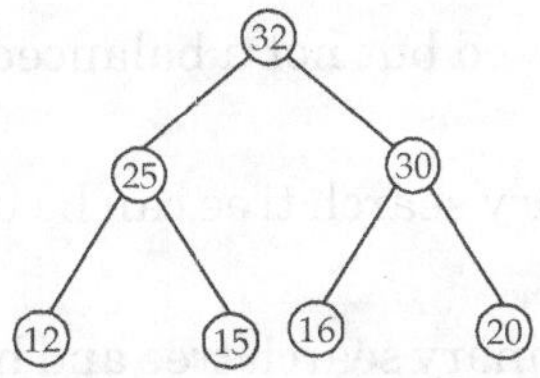

194. Assume that the operators +, –, are left associative and ^ is right associative. The order of precedence (from highest to lowest) is ^, , +, – . The postfix expression corresponding to the infix expression $a + b \times c - d \wedge e \wedge f$ is

(a) $abc \times + def \wedge\wedge -$ (b) $abc + de \wedge f \wedge -$

(c) $ab + c \; d - e \wedge f \wedge$ (d) $- + a \; bc \wedge\wedge def$

195. Consider the following C program

```
main ( )
{   int x, y, m, n ;
    scanf ("%d %d", &x, &y) ;
    /* Assume x > 0 and y > 0 */
        m = x ;    n = y ;
      while ( m != n)
                { if (m > n)
                        m = m − n;
               else
            n = n − m ;
                }
    printf ("% d", n) ;
}
```

The program computes

(a) $x \div y$ using repeated subtraction

(b) x mod y using repeated subtraction

(c) the greatest common divisor of x and y

(d) the least common multiple of x and y

196. What does the following algorithm approximate? (Assume m > 1, ∈ > 0).

```
x = m ;
y = 1 ;
while (x − y > ∈)
  {   x = (x + y) / 2 ;
      y = m / m ;
  }
print (x) ;
```

(a) log m (b) m^2

(c) $m^{1/2}$ (d) $m^{1/3}$

197. Consider the following C program segment :

```
struct CellNode {
   struct CellNode *leftChild ;
   int element ;
   struct CellNode *rightChild ;
   } ;
int DoSomething (struct CellNode *ptr)
{
   int value = 0 ;
   if (ptr ! = NULL)
   {  if (ptr − > leftChild ! = NULL)
     value = 1 + DoSomething   (ptr − > leftChild) ;
     if (ptr − > rightChild ! = NULL)
value  =  max (value, 1 + DoSomething
     (ptr − > rightChild)) ;
   }
return (value) ;
}
```

The value returned by the function DoSomething when a pointer to the root of a non-empty tree is passed as argument is

(a) The number of leaf nodes in the tree

(b) The number of nodes in the tree

(c) The number of internal nodes in the tree

(d) The height of the tree

198. Choose the best matching between the programming styles in Group 1 and their characteristics in Group 2.

Group - 1	Group - 2
P. Functional	1. Command-based, procedural
Q. Logic	2. Imperative, abstract data types
R. Object-oriented	3. Side-effect free, declarative, expression evaluation
S. Imperative	4. Declarative, clausal representation, theorem proving

Codes :

	P	Q	R	S
(a)	2	3	4	1
(b)	4	3	2	1
(c)	3	4	1	2
(d)	3	4	2	1

2003

199. Consider the following C function :

```
float f,(float x, int y)     {
float p, s; int i;
for (s = 1, p = 1, i = 1; i < y; i ++)
  {
    p* = x/i;
    s + = p;
  }
  return s;
  }
```

For large values of y, the return value of the function f best approximates

(*a*) X^y (*b*) e^x

(*c*) $\ln(1 + x)$ (*d*) X^X

200. Assume the following C variable declaration :

int *A [10], B [10][10];

Of the following expressions

I. A[2] II A [2] [3]

III. B [1] IV. B [2] [3]

which will not give compile-time errors if used as left hand sides of assignment statements in a C program ?

(*a*) I, II, and IV only (*b*) II, III, and IV only

(*c*) II and IV only (*d*) IV only

201. Let T(n) be the number of different binary search trees on n distinct elements.

Then $T(n) = \sum_{k=1}^{n} T(k-1)\, T(x)$,

where x is

(*a*) $n - k + 1$ (*b*) $n - k$

(*c*) $n - k - 1$ (*d*) $n - k - 2$

202. Suppose the numbers 7, 5, 1, 8, 3, 6, 0, 9, 4, 2 are inserted in that order into an initially empty binary search tree. The binary search tree uses the usual ordering on natural numbers. What is the in-order traversal sequence of the resultant tree ?

(*a*) 7 5 1 0 3 2 4 6 8 9

(*b*) 0 2 4 3 1 6 5 9 8 7

(*c*) 0 1 2 3 4 5 6 7 8 9

(*d*) 9 8 6 4 2 3 0 1 5 7

203. A data structure is required for storing a set of integers such that each of the following operations can be done in (log n) time, where n is the number of elements in the set.

I. Deletion of the smallest element

II. Insertion of an element if it is not already present in the set

Which of the following data structures can be used for this purpose ?

(*a*) A heap can be used but not a balanced binary search tree

(*b*) A balanced binary search tree can be used but not a heap

(*c*) Both balanced binary search tree and heap can be used

(*d*) Neither balanced binary search tree nor heap can be used

204. Let S be a stack of size $n \geq 1$. Starting with the empty stack, suppose we push the first n natural numbers in sequence, and then perform n pop operations. Assume that Push and pop operation take X seconds each, and Y seconds elapse between the end of one such stack operation and the start of the next operation. For $m \geq 1$, define the stack-life of m as the time elapsed from the end of Push(m) to the start of the pop operation that removes m from S. The average stack-life of an element of this stack is

(*a*) n (X + Y) (*b*) 3Y + 2X

(*c*) n (X + Y) – X (*d*) Y + 2X

205. Consider the following 2-3-4 tree (i.e., B-tree with a minimum degree of two) in which each data item is a letter. The usual alphabetical ordering of letters is used in constructing the tree

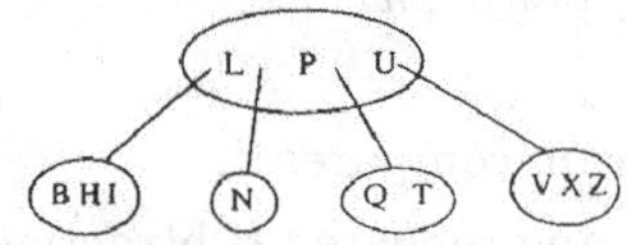

What is the result of inserting G in the above tree ?

(*a*)

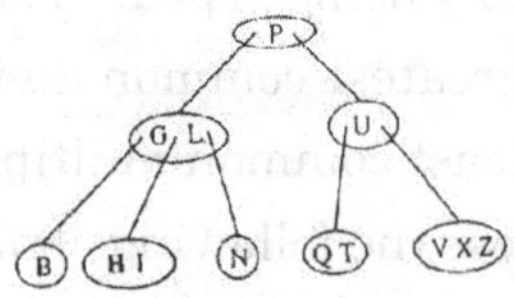

(*b*)

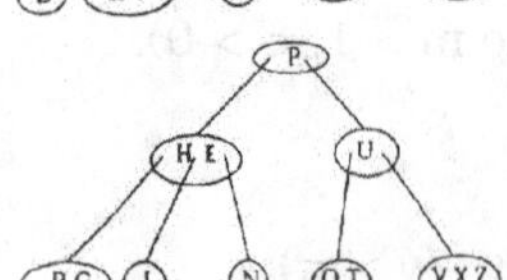

(*c*)

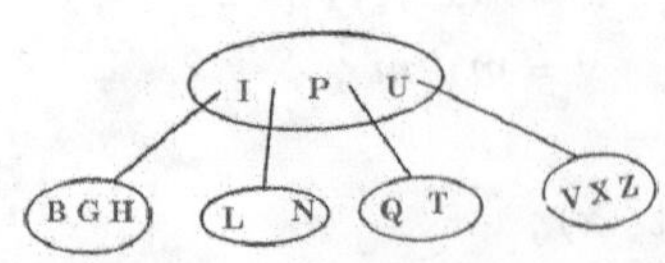

(*d*) None of these

206. In the following C program fragment, j,k n and TwoLog_n are interger variables, and A is an array of integers. The variable n is intialized to an niteger ≥ 3, and TwoLog_n is initialized to the value of $2*\lceil \log_2(n) \rceil$

```
for (k = 3; k < = n; k++)
        A [k} = 0;
for (k = 2; k < = TwoLog_n; k++)
        for (j = k + 1; j <= n; j++)
                A [j] = A [j] | | (j% k);
for (j =  3; j < = n; j++)
        if (!A[j]) printf ("%d ",j);
```

The set of numbers printed by this program fragment is

(a) $\{m \mid m \leq n, (\exists i)\ [m = i!]\}$

(b) $\{m \mid m \leq n, (\exists i)\ [m = i^2]\}$

(c) $\{m \mid m \leq n,$ m is prime$\}$

(d) { }

207. Consider the C program shown below :

```
# include <stdio.h>
#define print (x) printf ("%d", x)
int x;
void Q (int z) {
        z + = x; print (z);
}
void p (int *y) {
    int x = *y+2;
    Q (x); *y = x – 1;
    print (x)
}
main (void) {
    x = 5;
    p (&x);
    print (x);
}
```

The output of this program is

(a) 12 7 6 (b) 22 12 11

(c) 14 6 6 (d) 7 6 6

208. Consider the function f defined below.

```
struct item {
    int data;
    struct item * next;
};
int, f (struct item *p) {
return ((p = = NULL) | | (p – > next = =
NULL) | |
    ((P–> data < = p – > next – > data) &&
            f (p – > next)));
}
```

For a given linked list p, the function f returns 1 if and only if

(a) the list is empty or has exactly one element

(b) the elements in the list are sorted in non-decreasing order of data value

(c) the elements in the list are sorted in non-increasing order of data value

(d) not all elements in the list have the same data value.

2000

209. An $n \times n$ array v is defined as follows :

$v[i, j] = i - j$ for all $i, j,\ 1 \leq i \leq n,\ 1 \leq j \leq n$

The sum of the elements of the array v is

(a) 0 (b) $n - 1$

(c) $n^2 - 3n + 2$ (d) $n^2 (n + 1) /2$

210. The following C declarations

```
struct node {
    int i ;
    float j ;
} ;
struct node *s[10] ;
```

define s to be

(a) An array, each element of which is a pointer to a structure of type node

(b) A structure of 2 fields, each field being a pointer to an array of 10 elements

(c) A structure of 3 fields: an integer, a float, and an array of 10 elements

(d) An array, each element of which is a structure of type node

211. The most appropriate matching for the following pairs

X: m =malloc (5) ; m=NULL; 1 : using dangling pointers

Y: free (n) ; n-> value=5; 2 : using uninitialized pointers

Z: char *p; *p = 'a' ; 3 : lost memory

is

(a) X-1, Y-3, Z-2 (b) X-2, Y-1, Z-3

(c) X-3, Y-2, Z-1 (d) X-3, Y-1, Z-2

212. Aliasing in the context of programming languages refers to

(a) multiple variables having the same memory location

(b) multiple variables having the same value

(c) multiple variables having the same identifier

(d) multiple uses of the same variable

213. Consider the following C declaration

```
struct {
    short s [5]
    union {
        float y;
        long z;
    } u;
} t;
```

Assume that objects of the type short, float and long occupy 2 bytes, 4 bytes and 8 bytes, respectively. The memory requirement for variable *t*, ignoring alignment considerations, is

(*a*) 22 bytes (*b*) 14 bytes
(*c*) 18 bytes (*d*) 10 bytes

214. The number of tokens in the following C statement

```
printf ("i=%d, &i = %x", i, &i);
```

is

(*a*) 3 (*b*) 26
(*c*) 10 (*d*) 21

215. Suppose you are given an array *s*[1..*n*] and a procedure reverse (*s*, *i*, *j*) which reverses the order of elements in a between positions *i* and *j* (both inclusive). What does the following sequence do, where $1 \le k \le n$:

```
reverse (s, 1, k) ;
reverse (s, k + 1, n);
reverse (s,1, n) ;
```

(*a*) Rotates *s* left by *k* positions
(*b*) Leaves *s* unchanged
(*c*) Reverses all elements of *s*
(*d*) None of these

216. The value of *j* at the end of the execution of the following C program

```
int incr (int i)
{
    static int count = 0 ;
    count = count + i ;
    return (count) ;
}
main () {
    int i,j ;
    for (i = 0 ; i < = 4 ; i++)
            j = incr (i) ;
}
```

is

(*a*) 10 (*b*) 4
(*c*) 6 (*d*) 7

217. Consider the line $y = \frac{n}{m}x$, where n and m are positive integers.

(*a*) If $mq - np < 0$, then is the point (*p*, *q*) above the line, below the line, or on the line?

(*b*) Complete the following function, that returns true iff the line segment with endpoints (*p*, *q*) and (*r*, *s*) intersects the line $y = \frac{n}{m}x$, by writing the line number and the content of each box in your answer book.

```
1 : function clash (m, n, p, q, r, s : integer) :
    boolean ;
2 : begin
3 : clash : = false ;
4 : if (m * q – n * p) [    ] 0 then clash : = true;
5 : if (m * s – n * r) [    ] 0 then clash: = true;
6 : if (m* q – n * p) [    ] 0 and (m * s – n * r)
    [    ] 0 then clash : = true;
7 : if (m* q – n * p) [    ] 0 and (m * s – n * r)
    [    ]  0 then clash : = true;
8 : end ;
```

218. Suppose you are given arrays *p* [1.....N] and *q* [1......N] both uninitialized that is, each location may contain an arbitrary value), and a variable count, initialized to 0. Consider the following procedures set and iset :

```
set (i) {
    count  = count + 1;
            q [count] = i ;
            p [i] = count ;
}
is_set (i) {
    if (p [i] ≤ 0 or p [i] > count)
                                return false ;
            if (q [p [i] ] ≠ i)
                return false;
    return true ;
}
```

(*a*) Suppose we make the following sequence of calls :

set (7); set (3); set (9) ;

After these quence of calls, what is the value of count, and what do *q* [1], *q* [2], *q*[3], *p*[7], *p*[3] and *p*[9] contain?

(*b*) Complete the following statement "The first count elements of ________ contain values *i* such that set (________) has been called."

(*c*) Show that if set (*i*) has not been called for some *i*, then regardless of what *p* [*i*] contains, is_set (*i*) will return false.

219. A recursive program to compute Fibonacci numbers is shown below. Assume you are also given an array of [0 .... *m*] with all elements initialised to 0.

```
fib (n) {
      if (n > M) error ( ) ;
      if (n = = 0) return 1;
      if (n ==1) return 1;
   if ( [    ] ) ________ ________ (1)
   return [    ] ________ (2)
   t = fib (n – 1) + fib (n – 2);
   [    ] ____________ (3)
         return t ;
   }
```

(*a*) Fill in the boxes with expressions/statements to make fib ( ) store and reuse computed Fibonacci values. Write the box number and the corresponding contents in your answer book.

(*b*) What is the time complexity of the resulting program when computing fib (*n*)?

220. An array contains four occurrences of 0, five occurrences of 1, and three occurrences of 2 in any order.

The array is to be sorted using swap operations (elements that are swapped need to be adjacent).

(*a*) What is the minimum number of swaps needed to sort such an array in the worst case?

(*b*) Give an ordering of elements in the above array so that the minimum number of swaps needed to sort the array is maximum.

221. Consider the following porgram is pseudo-Pascal syntax.

```
Program main;
   var x : integer;
   procedure Q [z : integer) ;
         begin
               z : = z + x;
               writeln (z)
         end;
   procedure P (y : integer);
         var x : integer;
         begin
               x : = y + 2;
               Q (x);
               writeln (x)
         end;
   begin
         x : = 5;
         P (x) ;
         Q (x);
      writeln (x)
   end.
```

What is the output of the program, when

(*a*) The parameter passing mechanism is call-by-value and the scope rule is static scoping ?

(*b*) The parameter passing mechanism is call-by-reference and the scope rule is dynamic scoping?

1999

222. Given the programming constructs (*i*) assignment (*ii*) for loops where the loop parameter cannot be changed within the loop (*iii*) If-then-else (*iv*) forward goto (*v*) arbitrary goto (*vi*) non-recursive procedure call (*vii*) recursive procedure/function call (*viii*) repeat loop, which constructs will you not include in a programming language such that it should be possible to program the terminates (i.e. halting) function in the same programming language.

(*a*) (*ii*), (*iii*), (*iv*)
(*b*) (*v*), (*vii*), (*viii*)
(*c*) (*vi*), (*vii*), (*viii*)
(*d*) (*iii*), (*vii*), (*viii*)

223. Consider the following program in a language that has dynamic scoping

```
var x : real ;
procedure show
   begin print (x) ; end;
procedure small ;
   var x : real;
      begin x : = 0.125; show; end
begin x : = 0.25;
      show ; small
   end.
```

Then the output of the program is :

(*a*) 0.125 0.125
(*b*) 0.25 0.25
(*c*) 0.25 0.125
(*d*) 0.125 0.25

224. The number of tokens in the Fortran statement DO 10 I = 1.25 is

(*a*) 3
(*b*) 4
(*c*) 5
(*d*) None of these

225. Consider the following C function definition

```
int Trial (int a, int b, int c)
{
   if ((a > = b)&& (c < b) return b;
   else if (a > = b) return Trial (a, c, b);
   else return Trial (b, a, c) ;
}
```

The function Trial :

(*a*) finds the maximum of *a*, *b* and *c*
(*b*) finds the minimum of *a*, *b* and *c*
(*c*) finds the middle number of *a*, *b*, *c*
(*d*) none of the above

226. Suppose we have a function HALTS which when applied to any arbitrary function f and its arguments will say TRUE if function f terminates for those arguments and FALSE otherwise. Example : Given the following function definition.

FACTORIAL (N) = IF (N = 0) THEN 1 ELSE N*FACTORIAL (N-1)

Then HALTS (FACTORIAL 4) = TRUE and HALTS (FACTORIAL-5) = FALSE

Let us define the function FUNNY (f) = IF HALTS (f f) THEN not (f f) ELSE TRUE

(*a*) Show that FUNNY terminates for all functions f.

(*b*) Use (*a*) to prove (*by contradiction*) that it is not possible to have a function like HALTS which for arbitrary functions and inputs says whether it will terminate on that input or not.

227. (*a*) In binary tree, a full node is defined to be a node with 2 children. Use induction on the height of the binary tree to prove that the number of full nodes plus one is equal to the number of leaves.

(*b*) Draw the min-heap that results from insertion of the following elements in order into an initially empty min-heap : 7, 6, 5, 4, 2, 3, 1. Show the result after the deletion of the root of this heap.

228. (*a*) Show that the formula $[(\sim p \vee q) \Rightarrow (q \Rightarrow p)]$ is not a tautology.

(*b*) Let A be a tautology and B be any other formula. Prove that $(A \vee B)$ is a tautology.

229. What will be the output of the following program assuming that parameter passing is

(*i*) call by value

(*ii*) call by reference

(*iii*) call by copy restore

```
procedure P {x, y, z);
    begin y : = y + 1; z : = z + x end;
begin
        a : = 2 : b : = 3;
        P (a + b, a, a);
print (a)
end.
```

230. Consider the following Pascal program skeleton

```
program sort (...);
    var a, x, ...;
    procedure readarray ;
            var i, ....;
            begin
                    ... : = ...a ...
            end;
procedure exchange (...);
            begin
                    ... : = ... a ... ;
                    ... : = ... x .... ;
            end;
procedure qsort (....);
            var k, v, ....;
    function partition (...) ...;
                    var i, j, ... ;
                    begin
                    .... : = ... a .... ;
                    .... : = ... v ... ;
                    end ;
                    begin
                    :
end :
            begin
            :
            end.
```

Assume that at a given point in time during program execution, following procedures are active : sort, qsort (1, 9), qsort (1, 3), partition (1, 3), exchange (1, 3)

Show snaphots of the runtime stack with access links after each of the activations.

1998

231. Which of the following statements is false ?

(*a*) A tree with n nodes has $(n - 1)$ edges.

(*b*) A labelled rooted binary tree can be uniquely constructed given its postorder and preorder traversal results.

(*c*) A complete binary tree with n internal nodes has $(n + 1)$ leaves.

(*d*) The maximum number of nodes in a binary tree of height h is $(2^{h+1} - 1)$

232. A complete n-ary tree is one in which every node has O or n sons. If x is the number of internal nodes of a complete n-ary tree, the number of leaves in it is given by

(*a*) $x(n - 1) + 1$ (*b*) $xn - 1$

(*c*) $xn + 1$ (*b*) $x(n + 1)$

233. What value would the following function return for the input x = 95 ?

```
    Function fun (x : integer) : integer;
begin
    If x > 100 then fun : = x – 10
    else fun : fun (fun (x + 11) )
end;
```

(*a*) 89 (*b*) 90

(*c*) 91 (*d*) 92

234. What is the result of the following program ?

```
Program side-effect (input, output);
var x, result : integer :
Fuction f (var x : integer): integer;
begin
    x : x + 1; F : = x;
end
begin
    x : = 5
    result : = f(x)* f(x)
    writeln (result)
    end
```

(*a*) 5 (*b*) 25

(*c*) 36 (*d*) 42

235. Let A be a two-dimensional array declared as follows

A : array [1 .... 10] [1 ....15] of integer ;

Assuming that each integer takes one memory locations the array is stored in row-major order and the first element of the array is stored at location 100, what is the address of the element A [*i*] [*j*] ?

(*a*) $15i + j + 84$

(*b*) $15j + i + 84$

(*c*) $10i + j + 89$

(*d*) $10j + i + 89$

236. Faster access to non-local variables is achieved using an array of pointers to activation records, called a

(*a*) stack (*b*) heap

(*c*) display (*d*) activation tree

237. (*a*) Let p be a pointer as shown in the figure in a single linked list.

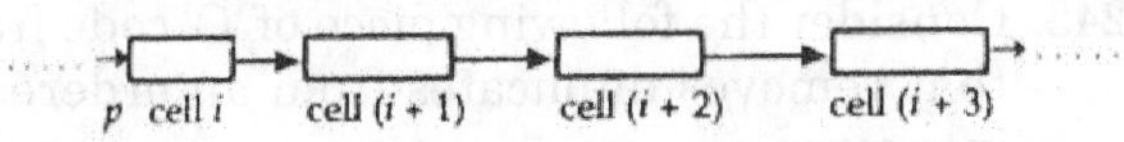

What do the following assignment statements achieve ?

q : = p → next

p → next : = q → next

p → next : = (q → next) → next

(p → next) → next : = q

(*b*) Compute the post fix equivalent of the following infix expression.

$$3 * \log (x + 1) - \frac{a}{2}$$

1997

238. Given the following Pascal-like program segment

```
Procedure A ;
    x, y : integer;
    Procedure B;
                x, z : real;
                S1
    end B ;
    Procedure C;
                i : integer;
                S2
    end C;
end A;
```

The variables accessible in S1 and S2 are

(*a*) *x* of A, *y*, *x* of B and *z* in S1 and *x* of B, *y* and *i* in S2

(*b*) *x* of B, *y* and *z* in S1 and *x* of B, *i* and *z* in S2

(*c*) *x* of B, *z* and *y* in S1 and *x* of A, *i* and *y* in S2

(*d*) None of the above

239. Let G be a graph with 100 vertices numbered 1 to 100. Two vertices i and *j* are adjacent if $| i - j | = 8$ or $| i - j | = 12$. The number of connected components in G is

(*a*) 8 (*b*) 4

(*c*) 12 (*d*) 25

240. Let $L = (a_1, a_2, ..., a_n)$ $n \geq 0$ be a list whose Pascal representation is

type list = record

next : ↑ list ; val : integer end

The following function returns a list in which a_{2i} and a_{2i-1}, $1 \leq i \leq \left\lceil \frac{n}{2} \right\rceil$ are interchanged. Complete the function by filling in the boxes. Write the line number and the content of the box in your answer-sheet.

```
1.  function change (p : ↑ list) : ↑ list ;
2.  var q. t : ↑ list ;
3.  begin
4.  if p = nil then change : = p
5.  else if p ↑ next = nil then change : = [    ]
6.  else begin
7.  q : p ↑ next ;
8.  [    ] : = q ;
9.  t : q ↑ next ;
10. [    ] : = p;
11. [    ] : = change (t)
12. end
13. end
```

241. Consider the following program in Pseudo-Pascal syntax.

```
program what :
        var z : integer
    procedure recur (x) ;
     begin if x ≤ 40 then
                   begin x : = x + z;
                             recur (x) ;
                           z : = x + 10
                   end
        end (*recur*)
  begin (*what*)
             z = 10;
           recur (z);
          writeln (z)
  end
```

(*a*) Suppose the parameter to the procedure 'recur' is passed by value.

(*i*) What value is printed by the program?

(*ii*) How many time is 'recur' called?

(*b*) What value is printed by the program if the parameter is passed by reference ?

242. Consider the following function.

```
Function F (n, m : integer) : integer ;
begin
  If (n < = 0) or (m < = 0) then F : = 1
  else
  F : = F (n – 1, m) + F (n, m – 1);
end;
```

Use the recurrence relation

$$\binom{n}{k} = \binom{n-1}{k} + \binom{n-1}{k-1}$$

to answer the following questions. Assume that n, m, are positive integers. Write only the answers without any explanation.

(*a*) What is the value of F (n, 2) ?

(*b*) What is the value of F (n, m) ?

(*c*) How many recursive calls are made to the function F, including the original call, when evaluating F (n, m) ?

243. A size-balanced binary tree is a binary tree in which for every node, the difference between the number of nodes in the left and right subtree is at most 1. The distance of a node from the root is the length of the path from the root to the node. The height of a binary tree is the maximum distance of a leaf node from the root.

(*a*) Prove, by using induction on h, that a size-balance binary tree of height h contains at least 2^h nodes.

(*b*) In a size-balanced binary tree of height h ≤ 1, how many nodes are at distance h – 1 from the root? Write only the answer without any explanations.

244. An array A contains $n \geq 1$ positive integers in the locations A [1], A[2], ..., A [n]. The following program fragment prints the length of a shortest sequence of consecutive elements of A, A [i], A [i + 1], ..., A[j] such that the sum of their values is ≥ M, a given positive number. It prints 'n + 1' if no such sequence exists. Complete the program by filling the boxes. In each case use the simplest possible expression. Write only the line number and the contents of the box.

```
1.  begin
2.          i : + 1; j : = 1;
3.      Sum : = [        ] ;
4.  min : n; finish : = false ;
5.      While not finish do
6.          If [        ] then
7.  If j = n then finish : = true.
8.                          else
9.                          begin
10.                         j : = j + 1;
11.                         sum : = [        ] ;
12.                         end
13.                 else
14.                 begin
15. If (j – i) < min then min : = j – 1;
16.                         sum : = sum – A [i];
17.                         i : = i + 1;
18.                 end
19.     writeln (min + 1);
20. end
```

245. Consider the following piece of 'C' code fragment that removes duplicates from an ordered list of integers.

```
struct node {
 int val;
struct node *next;};
typedef struct node Node;
Node*remove-duplicates (Node *head, int *j)
{
   Node *t1, *t 2;
   *j = 0;
   i 1 = head;
   if (t 1! = NULL) t2 = t1 → next;
   else return head :
```

```
    * j = 1;
    if (t2 = = NULL) return head;
    while t2 ! = NULL)
    {
    if (t1. val! = t2.val) ──────────► (S1)
    {
    (*j) ++; t1 → next = t2 ; t1 = t2 : ──────► (S2)
    }
          t2 = t2 → next ;
    }
    t1 → next = NULL;
    return head;
}
```

Assume the list contains n elements $(n - 2)$ in the following questions.

(a) How many times is the comparison in statement S1 made ?

(b) What is the minimum and maximum number of times statements marked S2 get executed ?

(c) What is the significance of the value in the integer pointed to by j when the function completes?

246. Consider the following program fragment in Pascal :

```
Program Main;
    var X : integer;
    procedure A;
          var Y : integer;
              procedure B;
                        var Z : integer;
                        procedure C ;
                                  var Z : integer;
                        begin (* procedure C*)
                                               :
                          end (*procedure C*)
begin (*procedure B*)
    :
    C ; (* call to C*)
    A ; (*call to A*)
    :
end (* procedure B*)
begin (* procedure A*)
    :
    B ; (*call to B *)
    :
end (* procedure
```

1996

247. The minimum number of interchanges needed to convert the array

89, 19, 40, 17, 12, 10, 2, 5, 7, 11, 6, 9, 70

into a heap with maximum element at the root is

(a) 0 (b) 1

(c) 2 (d) 3

248. The Fibonacci sequence $\{f_1, f_2, f_3 ....., f_n\}$ is defined by the following recurrence :

$$f_{n+2} = f_{n+1} + f_n, n^{3} 1; f_2 = 1 : f_1 = 1:$$

Prove by induction that every third element of the sequence is even.

249. A two dimensional array $A[1-n][1-n]$ of integers is partially sorted if

$\forall i, j \varepsilon [1 -- n-1] A[i][j] < A[i][j+1]$ and

$A[i][j] <$ $[A[i+1][j]$

Fill in the blanks :

(a) The smallest item in the array is at A [i] [j] where i = and j = ...

(b) The smallest item is deleted. Complete the following O(n) procedure to insert item x (which is guaranteed to be smaller than any item in the last row or column) still keeping A partially sorted.

```
procedureinsert (x integer)
var      j'j : integer ;
begin
(1) i : = 1; j : = A [i] [i] : = x;
(2) while (x >  or x > ) do
(3) if A [i + 1] [j] ∩ [i] [j] then begin
(4) A [i] [j] : = A [i + 1] [j]; i : = i + 1
(5) end
(6) else begin
(7)
(8) end
(9) A [i] [j] : =
end
```

250. Consider the following program that attempts to locate an element x in an array a [ ] using binary search. Assume N > 1. The program is erroneous. Under what conditions does the program fail ?

```
var       i.j.k : integer ; x : integer.
          a : = array ; [1 ... N] of integer;
begin     i : 1; = N ;
repeat    k : (i + j) div 2;
          if a [k] < x then i : = k
          else j : = k
```

```
until (a ] = x) or (i ∩ = j);
if (a [k] = x) then
writeln ('x is not in the array')
else
writeln ('x is not in the array')
end;
```

251. Consider the following program in pseudo-pascal syntax. What is printed by the program if parameter a in procedure test 1 is passed as

(*i*) call-by-reference parameter ?

(*ii*) call-by-value-result parameter ?

```
program Example (input, output);

var b : integer;
procedure test 2;
begin b : = 10 end
procedure test 1 (a : integer);
begin        a : 5;
writeln ('point 1 : 'a, b);
test 2;
Wrote;m ('point : 'a, b);
end ;
begin (*Example*)
b : = 3; test ] (b) ;
writeln ('point 3 : 'b)
end
```

1995

252. A binary tree T has n leaf nodes. The number of nodes of degree 2 in T is

(*a*) $\log_2 n$ (*b*) $n-1$

(*c*) n (*d*) 2^n

253. The minimum number of edges in a connected cyclic graph on *n* vertices is

(*a*) $n - 1$ (*b*) n

(*c*) $n + 1$ (*d*) None of these

254. A language with string manipulation facilities uses the following operations

head (s) : first character of a string

tail (s) : all but the first character of a string

contcat (s1, s2) : s1 s2

For the string acbc what will be the output of

Contcat (head(s), head (tail (tail(s))))

(*a*) *ac* (*b*) *bc*

(*c*) *ab* (*d*) *cc*

255. The postfix expression for the infix expression A + B * (C + D) / F + D * E is

(*a*) AB + CD + * F/D + E*

(*b*) ABCD + * F/DE * ++

(*c*) A *B + CD/F * DE ++

(*d*) A + * BCD/F* DE ++

256. Merge sort uses

(*a*) Divide and conquer strategy

(*b*) Backtracking approach

(*c*) Heuristic search

(*d*) Greedy approach

257. For merging two sorted lists of sizes *m* and *n* into a sorted list of size m + n, we require comparisons of

(*a*) O (*m*) (*b*) O (*n*)

(*c*) O (*m* + *n*) (*d*) O (log *m* + log *n*)

258. Which of the following statements is true ?

I. As the number of entries in a hash table increases, the number of collisions increases

II. Recursive programs are efficient

III. The worst case complexity for Quicksort is $O(n^2)$

IV. Binary search using a linear linked list is efficient

(*a*) I and II (*b*) II and III

(*c*) I and IV (*d*) I and III

1994

259. An unrestricted use of the "goto" statement is harmful because

(*a*) it makes it more difficult to verify programs

(*b*) it increases the running time of the programs

(*c*) it increases the memory required for the programs

(*d*) it results in the compiler generating longer machine code

260. The number of distinct simple graphs with upto three nodes is

(*a*) 15 (*b*) 11

(*c*) 7 (*d*) 9

261. In a compact single dimensional array representation for lower triangular matrices (i.e. all the elements above the diagonal are zero) of size n n, non-zero elements (i e elements of the lower triangle) of each row are stored one after another, starting from the first row, the index of the (i.j)th element of the lower triangular matrix in this new representation is

(a) $i + j$ (b) $i + j - 1$

(c) $j + \frac{i(i-1)}{2}$ (d) $i + \frac{j(j-1)}{2}$

262. The number of substrings (of all lengths inclusive) that can be formed from a character string of length n is

(a) n (b) n^2

(c) $\frac{n(n-1)}{2}$ (d) $\frac{n(n+1)}{2}$

263. Linked lists are not suitable data structures of which one of the following problems ?

(a) Insertion sort

(b) Binary search

(c) Radix sort

(d) Polynomial manipulation

264. In which one of the following cases is it possible to obtain different results for call-by reference and call-by-name parameter passing methods?

(a) Passing a constant value as a parameter

(b) Passing the address of an array as a parameter

(c) Passing an array element as a parameter

(d) Passing an array following statements is true?

265. Which one of the following statements is true ?

(a) Macro definitions cannot appear within other macro definitions in assembly language programs

(b) Overlaying is used to run a program which is longer than the address space of computer

(c) Virtual memory can be used to accommodate a program which is longer than the address space of a computer of a

(d) It is not possible to write interrupt service routines in a high level language

266. Which one of the following statements is false ?

(a) Optimal binary search tree construction can be performed efficiently using dynamic programming

(b) Breadth-first search cannot be used to find converted components of a graph

(c) Given the prefix and postfix walks over a binary tree, the binary tree cannot be uniquely constructed

(d) Depth-first search can be used to find connected components of a graph

267. The recurrence relation that arises in relation with the complexity of binary search is

(a) $T(n) = T(n/2) + k$, k a constant

(b) $T(n) = 2T(n/2) + k$, k a constant

(c) $T(n) = T(n/2) + \log n$

(d) $T(n) = T(n/2) + n$

268. Which of the following algorithm design techniques is used in the quicksort algorithm ?

(a) Dynamic programming

(b) Backtracking

(c) Divide and conquer

(d) Greedy method

1993

269. What is the scope of m declared in the main program ?

(a) PARAM, P, Q (b) PARAM, P

(c) PARAM, Q (d) P, Q

(e) None of the above

270. What does the following code do ?

```
var a, b : integer;
begin
    a : = a + b;
    b : = a – b;
    a : = a – b
end;
```

(a) exchanges a and b

(b) doubles a and stores in b

(c) doubles b and stores in a

(d) leaves a and b unchanged

(e) none of these

271. For the program segment given below, which of the following are true ?

```
program main (output);
type link = ^ data;
    data = record
                d : real;
                n : link
                    end;
```

```
var ptr : link;
begin
    new (ptr);
    ptr : = nil;
    .ptr^.d : = 5.2;
    write ln (ptr)
end.
```

(*a*) The program leads to compile time error

(*b*) The program leads to run time error

(*c*) The program outputs 5.2

(*d*) The program produces error relating to nil pointer dereferencing

(*e*) None of the above

272. Consider a simple connected graph G with n vertices and **n**-edges ($n > 2$). Then, which of the following statements are true ?

(*a*) G has no cycles.

(*b*) The graph obtained by removing any edge from G is not connected.

(*c*) G has at least one cycle.

(*d*) The graph obtained by removing any two edges from G is not connected.

(*e*) None of these

1992

273. Which of the following problems is not NP-hard?

(*a*) Hamiltonian circuit problem

(*b*) The 0/1 Knapsack problem

(*c*) Finding biconnected components of a graph

(*d*) The graph colouring problem

274. A 2-3 tree is a tree such that

(*a*) all internal nodes have either 2 or 3 children

(*b*) all paths from root to the leaves have the same length.

The number of internal nodes of a 2-3 tree having 9 leaves could be

(*a*) 4 (*b*) 5

(*c*) 6 (*d*) 7

275. A non-planar graph with minimum number of vertices has

(*a*) 9 edges, 6 vertices

(*b*) 6 edges, 4 vertices

(*c*) 10 edges, 5 vertices

(*d*) 9 edges, 5 vertices

276. Following algorithm (*s*) can be used to sort n integers in the range [1 ....n^3] in 0 (n) time

(*a*) Heapsort

(*b*) Quicksort

(*c*) Mergesort

(*d*) Radixsort

277. At a particular time of computation the value of a counting semaphore is 7. Then 20 P operations and 15 V operations were completed on this sempahore. The resulting value of the semaphore is

(*a*) 42 (*b*) 2

(*c*) 7 (*d*) 12

NUMERICAL TYPE QUESTIONS

2016

1. Consider the following directed graph:

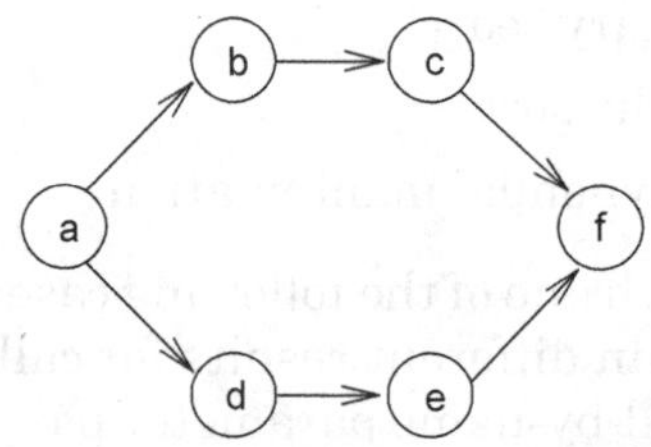

The number of different topological orderings of the vertices of the graph is ________.

2. Consider the following C program.

```
#include<stdio.h>
void mystery (int *ptra, int *ptrb) {
    int *temp;
    temp = ptrb;
    ptrb = ptra;
    ptra = temp;
}
int main () {
    int a=2016, b=0, c=4, d=42;
    mystery (&a, &b) ;
    if (a < c)
        mystery (&c, &a) ;
    mystery (&a, &d) ;
    printf("%d\n", a);
}
```

The output of the program is ______ .

3. Consider the weighted undirected graph with 4 vertices, where the weight of edge $\{i, j\}$ is given by the entry W_{ij} in the matrix W.

$$W = \begin{bmatrix} 0 & 2 & 8 & 5 \\ 2 & 0 & 5 & 8 \\ 8 & 5 & 0 & x \\ 5 & 8 & x & 0 \end{bmatrix}$$

The largest possible integer value of x, for which at least one shortest path between some pair of vertices will contain the edge with weight x is ______.

4. Let G be a complete undirected graph on 4 vertices, having 6 edges with weights being 1, 2, 3, 4, 5, and 6. The maximum possible weight that a minimum weight spanning tree of G can have is ______.

5. Breadth First Search (BFS) is started on a binary tree beginning from the root vertex. There is a vertex t at a distance four from the root. If t is the n-th vertex in this BFS traversal, then the maximum possible value of n is______

6. The value printed by the following program is______.

```
void f(int* p, int m){
    m = m + 5;
    *p = *p + m;
    return;
}
void main()
{
    int i=5, j=10;
    f(&i, j);
printf("%d", i+j);
}
```

7. A complete binary min-heap is made by including each integer in [1,1023] exactly once. The depth of a node in the heap is the length of the path from the root of the heap to that node. Thus, the root is at depth 0. The maximum depth at which integer 9 can appear is ______.

8. Consider the following program:

```
int f(int *p, int n)
{
    if (n <= 1) return 0;
    else return max(f(p+1,n-1),p[0]-
p[1]);
}
int main()
{
    int a[] = {3,5,2,6,4};
    printf("%d", f(a,5));
}
```

Note: max(x,y) returns the maximum of x and y. The value printed by this programis__________.

9. The number of ways in which the numbers 1, 2, 3, 4, 5, 6, 7 can be inserted in an empty binary search tree, such that the resulting tree has height 6, is__________.

Note: The height of a tree with a single node is 0.

10. Let Q denote a queue containing sixteen numbers and S be an empty stack. Head (Q) returns the element at the head of the queue Q **without** removing it from Q, Similarly Top (S) returns the element at the top of S **without** removing it from S, Consider the algorithm given below.

```
while Q is not Empty do
    if S is Empty OR Top (S) ≤ Head (Q) then
        x:=Dequeue (Q);
        Push(S; x);
    else
        x:= Pop(S);
        Enqueue (Q,x);
    end
end
```

The maximum possible number of iterations of the **while** loop in the algorithm is________.

11. The given diagram shows the flowchart for a recursive function A(n). Assume that all statements, except for the recursive calls, have O(1) time complexity. If the worst case time complexity of this function is $O(n^{\alpha})$, then the least possible value (accurate up to two decimal positions) of α is________.

Flowchart for Recursive Function A(n)

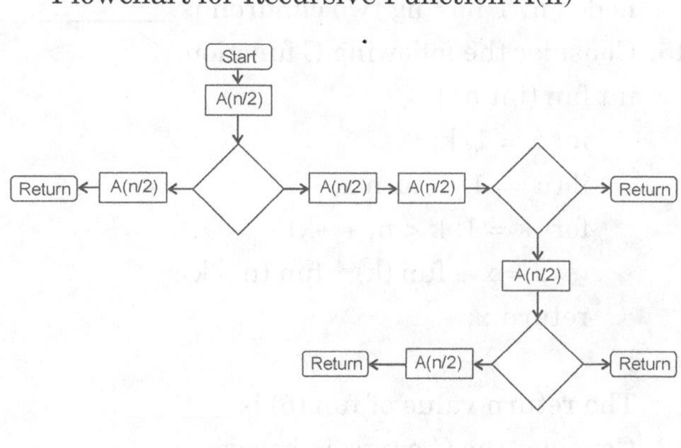

2015

12. The output of the following C program is ______.

```
void f1(int a, int b)
{
    int c;
    c =a; a=b; b=c;
}
void f2(int *a, int *b)
{
    int c;
    c =*a; *a=*b; *b=c;
}
int main ( )
{
    int a=4, b=5, c=6;
    f1(a, b);
    f2(&b, &c);
    printf("%d", c–a–b);
}
```

13. Consider the following C program segment.

```
while (first <= last)
{
    if(array[middle] < search)
        first = middle + 1;
    else if (array[middle] = = search)
            found = TRUE;
    else last = middle – 1;
    middle = (first + last)/2;
}
if (first > last) notPresent = TRUE;
```

The cyclomatic complexity of the program segment is ______.

14. A binary tree T has 20 leaves. The number of nodes in T having two children is ________.

15. Consider the following C function.

```
int fun (int n) {
    int x = 1, k;
    if (n == 1) return x;
    for (k = 1; k < n; + +k)
        x = x + fun (k) * fun (n – k);
    return x;
}
```

The return value of fun (5) is ______

16. Consider the C program below.

```
#include <stdio.h>
Int *A, stkTop;
Int stkFunc (int opcode, int val)
{
    Static int size =0, stkTop=0;
Switch (opcode) {
    Case -1 : Size = val; break;
    Case 0 : if (stkTop < size) A (stktop++] = val;
    break;
    Default : if (stktop) return A [--stkTop];
}
return -1;
}
int main ( )
{
int B[20] ; A = B; stkTop = -1;
stkFunc (-1, 10);
stkFunc (0, 5);
stkFunc (0, 10);
print f ("%d\n", stkFunc(1, 0) + stkfunc(1, 0);
}
```

The value printed by the above program is _____.

17. Consider a binary tree T that has 200 leaf nodes. Then, the number of nodes in T that have exactly two children are ____.

18. Suppose $c = \langle c[0], ..., c[k-1]\rangle$ is an array of length k, where all the entries are from the set {0, 1}. For any positive integers a and n, consider the following pseudo code.

DOSOMETHING (c, a, n)

$z \leftarrow 1$

for $i \leftarrow 0$ to $k - 1$

  do $z \leftarrow z^2 \bmod n$

  if $c[i] = 1$

  then $z \leftarrow (z \times a) \bmod n$

  return z

If $k = 4$, $c = \langle 1.0, 1, 1\rangle$, $a = 2$ and $n = 8$, then the output of DOSOMETHING (c, a, n) is _______.

19. Consider the following C program

```
# include < stdio.h >
int main ( )
{
    static int a [ ] = {10, 20, 30, 40, 50};
    static int * p [ ] = {a, a + 3, a + 4, a + 1, a + 2};
    int **ptr = p;
    ptr ++;
    print f ("%d %d", ptr – p, **ptr):
}
```

The output of the program is ________.

20. Consider the following C program

```
#include < stdio.h >
int main ( )
{
    int i, j, k = 0;
    j = 2*3/4 + 2.0/5 + 8/5;
    k – = – – j;
    for (i = 0; i < 5; i ++)
        {
            Switch (i + k)
        {
            case1 :
            case 2 : printf ("\ n % d", i + k)
            case 3 : printf ("\ n % d", i + k);
            default : print f ("\ n%d", i + k) ;
        }
    }
    Return 0 :
}
```

The number of times printf statement is executed is ______.

21. Consider the following C program.

```
#include < stdio.h >
int f1 (void);
int f2 (void);
int x = 10;

int main ( )
    {
        int x = 1;
        x + = f1 ( ) + f2 ( ) + f3 ( ) + f2 ( );
        print f ("%d", x);
        return 0;
    }
    int f1 ( ) {int x = 25; x ++; return x;}
    int f2 ( ) {static int x = 50; x + +; return x;}
    int f3 ( ) {x* = 10; return x};
```

The output of program is ________.

22. The graph shown below has 8 edges with distinct integer edge weights. The minimum spanning tree (MST) is of weight 36 and contains the edges: {(A, C), (B, C), (B, E), (E, F), (D, F)}. The edge weights of only those edges which are in the MST are given in the figure shown below. The minimum possible sum of weights of all 8 edges of this graph is ______.

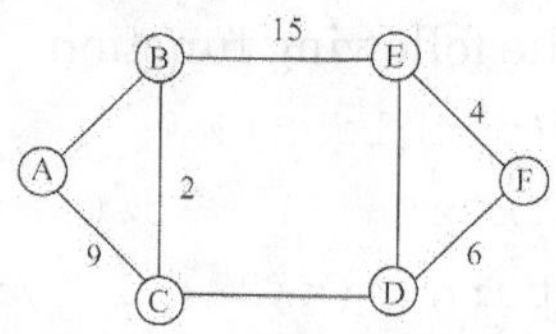

23. Let G be a connected planar graph with 10 vertices. If the number of edges on each face is three, then the number of edges in G is ______.

24. Let G be a connected undirected graph of 100 vertices and 300 edges. The weight of a minimum spanning tree of G is 500. When the weight of each edge of G is increased by five, the weight of a minimum spanning tree becomes ________.

2014

25. Consider an undirected graph G where self-loops are not allowed. The vertex set of G is (i, j): $1 \le i \le 12$, $1 \le j \le 12\}$. There is an edge between (a, b) and (c, d) if $|a - c| \le 1$ and $|b - d| \le 1$. The number of edges in the graph is ____________.

26. Consider the function `func` shown below:

```
int func(int num) {
int count = 0;
  while (num) {
        count++;
        num>>= 1;
  }
return (count);
}
```

The value returned by `func(435)` is ________.

27. Three processes A, B and C each execute a loop of 100 iterations. In each iteration of the loop, a process performs a single computation that requires t_c CPU milliseconds and then initiates a single I/O operation that lasts for t_{io} milliseconds. It is assumed that the computer where the processes execute has sufficient number of I/O devices and the OS of the computer assigns different I/O devices to each process. Also, the scheduling overhead of the OS is negligible. The processes have the following characteristics:

Process id	t_c	t_{io}
A	100 ms	500 ms
B	350 ms	500 ms
C	200 ms	500 ms

The processes A, B, and C are started at times 0, 5 and 10 milliseconds respectively, in a pure time sharing system (round robin scheduling) that uses a time slice of 50 milliseconds. The time in milliseconds at which process C would complete its first I/O operation is ________.

28. Consider the following function

```
double f(double x){
  if( abs(x*x - 3) < 0.01) return x;
  else return f(x/2 + 1.5/x);
}
```

Give a value q (to 2 decimals) such that f(q) will return q:_____.

29. The number of distinct minimum spanning trees for the weighted graph below is _____

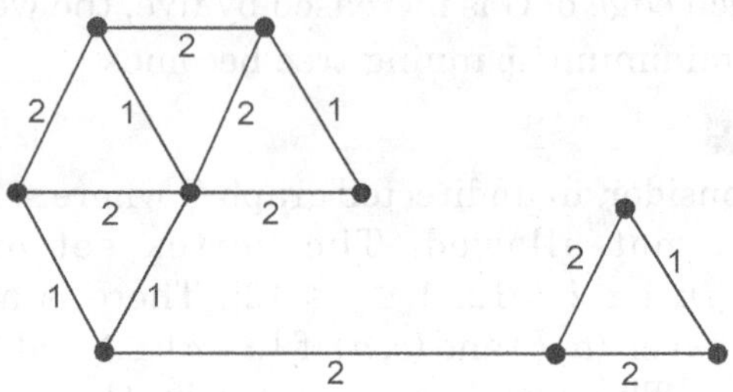

30. The minimum number of arithmetic operations required to evaluate the polynomial $P(X) = X^5 + 4X^3 + 6X + 5$ for a given value of X, using only one temporary variable is _____.

31. Suppose depth first seach is executed on the graph below starting at some unknown vertex. Assume that a recursive call to visit a vertex is made only after first checking that the vertex has not been visited earlier. Then the maximum possible recursion depth (including the initial call) is _________.

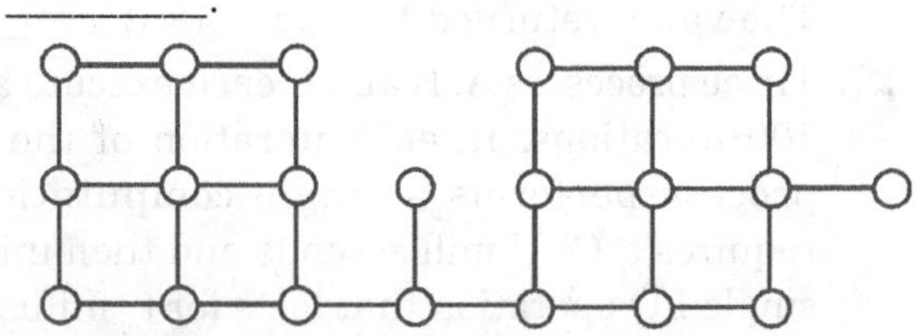

32. Consider a rooted n node binary tree represented using pointers. The best upper bound on the time required to determine the number of subtrees having exactly 4 nodes is $O(n^a \log^b n)$. Then the value of $a + 10b$ is_____

33. The minimum number of comparisons required to find the minimum and the maximum of 100 numbers is ___________.

34. The maximum number of edges in a bipartite graph on 12 vertices is _____.

35. Consider two strings A = "*qpqrr*" and B = "*pqprqrp*". Let x be the length of the longest common subsequence (not necessarily contiguous) between A and B and let y be the number of such longest common subsequences between A and B. Then $x + 10y$ =_____

36. Suppose P, Q, R, S, T are sorted sequences having lengths 20, 24, 30, 35, 50 respectively. They are to be merged into a single sequence by merging together two sequences at a time. The number of comparisons that will be needed in the worst case by the optimal algorithm for doing this is ______.

37. Consider the expression tree shown. Each leaf represents a numerical value, which can either be 0 or 1. Over all possible choices of the values at the leaves, the maximum possible value of the expression represented by the tree is ________.

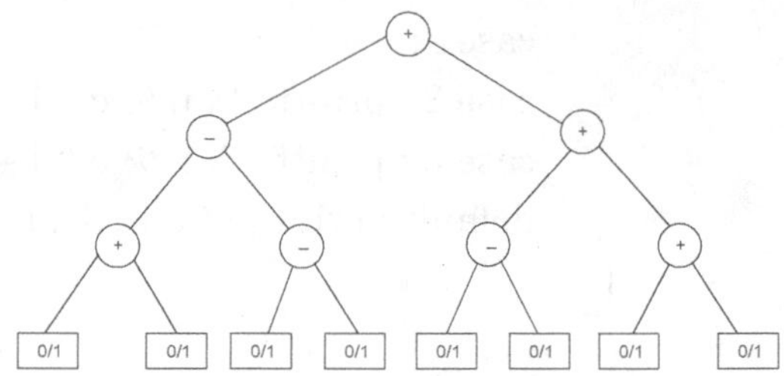

38. A cycle on n vertices is isomorphic to its complement. The value of n is _____.

39. Suppose you want to move from 0 to 100 on the number line. In each step, you either move right by a unit distance or you take a *shortcut*. A shortcut is simply a pre-specified pair of integers i, j with $i < j$. Given a shortcut i, j if you are at position i on the number line, you may directly move to j. Suppose $T(k)$ denotes the smallest number of steps needed to move from k to 100. Suppose further that there is at most 1 shortcut involving any number, and in particular from 9 there is a shortcut to 15. Let y and z be such that $T(9) = 1 + \min(T(y), T(z))$. Then the value of the product yz is ___________.

40. Suppose we have a balanced binary search tree T holding n numbers. We are given two numbers L and H and wish to sum up all the numbers in T that lie between L and H. Suppose there are m such numbers in T. If the tightest upper bound on the time to compute the sum is $O(n^a \log^b n + m^c \log^d n)$, the value of $a + 10b + 100c + 1000d$ is _____.

1992

41. Complexity of Kruskal's algorithm for finding the minimum spanning tree of an undirected graph containing n vertices and m edges if the edges are sorted is ....

42. Maximum number of edges in a planar graph with n vertices is ....

ANSWERS

MCQ Type Questions

1. (*d*)	**2.** (*d*)	**3.** (*d*)	**4.** (*a*)	**5.** (*c*)	**6.** (*c*)	**7.** (*a*)	**8.** (*c*)	**9.** (*c*)	**10.** (*a*)
11. (*d*)	**12.** (*b*)	**13.** (*d*)	**14.** (*c*)	**15.** (*c*)	**16.** (*b*)	**17.** (*a*)	**18.** (*a*)	**19.** (*b*)	**20.** (*a*)
21. (*d*)	**22.** (*d*)	**23.** (**b**)	**24.** (*a*)	**25.** (*d*)	**26.** (*c*)	**27.** (*c*)	**28.** (*c*)	**29.** (*a*)	**30.** (*b*)
31. (*c*)	**32.** (*c*)	**33.** (*b*)	**34.** (*b*)	**35.** (*d*)	**36.** (*b*)	**37.** (*a*)	**38.** (*d*)	**39.** (*a*)	**40.** (*a*)
41. (*c*)	**42.** (*b*)	**43.** (*d*)	**44.** (*b*)	**45.** (*c*)	**46.** (*d*)	**47.** (*b*)	**48.** (*c*)	**49.** (*b*)	**50.** (*d*)
51. (*a*)	**52.** (*c*)	**53.** (*c*)	**54.** (*b*)	**55.** (*c*)	**56.** (*a*)	**57.** (*c*)	**58.** (*d*)	**59.** (*c*)	**60.** (*a*)
61. (*a*)	**62.** (*d*)	**63.** (*b*)	**64.** (*c*)	**65.** (*c*)	**66.** (**c**)	**67.** (*c*)	**68.** (*d*)	**69.** (*a*)	**70.** (*a*)
71. (*b*)	**72.** (*a*)	**73.** (*a*)	**74.** (*a*)	**75.** (*c*)	**76.** (*c*)	**77.** (*b*)	**78.** (*b*)	**79.** (*b*)	**80.** (*b*)
81. (*c*)	**82.** (*b*)	**83.** (*a*)	**84.** (*c*)	**85.** (*b*)	**86.** (*a*)	**87.** (*a*)	**88.** (*d*)	**89.** (*)	**90.** (*a*)
91. (*)	**92.** (*b*)	**93.** (*b*)	**94.** (*c*)	**95.** (*d*)	**96.** (*c*)	**97.** (*b*)	**98.** (*d*)	**99.** (*b*)	**100.** (*b*)
101. (*c*)	**102.** (*b*)	**103.** (*a*)	**104.** (*c*)	**105.** (*d*)	**106.** (*a*)	**107.** (*d*)	**108.** (*b*)	**109.** (*a*)	**110.** (*d*)
111. (*b*)	**112.** (*c*)	**113.** (*d*)	**114.** (*d*)	**115.** (*a*)	**116.** (*c*)	**117.** (*d*)	**118.** (*b*)	**119.** (*b*)	**120.** (*a*)
121. (*b*)	**122.** (*c*)	**123.** (*a*)	**124.** (*c*)	**125.** (*d*)	**126.** (*b*)	**127.** (*a*)	**128.** (*d*)	**129.** (*d*)	**130.** (*b*)
131. (*c*)	**132.** (*c*)	**133.** (*d*)	**134.** (*a*)	**135.** (*a*)	**136.** (*d*)	**137.** (*b*)	**138.** (*b*)	**139.** (*d*)	**140.** (*d*)
141. (*a*)	**142.** (*b*)	**143.** (*a*)	**144.** (*d*)	**145.** (*a*)	**146.** (*d*)	**147.** (*c*)	**148.** (*c*)	**149.** (*b*)	**150.** (*a*)
151. (*a*)	**152.** (*b*)	**153.** (*d*)	**154.** (*c*)	**155.** (*d*)	**156.** (*a*)	**157.** (*d*)	**158.** (*d*)	**159.** (*a*)	**160.** (*c*)
161. (*c*)	**162.** (*b*)	**163.** (*a*)	**164.** (*b*)	**165.** (*c*)	**166.** (*d*)	**167.** (*c*)	**168.** (*c*)	**169.** (*c*)	**170.** (*d*)
171. (*d*)	**172.** (*d*)	**173.** (*a*)	**174.** (*c*)	**175.** (*a*)	**176.** (*c*)	**177.** (*c*)	**178.** (*c*)	**179.** (*b*)	**180.** (*a*)
181. (*d*)	**182.** (*d*)	**183.** (*a*)	**184.** (*c*)	**185.** (*d*)	**186.** (*d*)	**187.** (*b*)	**188.** (*b*)	**189.** (*c*)	**190.** (*a*)
191. (*a*)	**192.** (*c*)	**193.** (*a*)	**194.** (*a*)	**195.** (*c*)	**196.** (*c*)	**197.** (*d*)	**198.** (*d*)	**199.** (*c*)	**200.** (*d*)
201. (*a*)	**202.** (*b*)	**203.** (*b*)	**204.** (*d*)	**205.** (*c*)	**206.** (*b*)	**207.** (*a*)	**208.** (*d*)	**209.** (*a*)	**210.** (*a*)
211. (*d*)	**212.** (*a*)	**213.** (*c*)	**214.** (*c*)	**215.** (*a*)	**216.** (*a*)	**217.** (*)	**218.** (*)	**219.** (*)	**220.** (*)
221. (*)	**222.** (*b*)	**223.** (*c*)	**224.** (*c*)	**225.** (*c*)	**226.** (*)	**227.** (*)	**228.** (*)	**229.** (*)	**230.** (*)
231. (*c*)	**232.** (*a*)	**233.** (*c*)	**234.** (*c*)	**235.** (*b*)	**236.** (*d*)	**237.** (*)	**238.** (*c*)	**239.** (*b*)	**240.** (*)
241. (*c*)	**242.** (*)	**243.** (*)	**244.** (*)	**245.** (*)	**246.** (*)	**247.** (*c*)	**248.** (*)	**249.** (*)	**250.** (*)
251. (*)	**252.** (*b*)	**253.** (*b*)	**254.** (*c*)	**255.** (*b*)	**256.** (*a*)	**257.** (*c*)	**258.** (*d*)	**259.** (*a*)	**260.** (*b*)
261. (*c*)	**262.** (*d*)	**263.** (*b*)	**264.** (*b*)	**265.** (*b*)	**266.** (*a*)	**267.** (*a*)	**268.** (*c*)	**269.** (*c*)	**270.** (*a*)
271. (*b*, *d*)	**272.** (*c*, *d*)	**273.** (*c*)	**274.** (*a*, *d*)	**275.** (*)	**276.** (*d*)	**277.** (*c*)			

Numerical Type Questions

1. (6) **2.** (2016) **3.** (11) **4.** (7) **5.** (31) **6.** (30) **7.** (8) **8.** (3) **9.** (64)

10. (256) **11.** (2.32) **12.** (–5) **13.** (5) **14.** (19) **15.** (51) **16.** (15) **17.** (199) **18.** (0)

19. (140) **20.** (10) **21.** (230) **22.** (69) **23.** (24) **24.** (995) **25.** (506) **26.** (9 to 9)

27. (1000 to 1000) **28.** (1.72 to 1.74) **29.** (6 to 6) **30.** (7) **31.** (19) **32.** (1)

33. (148) **34.** (36 to 36) **35.** (34 to 34) **36.** (358 to 358) **37.** (6 to 6)

38. (5 to 5) **39.** (150) **40.** (110) **41.** O($m+n$) **42.** ($3n-6$)

EXPLANATIONS

MCQ TYPE QUESTIONS

1. $f(i, * p)$

```
void f(int, short);
    void main( )
{
    int i = 100;
    short s = 12;
    short * p = &s;
    f(i, * p);
}
```

2. Example :

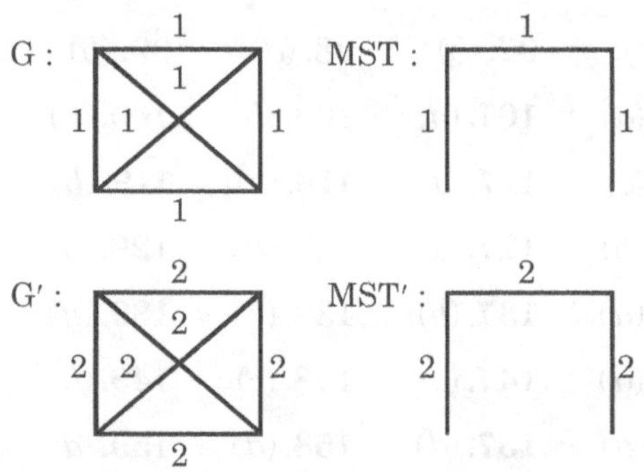

- Minimum spanning tree of G does not change.
- Shortest path between any pair of vertices does not change.

3. b ! = a

4.

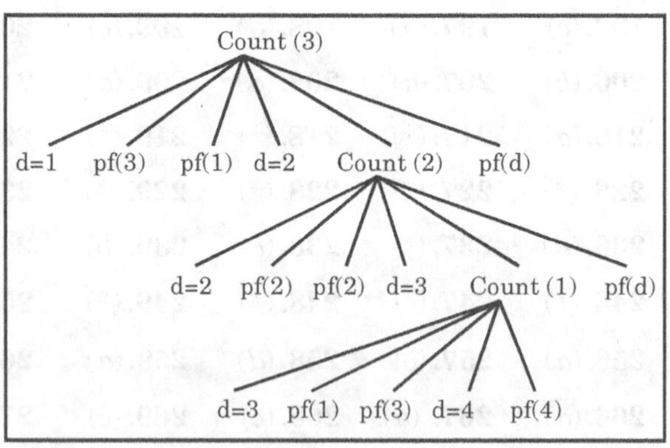

Output : 3 1 2 2 1 3 4 4 4

5.

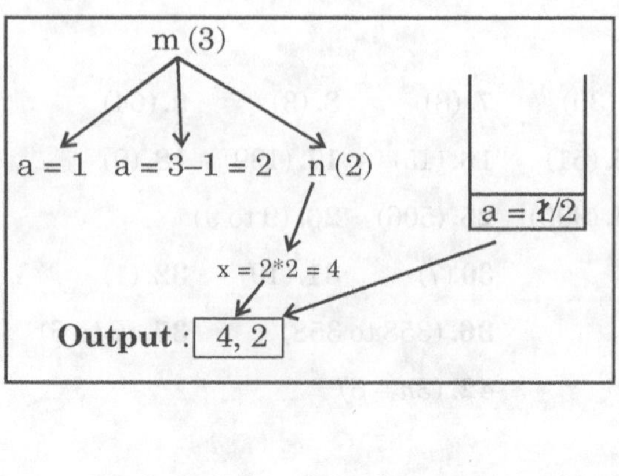

6. Both I and II

7. A Tree is called balanced, if the length of the paths from the root to all leaf nodes are all equal.

9.

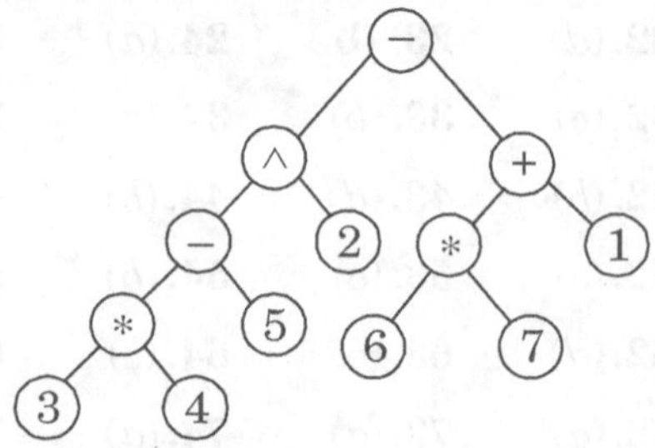

Given expression is 34 * 5 – 2 ∨ 6 7 * 1 + –

Now Converse it into preorder

1. Root
2. RST
3. LST

10. Both ENQUEUE and DEQUEUE operations can be performed in O(1) time.

11.

		Worst Case
Insertion sort	→	$O(n^2)$
Merge sort	→	$O(n \log n)$
Quick sort	→	$O(n^2)$

12. In a Binary heap

The re-fix takes log$n$ time

Here d is depth

Hence $O(d)$.

13. 1. Quicksort will take worst case, if the input is in ascending order i.e $\Theta(n^2)$

2. Insertion sort runs in $\Theta(n)$ time.

14. Dynamic programming

17. Maximum number of nodes with height $h \Rightarrow 2^{5+1} - 1 = 63$ nodes is $2^{h+1} - 1$

and minimum no. of nodes with height h is $h + 1$.

Hence $5 + 1 = 6$ nodes.

18. 1. 3, 5, 7, 8, 15, 19, 25

4. 4, 6, 7, 9, 18, 20, 25

All nodes are in ascending order inorder traversal of a binary search tree.

20. 2036, 2036, 2036,

It will return initial address for all three i.e 2036

21. $n \log(\log n)$

First for loop is running n times nested loops are running log (log n) times.

Hence total running time is $n \log(\log n)$

22. DCBA is the output

The condition will fail on encountering (' '-space), and printed character will be DCBA

23. A bridge can not be part of simple cycle

27. 1204

S_1 is

1	2	3	4
1	2	3	4

$P = S_1 + 2$

P = 0

1	2	0	4

28.

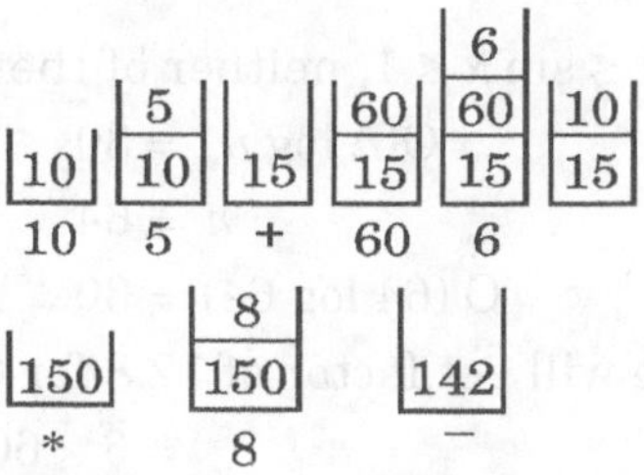

29. Program-X :

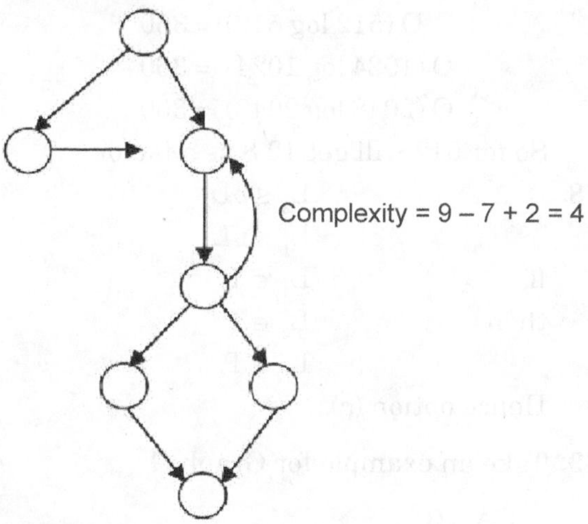

Program-Y :

Cyclomatic complexity = 10 – 8 + 2 = 4

Program Z :

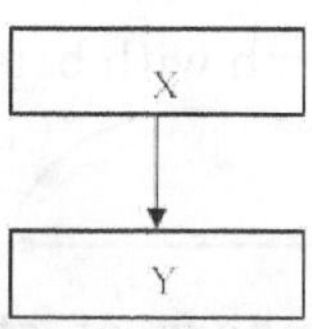

Total number of edges = X + Y + 1 ⇒ 20

Total number of vertices = 15

Hence cyclomatic complexity = 20 – 15 + 2 = 7

30.

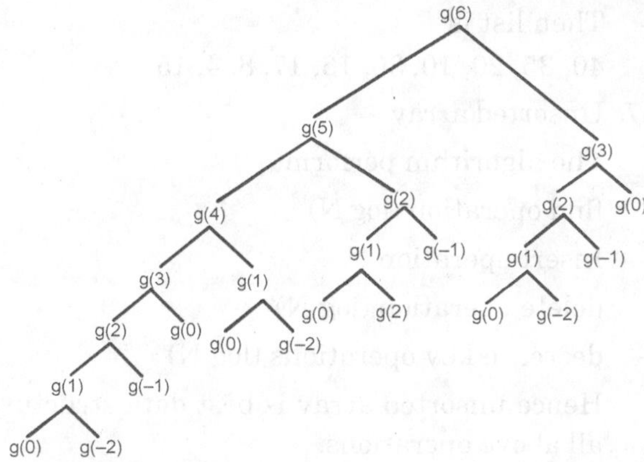

Total calls = 25

32. Prims algorithm is greedy method because it choose minimum distance node.

Floyd warshal's is dynamic because it changes the distance on each iteration.

Merge sort is divide and conquer because it divide the hole list is sublist and combine after sorting each sublist Hamiltonian cycle is based on backtracking.

33. The recurrence equation is

$$T(n) = T(n-1) + T(1) + cn$$

In quick sort, worst case divide the list into two list with 1 and $(n-1)$ elements each time.

34. Both insertion and deletion of a key is a binary search tree is Q(n) in worst case as both are worst case of BST will take Q(n) for insertion and deletion.

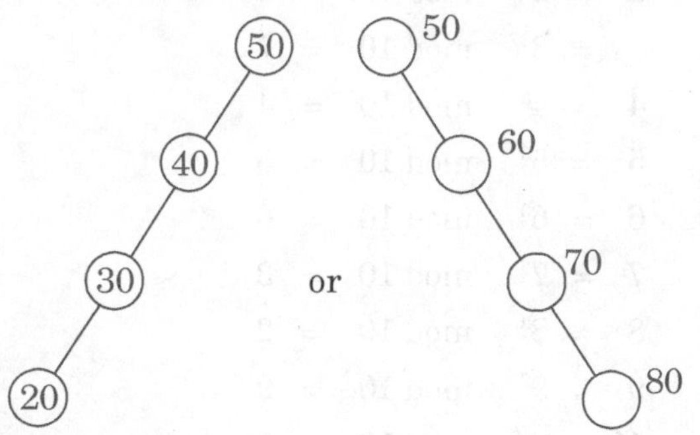

35. $d(u) - d(v) \neq 2$

36. The max heap is

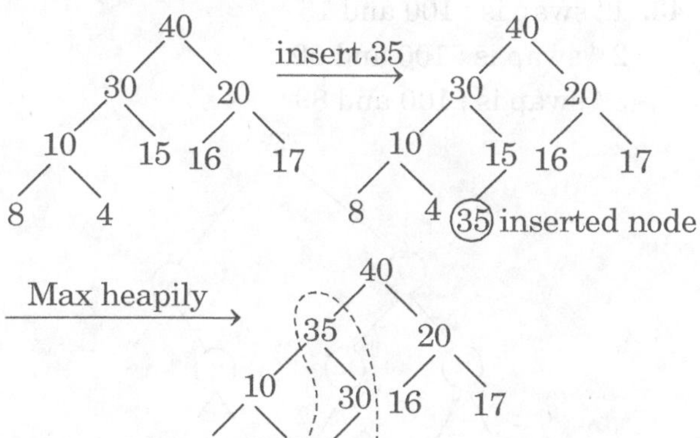

Then list is

40, 35, 20, 10, 30, 16, 17, 8, 4, 15

37. Unsorted array

The algorithm perform

find operation $(\log N)^{1/2}$

Insert operation N

delete operation $(\log N)^{1/2}$

decrease key operations $(\log N)^{1/2}$

Hence unsorted array is best data structure for all above operations.

38. Suppose a list contains n elements, consider first three element and find middle element which will be neither maximum nor minimum.

Hence it is $\Theta(1)$.

39. The subtrees are already Max-heap, so to make it half, we have to heapify the root, which takes $\Omega(\log n)$ time.

40. Q_1 is in NP and Q_2 is in NP-hard

41. Dijkstra use gready approach, warshals use dynamic programming approach, Binary search is based on divide and conquer and Back tracking is depth first search.

42. $h(i) = l^3 \bmod 10$

i = 1	=	1^3	mod 10	=	1
2	=	2^3	mod 10	=	8
3	=	3^3	mod 10	=	7
4	=	4^3	mod 10	=	4
5	=	5^3	mod 10	=	5
6	=	6^3	mod 10	=	6
7	=	7^3	mod 10	=	3
8	=	8^3	mod 10	=	2
9	=	9^3	mod 10	=	9
10	=	10^3	mod 10	=	0

Hence the hash function will be $h(i) = l^3 \bmod 10$

43. 1st swap is : 100 and 15

2nd swap is : 100 and 50

3rd swap is : 100 and 89

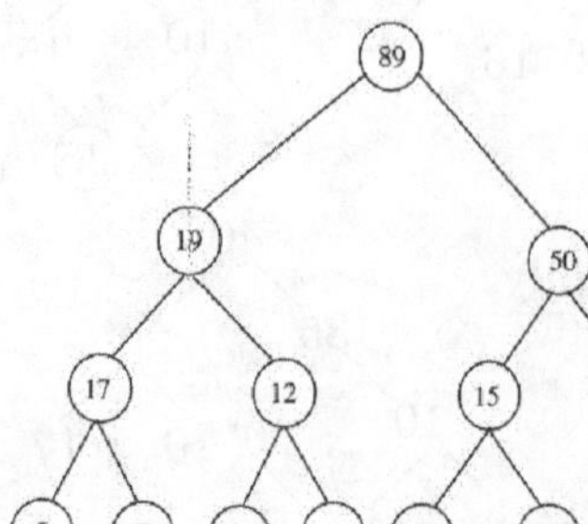

44.

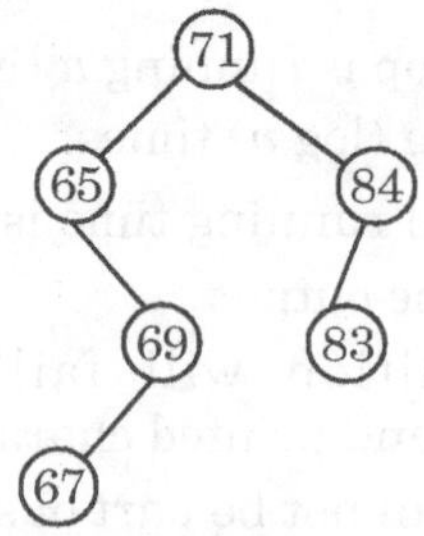

Lowest level element is 67.

45. I or III or IV but not II

as $$\sum_{i=0}^{n} i^3 \Rightarrow \frac{n^2(n+1)^2}{4},$$

this can be represent by $Q(n^4)$, $O(n^5)$ 4 $\Omega(n^3)$ but not $Q(n^5)$.

46. As $-1 \le \sin x \le 1$, neither of them is true

47.
$$O(n \log n) = 30s$$
$$n = 64$$
$$O(64 \log 64) = 30$$

Hence will get factor of 12.8 for 6 min

$$= 6 \times 60 = 360 \text{ s}$$
$$O(256 \log 256) = 360$$
$$O(512 \log 512) = 360$$
$$O(1024 \log 1024) = 360$$
$$O(2048 \log 2048) = 360$$

So for 512 will get 12.8 as a factor

48.
$$L_2 \le pL_4$$
$$L_1 \le pL_2$$

If $L_4 \in P$

then $L_2 \in P$

$L_1 \in P$,

Hence option (c).

49. Take an example for Graph G

A B

Then option A and D will be eliminated.

Let G is below graph

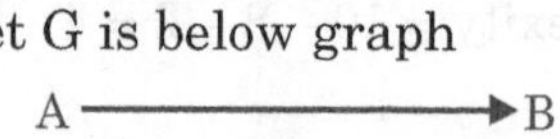

Then G_3 is a graph with below structure

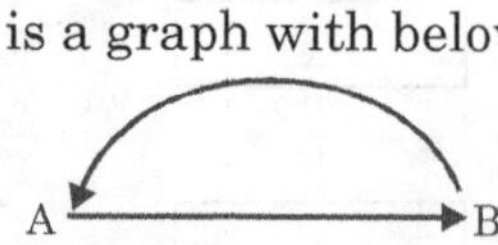

In G the numbers of strongly connected components are 2 where as in G_3 it is only one.

50. pi contains the address of i. So scanf("%d",pi) places the value entered in console into variable i.e So printf("%d\n", $i + 5$),prints 5 more than the value entered in console.

51. int Myx (int*E, un sin ged int sixe)

```
{
  int Y= 0 ;
  int Z ;
  int i, j, k ;
  for (i = 0; i < size ; i++)

      Y = Y + E[i]

  for (i = 0; i < size ; i++)
  for (j = i; j < size ; j++)
    {
    Z = 0
    for (k = i; k <= j ; k++)
        Z = Z + E[k];

    if (Z >Y) → Checks whether sum of
                elements of each subarry
    Y = Z ;     is greater than the sum of
                elements of array if so, that
                sum is assigned to Y, if not
                'Y' will be the sum of
                elements of complete array
    }
  return Y ;
}
```

Ultimately returns the maximum possible sum of elements in any sub array of given array E.

52. $i = 1, j = 1, k = 2$ to $n \Rightarrow n - 1$ times

$i = 1, j = 2, k = 3$ to $n \Rightarrow n - 2$ times

$i = 1, j = 3, k = 4$ to $n \Rightarrow n - 3$ times

:

$i = 1, j = n-2, k = n-1$ to $n \Rightarrow$ 2 times

$i = 1, j = n - 1, k = n$ to $n \Rightarrow$ 1 time

$i = 2, j = 2, k = 3$ to $n \Rightarrow n - 2$ times

$i = 2, j = 3, k = 4$ to $n \Rightarrow n - 3$ times

: :

: : $\Sigma (n - 1)$ times

$i = 2, j = n - 1, k = n$ to $n \Rightarrow$ 1 time

:

:

$i = n - 1, j = n - 1, k = n$ to $n \Rightarrow$ 1 time $\} \Sigma$ 1 times

$\therefore$ Total number of multiplications

$$\Rightarrow \Sigma 1 + \Sigma 2 + \Sigma 3 + ...\Sigma(n-1)$$

$$= \underset{S_1}{1} + \underset{S_2}{(1+2)} + \underset{S_3}{(1+2+3)} + ... + \underset{S_{n-1}}{(1+2+3+....n-1)}$$

$$= \sum_{i=1}^{n-1} S_i = \sum \frac{n(n-1)}{2}$$

$$= \frac{1}{2}\sum n^2 - \frac{1}{2}\sum n$$

$$= \frac{1}{2}\frac{n(n+1)(2n+1)}{6} - \frac{1}{2}\frac{n(n+1)}{2}$$

$$= \frac{(n-1)(n)(n+1)}{6}$$

53. According to havel-hakimi theorem

(1,1,1,1,1,1) is graphic iff<1,1,1,1,0> is graphic

(0,1,1,1,1) is graphic iff (0,1,1,0) is graphic

(0,0,1,1) is graphic iff (0,0,0) is graphic

Since (0,0,0) is graphic (1,1,1,1,1,1) is also graphic.

(The process is always finding maximum degree and removing it from degree sequence, subtract 1 from each degree for d times from right to left where d is maximum degree)

(2,2,2,2,2,2) is graphic iff (2, 2, 22 -1, 2 -1)

= (2, 2, 2,1,1) is graphic.

(1,1,2,2,2) is graphic iff (1,1,1,1) is graphic.

(1,1,1,1) is graphic iff (0,1,1)

(0,1,1) is graphic iff (0,0) is graphic.

Since (0,0) is graphic (2,2,2,2,2,2) is also graphic.

Consider option C now.

(3,3,3,1,0,0)→(0,0,1,3,3,3) is graphic iff (0,0,0,2,2) is graphic.

Note that before applying the havel-hakimi step degree sequence should be in non-increasing order.

(0,0,0,2,2) is graphic iff (0,0,-1,1) is graphic.

Since (0,0,–1,1) is not graphic (3,3,3,1,0,0) is also not graphic.

54. $^nC_3$ will stand for

$$= n * \frac{n\ 1}{2} \quad ... (i)$$

$$\frac{n-1}{3} \quad ... (ii)$$

Multiplying (*i*) by (*ii*), we get

$$\rho = n * \frac{(n-1)}{2} * \frac{(n-2)}{3}$$

55. Since the consumer will always execute wait(*s*) following by wait (*n*) due to which it goes to sleep by continuously decreasing value of *n*. After the consumer sleeps, the turn comes to producer which goes to sleep by executing wait(*s*). This process continues and causes dead lock.

56. X is declared as

"int X [32] [32] [8]"

57. Since enqueue means to add an item from the back called push, So it will take all the three instructions ie PUSH, POP & REVERSE, but DEQUEUE doesn't have to take any thing from PUSH, REVERSE because it removes item from front called POP. Hence, a queue will be implemented ENQUEUE takes 3 instructions, DEQUEUE takes 1 instruction.

58. When $f = 50$, the f^n will exhaust run time stack, because function will be called infinite times which results into an infinite loop at $j = 50$.

59. $y = \bar{x}b + xa$

'x' is working as selection line, where the two input lines are 'a' and 'b', so the function F(x, y, a,b) can be implemented using (2 × 1) multiplexer as follows:

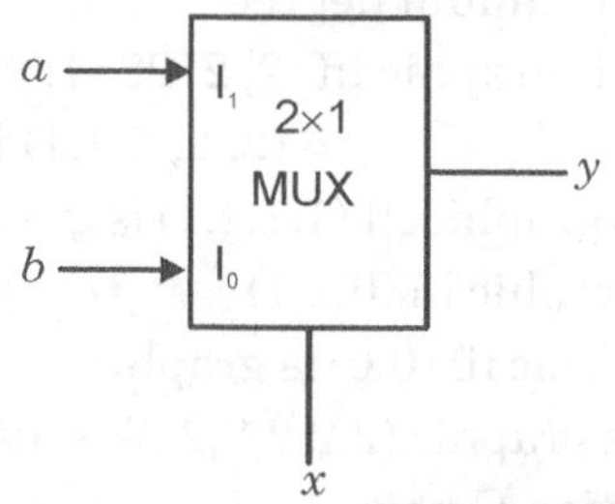

60. In the computation of given pseudo code for each row and column of Matrix A, each upper triangular element will be interchanged by its mirror image in the lower triangular and after that the same lower triangular element will be again re-interchanged by its mirror image in the upper triangular, resulting the final computed Matrix A same as input Matrix A.

61. In order Traversal of Ternary Tree is done as follows:

Left → Root → Middle → Right

So the nodes are visited in SQPTRWUV order.

62. The key to solving such questions is to understand or detect where/by what condition the value (or the counter) is getting incremented each time. Here, that condition is if

(tree → leftMostchild == Null)

⇒ Which means if there is no left most child of the tree (or the sub-tree or the current nodeas called in recursion)

⇒ Which means there is no child to that particular node (since if there is no left most child, there is no child at all).

⇒ Which means the node under consideration is a leaf node.

⇒ The function recursively counts, and adds to value, whenever a leaf node is encountered.

⇒ The function returns the number of leaf nodes in the tree.

63. By the logic of the algorithm it is clear that it is an attempted implementation of Binary Search. So option (c) is clearly eliminated. Let us now check for options (a) and (d).

A good way to do this is to create small dummy examples (arrays) and implement the algorithm as it is. One may make any array of choice. Running iterations of the algorithm would indicate that the loop exits when the x is not present. So option (a) is wrong. Also, when x is present, the correct index is indeed returned. (d) is also wrong.

Correct answer is (b). It is a correct implementation of Binary Search.

64. Let $n_1, n_2, \ldots.. n_k$ be the number of vertices respectively in K connected components of a forest G, then $n_1 -1$, $n_2 -1, \ldots\ldots, n_k -1$ be the number of edges respectively in K connected components and $n_1 + n_2 + \ldots.. + n_k = n$ (number of vertices in G)

Hence, number of edges in G = number of edges in K connected components

$$= (n_1 -1) + (n_2 -1) + \ldots\ldots + (n_k -1) = n - k$$

65. DFS visits each vertex once and as it visits each vertex, we need to find all of its neighbours to figure out where to search next. Finding all its neighbours in an adjacency matrix requires O(V) time, so overall the running time will be O(V^2).

66. Topological ordering of a directed graph is a linear ordering of its vertices such that for every directed edge uv from vertex u to vertex v, u comes before v in the ordering. Topological ordering is possible iff graph has no directed cycles.

(a) As the given graph doesn't contain any directed cycles, it has at least one topological ordering. So option (A) is false

(b) PQRS cannot be topological ordering because S should come before R in the ordering as there is a directed edge from S to R. SRQP cannot be topological ordering, because P should come before Q in the ordering as there is a directed edge from P to Q

(c) PSRQ and SPRQ are topological orderings as both of then satisfy the above mentioned topological ordering conditions.

(d) PSRQ is not the only one topological ordering as SPRQ is other possibility.

67. Partition algorithm for quick sort

```
Partition (A, P, q)// A [P, .....q]
x ← A [P] // pivot = A [P]
i ← P
for j = P + 1 to q
   do if A [j] ≤ x
      then i ← i + 1
         exchange A [i]↔ A [j]
exchange A [P] ↔ A [i]
return i [returning where pivot element is there after partitioning]
```

Recursively call the above algorithm for the two sub arrays [elements before and after pivot element] to complete the sorting.

x = pivot

1 2 3 4 5
i j — 2 ≤ 1 ? NO

1 2 3 4 5
i j — 3 ≤ 1 ? NO

1 2 3 4 5
i j — 4 ≤ 1 ? NO

1 2 3 4 5
i j — 5 ≤ 1 ? NO

exchange A [P] & A [i]

1 2 3 4 5
Pivot (1), ≥ Pivot (2 3 4 5) — Call recursively for this subarray

Pivot =x = A [B]

1 2 3 4 5
i j — 3 ≤ 2 ? NO

1 2 3 4 5
i j — 4 ≤ 2 ? NO

1 2 3 4 5
i j — 5 ≤ 2 ? NO

exchange A [P] & A [J]

1 2 3 4 5
Pivot (2), ≥ Pivot (3 4 5) — Call recursively for this

x = Pivot = A [P]

1 2 3 4 5
i j — 4 ≤ 3 ? NO

1 2 3 4 5
i j — 5 ≤ 3 ? NO

exchange A [P] & A [i]

1 2 3 4 5
Pivot (3), ≥ Pivot (4 5)

x = Pivot

1 2 3 4 5
i j — 5 ≤ 4 ? NO

exchange A [P] & A[i]

1 2 3 4 5
Pivot (4), ≥ Pivot (5)

∴ total 10 comparisons

↗ x = Pivot = A [P]

4 1 5 3 2

i j $1 \le 4$? Yes

i ← i +1exchange A[i] & A[j] & increment j

4 1 5 3 2

i j $5 \le 4$? NO

4 1 5 3 2

i j $3 \le 4$? Yes

i ← i +1 exchange A[i] & A[j] & increment j

4 1 3 5 2

i j $2 \le 4$? Yes

i ← i + 1

4 1 3 2 5

i j

exchange A[P] & A[i]

2 1 3 4 5

≤Pivot   Pivot   ≥Pivot

x = pivot = A (P)

2 1 3 |4| 5

i j $1 \le 2$? Yes

2 1 3 |4| 5

i j $3 \le 2$? NO

exchange A [P] & A[i]

1 (2) 3 4 5

Pivot

∴ 6 conparisons

68. The most important open question in complexity theory is whether the **P = NP** , which asks whether polynomial time algorithms actually exist for **NP**-complete and all **NP** problems (since a problem "C" is in NP-complete, iff C is in NP and every problem in NP is reducible to C in polynomial time). In the given question it is given that some polynomial time algorithm exists which computes the largest clique problem in the given graph which is known NP-complete problem. Hence P = NP = NP-Complete.

69.

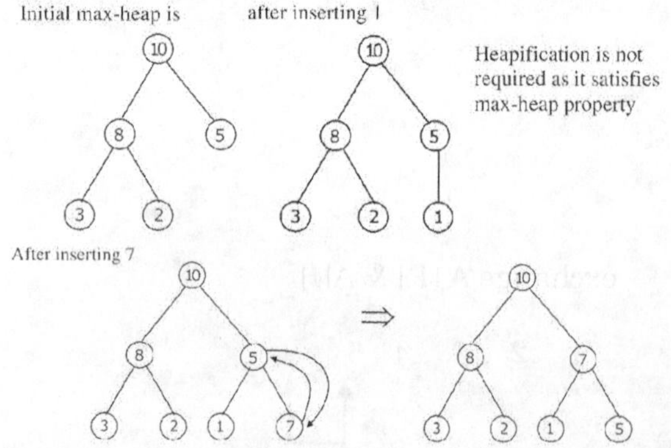

Hence level order traversal is 10, 8, 7, 3, 2, 1, 5

70. Since $f(n) = \log n$

$a = 2, b = 2$

finding $\log_b a$ using master's method = $\log_2 2 = 1$

Hence, $f(n) = n'$

So, $T(n) = O(n)$

71.

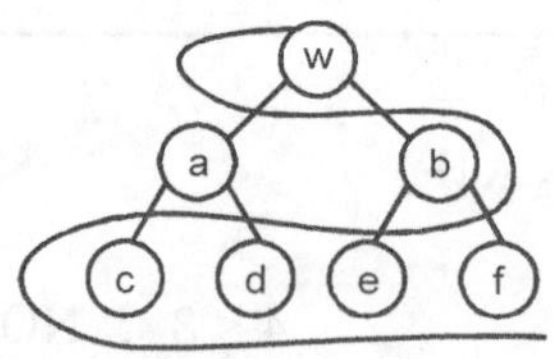

Shortest path from w to every vertex in graph.

72. The Worst case time complexity of quick sort is O (n^2). This will happen when the elements of the input array are already in order (ascending or descending), irrespective of position of pivot element in array.

73. A

P(First insertion in such a way that first 3 slots are unfilled) $= \dfrac{97C_1}{100C_1} = \dfrac{97}{100}$

B

P(second insertion in such a way that first

3 slots are unfilled) = $\frac{97C_1}{100C_1} = \frac{97}{100}$

(∵ chaining is used to resolve collision, so second insertion can be done at same index as first index]

C

P (Third insertion in such a way that first 3 slots are unfilled) = $\frac{97C_1}{100C_1} = \frac{97}{100}$

(∵ Third insertion can be done at same index as first or second index]

So total prob. P (A) × P (B) ×P(C)

$$= \frac{97}{100} \times \frac{97}{100} \times \frac{97}{100} = \frac{(97\times97\times97)}{100^3}$$

74. We know that $v + r = e + 2 \Rightarrow e = n + r - 2$ ...(1)

Where V = n(number of vertices);

r = number of faces and

e = number of edges

Given, $\delta \geq 3$ then $3n \leq 2e$

$$\Rightarrow e \geq \frac{3n}{2} \Rightarrow n + r - 2 \geq \frac{3n}{2} \text{ (using (1))}$$

$$\Rightarrow r \geq \frac{3n}{2} - n + 2 \Rightarrow r \geq \frac{n}{2} + 2$$

∴ Number of faces is atleast $\frac{n}{2} + 2$

75. To find the expected number of unordered cycles of length three.

To compute:

Look at all the possible triplets of 3 vertices out of 8 and see if they form a cycle.

Possible triplets: We are looking at unordered cycles, so it suffices to chose any 3 vertices out of the 8 in any order. This can be done in $^8C_3$ ways. If they have a cycle among them? To form a cycle between 3 chosen vertices, we need to form edges between all pairs

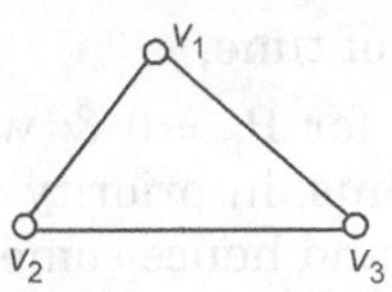

So, probability of this happening

$$= \frac{1}{2} \times \frac{1}{2} \times \frac{1}{2} = \frac{1}{8}$$

So, by definition of Expectation, which is if X is a random variable oveer sample space Ω

$$\lfloor F[x] = \sum_{x\in\Omega} x P(x)$$

Here $P(x) = \frac{1}{8} \forall x$

& x spans over all $^8C_3$ configurations

Hence, expected value = $^8C_3 \times \frac{1}{8} = 7$

Hence, the solution is (c)

76. P : Number of odd degree vertices is even

Q : Sum of degrees of all vertices is even

Q is true:

Reason: Calculating the sum of degrees of all vertices.

Take any edge, it is joining two vertices (not necessarily distinct), hence contribution 2 in the sum of degrees. Hence, for 'e' edges, the sum of degrees of all vertices is 2e (is even).

Note: It is volid even in case of self loops

P is also true:

Reason: We have established that sum of degrees of all vertices is even.

Let us assume, number of odd degree vertices is odd, so, the contribution of odd degree vertices in total sum is odd.

Now, the contribution of even degree vertices is also even (whether the number is even or odd).

So, total sum becomes odd, which is not possible. Hence P is true.

Note: Include vertex of degree zero in even degree vertices.

77. So, this is in $\theta(\log n)$

Hence Answer is (c)

The outer for-loop goes for $\frac{n}{2}+1$ iterations. The inner for-loop runs independent of the otuer loop. And for each inner iteration. $\frac{n}{2}$ gets added to k.

∴ Our answer = $\frac{n}{2}$ × # outer loops × #Inner loops per outer loop

Inner loops = $\theta(\log n)$ $[\because 2^{\theta(\log n)} = \theta(n)]$

∴ Our answer = $\frac{n}{2} + \left[\frac{n}{2}+1\right] \cdot \theta(\log n) = \theta(n^2 \log n)$

$L_1 = \{0^p 1^q 0^r \mid p, q, r \geq 0\}$

$L_2 = \{0^p 1^q 0^r \mid p, q, r \geq 0, p \neq r\}$

78. Sol. Option (*a*) : Suppose process X executes Exit X then it will wait for R, and then process Y executes Entry Y then it will wait for S. Since initially both binary semaphore are 0, no one will increment it and both process will stuck in dead lock.

Hence option (a) is wrong.

Option (*b*) : Here if process X executes for n times repeadetly it will set both semaphorse to 1 (since only two values are possible) and after that process Y executes. First time it passes the Entry Y and make both semaphores to 0. And on second time it finds both semaphores to 0 and cannot pass the Entry Y barrier. Hence it will stuck.

So option (*b*) is wrong.

Option (*d*) : Suppose first process X executes it sets R = 1 and then waits for S. Now after that process Y executes. It first sets S = 1 and then decrement R = 0. It comes again and then again sets S = 1 (i.e. it overlaps the value of S) and then wait for R.

Clearly here we lost one iteration of process X due to overlapping of value of S. and after $n-1$ iteration process X will stuck.

So option (*d*) is wrong.

Option (*c*) : Here take any sequence of operation of process X and process Y, first process X will wait for S which is increment by process Y and then process Y waits for R which is incremented by process X.

There is no sequence of operation in which the value of R or S overlaps.

Hence both process executes one after another.

So option (*c*) is correct.

To find : Tighest upper bound on number of swaps required to sort n numbers using selection sort.

79. Since, reference of p is passed as '*x*'

Thus, any change in value of *x* in *f* would be reflected globally.

The recursion can be broken down as:

$f\begin{pmatrix}5 & 5\\ x, & c\end{pmatrix}$

$\hookrightarrow x * f\begin{pmatrix}6 & 4\\ x, & c\end{pmatrix}$

$\hookrightarrow x * f\begin{pmatrix}7 & 3\\ x, & c\end{pmatrix}$

$\hookrightarrow x * f\begin{pmatrix}8 & 2\\ x, & c\end{pmatrix}$

$\hookrightarrow x * f\begin{pmatrix}9 & 1\\ x, & c\end{pmatrix}$

$\hookrightarrow 1$ [$\because c = 0$ in this code]

$\therefore$ Our answer $= x * x * x * x$

The final value of $x = 9$

$\therefore$ $9^4 = \boxed{6561}$

80. Given: n numbers

To find: Tighest upper bound on number of swaps required to sort n numbers using selection sort.

Nalysis: In selection sort, in the unsorted part of the array, we find the minimum element and swap it with the value placed at the index where the unsorted array starts.

Hence, for each element to put it in its sorted position, we will do some swaps. In each itenation, when we find the minimum and place it in its sorted position, we do only one swap.

There are *n* such iterations, since maximum number of positions to sort is n.

Hence, there are n. 0(1) swaps

$\Rightarrow$ 0(n) swaps.

$\therefore$ The solution is (*b*)

81. Given: A binary tree with n nodes

To find: Tighest upper bound on time complexity of inserting an object.

Nalysis: When inserting a new element, we need to find its position in the tree. The time for this operation is upper bounded by the height of the binary tree. Since, the tree is unbalanced, we don't need to perform balancing operations upon insertion, so only time consums is in finding its right position. The time consumed in finding the position is equal to height of the tree.

Max height of tree = 0(n)

[All elements are on one side of root & no root has two non empty subtrees]

$\Rightarrow$ Answer is (*c*)

82. Given: priority of a process α Waiting Time i.e. process scheduling is independent of the time it takes for a process to execute. Thus, options C & D can be discarded.

Now, initially when all the processes arrived simultaneously, waiting time for each process = 0. Any process can be scheduled first, say P_1.

After T units of time,

Waiting time for P_1 = 0 & waiting time for all others = T. Thus, in priority all other processes supercede P_1 and hence some other process gets scheduled now.

Now, at every time = kT (K > 0), if there is any process which has not been given CPU atleast once, gets scheduled. Once every process got scheduled one time each (for T time units) all processes have now the same waiting time = (n – 1) T where n = # processes.

Till now, the scheduling was Round-Robin with pre-emptions at periods of T.

The same analycis can be extended for further schedulings as all the processes have the same priority (= (n – 1)T) which was O, earlier.

Option (A) is incorrect because the scheduling is independent of the arrival time of the processes. Actually, all arrived at the same time & among all processes with same priority any one can get scheduled at an instant.

83. 1. We can use "Depth First Search" Algorithm, to check it there is a cycle is an undirected graph. It we encounter any "back edge" in "Depth first search" then given undirected graph has a cycle. Also, If there is a cycle in the Undirected graph, we must encounter a "back edge" in DFS. And, DFS can be done in $O(|E| + |V|)$ time for graph G = (V, E). So, it can is in F.

2. $P \leq NP$, So, it is also in NP.

3. NP - complete problem $A \in NP$. By, Definition Every problem in NP can be solved in polynomial time using non-deterministic turing machine.

So, Answer is (*a*) i.e. 1, 2, and 3 are true.

84. Given: A complete graph on n vertices?

To find: Time complexity of Bellman-Ford Single source shortest path.

Analysis:

Time complexity of Bellman-ford algorithm on a graph with *n* vertices and m edges is O(*nm*)

For a complete graph, $m = {}^nC_2 = 0(n^2)$ (Since, there is an edge between all pair of vertices)

∴ Time Complexity = $0(n^2 \cdot n) = 0(n^3)$

∴ Solution is (*c*)

Note : Include vertex of degree zero in even degree vertices.

85. (P) Let 'C' be a cycle. In the live graph L(C) :

(*i*) There will be an edge between two vertices corresponding to adjacent edges in the cycle.

(*ii*) Degree of each vertex in L(C) will be 2

(*iii*) L(C) will be connected.

Hence, L(C) will also be a cycle. So, (P) is TRUE

(Q) Let 'K_n' be a clique on '*n*' vertices. Consider line graph $L(K_n)$:

- $L(K_n)$ has n_{c2} vertices at least say e_1, e_2
- For $n > 3$, there will be two edges in "K_n" which do not share a vertex in "K_n".
- So, $V(e_1)$, $V(e_2)$ will not be adjacent in $L(K_n)$.
- Hence, $L(K_n)$ is not always a clique.

(Q) is FALSE.

(R) Let 'G' be a star graph consider line graphical

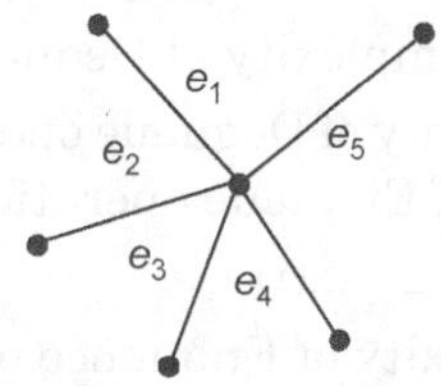

⇒ In L(G): $V(e_1)$, $V(e_2)$, $V(e_3)$, $V(e_4)$, $V(e_5)$ will "K5" form a clique because they all share a vertex.

A planar graph cannot have a "K5" minor. Hence L(G) is not a pllanar graph. Even though G is planar

So, R is FALSE.

(S) Let 'T' be the following tree, and L(T) is its line graph

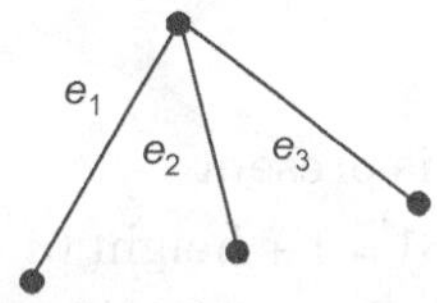

- In L(T): e_1, e_2, e_3 will form a $K_3(\Delta L_e)$ i.e., a 3-cycle.
- Tree is an acyclic graph i.e. doesn't have a cycle.
- So, L(T) is not a tree.

So, S is False

∴ Answer is "P" only.

86. Let the number of element is "K", they can be sorted in θ(k log k) time.

We try the options in decreasing order of complexity since, we need a tight band i.e. θ

i.e. $\theta(\log n) \cdot \theta\left(\frac{(\log n)}{\log\log n}\right), \theta\left(\sqrt{\log n}\right), \theta(1)$

So if $K \in \theta(\log n)$ time required for loop sort is. θ(k log k) i.e.

$\theta(\log n \times \log\log n)$, But this is not in $\theta(\log n)$

if $k \in \theta\left(\frac{\log n}{\log\log n}\right)$ time required for loop sort:

$$\theta\left(\frac{\log n}{\log\log n} \times \log\left(\frac{\log n}{\log\log n}\right)\right),$$

$$\text{i.e. } \theta\left(\log n \times \underbrace{\left[\frac{\log\left(\frac{\log n}{\log 1 > n}\right)}{\log\log n}\right]}_{\leq 1}\right)$$

87. Complexity of a sequence of '*n*' operations

= Total Complexity of Enqueue operations ($\propto$)

+ Total complexity of Dequeue operations (β)

total complexity of Dequeue operations (β) $\leq$ Total complexity of Enqueue operations ($\propto$).

$$\beta \leq \propto ...(i)$$

Total complexity of Enquence operations

$$(\propto) \leq n ...(2)$$

$\therefore$ Total complexity of n operations

$$= \propto + \beta$$
$$\leq \propto + \propto \text{ (from (1))}$$
$$\leq n + n \text{ (from (2))} \leq 2n.$$

88. $r = e - v + 2$ for bound + non bound

$r = e - v + 2 - 1$ for bounded

$r = 15 - 10 + 2 - 1$

$r = 6.$

90. If right child is present

B1 = 1 + height ($n \rightarrow$ right)

Other if both are present

B2 = 1 + max (h_1, h_2)

93.

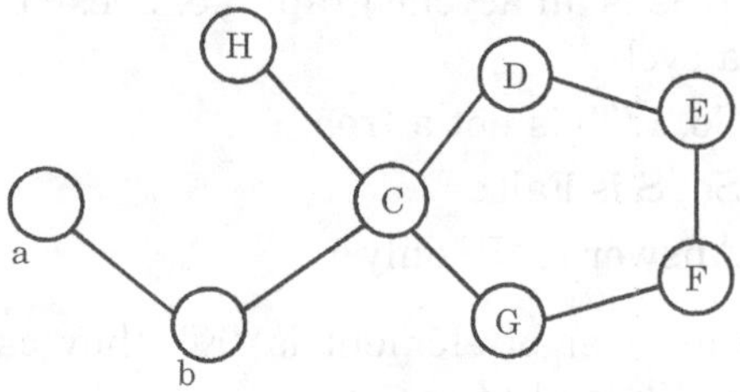

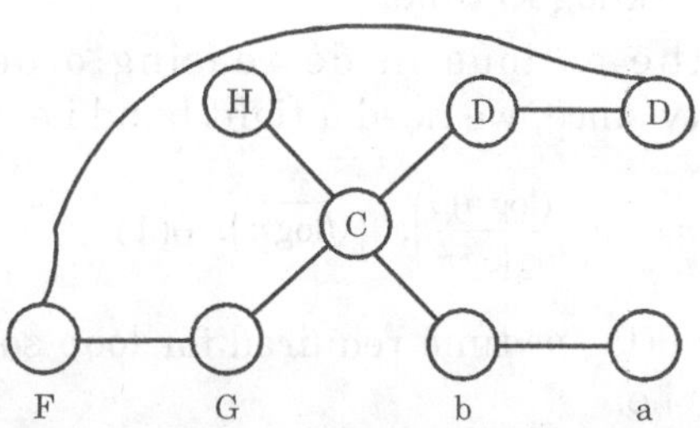

94. If B(n), XXA(n) and W(n) denote best case , average case and worst case time complexities of an algorithm P respectively then B(n) = O(A(n)), A(n) = O(W(n))

95. Let the three pegs be A,B and C, the goal is to move n pegs from A to C usingpeg B

The following sequence of steps are executed recursively

1. move $n - 1$ discs from A to B. This leaves disc n alone on peg A ..... T($n - 1$)
2. move disc n from A to C 1
3. move $n - 1$ discs from B to C so they sit on disc n T($n - 1$)

So, $\quad$ T(n) = 2T($n - 1$) + 1

96. The worst case running time of search in BST is log n where n is total number of elements in the tree. The total number of elements are n. 2^n thus search R. T. will be long (n. 2^n).

$$\log n \,.\, 2n = \log n + \log 2^n$$
$$\therefore \quad = \log n + n \log 2$$
$$= \theta(n)$$

97. If P ! = NP, then it implies that no NP-Complete problem can be solved in polynomial time which implies that the set P and the set NPC are disjoint.

98.

S	A	B	C	D	E	F	G	T
∞	∞	∞	∞	∞	∞	∞	∞	∞
4	[3]		7					
[4]	3		7					
4	3	[5]	7					
4	3	5	7	[6]				
4	3	5	7	6		8	10	
4	3	5	[7]	6	12	8	10	
4	3	5	7	6	12	[8]	10	
4	3	5	7	6	12	8	10	

SACET

100. Heap is a complete binary tree.

102.

K4

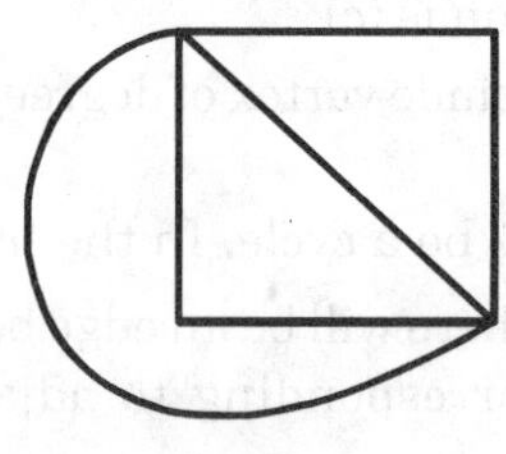

Q3

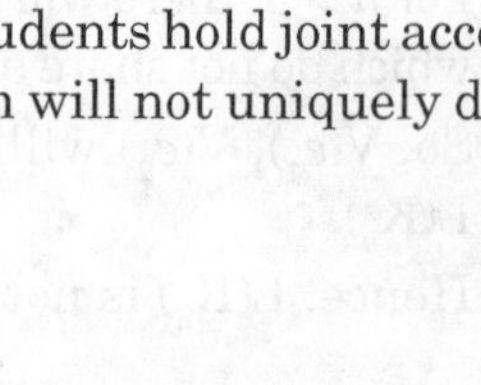

Both K4 and Q3 are planar

103. In case two students hold joint account then Bank Account_Num will not uniquely determine other attributes

104. T1 and T2 : checking same condition $a = 0$ hence, any one of T1 and T2 is redundant.

T3, T4 : in both case discriminant

(D) = $b^2 - 4ac = 0$.

Hence any one of it is redundant.

T5 : D > 0

T6 : D < 0

105. Load $R_1, a; R_1 \leftarrow M[a]$

Load $R_2, b; R_2 \leftarrow M[b]$

Sub $R_1, R_2; R_1 \leftarrow R_1 - R_2$

Load $R_2, c; R_2 \leftarrow M[c]$

Load $R_3, d; R_3 \leftarrow M[d]$

Add $R_2, R_3; R_2 \leftarrow R_2 + R_3$

Load $R_3, e; R_3 \leftarrow M[e]$

Sub $R_3\ R_2 : R_3 \leftarrow R_3 - R_2$

Add $R_1, R_3; R_1 \leftarrow R_1 + R_3$

Total 3 Registers are required minimum

106.

P_0	P_1	P_0	P_2

0 1 5 13 22

Average waiting time = $\frac{4+11}{3}$ = 5 ms

108. $7 \downarrow 3 \uparrow 4 \uparrow 3 \downarrow 2$

$\Rightarrow$ $7 \downarrow 3 \uparrow (4 \uparrow 3) \downarrow 2$ as $\uparrow$ is right associative

$\Rightarrow$ $7 \downarrow (3 \uparrow (4 \uparrow 3)) \downarrow 2$

$\Rightarrow$ $(7 \downarrow (3 \uparrow (4 \uparrow 3))) \downarrow 2$ as $\downarrow$ is left associative

110. Given :

```
# include < stdio.h>
void f (int * p, int * q){
{ p = q;
 * p = 2;
}
int i = 0, j = 1;
int main() {
{ f (& i, & j); → Passing the address of i, j
print f ("% d % n", i, j);
retur, 0;
}
```

Let address of i and j are 200, 400

means [$i = 0$] [$j = 0$]

200 400

in function f pRq are pointers that have address of i, j than by $p = q$ copy address of j in p

means initially [200] [400]

p q

after $p = q$ [400] [400]

p q

by * p it represent value of j now

then * p = 2 changes value of j

So after print f statement $i = 0, j = 2$.

111. P-2 means Requirment Capture in Domain Analysis.

Q-3 means Design considered as Structural and Behavioral modeling.

R-1 Implementation Modules are developed and integration are done between modules.

S-4 Maintenance is Performance Tuning after deployment of system.

112. a [ ] =

12	7	13	4	11	6

So $f(a, 6) \to$ first this call

Thus is the number stored in the array and we can access these by using *a-

$f(a, 6)$

$\downarrow$ 12

So $12 + f(a + 1), n - 1)$ {even}

$\downarrow$

$7 - f(a + 1, n - 1)$ {odd}

$\downarrow$

$13 - f(a + 1, n - 1)$ {odd}

$\downarrow$

$4 + f(a + 1, n - 1)$ {even}

$\downarrow$

$11 - f(a + 1, n - 1)$ {odd}

$\downarrow$

$6 + f(a + 1, 0)$ {even}

$\downarrow$

0{n = 0 then 0}

$= 12 + [7 - [13 - [4 + [11 - (6 + 0)]]]]$

$= 12 + [7 - [13 - [4 + [11 - 6]]]$

$= 12 + [7 - [13 - [4 + 5]]]$

$= 12 + (7 - (13 - 9))$

$= 12 + (7 - 4) = 12 + 3 = 15$

113. We assigned initial q = NULL, p = head

Now we checked 0 is there $p \to$ next $\neq$ NULL if it is then break means if we are at the end of linked-list.

Now we are at $p \to$ next = NULL and $q \to$ next = p and we are out of loop

Now we want p as a head and q is last node

Then we have to $p \to$ next = head means we assign first node as the next node of p and declare p = head means at head is p means **head = p**

Now it is ring because $q \to$ next = p till now

So declare $q \to$ next = NULL

then we have to write at blank line

$q \rightarrow$ next = NULL, $p \rightarrow$ next = head, head = p

Alternately

```
1.  typedef struct node
2.  {   int value;
3.  struct node * next;
4.  } Node;
5.  Node * move-to-front (Node * head)
6.  }
7.  Node * p, * q;
8.  if((head = = NULL) || (head -> next = = NULL))
9.  return head
10. q = NULL;
11. p = head;
12. while (p -> next ! = NULL)
13. {
14. q = p;
15. p = p -> next;
16. }
17. q -> next = NULL;

18. p -> next = head
19. head = p ;
20. return head
21. }
```

Line 1-4 declare the structure

Line 5 function definition

Line 7 declare two pointer variable of type NODE

Line 8 check whether list is empty or contain only 1 node

Line 10-11 if condition at line 8 fails, then it set p and q

Line 12-16 iteration till node with NULL is fetched and each time p and q gets update

e.g.

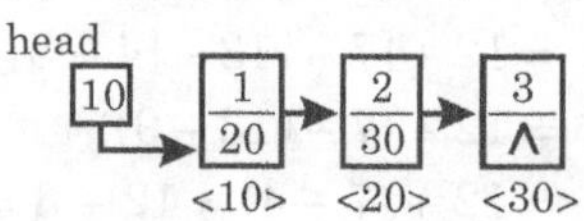

initially

q – NULL, 10, 20

p – 10, 20, 30 – loop terminate

Now, we have to move 3rd node at 1st place.

So,

Line 17 $\quad q \rightarrow$ next = NULL

i.e. $\quad 20 \rightarrow$ next = NULL

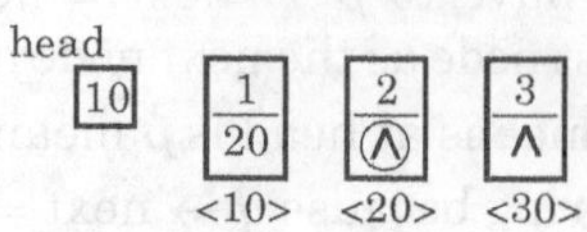

Line 18 $\quad p \rightarrow$ next = head

[∵ head = 10]

$30 \rightarrow$ next = 10

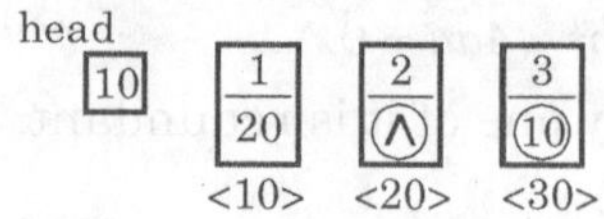

Line 19

head = p

head = 30

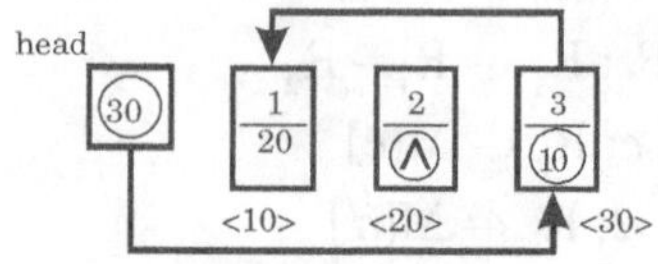

OR

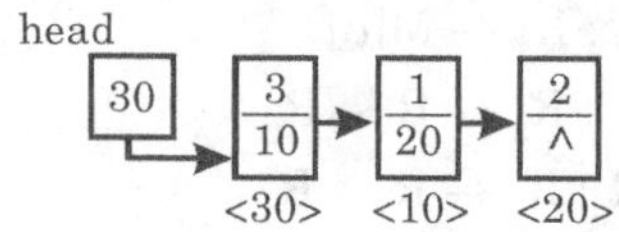

114. begin

if (a = = b) {S1; exit;}

else if (c = = d) {S2 ;}

else {S3; exit;}

S4;

end

115. Cyclomatic complexity always (number of comparisions +1)

So for A (number of comparisons + 1)

9 + 1 = 10

for B $\quad$ 9 + 1 = 10

When we summarise both, then

total number comparisions = 9 + 9 = 18

∴ $\quad$ Cyclomatic complexity = 18 + 1 = 19

116. B must be preferred on A as

$$0.0001\, n^2 < 10\, n \log_{10} n$$

$$\Rightarrow \quad 10^{-5}\, n < \log_{10} n$$

$$\Rightarrow \quad 10^{-5} < \log_{10} n^{1/n}$$

$$\Rightarrow \quad n\, 10^{-5} < \log_{10} n$$

We know $\quad \log_{10} n = k$

$$\Rightarrow \quad 10^k = t$$

$$\therefore \quad k > 10^{-5}\, 10k$$

$$\Rightarrow \quad k > 10^{k-5}$$

$$\Rightarrow \quad k - 5 > 0$$

$$\Rightarrow \quad k > 5$$

Then $\quad$ min k = 6

118. *Stack Positions :*

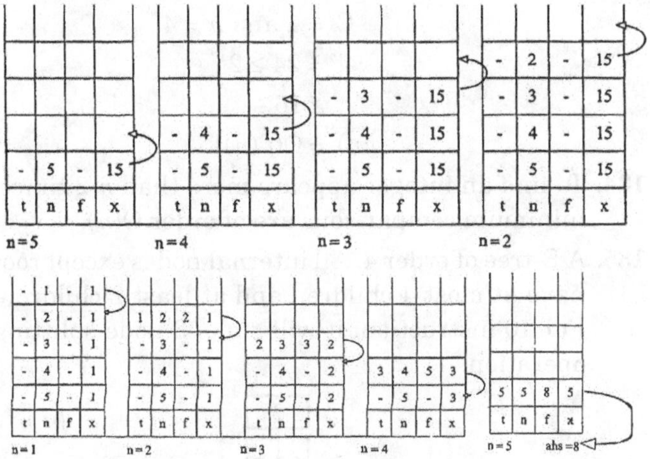

119.

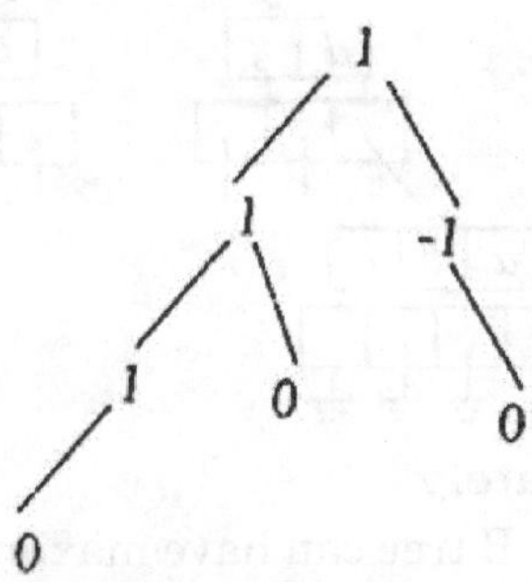

Maximum height = 3

120. If there are n elements, then in worst case, total swaps will be (n-1) in selection sort. So the number of swaps is $\theta(n)$.

Alternately

The selection sort is similar to bubble sort except it does not swap elements with every move. The sorting algorithm first finds the smallest element in the list and then puts it in to place in single swap. So n swap required for n elements.

121. In Bellman Ford shortest path algorithm, we choose a node first and then we find any negative weighted cycle is rechable from source.

122. If π_A is NP-hard, then it is NP-complete

Alternately

π_A be a problem (given) in class NP. we say that π_A is NP complete if the following statements are true about L.

(1) π_A is in NP

(2) For every π_A' in NP there is polynomial time reduction of π_A' to π_A.

123. Applying Master's Theorem

$cn > n^{\ln_3 1}$

$cn > n^0$

Now checking $af(n/b) \le kf(n)$ for some $k < 1$

$1*cm/3 \le kcn$

This is true for $k > 1/3$

Hence solution is $\theta(n)$.

124. In linear probing, if there is already an element then the new element is fed into the next blank value field in the table.

125. In Kruskal's Algorithm we choose on edge of G which has smallest weight among the edges of G. So (b, e) = 2, (e, f) = 3, (b, c) = 4, (a, c)= 8, (f,g) = 4 (c,d) = 5

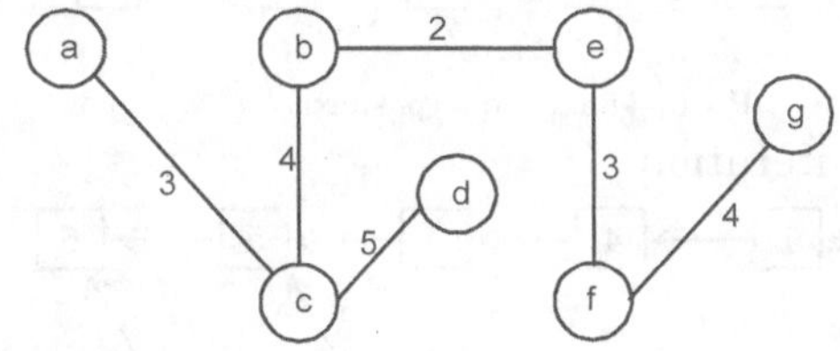

Alternately

Order the edges in non-decreasing order and pick edge one by one until all the nodes are completed with no edge making cycle on addition.

126. Average complexity of quick sort is θ (n log n).

127.

a = (x > y) ? ((x > z) ? x : z) : ((y > z ? y : z))

x = 3, y = 4, z = 2 satisfy the values, so we get a value 4.

128. Suppose 100[4] *b*[100] 4[1000]

C 1000

**ppz* + = 1

c = 5

z = 5

**py* + = 2

c = 7

y = 7

x + = 3

x + *y* + *z* = 22

129. Whenever character input is not return key (in) it accept character input ? 1 (c = getchar()) = ! (in) ? 2 for bringing all character after reverse functions so ?2 is putchar (c).

Alternately

To print reverse of the input, this programme basically collects the input in buffer with the help of some f^n (i.e. f^n is getcher ()) and by using stack, then where ↵ is pressed stack is popped off and characters are printed in reverse order as that of the process call, i.e. last process call to reverse is processed first because of stack.

130. In function rearrange the string of integer 1, 2, 3, 4, 5, 6, 7 converted in to 2, 1, 4, 3, 6, 5, 7 we can check this by execute this program.

Alternately

Initially

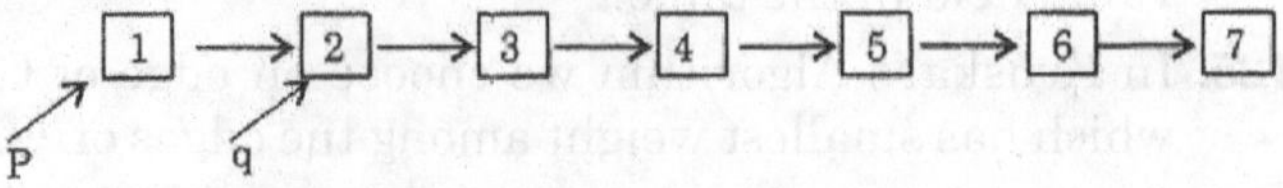

1st iteration of while

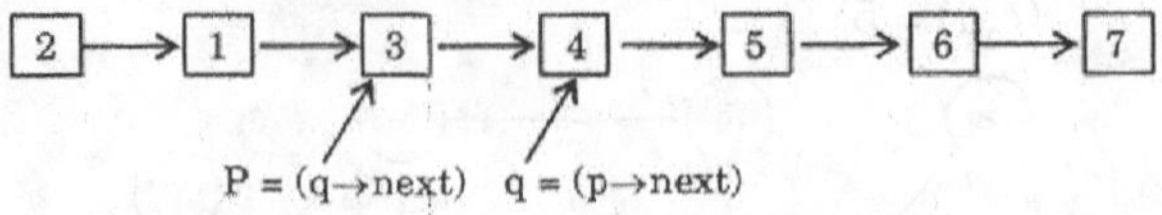

2nd iteration

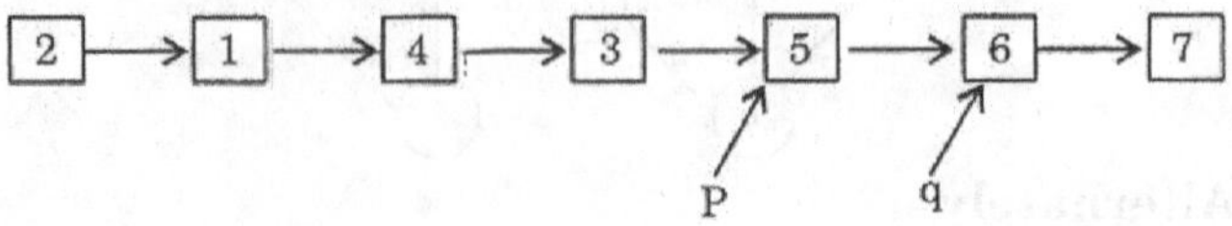

3rd iteration

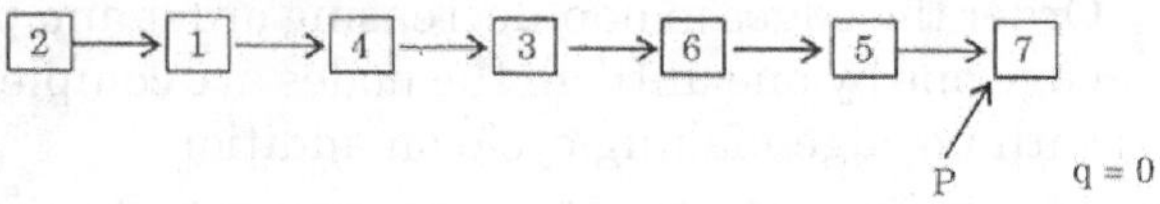

so loop terminates

131. The most efficient algorithm for finding the number of connected components (articulation point) in an undirected graph on n vertices and n edges using depth-first search takes $O(m + n)$ time. Assume $n \leq m$.

132. *Applying BFS Algorithms*

Starting from Q

Queue Q

Making Q's child's status 1.

Queue

Q | M | N | P

Making M's child 1 (which are not 1)

Status

Q	M	N	O	P	R
2	1	1		1	
2	2	1		1	1
2	2	2	1	1	1

Q | M | N | P | R

Making N's Child 1

Q | M | N | P | R | O

(other are already 1)

133.
$$h(n) = n^{\log n}$$
$$f(n) = 2^n$$
$$n \log n \leq C2^n$$

for all $n \geq n_o$

$C = 1$ and $n_o = 2$

$$2 \log 2 \leq 2^2$$

So $h(n) = O(f(n))$

$$g(n) = n!$$
$$f(n) = 2^n$$
$$n! \geq C2^n$$

for all $n \geq n_o$

$C = 1$ and $n = 4$

$$4! = 24 \geq 2^4$$
$$\geq 16$$
$$g(n) = \Omega(f(n))$$

134. To find an integer appears more than $n/2$ times, minimum comparisons are of order $O(n)$.

135. A B-tree of order 4. All internal nodes except root have at most 4 children and at least 2 children. For 10 instruction, it will stake 3 node splitting operation.

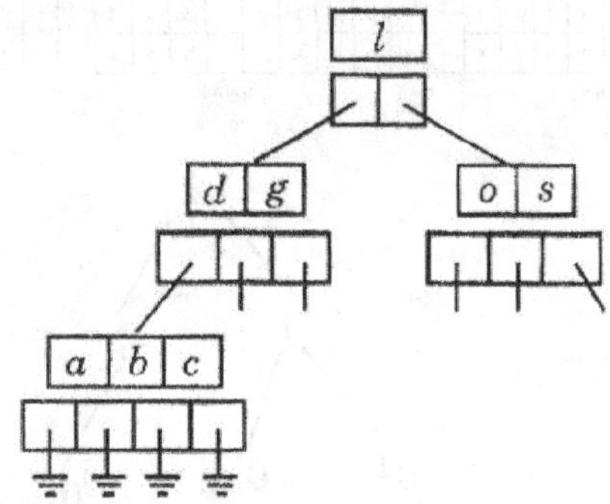

Alternately

Order 4-B tree can have maximum 3 keys in one node and each node have max 4 children so lets take values 84, 82, 29, 99, 65, 12, 50, 28, 58, 71

Inserting 84, 82, 29 [29, 82, 84]

Inserting 99

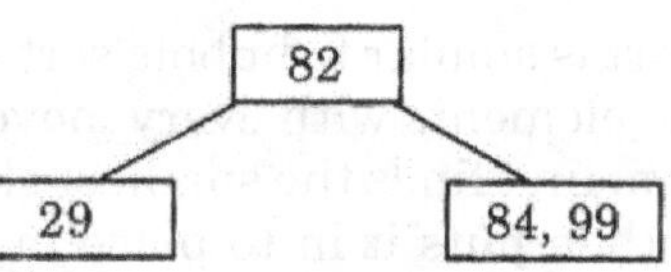

1st Splitting

Inserting 65, 12

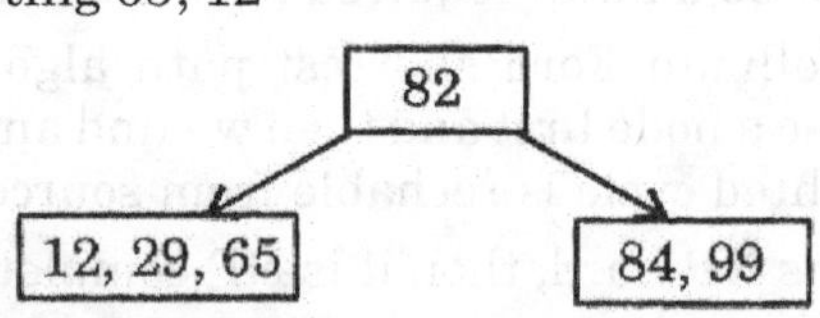

Inserting 50

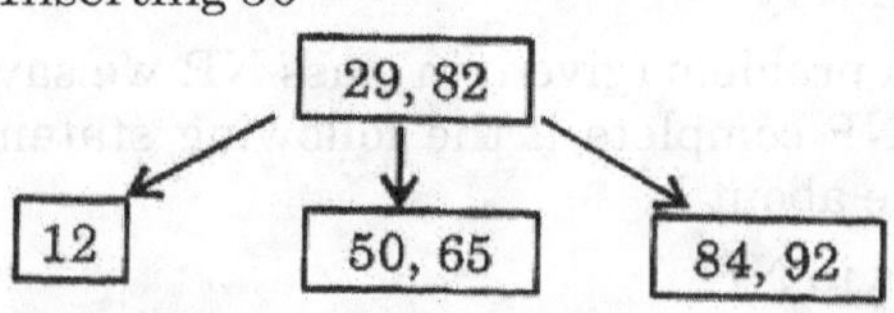

2nd Splitting

Inserting 28, 58

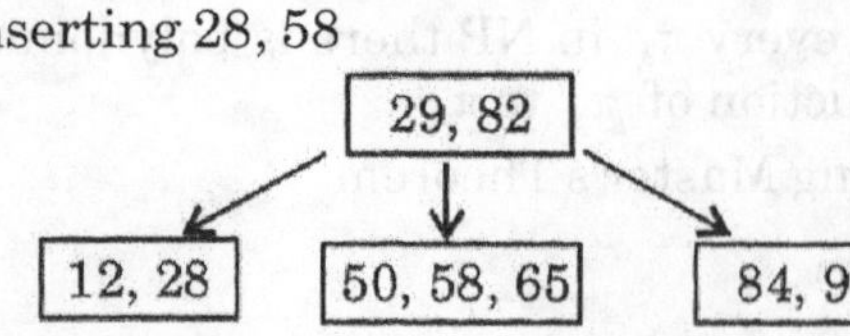

Inserting 71

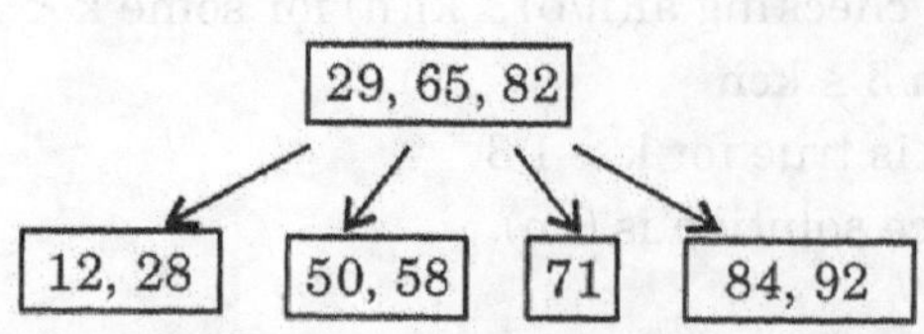

3rd Splitting

For any sequence of insertion, maximum spilliting is 3.

136. Minimum number of edges for a connected graph = n

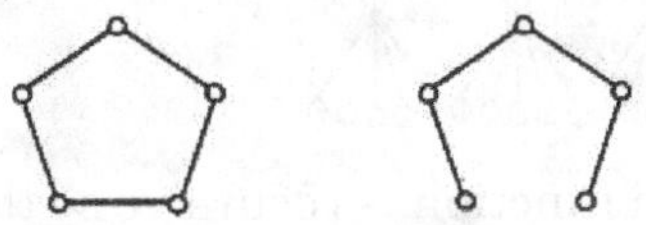

and for a connected tree = $n - 1$

Here given that $2n - 2$ edges and the edges of graph is partitioned into two edge disjoint trees. So there are two vertex disjoint paths between every pair of vertices.

137. In quicksort a set of number is reduced to sorting two smaller set. We take first element as key value and combine all other with this. A pivot element which splits list into two sublists each of which at least one fifth of element only (B), i.e.

$T(n) \le T(n/5) + T(4n/5) + n$ the problem.

Alternately

If one sublist contains 1/5 elements other contains 4/5 elements.

If T(n) number of comparisons for sorting n elements.

So, for 1/5 elements = $T(1/5n)$

and for 4/5 elements = $T(4n/5)$

So, $\quad T(n) \le T(n/5) + T(4n/5) + n.$

Here, n = time to spilt

138. Given a set S of n positive integer and a positive integer W. And also a algorithm Q solves in $0(x\text{W})$ time. So only (*b*) is false.

139. In given graph, the graph is directed and from vertex a to all the vertices there exist a weighted path so Dijkstra's single source shortest path algorithm when run from vertex a in the above graph it includes all the vertices. Dijkstra's don't work properly if the edge has negative weight. $(b, e), (c, h)$ are negative edges so algorithm results correct result only for b, c, d.

140. To find binary tree two of the orders, i.e. preorder, postorder and inorder should be given. By using only post order unique b –, tree cannot be found.

141. It takes only Θ (log (n)) time because it is not addition of n more elements in list.

142. Upper bound may be $\sqrt{n}$ times it gets executed.

Lower bound may be that if gets executed only once or twice.

143. Let T (m, n) be the total number of steps.

So $T(m, 0) = 0$ $T(m, n) = 1$ (n, m nod n) on average

$$T_n = \frac{1}{n} \sum_{0 \le k \le n} T(k,n)$$

$$T_n \approx 1 + \frac{1}{n}(T_0 T_1 + \ldots + T_{n-1})$$

$$T_n \approx S_n$$

$$S_n = 1 + \frac{1}{n}(S_0 S_1 + \ldots + S_{n-1})$$

$$S_n = 1 + \frac{1}{n+1}(S_0 S_1 + \ldots + S_n)$$

$$= 1 + \frac{1}{n+1}(n(S_{n-1}) + S_n)$$

$$= 1 + \frac{1}{n+1} = S_n + \frac{1}{n+1}$$

So $\quad T_n \approx \theta(\log_2 n + 0(1)$

$T \approx \theta\ (\log_2 n)$

144. Since, j increases in power of 2's.

if statement $j = j * 2$ executes k times, then

$2^k \le n$

$\Rightarrow \quad k \le \log_2 n$

Since k will be integer,

total number of comparison

$= \lfloor \log_2 n \rfloor + 1$ (when loop exits)

145. Evaluation will proceed as

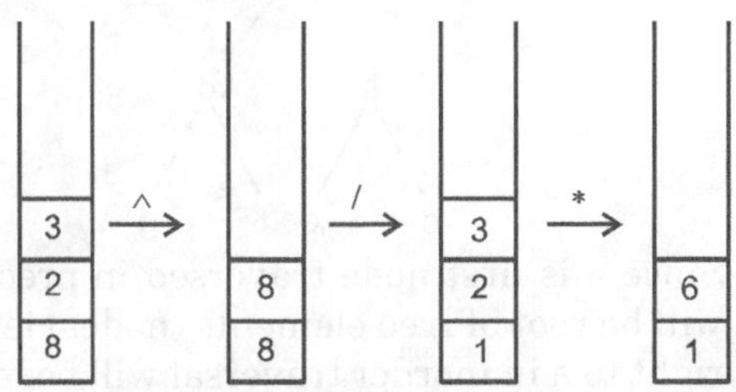

So after evaluation of first *top elements will be 6, 1.

146. *Calbing sequence will be*

Sequencereturns

$f(5) \qquad f(3) + 2 = 18$

↓ ↑

$f(3) \qquad f(2) + 5 = 16$

↓ ↑

$f(2) \qquad f(1) + 5 = 11$

↓ ↑

$f(1) \qquad f(0) + 5 = 6$

↓ ↑

$f(0) \qquad 1 = 1$

147. Since value = 1 only if nodes has no left as well as right node otherwise value = 0. Therefore it returns number of leg nodes in tree.

148. Maximum nodes in binary tree of height 0
$= 1 = (2^{0+1} - 1)$

Maximum nodes in binary tree of height 1
$= 3 = (2^{1+1} - 1)$

$\therefore$ Maximum nodes in binary tree of height h
$= (2^{h+1} - 1)$

149. 5 binary trees can be formed with three unlabeled nodes as shown below.

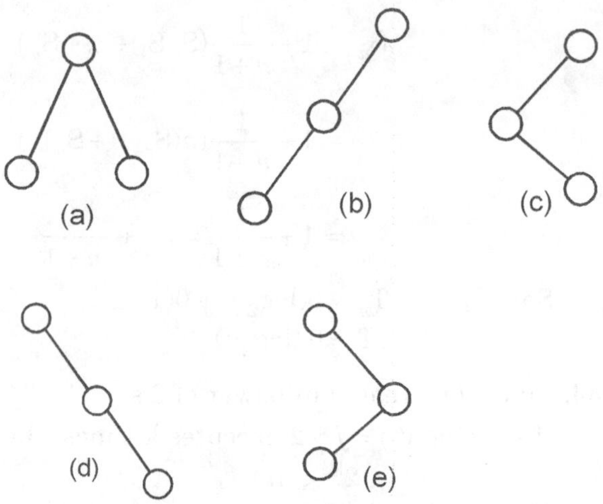

150. Merge sort has lowest worst – case complexity, i.e. $O(n \log n)$, whereas all remaining three has $O(n^2)$.

151. From given inorder and preorder traversal, the binary tree can be formed.

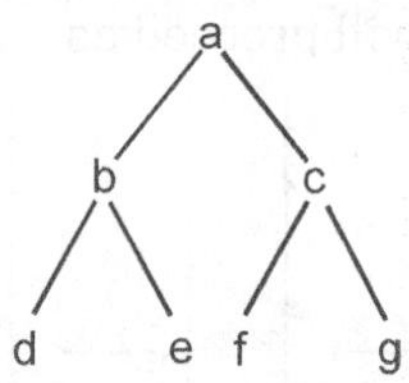

Since a is first node traversed in preorder, so it will be root of tree elements (nodes) left to a and right to a in inorder traversal will be left subtree and right subtree respectively of the tree.

In left subtree elements d, b, e since bcomes first in preorder, so b will be root of left subtree d is left to b in inorder, so it will be left child of d and e will be right child of d. Tree will be like

152. 1 will occupy location 0.

3 will occupy location 6.

8 hashed to location 0 which is already occupied, so it will be hashed to one location next to it (0) i.e. to location 1.

Since 10 also clashes, so it will be hashed to location 2.

153. In case of unweighted, undirected graphs, BFS gives the most time efficient computation for shortest path. It is guaranteed to find first shortest path.

154.

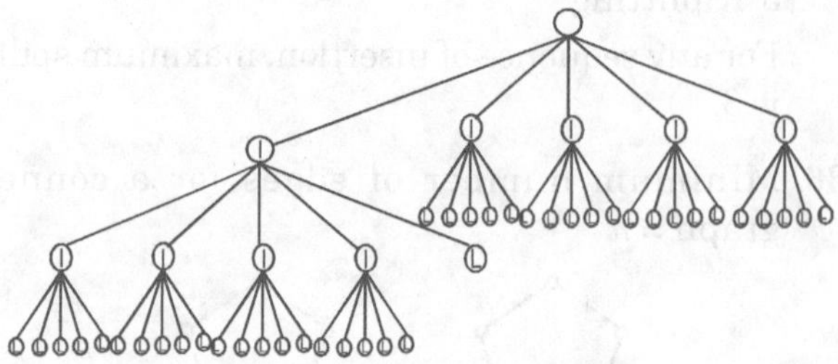

155. The given function is recursive so the equivalent recursion equation is

$$T(n) = 1 \quad n \le 2$$

$$T(n) = \lfloor \sqrt{n} \rfloor + n \quad n > 2$$

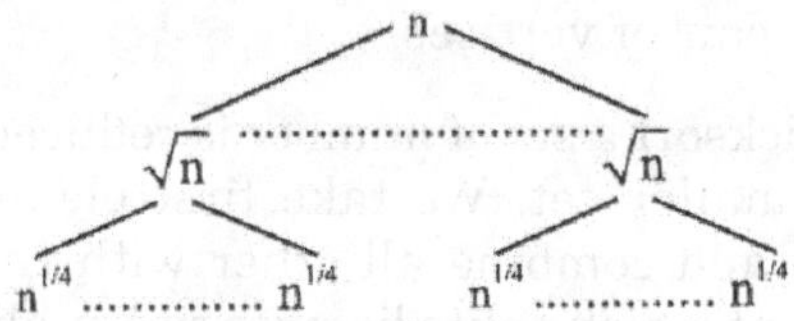

All the level sums are equal to n. The problem size at level k of the recursion tree is $n^{2^{-k}}$ and we stop recursing when this value is a constent. Setting $n^{2^{-k}} = 2$ and solving for k gives us

$$2^{-k} \log_2 n = 1$$

$$\Rightarrow \quad 2^k = \log_2 n$$

$$\Rightarrow \quad k = \log_2 \log_2 n$$

So $\quad T(n) = \theta(\log_2 \log_2 n)$

156. Since tree for Max Heap is binary tree and binary search is being performed.

157. e is need not to be present in every spanning tree since there may be edges (in cycle formed by adding e), which has same weight as e has.

158. Since,

$2n - c$ = average number of comparison needed.

$1.5\,n - 2$ = number of comparison in case.

$n \log_2 n$ = also doesn't conform with number of comparison needed.

159. Number of push operations will be minimum when m alternate insert and delete *op* are performed with n–m, incerts in the end.

For each alternate insert and delete *op* 1 push is needed

$\therefore \quad 2m$

Rest of the $n - m$ inserts need $n - m$ push

$\therefore$ Minimum push $= 2m + n^{-n}$

$= m + n$

Number of *pop* operations will be maximum when n insertions are done consecutively and then m deletions are performed.

For the first deletion, first n element have to be popped from S_1, then all the m deletions can be performed each by a single pop.

$\therefore$ Maximum $pop = n + m$

160. (*i*) will occur, if $i = n$ occurs before $j = n$ so that the while loop terminates till that time $j–1$ elements of b and n elements of a would have been inserted in c. $i = n$ would have occured only if i would have been incremented i.e,

$$a[i] < b[j] \text{ for the last } i.$$

$$\Rightarrow \quad a[n-1] < b[j]$$

$$\therefore \quad k = j - 1 + n$$

161. Only an extra variable t 1 has been added in work 2 instead of directly computing the subscript as in work 1. The output will be the same. S1 is true.

The addition of variables $t1$ and $t2$ will not improve the performance in any way. i.e. S2 is false.

162. S3 is true S4 is false S1 is false S5 is false

163. MAX Heap used to identity max element in O(1) time for to identity min element require O(n).

164. Minimum spanning tree will be formed when $\forall$ $i. \in. \{1, 2, ... n\}$

V_i is connected to V_{i+1}, as in that case each edge will have the minimum weight of 2.

For example, for $n = 4$, the minimum spanning tree is as follows :

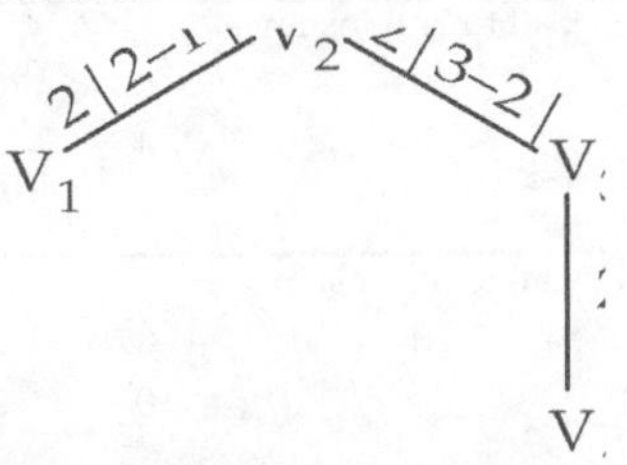

In such a tree, weight of tree consisting of $n–1$ edges each of weight 2 will be

$$2(n-1) = 2n - 2$$

165. In order to find minimum size of X capable of storing any kind of binary tree, the worst cose size of the tree has to be taken.

In the worst case size of the tree has to be taken.

In the worst case only a single node will contain the data at each level of the tree.

For example, for 4 data items, the worst case binary tree will be as follows

Generalizing the concept, for n vertices, the levels of tree that are required will be n.

Memory required at each level (starting from root) will be

$$2^0, 2^1, 2^2, \ldots\ldots 2^{n-1}$$

$$\therefore \text{ Minimum size} = 2^0 + 2^1 \ldots\ldots\ldots\ldots\ldots 2^{n-1}$$

$$= \frac{2^0(2^n - 1)}{2-1} = 2^{n-1}$$

168. If n is a power of 2, then

$$j = n + \frac{n}{2} + \frac{n}{2} + \ldots\ldots\ldots\ldots + \log_2 n \text{ term}$$

If n is not a power of 2, then there will be minor differences of 1 at $\frac{n}{2^i}$ wherever $\frac{n}{2^{i-1}}$ is odd.

Hence val (j) computed on the basis of $n = 2^n$ will give a fair answer

$$j = n + \frac{n}{2} + \ldots\ldots\ldots\ldots 1 \text{ G.P.}$$

$$= \frac{n\left(\left(\frac{1}{2}\right)^{\log n} - 1\right)}{\frac{1}{2} - 1}$$

$$= 2n\left(1 - \frac{1}{2^{\log n}}\right)$$

$$= 2n\left(1 - \frac{1}{n}\right) = 2(n-1) = \theta(n)$$

169. Let x contains n elements divie it by $n/2$ repeatedly so the recurrence become

$$T(1) = 1$$

$$T(n) = 2T(n/2) + 1$$

$$T(n) = O(n \log n)$$

170. Ordering the weights, the sequence obtained is 1, 1, 2, 2, 3, 3, 4, 4, 5, 6, 7

Now, in order to obtain minimum spanning tree using Kruskal's algorithm, we have to add edges with weights in increasing order such that weight of the spanning tree is minimum.

In option (*d*), weights of the edges are 1, 1, 2, 3, 2 which contradicts Kruskal's algorithm.

171.

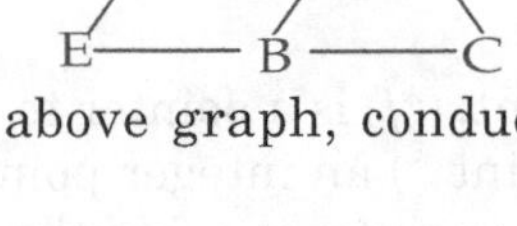

For the above graph, conducting depth First scarch:

Stack : A

Stack : DBC Tree : A

Stack : EBC Tree : A / D

Stack : BC Tree : A / D / E

Stack : BC

Stack : ϕ Tree :

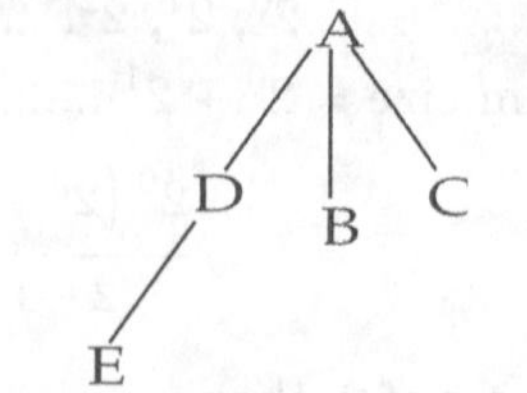

Considering leaf nodes E and C, the given condition is satisfied as their degrees are more than one. But none of (*a*), (*b*) or (*c*) hold.

But a cycle consisting of E and all its neighbour hold.

172. The statement inside the for loop is similar to X–OR operation such that the set obtained is $(X \cap Y') \cup (X' \cap Y)$.

It is equivalent to $(X - Y) \cup (Y - X)$.

173.

$$T(1) = 1$$

$$T(n) = 2T\left(\left[\sqrt{n}\right]\right) + 1$$

We know that $\log_2^2 = 1$

So, all the level sums are equal to $\log_2^2$. The problem size at level *k* of the recursion tree is $n^{2^{-k}}$ and we stop recursing this value is a constant. Setting $n^{2^{-k}} = 2$ and solving for *k* gives us $2^{-k} \log_2 n = 1 \Rightarrow 2^k = \log_2 n \Rightarrow k = \log \log_2 n)$

So $T(n) = \theta(\log \log n)$

174. $a_1, a_2 \ldots\ldots\ldots\ldots\ldots\ldots a_n$

$b_1, b_2 \ldots\ldots\ldots\ldots\ldots\ldots b_n$

In order to find out the largest span, check the sums of

$a_i + \ldots\ldots\ldots\ldots a_j$ and $b_i + \ldots\ldots\ldots\ldots b_j$ at each step.

If $a_1 + a_2 = b_1 + b_2$ go on, check $a_1 + a_2 + a_3$ and $b_1 + b_2 + b_3$.

If not, then check $a_2 + a_3$ and $b_2 + b_3$

Similarly a check is done at each of the *n* places during traversal. A separate variable has to be kept that contains the maximum span observed hitherto

Hence fastest algorithm computes with (~) (*n*) time and space.

175. S1 is true S_4 and S5 are false as the program will print 3 and 8. The option left is (*a*).

176. int (*f) (int*);

return type int, (*f) is a pointer to a function the argumen is (int *) an integer pointer So int (*f) (int*) means a pointer to a function that takes an integer pointer as argument and returns an integer.

177. The abstract data type (ADT) refers to a programmer defined data type together with a set of operations that can be performed on that data so the choice (*c*) is correct.

178. A common property of logic programming languages and functional languages is both are declarative because we declare any statement before we will use it.

179. Object oriented programming language is

Object based PL + Abstraction + Inheritance.

The last wo are must for any L to be OOPL.

180. Apply concept of hashing where hash function return index where to increment corresponding entry

Index = (no. – 51)

(no. is given no.)

So mapping goes through 0 — 49

Hence, an array of 50 numbers

181. Consider 'print *f*' statement in main ( )

Sum is initilize to 0

So final answer is always zero here

only option's have 0 in last digits are (*b*) and (*d*)

n	sum	K	J
2048	0	0	0
		8	204

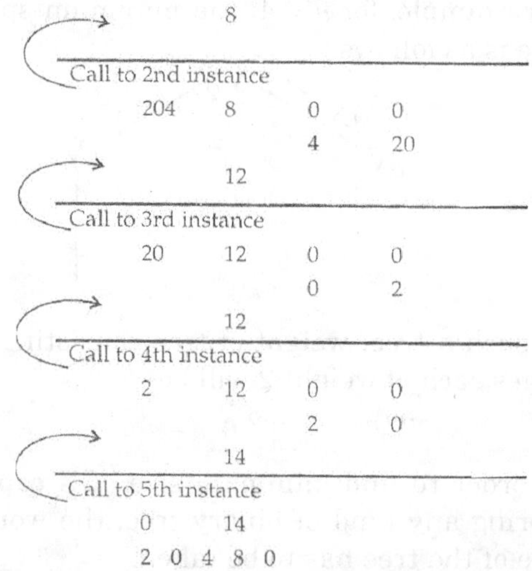

182. When we don't declare a function (specify the prototype), the default rules that the function (foo in our case) would have been assumed to be int, even though it really return a double. This will generates compiler warning and our program will have undefined behaviour is disastrous.

183. Inorder always have print in ascending order that why.

184. The goal of strecture programming is to determine the flow of control from program text (source program hence C is correct answer).

185. Since no print & instruction inside the body of the function and function will return nothing in the calling environment since (x, y) cannot be used as, the parameters are passed by value.

186.

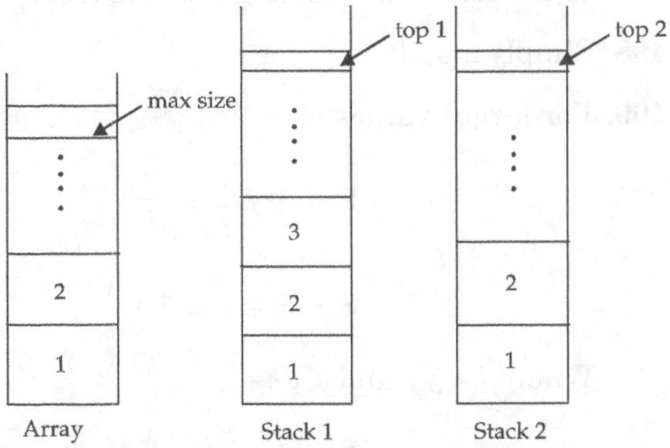

As insertion in stock starts from opposite end, then if A [1] is inserted into stock 1 and A [max size] is inserted into the other stock, stock 2 as all element of arrang are placed into stack

so, top + 1 = top 2

⇒ top 1 = top 2 – 1

187. Binary search tree formed affer inserting into empty binary search tree as

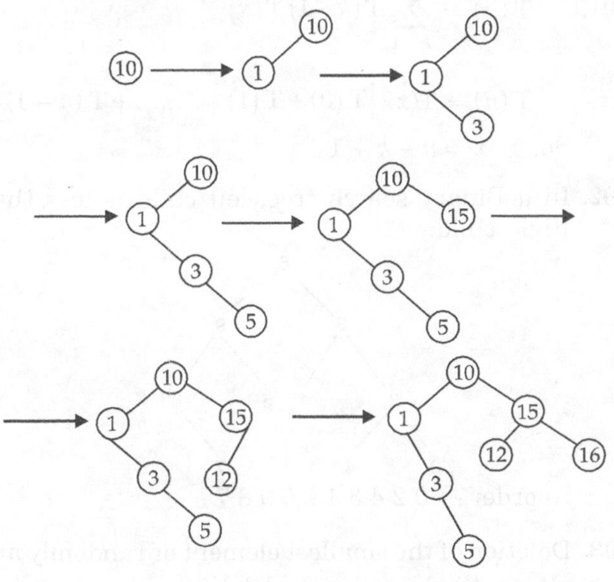

188. Stock is used to check whether aur arithmetic expression has balanced parenthesis or not the algorither are as follow :

1. If opening parenthesis is encountered PUSH into the Stock
2. If closing parenthesis is encounter POP from the stock
3. Check wether Stack is empty or not
4. If stock is empty' then Parenthesis are balanced else parenthesis are not balanced.

189. The program is

```
int f (int n)
{
Static int i = 1
    if (n z = 5) return n          ......... (1)
    n = n + i ;
    i ++ ;
    return f (n) ;
}
```

as 1 not full fill the condition of if statement so excute next instruction, the iteration will be as

iteration	n	i
1	1 + 1 = 2	2
2	2 + 2 = 4	2 + 1 + 3
3	4 + 3 = 7	i = 4

as 7 is greater than 5 so it will return to the main program.

190.

```
int n, rev ;
rev = 0 ;
while (n > 0)
{
rev = rev * 10 + n% 10 ;
n = n/10 ;
}
```

If $n = d_1 d_2 d_3 -- d_{m-i}$

then after intering into the loop

loop	n	rev
1	$d_1 d_2 .... d_{m-i-1}$	d_{m-i}
2	$d_1 d_2 .. d_{m-i-2} (d_{m-i})$	$(d_{m-i-1}) + (d_{m-i-1})$

After executing m times within the loop, rev will be

$$\text{rev} = d_m d_m d_{m-1} -- d_{in-i+1}.$$

191. *Given program is*

```
Chav P [20] ;
Chav * S = "string" ;
int length = strlen(s) ;
for (i = 0 ; i < length ; i + +)
p [i] = S [length – i] ;
print f ("% s", P) ;
```

After executing within the loop

P [0] = g

P [1] = n

P [2] = i

P [3] = r

P [4] = t

P [5] = s

length will be 6 from the statement

length = strlen (s) ;

so after that it will go not of the loop, then

P = gnirts

192. Single variable are used to access the queuce. So it is not possible to operate enqueue and deque operation with constant, as insertion and deletion takes from oposite end rear and front respectively.

193. Max Heap are those tree in which root node has larger value than that of the child and left sibling has larger value than right.

Given numbers are 32, 15, 20, 30, 12, 25, 16 then Mox Heap tree will be

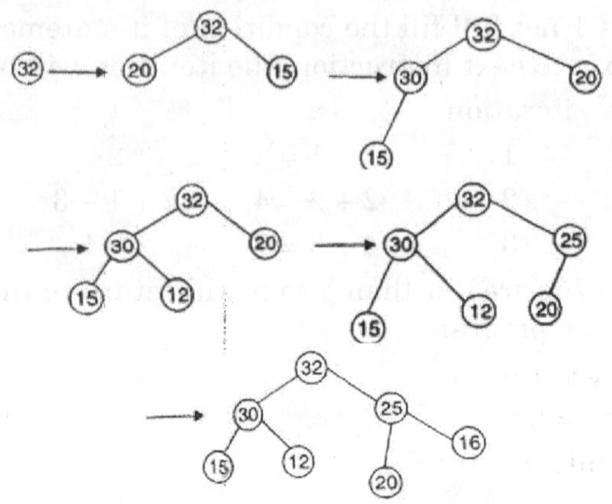

194. Given expression are

$$\{(a + (b \quad c)) - (d \,\hat{}\, (e \hat{} f))\}^*$$

The parrenthesis are arranged in this way because $\wedge$ is right associative so converting into postfix stepwise

$$\{(a + (b \quad c)) - (d \hat{}\, (e \hat{} f))\}$$
$$= (a + (bc\,)) - (def\hat{}\hat{}\,)$$
$$= (abc\,+) - (def\hat{}\hat{}\,)$$
$$= abc\;+ def\hat{}\hat{}\, -$$

This is same as (*a*).

195. This program will evaluate the greatest common divisor of X and Y.

196. Given program fragment in Pseudo language is

```
x = m ;
y = 1 ;
while (x – y > e)
x = (x + y) /2 ;
y = m/x ;
}
Print (x)
```

This program will find out the square root of m, suppose that m = 2

	X –	Y	X	Y
Ist looping	2		3/2 = 1.5	2/1.5 = 1.33
2nd looping	.16		$\frac{1.5+1.3}{2} = 1.415$	$\frac{2.0}{1.415} = 1.413$
3rd looping	0.02		1.414	1.414
4th looping	0			

as $x - y = 0$ exit from loop hence print 1.414 which is root of 2.

197. This count the number of edge from the root node to the leaf which is height of the tree.

198. Simply match.

199. For larger values of y

$$P = P * \frac{x}{i} = \frac{x}{i}$$

$$S = S + P = 1 + \frac{x}{i}$$

When $i < y$ and i ++

$$S = 1 + \frac{x}{i} + \frac{x}{i+1} + \ldots\ldots\ldots\ldots$$

$$= 1 + x + \frac{x}{2} + \frac{x}{3} + \ldots\ldots\ldots\ldots$$

Hence for larger value of y, ln (1 + *x*)

200. B [2] [3] gives element of second rows from third column.

201.
$$T(n) = \sum_{k=1}^{n} T(k-1)\,T(x)$$

$$T(n) = T(x)\left[T(0) + T(1) + \ldots\ldots + T(n-1)\right]$$

So, $x = n - k + 1$

202. In a Binary search tree, left child is less than Right child.

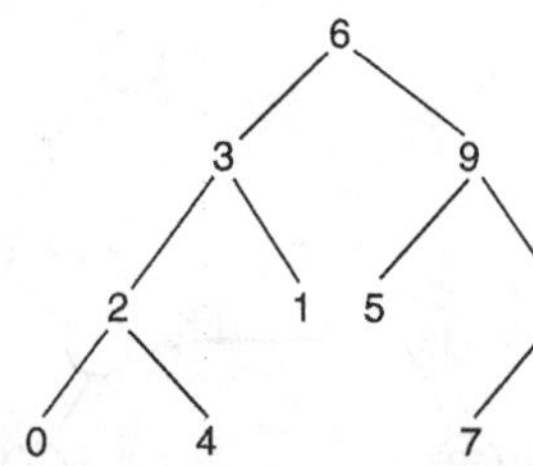

In order → 0 2 4 3 1 6 5 9 8 7

203. Deletion of the smallest element or randomly any element is insertion or deletion.

Complexity is O ($\log_2 n$).

204. Push & Pop take time = 2X

Delay between one push and one pop = Y

So, average stack life of an element

$$(m) = \frac{2X\,m + mY}{m}$$
$$= 2X + Y$$

205. Initially

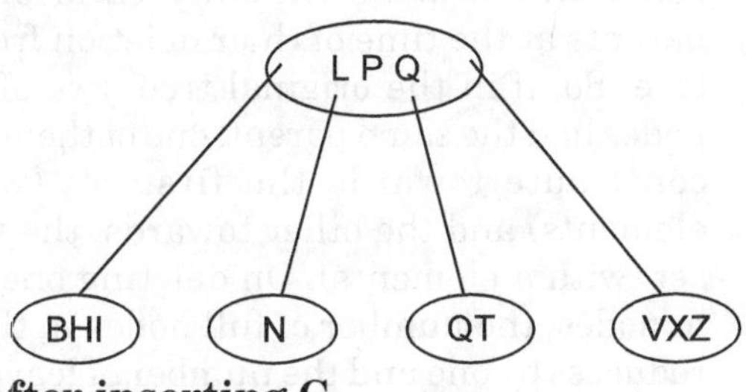

After inserting G.

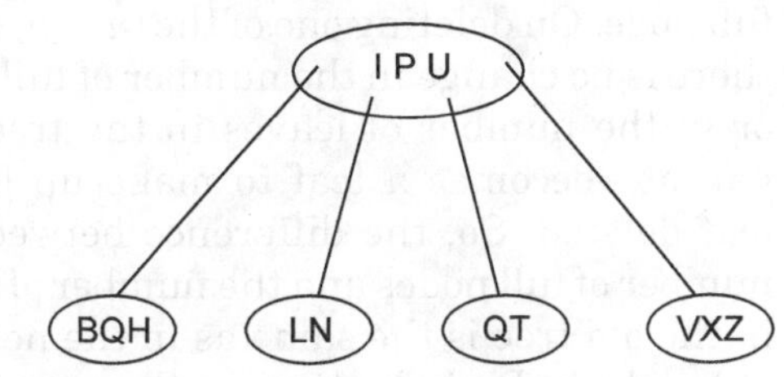

206. If (!A[j]) condition

If (A[j] == 0)

Prints the value. But no zero is the array.

207. $*y = \&x = 5$

$x = *y + 2 = 7$

Q (x) ;

$z = x = 7$

$z = z + x = 12$

print $(z) = 12$

$*y = x - 1 = 6$

print $(x) = 7$

print $(x) = 6$

208. For a given linked list p, the function f returns 1 if and only if not all elements in the list have the same data value because if p == NULL or p – > next == NULL or p – > data < = next – > data and p – > next.

217. (*a*) The point (p, q) is always below the line

(*b*)

4	=	
5	=	
6	<	>
7	>	<

or

Line 6 could also be > <

in which case line > must be < >

Note : At any place in lines 6 and 7,

≤ may be used instead of <, and

≥ may be used instead of >

218. (*a*) Count = 3

$q[1] = 7$

$q[2] = 3,$

$q[3] = 9$

$p[7] = 1,$

$p[3] = 2,$

$p[9] = 3$

(*b*) The first count elements of q contain values i such that set (*i*) has been called.

(*c*) Suppose $p[i]$ has a value < = 0 or > count, then is-set (*i*) returns false.

Otherwise consider q[p [*i*]]. Using (*b*), $q[p\ [i]]$ contains a value j such that set (*i*) has been called. Since set (*i*) has not been called, $q\ [p\ [i]]$ cannot be equal to i, and is set (*i*) returns false.

219. (*a*) (1) $f\,[n]\ ! = 0$

or

Expression like $f\,(n)$ ¹ 0 etc.

(2 $f[n]$

(3) $f[n] = t$

(*b*) O (n) or $(n + 1)$

Alternately

0 (n^2) in the log-cost model.

220. (*a*) 7

(*b*) 22210000 1111

Arrangements that satisfy one of the following two constraints are also correct.

(*i*) 1's in the first 4 positions and no 2's in the last 3 positions

or $\dfrac{1111}{\text{all ones}}$ 22020 $\dfrac{010}{\text{no two's}}$

(*ii*) 1's in the last 3 positions and no zeros in the first 4 positions

or $\dfrac{1212}{\text{no zeros}}$ 00020 $\dfrac{111}{\text{all ones}}$

221.

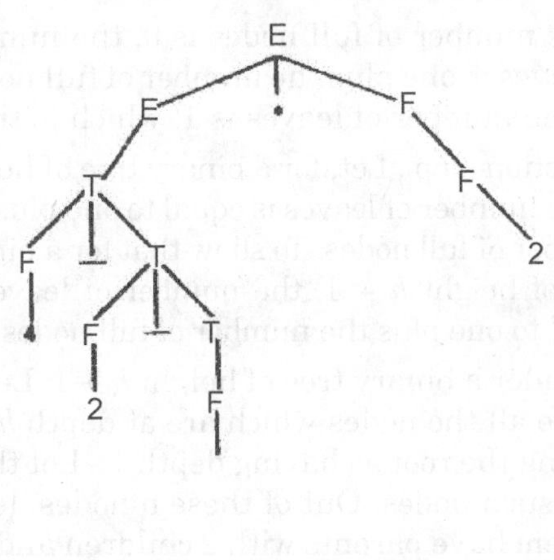

(*a*) 12

7

10

5

(*b*) 14

14

10

10

222. An arbitrary goto can lead to infinite loops as follows

Label1 : Goto Label2;

Label2 : Goto Label1;

Recursive procedure/functional calls may be non-terminating if the terminating condition is never satisfied.

A repeat loop can also lead to infinite loops if the condition to exit the loop is never satisfied.

223. When the procedure "show" is called from the main program, the value of the global variable $x - 0.25$ in this case- gets printed. When the same "show" is called from the procedure "small", the value of the local variable $x - 0.125$ in this case - gets printed.

224. The five tokens are "DO", "10", "I", "=" and "1.25".

226. (*a*) FUNNY terminates for all functions f. This is because if *f* does terminate, then HALTS (*ff*) would return true and FUNNY (*ff*) would return not (*ff*), the calculation of which takes finite time. And if f does not terminate, then HALTS (*ff*) returns false and FUNNY (*f*) would return true. So, in either case FUNNY terminates.

(*b*) Consider FUNNY (FUNNY). Since FUNNY terminates, HALTS (FUNNY FUNNY) would return true.

This would cause FUNNY (FUNNY) to be equated to not FUNNY (FUNNY) which is a contradiction.

227. (*a*) Basic Step : Height of binary tree = 1

Since number of full nodes is 0, the number of leaves is one plus the number of full nodes, i.e. the number of leaves is 1, which is true.

Induction step : Let, for a binary tree of height h, the number of leaves is equal to one plus the number of full nodes. To show that for a binary tree of height $h + 1$, the number of leaves is equal to one plus the number of full nodes.

Consider a binary tree of height $h + 1$. Let us delete all the nodes which are at depth $h + 1$ (taking the root as having depth 1). Let there be n such nodes. Out of these n nodes, let m of them have parents with 2 children and the remaining n-m be the only child of their parents at the time of their deletion from the tree. So, if in the original tree, two of the n nodes had the same parent, one of them would contribute towards the first set (with m elements) and the other towards the second set (with n elements). On deleting one of the m nodes, the number of full nodes in the tree reducess by one and the number of leaves also reduces by one—the parent—is no longer a full node. On deleting one of the $(n - m)$ nodes, there is no change in the number of full nodes or in the number of leaves in the tree—the parent—becomes a leaf to make up for the leaf deleted. So, the difference between the number of full nodes and the number of leaves in the old tree is the same as in the new tree of height h. By induction, in the new tree of height h, the number of leaves is one plus the number of full nodes. So, the tree of height $h + 1$ also has it s number of leaves as one more than the number of full nodes.

Hence, proved.

(*b*) The sequence of insertions modify the heap as below. Note that for every intermediate heap, the minimum node bubbles upto the root.

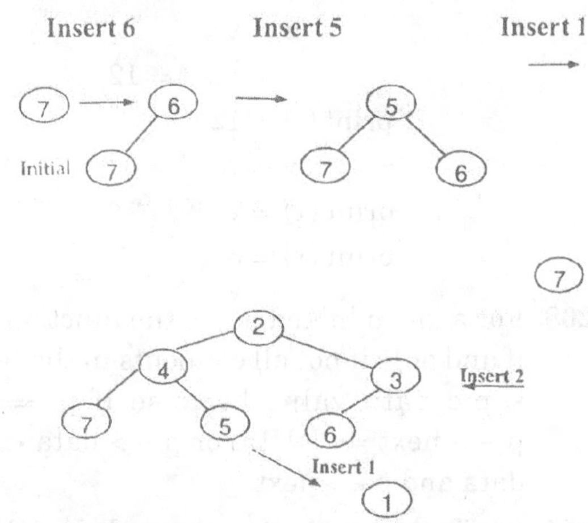

228. (*a*) The boolean expression can be simplified as below

$$[\,(\tilde{}p \vee q) \Rightarrow (q \Rightarrow p)\,]$$

i.e. $[(\tilde{}p \vee q) \Rightarrow (\tilde{}q \vee p)\,]$

i.e $[\tilde{}\,(\tilde{}p \vee q) \vee (\tilde{}q \vee p)]$

i.e. $[\,(p \vee \tilde{}q) \vee \tilde{}q \vee p\,]$

i.e. $[\tilde{}q \vee p\,]$

The above expression is false for $p = 0, q = 1$. So, it is not a tautology.

(*b*) Since A is a tautology, it is true for all possible inputs. So, A $\vee$ B will also be true for all possible inputs, regardless of whether B is true or not.

229. (*i*) In the case of call by value, the values of a and b in the main program don't change upon calling procedure P. So 2 is printed.

(*ii*) In the case of call by reference, only the second and third arguments to P - '*a*' and '*a*')- can be called reference. So, variables '*y*' and '*z*' is procedure P point to the same location as '*a*.' So, on executing y = $y + 1$, the value of a becomes 3. Then on executing $z = z + x$, the value of a becomes 3 + 5 = 8. So, 8 gets printed.

(*iii*) The final output is same as call by reference. So, 8 gets printed.

230.

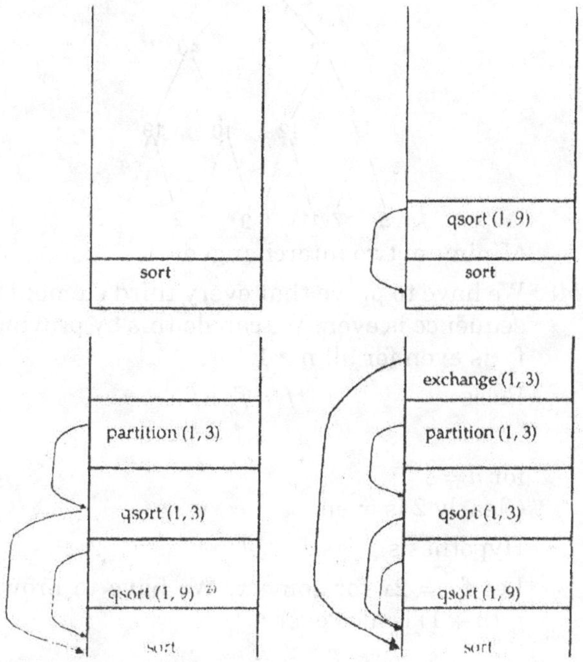

231. Consider the complete binary tree

Here Interval nodes = 3.

Leaves = 3.

232. If number of internal nodes is n–1, then leaves are maximum upto $n - 1 + 1$.

So, in n–ary tree if internal node is x, then numbers of leaves in it is given by

$= x\,(n–1) + 1$

233. fun (95) = fun (fun (106))

= fun (96) = fun (fun (107))= fun (97)

= fun (fun (108)) = fun (98)

= (fun (fun (109)) = fun (99)

= fun (fun (140)),

= fun (100) = fun (fun (111))

= fun (101) = 91.

234. $x := x + 1$

F = x ;

when $x = 5$,

$x := x+1 = 6$

F : = 6

So, F(x) * F(x) = 36

235. A [*i*] [*j*]th location = Starting address + (i – 1) × Number of columns × Size of one element + (j – 1) × Size of one element.

$= 100 + (i – 1)\,15 + (j – 1)$

$= 100 + 15i – 15 + j – 1 = 15i + j + 84$

236. Faster access to non-locals than with links can be obtained using an array α of pointers to a activation record is called display.

237. (*a*)

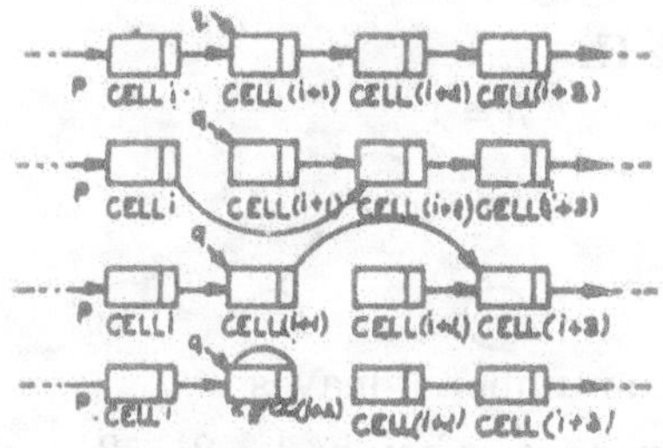

(*i*) $q : p \rightarrow$ next

(*ii*) $p \rightarrow$ next : = $q \rightarrow$ next

(*iii*) $q \rightarrow$ next : ($q \rightarrow$ next) $\rightarrow$ next

(*iv*) ($q \rightarrow$ next) $\rightarrow$ next : = q

(*b*) The post fix equivalent of expression

$$3 * \log (x + 1) - \frac{a}{2} \text{ is,}$$

$$3x_1 + \log * \frac{3}{2}$$

This is obtained by taking the mathematical function log as a unary operator.

238. From program we get, x of B, z and y in S_1 and x of A, i and y in S_2 are variables acceisble in S_1 and S_2.

239. $|i - j| = 8$ or $|i - j| = 12$

Number of connected components in G

= difference of value of $|i - j| = 12 - 8 = 4$

In other way, number of connected components in G = 100 – 12 × 8 = 4

241. (*a*) $\left(\frac{n-1}{n}\right)^k$

(*b*) $\left(\frac{n-1}{n}\right)^{k-1} (k + n - 1)$

242. (*a*) $F(n, 2) = \frac{n(n+3}{2}$

243. (*a*) If there is only 1 node *i.e.* the roof

$n = 1, h = 0$

$n = 2^0 = 1$

So it is true for $h = 0$

For $h = 1$, there are 3 cases

Case I. There are two nodes

1 root 1 leaf in the left subtree

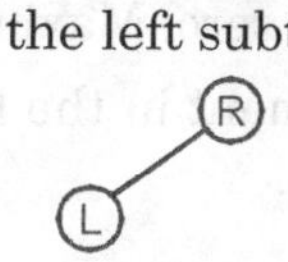

Case II. Two nodes, 1 root and 1 leaf in the right subtree

or

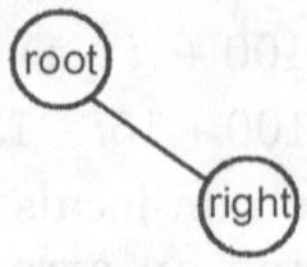

Case III. There are three nodes 1 root and 1 at leaf in each right and left subtree

Case I & II.

$h = 1$

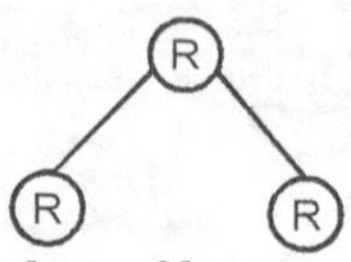

Maximum number of leaves of a binary tree at height 1 = $2^n = 2$

Since it can have 1 less node in either subtree

Number of leaves = 1

$\therefore$ Total nodes are at least = 2 (1 parent node + 1 leaf)

So relation holds for $h = 1$

Assuming that the relation is tree for height = h

$\therefore$ Number of nodes is atleast 2^n. Which the least number of nodes at height $(n - 1)$ + number of leaves at height h *i.e.*

Number of nodes at height $n.n_n = 2^n = (2^n + N_n)$, *where* N_n is the number of leaves at height h.

Now at height $(h + 1)$ the number of leaves are $= 2N_n$.

$\therefore$ Total Nodes at height $(n + 1)$ = Number of nodes at height h + Number of leaves at height $(\boldsymbol{h} + 1)$

$\therefore \quad n_n + 1 = n_n + 2\,N_n$

$= 2^h + 2\,N_n = 2\,(2^h - 1 + N_n)$

$\because \quad 2^{n-1} + N_n = 2^n = n_n$

$\therefore \quad n_{n+1} = 2\,(2^n) = 2^{n+1}$ (Hence proved)

(*b*) $\quad 2^{n-1} - 1 \le$ Node (at h – 1 height) $\le 2^n$

244. 3. Sum : = A [*j*]

6. if sum < M then

11. Sum : = Sum + A [*j*]

245. (*a*) $\dfrac{n\,(n-1)}{2}$

(*b*) Minimum → zero, Maximum → $(n - 1)$

(*c*) The last element in the list.

246.

Procedure C	← Top of the stack
Procedure B	
Procedure A	
Procedure B	
Procedure A	

247. With heap sort,

⇒ 89, (19) 40, 17, 12, 10, 2, 5, 7, 11, 6, 9, (70)

⇒ 89, 70 40, 17, 12, 10, (2), 5, 7, 11, 6, 9, (19)

⇒ 89, 70 40, 17, 12, 10, 19, 5, 7, 11, 6, 9, 2

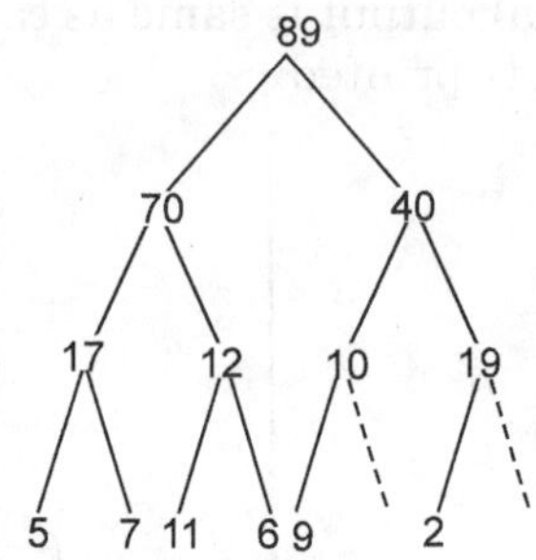

Minimum two interchanged.

248. We have to prove that every third element of the sequence is even. We can do this by proving that f_{3n} is even for all $n \ge 1$.

Basis $\quad f_3 = f_2 + f$

$= 1 + 1 = 2$

for $n = 1$

Clearly 2 is even

Hypothesis

Let $f_{3n} = 2x$ for some x. We have to prove that $f_3\,(n + 1)$ is also even

$$\begin{aligned} f_{3(n+1)} &= f_{3n+3} \\ &= f_{3n+2} + f_{3n+1} \\ &= f_{3n+1}\,f_{3n} + f_{3n+1} \\ &= 2\,.\,f_{3n+1} + f_{3n} \\ &= 2\,.\,f_{3n+1}\quad 2x = 2\,(f_{3n+1} + x) \end{aligned}$$

Hence by induction f_{3n} is even for all $n \ge 1$.

249. The question is in correct. Line 3 of the program should read

i f A [*i* + 1] [*j*] < A [*i*] [*j* + 1] then begin

The solution according to the question printed is

(*a*) *i* = 1 and j = 1

(*b*) Line 2while x > A [i + 1] [*j*] or x > A [*i*] [*j* + 1]

(*c*) Line 7A [*i*] [*j*] : = A [*i*] [*j* + 1]; *j* = *j* + 1;

(*d*) Line 9 A [*i*] [*j*] = x

250. The program segment does not terminate if the value *x* is greater than the largest value in the array *a*.

251. (*i*) call-by-reference

Point 1 : 5 5

Point 2 : 10 10

Point 3 : 10

(ii) Call-by-value
Point 1 : 5 3
Point 2 : 5 10
Point 3 : 5

252.

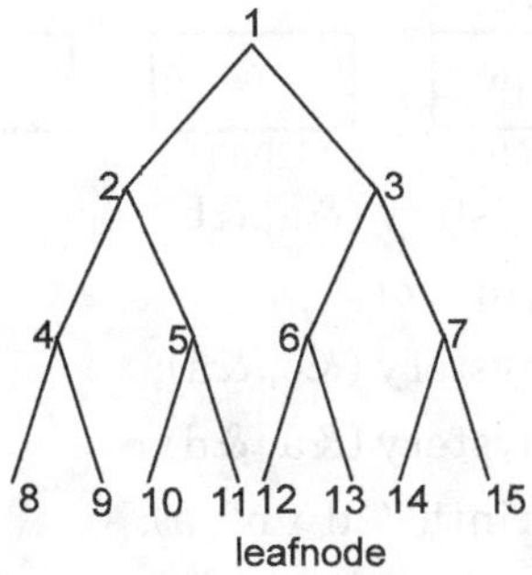

If leaf node = 8
Then nodes of degree = 7
So, if leaf node is n, then nodes of degree 2 in T is $(n-1)$

253. Any connected acyclic graph is a tree having n – 1 edges. Hence minimum number of edges in a connected cyclic graph is $(n-1) + 1 = n$. By adding an edge to a tree we will get a minimal connected cyclic graph.

$n = 6$
$e = 5$

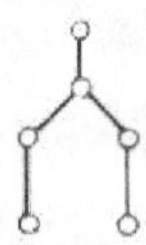

$n = 6$
$e = n = 6$

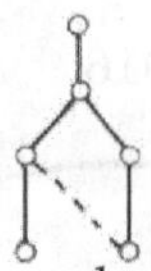

$(n-1)$ edges　　n edges
Tree Connected, cyclic, minimum

254. Consider s = acbc and
acbc acbc
Concat (head(s), head (tail (tail(s))))

255. $A + B * (C + D)/F + D * E$

$\Rightarrow A + B * (CD+)/F + D * E$

$\Rightarrow A + B * (CD+) * F/DE * +$

$\Rightarrow AB\,CD + * \quad F/DE * ++$

256. If we take example, 40, 30, 10, 12, 85, 48, 9, 16
Next step : 30, 40, 10, 12, 35, 48, 9, 16
Next step : 10, 12, 30, 40, 9, 16, 35, 48

257. We use merge sorting and finally we get comparison $O(m + n)$

258. * In worst case complexity is $O(n^2)$
* In best case complexity is $O(n \log n)$
In Hash table, = given value mode n

261. In array Row 1 is stored first, Row 2 next, Row 3 next, and so no.

Here Row 1 has one element. Row 2 has 2 elements. Row 3 has 3 elements, ..., Row $(i-1)$ has $(i-1)$ elements (non - zero).

Hence (i, j)th element present in the array only after presence of

1 element of row 1,

2 elements of row 2,

....

$(i-1)$ elements of row $(i-1)$ and

first $(i-1)$ elements of row i.

Hence the index of (i, j)th element in the array is

$1 + 2 + 3 + \ldots\ldots + (i-1) + j$

$$= \frac{(i-1)(i-1+1)}{2} + j = j + \frac{i(i-1)}{2}$$

Consider the following example,

$$\begin{matrix} R_1 \\ \\ R_2 \\ \\ R_3 \\ \\ R\,(i-1) \end{matrix} \begin{bmatrix} \underbrace{2}_{1} & 0 & 0 & \ldots & 0 \\ \\ \underbrace{2 \quad 3}_{2} & & 0 & \ldots & 0 \\ \\ \underbrace{1 \quad 3 \quad 4}_{3} & & & \ldots & x \\ \\ \underbrace{x \quad x \quad x \quad \ldots \quad x}_{i-1} \end{bmatrix}$$

262. Let S be the given string with a elements.

Let $S = x_1\ x_2\ x_3\ \ldots.\ x_n$

The number of substrings starting with x_1 is n.

The number of substrings starting with x_2 is $(n-1)$,

The number of substrings startring with x_n is 1.

Hence number of substring of

$$S = 1 + 2 + 3 + \ldots\ldots\ldots + n = \frac{n(n+1)}{2}$$

Consider the following example : S = abcd

a	*b*	*c*	*d*

Number of substrings

= 4 + 3 + 2 + 1

$$= \frac{4(4+1)}{2} = 10$$

↓	↓	↓	↓
a	*b*	*c*	*d*
ab	*bc*	*cd*	
abc	*bcd*		
abcd			

265. All (*a*), (*c*) and (*d*) are false. The difference between. (*b*) and (*c*) is vital.

For example 80386 processor has 32 bit address capacity (32 pins for address), hence it is capable of accessing $2^{32} = 2^2 \times 2^{30}$ 4GB $= 2^{12} \times 2^{20}$ = 4096 MB of main memory. But present day computers have at most 32 MB of RAM. The address space of 386 processor is 4 GB and hence virtual memory can be at most 4 GB. If a program is of 5 GB, we have to use only overlaying techineque.

268. If S is the given sequence for quicksort then it is divided into three subsequences S_1, S_2 and S_3 such that for some constant $k \in S$,

elements of $S_1 < k$,

elements of $S_2 = k$ and

elements of $S_3 > k$.

Then recursion is applied for S_1 and S_2 (S_2 is already sorted as all elements of S_2 are equal). Then recursion is applied for S_1 and S_3 (S_2 is already sorted as all elements of S_2 are equal)

QUICKSORT (S) = QUICKSORT (S_1) ∪ S_2 ∪ QUICKSORT (S_3)

Hence S is divided and recursion is applied. Thus quicksort falls under divide and conquer technique.

NUMERICAL TYPE QUESTIONS

1.

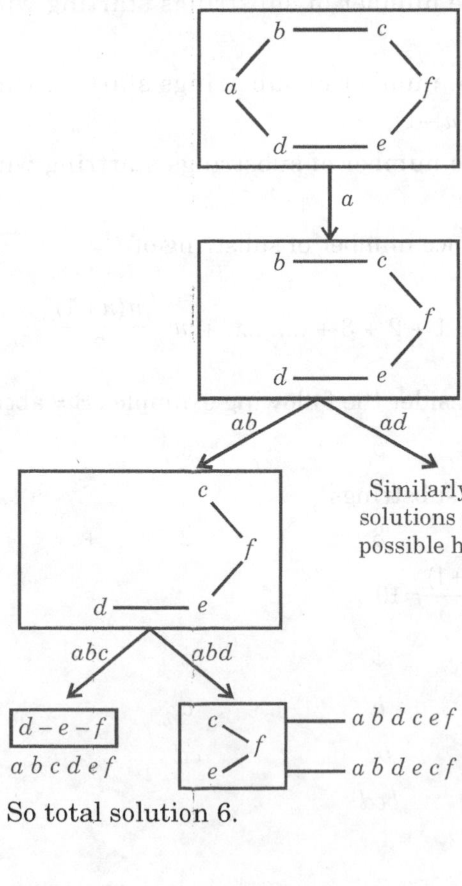

So total solution 6.

2.

```
int main ( )
{
    int a = 2016, b = 0, c = 4, d = 42;
```

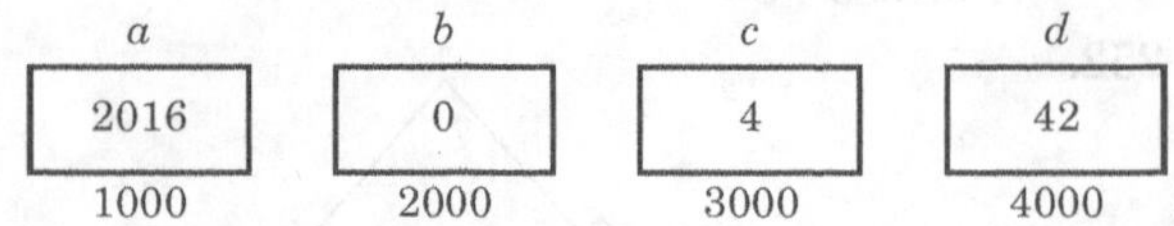


```
    mystery (&a, &b);
    if (a < c)
    mystery (&c, &a);
    mystery (&a, &d);
    printf("%d \ n", a);
}
void mystery (int * ptra, int * ptrb)
{
    int * temp;
    temp = ptrb;
    ptrb = ptra;
    ptra = temp;
}
```

Output → 2016.

3.

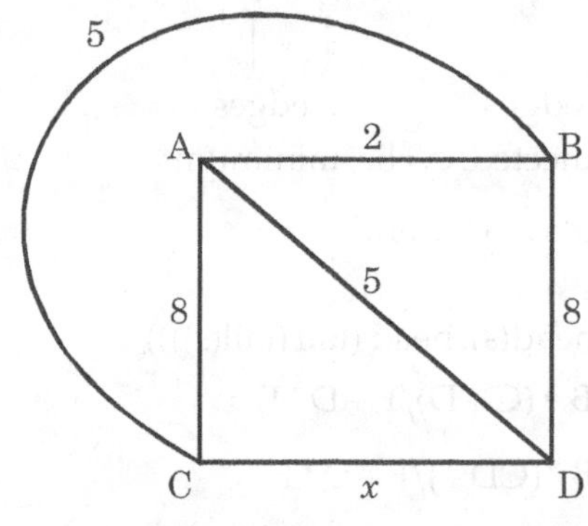

Smallest path between C & D is 12.

So maximum possible value of x is 11.

4.

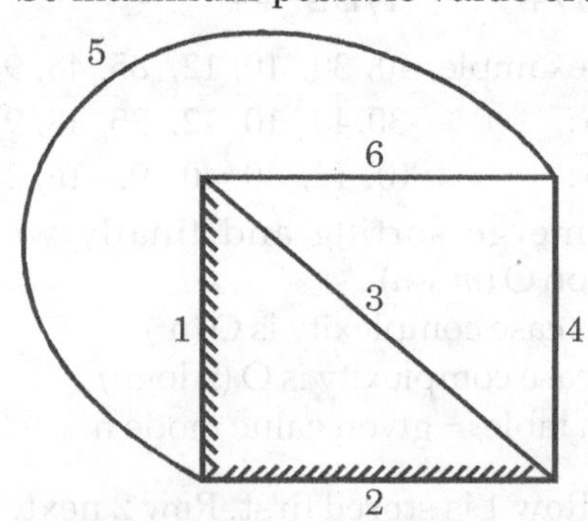

Here 3 can't be taken because it will produce a cycle so take 4.

This solution is 1 + 2 + 4 = 7

5. Maximum possible value of n for which we have complete tree and our 't' node is the last leaf node at height 4.

So, the maximum possible value of n

$= 1 + 2 + 4 + 8 + 16$

$= 31$

6.

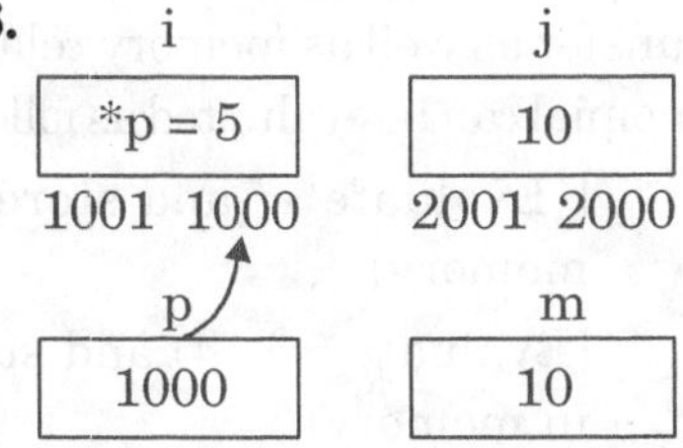

m = m + 5; // m = 15

*p = *p + m; // * p = *p + m = 5 + 15

*p = 20 (i.e., i = 20)

i + j = 20 + 10 = 30

So, the output of the given program is 30.

8. From the given program, we have

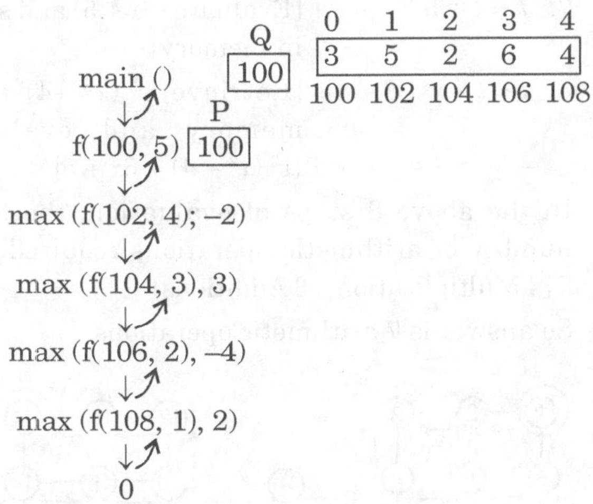

So, the value printed by the program is 3.

9. Formula is 2^n, here n is 6

$2^6 = 64$

The number of ways $= 2^n = 2^6 = 64$

(Here n = height of a tree = 6)

10. for $n = 16$.

Algorithm runs while loop $16 \times 16 = 256$.

12. The output is – 5

13. The cyclomatic complexity of given code segment is 5.

17. The number of nodes in a binary tree have exectly two childrens are $n - 1$ if n is number of leaf.

Hence (200 – 1) = 199 nodes

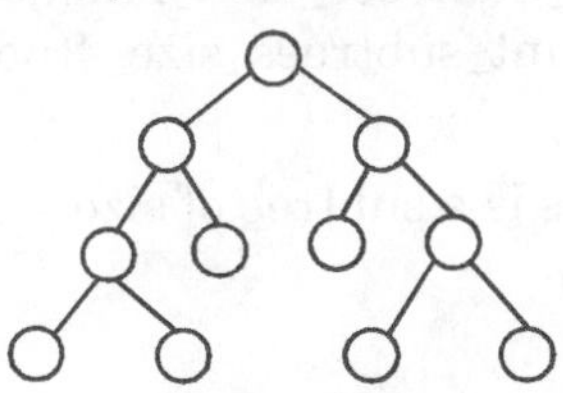

Number of leaf nodes is 6

Number of nodes have exectly two children is 5

18. C | i | 0 | 1 | 1 |

20 something

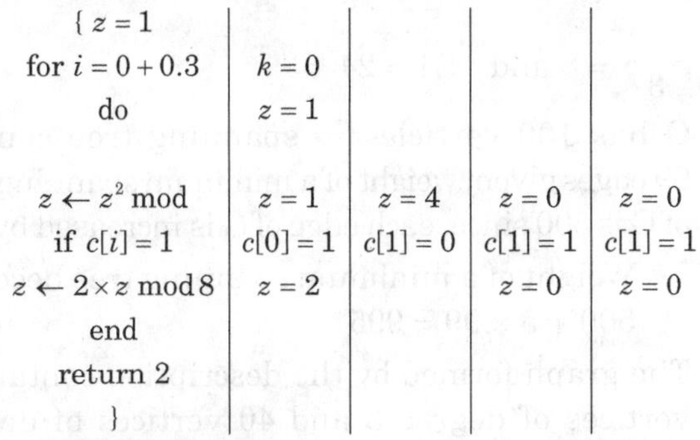

19.

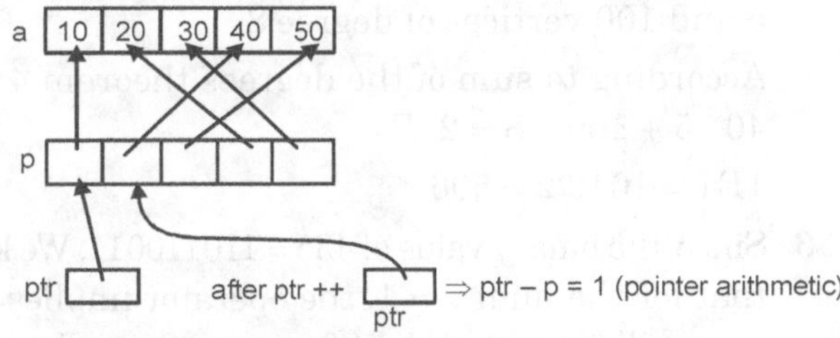

**ptr = 40

∴ printf(" %d%d", p + r – p, p + r) will print 140

20. j and k will be evaluated to 2 and -1 respectively.

In for loop :

When i = 0; 1 time printed (– 1)

When i = 1; 1 time printed (0)

When i = 2; 3 times printed (1, 1, 1)

When i = 3; 3 times printed (2, 2, 2)

When i = 4; 2 times printed (3, 3)

∴ on the whole printf is executed 10 times

21. In function main x will be updated as follows

$x = x + f_1() + f_2() + f_3() + f_2()\, x$

↓ ↓ ↓ ↓ ↓

1 26 51 100 52

Note : static variable in $f_2()$ will be initialized only once & it retains value in between function calls.

22. MST, The complete graph should be

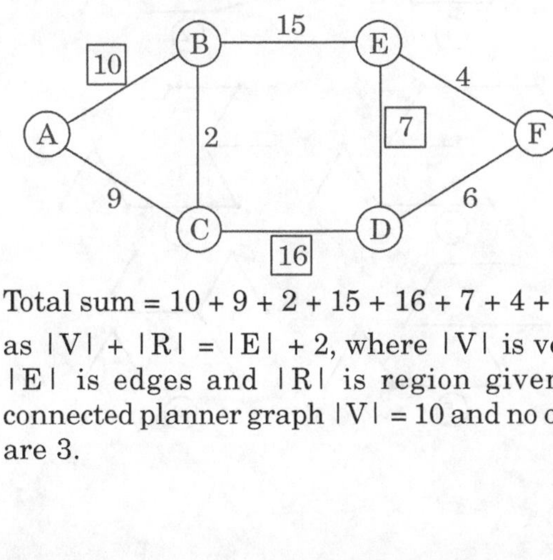

Total sum = 10 + 9 + 2 + 15 + 16 + 7 + 4 + 6 = 69.

23. as |V| + |R| = |E| + 2, where |V| is vertices, |E| is edges and |R| is region given for a connected planner graph |V| = 10 and no of edges are 3.

Then $3|R| = 2|E|$

and then $|R| = \frac{2}{3}|E|$

Hence

$$10 + \frac{2}{3}|E| = |E| + 2$$

$$\frac{|E|}{3} = 8 \text{ and } |E| = 24$$

24. G has 100 verticles ⇒ spanning tree contain 99 edges given, weight of a minimum spanning tree of G is 500 since, each edge of G is increased by five

∴ Weight of a minimum spanning tree becomes $500 + 5 \times 99 = 995$

25. The graph formed by the description contains 4 vertices of degree 3 and 40 vertices of degree 5 and 100 vertices of degree 8.

According to sum of the degrees theorem 4 *3 + 40* 5 + 100 * 8 = 2|E|

|E| = 1012/2 = 506

26. Since, the binary value of 435 = 110110011. We know that for the num > = 1, the operator implies that num will be shifted right for every time when loop is executed. Since, in the given code the loop is incremented 9 times and at last 10th time it is zero. That's why, count will be incremented 9 times.

Hence total count is **9**.

27. C would complete its first I/O operation in 1000 ms as it is using round robin scheduling (as per IIT).

But it is seems to be wrong.

28. When we take the value from 1·72 to 1·74, we will see that else condition will be true *i.e.* return $f(x/2 + 1.5/x)$;

That's why value to $f(q)$ such that it returns q is 1·72 to 1·74.

29. The MST are

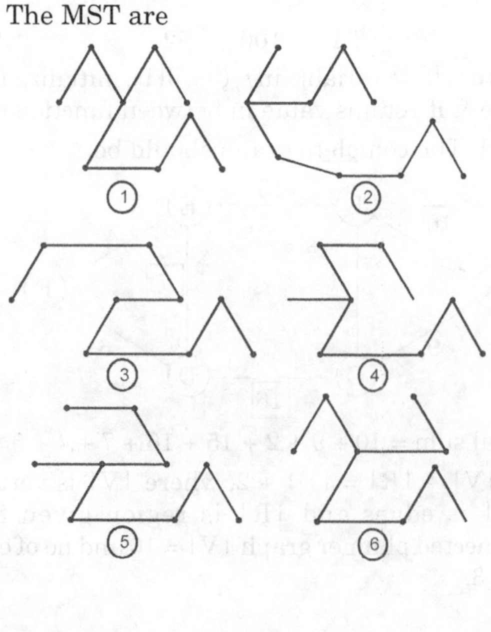

30. $P(x) = x^5 + 4x^3 + 6x + 5$ can be rewritten as follows

$P(x) = x^3 (x^2 + 4) + 6x + 5$

Now using only one temporary variable t and any number of data transfer as well as memory related operation the polynomial can be evaluated as follows

1. $t = x * x$ — [Evaluate x^2 and store in memory]
2. $t = t + 4$ — [Evaluate $(x^2 + 4)$ and store in memory]
3. $t = x^2$ — [Retinue x^2 from memory]
4. $t = t^*.X$ — [Evaluate x^3 and store in memory]
5. $t = t^*(x^2 + 4)$ — [Evaluate $x^3 (x^2 + 4)$ amd store in memory]
6. $t = 6^* x$ — [Evaluate $6x$ and store in memory]
7. $t = t + 5$ — [Evaluate $(6x + 5)$ and store in memory]
8. $t = t + x^3 (x^2 + 4)$ — [Retrieve $x^2 (x^2 + 4)$ from memory and evaluate $\{x^3 (x^2 + 4) + 6x + 5\}$

In the above 8 steps of evaluation, the total number of arithmetic operations required and 7 [4 Multiplications, 3 Additions]

So answer is 7 arithmetic operations.

31.

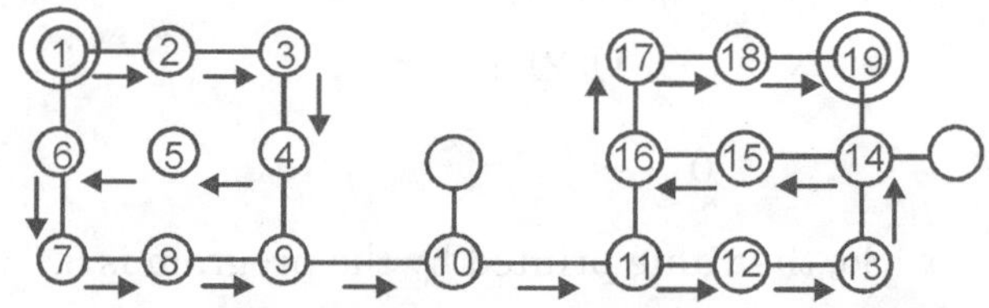

Suppose, we start DFS at vertex numbered as 1 and continue calling recursive function for DFS on subsequent nodes numbered in ascending order. The recursive calling sequence is shown as marked line in the above diagram which shows maximum possible recursion depth including the initial call is 19.

32.

```
int print_subtrees_size_4(node *n)
{
int size=0;
if(node==null)
return 0;
size=print_subtrees_size_4 (node->left) +
        print_subtrees_size_4(node ->right) + 1;
if(size ==4)
printf("this is a subtree of size 4");
return size;
}
```

The above function on taking input the root of a binary tree prints all the subtrees of size 4 in O(n) time

so a =1 , b = 0 and then a + 10 b =1

33. From the list of given n numbers [say n is even], Pick up first two elements, compare them assign Current – min = min of two numbers
Current – max = max of two numbers
From the remaining n – 2 numbers, take pairs wise and follow this process given below.

1. Compare two elements
Assign min = min of two numbers
max = max of two numbers
2. Compare min and current – min
Assign current – min
= min{current–min,min}
3. Compare max and current – max
Assign current – max
= max{current – max, max}

Repeat above procedure for all the remaining pairs of numbers. We can observe that each of pair requires 3 comparisons

1. for finding min and max
2. For updating current – min
3. for updating current – max

But for initial pair we need only one comparison not 3.

$$\therefore \text{ Total number of comparisons } = \frac{3(n-2)}{2}+1$$

$$= \frac{3n}{2}-3+1 = \frac{3n}{2}-2$$

Here n =100, so number of comparisons = 148.

34. Since each vertices in A meet with B. That's why total number of edges = 6 × 6 = 36.

35.

	•	p	q	p	r	q	r	p
	0	(0)	0	0	0	0	0	0
q	0	0↑	(↖1)	←1	←1	↖1	←1	←1
p	0	↖1	↑1	(↖2)	(←2)	←2	←2	↖2
q	0	↑1	↖2	↑2	↑2	(↖3)	←3	←3
r	0	↑1	↑2	↑2	↖3	(↑3)	↖4	←4
r	0	↑1	↑2	↑2	↖3	↑3	(↖4)	(←4)

Longest common subsequence : $qpqr$

$x + 10y = 4 + 10 \times 3 = 34$

36. 20, 24, 30, 35, 50

Step 1 : We take

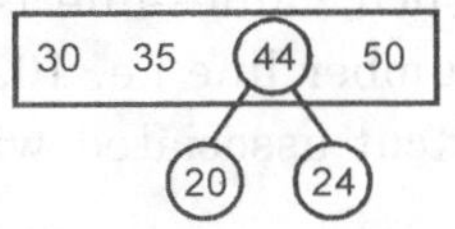

Comparisons = (20 + 24 – 1) Max = 43

Step 2 :

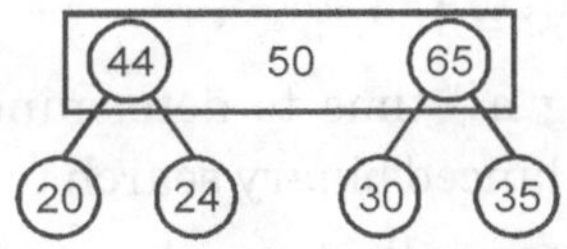

Total comparison = 43 + (65 – 44) = 64

Step 3 :

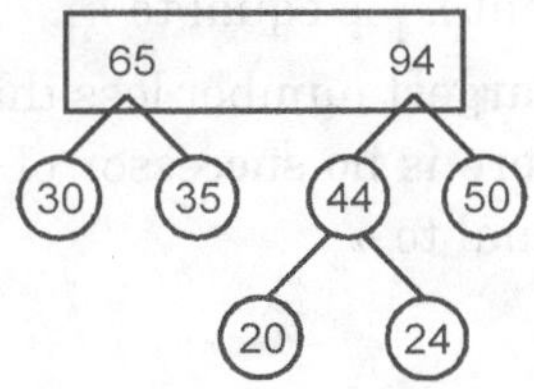

Total comparison = 64 + 19 = 83

Step 4 :

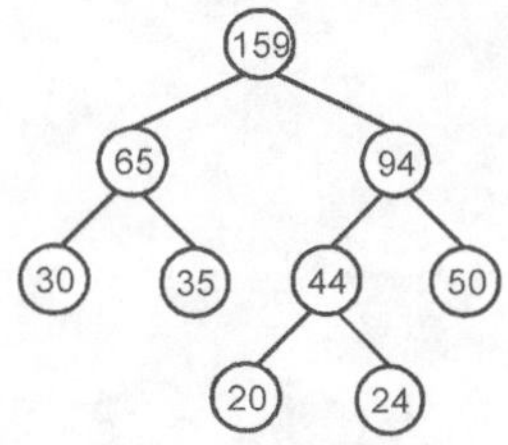

Total comparison = 93 + 65 = 158
= 158 + 93 + 64 + 43 = 358

37.

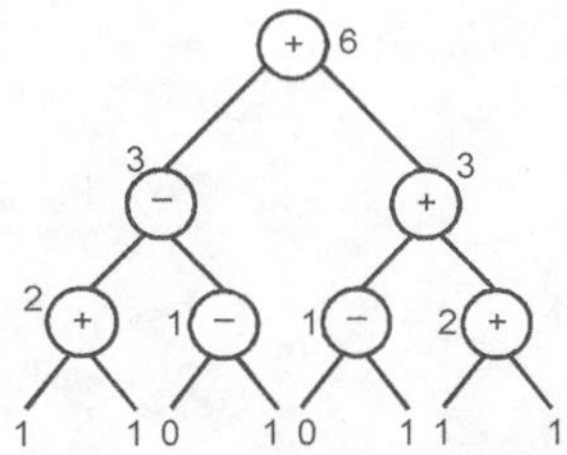

For ⊖, we can take maximum value 0 or 1, but ⊕ we can take maximum value 1, Max. value of tree will be 6.

38. When we take n = S, ie

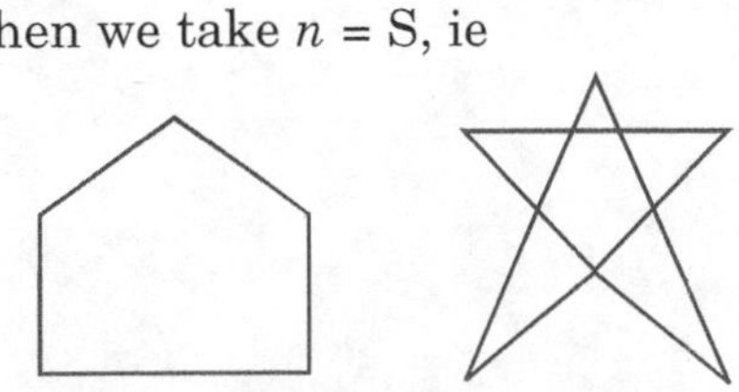

G G′

We can see that in this case G & G′ will be isomorphic to each other.

39. By definition, T(9) = Dist. From 9 to 100
As given, T(9) = 1+min (T(y), T()(z) = 1 + min (Dist.

from y to 100, Dist. From z to 100)

⇒ 1 = Dist. from 9 to y/Dist. From 9 to z

⇒ There are only two such values-one is the simple one step on number line i.e. 10, and the other is the shortcut associated with 9 i.e. 15.

⇒ Therefore, y and z are 10 and 15 (in any order)

⇒ Product yz = 150.

40. It takes (log n) time to determine numbers n_1 and n_2 in balanced binary search tree T such that

1. n_1 is the smallest number greater than or equal to L and there is no predecessor n'_1 of n_1 such that n'_1 is equal to n_1.
2. n_2 is the largest number less than or equal to H and there is no successor of n'_2 of n_2 such that is equal to n_2.

Since there are m elements between n_1 and n_2, it takes 'm' time to add all elements between n_1 and n_2.

So time complexity is O (log $n + m$)

So the given expression becomes

$$O(n^{\circ} \log' n + m' \log^{\circ} n)$$

And $a + 10b + 100c + 1000d = 0 + 10*1 + 100*1 + 1000*1 = 10 + 100 = 110$

Because $a = 0, b = 1, c = 1$ and $d = 0$

41. O ($m + n$) i.e. almost linear

In Kruskal's algorithm, edge e is considered with minimum weight, it is checked whether T + e has cycle or not, then the edge e is added recursively to the partial spanning tree T. There are various types of implementation, according to that order differs.

42. $3n - 6$

4 CHAPTER Theory of Computation

MCQ TYPE QUESTIONS

2016

1. Which of the following languages is generated by the given grammar?

$$S \rightarrow aS \mid bS \mid \varepsilon$$

(*a*) $\{a^n b^m \mid n, m \geq 0\}$

(*b*) $\{w \in \{a, b\}^* \mid w$ has equal number of a's and b's$\}$

(*c*) $\{a^n \mid n \geq 0\} \cup \{b^n \mid n \geq 0\} \cup \{a^n b^n \mid n \geq 0\}$

(*d*) $\{a, b\}^*$

2. Which of the following decision problems are undecidable?

I. GivenNFAs N_1 and N_2, is $L(N_1) \cap L(N_2) = \Phi$?

II. Given a CFG $G = (N, \Sigma, P, S)$ and a string $x \in \Sigma^*$, does $x \in L(G)$?

III. Given CFGs G_1 and G_2, is $L(G_1) = L(G_2)$?

IV. Given a TM M, is $L(M) = \Phi$?

(*a*) I and IV only (*b*) II and III only

(*c*) III and IV only (*d*) II and IV only

3. Which one of the following regular expressions represents the language: *the set of all binary strings having two consecutive 0s and two consecutive* 1s?

(*a*) $(0 + 1)^*0011 (0 + 1)^* + (0 + 1)^*1100 (0 + 1)^*$

(*b*) $(0 + 1)^*(00 (0 + 1)^* 11 + 11(0 + 1)^*00) (0 + 1)^*$

(*c*) $(0 + 1)^*00 (0 + 1)^* + (0 + 1)^* 11 (0 + 1)^*$

(*d*) $00(0 + 1)^* 11 + 11(0 + 1)^*00$

4. Consider the following context-free grammars:

$G_1 : S \rightarrow aS \mid, B \rightarrow b \mid bB$

$G_2 : S \rightarrow aA \mid bB, A \rightarrow aA \mid B \mid \varepsilon, B \rightarrow bB \mid \varepsilon$

Which one of the following pairs of languages is generated by G_1 and G_2, respectively?

(*a*) $\{a^m b^n \mid m > 0$ or $n > 0\}$ and $\{a^m b^n \mid m > 0$ and $n > 0\}$

(*b*) $\{a^m b^n \mid m > 0$ and $n > 0\}$ and $\{a^m b^n \mid m > 0$ or $n \geq 0\}$

(*c*) $\{a^m b^n \mid m \geq 0$ or $n > 0\}$ and $\{a^m b^n \mid m > 0$ and $n > 0\}$

(*d*) $\{a^m b^n \mid m \geq 0$ and $n > 0\}$ and $\{a^m b^n \mid m > 0$ or $n > 0\}$

5. Consider the transition diagram of a PDA given below with input alphabet $\Sigma = \{a,b\}$ and stack alphabet $\Gamma = \{X,Z\}$. Z is the initial stack symbol. Let L denote the language accepted by the PDA.

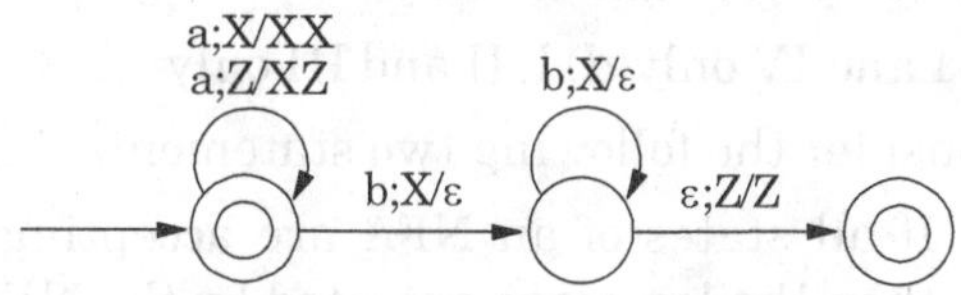

Which one of the following is TRUE?

(*a*) $L = \{a^n b^n \mid n \geq 0\}$ and is not accepted by any finite automata

(*b*) $L = \{a^n \mid n \geq 0\} \cup \{a^n b^n \mid n \geq 0\}$ and is not accepted by any deterministic PDA

(*c*) L is not accepted by any Turing machine that halts on every input

(*d*) $L = \{a^n \mid n \geq 0\} \cup \{a^n b^n \mid n \geq 0\}$ and is deterministic context-free

6. Let X be a recursive language and Y be a recursively enumerable but not recursive language. Let W and Z be two languages such that $\overline{Y}$ reduces to W, and Z reduces to $\overline{X}$ (reduction means the standard many-one reduction). Which one of the following statements is **TRUE**?

(*a*) W can be recursively enumerable and Z is recursive.

(*b*) W can be recursive and Z is recursively enumerable.

(*c*) W is not recursively enumerable and Z is recursive.

(*d*) W is not recursively enumerable and Z is not recursive.

7. Language L_1 is defined by the grammar:

$S_1 \rightarrow aS_1b \mid \varepsilon$

Language L_2 is defined by the grammar:

$S_2 \rightarrow abS_2 \mid \varepsilon$

Consider the following statements:

P: L_1 is regular

Q: L_2 is regular

Which one of the following is TRUE?

(*a*) Both P and Q are true

(*b*) P is true and Q is false

(*c*) P is false and Q is true

(*d*) Both P and Q are false

8. Consider the following types of languages: L_1 : Regular, L_2 : Context-free, L_3 : Recursive, L_4 : Recursively enumerable. Which of the following is/are TRUE?

I. $\bar{L}_3 \cup L_4$ is recursively enumerable

II. $\bar{L}_2 \cup L_3$ is recursive

III. $L_1^* \cap L_2$ is context-free

IV. $L_1 \cap \bar{L}_2$ is context-free

(*a*) I only (*b*) I and III only

(*c*) I and IV only(*d*) I, II and III only

9. Consider the following two statements:

I. If all states of an NFA are accepting states then the language accepted by the NFA is Σ^*.

II. There exists a regular language A such that for all languages B, $A \cap B$ is regular.

Which one of the following is CORRECT?

(*a*) Only I is true

(*b*) Only II is true

(*c*) Both I and II are true

(*d*) Both I and II are false

10. Consider the following languages:

$L_1 = \{a^n b^m c^{n+m} : m, n = \geq 1\}$

$L_2 = \{a^n b^n c^{2n} : n \geq 1\}$

Which one of the following is TRUE?

(*a*) Both L_1 and L_2 are context-free

(*b*) L_1 is context-free while L_2 is not context-free

(*c*) L_2 is context-free while L_1 is not context-free

(*d*) Neither L_1 nor L_2 is context-free

11. Consider the following languages.

$L_1 = \{\langle M \rangle \mid$ M takes at least 2016 steps on some input$\}$,

$L_2 = \{\langle M \rangle \mid$ M takes at least 2016 steps on all inputs$\}$ and

$L_3 = \{\langle M \rangle \mid$ M accepts $\varepsilon\}$,

where for each Turing machine M, $\langle M \rangle$ denotes a specific encoding of M. Which one of the following is TRUE?

(*a*) L_1 is recursive and L_2, L_3 are not recursive

(*b*) L_2 is recursive and L_1, L_3 are not recursive

(*c*) L_1, L_2 are recursive and L_3 is not recursive

(*d*) L_1, L_2, L_3 are recursive

12. Which one of the following grammars is free from left recursion?

(*a*) $S \to AB$
$A \to Aa \mid b$
$B \to c$

(*b*) $S \to Ab \mid Bb \mid c$
$A \to Bd \mid \varepsilon$
$B \to e$

(*c*) $S \to Aa \mid B$
$A \to Bb \mid Sc \mid \varepsilon$
$B \to d$

(*d*) $S \to Aa \mid Bb \mid c$
$A \to Bd \mid \varepsilon$
$B \to Ae \mid \varepsilon$

13. A student wrote two context-free grammars G1 and G2 for generating a single C-like array declaration. The dimension of the array is at least one. For example,

int a[10][3];

The grammars use D as the start symbol, and use six terminal symbols **int ; id [ ] num.**

Grammar G1Grammar G2

D → **intL;** D → **intL;**

L → **id[E** L → **idE**

E → **num]** E → **E[num]**

E → **num][E** E → **[num]**

Which of the grammars correctly generate the declaration mentioned above?

(*a*) Both G1 and G2 (*b*) Only G1

(*c*) Only G2 (*d*) Neither G1 nor G2

2015

14. For any two languages L_1 and L_2 such that L_1 is context-free and L_2 is recursively enumerable but not recursive, which of the following is/are necessarily true ?

I. $\bar{L}_1$ (complement of L_1) is recursive

II. $\bar{L}_2$ (complement of L_2) is recursive

III. $\bar{L}_1$ is context – free

IV. $\bar{L}_1 \cup L_2$ is recursively enumerable

(*a*) I only (*b*) III only

(*c*) III and IV only (*d*) I and IV only

15. Consider the NPDA $\langle Q = \{q_0, q_1, q_2\}, \Sigma = \{0, 1\}, \Gamma = \{0, 1, \Gamma\} \perp \delta, q_0, \perp, F = \{q_2\} \rangle$, where (as per usual convention) Q is the set of states, Σ is the input alphabet, δ is the stack alphabet, δ is the state transition function, q_0 is the initial state, $\perp$ is the initial stack symbol, and F is the set of accepting states. The state transition is as follows :

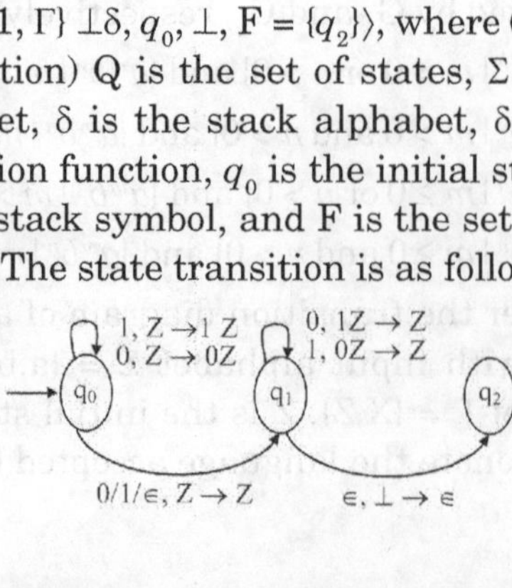

Which one of the following sequences must follow the string 101100 so that the overall string is accepted by the automation ?

(*a*) 10110 (*b*) 10010

(*c*) 01010 (*d*) 01001

16. Consider the following statements

I. The complement of every Turing decidable language is Turing decidable

II. There exists some language which is in NP but is not turing decidable

III. If L is a language in NP, L is turing decidable

Which of the above statements is/are true?

(*a*) Only I (*b*) Only III

(*c*) Only I and II (*d*) Only I and III

17. Consider the alphabet $\Sigma = \{0.1\}$, the null/empty string λ and the sets of strings X_0, X_1, and X_2 generated by the corresponding non-terminals of regular grammar. X_0, X_1, and X_2 are related as follows:

$X_0 = 1X_1$

$X_1 = 0X_1 + 1X_2$

$X_2 = 0X_1 + \{\lambda\}$

Which one of the following choices precisely represents the strings in X_0?

(*a*) $10(0^* + (10)^*)1$

(*b*) $10(0^* + (10)^*)^*1$

(*c*) $1(0 + 10)^*1$

(*d*) $10(0 + 10^*)^*1 + 110(0 + 10)^*1$

18. Which of the following languages is/are regular?

L_1 : $\{wxw^R \mid w, x \in \{a, b\}^*$ and $|w|, |x| > 0\}$, w^R is the reverse of string w

L_2 : $\{a^nb^m \mid m \neq n$ and $m, n \geq 0\}$

L_3 : $\{a^pb^qc^r \mid p, q, r \geq 0\}$

(*a*) L_1 and L_3 only (*b*) L_1 only

(*c*) L_2 and L_3 only (*d*) L_3 only

19. Let L be the language represented by the regular expression $\sum^*0011\sum^*$ where $\Sigma = \{0,1\}$.

What is the minimum number of states in a DFA that recognizes $\overline{L}$ (complement of L) ?

(*a*) 4 (*b*) 5

(*c*) 6 (*d*) 8

20. Consider the following grammar G

$S \rightarrow F|H$

$S \rightarrow p|c$

$S \rightarrow d|c$

where S, F, and H are non-terminal symbols, *p*, *d*, and *c* are terminal symbols. Which of the following statements(s) is/are correct?

S1 : LL(1) can parse all strings that are generated using grammar G

S2 : LR(1) can parse all strings that are generate using grammar G

(*a*) Only S1 (*b*) Only S2

(*c*) Both S1 and S2 (*d*) Neither S1 nor S2

21. Which of the following languages are context-free?

$L_1 = \{a^mb^na^nb^m \mid m, n \geq 1\}$

$L_2 = \{a^mb^na^mb^n \mid m, n \geq 1\}$

$L_3 = \{a^mb^n \mid m = 2n + 1\}$

(*a*) L_1 and L_2 only (*b*) L_1 and L_3 only

(*c*) L_2 and L_3 only (*d*) L_3 only

2014

22. Which one of the following is TRUE?

(*a*) The language $L = \{a^n b^n \mid n \geq 0\}$ is regular.

(*b*) The language $L = \{a^n \mid n$ is prime$\}$ is regular.

(*c*) The language L = {w | w has 3*k* + 1b's for some $k \in \mathbb{N}$ with $\Sigma = \{a, b\}$ } is regular.

(*d*) The language $L = \{ww \mid w \in \Sigma^*$ with $\Sigma = \{0,1\}\}$ is regular.

23. Consider the finite automaton in the following figure.

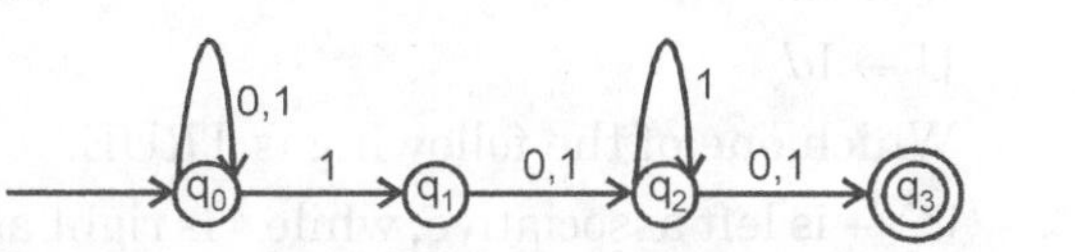

What is the set of reachable states for the input string 0011?

(*a*) $\{q_0, q_1, q_2\}$ (*b*) $\{q_0, q_1\}$

(*c*) $\{q_0, q_1, q_2, q_3\}$ (*d*) $\{q_3\}$

24. Let L be a language and $\overline{L}$ be its complement. Which of the following is NOT a viable possibility?

(*a*) Neither L nor $\overline{L}$ is recursively enumerable (r.e.).

(*b*) One of L and $\overline{L}$ is r.e. but not recursive; the other is not r.e.

(*c*) Both L and $\overline{L}$ are r.e. but not recursive.

(*d*) Both L and $\overline{L}$ are recursive.

25. Which of the regular expressions given below represent the following DFA?

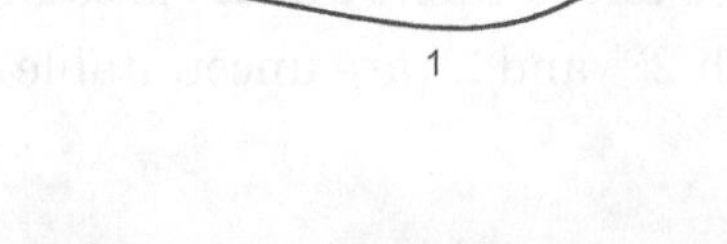

I. 0*1(1 + 00*1)*
II. 0*1*1 + 11*0*1
III. (0 + 1)*1
(a) I and II only (b) I and III only
(c) II and III only (d) I, II, and III

26. If $L_1 = \{a^n \mid n \geq 0 \mid\}$ and $L_2 = \{b^n \mid n \geq 0 \mid\}$, consider
I. $L_1 \cdot L_2$ is a regular language
II. $L_1 \cdot L_2 = \{a^n b^n \mid n \geq 0\}$
Which one of the following is CORRECT?
(a) Only (I) (b) Only (II)
(c) Both (I) and (II) (d) Neither (I) nor (II)

27. Let $A \leq_m B$ denotes that language A is mapping reducible (also known as many-to-one reducible) to language B. Which one of the following is FALSE?
(a) If $A \leq_m B$ and B is recursive then A is recursive
(b) If $A \leq_m B$ and A is undecidable then B is undecidable
(c) If $A \leq_m B$ and B is recursively enumerable then A is recursively enumerable
(d) If $A \leq_m B$ and B is not recursively enumerable then A is not recursively enumerable

28. Consider the grammar defined by the following production rules, with two operators $*$ and $+$
$S \rightarrow T * P$
$T \rightarrow U \mid T * U$
$P \rightarrow Q + P \mid Q$
$Q \rightarrow Id$
$U \rightarrow Id$
Which one of the following is TRUE?
(a) + is left associative, while * is right associative
(b) + is right associative, while * is left associative
(c) Both + and * are right associative
(d) Both + and * are left associative

29. Let $L_1 = (w \in \{0, 1\}^* \mid$ w has least as many occurrences of (110)'s as (011)'s}. Let $L_2 = \{w \in \{0, 1\}^* \mid$ w has at least as many occurrences of (000)'s as (111)'s}. Which one of the following is TRUE?
(a) L_1 is regular but not L_2
(b) L_2 is regular but not L_1
(c) Both L_1 and L_2 are regular
(d) Neither L_1 nor L_2 are regular

30. Let Σ be a finite non-empty alphabet and let 2^{Σ^*} be the power set of Σ^*. Which one of the following is **TRUE**?
(a) Both 2^{Σ^*} and Σ^* are countable
(b) 2^{Σ^*} is countable Σ^* is uncountable
(c) 2^{Σ^*} is uncountable and Σ^* is countable
(d) Both 2^{Σ^*} and Σ^* are uncountable

31. Which one of the following problems is undecidable?
(a) Deciding if a given context-free grammar is ambiguous.
(b) Deciding if a given string is generated by a given context-free grammar.
(c) Deciding if the language generated by a given context-free grammar is empty.
(d) Deciding if the language generated by a given context-free grammar is finite.

32. Consider the following languages over the alphabet $\Sigma = \{0, 1, c\}$:
$L_1 = \{0^n 1^n \mid n \geq 0\}$
$L_2 = \{wcw^r \mid w \in \{0, 1\}^*\}$
$L_3 = \{ww^r \mid w \in \{0, 1\}^*\}$
Here w^r is the reverse of the string w. Which of these languages are deterministic Context-free languages?
(a) None of the languages
(b) Only L_1
(c) Only L_1 and L_2
(d) All the three languages

33. Consider the decision problem 2CNFSAT defined as follows :
$\{\phi \mid \phi$ is a satisfiable propositional formula in CNF with at most two literal per clause$\}$
For example, $\phi = (x_1 \vee x_2) \wedge (x_1 \vee \overline{x_3}) \wedge (x_2 \vee x_4)$ is a Boolean formula and it is in 2CNFSAT.
The decision problem 2CNFSAT is
(a) NP-Complete.
(b) solvable in polynomial time by reduction to directed graph reachability.
(c) solvable in constant time since any input instance is satisfiable.
(d) NP-hard, but not NP-complete.

2013

34. Which of the following statements is/are **FALSE**?
1. For every non-deterministic Turing machine, there exists an equivalent deterministic Turing machine.
2. Turing recognizable languages are closed under union and complemen-tation.
3. Turing decidable languages are closed under intersection and complemen-tation.
4. Turing recognizable languages are closed under union and intersection.

(a) 1 and 4 only (b) 1 and 3 only
(c) 2 only (d) 3 only

35. Consider the DFA A given below.

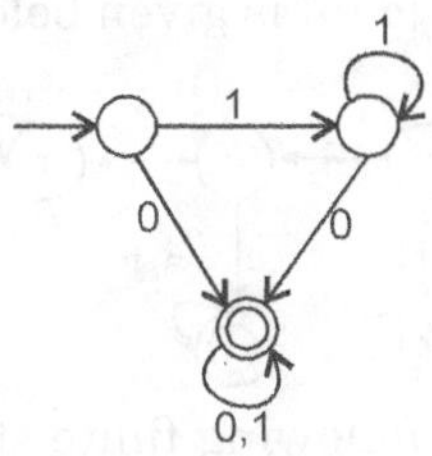

Which of the following are ***FALSE***?

1. Complement of L(A) is context-free.
2. L(A) = L((11 *0+0)(0 + 1)*0*1*)
3. For the language accepted by A, A is the minimal DFA.
4. A accepts all strings over {0, 1} of length at least 2.

(*a*) 1 and 3 only (*b*) 2 and 4 only

(*c*) 2 and 3 only (*d*) 3 and 4 only

36. Which of the following is/are undecidable?

1. G is a CFG. Is L(G) = Φ?
2. G is a CFG. Is L(G) = Σ*?
3. M is a Turing machine. Is L(M) regular?
4. A is a DFA and N is an NFA. Is L(A) = L(N)?

(*a*) 3 only (*b*) 3 and 4 only

(*c*) 1, 2 and 3 only (*d*) 2 and 3 only

2012

37. Given the language $L = \{ab, aa, baa\}$, which of the following strings are in L^*?

1. abaabaaabaa
2. aaaabaaaa
3. baaaaabaaaab
4. baaaaaba

(*a*) 1, 2 and 3 (*b*) 2, 3 and 4

(*c*) 1, 2 and 4 (*d*) 1, 3 and 4

38. Consider a random variable X that takes values +1 and – 1 with probability 0.5 each. The values of the cumulative distribution function F(x) at x = – 1 and + 1 are

(*a*) 0 and 0.5 (*b*) 0 and 1

(*c*) 0.5 and 1 (*d*) 0.25 and 0.75

39. What is the complement of the language accepted by the NFA shown below?

Assume Σ = {a} and ε is the empty string.

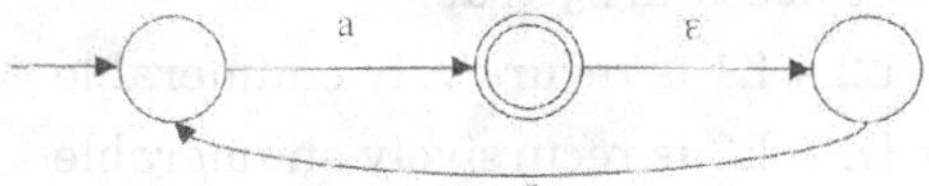

(*a*) ∅ (*b*) {ε}

(*c*) a (*d*) {a, ε}

40. Consider the following logical inferences.

I_1 : If it rains then the cricket match will not be played.
The cricket match was played.
Inference : There was no rain.

I_2 : If it rains then the cricket match will not be played.
It did not rain.
Inference : The cricket match was played.

Which of the following is TRUE?

(*a*) Both I_1 and I_2 are correct inferences

(*b*) I_1 is correct but I_2 is not a correct inference

(*c*) I_1 is not correct but I_2 is a correct inference

(*d*) Both I_1 and I_2 are not correct inferences

41. Consider the set of strings on {0, 1} in which, *every substring of 3 symbols* has at most *two* zeros. For example, 001110 and 011001 are in the language, but 100010 is not. All strings of length less than 3 are also in the language. A partially completed DFA that accept this language is shown below.

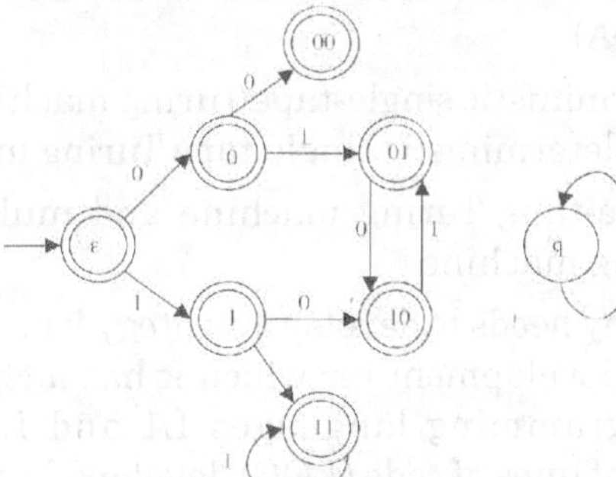

The missing arcs in the DFA are

(*a*)

	00	01	10	11	q
00	1	0			
01				1	
10	0				
11			0		

(*b*)

	00	01	10	11	q
00		0			1
01		1			
10				0	
11		0			

(*c*)

	00	01	10	11	q
00		1			0
01		1			
10			0		
11		0			

(*d*)

	00	01	10	11	q
00		1			0
01				1	
10	0				
11			0		

2011

42. Let P be a regular language and Q be a context-free language such that $Q \subseteq P$. (For example, let P be the language represented by the regular expression p^*q^* and Q be $[p^nq^n \mid n \in N]$. Then which of the following is **ALWAYS** regular?

(a) $P \cap Q$ (b) $P - Q$

(c) $\Sigma^* - P$ (d) $\Sigma^* - Q$

43. The lexical analysis for a modern computer language such as Java needs the power of which one of the following machine models in a necessary and sufficient sense?

(a) Finite state automata

(b) Deterministic pushdown automata

(c) Non-deterministic pushdown automata

(d) Turing machine

44. Which of the following pairs have DIFFERENT expressive power?

(a) Deterministic finite automata (DFA) and Non-deterministic finite automata (NFA)

(b) Deterministic push down automata (DPDA) and Non-deterministic push down automata (NPDA)

(c) Deterministic single-tape Turing machine and Non-deterministic single-tape Turing machine

(d) Single-tape Turing machine and multi-tape Turing machine

45. A company needs to develop a strategy for software product development for which it has a choice of two programming languages L1 and L2. The number of lines of code (LOC) developed using L2 is estimated to be twice the LOC developed with L1. The product will have to be maintained for five years. Various parameters for the company are given in the table below.

Parameter	Language L1	Language L2
Man years needed for development	LOC/10000	LOC/10000
Development Cost per man year	₹10,00,000	₹7,50,000
Maintenance time	5 years	5 years
Cost of maintenance per year	₹10,00,000	₹50,000

Total cost of the project includes cost of development and maintenance. What is the LOC for L1 for which the cost of the project using L1 is equal to the project using L2?

(a) 4000 (b) 5000

(c) 4333 (d) 4667

46. A deterministic finite automaton (DFA) D with alphabet $\Sigma = \{a, b\}$ is given below.

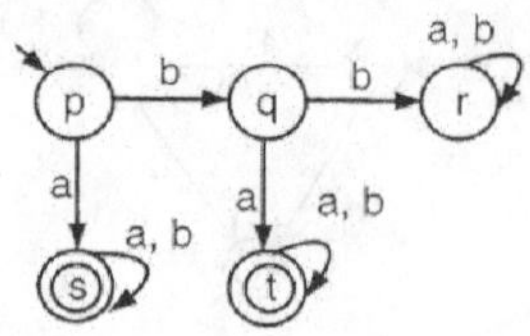

Which of the following finite state machines is a valid minimal DFA which accepts the same language as D?

(a) 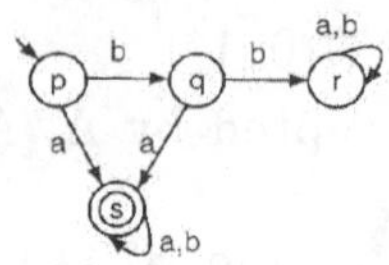

(b) 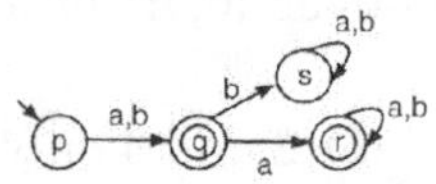

(c) 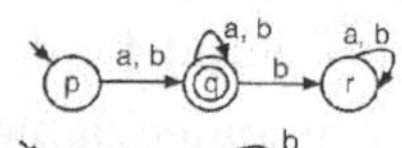

(d) 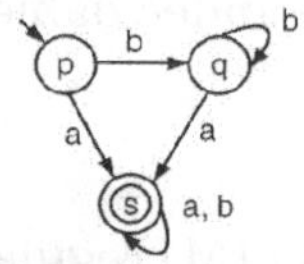

47. Definition of a language L with alphabet {a} is given as following.

$L = \{a^{nk} \mid k < 0, \text{and } n \text{ is a positive integer constant}\}$

What is the minimum number of states needed in a DFA to recognize L?

(a) $k + 1$ (b) $n + 1$

(c) 2^{n+1} (d) 2^{k+1}

48. Consider the languages L1, L2 and L3 as given below.

$L1 = \{0^p\, 1^q \mid p, q \in N\}$

$L2 = \{0^p\, 1^q \mid p, q \in N \text{ and } p = q\}$ and

$L3 = \{0^p\, 1^q\, 0^r \mid p, q, r \in N \text{ and } p = q = r\}$. Which of the following statements is NOT TRUE?

(a) Push Down Automate (PDA) can be used to recognize L1 and L2

(b) L1 is a regular language

(c) All the three languages are context free

(d) Turing machines can be used to recognize all the languages

2010

49. Let L1 be a recursive language. Let L2 and L3 be languages that are recursively enumerable but not recursive. Which of the following statements is not necessarily true?

(a) L2 – L1 is recursively enumerable

(b) L1 – L3 is recursively enumerable

(c) $L2 \cap L3$ is recursively enumerable

(d) $L2 \cup L3$ is recursively enumerable

50. Let L = {$w \in (0+1)^* \mid w$ has even number of 1s}, i.e., L is the set of all bit strings with even number of 1s. Which one of the regular expressions below represents L?

(*a*) (0*10*1)* (*b*) 0* (10*10*)*
(*c*) 0* (10*1)*0* (*d*) 0* 1(10*1)*10*

51. Consider the languages

$L1 = \{0^i1^j \mid i \neq j\}$,
$L2 = \{0^i1^j \mid i = j\}$,
$L3 = \{0^i1^j \mid i = 2j + 1\}$,
$L4 = \{0^i1^j \mid i \neq 2j\}$.

Which one of the following statements is true?

(*a*) Only L2 is context free
(*b*) Only L2 and L3 are context free
(*c*) Only L1 and L2 are context free
(*d*) All are context free

52. Let w be any string of length n in {0, 1}*.
Let L be the set of all substrings of w.
What is the minimum number of states in a non-deterministic finite automaton that accepts L?

(*a*) $n - 1$ (*b*) n
(*c*) $n + 1$ (*d*) 2^{n-1}

2009

53. S → aSa | bSb | a | b
The language generated by the above grammar over the alphabet {a, b} is the set of

(*a*) all palindromes.
(*b*) all odd length palindromes.
(*c*) strings that begin and end with the same symbol.
(*d*) all even length palindromes.

54. Which one of the following languages over the alphabet {0, 1} is described by the regular expression (0 + 1)*0(0 + 1) * 0(0 + 1)*?

(*a*) The set of all strings containing the substring 00
(*b*) The set of all strings containing at most two 0's.
(*c*) The set of all strings containing at least two 0's.
(*d*) The set of all strings that begin and end with either 0 or 1.

55. Which one of the following is FALSE ?

(*a*) There is a unique minimal DFA for every regular language.
(*b*) Every NFA can be converted to an equivalent PDA.
(*c*) Complement of every context-free language is recursive.
(*d*) Every nondeterministic PDA can be converted to an equivalent deterministic PDA.

56. Match all items in Group 1 with correct options from those given in Group 2.

Group 1	Group 2
P. Regular expression	**1.** Syntax analysis
Q. Pushdown automata	**2.** Code generation
R. Dataflow analysis	**3.** Lexical analysis
S. Register allocation	**4.** Code Optimization

Codes :

(*a*) P -4, Q -1, R -2, S -3
(*b*) P -3, Q -1, R -4, S -2
(*c*) P -3, Q -4, R -1, S -2
(*d*) P -2, Q -1, R -4, S -3

57. Given the following state table of an FSM with two states A and B, one input and one output:

Present State A	Present State B	Input State C	Next State A	Next State B	Output
0	0	0	0	0	1
0	1	0	1	0	0
1	0	0	0	1	0
1	1	0	1	0	0
0	0	1	0	1	0
0	1	1	0	0	1
1	0	1	0	1	1
1	1	1	0	0	1

If the initial state is A = 0, B = 0, what is the minimum length of an input string which will take the machine to the state A= 0, B = 1 with Output = 1?

(*a*) 3 (*b*) 4
(*c*) 5 (*d*) 6

58. Let $= L_1 \cap L_2$, where L_1 and L_2 are languages as defined below:

$L_1 = \{a^m b^m c\, a^n b^n \mid m, n^3 \geq 0\}$

$L_2 = \{a^i b^i c^k \mid i, j, k \geq 0\}$

The L is

(*a*) not recursive
(*b*) regular
(*c*) context-free but not regular
(*d*) recursively enumerable but not context-free.

59. In the following figure, DFA accepts the set of all strings over {0,1} that

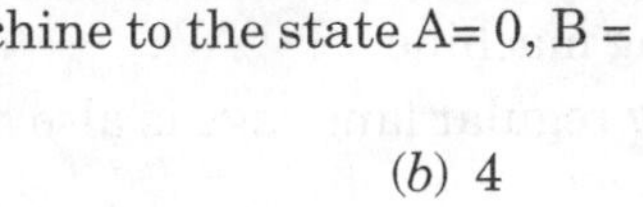

(*a*) begin either with 0 or 1.
(*b*) end with 0.
(*c*) end with 00.
(*d*) contain the substring 00.

2008

60. Which of the following is true for the language $\{a^p \mid p \text{ is a prime}\}$?

(a) It is not accepted by a Turing Machine
(b) It is regular but not context-free
(c) It is context-free but not regular
(d) It is neither regular nor context-free, but accepted by a Turing machine

61. Which of the following are decidable?

I. Whether the intersection of two regular languages is infinite
II. Whether a given context-free language is regular
III. Whether two push-down automata accept the same language
IV. Whether a given grammar is context-free

(a) I and II (b) I and IV
(c) II and III (d) II and IV

62. If L and $\overline{L}$ are recursively enumerable, then L is

(a) regular (b) context-free
(c) context-sensitive (d) recursive

63. Which of the following statements is false?

(a) Every NFA can be convrted to an equivalent DFA
(b) Every non-deterministic Turing machine can be converted to an equivalent deterministic Turing machine
(c) Every regular language is also a context-free language
(d) Every subset of a recursively enumerable set is recursive

64. Given below are two finite state automata (→ indicates the start state and F indicates a final state)

Y:

	a	b
→1	1	2
2(F)	2	1

Z:

	a	b
→1	2	2
2(*f*)	1	1

Which of the following represents the product automaton Z × Y ?

(a)

	a	b
→ P	S	R
Q	R	S
R(F)	Q	P
S	Q	P

(b)

	a	b
→ P	S	Q
Q	R	S
R(F)	Q	P
S	P	Q

(c)

	a	b
→ P	Q	S
Q	R	S
R(F)	Q	P
S	Q	P

(d)

	a	b
→ P	S	Q
Q	S	R
R(F)	Q	P
A	Q	P

65. Which of the following statements are true?

I. Every left-recursive grammar can be converted to a right-recursive grammar and vice-versa
II. All ε-productions can be removed from any context-free grammar by suitable transformations
III. The language generated by a context-free grammar all of whose productions are of the form X → w or X → wY (where, w is a string of terminals and Y is a non-terminal), is always regular
IV. The derivation trees of strings generated by a context-free grammar in Chomsky Normal From are always binary trees

(a) I, II, III and IV (b) II, III and IV only
(c) I, III and IV only (d) I, II and IV only

66. Match the following

List - I

E. Checking that identifiers are declared before their use
F. Number of formal para-meters in the declaration of a function agrees with the number of actual parameters in a use of that function
G. Arithmetic expressions with matched pairs of
H. Palindromes

List - II

P. $L = \{a^n b^m c^n d^m \mid n \geq 1, m \geq 1\}$
Q. $X \rightarrow X\,b\,X \mid X\,c\,X \mid d\,X\,f \mid g$
R. $L = \{wcw \mid w \in (a \mid b)^*\}$
S. $X \rightarrow b\,X\,b \mid c\,X\,c \mid \varepsilon$

Codes :

(a) E – P, F – R, G – Q, H – S
(b) E – R, F – P, G – S, H – Q
(c) E – R, F – P, G – Q, H – S
(d) E – P, F – R, G – S, H – Q

67. Match the following NFAs with the regular expressions they correspond to.

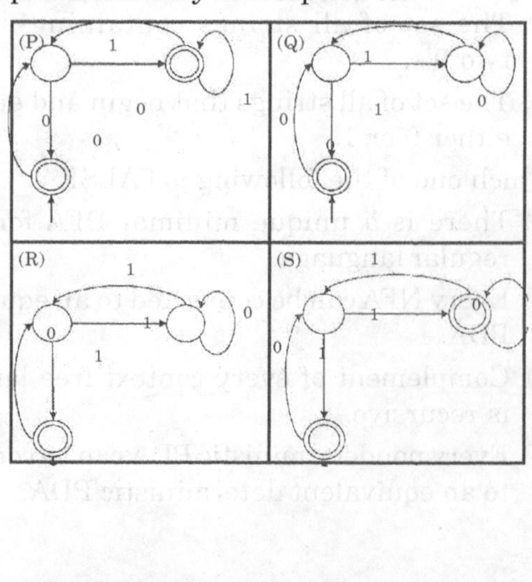

1. $\varepsilon + 0(01^*1 + 00)^*01^*$
2. $\varepsilon + 0(10^*1 + 00)^*0$
3. $\varepsilon + 0(10^*1 + 10)^*1$
4. $\varepsilon + 0(10^*1 + 10)^*10^*$

Codes :

(a) P – 2, Q – 1, R – 3, S – 4
(b) P – 1, Q – 3, R – 2, S – 4
(c) P – 1, Q – 2, R – 3, S – 4
(d) P – 3, Q – 2, R – 1, S – 4

68. Which of the following are regular sets?

I. $\{a^n b^{2m} \mid n \geq 0, m \geq 0\}$
II. $\{a^n b^m \mid n = 2m\}$
III. $\{a^n b^m \mid n \neq m\}$
IV. $\{xcy \mid x, y \in \{a, b\}^*\}$

(a) I and IV only (b) I and III only
(c) I only (d) IV only

2007

69. Which of the following problems is undecidable ?

(a) Membership problem for CFGs.
(b) Ambiguity problem for CFGs.
(c) Finiteness problem for FSAs
(d) Equivalence problem for FSAs

70. Which of the following is **TRUE**?

(a) Every subset of a regular set is regular
(b) Every finite subset of a non-regular set is regular
(c) The union of two non-regular sets is not regular
(d) Infinite union of finite sets is regular

71. A minimum state deterministic finite automaton accepting the language

$L = \{w \mid w \in \{0,1\}^*$, number of 0s and 1s in w are divisible by 3 and 5, respectively$\}$ has

(a) 15 states (b) 11 states
(c) 10 states (d) 9 states

72. The language $L = \{0^i 21^i \mid i \geq 0\}$ over the alphabet $\{0, 1, 2\}$ is

(a) not recursive
(b) is recursive and is a deterministic CFL
(c) is a regular language
(d) is not a deterministic CFL but a CFL

73. Which of the following languages is regular ?

(a) $\{ww^R \mid w \in \{0,1\}^+\}$
(b) $\{ww^R x \mid x, w \in \{0,1\}^+\}$
(c) $\{wxw^R \mid x, w \in \{0,1\}^+\}$
(d) $\{xww^R \mid x, w \in \{0,1\}^+\}$

2006

74. Let S be an NP-complete problem Q and R be two other problems not known to be in NP. Q is polynomial-time reducible to S and S is polynomial-time reducible to R.

Which of the following statements is true ?

(a) R is NP-complete
(b) R is NP-hard
(c) Q is NP-complete
(d) Q is NP-hard

75. Let $L_1 = \{0^{n+m} 1^n 0^m \mid n, m \geq 0\}$,
$L_2 = \{0^{n+m} 1^{n+m} 0^m \mid n, m \geq 0\}$, and
$L_3 = \{0^{n+m} 1^{n+m} 0^{n+m} \mid n, m \geq 0\}$.

Which of these languages are NOT context free?

(a) L_1 only (b) L_3 only
(c) L_1 and L_2 (d) L_2 and L_3

76. If s is a string over $(0 + 1)^*$, then let $n_0(s)$ denote the number of 0's in s and $n_1(s)$ the number of 1's in s. Which one of the following languages is not regular?

(a) $L = \{s \in (0 + 1)^* \mid n_0(s)$ is a 3-digit prime$\}$
(b) $L = \{s \in (0 + 1)^* \mid$ for every prefix s' of s, $|n_0(s') - n_1(s')| \leq 2\}$
(c) $L = \{s \in (0 + 1)^* \mid |n_0(s) - n_1(s) \leq 4\}$
(d) $L = \{s \in (0 + 1)^* \mid n_0(s) \bmod 7 = n_1(s) \bmod 5 = 0\}$

77. For $s \in (0 + 1)^*$ let $d(s)$ denote the decimal value of s (e.g. $d(101) = 5$).

Let $L = \{s \in (0 + 1)^* \mid d(s) \bmod 5 = 2$ and $d(s) \bmod 7 \neq 4\}$

Which one of the following statements is true ?

(a) L is recursively enumerable, but not recursive
(b) L is recursive, but not context-free
(c) L is context-free, but not regular
(d) L is regular

78. Consider the following statements about the context-free grammar :

$G = \{S \to SS, S \to ab, S \to ba, S \to \in\}$

I. G is ambiguous
II. G produces all strings with equal number of a's and b's
III. G can be accepted by a deterministic PDA.

Which combination below expresses all the true statements about G ?

(a) I only (b) I and III only
(c) II and III only (d) I, II, and III

79. Let L_1 be regular language, L_2 be a deterministic context-free language and L_3 a recursively enumerable, but not recursive, language. Which one of the following statements is false ?

(*a*) $L_1 \cap L_2$ is a deterministic CFL

(*b*) $L_3 \cap L_1$ is recursive

(*c*) $L_1 \cup L_2$ is context free

(*d*) $L_1 \cap L_2 \cap L_3$ is recursively enumerable

80. Consider the circuit shown below.

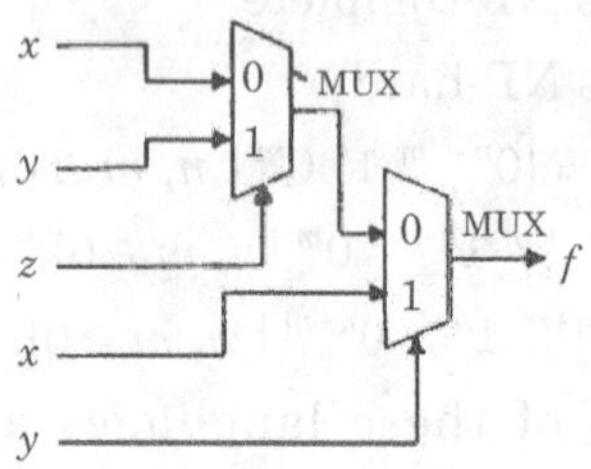

Which one of the following options correctly represents $f(x, y, z)$?

(*a*) $x\bar{z} + xy + \bar{y}z$ (*b*) $x\bar{z} + xy + \overline{yz}$

(*c*) $xz + xy + \overline{yz}$ (*d*) $xz + x\bar{y} + \bar{y}z$

81. Consider the regular language $L = (111 + 11111)^*$. The minimum number of states in any DFA accepting this languages is

(*a*) 3 (*b*) 5

(*c*) 8 (*d*) 9

2005

82. Consider three decision problems P_1, P_2 and P_3. It is known that P_1 is decidable and P_2 is undecidable. Which one of the following is TRUE?

(*a*) P_3 is decidable if P_1 is reducible to P_3

(*b*) P_3 is undecidable if P_3 is reducible to P_2

(*c*) P_3 is undecidable if P_2 is reducible to P_3

(*d*) P_3 is decidable if P_3 is reducible to P_2's complement

83. Consider the machine M:

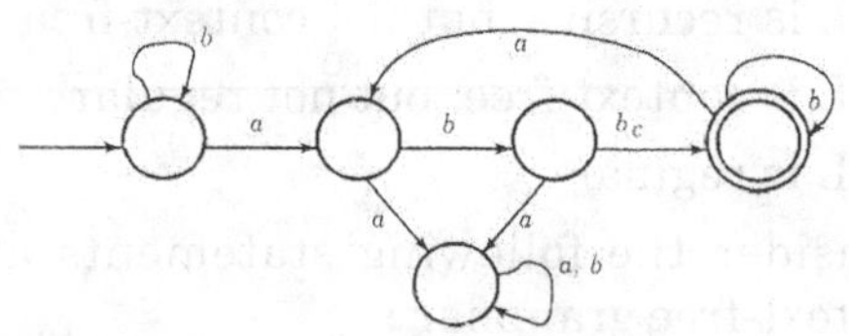

The language recognized by M is

(*a*) $\{w \in \{a, b\}^* /$ every a in w is followed by exactly two b's$\}$

(*b*) $\{w \in \{a, b\}^*$ every a in w is followed by at least two b'$\}$

(*c*) $\{w \in \{a, b\}^*$ w contains the substrzing 'abb' $\}$

(*d*) $\{w \in \{a, b\}^*$ w does not contain 'aa' as a substring$\}$

84. Let N_f and N_p denote the classes of languages accepted by non-deterministic finite automata and non-deterministic push-down automata, respectively. Let D_f and D_p denote the classes of languages accepted by deterministic finite automata and deterministic push-down automata, respectively.

Which one of the following is TRUE?

(*a*) $D_f \subset N_f$ and $D_p \subset N_p$

(*b*) $D_f \subset N_f$ and $D_p = N_p$

(*c*) $D_f = N_f$ and $D_p = N_p$

(*d*) $D_f = N_f$ and $D_p \subset N_p$

85. Consider the languages

$L1 = \{a^n b^n c^m \mid n, m > 0\}$ and $L_2 = \{a^n b^m c^m \mid n, m > 0\}$

Which one of the following statements is FALSE?

(*a*) $L_1 \cap L_2$ is a context-free language

(*b*) $L_1 \cup L_2$ is a context-free language

(*c*) L_1 and L_2 are context-free languages

(*d*) $L_1 \cap L_2$ is a context sensitive language

86. Consider the languages

$L_1 = \{ww^R \mid w \in \{0, 1\}^*\}$

$L_2 = \{w \# w^R \mid w \in \{0, 1\}^*\}$,

where # is a special symbol

$L_3 = \{ww \mid w \in \{0, 1\}^*\}$

Which one of the following is TRUE?

(*a*) L_1 is a deterministic CFL

(*b*) L_2 is a deterministic CFL

(*c*) L_3 is a CFL, but not a deterministic CFL

(*d*) L_3 is a deterministic CFL

2004

87. The problems 3-SAT and 2-SAT are

(*a*) both in P

(*b*) both NP-complete

(*c*) NP-complete and in P respectively

(*d*) undecidable and NP-complete respectively

88. The following finite state machine accepts all those binary strings in which the number of 1's and 0's are respectively

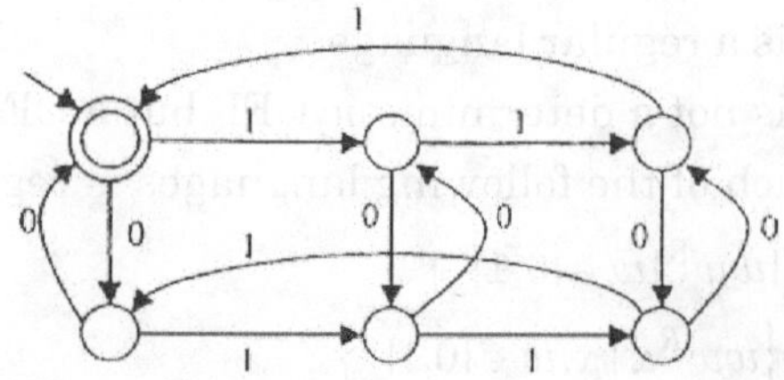

(*a*) divisible by 3 and 2

(*b*) odd and even

(*c*) even and odd

(*d*) divisible by 2 and 3

89. The language $\{a^m b^n c^{m+n} \mid m, n \geq 1\}$ is

(*a*) regular

(*b*) context-free but not regular

(*c*) context sensitive but not context free

(*d*) type-0 but not context sensitive

90. Consider the following grammar G:

$$S \to bS \mid aA \mid b$$
$$A \to bA \mid aB$$
$$B \to bB \mid aS \mid a$$

Let $N_a(w)$ and $N_b(w)$ denote the number of a's and b's in a string w respectively. The language $L(G) \subseteq \{a, b\}^+$ generated by G is

(*a*) $\{w \mid N_a(w) > 3N_b(w)\}$

(*b*) $\{w \mid N_b(w) > 3N_b(w)\}$

(*c*) $\{w \mid N_a(w) = 3k, k \in \{0, 1, 2, ...\}\}$

(*d*) $\{w \mid N_b(w) = 3k, k \in \{0, 1, 2, ...\}\}$

91. L_1 is a recursively enumerable language over Σ. An algorithm A effectively enumerates its words as $w_1, w_2, w_3, ...$ Define another language L_2 over $\Sigma \cup \{\#\}$ as $\{w_i\#w_j : w_i, w_j \in L_1, i < j\}$. Here # is a new symbol. Consider the following assertions.

S_1 : L_1 is recursive implies L_2 is recursive

S_2 : L_2 is recursive implies L_1 is recursive

Which of the following statements is true ?

(*a*) Both S_1 and S_2 are true

(*b*) S_1 is true but S_2 is not necessarily true

(*c*) S_2 is true but S_1 is not necessarily true

(*d*) Neither is necessarily true

2003

92. Ram and Shyam have been asked to show that a certain problem Π is NP-complete. Ram shows a polynomial time reduction from the 3-SAT problem to Π, and Shyam shows a polynomial time reduction from Π to 3-SAT. Which of the following can be inferred from these reductions ?

(*a*) Π is NP-hard but not NP-complete

(*b*) Π is in NP, but is not NP-complete

(*c*) Π is NP-complete

(*d*) Π is neither NP-hard, nor in NP

93. Nobody knows yet if P = NP.

Consider the language L defined as follows :

$$L = \begin{cases} (0+1)^* & \text{if } P = NP \\ \phi & \text{otherwise} \end{cases}$$

Which of the following statements is true ?

(*a*) L is recursive

(*b*) L is recursively enumerable but not recursive

(*c*) L is not recursively enumerable

(*d*) Whether L is recursive or not will be known after we find out if P = NP

94. If strings of a language L can be effectively enumerated in lexicographic (i.e., alphabetic) order, which of the following statements is true?

(*a*) L is necessarily finite

(*b*) L is regular but not necessarily finite

(*c*) L is context free but not necessarily regular

(*d*) L is recursive but not necessarily context free

95. Consider the following deterministic finite state automaton M.

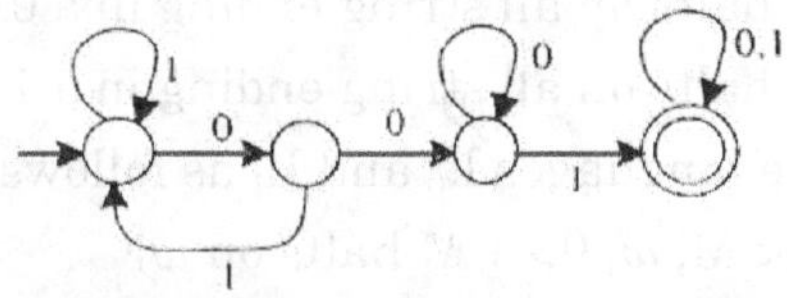

Let S denote the set of seven bit binary strings in whichthe first, the fourth, and the last bits are 1. The number of strings in S that are accepted by M is

(*a*) 1 (*b*) 5

(*c*) 7 (*d*) 8

96. Let G = ({S}, {*a*, *b*} R,S) be a context free grammar where the rule set R is

$$S \to a\,S\,b \mid S\,S \mid \varepsilon$$

Which of the following statements is true ?

(*a*) G is not ambiguous

(*b*) There exist x, y, $\in$ L (G) such that xy $\notin$ L(G)

(*c*) There is a deterministic pushdown automaton that accepts L(G)

(*d*) We can find a deterministic finite state automaton that accepts L(G)

97. Consider two languages L_1 and L_2 each on the alphabet Σ.

Let $f : \Sigma \to \Sigma$ be a polynomial time computable bijection such that $(\forall x)\,[x \in L_1 \text{ iff } f(x) \in L_2]$. Further, let f^{-1} be also polynomial time computable.

Which of the following CANNOT be true ?

(*a*) $L_1 \in P$ and L_2 is finite

(*b*) $L_1 \in NP$ and $L_2 \in P$

(*c*) L_1 is undecidable and L_2 is decidable

(*d*) L_1 is recursively enumerable and L_2 is recursive

98. A single tape Turing Machine M has two states q0 and q1, of which q0 is the starting state. The tape alphabet of M is {0, 1, B} and its input alphabet is {0, 1}. The symbol B is the blank symbol used to indicate end of an input string. The transition function of M is described in the following table

	0	1	B
*q*0	*q*1, 1, R	*q*1, 1, R	Halt
*q*1	*q*1, 1, R	*q*0, 1, L	*q*0, B, L

The table is interpreted as illustrated below.

The entry (q1, 1, R) in row q0 and column 1 signifies that if M is in state q0 and reads 1 on the current tape square, then it writes 1 on the same tape square, moves its tape head one position to the right and transitions to state q1. Which of the following statements is true about M ?

(a) M does not halt on any string in $(0 + 1)^+$

(b) M does not halt on any string in $(00 + 1)^*$

(c) M halts on all string ending in a 0

(d) M halts on all string ending in a 1

99. Define languages L_0 and L_1 as follows:

L_0 = {< M, w, 0> | M halts on w}

L_1 = {< M, w, 1> | M does not halts on w}

Here < M, w, i> is a triplet, whose first component. M is an encoding of a Turing Machine, second component, w, is a string, and third component, i, is a bit.

Let $L = L_0 \cup L_1$. Which of the following is true ?

(a) L is recursively enumerable, but $\overline{L}$ is not

(b) $\overline{L}$ is recursively enumerable, but L is not

(c) Both L and $\overline{L}$ are recursive

(d) Neither L nor $\overline{L}$ is recrusively enumerable

100. Consider the NFA M shown below.

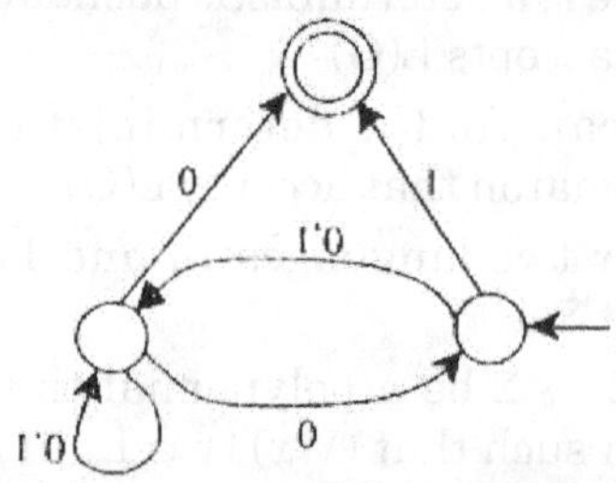

Let the language accepted by M be L. Let L_1 be the language accepted by the NFA M_1, obtained by changing the accepting state of M to a non-accepting state and by changing the non-accepting state of M to accepting states.

Which of the following statements is true ?

(a) $L_1 = \{0, 1\}^* - L$ (b) $L_1 = \{0, 1\}^*$

(c) $L_1 \subseteq L$ (d) $L_1 = L$

2002

101. The language accepted by a Pushdown Automation in which the stack is limited to 10 items is best described as

(a) Context Free

(b) Regular

(c) Deterministic Context Free

(d) Recursive

102. In the C language

(a) At most one activation record exists between the current activation record and the activation record for the main

(b) The number of activation records between the current activation record and the activation record for the main depends on the actual function calling sequence.

(c) The visibility of global variables depends on the actual function calling sequence.

(d) Recursion requires the activation record for the recursive function to be saved on a different stack before the recursive function can be called.

103. The smallest finite automation which accepts the language {x | length of x is divisible by 3} has

(a) 2 states (b) 3 states

(c) 4 states (d) 5 states

104. Which of the following is true?

(a) The complement of a recursive language is recursive.

(b) The complement of a recursively enumerable language is recursively enumerable.

(c) The complement of a recursive language is either recursive or recursively enumerable.

(d) The complement of a context-free language is context- free.

105. The C language is

(a) A context free language

(b) A context sensitive language

(c) A regular language

(d) Parasble fully only by a Turing machine

106. The Finite state machine described by the following state diagram with A as starting state, where an arc label is x/y and x stands for 1-bit input and y stands for 2- bit output

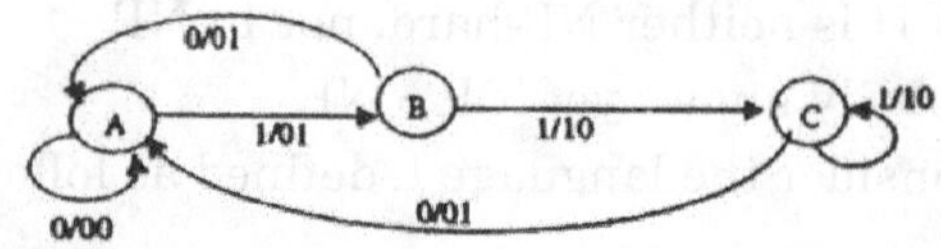

(a) Outputs the sum of the present and the previous bits of the input.

(b) Outputs 01 whenever the input sequence contains 11

(c) Outputs 00 whenever the input sequence contains 10

(d) None of these

2001

107. Consider a DFA over $\Sigma = \{a, b\}$ accepting all strings which have number of a's divisible by 6 and number of b's divisible by 8. What is the minimum number of states that the DFA will have ?

(*a*) 8 (*b*) 14

(*c*) 15 (*d*) 48

108. Consider the following two statements :

S1 : $\{0^{2n} \mid n \geq 1\}$ is a regular language

S2 : $\{0^m 1^n 0^{m+n} \mid m \geq 1 \text{ and } n \geq 1\}$ is a regular language

Which of the following statements is correct ?

(*a*) Only S1 is correct

(*b*) Only S2 is correct

(*c*) Both S1 and S2 are correct

(*d*) None of S1 and S2 is correct

109. Which of the following statements is true ?

(*a*) If a language is context free it can always be accepted by a deterministic push-down automaton

(*b*) The union of two context free languages is context free

(*c*) The intersection of two context free languages is context free

(*d*) The complement of a context free language is context free

110. Consider the following languages

L1 = $\{ ww \mid w \in \{a, b\}^* \}$

L2 = $\{ ww^R \mid w \in \{a, b\}^*$, w^R is the reverse of w$\}$

L3 = $\{ 0^{2i} \mid$ i is an integer $\}$

L4 = $\{ 0^{i^2} \mid$ i is an integer $\}$

Which of the languages are regular ?

(*a*) Only L1 and L2 (*b*) Only L2, L3, and L4

(*c*) Only L3 and L4 (*d*) Only L3

111. Consider the following problem X.

Given a Turing machine M over the input alphabet S, any state q of M and a word $w \in \Sigma^*$, does the computation of M on w visit the state q ?

Which of the following statements about X is correct?

(*a*) X is decidable

(*b*) X is undecidable but partially decidable

(*c*) X is undecidable and not even partially decidable.

(*d*) X is not a decision problem

2000

112. Let S and T be languages over $\Sigma = \{a, b\}$ represented by the regular expresions $(a + b^*)^*$ and $(a + b)^*$, respectively. Which of the following is true ?

(*a*) $S \subset T$ (*b*) $T \subset S$

(*c*) $S = T$ (*d*) $S \cap T = \phi$

113. Let L denotes the language generated by the grammar S → 0S0/00.

Which of the following is true ?

(*a*) $L = 0^+$

(*b*) L is regular but not 0^+

(*c*) L is context free but not regular

(*d*) L is not context free

114. What can be said about a regular language L over $\{a\}$ whose minimal finite state automaton has two states ?

(*a*) L must be $\{a^n \mid n \text{ is odd}\}$

(*b*) L must be $\{a^n \mid n \text{ is even}\}$

(*c*) L must be $\{a^n \mid \geq 0\}$

(*d*) Either L must be $\{a^n \mid n \text{ is odd}\}$, or L must be $\{a^n½n \text{ is even}\}$

115. Consider the following decision problems

(P1) Does a given finite state machine accept a given string

(P2) Does a given context free grammar generate an infinite number of stings

Which of the following statements is true ?

(*a*) Both (P1) and (P2) are decidable

(*b*) Neither (P1) nor (P2) are decidable

(*c*) Only (P1) is decidable

(*d*) Only (P2) is decidable

116. Given the following expression grammar :

E → E * F/ F + E | F

F → F — F/ *id*

Which of the following is true ?

(*a*) * has higher precedence than +

(*b*) – has higher precedence than *

(*c*) + and – have same precedence

(*d*) + has higher precedence than *

117. (*a*) Construct as minimal finite state machine that accepts the language, over, {0,1}, of all strings that contain neither the substring 00 nor the substring 11.

(*b*) Consider the grammar

S → *a*S A*b*

S → ε

A → *b*A

A → ε

where S, A are non-terminal symbols with S being the start symbol ; *a*, *b* are terminal symbols and ε is the empty string. This grammar generates strings of the form $a^i b^j$ for some $i, j \geq 0$, where i and j satisfy some condition. What is the condition on the values of i and j?

118. A pushdown automaton (*pda*) is given in the following extended notation of finite state diagrams:

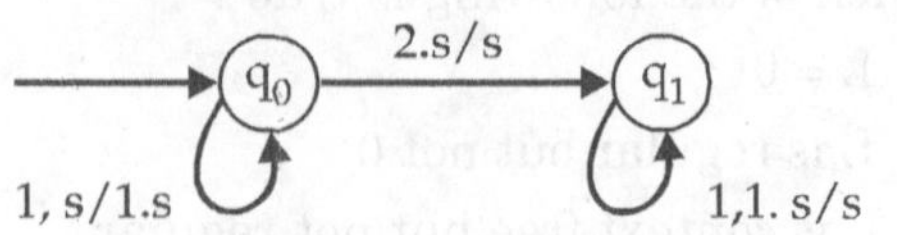

The nodes denote the states while the edges denote the moves of the *pda*. The edge labels are of the form d, *s/s'* where *d* is the input symbol read and *s*, *s'* are the stack contents before and after the move. For example, the edge labeled 1, *s*/1.*s* denotes the move from state q_0 to q_0 in which the input symbol 1 is read and pushed to the stack.

(*a*) Introduce two edges with appropriate labels in the above diagram so that the resulting *pda* accepts the language

$\{x2x^R \mid x \in \{0, 1\}^*, x^R$ denotes reverse of $x\}$, by empty stack.

(*b*) Describe a nondeterministic *pda* with three states in the above notation that accept the language

$\{0^n1^m \mid n \leq m \leq 2n\}$ by empty stack.

1999

119. Consider the regular expression (0 + 1) (0 + 1) .... *n* times. The minimum state finite automation that recognizes the language represented by this regular expression contains

(*a*) *n* states (*b*) *n* + 1 states

(*c*) *n* + 2 states (*d*) None of these

120. Context-free languages are closed under

(*a*) Union, intersection

(*b*) Union, Kleene closure

(*c*) Intersection, complement

(*d*) Complement, Kleene Closure

121. Let L_D be the set of all languages accepted by a PDA by final state and L_E the set of all languages accepted by empty stack. Which of the following is true ?

(*a*) $L_D = L_E$ (*b*) $L_D \supset L_E$

(*c*) $L_E = L_D$ (*d*) None of these

122. If n is a power of 2, then the minimum number of multiplications needed to compute a* is

(*a*) $\log_2 n$ (*b*) $\sqrt{n}$

(*c*) $n - 1$ (*d*) n

123. If L1 is context free language and L2 is a regular language which of the following is/are false ?

(*a*) L1 – L2 is not context free

(*b*) L1 ∩ L2 is context free

(*c*) ~L1 is context free

(*d*) ~L2 is regular

124. If T_1 = O (1), give the correct matching for the following pairs

(M) $T_n = T_{n-1} + n$	(U) $T_n = O(n)$
(N) $T_n = T_{n/2} + n$	(V) $T_n = O(n\log n)$
(O) $T_n = T_{n/2} + n\log n$	(W) $T_n = O(n^2)$
(P) $T_n = T_{n-1} + \log n$	(X) $T_n = O(\log^2 n)$

(*a*) M-W, N-V, O-U, P-X

(*b*) M-W, N-U, O-X, P-V

(*c*) M-V, N-W, O-X, P-U

(*d*) M-W, N-U, O-V, P-X

125. Show that the language L $\{xcx \mid x \in \{0, 1\}^*$ and c is a terminal symbol$\}$ is not context free c is not 0 or 1.

1998

126. If the regular set A is represented by A = (01 + 1)* and the regular set 'B' is represented by B = ((01)* 1*)*, which of the following is true ?

(*a*) A ⊂ B

(*b*) B ⊂ A

(*c*) A and B are incomparable

(*d*) A = B

127. Which of the following set can be recognized by a Deterministic Finite-state Automaton ?

(*a*) The numbers 1, 2, 4, 8, ... 2^n, ... written in binary.

(*b*) The numbers 1, 2, 4, ..., 2^n, ... written in unary.

(*c*) The set of binary string in which the number of zeros is the same as the number of ones.

(*d*) The set {1, 101, 11011, 1110111, ...}

128. Regarding the power of recognition of languages, which of the following statements is false ?

(*a*) The non-deterministic finite-state automata are equivalent to deterministic finite-state automata.

(*b*) Non-deterministic Push-down automata are equivalent to deterministic Push-down automata.

(*c*) Non-deterministic Turing machines are equivalent to deterministic Push-down automata.

(*d*) Non-deterministic Turing machines are equivalent to derterministic Turing machines.

(*e*) Multi-tape Turing machines are equivalent to Single-tape Turing machines.

129. The string 1101 does not belong to the set represented by

(*a*) 110* (0 + 1) (*b*) 1 (0 + 1)* 101

(*c*) (10)* (01)* (00 + 11)* (*d*) (00 + (11)* 0)*

130. How many substrings of different lengths (non-zero) can be found formed from a character string of length n ?

(a) n (b) n^2

(c) 2^n (d) $\frac{n(n+1)}{2}$

131. Let L be the set of all binary strings whose last two symbols are the same. The number of states in the minimum state deterministic finite 0 state automaton accepting L is

(a) 2 (b) 5

(c) 8 (d) 3

132. Which of the following statements is false ?

(a) Every finite subset of a non-regular set is regular

(b) Every subset of a regular set is regular

(c) Every finite subset of a regular set is regular

(d) The intersection of two regular sets is regular

133. Design a deterministic finite state automaton (using minimum number of states) that recognizes the following language

L = {w ∈ {0, 1}* | w interpreted as binary number (ignoring the leading zeros) is divisible by five.

134. Let M = $(\{q_0, q_1\}, \{0, 1\}, \{z_0, X\}, \delta, q_0, z_0, \phi)$ be a Pushdown automaton where δ is given by

$$\delta(q_0, 1, z_0) = \{(q_0, x z_0)\}$$
$$\delta(q_0, \in, z_0) = \{(q_0, \in)\}$$
$$\delta(q_0, 1, X) = \{(q_0, XX)\}$$
$$\delta(q_1, 1, X) = \{(q_1, \in)\}$$
$$\delta(q_0, 0, X) = \{(q_1, X)\}$$
$$\delta(q_1, 0, z_0) = \{(q_0, z_0)\}$$

(a) What is the language accepted by this PDA by empty store ?

(b) Describe informally the working of the PDA.

1997

135. Which one of the following regular expressions over {0, 1} denotes the set of all strings not containing 100 as a substring ?

(a) 0* (1 + 0)* (b) 0*1010*

(c) 0*1*01 (d) 0* (10 + 1)*

136. Which one of the following is not decidable ?

(a) Given a turing machine M, a string s and an integer k, M accepts s within k steps

(b) Equivalence of two given turing machines

(c) Language accepted by a given finite state machine is not empty

(d) Language generated by a context free grammar is non empty.

137. Which of the following languages over {a, b, c} is accepted by a deterministic pushdown automata?

(a) $\{w \subset w^R \mid w \in \{a, b\}^*\}$

(b) $\{ww^R \mid w \in \{a, b, c\}^*\}$

(c) $\{a^n b^n c^n \mid n \geq 0\}$

(d) {w | w is a palindrome over {a, b, c}}

Note : w^R is the string obtained by reversing 'w'.

138. Construct a finite state machine with minimum number of states, accepting all strings over (a, b) such that the number of a's is divisible by two and the number of b's is divisible by three.

139. Given that L is a language accepted by a finite state machine, show that L^P and L^R are also accepted by some finite state machines, where

L^P = {s | ss¢ ∈ L some string. s'}.

LR = {s | s obtainable by reversing some string in L}.

140. A language L is a subset of Pascal with the following constructs :

(a) Expressions involving the operators '+' and '<' only

(b) Assignment statements

(c) 'while' statements and

(d) Compound statements with syntax 'begin ... end'.

Give an unambiguous grammar for L.

1996

141. Which two of the following four regular expressions are equivalent ? (ε is the empty string).

(i) (00) * (ε + 0) (ii) (00)*

(iii) 0* (iv) 0 (00)*

(a) (i) and (ii) (b) (ii) and (iii)

(c) (i) and (iii) (d) (iii) and (iv)

142. Which of the following statements is false ?

(a) The Halting problem of Turing machines is undecidable.

(b) Determining whether a context-free grammar is ambiguous is undecidable.

(c) Given two arbitrary context-free grammars G_1 and G_2 it is undecidable whether $L(G_1) = L(G_2)$.

(d) Given two regular grammars G_1 and G_2 it is undecidable whether $L(G_1) = L(G_2)$.

143. Let $L \subseteq \Sigma^*$ where $\Sigma = \{a, b\}$: Which of the following is true ?

(a) L = {x | x has an equal number of a's and b's} is regular

(b) $L = \{a^n b^n \mid n \geq 1\}$ is regular

(c) L = {x | x has more a's than b's} is regular

(d) $L = \{a^m b^n \mid m \geq, n \geq 1\}$ is regular

144. Consider the following floating point number representation.

31 24	23 0
Exponent	Mantissa

The exponent is in 2's complement representation and mantissa is in the sign magnitude representation. The range of the magnitude of the normalised numbers in this representation is

(*a*) 0 to 1   (*b*) 0.5 to 1

(*c*) 2^{-23} to 0.5   (*d*) 0.5 to $(1 - 2^{-23})$

145. If L_1 and L_2 are context free languages and R a regular set, one of the languages below is not necessarily a context free language. Which one?

(*a*) $L_1 L_2$ (*b*) $L_1 \cap L_2$

(*c*) $L_1 \cap R$ (*d*) $L_1 \cup L_2$

146. Define a context free language $L \leq \{0 ; 1\}$ init (L) = {u/uv $\in$ L for some v in { {0, 1}}

(in other words, init (L) is the set of prefixes of L)

Let L {w/w is is nonempty and has on equal number of 0's and 1's

Then init (L) is

(*a*) the set of all binary strings with unequal number of 0's and 1's}

(*b*) the set of all binary strings including the null string

(*c*) the set of all binary strings with exactly one more 0's than the number of 1's or one more 1 than the number of 0's

(*d*) none of the above

147. Let G be a context-free grammar where G = ({S, A, B, C}, {*a*, *b*, *d*}, P, S) with the productions in P given below.

$$S \to ABAC$$
$$A \to aA \mid \varepsilon$$
$$B \to bB \to \varepsilon$$
$$C \to d$$

(ε denoted the null string). Transform the grammar G to an equivalent context-free grammar G that has no ε productions and no unit productions. (A unit production is of the form $x \to y$, and y are non terminals).

148. Given below are the transition diagrams (Figure) for two finite state machines M1 and M2 recognising languages L_1 and L_2 respectively.

(*a*) Display the transition diagram for a machine that recognizes $L_1 L_2$, obtained from transition dia-grams for M_1 and M_2 by adding only & transitions and no new states.

(*b*) Modify the transition diagram obtained in part (*a*) obtain a transition diagram for a machine that recognizes $(L_1 L_2)$ by adding only e tranitions and no new states.

(Final states are enclosed in double circles)

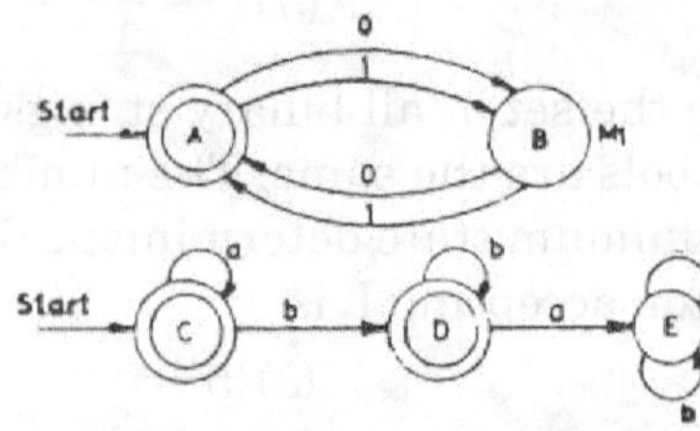

149. Consider the syntax-directed translation schema (SETS) shown below

E → E + E {print "+"}

E → E * E {print "."}

E → *id* {print *id*. name}

E → (E)

An LR — parser executes the actions asssociated with the productions immediately after a reduction by the corresponding production. Draw the parse tree and write the translation for the sentence. $(a + b) * (c + d)$, using SDTS given above.

1995

150. Consider a grammar with the following productions

S → *a α b* | *b α c* | *a*B

S → *α* S | *b*

S → *α bb* | *ab*

S *α* → *bdb* | *b*

The above grammar is

(*a*) Context free   (*b*) Regular

(*c*) Context sensitive   (*d*) LR (k)

151. If the proposition $\neg p \Rightarrow v$ is true, then the truth value of the proposition $\neg p \vee (p \Rightarrow q)$, where $\neg$ is negation, 'V' is inclusive or and $\Rightarrow$ is implication, is

(*a*) true   (*b*) multiple-valued

(*c*) false   (*d*) cannot be determined

152. Which of the following definitions below generates the same language as L,

where $L = \{x^n y^n$ such that $n >= 1\}$?

I. E → x E y | *xy*

II. $xy \mid (x^+ xyy^+)$

III. $x^+ y^+$

(*a*) I only   (*b*) I and II

(*c*) II and III   (*d*) II only

153. A finite state machine with the following state table has a single input x and a single out z.

present stat	next state, z	
	$x = 1$	$x = 0$
A	D, 0	B, 0
B	B, 1	C, 1
C	B, 0	D, 1
D	B, 1	C , 0

If the initial state is unknown, then the shortest input sequence to reach the final state C is

(*a*) 01 (*b*) 10

(*c*) 101 (*d*) 110

154. Let $\Sigma = \{0, 1\}$, $L = \Sigma^*$ and $R = \{0^n 1^n$ such that $n > 0\}$ Then the languages $L \cup R$ and R are respectively

(*a*) Regular, Regular

(*b*) Not Regular, Regular

(*c*) Regular, Not Regular

(*c*) Not Regular, Not Regular

1994

155. Generation of intermediate code based on an abstract machine model is useful in compilers because

(*a*) it makes implementation of lexical analysis and syntax analysis easier

(*b*) Syntax-directed translations can be written for intermediate code generation

(*c*) it enhances the portability of the front end of the compiler

(*d*) it is not possible to generate code for real machines directly from high level language programs

156. Which of the following conversions is not possible (algorithmically)?

(*a*) Regular grammar to context-free grammar

(*b*) Non-deterministic FSA to deterministic FSA

(*c*) Non-deterministic PDA to deterministic PDA

(*d*) Non-deterministic Turing machine to deterministic Turing machine

157. Which of the following features cannot be captured by context-fee grammars?

(*a*) Syntax of if-then-else statements

(*b*) Syntax of recursive procedures

(*c*) Whether a variable has been declared before its use

(*d*) Variable names of arbitrary lenth

1992

158. Which of the following predicate calculus statements is/are valid?

(*a*) $(\forall x) P(x) \vee (\forall x) Q(x) \rightarrow (\forall x) \{P(x) \vee Q(x)\}$

(*b*) $(\exists x) P(x) \wedge (\exists x) Q(x) \rightarrow (\exists x) \{P(x) \wedge Q(x)\}$

(*c*) $(\forall x) \{P(x) \vee Q(x)\} \rightarrow (\forall x) P(x) \vee (\forall x) Q(x)$

(*d*) $(\exists x) \{P(x) \vee Q(x)\} \rightarrow \sim(\forall x) P(x) \vee (\exists x) Q(x)$

159. Which of the following is/are tautology?

(*a*) $a \vee b \rightarrow b \wedge c$ (*b*) $a \wedge b \rightarrow b \vee c$

(*c*) $a \vee b \rightarrow (b \rightarrow c)$ (*d*) $a \rightarrow b \rightarrow (b \rightarrow c)$

160. Which of the following regular expression identities are true?

(*a*) $r(^*) = r^*$ (*b*) $(r^* s^*) = (r + s)^*$

(*c*) $(r + s)^* = r^* + s^*$ (*d*) $r^* s^* = r^* + s^*$

161. If G is a context-free grammar and w is a string of length l in L (G), how long is a derivation of w in G, if G is chomsky normal form?

(*a*) $2l$

(*b*) $2l + 1$

(*c*) $2l - 1$

(*d*) l

162. Context-free languages are

(*a*) closed under union

(*b*) closed under complementation

(*c*) closed under intersection

(*d*) closed under Kleene closure

163. In which of the cases stated below is the following statement true?

"For every nondeterministric machine M_1 there exists an equivalent deterministic machine M_2 recognizing the same language."

(*a*) M_1 is nondeterministic finite automaton

(*b*) M_1 is a nondeterministic PDA

(*c*) M_1 is a nondeterministic Turing machine

(*d*) For no machine M_1 use the above statement True.

NUMERICAL TYPE QUESTIONS

2016

1. The number of states in the minimum sized DFA that accepts the language defined by the regular expression

$(0 + 1)^* (0 + 1) (0 + 1)^*$ is ________.

2015

2. 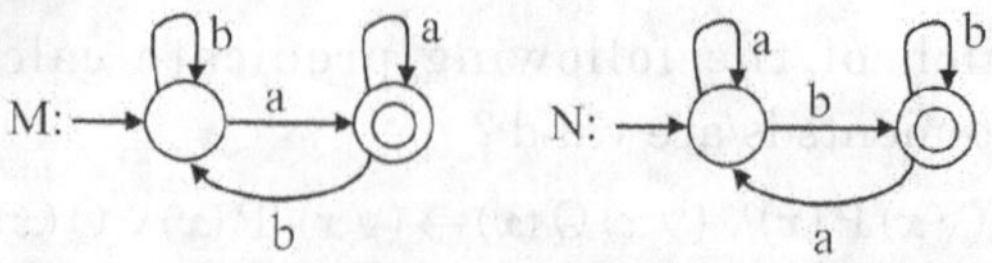

Consider the DFAs M and N given above. The number of states in a minimal DFA that accepts the languages L(M) ∩ L(N) is ________.

3. The number of states in the minimal deterministic finite automaton corresponding to the regular expression (0 + 1) * (10) is __________

2014

4. The length of the shortest string NOT in the language (over Σ = {*a*,*b*}) of the following regular expression is _________.

$a^*b^*(ba)^*a^*$

1994

5. The Hasse diagrams of all the lattices with upto four elements are .... (Write all the relevant Hasse diagrams).

6. The regular expression for the language recognized by the finite state automaton of given Figure is ....

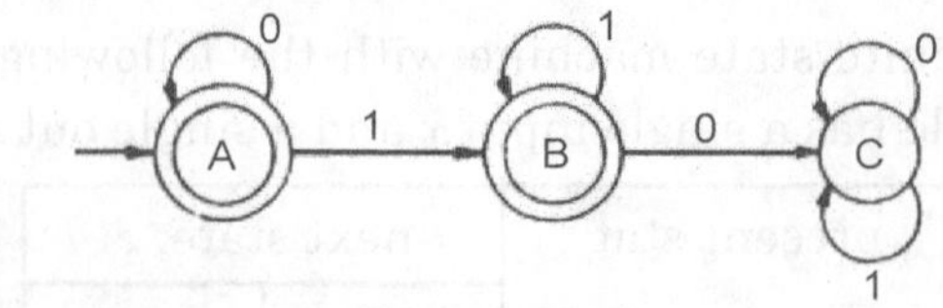

7. State True or False with one line explanation

A FSM (Finite State Machine) can be designed to add two integers of any arbitrary length (arbitrary number of digits).

8. Match the following :

(*i*) Backus-Naur form	(*a*) Regular expressions
(*ii*) Lexical analysis	(*b*) LALR (I) grammars
(*iii*) YACC	(*c*) LL (I) grammars
(*iv*) Recursive-descent parsing	(*d*) General context-free grammars

ANSWERS

MCQ Type Questions

1. (*d*)	2. (*c*)	3. (*b*)	4. (*d*)	5. (*d*)	6. (*c*)	7. (*c*)	8. (*d*)	9. (*d*)	10. (*b*)
11. (*c*)	12. (*b*)	13. (*a*)	14. (*d*)	15. (*b*)	16. (*d*)	17. (*c*)	18. (*a*)	19. (*b*)	20. (*d*)
21. (*b*)	22. (*c*)	23. (*a*)	24. (*c*)	25. (*b*)	26. (*a*)	27. (*d*)	28. (*b*)	29. (*a*)	30. (*c*)
31. (*a*)	32. (*c*)	33. (*b*)	34. (*a*)	35. (*d*)	36. (*d*)	37. (*c*)	38. (*c*)	39. (*b*)	40. (*b*)
41. (*d*)	42. (*c*)	43. (*a*)	44. (*b*)	45. (*b*)	46. (*a*)	47. (*b*)	48. (*c*)	49. (*b*)	50. (*b*)
51. (*d*)	52. (*c*)	53. (*b*)	54. (*c*)	55. (*d*)	56. (*b*)	57. (*a*)	58. (*c*)	59. (*c*)	60. (*b*)
61. (*c*)	62. (*c*)	63. (*d*)	64. (*b*)	65. (*c*)	66. (*a*)	67. (*b*)	68. (*c*)	69. (*b*)	70. (*b*)
71. (*a*)	72. (*b*)	73. (*c*)	74. (*c*)	75. (*d*)	76. (*b*)	77. (*b*)	78. (*d*)	79. (*d*)	80. (*a*)
81. (*d*)	82. (*a*)	83. (*b*)	84. (*d*)	85. (*a*)	86. (*b*)	87. (*c*)	88. (*a*)	89. (*b*)	90. (*c*)
91. (*b*)	92. (*c*)	93. (*d*)	94. (*a*)	95. (*a*)	96. (*d*)	97. (*c*)	98. (*d*)	99. (*a*)	100. (*c*)
101. (*b*)	102. (*a*)	103. (*c*)	104. (*a*)	105. (*a*)	106. (*a*)	107. (*c*)	108. (*a*)	109. (*b*)	110. (*d*)
111. (*b*)	112. (*c*)	113. (*b*)	114. (*d*)	115. (*a*)	116. (*b*)	117. (*)	118. (*)	119. (*c*)	120. (*c*)
121. (*a*)	122. (*a*)	123. (*a, c*)	124. (*b*)	125. (*)	126. (*d*)	127. (*a*)	128. (*b*)	128. (*c*)	130. (*c*)
131. (*b*)	132. (*a*)	133. (*)	134. (*)	135. (*b*)	136. (*a*)	137. (*a*)	138. (*)	139. (*)	140. (*)
141. (*c*)	142. (*d*)	143. (*d*)	144. (*d*)	145. (*b*)	146. (*b*)	147. (*)	148. (*)	149. (*)	150. (*c*)
151. (*d*)	152. (*a*)	153. (*b*)	154. (–)	155. (*a*)	156. (*c*)	157. (*c*)	158. (*a*)	159. (*)	160. (*)
161. (*)	162. (*a*)	163. (*a, c*)							

Numerical Type Questions

1. (2)	2. (1)	3. (3)	4. (3)	5. (*)	6. (*)	7. (*)	8. (*)

EXPLANATIONS

MCQ TYPE QUESTIONS

1. $S \to aS \mid bS \mid$

$S \to \varepsilon, S \to a, S \to b, S \to aa$

$S \to ab, S \to ba, S \to bb$ ......

Hence $\{a, b\}^*$.

2. $L[N_1] \cap L[N_2] \neq \phi$ – undecidable

$x \in L(G)$ – decidable

$L(G_1) = L(G_2)$ – decidable

$L[M] = \phi$ is also undecidable.

3. $(0 + 1)^* (00(0 + 1)^* 11 + 11(0 + 1)^*00) (0 + 1)^*$

4. a can be 0.

b can't be 0.

5. String will be of form a^nb^n

7. From the given question

$L_1 : S_1 \to aS_1 b \mid \varepsilon$

$L_2 : S_2 \to abS_2 \mid \varepsilon$

$L_1 : \{a^n b^n \mid n > 0\} \to$ CFL

$L_2 : (ab)^* \to$ RL

So, the given statements P is false and Q is true.

8. From the given question

L_1 : Regular

L_2 : CFL (Context-free)

L_3 : Recursive language

L_4 : REL (Recursively enumerable.)

(i) $\bar{L}_3$ is Recursive

$\bar{L}_3 \cup L_4$ is REL (Recursively enumerable)

(ii) $\bar{L}_2$ is recursive

$\bar{L}_3$ is recursive

$\Rightarrow \bar{L}_2 \cup L_3$ is also recursive

(iii) L_1^* is regular

L_2 is CFL (Context-free)

$\Rightarrow L_1^* \cup L_2$ is CFL

Since CFL is closed under the intersection with RL

$\therefore$ RL $\cap$ CFL is CFL

(iv) L_1 is RL

$\bar{L}_2$ is recursive

$\Rightarrow L_1 \cup \bar{L}_2$ is CFL is not possible

So, the statements (i), (ii) and (iii) are correct.

9. Both I and II are false.

10. Given language is

L_1: $\{a^n b^m c^{n+m} \mid m, n \geq 1\}$ – CFL

L_2: $\{a^n b^n c^{2n} \mid n \geq 1\}$ – CSL

So, from the above language is is clear that L_1 is context-free language (CFL) but L_2 is not context-free language (CFL)

11. From the given language.

L_1 is Recursive

L_2 is Recursive

and L_3 is Not Recursive

12. From option (b)

$$\left.\begin{array}{l} S \to Ab \mid Bb \mid \in \\ A \to Bd \mid \in \\ B \to e \end{array}\right\} \text{Generates finite language}$$

No Recursion at all

So, the given option (b) is free from left recursion.

13.

Grammar$_1$:	**Grammar$_2$:**
D → int L;	D → int L;
L → id [E	L → id E
E → num]	E → E[num]
E → num][E	E → [num]

int a[10] [3];

From Grammar$_1$:

D → int L;		D → int L;
→ int id [E];	**(or)**	→ int a[E];
→ int a [num];		→ int a [num] [E
		→ int a [num] [num]
		→ int a [10] [3];

From Grammar$_2$:

D → int L;

→ int id E;

→ int a E[num];

→ int a [num] [num];

→ int a [10] [3];

$\therefore$ Both G_1 and G_2 generates the string.

int a[10] [3];

Hence, both the grammars G_1 and G_2 generate the declaration.

14. By the property.

If L_1 is context free, $\bar{L}_1$ is recursive.

If L_2 is recursively enumerable and $\overline{L}_1$ is recursive then union of recursive and recursively enumerable language is recursively enumerable.

II and III are false because complement of a context free language is not context free and complement of a recursively enumerable language is not recursive.

15. The overall string accepted by automata is 10010

16. By property,

Complement of every Turing decidable language is also turing decidable

If L is in NP, L is Turing decidable.

17.

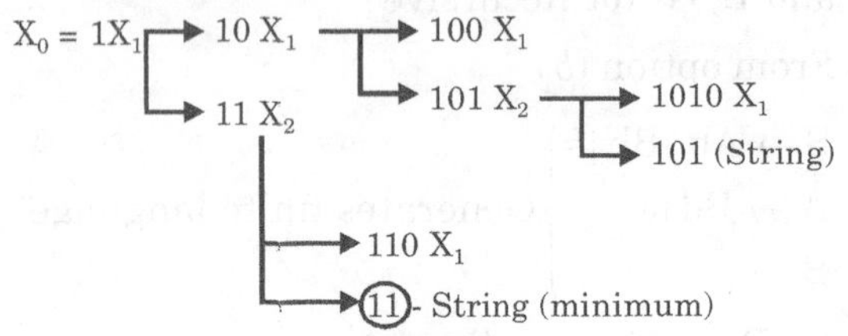

All string are starting with 1 with min string 11. which can be generated by 1(0* + 10)*1.

18. $L_1 = \{W \times W^R \mid W, x \in (a,b)^*, |W|, |X| > 0\}$

W^R is reverse of string of W

It can not be regular, because we can not compare W is regular expression.

$L_2 = \{a^n b^m \mid m \neq n, \text{and } m, n \geq 0\}$ is also not regular due to comparision in a and b

$L_3 = \{a^p b^q c^r \mid p, q, r \geq 0\}$

Here a, b, c are independent and regular exp is $a^*b^*c^*$. Hence L_3 is regular.

21. $a^m b^n a^n b^m \Rightarrow$ This one is CFL

$a^m b^n a^m b^n \Rightarrow$ by pumping lemma this one is not CFL.

$\{a^m b^n \mid m = 2n+1\}$ This is CFL.

22. (*a*) $L = \{a^n b^n \mid n \geq 0\}$ is a CFL but not regular, it requires memory for the representation.

(*b*) $L = \{a^n \mid n \text{ is prime}\}$ is neither regular nor CFL

(*c*) $L = \{w \mid w \text{ has } 3K + 1b\text{'s for some } k \in N \text{ with}\}$

$\Sigma = \{a, b\}$

is a regular language, since the total count of b's are multiple of 3 plus one. The regular expression is $a^*ba^*(a^*ba^*ba^*ba^*)^*$
$+ (a^*ba^*ba^*ba^*)^*a^*ba^*$

(*d*) $L = \{ww \mid w \in \Sigma^* \text{with } \Sigma = \{0,1\}\}$ is neither regular nor CFL

23.
$$\begin{aligned}\delta(q_0, 0011) &= \delta(q_0, 011)\\ &= \delta(q_0, 11)\\ &= \delta(\{q_0, q_1\}, 1)\\ &= \delta(q_0, 1) \cup \delta(q_1, 1)\\ &= \{q_0, q_1\} \cup \{q_2\}\\ &= \{q_0, q_1, q_2\}\end{aligned}$$

24. Recursive languages are closed under complement. If a language L is recursive enumerable but not recursive then its complement is not a recursive enumerable, so both L and $\overline{L}$ are recursive enumerable but not recursive is not a viable possibility.

25. Given DFA will accept all the strings over ε ={0,1} which are ending with 1.

0*1(1+ 00*1)* and(0 +1)*1, are the regular expressions for ending with 1.

26. $L_1 . L_2$ will be regular language, concatenation of two regular language is language.

It will be like $L_1 . L_2 \neq \{a^n b^n \mid n \geq 0\}$

It will be like $L_1 . L_2 = \{a^n b^m \mid n, m \geq 0\}$

That's why only (I) will satisfy.

27. Since $A \leq_m B$ and since B is not enumerable recursively creates a situation for A to not to be recursively enumerable.

28. $S \rightarrow T * P$

$T \rightarrow U/T * U$

$P \rightarrow Q + P/Q$

$Q \rightarrow ID$

$U \rightarrow ID$

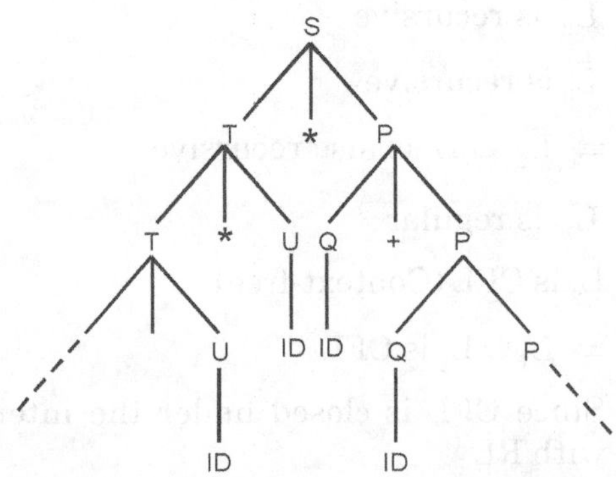

29. L_1 is regular because we can design FA for L_1 but we can not design FA for L_2. Hence L_1 is regular but not L_2.

30. 2^{ε^*} is the power set of ε*

ε* is countabily infinite

The power set of countabily infinite set is uncountable.

So 2^{ε^*} is uncountable, and ε* is countable.

31. There were algorithms to find the membership of CFG (using CYK algorithm) and finiteness of CFG (using CNF graph) and emptiness. But there is no algorithm for ambiguity of CFG, so it is undecidable.

32. For the languages L_1 and L_2 we can have deterministic push down automata, so they are DCFL's, but for L_3 only non-deterministic PDA possible. So the language L_3 is not a deterministic CFL.

33. 2 SAT is in P. This we can prove by reducing 2 SAT to directed graph reachability problem which is known to be in P.

<u>Procedure for reducing 2 SAT to reachability problem:</u>

1. Let φ be CNF with clauses of length 2 and let P be the set of propositional variables(literals) in φ
2. Build a graph G = (V,E) with V= P∪{¬p | p∈P} and (*x*, *y*)∈ E iff there is a clause in φ that is equivalent to *x*→*y* (all the clauses are converted to equivalent implications and the graph built is called as implication graph)
3. Observe that φ is unsatisfiable iff there is a p∈P such that there is both a path from p to ¬p and from ¬p to p in G.

   This condition can be tested by running the reachability algorithm several times.

34. 1. TRUE. Non deterministic turing machine can be simulated by a Deterministic turing machine with exponential time.

2. Turing Recognizable languages are "not" closed under complementation. For any Toring recognizable language, the toring machine 'T' recognizing 'L', may not terminate on inputs $x \notin L$.

   Hence this is FALSE

3. Toring Decidable languages are CLOSED under unioin and complementation. It is easy to construct a turing machine to decide $L_1 \cup L_2$, L_1' if L_1, L_2 are turing decidable.

   So, this is TRUE.

   (*c*) is the only option which contains (2).

35. Given: DFA :

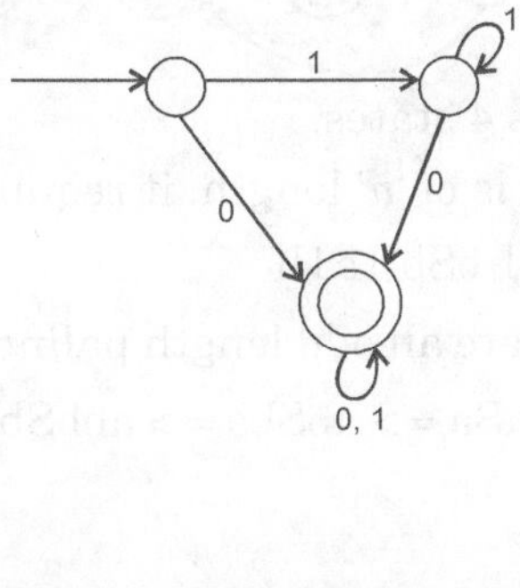

Q: Which are False?

1. Complement of L(A) is context free – <u>True</u>

   – As there exist a DFA, L(A) is regular. Regular languages are closed under complemer,

   ∴ Complement of L(A) is regular and therefore context free.

2. $L(A) = L((11^* 0 + 0)(0 + 1)^* 0^* 1^*)$ – True

   – As $L(A) = L((11^* 0 + 0)(0 + 1)^*)$ is equivalent to $L((11^*0 + 0)(0 + 1)^* 0^* 1^*)$

3. For the language accepted by A,

   A is minimal DFA – <u>FALSE</u>

   – Minimal DFA is

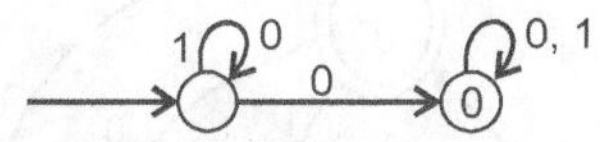

4. A accepts all strings over {0, 1} of length at least 2 – <u>FALSE</u>

   – The given DFA A accepts the string "0" which is of length less than

Ans. (*d*) 3/4 only FALSE.

36. Which are/is undecidable

1. G is CFG. Is L(G) = φ?

   – Decidable

2. G is a CFG. Is $L(G) = \Sigma^*$?

   – Undecidable

3. M is a turing machine. Is L(M) regular?

   – Undecidable (Present in all options)

4. A is a DFA and N is a NFA.

   Is L(A) = L(N)?

   – Decidable

Ans. (*d*) 2 and 3 only.

PS. Refer closere properties (wiki)

37. L = {*ab*, *aa*, *baa*}

Let S1 = *ab*, S2 = *aa*

and S3 = *baa*

abaabaaabaa can be written as S1 S2 S3 S1 S2

aaaabaaaa can be written as S1 S1 S3 S1

baaaabaa can be written as S3 S2 S1 S2

38. The cumulative distribution function

$$F(x) = P(X \leq x)$$

$$F(-1) = P(X \leq -1)$$
$$= P(X = -1) = 0.5$$

$$F(+1) = P(X \leq +1)$$
$$= P(X = -1) + P(X = +1)$$
$$= 0.5 + 0.5 = 1$$

39. Language accepted by NFA is a^+, so complement of this language is $\{\varepsilon\}$

40. $I_1 : R \rightarrow \sim C \quad = \sim R V \sim C$

$$\frac{\begin{array}{c} C \\ -R \end{array}}{} \quad \text{(there was no rain)}$$

$I_2 : R \rightarrow C \quad = \sim R v \sim C$

$$\frac{\begin{array}{cc} \sim R & \sim R \end{array}}{-RvC}$$

(I_1 is correct and I_2 is not correct inference)

41. The complete DFA is

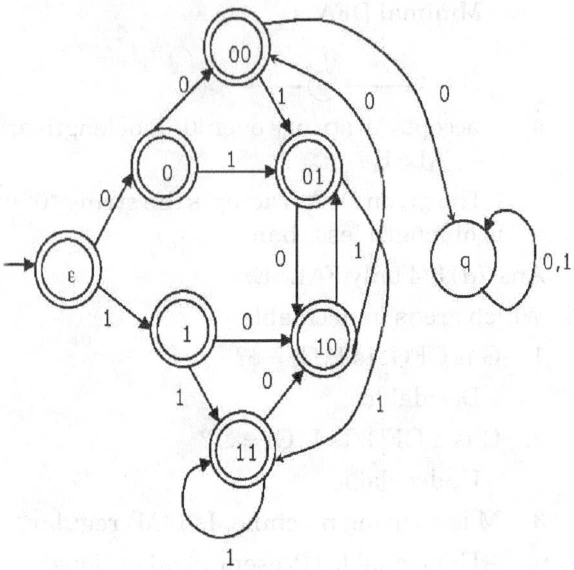

42. $\Sigma^* - P$ is the complement of P so it is always regular,

Since regular languages are closed under complementation

43. Lexical Analysis is implemented by finite automata

44. NPDA is more powerful than DPDA.

Hence answer is (*b*)

45. LOC L1 = x

L2 = $2x$

Total cost of project

$$= \frac{x}{10000} \times 1000000 + 5 \times 100000$$

$$= \frac{2x}{10000} \times 750000 + 50000 \times 5$$

$100x + 500000 = 150x + 250000$

$\Rightarrow \quad 50\,x = 500000 - 250000$

$\therefore \quad x = \dfrac{250000}{50} = 5000$

46. Options (*b*) and (*c*) will accept the string b

Option (*d*) will accept the string "bba"

Both are invalid strings.

So minimized DFA is option *a*

47. Let $n = 3$ and $k = 1$

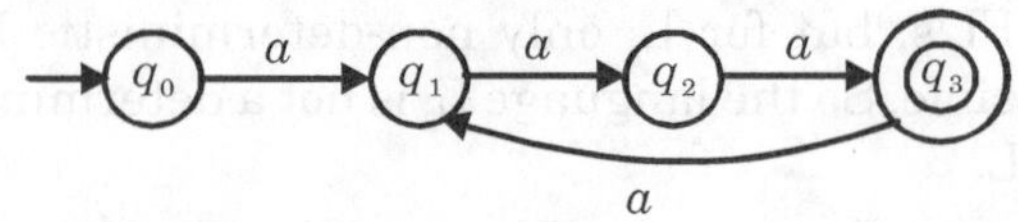

48. L1 : regular language

L2 : context free language

L3 : context sensitive language

49. L1 is recursive and L2, L3 are recursively enumerable. So $L1 \cap L3$ and $L2 \cup L3$ can recursively enumerable and also L2 – L1 can recursively enumerable. But we can't say that **L1-L3** is also **recursively enumerable.**

50. Every string should contain even number of 1's min string are

$\in$, 0, 11, 101, 1010, 0101, 0110, ...

We can't get it by

0* (10 * 1) 0* and 0 * 1 (10 * 1)* 10*

because these don't give $\in$ and 0 string.

51. Since L1, L2, L3, L4 can be recognised by push down automata, so these all are context-free grammer.

52. w be any string of length n in $\{0, 1\}^*$ and L is substring of L

means if **101** is the w

Then L = 01, 10, 01, 11

Then

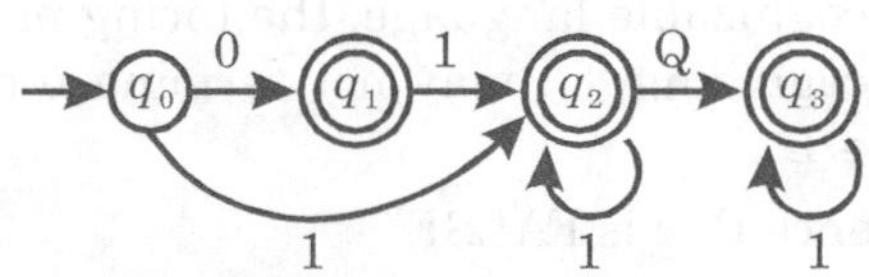

Then it should be $n + 1$, where n is length of the string.

Alternately

Let $w = 101$

$\therefore$ sub strings = 1, 0, 10, 11, 01, 101

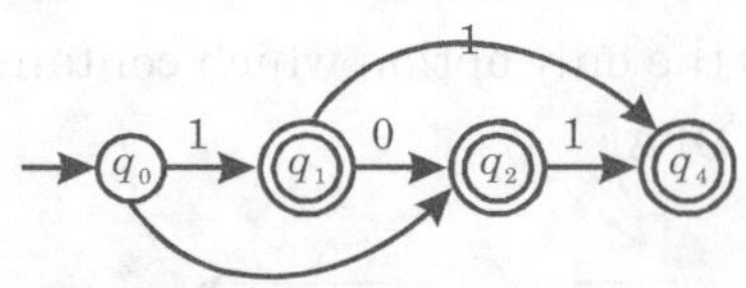

It requires 4 states.

If a string is of 'n' length, it requires $n + 1$ states

53. S –> aSa | bSb | a | b

will generate all odd length palindromes

e.g. S => aSa => abSba => abbSbba => abbababba

54. R.E. = (0+1)*0(0+1)*0(0+1)*

Accepting Language will be

L = {00, 000, 100, 001, 010, 0000, 0001, 1000, 1001, 0100, 1100, 0010, 0011, 0110, 0101, 1010, ...}

atleast two zeros.

55. (*a*) There is a unique minimal DFA for every regular language. TRUE

(*b*) Every NFA can be converted to an equivalent PDA. TRUE

(*c*) Complement of every context-free language is recursive. TRUE

Because context-free language is not closed under Complementation.

(*d*) Every nondeterministic PDA can be converted to an equivalent deterministic PDA. FALSE

Because ww^R can not be accepted by deterministic PDA but nondeterministic PDA can accept it. So there does not exist any equivalent deterministic PDA.

56. Regular expression denote structure of data specially text string-lexical analyser break input text into logical unit such as identifiers.

Push down automater- Syntax analysis. Study with the help of syntax.

Data flow analysis – Code optimization

Register allocation – Lexical analysis

57.

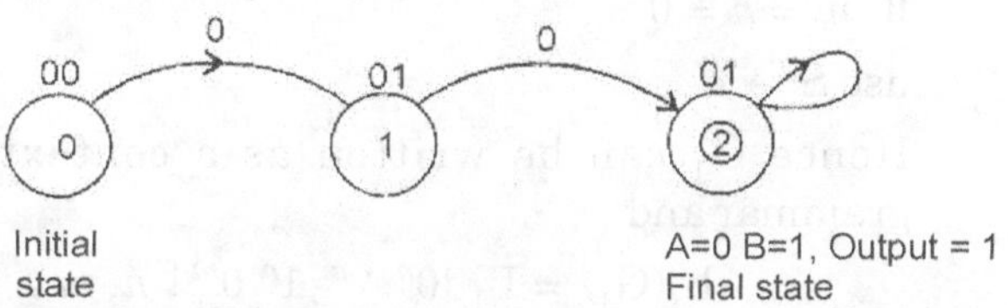

Hence 3 stakes required

Alternately

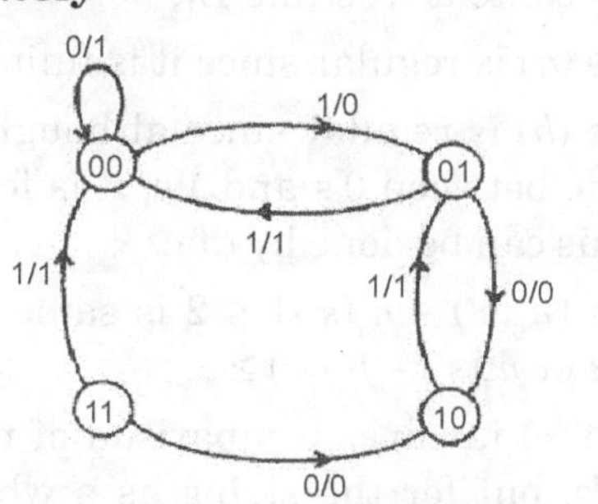

Fom state 00 to 01 with output 1 required minimum 3 length of string i.e. 101.

58. Intersection of two regular language is regular

Given : $L_1 = \{a^m b^m c a^n b^n \mid m, n \geq 0\}$

If $\begin{matrix} n=1 \\ m=1 \end{matrix}$ { a, b, c, a, b} not regular

If n/1 a^m, b^m c a^n b^n is regular

59. Let A be the starting state

A to A input 1 0 output 0 0

B to A input 1 0 output 0 0

C to A input 1,0 output 0 0

so end with 0 0

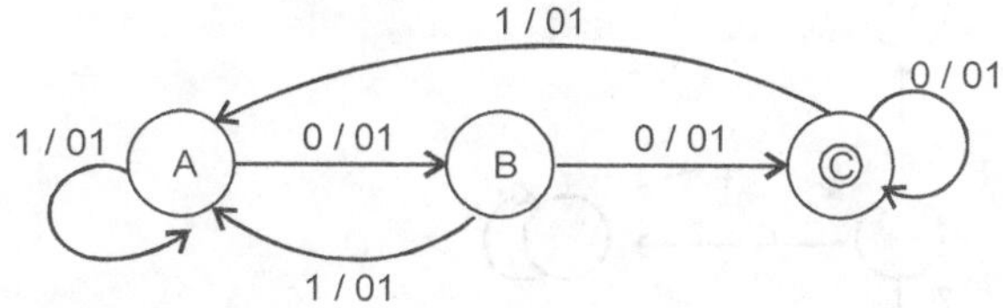

Alternately

R.E. = (0 + 1)* 00

60. L = a^P | p is prime.

L is not be regular, can be proved by pumping Lemma, so it cannot be context free language.

61. Intersection of two regular languages can be determined by a given algorithm, it can be determined whether a given grammer is context free.

Context free grammar should have all productions of the type

$$A \rightarrow x$$

where, $A \in V_N$ {set of varibale}

$\alpha \in (V_N \text{ U} z)^*$ {z = set of terminal}

62. If a language is recursively enumerable, and its complement is also, then the language is recursive.

63. I, II and III are true

Instead true statement is, "every recursive set is recursively enumerable".

64.

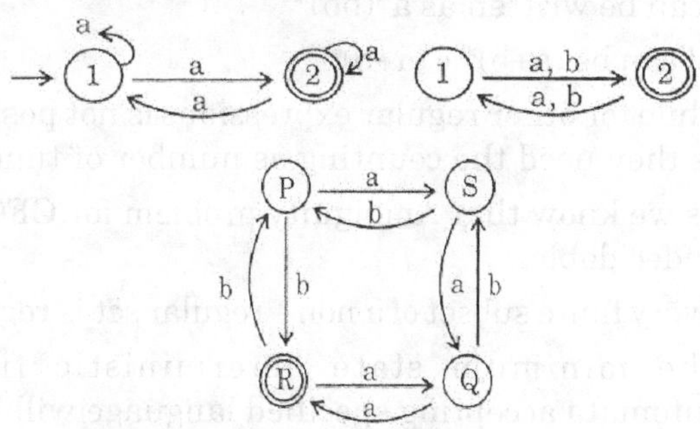

65. Statement III is false. In a context free grammar, right side of the productions should either have single terminal or one non-terminal followed by terminal or λ.

66. Here X → b *x* b | c *x* c | ε surely repesent palindrome and x → x b x | | x c x | d x f | g Arithmetic expressions with match pair are simple & L = {wcw/wε (a/b)*}checking that identifier are declared before their use.

67. 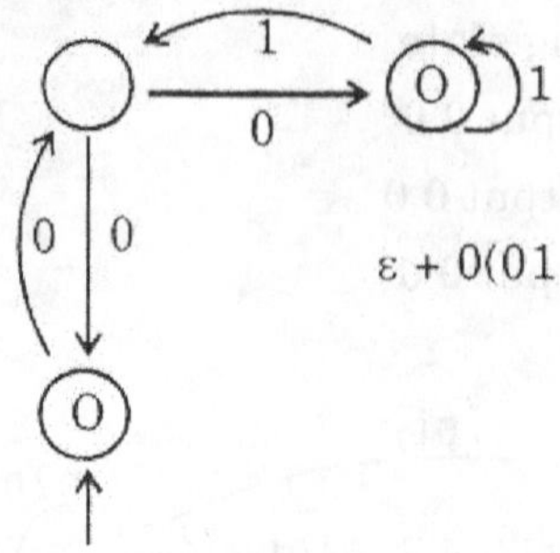

$\varepsilon + 0(01 * 1 + 00) * 01 *$

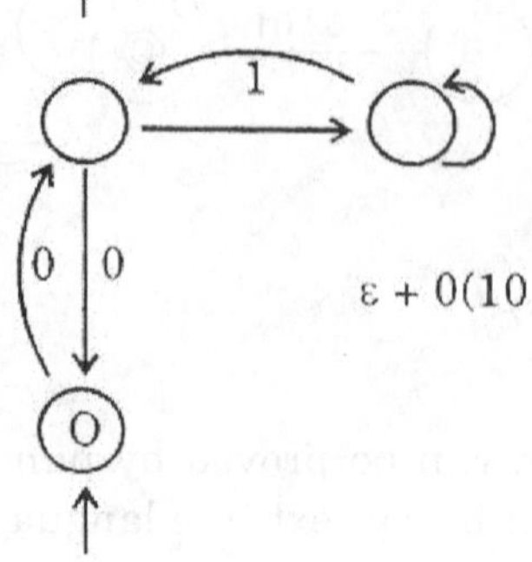

$\varepsilon + 0(10 * 1 + 00) * 0$

Alternately

Converting NFA into regular expression.

P says ε moves or 0, followed by zero and 1*1 or 00 any number of times followed by zero, again followed by 1 any times.

$$P \to \varepsilon + 0\,(01 * 1 + 0\,0)^*\, 01^*$$

Similarly for Q, R & S.

68. Only $\{a^n b^{2m} \mid n \geq 0, m \geq 0\}$

& $\{x_{cy}$, x, y ε (a, b)*} are regular sets.

Alternately

In a regular language, counting of numbers is not possible but counting that a input is repeated even times or odd times is possible; to get the number (even / odd say 4/7) is not possible.

I can be written as a*(bb)*

IV can be (a+b)* c (a+b)*

while for other regular expressions is not possible as they need the counting as number of times.

69. As we know that Ambiguity problem for CFGs is undecidable.

70. Every finite subset of a non – regular set is regular.

71. The minimum state deterministic finite automata accepting specified language will have 15 states.

72. Language $L = \{ 0^i\, 21^i \mid i \geq 0\}$ over alphabet { 0, 1, 2} is recursive and is a deterministic CFL (every CFL is recursive)

73. language $L = \{wxw^R \mid x_1\, w \in \{0, 1\}^+ \}$ is a regular language.

74. **Note :** If $P_1 \leq_p P_2$ then P_1 is Np-complete ⇒ P_2 is Np-complete.

Given, S is Np-complete.

$Q \leq_p S$ and $S \leq_p R$

Since $S \leq_p R$

S is Np-complete ⇒ R is Np-complete

∴ (*a*) is true.

75. In L_1, L_2 and L_3, only L_1 can be written as a context free language, the production for L_1 are

$$S \to 0\,S0 \mid 0A1 \mid \in$$
$$A \to 0A1 \mid \in$$

to generate $0^{n+m}\ 1^n\ 0^m$

i. e. $0^m\ 0^n\ 1^n 0^m$

first we apply, $S \to 0S0$, *m* times

So $S \xrightarrow{*} 0^m\ S\ 0^m$

Now we apply, $S \longrightarrow 0A1$

$S \xrightarrow{*} 0^m\ 0\ A\ 1\ 0^m$

Now apply, $A \to 0A1$, $(n-1)$ times

$S \xrightarrow{*} 0^m\ 0\ 0^{n-1}\ A\ 1^{n-1}\ 10^m$

i.e. $S \xrightarrow{*} 0^m\ 0^n\ A\ 1^n\ 0^m$

Now $A \longrightarrow \in$

$S \xrightarrow{*} 0^m\ 0^n\ 1^n\ 0^m$

If $m = 0$ and $n \neq 0$

start from $S \to 0A1$

If $m \neq 0$ and $n = 0$

start from $S \to 0S0$ and never use

$S \to 0A1$

If $m = n = 0$

use $S \to \in$

Hence G_1 can be written as a context free grammar and

$$L_1(G_1) = L_1\ \{0^{n+m}\ 1^n\ 0^m \mid n, m \geq 0\}$$

For L_2 and L_3 we can not generate a grammer that is context free like L_1,

76. Choice (*a*) is regular since it is finite.

Choice (*b*) is regular since although comparison is made between 0's and 1's, it is for all prefixes and this can be done by dfa.

Note : $|n_0(s') - n_1(s')| \leq 2$ is same as $n_0(s') - n_1(s') \geq 2$ or $n_1(s') - n_0(s') \geq 2$.

Choice (*c*) involves comparison of number of 0's and 1's, but for the string as a whole, and this cannot be done by a dfa, since it has finite memory and has no stack for counting upto infinity. Therefore, choice (*c*) is not regular.

Choice (*d*) is regular since $n_0(s) \bmod 7 = n_1(s) \bmod 5 = 0$ means number of 0's is divisible by 7 and number of 1's is divisible by 5 and this can be accepted by a dfa with 7 × 5 = 35 states.

A dfa that will accept the language of choice (*b*) is shown below :

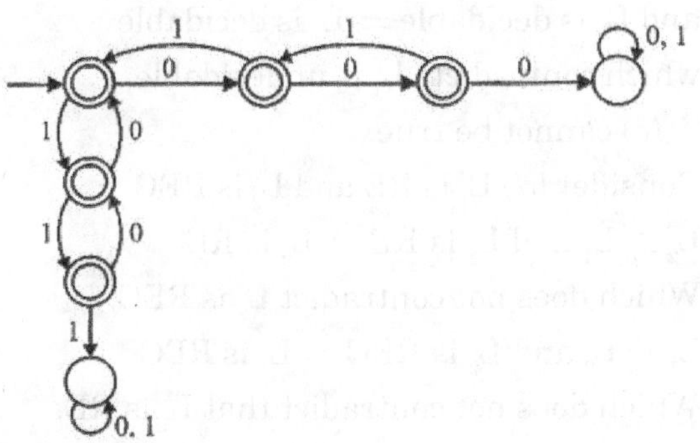

77. By observation, all the numbers of the form $5x + 2$, $x \in N$ except of the form $7(5n + 4) + 4n \in N$, belong to the language, Since we have an algorithm to check whether a given number belongs to L or not. It is recursive.

78. Let's take a string *abba* generated by G. The two leftmost derivations are

(i) $S \to SS \to \epsilon S \to \epsilon SS \to SS \to abS \to abba$

(ii) $S \to SS \to abS \to abba$

Hence G is ambiguous

As any replacement of S with terminals will add equal number of *a*'s and *b*'s to the string

Hence All strings generated by G will have equal number of *a*'s and *b*'s

G is also accepted by a deterministic PDA.

79. Since L_1 may or may not be content – free, hence options (*a*) and (*c*) are ruled out.

Since L_3 is not recursive, hence option *(b)* is also ruled out.

80. Output of the top MUX

$$M_1 = x\bar{z} + \bar{y}z$$

Output of the second MUX

$$M_2 = M_1\bar{y} + xy$$

$$= (x\bar{z} + \bar{y}z)\,\bar{y} + xy$$

$$= x\bar{y}\bar{z} + \bar{y}z + xy$$

$$= \bar{y}z + x\bar{y}\bar{z} + xy\,(z + \bar{z})$$

$$= \bar{y}z + x\bar{y}\bar{z} + xy\bar{z} + xy\bar{z} + xyz$$

$$= \bar{y}z + x\bar{z}\,(\bar{y} + y) + xy\,(z + \bar{z})$$

$$= \bar{y}z + x\bar{z} + xy$$

82. Note that in general if $L_1 \leq L_2$, L_2 decidable $\Rightarrow L_1$ decidable and L_1 undecidable $\Rightarrow L_2$ is undecidable.

Given that P_1 is decidable and P_2 is undecidable.

Consider (*a*) P_3 is decidable if P_1 is reducible to P_3

i.e. $P_1 \leq_p P_3$

and if P_1 is undecidable, then P_3 would be undecidable.

But it is given that P_1 is decidable, therefore we cannot use this theorem.

(*a*) is false.

Consider (*b*) P_3 is undecidable if P_3 is reducible to P_2

i.e. $P_3 \leq_p P_2$

Now if P_3 is undecidable then P_2 is undecidable but nothing is given regarding P_3.

Also if P_2 is decidable, then P_3 would be decidable, but it is given that P_2 is undecidable, so we can't use this.

(*b*) is false.

Consider (*c*) P_3 is undecidable if P_2 is reducible to P_3

i.e. $P_2 \leq_p P_3$

Now if P_2 is undecidable, this would mean P_3 is undecidable. Since it is given that P_2 is undecidable, therefore, surely P_3 is undecidable is correct.

Choice (*c*) is correct.

83. (*a*) and (*d*) are two possible solutions but best is (*b*).

Why (a) is wrong : Run this string on DFA

a b b b : is stop in final stage while it have three **b**.

Why not (c) : As **a b b a a** have substring **'a b b'** but, don't stop at final state.

84. There is a language ww^R which is N.C.F.L. but not D.C.F.L.

There is no language which is accepted by D.F.A. and not by N.D.F.A. or vice versa.

85. Result of these two grammar is only the case where $a = b = c$.

86. L_1 is CFL but not a DCFL, since accepting wwR necessarily involves finding the middle of the string, which involves non-determinism.

∴ (*a*) is false.

L_2 is a DCFL is true since "#" is a special symbol and middle of string can now be surely found by using "#", thereby eliminating the need for non-deterministic guessing. So (*b*) is true.

L_3 is a CSL and not a CFL. So (*c*) is false.

L_3 is not a DCFL either. So (*d*) is false.

87. 3 SAT and 2 SAT problem is NP complete and in P respectively.

88. This automata accept 10 11 11 0 1 and checking for other input it is clear that it accept number divisible by 3 and 2.

89. $L = \{a^m b^n c^{m+n} \mid m, n \geq 1\}$

The given language is context free but not regular language

90. $S \rightarrow bs \mid a \mid b$

$A \rightarrow bA \mid a\mathbf{B}$

$B \rightarrow bB \mid aS \mid a$

This grammar will execute

$\{w \mid Na(w) = 3k \quad k \in \{0, 1, 2, ...\}\}.$

92. 2 SAT is NP-complete

93. The most famous unsolved problem in computer science is

whether P = NP or P ¹ NP

94. Lexico graphic is a sequence of number at no repetition.

95.

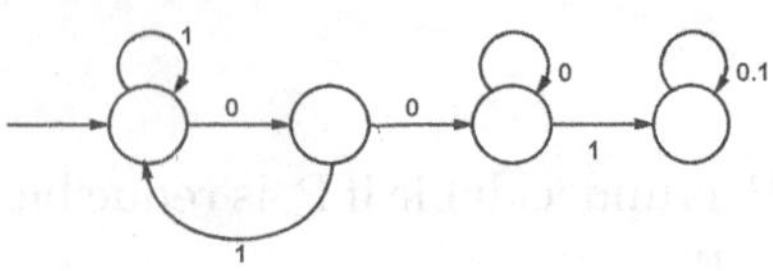

S denote the set of seven bit binary strings in which the first, fourth and last bits are 1.

	1	2	3	4	5	6	7
⇒	1	0	0	1	0	0	1

So number of strings in S that are accepted by M is one.

96.

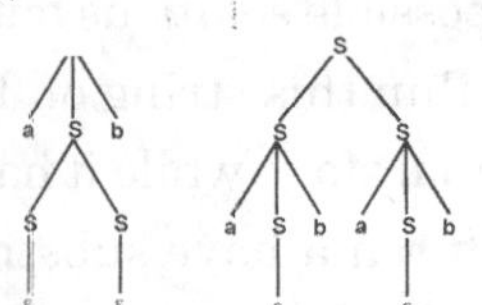

$S \rightarrow aSb \mid SS \mid \in$

Hence, S is ambiguous

So, we can find a deterministic finite state automation that accepts L (G).

97. Since f is polynomial time computable,

$$L_1 \leq_p L_2 \qquad ...(i)$$

Since f^{-1} is also polynomial time computable,

$$L_2 \leq_p L_1 \qquad ...(ii)$$

Now consider (*a*) $L_1 \in P$ and L_2 is finite.

From (*ii*) we can say that $h_1 \in p \Rightarrow h_2 \in P$

Now $L_2 \in P$ and L_2 is finite is not contradictary.

∴ (*a*) can be true.

Choice (*b*) $L_1 \in NP$ and $L_2 \in P$

Now $L_2 \leq_p L_1$

and $L_1 \in NP \Rightarrow L_2 \in NP$ which does not controdict $L_2 \in P$.

$$L_1 \leq_p L_2$$

and $L_2 \in P \Rightarrow L_1 \in P$ which does not contradict $L_1 \in NP$.

∴ (*b*) can be true.

Consider (*c*) L_1 undecidable and L_2 is decidable.

Now $L_1 \leq_p L_2$

and L_2 is decidable ⇒ L_1 is decidable

which contradicts L_1 is undecidable.

∴ (*c*) cannot be true.

Consider (*d*) L_1 is RE and L_2 is REC

$L_2 \leq_p L_1$ and L_1 is RE ⇒ L_2 is RE

Which does not contradict L_2 is REC.

$L_1 \leq_p L_2$ and L_2 is REC ⇒ L_1 is REC

Which does not contradict that L_1 is RE.

∴ (*d*) can be true.

98.

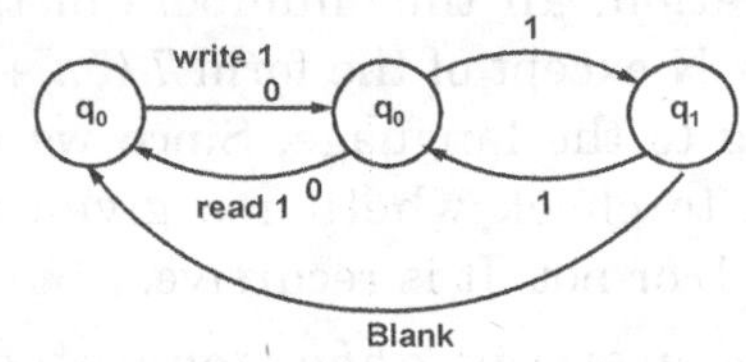

99. If $L_0 \cup L_1$ is recursively enumerable, it means we can find out for all $\omega \in \Sigma^*$, whether M halts or does not halt. This means that if $L_0 \cup L_1$ is recursively enumerable, the halting problem would be decidable. But we know, that halting problem is undecidable.

Therefore $L = L_0 \cup L_1$ is not RE.

Since $\bar{L} = (L_0 \cup L_1)^c = L_0^c \cap L_1^c = \phi$, which is regular language and hence is RE.

Therefore, $\bar{L}$ is RE.

So correct choice is (*d*) which is $\bar{L}$ is RE but L is not.

100.

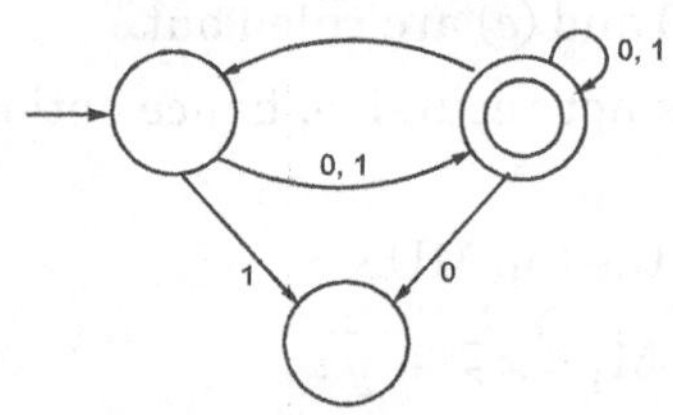

$$L = (0|1)\,01$$

$$= (0|1)\,(0,1)*0$$

Changing accepting state to non-accepting state and changing the non-accepting state to accepting state is know as h_1.

$$L = (0|1)\,(0,1)* = 0\,(0|1)\,(0,1)*$$

We find from both language L and L_1.

So $L_1 \subseteq L$

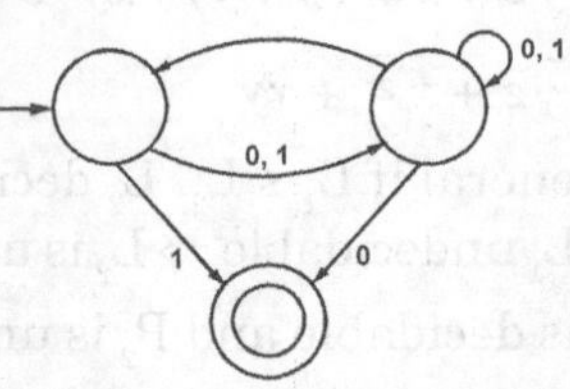

101. Stack function is a type of recursion so, pushdown automata accept the recursive language.

102. Information needed by a single execution of a procedure is managed using a contiguous block of storage called an *activation record*, or *frame*, consisting of the collection of fields. Pascal and C uses all these fields. Often register can take the place of one of one or more of them. It customary to push the activation record of a procedure on the run-time slack when the procedure is called and to popu the activation record off the stack when control returns to the caller.

103.

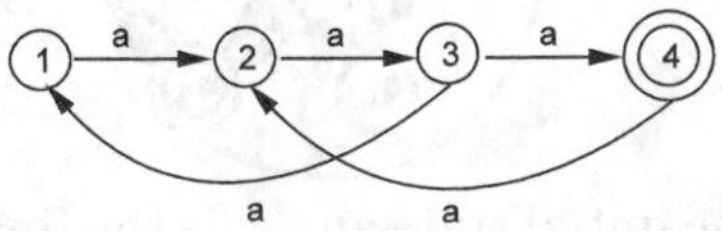

106. Start from A, B, C, we get output at A is 00 and input is sequence of 10.

A to A $\rightarrow$ input = 10,output = 00

B to A $\rightarrow$ input = 10,output = 00

C to A $\rightarrow$ input = 10,output = 00

107. A′ S is divisible by 6

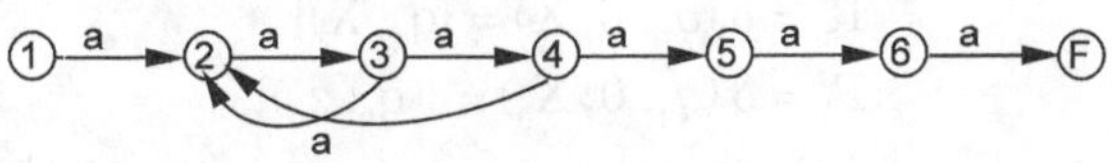

a′S divisible by 6

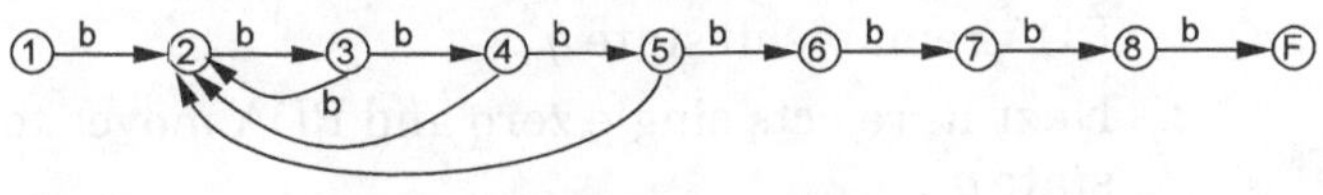

b′S divisible by 8

Total no of state = 9 + 7 – 1 = 15

108.
$$S = \{0^{2n} | n \geq 1\} \text{ is a regular language}$$
$$= 00,\ 0000,\ 000000,\ \ldots\ldots\ldots\ldots$$
regular language
$$S_2 = \{0^m 1^n 0^{m+n} | mZ_1 \text{ and } nZ_1\}$$
$$= 0100, 00110000, 000111000000$$

109. * If language is context free, then it is not surety that it is accepted by POA

* Intersection of two context free is context free is not always happen

* **Couplement of context free** is not context free.

110. * 0^{2i} will regular when $i \geq 1$ [integer $\rightarrow 0 - n$]

* 0^{i2} will not regular when $i \geq 1$

* (a, b) * is not regular.

* (a, b) * (b, a) * not is regular.

[0^{i^2}, 0^{i^3}, 0^{2^n}, is not regular]

111. Indirect–passing array as parameter.

Indexed address kg–Address field of the instruction defines the beggining address of a data array

Base Register–It is used in computers to facilitate the relocation of programs in rolemery.

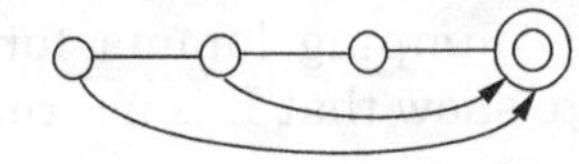

117. (*a*)

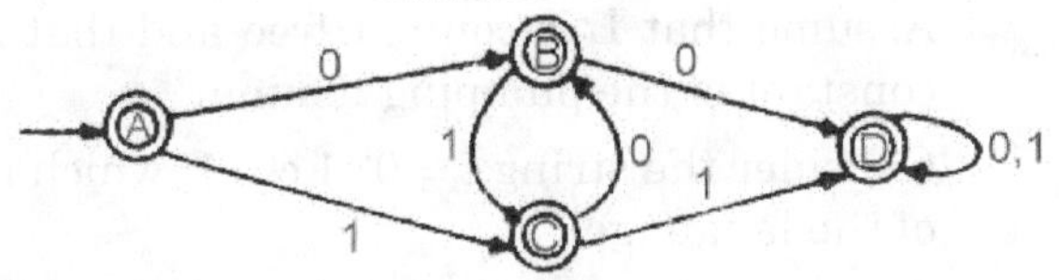

(*b*) $j \geq i$ or equivalent condition.

118. (*a*)

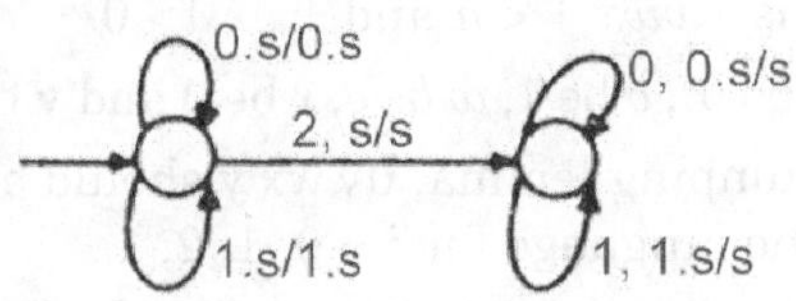

(*b*)

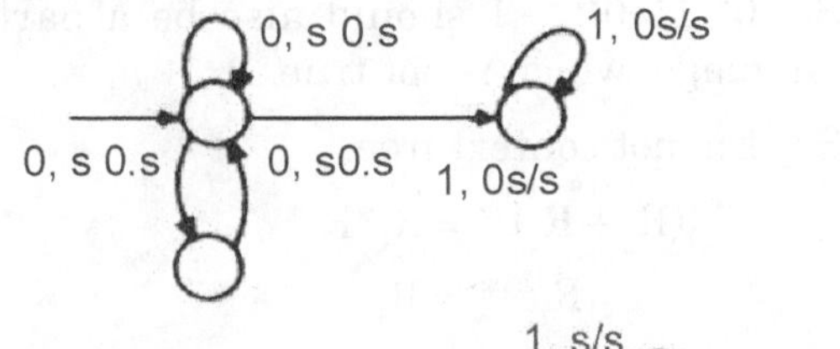

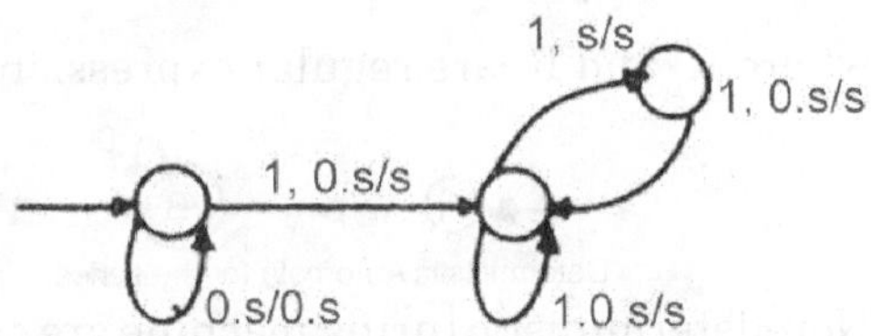

119. The finite state automation must basically accept any n bit string. So, we need $n + 1$ states for counting through 0 to n and finally a termination state. Totally, we need $n + 2$ states.

121. The two sets are the same.

122. We first multiply a with itself to get a^2, then a^2 with itself to get a^4 and so on until we get a^n. This would take $\log_2 n$ multiplications since n is a power of 2.

123. Intersection of a content free language and a regular language is context free. L1 – L2 is the same as L1 ∩ ~L2. Also ~L2 is regular, as complement of a regular language is regular. So L1 - L2 is context free. So (*a*) is false.

The complement of a context free language need not be context free. So (*c*) is false.

(*b*) and (*d*) are true.

124.
$$\text{(M) } T_n = T_{n-1} + n$$
$$= T_{n-2} + (n-1) + n$$
$$= 1 + 2 + 3 + \ldots\ldots + n$$
$$= O(n^2)$$

(N) Put $n = 2^m$

Then, $T_m = T_{m-1} + 2^m$
$= 1 + 2 + 4 + ... + 2^m$
$= 2^{m+1} - 1$
$= 2.n$
$= O(n)$

125. We use the pumping lemma for context free languages to show that L is not context free.

Assume that L is context free and that n is the constant of the pumping lemma.

Consider the string $z = 0^n\ 1\ c0^n\ 1$, which is a part of the language.

So, z can be written as uvwxy satisfying the conditions $|\ vwx\ | < n$ and $|\ vx\ | > 0$.

So, let u be 0^n, v be 1, w be c, x be 0 and y be 0^{n-1} 1.

By the pumping lemma, uv^iwx^iy should also be a part of the language for $i = 0, 1, 2, ...$

So, $0^n\ 11c0^{n+1}\ 1$ should also be a part of the language, which is not true.

So, 1 is not context free.

126. $(R_1 + R_2)^* = R_1^*R_2^*$
$(R_1^*)^* = R_1^*$,

where R_1 and R_2 are regular expressions.

127.

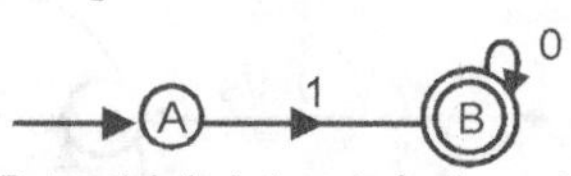

Deterministic Automata for the series

128. Non-deterministic turing machine are equivalent to deterministic push down automata.

129. (*a*) $110^*\ (0 + 1) = 1100, 1101$

(*b*) $1\ (0 + 1)^*\ 101 = 10^*\ 1^*\ 101$
$= 101101$

(*c*) $(10)^*\ (01)^*\ (00 + 01)^*$
$= (10)^*\ (01)^*\ (00)^*\ (01)^*$
$= 10\ 01\ 0001$

(*d*) $(00 + (11)^*\ 0)^*$
$= (00)^*\ (11)^*\ 0)^*$
$= (00)^*\ (110)^*$
$= 00\ 110110$

From above calculation (*c*) does not belong to 1101.

130. Number of substring = $2n$.

where, n = length of character string.

131.

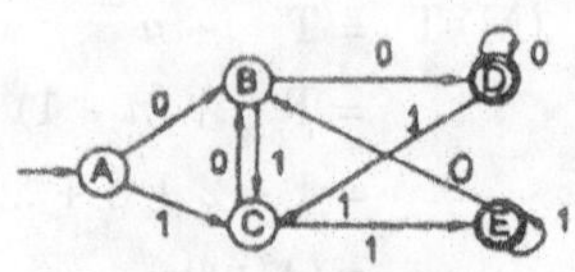

A to D → $\underline{00}$, $1\underline{00}$, $11\underline{00}$, $011\underline{00}$

A to E → $\underline{11}$, $0\underline{11}$, $00\underline{11}$, $100\underline{11}$

From above example we see A to D end with 00 and A to E end with 11.

So, number of state for deterministic finite state automation accepting L is **A, B, C, D, E** means 5.

132. A non-regular set is a subset of itself.

133. (*b*) → $(1^k\ 1^*\ 01^k)^*$

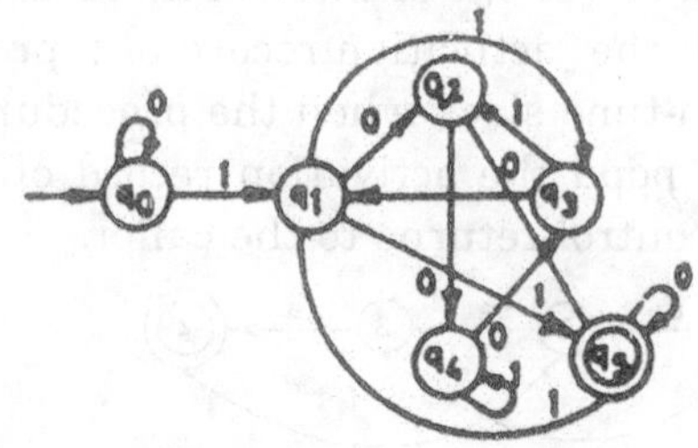

Here q_0 is the initial state and q_5 is the final state. The subscript of the states q_1, q_2, q_3, q_4, q_5 gives the residue 1, 2, 3, 4, 0 respectively.

134. Let
$R_1 = \delta(q_0, 1, z_0) = \{(q_0, X_{z0})\}$
$R_2 = \delta(q_0, \in z_0) = \{(q_0, \in)\}$
$R_3 = \delta(q_0, 1, X) = \{(q_0, XX)\}$
$R_4 = \delta(q_1, 1, X) = \{(q_1, \in)\}$
$R_5 = \delta(q_0, 0, X) = \{q_1, X)\}$
$R_6 = \delta(q_1, 0, X_0) = \{(q_0, z_0)\}$.

1. R_1 and R_2 consumes n (> 1) number of 1's and pushing equal number of X's on the stack, the PDA remains in state q_0.
2. Next R_5 rejects single zero and PDA moves to state q_1.
3. Next R_4, consumes n number of 1's and popping equal number of X's from the stack and leaving PDA in state q_1.
4. Now R_6, rejects one more zero, moving PDA to state q_0.
5. Using R_2, we can empty the stack.

∴ L (m) $\{1^n\ 0\ 1^n\ 0 : n > 1\}$.

135. $0^*\ (1^+\ 0)^* = 0110, 00110, 0110110, 000110, 0110110$

$0^*1010^* \rightarrow 01010, 0010100, 000101000$

$0^*\ 1^*\ 01 \rightarrow 0101, 001101, 00011101$

$0^*\ (10 + 1)^* \rightarrow 010, 01, 001010, 0011, 00010100, 000111, 001010, 0011$

Only $0^*\ 1010^*$ contains 100 as a substring.

136. It is not possible for turning machine M accepts a string within K steps because length of string is not given.

137. Deterministic Push down Automata. DFA is special case of the NFA in which for each state there is a unique transition on each symbol.

(*a*) wCw^R means $w = w^R$

In DPA we used stack . If we take *a*, *b*, *c*. for input then w^R = *cba*, it matches. So, wCw^R accepted by DPA.

In case of ww^R, we have not information at which steps data be reversed.

141. From options given, we see that $(00)^*$ $(\in + 0)$ and 0^* is equivalent.

142. If $L(G_1) \leq L(G_2)$, then two regular grammars G_1 and G_2

It is decidable whether $L(G_1) = L(G_2)$

143. $L \leq \Sigma*$ where $\Sigma = \{a, b\}$

It is function of regular function,

$$\Sigma^* = (a, b)^*$$

or we write $a^m\, b^n$, $m > 1$, $n > 1$

144.

31 — 24	23 — 0
Exponent	Mantissa

0.5 to $(1–2^{-23})$

Mantissa = **0–23**

145. Intersection of few context free language is not necessary a context free language.

147. Let us first eliminate $A \to \in$

We get the following rules

$$S \to ABC \mid BAC \mid BC$$
$$A \to a$$

By eliminating $B \to \in$ we get following rules

$$S \to AC \mid AAC \mid C$$
$$B \to b$$

Hence, after eliminating $\in$, grammar becomes :

$$S \to ABAC \mid ABC \mid BAC \mid BC \mid AC \mid AAC \mid C$$
$$A \to aA \mid a$$
$$B \to bB \mid b$$
$$C \to d$$

Now the eliminate unit production $S \to C$

$$S \to ABAC \mid ABC \mid BAC \mid BC \mid AC \mid AAC \mid d$$
$$A \to aA \mid a$$
$$B \to bB \mid b$$
$$C \to d$$

148. (*a*)

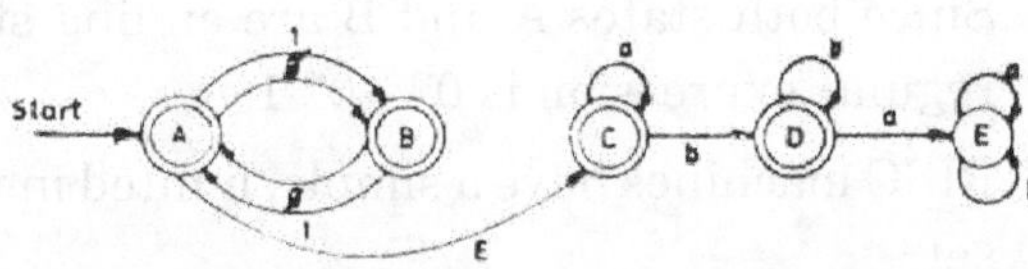

(*b*)

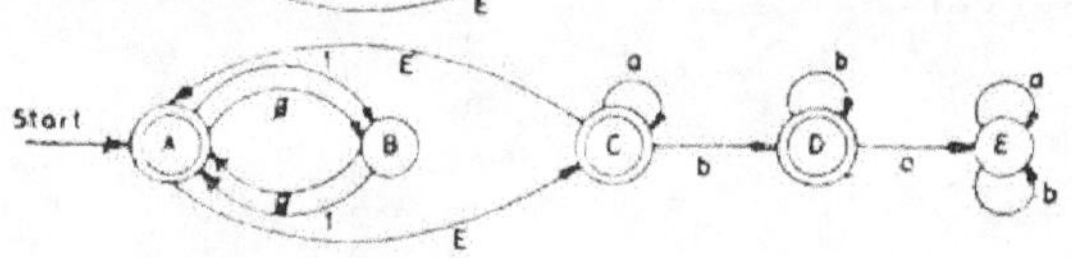

149. Parse tree is given as

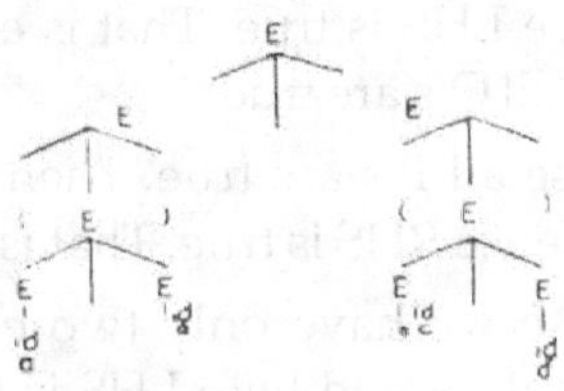

Translation $ab + cd$

150. $S \to \alpha S \quad \to \alpha\alpha S \quad \to \alpha\alpha\alpha bb$

$S \to \alpha ab$

$S \to \alpha S$

$\to \alpha\alpha S$

$\to \alpha\alpha ab$

Some language cannot generated by any grammar.

151. $\neg p \Rightarrow V$

$\Rightarrow$ pVV is true

Then $\neg pV(\neg pVq)$

It cannot be determined.

152. $E \Rightarrow XEY \mid XY$

$E \Rightarrow XEY$

$\Rightarrow XXEYY$

$\Rightarrow XXXYYY$

$\Rightarrow X^n\overline{Y}^n$

153.

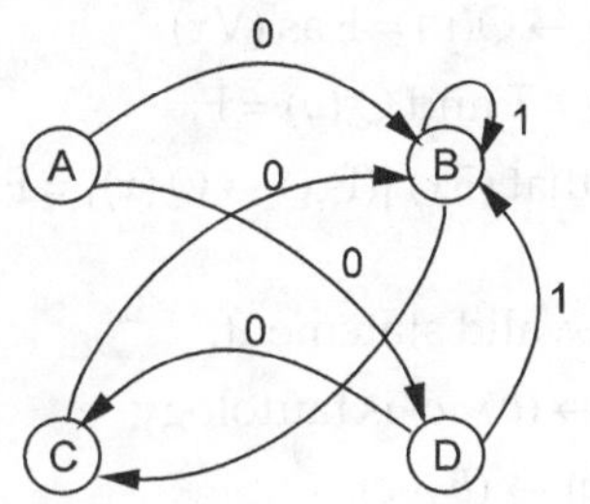

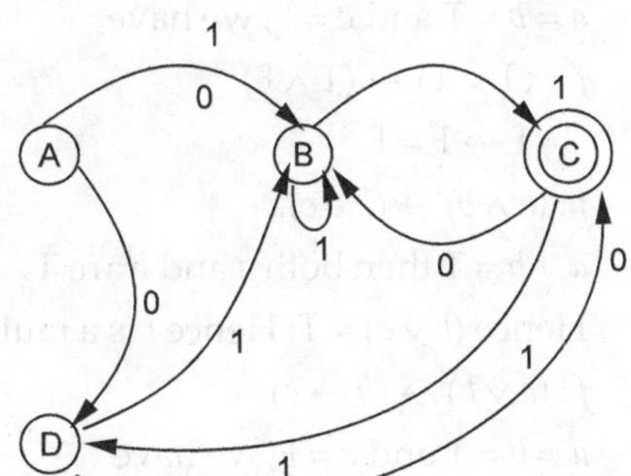

154. Given, ${}^1R = \{0^n\, 1^n$, such that $n > 0\}$

If $n = 1$, R = 01 not a regular

If $n > 1$ we said $R = 0^n\, 1^n$ is regular.

158. (*a*) and (*d*) are valid and (*b*) and (*bc*) are invalid.

If we want to prove $p \to q$; it is enough to prove if $p = T$ then $q = T$.

(*a*) $(\forall x) P(x) \vee (\forall x) Q(x) \to (\forall x), (P(x) \vee Q(x))$

Suppose LHS is true. That is either all P's are true or all Q's are true.

Suppose all P's are true. Then all (P V Q) are true. Hence RHS is true. That is (*a*) is valid.

(*b*) Suppose we have only two elements in our universal set and here LHS is true but RHS is false. Hence (*b*) is invalid.

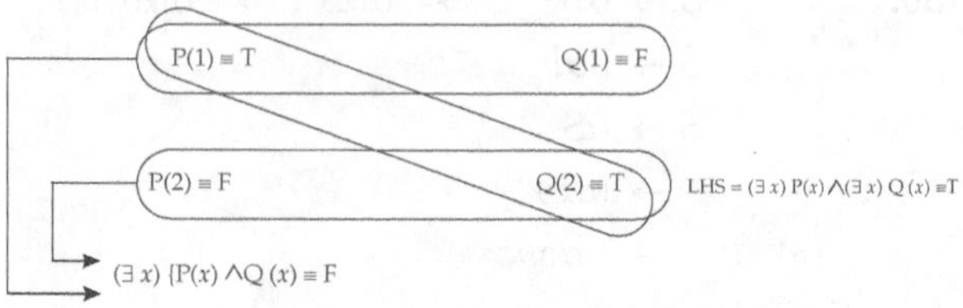

(*c*) Let $P_1 = Q_2 = T$ and $P_2 = Q_1 = .F.$

Then for every x at least P or Q is true and not all P and not all Q are true.

Hence $(\forall x) \{P(x) \vee Q(x)\} = T$

and $(\forall x) P(x) = F$ and $(\forall x) Q(x) = F$.

(*d*) Let RHS be false. Then

$\sim (\forall x) P(x) \vee (\exists x) Q(x) = F.$

That is $\sim (\forall x) P(x) = F$ and $(\exists x) Q(x) = F$.

Hence $(\forall x) P(x) = T$ and $(\exists x) Q(x) = F$.

Let $Q(Y) = F$.

Hence $P(y) \to Q(y) = F$ as $(\forall x)$

$P(x) = T$ and $Q(y) = F$.

This implies that $(\exists x) \{(P x) \to Q(x)\} = F$. That is LHS is false

Hence (*d*) is a valid statement.

159. (*b*) $(a \wedge b) \to (b \vee c)$ is tautology

(*a*) $f: (a \vee b) \to (b \wedge c)$.

For $a = b = T$ and $c = F$, we have

$f = (T \vee T) \to (T \wedge F)$

$= T \to F = F$

(*b*) $f: (a \wedge b) \to (b \vee c)$.

If $a \vee b = T$ then both *a* and *b* are T.

Hence $(b \vee c) = T$. Hence f is a tautology.

(*c*) $f: (a \vee b) \to (b \to c)$.

For $a = b = T$ and $c = F$, we have

$f = (T \vee T) \to (T \to F) = T \to F = F$

(*d*) $f: (a \to b) \to (b \to c)$.

For $a = F, b = T$ and $c = F$,

We have

$f = (F \to T) \to (T \to F) = T \to F = F$

NUMERICAL TYPE QUESTIONS

1. 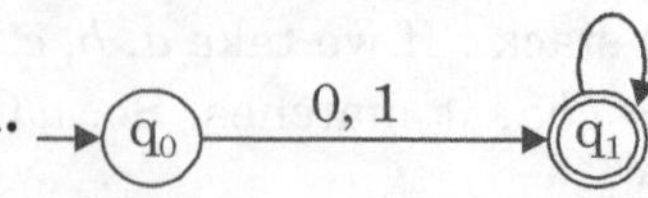

Given regular expression

$(r) = (0 + 1)^* (0 + 1) (0 + 1)^*$

$= 2$

So, the number of states in minimal DFA is 2.

2. $L(M) \cap L(N) = \Sigma^* - (\Sigma^* - L(M) \cup (\Sigma^* - L(N))$

$\Sigma^* - L(M) \Rightarrow$ 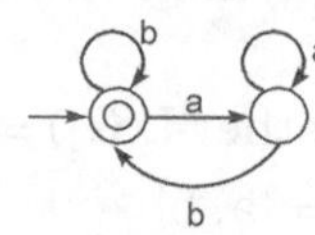

$\Sigma^* - L(N) \Rightarrow$ 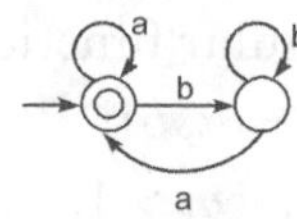

M accept all string end with a and N accept all string end with *b*. The intersection of both will accept empty language.

Hence

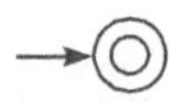

Then no. of state is 1.

3. 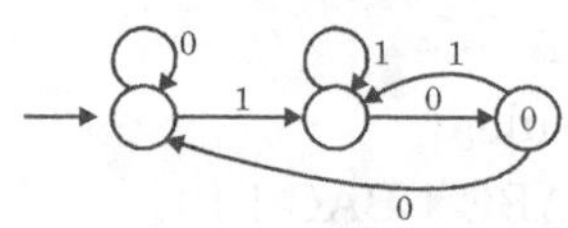

Ans = 3

4. R .E = a*b* (ba) *a*

Length 0 is present as it accepts ∈ all length 1 strings are present (a,b) also aa, ab, ba, bb are present, But 'bab ' is not present. So it is 3.

6. Since only A and B are end states we need not travers through 0 and reach the state C for finding regular expression.

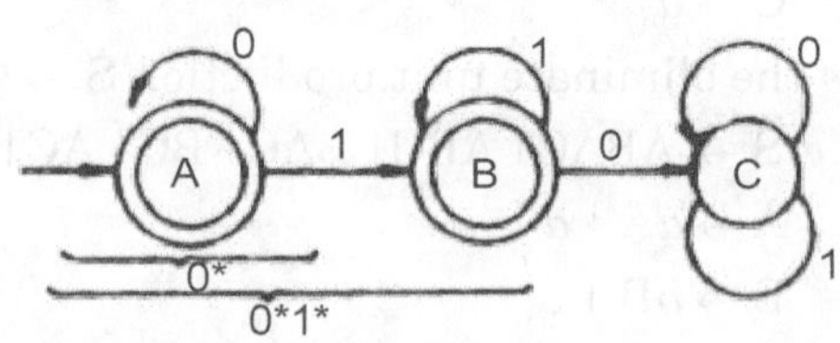

Since both states A and B are ending state, the regular expression is 0* --0* 1.

7. RISC machines have a simple, limited instruction set.

5

CHAPTER

Compiler Design

MCQ TYPE QUESTIONS

2016

1. Consider the following Syntax Directed Translation Scheme (SDTS), with non-terminals {S, A} and terminals **{a, b}**.

S → **aA** { print 1 }

S → **a** { print 2 }

A → **Sb** { print 3 }

Using the above SDTS, the output printed by a bottom-up parser, for the input **aab** is:

(*a*) 1 3 2 (*b*) 2 2 3

(*c*) 2 3 1 (*d*) syntax error

2. Match the following :

(P) Lexical analysis	(i) Leftmost derivation
(Q) Top down parsing	(ii) Type checking
(R) Semantic analysis	(iii) Regular expressions
(S) Runtime environments	(iv) Activation records

(*a*) P ↔ i, Q ↔ ii, R ↔ iv, S ↔ iii

(*b*) P ↔ iii, Q ↔ i, R ↔ ii, S ↔ iv

(*c*) P ↔ ii, Q ↔ iii, R ↔ i, S ↔ iv

(*d*) P ↔ iv, Q ↔ i, R ↔ ii, S ↔ iii

2015

3. Which one of the following is TRUE at any valid state in shift – reduce parsing ?

(*a*) Viable prefixes appear only at the bottom of the stack and not inside

(*b*) Viable prefixes appear only at the top of the stack and not inside

(*c*) The stack contains only a set of viable prefixes

(*d*) The stack never contains viable prefixes

4. For computers based on three-address instruction formats, each address field can be used to specify which of the following.

S1 : A memory operand

S2 : A processor register

S3 : An implied accumulator register

(*a*) Either S1 or S2

(*b*) Either S2 or S3

(*c*) only S2 and S3

(*d*) All of S1, S2 and S3

5. A variable x is said to be live at a statement S_i in a program if the following three conditions hold simultaneously :

I. There exists a statement S_j that uses x

II. There is a path from S_i to S_j in the flow graph corresponding to the program

III. The path has no intervening assignment to x including at S_i and S_j

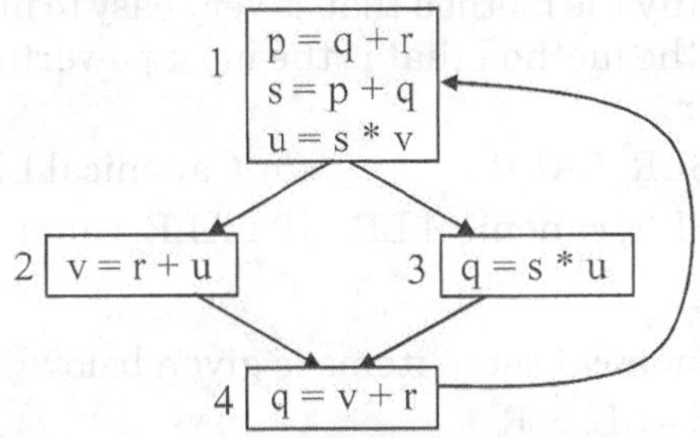

The variables which are live at the statement in basic block 2 and at the statement in basic block 3 of the above control flow graph are

(*a*) *p*, *s*, *u* (*b*) *r*, *s*, *u*

(*c*) *r*, *u* (*d*) *q*, *v*

6. In the context of abstract-syntax-tree (AST) and control-flow-graph (CFG), which one of the following is TRUE?

(*a*) In both AST and CFG, let node, N_2 be the successor of node N_1. In the input program, the code corresponding to N_2 is present after the code corresponding in N_1.

(*b*) For any input program, neither AST nor CFG will contain a cycle

(*c*) The maximum number of successors of a node in an AST and a CFG depends on the input program

(*d*) Each node is AST and CFG corresponds to at most one statement in the input program

7. Match the following :

(P) Lexical analysis	1. Graph coloring
(Q) Parsing	2. DFA minimization
(R) Register allocation	3. Post-order traversal
(S) Expression evaluation	4. Production tree

(*a*) P – 2, Q – 3, R – 1, S – 4

(*b*) P – 2, Q – 1, R – 4, S – 3

(*c*) P – 2, Q – 4, R – 1, S – 3

(*d*) P – 2, Q – 3, R – 4, S – 1

8. Consider the intermediate code given below.

1. i = 1
2. j = 1
3. t1 = 5 * i
4. t2 = t1 + j
5. t3 = 4 * t2
6. t4 = t3
7. a[t4] = –1
8. j = j + 1
9. if j <= 5 goto (3)
10. i = i + 1
11. if i < 5 goto 2

The number of nodes and edges in the control-flow-graph constructed for the above code, respectively, are

(*a*) 5 and 7 (*b*) 6 and 7
(*c*) 5 and 5 (*d*) 7 and 8

9. Among simple LR (SLR), canonical LR, and look ahead LR (LALR), which of the following pairs identify the method that is very easy to implement and the method that is the most powerful, in that order

(*a*) SLR. LALR (*b*) Canonical LR, LALR
(*c*) SLR, canonical LR (*d*) LALR, canonical LR

2014

10. A canonical set of items is given below

$S \rightarrow L. > R$
$Q \rightarrow R.$

On input symbol < the set has

(*a*) a shift-reduce conflict and a reduce-reduce conflict.
(*b*) a shift-reduce conflict but not a reduce-reduce conflict.
(*c*) a reduce-reduce conflict but not a shift-reduce conflict.
(*d*) neither a shift-reduce nor a reduce-reduce conflict.

11. Which one of the following is NOT performed during compilation?

(*a*) Dynamic memory allocation
(*b*) Type checking
(*c*) Symbol table management
(*d*) Inline expansion

12. One of the purposes of using intermediate code in compilers is to

(*a*) make parsing and semantic analysis simpler.
(*b*) improve error recovery and error reporting
(*c*) increase the chances of reusing the machine-independent code optimizer in other compliers.
(*d*) improve the register allocation.

13. Consider the basic block given below.

$a = b + c$
$c = a + d$
$d = b + c$
$e = d - b$
$a = e + b$

The minimum number of nodes and edges present in the DAG representation of the above basic block respectively are

(*a*) 6 and 6 (*b*) 8 and 10
(*c*) 9 and 12 (*d*) 4 and 4

2013

14. Consider the languages $L_1 = \Phi$ and $L_2 = \{a\}$. Which one of the following represents $L_1 L_2^* \cup L_1^*$?

(*a*) $\{\varepsilon\}$ (*b*) Φ
(*c*) a^* (*d*) $\{\varepsilon, a\}$

15. What is the maximum number of reduce moves that can be taken by a bottom-up parser for a grammar with no epsilon- and unit-production (i.e., of type $A \rightarrow \varepsilon$ and $A \rightarrow a$) to parse a string with n tokens?

(*a*) $n/2$ (*b*) $n - 1$
(*c*) $2n - 1$ (*d*) 2^n

16. Consider the following languages.

$L_1 = \{0^p 1^q 0^r \mid p, q, r \geq 0\}$
$L_2 = \{0^p 1^q 0^r \mid p, q, r \geq 0, p \neq r\}$

Which one of the following statements is FALSE?

(*a*) L_2 is context-free.
(*b*) $L_1 \cap L_2$ is context-free.
(*c*) Complement of L_2 is recursive.
(*d*) Complement of L_1 is context-free but not regular.

17. Consider the following two sets of LR(1) items of an LR(1) grammar.

X → c.X, c/d	X → c.X, $
X → .cX, c/d	X → .cX, $
X → .d, c/d	X → .d, $

Which of the following statements related to merging of the two sets in the corresponding LALR parser is/are **FALSE**?

1. Cannot be merged since look aheads are different.
2. Can be merged but will result in S-R conflict.
3. Can be merged but will result in R-R conflict.
4. Cannot be merged since goto on c will lead to two different sets.

(*a*) 1 only (*b*) 2 only
(*c*) 1 and 4 only (*d*) 1, 2, 3 and 4

2012

18. Which of the following problems are decidable?

1. Does a giv.en program ever produce an output?
2. If L is a context-free language, then, is $\overline{L}$ also context-free?

3. If L is a regular language, then, is $\bar{L}$ also regular?
4. If L is a recursive language, then, is $\bar{L}$ also recursive?

(a) 1, 2, 3, 4 (b) 1, 2
(c) 2, 3, 4 (d) 3, 4

19. Consider the program given below, in a block-structured pseudo-language with lexical scoping and nesting of procedures permitted.

```
Program main;
  Var ---
  Procedure A1;
    Var ...
    Call A2;
  End A1
  Procedure A2;
    Var ...
    Procedure A21;
      Var ...
      Call A1;
    End A21
    Call A21;
  End A2
  Call A1;
End main.
```

Consider the calling chain:

Main → A1 → A2 → A21 → A1

The correct set of activation records along with their access links is given by

(a)

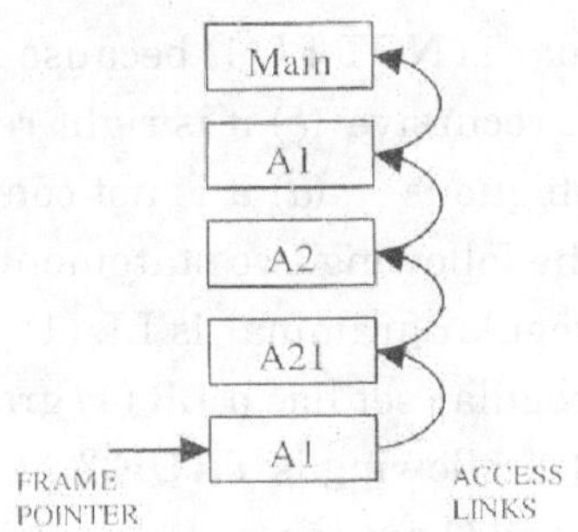

(b)

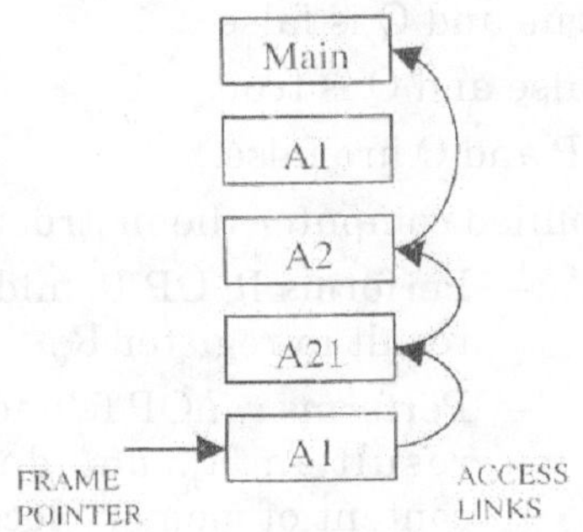

(c)

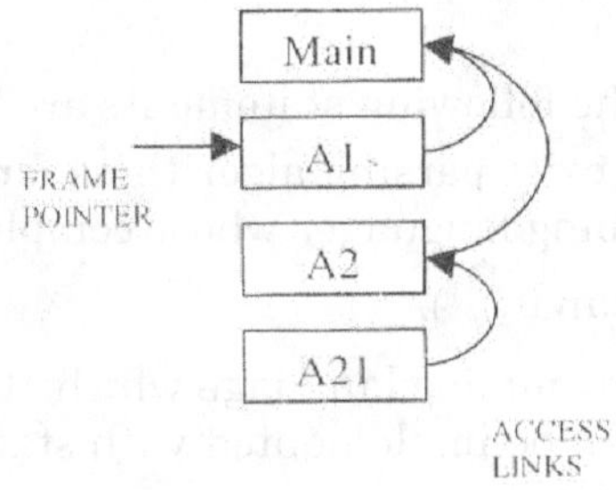

(d)

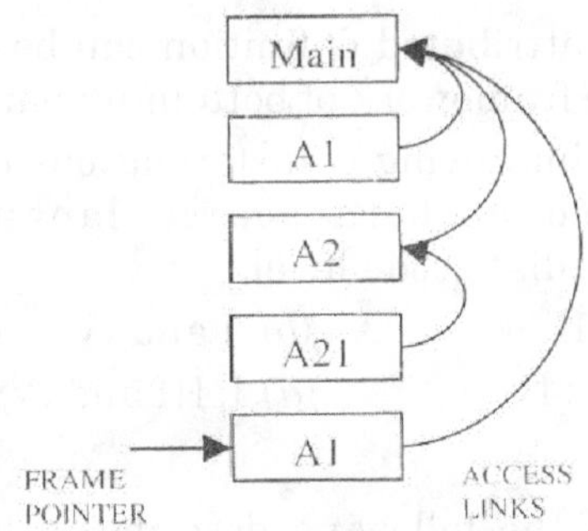

2011

20. In a compiler, keywords of a language are recognized during

(a) parsing of the program
(b) the code generation
(c) the lexical analysis of the program
(d) dataflow analysis

2010

21. Which data structure in a compiler is used for managing information about variables and their attributes?

(a) Abstract syntax tree
(b) Symbol table
(c) Semantic stack
(d) Parse table

22. Which languages necessarily need heap allocation in the runtime environment?

(a) Those that support recursion
(b) Those that use dynamic scoping
(c) Those that allow dynamic data structures
(d) Those that use global variables

23. The grammar S → aSa | bS | c is

(a) LL(1) but not LR(1)
(b) LR(1) but not LL(1)
(c) Both LL(1) and LR(1)
(d) Neither LL(1) nor LR(1)

2009

24. What of the following statements are TRUE ?

I. There exist parsing algorithms for some pro gramming languages whose complexities are less than $\theta(n^3)$.

II. A programming language which allows recur sion can be implemented with static storage allocation.

III. No L-attributed definition can be evaluated in the framework of bottom-up parsing.

IV. Code improving transformations can be per formed at both source language and itermediate code level.

(*a*) I and II (*b*) I and IV

(*c*) III and IV (*d*) I, III and IV

2008

25. Which of the following describes a handle (as applicable to LR-parsing) appropriately?

(*a*) It is the position in a sentential form where the next shift or reduce operation will occur

(*b*) It is a non-terminal whose production will be used for reduction in the next step

(*c*) It is a production that may be used for reduction in a future step along with a position in the sentential form where the next shift or reduce operation will occur

(*d*) It is the production p that will be used for reduction in the next step along with a position in the sentential form where the right hand side of the production may be found

26. Some code optimizations are carried out on the intermediate code because

(*a*) they enhance the portability of the compiler to other target processors

(*b*) program analysis is more accurate on intermediate code than on machine code

(*c*) the information from dataflow analysis cannot otherwise be used for optimization

(*d*) the information from the front end cannot otherwise be used for optimization

27. Which of the following are true?

I. A programming language which does not permit global variables of any kind and has no nesting of procedures/functions, but permits recursion can be implemented with static storage allocation

II. Multi-level access link (or display) arrangment is needed to arrange activation records only if the programming language being implemented has nesting of procedures/functions

III. Recursion in programming languages cannot be implemented with dynamic storage allocation

IV. Nesting of procedures/functions and recursion require a dynamic heap allocation scheme and cannot be implemented with a stack-based allocation scheme for activation records

V. Programming languages which permit a function to return a function as its result cannot be implemented with a stack-based storage allocation scheme for activation records

(*a*) II and V only (*b*) I, III and IV only

(*c*) I, II and V only (*d*) I, III and V only

28. An LALR(1) parser for a grammar G can have shift-reduce (S-R) conflicts if and only if

(*a*) the SLR(1) parser G has S-R conflicts

(*b*) The LR(1) paser for G has S-R conflicts

(*c*) The LR(0) parser for G has S-R conflicts

(*d*) The LALR(1) parser for G has reduce-reduce conflicts

2007

29. Which one of the following is a top-down parser?

(*a*) Recursive descent parser

(*b*) Operator precedence parser

(*c*) An LR(k) parser

(*d*) An LALR(k) parser

30. Consider the grammer with non-terminals N = {S, C, S_1}, terminals T = {*a*, *b*, *i*, *t*, *e*}, with S as the start symbol, and the following set of rules

$$S \rightarrow iCtSS_1 \mid a$$
$$S_1 \rightarrow eS \mid \varepsilon$$
$$C \rightarrow b$$

The grammar is **NOT** LL(1) because :

(*a*) It is left recursive (*b*) it is right recursive

(*c*) it is ambiguous (*d*) it is not context-free

31. Consider the following two statements :

P : Every regular grammar is LL (1)

Q : Every regular set has a LR (1) grammar

Which of the following is **TRUE** ?

(*a*) Both P and Q are true

(*b*) P is true and Q is false.

(*c*) P is false and Q is true.

(*d*) Both P and Q are false.

32. In a simplified computer the instructions are :

OP R_j, R_i – Performs R_j OP R_i and stores the result in register R_i.

OP *m*, R_i – Performs *val* OP R_i and stores the result in R_i. *val* denotes the content of memory location *m*.

MOV *m*, R_i – Moves the content of memory location *m* to register R_i.

MOV R_i,*m* – Moves the content of register R_i to memory location *m*.

The computer has only two registers, and OP is either ADD or SUB. Consider following basic block :

$t_1 = a + b$
$t_2 = c + d$
$t_3 = e - t_2$
$t_4 = t_1 - t_3$

Assume that all operands are initially in memory. The final value of the computation should be in memory. What is the minimum number of MOV instructions in the code generated for this basic block?

(*a*) 2 (*b*) 3
(*c*) 5 (*d*) 6

2006

33. Consider the following grammar :

S → S*E
S → E
E → F + E
E → F
F → *id*

Consider the following LR(0) items corresponding to the grammar above :

(*i*) S → S * .E (*ii*) E → F. + E
(*iii*) E → F + .E

Given the items above, which two of them will appear in the same set in the canonical sets-of-items for the grammar ?

(*a*) (*i*) and (*ii*) (*b*) (*ii*) and (*iii*)
(*c*) (*i*) and (*iii*) (*d*) None of these

34. Consider the following translation scheme :

S → ER
R → *E {print ("*"); R | ε
E → F + E {print ('+'); | F
F → (S) | *id* {print (*id*. value);}

Here *id* is a taken that represents an integer and *id. value* represents the corresponding integer value. For an input '2 * 3 + 4', this translation scheme prints

(*a*) 2 * 3 + 4 (*b*) 2 * + 3 4
(*c*) 2 3 * 4 + (*d*) 2 3 4 + *

35. Consider the following C code segment :

```
for (i = 0; i < N ; i ++ )
        for (j = 0; j < N ; j ++)
        if(i % 2)
                {x + = (4 * j + 5 * i);
                y + = (7 + 4 * j);
                }
        }
}
```

Which one of the following is false ?

(*a*) The code contains loop-in variant computation
(*b*) There is scope of common sub-expression elimination in this code
(*c*) There is scope of strength reduction in this code
(*d*) There is scope of dead code elimination in this code

2005

36. The grammar A → AA | (A) | e is not suitable for predictive-parsing because the grammar is

(*a*) ambiguous (*b*) left-recursive
(*c*) right-recurisve (*d*) an operator-grammar

37. Consider the grammar

E → E + *n* | E *n* | *n*

For a sentence *n* + *n n*, the handles in the right-sentential form of the reduction are

(*a*) *n*, E + *n* and E + *n n*
(*b*) *n*, E + *n* and E + E *n*
(*c*) *n*, *n* + *n* and *n* + *n n*
(*d*) *n*, E + *n* and E *n*

38. Consider the grammar :

S → (S) | *a*

Let the number of states in SLR (1), LR (1) and LALR (1) parsers for the grammar be n_1, n_2 and n_3 respectively. Which of the following relationship holds good ?

(*a*) $n_1 < n_2 < n_3$ (*b*) $n_1 = n_3 < n_2$
(*c*) $n_1 = n_2 = n_3$ (*d*) $n_1 \geq n_3 \geq n_2$

39. Consider line number 3 of the following C-program :

```
int main () {  /* Line 1 */
imt I, N;      /* Line 2 * /
fro (I = 0, I < N, I + +);/* Line 3 */
}
```

Identify the compiler's response about this line while creating the object –module

(*a*) No compilation error
(*b*) Only a lexical error
(*c*) Only syntactic errors
(*d*) Both lexical and syntactic errors

Linked Answer Q. 40 - 41

Consider the following expression grammar :

The semantic rules for expression calculation are stated next to each grammar production.

E → numberE.val = number. val
| E '+' EE$^{(1)}$. val = E$^{(2)}$. val + E$^{(3)}$. val
| E '×' EE$^{(1)}$. val = E$^{(2)}$. val × E$^{(3)}$. val;

40. The above grammar and the semantic rules are fed to a yacc tool (which is an LALR (1) parser generator) for parsing and evaluating arithmetic expressions. Which one of the following is true about the action of yacc for the given grammar?

(*a*) It detects recursion and eliminates recursion

(*b*) It detects reduce-reduce conflict, and resolves

(*c*) It detects shift-reduce conflict, and resolves the conflict in favor of a shift over a reduce action

(*d*) It detects shift-reduce conflict, and resolves the conflict in favor of a reduce over a shift action

41. Assume the conflicts in Part (*a*) of this question are resolved and an LALR (1) parser is generated for parsing arithmetic expressions as per the given grammar. Consider an expression $3 \times 2 + 1$. What precedence and associativity properties does the generated parser realize?

(*a*) Equal precedence and left associativity; expression is evaluated to 7

(*b*) Equal precedence and right associativity; expression is evaluated to 9

(*c*) Precedence of '×' is higher than that of '+', and both operators are left associative; expression is evaluated to 7

(*d*) Precedence of '+' is higher than that of '×', and both operators are left associative; expression is evaluaterd to 9

2004

42. Which of the following grammar rules violate the requirements of an operator grammar ? P, Q, R are nonterminals, and *r*, *s*, *t* are terminals.

(*i*) $P \rightarrow Q\ R$ (*ii*) $P \rightarrow Q\ s\ R$

(*iii*) $P \rightarrow \varepsilon$ (*iv*) $P \rightarrow Q\ t\ R\ r$

(*a*) (*i*) only (*b*) (*i*) and (*iii*) only

(*c*) (*ii*) and (*iii*) only (*d*) (*iii*) and (*iv*) only

43. Consider a program P that consists of two source modules M_1 and M_2 contained in two different files. If M_1 contains a reference to a function defined in M_2, the reference will be resolved at

(*a*) Edit-time (*b*) Compile-time

(*c*) Link-time (*d*) Load-time

44. Consider the grammar rule $E \rightarrow E_1 - E_2$ for arithmetic expressions. The code generated is targeted to a CPU having a single user register. The subtraction operation requires the first operand to be in the register. If E_1 and E_2 do not have any common subexpression, in order to get the shortest possible code

(*a*) E_1 should be evaluated first

(*b*) E_2 should be evaluated first

(*c*) Evaluation of E_1 and E_2 should necessarily be interleaved

(*d*) Order of evaluation of E_1 and E_2 is of no consequence

45. Consider the grammar with the following translation rules and E as the start symbol :

$E \rightarrow E_1\ \#\ T\{\ E.value = E_1.value * T.value\ \}$
$\quad\mid T\{\ E.value = T.value\ \}$
$T \rightarrow T_1\ \&\ F\{\ T.value = T_1.value + F.value\ \}$
$\quad\mid F\{\ T.value = F.value\}$
$F \rightarrow num\{\ F.value = num.value\ \}$

Compute E value for the root of the parse tree for the expression :

2 # 3 & 5 # 6 & 4.

(*a*) 200 (*b*) 180

(*c*) 160 (*d*) 40

2003

46. Which of the following suffices to convert an arbitrary CFG to an LL(1) grammar ?

(*a*) Removing left recursion alone

(*b*) Factoring the grammar alone

(*c*) Removing left recursion and factoring the grammar

(*d*) None of these

47. Assume that the SLR parser for a grammar G has n_1 states and the LALR parser for G has n_2 states. The relationship between n_1 and n_2 is

(*a*) n_1 is necessarily less than n_2

(*b*) n_1 is necessarily equal to n_2

(*c*) n_1 is necessarily greater than n_2

(*d*) none of these

48. In a bottom-up evaluation of a syntax directed definition, inherited attributes can

(*a*) always be evaluated

(*b*) be evaluated only if the definition is L-attributed

(*c*) be evaluated only if the definition has synthesized attributes

(*d*) never be evaluated

49. Which of the following statements is FALSE ?

(*a*) In statically typed language, each variable in a program has a fixed type

(*b*) In un-typed languages, values do not have any types

(*c*) In dynamically typed languages, variables have no types

(*d*) In all statically typed languages, each variable in a program is associated with values of only a single type during the execution of the program

50. Consider the grammar shown below :

$S \to i\,E\,t\,S\,S' \mid a$

$S' \to e\,S \mid \varepsilon$

$E \to b$

In the predictive parse table. M, of this grammar, the entries M[S', *e*] and M[S', $] respectively are

(*a*) {$S' \to e\,S$} and {$S' \to e$}

(*b*) {$S' \to e\,S$} and { }

(*c*) {$S' \to \varepsilon$} and {$S' \to \varepsilon$}

(*d*) {$S' \to e\,S, S\,\varepsilon$} and {$S' \to \varepsilon$}

51. Consider the grammar shown below :

$S \to C\,C$

$C \to c\,C \mid d$

The grammar is

(*a*) LL (1)

(*b*) SLR (1) but not LL (1)

(*c*) LALR (1) but not SLR (1)

(*d*) LR (1) but not LALR (1)

52. Consider the translation scheme shown below :

$S \to T\,R$

$R \to +\,T$ {print ('+');} R | ε

$T \to$ num {print (num.val);}

Here num is a token that represents an integer and num.val represents the corresponding integer value. For an input string '9 + 5 + 2', this translation scheme will print

(*a*) 9 + 5 + 2 (*b*) 9 5 + 2 +

(*c*) 9 5 2 + + (*d*) + + 9 5 2

53. Consider syntax directed definition shown below :

$S \to id := E$ {gen (*id*.place = E.place;);}

$E \to E_1 + E_2$ {t = newtemp ( );
gen ($t = E_1$. place + E_2.place;);
E.place = t}

$E \to id$ {E.place = *id*.place;}

Here, gen is a function that generates the output code, and newtemp is a function that returns the name of a new temporary variable on every call. Assume that t_i's are the temporary variable names generated by newtemp.

For the statement 'X: = Y + Z', the 3-address code sequence generated by this definition is

(*a*) X = Y + Z

(*b*) t_1 = Y + Z; X t_1

(*c*) t_1 = Y; $t_2 = t_1$ + Z; X = t_2

(*d*) t_1 = Y; t_2 = Z; $t_3 = t_1 + t_2$; X = t_3

Common Data Q. 54 - 55

The following program fragment is written in a programming language that allows variables and does not allow nested declarations of functions.

```
global int i = 100, j =5;
void P (x) {
    int i = 10;
    print (x + 10);
    i = 200;
    j = 20;
    print (x);
}
main ( ) {P (i + j);}
```

54. If the programming language uses static scoping and call by need parameter passing mechanism, the values printed by the above program are

(*a*) 115, 220 (*b*) 25, 220

(*c*) 25, 15 (*d*) 115, 105

55. If the programming language uses dynamic scoping and call by name parameter passing mechanism, the values printed by the above program are

(*a*) 115, 220 (*b*) 25, 220

(*c*) 25, 15 (*d*) 115, 105

56. Consider the following class definitions in a hypothetical Object Oriented language that supports inheritance and uses dynamic binding. The language should not be assumed to be either Java or C ++, though the syntax is similar.

```
Class P {                    Class Q subclass of P {
    void f (int i) {             void f (int i) {
        print (i);                   print (2*i);
    }                            }
}                            }
```

Now consider the following program fragment:

```
P x = new Q ( );
Q y = new Q ( );
P z = new Q ( );
x.f(1); ((P) y).f(1); z.f(1);
```

Here ((P) *y*) denotes a typecast of *y* to P. The output produced by executing the above program fragment will be

(*a*) 1 2 1 (*b*) 2 1 1

(*c*) 2 1 2 (*d*) 2 2 2

57. Which of the following is NOT an advantage of using shared, dynamically linked libraries as opposed to using statically linked libraries ?

(*a*) Smaller sizes of executable files

(*b*) Lesser overall page fault rate in the system

(*c*) Faster program startup

(*d*) Existing programs need not be re-linked to take advantage of newer versions of libraries

2000

58. Which of the following derivations does a top-down parser use while parsing an input string? The input is assumed to be scanned in left to right order.

(*a*) Leftmost derivation

(*b*) Leftmost derivation traced out in reverse

(*c*) Rightmost derivation

(*d*) Rightmost derivation traced out in reverse

59. Consider the syntax directed translation scheme (SDTS) given in the following. Assume attribute evaluation with bottom-up parsing, i.e., attributes are evaluated immediately after a reduction.

$E \rightarrow E_1 * T \quad \{E.val = E_1.val * T.val\}$

$E \rightarrow T \{E.val = T.val\}$

$T \rightarrow F - T_1 \{T.val = F.val - T_1.val\}$

$T \rightarrow F \quad \{T.val = F.val\}$

$F \rightarrow 2 \quad \{F.val = 2\}$

$F \rightarrow 4 \quad \{F.val = 4\}$

(*a*) Using this SDTS, construct a parse tree for the expression

$4 - 2 - 4 * 2$

and also compute its E . val.

(*b*) It is required to compute the total number of reductions performed to parse a given input. Using synthsized attributes only, modify the SDTS given, without changing the grammar, to find E.red, the number of reductions performed while reducing an input to E.

1999

60. Let L be a set with a relation R which is transitive, anti-symmetric and reflexive and for any two elements a, b ∈ L let the least upper bound lub (*a*, b) and the greatest lower bound glb (*a*, b) exist. Which of the following is/are true ?

(*a*) L is a poset (*b*) L is a boolean algebra

(*c*) L is a lattice (*d*) None of these

61. A grammar that is both left and right recursive for a non-terminal, is

(*a*) Ambiguous

(*b*) Unambiguous

(*c*) Information is not sufficient to decide whether it is ambiguous or unambiguous

(*d*) None of these

62. Let synthesized attribute val give the value of binary number generated by S in the following grammar. For example, on input 101, 101, S.val = 5.625.

S → LL\L

L → LB\B

B → 0\1

Write S-attributed values corresponding to each of the productions to find S.val.

1998

63. In a resident – OS computer, which of the following systems must reside in the main memory under all situations ?

(*a*) Assembler (*b*) Linker

(*c*) Loader (*d*) Compiler

64. Which of the following statements is true ?

(*a*) SLR parser is more powerful than LALR.

(*b*) LALR parser is more powerful than Canonical LR parser.

(*c*) Canonical LR parser is more powerful than LALR parser.

(*d*) The parsers SLR, Canonical CR, and LALR have the same power.

65. Type checking is normally done during

(*a*) lexical analysis

(*b*) syntax analysis

(*c*) syntax directed translation

(*d*) code optimization

66. A linker reads four modules whose lengths are 200, 800, 600 and 500 words, respectively. If they are loaded in that order, what are the relocation constants ?

(*a*) 0, 200, 500, 600

(*b*) 0, 200, 1000, 1600

(*c*) 200, 500, 600, 800

(*d*) 200, 700, 1300, 2100

67. (*a*) Let $G_1 = (N, T, P, S_1)$ be a CFG where,

$N = \{S_1, A, B\} T = \{a, b\}$ and

P is given by

$S_1 \rightarrow a, S_1 b \qquad S_1 \rightarrow a B b$

$S_1 \rightarrow a A b \qquad B \rightarrow Bb$

$A \rightarrow a A \qquad B \rightarrow b$

$A \rightarrow a$

What is $L(G_1)$?

(*b*) Use the grammar in Part (*a*) to give a CFG for $L_2 = \{a^i b^j a^k b^1 \mid i, j, k, 1 \,^3\, 1, i = j \text{ or } k = 1\}$ by adding not more than 5 production rules.

(*c*) Is L_2 inherently ambiguous ?

68. (*a*) An identifier in a programming language consists of upto six letters and digits of which the first character must be a letter. Derive a regular expression for the identifier.

(*b*) Build an LL (1) parsing table for the language defined by the LL(1) grammar with productions

Program → begin d semi X end

X → d semi X | sY

Y → semi s Y | ∈

69. Let the attribute 'val' give the value of a binary number generated by S in the following gramar

S → L. L | L

L → LB | B

B → 0 | 1

For example, an input 101.101 give S.val = 5.625

Construct a syntax directed translation scheme using only synthesized attributes, to determine S.val.

1997

70. In the following grammar

$$X ::= X \oplus \frac{Y}{Y}$$

$$Y :: Z * \frac{Y}{Z}$$

Z : : = id

Which of the following is true ?

(*a*) '⊕' is left associative while '*' is right associative

(*b*) Both '⊕' and '*' are left associative

(*c*) '⊕' is right associative while '*' is left associative

(*d*) None of these

71. A language L allows declaration of arrays whose sizes are not known during compilation. It is required to make efficient use of memory. Which one of the following is true ?

(*a*) A compiler using static memory allocation can be written for L

(*b*) A compiler cannot be written for L; an interpreter must be used.

(*c*) A compiler using dynamic memory allocation can be written for L

(*d*) None of the above.

72. Given $\Sigma = \{a, b\}$, which one of the following sets is not countable ?

(*a*) Set of all strings over Σ

(*b*) Set of all languages over Σ

(*c*) Set of all regular languages over Σ

(*d*) Set of all languages over Σ accepted by Turning machines

73. Consider the grammar

S → *b*S*e*

S → PQR

P → *b*P*c*

P → ε

Q → *c*Q*d*

Q → ε

R → *d*R*e*

R → ε

where S, P, Q, R are non-terminal symbols with S being the start symbol ; *b, c, d, e* are terminal symbols and 'ε' is the empty string. This grammar generates strings of the form b^i, c^j, d^k, e^m for some $i, j, k, m \le 0$.

(*a*) What is the condition on the values of *i, j, k, m*?

(*b*) Find the smallest string that has two parse trees.

74. The language L, defined by the following grammar, allows use of real or integer data in expressions and assignment statements.

⟨assign – stmt⟩ : : ⟨LHS⟩ : = ⟨E⟩

⟨E⟩ : : = ⟨E⟩ + ⟨T⟩ | ⟨T⟩

⟨T⟩ : : = ⟨T⟩ * ⟨V⟩ | ⟨V⟩

⟨V⟩ : : = *id* | (⟨E⟩)

⟨LHS⟩ : : *id*

It is required to convert expression and assignment strings of L into postfix strings that use the type-specific operations (+, *i*) (+, *r*), (*, *i*), (*, *r*), (: =, *i*) and (: =, *r*)

Write a syntax directed translation scheme to convert expression and assignment strings into the post-fix form. You may assume that the name and type of a variable can be obtained by making the function calls' give-type (*id*) and give-name (*id*)* respectively.

1996

75. The pass numbers for each of the following activities

(*i*) object code generation

(*ii*) literals added to literal table

(*iii*) listing printed

(*iv*) address resolution of local symbols that occur in a two pass assembler respectively are

(*a*) 1, 2, 1, 2 (*b*) 2, 1, 2, 1

(*c*) 2, 1, 1, 2 (*d*) 1, 2, 2, 2

76. The grammar whose productions are

→ if id then < stmt >

→ if id then < stmt > else <stmt >

→ id : = id

is ambiguous because

(*a*) the sentence if *a* then if *b* then *c* : = *d*

(*b*) the left most and right most derivations of the sentence if *a* then if *b* then *c* : = *d* give rise top different parse tress

(*c*) the sentence if *a* then if *b* then *c* : = *d* else *c* : = *f* has more than two parse trees

(*d*) the sentence if a then if then *c* := *d* else *c* : = *f* has two parse trees.

77. Which of the following macros can put a macro assembler into an infinite loop ?

(i)
```
MACRO        M1, X
IF EQ, X :if X = 0 then ....
M1 X + 1
ENDC
IF NE, X :if X ≠ O then .....
WORD X :address (X) is stored here
ENDC
ENDM
```

(ii)
```
MACRO M2, X
IF EQ, X
M2 X
ENDC
IF NE, X
WORD X + 1
ENDC
ENDM
```

(a) (ii) only (b) (i) only

(c) both (i) and (ii) (d) none of these

78. The correct matching for the following pairs is

(A) Activation record	(1) Linking loader
(B) Location counter	(2) Garbage collection
(C) Reference counts	(3) Subroutine call
(D) Address relocation	(4) Assembler

(a) A–3, B–4, C– 1, D–2

(b) A–4, B–3, C–1, D–2

(c) A–4, B–3, C–2, D–1

(d) A–3, B–4, C–2, D–1

1995

79. In the following Pascal program segment, what is the value of X after the execution of the program segment ?

X : = –10; y: = 20;

If X > Y, then if X < 0 then X : = *abs* (X) else X : = 2* X;

(a) 10 (b) –20

(c) –10 (d) None of these

80. In some programming languages, an identifier is permitted to be a letter following by any number of letters or digits. If L and D denote the sets of letters and digits respectively, which of the following expressions defines an identifier ?

(a) $(L \cup D)^+$ (b) $L(L \cup D)^*$

(c) $(L.D)^*$ (d) $L.(L.D)^*$

81. What are *x* and *y* in the following macro definition?

```
macro        Add x, y
             Load y
             Mul x
             Store y
end macro
```

(a) Variables

(b) Identifiers

(c) Actual parameters

(d) Formal parameters

82. What is the distance of the following code ? 000000, 010101, 000111, 011001, 111111

(a) 2 (b) 3

(c) 4 (d) 1

83. Which of the following strings can definitely be said to be tokens without looking at the next input character while compiling a Pascal progam ?

I. begin

II. program

III. < >

(a) I (b) II

(c) III (d) All of these

84. A linker is given object modules for a set of programs that were compiled separately. What information need not be included in an object module ?

(a) Object code

(b) Relocation bits

(c) Names and locations of all external symbols defined in the object module

(d) Absolute addresses of internal symbols

85. Assume that X and Y are nonzero positive integers. What does the following Pascal program segment do ?

```
while     X < > Y do
if        X > Y then
              X : = X – Y
else
              Y : = Y – X;
write (X);
```

(a) Computes the LCM of two numbers

(b) Divides the larger number by the smaller number

(c) Computes the GCD of two numbers

(d) None of the above

86. A shift reduce parser carries out the actions specified within braces immediately after reducing with the corresponding rule of grammar

$S \rightarrow xxW$ {print "1"}

$S \rightarrow y$ {print "2"}

$W \rightarrow Sz$ {print "3"}

What is the translation of *xxxxyzz* using the syntax directed translation scheme described by the above rules ?

(*a*) 23131 (*b*) 11233

(*c*) 11231 (*d*) 33211

87. A variant record in Pascal is defined by

```
type varirec        = record
                      number : integer;
                      case (var1, var2) of
                      var1 : (x, y : integer);
                      var2 : (p.q. : real)
           end
    end
```

Suppose an array of 100 records was declared on a machine which uses 4 bytes for an integer and 8 bytes for a real. How much space would the compiler have to reserve for the array ?

(*a*) 2800 (*b*) 2400

(*c*) 2000 (*d*) 1200

1994

88. FORTRAN implementation do not permit recursion because

(*a*) they use static allocation for variables

(*b*) they use dynamic allocation for variables

(*c*) stacks are not available on all machines

(*d*) it is not possible to implement recursion on all machines

1993

89. The value of *m*, output by the program PARAM is

(*a*) 1, because *m* is a local variable in *P*

(*b*) 0, because *m* is the actual parameter that corresponds to the formal parameter *y* in *p*

(*c*) 0, because both *x* and *y* are just reference to *m*, and *y* has the value 0

(*d*) 1, because both *x* and *y* are just references to m which gets modified in procedure *P*

(*e*) none of the above

90. The value of n, output by the program PARAM is

(*a*) 0, because *n* is the actual parameter corresponding to x in procedure Q.

(*b*) 0, because *n* is the actual parameter to *y* in procedure Q.

(*c*) 1, because *n* is the actual parameter corresponding to *x* in procedure Q.

(*d*) 1, because *n* is the actual parameter corresponding to *y* in procedure Q.

(*e*) none of the above

1992

91. For a context-free grammar, FOLLOW (A) is the set of terminals that can appear immediately to the right of non-terminal A in some "sentential" form. We define two sets LFOLLOW (A) and RFOLLOW (A) by replacing the word "sentential" by "left most sentential" and "right most sentential" respectively in the definition of FOLLOW (A).

Which of the following statements is/are true?

(*a*) FOLLOW (A) and FOLLOW (A) may be different.

(*b*) FOLLOW (A) and RFOLLOW (A) are always the same.

(*c*) All the three sets are identical.

(*d*) All the three sets are different.

92. Consider the SLR (1) and LALR (1) parsing tables for a context free grammar. Which of the following statements is/are true ?

(*a*) The go to part of both tables may be different.

(*b*) The shift entries are identical in both the tables.

(*c*) The reduce entries in the tables may be different.

(*d*) The error entries in the tables may be different.

NUMERICAL TYPE QUESTIONS

2016

1. Consider the following code segment.

```
x = u – t;
y = x * v;
x = y + w;
y = t – z;
y = x * y;
```

The minimum number of *total* variables required to convert the above code segment to *static single assignment* form is _______ .

2015

2. The least number of temporary variables required to create a three-address code in static single assignment form for the expression $q + r/3 + s - t * 5 + u * v/w$ is ______.

1995

3. What is the value of X printed by the following program ?

```
program COMPUTE (input, output);
var
    X : integer;
procedure FIND (X: real);
    begin
```

1993

4. Note: For sub-questions 7.1 to 7.3, refer to the Pascal program shown below

```
    Program PARAM (input, ouput);
    var m, n : integer;
    procedure P (var x, y : integer);
        var m : integer;
        begin
            m : = 1;
            x : = y + 1
        end;
    procedure Q (x : integer; var y : integer);
        begin
            x : = y + 1;
        end;
    begin
        m : = 0; P (m, m); write (m);
        n : = 0; Q (n*1, n); write (n)
    end
```

ANSWERS

MCQ Type Questions

1. (*c*)	**2.** (*b*)	**3.** (*c*)	**4.** (*a*)	**5.** (*c*)	**6.** (*c*)	**7.** (*c*)	**8.** (*b*)	**9.** (*c*)	**10.** (*d*)
11. (*a*)	**12.** (*c*)	**13.** (*a*)	**14.** (*d*)	**15.** (*a*)	**16.** (*d*)	**17.** (*d*)	**18.** (*d*)	**19.** (*d*)	**20.** (*c*)
21. (*b*)	**22.** (*c*)	**23.** (*c*)	**24.** (*c*)	**25.** (*d*)	**26.** (*a*)	**27.** (*d*)	**28.** (*b*)	**29.** (*a*)	**30.** (*c*)
31. (*a*)	**32.** (*b*)	**33.** (*c*)	**34.** (*d*)	**35.** (*b*)	**36.** (*b*)	**37.** (*d*)	**38.** (*b*)	**39.** (*c*)	**40.** (*c*)
41. (*c*)	**42.** (*a*)	**43.** (*c*)	**44.** (*b*)	**45.** (*c*)	**46.** (*c*)	**47.** (*b*)	**48.** (*c*)	**49.** (*a*)	**50.** (*a*)
51. (*d*)	**52.** (*d*)	**53.** (*c*)	**54.** (*d*)	**55.** (*a*)	**56.** (*d*)	**57.** (*d*)	**58.** (*a*)	**59.** (*)	**60.** (*a, c*)
61. (*c*)	**62.** (*)	**63.** (*c*)	**64.** (*c*)	**65.** (*c*)	**66.** (*b*)	**67.** (*)	**68.** (*)	**69.** (*)	**70.** (*a*)
71. (*c*)	**72.** (*b*)	**73.** (*)	**74.** (*)	**75.** (*b*)	**76.** (*d*)	**77.** (*a*)	**78.** (*b*)	**79.** (*c*)	**80.** (*b*)
81. (*d*)	**82.** (*a*)	**83.** (*c*)	**84.** (*d*)	**85.** (*c*)	**86.** (*a*)	**87.** (*c*)	**88.** (*d*)	**89.** (*d*)	**90.** (*a*)
91. (*)	**92.** (*b*)								

Numerical Type Questions

1. (7)	**2.** (8)	**3.** (*a*)	**4.** (*)

EXPLANATIONS

MCQ TYPE QUESTIONS

1.

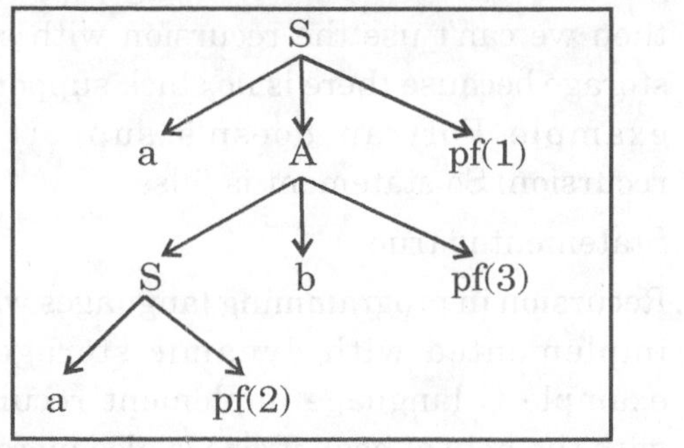

3. In shift reduce parser, the stack contains only a set of variable prefix.

4. In three address instruction format, each address field can be used to specify memory operand and processor register

e.g. $R = R_1 + R_2$

7. The match are as follows

Lexical analysis – DFA minimization

Parsing – Production Tree

Register allocation – Graph coloring

expression evaluation – Post order traversal

9. SLR and CLR are easy to implement. CLR is more powerful to any of the parsac.

10.

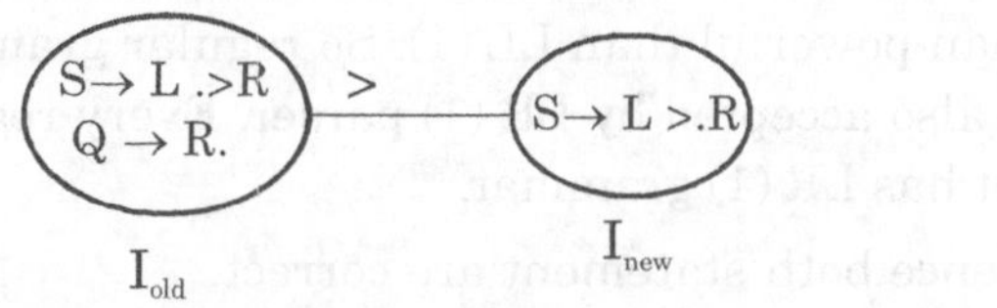

Form above diagram, we can see that there is no shift-reduce or reduce-reduce conflict.

11. At compilation time dynamic memory allocation is not feasible.

12. Intermediate code is machine independent code which makes it easy to retarget the compiler to generate code for newer and different processors.

13. The given basic block can be rewritten as

$a = b + c$	$a = b + c$
$c = a + d$	$c = b + c + d$
$d = b + c \Rightarrow$	$d = b + b + c + d = 2b + c + d$
$e = d - b$	$e = b + b + c + d - b = b + c + d$
$a = e + b$	$a = b + b + c + d = 2b + c + d$

From above simplification it is visible that e is same as c and final value of a is same as d. So the final basic block can be written as follows:

$a = b + c$

$c = a + d$

$d = 2b + c + d$

$e = c$

$a = d$

The DAG generated for the above basic block in as

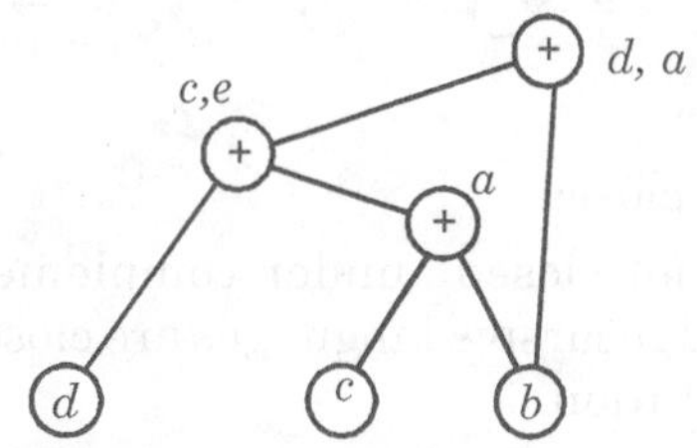

Maximum number of modes and edges in above DAG is (6,6)

14. $L_2^* \cup L_1^* = (L_1 \cdot L_2) \cup L_1^*$

We know that $\phi \cdot L = \phi$ for all languages L.

This is because,

Suppose $\exists a$ string $s \in \phi \cdot L$

$\Rightarrow \exists s'$ such that $s = s' \cdot s''$

and $s' \in \phi$ & $s'' \in L$

But $s' \notin \phi$

$\because$ ϕ is an empty language

$\therefore$ $\phi \cdot L = \phi$.

also $\{\in\} \subseteq L^*$ for all languages L. as it means that take letters from the language and concatenate them 'O' time creating a length string which can be done for all language.

$\therefore$ E is in ϕ^*

$L_1 \quad L_2 = f$

& $L_1^* = \{\in\}$

$\therefore$ $\phi \cup \{E\} = \{\in\}$

16. (*a*) L_2 is context free – <u>TRUE</u>

– We can accept or reject L_2 with single stack.

– Insert P O'S into stack skip q 1's

For each 0 corresponding to r, remove 0 from stack.

(*b*) $L_1 \cap L_2$ is context free – <u>TRUE</u>

– Here $L_1 \cap L_2 = L_2$ which is context free.

(*c*) Complement of L_2 is recursive – <u>TRUE</u>

– L_2 is CFL ($\because$ Given)

– Complement of CFL may or may not be CFL.

– Complement of CFL is definately recursive.

(*d*) Complenent of L1 is context free but not Regular – FALSE.

$L_1 = \{0^p \, 1^q \, 0^r \mid p, q, r \geq 0\}$

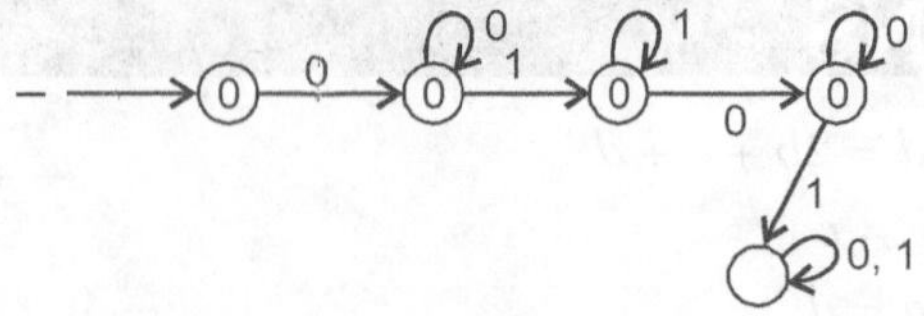

– which is regular?

– $\overline{L_1}$ = 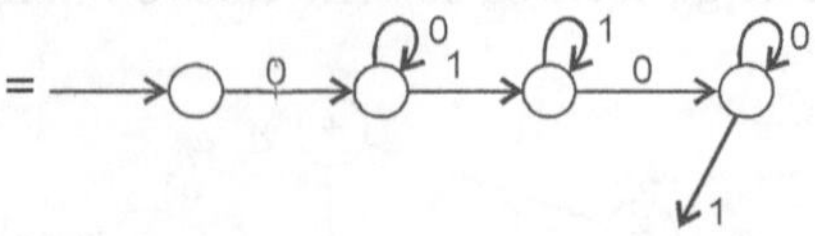 → Regular

Regular are closed

18. CFL's are not closed under complementation. Regular and recursive languages are closed under complementation.

20. Any identifier is also a token so it is recognized in lexical Analysis

21. Symbol table is a Data structure containing record for each identifier, with fields for the attribute of the identifier.

The symbols entered into symbol table are nothing but identifier and operators. It contain information about variables and their attribute.

22. When dynamic data structure is used, heap should be used for runtime environment.

23. It is LL(1) and LR(1)

because in $S \to aSa$

$S \to bS$

$S \to c$

S	a	b	c
	$s \to sSa$	$s \to bS$	$s \to c$

no multiple entries for 1 iteration, so it is LL(1) grammer

mean by LR(1) that it is Left shift Reduced grammer and so it is also LR(1).

Hence it is both LL(1) and LR(1)

24. It is not necessary there exists parsing algo for some programming language whose complexities are less than $\theta(n^3)$

A programming language which allow recursion can be implemented with static storage allocation.

25. According to definition, handle is a production rule $A \to \beta$ and a position in the sentential form where string β may be found and replaced to produce the previous right sentiential form in a reightmost derivation of sentiential form.

26. Code optimizations are carried out on the intermediate code so that same source code can be converted to machine language of the target machine depending upon the back end tools. It also increases the probability of the compiler, i.e. compiler can generate machine code of different machine codes.

27. Consider each statement separately

I. If a programming language doesn't permit global variables and no nesting procedures then we can't use the recursion with static storage because there is no stack support for example Fortran doesn's support the recursion. So statement is false.

II. Statement is true.

III. Recursion in programming languages will be implemented with dynamic storage for example C language implement recursion with the help of heap if size is also increases because heap stores the all activation record of a recursion. So statement if false.

IV. Statement is false because we can implement recursion either with the help of heap or a stack.

V. Statement is true.

28. An LALR(1) parser for a grammer G can have shift reduce S – R confilict if and only if the LR(1) parser for G has S – R conflicts.

29. Recursive descent parser is a kind of top – down parser.

30. It is ambiguous

31. Regular grammar is well recognised by LL(1) parsers and LR (1) parser is stronger and more than powerful than LL (1). So regular grammar is also accepted by LR (1) parser. Every regular set has LR (1) grammar.

Hence both statement are correct.

32. Instructions will be following :

MOV	b,	R_1
ADD	a,	R_1
MOV	d,	R_2
ADD	c,	R_2
SUB	e,	R_2
SUB	R_1,	R_2
MOV	R_2,	t_4

It takes 3 MOV instructions.

33. $S \to S * \bullet E$

$S \to \bullet E$

$E \to F + \bullet E$

Hence $S \to S * \bullet E$ and $E \to F + \bullet E$

belong to the same set of canonical LR (0) items because in both productions the dot is left to E.

34.

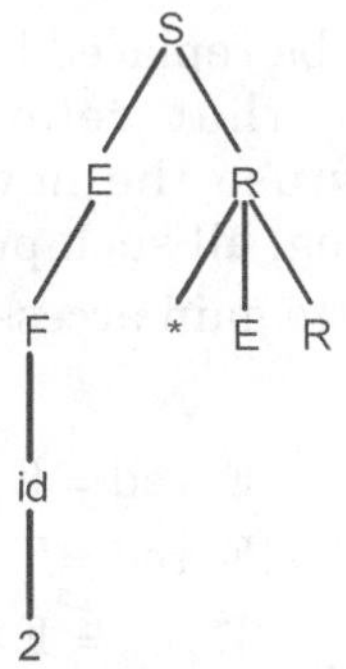

So an inoput 2 * 3 + 4 it prints

234+*

35. The code can be converted to the following in order to reduce the number of cycles needed for execution

for (i = 0, i < N, i ++)

if (i % 2)

for (j = 0; j < N, j ++)

{ x + = (4 * j + 5 * c);

{ y + = (7 + 4 * j); }

∴ The only false statement is B since no sub expression can be eliminated

36. Production

A ⟶ AA

is left-recursive and any grammar which have left-recursive is not predictive-parsing compatible.

37. Derive the sentence

E → E * n → E + n * n → n + n * n

Then handle is always substring, where reduction gives us previous right-sentential form.

$\underline{n}$ + n * n ,

Here, handle is underlined

If we reduce, we get $\underline{E + n}$ * n

(consider this is same as previous right-sentential form)

$\underline{E * n}$

E

n , E + n , E * n

38. Always the case SLR and LALR have same number of states.

while LR have more states than these two.

Because for any Bottom-up paring number of 'CORES' is always same while for LR() only other thing is lookahead is different.

39. Consider 'fro' is also legel identifier, so loxical error is not generated.

40. E → number |E′ + E′|E′ × E′

Then Y_{yacc} compiler detects shift-reduce conflict, and resolves the conflict in favor of a shift over a reduce action.

Consider following configuration where shift-reduce conflict occurs

Stack	Input
... E + Ex	E...$

41. With look ahead, we would prefer to shift because the look ahead has higher precedence than X over + and both operation are left associative. So expression $3 \times 2 + 1 = 6 + 1 = 7$ will be evaluated.

42. P → QR

P → Q SR

P → e

P → Q t R r

P → QR violate the condition of operator because no terminal symbol.

43. Linking between the different files during the compilation is done during the link time.

44. To optimise the solution, evaluate the expression E_2. Then E_1 can calculated and finally E_1 will be one of operands that will be in register and subtraction can be performed directly. But if opposite is followed, then make move store operations.

45. The parse tree will be

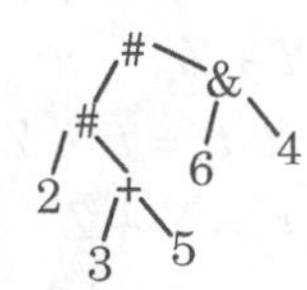

is multication

& is addition

so converting

This parse tree to multiplication and addition.

This will evaluated as

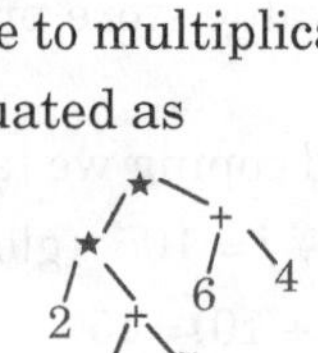

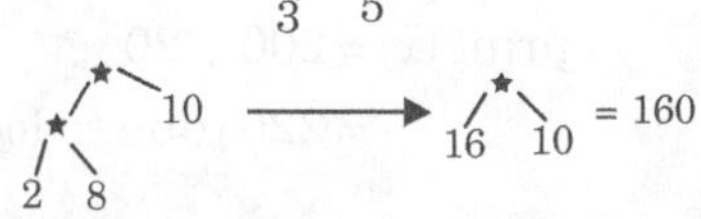

46. LL (1) grammar is top down parsing. It is used in removing left recursion and factoring the grammar.

47. Number of state in SLR is always same as number of state in LALR parser.

48. A syntax-directed definition is a generalization of a context free grammar in which each grammar or symbol has an associated into two subsets called the synthesized and inherited attributes of that grammar symbol.

49. Static type language like C, PASCAL have variable not fixed type.

50. $S \rightarrow iE\ tSS' \backslash a$

$S' \Rightarrow eS \mid a$

$E \rightarrow b$

This is left factor grammar

Thus we may expand S to ibtSS' on input i and wait untill ibtS has been seen to decide whether to expand $S' \rightarrow eS \mid \in$

51. $S \rightarrow CC$

$s \rightarrow CC \mid d$ is example of cononical LR grammar. Cannonical LR grammar is called LR (1) grammar. Every SLR (1) is in LR (1) grammar.

52. $S \rightarrow TR$

$R \rightarrow + T$ {Print ('+') ; } R | ∈

$T \rightarrow$ num {print (num. val) ;}

53. This is three-address code generation. Three address code is a sequence of statement of the general form.

X : Y opZ

where, X, Y and Z are name, const or compiler-generated temporaries op stands for any operator such as fixed or floating point arithmatic operation or a logical operator on boolean value data.

OR X : Y + Z

$t = Y, t_2 = t_1 + Z = Y + Z$

$X = t_2 = Y + Z$

54. P $(i + j)$ $x = i + j = 105$ (global value of i and j)

print $(x + 10) = 115$

print $(x) = 105$

because static value store previous value stored at place of x.

55. By dynamic and coping we take local value

P $(i + j)$, $x = i + j = 105$ (global value of i and j)

print $(x + 10) = 15$

print $(x) = 200 + 20$

$= 220$ (due to local value)

56. $x . f(1)$

$f(1)$ copy to f (int i)

So $i = 1$

print $(2 * i) = 2$

Same as, ((P) y) . $f(1)$; $z . f(1) = 2$

57. With dynamic linking, a stub is included in the image for each library routine reference. The stub is a small piece of code that indicates how to locate the appropriate memory-resident library routine, or how to load the library if the routine is not already present.

A library may be replaced by a new version and all programs that reference library will automatically use the new version. Without dynamic linking, all such programs would need to be relinked to gain access to the new library.

59. (*a*) E.val = 12

(*b*) $E \rightarrow E_1 * T$ {E. red = E_1 red + T. red + 1}

$E \rightarrow T$ {E. red = T. red + 1}

$T \rightarrow F{-}T_1$ {T. red = F. red + T_1. red + 1}

$T \rightarrow F$ {T. red = F red + 1}

$F \rightarrow 2$ {F. red = 1}

$F \rightarrow 4$ {F. red = 1}

60. By definition of poset and lattice.

61. The grammar $A \rightarrow AA$, $A \rightarrow a$ is ambiguous. It is left and right recursive.

The grammar $A \rightarrow A\ B$, $B \rightarrow yB$, $A \rightarrow a$, $B \rightarrow b$ is not ambiguous though it is left and right recursive.

62. $S \rightarrow L_1 . L_2$ {S.val ← L_1.val + $\frac{L_2.\text{val}}{2^{L_2.\text{length}}}$

$S \rightarrow L$ {S. val ← L. val}

$L \rightarrow L_1\ B$ {L.val ← L_1.val * 2 + B.val; L. length ← L_1.length + 1}

$L \rightarrow B$ {L.val ← B.val; L. length ← 1}

$B \rightarrow 0$ {B.val ← 0} | 1{B.val ← 1}

The attribute length keeps track of the length of the bit sequence corresponding to L. We then just use the formula specified in the first translation to compute the value of the binary string.

63. **Loader.** A program called loader performs the two functions of loading and link-editing the process of loading consists of taking *relocatable machine code*, altering the relocatable addresses and placing the altered instruction and data in memory at the proper locations.

Link editor. The link-editor allows us to make a single program from several files of relocatable machine code. These files may have been result of several different compilations and one or more may be library files of routines provided by the system and available to any program that needs them.

64. LR is powerful than LALR parsers and LALR are powerful than SLR parsers.

65. **Type checking.** A compiler must check that the source program follows both the syntactic and semantic conventions of the source language. This checking called static checking. Type checks is part of static checks. In type checking, a compiler should report an error if an operator is applied to an incompatible operand;

e.g. An array variable and a function variable are added together.

* A type checker verifies that the type of a construct mathes that expected by its content.
* Type checker implements a type system. The type system are specified in a syntax-directed manner.

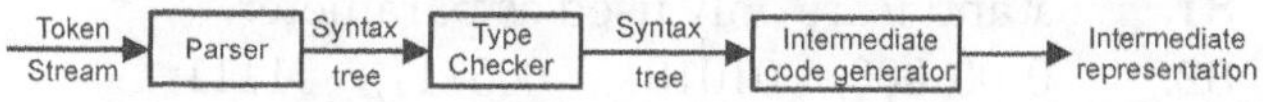

Position of type checker

66. Relocation constant = Final loading address – Original loading address

0	200	1000	1600

0 1 2 3 4

67. (*a*) Let $P_1 : S_1 \to a\, S_1\, b$ $\quad P_2 = S_1 \to aBb$

$P_3 : S_1 \to aAb$ $\quad P_4 = B \to Bb$

$P_5 : A \to aA$ $\quad P_6 = B \to b$

$P_7 : A \to a.$

(*i*) Repeated applications of P_1 contributes equal number of *a*'s and *b*'s and proceeding S_1 and succeeding S_1 respectively.

(*ii*) P_3 adds *a* pair *a*, *b* then P_5, P_7 contributes 5 or more *a*'s to the final sentential form. Hence in this case it will be of the form $a^n b^m$ *s.t.* $n > m + 2$.

(*iii*) P_2 adds *a* pair *a*, *b* then P_4, P_6 contributes 2 or more *b*'s to the final sentential form. Hence in this case it will be of the form $a^n b^m$, where $m > n + 2$.

$\therefore \quad L(G_1) = \{a^n b^m : n, m > 1, \mid n - m \mid > 1\}$

(*b*) Let $G_2 = \{N, T, P, S\}$

where $N = \{S_1, A, B\}$, $T = \{a, b\}$ and P is given by

$P_1 : S_1 \to aS_1\, baS_1\, b$

$P_2 : S_1 \to aAb$

$P_3 : A \to aAb$

$P_4 : A \to ab$

$P_5 : S_1 \to aBb$

$P_6 : B \to aBb$

$P_7 : B \to ab.$

Here P_1, P_2, P_4, P_6, P_7 have been added.

(*c*) No, it is not inherently ambiguous.

68. (*a*) The regular expression of an identifier with first character a letter and remaining five characters as digits and letters is

(letter) (digit + letter) (digit + letter) (digit + letter) (digit + letter) (digit + letter)

Some programming language compilers provide a separate function to truncate the identifier name upto a fixed length of string. In that case the regular expression can be written as

(letter) (digit + letter)* ...

(*b*)

Stack symbol	Current Input symbol					
	begin	*d*	semi	*s*	end	#
Program	1	–	–	–	–	–
X	–	2	–	3	–	–
Y	–	–	4	–	5	–
begin	pop	–	–	–	–	–
d	–	pop	–	–	–	–
semi	–	–	pop	–	–	–
s	–	–	–	pop	–	–
end	–	–	–	–	pop	–
#	–	–	–	–	–	accept

Where the digits in the first three rows of the table indicate the production number whose R.H.S. is to be used. The productions are numbered as follows :

0. S′ → Program #
1. Program → begin d Semi X end
2. X → d Semi X
3. X → *s*Y
4. Y → Semi *s*Y
5. Y → ε

The grammar has been augmented with the zeroth production so that # denotes the end of the input string.

69. The translation elements of the productions will be different for parsing a string before decimal (also without decimal and after decimal. SDTS itself cannot take a decision which translation element is to be used. So for the same grammar the following two SDTS can be constructed.

(*a*) For parsing before decimal (also without decimal)

S → L.S. Val

S → L.L. $\quad$ S. Val ← L. Val + L. Val

L → LB $\quad$ L Val ← L. Val * 2 + B. Val

L → B $\quad$ L. Val ← B. Val

B → 1 $\quad$ B. Val ← 0

B → 1 $\quad$ B. Val ← 1

(*b*) For parsing after decimal

S → L $\quad$ S. Val ← L. Val

S → L.L. $\quad$ S. Val ← L. Va + L. Val, count ← 1

2 → LB $\quad$ L. Val ← L. Val + B. Val/2 count, count ← count + 1

$L \rightarrow B$ L. Val $\leftarrow$ B. Val

$B \rightarrow 0$ B. Val $\leftarrow 0$

$B \rightarrow 1$ B. Val $\leftarrow 1$

70. From given option we find that ⊕ is left associative while '*' is right associative.

71. A compiler have facility for using dynamic memory allocation for language L.

72. Given, $\Sigma = \{a, b\}$

Set of all language over Σ is infinite, so it is not countable

75. In two pass assembler,

Purpose : Generate object program.

1. Substitute the corresponding address for each symbol.
2. Generate instruction, which are opcode are substituted for machine instruction.
3. Data is generated.
4. Some pseudo operations are also executed.

76. → if id then < stmt >

→ if id then < stmt > else < stmt >

→ *id* : = *id* is ambiguous because.

if a then if b then c : = d else c : = f has few parse trees.

77. If is an conditional branch pseudo-up. It performs an arithmetic test and branches only if the tested condition is true.

78. Address record used in assembler.

In the case of subroutine call, Location counter is used for need intruction.

* Linking loader is used for reference counts.

* Garbage collection is used for address relocation.

79. X: = –10 ; Y : = 20 ;

If X > Y

then if X < 0

then X : = *abs* (X) else

X : = 2*X

Here X < 0

X : = *abs* (X)

= –10

80. Identifier–Language use identifiers as names of variables, arrays, functions. A gramar for an language often treats an identifier as a token. Each time an identifier appears in the input.

Example : Count = Count + increment :

id = *id* + *id* this token stream is used for parsing.

81. *x* and *y* are only used as parameter.

82. 0 00 000, 010101, 000111, 11111

For distance of any code we take exclusive or expression.

000 000	010 101	000 111
010 101	000 111	111 111
010 101	010 101	111 000

Number of one is in exclusive or operation = distance code

We take distance of minimum = 2.

83. <> used in expression for using the token.

84. Linker–Resolves symbolic references between object decks.

85. This is method for greatest common division (GCD) of two numbers.

86. $S \rightarrow XXW$ {Print + 1}

$S \rightarrow Y$ {Print + 2}

$W \rightarrow SZ$ {Print + 3}

Translation of XXXXYZZ

$S \rightarrow XXW$ 1

$\rightarrow XXSZ$ 3

$\rightarrow XXXXWZ$ 1

$\rightarrow XXXXSZZ$ 3

$\rightarrow XXXXYZZ$ 2

Syntax directed translation scheme described by 23131

87. Array → [] []

Space for compliler to reserve the word

$= [(8 \times 4) - (8 + 4)] \times 100$

$= (32 - 12) \times 100$

$= 2000$

NUMERICAL TYPE QUESTION

3. Writenln is used for write output lines. So, X = 2

6 CHAPTER

Operating System

MCQ TYPE QUESTIONS

2016

1. Consider an arbitrary set of CPU-bound processes with unequal CPU burst lengths submitted at the same time to a computer system. Which one of the following process scheduling algorithms would minimize the average waiting time in the ready queue?

(*a*) Shortest remaining time first

(*b*) Round-robin with time quantum less than the shortest CPU burst

(*c*) Uniform random

(*d*) Highest priority first with priority proportional to CPU burst length

2. Consider the following proposed solution for the critical section problem. There are n processes: $P_0 \ldots P_{n-1}$, In the code, function pmax returns an integer not smaller than any of its arguments. For all *i*, t [i] is initialized to zero,

Code for P_i:

```
do {
    c[i]=1; t[i] = pmax (t [0] ,...,t [n-1] ) + 1; c[i]=0;
    for every j ≠ i in {0,..., n – 1} {
        while (c[j]) ;
        while (t [ j] != 0 && t[j] <= t[i]) ;
    }
    Critical Section ;
    t[i] = 0;
    Remainder Section;
} while (true) ;
```

Which one of the following is **TRUE** about the above solution?

(*a*) At most one process can be in the critical section at any time

(*b*) The bounded wait condition is satisfied

(*c*) The progress condition is satisfied

(*d*) It cannot cause a deadlock

3. Consider the following two phase locking protocol. Suppose a transaction T accesses (for read or write operations) , a certain set of objects $\{O_1,..., O_k\}$. This is done in the following manner:

Step 1. T acquires exclusive locks to $O_1, ..., O_k$ in increasing order of their addresses.

Step 2. The required operations are performed.

Step 3. All locks are released.

This protocol will

(*a*) guarantee serializability and deadlock-freedom

(*b*) guarantee neither serializability nor deadlock-freedom

(*c*) guarantee serializability but not deadlock-freedom

(*d*) guarantee deadlock-freedom but not serializability

4. In which one of the following page replacement algorithms it is possible for the page fault rate to increase even when the number of allocated frames increases?

(*a*) LRU (Least Recently Used)

(*b*) OPT (Optimal Page Replacement)

(*c*) MRU (Most Recently Used)

(*d*) FIFO (First In First Out)

5. Consider the following two-process synchronization solution.

Process 0

```
--------
Entry: loop while (turn == 1);
critical section)
Exit: turn=1;
```

Process 1

```
--------
Entry: loop while (turn == 0);
critical section)
Exit: turn=0;
```

The shared variable turn is initialized to zero. Which one of the following is TRUE?

(*a*) This is a correct two-process synchronization solution

(*b*) This solution violates mutual exclusion requirement

(*c*) This solution violates progress requirement

(*d*) This solution violates bounded wait requirement

2015

6. Consider a main memory with five page frames and the following sequence of page references : 3, 8, 2, 3, 9, 1, 6, 3, 8, 9, 3, 6, 2, 1, 3. Which one of the following is true with respect to page replacement policies First In First Out (FIFO) and Least Recently Used (LRU) ?
   (a) Both incur the same number of page faults.
   (b) FIFO incurs 2 more page faults than LRU
   (c) LRU incurs 2 more page faults than FIFO
   (d) FIFO incurs 1 more page faults than LRU

7. A system has 6 identical resources and N processes competing for them. Each process can request atmost 2 resources. Which one of the following values of N could lead to a deadlock?
   (a) 1 (b) 2
   (c) 3 (d) 4

8. Consider six memory partitions of sizes 200 KB, 400 KB, 600 KB, 500 KB, 300 KB and 250 KB, where KB refers to kilobyte. These partitions need to be allotted to four processes of sizes 357 KB, 210KB, 468 KB and 491 KB in that order. If the best fit algorithm is used, which partitions are NOT allotted to any process?
   (a) 200KB and 300 KB (b) 200KB and 250 KB
   (c) 250KB and 300 KB (d) 300KB and 400 KB

9. The maximum number of processes that can be in Ready state for a computer system with n CPUs is
   (a) n (b) n^2
   (c) 2^n (d) Independent of n

10. Consider the following policies for preventing deadlock in a system with mutually exclusive resources.
    I. Processes should acquire all their resources at the beginning of execution. If any resources acquired so far are released.
    II. The resources are numbered uniquely, and processes are allowed to request for resources only in increasing resource numbers.
    III. The resources are numbered uniquely, and processes are allowed to request for resources only in decreasing resource numbers.
    IV. The resources are numbered uniquely. A process is allowed to request only for a resource with resource number larger than its currently held resources.

    When of the above policies can be used for preventing deadlock ?
    (a) Any one of I and III but not II or IV
    (b) Any one of I, III, and IV but not II
    (c) Any one of II and III but not I or IV
    (d) Any one of I, II, III, and IV

11. For the processes listed in the following table, which of the following scheduling schemes will the lowest average turnaround time ?

Process	Arrival Time	Processing Time
A	0	3
B	1	6
C	4	4
D	6	2

    (a) First Come First Serve
    (b) Non-preemptive Shortest Job First
    (c) Shortest Remaining Time
    (d) Round Robin with Quantum value two

2014

12. Which one of the following is **FALSE**?
    (a) User level threads are not scheduled by the kernel.
    (b) When a user level thread is blocked, all other threads of its process are blocked.
    (c) Context switching between user level threads is faster than context switching between kernel level threads.
    (d) Kernel level threads cannot share the code segment.

13. A computer has twenty physical page frames which contain pages numbered 101 through 120. Now a program accesses the pages numbered 1, 2, .,.100 in that order, and repeats the access sequence THRICE. Which one of the following page replacement policies experiences the same number of page faults as the optimal page replacement policy for this program?
    (a) Least-recently-used
    (b) First-in-first-out
    (c) Last-in-first-out
    (d) Most-recently-used

14. Which of the following statements are CORRECT?
    1. Static allocation of all data areas by a compiler makes it impossible to implement recursion.
    2. Automatic garbage collection is essential to implement recursion.
    3. Dynamic allocation of activation records is essential to implement recursion.
    4. Both heap and stack are essential to implement recursion.

    (a) 1 and 2 only (b) 2 and 3 only
    (c) 3 and 4 only (d) 1 and 3 only

2013

15. Three concurrent processes *X*, *Y*, and *Z* execute three different code segments that access and update certain shared variables. Process *X* executes the *P* operation (i.e., wait) on semaphores *a*, *b* and *c*; process *Y* executes the *P* operation on semaphores *b*, *c* and *d*; process *Z* executes the *P* operation on semaphores *c*, *d*, and *a* before entering the respective code, segments. After completing the execution of its code segment, each process invokes the *V* operation **(i.e., signal)** on its three semaphores. All semaphores are binary semaphores initialized to one. Which one of the following represents a deadlock-free order of invoking the *P* operations by the processes?

(*a*) X: P (*a*) P (*b*) P (*c*)
Y: P (*b*) P (*c*) P (*d*)
Z: P (*c*) P (*d*) P (*a*)

(*b*) X: P (*b*) P (*a*) P (*c*)
Y: P (*b*) P (*c*) P (*d*)
Z: P (*a*) P (*c*) P (*d*)

(*c*) X: P (*b*) P (*a*) P (*c*)
Y: P (*c*) P (*b*) P (*d*)
Z: P (*a*) P (*c*) P (*d*)

(*d*) X: P (*a*) P (*b*) P (*c*)
Y: P (*c*) P (*b*) P (*d*)
Z: P(*c*) P (*d*) P (*a*)

16. A shared variable *x*, initialized to zero, is operated on by four concurrent processes *W, X, Y, Z* as follows. Each of the processes *W* and *X* reads *x* from memory, increments by one, stores it to memory, and then terminates. Each of the processes *Y* and *Z* reads *x* from memory, decrements by two, stores it to memory, and then terminates. Each process before reading *x* invokes the *P* operation (i.e., wait) on a counting semaphore *S* and invokes the *V* operation (i.e., signal) on the semaphore *S* after storing *x* to memory. Semaphore S is initialized to two. What is the maximum possible value of *x* after all processes complete execution?

(*a*) –2 (*b*) –1
(*c*) 1 (*d*) 2

2012

17. A process executes the code

```
fork () ;
fork () ;
fork () ;
```

The total number of child processes created is

(*a*) 3 (*b*) 4
(*c*) 7 (*d*) 8

18. Consider the virtual page reference string

1, 2, 3, 2, 4, 1, 3, 2, 4, 1

on a demand paged virtual memory system running on a computer system that has main memory size of 3 page frames which are initially empty. Let LRU, FIFO and OPTIMAL denote the number of page faults under the corresponding page replacement policy. Then

(*a*) OPTIMAL < LRU < FIFO
(*b*) OPTIMAL < FIFO < LRU
(*c*) OPTIMAL = LRU
(*d*) OPTIMAL = FIFO

19. Consider the 3 processes, P1, P2 and P3 shown in the table.

Process	Arrival time	Time Units Required
P1	0	5
P2	1	7
P3	3	7

The completion order of the 3 processes under the policies FCFS and RR2 (round robin scheduling with CPU quantum of 2 time units) are

(*a*) **FCFS:** P1, P2, P3 **RR2:** P1, P2, P3
(*b*) **FCFS:** P1, P3, P2 **RR2:** P1, P3, P2
(*c*) **FCFS:** P1, P2, P3 **RR2:** P1, P3, P2
(*d*) **FCFS:** P1, P3, P2 **RR2:** P1, P2, P3

20. Consider the following transactions with data items P and Q initialized to zero :

T_1 : read (P);
read (Q);
if P = 0 then Q : = Q + 1;
write (Q)

T_2 : read (Q);
read (P);
if Q = 0 then P : = P + 1;
write (P).

Any non-serial interleaving of T_1 and T_2 for concurrent execution leads to

(*a*) a serializable schedule
(*b*) a schedule that is not conflict serializable
(*c*) a conflict serializable schedule
(*d*) a schedule for which a precedence graph cannot be drawn

2011

21. A thread is usually defined as a "light weight process" because an operating system (OS) maintains smaller data structures for a thread than for a process. In relation to this, which of the following is **TRUE**?

(*a*) On per-thread basis, the OS maintains *only* CPU register state (*b*) The OS does not maintain a separate stack for each thread

(*c*) On per-thread basis, the OS does maintain virtual memory state

(*d*) On per-thread basis, the OS maintains *only* scheduling and accounting information

22. A company needs to develop digital signal processing software for one of its newest inventions. The software is expected to have 40000 lines of code. The company needs to determine the effort in person-months needed to develop this software using the basic COCOMO model. The multiplicative factor for this model is given as 2.8 for the software development on embedded systems, while the exponentiation factor is given as 1.20. What is the estimated effort in person-months?

(*a*) 234.25 (*b*) 932.50
(*c*) 287.80 (*d*) 122.40

23. On a non-pipelined sequential processor, a program segment, which is a part of the interrupt service routine, is given to transfer 500 bytes from an I/O device to memory.

```
       Initialize the address register
       Initialize the count to 500
LOOP : Load a byte from device
       Store in memory at address given by
       address register
       Increment the address register
       Decrement the count
       If count ! = 0 go to LOOP
```

Assume that each statement in this program is equivalent to a machine instruction which takes one clock cycle to execute if it is a non-load/store instruction. The load-store instructions take two clock cycles to execute.

The designer of the system also has an alternate approach of using the DMA controller to implement the same transfer. The DMA controller requires 20 clock cycles for initialization and other overheads. Each DMA transfer cycle takes two clock cycles to transfer one byte of data from the device to the memory.

What is the approximate speedup when the DMA controller based design is used in place of the interrupt driven program based input-output?

(*a*) 3.4 (*b*) 4.4
(*c*) 5.1 (*d*) 6.7

24. Let the page fault service time be 10 ms in a computer with average memory access time being 20 ns. If one page fault is generated for every 10^6 memory accesses, what is the effective access time for the memory?

(*a*) 21 ns (*b*) 30 ns
(*c*) 23 ns (*d*) 35 ns

2010

25. Consider the methods used by processes P1 and P2 for accessing their critical sections whenever needed, as given below. The initial values of shared boolean variables S1 and S2 are randomly assigned.

Method used by P1	Method used by P2
while (S1 = = S2) ; Critical Section S1 = S2 ;	while (S1 ! = S2) ; Critical Section S2 = not (S1) ;

Which one of the following statements describes the properties achieved?

(*a*) Mutual exclusion but not progress

(*b*) Progress but not mutual exclusion

(*c*) Neither mutual exclusion nor progress

(*d*) Both mutual exclusion and progress

26. A system uses FIFO policy for page replacement. It has 4 page frames with no pages loaded to begin with. The system first accesses 100 distinct pages in some order and then accesses the same 100 pages but now in the reverse order. How many page faults will occur?

(*a*) 196 (*b*) 192
(*c*) 197 (*d*) 195

27. Which of the following statements are true?

I. Shortest remaining time first scheduling may cause starvation

II. Preemptive scheduling may cause starvation

III. Round robin is better than FCFS in terms of response time

(*a*) I only (*b*) I and III only
(*c*) II and III only (*d*) I, II and III

28. The following program consists of 3 concurrent processes and 3 binary semaphores. The semaphores are initialized as

S0 = 1, S1 = 0, S2 = 0.

Process P0	Process P1	Process P2

while (true) {
wait (S0);
print '0';
release (S1);
release (S2);
}
	wait (S1);
	release (S0);
		wait (S2)
		release (S0);

How many times will process P0 print '0'?

(*a*) at least twice (*b*) exactly twice
(*c*) exactly thrice (*d*) exactly once

29. A system has n resources $R_0...R_{n-1}$, and k processes $P_0..P_{k-1}$. The implementation of the resource request logic of each process P_i, is as follows:

```
if (i % 2 ==0) {
    if (i < n) request R_i ;
    if (i + 2 < n) request R_{i+2} ;
}
else {
    if (i < n) request R_{n-i} ;
    if (i + 2 < n) request R_{n-i-2};
}
```

In which one of the following situations is a deadlock possible?

(*a*) n = 40, k = 26 (*b*) n = 21, k = 12

(*c*) n = 20, k = 10 (*d*) n = 41, k = 19

2009

30. In which one of the following page replacement policies, Belady's anomaly may occur ?

(*a*) FIFO (*b*) Optimal

(*c*) LRU (*d*) MRU

31. The essential content (s) in each entry of a page table is/are

(*a*) virtual page number.

(*b*) page frame number.

(*c*) both virtual page number and page frame number

(*d*) access right information.

32. Consider a system with 4 types of resources R1 (3 units), R2 (2 units), R3 (3 units), R4 (2 units). A non-preemptive resource allocation policy is used. At any given instance, a request is not entertained if it cannot be completely satisfied. Three processes P1, P2, P3 request the resources as follows if executed independently.

Process P1 :	Process P2 :	Process P3 :
t = 0: requests 2 units of R2	t = 0: requests 2 units of R3	t = 0: requests 1 units of R4
t = 1: requests 1 units of R3	t = 2: requests 1 units of R4	t = 2: requests 2 units of R1
t = 3: requests 2 units of R1	t = 4: requests 1 units of R1	t = 5: requests 2 units of R1
t = 5: releases 1 units of R2 and 1 unit of R1	t = 6: releases 1 units of R3 t = 8: Finishes	t = 7: requests 1 units of R2 t = 8: requests 1 units of R3
t = 7: releases 1 units of R3		t = 9: Finishes
t = 8: requests 2 units of R4		
t = 10: Finishes		

Which one of the following statements is TRUE if all three processes run concurrently starting at time t = 0 ?

(*a*) All processes will finish without any deadlock.

(*b*) Only P1 and P2 will be in deadlock.

(*c*) Only P1 and P3 will be in deadlock.

(*d*) All three processes will be in deadlock.

33. Consider a disk system with 100 cylinders. The requests to access the cylinders occur in following sequence:

4, 34, 10, 7, 19, 73, 2, 15, 6, 20

Assuming that the head is currently at cylinder 50, what is the time taken to satisfy all requests if it takes 1 ms to move from one cylinder to adjacent one and shortest seek time first policy is used ?

(*a*) 95 ms (*b*) 119 ms

(*c*) 233 ms (*d*) 276 ms

34. In the following process state transition diagram for a uniprocessor system, assume that there are always some processes in the ready state:

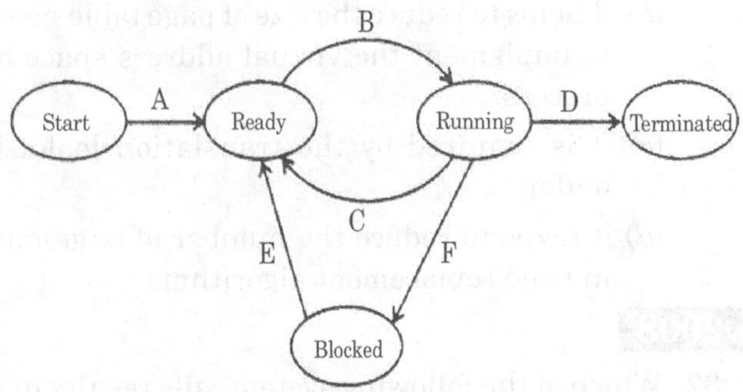

Now consider the following statements:

I. If a process makes a transition D, it would result in another process making transition A immediately.

II. A process P2 in blocked state can make transition E while another process P1 is in running state.

III. The OS uses preemptive scheduling.

IV. The OS uses non-preemptive schedulig.

Which of the above statements are TRUE ?

(*a*) I and II (*b*) I and III

(*c*) II and III (*d*) II and IV

35. The enter_CS ( ) and leave_CS ( ) functions to implement critical section of a process are realized using test-and-set instruction as follows:

```
void enter_CS (X)
{
    while (test-and-set (X));
}
void leave_CS(X)
{
    X = 0;
}
```

In the above solution, X is a memory location associated with the CS and is initialized to 0. Now consider the following statements:

I. The above solution to CS problem is deadlock free.

II. The solution is starvation free.

III. The processes enter CS is FIFO order.

IV. More than one process can enter CS at the same time.

Which of the above statements are TRUE ?

(*a*) I only

(*b*) I and II

(*c*) II and III

(*d*) IV only

36. A multilevel page table is preferred in comparison to a single level page table for translating virtual address to physical address because

(*a*) it reduces the memory access time to read or write a memory location.

(*b*) it helps to reduce the size of page table needed to implement the virtual address space of a process.

(*c*) it is required by the translation lookaside buffer.

(*d*) it helps to reduce the number of page faults in page replacement algorithms.

2008

37. Which of the following system calls results in the sending of SYN packets?

(*a*) socket (*b*) bind

(*c*) listen (*d*) connect

38. The data blocks of a very large file in the Unix file system are allocated using

(*a*) contiguous allocation

(*b*) linked allocation

(*c*) indexed allocation

(*d*) an extension of indexed allocation

39. The P and V operations on counting semaphores, where is a counting semaphore, are defined as follows

P(s) : s =s – 1;
if s < 0 then wait;
V(s) : s = s + 1;
if s < = 0 then wakeup a process waiting on s;

Assume that P_b and V_b, the wait and signal operations on binary semaphores are provided. Two binary semaphores x_b and y_b are used to implement the semaphore operations P(s) and V(s) as follows

```
P (s): Pb (xb);
    s = s – 1;
    if (s < 0)
    {
    Vb (Xb);
    Pb (yb);
    }
    else Vb (Xb);
V (s) : Pb (Xb);
    s = s + 1;
    if (s < = 0) Vb(yb);
    Vb(Xb);
```

The initial values of x_b and y_b are respectively

(*a*) 0 and 0 (*b*) 0 and 1

(*c*) 1 and 0 (*d*) 1 and 1

40. Which of the following statements about synchronous and asynchronous I/O is NOT true?

(*a*) An ISR is invoked on completion of I/O in synchronous I/O but not in asynchronous I/O

(*b*) In both synchronous and asynchronous I/O, an ISR (Interrupt Service Routine) is invoked after completion of the I/O

(*c*) A process making a synchronous I/O call waits until I/O is complete, but a process making an asynchronous I/O call does not wait for completion of the I/O

(*d*) In the case of synchronous I/O, the process waiting for the completion of I/O is woken up by the ISR that is invoked after the completion of I/O

41. Which of the following is NOT true of deadlock prevention and deadlock avoidance schemes?

(*a*) In deadlock prevention, the request for resources is always granted if the resulting state is safe

(*b*) In deadlock avoidance, the request for resources is always granted if the resulting state is safe

(*c*) Deadlock avoidance is less restrictive than deadlock prevention

(*d*) Deadlock avoidance requires knowledge of resource requirements a *priori*

42. A process executes the following code

for (i = 0; i < n; i++) for k ();

The total number of child processes created is

(a) n (b) $2^n - 1$

(c) 2^n (d) $2^{n+1} - 1$

43. A processor uses 36 bit physical addresses and 32 bit virtual addresses, with a page frame size of 4 Kbytes. Each page table entry is of size 4 bytes. A three level page table is used for virtual-to-physical address translation, where the virtual address is used as follows

- bits 30-31 are used to index into the first level page table,
- bits 21-29 are used to index into the second level page table,
- bits 12-20 are used to index into the third level page table, and
- bits 0-11 are used as offset within the page.

The number of bits required for addressing the next level page table (or page frame) in the page table entry of the first, second and third level page tables are respectively

(a) 20, 20 and 20 (b) 24, 24 and 24

(c) 24, 24 and 20 (d) 25, 25 and 24

2007

44. Group 1 contains some CPU scheduling algorithms and Group 2 contains some applications. Match entries in Group 1 to entries in Group 2.

Group 1	Group 2
P. Gang Scheduling	1. Guaranteed Scheduling
Q. Rate Monotonic Scheduling	2. Real-time Scheduling
R. Fair Share Scheduling	3. Thread Scheduling

Codes :

	P	Q	R
(a)	3	2	1
(b)	1	2	3
(c)	2	3	1
(d)	1	3	2

45. Consider the following statements about user level threads and kernel level threads. Which one of the following statements is FALSE ?

(a) Context switch time is longer for kernel level threads than for user level threads.

(b) User level threads do not need any hardware support

(c) Related kernel level threads can be scheduled on different processors in a multiprocessor system

(d) Blocking one kernel level thread blocks all related threads

46. An operating system uses Shortest Remaining Time first (SRT) process scheduling algorithm. Consider the arrival times and execution times for the following processes :

Process	Execution time	Arrival time
P1	20	0
P2	25	15
P3	10	30
P4	15	45

What is the total waiting time for process P2 ?

(a) 5 (b) 15

(c) 40 (d) 55

47. A virtual memory system uses first In First Out (FIFO) page replacement policy and allocates a fixed number of frames to a process. Consider the following statements :

P : Increasing the number of page frames allocated to a process sometimes increases the page fault rate.

Q : Some programs do not exhibit locality of reference.

Which one of the following is **TRUE** ?

(a) Both P and Q are true, and Q is the reason for P.

(b) Both P and Q are true, but Q is not the reason for P.

(c) P is false, but Q is true.

(d) Both P and Q are false.

48. A single processor system has three resource types X, Y, and Z, which are shared by three processes. There are 5 units of each resource type. Consider the following scenario, where the column ***alloc*** denotes the number of units of each resource type allocated to each process, and the column ***request*** denotes the number of units of each resource type requested by a process in order to complete execution. Which of these processes will finish **LAST**?

	alloc	*request*
	X Y Z	X Y Z
P0	1 2 1	1 0 3
P1	2 0 1	0 1 2
P2	2 2 1	1 2 0

(a) P0

(b) P1

(c) P2

(d) None of the above, since the system is in a deadlock.

49. Two processes, P1 and P2, need to access a critical section of code. Consider the following synchronization construct used by the processes :

/* P1 */	/* P2 */
while (true) {	While (true) {
wants1 = true ;	wants2 = true ;
while (wants2 ==	while (wants1 ==
true);	true);
/ *Critical	/ * Critical
Section * /	Section * /
wants 1 = false ;	wants 2 = false ;
}	}
/*Remainder section	*/ / *Remainder section*

Here, wants1 and want s2 are shared variables, Which are initialized to false. Which one of the following statements is **TRUE** about the above construct ?

(*a*) It does not ensure mutual exclusion.

(*b*) It does not ensure bounded waiting.

(*c*) It requires that processes enter the critical section in strict alternation.

(*d*) It does not prevent deadlocks, but ensures mutual exclusion.

2006

50. Consider three CPU-intensive processes, which require 10, 20, and 30 time units and arrive at times 0, 2, and 6, respectively. How many context switches are needed if the operating system implements a shortes remaining time first scheduling algorithm ? Do not count the context switches at time zero and at the end.

(*a*) 1 (*b*) 2

(*c*) 3 (*d*) 4

51. The atomic fetch-and-set x, y instruction unconditionally sets the memory location x to 1 and fetches the old value of x in y without allowing any intervening access to the memory location x. Consider the following implementation of P and V functions on a binary semaphore S.

```
void p (binary_semaphore *S)
{
unsigned y;
unsigned *x = & (S->value);
}
    do
    {
    fetch – and – set x, y;
    } while (y);
}
void V (binary_semaphore *S) {
        {S–> value = 0;
}
```

Which one of the following is true ?

(*a*) The implementation may not work if context switching is disabled in P

(*b*) Instead of using fetch-and-set, a pair of normal load/store can be used

(*c*) The implementation of V is wrong

(*d*) The code does not implement a binary semaphore

52. A CPU generates 32-bit virtual addresses. The page size is 4 kB. The processor has a translation look-aside buffer (TLB) which can hold a total of 128 page table entries and is 4-way set associative. The minimum size of the TLB tag is

(*a*) 11 bits (*b*) 13 bits

(*c*) 15 bits (*d*) 20 bits

53. Consider three processes (process id 0, 1, 2, respectively) with compute time bursts 2, 4, and 8 time units. All processes arrive at time zero. Consider the longest remaining time first (LRTF) scheduling algorithm. In LRTF ties are broken by giving priority to the process with the lowest process id. The average turn around time is

(*a*) 13 units (*b*) 14 units

(*c*) 15 units (*d*) 16 units

54. Consider three processes, all arriving at time zero, with total execution time of 10, 20, and 30 units, respectively. Each process spends the first 20% of execution time doing I/O, the next 70% of time doing computation, and the last 10% of time doing I/O again. The operating system uses a shortest remaining compute time first scheduling algorithm and schedules a new process either when the running process gets blocked on I/O or when the running process finishes its compute burst. Assume that all I/O operations can be overlapped as much as possible. For what percentage of time does the CPU remain idle ?

(*a*) 0% (*b*) 10.6%

(*c*) 30.0% (*d*) 89.4%

55. Consider the following snapshot of a system running n processes. Process i is holding x_i instances of a resource R, for $1 \le i \le n$. Currently, all instances of R are occupied. Further, for all i, process i has placed a request for an additional y_i instances while holding the x_i instances it already has. There are exactly two processes p and q such that $y_p = y_q = 0$. Which one of the following can serve as a necessary condition to guarantee that the system is not approaching a deadlock?

(*a*) $\min(x_p, x_q) < \max_{k \ne p,q} y_k$

(*b*) $x_p + x_q \ge \min_{k \ne p, q} y_k$

(*c*) $\max(x_p, x_q) > 1$

(*d*) $\min(x_p, x_q) > 1$

2005

56. Suppose n processes, P_1,...., P_n share m identical resource units, which can be reserved and released one at a time. The maximum resource requirement of process P_i is s_p where $s_i > 0$. Which one of the following is a sufficient condition for ensuring that deadlock does not occur?

(a) $\forall i, s_i < m$ (b) $\forall i, s_i < n$

(c) $\sum_{i=1}^{n} s_i < (m+n)$ (d) $\sum_{i=1}^{n} s_i (m * n)$

57. Consider the following code fragment:

if (fork ( ) = = 0)

{$a = a + 5$; print f ('% d, % d/m" , a, and a);}

else {$a - 5$; print f ('% d, % d/n" , a, & a);

Let u,n be the values printed by the parent process, and x,y be the values printed by the child process. Which one of the following is TRUE?

(a) $u = x + 10$ and $v = y$

(b) $u = x + 10$ and $v \neq y$

(c) $u + 10 = x$ and $v = y$

(d) $u + 10 = x$ and $v \neq y$

2004

58. Consider the following statements with respect to user-level threads and kernel-supported threads

(i) Context switch is faster with kernel-supported threads

(ii) For user-level threads, a system call can block the entire process

(iii) Kernel-supported threads can be scheduled independently

(iv) User-level threads are transparent to the kernel

Which of the above statements are true ?

(a) (ii), (iii) and (iv) only

(b) (ii) and (iii) only

(c) (i), and (iii) only

(d) (i) and (ii) only

59. The minimum number of page frames that must be allocated to a running process in a virtual memory environment is determined by

(a) the instruction set architecture

(b) page size

(c) physical memory size

(d) number of processes in memory

60. Consider the following set of processes, with the arrival times and the CPU-burst times given in milliseconds

Process	Arrival Time	Burst Time
P1	0	5
P2	1	3
P3	2	3
P4	4	1

What is the average turnaround time for these processes with the preemptive shortest remaining processing time first (SRPT) algorithm ?

(a) 5.50 (b) 5.75

(c) 6.00 (d) 6.25

61. Consider a system with a two-level paging scheme in which a regular memory access takes 150 nanoseconds, and servicing a page fault takes 8 milliseconds. An average instruction takes 100 nanoseconds of CPU time, and two memory accesses. The TLB hit ratio is 90%, and the page fault rate is one in every 10,000 instructions. What is the effective average instruction execution time ?

(a) 645 nanoseconds (b) 1050 nanoseconds

(c) 1215 nanoseconds (d) 1230 nanoseconds

62. Consider two processes P_1 and P_2 accessing the shared variables X and Y protected by two binary semaphores S_X and S_Y respectively, both initialized to 1. P and V denote the usual semaphone operators, where P decrements the semaphore value, and V increments the semaphore value. The pseudo-code of P_1 and P_2 is as follows :

P_1 :	P_2 :
while true do {	while true do {
L_1 :	L_3 : ....
L_2 :	L_4 : ....
X = X + 1;	Y = Y + 1;
Y = Y – 1;	X = Y – 1;
V(S_X);	V(S_Y);
V(S_Y); }	V(S_X); }

In order to avoid deadlock, the correct operators at L_1, L_2, L_3 and L_4 are respectively

(a) P(S_Y), P(S_X); P(S_X), P(S_Y)

(b) P(S_X), P(S_Y); P(S_Y), P(S_X)

(c) P(S_X), P(S_X); P(S_Y), P(S_Y)

(d) P(S_X), P(S_Y); P(S_X), P(S_Y)

63. A Unix-style *i*-node has 10 direct pointers and one single, one double and one triple indirect pointers. Disk block size is 1 Kbyte, disk block address is 32 bits, and 48-bit integers are used. What is the maximum possible file size ?

(a) 2^{24} bytes (b) 2^{32} bytes

(c) 2^{34} bytes (d) 2^{48} bytes

2003

64. Using a larger block size in a fixed block size file system leads to

(*a*) better disk throughput but poorer disk space utilization

(*b*) better disk throughput and better disk space utilization

(*c*) poorer disk throughput but better disk space utilization

(*d*) poorer disk throughput and poorer disk space utilization

65. In a system with 32 bit virtual addresses and 1 kB page size, use of one-level page tables for virtual to physical address translation is not practical because of

(*a*) the large amount of internal fragmentation

(*b*) the large amount of external fragmentation

(*c*) the large memory overhead in maintaining page tables

(*d*) the large computation overhead in the translation process

66. A uni-processor computer system only has two processes, both of which alternate 10ms CPU bursts with 90ms I/O bursts. Both the processes were created at nearly the same time. The I/O of both processes can proceed in parallel. Which of the following scheduling strategies will result in the least CPU utilization (over a long period of time) for this system?

(*a*) First come first served scheduling

(*b*) Shortest remaining time first scheduling

(*c*) Static priority scheduling with different priorities for the two processes

(*d*) Round robin scheduling with a time quantum of 5 ms.

Common Data Q. 67 - 68

A processor uses 2-level page tables for virtual to physical address translation. Page tables for both levels are stored in the main memory. Virtual and physical addresses are both 32 bits wide. The memory is byte addressable. For virtual to physical address translation, the 10 most significant bits of the virtual address are used as index into the first level page table while the next 10 bits are used as index into the second level page table. The 12 least significant bits of the virtual address are used as offset within the page. Assume that the page table entries in both levels of page tables are 4 bytes wide. Further, the processor has a translation look-aside buffer (TLB), with a hit rate of 96%. The TLB caches recently used virtual page numbers and the corresponding physical page numbers. The processor also has a physically addressed cache with a hit rate of 90%. Main memory access time is 10 ns, cache access time is 1 ns, and TLB access time is also 1 ns.

67. Assuming that no page faults occur, the average time taken to access a virtual address is approximately (to the nearest 0.5 ns)

(*a*) 1.5 ns (*b*) 2 ns

(*c*) 3 ns (*d*) 4 ns

68. Suppose a process has only the following pages in its virtual address space: two contiguous code pages starting at virtual address 0×00000000, two contiguous data pages starting at virtual address 0×00400000, and a stack page starting at virtual address 0×FFFFF000. The amount of memory required for storing the page tables of this process is

(*a*) 8 kB (*b*) 12 kB

(*c*) 16 kB (*d*) 20 kB

Common Data Q. 69 - 70

Suppose we want to synchronize two concurrent processes P and Q using binary semaphores S and T. The code for the processes P and Q is shown below.

Process P:	Process Q:
while (1) {	while (1) {
W:	Y:
print '0';	print '1'
print '0';	print '1'
X:	Z:
}	}

Synchronization statements can be inserted only at points W, X, Y and Z

69. Which of the following will always lead to an output staring with '001100110011' ?

(*a*) P(S) at W, V(S) at X, P(T) at Y, V(T) at Z, S and T initially 1

(*b*) P(S) at W, V(T) at X, P(T) at Y, V(S) at Z, S initially 1, and T initially 0

(*c*) P(S) at W, V(T) at X, P(T) at Y, V(S) at Z, S and T initially 1

(*d*) P(S) at W, V(S) at X, P(T) at Y, V(T) at Z, S initially 1, and T initially 0

70. Which of the following will ensure that the output string never contains a substring of the form 0.1"0 or 10"1 where *n* is odd ?

(*a*) P(S) at W, V(S) at X, P(T) at Y, V(T) at Z, S and T initially 1

(*b*) P(S) at W, V(T) at X, P(T) at Y, V(S) at Z, S and T initially 1

(*c*) P(S) at W, V(S) at X, P(S) at Y, V(S) at Z, S initially 1

(*d*) V(S) at W, V(T) at X, P(S) at Y, P(T) at Z,S and T initially 1

2001

71. Consider a set of n tasks with known runtimes $r_1, r_2, \ldots r_n$ to be run on a uniprocessor machine. Which of the following processor scheduling algorithms will result in the maximum throughput?

(*a*) Round-Robin

(*b*) Shortest-Job-First

(*c*) Highest-Response-Ratio-Next

(*d*) First-Come-First-Served

2000

72. Let *m* [0] .... *m* [4] be mutexes (binary semaphores) and P [0] ... P [4] be processes.

Suppose each process P[*i*] executes the following:

wait (*m* [*i*]); wait (*m* [(*i* + 1) mode 4]);

....

release (*m* [i]) ; release (*m*[(*i* + 1) mod 4]);

This could cause

(*a*) Thrashing

(*b*) Deadlock

(*c*) Starvation, but not deadlock

(*d*) None of these

73. Suppose the time to service a page fault is on the average 10 milliseconds, while a memory access takes 1 microsecond. Then a 99.99% hit ratio results in average memory access time of

(*a*) 1.9999 milliseconds (*b*) 1 millisecond

(*c*) 9.999 microseconds (*d*) 1.9999 microseconds

74. Which of the following is NOT a valid deadlock prevention scheme?

(*a*) Release all resources before requesting a new resource

(*b*) Number the resources uniquely and never request a lower numbered resource than the last one requested

(*c*) Never request a resource after releasing any resource

(*d*) Request and all required resources be allocated before execution

75. (*a*) Fill in the boxes below to get a solution for the readers-writers problem, using a single binary semaphore, mutex (initialized to 1) and busy waiting. Write the box numbers (1, 2 and 3), and their contents in your answer book.

```
        int R = 0, W = 0;
            Reader ( ) {
L1:                 wait (mutex) ;
                    if (W==0) {
                        R = R + 1;
                        [          ] ________ (1)
                    }
                    else {
                        [          ] ________ (2)
                        goto L1;
                    }
                    .... /* do the read */
                    wait (mutex)
                    R = R – 1;
                    signal (mutex) ;
            }
            Writer ( ) {
L2 :                wait (mutex);
                    if ([          ]) { ____ (3)
                        signal (mutex);
                        goto L2;
                    }
                    W =1;
                    signal (mutex) ;
                    .... /*do the write */
                    wait (mutex)
                    W = 0;
                    signal (mutex); (4)
```

(*b*) Can the above solution lead to starvation of writers?

1999

76. Listed below are some operating system abstractions (in the left column) and the hardware components (in the right column)?

(A) Thread	1. Interrupt
(B) Virtual address space	2. Memory
(C) File system	3. CPU
(D) Signal	4. Disk

(*a*) (A)–2, (B)–4, (C)–3, (D)–1

(*b*) (A)–1, (B)–2, (C)–3, (D)–4

(*c*) (A)–3, (B)–2, (C)–4, (D)–1

(*d*) (A)–4, (B)–1, (C)–2, (D)–3

77. Which of the following disk scheduling strategies is likely to give the best through put?

(*a*) Farthest cylinder next

(*b*) Nearest cylinder next

(*c*) First come first served

(*d*) Elevator algorithm

78. System calls are usually invoked by using

(*a*) a software interrupt

(*b*) polling

(*c*) an indirect jump

(*d*) a privileged instruction

79. For the schedule given below, which of the following is correct

1	Read A	
2		Read B
3	Write A	
4		Read A
5		Write A
6		Write B
7	Read B	
8	Write B	

(*a*) This schedule is serialisable and can occur in a scheme using 2PL protocol.

(*b*) This schedule is serialisable but cannot occur in a scheme using 2PL protocol.

(*c*) This schedule is not serialiable but can occur in a scheme using 2PL protocol.

(*d*) This schedule is not serialisable and cannot occur in a scheme using 2PL protocol.

80. Which of the following is/are advantages of virtual memory ?

(*a*) Faster access to memory on an average.

(*b*) Processes can be given protected address spaces.

(*c*) Linker can assign addresses independent of where the program will be loaded in physical memory.

(*d*) Programs larger than the physical memory size can be run.

81. Which of the following actions is/are typically not performed by the operating system when switching context from process A to process B ?

(*a*) Saving current register values and restoring saved register values for process B.

(*b*) Changing address translation tables.

(*c*) Swapping out the memory image of process A to the disk.

(*d*) Invalidating the translation look-aside buffer.

82. Raid configurations of disks are used to provide

(*a*) Fault-tolerance (*b*) High speed

(*c*) High data density (*d*) None of these

83. A certain computer system has the segmented paging architecture for virtual memory. The memory is byte addressable. Both virtual and physical address spaces contain 2^{16} bytes each. The virtual address space is divided into 8 non-overlapping equal size segments. The memory management unit (MMU) has a hardware segment table, each entry of which contains the physical address of the page table for the segment. Page table are stored in the main memory and consists of 2 byte page table entries.

(*a*) What is the minimum page size in bytes so that the page table for a segment requires at most one page to store it ? Assume that the page size can only be a power of 2

(*b*) Now suppose that the page size is 512 bytes. It is proposed to provide a TLB (translation look-aside buffer) for speeding up address translation. The proposed TLB will be capable of storing page table entries for 16 recently referenced virtual pages, in a fast cache that will use the direct mapping scheme. What is the number of tag bits that will need to be associated with each cache entry ?

(*c*) Assume that each page table entry contains (besides other information) 1 valid bit, 3 bits for page protection and 1 dirty bit. How many bits are available in page table entry for storing the aging information for the page ? Assume that the page size is 512 bytes.

1998

84. Which of the following is an example of a spooled device ?

(*a*) The terminal used to enter the input data for the C program being executed

(*b*) An output device used to print the output of a number of jobs.

(*c*) The secondary memory device in a virtual storage system.

(*d*) The swapping area on a disk used by the swapper.

85. When the result of a computation depends on the speed of the processes involved there is said to be

(*a*) cycle steating (*b*) rare condition

(*c*) a time lock (*d*) a deadlock

86. A counting semaphore was initialized to 10. Then 6 P (wait) operations and 4 V (signal) operations were completed on this semaphore. The resulting value of the semaphore is

(*a*) 0 (*b*) 8

(*c*) 10 (*d*) 12

87. A computer has six tape drives, with n processes competing for them. Each process may need two drives. What is the maximum value of n for the system to be deadlock free ?

(*a*) 6 (*b*) 5

(*c*) 4 (*d*) 3

88. The overlay tree for a program is as shown below

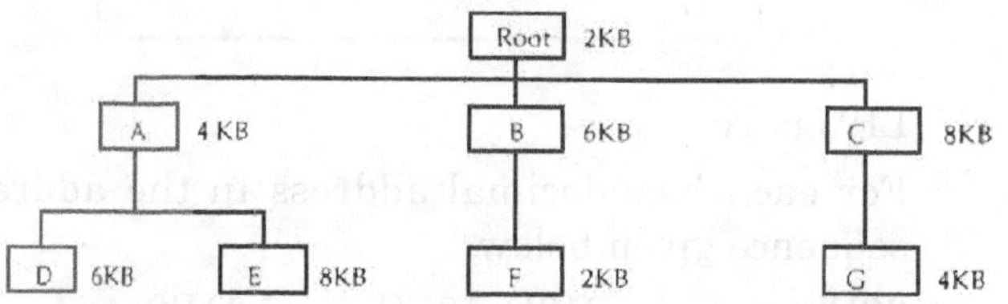

What will be the size of the partition (in physical memory) required to load (and run) this program?

(*a*) 12 KB (*b*) 14 KB

(*c*) 10 KB (*d*) 8 KB

89. Consider n processes sharing the CPU in a round-robin fashion. Assuming that each process switch takes s seconds, what must be the quantum size q such that the overhead resulting from process switching is minimized but, at the same time each process is guaranteed to get its turn at the CPU at least every t seconds ?

(*a*) $q \le \frac{t-ns}{n-1}$ (*b*) $q \ge \frac{t-ns}{n-1}$

(*c*) $q \le \frac{t-ns}{n+1}$ (*d*) $q \ge \frac{t-ns}{n+1}$

90. If an instruction takes i microseconds and a page fault takes an additional j microseconds, the effective instruction time if on the average a page fault occurs every k instruction is

(*a*) $i + \frac{j}{k}$ (*b*) $i + j * k$

(*c*) $\frac{i+j}{k}$ (*d*) $(i + j) * k$

1997

91. Locality of reference implies that the page reference being made by a process

(*a*) will always be to the page used in the previous page reference

(*b*) is likely to be to one of the pages used in the last few page references

(*c*) will always be to one of the pages existing in memory

(*d*) will always lead to a page fault.

92. The correct matching for the following pairs is

(A) Disk scheduling (1) Round robin

(B) Batch processing (2) SCAN

(C) Time sharing (3) LIFO

(D) Interrupt processing (4) FIFO

(*a*) A—3, B—4, C—2 and D—1

(*b*) A—4, B—3, C—2 and D—1

(*c*) A—2, B—4, C—1 and D—3

(*d*) A—3, B—4, C—3 and D—2

93. I/O redirection

(*a*) implies changing the name of a file

(*b*) can be employed to use an existing file as input file for a program

(*c*) implies connection 2 programs through a pipe

(*d*) none of the above

94. When an interrupt occurs, an operating system

(*a*) ignores the interrupt

(*b*) always changes state of interrupted process after processing the interrupt

(*c*) always resumes execution of interrupted process after processing the interrupt.

(*d*) may change state of interrupted process to 'blocked' and schedule another process

95. Thrashing

(*a*) reduces page I/O

(*b*) decreases the degree of multiprogramming

(*c*) implies excessive page I/O

(*d*) improves the system performance

96. Dirty bit for a page in a page table

(*a*) helps avoid unnecessary writes on a paging device

(*b*) helps maintain LRU information

(*c*) allows only read on a page

(*d*) none of the above

97. An operating system contains 3 user processes each requiring 2 units of resource R. The minimum number of units of R such that no deadlocks will ever arise is

(*a*) 3 (*b*) 5

(*c*) 4 (*d*) 6

98. Each process Pi, *i* = 1 ..... 9 is coded as follows

```
repeat
    P (mutex)
    {critical section}
    v (mutex)
forever
```

The code for P_{10} is identical except that it uses *v* (mutex) in place of P (mutex). What is the largest number of processes that can be inside the critical section at any moment

(*a*) 1 (*b*) 2

(*c*) 3 (*d*) none of above

1996

99. The process state transition diagram given in Figure is representative of

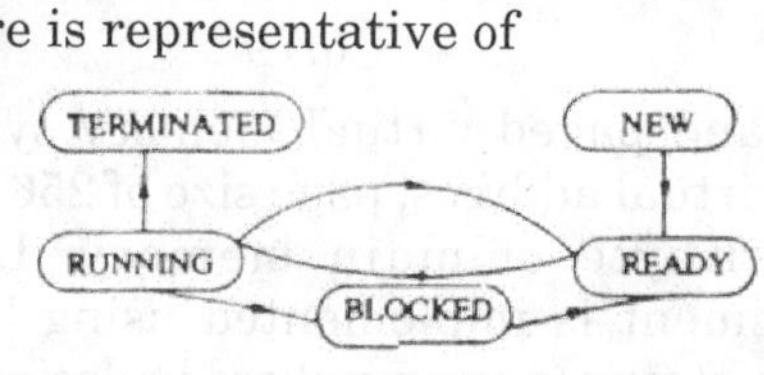

(a) a batch operating system

(b) an operating system with a preemptive scheduler

(c) an operating system with a non-preemptive scheduler

(d) a uni-programmed operating system

100. A critical section is a program segment

(a) which should run in a certain specified amount of time

(b) which avoids deadlocks

(c) where shared resources are accessed

(d) which must be enclosed by a pair of semaphore operations, P and V

101. Which of the following is an example of spooled device?

(a) A line printer used to print the output of a number of jobs.

(b) A terminal used to enter input data to a running program.

(c) A secondary storage device in a virtual memory system.

(d) A graphic display device.

102. A 1000 K byte memory is managed using variable partitions but to compaction. It currently has two partitions of sizes 200 K bytes and 260 Kbytes respectively. The smallest allocation request in Kbytes that could be denied is for

(a) 151 (b) 181

(c) 231 (d) 541

103. A solution to the Dining Philosophers Problem which avoids deadlock is

(a) ensure that all philosophers pick up the left fork before the right fork

(b) ensure that all philosophers pick up the right fork before the left fork

(c) ensure that one particular philospher picks up the left fork before the right fork, and that allother philosphers pick up the right fork before the left fork

(d) none of the above

104. Four jobs to be executed on a single processor system arrive at time 0^+ in the order A, B, C, D. Their burst CPU time requirements are 4, 1, 8, 1 time units respectively. The completion time of A under round robin scheduling with time slice of one time unit is

(a) 10 (b) 4

(c) 8 (d) 9

105. A demand paged virtual memory system uses 16 bit virtual address, page size of 256 bytes, and has 1 Kbyte of main memory. LRU page replacement is implemented using list, whose current status (page numbers in decimal) is

17	1	63

↑

LRU page

For each hexadecimal address in the address sequence given below,

00FF, 010D, 10FF, 11B0

indicate, (i) the new status of the list

(ii) page faults, if any, and

(iii) page replacements, if any.

106. A computer system uses the Banker's Algorithm to deal with deadlocks. Its current state is shown in the tables below, where P0, P1, P2 are processes, and R0, R1, R2 are resources types.

	Maximum Need				Current Allocation			Available		
	R0	R1	R2		R0	R1	R2	R0	R1	R2
P0	4	1	2	P0	1	0	2	2	2	0
P1	1	5	1	P1	0	3	1			
P2	1	2	3	P2	1	0	2			

(a) Show that the system can be in this state.

(b) What will system do on a request by process P_0 for one unit of resource type R_1 ?

107. A file system with a one-level directory structure is implemented on a disk with disk block size of 4 K bytes. The disk is used as follows :

Disk-block 0 : File Allocation Table, consisting of one 8 bit entry per date block, representing the data block address of the next date block in the file,

Disk block 1 : Directory, with one 32 bit entry per file :

Disk block 2 : Data block 1;

Disk block 3 : Data block 2 ; etc.

(a) What is the maximum possible number of files?

(b) What is the maximum possible file size in blocks?

1995

108. In a paged segmented scheme of memory management, the segment table itself must have a page table because

(a) the segment table is often too large to fit in one page

(b) each segment is spread over a number of pages

(c) segment tables point to page table and not to the physical locations of the segment

(d) the processor's description base register points to a page table

109. Which of the following page replacement algorithms suffers from Belady's anamoly ?

(*a*) Optimal replacement

(*b*) LRU

(*c*) FIFO

(*d*) Both (*a*) and (*c*)

110. Which scheduling policy is most suitable for a time-shared operating system ?

(*a*) Shortest Job First

(*b*) Round Robin

(*c*) First Come First Serve

(*d*) Elevator

111. The sequence .... is an optimal nonpreemptive scheduling sequence for the following jobs which leaves the CPU idle for .... unit (s) of time.

Job	Arrival Time	Burst Time
1	0.0	9
2	0.6	5
3	1.0	1

(*a*) {3, 2, 1}, 1 (*b*) {2, 13}, 0

(*c*) {3, 2, 1}, 0 (*d*) {1, 2, 3}, 5

1994

112. A memory page containing a heavily used variable that was initialized very early and is in constant use is removed when

(*a*) LRU page replacement algorithm is used

(*b*) FIFO page replacement algorithm is used

(*c*) LFU page replacement algorithm is used

(*d*) None of the above

113. Which of the following permutations can be obtained in the output (in the same order) using a stack assuming that the input is the sequence 1, 2, 3, 4, 5 in that order ?

(*a*) 3, 4, 5, 1, 2 (*b*) 3, 4, 5, 2, 1

(*c*) 1, 5, 2, 3, 4 (*d*) 5, 4, 3, 1, 2

1993

114. A simple two-pass assembler does the following in the first pass

(*a*) It allocates space for the literals.

(*b*) It computes the total length of the program.

(*c*) It builds the symbol table for the symbols and their values.

(*d*) It generates code for all the load and store register instructions.

(*e*) None of the above

115. A part of the system software, which under all circumstances must reside in the main memory, is

(*a*) text editor (*b*) assembler

(*c*) linker (*d*) loader

(*e*) none of these

116. The root directory of a disk should be placed

(*a*) at a fixed address in main memory

(*b*) at a fixed location on the disk

(*c*) anywhere on the disk

(*d*) at a fixed location on the system disk

(*e*) anywhere on the system disk.

117. Consider a system having m resources of the same type. These resources are shared by 3 processes A, B and C, which have peak demands of 3, 4 and 6 respectively. For what value of m deadlock will not occur ?

(*a*) 7 (*b*) 9

(*c*) 10 (*d*) 13

(*e*) 15

118. Assume that the following jobs are to be executed on a single processor system

Job Id	CPU Burst time
p	4
q	1
r	8
s	1
t	2

The jobs are assumed to have arrived at time 0^+ and in the order *p*, *q*, *r*, *s*, *t*. Calcuclate the departure time (completion time) for job *p* if scheduling is round robin with time slice 1.

(*a*) 4 (*b*) 10

(*c*) 11 (*d*) 12

(*e*) None of the above

1992

119. Bit-slice processors

(*a*) can be cascaded to get any desired word length processor

(*b*) speed of operation is independent of the word length configured

(*c*) don't contain anything equivalent of program counter in a 'normal' microprocessor

(*d*) contain only the data path of a 'normal' CPU

120. A computer system has 6 tape drives, with n process completing for them. Each process may need 3 tape drives. The maximum value of n for which the system is guaranteed to be deadlock free is

(*a*) 2 (*b*) 3

(*c*) 4 (*d*) 1

NUMERICAL TYPE QUESTIONS

2016

1. Consider a computer system with 40-bit virtual addressing and page size of sixteen kilobytes. If the computer system has a one-level page table per process and each page table entry requires 48 bits, then the size of the per-process page table is ______ megabytes.

2. Consider a disk queue with requests for I/O to blocks on cylinders 47, 38, 121, 191, 87, 11, 92, 10. The C-LOOK scheduling algorithm is used. The head is initially at cylinder number 63, moving towards larger cylinder numbers on its servicing pass. The cylinders are numbered from 0 to 199. The total head movement (in number of cylinders) incurred while servicing these requests is ______.

3. Consider a computer system with ten physical page frames. The system is provided with an access sequence (a_1, a_2,..., a_{20}, a_1, a_2,...., a_{20}), where each a_i is a distinct virtual page number. The difference in the number of page faults between the last-in-first-out page replacement policy and the optimal page replacement policy is ______ .

4. Suppose the functions F and G can be computed in 5 and 3 nanoseconds by functional units U_F and U_G, respectively. Given two instances of U_F and two instances of U_G, it is required to implement the computation $F(G(X_i))$ for $1 \le i \le 10$. Ignoring all other delays, the minimum time required to complete this computation is______nanoseconds.

5. Consider the following processes, with the arrival time and the length of the CPU burst given in milliseconds. The scheduling algorithm used is preemptive shortest remaining-time first.

Process	Arrival Time	Burst Time
P_1	0	10
P_2	3	6
P_3	7	1
P_4	8	3

The average turn around time of these processes is__________milliseconds.

6. Consider a non-negative counting semaphore S. The operation P(S) decrements S, and V(S) increments S. During an execution, 20 P(S) operations and 12 V(S) operations are issued in some order. The largest initial value of S for which at least one P(S) operation will remain blocked is________.

7. A file system uses an in-memory cache to cache disk blocks. The miss rate of the cache is shown in the figure. The latency to read a block from the cache is 1 ms and to read a block from the disk is 10 ms. Assume that the cost of checking whether a block exists in the cache is negligible. Available cache sizes are in multiples of 10 MB.

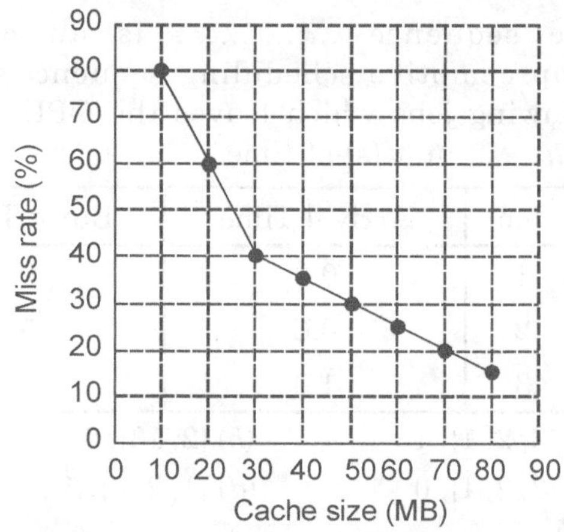

The smallest cache size required to ensure an average read latency of less than 6 ms is____ MB.

2015

8. Consider a uniprocessor system executing three tasks T_1, T_2 and T_3, each o which is composed of an infinite sequence of jobs (or instances) which arrive periodically at intervals of 3, 7 and 20 milliseconds, respectively. The priority of each task is the inverse of its period, and the available tasks are scheduled in order of priority, with the highest priority task scheduled first. Each instance of T_1, T_2 and T_3 requires an execution time of 1, 2 and 4 milliseconds, respectively. Given that all tasks initially arrive at the beginning of the 1st millisecond and task preemptions are allowed, the first instance of T_3 completes its execution at the end of ________ milliseconds.

9. Suppose the following disk request sequence (track numbers) for a disk with 100 tracks is given: 45, 20, 90, 10, 50, 60, 80, 25, 70. Assume that the initial position of the R/W head is on track 50. The additional distance that will be traversed by the R/W head when the Shortest Seek Time First (SSTF) algorithm is used compared to the SCAN (Elevator) algorithm (assuming that SCAN algorithm moves towards 100 when it starts execution) is ______ tracks.

2014

10. Assume that there are 3 page frames which are initially empty. If the page reference string 1, 2, 3, 4, 2, 1, 5, 3, 2, 4, 6, the number of page faults using the *optimal replacement policy* is ________.

11. A system uses 3 page frames for storing process pages in main memory. It uses the Least Recently Used (LRU) page replacement policy. Assume that all the page frames are initially empty. What is the total number of page faults that will occur while processing the page reference string given below?

4, 7, 6, 1, 7, 6, 1, 2, 7, 2

12. A system contains three programs and each requires three tape units for its operation. The minimum number of tape units which the system must have such that deadlocks never arise is ________.

13. An operating system uses *shortest remaining time first* scheduling algorithm for pre-emptive scheduling of processes. Consider the following set of processes with their arrival times and CPU burst times (in milliseconds):

Process	Arrival Time	Burst Time
P1	0	12
P2	2	4
P3	3	6
P4	8	5

The average waiting time (in milliseconds) of the processes is ________.

1992

14. Many of the advanced microprocessors prefetch instructions and store it in an instruction buffer to speed up processing. This speed up is achieved because ....

ANSWERS

MCQ Type Questions

1. (*a*)	**2.** (*a*)	**3.** (*a*)	**4.** (*d*)	**5.** (*c*)	**6.** (*a*)	**7.** (*d*)	**8.** (*a*)	**9.** (*d*)	**10.** (*d*)
11. (*c*)	**12.** (*d*)	**13.** (*d*)	**14.** (*d*)	**15.** (*b*)	**16.** (*d*)	**17.** (*c*)	**18.** (*b*)	**19.** (*c*)	**20.** (*b*)
21. (*a*)	**22.** (*a*)	**23.** (*a*)	**24.** (*b*)	**25.** (*a*)	**26.** (*a*)	**27.** (*d*)	**28.** (*a*)	**29.** (*b*)	**30.** (*a*)
31. (*b*)	**32.** (*a*)	**33.** (*b*)	**34.** (*c*)	**35.** (*a*)	**36.** (*b*)	**37.** (*d*)	**38.** (*d*)	**39.** (*c*)	**40.** (*b*)
41. (*a*)	**42.** (*b*)	**43.** (*b*)	**44.** (*a*)	**45.** (*d*)	**46.** (*b*)	**47.** (*b*)	**48.** (*c*)	**49.** (*d*)	**50.** (*b*)
51. (*a*)	**52.** (*a*)	**53.** (*a*)	**54.** (*b*)	**55.** (*a*)	**56.** (*c*)	**57.** (*b*)	**58.** (*b*)	**59.** (*a*)	**60.** (*a*)
61. (*d*)	**62.** (*d*)	**63.** (*b*)	**64.** (*d*)	**65.** (*a*)	**66.** (*a*)	**67.** (*c*)	**68.** (*c*)	**69.** (*b*)	**70.** (*b*)
71. (*b*)	**72.** (*b*)	**73.** (*d*)	**74.** (*c*)	**75.** (*)	**76.** (*c*)	**77.** (*b*)	**78.** (*a*)	**79.** (*d*)	**80.** (*b, d*)
81. (*c, d*)	**82.** (*a*)	**83.** (*)	**84.** (*b*)	**85.** (*b*)	**86.** (*b*)	**87.** (*b*)	**88.** (*b*)	**89.** (*b*)	**90.** (*a*)
91. (*b*)	**92.** (*c*)	**93.** (*b*)	**94.** (*d*)	**95.** (*c*)	**96.** (*a*)	**97.** (*c*)	**98.** (*d*)	**99.** (*b*)	**100.** (*c*)
101. (*a*)	**102.** (*b*)	**103.** (*b*)	**104.** (*d*)	**105.** (*)	**106.** (*)	**107.** (*)	**108.** (*a*)	**109.** (*c*)	**110.** (*b*)
111. (*a*)	**112.** (*b*)	**113.** (*b*)	**114.** (*a, b, c*)	**115.** (*d*)	**116.** (*b*)	**117.** (*d*, e)	**118.** (*c*)	**119.** (*)	**120.** (*a*)

Numerical Type Questions

1. (384 MB)	**2.** (346)	**3.** (1)	**4.** (30)	**5.** (8.25)	**6.** (7)	**7.** (30)	**8.** (12)	**9.** (10)	**10.** (7)
11. (6)	**12.** (7)	**13.** (5.5)	**14.** (*)						

EXPLANATIONS

MCQ TYPE QUESTIONS

1. Shortest remaining time first minimizes the average waiting time in the ready queue.

6. 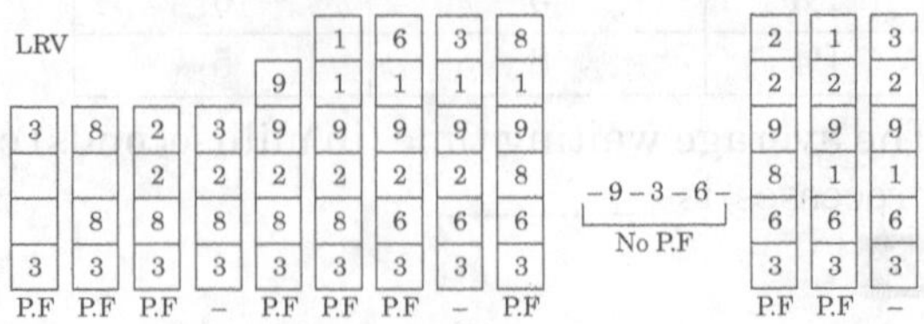

Total page fault = 9

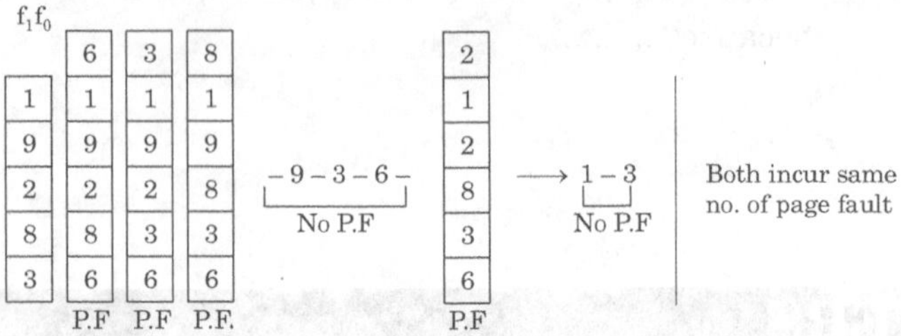

5- Page fault

Total page fault = 9

8. Consider the memory partition and using best fit algorithm

200	400	600	500	300	250
	357	491	468		201

Hence 200 and 300 are not alloted to any process.

9. The maximum number of processor is not dependent upon number of CPU's.

10. For deadlock prevention we need to dissatisfy any of the necessary condition for deadlock
    1. For hold and wait if we are disatisfy it can be hold or wait for hold ... before process start os assign all resources. While executing if process making new resource request it has to release all its assign resources that is waiting for release resources.
    2. If we are dissatisfy circular wait condition suppose there are five resources uniquely numbered r1 to r5 and there five processes p1 to p5 suppose p2 hold r1 ,and requesting for r2,and r2 hold by p3 and wait for r3, r3 hold by p4 wait for r4 which is hold by p5 and wait for r5 which is held by p1 (this is happening in circular manner) (condition to come out from circular wait is a process can hold the resource and request for new resource only when holding resource id is lesser then requesting resource id) in above p1 is violating condition.
    3. If we dissatisfy preemption if a process hold some resources requesting for new resources and that requesting resources are busy with some other process requesting process voluntarily release its held resources.
    4. Answer, according to 1 and 3 above statements first option is correct.

    According to above second statement second option is correct.

    According to above second statement if we implement the logic in reverse order third option is also correct.

    According to second statement condition fourth option is also correct.

11. Given Snapshot

Process	AT	BT
A	0	3
B	1	6
C	4	4
D	6	2

(*i*) FcFs

Process	AT	BT	LT	TAT
A	0	3	3	3
B	1	6	9	8
C	4	4	13	9
D	6	2	15	9

$$\frac{29}{4} = 7.25$$

Gantt chart

A	B	C	D

0 3 9 13 15

(*ii*) SJF

Process	AT	BT	LT	TAT
A	0	3	3	3
B	1	6	9	8
C	4	4	15	11
D	6	2	11	5

$$\frac{27}{4} = 6.75$$

Gantt chart

A	B	D	C

0 3 9 11 15

B – 6 C – 9

D – 2

(*iii*) SRTF

Process	AT	BT	CT	TAT
A	0	3	3	3
B	1	6	15	14
C	4	4	8	4
D	6	2	10	4

$$\frac{25}{4} = 6.25$$

Gantt chart

A	A	B	C	C	D	B

0 1 3 4 6 8 10 15

A – 2 B – 5 C – 2 B – 5 B – 5

B – 6 C – 4 B – 5 D – 2

D – 2

(*iv*) R.Q (Q = 2)

Process	AT	BT	CT	TAT
A	0	3	5	5
B	1	6	15	14
C	4	4	13	9
D	6	2	11	5

$$\frac{33}{4} = 8.25$$

Gantt Chart

R. Q

A	B	A	C	B	D	C	B

0 2 4 5 7 9 11 13 15

12. User threads are supported above the kernel and a managed without kernel support. The thread function library to implement user level threads usually runs on top of the system in user mode. Thus these threads with in a process are invisible to the operating system. Since the kernel is unaware of the existence of such threads; when one user level thread is blocked in the kernel all other threads of its process are blocked. So options (*a*) and (*b*) are true. (*c*) The OS is aware of kernel level threads. Kernel threads are scheduled by the OS's scheduling algorithms and require a "lightweight" context switch to switch between (that is, registers, PC and SP must be changed, but the memory context remains the same among kernel threads in the (same process). User level threads are much faster to switch between as there is not context switch.(*d*) False Kernel level threads within the same process share code section, data section and other operating system resources such as open files and signals.

13. Physical page frames are 20 contain pages numbered 101 to 120.

Program accessed page numbered 1, 2, - - - - 100 in that order and repeat thrice.

14. To implement recursion, activation record should be implemented by providing dynamic memory allocation. This dynamic allocation is done from runtime stack. Heap is essential to allocate memory for data structures at run-time, not for recursion. So statement 1 and 3 are correct.

15. (*b*) Correct

(*a*)

X	Y	Z
P(*a*)	P(*b*)	P(*c*)
P(*b*)	P(*c*)	P(*d*)
P(*c*)	P(*d*)	P(*a*)

wrong answer because:

suppose X execute first & executed P(*a*) & P(*b*) then process switches to Z, then Z executed P(*c*), P(*d*) & wait for P(*a*) then again process switches to X & X then wait for P(*c*).

so, X is waiting for C which is occupied by Z & Z is waiting for X so no one can execute & deadlock occur.

(*b*) Correct

X	Y	Z
P(*b*)	P(*b*)	P(*a*)
P(*a*)	P(*c*)	P(*c*)
P(*c*)	P(*d*)	P(*d*)

Correct because all process does not have reverse call for wait on any variable.

(*c*)

X	Y	Z
P(*b*)	P(*c*)	P(*a*)
P(*a*)	P(*b*)	P(*c*)
P(*c*)	P(*d*)	P(*d*)

wrong answer because sequence of P(*b*) & P(*c*) are reverse or opposite in X & Y respectively so deadlock may occur.

(*d*)

X	Y	Z
P(*a*)	P(*c*)	P(*c*)
P(*b*)	P(*b*)	P(*d*)
P(*c*)	P(*d*)	P(*a*)

wrong answer because sequence of P(*c*) & P(*a*) are opposite in Z & X. so deadlock may occur.

16. A shared variable x_1 initialized to zero, is opereated on by four concurrent processes W, X, Y, Z as follows. Each of the processes W and X reads X from memory, increments by one. Stores it to memory and the terminates. Each of processes Y and z reads x from memory, decrements by two, stores it to memory and then terminates. Each process before reading x invokes the P operation (i.e. wait) on a counting semaphore S and invokes the V operation (i.e. signal) on the semaphore s after storing x to memory. Semaphore S is initalized to two. What is the maximum possible value of x after all processes complete execution?

⇒ x , w reads x and increment x by 1.

y, z reads x and decrement by 2.

Start with x. will perform P(s) then s = 1. read $x = 0$ $x = x + 1 = 1$

then y will perform P(s) then s = 0. read $x = 0$

$x = x - 2 = -2$, then store $x \cdot v(s)$, $s = 1$

then z will perform P(s) there s = 0, read $x = -2$

$x = x - 2 = -4$, then store x, $v(s)$, $s = 1$

then x will store $x \cdot v(s)$, $s = 2$, $x = 1$

then w will perform P(s), $s = 1$, read $x = 1$

$x = x + 1 = 2$, store x, $v(s)$, $s = 2$, $\boxed{x = 2}$

17. If fork is called n times, there will be total 2^n running processes including the parent process. So, there will be $2^n - 1$ child processes.

18. 1, 2, 3, 2, 4, 1, 3, 2, 4, 1

LRU	1	1	1	1	3	2	4	1	3	2
		2	2	3	2	4	1	3	2	4
			3	2	4	1	3	2	4	1
	F	F	F		F	F	F	F	F	F = 9
FIFO	1	1	1	1	2	3	3	4	4	4
		2	2	2	3	4	4	1	1	1
			3	3	4	1	1	2	2	2
	F	F	F		F	F		F		= 6
OPTIMAL	1	1	1	1	4	4	4	2	2	2
		2	2	2	1	1	1	1	1	1
			3	3	3	3	3	4	4	4
	F	F	F	NF	F			F		= 5

Optimal < FIFO < LRU

5 < 6 < 9

19. FCFS will complete in

P_1 P_2 P_3

and Round Robin

P_1 P_3 P_2

P_1	P_2	P_1	P_3	P_2	P_1	P_3

0 2 4 6 8 10 11 13

20. Let S be a non-serial schedule, without loss of generality assume that T1 has started earlier than T2. The first instruction of T1 is read (P) and the last instruction of T2 is write (P), so the precedence graph for S has an edge from T1 to T2, now since S is a non-serial schedule the first instruction of T2 (read(Q)) should be executed before last instruction of T1 (write(Q)) and since read and write are conflicting operations, the precedence graphs for S also contains an edge from T2 to T1, So we will have a cycle in the precedence graph which implies that any non serial schedule with T1 as the earliest transaction will not be conflict serializable.

In a similar way we can show that if T2 is the earliest transaction then also the schedule is not conflict serializable.

22. Effort person per month = a.(KDSI)^B

KDSI = kilo LOC

$= 2.8 \times (40)^{1.20}$

$= 2.8 \times 83.6511$

= 234.22 person per month

23. Number of clock cycles required by using load-store approach

$= 2 + 500 \times 7 = 3502$

and that of by using DMA

$= 20 + 500 \times 2 = 1020$

$$\text{Required speed up} = \frac{3502}{1020} = 3.4$$

24. P = page fault rate

EA = p × page fault service time

+ (1 – p) × Memory access time

$$= \frac{1}{10^6} \times 10 \times 10^6 + \left(1 - \frac{1}{10^6}\right) \times 20$$

$\cong$ 29.9 ns

25. Both process can't be in critical section simulteneously, so they should be in mutual exclusion.

26. Initially all pages are bring in physical memory and all are different, so that all time page fault occur.

So, 100 page fault after that in reverse order pages required.

So we see that 4 pages at last already in memory.

So there is no page fault for these.

So only 100 – 4 = 96 page faults occur.

∴ Total page faults = 100 + 96 = 196

27. SRTF (Shortest Remaining Time First)

Preemptive may cause of starvation and RR (Round Robin) is better than FCFS in response time because in RR if some process comes letter, then after some time it brings in process but in FCFS it is not upto finishing of First process.

Alternately

I. In SRTF case, if processes with small processing time keep on coming, then processes with higher processing time has to wait and may starve.

II. In preemptive scheduling, if processes of high priority keep on coming, then processes with low priority may starve.

III. In RR, every process is served for a quantam time period but it is not in FCFS.

Thus all I, II and III are true.

28. ,Initial P1 and P2 does not go because they are not using semaphore initially. P0 uses semaphore whose value S0 = 1, and P1 and P2 uses S1 = S2 = 0, So initially P0 executes so it prints '0'.

Now, it release S1 and S2 means value of these now 1 = S1 = S2. Then process P1 & P2 executes after that they Release. So and it is S0 = 1 again. Then this prints '0' again means at least twice **0** print.

Alternately

- Initially P1 and P2 can't proceed because S1 and S2 are 0.
- P0 will proceed and print '0' then it release S1 and S2.
- Either of S1 and S2 will release so it prints '0' again.

29. If $n = 21, k = 12$

(if (i%2 = = 0) {if ($i < n$) Request Ri;

if ($i + 2 < n$) Request R_{i+2};

else (if ($i<n$) Request R_{n-i}, if (i+2<n) Request (R_{n-i-2i})

We seen that if value of k = 11, 12.

Now first $k = 11$ means $p_{11-1} = p_{10} = p_i \Rightarrow i = 10$

then according to logic

initially it goes if block because (i%2 = 0)

(10%2 = = 0)

then it Request R_{10}, R_{10+2} (R_{12})

$\Rightarrow R_{10}, R_{12}$ Resources

if now next k = 12 then i = 11

Now it goes in else block and

Request R_{n-i}, R_{n-i-2}

$\Rightarrow R_{21-11}, R_{21-11-2}$

$\Rightarrow R_{10}, R_8$

then it also Request R_{10} then

both k = 11, k = 12 request R_{10}.

It is problem of dead lock.

30. FIFO may have Belady's Anamoly

e.g. in FIFO for three frames the reference string

1, 2, 3, 4, 1, 2, 5, 1, 2, 3, 4, 5

There are 9 page faults and for four frames for the reference string there will be 10 faults.

31. Page frame number is essential content in each entry of the page table.

Alternately

The page table has the ability to mark on entry invalid through a valid invalid bit or special value of protection bit, which is often called page frame number.

32. *At resource use*

t = 0 R2 - 2units R3 - 2 units R4 - 1units

t = 2 R2 - 2units R3 - 3 units R4 - 2 units R1- 1units

t = 3 R2 - 2units R3 - 3 units R4 -2 units<u>R1- 4 units</u>

t = 4 R2 - 2units R3 - 3 units R4 - 2units<u>R1- 5 units</u>

t = 5 R2 - 1 units R3 - 3units R4 - 2unitsR 1-2units

t = 6 R2 - 1units R3 - 2 units R4 - 2units R1-2units

t = 7 R2- 2 units R3 - 1 units R4 - 2unitsR 1- 2units

t = 8 R2 - 2 units R3- 1 units <u>R4- 3 units</u> R1- 1units

t = 9

Underline show that at that time requirement of resource is less than avaiability but it does not cause dead lock. All process finsh without any dead lock.

33. Requests : 4, 34, 10, 7, 19, 73, 2, 15, 6, 20

Current Position of head is 50.

Current	50	34	20	19	15	10	7	6	4	2
Next Access	34	20	19	15	10	7	6	4	2	73
Difference	16	14	1	4	5	5	1	2	2	71

Total time = 16 + 14 + 1 + 4 + 5 + 3 + 1 + 2 + 2 + 71

= 119 ms

34. In premptive sheduling the process which allocated the CPU keeps it and release it only whne it switching to wating state. Also a process P_2 in blocked state can make transition E while other process P_1 in running.

Alternately

A process P_2 in blocked state can make transition E while another P_1 is in running state.

OS uses preemptive Scheduling.

35. In given program the process test -and-set in critical section and in function leaves _CS initialise memory location x to zero. So this process is dead lock free.

36. Most computer system support a large logical address space (2^{32} to 2^{64}). The page table become excessively large for example.

Consider a system with a 32 bit logical address space. If page size 4K(2^{12}), then page table may consist 1 million page. For this we use multilevels page table.

37. Connect result in sending SYN packets (TCP handshaking).

38. Index allocation cannot allocate very large file.

39. P(I) : $P_6(x_1)$; S = S – 1; if (S < 0) {$V_6(K_6)$; $p_6(y_5)$;}

else $V_6(x_6)$; value of $x_6 = 1$ satisfy

V(S) : $P_6(x_6)$; $P_6(x_6)$; S = S + 2 ;

if (S < = 0) $V_6(y_6)$; $V_6(x_5)$;

$Y_6 = 0$ satisfy

40. ISR is invoked after completion of I/O irrespective of the type of I/O.

41. In deadlock avoidance, the request for resources is granted if only the state guarantees deadlock would never occur (safe state)

Deadlock prevention provides a set of methods that ensures that at least one of the necessary condition cannot hold – (mutual exclusion, hold & wait, no preemption & circular wait). These methods prevents deadlock by constraining how request can be made.

42. Number of child processes $2^n - 1$

43. Number of bits required for first lent = 24

Number of bits required for second lent = 24

Number of bits required for third lent = 24

44.

Group I	Group 2
P. Gang Scheduling	3. Thread Scheduling
Q. Rate Monotonic Scheduling	2. Real-time Scheduling
R. Fair Show Scheduling	1. Guaranteed Scheduling

45. Blocking one kernel level thread doesn't block all related threads.

46. Gant chart of scheduling can be given as

P_1	P_2	P_3	P_2	P_4
0 – 20	20 – 30	30 – 40	40 – 55	55 – 70

Waiting time of process, P_2 = (20 – 15) + 10 = 15

47. Both P and Q are true But Q is not the reason for P because page fault is concerned with pages present in frame not with pages nearly the page accessed recently.

48. In present situation free resources are 0.12, so P_1 can be processed, after this resources will be 213 so P_0 can be processed therefore P_2 will be last to be processed.

49. Since there is no way to synchronize two statementwants 1 = true (in P_1) and wants 2 = true (in P_2).

So both of them may get executed one after other. In this situation there will be a dead lock.

But if only of the two is true, other will not go beyond cuhile loop, hence ensure nutual exclusion.

50. Context-Switches will be needed only at the time of switching over to some other process. Following table shows **time remaining** for three processes at different instants of time.

Time/Processes →	I	II	III	Process continued
0	10	-	-	I
2	8	20	-	I
6	4	20	30	I
10	0	20	30	II
30	0	0	30	III
60	0	0	0	-

Hence context-witches are needed only at times 10 and 30.

51. The P and V function is as follows :

```
1. void P (binary-semaphore * S) {
2. unsigned y;
3. unsigned * x = & (S → value);}
4. do {
5. fetch-and-set x, y;
6. } while (y);
7. }
8. void V (binary-semaphore *S) {
9. {S → value = 0;}
10. }
```

fetch-and-set instruction always sets the memory location $x = 1$ and fetches the old value of x into y. The binary-semphore * S takes only two values either 0 and 1. When we initiliaze S = 0 then in statement 3 this value will be start at location x and fetch-and-set instruction charge the value of $x = 0$ to $x = 1$ and y becomes 0. If there are more than two processes and context switching between processes is disabled in P then this implementation doesn't work properly and can't synchronize the processes.

52. *Number of bits required for various purposes in the 32 bit address is as follows :*

To find memory cell out of 4-way associative memory – 2 bits are needed.

To find page out of 128 page table entries - 7 bits are needed.

To find required byte in the page of size 4 kB – 12 bits are needed.

Total bits consumed in this way = 21

TLB tag's minimum size = 32 – 21 = 11 bits

53.

Process	id	Arrival time	CPU Burst
P_0	0	0	2
P_1	1	0	4
P_2	2	0	8

Remaining Time

P_0	2
P_1	4
P_2	8

The Gannt chart for LRTF scheduling algorithm

P_0	P_1	P_2	P_2	P_2	P_2	P_2	P_1	P_2	P_1	P_2	P_0	P_1	P_2

0 12 3 4 5 6 7 8 9 10 11 12 13 14

Turn around time for $P_0 = 12 - 0 = 12$

Turn around time for $P_1 = 13 - 1 = 12$

Turn around time for $P_2 = 14 - 2 = 12$

Average Turn around Time = $36/3 = 12 \approx 13$

55. Total number of processes = n

Process i is holding x_i instances of a resource R for $1 \leq i \leq n$

Process i holding resource x_i and additional required y_i

There are two processes p and q such that $y_p = y_q = 0$

For no dead lock can occur

$\min(x_p, x_q) < (\max_{k \neq p,q} yk)$

56. There are n process $P_1, P_2, ..., P_n$.

Number of identical resources = m

The maximum resource requirement for a process P_2 is S_P where $S_i > 0$

If all processes is in safe state or system can allocate resources to each process P_i in some order and still avoid a dead lock. We can avoid the dead lock if each P_i can still request can be satisfied by the current avialable resources plus the resources held by process P_j such that $j < i$ The maximum resource requirement of n processes is $\sum_{i=1}^{n} S_i$ and this amout must less than $m + n$ so

$$\sum_{i=1}^{n} S_i < (m+n)$$

57. Here, we follow concept of copy on write

So, we have two different pages one for child and one for parent.

Because value of v and y are different, so they read (assume value 10), then child increases to '15' and parent decrement to '5'.

58. Consider the each statement

(*i*) Statement is false because there is no connection between kernel-supported threads and context switch.

(*ii*) Statement is true because it is the drawback of user-level threads blocking system call can block the entire process.

(*iii*) Statement is true because kernel-supported threads having own memory area and scheduled independently by the operating system.

(*iv*) Statement is false because kernel is unware about user level threads and there is no kernel support to user-level threads.

59. If the processes are in the memory, page frames is created in the virtual memory to minimize the system load and to improve the preformance.

60.

Process	Arrival Time	Burst Time
P1	0	5
P2	1	3
P3	2	3
P4	4	1

P_1	P_2	P_2	P_2	P_4	P_3	P_3	P_3	P_1	P_1	P_1	P_1
1	2	3	4	5	6	7	8	9	10	11	12

Gantt chart for scheduling.

Turn arround time for

$P_1 = 12$

$P_2 = 4 - 1$

$= 3$

$P_3 = 6$

$P_4 = 1$

Average turn around time

$$= \frac{P_1 + P_2 + P_3 + P_4}{4}$$

$$= \frac{12 + 3 + 6 + 1}{4}$$

$$= 5.5$$

61. First P_1 issue signal wait(x) at that time process P_2 issue wait(y) and when P_1 issue wait(y) then process P_2 issue wait (x); so correct sequence is

$P(S_x), P(S_y)$; $P(S_x), P(S_Y)$

62. S_x and S_y are two binary semaphore if assume P means wait or V means signal then for two process P_1 and P_2 we take alternate then there in no chance of dead lock.

The code is as follows :

P_1	P_2
while true do {	while true do {
$L_1 : P(S_x)$	$L_3 : P(S_x)$
$L_2 : P(S_y)$	$L_4 : P(S_y)$
$x = x + 1;$	$y = y + 1;$
$y = y - 1;$	$x = y - 1;$
$V(S_x);$	$V(S_y);$
$V(S_y);\}$	$V(S_x);\}$

63. Disk block address = 32 bit

It can address 2^{32} location, i.e. 2^{32} byte, so size of file is 2^{32}. Hence correct answer is 2^{32}.

64. Throughput → one measure of work is the number of processes that are completed per time unit, called throughput.

CPU Utilization : We want to keep CPU as busy as possible. In case of larger block size and fixed block size file system, CPU utilization is poorer and throughput is also decresead.

65. Number of page $= \frac{2^{32}}{2^{12}} = 2^{20}$

Hence, number of pages is much in number, thus, chances to internal fragmentation due to size of pages is larger, then overhead is reduced.

66. CPU utilization is always least when we take First Come First Serve.

CPU utilization is maximum when we take Round Robin Scheduling.

67. TLB hit ratio = 96 %

TLB access time = 1 ns

Virtual page hit ratio = 90 %

Main memory access time = 10 ns

For no page faults Average time

= hit ratio × cache acess time

+ (1 – hit ratio) × memory access time

$= 0.9 \times 1 + 0.1 \times 10$

= 1.9 ns

≅ 2ns

68. Total amount of memory required for starting the page tables of this process

$$= 4 \times 2^{12} \text{ byte}$$
$$= 4 \times 4 \times 2^{10} \text{ byte}$$
$$= 16 \text{ kB}$$

69. To get the expected output, The sequence of process is P, Q, P, Q, P, Q and so on we must initialize S = 1 and T = 0.

70. If the output string never contains a substring of the from 01^n0 or 10^n1 where n is odd then the procedures becomes.

S = 1

Process P:	Process Q:
While (1){	While (1){
W : P(S)	Y : P(S)
print '0';	print '1';
print '0';	print '1';
X : V (S)	Z : V(S)
}	}

71. Throughput. If the CPU is busy executing processor, then work is being done. One measure of work is the number of process that are coupleted per time unit called throughput. By increasing the number of processors, we hope to get more work done in shorter period of time.

* For uniprocessor first come first served give maximum throughput, but in case of known untime shortest job first is used.
* If multiprocess then round robin scheduling is the best.
* In the case of turnaround shortest job first is the best.

75. (*a*) (1) signal (mutex)

(2) signal (mutex)

(3) R! = 0 or W! = 0

or

not (R = 0 and W = 0)

76. Threads refer to the execution of different processes simultaneously in the CPU. Virtual address space is implemented in memory. The file-system in the way in which data in a disk is organized. A signal is acted upon using the mechanism of interrupts.

77. Nearest cylinder nect gives the best through put because: First nearest cylinder gives first ouput.

78. System calls, State changes can be caused by program commands, which are referred to as system calls and are implemented using software interrupts or automatically following certain events.

79. The schedule is not serializable

80. Virtual memory is in fact stored in the secondary storage, which increases memory access time.

Processes can be given larger protected address spaces in virtual memory than is possible by just segmenting real memory.

A linker always assigns addresses independent of where the program is loaded in physical memory, so it is not a particular advantage of virtual memory.

Programs larger than physical memory size can be run as pages of the program can be swapped from virtual memory to physical memory as and when required.

81. Context switch does involve saving current register values and restoring saved register values for process B.

Address translation tables are changed and new ones for the incoming process are loaded.

C and D are typically not done on a context switch.

82. RAID configurations provide redundancy data store in the disk and thus improve fault tolerance.

83. (*a*) Let the minimum page size be $z2^n$ bytes.

Each segment is of size $\frac{2^{16}}{8} = 2^{13}$ bytes.

So, the page table must address a memory space of 2^{13} bytes. The number of pages in this memory space for one segment is 2^{13-n} bytes. Also, since each page table entry is 2 bytes long, the number of page table entries in the page table is 2^{n-1}.

Equating the two,

$$2^{13-n} = 2_{n-1}$$

or $$n = 7$$

So, minimum page size is 2^7 bytes.

(*b*) We assume that there is only one TLB for all the segments. So, the TLB would have pages which may be anywhere in the entire address space of 2^{16} bytes. Since, the page size is 2^9 bytes, the number of pages is $2^{16-9} = 2^7$.

So, we need 7 bytes for identifying the age. We may also need 3 bits for page protection, 1 valid bit and 1 dirty bit. So the number of tag bits is 7 + 3 + 1 + 1 = 12.

(*c*) Each page table entry has 16 bits, out of which 7 bits are used for addressing the page, and there is one valid bit, one dirty bit and 3 bits for page protection. This leaves 4 bits for storing the aging information.

84. The output device used to print the output of a number of jobs executed like bates processing.

Spool Device. In spool device, number of jobs executed like batch processing.

e.g. Printer.

85. A situation like this, where several processes access and manipulate the same data conveniently and the outcome of the execution depends on the particular order in which the access take place is called a race condition.

86. 6P (Wait) operations will change the value to 4 and 4V (signal) operations will make it to 8.

87. Tape drive = 6

Each process needs = 2

There are n number of process.

For deedlock free, $n = 6 - 1 = 5$.

88. Required physical memory for run the program is maximum load of any overlay tree

= size of D + size of E

= 6 KB + 8KB = 14 KB

89. In Round Robin scheduling every one get quantum time for executing.

number of process = n

Each process takes S second, so total time taken by process = nS

For process switching is minimized.

For quantum size $q \geq t$-total time taken by process number of process –1.

So, $$q \geq = \frac{t - nS}{n-1}$$

where, t = total time.

90. Effective instruction for k instructions

$= i \times k + j$

Effective instruction for 1 instruction

$$= \frac{i \times k + j}{k} = \text{i} + \frac{j}{k}$$

91. Locality of references implies to cache memory, in which condition we get that are of the pages used in last few page references.

92. (*a*) SCAN is case of disk scheduling in which disk arm starts at one end of the disk and moves towards the other end, servicing request as it reaches each cylinder, until it gets to the other end of the disk. At the other end, the direction of head movement is reversed and servicing continues. The head continuously scans back and forth across the disk. SCAN algorithm is sometimes called *elevator algorithm*.

(*b*) **Batch processing :** Batch processing look like queus. It works like first in first out.

(*c*) **Time sharing.** In the case of Round Robin, it works like time sharing processing. It takes quantum of time for each process.

(*d*) **LIFO** is used like a interrupt processes. In the case of interrupt processing, last in first out method is used.

93. I/O redirection. The common shells have a simple syntax for changing what files are open for standard I/O streams of a process. Changing a standard file is called *I/O redirection*. The subsequent command forces all output and all error messages to be redirected to a file without the ampers and error message appear on the terminals.

94. When an interrupt occurs, an operating system changed their state and process have goto, wait or blocked or in ready queue.

95. In thrashing, paging activity is more comparegion to executing high paging activity is called thrashing.

96. Dirty bit. If no free frames, then two page transfers one page out and one page in are required. In this situation effectively doubles the page fault service time, which will increase the effective access time accordingly.

This overhead can be reduced by the use of a modify (dirty) bit. Each page or frame may have a modify bit associated with it in the hardware. The modify bit or dirty bit for a page is set by the hardware whenever anyword or byte in the page is written into indicating that page has been modified.

97. Number of users = 3

Energy one need of resources = 2.

So, minimum number of resources for no dead lock is = 4

because Ist user = 2

2nd user = 1

3rd user = 1

Ist user used the resource, then transfer the next process.

98. A process must execute wait (mutex) before entering the monitor and must execute signal (mutex) after leaving the monitor.

Since a signaling process must wait until the resumed process either leaves or waits, an additional semaphore next is introduced, initialized to 0. On which the signaling process may suspended themselves.

P = 1 to 9.

If P = 9 (for max)

then P (mutex) = 8

then V (mutex) = 8 + 1 = 9

99. Preemptive Scheduling. In pre-emptive scheduling, the process which is allocated the CPU keeps it and releases it only when it switching to a waiting state.

100. Critical section. A critical section is a segment of code in which a process may be reading common variables, updating a table etc.

101. Spool device. Spooling is a process in which high speed hardware can be used to temporarily store the data transferred by processor to the Input/Output device. When Input/Output device is free, the transferred data is send to the device, thus spooling can keep both the **CPU** and Input Output devices working at much higher rates.

102. Memory size of variable partition are 200 K bytes and 260 K bytes.

So, total memory left = 1000 (200 + 260) = 540.

So, 541 Kbytes could denied for reqeust.

103. Dining Philosophers Problem.

Representation of the need to allocate several processes in a dead lock and startvation free manner. Its simple solution by *semaphore.*

Solution to the Dining - Philosophers problem that ensures freedom from dead lock.

* Allow at most four philosophies to be sitting simultaneously at the table.
* Allow a philospher to pickup her chopstics only if both chopstics are available.
* Use an asymmetric solution, that is, an odd philospher picks up first her left chopstick, where as an even philospher picks up her right chop stick and then her left chopstick.

104.

Jobs	Burst time
A	4
B	1
C	8
D	1

1	2	3	4	5	6	7	8	9
A	B	C	D	A	C	A	C	A

105.

Virtual page number	page offsee	Virtual address
8 bits	8 bits	

Page offset corresponds to the 8 lsbs of virtual address. The hexadecimal address sequence is

OOFF, OIOD, IOFF, IIBO

The last two hexadecimal digits (corresponding) to 8 lsb's of equivalent binary address) gives page offset. Hence the page reference string is

ϕϕ, ϕ1, 1ϕ, 11 (Hexadecimal)

or ϕ, 1, 16, 17 (decimal)

number of pages that the physical memory can contain

$$= \frac{\text{Physical Memory Size}}{\text{Page Size}} = \frac{1 \times 20^{10}}{256} = 4$$

Page Input	Physical Memory Pages 1	2	3	4	Page fault
Initially	17	1	63	—	
0	17	1	63	0	Page fault
1	17	1	63	0	No page fault
—	17	63	0	1	
16	63	0	1	16	Page fault
17	0	1	16	17	Page fault

New status of the list is

0, 1, 16, 17

↑

LRU Page

Number of page faults 3

Number of page replacement 2

(corresponding to page 16 and 17)

106. (*a*) We can prove that the system can be in the given state provided there is a safe sequence. One such safe sequence is P1, P2, P0.

(*b*) If P0 is given one unit of resource type R1, the system will move to unsafe state such that no process will be able to complete. Hence the request should be denied.

107. (*a*) As there must be at least one directory entry per file,

Maximum number of files

$$= \frac{\text{Directory size}}{\text{Directory entry size}} = \frac{4\,\text{kB}}{32\,b} = 1024$$

(*b*) A single file can occupy at most as many data blocks as can be addressed by 8 bit FAT entries.

Number of distinct FAT entry representations = 28 = 256

As some x of these representations must be used to indicate end of file, unusual block, bad block, etc. Maximum possible file size = 256 – x blocks. For blocks of small x, or $(256 - x)\ x\ 4$ K bytes.

108. Segmentation may be cause of external fragmentation. A segment table kept in register and used quickly. In segment table, the addition to the base and compression with the limit can be done simultaneously to same time.

109. Belady amamly–Number of page fault occur more when we increase the page frame, generally page fault decrease when the page frame increases. It happen unexpected. So it is called Belady anamolies.

110. Round Bobin–A small unit of time, quantum is selected. Each process in the ready queue is allotted the CPU for this quantum.

111. For preemptive scheduling

Job (P)	Arrival time	Burst time
1	0.0	9
2	0.6	5
3	1.0	1

Gantt Chart–

P_1	P_2	P_3	P_2	P_1

0 0.6 1 2 6.6 15

113. The PUSH and POP operations are listed below :

The input string is 1, 2, 3, 4, 5

Operation	Stack	Putput String
PUSH	1	
PUSH	(Top) 1, 2 (Bottom))	
PUSH	1, 2, 3	
POP	1, 2	3
PUSH	1, 2, 4	
POP	1, 2	3, 4
PUSH	1, 2, 5	
POP	1, 2	3, 4, 5
POP	1	3, 4, 5, 2
POP		3, 4, 5, 2, 1

If 1, 5 are output then 4, 3, 2 must be the remaining output string since when we can POP 5, then the input string 2, 3, 4 must have been already PUSHed into and when it is POPed out we will get 4, 3, 2

(*a*) 3, 4, 5, 1, 2 is wrong (3, 4, 5, 2, 1 is correct)

(*c*) 1, 5, 2, 3, 4 is wrong (1, 5, 4, 3, 2 is correct)

(*d*) 5, 4, 3, 1, 2 is wrong (5, 4, 3, 2, 1 is correct)

NUMERICAL TYPE QUESTIONS

1. V.A. :

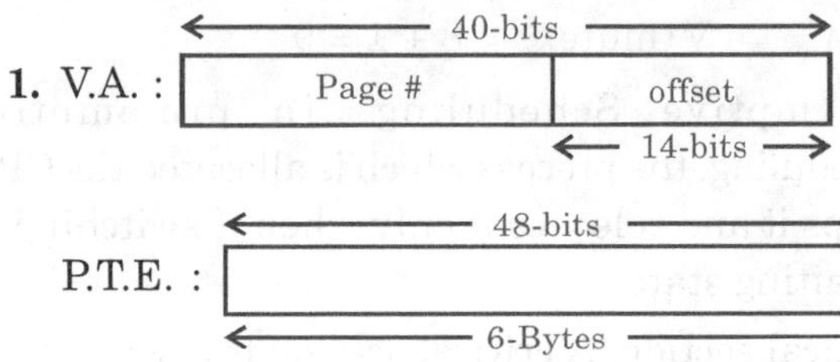

P.T. size = #entries in P.T. * P.T.E. size

$$= \frac{2^{40}}{2^{14}} * 6 = 2^{26} * 6$$

= 64 MB × 6 = 384 MB

2.

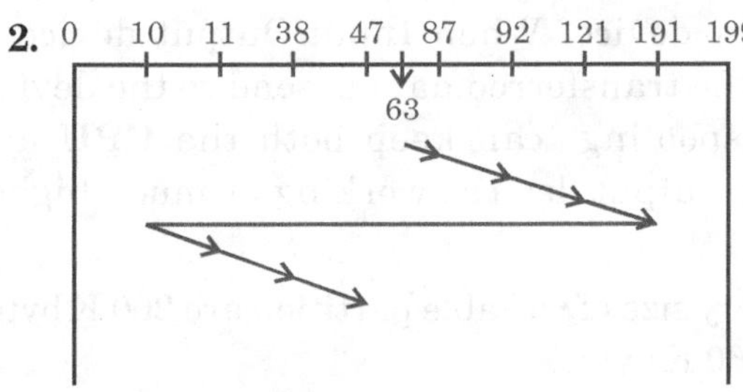

Total head movement

= (191 – 63) + (191 – 10) + (47 – 10)

= 128 + 181 + 37

= 346

3. Frame size = 10

Sequence $\{a_1, a_2, ..., a_{20}, a_1, a_2, ..., a_{20}\}$

⇒ Find difference of page fault of LIFO & optimal page replacement policy.

Consider a small case :

Frame size = 2

Sequence = $a_1 a_2 a_3 a_4 a_1 a_2 a_3 a_4$

LIFO :

a_1	a_2	a_3	a_4	a_1	a_2	a_3	a_4
	a_2	a_3	a_4	a_4	a_2	a_3	a_4
a_1	a_1	a_1	a_1	a_1	a_1	a_1	a_1
F	F	F	F	H	F	F	F

⇒ 7 faults

Optional :

a_1	a_2	a_3	a_4	a_1	a_2	a_3	a_4
	~~a_2~~	~~a_3~~	a_4	a_4	a_4	a_4	a_4
a_1	a_1	a_1	a_1	~~a_1~~	~~a_2~~	a_3	a_3
F	F	F	F	H	F	F	H

$\Rightarrow$ 6 faults

Difference = LIFO page faults – Optimal page faults

= 7 – 6

= 1

Similarly for :

Frame size = 10

Sequence = $a_1\, a_2\, a_3\, a_4 \ldots\ldots a_{20}\, a_1\, a_2\, a_3 \ldots a_{20}$

Difference = LIFO page faults – Optimal page faults

= 31 – 30

= 1

4. From the given question

5*G + 3*F = 3*5 + 5*3 = 30 ns

8. Gantt chart is

T_1^1	T_2^1	T_1^2	T_3^1	T_1^3	T_2^2	T_1^4	T_3^1	T_1^5

0 1 3 4 6 7 9 10 12

all tasks are arriving at beginning of 1 ms means at 0. T_1 has highest priority, then T_2 and the T_3. Hence first instance of T_1 by end of 12.

9. Using SSTF algorithm, total head moments are

5 + 15 + 10 + 10 + 10 + 65 + 5 + 10 = 130

using SCAN algorithm total head moments are

10 + 10 + 10 + 10 + 10 + 55 + 20 + 5 + 10 = 140

Hence additional distance covered = 140 – 130 = 10

10.

1	2	3	4	2	1	5	3	2	4	
		3	4	4	4	4	4	4	4	4
	2	2	2	2	2	2	2	2	2	6
1	1	1	1	1	1	5	3	3	3	3
F	F	F	F	H	H	F	F	H	H	F

7 page faults

11. Page reference string is

4, 7, 6, 1, 7, 6, 1, 2, 7, 2

Implementing LRU using 3 page frames

~~4~~ 1
~~2~~ 2
~~6~~ 7

Total page faults = 6

12.

Maximum	Allocate	Need	Available
$P_1 - 3$	2	1	1
$P_2 - 3$	2	1	
$P_3 - 3$	2	1	

With the above given data, after allocating 2 units of tape to each process, with 1 available unit any of the 3 process can be satisfied in such a way, that No dead lock will be there. So answer is 7 tape units.

13. The Gantt chart for SRTF scheduling algorithm is as follows:

P_1	P_2	P_3	P_4	P_1

0 2 6 12 17 27

$$\text{Average waiting time} = \frac{15+0+3+4}{4} = \frac{22}{4} = 5.5$$

14. Pretech is done during cycles that do not use buses.

7

CHAPTER

Databases

MCQ TYPE QUESTIONS

2016

1. Which of the following is **NOT** a superkey in a relational schema with attributes V, W, X, Y, Z and primary key V Y?

(*a*) VXYZ (*b*) VWXZ

(*c*) VWXY (*d*) VWXYZ

2. Which one of the following is **NOT** a part of the ACID properties of database transactions?

(*a*) Atomicity (*b*) Consistency

(*c*) Isolation (*d*) Deadlock-freedom

3. A database of research articles in a journal uses the following schema.

(VOLUME, NUMBER, STARTPAGE, ENDPAGE, TITLE, YEAR, PRICE)

The primary key is (VOLUME, NUMBER, STARTPAGE, ENDPAGE) and the following functional dependencies exist in the schema.

(VOLUME, NUMBER, STARTPAGE, ENDPAGE) → TITLE

(VOLUME, NUMBER) → YEAR

(VOLUME, NUMBER, STARTPAGE, ENDPAGE) → PRICE

The database is redesigned to use the following schemas.

(VOLUME, NUMBER, STARTPAGE, ENDPAGE, TITLE, PRICE)

(VOLUME, NUMBER, YEAR)

Which is the weakest normal form that the new database satisfies, but the old one does not?

(*a*) 1NF (*b*) 2NF

(*c*) 3NF (*d*) BCNF

4. Consider that B wants to send a message m that is digitally signed to A. Let the pair of private and public keys for A and B be denoted by K_x^- and K_x^+ for x = A, B, respectively. Let $K_x(m)$ represent the operation of encrypting m with a key K_x and H(m) represent the message digest. Which one of the following indicates the **CORRECT** way of sending the message m along with the digital signature to A?

(*a*) $\{m, K_B^+(H(m))\}$ (*b*) $\{m, K_B^-(H(m))\}$

(*c*) $\{m, K_A^-(H(m))\}$ (*d*) $\{m, K_A^+(H(m))\}$

5. Suppose a database schedule S involves transactions $T_1, ..., T_n$. Construct the precedence graph of S with vertices representing the transactions and edges representing the conflicts. If S is serializable, which one of the following orderings of the vertices of the precedence graph is guaranteed to yield a serial schedule?

(*a*) Topological order

(*b*) Depth-first order

(*c*) Breadth-first order

(*d*) Ascending order of transaction indices

6. Anarkali digitally signs a message and sends it to Salim. Verification of the signature by Salim requires

(*a*) Anarkali's public key

(*b*) Salim's public key

(*c*) Salim's private key

(*d*) Anarkali's private key

7. A binary relation R on N N is defined as follows: (a,b)R(c,d) if $a \le c$ or $b \le d$. Consider the following propositions:

P : R is reflexive

Q : R is transitive

Which one of the following statements is TRUE?

(*a*) Both P and Q are true

(*b*) P is true and Q is false

(*c*) P is false and Q is true

(*d*) Both P and Q are false

8. Consider the following database schedule with two transactions, T_1 and T_2.

$S = r_2(X); r_1(X); r_2(Y); w_1(X); r_1(Y); w_2(X); a_1; a_2$

where $r_i(Z)$ denotes a read operation by transaction T_i on a variable Z, $w_i(Z)$ denotes a write operation by T_i on a variable Z and a_i denotes an abort by transaction T_i.

Which one of the following statements about the above schedule is TRUE?

(*a*) S is non-recoverable

(*b*) S is recoverable, but has a cascading abort

(*c*) S does not have a cascading abort

(*d*) S is strict

2015

9. SELECT operation in SQL is equivalent to
   (a) the selection operation in relational algebra
   (b) the selection operation in relational algebra, except that SELECT in SQL retains duplicates
   (c) the projection operation in relational algebra
   (d) the projection operation in relational algebra, except that SELECT in SQL retains duplicates

10. Consider the following transaction involving two bank account x and y.
    read (x); $x := x - 50$; write (x); read (y); $y := y + 50$; write (y)
    The constraint that the sum of the accounts x and y should remain constant is that of
    (a) Atomicity (b) Consistency
    (c) Isolation (d) Durability

11. Consider two relations R_1(A, B) with the tuples (1.5), (3, 7) and R_2(A, C) = (1, 7), (4, 9). Assume that R(A, B, C) is the full natural outer join of R_1 and R_2. Consider the following tuples of the form (A, B, C): a = (1.5, null), b = (1, null, 7) c = (3, null, 9), d = (4, 7, null), e = (1, 5, 7), f = (3, 7, null), g = (4, null, 9). Which one of the following statements is correct?
    (a) R contains a, b, e, f, g but not c, d.
    (b) R contains all of a, b, c, d, e, f, g
    (c) R contains e, f, g but not a, b
    (d) R contains e but not f, g.

12. Consider a simple checkpointing protocol and the following set of operations in the log.
    (Start, T4); (write, T4, y, 2, 3); (Start, T1); (commit, T4); (write, T1, z, 5, 7);
    (checkpoint);
    (Start,T_2); (write, T2, x,1, 9); (commit, T2); (start, T3), (write,T3, z, 7, 2);
    If a crash happens now and the system tries to recover using both undo and redo operations, what are the contents of the undo lists and the redo list?
    (a) Undo T3, T1; Redo T2
    (b) Undo T3, T1; Redo T2, T4
    (c) Undo: none; redo :T2, T4, T3, T1
    (d) Undo T3, T1; T4; Redo :T2

13. Consider the relation X(P, Q, R, S, T, U) with the following set of functional dependencies
    F = {
    {P, R} → {S, T}
    {P, S, U} → {Q,R}

    Which of the following is the trivial functional dependency in F^+, where F^+ is closure of F ?
    (a) {P, R} → {S, T} (b) {P, R} → {R,T}
    (c) {P, S} → {S} (d) {P, S, U} → {Q}

14. Two processes X and Y need to access a critical section. Consider the following synchronization construct used by both the processes

Process X	Process Y

/* other code for process X*/
while (true)
{
var P = true;
while (var Q == true)
{
/* critical section */
varP = false;
}
}
/* other code for process X*/
	/* other code for process Y*/
	while (true)
	{
	var Q = true;
	while (var P == true)
	{
	/* critical section */
	varQ = false;
	}
	}
	/* other code for process X*/

    Here, varP and varQ are shared variables and both are initialized to false. Which one of the following statements is true ?
    (a) The proposed solution prevents deadlock but fails to guarantee mutual exclusion
    (b) The proposed solution guarantees mutual exclusion but fails to prevent deadlock
    (c) The proposed solution guarantees mutual exclusion and prevents deadlock
    (d) The proposed solution fails to prevent deadlock and fails to guarantee mutual exclusion

15. Consider the following relation
    Cinema (theater, address, capacity)
    Which of the following options will be needed at the end of the SQL query
    SELECT P1. address
    FROM Cinema P1
    Such that it always finds the addresses of theaters with maximum capacity ?
    (a) WHERE P1. Capacity> = All (select P2. Capacity from Cinema P2)
    (b) WHERE P1. Capacity> = Any (select P2. Capacity from Cinema P2)
    (c) WHERE P1. Capacity> = All (select max(P2. Capacity) from Cinema P2)
    (d) WHERE P1. Capacity> = Any (select max (P2. Capacity) from Cinema P2)

16. Consider the following partial Schedule S involving two transactions T1 and T2. Only the read and write operations have been shown. The read operation on data item P is denoted by read (P) and the write operation on data item P is denoted by write (P).

Time Instance	Transaction-id	
	T1	T2
1	read(A)	
2	write(A)	
3		read(C)
4		write(C)
5		read(B)
6		write(B)
7		read(A)
8		commit
9	read (B)	

Schedule S

Suppose that the transaction T1 fails immediately after time instance 9. Which one of the following statements is correct ?

(*a*) T2 must be aborted and then both T1 and T2 must be re-started to ensure transaction atomicity

(*b*) Schedule S is non-recoverable and cannot ensure transaction atomicity

(*c*) Only T2 must be aborted and then re-started to ensure transaction atomicity

(*d*) Schedule S is recoverable and can ensure atomicity and nothing else needs to be done

2014

17. Consider the relation scheme R = (E, F, G, H, I, J, K, L, M, N) and the set of functional dependencies {{E,F} → {G}, {F} → {I, J}, {E,H} → {K, L}, {K} → {M}, {L} → {N}} on R. What is the key for R?

(*a*) {E, F} (*b*) {E, F, H }

(*c*) {E, F, H, K, L} (*d*) {E}

18. Given the following statements:

S1 : A foreign key declaration can always be replaced by an equivalent check assertion in SQL.

S2 : Given the table R(a,b,c) where a and b together form the primary key, the following is a valid table definition.

```
CREATE TABLE S (
a INTEGER,
d INTEGER,
e INTEGER,
PRIMARY KEY (d),
FOREIGN KEY (a) references R)
```

Which one of the following statements is CORRECT?

(*a*) S1 is TRUE and S2 is FALSE

(*b*) Both S1 and S2 are TRUE

(*c*) S1 is FALSE and S2 is TRUE

(*d*) Both S1 and S2 are FALSE

19. Consider the following four schedules due to three transactions (indicated by the subscript) using *read* and *write* on a data item x, denoted by r(x) and w(x) respectively. Which one of them is conflict serializable?

(*a*) $r_1(x); r_2(x); w_1(x); r_3(x); w_2(x)$

(*b*) $r_2(x); r_1(x); w_2(x); r_3(x); w_1(x)$

(*c*) $r_3(x); r_2(x); r_1(x); w_2(x); w_1(x)$

(*d*) $r_2(x); w_2(x); r_3(x); r_1(x); w_1(x)$

20. Given the following two statements:

S1: Every table with two single-valued attributes is in 1NF, 2NF, 3NF and BCNF

S2: AB → C, D → E, E → C is a minimal cover for the set of functional dependencies AB → C, D → E, AB → E, E → C.

Which one of the following is CORRECT?

(*a*) S1 is TRUE and S2 is FALSE.

(*b*) Both S1 and S2 are TRUE.

(*c*) S1 is FALSE and S2 is TRUE.

(*d*) Both S1 and S2 are FALSE.

21. Given the following schema:

employees(emp-id, first-name, last-name, hire-date, dept-id, salary)

departments(dept-id, dept-name, manager-id, location-id)

You want to display the last names and hire dates of all latest hires in their respective departments in the location ID 1700. You issue the following query:

```
SQL>SELECT last-name, hire-date
    FROM employees
    WHERE (dept-id, hire-date) IN
    (SELECT dept-id, MAX(hire-date)
    FROM employees JOIN departments USING(dept-id)
    WHERE location-id = 1700
    GROUP BY dept-id);
```

What is the outcome?

(*a*) It executes but does not give the correct result.

(*b*) It executes and gives the correct result.

(*c*) It generates an error because of pairwise comparison.

(*d*) It generates an error because the GROUP BY clause cannot be used with table joins in a sub-query.

22. Consider the following schedule S of transactions T1, T2, T3, T4:

T1	T2	T3	T4
	Reads(X)		
		Writes (X)	
		Commit	
Writes (X)			
Commit			
	Writes(Y)		
	Reads(Z)		
	Commit		
			Reads(X)
			Reads(Y)
			Commit

Which one of the following statements is CORRECT?

(*a*) S is conflict-serializable but not recoverable
(*b*) S is not conflict-serializable but is recoverable
(*c*) S is both conflict-serializable and recoverable
(*d*) S is neither conflict-serializable nor is it recoverable

23. Consider a join (relation algebra) between relations r(R) and s(S) using the nested loop method. There are 3 buffers each of size equal to disk block size, out of which one buffer is reserved for intermediate results. Assuming size(r(R))<size(s(S)), the join will have fewer number of disk block accesses if

(*a*) relation r(R)is in the outer loop.
(*b*) relation s(S)is in the outer loop.
(*c*) join selection factor between r(R) and s(S) is more than 0.5
(*d*) join selection factor between r(R) and s(S) is less than 0.5

24. SQL allows duplicate tuples in relations, and correspondingly defines the multiplicity of tuples in the result of joins. Which one of the following queries always gives the same answer as the nested query shown below:

select * from R where a in (select S.a from S)

(*a*) select R.* from R, S where R.a = S . a
(*b*) select distinct R.* from R,S where R.a = S.a
(*c*) select R.* from R,(select distinct a from S) as S1 where R.a = S1.a
(*d*) select R.* from R, S where R.a = S.a and is unique R

25. *A prime attribute* of a relation scheme R is an attribute that appears

(*a*) in all candidate keys of R.
(*b*) in some candidate key of R.
(*c*) in a foreign key of R.
(*d*) only in the primary key of R.

26. Consider the transactions T1, T2, and T3 and the schedules S1 and S2 given below.

T1 : r1 (X) ; r1 (Z) ; w1 (X) ; w1 (Z)
T2 : r2 (Y) ; r2 (Z) ; w2 (Z)
T3 : r3 (Y) ; r3 (X) ; w3 (Y)
S1: r1(X); r3(Y); r3(X); r2(Y); r2(Z); w3(Y); w2(Z); r1(Z); w1(X); w1(Z)
S2: r1(X); r3(Y); r2(Y); r3(X); r1(Z); r2(Z); w3(Y); w1(X); w2(Z); w1(Z)

Which one of the following statements about the schedules is TRUE?

(*a*) Only S1 is conflict-serializable.
(*b*) Only S2 is conflict-serializable.
(*c*) Both S1 and S2 are conflict-serializable.
(*d*) Neither S1 nor S2 is conflict-serializable.

27. Consider the relational schema given below, where eId of the relation dependent is a foreign key referring to empId of the relation employee. Assume that every employee has at least one associated dependent in the dependent relation.

employee (<u>empId</u>, empName, empAge)
dependent (<u>depId, eId</u>, depName, depAge)

Consider the following relational algebra query : Π_{empId} (employee) – Π_{empId} (employee ><$_{\text{(empId = eID) Ù (emp Age £ depAge)}}$ dependent)

The above query evaluates to the set of empIds of employees whose age is greater than that of

(*a*) some dependent.
(*b*) all dependents.
(*c*) some of his/her dependents
(*d*) all of his/her dependents

28. Consider the following relational schema:

employee (<u>empId</u>, empName, empDept)
customer (<u>custId</u>, custName, sales RepId, rating)

salesRepId is a foreign key referring to empId of the employee relation. Assume that each employee makes a sale to at least one customer. What does the following query return?

```
SELECT empName
FROM employee E
WHERE NOT EXISTS (SELECT custId
                  FROM customer C
                  WHERE C.salesRepId = E. empId
                  AND C. rating < > 'GOOD');
```

(*a*) Names of all the employees with at least one of their customers having a 'GOOD' rating.
(*b*) Names of all the employees with at most one of their customers having a 'GOOD' rating.
(*c*) Names of all the employees with none of their customers having a 'GOOD' rating.
(*d*) Names of all the employees with all their customers having a 'GOOD' rating.

2013

29. An index is clustered, if

(*a*) it is on a set of fields that form a candidate key.
(*b*) it is on a set of fields that include the primary key.
(*c*) the data records of the file are organized in the same order as the data entries of the index.
(*d*) the data records of the file are organized not in the same order as the data entries of the index.

30. Consider the following relational schema.

Students(rollno: integer, sname: string)

Courses(courseno: integer, cname: string)

Registration(rollno: integer, conrseno: integer, percent: real)

Which of the following queries are equivalent to this query in English?

"Find the distinct names of all students who score more than 90% in the course numbered 107"

(I) SELECT DISTINCT S.sname
FROM Students as S, Registration as R
WHERE R.rollno = S.rollno AND R.courseno = 107 AND R.percent>90

(II) Π σ name (σ courseno=107 ^ percent > 90 (Registra-tion ∞ Students))

(III){T | $\exists$ S $\in$ Students, $\exists$ R $\in$ Registration (S.rollno = R.rollno ^ R.courseno=107^ R. percent > 90 ^ T.sname = S.sname))

(IV){<S_N> | $\exists S_R \exists R_P$ (<S_R, S_N> $\in$ Students ^ < S_R, 107, R_P> $\in$ Registration ^ R_P>90)}

(*a*) I, II, III and IV (*b*) I, II and III only

(*c*) I, II and IV only (*d*) II, III and IV only

31. The preorder traversal sequence of a binary search tree is 30, 20, 10, 15, 25, 23, 39, 35, 42. Which one of the following is the postorder traversal sequence of the same tree?

(*a*) 10, 20, 15, 23, 25, 35, 42, 39, 30

(*b*) 15, 10, 25, 23, 20, 42, 35, 39, 30

(*c*) 15, 20, 10, 23, 25, 42, 35, 39, 30

(*d*) 15, 10, 23, 25, 20, 35, 42, 39, 30

2012

32. Which of the following statements are TRUE about an SQL query?

P : An SQL query can contain a HAVING clause even if it does not have a GROUP BY clause

Q : An SQL query can contain a HAVING clause only if it has a GROUP BY clause

R : All attributes used in the GROUP BY clause must appear in the SELECT clause

S : Not all attributes used in the GROUP BY clause need to appear in the SELECT clause

(*a*) P and R (*b*) P and S

(*c*) Q and R (*d*) Q and S

33. Given the basic ER and relational models, which of the following is **INCORRECT**?

(*a*) An attribute of an entity can have more than one value

(*b*) An attribute of an entity can be composite

(*c*) In a row of a relational table, an attribute can have more than one value

(*d*) In a row of a relational table, an attribute can have exactly one value or a NULL value

34. Which of the following is TRUE?

(*a*) Every relation in 3NF is also in BCNF

(*b*) A relation R is in 3NF if every non-prime attribute of R is fully functionally dependent on every key of R

(*c*) Every relation in BCNF is also in 3NF

(*d*) No relation can be in both BCNF and 3NF

35. Suppose R_1(A, B) and R_2 (C, D) are two relation schemas. Let r_1 and r_2 be the corresponding relation instances. B is a foreign key that refers to C in R_2. If data in r_1 and r_2 satisfy referential integrity constraints. which of the following is **ALWAYS TRUE**?

(*a*) $\Pi_B(r_1) - \Pi_C(r_2) = \varnothing$

(*b*) $\Pi_C(r_2) - \Pi_B(r_1) = \varnothing$

(*c*) $\Pi_B(r_1) = \Pi_C(r_2)$

(*d*) $\Pi_B(r_1) - \Pi_C(r_2) \neq \varnothing$

2011

36. Database table by name Loan_Records is given below.

Borrower	Bank_Manager	Loan_Amount
Ramesh	Sunderajan	10000.00
Suresh	Ramgopal	5000.00
Mahesh	Sunderajan	7000.00

What is the output of the following SQL query?

```
SELECT count (*)
FROM (
    (SELECT Borrower, Bank_Manager FROM Loan_Records) AS S
    NATURAL JOIN
    (SELECT Bank_Manager, Loan_Amount FROM Loan_Records) AS T );
```

(*a*) 3 (*b*) 9

(*c*) 5 (*d*) 6

37. Consider a relational table *r* with sufficient number of records, having attributes $A_1, A_2, \ldots A_n$ and let $1 \le p \le n$. Two queries Q_1 and Q_2 are given below.

Q1 : $\pi_{A_1 \cdots Ap} (\sigma_{Ap = c} (r))$ where c is a constant

Q2 : $\pi_{A_1 \cdots Ap} (\sigma_{c_1 \le Ap \le c_2} (r))$ where c_1 and c_2 are constants

The database can be configured to do ordered indexing on A_p or hashing on A_p. Which of the following statements is TRUE?

(a) Ordered indexing will always outperform hashing for both queries

(b) Hashing will always outperform ordered indexing for both queries

(c) Hashing will outperform ordered indexing on Q1, but not on Q2

(d) Hashing will outperform ordered indexing on Q2, but not on Q1

38. Consider a database table T containing two columns X and Y each of type integer. After the creation of the table, one record (X = 1, Y = 1) is inserted in the table.

Let MX and MY denote the respective maximum values of X and Y among all records in the table at any point in time. Using MX and MY, new records are inserted in the table 128 times with X and Y values of MX and MY change.

What will be the output of the following SQL query after the steps mentioned above are carried out?

SELECT Y FROM T WHERE X = 7;

(a) 127 (b) 255

(c) 129 (d) 257

2010

39. One of the header fields in an IP datagram is the Time-to-Live (TTL) field. Which of the following statements best explains the need for this field?

(a) It can be used to prioritize packets

(b) It can be used to reduce delays

(c) It can be used to optimize throughput

(d) It can be used to prevent packet looping

40. Which one of the following is not a client-server application?

(a) Internet chat (b) Web browsing

(c) E-mail (d) Ping

41. Consider a B^+-tree in which the maximum number of keys in a node is 5. What is the minimum number of keys in any non-root node?

(a) 1 (b) 2

(c) 3 (d) 4

42. A relational schema for a train reservation database is given below.

Table: Passenger

pid	pname	Age
0	'Sachin'	65
1	'Rahul'	66
2	'Sourav'	67
3	'Anil'	69

Table: Reservation

pid	class	tid
0	'AC'	8200
1	'AC'	8201
2	'SC'	8201
5	'AC'	8203
1	'SC'	8204
3	'AC'	8202

Passenger (pid, pname, age)

Reservation (pid, class, tid)

What pids are returned by the following SQL query for the above instance of the tables?

```
SELECT   pid
FROM     Reservation
WHERE    class = 'AC' AND
         EXISTS(SELECT *
                    FROM Passenger
                    WHERE age > 65 and
                    Passenger. pid =
                    Reservation. pid)
```

(a) 1, 0 (b) 1, 2

(c) 1, 3 (d) 1, 5

43. Which of the following concurrency control protocols ensure both conflict serializability and freedom from deadlock?

I. 2-phase locking

II. Time-stamp ordering

(a) I only (b) II only

(c) Both I and II (d) Neither I nor II

44. Consider the following schedule for transactions T1, T2 and T3:

T1	T2	T3
Read (X)		
	Read (Y)	
		Read (Y)
	Write (Y)	
Write (X)		
		Write (X)
	Read (X)	
	Write (X)	

Which one of the schedules below is the correct serialization of the above?

(a) T1 → T3 → T2 (b) T2 → T1 → T3

(c) T2 → T3 → T1 (d) T3 → T1 → T2

45. The following functional dependencies hold for relations R (A, B, C) and S (B, D, E):
$B \rightarrow A$,
$A \rightarrow C$
The relation R contains 200 tuples and the relations S contains 100 tuples. What is the maximum number of tuples possible in the natural join $R \bowtie S$?
(*a*) 100 (*b*) 200
(*c*) 300 (*d*) 2000

2009

46. Consider two transactions T_1 an T_2, and four schedules S_1, S_2, S_3, S_4 of T_1 and T_2 as given below :
$T_1 : R_1 [x]\ W_1 [x]\ W_1 [y]$
$T_2 : R_2 [x]\ R_2 [y]\ W_2 [y]$
$S_1 : R_1 [x] R_2 [x] R_2 [y] W_1 [x] W_1 [y] W_2 [y]$
$S_2 : R_1 [x] R_2 [x] R_2 [y] W_1 [x] W_2 [y] W_1 [y]$
$S_3 : R_1 [x] W_1 [x] R_2 [x] W_1 [y] R_2 [y] W_2 [y]$
$S_4 : R_4 [x] R_2 [y] R_1 [x] W_1 [x] W_1 [y] W_2 [y]$
Which of the above schedules are conflict-serializable ?
(*a*) S_1 adn S_2 (*b*) S_2 and S_3
(*c*) S_3 only (*d*) S_4 only

47. The following key values are inserted into a B+ –tree in which order of the internal nodes is 3, and that of the leaf nodes is 2, is the sequence given below. The order of internal nodes in the maximum number of tree pointers in each node, and the order of leaf nodes is the maximum number of data items that can be stored in it. The B+ –tree is initially empty.
10, 3, 6, 8, 4, 2, 1
The maximum number of times leaf nodes would get split up as a result of these insertions is
(*a*) 2 (*b*) 3
(*c*) 4 (*d*) 5

48. Let R and S be relational schemes such that
$R = \{a, b, c\}$ and $S = \{c\}$.
Now consider the following queries on the database:
I. $\pi_{R-S}(r) - \pi_{R-S}(\pi_{R-S}(r) \times s - \pi_{R-S,S}(r))$
II. $\{t \mid t \in \pi_{R-S}(r) \wedge \forall u \in r\ (\exists v \in s\ (u = v[s] \wedge t = v[R-S]))\}$
III. $\{t \mid t \in \pi_{R-S}(r) \wedge \forall v \in r\ (\exists u \in s\ (u = v[s] \wedge t = v[R-S]))\}$
IV. Select R. a, R. b
from R, S
where R.c = S.c

Which of the above queries are equivalent ?
(*a*) I and II (*b*) I and III
(*c*) II and IV (*d*) III and IV

2008

49. A clustering index is defined on the fields which are of type
(*a*) non-key and ordering
(*b*) non-key and non-ordering
(*c*) key and ordering
(*d*) key and non ordering

50. Let R and S be two relations with the following schema
R(P, Q, R1, R2, R3)
S (P, Q, S1, S2)
where {P, Q} is the key for both schemas. Which of the following queries are equivalent?
I. $\Pi_P(R \bowtie S)$
II. $\Pi_P(R) \bowtie \Pi_P(S)$
III. $\Pi_P(\Pi_{P,Q}(R) \cap \Pi_{P,Q}(S))$
IV. $\Pi_P(\Pi_{P,Q}(R) - (\Pi_{P,Q}(R) - \Pi_{P,Q}(S)))$
(*a*) Only I and II (*b*) Only I and III
(*c*) Only I, II and III (*d*) Only I, III and IV

51. Consider the following relational schemes for a library database:
Book (Title, Author, Catalog_no, Publisher, Year, Price)
Collection (Title, Author, Catalog_no)
With the following functional dependencies:
I. Title Author → Catalong_no
II. Catalog_no → Title Author Publisher Year
III. Publisher Title Year → Price
Assume {Autho, Title} is the key for both schemes. Which of the following statements is true?
(*a*) Both Book and Collection are in BCNF
(*b*) Both Book and Collection are in 3 NF only
(*c*) Book is in 2NF and Collection is in 3NF
(*d*) Both Book and Collection are in 2NF only

52. Consider a file of 16384 records. Each record is 32 bytes long and its key field is of size 6 bytes. The file is ordered on a non-key field, and the file organization is unspanned. The file is stored in a file system with block size 1024 bytes, and the size of a block pointer is 10 bytes. If the secondary index is buit on the key field of the file, and a multi-level index scheme is used to store the secondary index, the number of first-level and second-level blocks in the multi-level index are respectively
(*a*) 8 and 0 (*b*) 128 and 6
(*c*) 256 and 4 (*d*) 512 and 5

2007

53. Information about a collection of students is given by the relation **studInfo** (studId, name, sex). The relation **enroll** (studId, courseId) gives which student has enrolled for (or taken) what course (s). Assume that every course is taken by at least one male and at least one female student. What does the following relational algebra expression represent ?

$\Pi_{courseId}((\Pi_{studId}(\sigma_{sex=\text{"female"}}(studInfo)) \; \Pi_{courseId}(enroll)) - enroll)$

(*a*) Courses in which all the female students are enrolled.

(*b*) Courses in which a proper subset of female students are enrolled.

(*c*) Courses in which only male students are enrolled.

(*d*) None of these.

54. Consider the relation **employee** (name, sex, supervisorName(with *name* as the key. *supervisor Name* gives the name of the supervisor of the employee under consideration. What does the following Tuple Relational Calculus query produce?

{e. name | employee (e) ∧

(∀ x) [¬ employee (x) ∨ x.supervisorName

≠ e.name ∨ x. sex = "male"]}

(*a*) Names of employees with a male supervisor.

(*b*) Names of employees with no immediate male subordinates.

(*c*) Names of employees with no immediate female subordinates.

(*d*) Names of employees with a female supervisor.

55. Consider the table **employee** (empId, name, department, salary) and the two queries Q_1, Q_2 below. Assuming that department 5 has more than one employee, and we want to find the employees who get higher salary than anyone in the department 5, which one of the statements is **TRUE** for any arbitrary employee table ?

```
Q1 : Select e.empId
     From employee e
     Where not exists
     (Select * From employee s Where s.
     department = "5" and s. salary > = e.salary)
Q2 : Select e. empId
     From employee e
     Where e. salary > Any
     (Select distinct salary From employee s
     Where s. department = "5")
```

(*a*) Q_1 is the correct query.

(*b*) Q_2 is the correct query.

(*c*) Both Q_1 and Q_2 produce the same answer.

(*d*) Neither Q_1 nor Q_2 is the correct query.

56. Which one of the following statements is FALSE ?

(*a*) Any relation with two attributes is in BCNF.

(*b*) A relation in which every key has only one attribute is in 2NF.

(*c*) A prime attribute can be transitively dependent on a key in a 3NF relation.

(*d*) A prime attribute can be transitively dependent on a key in a BCNF relation.

57. The order of a leaf node in a B^+ –tree is the maximum number of (value, data record pointer) pairs it can hold. Given that the block size is 1K bytes, data record pointer is 7 bytes long, the value field is 9 bytes long and a block pointer is 6 bytes long, what is the order of the leaf node?

(*a*) 63 (*b*) 64

(*c*) 67 (*d*) 68

58. Consider the following schedules involving two transactions. Which one of the following statements is **TRUE** ?

$S_1 : r_1(X); r_1(Y); r_2(X); r_2(Y); w_2(Y); w_1(X)$

$S_2 : r_1(X); r_2(X); r_2(Y); w_2(Y); r_1(Y); w_1(X)$

(*a*) Both S_1 and S_2 are conflict serializable.

(*b*) S_1 is conflict serializable and S_2 is not conflict serializable.

(*c*) S_1 is not conflict serializable and S_2 is conflict serializable.

(*d*) Both S_1 and S_2 are not conflict serializable.

2006

59. Consider the following log sequence of two transactions on a bank account, with initial balance 12000, that transfer 2000 to a mortgage payment and, then apply a 5% interest.

1. T1 start
2. T1 B old = 12000 new = 10000
3. T1 M old = 0 new = 2000
4. T1 commit
5. T2 start
6. T2 B old = 10000 new = 10500
7. T2 commit

Suppose the database system crashed just before log record 7 is written. When the system is restarted, which one statement is true of the recovery procedure?

(*a*) We must redo log record 6 to set B to 10500

(*b*) We must undo log record 6 to set B to 10000 and then redo log records 2 and 3

(*c*) We need not redo log records 2 and 3 because transaction T1 has committed

(*d*) We can apply redo and undo operations in arbitrary order because they are idempotent

60. Consider the relation account (customer, balance) where customer is a primary key and there are no null values. We would like to rank customers according to decreasing balance. The customer with the largest balance gets rank 1. Ties are not broken but ranks are skipped: if exactly two customers have the largest balance they each get rank 1 and rank 2 is not assigned.

Query 1 : select A. customer, count (B. customer) from account A, account B where A. balance < = B. balance group by A. customer

Query 2 : select A. customer, 1 + count (B. customer) from account A, account B where A. balance < B. balance 7group by A. customer

Consider these statements about Query 1 and Query 2.

1. Query 1 will produce the same row set as Query 2 for some but not all databases
2. Both Query 1 and Query 2 are correct implementations of the specification
3. Query 1 is a correct implementation of the specification but Query 2 is not
4. Neither Query 1 nor Query 2 is a correct implementation of the specification
5. Assigning rank with a pure relational Query takes less time than scanning in decreasing balance order and assigning ranks using ODBC

Which two of the above statements are correct ?

(*a*) 2 and 5 (*b*) 1 and 3

(*c*) 1 and 4 (*d*) 3 and 5

61. Consider the relation enrolled (student, course) in which (student, course) is the primary key, and the relation paid (student, amount) where student is the primary key. Assume no null values and no foreign keys or integrity constraints. Given the following four queries :

Query 1 : select student form enrolled where student in (select student form paid)

Query 2 : select student from paid where student in (select student from enrolled)

Query 3 : select E. student from enrolled E, paid P where E. student = P. student

Query 4 : Select student from paid where exists (select * from enrolled where enrolled.student = paid. student)

Which one of the following statements is correct ?

(*a*) All queires return identical row sets for any database

(*b*) Query 2 and Query 4 return identical row sets for all databases but there exist databases for which Query 1 and Query 2 return different row sets

(*c*) There exist databases for which Query 3 returns strictly fewer rows than Query 2

(*d*) There exist databases for which Query 4 will encounter an intergrity violation at runtime

62. Consider the relation enrolled (student, course) in which (student, course) is the primary key, and the relation paid (student, amount) where student is the primary key. Assume no null values and no foreign keys or integrity constraints. Assume that amounts 6000, 7000, 8000, 9000 and 10000 were each paid by 20% of the students. Consider these query plans (Plan 1 on left, Plan 2 on right) to "list all courses taken by students who have paid more than *x*."

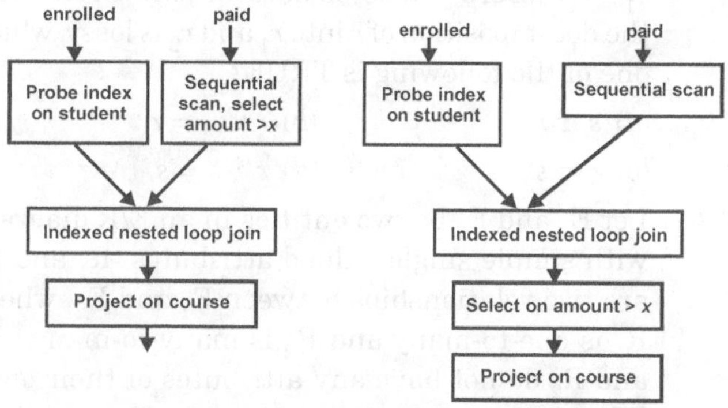

A disk seek takes 4 ms, disk data transfer bandwidth is 300 MB/s and checking a tuple to see if amount is greater than *x* takes 10 μs. Which of the following statements is correct ?

(*a*) Plan 1 and Plan 2 will not output identical row sets for all databases

(*b*) A course may be listed more than once in the output of Plan 1 for some databases

(*c*) For *x* = 5000, Plan 1 executes faster than Plan 2 for all databases

(*d*) For *x* = 9000, Plan 1 executes slower than Plan 2 for all databases

63. The following functional dependencies are given: $AB \rightarrow CD$, $AF \rightarrow D$, $DE \rightarrow F$, $C \rightarrow G$, $F \rightarrow E$, $G \rightarrow A$.

Which one of the following options is false ?

(*a*) $\{CF\}^+ = \{ACDEFG\}$ (*b*) $\{BG\}^+ = \{ABCDG\}$

(*c*) $\{AF\}^+ = \{ACDEFG\}$ (*d*) $\{AB\}^+ = \{ABCDFG\}$

2005

64. Which one of the following is a key factor for preferring B⁺-trees to binary search trees for indexing database relations?

(*a*) Database relations have a large number of records

(*b*) Database relations are sorted on the primary key

(*c*) B⁺ -trees require less memory than binary search trees

(*d*) Data transfer from disks is in blocks

65. Which one of the following statements about normal forms is FALSE?

(a) BCNF is stricter than 3NF

(b) Lossless, dependency-preserving decomposition into 3NF is always possible

(c) Lossless, dependency-preserving decomposition into BCNF is always possible

(d) Any relation with two attributes is in BCNF

66. Let r be a relation instance with schema

$$R = (A, B, C, D).$$

We define $r_1 = \Pi_{A,B,C}(r)$ and $r_2 = \Pi_{A,D}(r)$. Let $s = r_1 * r_2$, where * denotes natural join. Given that the decomposition of r into r_1 and r_2 is lossy, which one of the following is TRUE?

(a) $s \subset r$ (b) $r \cup s = r$

(c) $r \subset s$ (d) $r * s = s$

67. Let E_1 and E_2 be two entities in an E/R diagram with simple single-valued attributes. R_1 and R_2 are two relationships between E_1 and E_2, where R_1 is one-to-many and R_2 is many-to-many. R_1 and R_2 do not have any attributes of their own. What is the minimum number of tables required to represent this situation in the relational model?

(a) 2 (b) 3

(c) 4 (d) 5

68. The following table has two attributes A and C where A is the primary key and C is the foreign key referencing A with on-delete cascade.

A	C
2	4
3	4
4	3
5	2
7	2
9	5
6	4

The set of all tuples that must be additionally deleted to preserve referential integrity when the tuple (2, 4) is deleted is

(a) (3, 4) and (6, 4) (b) (5, 2) and (7, 2)

(c) (5, 2) (7, 2) and (9, 5) (d) (3, 4) (4, 3) and (6, 4)

69. The relation book (title, price) contains the titles and prices of different books. Assuming that no two books have the same price, what does the following SQL ?

```
select title
from book as B
where (select count (*)
from book as T
where T. price > B. price) < 5
```

(a) Titles of the four most expensive books

(b) Title of the fifth most inexpensive book

(c) Title of the fifth most expensive book

(d) Titles of the five most expensive books

70. Consider a relation scheme

R = (A, B, C, D, E, H) on which the following functional dependencies hold :

$\{A \rightarrow B,\ BC \rightarrow D,\ E \rightarrow C,\ D \rightarrow A\}$.

What are the candidate keys of R?

(a) AE, BE (b) AE, BE, DE

(c) AEH, BEH, BCH (d) AEH, BEH, DEH

2004

71. Let R_1 ($\underline{A}$, B, C) and R_2 ($\underline{D}$, E) be two relation schema, where the primary keys are shown underlined, and let C be a foreign key in R_1 referring to R_2. Suppose there is no violation of the above referential integrity constraint in the corresponding relation instances r_1 and r_2. Which one of the following relational algebra expressions would necessarily produce an empty relation ?

(a) $\Pi_D(r_2) - \Pi_C(r_1)$ (b) $\Pi_C(r_1) - \Pi_D(r_2)$

(c) $\Pi_D(r_1 \bowtie_{C \neq D} r_2)$ (d) $\Pi_C(r_1 \bowtie_{C = D} r_2)$

72. Consider the following relation schema pertaining to a students database:

Student (rollno, name, address)

Enroll (rollno, courseno, coursename)

where the primary keys are shown underlined. The number of tuples in the Student and Enroll tables are 120 and 8 respectively. What are the maximum and minimum number of tuples that can be present in (Student * Enroll), where '*' denotes natural join ?

(a) 8, 8 (b) 120, 8

(c) 960, 8 (d) 960, 120

73. It is desired to design an object-oriented employee record system for a company. Each employee has a name, unique id and salary. Employees belong to different categories and their salary is determined by their category. The functions get Name, getId and compute Salary are required. Given the class hierarchy below, possible locations for these functions are:

(i) getId is implemented in the superclass

(ii) getId is implemented in the subclass

(iii) getName is an abstract function in the superclass

(iv) getName is implemented in the superclass

(v) getName is implemented in the subclass

(*vi*) getSalary is an abstract function in the superclass

(*vii*) getSalary is implemented in the superclass

(*viii*) getSalary is implemented in the subclass

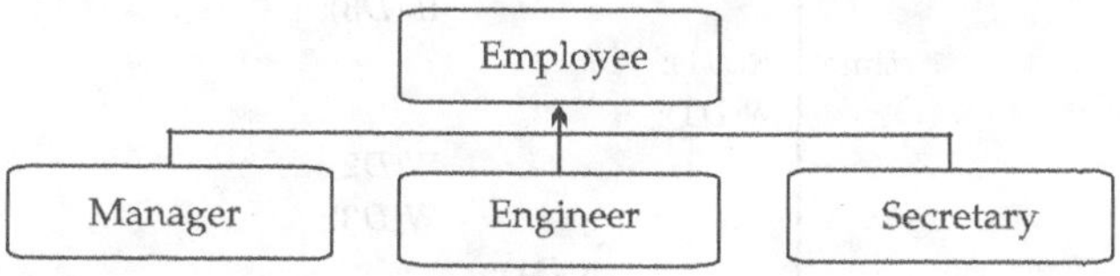

Choose the best design

(*a*) (*i*), (*iv*), (*vi*), (*viii*)

(*b*) (*i*), (*iv*), (*vii*)

(*c*) (*i*), (*iii*), (*v*), (*vi*), (*viii*)

(*d*) (*ii*), (*v*), (*viii*)

74. The relation scheme Student Performance (name, courseNo, rollNo, grade) has the following functional dependencies:

name, courseNo → grade

rollNo, courseNo → grade

name → rollNo

rollNo → name

The highest normal form of this relation scheme is

(*a*) 2 NF (*b*) 3 NF

(*c*) BCNF (*d*) 4NF

75. Consider the relation Student (name, sex, marks), where the primary key is shown underlined, pertaining to students in a class that has at least one boy and one girl. What does the following relational algebra expression produce? (Note: r is the rename operator).

$$P_{name}(r_{sex=female}(\text{Student})) - \Pi_{name}(\text{Student} \underset{(sex=female \wedge x=male \wedge marks \leq m)}{\bowtie} r_{n,x,m}(\text{Student}))$$

(*a*) names of girl students with the highest marks

(*b*) names of girl students with more marks than some boy student

(*c*) names of girl students with marks not less than some boy students

(*d*) names of girl students with more marks than all the boy students

76. The order of an internal node in a B⁺ tree index is the maximum number of children it can have. Suppose that a child pointer takes 6 bytes, the search field value takes 14 bytes, and the block size is 512 bytes. What is the order of the internal node?

(*a*) 24 (*b*) 25

(*c*) 26 (*d*) 27

77. The employee information in a company is stored in the relation

Employee (name, sex, salary, deptName)

Consider the following SQL query

```
select deptName
from Employee
where sex='M'
group by deptName
having avg (salary) >
    (select avg (salary) from Employee)
```

It returns the names of the department in which

(*a*) the average salary is more than the average salary in the company

(*b*) the average salary of male employees is more than the average salary of all male employees in the company

(*c*) the average salary of male employees is more than the average salary of employees in the same department

(*d*) the average salary of male employees is more than the average salary in the company

2003

78. Which of the following scenarios may lead to an irrecoverable error in a database system ?

(*a*) A transaction writes a data item after it is read by an uncommitted transaction

(*b*) A transaction reads a data item after it is read by an uncommitted transaction

(*c*) A transaction reads a data item after it is written by a committed transaction

(*d*) A transaction reads a data item after it is written by an uncommitted transaction

79. Consider the following SQL query

select distinct $a_1, a_2, \ldots\ldots, a_n$

from $r_1, r_2, \ldots\ldots, r_m$

where P

For an arbitrary predicate P, this query is equivalent to which of the following relational algebra expressions ?

(*a*) $\Pi_{a_1, a_2, \ldots, a_n} \sigma_p (r_1 \times r_2 \times \ldots \times r_m)$

(*b*) $\Pi_{a_1, a_2, \ldots, a_n} \sigma_p (r_1 \bowtie r_2 \bowtie \ldots \bowtie r_m)$

(*c*) $\Pi_{a_1, a_2, \ldots, a_n} \sigma_p (r_1 \cup r_2 \cup \ldots \cup r_m)$

(*d*) $\Pi_{a_1, a_2, \ldots, a_n} \sigma_p (r_1 \cap r_2 \cap \ldots \cap r_m)$

80. Consider the following functional dependencies in a database :

Data_of_Birth → Age
Age → Eligibility
Name → Roll_number
Roll_number → Name
Course_number → Course_name
Course_number → Instructor
(Roll_number, Course_number) → Grade

The relation (Roll_number, Name, Date_of_birth, Age) is

(*a*) in second normal form but not in third normal form
(*b*) in third normal form but not in BCNF
(*c*) in BCNF
(*d*) none of these

81. Consider the set of relations shown below and the SQL query that follows :

Students : (Roll_number, Name, Date_of _birth)
Courses : (Course_number, Course_name, Instructor)
Grades : (Roll_number, Course_number, Grade)

select distinct Name
from Students, Courses, Grades
where Students. Roll_number = Grades. Roll_number
and Courses. Instructor = Korth
and Courses. Course_number = Grades. Course_number
and Grades.grade = A

Which of the following sets is computed by the above query ?

(*a*) Names of students who have got an A grade in all courses taught by Korth
(*b*) Names of students who have got an A grade in all courses
(*c*) Name of students who have got an A grade in at least one of the courses taught by Korth
(*d*) None of these

82. Consider three data items D1, D2, and D3, and the following execution schedule of transactions T_1, T_2, and T_3. In the diagram, R(D) and W(D) denote the actions reading and writing the data item D respectively.

time ↓	T_1	T_2	T_3
		R (*D*3);	
		R (*D*2);	
		W (*D*2);	
			R (*D*2);
			R (*D*3);
	R(*D*1);		
	W(*D*1);		
			W(*D*2);
			W(*D*3);
		R(*D*1);	
	R(*D*2);		
	W(*D*2);		
		W(*D*1);	

(*a*) The schedule is serializable as T2; T3; T1
(*b*) The schedule is serializable as T2; T1; T3
(*c*) The schedule is serializable as T3; T2; T1
(*d*) The schedule is not serializable

2001

83. R (A, B, C, D) is a relation. Which of the following does not have a lossless join, dependency preserving BCNF decomposition ?

(*a*) A → B, B → CD
(*b*) A → B, B → C, C → D
(*c*) AB → C, C → AD
(*d*) A → BCD

84. Suppose the adjacency relation of vertices in a graph is represented in a table Adj(X, Y). Which of the following queries cannot be expressed by a relational algebra expression of constant length?

(*a*) List all vertices adjacent to a given vertex
(*b*) List all vertices which have self loops
(*c*) List all vertices which belong to cycles of less than three vertices
(*d*) List all vertices reachable from a given vertex

85. Let *r* and *s* be two relations over the relation schemes R and S respectively, and let A be an attribute in R. Then the relational algebra expression $\sigma_{A=a}(r \bowtie s)$ is always equal to

(*a*) $\sigma_{A=a}(r)$ (*b*) r
(*c*) $\sigma_{A=a}(r) \bowtie s$ (*d*) none of these

2000

86. B⁺-trees are preferred to binary trees in databases because

(*a*) Disk capacities are greater than memory capacities
(*b*) Disk access is much slower than memory access
(*c*) Disk data transfer rates are much less than memory data transfer rates
(*d*) Disks are more reliable than memory

87. Given the relations
employee (name, salary, deptno), and
department (deptno, deptname, address)
which of the following queries cannot be expressed using the basic relational algebra operations (6, π, , ⋈, ∪, ∩, –)?

(*a*) Department address of every employee
(*b*) Employees whose name is the same as their department name
(*c*) The sum of all employee salaries
(*d*) All employees of a given department

88. Given the following relation instance

X	Y	Z
1	4	2
1	5	3
1	6	3
3	2	2

Which of the following functional dependencies are satisfied by the instance?
(*a*) $XY \to Z$ and $Z \to Y$ (*b*) $YZ \to X$ and $Y \to Z$
(*c*) $YZ \to X$ and $X \to Z$ (*d*) $XZ \to Y$ and $Y \to X$

89. Given relations *r* (*w*, *x*) and *s* (*y*, *z*), the result of
select distinct *w*, *x*
from *r*, *s*
is guaranteed to be same as r, provided
(*a*) *r* has no duplicates and *s* is non-empty
(*b*) *r* and *s* have no duplicates
(*c*) *s* has no duplicates and *r* is non-empty
(*d*) *r* and *s* have the same number of tuples

90. In SQL, relations can contain null values, and comparisons with null values are treated as unknown. Suppose all comparisons with a null value are treated as false. Which of the following pairs is not equivalent ?
(*a*) $x = 5$ not (not ($x = 5$))
(*b*) $x = 5x > 4$ and $x < 6$, where x is an integer
(*c*) $x \neq 5$ not ($x = 5$)
(*d*) None of the above

91. (*a*) Suppose you are given an empty B+-tree where each node (leaf and internal) can store up to 5 key values. Suppose values 1, 2, ..., 10 are inserted, in order, into the tree. Show the tree pictorially
(*i*) After 6 insertions, and
(*ii*) After all 10 insertions
Do NOT show intermediate stages.

(*b*) Suppose instead of splitting a node when it is full, we try to move a value to the left sibling. If there is no left sibling, or the left sibling is full, we split the node. Show the tree after values, 1, 2, ...9 have been inserted. Assume, as in (*a*) that each node can hold up to 5 keys.

(*c*) In general, suppose a B^+ - tree node can hold a maximum of *m* keys, and you insert a long sequence of keys in increasing order. Then what approximately is the average number of keys in each leaf level node.
(*i*) In the normal case, and
(*ii*) With the insertion as in (*b*).

92. Consider a bank database with only one relation transaction (transno, acctno, date, amount)
The amount attribute value is positive for deposits and negative for withdrawals.
(*a*) Define an SQL view TP containing the information (*acctno*, T1.date, T2.amount) for every pair of transactions T1, T2 such that T1 and T2 are transactions on the same account and the date of T2 is ≤ the date of T1.
(*b*) Using only the above view TP, write a query to find for each account the minimum balance it ever reached (not including the 0 balance when the account is created). Assume there is at most one transaction per day on each account, and each account has had at least one transaction since it was created.
To simplify your query, break it up into 2 steps by defining an intermediate view V.

1999

93. Let R = (*a*, *b*, *c*, *d*, *e*, *f*) be a relation scheme with the following dependencies $c \to f$, $e \to a$, $ec \to d$. $a \to b$. Which of the following is a key for R ?
(*a*) CD (*b*) EC
(*c*) AE (*d*) AC

94. Which of the following is correct ?
(*a*) B-trees are for storing data on disk and B* trees are for main memory.
(*b*) Range queries are faster on B* trees.
(*c*) B-trees are for primary indexes and B* trees are for secondary indexes.
(*d*) The height of a B* tree is independent of the number of records.

95. Consider the schema R = (S T U V) and the dependencies $S \to T$, $T \to U$. $U \to V$ and $V \to S$. Let R = (R1 and R2) be a decomposition such that $R1 \cap R2 = \varnothing$. The decomposition is
(*a*) not in 2NF
(*b*) in 2NF but not 3NF
(*c*) in 3NF but not in 2NF
(*d*) in both 2NF and 3NF

96. The minimum number of record movements required to merge five files A (with 10 records), B (with 20 records), C (with 15 records), D (with 15 records), D (with 5 records) and E (with 25 records) is
(*a*) 165 (*b*) 90
(*c*) 75 (*d*) 65

97. Which of the following is/are correct ?

(*a*) An SQL query automatically eliminates duplicates
(*b*) An SQL query will not work if there are no indexes on the relations
(*c*) SQL permits attribute names to be repeated in the same relation
(*d*) None of these

98. Consider the set of relations

EMP (Employee-no. Dept-no, Employee-name; Salary)
DEPT (Dept-no. Dept-name, Location)

Write an SQL query to :

(*a*) Find all employee names who work in departments located at 'Calcutta' and whose salary is greater than ₹ 50,000
(*b*) Calculate, for each department number, the number of employees with a salary greater than ₹ 1,00,000.

1998

99. Which normal form is considered adequate for normal relational database design ?

(*a*) 2 NF (*b*) 5NF
(*c*) 4NF (*d*) 3 NF

100. There are five records in a database.

Name	Age	Occupation	Category
Rama	27	CON	A
Abdul	22	ENG	A
Jeniffer	28	DOC	B
Maya	32	SER	D
Dev	24	MUS	C

There is an index file associated with this and it contains the values 1, 3, 2, 5 and 4. Which one of the fields is the index built from ?

(*a*) Age (*b*) Name
(*c*) Occupation (*d*) Category

101. Which of the following query transformations (i.e. replacing the l.h.s. expression by the r.h.s. expression) is incorrect ? R_1 and R_2 are relations, C_1, C_2 are selection conditions and A_1, A_2 are attributes of R_1.

(*a*) $\sigma_{c_1}(\sigma_{c_1}(R_1)) \rightarrow \sigma_{c_2}(\sigma_{c_2}(R_1))$
(*b*) $\sigma_{c_1}(\pi_{A_1}(R_1)) \rightarrow \pi_{A_1}(\sigma_{c_1}(R_1))$
(*c*) $\sigma_{c_1}(R_1 \cup R_2) \rightarrow \sigma_{c_1}(R_1) \cup \sigma_{c_1}(R_2)$
(*d*) $\pi_{A_2}(\sigma_{c_1}(R_1)) \rightarrow \sigma_{c_1}(\pi_{A_2}(R_1))$

102. Suppose the domain set of an attribute consists of signed four digit numbers. What is the percentage of reduction in storage space of this attribute if it is stored as an integer rather than in character form?

(*a*) 80% (*b*) 20%
(*c*) 60% (*d*) 40%

103. (*a*) Suppose we have a database consisting of the following three relations.

FREQUENTS (student, parlor) giving the parlors each student visits.

SERVES (parlor, ice-cream) indicating what kind of ice-creams each parlor serves.

LIKES (student, ice-cream) indicating what ice-creams each student likes.

(Assume that each student likes at least one ice-cream and frequents at least one parlor).

Express the following in SQL

Print the students that frequent at least one parlor that serves some ice-cream that they like.

(*b*) In a computer system where the 'best-fit' algorithm is used for allocating 'jobs' to 'memory partitions', the following situation was encountered

Partitions sizes in KB	4K 8K 20K 2K
Jobs sizes in KB	2K 14K 3K 6K 6K 10K 20K 2K
Time for execution	4 10 2 1 4 1 8 6

When will the 20K job complete ?

104. Consider the following database relations containing the attributes

Book – id
Subject – Category – of – book
Name – of – Author
Nationality – of – Author

with book – id as the primary key.

(*a*) What is the highest normal form satisfied by this relation ?
(*b*) Suppose the attributes Book - title and Author - address are added to the relation, and the primary key is changed to {Name - of - Author, Book - title}, what will be the highest normal form satisfied by the relation ?

105. Consider the following relational database schemes

COURSES (Cno. name)
PRE-REQ (Cno, pre – Cno)
COMPLETED (student – no, Cno)

COURSES gives the number and name of all the available courses.

PRE-REQ gives the information about which courses are pre-requisites for a given course.

COMPLETED indicates what courses have been completed by students.

Express the following using relational algebra

List all the courses for which a student with student-no 2310 has completed all the pre-requisites.

1997

106. For a database relation R (*a*, *b*, *c*, *d*), where the domains of *a*, *b*, *c*, *d* include only atomic values, only the following functional dependencies and those that can be inferred from them hold :

$a \to c$

$b \to d$

The relation is

(*a*) in first normal form but not in second normal form

(*b*) in second normal form but not in third normal form

(*c*) in third normal form

(*d*) none of the above

107. Let R (*a*, *b*, *c*) and S (*d*, *e*, *f*) be two relations in which *d* is the foreign key of S that refers to the primary key of R. Consider the following four operations R and S

(A) Insert into R (B) Insert into S

(C) Delete from R (D) Delete from S

Which of the following is true about the referential integrity constraint above ?

(*a*) None of (*a*), (*b*), (*c*) or (*d*) can cause its violation

(*b*) All of (*a*), (*b*), (*c*) and (*d*) can cause its violation

(*c*) Both (*a*) and (*d*) can cause its violation

(*d*) Both (*b*) and (*c*) can cause its violation

108. A B^+ – tree of order *d* is a tree in which each internal node has between *d* and 2*d* key values. An internal node with M key values M + 1 children. The root (if it is an internal node) has between 1 and 2*d* key values. The distance of a node from the root is the length of the path from the root to the node. All leaves are at the same distance from the root. The height of the tree is the distance of a leaf from the root.

(*a*) What is the total number of key values in the internal nodes of a B^+ – tree with l leaves ($1 \geq 2$)?

(*b*) What is the maximum number of internal nodes in a B^+ – tree of order 4 with 52 leaves ?

(*c*) What is the minimum number of leaves in a B^+ – tree of order *d* and height *h* ($h \geq 1$) ?

1996

109. A library relational database system uses the following schema

USERS (User #, User Name, Home Town)

BOOKS (*Book* # Book Title, Author Name)

ISSUED (*Book* #, User #, Date)

Explain in one English sentence, what each of the following relational algebra queries is designed to determine

(*a*) σ User # =6 (11 User #, Book Title ((USERS ISSUED) BOOKS))

(*b*) σ Author Name (BOOKS (σ Home Town) = Delhi (USERS ISSUED)))

1995

110. Let R be a symmetric and transitive relation on a set A. Then

(*a*) R is reflexive and hence an equivalence relation.

(*b*) R is reflexive and hence a partial order.

(*c*) R is reflexive and hence not an equivalence relation.

(*d*) None of the above

NUMERICAL TYPE QUESTIONS

2016

1. The attributes of three arithmetic operators in some programming language are given below.

Operator	Precedence	Associativity	Arity
+	High	Left	Binary
—	Medium	Right	Binary
*	Low	Left	Binary

The value of the expression **2 – 5 + 1 – 7*3** in this language is ______ .

2. Consider the following database table named water_schemes :

water_schemes		
scheme_no	**district_name**	**capacity**
1	Ajmer	20
1	Bikaner	10
2	Bikaner	10
3	Bikaner	20
1	Churu	10
2	Churu	20
1	Dungargarh	10

The number of tuples returned by the following SQL query is______.

```
with total(name, capacity) as
select  district_name, sum(capacity)
from water_schemes
group by district_name
with total_avg(capacity) as
select avg(capacity)
from  total
select name
from total, total_avg
where total.capacity =
total_avg.capacity
```

2015

3. Consider the following relations :

Students

Roll Number	Student Name
1	Raj
2	Rohit
3	Raj

Performance

Roll Number	Course	Marks
1	Math	80
1	English	70
2	Math	75
3	English	80
2	Physics	65
3	Math	80

Consider the following SQL query.

SELECT S. Student_Name, sum (P.Marks)

FROM Student S, Performance P

WHERE S.Roll_No = P.Roll_No

GROUP BY S.Student_Name

The number of rows that will be returned by the SQL query is _______.

4. Consider an Entity-Relationship (ER) model in which entity sets E_1 and E_2 are connected by an $m : n$ relationship R_{12}. E_1 and E_3 are connected by a $1 : n$ (1 on the side of E_1 and n on the side of E_3) relationship R_{13}.

E_1 has two single-valued attributes a_{11} and a_{12} of which a_{11} is the key attribute. E_2 has two single-valued attributes a_{21} and a_{22} of which a_{21} is the key attribute. E_3 has two single-valued attributes a_{31} and a_{32} of which a_{31} is the key attribute. The relationships do not have any attributes.

If a relational model is the derived from the above ER model, then the minimum number of relations that would be generated if all the relations are in 3NF is _______.

5. With reference to the B+ tree index of order 1 shown below, the minimum number of nodes (including the Root node) that must be fetched in order to satisfy the following query: "Get all records with a search key greater than or equal to 7 and less than 15" is ________

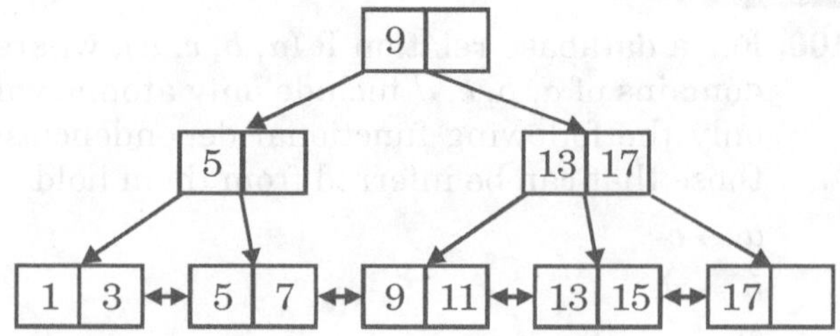

6. Consider a B+ tree in which the search Answer is 12 bytes long, block size is 1024 bytes, record pointer is 10 bytes long and block pointer is 8 bytes long. The maximum number of keys that can be accommodated in each non-leaf node of the tree is ____ .

2014

7. The maximum number of superkeys for the relation schema R(E,F,G,H) with E as the key is _____.

8. Given an instance of the STUDENTS relation as shown below:

StudentID	StudentName	StudentEmail	StudentAge	CPI
2345	Shankar	Shankar@math	X	9.4
1287	Swati	Swati@ee	19	9.5
7853	Shankar	Shankar@cse	19	9.4
9876	Swati	Swati@mech	18	9.3
8765	Ganesh	Ganesh@civil	19	8.7

For (StudentName, StudentAge) to be a key for this instance, the value X should NOT be equal to ______.

1994

9. State True or False with reason

There is always a decomposition into Boyce-Codd normal form (BCNF) that is lossless and dependency preserving.

10. An instance of a relational scheme R (*A*, B, C) has distinct values for attribute A.

Can you conclude that A is a candidate key for R?

11. Give a relational algebra expression using only the minimum number of operators from $(\cup, -)$ which is equivalent to $R \cap S$.

12. Every subset of a countable set is countable.

State whether the above statement is true or false with reason.

13. State True or False with reason

Logical data independence is easier to achieve than physical data independence

ANSWERS

MCQ Type Questions

1. (b)	2. (d)	3. (2NF)	4. (b)	5. (a)	6. (a)	7. (a)	8. (c)	9. (d)	10. (b)
11. (c)	12. (a)	13. (c)	14. (a)	15. (a)	16. (b)	17. (b)	18. (d)	19. (d)	20. (a)
21. (b)	22. (c)	23. (a)	24. (c)	25. (b)	26. (a)	27. (d)	28. (d)	29. (c)	30. (a)
31. (d)	32. (c)	33. (c)	34. (c)	35. (a)	36. (c)	37. (c)	38. (a)	39. (d)	40. (b)
41. (b)	42. (c)	43. (b)	44. (a)	45. (a)	46. (b)	47. (b)	48. (c)	49. (a)	50. (c)
51. (c)	52. (c)	53. (b)	54. (c)	55. (b)	56. (d)	57. (b)	58. (c)	59. (c)	60. (c)
61. (a)	62. (c)	63. (c)	64. (d)	65. (c)	66. (c)	67. (b)	68. (c)	69. (d)	70. (d)
71. (b)	72. (c)	73. (c)	74. (a)	75. (a)	76. (c)	77. (d)	78. (d)	79. (a)	80. (a)
81. (c)	82. (c)	83. (c)	84. (c)	85. (c)	86. (b)	87. (c)	88. (b)	89. (a)	90. (c)
91. (*)	92. (*)	93. (b)	94. (b)	95. (d)	96. (b)	97. (d)	98. (*)	99. (d)	100. (c)
101. (a)	102. (c)	103. (*)	104. (*)	105. (*)	106. (a)	107. (d)	108. (*)	109. (*)	110. (d)

Numerical Type Questions

1. (9)	2. (2)	3. (2)	4. (4)	5. (5)	6. (50)	7. (8 to 8)	8. (19 to 19)	9. (*)
10. (*)	11. (*)	12. (True)	13. (*)					

EXPLANATIONS

MCQ TYPE QUESTIONS

1. Super key

= Candidate key + Other Attribute of set

= Primary key + Other Attribute of set.

Given, Primary key = VY

So, VXYZ, VWXY, VWXYZ are super keys except VWXZ.

2. A C I D

D → Durability

I → Isolation

C → Consistency

A → Atomicity

3. It is 2NF because initially it contains partial dependency.

5. If a schedule(s) is serializable, the topological order of a graph (also called precedence graph) yields a serial schedule.

6. Sign is sender's private key and the receiver side verification of the signature is done with sender public key.

7. A binary relation R on N × N is defined as (a, b) R(C, d)

Reflexive: (a, a) R(a, a)

Since $a \le a$, and $a \le a$

Transitive: (a, b) R (c, d) and (c, d) R(m, n) then (a, b) R(m, n)

Suppose (a, b) R(c, d)

$\Rightarrow$ $a \le c$ and $b \le d$

and (c, d) R(m, n)

$\Rightarrow$ $c \le m$, $d \le n$

Since $a \le c$, and $c \le m$ so $a \le m$

$b \le d$ and $d \le n$, so $b \le n$

$\therefore$ (a, b) R(m, n)

(OR)

P. we have $a \le a$ and $b \le b$

$\Rightarrow$ (a, b) R(a, b)

$\Rightarrow$ R is reflexive

$\therefore$ P is true

Q. Let (a, b) R(c, d) and (c, d) R (e, f)

$\Rightarrow$ $\{a \le c \text{ and } b \le d\}$ and $\{c \le e \text{ and } d \le f\}$

$\Rightarrow$ $\{a \le e \text{ and } b \le f\}$

$\Rightarrow$ (a, b) R (e, f)

$\Rightarrow$ R is transitive

Hence both the statements P and Q are true.

8. As there is no dirty-read in the given schedule, the schedule is both recoverable and cascadeless.

9. The select operation is SQL is same as The projection operation is relational algebra except that SELECT is SQL retain duplicate.

10. Consistency : Consistancy properly ensure that any transaction will bring the database from one valid state to another

read (x);	
x : = x – 50;	
write (x) ;	
	read (y);
	y : = y + 50;
	write (y)

12. Undo T_3, T_{ij} Redo T_2

T_1 and T_3 will be undo, the transaction after checkpoint is T_2 which must be redo.

13. {P, S} → {S}

On finding closure of F^+, we can define {P, S} → {S} is trival functional dependency.

14. Var P = Var Q = FALSE Initially.

Assume that, process X is willing to enter into critical section. So it makes $V_{ar}P$ = True, then if processor switches to process Y, then process Y can enter into critical section.

After entering into the critical section, then if processor switches to process X, then process X also can enter into the critical section.

It is clearly showing that both are in critical section at a time which leads to "failing to guarantee material exclusion"

To enter into the critical section process X is not waiting for process Y and vice versa. So we can "Prevent Deadlock" so, overall, option (*a*) is correct (or) TRUE.

15. Inner query collects capacities of all the theatres and in outer query we are filtering the tuples with the condition "capacity>=All". So the theatres which are having maximum capacity will be satisfy the conductivity and they will.

16. T_2 is reading the value written by T_1 and getting committed before T_1 commits. So it is non-recoverable schedule.

17. R (EFGHI, JKLMN)

F = {

EF → G

F → IJ

EH → KL

K → M

L → N

}

$(EF)^+$ = EFGIJ, E & F

Together functionally derive GIJ and if we observe given FDs, H can't be determined by any other attributes. So H must be part of all the (candidate) keys. H along with E determines K and L, K & L functionally determine M and N respectively.

∴ $(EFH)^+$ = EFGIJHKLMN

∴ EFH is the only candidate for key.

18. S_1 : Manger (<u>Name</u>, Dept ID)

Department (DeptName, <u>Deptid</u>)

In given relation Manager DeptID is a foreign key referencing Deptid (P.K) of relation Department. Let's declare the foreign key by an equivalent check assertion as follows:-

```
CREATE TABLE Manager (
    Name Varchar (10)
    DeptID INT (6) check (DeptID IN (select
                     Deptid from Department)),
    PRIMARY KEY (Name)
    );
```

The above use of check assertion is good to declare the foreign key as far as insertion is considered for relation manager (will not insert any tuple in Manager containing such DeptID value which is not present in any tuple of Department).

But the above declaration will fail to implement changes done in Department relation in terms of deletion & updation. For an instance if a deptid present in Department gets deleted, then respective reference in Manager should also be deleted.

∴ S_1 is false

S_2 : The given table definition is not valid due to invalid foreign key declaration. Attribute a is declared as foreign key which is a single valued attribute and it is referencing the primary key (<u>ab</u>) of relation R (<u>a, b</u>, c), which is a composite key.

A single value attribute cannot refer a composite key.

S_2 is false.

19. If there is a cycle in precedence graph, then the schedule is not conflict serializable.

(*a*)

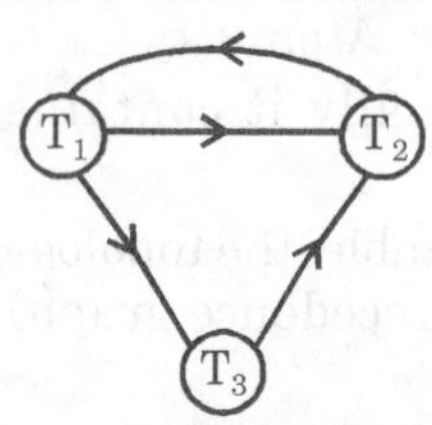

Not conflict serializable

(*b*)

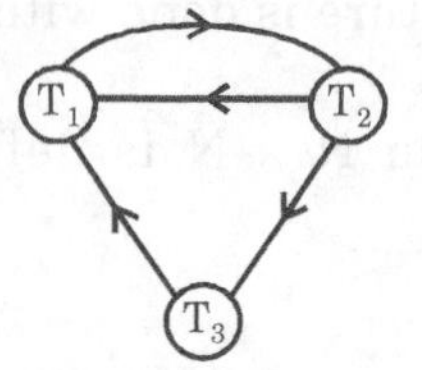

Not conflict serializable

(c) 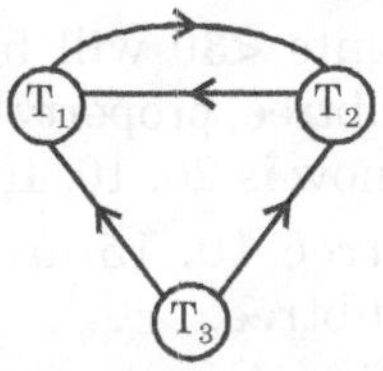

Not conflict serializable

(d) 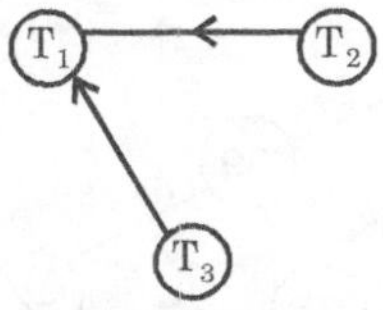

it is conflict equivalent to

$T_2 \rightarrow T_3 \rightarrow T_1$ &

$T_3 \rightarrow T_2 \rightarrow T_1$

20. S :True

Consider any table R with two attributes R (A.B)

The possible FD sets are

F_1 {

$A \rightarrow B$

}

Key :A and is in BCNF

F_2 {

$B \rightarrow A$

}

Key : B and is in BCNF

F_3 = {

$A \rightarrow B$

$B \rightarrow A$

}

Key : A & B it is in BCNF

F_4 = {

}

Key : AB and is in BCNF

If a table is in BCNF it is also in 1NF, 2NF and 3NF also

S_2 : False

First FD set cannot cover second FD set because in second FD set AB can functionally derive E but that is not happing in first FD set.

21. In the inner sub query, "employees" and "departments" tables are joined by "using" clause (first Cartesian product of those two tables will be done and then and wherever these is a match on the dept-ids that tuple will be filtered). After this, the tuples of the resultant table will be filtered by using the condition "location-id=1700" and then will grouped on deptid(all the tuples having equal values under dept-id will come into one group). After grouping, the columns dept-id in location-id 1700 and maximum of hire dates in that respective dept-id will be selected. Format of the tuples in the resultant table will be dept-id in location-id 1700 along with the latest hire date in the respective dept (two columns). Outer query takes each tuple from "employees" table and it will check whether dept-id and hire-date pair for this tuple is contained in the table given by inner sub query. If this is the case it will display the last-name of respective employee

IN operator compares one or multiple expressions on the left side of the operator to a set of one or more values on the right side of the operator. When using multiple expressions (like 2 columns - pair wise comparison), the number and data types of expressions in the list must match on both sides of the operator.

22. Since, the graph contains no cycle, that's why it is called conflict serializable.

Since, in this schedule, transaction reads data item previously written by former transactions. The commit operation of former transactions occur before later transactions, hence it is recoverable also. That's why 'S' is both conflict serializable and recoverable.

23. A join between r(R) and s (S) using nested loop method will be as follows.

For each tuple r in R do

For each tuple s in S do

If r and s satisfy the join condition then output the tuple <r, s>

This algorithm will involve $n_r * b_s + b_r$ block transfers and $n_r + b_r$ seeks, where b_r and b_s are number of blocks in relations R and S respectively and n_r is number of tuple in relation R. Now to have less block accesses, n_r should be less and it is already given that $|R| < |S|$. Relation r(R) should be in the outer loop to have fewer number of disk block accesses.

24. When we execute query R * from (select distinct from S) as S_1 where $R \cdot a = S_1 \cdot a$, it will give the same results.

25. A prime attribute or key attribute of a relation scheme R is an attribute that appears in any of the candidate key of R, remaining attributes are known as non-prime or non-key tribute.

26. Precedence graph for S_1 & S_2 are as follows

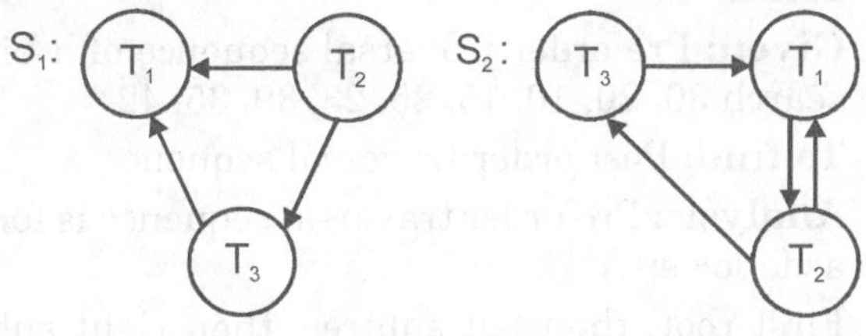

No cycle Cycle

$\therefore$ Only S_1 is conflict serializable.

27.

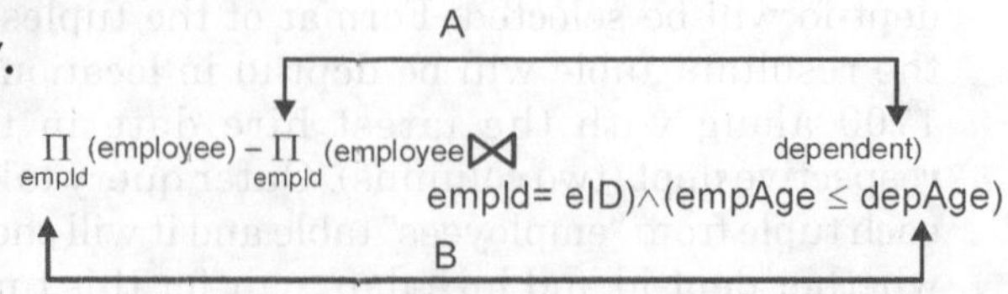

Part A of the above given relational algebra query will give the set of empIds of those employees whose age is less than or equal to the age of some of his/her dependents. Now when set of empIds of all employees minus set of empIds obtained from part A is done, then we get the set of empIds of employees whose age is greater than that of all of his/her dependents.

28. The outer query will return the value (names of employees) for a tuple in relation E, only if inner query for that tuple will return no tuple (usage of NOT EXISTS).

The inner query will run for every tuple of outer query. It selects cust-id for an employee E, if rating of customer is NOT good. Such an employee should not be selected in the output of outer query. So the query will return the names of all those employees whose all customers have GOOD rating.

29. **Clustered Index:** Sorts and store the data rows in the table or view based on their key values the column on which clustered index is created need not be primary key but it should always be not null.

30. Find the distinct names of all students who score more than 90% in the course no. 107.

1. SQL query

Condition would give all S. name having score > 90 and attending course no. 107 and DISTINCT S.sname will give distinct student names.

TRUE

2. Relational Algebra

πsname gives projection of all students meeting the condition and 'π' gives DISTINCT value.

TRUE

3. Tuple Calculus

gives DISTINCT student name having score > 90 and course no. is 107. TRUE

4. Domain Calculus

domain calculus is equivalent to relational algebra and provide distinct value for the query.

TRUE

31. **Given:** Pre order traversal sequence of a binary search 30, 20, 10, 15, 25, 23, 39, 35, 42

To find: Post order traversal sequence

Analysis: Pre order traversal sequence is formed as follows:

First root, then left subtree, then right subtree and then recursively do this. This means 30 is the root. constructing tree for this:

(we also know, all elements <30 will be in left subtree and > 30 in right subtree, property of binary search tree) Left subtree now is 20, 10, 15, 25

⇒ 20 is root of left subtree 10, 15 are its left subtree, 23, 25 its right subtree.

Going like this, use can construct the tree.

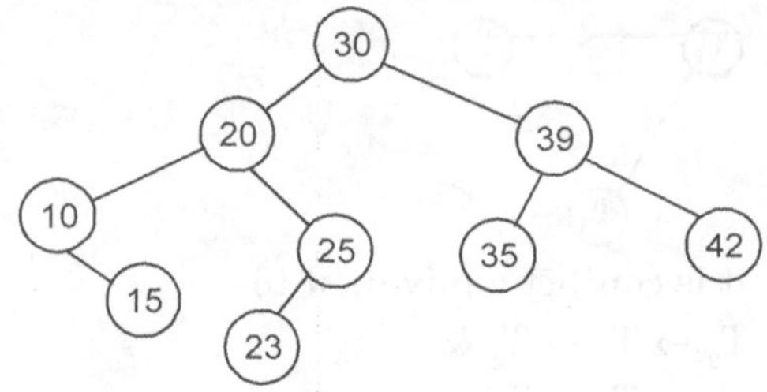

Getting the order:

Moving to left subtree of tree rooted at 30

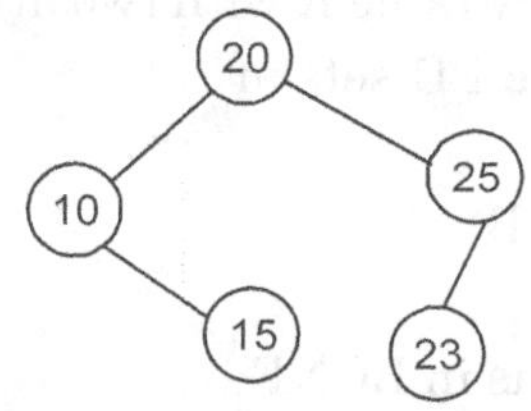

Moving to left subtree

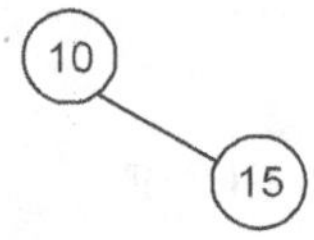

Left subtree is empty, so going to right subtree

Left is right subtree and are empty, so print root

Going back from right subtree

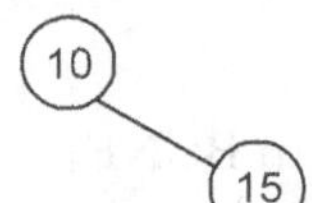

Print root (10)

Backing from left subtree, going to right subtree

Processed←

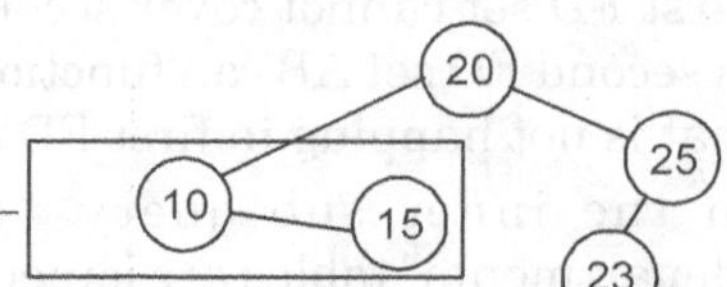

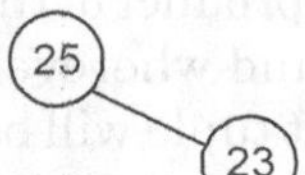

Similarly, here, we will print (23), (25) & go back to original root. Then move to its right subtree

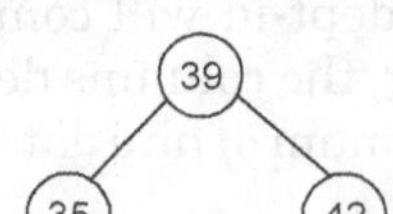

Here, print order is (35), (42), (39) and at last root (30).

Hence, the order is:

15, 10, 23, 25, 20, 35, 42, 39, 30.

So, the answer is (*d*).

33. Row cannot have attribute more than one value.

34. Option A is false since BCNF is stricter than 3NF

Option B is false since the definition given here is of 2NF

Option C is true, since BCNF is stricter than 3NF, every relation in BCNF satisfies all the properties of 3NF.

35. Foreign key should refer to existing keys so:

$$\pi_B(r_1) - \pi_C(r_2) = \phi$$

36. S

Borrower	Bank_Manager
Ramesh	Sunderajan
Suresh	Ramgopal
Mahesh	Sunderjan

T

Bank_Manager	Loan_Amount
Sunderajan	10000.00
Ramgopal	5000.00
Sunderjan	7000.00

After executing the given query, the output would be

Borrower	Bank_Manager	Loan_Amount
Ramesh	Sunderajan	10000.00
Ramesh	Sunderajan	7000.00
Suresh	Ramgopal	5000.00
Mahesh	Sunderajan	10000.00
Mahesh	Sunderajan	7000.00

38.

X	Y
1	1
2	3
3	7
4	15
5	31
6	63
7	127

39. It can be used to prevent packet looping because when Time-to-Live field reaches to '0' means when there is no any type of acknowledgement received, then TTL decrementet continuously and when it reaches '0', then it stop looping of packet.

41. Minimum number of keys = $\left\lfloor \frac{n}{2} \right\rfloor = \left\lfloor \frac{5}{2} \right\rfloor = 2$

42. SELECT pid

FROM Reservation

WHERE class = 'AC'

EXISTS (SELECT * FROM Passanger WHERE age > 65 AND Passanger pid = Reservation. pid

Query A select where age > 65 and Passanger. pid matches with Reservation. pid

means Rahul, Sourav and Anil

Now we check in Query B from Reservation that class should 'AC' and Exit in Rahul, Sourav, Anil, So that class of Rahul and Anil is AC.

So pid is 1 & 3.

43. 2-phase locking not ensure deadlock but it can ensure conflict serialization some how

but Time-stamp locking can ensure both conflict searialization and deadlock.

44. By using the precedence graph we solve thus problem

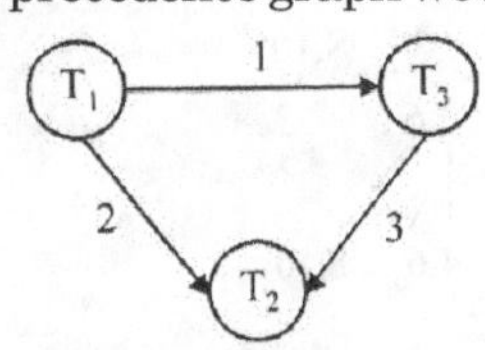

1. Read (x) in T_1 is followed by write (x) in T_2
2. Read (x) in T_1 is followed by write (x) in T_3
3. Read (y) in T_3 is followed by write (y) in T_2

So it in clear from precedence graph

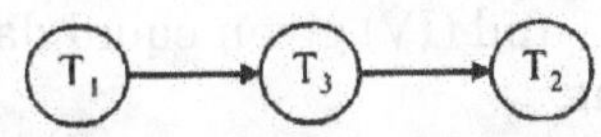

45. B → A where R (A, B, C) and S (B, D, E)

A → C

R contains 200 tuples

S contains 100 tuples

Natural join ⋈ = R ⋈ S = π[σ (R × S)]

So R = 200 tuples and S = 100 tuples.

So R ⋈ S = 100

[common in both or we can say Distinct equality b/w All common Attribute]

46.

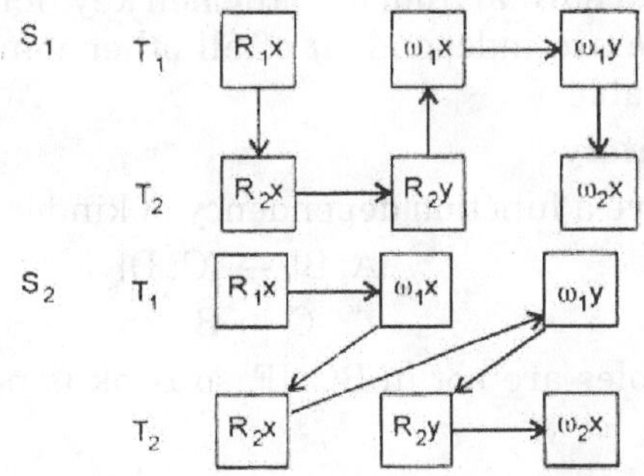

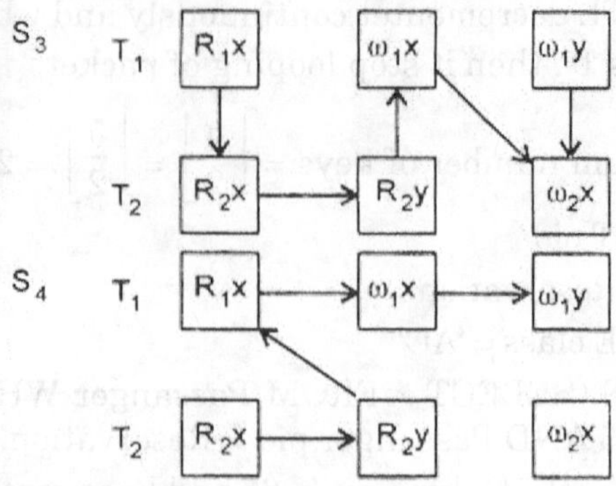

Clearly S_2 and S_3 are conflict - serializable.

47.

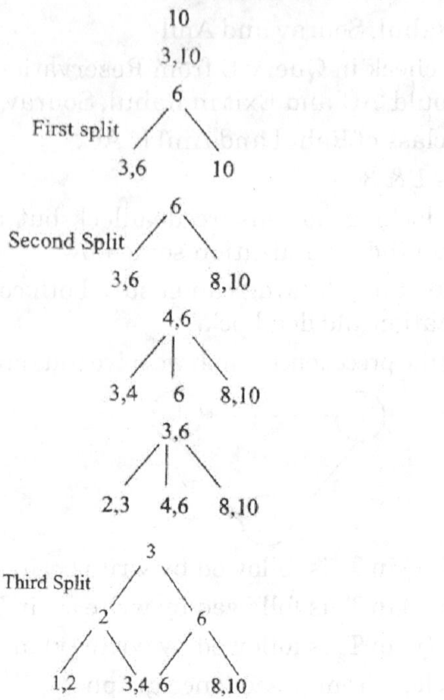

48. Query (II) and (IV) given equal data so they are equivalent.

49. Clustering index in unique and is created automatically when primary key is declared it is ordered.

50. I, II and III express following quering select P from the join (natural) of R and S, Which can be expressed as select P, then joining (II) or selecting P from the union of R & S by first selecting R & Q (key values).

51. A table in the second normal from if all the non key fields fully dependent on whole key. A table is in third normal from if all the non key fields of the table are independent of all other non key field of table.

Alternately

If we have a function dependency of kind

$$\{A, B\} \rightarrow \{C, D\}$$
$$C \rightarrow B$$

then Tables are not in BCNF, so Book is not in BCNF.

If a non key value is depndent on other non key, then table is not in 3NF, of Book is also not in 3NF and collection is in 3NF.

52. Block size is given 1024 so first level and second level multiplication must be 2^{10}, so only (c) satisfy $2^8 \times 22 = 2^{10}$.

54. The query

$\{e\cdot$ name | employee $(e) \wedge (\forall x)$ [⌈ employee (x)] $vx\cdot$ supervisor Name $\neq e\cdot$ name v xssex = "male"]}

computes the names of employees with no immediate female subordinates.

55. Query Q_1 doesn't give correct result because it contain not exists clause which lead to wrong answer. Q_2 is correct.

56. In BCNF, a prime attribute cannot be transitively dependent on a key.

57. Let the order be n

So, $n \times 7 + (n - 1)\,9 = 1024$

$\Rightarrow \quad 16\,n = 1033$

$\Rightarrow \quad n = \left\lceil \dfrac{1033}{16} \right\rceil = 64$

58. Here S_1 is not conflict serializable whereas S_2 is conflict serializable.

59. Once a transaction commits, the changes made by it to the database get permanent and there is no effect of system failure over the data. Since T_2 is not allowed to commit, we must undo log record 6.

60. Lets take an example of the balances

1	20	1
2.	21	2
3.	21	2
4.	21	2
5.	22	5

Query 1 will assign rank 4 to account (4) which is wrong.

61. All queries give one and the same output.

62. In Plan 1, first the records from 'paid' is selected and then they are joined. On the other hand in Plan 2, all the records from 'paid' are joined and then the records are checked.

As join is an iterative and relatively expressive process. Plan 1 will execute faster though the output will be the same.

63. The algorithm used is (for α^+)

result $= \alpha$,

While (changes to result) do

for each functional dependency $\beta \rightarrow \gamma$ in F

do begin

if $\beta \subseteq$ result, then

result = result $\upsilon\gamma$,

end

For (C), $\{AF\}^+ = \{AFDE\}$

64. Because data transfer take place in the form of block's frame disk, so, any data structure which store as large as can, information in a single block is more efficient.

65. Note that B.C.N.F. is not dependency-preserving in all cases.

66. *s* have more tuples than required one

it have all tuples in *r* but some which are not is *r* also.

So, $r \subset s$

67. One table for E_1;

One table for E_2;

One table for R_2

* Remember that only one to many relationship can be represented with entity set from one's side, because each entity in this entity set can be associated with at most one entity of another set.

68. When (2, 4) is deleted any record that have '2' in the foreign key must have to be deleted.

Here, records are < 5, 2 >, <7, 2>

Then because of cascade any record that have 5 or 7 as foreign key must be deleted. There is no record that have 7 as foreign key (9, 5) is gone to delete. Now, any record that have 9 has an foreign key have to delete but there is no one.

69. The given SQL query compute "Titles of the five most expensive books".

70. When we consider

$$A = \{A, B\}$$
$$B = \{B\}$$

and $$H = \{H\}$$

$$\{A, B, H\} = \{A, B, C, D, E, H\}$$
$$\{B, E, H\} = \{A, B, C, D, F, H\}$$
$$\{D, E, H\} = \{A, B, C, D, E, H\}$$

and no one option can generate this result.

71. – empty table is generated by the query

$$\pi_C (r_1) - \pi_D (r_2)$$

72. Maximum number of tupte is minimum of these two, is 8.

$$120 \times 8 = 960$$

73. It should not be visible to outside world and should be extracted through super class. Name can be duplicate should be implemented in sub class. Salary is dependent on category should be implemented in subclass.

74. Given functional dependeney are

name, course no. → grade ;
roll no, course no → grade
name → roll no.
roll no. → name

from the function it is clear that there is no repetation of attributes hence it is in 1 NF. There is no partial dependency hence it is 2NF. and

name → roll no.
roll no → name

So there is transitive dependeney it is not in 3NF so heighest normal from of this relation is 2NF.

75. Relation is

Student (name, sex, marks)

expression for query is

$$\pi_{\text{name}} (\sigma_{\text{six=female}}(\text{student})) - \pi_{\text{name}} (\text{student} \underset{\substack{(\text{sex = female} \\ \wedge X = \text{male} \\ \wedge \text{marks} \leq m)}}{\bowtie} \rho_{n, x, m}(\text{student}))$$

this will retrience the name of girl student with more marks than all the boy student.

76. Child pointer takes b byte

Search field= 14 byte

block size= 512 byte

The order of internal node is 9 + 14 + 3 = 26

77. Given relation is

Employee (<u>Name</u>, Sex, Salary, deptName)

SQL query is

```
Select deptName,
  from Employee
    Where Sex = 'M'
group by deptName
  having avg (Salary) > (Select avg (Salary) from
                    Employee)
```

This will retrieve the department in which average salary of male employee is more than the average salary in the company.

78. If data is uncommitted, then transactions reads a data after write always give error.

79. SQL form the cartesian product of the relation named in the form cluase, perform a relational algebra selection using the where clause predicate and then projects the result onto the attributes of the select clause.

80. Date–of–Birth → Age

Age → Eligibility

Name → Roll-number,

Roll Number → Name

Course – Number → Course–Name

Course – Name → Instructor

(Roll Number, Course – number) → Grade

From given relation,

Date–of–Birth → Eligibility (By transitively)

Course–Number → Instructor (By transtively)

So, it is not in 3rd Normal form because in third normal form relation, every non prime attribute is non-transitively and fully dependent on the every candidate key.

In 2nd Normal from, all non-prime attributes are fully functionally dependent on the relation keys.

81. There are three relations

Select distinct name, select the name of students and then there are three predicates

Courses. instructor = korth specify the courses taught by korth.

The other two predicate specify that student can earn a grade at least A from causes so the SQL query compute.

Name of students who have got an A grade in at least one of the courses taught by korth.

82.

T_1	T_2	T_3
	R (D3);	
	R (D2);	
	W (D2);	
		R (D2);
		W (D1);
R (D1);		
W (D1);		
R (D2);	R (D1);	W (D2);
W (D2);	W (D1);	W (D3);

In transation T_3 R(D2) is conflict with original R (D2), because R (D2) is read W (D2).

Again an transaction T_2, R (D1) is conflict with R (D1) in T_1 because it read (D1) as W (D1)

In transaction T_1, R(D2) conflicts with R(D2) in T_2, because it is W(D2) in T_2.

So, finally transaction is conflict serialization schedule as T_3 ; T_2; T_1.

83. R (A, B, C, D) is relation, and R(A), R(B), R(C), and R(D) is decomposition, then

$R_1 \cap R_2 \to R_1$ $\quad R_1 \cup R_2 \cup R_3 \cup R_4 = R$

$R_1 \cap R_2 \to R_2$

$A \to B$, $B \to C$, so $A \to C$

$B \to C$, $C \to D$, so $B \to D$

$A \to B, A \to C, A \to BC$

$B \to C$, $B \to D$, $B \to CD$, so, its multivalued dependency so it is in BC at E].

84. Adjancy matrix. Graphs represented in two ways

(*a*) **Sequential.** This form uses a square table within rows and column, where n is number of vertices. This table is called adjancy matrix. If diagonal elements are zero indicating no "self edges".

85. $s_A = a\,(r \bowtie S)$ $\quad$ [$\bowtie$= natural join]

$= s_A = a^{(r)}$

Because we have to select A = a in relation ($\gamma \bowtie$ S). But A is attribute of R and γ is relation of R. so are write.

$$A = \widehat{a(\gamma \bowtie S) = \sigma_A} = a(\gamma) \bowtie S$$

γ	B
1	*Prawd*
2	*Mourye*
3	*Sign*
4	*Nag*

A	B
1	*Delhi*
2	*Patna*
3	*Salgram*
4	*Dehri*

$\sigma_{A=1}(\gamma \bowtie S) =$ | 1 | Prawd | Delhi |

$\sigma^{A=1}_{(\gamma)} =$ | 1 | Pramal |, $\gamma^{(\gamma)\bowtie S}_{A=1} =$ | 1 | Prawd | Delhi |

91. (*a*)

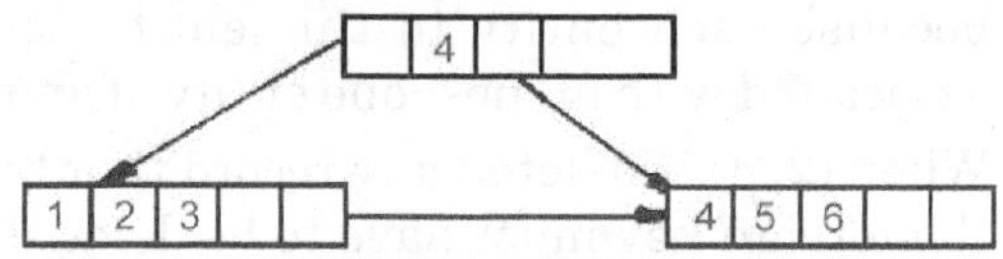

(*b*)

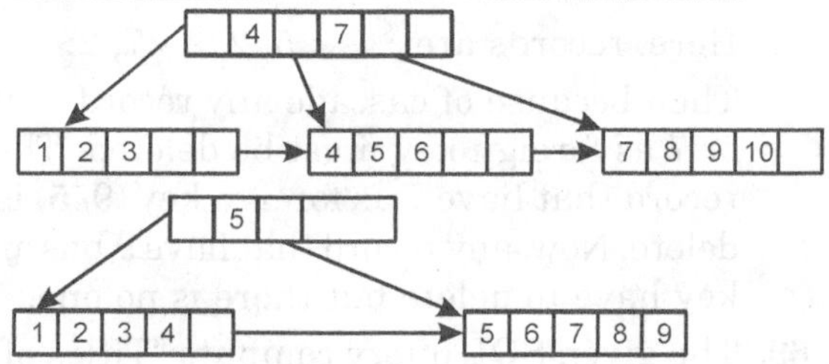

(*c*) (*i*) $\left\lceil \dfrac{m}{2} \right\rceil$ or $\dfrac{m}{2}$

(*ii*) m

92. (*a*) Create view TP (*a*cctno, date, amount)
as select T1. acctno, T1. date,
T2. amount from transaction T1,
transaction T2
where T1.acctno = T2.acctno
and T2. date < = T1 date

(*b*) Create view V (acctno, date, balance)
as select acctno, date, sum (amount)
from TP
group by acctno, date
Select acctno, min (balance)
from V
group by acctno.

93. EC is the key as

$E \to A \to B$, so $EC \to B$

$C \to F$, so $EC \to F$

Also, $\quad EC \to D$ and $EC \to EC$

Hence, taking all the above, $EC \to ABCDE$

94. In a B^+ tree, the leaf nodes are linked together to provide ordered access- hence, range queries are faster for B^+ tress.

96. Keep the records of A fixed and insert the records of the other files in A in sorted order. This would require 20 + 15 + 5 + 25 = 65 record movements.

97. An SQL query automatically not eliminates duplicates.

* An sql query will work if index are not given on the relation.
* SQL not permit attribute n axes for fepetition

98. (*a*) select Employee_name from EMP, DEPT where Location = "Calcutta" and Salary > 50000 and EMP. Dept-no = DEPT.Dept-no.

(*b*) select Dept-no, count (*) from EMP, DEPT where EMP. Dept-no = DEPT. Dept-no and Salary > 100000.

99. **NF.** A relation R is third normal form (3NF) if and only if it is 2NF and every non key attribute is non transitively dependent on the primary key.

Main Functions of 3NF

(1) A relation R is in 3NF with respect to F of functional dependency if all function at dependencies in F^+ of the form $\alpha \to \beta$, where $\alpha \le R$ and $\beta \le R$ atleast one of the following folds.

* $\alpha \to \beta$ is trial functional dependency.
* α is superkey of R.

(2) In 3NF, we find lossless join, dependency per serving decomposition.

100. We find from question, index file associated and contains the values of 1, 3, 2, 5, 4, we get **Index filed from occupation.** One to this conflicting never occur.

101. Condition C_1 may be different from C_2.

102. Maximum signed form digit number (± 9999) can be stored in two bytes as integer and will require 5 bytes storage space.

103. (*a*) We have the relations

FREQUENTS (student, parlor)
SERVES (parlor, ice-cream)
LIKES (student, ice-cream)

We have the SQL as

```
Select Student
From FREQUENTS
where Parlor
= (Select Parlor)
from SERVES
where ice-cream
= (Select ice-cream
from LIKES
where LIKE student = Frequents. Students)).
```

(*b*) The 20 K partition will be occupied by the 14 K job which will require 10 units of time for execution. After its completion the 10 K job will be occupying this 20K partition. And on its completion 20 K will be taking up the partition. Hence total time = 10 + 1 + 8 = 19 Units

Other jobs will be occupying the other partitions.

104. (*a*) Following diagram shows the functional dependencies in the relation :

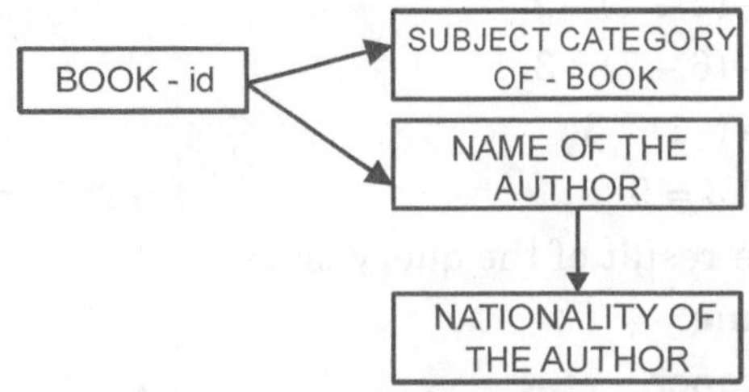

Nationality of the Author transitively depends on Book -id, primary key. So it can't be in the 3NF but is in the 2NF.

(*b*) Following diagrams shows the functional dependencies in the relation :

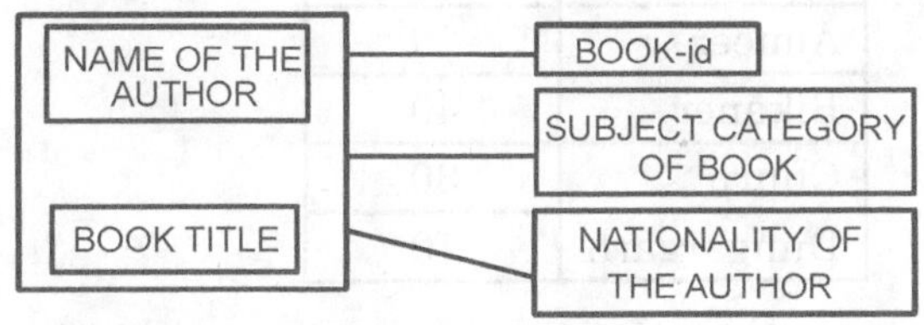

The above relation is in 3NF.

105. (Completed where Student. number = 2310 and C_{n0} = (Pre – REQ
where C_{n0} = (COMPLETED)
where student number = (2310) [C_{n0}])
[Pre – C_{n0}] [C_{n0}].

106. A relation R is in first normal form (1NF) if the domains of all attributes of R are atomic. A domain is atomic if elements of the domain are considered to be indivisible units.

Given, $a \to c$ $\quad a^+ = \{a, c\}$ $\quad b^+ = \{b, d\}$
$b \to d$ It is Ist normal form (It have no key] so, it is not in 2 NF.

107. For referential integrity constraint

(*b*) Insert Into S (*c*) Deletes from R

because R (*a*, *b*, *c*) is primary key. If we insert into S, not change value of R (*a*, *b*, *c*) and when delete from R, then we have need to delete from S also.

109. (*a*) Titles of the books issued to user 6

(*b*) Names of the authors of books that are issued to users who are from Delhi.

110. Symmetrical Relation. (*a*, *b*) and (*b*, *a*) must implies in relation R.

Transitive. (*a*, *b*), (*b*, *c*) then (*a*, *c*) should be granted in relation R

Reflexive. (*a*, *a*) must be in Relation R.

Equivalence relation. A binary relation on a set is said to be an equivalence relation if it is reflexive, symmetric and transitive.

Partial order. A binary relation is said to be partial order relation if it is reflexive, antisymmetric and transitive.

NUMERICAL TYPE QUESTIONS

1. $2 - (5 + 1) - 7 * 3$

$2 - (6 - 7) * 3$

$2 - (-1) * 3$

$3 * 3 = 9$

2. The result of the query is:

name

Bikaner

churu

Total	
District name	**Capacity**
Ajmeer	20
Bikaner	40
Churu	30
Dungargarh	10

$$\text{Total} - \text{Average} = \frac{\text{Capacity of (Ajmer + Bikaner + Churu + Dungargarh)}}{4}$$

$$= \frac{20+40+30+10}{4}$$

$$= \frac{110}{4} = 25$$

Total – avg capacity
25

So, the number of tables returned by the given SQL query is 2.

3. The output is

Raj	310
Rohit	140

Hence no of rows returned are 2

4. The E–R diagram is

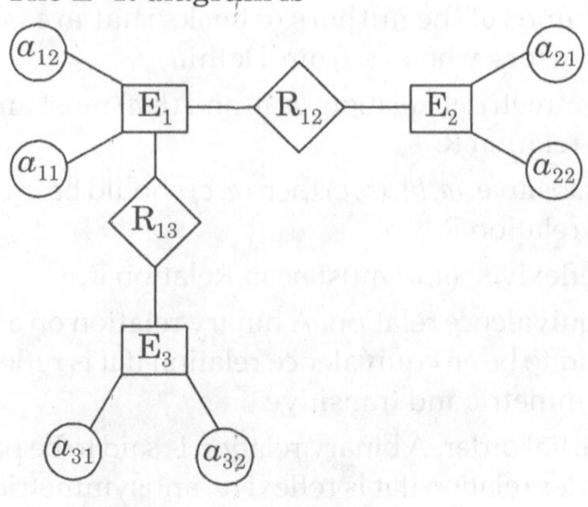

5. In given B⁺ tree

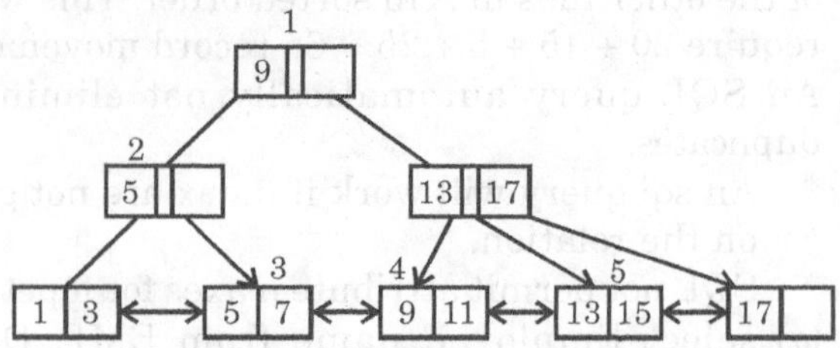

So to find greater than or equal to 7 and less than 15. It will fatch 5 nodes.

As shown in above diagram it may be

1 – 2 – 3 – 4 – 5

or

1 – 6 – 5 – 4– 3

Ans = 5

6. Suppose that 'k' is order of the non-leaf node

$$k(8) + (k - 1)\,12 \le 1024$$

$$20\,k \le 1036$$

$$k \le \left[\frac{1036}{20}\right] \Rightarrow k \le 51$$

As the order is 51, maximum we can store 50 keys.

7. Since the number of super keys is given by 2^{n-1} where n is number of attributes.

Hence, total number of super keys with n attributes are= $2^{n-1} = 2^{4-1} = 2^8$

8. If we put value of student age to be 19, then student name, student age will not be key, that's why value of x should not be equal to 19 because it may be same for another student.

10. No A may have null value

12. True

Let A be any countable set and BCA be subset.

If B is finite, there is nothing to prove.

If B is infinity, then A is countable infinite (is denumerable). Then we can write A as an infinite sequence $< a_1, a_2, a_3, a_n$.

Let n_1 be the least positive integer such that $a_{n1} \in B$.

Again let n_2 be least positive integer greater than n, such that $a_{n2} \in B$ and so on.

Then it is evident that the mapping $f : N \to B$: $f(k) = ank$.

Hence B is countable

13. True

8 CHAPTER Computer Networks

MCQ TYPE QUESTIONS

2016

1. Which one of the following protocols is **NOT** used to resolve one form of address to another one?

(*a*) DNS (*b*) ARP

(*c*) DHCP (*d*) RARP

2. Which of the following is/are example (s) of stateful application layer protocols?

(*i*) HTTP (*ii*) FTP

(*iii*) TCP (*iv*) POP3

(*a*) (*i*) and (*ii*) only (*b*) (*ii*) and (*iii*) only

(*c*) (*ii*) and (*iv*) only (*d*) (*iv*) only

3. In an Ethernet local area network, which one of the following statements is TRUE?

(*a*) A station stops to sense the channel once it starts transmitting a frame.

(*b*) The purpose of the jamming signal is to pad the frames that are smaller than the minimum frame size.

(*c*) A station continues to transmit the packet even after the collision is detected.

(*d*) The exponential backoff mechanism reduces the probability of collision on retransmissions.

4. Identify the correct sequence in which the following packets are transmitted on the network by a host when a browser requests a webpage from a remote server, assuming that the host has just been restarted.

(*a*) HTTP GET request, DNS query, TCP SYN

(*b*) DNS query, HTTP GET request, TCP SYN

(*c*) DNS query, TCP SYN, HTTP GET request

(*d*) TCP SYN, DNS query, HTTP GET request

5. For the IEEE 802.11 MAC protocol for wireless communication, which of the following statements is/are TRUE?

I. At least three non-overlapping channels are available for transmissions.

II. The RTS-CTS mechanism is used for collision detection.

III. Unicast frames are ACKed.

(*a*) All I, II, and III (*b*) I and III only

(*c*) II and III only (*d*) II only

2014

6. Consider the following three statements about link state and distance vector routing protocols, for a large network with 500 network nodes and 4000 links.

S1: The computational overhead in link state protocols is higher than in distance vector protocols.

S2: A distance vector protocol (with split horizon) avoids persistent routing loops, but not a link state protocol.

S3: After a topology change, a link state protocol will converge faster than a distance vector protocol.

Which one of the following is correct about S1, S2, and S3?

(*a*) S1, S2, and S3 are all true

(*b*) S1, S2, and S3 are all false.

(*c*) S1 and S2 are true, but S3 is false

(*d*) S1 and S3 are true, but S2 is false.

7. Which one of the following are used to generate a message digest by the network security protocols?

P. RSA Q. SHA-1

R. DES S. MD5

(*a*) P and R only (*b*) Q and R only

(*c*) Q and S only (*d*) R and S only

8. Identify the correct order in which the following actions take place in an interaction between a web browser and a web server.

1. The web browser requests a webpage using HTTP.
2. The web browser establishes a TCP connection with the web server.
3. The web server sends the requested webpage using HTTP.
4. The web browser resolves the domain name using DNS.

(*a*) 4, 2, 1, 3 (*b*) 1, 2, 3, 4

(*c*) 4, 1, 2, 3 (*d*) 2, 4, 1, 3

9. Which one of the following is TRUE about the interior gateway routing protocols – Routing Information Protocol (RIP) and Open Shortest Path First (OSPF)?

(*a*) RIP uses distance vector routing and OSPF uses link state routing

(*b*) OSPF uses distance vector routing and RIP uses link state routing

(*c*) Both RIP and OSPF use link state routing

(*d*) Both RIP and OSPF use distance vector routing

10. Which one of the following socket API functions converts an unconnected active TCP socket into a passive socket?

(*a*) connect (*b*) bind

(*c*) listen (*d*) accept

11. Consider the store and forward packet switched network given below. Assume that the bandwidth of each link is 10^6 bytes / sec. A user on host A sends a file of size 10^3 bytes to host B through routers R1 and R2 in three different ways. In the first case a single packet containing the complete file is transmitted from A to B. In the second case, the file is split into 10 equal parts, and these packets are transmitted from A to B. In the third case, the file is split into 20 equal parts and these packets are sent from A to B. Each packet contains 100 bytes of header information along with the user data. Consider only transmission time and ignore processing, queuing and propagation delays. Also assume that there are no errors during transmission. Let T1, T2 and T3 be the times taken to transmit the file in the first, second and third case respectively. Which one of the following is CORRECT?

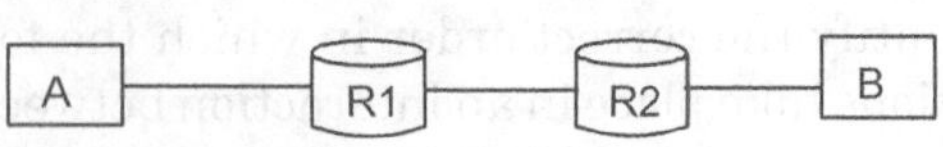

(*a*) T1 < T2 < T3

(*b*) T1 > T2 > T3

(*c*) T2 = T3, T3 < T1

(*d*) T1 = T3, T3 > T2

12. An IP machine Q has a path to another IP machine H via three IP routers R1, R2, and R3.

Q–R1–R2–R3–H

H acts as an HTTP server, and Q connects to H via HTTP and downloads a file. Session layer encryption is used, with DES as the shared key encryption protocol. Consider the following four pieces of information:

[I1] The URL of the file downloaded by Q

[I2] The TCP port numbers at Q and H

[I3] The IP addresses of Q and H

[I4] The link layer addresses of Q and H

Which of I1, I2, I3, and I4 can an intruder learn through sniffing at R2 alone?

(*a*) Only I1 and I2 (*b*) Only I1

(*c*) Only I2 and I3 (*d*) Only I3 and I4

13. In the following pairs of OSI protocol layer/sub-layer and its functionality, the INCORRECT pair is

(*a*) Netwrok layer and Routing

(*b*) Data Link Layer and Bit synchronization

(*c*) Transport layer and End-to-end process communication

(*d*) Medium Access Control sub-layer and Channel sharing

14. Host A (on TCP/IP v4 network A) sends an IP datagram D to host B (also on TCP/IP v4 network B). Assume that no error occurred during the transmission of D. When D reaches B, which of the following IP header field(s) may be different from that of the original datagram D?

(*i*) TTL (*ii*) Checksum

(*iii*) Fragment Offset

(*a*) (*i*) only (*b*) (*i*) and (*ii*) only

(*c*) (*ii*) and (*iii*) only (*d*) (*i*), (*ii*) and (*iii*)

15. An IP router with a Maximum Transmission Unit (MTU) of 1500 bytes has received an IP packet of size 4404 bytes with an IP header of length 20 bytes. The values of the relevant fields in the header of the third IP fragment generated by the router for this packet are

(*a*) MF bit: 0, Datagram Length: 1444; Offset: 370

(*b*) MF bit: 1, Datagram Length: 1424; Offset: 185

(*c*) MF bit: 1, Datagram Length: 1500; Offset: 370

(*d*) MF bit: 0, Datagram Length: 1424; Offset: 2960

16. Suppose that everyone in a group of N people wants to communicate secretly with the N-1 others using symmetric key cryptographic system. The communication between any two persons should not be decodable by the others in the group. The number of keys required in the system as a whole to satisfy the confidentiality requirement is

(*a*) 2N (*b*) N(N-1)

(*c*) N(N-1)/2 (*d*) $(N-1)^2$

17. Which one of the following fields of an IP header is NOT modified by a typical IP router?

(a) Checksum (b) Source address

(c) Time to Live (TTL) (d) Length

18. Suppose two hosts use a TCP connection to transfer a large file. Which of the following statements is/are FALSE with respect to the TCP connection ?

I. If the sequence number of a segment is m, then the sequence number of the subsequent segment is always m + 1.

II. If the estimated round trip time at any given point of time is *t* sec the value of the retransmission timeout is always set to greater than or equal to t sec.

III. The size of the advertised window never changes during the curse of the TCP connection.

IV. The number of unacknowledged bytes at the sender is always less than or equal to the advertised window.

(a) III only (b) I and III only

(c) I and IV only (d) II and IV only

19. In one of the pairs of protocols given below, both the protocols can use multiple TCP connections between the same client and the server. Which one is that ?

(a) HTTP, FTP

(b) HTTP, TELNET

(c) FTP, SMTP

(d) HTTP, SMTP

20. Identify the correct order in which a server process must invoke the function calls accept, bind, listen, and recv according to UNIX socket APL

(a) listen, accept, bind recv

(b) bind, listen, accept, recv

(c) bind, accept, listen, recv

(d) accept, listen, bind recv

21. Which one of the following statements is NOT correct about HTTP cookies?

(a) A cookie is a piece of code that has the potential to compromise the security of an internet user

(b) A cookie gains entry to the user's work area through an HTTP header

(c) A cookie has an expiry date and time

(d) Cookies can be used to track the browsing pattern of a user at a particular site

22. Host A sends a UDP datagram containing 8880 bytes of user data to host B over an Ethernet LAN. Ethernet frames may carry data up to 1500 bytes (i.e. MTU = 1500 bytes). Size of UDP header is 8 bytes and size of IP heard is 20 bytes.There is no option field in IP header. How many total number of IP fragments will be transmitted and what will be the contents of offset field in the last fragment?

(a) 6 and 925 (b) 6 and 7400

(c) 7 and 1110 (d) 7 and 8880

23. Consider the following routing table at an IP router:

Network No.	Net Mask	Next Hop
128.96.170.0	255.255.254.0	Interface 0
128.96.168.0	255.255.254.0	Interface 1
128.96.166.0	255.255.254.0	R2
128.96.164.0	255.255.252.0	R3
0.0.0.0	Default	R4

For each IP address in Group I identify the correct choice of the next hop from Group II using the entries from the routing table above.

Group I	Group II
i. 128.96.171.92	a. Interface 0
ii. 128.96.167.151	b. Interface 1
iii. 128.96.163.151	c. R2
iv. 128.96.165.121	d. R3
	e. R4

(a) i – a, ii – c, iii – e, iv – d

(b) i – a, ii – d, iii – b, iv – e

(c) i – b, ii – c, iii – d, iv – e

(d) i – b, ii – c, iii – e, iv – d

24. Assume that the bandwidth for a TCP connection is 1048560 bits/sec. Let α be the value of RTT in milliseconds. (rounded off to the nearest integer) after which the TCP window scale option is needed. Let β be the maximum possible window size the window scale option. Then the values of α and β are

(a) 63 milli seconds, 65535×2^{14}

(b) 63 milli seconds, 65535×2^{16}

(c) 500 milliseconds, 65535×2^{14}

(d) 500 milliseconds, 65535×2^{16}

25. Consider the following statements.

I. TCP connections are full duplex

II. TCP has no option for selective acknowledgment

III. TCP connections are message streams

(*a*) Only I is correct

(*b*) Only I and III are correct

(*c*) Only II and III are correct

(*d*) All of I, II and III are correct

26. Consider a CSMA/CD network that transmits data at a rate of 100 Mbps (10^8 bits second) over a 1 km(kilometer) cable with no repeaters. If the minimum frame size required for this network is 1250 bytes, what is the signal speed (km/sec) in the cable ?

(*a*) 8000 (*b*) 10000

(*c*) 16000 (*d*) 20000

2013

27. Match the problem domains in GROUP I with the solution technologies in GROUP II.

GROUP I

(P) Service oriented computing

(Q) Heterogeneous communicating systems

(R) Information representation

(S) Process description

GROUP II

(1) Interoperability

(2) BPMN

(3) Publish-find-bind

(4) XML

(*a*) P-1, Q-2, R-3, S-4 (*b*) P-3, Q-4, R-2, S-1

(*c*) P-3, Q-1, R-4, S-2 (*d*) P-4, Q-3, R-2, S-1

28. The transport layer protocols used for real time multimedia, file transfer, DNS and email, respectively are:

(*a*) TCP, UDP, UDP and TCP

(*b*) UDP, TCP, TCP and UDP

(*c*) UDP, TCP, UDP and TCP

(*d*) TCP, UDP, TCP and UDP

29. Using public key cryptography, X adds a digital signature σ to message M, encrypts <M, σ>, and sends it to Y, where it is decrypted. Which one of the following sequences of keys is used for the operations?

(*a*) Encryption: X's private key followed by Y's private key; Decryption: X's public key followed by Y's public key.

(*b*) Encryption: X's private key followed by Y's public key; Decryption: X's public key followed by Y's private key.

(*c*) Encryption: X's public key followed by Y's private key; Decryption: Y's public key followed by X's private key.

(*d*) Encryption: X's private key followed by Y's public key; Decryption: Y's private key followed by X's public key.

30. Assume that source S and destination D are connected through two intermediate routers labeled R. Determine how many times each packet has to visit the network layer and the data link layer during a transmission from S to D.

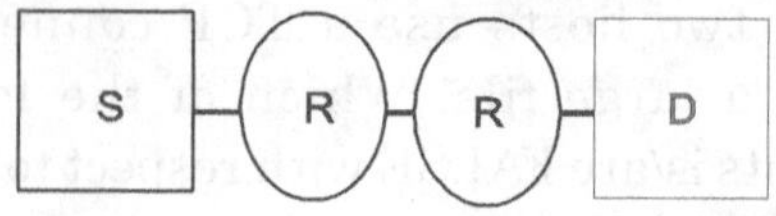

(*a*) Network layer - 4 times and Data link layer - 4 times

(*b*) Network layer - 4 times and Data link layer - 3 times

(*c*) Network layer - 4 times and Data link layer - 6 times

(*d*) Network layer - 2 times and Data link layer - 6 times.

31. Determine the maximum length of the cable (in km) for transmitting data at a rate of 500 Mbps in an Ethernet LAN with frames of size 10,000 bits. Assume the signal speed in the cable to be 2,00,000 km/s.

(*a*) 1 (*b*) 2

(*c*) 2.5 (*d*) 5

32. In an IPv4 datagram, the M bit is 0, the value of HLEN is 10, the value of total length is 400 and the fragment offset value is 300. The position of the datagram, the sequence numbers of the first and the last bytes of the payload, respectively are

(*a*) Last fragment, 2400 and 2789

(*b*) First fragment, 2400 and 2759

(*c*) Last fragment, 2400 and 2759

(*d*) Middle fragment, 300 and 689

2012

33. In the IPv4 addressing format, the number of networks allowed under Class C addresses is

(*a*) 2^{14} (*b*) 2^7

(*c*) 2^{21} (*d*) 2^{24}

34. Which of the following transport layer protocols is used to support electronic mail?

(*a*) SMTP (*b*) IP

(*c*) TCP (*d*) UDP

35. The protocol data unit (PDU) for the application layer in the Internet stack is

(*a*) Segment (*b*) Datagram

(*c*) Message (*d*) Frame

36. Consider an instance of TCP's Additive Increase Multiplicative Decrease (AIMD) algorithm where the window size at the start of the slow start phase is 2 MSS and the threshold at the start of the first transmission is 8 MSS. Assume that a timeout occurs during the fifth transmission. Find the congestion window size at the end of the tenth transmission.

(*a*) 8 MSS (*b*) 14 MSS

(*c*) 7 MSS (*d*) 12 MSS

37. Consider a source computer (S) transmitting a file of size 10^6 bits to destination computer (D) over a network of two routers (R_1 and R_2) and three links (L_1, L_2, and L_3), L1 connects S to R_1 : L_2 connects R_1 to R_2; and L_3 connects R_2 to D. Let each link be of length 100 km. Assume signals travel over each link at a speed of 10^8 meters per second. Assume that the link bandwidth on each link is 1 Mbps. Let the file be broken down into 1000 packets each of size 1000 bits. Find the total sum of transmission and propagation delays in transmitting file from S to D?

(*a*) 1005 ms

(*b*) 1010 ms

(*c*) 3000 ms

(*d*) 3003 ms

38. An Internet Service Provider (ISP) has the following chunk of CIDR-based IP addresses available with it: 245.248.128.0/20. The ISP wants to give half of this chunk of addresses to Organization A, and a quarter to Organization B, while retaining the remaining with itself. Which of the following is a valid allocation of addresses to A and B?

(*a*) 245.248.136.0/21 and 245.248.128.0/22

(*b*) 245.248.128.0/21 and 245.248.128.0/22

(*c*) 245.248.132.0/22 and 245.248.132.0/21

(*d*) 245.248.136.0/24 and 245.248.132.0/21

2011

39. Which one of the following is NOT desired in a good Software Requirement Specifications (SRS) document?

(*a*) Functional Requirements

(*b*) Non-Functional Requirements

(*c*) Goals of Implementation

(*d*) Algorithms for Software Implementation

40. HTML (Hyper Text Markup Language) has language elements which permit certain actions other than describing the structure of the web document. Which one of the following actions is NOT supported by pure HTML (without any server or client side scripting) pages?

(*a*) Embed web objects from different sites into the same page

(*b*) Refresh the page automatically after a specified interval

(*c*) Automatically redirect to another page upon download

(*d*) Display the client time as part of the page

41. Let the time taken to switch between user and kernel modes of execution be t_1 while the time taken to switch between two processes be t_2. Which of the following is **TRUE**?

(*a*) $t_1 > t_2$

(*b*) $t_1 = t_2$

(*c*) $t_1 < t_2$

(*d*) nothing can be said about the relation between t_1 and t_2

42. Consider different activities related to email.

m1 : Send an emial from a mail client to a mail server

m2 : Download an email from mailbox to a mail client

m3 : Checking email in a web browser

Which is the application level protocol used in each activity?

(*a*) m1 : HTTP m2 :SMTP m3 : POP

(*b*) m1 : SMTP m2 :FTP m3 : HTTP

(*c*) m1 : SMTP m2 :POP m3 : HTTP

(*d*) m1 : POP m2 :SMTP m3 : IMAP

43. A layer-4 firewall (a device that can look at all protocol headers up to the transport layer) **CANNOT**

(*a*) block entire HTTP traffic during 9:00 PM and 5:00 AM

(*b*) block all ICMP traffic

(*c*) stop incoming traffic from a specific IP address but allow outgoing traffic to the same IP address

(*d*) block TCP traffic from a specific user on a multi-user system during 9:00 PM and 5:00 AM

2010

44. One of the header fields in an IP datagram is the Time-to-Live (TTL) field. Which of the following statements best explains the need for this field?

(a) It can be used to prioritize packets

(b) It can be used to reduce delays

(c) It can be used to optimize throughput

(d) It can be used to prevent packet looping

45. Which one of the following is not a client-server application?

(a) Internet chat

(b) Web browsing

(c) E-mail

(d) Ping

46. Suppose computers A and B have IP addresses 10.105.1.113 and 10.0105.1.91 respectively and they both use the same netmask N. Which of the values of N given below should not be used if A and B should belong to the same network?

(a) 255.255.255.0 (b) 255.255.255.128

(c) 255.255.255.192 (d) 255.255.255.224

2009

47. In the RSA public key cryptosystem, the private and public keys are (e, n) and (d, n) respectively, where $n = p * q$ and p and q are large primes. Besides, n is public and p and q are private. Let M be a integer such that $0 < M < n$ ad $\phi(n) = (p-1)(q-1)$.

Now cosider the following equatios.

I. $M' = M^e \bmod n$

$M = (M')^d \bmod n$

II. ed $\equiv 1 \bmod n$

III. ed $\equiv 1 \bmod \phi n$

IV. $M' = M^e \bmod \phi(n)$

$M = (M')^d \bmod \phi(n)$

While of the above equations correctly represent RSA cryptosystem ?

(a) I and II (b) I and III

(c) II and IV (d) III and IV

48. Which opening a TCP connection, the initial sequence number is to be derived using a time-of-day (ToD) clock that keeps running even when the host is down. The low order 32 bits of the counter of the ToD clock is to be used for the initial sequence numbers. The clock counter increments once per millisecond. The maximum packet lifetime is given to be 64s.

Which one of the choices given below is closest to the minimum permissible rate at which sequence numbers used for packets of a connection can increase ?

(a) 0.015/s (b) 0.064/s

(c) 0.135/s (d) 0.327/s

49. Let $G(x)$ be the generator polynomial used for CRC checking. What is the condition that should be satisfied by $G(x)$ to detect odd number of bits in error?

(a) $G(x)$ contains more than two terms.

(b) $G(x)$ does not divide $1 + x^k$, for any k not exceeding the frame length.

(c) $1 + x$ is a factor of $G(x)$.

(d) $G(x)$ has an odd number of terms.

2008

50. What is the maximum size of data that the application layer can pass on to the TCP layer below?

(a) Any size

(b) 2^{16} bytes – size of TCP header

(c) 2^{16} bytes

(d) 1500 bytes

51. In the slow start phase of the TCP congestion control algorithm, the size of the congestion window

(a) does not increase

(b) increases linearly

(c) increases quadratically

(d) increases exponentially

52. If a class B network on the Internet has a subnet mask of 255.255.248.0, what is the maximum number of hosts per subnet?

(a) 1022 (b) 1023

(c) 2046 (d) 2047

53. A computer on a 10 Mbps network is regulated by a token bucket. The token bucket is filled at a rate of 2Mbps. It is initially filled to capacity with 16 megabits. What is the maximum duration for which the computer can transmit at the full 10 Mbps?

(a) 1.6 seconds (b) 2 seconds

(c) 5 seconds (d) 8 seconds

54. A client process P needs to make a TCP connection to a server process S. Consider the following situation: the server process S executes a socket (), a bind () and a listen () system call in that order, following which it is preempted. Subsequently, the client process P executes a socket () system call followed by connect () system call to connect to the server proccess S. The server process has not executed any accept () system call. Which one of the following events could take place?

(a) connect () system call returns successfully
(b) connect () system call blocks
(c) connect () system call returns an error
(d) connect () system call results in a core dump

2007

55. In Ethernet when Manchester encoding is used, the bit rate is

(a) Half the baud rate
(b) Twice the baud rate
(c) Same as the baud rate
(d) None of these

56. Which one of the following uses UDP as the transport protocol ?

(a) HTTP (b) Telnet
(c) DNS (d) SMTP

57. There are n stations in a slotted LAN. Each station attempts to transmit with a probability p in each time slot. What is the probability that **ONLY** one station transmits in a given time slot ?

(a) $np(1-p)^{n-1}$ (b) $(1-p)^{n-1}$
(c) $p(1-p)^{n-1}$ (d) $1-(1-p)^{n-1}$

58. In a token ring network the transmission speed is 10^7 bps and the propagation speed is 200 metres / μs. The 1 –bit delay in this network is equivalent to :

(a) 500 metres of cable.
(b) 200 metres of cable.
(c) 20 metres of cable.
(d) 50 metres of cable.

59. The address of a class B host is to be split into subnets with a 6 – bit subnet number. What is the maximum number of subnets and the maximum number of hosts in each subnet ?

(a) 62 subnets and 262142 hosts.
(b) 64 subnets and 262142 hosts.
(c) 62 subnets and 1022 hosts.
(d) 64 subnets and 1024 hosts.

60. The message 11001001 is to be transmitted using the CRC polynomial $x^3 + 1$ to protect it from errors. The message that should be transmitted is :

(a) 11001001000 (b) 11001001011
(c) 11001010 (d) 110010010011

61. The distance between two stations M and N is L kilometres. All frames are K bits long. The propagation delay per kilometre is t seconds. Let R bits/second be the channel capacity. Assuming that processing delay is negligible, the *minimum* number of bits for the sequence number field in a frame for maximum utilization, when the *sliding window protocol* is used, is:

(a) $\left\lceil \log_2 \frac{2LtR + 2K}{K} \right\rceil$ (b) $\left\lceil \log_2 \frac{2LtR}{K} \right\rceil$

(c) $\left\lceil \log_2 \frac{2LtR + K}{K} \right\rceil$ (d) $\left\lceil \log_2 \frac{2LtR + K}{2K} \right\rceil$

62. Match the following :

P. SMTP 1. Application layer
Q. BGP 2. Transport layer
R. TCP 3. Data link layer
S. PPP 4. Network layer
5. Physical layer

Codes :

	P	Q	R	S
(a)	2	1	3	5
(b)	1	4	2	3
(c)	1	4	2	5
(d)	2	4	1	3

2006

63. Station A uses 32 byte packets to transmit messages to Station B using a sliding window protocol. The round trip delay between A and B is 80 milliseconds and the bottleneck bandwidth on the path between A and B is 128 kbps. What is the optimal window size that A should use ?

(a) 20 (b) 40
(c) 160 (d) 320

64. Two computers C1 and C2 are configured as follows. C1 has IP address 203. 197.2.53 and netmask 255. 255. 128.0. C2 has IP address 203.197.75.201 and netmask 255. 255.192.0. Which one of the following statements is true ?

(a) C1 and C2 both assume they are on the same network
(b) C2 assumes C1 is on same network, but C1 assumes C2 is on a different network
(c) C1 assumes C2 is on same network, but C2 assumes C1 is on a different network
(d) C1 and C2 both assume they are on different networks

65. Station A needs to send a message consisting of 9 packets to Station B using a sliding window (window size 3) and go-back-*n* error control strategy. All packets are ready and immediately available for transmission. If every 5th packet that A transmits gets lost (but no acks from B ever get lost), then what is the number of packets that A will transmit for sending the message to B ?

(*a*) 12 (*b*) 14

(*c*) 16 (*d*) 18

2005

66. The address resolution protocol (*ARP*) is used for

(*a*) Finding the IP address from the DNS

(*b*) Finding the IP address of the default gateway

(*c*) Finding the IP address that corresponds to a MAC address

(*d*) Finding the MAC address that corresponds to an IP address

67. The maximum window size for data transmission using the selective reject protocol with *n*–bit frame sequence numbers is

(*a*) 2^n (*b*) 2^{n-1}

(*c*) $2^n - 1$ (*d*) 2^{n-2}

68. In a network of LANs connected by bridges, packets are sent from one LAN to another through intermediate bridges. Since more than one path may exist between two LANs, packets may have to be routed through multiple bridges. Why is the spanning tree algorithm used for bridge-routing?

(*a*) For shortest path routing between LANs

(*b*) For avoiding loops in the routing paths

(*c*) For fault tolerance

(*d*) For minimizing collisions

69. An organization has a class B network and wishes to form subnets for 64 departments. The subnet mask would be

(*a*) 255.255.0.0 (*b*) 255.255.64.0

(*c*) 255.255.128.0 (*d*) 255.255.252.0

70. In a packet switching network, packets are routed from source to destination along a single path having two intermediate nodes. If the message size is 24 bytes and each packet contains a header of 3 bytes, then the optimum packet size is

(*a*) 4 (*b*) 6

(*c*) 7 (*d*) 9

71. Suppose the round trip propagation delay for a 10 Mbps Ethernet having 48-bit jamming signal is 46.4 ms. The minimum frame size is

(*a*) 94 (*b*) 416

(*c*) 464 (*d*) 512

2004

72. Choose the best matching between Group 1 and Group 2.

Group – 1	Group – 2
P. Data link layer	1. Ensures reliable trans-port of data over a physical point-to-point link
Q. Network layer	2. Encodes/decodes data for physical trans-mission
R. Transport layer	3. Allows end-to-end communication between two processes
	4. Routes data from one network node to the next

Codes :

	P	Q	R
(*a*)	1	4	3
(*b*)	2	4	1
(*c*)	2	3	1
(*d*)	1	3	2

73. Which of the following is NOT true with respect to a transparent bridge and a router ?

(*a*) Both bridge and router selectively forward data packets

(*b*) A bridge uses IP addresses while a router uses MAC addresses

(*c*) A bridge builds up its routing table by inspecting incoming packets

(*d*) A router can connect between a LAN and a WAN

74. How many 8-bit characters can be transmitted per second over a 9600 baud serial communication link using asynchronous mode of transmission with one start bit, eight data bits, two stop bits, and one parity bit ?

(*a*) 600 (*b*) 800

(*c*) 876 (*d*) 1200

75. A and B are the only two stations on an Ethernet. Each has a steady queue of frames to send. Both A and B attempt to transmit a frame, collide, and A wins the first backoff race. At the end of this successful transmission by A, both A and B attempt to transmit and collide. The probability that A wins the second backoff race is

(*a*) 0.5 (*b*) 0.625

(*c*) 0.75 (*d*) 1.0

76. The routing table of a router is shown below:

Destination	Subnet Mask	Interface
128.75.43.0	255.255.255.0	Eth0
128.75.43.0	255.255.255.128	Eth1
192.12.17.5	255.255.255.255	Eth3
default		Eth2

On which interfaces will the router forward packets addressed to destinations 128.75.43.16 and 192.12.17.10 respectively?

(*a*) Eth1 and Eth2

(*b*) Eth0 and Eth2

(*c*) Eth0 and Eth3

(*d*) Eth1 and Eth3

Common Data Q. 77 - 78

Consider three IP networks A, B and C. Host H_A in network A sends messages each containing 180 bytes of application data to a host H_C in network C. The TCP layer prefixes a 20 byte header to the message. This passes through an intermediate network B. The maximum packet size, including 20 byte IP header, in each network is

A : 1000 bytes

B : 100 bytes

C : 1000 bytes

The network A and B are connected through a 1 Mbps link, while B and C are connected by a 512 Kbps link (*bps* = bits per second).

77. Assuming that the packets are correctly delivered, how many bytes, including headers, are delivered to the IP layer at the destination for one application message, in the best case? Consider only data packets.

(*a*) 200 (*b*) 220

(*c*) 240 (*d*) 260

78. What is the rate at which application data is transferred to host H_C? Ignore errors, acknowledgements, and other overheads.

(*a*) 325.5 Kbps (*b*) 354.5 Kbps

(*c*) 409.6 Kbps (*d*) 512.0 Kbps

2003

79. Which of the following assertions is FALSE about the Internet Protocol (IP)?

(*a*) It is possible for a computer to have multiple IP addresses

(*b*) IP packets from the same source to the same destination can take different routes in the network

(*c*) IP ensures that a packet is discarded if it is unable to reach its destination within a given number of hops

(*d*) The packet source cannot set the route of an outgoing packets; the route is determined only by the routing tables in the routers on the way

80. Which of the following functionalities must be implemented by a transport protocol over and above the network protocol?

(*a*) Recovery from packet losses

(*b*) Detection of duplicate packets

(*c*) Packet delivery in the correct order

(*d*) End to end connectivity

81. The subnet mask for a particular network is 255.255.31.0. Which of the following pairs of IP addresses could belong to this network?

(*a*) 172.57.88.62 and 172.56.87.233

(*b*) 10.35.28.2 and 10.35.29.4

(*c*) 191.203.31.87 and 191.234.31.88

(*d*) 128.8.129.43 and 128.8.161.55

82. A 2 km long broadcast LAN has 10^7 bps bandwidth and uses CSMA/CD. The signal travels along the wire at 2×10^8 m/s. What is the minimum packet size that can be used on this network?

(*a*) 50 bytes (*b*) 100 bytes

(*c*) 200 bytes (*d*) None of these

83. Host A is sending data to host B over a full duplex link. A and B are using the sliding window protocol for flow control. The send and receive window sizes are 5 packets each. Data packets (sent only from A to B) are all 1000 bytes long and the transmission time for such a packet is 50 μs. Acknowledgement packets (sent only from B to A) are very small and require negligible transmission time. The propagation delay over the link is 200 μs. What is the maximum achievable throughput in this communication?

(*a*) 7.69×10^6 bps

(*b*) 11.11×10^6 bps

(*c*) 12.33×10^6 bps

(*d*) 15.00×10^6 bps

NUMERICAL TYPE QUESTIONS

2016

1. An IP datagram of size 1000 bytes arrives at a router. The router has to forward this packet on a link whose MTU (maximum transmission unit) is 100 bytes. Assume that the size of the IP header is 20 bytes.

   The number of fragments that the IP datagram will be divided into for transmission is _______.

2. For a host machine that uses the token bucket algorithm for congestion control, the token bucket has a capacity of 1 megabyte and the maximum output rate is 20 megabytes per second. Tokens arrive at a rate to sustain output at a rate of 10 megabytes per second. The token bucket is currently full and the machine needs to send 12 megabytes of data. The minimum time required to transmit the data is ______ seconds.

3. A sender uses the Stop-and-Wait ARQ protocol for reliable transmission of frames. Frames are of size 1000 bytes and the transmission rate at the sender is 80 Kbps (1Kbps = 1000 bits/second). Size of an acknowledgement is 100 bytes and the transmission rate at the receiver is 8 Kbps. The one-way propagation delay is 100 milliseconds.

   Assuming no frame is lost, the sender throughput is ______ bytes/second.

4. A network has a data transmission bandwidth of 20×10^6 bits per second. It uses CSMA/CD in the MAC layer. The maximum signal propagation time from one node to another node is 40 microseconds. The minimum size of a frame in the network is______bytes.

5. Consider a 128×10^3 bits/second satellite communication link with one way propagation delay of 150 milliseconds. Selective retransmission (repeat) protocol is used on this link to send data with a frame size of 1 kilobyte. Neglect the transmission time of acknowledgement. The minimum number of bits required for the sequence number field to achieve 100% utilization is_________.

2014

6. Consider a token ring network with a length of 2km having 10 stations including a monitoring station. The propagation speed of the signal is 2×10^8 m/s and the token transmission time is ignored. If each station is allowed to hold the token for 2 μsec, the minimum time for which the monitoring station should wait (in μsec) before assuming that the token is lost is ______.

7. Consider a selective repeat sliding window protocol that uses a frame size of 1 KB to send data on a 1.5 Mbps link with a one-way latency of 50 msec. To achieve a link utilization of 60%, the minimum number of bits required to represent the sequence number field is ______.

8. In the diagram shown below, L1 is an Ethernet LAN and L2 is a Token-Ring LAN. An IP packet originates from sender S and traverses to R, as shown. The links within each ISP and across the two ISPs, are all point-to-point optical links. The initial value of the TTL field is 32. The maximum possible value of the TTL field when R receives the datagram is ___________ .

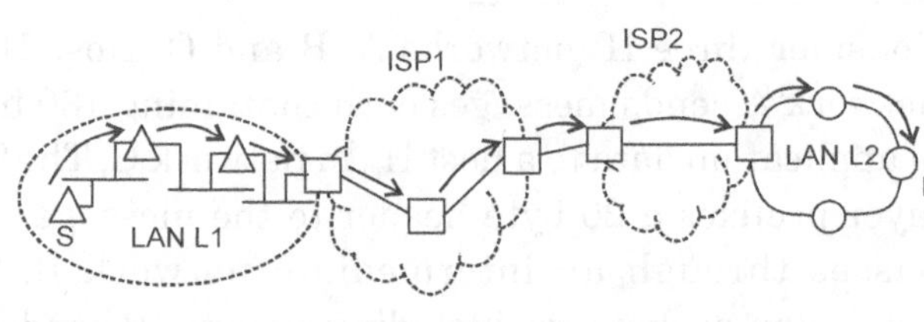

9. An IP router implementing Classless Inter-domain routing (CIDR) receives a packet with address 131.23.151.76. The router's routing table has the following entries:

Prefix	Output Interface Identifier
131.16.0.0/12	3
131.28.0.0/14	5
131.19.0.0/16	2
131.22.0.0/15	1

   The identifier of the output interface on which this packet will be forwarded is _____.

10. Every host in an IPv4 network has a 1-second resolution real-time clock with battery backup. Each host needs to generate up to 1000 unique identifiers per second. Assume that each host has a globally unique IPv4 address. Design a 50-bit globally unique ID for this purpose. After what period (in seconds) will the identifiers generated by a host wrap around?

11. Suppose that the stop-and-wait protocol is used on a link with a bit rate of 64 kilobits per second and 20 milliseconds propagation delay. Assume

that the transmission time for the acknowledgement and the processing time at nodes are negligible. Then the minimum frame size in bytes to achieve a link utilization of at least 50% is ________.

12. Consider a LAN with four nodes S_1, S_2, S_3 and S_4. Time is divided into fixed-size slots, and a node can begin its transmission only at the beginning of a slot. A collision is said to have occurred if more than one node transmit in the same slot. The probability of generation of a frame in a time slot by S_1, S_2, S_3 and S_4 are 0.1, 0.2, 0.3 and 0.4, respectively. The probability of sending a frame in the first slot without any collision by any of these four stations is ________.

13. A link has a transmission speed of 10^6 bits/sec. It uses data packets of size 1000 bytes each. Assume that the acknowledgement has negligible transmission delay, and that its propagation delay is the same as the data propagation delay. Also assume that the processing delays at the nodes are negligible. The efficiency of the stop-and-wait protocol in this setup is exactly 25%. The value of the one-way propagation delay (in milliseconds) is ________.

14. Consider a network connected two systems located 8000 kilometers apart. The bandwidth of the network is 500×10^6 bits per second. The propagation speed of the media is 4×10^6 meters per second. It is needed to design a Go-Back-N sliding window protocol for this network. The average packet size is 10^7 bits. The network is to be used to its full capacity.

Assume that processing delays at nodes are negligible. Then the minimum size in bits of the sequence number field has to be ________.

15. In the network 200.20.11.144/27, the fourth octet (in decimal) of the last IP address of the network which can be assigned to a host is ________.

16. Two hosts are connected via a packet switch with 10^7 bits per second links. Each link has a propagation. Delay of 20 microseconds. The switch begins forwarding a packet 35 microseconds after it receives the same. If 1000 bits of data are to be transmitted between the two hosts using a packet size of 5000 bits, the time elapsed between the transmission of the first bit of data and the reception of the last of the data in microsecond is ________.

1992

17. A simple and reliable data transfer can be accomplished by using the 'handshake protocol'. It accomplishes reliable data transfer because for every data item sent by the transmitter ....

ANSWERS

MCQ Type Questions

1.(a)	**2.**(c)	**3.**(d)	**4.**(c)	**5.**(b)	**6.**(d)	**7.**(c)	**8.**(a)	**9.**(a)	**10.**(c)
11.(d)	**12.**(c)	**13.**(b)	**14.**(d)	**15.**(a)	**16.**(c)	**17.**(b)	**18.**(b)	**19.**(a)	**20.**(b)
21.(a)	**22.**(c)	**23.**(a)	**24.**(c)	**25.**(a)	**26.**(d)	**27.**(b)	**28.**(c)	**29.**(d)	**30.**(c)
31.(b)	**32.**(c)	**33.**(c)	**34.**(c)	**35.**(c)	**36.**(c)	**37.**(a)	**38.**(a)	**39.**(d)	**40.**(d)
41.(c)	**42.**(c)	**43.**(a)	**44.**(d)	**45.**(d)	**46.**(d)	**47.**(b)	**48.**(b)	**49.**(c)	**50.**(a)
51.(d)	**52.**(c)	**53.**(b)	**54.**(c)	**55.**(b)	**56.**(c)	**57.**(a)	**58.**(c)	**59.**(c)	**60.**(b)
61.(b)	**62.**(b)	**63.**(b)	**64.**(c)	**65.**(c)	**66.**(d)	**67.**(b)	**68.**(b)	**69.**(d)	**70.**(d)
71.(c,d)	**72.**(a)	**73.**(b)	**74.**(b)	**75.**(b)	**76.**(c)	**77.**(c)	**78.**(b)	**79.**(a)	**80.**(d)
81.(c)	**82.**(d)	**83.**(b)							

Numerical Type Questions

1. (13) **2.** (1.1) **3.** (2500) **4.** (200) **5.** (4) **6.** (28μs to 30μs)

7. (5) **8.** (26 to 26) **9.** (1) **10.** (256) **11.** (160) **12.** (0.40–0.46)

13. (12) **14.** (8) **15.** (158) **16.** (1575) **17.** (*)

EXPLANATIONS

MCQ TYPE QUESTIONS

1. In DNS (mapping of IP address & URL)

IP address	URL
197.12.0.7	www.xyz.com

2. FTP and POP3 are non-HTTP protocols

These are stateful application layer protocols.

3. According to the concept of binary exponential backoff algorithm the exponential backoff mechanism reduces the probability of collision on retransmissions.

4. Theere are following steps in which packets are transmitted on the network by a host when a browser requests a webpage from a remote server :

Step 1 : The client(browser) initiates a DNS query for remote server. It may be that they already have this server in their DNS cache, in which case the client may simply send a TCP SYN directly to the application server.

Step 2 : The client will next send a connection request to the application server. This will be a TCP SYN packet, the first in the TCP three-way handshake.

Step 3 : Next, after the TCP connection has been established, the client will request data from the server. In the web-based application, the client performs an HTTP GET.

5. In case of IEEE 802.11 MAC protocol for wireless communication RTS and CTS mechanism is used for collision avoidance, not for collision detection.

6. Statement S1

The Distance Vector routing protocols rely on the information from their directly connected neighbours in order to calculate and accumulate route information. Distance Vector routing protocols require very little overhead as compared to Link State routing protocols as measured by memory and processor power while the Link State routing protocols do not rely solely on the information from the neighbours or adjacent router in order to calculate route information. Instead, Link State routing protocols have a system of databases that they use in order to calculate the best route to destinations in the network. This is TRUE

Statement S3

Distance Vector exchanges the routing updates periodically whether the topology is change or not, this will maximize the convergence time which increases the chance of routing loops while the Link State routing protocols send triggered change based updates when there is a topology change. After initial flood, pass small event based triggered link state updates to all other routers. This will minimize the convergence time that's why there is no chance of routing loops. This is TRUE.

7. RSA and DES are for Encryption where MD5 and SHA – 1 are used to generate Message Digest.

8. First of all the browser must now know what IP to connect to. For this purpose browser takes help of Domain name system (DNS) servers which are used for resolving hostnames to IP addresses. As browser is an HTTP client and as HTTP is based on the TCP/IP protocols, first it establishes a TCP connection with the web server and requests a webpage using HTTP, and then the web server sends the requested webpage using HTTP. Hence the order is 4, 2, 1, 3 .

9. We know that RIP uses distance vector routing and QSPF uses link state routing.

10. Listen connects an unconnected active TCP socket into a passive socket.

11. Bandwidth of link is 10^6 bytes/sec

File size = 10^3 bytes

T_1 & T_3 will take same time and $T_3 > T_2$ means T_3 will take more time then T_2.

12. $Q - R_1 - R_2 - R_3 - H$

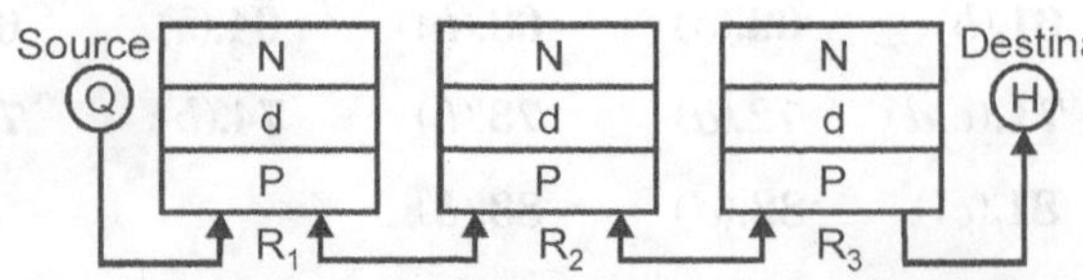

P-Physical Layer, d-data link layer, N-Network layer

Since, the router R_1 contains TCP part numbers of Q and R_2 contains the TCP part numbers of H at Data link layer, and with both routers contains IP addresses of Q and H at Network layer. So, only statement I_2 and I_3 will be true.

13. (*a*) One of the main functionality of Network Layer is Routing. So Option (a) is CORRECT.

(*b*) Bit Synchronization is always handled by Physical Layer of OSI model but not Data Link Layer. So Option (*b*) is INCORRECT.

(*c*) End – to – End Process Communication is handled by Transport Layer. So Option (c) is CORRECT.

(*d*) MAC sub layer have 3 types of protocols (Random, Controlled and Channelized Access).

14. While an IP Datagram is transferring from one host to another host, TTL, Checksum and Fragmentation Offset will be changed.

15.

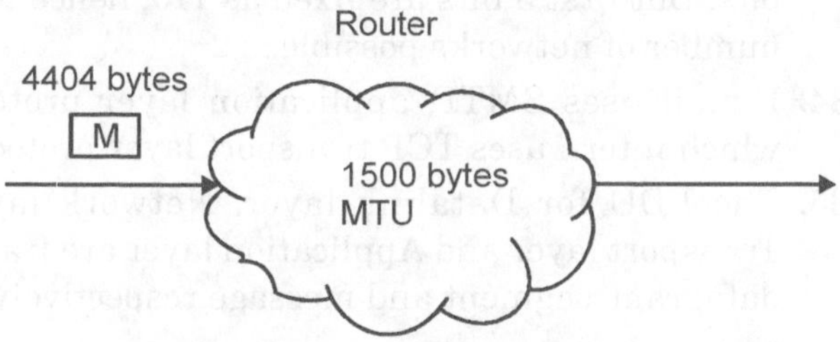

Data length	1480	1480	1444
	+	+	
Header length	20	20	
MF	1	1	0

16. If there are N-people, then total no of key required are N(N – 1)/2.

17. In a IP header, the source address is never modified checksum, TTL and length may vary for each router.

18. In a TCP connection

- If the sequence number of a segments is *m*. Then it is not necessary the subsequent segment is *m* + 1, because it depend upon no of packet sent is current segment.
- Advertise window can not be fixed it may change on changing the capacity of receiver window.

19. HTTP and FTP both can use multiple TCP connection between same client and server.

20. bind, listen, accept, recv

22. 7 and 1110

23. Network ranges are

0 · 0 · 0 · 0 – default

128 · 96 · 164 · 0 to 128 · 96 · 165 · 0 — R_3

128 · 96 · 166 · 0 to 128 · 96 · 167 · 255 — R_2

128 · 96 · 168 · 0 to 128 · 96 · 169 · 255 — interface 1

128 · 96 · 170 · 0 to 128 · 96 · 171 · 255 — interface 0

Ans = A

A – 1
B – 3
C – 5
D – 4

25. TCP connections are full duplex. It allow to send and receive packets at same time.

TCP allow for selective acknowledgement depend upon cengestion window and there are not message stream.

26. Given L = 1250 Bytes

B = 100 mbps

d = 1 km

V = ?

In CSMA/CD, $L = 2\times\frac{d}{v}\times B$

$$\Rightarrow \quad V = \frac{2dB}{L} = \frac{2\times10^3\times10^8}{10^4}$$

$$\Rightarrow \quad V = 20{,}000 \text{ km/sec}$$

27. Service Oriented Computing (SOC) : Publish-Find-BIND

Heterogeneous Comm. System: Interpretability

Information Representation: XML

Process description: BPMN

Reference: Wikipedia .org/wiki/XML/Bussines_ Process_ Model_and_Notation

Trick: Info representation mapped to XML in only one option.

28. 1. Real Time Multimedia: Can be unreliable but have to be fast so UDP

2. File Transfer: Has to be secure & reliable so uses TCP

3. **DNS:** Work or part 953, can be both TCP and UDP
4. **Email:** uses TCP, for reliability

∴ UDP, TCP, TCP/UDP, TCP

29. Given: X encrypts a message and send it to Y.

To find: Correction encryption - decryption order

Analysis: To make sure that Y receives the message & is able to decrypt it and no one else is able to X. The message over the network should be encrypted by Y's public key.

So, order of encryption is X's private key, Y's public key. On receiving the encrypted message, Y will have to decrypt it using its private key & then use X's public key for signature. So, order of decryption is Y's private key followed by X's public key.

So, the answer is (*d*)

30. Assume the source S & destination D are connected through two intermediate routers labled R. Determine how many times each packet has to visit the network layer and data link layer during a transmission from S to D.

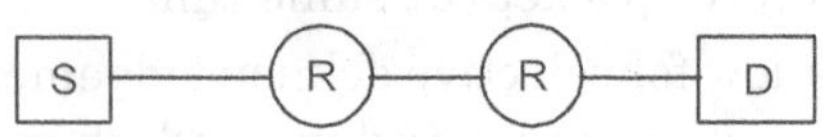

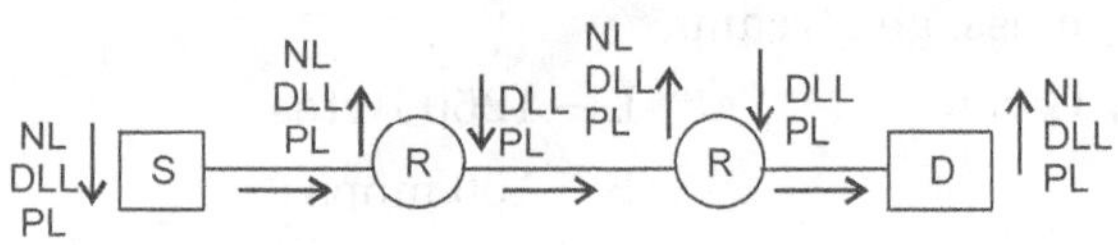

⇒ Network Layer 4 times

⇒ Data link layer 6 times

31. Propagation time = Transmission time + collision signal time (Acknowledge)

$$\frac{\text{Frame size}}{\text{Propagation Time}} = \frac{\text{Length}}{\text{Signal Speed}} + \frac{\text{Length}}{\text{Signal Speed}}$$

$$\frac{10000 \text{ bit}}{500 \times 10^6 \text{bits/sec}} = \frac{2 \times \text{Length}}{2 \times 10^5 \text{ km/sec}}$$

$$\boxed{\text{Length} = 2\text{km}}$$

* An ethernet node must be transmitting a frame for the slot time for a collision with that frame to detected.

32. Since M bit is 0, so there is no fragments after this fragment. Hence this <u>fragment is the "last fragment</u>" Tow, H LEN defines the length of Header in datagram. Since H LEN is 10 so size of header is 10 * 4 = 40B.

Length of data = Total length – Leader length = 400 – 40 = 360 B.

Few, fragment offset of data in original datagram is measured in units of 8B. So to find first Byte of this fragment,

$$\frac{\text{first Byte}}{\text{B}} = \text{fragment offset}$$

⇒ <u>first Byte</u> = 300 ∗ 8 = <u>"2400"</u> B

since length of data is 360B

so last Byte on this datagram will be <u>"2759"</u> B

i.e. "first last" 2400 – 2759 (360B length)

33. For class C address, size of network field is 24 bits. But first 3 bits are fixed as 110; hence total number of networks possible is 2^{21}

34. E-mail uses SMTP, application layer protocol which intern uses TCP transport layer protocol.

35. The PDU for Datalink layer, Network layer, Transport layer and Application layer are frame, datagram, segment and message respectively.

37.

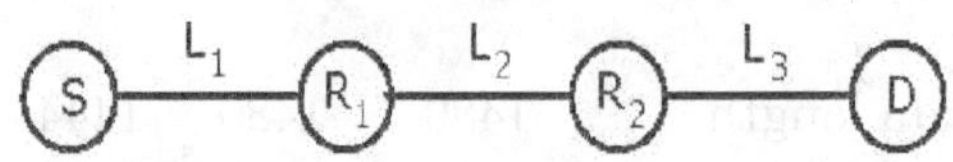

Transmission delay for 1 packet from each of S, R_1 and R_2 will take 1ms

Propagation delay on each link L_1, L_2 and L_3 for one packet is 1ms

Therefore the sum of transmission delay and propagation delay on each link for one packet is 2ms.

38.

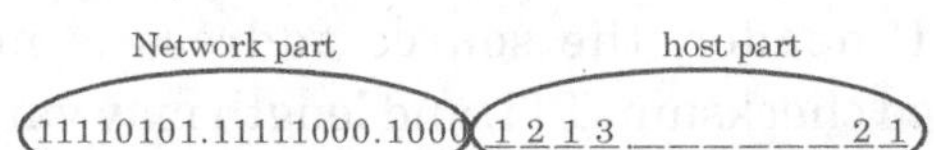

Since half of 4096 host addresses must be given to organization A, we can set 12th bit to 1 and include that bit into network part of organization A, so the valid allocation of addresses to A is 245.248.136.0/21

Now for organization B, 12th bit is set to '0' but since we need only half of 2048 addresses, 13th bit can be set to '0' and include that bit into network part of organization B so the valid allocation of addresses to B is 245.248.128.0/2.

41. Process switching also involves mode changing.

42. Sending an email will be done through user agent and message transfer agent by SMTP, downloading an email from mail box is done through POP, checking email in a web browser is done through HTTP

43. Since it is a layer 4 firewall it cannot block application layer protocol like HTTP.

44. It can be used to prevent packet looping because when Time-to-Live field reaches to '0' means when there is no any type of acknowledgement received, then TTL decrementet continuously and when it reaches '0', then it stop looping of packet.

45. Internet chat, web browsing and E-mail all are client-server application. Ping is a utility. It is mainly used to check the connection between two computer, there is a chance both are client or one is client and another server. In chat system first user authentication required and it requires server.

46. Given : 10.105.1.113 and 10.105.1.91

When these are in same network, then AND with netmask give the address of same ID otherwise these are in different class in these only AND with 255.255.255.224 are in different class

This is 96 and 64. Then these are different ID means 10.105.1.96 and 10.105.1.64 are different ID. So this is not in same network.

Alternately

10.105.1.113	→ 00001010	01101001	00000001	01110001
	→ 11111111	11111111	11111111	11100000
	00001010	01101001	00000001	01100000
	10 .	105 .	1 .	96

When we do the similar operation with 2nd IP, it gives 10.105.1.64

Here, it gives different IP

but for the rest it gives same IP.

47. In RSA public key cryptography, a public key provide for every one but they have their seprate private key.

According to formula of public key cryptography

I. $M' = M^e$ mod, $M = (M')^d$ mod n

IV. $M' = M^e \bmod \phi(n)$, $M = (M')^d \bmod \phi(n)$

represent RSA cryptosystem.

48. *Sequence number* : Frame from a sending station are numbered sequentially we need to set a limit.

49. When polynomial code method is employed, the sender and receiver must agree upon a generator polynomial G(x). Both high and low order bit of the generator must be 1 .

So $1 + x$ is a factor of G(x).

Alternately

For odd number of bits error, error function will be having a factor of $(1 + x^2 + x^4 + ...)$ which can not be divided by the generator having $(1 + x)$ as a factor.

50. Application layer just takes the data from user, pass it on the TCP layers below. It is the work of other TCP layer to actually disintegrate the data into packets accroding to network parameters to transmit in the network and assemble different packets on receiving them and handling it to the application layer. So, application layer doesnot bother about size.

51. Congestion window increases exponentially.

52. Starting address : 255. 255. 248. 0

End address : 255. 255. 255. 254.

53. Let duration is t sec.

$\therefore \quad 16 + 2t = 10 \times t$

$\Rightarrow \quad t = 2$ sec

54. As there is no accept() at server side, the connect() at client could not get anything that can respond to its requests, so error occurs.

55. In Manchester encoding, bit rate is twice the baud rate.

56. DNS uses UDP as the transport protocal.

57. Let 1 : event when station 1 transmits

2 : event when station 2 transmits

N : event when station N transmits

Given : $P(i) = P \quad 1 \le i \le N$

$P(\bar{i}) = (1 - p) \quad (\le i \le N)$

Probability that only one station transmits is given as

$$P(1\,\bar{2}\,\bar{3}\,....\,\bar{N} \cup \bar{1}\,2\,\bar{3}\,\bar{4}\,....\,\bar{N} \cup \bar{1}\,\bar{2}\,3\,\bar{4}\,5\,....\,\bar{N} \cup ....)$$

$$= P(1\,\bar{2}\,\bar{3}\,....\,\bar{N}) + P(\bar{1}\,2\,\bar{3}\,\bar{4}\,....\,\bar{N}) + P(\bar{1}\,\bar{2}\,3\,\bar{4}\,\bar{5}\,....\,\bar{N}) + ...$$

Since all events are mutually exclusive, hence probability

$$= P(1)\,P(\bar{2})\,P(\bar{3})\,....\,P(\bar{N}) + P(\bar{1})\,P(2)\,P(\bar{3})\,P(\bar{4})\,....\,P(\bar{N}) + P(\bar{1})\,P(\bar{2})\,P(3)\,P(\bar{4})\,P(\bar{5})\,....\,P(\bar{N}) + ...$$

Since all events are independent, hence probability

$= p\,(1-p)\,(1-p)\,....\,(1-p) + (1-p)\,p\,(1-p)\,....$
$(1-p) + (1-p)\,(1-p)\,p\,(1-p)\,....\,(1-p) + ...$
$= n\,p\,(1-p)^{n-1}$

58. 10^7 bits needs 1 second

$\therefore$ 1 bits needs $\frac{1}{10^7}$ second $= \frac{1}{10}$ μs.

Since 1 μs corresponds to 200 metre cable.

$\therefore$ $\frac{1}{10}$ μs corresponds to 20 metre cable.

59. Maximum number of subnets

$$= 2^6 - 2 = 62$$

Maximum number of host in each subnet

$$= 2^{10} - 2 = 1022$$

60. $P(x) = 11001001$

divisor $D(x) = 1001$ and CRC remainder is 011 so the transmitted message is 11001001011.

61. Total propagation delay = Lt sec.

Roundtrip time = 2 Lt = 2 Lt sec

Number of bits transmitted in roundtrip

= 2 LtR bits

$$\text{Number of frames} = \frac{2LtR}{K}$$

Let number of bits in sequent numbers be b.

$$\therefore \quad 2^b = \frac{2LtR}{K}$$

$$\Rightarrow \quad b = \left\lceil \log_2 \frac{2LtR}{K} \right\rceil$$

62. TCP protocol works on Transport layer.

SMTP protocol works on Application layer.

PPP Protol works on Data link layer.

BGP protol works on Physical layer.

63. Band width delay product

= Round trip delay × bottle neck bind width

$= 80 \times 128 \times 10^{-3} \times 1024$ bits

$= \frac{80 \times 128 \times 10^{-3} \times 1024}{8}$ bytes

$\therefore$ Optimal size window

$$= \frac{80 \times 128 \times 10^{-3} \times 1024}{8 \times 32} = 40$$

64. The two computer C1 and C2 are configured as follows :

	C1	C2
IP Address	203.197.2.53	203.197.75.201
AND		AND
Netmask	255.255.128.0	255.255.192.0
	203.197.0.0	203.197.64.0
	Network Address	Network Address

203.197.2.53 → 203.197.0000010.00111001
255.255.192.0 →255.255.11000000.00000000

203.197.0.0   203.197.0.0

203.197.75.201
255.255.128.0

203.192.0.0

$\therefore$ C1 assumes C2 is on same network but C2 assumes C1 is on different network.

65.

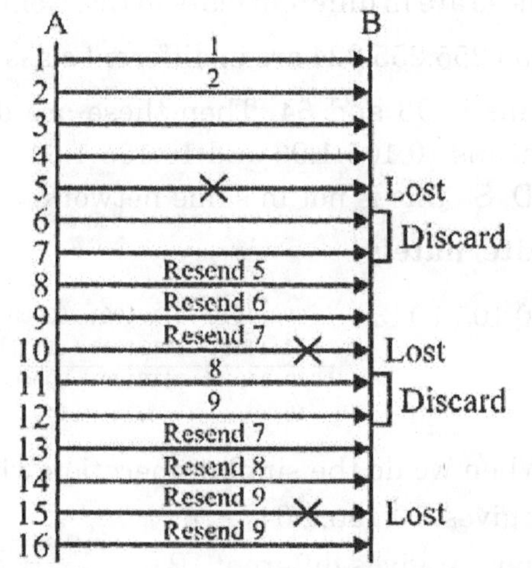

66. The Address Resolution Protocol (ARP), allows a host to find the MAC (Physical) address of a target host on the same physical network, given only the targets IP address.

67. Stalling networks assume here window size of 8, i.e., (0 – 7)

1. Station A under frame 0 through 6 to station B
2. Station B receives all seven frames, and ack with R R 7 (Receive Ready 7)
3. R R 7 is lost
4. A times out and retransmit frame O.
5. B has already advanced its receive window to accept frames 7, 0, 1, 2, 3, 4 and 5 thus it assume that 7 has been lost and this is a new frame O.

To overcome this problem, the maximum windows size is 2^{n-1}

68. The spanning tree approach is a mechanism in which bridges automatically develop a routing table and update that table in response to changing topology. The algorithm consists of three mechanisms.

1. Frame Forwarding
2. Address Learning
3. Loop resolution

69. Since, we have to support 64 department so our first

1 1 1 1 1 1 0 0

= 252

70. Consider optimum packet size which required minimum number of packet and does not waste any space.

Here consider each packet header because they are all work on packet switching network.

3 bytes is header size;

9 – 3 = 6 is data size

24/6 = 4 are the required packet

For case 1 : 24 packets are required

For case 2 : 8 packets are required

For case 3 : 6 packets are required

71. Question have certain ambiguity. If we consider 46.4 μs total (round) propagation time with 48 bit jamming signal transmission time.

Because now we have to subtract transmission time of 48 bit signal from Round propagation time to get actual round propagation time and this is 51.2 μs and hence answer is 512 bit.

72. P — 1; Q — 4; R — 3

By the definition and function of data link layer, Network layer and Transport layer.

73. Choice (*b*) is not true.

A bridge operates at layer 2 (Data Link Layer) so it uses MAC address while routes operates at layer 3 (Network Layer) so it uses IP addresses.

74. 8-bits characters

$$= \frac{9600}{\text{(start bit + data bit + end bit + parity bit)}}$$

$$= \frac{9600}{12} = 800$$

75. There are two condition when A will win the first back-off (0, 1). In second back-off there are four condition (0, 1, 2, 3) [22 – 1 = 4 – 1 = 3]. If A choose 10 in first then required probability

$$= \frac{1}{2}\cdot\frac{3}{4}+\frac{1}{2}\cdot\frac{1}{2} = \frac{3}{8}+\frac{1}{4} = \frac{5}{8} = 0.625$$

76. 128.75.43.16 lies in the range of Eth 0 and 192.12.17.10 lies in the range of Eth 3, hence correct answer is Eth 0 and Eth 3.

77. 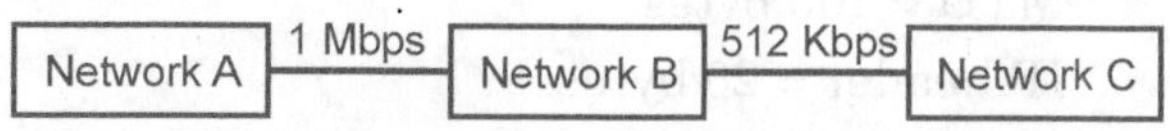

As 3 packets are formed, number of bytes delivered correctly including headers to the destination for one application message in best case

= 180 + 20 + 20 = 240 bytes.

78. Ignoring errors, i.e. noise, we have

B = 2 H (Nyquist theorem)

= 354.5 kbps

79. Every computer has a fixed IP addresses.

80. Transport protocol is called end to end connecting layer.

81. Subnet mask 255.255.31.0 shows class C network So, class C network. IP address is

191.203.31.87 and 191.234.31.88

82. Short message are called *packet*

Given : length = 2 km = 2000 m

$$\lambda = 10^7 \text{ bps}$$

$$v = 2 \times 10^8 \text{ m/s}$$

$$s = vt$$

$$\therefore \quad t = \frac{2 \times 10^3}{2 \times 10^8} = 10^{-5} \text{ sec} = 10 \text{ μ sec.}$$

Total number of packets

$$= 10^7 \times 10 \times 10^{-6} = 100 \text{ bits}$$

$$= 12 \text{ byte}$$

83. Given :

Window size = 5 packet

Packet size = 1000 bytes

= 2^{10} (approx. 10 bits)

Window size = 5000 byte (13 bits approx.)

Transmission time = 5 × 50 = 250 μ sec

Propagation delay = 200 μ sec

Total time = 250 + 200 μ sec

= 450 μ sec

Maximum achievable throughput

$$= \frac{5000}{450} \times 10^6 \text{ bps}$$

$$= 11.11 \times 10^6 \text{ bps}$$

NUMERICAL TYPE QUESTIONS

1. IP datagram = 1000 bytes.
   MTU = 100 bytes
   IP header = 20 bytes.

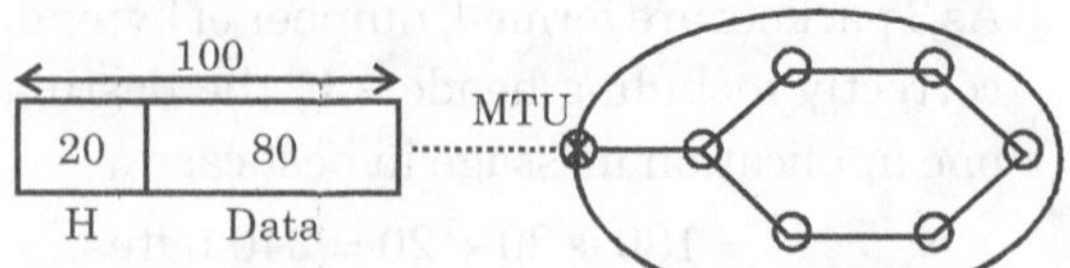

Number of fragments $\Rightarrow \left[\dfrac{1000}{80}\right]$

$\Rightarrow [12.4] \Rightarrow 13$

2. C + ps = mS

$$S = \frac{1MB}{(20-10)MBPs} = 0.1 \text{ sec.}$$

Data transmission in 0.1 sec.
$= 0.1 \times$ output data rate
$= 2$ MB.

Data Remaining = (12 MB – 2 MB) = 10 MB.

To transmit 1 MB $\xrightarrow{\text{takes}}$ 0.1 sec.

10 MB $\longrightarrow 10 \times 0.1$ sec.

Total time = 1 + 0.1 = 1.1 sec.

3. $$\text{Throughput} = \frac{\text{output}}{\text{time}} = \frac{L}{T_{data} + T_{ack} + 2P_d}$$

$$T_d = \frac{1000 \times 8}{80 \times 1000} = \frac{1}{10} \text{ sec} = 100 \text{ ms}$$

$$T_{ack} = \frac{100 \times 8}{8 \times 1000}$$

$$= \frac{1}{10} \text{ sec} = 100 \text{ ms}$$

$$= \frac{1000}{100 + 100 + 2 \times 100} = 2500$$

4. From the given data
   The size of a frame(L) = ?
   Transmission bandwidth (B) = 20 Mbps
   Propagation time (T_p) = 40 microse conds
   T_x = L/B = 100 ms
   $T_x = 2T_p$
   The minimum size of a frame
   $(L_{min}) = 2T_p B = 2(40)(20)/8 = 200$ Bytes

5. From the given question, we have 5 step problem
   1. Calculate RTT = $2(T_P)$
   2. Calculate BR, window size in bits
   3. Calculate W = window in packets = BR/L
   4. For selective repeat, ASN is set to 2W
   5. Sequence number, k

Bandwidth (B) = 128×10^3 bps
Propagation delay (T_P) = 150 msec
Packet size(L) = 1 kilobyte

$$\text{Transmission delay } (T_t) = \frac{L}{B}$$

$$T_t = \frac{1 \times 8 \times 10^3 \text{ bits}}{128 \times 10^3 \text{ bps}}$$

$$\Rightarrow \quad T_t = \frac{1}{16} \text{ sec}$$

T_t = 64 msec
W_S = sender window size

$$\eta = \frac{W_c \times T_t}{T_t + 2T_p}$$

$$1 = \frac{W_S \times 64}{64 + 2 \times 150}$$

$$\frac{364}{64} = W_S$$

$W_S = 5.6875$

$W_S + W_R$ = Available sequence numbers for SR,
$W_S = W_R$ (Here W_R = receiver window size)
ASN $= 2 \times W_S$
ASN $= 2 \times 5.6875$
ASN = 11.375

No. of bits in the sequence number
$= \lceil \log_2 \text{ASN} \rceil$
$= \lceil \log_2 11.375 \rceil = 4$

So, the minimum number of bits required for the sequence number field to achieve 100% utilization is 4.

6. Given Length (d) = 2 Km
   No. of Stations (m) = 10
   Propagation Speed (v) = 2×10^8 m/s
   THT = 2μs
   So, Max. TRT = T_P in the Ring + No. of Active Stations * THT
   $= 10 \times 10^{-6} + 10 \times 2 \times 10^{-6} = 30$ μs

7. Given L = 1KB

B = 1.5Mbps

T = 50ms

$\eta = 60\%$

Efficiency formula for SR protocol is

$$\eta = \frac{W}{1+2a} \Rightarrow \frac{60}{100} = \frac{W}{1+2a} \qquad \left(\because a = \frac{T_p}{T_x}\right)$$

$$T_x = \frac{L}{B} = \frac{8\times10^3}{1.5\times10^6} = 5.3 \text{ ms}$$

$$a = \frac{T_p}{T_x} = \frac{50}{5.3} = \frac{500}{53} = 9.43$$

$$\Rightarrow \frac{60}{100} = \frac{W}{19.86} \Rightarrow W = 11.9 \approx 12$$

$\Rightarrow W = 2^{n-1} = 12$

$\Rightarrow 2^n = 24$

$\Rightarrow 2^n = 24 \approx 2^5 \Rightarrow n = 5$

8. From S to R_1, there are 10 nodes but only 6 of them will decrement the TTL value. That's why, the maximum value of TTL field when R receives datagram is 32 – 6 = 26.

9. Given address 131.23. 151.76. coming to the first field of given routing table

$\Rightarrow$ 131.16. 0.0/12

131.0001 0111.151.76

131.0001 0000.0.0 ($\because$ given mask bits = 12)

$\Rightarrow$ 131.16.0.0 Matched

Coming to the 2nd field of given Routing table

$\Rightarrow$ 131.28.0.0/14

131.0001 0111. 151. 76

131.0001 0100.0.0 ($\because$ given mask bits = 14)

$\Rightarrow$ 131.20.0.0 not matched

Coming to the 3rd field of given Routing table

Error ! Not a valid link 131.19.0.0/16

131.0001 0111.151.76

131.0001 0111.0.0 ($\because$ given mask bits = 16)

$\Rightarrow$ 131.23.0.0 Not matched

Coming to the 4th field of given Routing table

$\Rightarrow$ 131.22.0.0/15

131.0001 0111.151.76

131.0001 0110.0.0 ($\because$ given mask bits = 15)

$\Rightarrow$ 131.22.0.0 Matched

We are getting 1st and 4th entries are matched so among them we have to picked up the longest mask bit, so output interface identifier is 1.

10. Given that each host has a globally unique IPv4 Address and we have to design 50 – bit unique Id. So, 50 – bit in the sense (32 + 18). So, It is clearly showing that IP Address (32 – bit) followed by 18 bits.

1000 unique Ids => 1Sec

2^{18} unique Ids => $2^{18} / 1000 = 2^8 = 256$

11. Given Bit rate = 64 kbps, T_p = 20 ns

L ≥ BR then

$L = 64 \times 10^3 \times 20 \times 10^{-3}$

= 1280 bits

= 160 byte

13. The efficiency of stop-and-wait protocol is 25%, then

$$\frac{1}{4} = \frac{1}{1+2a} \text{ i.e } 1 + 2a = 4$$

$$a = \frac{3}{2}$$

Now, $$T_X = \frac{8\times10^3}{10^6} = 8\text{ms}$$

as $$a = \frac{3}{2} \Rightarrow \frac{T_P}{T_X}$$

$2T_P = 3T_X$

$2T_P = 3 \times 8$

$T_P = 12$ ms

14. Given,

$$\left.\begin{matrix} L = 10^7 \text{ bits} \\ B = 500\times10^6 \text{ bps}\end{matrix}\right\} T_x$$

$$\Rightarrow \frac{L}{B} = \frac{10\times10^6}{500\times10^6} = 0.02 \text{ sec}$$

$$\left.\begin{matrix} d = 8000 \text{ km} \\ v = 4\times10^6 \text{ m/s}\end{matrix}\right\} \Rightarrow T_p$$

$$\frac{d}{v} = \frac{8\times10^6}{4\times10^6} = 2 \text{ sec}$$

$\eta = 100\%$

$n = ?$

$$\therefore \quad a = \frac{T_p}{T_n} = \frac{2}{0.02} = 100$$

Given Protocol, Go back N protocol.

So $$\eta = \frac{w}{1+2a}$$

where $w = 2^n - 1$

$$\frac{100}{100} = \frac{w}{1+2a}$$

$\Rightarrow$ $w = 1 + 2a$

$\Rightarrow$ $2^{n-1} = 1 + 2(100)$

$\Rightarrow$ $2^n - 1 = 201$

$\Rightarrow$ $2^n = 202$

$\Rightarrow$ $2^n = 2^8$

$\Rightarrow$ $n = 8$

15. Given IP address 200.20.11.144/27,

To find out the loss address in a block, we have to set $(32 - n)$ no. of right most bits to 1.

$$n = 27$$

$$32 - n = 32 - 27 = 5$$

200.20.11.10010000

200.20.11.10011111

200.20.11.159

$\therefore$ CIDR Address range is

200.20.11.128/27-200.20.11.159/27

But w.r.t. the question, the value of the last octet of last host in this network is 200.10.11.158.

17. Receiver sends back acknowledge

SOLVED PAPER - 2017

INSTRUCTIONS

1. Total of 65 questions carrying 100 marks, out of which 10 questions carrying a total of 15 marks are in General Aptitude (GA)
2. The Engineering Mathematics will carry around **15% of the total marks,** the General Aptitude section will carry **15% of the total marks** and the **remaining 70% of the total marks.**
3. **Types of Questions**
   (*a*) **Multiple Choice Questions (MCQ)** carrying 1 or 2 marks each in all papers and sections. These questions are objective in nature, and each will have a choice of four options, out of which the candidate has to mark the correct answer(s).
   (*b*) **Numerical Answer Questions** of 1 or 2 marks each in all papers and sections. For these questions the answer is a real number, to be entered by the candidate using the virtual keypad. No choices will be shown for these type of questions.
4. For **1-mark** multiple-choice questions, **1/3 marks** will be deducted for a wrong answer. Likewise, for **2-marks** multiple-choice questions, **2/3** marks will be deducted for a wrong answer. There is no negative marking for numerical answer type questions.

Chapter-Wise Analysis

#	Chapters	Marks		
		1	2	Total
1	General Aptitude	5	5	15
2	Engineering Mathematics	5	6	17
3	Digital Logic	3	2	7
4	Computer Organization and Architecture	1	3	7
5	Data Structures and Algorithms	6	6	18

#	Chapters	Marks		
		1	2	Total
6	Theory of Computation	3	3	9
7	Compiler Design	2	2	6
8	Operating System	2	3	8
9	Databases	2	3	8
10	Computer Networks	1	2	5

TECHNICAL SECTION

(Q.1 – 25) : Carry One Mark Each

1. The representation of the value of a 16-bit unsigned integer X in hexadecimal number system is BCA9. The representation of the value of X in octal number system is

(a) 571244 (b) 736251

(c) 571247 (d) 136251

2. In a file allocation system, which of the following allocation scheme(s) can be used if no external fragmentation is allowed?

I. Contiguous

II. Linked

III. Indexed

(a) I and III only

(b) II only

(c) III only

(d) II and III only

3. A circular queue has been implemented using a singly linked list where each node consists of a value and a single pointer pointing to the next node. We maintain exactly two external pointers FRONT and REAR pointing to the front node and the rear node of the queue, respectively. Which of the following statements is/are CORRECT for such a circular queue, so that insertion and deletion operation can be performed in O(1) time?

I. Next pointer of front node points to the rear node.

II. Next pointer of rear node points to the front node.

(a) I only (b) II only

(c) Both I and II (d) Neither I nor II

4. Identify the language generated by the following grammar, where S is the start variable.

$S \rightarrow XY$

$X \rightarrow aX \mid a$

$Y \rightarrow aYb / \in$

(a) $\{a^m b^n \mid m \geq n, n > 0\}$

(b) $\{a^m b^n \mid m \geq n, n \geq 0\}$

(c) $\{a^m b^n \mid m > n, n \geq 0\}$

(d) $\{a^m b^n \mid m > n, n > 0\}$

5. The minimum possible number of states of a determinstic finite automaton that accepts the regular language

$L = \{w_1 a w_2 \mid w_2, w_2 \in \{a, b\}^*, |w_1| = 2, |w_2| \geq 3\}$ is ______ .

6. Match the following according to input (from the left column) to the complier phase (in the right column) that processes it.

List I	List II
(P) Syntax tree	(i) Code generator
(Q) Character stream	(ii) Syntax analyzer
(R) Intermediate representation	(iii) Semantic analyzer
(S) Token stream	(iv) Lexical analyzer

(a) P → (ii), Q → (iii), R → (iv), S → (i)

(b) P → (ii), Q → (i), R → (iii), S → (iv)

(c) P → (iii), Q → (iv), R → (i), S → (ii)

(d) P → (i), Q → (iv), R → (ii), S → (iii)

7. If $f(x) = R \sin\left(\frac{\pi x}{2}\right) + S$, $f'\left(\frac{1}{2}\right) = \sqrt{2}$ and $\int_0^1 f(x)\,dx = \frac{2R}{\pi}$, then the constants R and S are. respectively.

(a) $\frac{2}{\pi}$ and $\frac{16}{\pi}$ (b) $\frac{2}{\pi}$ and 0

(c) $\frac{4}{\pi}$ and 0 (d) $\frac{4}{\pi}$ and $\frac{16}{\pi}$

8. An ER model of a database consists of entity types A and B. These are connected by a relationship R which does not have its own attribute. Under which one of the following conditions, can the relational table for R be merged with that of A?

(a) Relationship R is one-to-many and the participation of A in R is total.

(b) Relationship R is one-to-many and the participation of A in R is partial.

(c) Relationship R is many-to-one and the participation of A in R is partial.

(d) Relationship R is many-to-one and the participation of A in R is partial.

9. Given the following binary number in 32-bit (single precision) IEEE-754 format:

00111110011011010000000000000000

The decimal value closest to this floating-point number is

(a) 1.45×10^1 (b) 1.45×10^{-1}

(c) 2.27×10^{-1} (d) 2.27×10^1

10. Let L_1, L_2 be any two context-free language and R be any regular language. Then which of the following is are CORRECT?

I. $L_1 \cup L_2$ is context-free

II. $\overline{L_1}$ is context-free

III. $L_1 - R$ is context-free

IV. $L_1 \cap L_2$ is context-free

(*a*) I, II and IV only (*b*) I and III only

(*c*) II and IV only (*d*) I only

11. Consider a quadratic equation $x^2 - 13x + 36 = 0$ with coefficients in a base *b*. The solution of this equation in the same base *b* are $x = 5$ and $x = 6$. Then $b =$ _____ .

12. Consider the following table T_1 and T_2.

T_1

P	Q
2	2
3	8
7	3
5	8
6	9
8	5
9	8

T_2

R	S
2	2
8	3
3	2
9	7
5	7
7	2

In table T_1, P is the primary key and Q is the foregein key referencing R in table T_2 with on-delete cascade and on-update cascade. In table T_2. R is the primary key and S is the foreign key referencing P in table T_1 with on-delet set NULL and on-update cascade. In order to delete record (3, 8) from table T_1, the number of additional records that need to be deleted from table T_1 is _____ .

13. Consider socket API on a Linux machine that supports connected UDP sockets. A connected UDP socket is a UDP socket on which connect function has already been called. Which of the following statement is/are CORRECT?

I. A connected UDP socket can be used to communicate with multiple peers simultaneously.

II. A process can successfully call connect function again for an already connected UDP socket.

(*a*) I only (*b*) II only

(*c*) Both I and II (*d*) Neither I nor II

14. G is an undirected graph with *n* vertices and 25 edges such that each vertex of G has degree at least 3. Then the maximum possible value of *n* is _____ .

15. Consider the set X = {*a, b, c, d, e*} under the partial ordering

$R = \{(a, a), (a, b), (a, c), (a, d), (a, e), (b, b), (b, c), (b, e), (c, c), (c, e), (d, d), (d, e), (e, e)\}$.

The Hase diagram of the partial order (X, R) is shown below :

List II

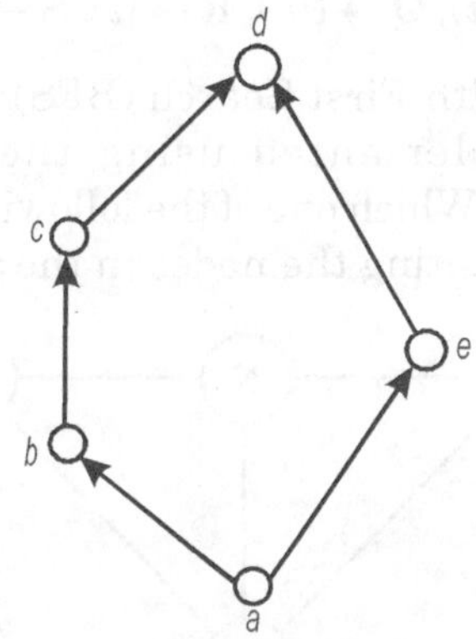

The minimum number of ordered pairs that need to be added to R to make (X, R) a lattice is _____.

16. Which of the following statements about parser is/are CORRECT?

I. Canonical LR is more powerful than SLR.

II. SLR is more powerful than LALR.

III. SLR is more powerful than Canonical LR.

(*a*) I only (*b*) II only

(*c*) III only (*d*) II and III only

17. Let $P = \begin{bmatrix} 1 & 1 & -1 \\ 2 & -3 & 4 \\ 3 & -2 & 3 \end{bmatrix}$ and

$Q = \begin{bmatrix} -1 & -2 & -1 \\ 6 & 12 & 6 \\ 5 & 10 & 5 \end{bmatrix}$ be two matrices.

Then the rank of P + Q is _____ .

18. Match the following

List–I

(P) Static char var;

(Q) m = malloc (10); m = NULL;

(R) char *ptr [10];

(S) register int var 1;

List–II

(*i*) Sequence of memory locations to store addresses

(*ii*) A variable located in data section of memory

(*iii*) Request to allocate a CPU register to store data

(*iv*) A lost memory which cannot be freed

(*a*) P → (*ii*), Q → (*iv*), R → (*i*), S → (*iii*)
(*b*) P → (*ii*), Q → (*i*), R → (*iv*), S → (*iii*)
(*c*) P → (*ii*), Q → (*iv*), R → (*iii*), S → (*i*)
(*d*) P → (*iii*), Q → (*iv*), R → (*i*), S → (*ii*)

19. The Breadth First Search (BFS) algorithm has been implemented using the queue data structure. Which one of the following is a possible order of visiting the nodes in the graph below?

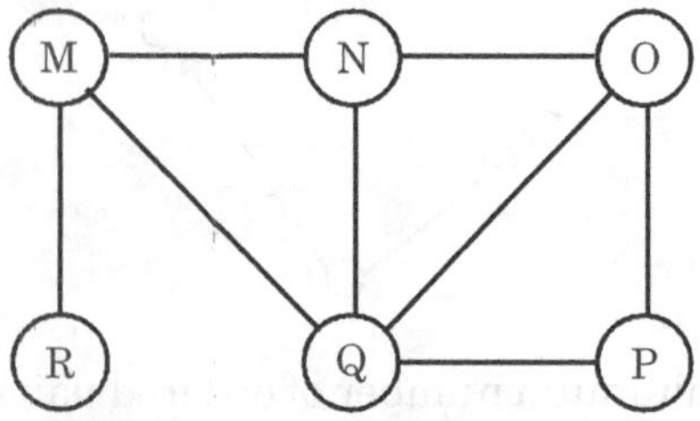

(*a*) MNOPQR (*b*) NQMPOR
(*c*) QMNROP (*d*) POQNMR

20. Let *p*, *q*, *r* denote the statements *"It is raining"*. *"It is cold"*, and *"It is pleasant"*, respectively. Then the statement *"It is nor raining and it is pleasant, and it is not pleasant only if it is raining and it is cold"* is represented by

(*a*) $(\neg p \wedge r) \wedge (\neg r \rightarrow (p \wedge q))$
(*b*) $(\neg p \wedge r) \wedge ((p \wedge q) \rightarrow \neg r)$
(*c*) $(\neg p \wedge r) \vee ((p \wedge q) \rightarrow \neg r)$
(*d*) $(\neg p \wedge r) \vee (r \rightarrow (p \wedge q))$

21. Consider the following function implemented in C:

```
void printxy (int x, int y)
{
   int* ptr ;
      x = 0 ;
        ptr= &x ;
          y=*ptr ;
   *ptr = 1;
   printf ("'% d, % d", x, y);
}
```

The output of invoking printexy (1, 1) is

(*a*) 0, 0 (*b*) 0, 1
(*c*) 1, 0 (*d*) 1, 1

22. Match the algorithms with their time complexities:

List I : Algorithm

(P) Towers of Hanoi with *n* disks
(Q) Binary search given *n* sorted numbers
(R) Heap sort given *n* numbers at the worst case
(S) Addition of two $n \times n$ matrices

List II : Time Complexity

(*i*) $\Theta(n^2)$
(*ii*) $\Theta(n \log n)$
(*iii*) $\Theta(2^n)$
(*iv*) $\Theta(\log n)$

(*a*) P → (*iii*), Q → (*iv*), R → (*i*), S → (*ii*)
(*b*) P → (*iv*), Q → (*iii*), R → (*i*), S → (*ii*)
(*c*) P → (*iii*), Q → (*iv*), R → (*ii*), S → (*i*)
(*d*) P → (*iv*), Q → (*iii*), R → (*ii*), S → (*i*)

23. Consider the following about the routing protocols. Routing Information Protocol (RIP) and Open Shortest Path First (OSPF) in an IPv4 network.

I. RIP uses distance vector routing
II. RIP packets are sent using UDP
III. OSPF packets are sent using TCP?
IV. OSPF operation is based on link-state routing

Which of the statement above are CORRECT?

(*a*) I and IV only
(*b*) I, II and III only
(*c*) I, II and IV only
(*d*) II, III and IV only

24. The maximum number of IPv4 router addresses that can be listed in the record route (RR) oprion field of an IPv4 header is ______.

25. Which of the following is/are shared by all the threads in a process?

I. Program contact
II. Stack
III. Address space
IV. Registers

(*a*) I and II only (*b*) III only
(*c*) IV only (*d*) III and IV only

(Q.26 – 55) : Carry Two Marks Each

26. P and Q are considering to apply for a job. The probability that P applies for the job is $\frac{1}{4}$, the probability that P applies for the job given that Q applies for the job is $\frac{1}{2}$, and the probability that Q applies for the job given that P applies for the job is $\frac{1}{3}$. Then the probability that P does not apply for the job given that Q does not apply for the job is

(*a*) $\frac{4}{5}$ (*b*) $\frac{5}{6}$

(*c*) $\frac{7}{8}$ (*d*) $\frac{11}{12}$

27. Consider the following expression grammar G :

E → E – T I T
T → T + F I F
F → (E) I id

Which of the following grammars is not left recursive, but is equivalent to G?

(*a*) E → E – T I T
T → T + F I F
F → (E) I id

(*b*) E → TE′
E′ → – TE′ I ∈
T → T + F I F
F → (E) I id

(*c*) E → TX
X → – TX I ∈
T → FY
Y → + FY I ∈
F → (E) I id

(*d*) E → TX I (TX)
X → – TX I+ TX I ∈
T → id

28. Consider a binary code that consists of only four valid codewords as given below:

00000, 01011, 10101, 11110

Let the minimum Hamming distance of the code be p and the maximum number of erroneous bits that can be corrected by the code be q. Then the values of p and q are

(*a*) $p = 3$ and $q = 1$
(*b*) $p = 3$ and $q = 2$
(*c*) $p = 4$ and $q = 1$
(*d*) $p = 4$ and $q = 2$

29. Consider the following C Program.

```
#include<stdio.h>
#include<string.h>
{
  int main()
  char*c = "GATECSIT2017";
  char* p=c;
  printf("%d",int)strlen(c+2[p]-6[p]-1));
  return 0;
}
```

The ouput of the program is _____.

30. In a two-level cache system, the access times of L_1 cache and L_2 are 1 and 8 clock cycles, respectively. The miss penalty from the L_2 cache to main memory is 18 clock cycles. The miss rate of L_1 cache is twice that of L_2. The average memory access time (AMAT) of this cache system is 2 cycles. The miss rates of L_1 and L_2 respectively are :

(*a*) 0.111 and 0.056 (*b*) 0.056 and 0.111
(*c*) 0.0892 and 0.1784 (*d*) 0.1784 and 0.0892

31. If the ordinary generating function of a sequence $\{a_n\}_{n=0}^{\infty}$ is $\frac{1+z}{(1-z)^3}$. then $a_3 - a_0$ is equal to ______.

32. Let δ denote the transition function and $\hat{\delta}$ denote the extended transition function of the ε-NFA whose transition table is given below:

δ	ε	a	b
$\to q_0$	$\{q_z\}$	$\{q_1\}$	$\{q_0\}$
q_1	$\{q_2\}$	$\{q_2\}$	(q_3)
q_2	$\{q_0\}$	Φ	Φ
q_3	Φ	Φ	$\{q_2\}$

Then $\hat{\delta}(q_2, aba)$ is

(*a*) ϕ (*b*) (q_0, q_1, q_3)
(*c*) (q_0, q_1, q_2) (*d*) (q_0, q_2, q_3)

33. Consider the following database table named top_scorer

top_scorer

Player	Country	Goals
Klose	Germany	16
Ronaldo	Brazil	15
G Muller	Germany	14
Fontaine	France	13
Pele	Brazil	12
Klinsmann	Germany	11
Kocsis	Hungary	11
Batistuta	Argentina	10
Cubillas	Peru	10
Lato	Poland	10
Lineker	England	10
T Muller	Germany	10
Rahn	Germany	10

Consider the following SQL query we get

SELECT ta. player FROM top_score as ta
WHERE ta.goals > ALL (SELECT tb.goals
FROM top_scorer as tb
WHERE tb.country = 'Spain')
AND ta.goals> ANY (SELECT tc.goals
FROM top_scorer as tc
WHERE tc.country = 'Germany')

The number of tuples returned by the above SQL query is ______

34. In a B+ tree, if the search value is 8 bytes long, the block size is 512 bytes and the block pointer size is 2 bytes, then the maximum order of the B+ tree is ______ .

35. Given $f(w, x, y, z) = \Sigma_m(0, 1, 2, 3, 7, 8, 10) + \Sigma_d(5, 6, 11, 15)$, where *d* represents the *don't-care* condition in Karnaugh maps. Which of the following is a minimum product-of-sums (POS) form of $f(w, x, y, z)$?

(a) $f = (\overline{w} + \overline{z})(\overline{x} + z)$

(b) $f = (\overline{w} + z)(x + z)$

(c) $f = (w + z)(\overline{x} + z)$

(d) $f = (w + \overline{z})(\overline{x} + z)$

36. The next state table of a 2-bit saturating up-counter is given below.

Q_1	Q_0	Q_1^+	Q_0^+
0	0	0	1
0	1	1	0
1	0	1	1
1	1	1	1

The counter is built as a synchronous sequential circuit using T flip-flops. The expression for T_1 and T_0 are

(a) $T_1 = Q_1Q_0$ $\quad T_0 = \bar{Q}_1\bar{Q}_0$

(b) $T_1 = \bar{Q}_1\bar{Q}_0$ $\quad T_0 = \bar{Q}_1 + \bar{Q}_0$

(c) $T_1 = Q_1 + Q_0$ $\quad T_0 = \bar{Q}_1 + \bar{Q}_0$

(d) $T_1 = \bar{Q}_1Q_0$ $\quad T_0 = Q_1 + Q_0$

37. Consider the recurrence function

$$T(n) = \begin{cases} 2T(\sqrt{n}) + 1, & n > 2 \\ 2, & 0 < n \leq 2 \end{cases}$$

Then T(n) in terms of Θ notation is

(a) $\Theta(\log \log n)$ (b) $\Theta(\log n)$

(c) $\Theta(\sqrt{n})$ (d) $\Theta(n)$

38. A message is made up entirely of characters from the set X = {P, Q, R, S, T}. The table of probabilities for each of the characters is shown below :

Character	Probability
P	0.22
Q	0.34
R	0.17
S	0.19
T	0.08
Total	1.00

If a message of 100 characters over X is encode using Huffman coding, then the expected length of the encoded message in bits is ______ .

39. Consider the following C Program.

```
# include<stdio.h>
int main ()
{
  int m = 10 ;
   int n,n1 ;
     n = ++m ;
    n1 = m++ ;
    n - -  ;
    - -n1 ;
    n -= n1 ;
   printf ("%d", n) ;
   return 0 ;
}
```

The output of the program is ______ .

40. If *w, x, y, z* are Boolean variables, then which one of the following is INCORRECT?

(a) $wx + w(x + y) + x(x + y) = x + wy$

(b) $\overline{w\overline{x}(y + \overline{z})} + \overline{w}x = \overline{w} + x + \overline{y}z$

(c) $(w\overline{x}(y + x\overline{z}) + \overline{w}\overline{x})y = x\overline{y}$

(d) $(w + y)(wxy + wyz) = wxy + wyz$

41. For any discrete random variable X with probability mass function

$P(X = j) = p_j,\ p_j \geq 0.\ j \in \{0......N\}$, and $\sum_{j=0}^{N} p_j = 1$,

define the polynomial function $g_x(z) = \sum_{j=0}^{N} p_j z^j$.

For a certain discrete random variable Y, there exists s scalar β ∈ [0, 1] such that $g_y(z) = (1 - \beta + \beta z)^N$. The expectation of Y is

(a) $N\beta(1 - \beta)$

(b) $N\beta$

(c) $N(1 - \beta)$

(d) Not expressible in terms of N and β alone

42. Consider the set of processes with arrival time (in milliseconds), CPU burst time (in milliseconds). and priority (0 is the highest priority) shown below. None of the processess have I/O burst time.

Process	Arrival Time	Burst Time	Priority
P_1	0	11	2
P_2	5	28	0
P_3	12	2	3
P_4	2	10	1
P_5	9	16	4

The average waiting time (in milliseconds) of all the processes using preemptive priority scheduling algorithm is ________.

43. Consider a machine with a byte addressable main memory of 2^{32} bytes divided into blocks of size 32 bytes. Assume that a direct mapped cache having 512 cache lines is used with this machine. The size of the tag field in bits is ________.

44. Consider two hosts X and Y, connected by a single direct link of rate 10^6 bits/sec. The distance between the two hosts is 10,000 km and the propagation speed along the link is 2×10^8 m/sec. Host X sends a file of 50,000 bytes as one large message to host Y continuously. Let the transmission and propagation delays be p milliseconds and q milliseconds, respectively.

Then the values of p and q are

(*a*) $p = 50$ and $q = 100$

(*b*) $p = 50$ and $q = 400$

(*c*) $p = 100$ and $q = 50$

(*d*) $p = 400$ and $q = 50$

45. If a random variable X has a Poisson distribution with mean 5, then the expectation $E[(X + 2)^2]$ equals ________.

46. Consider the following snippet of a C program. Assume that swap (&x, &y) exchanges the contents of x and y.

```
int main()
{
  int array[] = {3, 5, 1, 4, 6, 2};
  int done = 0;
  int i;
  while {done == 0)
  {
   done = 1;
   for (i = 0; j<=4; i++)
   {
     if (array[i] < array[i+1])
     {
       swap (&array[i], &array[i+1]);
     }
   }
   for (i=5, i>=1; i--)
   {
     if (array[i] > array[i-1])
     {
       swap (&array[i], &array[i-1]);
       done = 0;
     }
   }
  }
  printf{"%d",array[3]);
}
```

The output of the program is _____.

47. A system shares 9 tape drives. The current allocation and maximum requirement of tape drives for three processes are shown below :

Process	**Current Allocation**	**Maximum Requirement**
P1	3	7
P2	1	6
P3	3	5

Which of the following best describes current state of the system?

(*a*) Safe, Deadlocked

(*b*) Safe, Not Deadlocked

(*c*) Not Safe, Deadlocked

(*d*) Not Safe, Not Deadlocked

48. Consider the following C function.

```
int fun(int n)
{
    int i, j;
    for(i = 1; i <= n; i++)
    {
      for(j = 1; j <n; j += i)
      {
        printf (" %d %d", i,j);
      }
    }
}
```

Time complexity of fun in terms of Θ notation is

(*a*) $\Theta(n\sqrt{n})$ (*b*) $\Theta(n^2)$

(*c*) $\Theta(n \log n)$ (*d*) $\Theta(n^2 \log n)$

49. Let L(R) be the language represented by regular expression R. Let L(G) be the language generated by a context free grammer G. Let L(M) be the language accepted by a Turing machine M. Which of the following decision problems are undecidable?

I. Given a regular expression R and a string w, is $w \in L(R)$?

II. Given a context-free grammer G, is $L(G) = \Phi$?

III. Given a context-free grammer G, is $L(G) = \Sigma*$ for some alphabet Σ?

IV. Given a Turing machine M and a string w, is $w \in L(M)$?

(*a*) I and IV only
(*b*) II and III only
(*c*) II, III and IV only
(*d*) III and IV only

50. If the characteristic polynomial of a 3×3 matrix M over $\mathbb{R}$ (the set of real numbers) is $\lambda^3 - 4\lambda^2 + a\lambda + 30$, $a \in \mathbb{R}$, and one eigenvalue of M is 2, then the largest among the absolute values of the eigenvalues of M is ________.

51. Consider the following languages.

$$L_1 = \{a^p \mid p \text{ is a prime number}\}$$

$$L_2 = \{a^n b^m c^{2m} \mid n \geq 0, m \geq 0\}$$

$$L_3 = \{a^n b^n c^{2n} \mid n \geq 0\}$$

$$L_4 = \{a^n b^n \mid n \geq 1\}$$

Which of the following are CORRECT?

I. L_1 is context-free but not regular.

II. L_2 is not context-free.

III. L_3 is not context-free but recursive.

IV. L_4 is deterministic context-free.

(*a*) I, II and IV only
(*b*) II and III only
(*c*) I and IV only
(*d*) III and IV only

52. Two transactions T_1 and T_2 are given as

$$T_1 : r_1(X)w_1(X)r_1(Y)w_1(Y)$$

$$T_2 : r_2(Y)w_2(Y)r_2(Z)w_2(Z)$$

where $r_i(V)$ denotes a *read* operation by transaction T_i on a variable V and $w_1(V)$ denotes a *write* operation by transaction T_i on a variable V. The total number of conflict serializable schedules that can be formed by T_1 and T_2 is ______ .

53. The read access times and the hit ratios for different caches in a memory hierarchy are as given below.

Code	Read access time (in nanoseconds)	Hit ratio
I-cache	2	0.8
D-cache	2	0.9
L2-cache	8	0.9

The read access time of main memory is 90 nanoseconds. Assume that the caches use the referred word-first read policy and the write back policy. Assume that all the caches are direct mapped caches. Assume that the dirty bit is always 0 for all the blocks in the caches. In execution of a program. 60% of memory reads are for instruction fetch and 40% are for memory operand fetch. The average read access time in nanoseconds (up to 2 decimal places) is ________.

54. Consider the C program fragment below which is meant to divide x by y using repeated subtractions. The variables `x, y, q` and `r` are all `unsigned int`.

```
while (r >= y)
{
        r = r - y;
        q = q + 1;
}
```

Which of the following conditions on the variables `x, y, q` and `r` before the execution of the fragment will ensure that the loop terminates in a state satisfying the condition `x==(y*q + r)`?

(*a*) `(q == r) && (r == 0)`
(*b*) `(x > 0) && (r == x) && (y > 0)`
(*c*) `(q == 0) && (r == x) && (y > 0)`
(*d*) `(q == 0) && (y > 0)`

55. The pre-order traversal of a binary search tree is given by 12, 8, 6, 2, 7, 9, 10, 16, 15, 19, 17, 20. Then the post-order traversal of this tree is :

(*a*) 2, 6, 7, 8, 9, 10, 12, 15, 16, 17, 19, 20
(*b*) 2, 7, 6, 10, 9, 8, 15, 17, 20, 19, 16, 12
(*c*) 7, 2, 6, 8, 9, 10, 20, 17, 19, 15, 16, 12
(*d*) 7, 6, 2, 10, 9, 8, 15, 16, 17, 20, 19, 12

GENERAL APTITUDE

(Q.1 – 5) : Carry One Mark Each

1. A test has twenty questions worth 100 marks in total. There are two types of questions. Multiple choice questions are worth 3 marks each and essay questions are worth 11 marks each. How many multiple choice questions does the exam have ?

(*a*) 12 (*b*) 15
(*c*) 18 (*d*) 19

2. Choose the option with words that are not synonyms.

(*a*) aversion, dislike
(*b*) luminous, radiant
(*c*) plunder, loot
(*d*) yielding, resistant

3. There are five buildings called V, W, X, Y and Z in a row (not necessarily in that order). V is to the West of W. Z is to the East of X and the West of V. W is to the West of Y. Which is the building in the middle ?

(*a*) V (*b*) W
(*c*) X (*d*) Y

4. There are 3 red socks, 4 green socks and 3 blue socks. You choose 2 socks. The probability that they are of the same colour is

(*a*) 1/5 (*b*) 7/30
(*c*) 1/4 (*d*) 4/15

5. Saturn is _____ to be seen on a clear night with the naked eye.

(*a*) enough bright
(*b*) bright enough
(*c*) as enough bright
(*d*) bright as enough

(Q.6 – 10) : Carry Two Marks Each

6. "We lived in a culture that denied any merit to literary works, considering them important only when they were handmaidens to somethings seemingly more urgent – namely ideology. This was a country where all gestures, even the most private, were interprated in political terms."

The author's belief that ideology is not as important as literature is revealed by the word :

(*a*) 'culture' (*b*) 'seemingly'
(*c*) 'urgent' (*d*) 'political'

7. An air pressure contour line joins locations in a region having the same atmospheric pressure. The following is an air pressure contour plot is a geographical region. Contour lines are shown at 0.05 bar intervals in this plot.

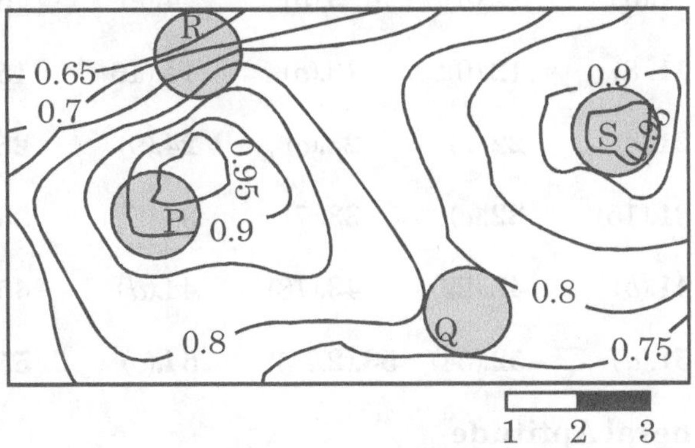

If the possibility of a thunderstorm is given by how fast air pressure rises or drops over a region, which of the following regions is most likely to have a thunderstorm ?

(*a*) P (*b*) Q
(*c*) R (*d*) S

8. The number of roots of $e^x + 0.5x^2 - 2 = 0$ in the range [–5, 5] is

(*a*) 0
(*b*) 1
(*c*) 2
(*d*) 3

9. There are three boxes. One contains apples another contains oranges and the last one contains both apples and oranges. All three are known to be incorrectly labelled. If you are permitted to open just one box and then pull out and inspect only one fruit, which box would you open to determine the contents of all three boxes?

(*a*) The box labelled 'Apples'
(*b*) The box labelled 'Apples and Oranges'
(*c*) The box labelled 'Oranges'
(*d*) Cannot be determined

10. X is a 30 digit number starting with the digit 4 followed by the digit 7. Then the number X^3 will have

(*a*) 90 digits
(*b*) 91 digits
(*c*) 92 digits
(*d*) 93 digits

ANSWERS

Techanical Section

1.(*d*)	**2.**(*d*)	**3.**(*b*)	**4.**(*c*)	**5.**(8)	**6.**(*c*)	**7.**(*c*)	**8.**(*c* & *d*)	**9.**(*c*)	**10.**(*b*)
11.(8)	**12.**(0)	**13.**(*b*)	**14.**(16)	**15.**(0)	**16.**(*a*)	**17.**(2)	**18.**(*a*)	**19.**(*d*)	**20.**(*a*)
21.(*c*)	**22.**(*c*)	**23.**(*c*)	**24.**(9)	**25.**(*b*)	**26.**(*a*)	**27.**(*c*)	**28.**(*a*)	**29.**(2)	**30.**(*a*)
31.(15)	**32.**(*c*)	**33.**(7)	**34.**(52)	**35.**(*a*)	**36.**(*b*)	**37.**(*b*)	**38.**(225)	**39.**(0)	**40.**(*c*)
41.(*b*)	**42.**(29)	**43.**(18)	**44.**(*d*)	**45.**(54)	**46.**(3)	**47.**(*b*)	**48.**(*c*)	**49.**(*d*)	**50.**(5)
51.(*d*)	**52.**(54)	**53.**(2.74)	**54.**(*c*)	**55.**(*b*)					

General Aptitude

1.(*b*)	**2.**(*d*)	**3.**(*a*)	**4.**(*d*)	**5.**(*b*)	**6.**(*c*)	**7.**(*c*)	**8.**(*c*)	**9.**(*a*)	**10.**(*a*)

EXPLANATIONS

TECHNICAL SECTION

1. The 16 bit is further divided into:

$$X = (B\ \ C\ \ A\ \ 9)_{16}$$

for octal number divide from the right in to 3 bits and derive the below number

$$= 1\ 011\ 111\ 001\ 010\ 101\ 001$$

$$= (1\quad 3\quad 6\quad 2\quad 5\quad 1)_8$$

2. Only as linked and indexed allocations are non cantagious, they will not suffer from external fragmentation.

3.

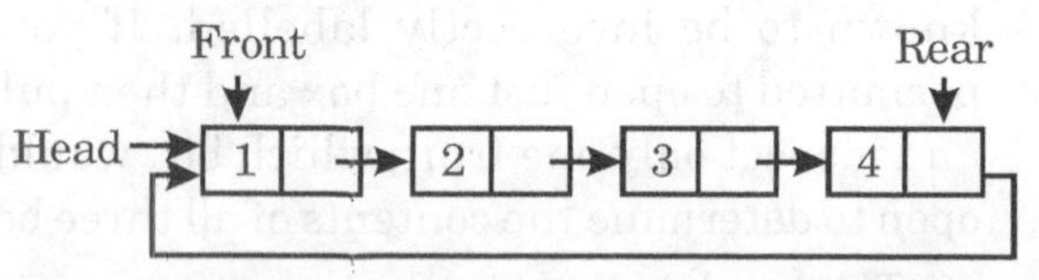

As in a queue, insertion is done from REAR and deletion is done from FRONT. As the next pointer of REAR node is pointing to the FRONT node, it leads both insertion and deletion operations in O(1) time.

4. As given:

$$S \rightarrow XY$$

$$X \rightarrow aX|a \Rightarrow X \rightarrow \{a^m | m \geq 1\}$$

$$Y \rightarrow aYb|\in \Rightarrow Y \rightarrow \{a^n b^n | n \geq 0\}$$

$$S \rightarrow XY \Rightarrow S \rightarrow \{a^m b^n | m > n,\ n \geq 0\}$$

$m > n$ because at least 1 will be attached on left of $a^n b^n$.

Hence the language generated here is

$$\{a^m b^n \mid m > n, n \geq 0\}$$

5. Given the regular language is :

Min DFA for L

$$= \{w_1 a w_2 | w_1, w_2 \in \{a,b\}^*, |w_1| = 2, |w_2| \geq 3\}$$

Hence the regular expression for L is

$$(a + b)\ (a + b)\ a\ (a + b)\ (a + b)(a + b)\ (a + b)^*$$

The minimal DFA is

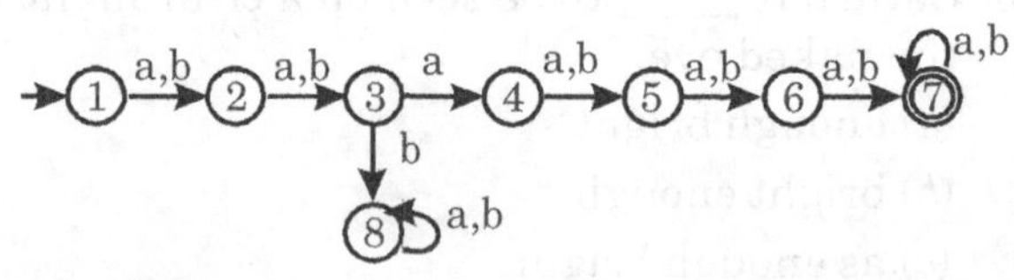

Hence the minimum possible number of states of DFA is 8.

6. According to the compiler phase process, we get the below structure:

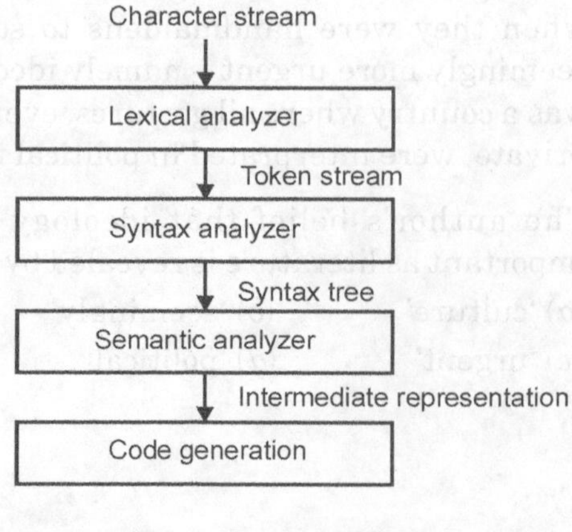

7. Given,

$$f(x) = R\sin\left(\frac{\pi x}{2}\right) + S, \quad ...(1)$$

Given $$f'\left(\frac{1}{2}\right) = \sqrt{2} \quad ...(2)$$

$$\int_0^1 f(x)dx = \frac{2R}{\pi} \quad ...(3)$$

Now we need to find R and S.

$$f'(x) = R\cos\left(\frac{\pi x}{2}\right)\frac{\pi}{2}$$

$$f'\left(\frac{1}{2}\right) = R\cos\left(\frac{\pi}{4}\right)\times\frac{\pi}{2} = \sqrt{2}$$

$$\Rightarrow \frac{R}{\sqrt{2}}\times\frac{\pi}{2} = \sqrt{2}$$

$$\Rightarrow R = \frac{4}{\pi}$$

Now, $$\int f(x)dx = \int R\sin\frac{\pi x}{2} + S$$

Putting $R = \frac{4}{\pi}$ we get

$$\int f(x)dx = \int\frac{4}{\pi}\sin\left(\frac{\pi x}{2}\right)dx + \int S\,dx$$

$$= \frac{4}{\pi}\times -\frac{\cos\left(\frac{\pi x}{2}\right)}{\frac{\pi}{2}} + Sx$$

$$= \frac{-8}{\pi^2}\cos\left(\frac{\pi x}{2}\right) + Sx$$

Putting limit 0 and 1

$$\int_0^1 f(x)dx = \frac{-8}{\pi^2}\left(\cos\frac{\pi}{2} - \cos(0)\right) + S(1-0)$$

$$= \frac{2R}{\pi}$$

$$\Rightarrow \frac{-8}{\pi^2}(0-1) + S = \frac{2R}{\pi}$$

Put $R = \frac{4}{\pi}$ and solve for S

$$\Rightarrow S = 0$$

So, $R = \frac{4}{\pi}$ and $S = 0$ is answer.

8. There are 2 entities sets A, B

1 relationship set R

As relation R merges with that of A

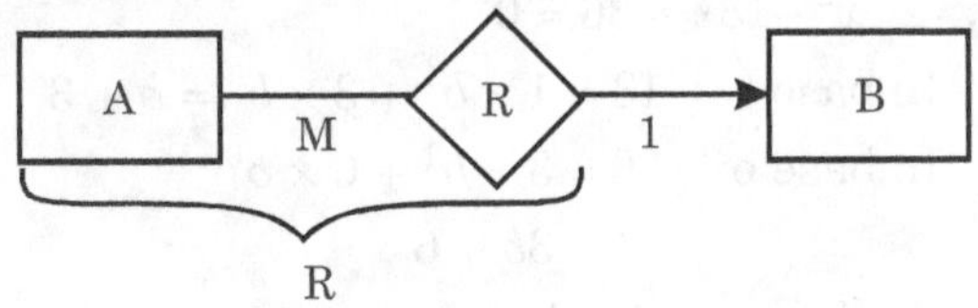

As many to one relationship set can merge towards entity set 'A'

The partipation towards A side can be total/partial

9. The 32- bit number is further divided as below:

1 bit	8 bit	23 bit
0	01111100	1101101000...
S	BE	M

Step 1. Sing = 0

= +ve

Step 2. AE = BE – Bias

2 2 2 2 2 2 2 2

BE = 0 1 1 1 1 1 0 0

Bias = 0 1 1 1 1 1 1 1

AE = 1 1 1 1 1 1 0 1

AS sign of AE is negative so take two complement of AE.

i.e., 00000010

1

00000011

⇒ – 3

Step 3.Mantissa

Hence normal Mantissa = 1.M = 1.1101101

Data + 1.1101101×2^{-3} {$\pm M \times B^{\pm e}$}

Now mantissa is aligned to right upto 3 times

↓

+0.0011101101

↓

0.228

↓

Hence 2.28×10^{-1}

10. As given :

I. $L_1 \cup L_2$ is context- free = CFL ∪ CFL = CFL.

So True.

II. $\overline{L}_1$ is context-free = $\overline{CFL}$ = CSL but not CFL.

So False.

III. L_1 –R is context-free = CFL ∩ $\overline{\text{Regular}}$ = CFL.

So,True

IV. $L_1 \cap L_2$ is context-free = $CFL \cap CFL = CSL$.

So, False

11. $x^2 - 13x + 36 = 0$

In base b $\quad 13 = 1 \times b^1 + 3 \times b^0 = b + 3$

In base b $\quad 36 = 3 \times b^1 + 6 \times b^0$

$= 3b + 6$

So the equation becomes

$x^2 - (b + 3)x + (3b + 6) = 0$

Now since it is given that x = 5 is a solution , so

$5^2 - (b + 3)\,5 + (3b + 6) = 0$

$\Rightarrow \quad -2b + 16 = 0$

$\Rightarrow \quad b = 8$

Same can be obtained by putting $x = 6$ also.

12. As we have the primary key of one table as foreign key of another table, from these tables :

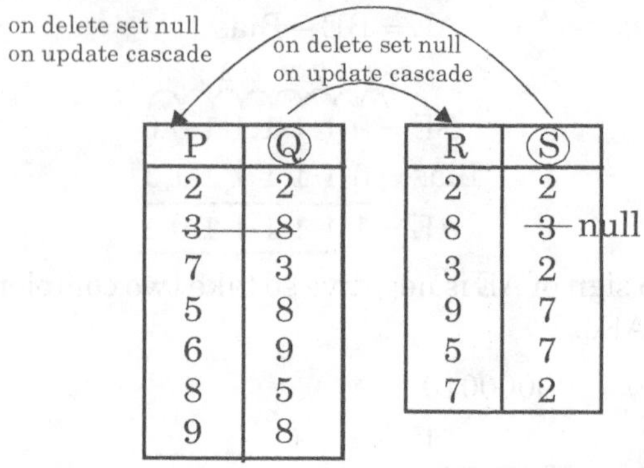

No other record need to delete because of deletion of (3, 8) record from T_1

13. Bind () function is used to create local address

Connect () function specifies remote address. An unconnected UDP socket is just a Bind () function. But a connected UDP socket is connect () function which behaves like a TCP.

14. In the undirected graph G, we have n vertices and 25 edges

Hence

$n \leq ?$

$e = 25$

As each vertex has at least 3 degree

and $\quad 2e = \Sigma\text{degree}$

i.e., $\quad 2e \geq 3n$

$n \leq 2e/3$

$\Rightarrow \quad n \leq \frac{2 \times 25}{3} \leq 16.66$

$\therefore$ n is at the maximum possible value of 16.

15. There is no need to add any ordered pair as the given hasse diagram is already a lattice.

16. Among all the LR(k) parsers, cononical LR is the most powerful parsers.

17. By adding both P and Q

$$P + Q = \begin{bmatrix} 0 & -1 & -2 \\ 8 & 9 & 10 \\ 8 & 8 & 8 \end{bmatrix}$$

Magnitude of P & Q

$|P+Q| = -16 + 16 = 0$

So rank $\neq 3$

rank < 3

Take the 2×2 minor $\begin{bmatrix} 0 & -1 \\ 8 & 9 \end{bmatrix} = 8 \neq 0$

So, rank of P + Q is 2

18. This refers to a variable located in data section of memory.

static chr var; : Initialization of a variable located in data section of memory.

***m* = malloc (10); *m* = NULL; :** A lost memory which can't be freed because free (m) is missed in code.

char * ptr[10]; : Sequence of memory locations to store addresses.

register int var 1; : Request to allocate a CPU register to store data.

19. While considering each option, we can see that:

- After vertices 'M' and 'N', vertex 'O' can't be traversed.
- After visting vertex 'M', vertex 'O' should be traversed.
- After 'N' either of the vertices 'O' or 'P' should be traversed

Hence we derive the below order of visiting the nodes

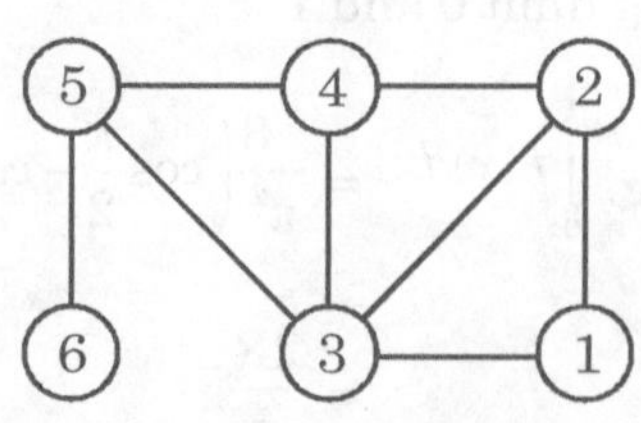

20. As given :

p : "It is raining"

q : "It is cold", and

r : "It is pleasant",

So the correct representation of "*It is not raining and it is pleasant, and it is not pleasant only if it is raining and it is cold*" is

$\neg p \wedge r \wedge \neg$ r only if $p \wedge q$

$\equiv (\neg p \wedge r) \wedge (\neg r \rightarrow (p \wedge q))$

21. print $xy(1, 1)$

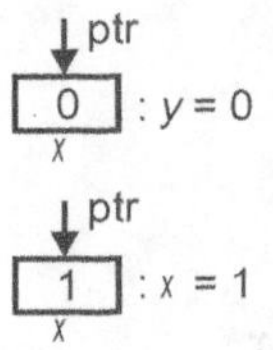

As the last line is printf (" % d, % d", x, y)
the output will be (1, 0)

22. As per the given algorithms and time complexities we derive:

Towers of Hanoi with n disks

$$= 2T(n-1) + 1 = \Theta(2^n)$$

Binary search given n sorted numbers

$$= T(n/2) + 1 = \Theta(\log n)$$

Heap sort given n numbers at the worst case

$$= 2T(n/2) + n = \Theta(n \log n)$$

Addition of two $n \times n$ matrices

$$= 4T(n/2) + 1 = \Theta(n^2)$$

23. As we know:

- RIP uses distance vector routing.
- OSPF uses link-state routing protocols.
- RIP uses UDP as transport protocol.
- OSPF neither uses TCP nor UDP.

[Link state packet should be given to all routers in subnet so it's not possible with TCP. These link state packets should be reliable at that same time which is not possible with UDP.]

24. In IPv4, 40 bytes are alloted for options and padding.

and maximum nine routers addresses are allowed.

Each IPv4 address is 32 bits or 4 bytes

Hence $4 \times 9 = 36$ bytes

The remaining byte are used for the option.

25. Only address space is shared by all the threads in a process, the other entities such as stack , PC, resisters are not shared as each thread has its own.

26. Given that

$$p(P) = \frac{1}{4} \quad ...(i)$$

$$p(P \mid Q) = \frac{1}{2} \quad ...(ii)$$

$$p(Q \mid P) = \frac{1}{3} \quad ...(iii)$$

$$p(\overline{P} \mid \overline{Q}) = ?$$

First solve for $p(Q)$ and $p(P \cap Q)$ from equation (*ii*) and (*iii*) as follows :

From equation (*ii*)

$$p(P \mid Q) = \frac{p(P \cap Q)}{p(Q)} = \frac{1}{2} \quad ...(iv)$$

From equation (*iii*) $p(Q \mid P) = \dfrac{p(P \cap Q)}{p(P)} = \dfrac{1}{3}$

$$\Rightarrow \quad p(P \cap Q) = \frac{1}{3} \times p(P)$$

$$= \frac{1}{3} \times \frac{1}{4} = \frac{1}{12}$$

Substitute in equation (*iv*) get

$$p(Q) = \frac{p(P \cap Q)}{1/2} = \frac{1/12}{1/2}$$

$$= \frac{2}{12} = \frac{1}{6}$$

$$p(P) = \frac{1}{4}$$

$$p(Q) = \frac{1}{6}$$

and $\quad p(P \cap Q) = \dfrac{1}{12}$

we need to find

$$p(\overline{P} \mid \overline{Q}) = \frac{p(\overline{P} \cap \overline{Q})}{p(\overline{Q})}$$

$$= \frac{1 - (P \cup Q)}{1 - p(Q)}$$

$$= 1 - \frac{[p(P) + p(Q) - p(P \cap Q)]}{1 - p(Q)}$$

$$= \frac{1 - \left[\frac{1}{4} + \frac{1}{6} - \frac{1}{12}\right]}{1 - \frac{1}{6}} = \frac{\frac{2}{3}}{\frac{5}{6}} = \frac{4}{5}$$

$$p(\overline{P} \mid \overline{Q}) = \frac{4}{5}$$

27.

$$E \rightarrow E - T \mid T$$
$$T \rightarrow T + F \mid F$$
$$F \rightarrow (E) \mid id$$

There are 2 left recurssion and both have to be removed.

$$E' \rightarrow - TE' \mid \in$$
$$E \rightarrow TE'$$
$$T' \rightarrow + FT' \mid \in$$
$$Y \rightarrow FT'$$
$$F \rightarrow (E) \mid id$$

Now by putting E′ as X and T′ as Y,

$$E \rightarrow TX$$
$$X \rightarrow -TX \mid \in$$
$$T \rightarrow FY$$
$$Y \rightarrow +FY \mid \in$$
$$F \rightarrow (E) \mid id$$

So option (*c*) is correct

28. By question, codewords are

00000
01011
10101
11110

Minimum hamming distance = min (hamming distance between every 2 pair) = 3

for correcting errors, we know that

$$2d + 1 = 3$$
$$\Rightarrow \quad d = 1$$

29. (C + 2[p] – 6[p] – 1)

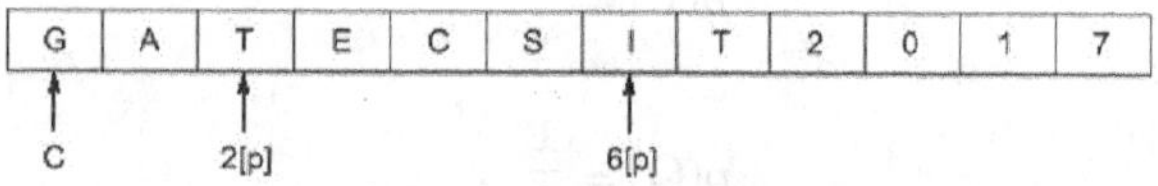

$$C + \text{'T'} - \text{'I'} - 1$$
$$= C + 11 - 1$$
$$= C + 10$$

Finally printf will print '2'.

30. Given data

Hit time L_1 = 1 cycle

Hit time L_2 = 8 cycles

Miss penality L_2 = 18 cycles

Tavg = 2 ns

Miss rate $L_1 = 2x$

Miss rate $L_2 = x$

- Tavg = Hit time L_1 + (Miss rate L_1 × Miss penality L_1)

  T_{avg} = 2ns
- Miss penality L_1 = Hit time L_2 + (Miss rate L_2 × Miss penality L_2)
- Substitute the above data and verifying with respect to the given options.
- $L_1 = 0.111$ $\quad L_2 = 0.056$

31. Then generating function $\{a_n\}_{n=0}^{\infty}$ is $\dfrac{1+z}{(1-z)^3}$

$$A(z) = \sum a_r z^r$$
$$= \frac{1+z}{(1-z)^3}$$

We can replace z by x, we get

$$A(x) = \sum a_r x^r$$
$$= \frac{1+x}{(1-x)^3}$$
$$= \frac{1}{(1-x)^3} + \frac{x}{(1-x)^3}$$
$$= \sum_{r=0}^{\infty} {}^{3-1+r}C_r x^r + x \sum_{r=0}^{\infty} {}^{3-1+r}C_r x^r$$
$$= \sum_{r=0}^{\infty} {}^{r+2}C_2 x^r + \sum_{r=0}^{\infty} {}^{r+2}C_2 x^{r+1}$$

$${}^2C_2 x^0 + {}^3C_2 x^1 + {}^4C_2 r^2 + {}^5C_2 x^3 \ldots\ldots\ldots$$
$$+ {}^2C_2 x^1 + {}^3C_2 x^2 + {}^4C_2 x^3 + \ldots\ldots\ldots$$

Now we read to find a_0 and a_3 which are coefficient of x^0 and x^3 respectively.

$$a_0 = \text{Coefficient } x^0$$
$$= {}^2C_2 = 1$$
$$a_3 = \text{Coefficient } x^3$$
$$= {}^5C_2 + {}^4C_2 = 16$$

So, $\quad a_3 - a_0 = 16 - 1 = 15$

32. Draw the table from state diagram, we get,

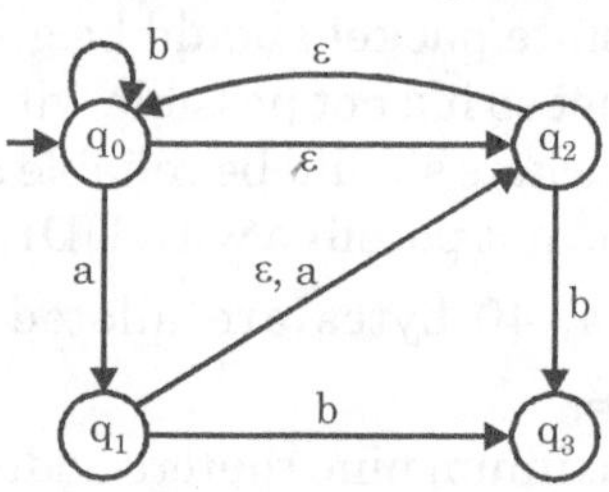

$\hat{\delta}(q_2, aba)$ = All states reachable from q_2 by "*aba*"

If *aba* is broken as ε.a.ε.ε.b.a. Then from q_2 we can reach q_1 and from there by null transition we can reach state q_2 as well as q_0.

$$\hat{\delta}(q_2, aba) = (q_0, q_1, q_2\}$$

33. Select ta.player

FROM top_scorer as ta

WHERE ta.goals > ALL (SELECT tb.goals)

FROM top_scorer as tb

WHERE tb.country = 'Spain')

AND ta.goals > ANY (SELECT tc. goals

FROM top_scorer as tc

WHERE tc.country = 'Germany')

So number of tuples in result 7.

34. B^+ tree

Search key : 8 bytes

Block size : 512 bytes

Block pointer : 2 bytes

Maximum order of B^+ tree node??

$P \times B_P + (P-1) \times \text{Key} \le \text{Block size}$

$$P \times 2 + (P-1)8 \le 512$$

$$10P \le 520$$

$$P = \left[\frac{520}{10}\right] = 52$$

Maximum order of B^+ tree is 52

35. Given

$f(w, x, y, z) = \Sigma_m(0, 1, 2, 3, 7, 8, 10) + d(5, 6, 11, 15)$

$= \pi_M (4, 9, 12, 13, 14). d(5, 6, 11, 15)$

draw K-map

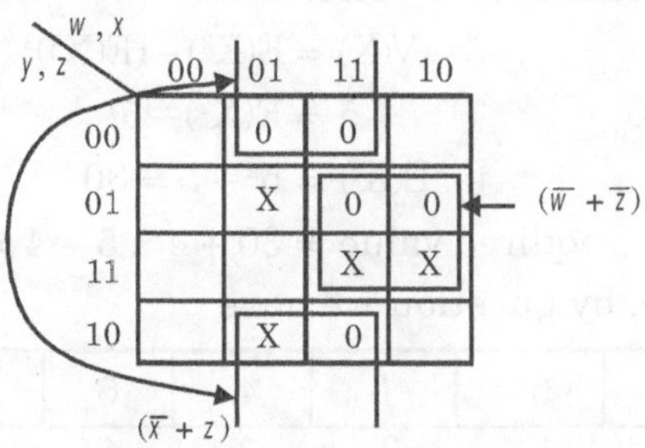

$f(w, x, y, z) = (\bar{w} + \bar{z})(\bar{x} + z)$]

This is minimum POS form of $f(w, x, y, z)$

36. State table showing input of flip-flope

FF inputs

Q_1	Q_0	Q_1^+	Q_0^+	T_1	T_0
0	0	0	1	0	1
0	1	1	0	1	1
1	0	1	1	0	1
1	1	1	1	0	0

From the table

$$T_1(Q_1, Q_0) = \overline{Q}_1 Q_0$$

$$T_2(Q_1, Q_0) = \overline{Q}_1 \overline{Q}_0 + \overline{Q}_1 Q_0 + Q_1 \overline{Q}_0$$

minimize T_2

$$= \overline{Q}_1 + \overline{Q}_0$$

37. $T(n) = 2T(\sqrt{n}) + 1 \quad n > 2$ ...(*i*)

$T(n) = 2T(\sqrt[2]{n}) + 1$ ...(*ii*)

Put (*ii*) in (*i*)

$T(n) = 2 * 2T(\sqrt[2]{n}) + 2$

$T(n) = 2^2 T(\sqrt[2]{n}) + 2$ ...(*iii*)

$T(\sqrt[2]{n}) = 2T(\sqrt[3]{n}) + 1$ ...(*iv*)

Substituting (*iv*) in (*iii*)

$$T(n) = 2^3 T(\sqrt[3]{n}) + 3$$

Running the same till K times,

$$T(n) = 2^K T(\sqrt[K]{n}) + K$$

$$\sqrt[K]{n} = 2$$

$$K = \log_2 n$$

Solving this will give

$$T(n) = \Theta(\log n)$$

39. By given C program, we have :

1. int m = 10; // m = 10
2. int n, n1 ;
3. n = ++m; // n = 11
4. n1 = m++; // n1 = 11, m = 12
5. n – –; // n =10
6. – – n1 ; // n1 = 10
7. n – = n1 ; // n = 0
8. printf ("%d", n);

Now, by above steps, we get output = 0

40. $\left(w\bar{x}\left(y + x\bar{z}\right) + \overline{w}\overline{x}\right)y = \bar{x}y$

$\left(w\bar{x}y + \overline{w}\overline{x}\right)y$

$w\bar{x}y + \overline{w}\overline{x}y$

$\bar{x}y\left(w + \bar{w}\right)$, since $\left(w + \bar{w}\right)$ evaluate to 1

$\bar{x}y \ne x\bar{y}$ False

41. $g_Y(z) = ((1-\beta) + \beta z)^N$ Scalar $\beta \in [0,1]$

If $g_Y(z)$ is expanded, we would get a bionomial distribution with $n = N$ and $p = \beta$

So the $E[Y] = np = N\beta$

42. As given in the table

Process	Arrival Time	Burst Time	Priority	C.T.	T.A.T.	W.T.
P_1	0	11	2	49	49	38
P_2	5	28	0 (high)	33	28	0
P_3	12	2	3	51	39	37
P_4	2	10	1	40	38	28
P_5	9	16	4	67	58	42
					Total	145

P_1	P_4	P_2	P_4	P_1	P_3	P_5

0 2 5 33 40 49 51 67

Hence

$$\text{Average waiting time} = \frac{145}{5} = 29 \text{ Ms}$$

43. From the given question:

MM size = 2^{32} B, Block size = 32 B

Direct CM

lines = 512

Address format is (32 bit)

Tag	LO	WO
18 bit	$\log_2 512$ = 9 bit	$\log_2 32$ = 5 bit

Hence Tag field = 18

44. Transmission time is ratio of Data size to Bandwidth

$$\text{Transmission time} = \frac{\text{Data size}}{\text{Bandwidth}}$$

$$= \frac{50000 \times 8 \text{ bits}}{10^6 \text{ bits/sec}}$$

$$= 400 \text{ m sec}$$

Also

$$\text{Propagation time} = \frac{\text{Distance}}{\text{Velocity}}$$

$$= \frac{10000 \times 10^3 \text{ m}}{2 \times 10^8 \text{ m/sec}}$$

$$= \frac{10^3 \times 10^{-4}}{2}$$

$$= 50 \text{ msec}$$

45. We know that in Poisson distribution representation

$$E(X) = V(X) = \lambda$$

Given $\lambda = 5$

$$E(X) = V(X) = 5$$

We need $E[(X + 2)^2]$

$$= E(X^2 + 4x + 4)$$

$$= E(X^2) + 4E(X + 4)$$

To find $E(X^2)$ we write,

$$V(X) = E(X^2) - (E(X))^2$$

$$5 = E(X^2) - 5^2$$

So, $E(X^2) = 5^2 + 5 = 30$

$$\text{required value} = 30 + 4 \times 5 + 4 = 54$$

46. Here, by question we have

3	5	1	4	6	2
0	1	2	3	4	5

For first for loop

($i = 0$) 5 3 1 4 6 2
($i = 1$) 5 3 1 4 6 2
($i = 2$) 5 3 4 1 6 2
($i = 3$) 5 3 4 6 1 2
($i = 4$) 5 3 4 6 2 1

For second for loop

($i = 5$) 5 3 4 6 2 1
($i = 4$) 5 3 4 6 2 1
($i = 3$) 5 3 6 4 2 1
($i = 2$) 5 6 3 4 2 1
($i = 1$) 6 5 3 4 2 1

Now since done is '0', So for loop will executed again and so.

for first for loop :

($i = 0$) 6 5 3 4 2 1
($i = 1$) 6 5 3 4 2 1
($i = 2$) 6 5 4 3 2 1
($i = 3$) 6 5 4 3 2 1
($i = 4$) 6 5 4 3 2 1

for second for loop :

($i = 5$) 6 5 4 3 2 1
($i = 4$) 6 5 4 3 2 1
($i = 3$) 6 5 4 3 2 1
($i = 2$) 6 5 4 3 2 1
($i = 1$) 6 5 4 3 2 1

Value of done is still '0', hence the for loop will execute again.

First for loop :

This time there will be no change by the for loop. The value of done is '1'. Hence the loop terminates as

6	5	4	3	2	1
0	1	2	3	4	5

The output of the program will be '3'

47. Draw the table

Process	Current Allocation	Maximum Requirement	Remaining Need	Current Available
P1	3	7	4	9 – 7 = 2
P2	1	6	5	5
P3	3	5	2	8
				9

From table

Safe sequence ⇒ P3 → P1 → P2

Safe and Not deadlocked

48. By the given C function

First loop will execute 'n' times and the inner loop will execute $\Theta(n\log n)$ times.

Hence the complexity will be $\Theta(n\log n)$

49. I. Membership of regular language (Decidable)

II. Emptiness of CFL (Decidable)

III. L = E* problem of CFL (Undecidable)

IV. Membership of RE language (Undecidable)

So, only III and IV are undecidable. So correct answer is (*d*).

50. $$f(\lambda) = \lambda^3 - 4\lambda^2 + a\lambda + 30 = 0$$

Given $m = 2$ will be one root of polynomial

So, $2^3 - 4 \times 2^2 + a \times 2 + 30 = 0$

$\Rightarrow 8 - 16 + 2a + 30 = 0$

$\Rightarrow a = -11$ (satisfy the equation)

So, the equation is $\lambda^3 - 4\lambda^2 - 11\lambda + 30 = 0$

Divided polynomials by $(\lambda - 2)$

$$\frac{\lambda^3 - 4\lambda^2 - 11\lambda + 30}{\lambda - 2} = \lambda^2 - 2\lambda - 15$$

roots of $\lambda^2 - 2\lambda - 15 = 0$ are

$$\lambda = \frac{2 \pm \sqrt{4+60}}{2}$$

$$= \frac{2+8}{2} = 5 \text{ and } -3$$

$\lambda_1 = 2$ $\lambda_2 = 5$ $\lambda_3 = 3$ the maximum absolute eigen value is 5.

51. $L_1 = \{a^p \mid p \text{ prime}\}$ is a CSL but not CFL (Prime number checking involve divsion)

$L_2 = \{a^n b^m c^{2m} \mid n \ge 0, m \ge 0\}$ is CFL (one comparision)

$L_3 = \{a^n b^n c^{2n} \mid n \ge 0\}$ is CSL (two comparision)

$L_4 = \{a^n b^n \mid n \ge 1\}$ is a DCFL

I. L_1 is CFL but not regular is false.

II. L_2 is not CFL is false.

III. L_3 is not CFL but recursive is true since every CSL is recursive.

IV. L_4 is DCFL is true.

Only III and IV are true and correct.

52. $T_1 : r_1(X)\, w_1(X)\, r_1(Y)\, w_1(Y)$

$T_2 : r_2(Y)\, w_2(Y)\, r_2(Z)\, w_2(Z)$

(*i*) Number of conflict serializable on $T_1 \to T_2$: 1

$r_1(X)\, w_1(X)\, r_1(Y)\, w_1(Y) r_2(Y)\, w_2(Y)\, r_2(Z) w_2(Z)$

(*ii*) Number of conflict seralizable on $T_2 \to T_1$:53

$S : r_2(Y)\, w_2(Y)\, r_1(Y)\, w_1(Y)$

$r_1(X)\, w_1(X)$ must be before $r_1(Y)$

so that $(r_2(Y)\, w_2(Y))\, (r_1(X)\, w_1(X))$ can place.

$${}^4C_2 = \frac{4!}{2! \times 2!} = 6 \text{ ways}$$

1. $r_2(Y)\, w_2(Y)\, r_1(X)\, w_1(X)\, r_1(Y)\, w_1(Y)$

   $r_2(Z)\, w_2(Z)$ can place in ${}^6C_2 = \frac{6!}{4! \times 2!}$ =15 ways

   Like wise

2. $r_2(Y)\, r_1(X)\, w_1(X)\, w_2(Y)\, r_1(Y)\, w_1(Y)$

   $r_2(Z)\, w_2(Z)$ can place in ${}^4C_2$ = 6 ways

3. $r_2(Y)\, r_1(X)\, w_2(Y)\, w_1(X)\, r_1(Y)\, w_1(Y)$

   $r_2(Z)\, w_2(Z)$ can place in ${}^5C_2$ = 10 ways

4. $r_1(X)\, w_1(X)\, r_2(Y)\, w_2(Y)\, r_1(Y)\, w_1(Y)$

   $r_2(Z)\, w_2(Z)$ can place in ${}^4C_2$ = 6 ways

5. $r_1(X)\, r_2(Y)\, w_2(Y)\, w_1(X)\, r_1(Y)\, w_1(Y)$

   $r_2(Z)\, w_2(Z)$ can place in ${}^5C_2$ = 10 ways

6. $r_1(X)\, r_2(Y)\, w_1(X)\, w_2(Y)\, r_1(Y)\, w_1(Y)$

   $r_2(Z)\, w_2(Z)$ can place in ${}^4C_2$ = 6 ways

So total no of conflict serializable schedules of T_1 and T_2 = 53 +1 = 54 ways

53. Tavg= $H_1T_1 + (1 - H_1)H_2(T_2 + T_1) + (1 - H_1)(1 - H_2) H_3(T_3 + T_2 + T_1) + (1 - H_1)(1 - H_2)(1 - H_3) H_4(T_4 + T_3 + T_2 + T_1)$

Put data

Tavg = $(0.8 \times 2) + (1 - 0.8)\ 0.9 \times (2 + 2) + (1 - 0.8)(1 - 0.9)\ 0.9 \times (8 + 2 + 2) + (1 - 0.8)(1 - 0.9)(1 - 0.9) \times (90 + 8 + 2 + 2)$

$= 1.6 + 0.72 + 0.216 + 0.204 = 2.32 + 0.420$

$= 0.740 = 2.74$ ns

55. Given

Preorder : 12, 8, 6, 2, 7, 9, 10, 16, 15, 19, 17, 20

Inorder: 2, 6, 7, 8, 9, 10, 12, 15, 16, 17, 19, 20

Tree will be, formed as

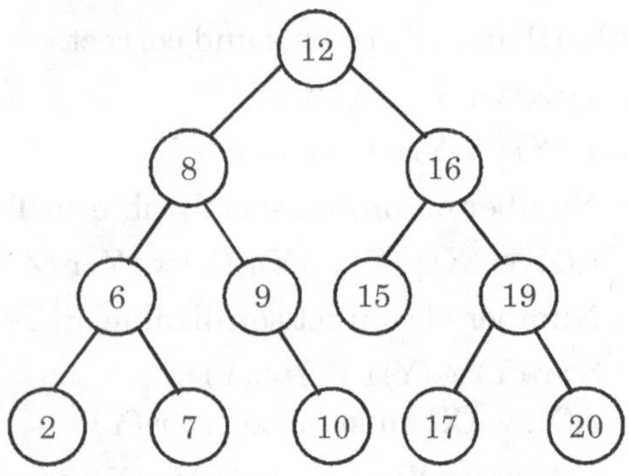

Postorder will be,

2, 7, 6, 10, 9, 8, 15, 17, 20, 19, 16, 12

GENERAL APTITUDE

1. Let number of multiple choice question be 'x'

$\therefore$ Total number of essay type question = $20 - x$

Now according to question

$x \times 3 + (20 - x)11 = 100$

$\therefore \quad 3x + 220 - 11x = 100$

$\therefore \quad 220 - 100 = 8x$

$\therefore \quad x = \frac{120}{8}$

$\therefore \quad x = 15$

$\therefore$ Opation (b) is correct

3. From the given condition of sequence we get following order of building in

X, Z, V, W, Y

Hence 'V' building is in the middle

$\therefore$ Option (a) is correct

5. Saturn is bright enough to be seen on a clear night with the naked eye.

$\therefore$ Option (b) is correct

2. Aversion means a strong dislike or dinclination. Hence aversion is synonyms of dislike.

Aversion means giving of light which is synonym of radiant plunder means loot while yielding and resistant are not synonyms of each other.

$\therefore$ Option (d) is correct.

4. $n(R) = 3$

$n(G) = 4$

$n(B) = 3$

Probability that 2 socks choosen are of both Red or Both Green or Both blue

$$\text{Same colour} = \frac{3}{10} \times \frac{2}{9} + \frac{4}{10} \times \frac{3}{9} + \frac{3}{10} \times \frac{2}{9}$$

$$= \frac{6}{90} + \frac{12}{90} + \frac{6}{10} = \frac{24}{90} = \frac{4}{15}$$

$\therefore$ Option (d) is correct.

6. The author's belief that ideology is not as important as literature is revealed by the word 'urgent' in above paragraph.

$\therefore$ Option (c) is correct.

8. $e^x + 0.5x^2 - 2 = 0$

Differention w.r.t to 'x' we get

$e^x + x = 0$

$\therefore$ Hence 'x' has total number of root which lies in the range [– 5,5] is '2'.

SOLVED PAPER - 2018

INSTRUCTIONS

1. Total of 65 questions carrying 100 marks, out of which 10 questions carrying a total of 15 marks are in General Aptitude (GA)
2. The Engineering Mathematics will carry around **15% of the total marks,** the General Aptitude section will carry **15% of the total marks** and the **remaining 70% of the total marks.**
3. **Types of Questions**
   (*a*) Multiple Choice Questions (MCQ) carrying 1 or 2 marks each in all papers and sections. These questions are objective in nature, and each will have a choice of four options, out of which the candidate has to mark the correct answer(s).
   (*b*) Numerical Answer Questions of 1 or 2 marks each in all papers and sections. For these questions the answer is a real number, to be entered by the candidate using the virtual keypad. No choices will be shown for these type of questions.
4. For **1-mark** multiple-choice questions, **1/3 marks** will be deducted for a wrong answer. Likewise, for **2-marks** multiple-choice questions, **2/3** marks will be deducted for a wrong answer. There is no negative marking for numerical answer type questions.

Chapter-Wise Analysis

#	Chapters	Marks		
		1	2	Total
1	General Aptitude	5	5	15
2	Engineering Mathematics	5	7	19
3	Theory of Computation	1	2	5
4	Digital Logic	2	1	4
5	Computer Organization & Architecture	3	4	11
6	Programming & Data Structures	4	4	12
7	Algorithm	1	3	7

#	Chapters	Marks		
		1	2	Total
8	Compiler Design	2	2	6
9	Operating System	4	3	10
10	Data Bases	0	2	4
11	Computer Networks	3	2	7
12	*Software Engineering	0	0	0
13	*Web Technology	0	0	0

GENERAL APTITUDE

1. "From where are they bringing their books? ______ bringing ______ books from ______."

The words that best fill the blanks in the above sentence are

(*a*) Their, they're, there

(*b*) They're, their, there

(*c*) There, their, they're

(*d*) They're, there, there

2. "A ______ investigation can sometimes yield new facts, but typically organized ones are more successful."

The word that best fills the blank in the above sentence is

(*a*) meandering (*b*) timely

(*c*) consistent (*d*) systematic

3. The area of a square is d. What is the area of the circle which has the diagonal of the square as its diameter?

(*a*) πd (*b*) πd^2

(*c*) $\frac{1}{4}\pi d^2$ (*d*) $\frac{1}{2}\pi d$

4. What would be the smallest natural number which when divided either by 20 or by 42 or by 76 leaves a remainder of 7 in each case?

(*a*) 3047 (*b*) 6047

(*c*) 7987 (*d*) 63847

5. What is the missing number in the following sequence?

2, 12, 60, 240, 720, 1440, ______, 0

(*a*) 2880 (*b*) 1440

(*c*) 720 (*d*) 0

6. In appreciation of the social improvements completed in a town, a wealthy philanthropist decided to gift Rs. 750 to each male senior citizen in the town and Rs. 1000 to each female senior citizen. Altogether, there were 300 senior citizens eligible for this gift. However, only 8/9th of the eligible men and 2/3rd of the eligible women claimed the gift. How much money (in Rupees) did the philanthropist give away in total?

(*a*) 1,50,000 (*b*) 2,00,000

(*c*) 1,75,000 (*d*) 1,51,000

7. In $pqr \neq 0$ and $p^{-x} = \frac{1}{q}, q^{-y} = \frac{1}{r}, r^{-z} = \frac{1}{p}$, what is the value of the product xyz?

(*a*) -1 (*b*) $\frac{1}{pqr}$

(*c*) 1 (*d*) pqr

8. In a party, 60% of the invited guests are male and 40% are female. If 80% of the invited guests attended the party and if all the invited female guests attended, what would be the ratio of males of females among the attendees in the party?

(*a*) 2 : 3 (*b*) 1 : 1

(*c*) 3 : 2 (*d*) 2 : 1

9. In the figure below, ∠DEC + ∠BFC is equal to ___.

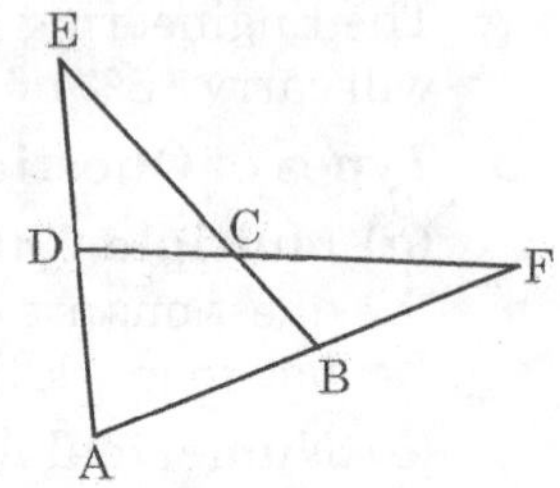

(*a*) ∠BCD − ∠BAD

(*b*) ∠BAD + ∠BCF

(*c*) ∠BAD + ∠BCD

(*d*) ∠CBA + ∠ADC

10. A six sided unbiased die with four green faces and two red faces is rolled seven times. Which of the following combinations is the most likely outcome of the experiment?

(*a*) Three green faces and four red faces.

(*b*) Four green faces and three red faces.

(*c*) Five green faces and two red faces.

(*d*) Six green faces and one red face.

COMPUTER SCIENCE

1. Which one of the following is a closed form expression for the generating function of the sequence $\{a_n\}$, where $a_n = 2n + 3$ for all $n = 0, 1, 2, ...$?

(*a*) $\frac{3}{(\ -\ )^2}$ (*b*) $\frac{3x}{(\ -\ )^2}$

(*c*) $\frac{2-x}{(\ -\ )^2}$ (*d*) $\frac{3-x}{(\ -\ )^2}$

2. Consider the following C program:

```
#include <stdio.h>
struct ournode {
    char x, y, z;
};
int main () {
    struct ournode p = {'1', '0', 'a' + 2};
    struct ournode *p = &q;
    printf("%c, %c", *((char*) q + 1), *((char*) q + 2));
    return 0;
}
```

The output of this program is:

(*a*) 0, c (*b*) 0, a + 2

(*c*) '0', 'a + 2' (*d*) '0', 'c'

3. A queue is implemented using a non-circular singly linked list. The queue has a head pointer and tail pointer, as shown in the figure. Let n denote of number of nodes in the queue. Let enqueue be implemented by inserting a new node at the head and dequeue be implemented by deletion of a node from the tail.

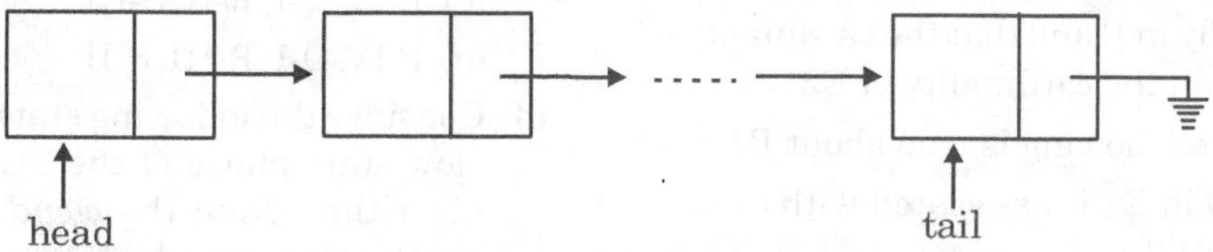

Which one of the following is the time complexity of the most time-efficient implementation of enqueue and dequeue, respectively, for this data structure?

(*a*) $\theta(1), \theta(1)$ (*b*) $\theta(1), \theta(n)$

(*c*) $\theta(n), \theta(1)$ (*d*) $\theta(n), \theta(n)$

4. Let $\oplus$ and $\odot$ denote the Exclusive OR and Exclusive NOR operations, respectively. Which one of the following is NOT CORRECT?

(*a*) $\overline{P \oplus Q} = P \odot Q$

(*b*) $\bar{P} \oplus Q = P \odot Q$

(*c*) $\bar{P} \oplus \bar{Q} = PQ\oplus$

(*d*) $(P \oplus \bar{P}) \oplus Q = (P \odot \bar{P}) \odot \bar{Q}$

5. Consider the following processor design characteristics:

I. Register-to-register arithmetic operations only.

II. Fixed-length instruction format.

III. Hardwired control unit.

Which of the characteristics above are used in the design of a RISC processor?

(*a*) I and II only (*b*) II and III only

(*c*) I and III only (*d*) I, II and III

6. Let N be an NFA with n states, Let k be the number of states of a minimal DFA which is equivalent to N. Which one of the following is necessarily true?

(*a*) $k \geq 2^n$ (*b*) $k \geq n$

(*c*) $k \leq n^2$ (*d*) $k \leq 2^n$

7. The set of all recursively enumerable language is

(*a*) closed under complementation

(*b*) closed under intersection

(*c*) a subset of the set of all recursive languages

(*d*) an uncountable set

8. Which one of the following statements is FALSE?

(*a*) Context-free grammar can be used to specify both lexical and syntax rules.

(*b*) Type checking is done before parsing.

(*c*) High-level language programs can be translated to different intermediate Representations.

(*d*) Arguments to a function can be passed using the program stack.

9. The following are some events that occur after a device controller issues an interrupt while process L is under execution.

(P) The processor pushes the process status of L onto the control stack.

(Q) The processor finishes the execution of the current instruction.

(R) The processor executes the interrupt service routine.

(S) The processor pops the process status of L from the control stack.

(T) The processor loads the new PC value based on the interrupt.

Which one of the following is the correct order in which the events above occur?

(*a*) QPTRS (*b*) PTRSQ

(*c*) TRPQS (*d*) QTPRS

10. Consider a process executing on an operating system that uses demand paging. The average time for a memory access in the system is M units if the corresponding memory page is available in memory and D units if the memory access causes a page fault. It has been experimentally measured that the average time taken for a memory access in the process is X units.

Which one of the following is the correct expression for the page fault rate experienced by the process?

(*a*) (D – M)/(X – M)

(*b*) (X – M)/(D – M)

(*c*) (D – X)/(D – M)

(*d*) (X – M)/(D – X)

11. In an Entity-Relationship (ER) model, suppose R is a many-to-one relationship from entity set E1 to entity set E2. Assume that E1 and E2 participate totally in R and that the cardinality of E1 is greater than the cardinality of E2.

Which one of the following is true about R?

(*a*) Every entity in E1 is associated with exactly one entity in E2.

(*b*) Some entity in E1 is associated with more than one entity in E2.

(*c*) Every entity in E2 is associated with exactly one entity in E1.

(*d*) Every entity in E2 is associated with at most one entity in E1.

12. Consider the following two tables and four queries in SQL.

Book (isbn, bname), Stock (isbn, copies)

Query 1:

SELECT B.isbn, S copies
FROM Book B INNER JOIN Stock S
ON B. isbn = S.isbn;

Query 2:

SELECT B. isbn, S.copies
FROM Book B LEFT OUTER JOIN Stock S
ON B. isbn = S.isbn;

Query 3:

SELECT B. isbn, S.copies
FROM Book B RIGHT OUTER JOIN Stock S
ON B. isbn = S.isbn;

Query 4:

SELECT B. isbn, S.copies
FROM Book B FULL OUTER JOIN Stock S
ON B. isbn = S.isbn;

Which one of the queries above is certain to have an output that is superset of the outputs of the other three queries?

(*a*) Query 1 (*b*) Query 2

(*c*) Query 3 (*d*) Query 4

13. Match the following:

Field	Length in bits
P. UDP Header's Port Number	I. 48
Q. Ethernet MAC Address	II. 8
R. IPv6 Next Header	III. 32
S. TCP Header's Sequence Number	IV. 16

(*a*) P-III, Q-IV, R-II, S-I

(*b*) P-II, Q-I, R-IV, S-III

(*c*) P-IV, Q-I, R-II, S-III

(*d*) P-IV, Q-I, R-III, S-II

14. Consider the following statements regarding the slow start phase of the TCP congestion control algorithm. Note the *cwnd* stands for the TCP congestion window and MSS denotes the Maximum Segment Size.

(*i*) The *cwnd* increases by 2 MSS on every successful acknowledgment.

(*ii*) The *cwnd* approximately doubles on every successful acknowledgment.

(*iii*) The *cwnd* increases by 1 MSS every round trip time.

(*iv*) The *cwnd* approximately doubles every round trip time.

Which one of the following is correct?

(*a*) Only (*ii*) and (*iii*) are true

(*b*) Only (*i*) and (*iii*) are true

(*c*) Only (*iv*) is true

(*d*) Only (*i*) and (*iv*) are true

15. Two people. P and Q, decide to independently roll two identical dice, each with 6 faces, Numbered 1 to 6. The person with the lower number wins. In case of a tie, they roll the dice repeatedly until there is no tie. Define a trial a throw of the dice by P and Q, Assume that all 6 numbers on each dice are equi-probable and that all trials are independent. The probability (rounded to 3 decimal places) that one of them wins on the third trial is _____.

16. The value of $\int_0^{\pi/4} x\cos(\quad)\,dx$ correct to three decimal places (assuming that $\pi = 3.14$) is _____.

17. Consider a matrix $A = uv^T$ where $u = \begin{pmatrix} \\ \end{pmatrix}$ $\begin{pmatrix} \\ \end{pmatrix}$. Note that v^T denotes the transpose of v. The largest eigenvalue of A is _____.

18. The chromatic number of the following graph is _____.

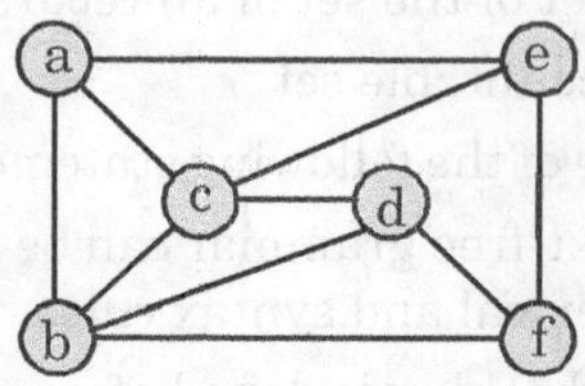

19. Let G be a finite group on 84 elements. The size of a largest possible proper subgroup of G is _____.

20. The post order traversal of a binary tree is 8, 9, 6, 7, 4, 5, 2, 3, 1. The inorder traversal of the same tree is 8, 6, 9, 4, 7, 2, 5, 1, 3. The height of a tree is the length of the longest path from the root to any leaf. The height of the binary tree above is ______.

21. Consider the following C program:

```
#include <stdio.h>
int counter = 0;
int calc (int a, int b) {
    int c;
    counter ++;
    if (b = = 3) return (a*a*a);
    else {
        c = calc (a b/3);
        return (c*c*c);
    }
}
int main ( ) {
    calc(4, 81);
    print("%%d", counter);
}
```

The output of this program is ______.

22. Consider the sequential circuit shown in the figure, where both flip-flops used are positive edge-triggered D flip-flops.

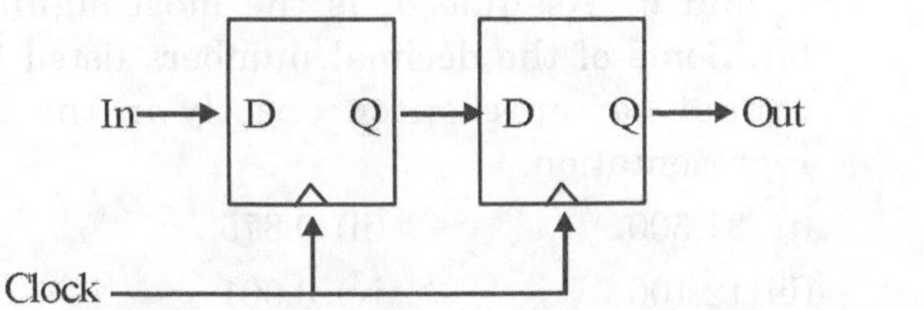

The number of states in the state transition diagram of the circuit that have a transition back to the same state on some value of "in" is ______.

23. A 32-bit wide main memory unit with a capacity of 1 GB is built using 256 M × 4 bit- DRAM chips. The number of rows of memory cells in the DRAM chip is 2^{14}. The time taken to perform one refresh operation is 50 nanoseconds. The refresh period is 2 milliseconds. The percentage (rounded to the closest integer) of the time available for performing the memory read/write operations in the main memory unit is ______.

24. Consider a system with 3 processes that share 4 instance of the same resource type. Each process can request a maximum of K instances. Resource instances can be requested and released only one at a time. The largest value of K that will always avoid deadlock is ______.

25. Consider a long-lived TCP session with an end-to-end bandwidth of 1 Gbps (= 10^9 bits-per-second). The session starts with a sequence number of 1234. The minimum time (in seconds, rounded to the closest integer) before this sequence number can be used again is ______.

26. Consider a matrix P whose only eigenvectors are the multiples of $\begin{bmatrix} \\ \end{bmatrix}$.

Consider the following statements:

I. P does not have an inverse.

II. P has a repeated eigenvalue.

III. P cannot be diagonalized.

Which one of the following options is correct?

(*a*) Only I and III are necessarily true

(*b*) Only II is necessarily true

(*c*) Only I and II are necessarily true

(*d*) Only II and III are necessarily true

27. Let N be the set of natural numbers. Consider the following sets:

P. Set of rational numbers (positive and negative).

Q. Set of functions from {0, 1} to N.

R. Set of functions from N to {0, 1}.

S. Set of finite subsets of N.

Which of the sets above are countable?

(*a*) Q and S only

(*b*) P and S only

(*c*) P and R only

(*d*) P, Q and S only

28. Consider the first-order logic sentence

$$\varphi \equiv \exists\ \exists\ \exists\ \forall\ \forall\ \ \forall\ \forall\ \psi(s,t,u,v,w,x,y)$$

where $\psi(s, t, u, v, w, x, y)$ is a quantifier-free first-order logic formula using only predicate symbols and possibly equality, but no function symbols. Suppose φ has a model with a universe containing 7 elements.

Which one of the following statements is necessarily true?

(*a*) There exists at least one model of φ with universe of size less than or equal to 3.

(*b*) There exists no model of φ with universe of size less than or equal to 3.

(*c*) There exists no model of φ with universe of size greater than 7.

(*d*) Every model of φ has a universe of size equal to 7.

29. Consider the following C program:

```
#include <stdio.h>
void fun1 (char *s1, char *s2) {
    char *tmp;
    tmp = s1;
    s1 = s2;
    s2 = tmp;
}
void fun2 (char **s1, char **s2) {
    char *tmp;
    tmp = *s1;
    *s1 = *s2;
    *s2 = tmp;
}
int main () {
    char *str 1 = "Hi", *str2 = "Bye";
    fun1 (str1, str2); print f("%s %s, str1, str2);
    fun2 (&str1, &str2); print f("%s %s, str1, str2);
    return 0;
}
```

The output of the program above is

(*a*) Hi Bye Bye Hi (*b*) Hi Bye Hi Bye

(*c*) Bye Hi Hi Bye (*d*) Bye Hi Bye Hi

30. Let G be a simple undirected graph. Let T_D be a depth first search tree of G. Let T_B be a breadth first search tree of G. Consider the following statements:

I. No edge of G is a cross edge with respect to T_D. (A cross edge in G is between two nodes neither of which is an ancestor of the other in T_D).

II. For every edge (u, v) of G, if u is at depth i and v is at depth j in T_B, then $|i - j| = 1$.

Which of the statements above must necessarily be true?

(*a*) I only (*b*) II only

(*c*) Both I and II (*d*) Neither I nor II

31. Assume that multiplying a matrix G_1 of dimension p × q with another matrix G_2 of of dimension q × r requires *pqr* scalar multiplications. Computing the product of *n* matrices $G_1G_2G_3...G_n$ can be done by parenthesizing in different ways. Define $G_i\ G_{i+1}$ as an explicitly computed pair for a given paranthesization if they are directly multiplied. For example, in the matrix multiplication chain $G_1G_2G_3G_4G_5G_6$ using parenthesization $(G_1(G_2G_3))(G_4(G_5G_6))$. G_2G_3 and G_5G_6 are the only explicitly computed pairs.

Consider a matrix multiplication chain $F_1F_2F_3F_4F_5$, where matrices F_1, F_2, F_3, F_4 and F_5 are of dimensions 2 × 25, 25 × 3, 3 × 16, 16 × 1 and 1 × 1000, respectively. In the parenthesization of $F_1F_2F_3F_4F_5$ that minimizes the total number of scalar multiplications, the explicitly computed pairs is/are

(*a*) F_1F_2 and F_3F_4 only (*b*) F_2F_3 only

(*c*) F_3F_4 only (*d*) F_1F_2 and F_4F_5 only

32. Consider the following C code. Assume that unsigned long int type length is 64 bits.

```
unsigned long int fun (unsigned long int n) {
    unsigned long int i, j = 0, sum = 0;
    for (i = n; i > 1; i = i/2) j++;
    for (; j > 1; j = j/2) sum ++;
    return (sum);
}
```

The value returned when call fun with the input 2^{40} is

(*a*) 4 (*b*) 5

(*c*) 6 (*d*) 40

33. Consider the unsigned 8-bit fixed point binary number representation below:

$$b_7\, b_6\, b_5\, b_4\, b_3 \,.\, b_2\, b_1\, b_0$$

where the position of the binary points is between b_3 and b_2. Assume b_7 is the most significant bit. Some of the decimal numbers listed below cannot be represented exactly in the above representation:

(i) 31.500 (ii) 0.875

(iii) 12.100 (iv) 3.001

Which one of the following statements is true?

(*a*) None of (i), (ii), (iii), (iv) can be exactly represented.

(*b*) Only (ii) cannot be exactly represented.

(*c*) Only (iii) and (iv) cannot be exactly represented.

(*d*) Only (i) and (ii) cannot be exactly represented.

34. The size of the physical address space of a processor is 2^P bytes. The word length is 2^W bytes. The capacity of cache memory is 2^N bytes, The size of each cache block is 2^M words. For a K-way set-associative cache memory, the length (in number of bits of the tag field is

(*a*) $P - N - \log_2 K$

(*b*) $P - N + \log_2 K$

(*c*) $P - N - M - W - \log_2 K$

(*d*) $P - N - M - W + \log_2 K$

35. Consider the following languages:

I. $\{a^m b^n c^p d^q \mid m + p = n + q$, where $m, n, p, q \geq 0\}$

II. $\{a^m b^n c^p d^q \mid m = n$ and $p = q$, where $m, n, p, q \geq 0\}$

III. $\{a^m b^n c^p d^q \mid m = n = p$ and $p \neq q$, where $m, n, p, q \geq 0\}$

IV. $\{a^m b^n c^p d^q \mid mn = p + q$, where $m, n, p, q \geq 0\}$

Which of the language above are context-free?

(*a*) I and IV only (*b*) I and II only

(*c*) II and III only (*d*) II and IV only

36. Consider the following L(G) denotes the language generated by a grammar G. L(M) denotes the language accepted by a machine M.

I. For an unrestricted grammar G and a string w, whether $w \in$ L(G).

II. Given a Turing Machine M, whether L(M) is regular.

III. Given two grammars G_1 and G_2, whether $L(G_1) = L(G_2)$.

IV. Given an NFAN, whether there is a deterministic PDA P such that N and P accept the same language.

Which one of the following statements is correct?

(*a*) Only I and II are undecidable

(*b*) Only III is undecidable

(*c*) Only II and IV are undecidable

(*d*) Only I, II and III are undecidable

37. A lexical analyzer uses the following patterns to recognize three tokens T_1, T_2 and T_3 over the alphabet {a, b, c}.

T_1 : a? (b | c)*a

T_2 : b? (a | c)*b

T_3 : c? (b | a)*c

Note that 'x?' means 0 or 1 occurrence of the symbol x. Note also that the analyzer outputs the token that matches the longest possible prefix.

If the string bbaacabc is processed by the analyzer, which one of the following is the sequence of tokens it outputs?

(*a*) $T_1T_2T_3$ (*b*) $T_1T_1T_3$

(*c*) $T_2T_1T_3$ (*d*) T_3T_3

38. Consider the following parse tree for the expression a#bcd#e#f, involving two binary operators $ and #.

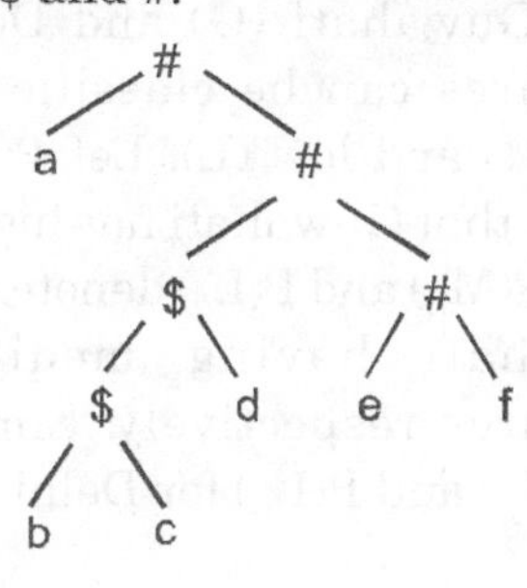

Which one of the following is correct for the given parse tree?

(*a*) $ has higher precedence and is left associative; # is right associative

(*b*) # has higher precedence and is left associative; $ is right associative

(*c*) $ has higher precedence and is left associative; # is left associative

(*d*) # has higher precedence and is right associative; $ is left associative

39. In a system, there are three types of resources: E, F and G. Four processes P_0, P_1, P_2 and P_3 execute concurrently. At the outset, the processes have declared their maximum resource requirements using a matrix named Max as given below. For example Max[P_2,F] is the maximum number of instances of F that P_2 would require. The number of instances of the resources allocated to the various processes at any given state is given by a matrix named Allocation.

Consider a state of the system with the Allocation matrix as shown below and in which 3 instances of E and 3 instances of F are the only resources available.

Allocation			
	E	F	G
P_0	1	0	1
P_1	1	1	2
P_2	1	0	3
P_3	2	0	0

Max			
	E	F	G
P_0	4	3	1
P_1	2	1	4
P_2	1	3	3
P_3	5	4	1

From the perspective of deadlock avoidance, which one of the following is true?

(*a*) The system is in safe state.

(*b*) The system is not in safe state, but would be safe if one more instance of E were available.

(*c*) The system is not in safe state, but would be safe if one more instance of F were available.

(*d*) The system is not in safe state, but would safe if one more instance of G were available.

40. Consider the following solution to the producer-consumer synchronization problem. The shared buffer size is N. Three semaphores empty, full and mutex are defined with respective initial values of 0, N and 1. Semaphore empty denotes the number of available slots in the buffer, for the consumer to read from. Semaphore full denotes the number of available slots in the buffer, for the producer to write to. The placeholder variables, denoted by P, Q, R and S, in the code below can be assigned either empty or full. The valid semaphore operations are: wait ( ) and signal ( ).

Producer	**Consumer**

do {
  wait (P);
  wait (mutex);
  //Add item to buffer
  signal (mutex);
  signal (Q);
} while (1);
	do {
	  wait (R);
	  wait (mutex);
	  //Consume item from buffer
	  signal (mutex);
	  signal (S);
	} while (1);

Which one of the following assignment to P, Q, R and S will yield the correct solution?

(*a*) P : full, Q : full, R: empty, S: empty
(*b*) P : empty, Q : empty, R: full, S: full
(*c*) P : full, Q : empty, R: empty, S: full
(*d*) P : empty, Q : full, R: full, S: empty

41. Consider the relations $r(A, B)$ and $s(B, C)$, where $s.B$ is a primary key and $r.B$ is a foreign key referencing $s.B$. Consider the query

$Q : r \bowtie (\sigma_{B<5}(s))$

Let LOJ denote the natural left outer-join operation. Assume that r and s contain no null values.

Which one of the following queries is not equivalent to Q?

(*a*) $\sigma_{B<5}(r \bowtie s)$
(*b*) $\sigma_{B<5}(r \text{LOJ } s)$
(*c*) $r\text{LOJ}(\sigma_{B<5}(S))$
(*d*) $\sigma_{B<5}(r)$ LOJ s

42. Consider the following relational schemas. For each schema, all non-trivial functional dependencies are listed. The underlined attributes are the respective primary keys.

Schema I: Registration (<u>rollno</u>, courses)
Field 'courses' is a set-valued attribute containing the set of courses a student has registered for.
Non-trivial functions dependency:
rollno → courses

Schema II: Registration (<u>rollno</u>, courseid, email)
Non-trivial functional dependencies.
rollno, courseid → email
email → rollno

Schema III: Registration (<u>rollno</u>, <u>courseid</u>, marks, grade)
Non-trivial functional dependencies.
rollno, courseid → marks, grade
marks → grade

Schema IV: Registration (<u>rollno</u>, <u>*courseid*</u>, credit)
Non-trivial functional dependencies.
rollno, courseid → credit
courseid → credit

Which one of the relational schemas above is in 3NF but not in BCNF?

(*a*) Schema I
(*b*) Schema II
(*c*) Schema III
(*d*) Schema IV

43. Let G be a graph with 100! vertices, with each vertex labelled by a distinct permutation of the numbers 1, 2, ... 100. There is an edge between vertices u and v if and only if the label of u can be obtained by swapping two adjacent numbers in the label of v. Let y denote the degree of a vertex in G and z denote the number of connected components is G.

Then, $y + 10z$ = ______.

44. Consider Guwahati (G) and Delhi (D) whose temperatures can be classified as high (H), medium (M) and low (L). Let $P(H_G)$ denote the probability that Guwahati has high temperature. Similarly, $P(M_G)$ and $P(L_G)$ denotes the probability of Guwahati having medium and low temperatures respectively. Similarly, we use $P(H_D)$, $P(M_D)$ and $P(L_D)$ for Delhi.

The following table gives the conditional probabilities for Delhi's temperature given Guwahati's temperature.

	H_D	M_D	L_D
M_G	0.40	0.48	0.12
M_G	0.10	0.65	0.25
L_G	0.01	0.50	0.49

Consider the first row in the table above. The first entry denotes that if Guwahati has high temperature (H_G) then the probability of Delhi also having a high temperature (H_D) is 0.40; i.e, $P(H_D \mid H_G) = 0.40$. Similarly, the next two entries are $P(M_D \mid H_G) = 0.48$ and $P(L_D \mid H_G) = 0.12$. Similarly for the other rows.

If it is known that $P(H_G) = 0.2$, $P(M_G) = 0.5$ and $P(L_G) = 0.3$, then the probability (correct to two decimal places) that Guwahati has high temperature given that Delhi has high temperature is ______.

45. Consider the following program written in pseudo-code. Assume that *x* and *y* are integers:

```
Count (x, y) {
    if (y ! = 1) {
        if (x ! = 1) {
            print ("*");
            Count (x/2, y);
        }
        else {
            y = y – 1;
            Count (1024, y);
        }
    }
}
```

The number of times that the print statement is executed by the call Count (1024, 1024) is _____.

46. The number of possible min-heaps containing each value from {1, 2, 3, 4, 5, 6, 7} exactly once is _____.

47. Consider the following undirected graph G:

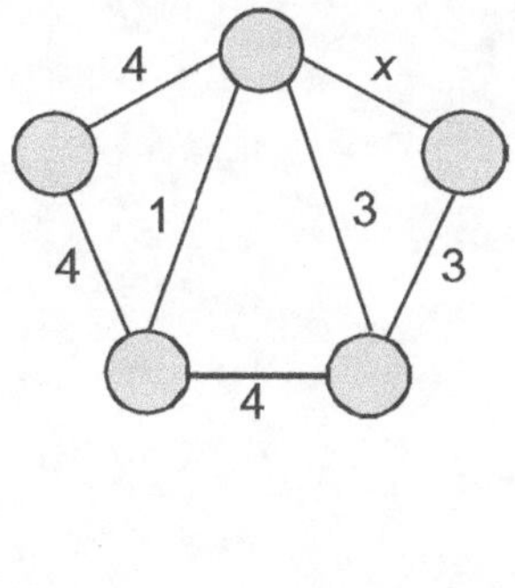

Choose a value of *x* that will maximize the number of minimum weight spanning trees (MWSTs) of G. The number of MWSTs of G for this value of *x* is _____.

48. Consider the weights and values of items listed below. Note that there is only one unit of each item.

Item Number	Weight in (Kgs)	Value in(Rupees)
1	10	60
2	7	28
3	4	20
4	2	24

The task is to pick subset of these items such that their total weight is not more than 11 Kgs and their total value is maximized. Moreover, no item may be split. The total value of items picked by an optimal algorithm is denoted by V_{opt}. A greedy algorithm sorts the items by their value-to-weight ratios in descending order and packs them greedily, starting from the first item in the ordered list. The total value of items picked by the greedy algorithm is denoted by V_{greedy}.

The value of $V_{opt} - V_{greedy}$ is ______.

49. Consider the minterm list form of a Boolean function F given below:

$F(P, Q, R, S) = \Sigma m(0, 2, 5, 7, 9, 11) + d(3, 8, 10, 12, 14)$

Here, *m* denotes a minterm and *d* denotes a don't care term. The number of essential prime implicants of the function F is _____.

50. The instruction pipeline of a RISC processor has the following stages. Instruction Fetch (IF), Instruction Decode (ID), Operand Fetch (OF), Perform Operation (PO) and Writeback (WB). The IF, ID, OF and WB stages take 1 clock cycle each for every instruction. Consider a sequence of 100 instructions. In the PO stage, 40 instructions take 3 clock cycles each, 35 instructions take 2 clock cycles each, and the remaining 25 instructions take 1 clock cycle each. Assume that there are no data hazards and no control hazards. The number of clock cycles required for completion of execution of the sequence of instructions is _____.

51. A processor has 16 integer registers (R0, R1, ..., R15) and 64 floating point registers (F0, F1, ..., F63). It uses a 2-byte instruction format. There are four categories of instructions: Type-1, Type-2, Type-3 and Type-4. Type-1 category consists of four instructions, each with 3 integer register operands (3Rs). Type-2 category consists of eight instructions, each with 2 floating point register operands (2F2). Type-3 category consists of fourteen instructions, each with one integer register operand and one floating point register operand (1R + 1F). Type-4 category consists of N instructions, each with a floating point register operand (IF).

The maximum value of N is ______.

52. Given a language L, define L^i as follows:

$$L^0 = \{\in\}$$

$$L^i = L^{i-1}.\, L \text{ for all } i > 0$$

The order of a language L is defined as the smallest k such that $L^k = L^{k+1}$.

Consider the language L_1 (over alphabet 0) accepted by the following automation.

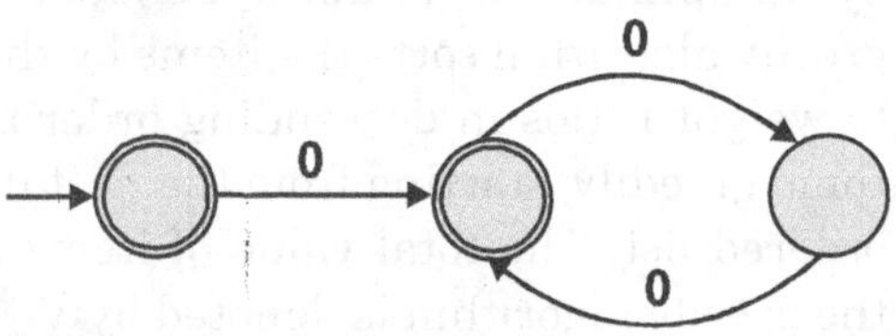

The order of L_1 is ______.

53. Consider a storage disk with 4 platters (numbered as 0, 1, 2 and 3), 200 cylinders (numbered as 0, 1, ..., 199) and 256 sectors per track (numbered as 0, 1, ..., 255). The following 6 disk requests of the form [sector number, cylinder number, platter number] are received by the disk controller at the same time:

[120, 72, 2], [180, 134, 1], [60, 20, 0], [212, 86, 3,], 56, 116, 2], [118, 16, 1]

Currently the head is positioned at sector number 100 of cylinder 80 and is moving towards higher cylinder numbers. The average power dissipation in moving the head over 100 cylinders is 20 milliwatts and for reversing the direction of the head movement once is 15 milliwatts. Power dissipation associated with rotational latency and switching of head between different platters is negligible.

The total power consumption in milliwatts to satisfy all of the above disk requests using the Shortest Seek Time First scheduling algorithm is ______.

54. Consider an IP packet with a length of 4500 bytes that includes a 20-byte IPv4 header and a 40-byte TCP header. The packet is forwarded to an IPv4 router that supports a Maximum Transmission Unit (MTU) of 600 bytes. Assume that the length of the IP header in all the outgoing fragments of this packet is 20 bytes. Assume that the fragmentation offset value stored in the first fragment is 0.

The fragmentation offset value stored in the third fragment is ______.

55. Consider a simple communication system where multiple nodes are connected by a shared broadcast medium (like Ethernet or wireless). The nodes in the system use the following carrier-sense based medium access protocol. A node that receives a packet to transmit will carrier-sense the medium for 5 units of time. If the node does not detect any other transmission in this duration, it starts transmitting its packet in the next time unit. If the node detects another transmission, it waits until this other transmission finishes, and then begins to carrier-sense for 5 time units again. Once they start to transmit, nodes do not perform any collision detection and continue transmission even if a collision occurs. All transmissions last for 20 units of time. Assume that the transmission signal travels at the speed of 10 meters per unit time in the medium. Assume that the system has two nodes P and Q, located at a distance d meters from each other. P starts transmitting a packet at time t = 0 after successfully completing its carrier-sense phase. Node Q has a packet to transmit at time t = 0 and begins to carrier-sense the medium.

The maximum distance d(in meters, rounded to the closest integer) that allows Q to successfully avoid a collision between its proposed transmission and P's ongoing transmission is ______.

ANSWERS

General Aptitude (GA)

1. (*b*)	**2.** (*a*)	**3.** (*d*)	**4.** (*c*)	**5.** (*b*)	**6.** (*b*)	**7.** (*c*)	**8.** (*b*)	**9.** (*a*)	**10.** (*c*)

Technical Section

1. (*d*)	**2.** (*a*)	**3.** (*b*)	**4.** (*d*)	**5.** (*d*)	**6.** (*d*)	**7.** (*b*)
8. (*b*)	**9.** (*a*)	**10.** (*b*)	**11.** (*a*)	**12.** (*d*)	**13.** (*c*)	**14.** (*c*)
15. 0.023	**16.** 0.289	**17.** 3	**18.** (3)	**19.** 42	**20.** 4	**21.** 4
22. 2	**23.** (60)	**24.** 2	**25.** 34	**26.** (*d*)	**27.** (*d*)	**28.** (*a*)
29. (*a*)	**30.** (*a*)	**31.** (*c*)	**32.** (*b*)	**33.** (*c*)	**34.** (*b*)	**35.** (*b*)
36. (*d*)	**37.** (*d*)	**38.** (*a*)	**39.** (*a*)	**40.** (*c*)	**41.** (*c*)	**42.** (*b*)
43. 109	**44.** 0.60	**45.** 10230	**46.** 80	**47.** 4	**48.** 16	**49.** 3
50. 219	**51.** 32	**52.** 2	**53.** 85	**54.** 144	**55.** 50	

EXPLANATIONS

GENERAL APTITUDE

1. They're used for pointing group.
Their is pointing people.
There is used for place.

2. Meandering : wandering aimlessly/indirect.

3.

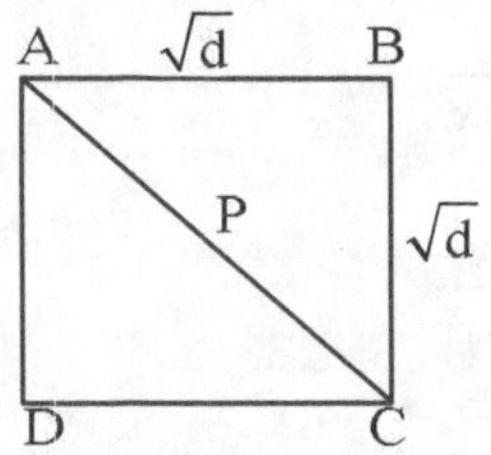

Area of square = d

Side one side of square = $\sqrt{d}$

Now Diagonal of square (AC) = $\sqrt{d + [illegible]} = \sqrt{2d}$

Now, Area of circle = πr^2

$$= \pi\left([illegible] \right)^2 \left(\because r = [illegible] \right)$$

$$= \pi\frac{d}{2}$$

$$= \frac{1}{2}\pi d$$

4. Number is divided by either by 20 or 42 or by 76
K × LCM (20, 42, 76) + constant difference
= 7890 K + 7 (K is natural number)
Least number will be 7890 + 7 = 7897.

5. 2, 12, 60, 240, 720, 1440, 1440, 0

(2 × 6), (12 × [illegible]), ([illegible] × [illegible]), ([illegible] × [illegible]), ([illegible] × 2), (1440 × 1), (1440 × 0)

−1, −1, −1, −1, −1, −1

So, 1440 must be answer.

6. Male (M) + Female (F) = 300

$$\text{Total money} = \frac{8}{9}M \times [illegible] + \frac{2}{3}F \times 1000 \quad ...(i)$$

$$= \frac{6000}{9}M + \frac{6000}{9}F = \frac{6000}{9}(M + F)$$

From equation (i) we get,

$$\text{Total money} = \frac{6000 \times 300}{9} = 2,00,000$$

7. $p^x = q \Rightarrow x \log p = \log q$

and $q^y = r \Rightarrow y \log q = \log r$

and $z^2 = p \Rightarrow z \log r = \log p$

$\therefore \quad xyz = \frac{\log q}{\log p} \times \frac{\log r}{\log q} \times \frac{\log p}{\log r} = 1$

8. Let total number of people are 100.

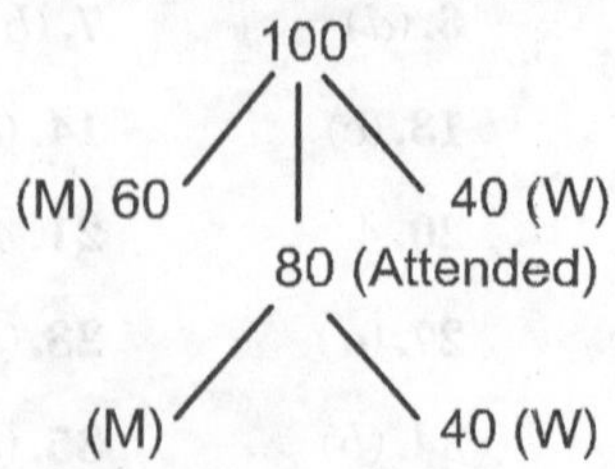

So, male attended the party 80 – 40 = 40

Ratio of male to female who attended the party

M : W = 40 : 40

= 1 : 1

9.

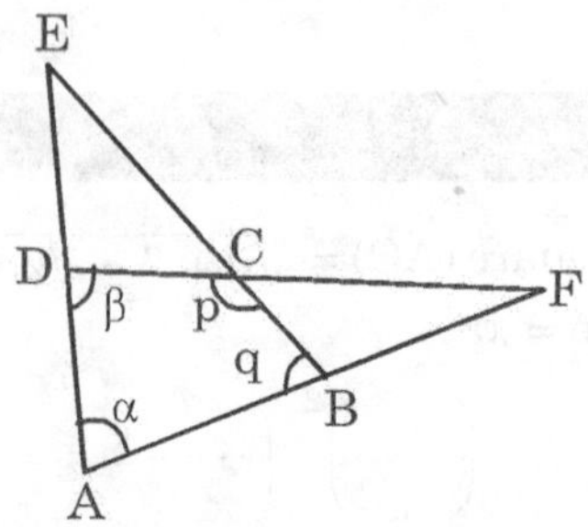

$\angle E + \angle F = ?$

$\alpha + q + E = 180$ ....(i)

and $\alpha + \beta + F = 180$ ....(ii)

and $\alpha + \beta + p + q = 360$ ....(iii)

Adding equations (i) and (ii) and equating it to (iii) we get

$\alpha + q + E + \alpha + \beta + F = \alpha + \beta + p + q$

$\therefore \quad E + F = p - \alpha$

10. Four green, two red face

$P(G) = \frac{4}{6} = \frac{2}{3}$

$q(R) = 1 - P(G)$

$= \frac{1}{3}$

$n = 7$

Now from options

From option (a), $P(G = 3) = {}^7C_3 \left(\right)^{\,} \left(\right)^4$

$\frac{35 \times 2^3}{(\ )^7} = \frac{35 \times 2^3}{(\ )^7}$

From option (b), $P(G = 4) = {}^7C_4 \left(\right) \left(\right)^3$

$\frac{35 \times 2^4}{(\ )^7} = \frac{35 \times 2^4}{(\ )^7}$

From option (c), $P(G = 5) = {}^7C_5 \left(\right) \left(\right)^2$

$\frac{21 \times 2^5}{(\ )^7} = \frac{42 \times 2^4}{(\ )^7}$

From option (d), $P(G = 6) = {}^7C_6 \left(\right) \left(\right)$

$\frac{7 \times 2^6}{(\ )^7} = \frac{28 \times 2^4}{(\ )^7}$

Option c is maximum value.

COMPUTER SCIENCE

1. Given, $a_n = 2n + 3$

Since generating function for 1 is $\frac{1}{1-x}$ and n is $\frac{x}{(\ -\ )^2}$, the generating function for a_n is

$A(x) = \frac{2x}{(\ -\ )^2} + \frac{3}{1-x}$

$\frac{2x + \ (\ -\ )}{(1-x)^2} = \frac{\ - x}{(1-x)^2}$

which is option (d).

4. (A) $\overline{P \oplus Q} = P \odot Q$ true

(B) $\bar{P} \oplus Q = P \odot Q$ true

(C) $\bar{P} \oplus \bar{Q} = P \oplus Q$ true

(D) $(P \oplus \bar{P}) \oplus Q = (P \odot \bar{P}) \odot \bar{Q}$ false

$(P \oplus \bar{P}) \oplus Q = 1 \oplus Q = \bar{Q}$

$(P \odot \bar{P}) \odot \bar{Q} = 0 \oplus \bar{Q} = Q$

$(P \oplus \bar{P}) \oplus Q \neq (P \odot \bar{P}) \odot \bar{Q}$

5. RISC processor characteristics:

1. It supports mode registers, so ALU operations are performed only on a register data.
2. It support fixed length instructions.
3. It uses hard-wired control unit.

6. n is number of states of given nfa (may not be minimal) k is number of states of equivalent min dfa. First we convert nfa to dfa using subset construction algorithm and we get an equivalent dfa which will have almost 2^n states. Then we can convert this dfa to a minimal dfa and get a minimal dfa with k states where $k \le 2^n$.

7. The set of RE languages is closed under intersection, not closed under complementation, is not subset of set of REC language and is a countable set.

8. Type checking is done before parsing is clearly false because in compiler type checking is done after parsing phase.

9. Processor required to handle the interrupt:

1. Processor finishes the execution of the current instruction.
2. Processor pushes the process status of L onto the control stack.
3. Processor loads the new PC value based on the interrupt.
4. Processor executes the interrupt service routine.
5. Processor pops the process status of "L" from the control stack.

10. EMAT = P * S + (1 – P) * M

X = P * D + (1 – P) * M

X = P * D + M – P * M

X – M = P (D – M)

$$P = \frac{X - M}{D - M}$$

11. 

E1 entries > E2 entities

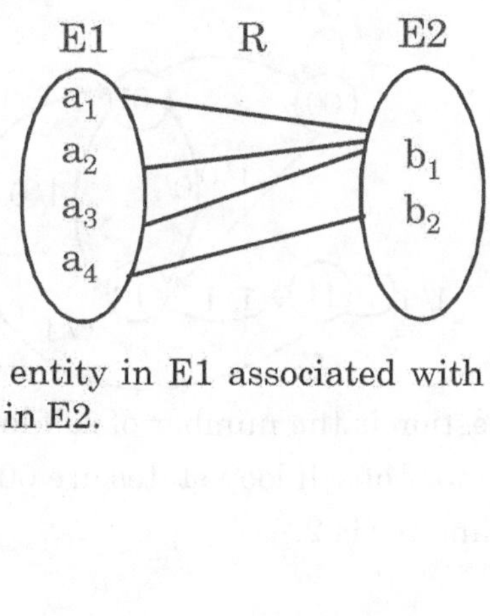

Every entity in E1 associated with exactly one entity in E2.

12.

Book

isbn	bname
2	A
4	B
6	C
8	D
10	E

Stock

isbn	copies
4	100
6	200
10	200
12	400

Query 1:

isbn	copies
4	100
6	200
10	200

Query 2:

isbn	copies
4	100
6	200
10	200
2	Null
8	Null

Query 3:

isbn	copies
4	100
6	200
10	200
12	400

Query 4:

isbn	copies
4	100
6	200
10	200
2	Null
8	Null
12	400

Query 4 is full outer join so that full order join record set superset of records compare to inner join, left outer join & right outer join.

13. UDP Header's Port Number ⇒ 16 bit

Ethernet MAC Address ⇒ 48 bit

IPv6 Next Header ⇒ 8 bit

TCP Header's Sequence Number ⇒ 32 bit

14. *cwnd* approximately doubles every round trip time.

15. P(one of them wins in 3rd trial)

= P(1st trial is Tie) × P (IInd trial is Tie) × P(one of them wins 3rd trial)

P(Tie in any trial)

= P(P = 1 and Q = 1) + P(P = 2 and Q = 2) + ... + P(P = 6 and Q = 6)

$$= \frac{6}{36} = \frac{1}{6}$$

∴ P(one of them wins) = 1 – P(Tie)

$$= 1 - \frac{1}{6} = \frac{5}{6}$$

So, required probability

$$= \frac{1}{6} \times \frac{1}{6} \times \frac{5}{6} = \frac{5}{216} = 0.023$$

(rounded to 3 decimal places)

16. $\int_0^{\pi/4} x\cos(\quad)\,dx$

Let, $t = x^2$

$\therefore \quad \frac{dt}{dx} = 2x$

$dt = 2x\,dx$

$\Rightarrow \quad xdx = xdx = \frac{dt}{2}$

when $x = 0 \Rightarrow t = 0$ and when $x = \frac{\pi}{4} \Rightarrow t = \left(\quad\right)^2$

So required integral reduce to

$$\int_0^{(\pi\quad)^2} \cos t\,dt = [\sin t]_0^{(\pi/4)^2}$$

$$= \sin\left(\quad\right)^2 - \sin(0)$$

$$= \sin\left(\quad\right)^2 = 0.28898$$

$\simeq 0.289$

(rounded to 3 decimal places)

17. $u = \left(\quad\right) \quad \left(\quad\right)$

$A = uv^T$

$= \left(\quad\right)[\quad]$

$= \left[\quad\right]$

Now $|A - \lambda I| = 0$

$$\left|\left[\quad\right] \left[\quad\right]\right| = 0$$

$$\begin{vmatrix} 1-\lambda & 1 \\ 2 & 2-\lambda \end{vmatrix} = 0$$

$\therefore \quad (1-\lambda)(2-\lambda) - 2 = 0$

$\lambda^2 - 3\lambda = 0$

$\lambda(\lambda - 3) = 0$

$\lambda = 0$ or $\lambda = 3$

$\therefore$ The largest eigen value is 3.

18.

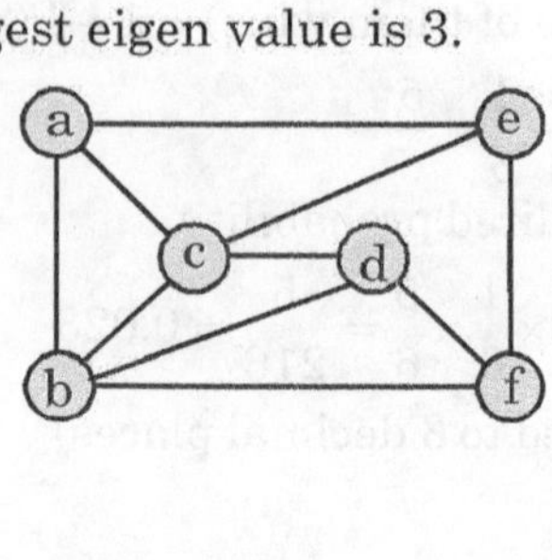

Since the largest complete sub graph is K_3, chromatic number is atleast 3. We can try for a chromatic number of 3 by using 3 colors, as follows:

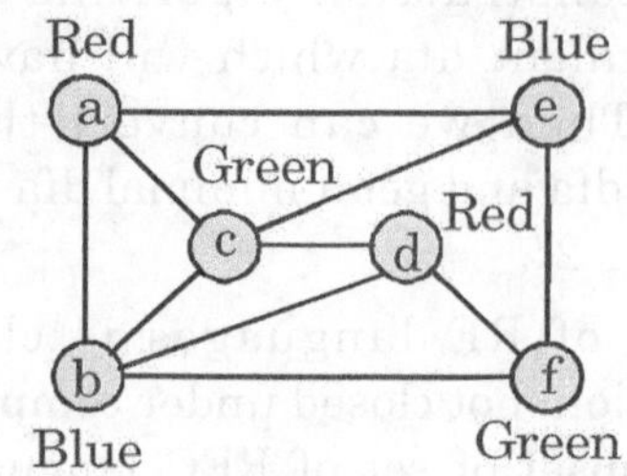

Since we have successfully, properly coloured all vertices with only 3 colors, the chromatic number of this graph is 3.

19. Given $|G| = 84$

By Lagrang's theorem any subgroup size is a divisor of 84.

But a proper subgroup cannot have same size as group.

So largest divisor of 84, other than 84 is 42.

So, largest proper subgroup can have in size of 42.

22.

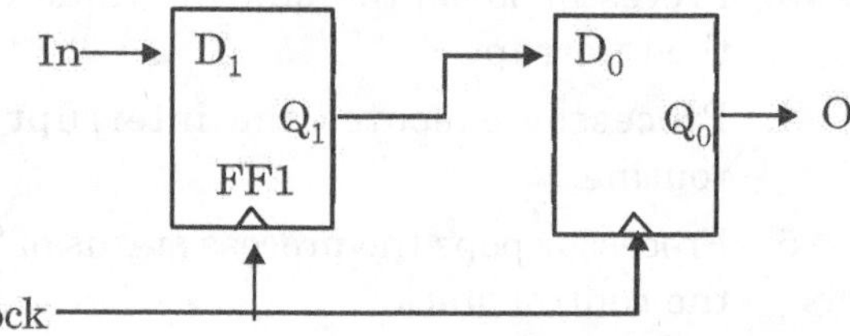

State Table:

P.S		Input	FF Inputs		N.S		
Q_1	Q_0	x	D_1=x	D_0=Q_1	Q_1	Q_0	Out = Q_0
0	0	0	0	0	0	0	0
0	0	1	1	0	1	0	0
0	1	0	0	0	0	0	0
0	1	1	1	0	1	0	0
1	0	0	0	1	0	1	1
1	0	1	1	1	1	1	1
1	1	0	0	1	0	1	1
1	1	1	1	1	1	1	1

State Transition Diagram:

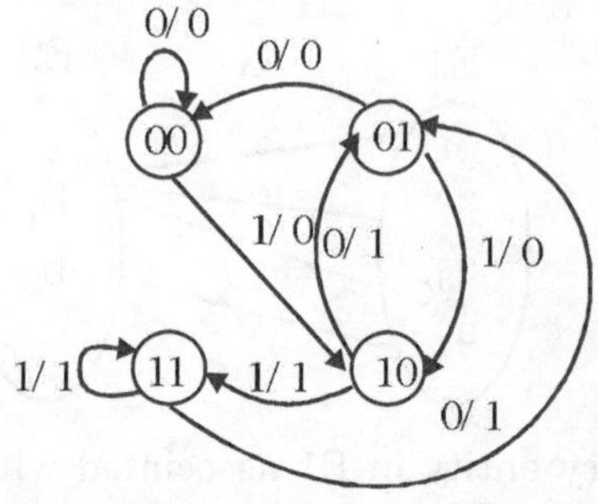

The question is the number of self loop states.

The number of self loop states are 00 and 11.

Hence answer is 2.

24. P_1 P_2 P_3

| | | No deadlock

|

Maximum each process can request for 2 resources so, that there will not be any deadlock, because we, have only 4 resource available.

So, K value is '2'.

25. 1 sec = 10^9 bits

$$\frac{2^{32} \times 8}{10^9} = 2^{32} \text{ bytes}$$

$\Rightarrow$ 34.35 sec

26. Only Eigen vector is $\begin{bmatrix} \\ \end{bmatrix}$ multiples means that eigen value is repeated since if eigen values were distinct we will get one more independent eigen vector. So, II P has repeated eigen values is true. I need not be true since $\begin{bmatrix} & \\ & \end{bmatrix}$ has repeated eigen values and yet it is invertible. III is true since if matrix has repeated eigen values then it cannot be diagonalizable.

27. P : Set of rational number $\rightarrow$ countable

Q : Set of functions from {0, 1} to N $\rightarrow$ N

0	1

$N \times N$

0 can be assigned in N ways

1 can be assigned in N ways

There are N $\times$ N functions, cross product of countable set in countable.

R : Set of functions from N to {0, 1}

1	2	3	4	5	6				

Each of thus boxes can be assigned to 0 or 1 so each such function is a binary number with infinite number of bits.

Example: 0000 ..... is the binary number corresponding to 0 is assigned to all boxes and so on.

Since each such binary number represents a subset of N (the set of natural numbers) by characteristic function method, therefore, the set of such function is same as power set of N which is uncountable due to Cantor's theorem, which says that power set of a countably infinite set is always uncountably infinite.

S : Set of finite subsets of N $\rightarrow$ countably infinite since we are counting only finite subsets.

So, P, Q and S are countable.

33. Binary code: $(b_7\, b_6\, b_5\, b_5\, b_3 \,.\, b_2\, b_1\, b_0)_2$

$(31.5)_{10} = (11111,1)_2$

$(0.875)_{10} = (0.111)_2$

$(12.100)_{10} = (01100.000110....)_2$

$\downarrow$

only 3 bits of fraction space available

So can't be stored.

$(3.001)_{10} = (00011.000000.....)_2$

It is also not accurate storage.

34. MM space = 2^P bytes

Physical Address (PA) size = P bits

CM size = 2^N bytes

Block size = 2^M words

$= 2^M$ words * 2^W bytes/word

$= 2^{(M+W)}$ bytes

$$\text{Number of lines} = \frac{\text{CMsize}}{\text{Block size}} \Rightarrow \frac{2^N}{2^{M+W}}$$

$\Rightarrow 2^{N-M-W}$

$$\text{Number of sets} = \frac{\text{Number in cm}}{\text{P - way}}$$

$$= \frac{2^{N-M-W}}{K}$$

Address format

$\longrightarrow$ PA $\longrightarrow$

P bits

tag	*so*	*wo*

$$\log_2 \frac{2^{N-M-W}}{K} \qquad \log_2 2^{M+W}$$

$\downarrow$ $\qquad$ $\downarrow$

$$\log_2 \frac{2^{N-M-W}}{\log_2 K} \qquad (M+W)\,bits$$

$\downarrow$

$$\log_2 2^{N-M-W} - \log_2 K$$

$\Rightarrow (N - M - W - \log_2 K)$

$\therefore$ Tag size

$\Rightarrow P - (M + W - \log_2 K + M + W)$

$\Rightarrow P - N + \log_2 K$

35. I. $\{a^m b^n c^p d^q \mid m + p = n + q\}$ is clearly CFL since, we can rearrange the equation as m – n + p – q = 0 which can be done by push, pop, push and pop and check if stack is empty at end.

II. $\{a^m b^n c^p d^q \mid m = n \text{ and } p = q\}$ is clearly CFL since, one comparison at a time can be done by pda.

III. $\{a^m b^n c^p d^q \mid m = n = p \text{ and } p \neq q\}$ is not CFL since m = n = p is a double comparison which cannot be done by PDA.

IV. $\{a^m b^n c^p d^q \mid mn = p + q\}$ is not a CFL, since mn involves multiplying number of a's and number b's which cannot be done by a PDA.

So, only I and II are CFL's.

36. I. Membership problem RE → undecidable

II. Regularity problem for RE → undecidable

III. Equivalence problem for RE → undecidable

IV. Since DPDA P exists for every *nfa* N and equivalent to it, this problem is trivially decidable.

37. Ans is T_3T_3 because from first T_3 [bbaac] is taken from second T_3 [abc] is taken longest possible prefix.

Hence T_3T_3 token output.

38. If any given parse tree or syntax free low level operations having higher precedence than upper level operators,

Hence here $ is higher precedence than # $ is left associative because in the sub expression b $ c $ d, b $ c will be evaluated first as per given tree.

As per the given tree structure right # if higher precedence than left #.

Hence it is right associative.

39.

Max need			
	E	F	G
P_0	4	3	1
P_1	2	1	4
P_2	1	3	3
P_3	5	4	1

Current allocation			
	E	F	G
P_0	1	0	1
P_1	1	1	2
P_2	1	0	3
P_3	2	0	0

Current available			
	E(3)	F(3)	G(0)
P_0	4	3	1
P_1	5	3	4
P_2	6	4	6
P_3	8	4	6

Remaining need			
	E	F	G
P_0	3	3	0
P_1	1	0	2
P_2	0	3	0
P_3	3	4	1

Safe sequence: P_0, P_2, P_1, P_3

Safe state

40. Full = N, empty = 0, mutex = 1

- Initially buffer will be empty, so consumer should not start first, so option b, D are eliminated.
- With option A consumer will never consume the item, so it is wrong.
- Option 'c' is correct answer which proper functionality of produce and consumer.

41.

R

A	B
a_1	2
a_2	4
a_3	4
a_4	6
a_5	6

B	C
2	c_1
4	c_2
4	c_2
8	c_2

⇑ Foreign key ⇑ Primary key

Given query: $r \bowtie (\sigma_{B<5}(s))$

A	B	C
a_1	2	c_1
a_2	4	c_1
a_3	4	c_1

A : $\sigma_{B<5}(r \bowtie s)$

A	B	C
a_1	2	c_1
a_2	4	c_1
a_3	4	c_1

B : $\sigma_{B<5}$ (r ⟗ s)

A	B	C
a_1	2	c_1
a_2	4	c_1
a_3	4	c_1

C : r ⟗ ($\sigma_{B<5}$ (s))

A	B	C
a_1	2	c_1
a_2	4	c_1
a_3	4	c_1
a_4	6	Null
a_5	6	Null

D : $\sigma_{B<5}$ (r) ⟗ s

A	B	C
a_1	2	c_1
a_2	4	c_1
a_3	4	c_1

Option "C" query result not equal to given query.

42. Schema II : Registration (rollno, courseid, email)

Primary key [rollno, courseid]

Non-trivial functional dependencies:

{rollno, courseid → email

email → rollno}

candidate keys {rollno, courseid,}

email courseid}

Given relation is in 3NF but not in BCNF.

43. The graph has 100! vertices which each vertex labelled by one of the 100! permutation.

Let us find degree of each vertex.

Let us take a vertex whose labelling is say 1, 2, 3, 4,....100.

Now it will be connected to all vertices where exactly 2 of the adjacent numbers all swapped.

The two swapped numbers could be (1, 2), (2, 3), (3, 4) .... etc. upto (99, 100) which makes for 99 edges for each such vertex.

So the graph is a regular graph with each vertex connected to 99 other vertices.

So $y = 99$

The number of connected components = z = 1 since we can go from any vertex to any other vertex by only swapping 2 adjacent number at a time, many times i.e. there is a path from any vertex to any other vertex.

Graph is connected.

So $z = 1$

So $y + 10z = 99 + 10 \times 1 = 109$

44. The condition probability table given is

	H_D	M_D	L_D
M_G	0.40	0.48	0.12
M_G	0.10	0.65	0.25
L_G	0.01	0.50	0.49

$P(H_G) = 0.2$

$P(M_G) = 0.5$

$P(L_G) = 0.3$

Drawing the tree diagram for HD we get.

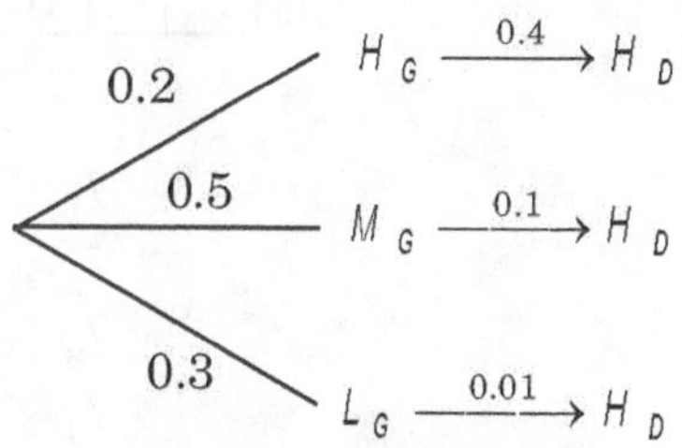

$$P(H_G \mid H_D) = \frac{P(H_G \cap H_D)}{P(\quad)}$$

From diagram,

$$P(H_G \cap H_D) = 0.2 \times 0.4$$

$$P(H_D) = 0.2 \times 0.4 + 0.5 \times 0.1 + 0.3 \times 0.01$$
$$= 0.133$$

Required probability, $P(H_G \mid H_D)$

$$= \frac{0.2 \times 0.4}{0.133} = 0.60$$

(rounding upto 2 decimal place)

49. $F(P, Q, R, S) = \Sigma m(0, 2, 5, 7, 9, 11) + d(3, 8, 10, 12, 14)$

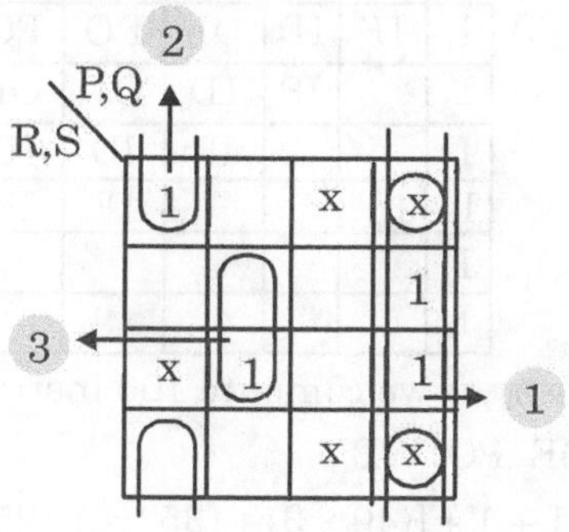

Number of EPI = 3

50.

	IF	ID	OF	PO	WB
Type(I_1)	1	1	1	3	1
Type(I_2)	1	1	1	2	1
Type(I_3)	1	1	1	1	1

$I_1 : 1 + 1 + 1 + 3 + 1 = 7$

I_2 :, I_3 : } usually takes cycles each due to overlapping but I_1(PO) takes 2 cycles to add "1" cycle extra

(2 + 1)

$\Rightarrow$ 7 + 8 + 1 = 10

	1	2	3	4	5	6	7	8	9	10
I_1	IF	ID	OF	PO	PO	PO	WB			
I_2		IF	ID	OF	OF	OF	PO	PO	WB	
I_3			IF	ID	ID	ID	OF	OF	PO	PO

	IF	*ID*	*OF*	*PO*	*WB*
I_1	1	1	1	3	1
I_2	1	1	1	3	1
I_3	1	1	1	2	1
I_4	1	1	1	2	1
I_5	1	1	1	1	1
I_6	1	1	1	1	1

If Type 1 – 2 instruction

Type 2 – 2 instruction

Type 3 – 2 instruction

$I_1 : 1 + 1 + 1 + 3 + 1 = 7$

I_2 : 1 + 2 extra cycles = 3

I_3 : 1 + 1 extra cycles = 2

I_4 : 1 + 1 extra cycles = 2

I_5 : 1 extra cycles = 1

I_6 : 1 extra cycles = 1

= 16

	1	2	3	4	5	6	7	8	9	10	11	12	13	14	15	16
I_1	IF	ID	OF	PO	PO	PO	WB									
I_2		IF	ID	OF	OF	OF	PO	PO	PO	WB						
I_3			IF	ID	ID	ID	OF	OF	OF	PO	PO	WB				
I4				IF	IF	IF	ID	ID	ID	OF	OF	PO	PO	WB		
I_5							IF	IF	IF	ID	ID	OF	OF	PO	WB	
I_6										IF	IF	ID	ID	OF	PO	WB

In this way, if we compute 100 instruction number of cycles required is

If ID OF PO WB

$\Rightarrow$ 1 + 1 + 1 + [(40 × 3) + (35 × 2) (25 × 1)] + 1

$\Rightarrow$ 219

51. Instruction size = 16 bit

Type I instruction design:

16 bit

opcode	IR	IR	IR
4 bit	4 bit	4 bit	4 bit

Number of operations = 2^4

= 16

↓

Face opcodes = 16 – 4 = 12

Type II instruction design:

16 bit

opcode	FR	FR
4 bit	6 bit	6 bit

Face opcodes after type 1 instruction = 12

Face opcodes after type 2 instruction = 12 – 8 = 4

Type III instruction design:

16 bit

opcode	IR	FR
6 bit	4 bit	4 bit

Expand opcode size = 6 bit

↓

Number of opcodes $= 4 \times 2^2 = 16$

∴ Number of free opcodes after type 3 instruction

= 16 – 14 = 2

Type IV instruction design:

16 bit

opcode	*FR*
10 bit	6 bit

Expand opcodes size = 10 bit

↓

Number of opcodes $= 2 \times 2^4 = 2^5 = 32$

52. We need to find smallest value of k which satisfies

$$L_1^k = L_1^{k+1}$$

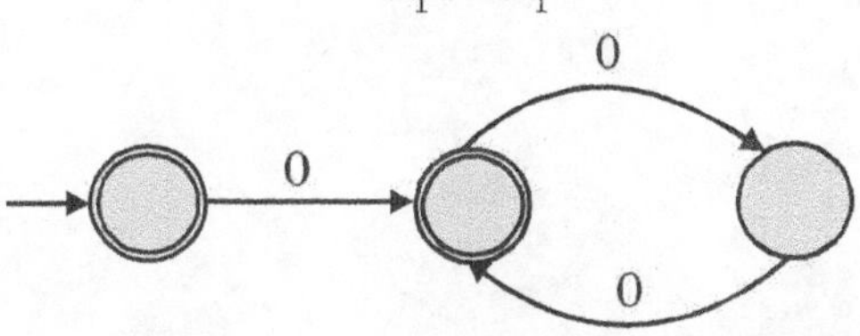

$$L_1 = \in(00)^*$$

Try $k = 0$ $\quad L_1^0 = L_1^1$

$\Rightarrow$ $\quad \in = L_1$ which is false.

So order is not 0.

Try k = 1: $\quad L_1^1 = L_1^2$

$\Rightarrow$ $\quad L_1^2 = L_1$

Now, $\quad L_1^2 = (\in + 0(00)^*)(\in + 0(00)^*)$

$$= \in + 0(00)^* + 00(00)^* = 0^*$$

Clearly $\quad L_1^2 \neq L_1$

So order is not 1.

Try k = 2: $\quad L_1^2 = L_1^3$

Now, $\quad L_1^3 = L_1^2 . L_1$

$$= 0^*(\in + 0(00)^*) = 0^*$$

Clearly $\quad L_1^3 = L_1^2 = 0^*$

(So order of L_1 is 2)

53.

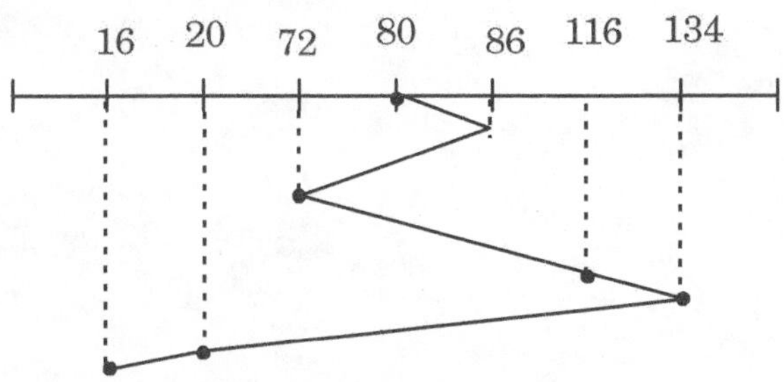

(86 – 80) + (86 – 72) + (134 – 72)

+ (134 – 16) 62 + 118 + 14

= 200

100 → 20

200 → ?

$$\frac{200}{100} \times 20 = 40$$

3 direction changes 3 × 15 = 45

40 + 45 = 85

54.

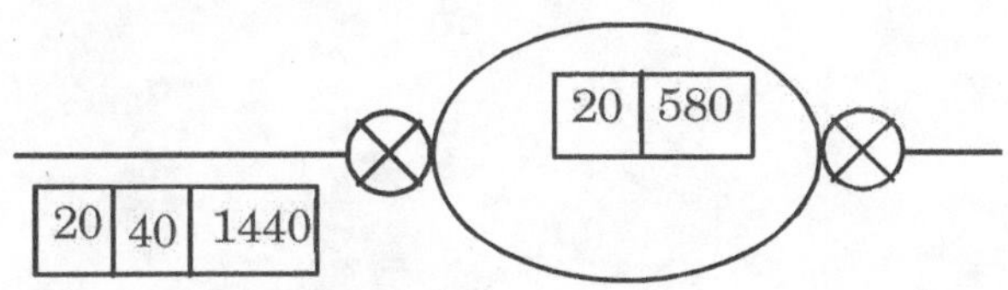

Fragment Bytes

1st		2nd		3rd		4th	
20	576	20	576	20	576	20	576

Fragment Offset

(0 – 71) (72 – 143) (144 – 215) (216 – 287)

■■

SOLVED PAPER - 2019

INSTRUCTIONS

1. Total of 65 questions carrying 100 marks, out of which 10 questions carrying a total of 15 marks are in General Aptitude (GA)
2. The Engineering Mathematics will carry around **15% of the total marks,** the General Aptitude section will carry **15% of the total marks** and the **remaining 70% of the total marks.**
3. **Types of Questions**

   (*a*) **Multiple Choice Questions (MCQ)** carrying 1 or 2 marks each in all papers and sections. These questions are objective in nature, and each will have a choice of four options, out of which the candidate has to mark the correct answer(s).

   (*b*) **Numerical Answer Questions** of 1 or 2 marks each in all papers and sections. For these questions the answer is a real number, to be entered by the candidate using the virtual keypad. No choices will be shown for these type of questions.
4. For **1-mark** multiple-choice questions, **1/3 marks** will be deducted for a wrong answer. Likewise, for **2-marks** multiple-choice questions, **2/3** marks will be deducted for a wrong answer. There is no negative marking for numerical answer type questions.

Chapter-Wise Analysis

#	Chapters	Marks		
		1	2	Total
1	General Aptitude	5	5	15
2	Engineering Mathematics	7	4	15
3	Theory of Computation	2	3	8
4	Digital Logic	4	2	8
5	Computer Organization & Architecture	1	1	3
6	Programming & Data Structures	4	6	16
7	Algorithm	1	1	3

#	Chapters	Marks		
		1	2	Total
8	Compiler Design	2	3	8
9	Operating System	1	4	9
10	Data Bases	2	2	6
11	Computer Networks	1	4	9
12	* Software Engineering	0	0	0
13	* Web Technology	0	0	0

GENERAL APTITUDE

1. Ten friends planned to share equally the cost of buying a gift for their teacher. When two of them decided not to contribute, each of the other friends had to pay Rs. 150 more. The cost of the gift was Rs. ______.

(1) 666 (2) 6000
(3) 3000 (4) 12000

2. A court is to a judge as ________ is to a teacher.

(1) a student (2) a syllabus
(3) a school (4) a punishment

3. The search engine's business model ________ around the fulcrum of trust.

(1) bursts (2) revolves
(3) plays (4) sinks

4. Two cars start at the same time from the same location and go in the same direction. The speed of the first car is 50 km/h and the speed of the second car is 60 km/h. The number of hours it takes for the distance between the two cars to be 20 km is ______.

(1) 2 (2) 1
(3) 6 (4) 3

5. The expenditure on the project _______ as follows: equipment Rs. 20 lakhs, salaries Rs. 12 lakhs, and contingency Rs. 3 lakhs.

(1) break (2) break down
(3) breaks down (4) breaks

6. In the given diagram, teachers are represented in the triangle, researchers in the circle and administrators in the rectangle. Out of the total number of the people, the percentage of administrators shall be in the range of _______.

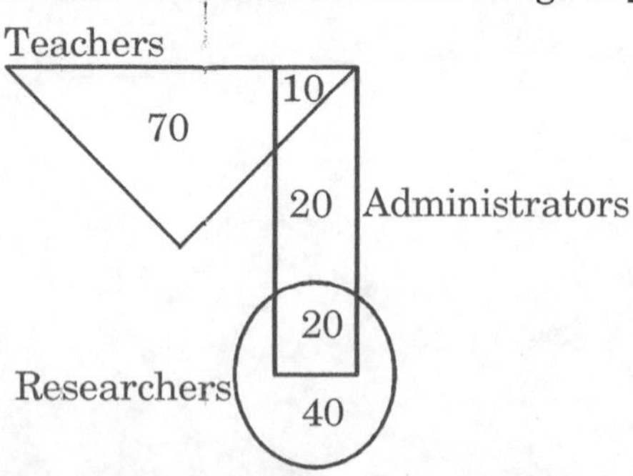

(1) 0 to 15
(2) 31 to 45
(3) 46 to 60
(4) 16 to 30

7. In a college, there are three student clubs. Sixty students are only in the Drama club, 80 students are only in the Dance club, 30 students are only in the Maths club, 40 students are in both Drama and Dance clubs, 12 students are in both Dance and Maths clubs, 7 students are in both Drama and Maths clubs, and 2 students are in all the clubs. If 75% of the students in the college are not in any of these clubs, then the total number of students in the college is _______.

(1) 975 (2) 1000
(3) 225 (4) 900

8. Three of the five students allocated to a hostel put in special requests to the warden. Given the floor plan of the vacant rooms, select the allocation plan that will accommodate all their requests.

Request by X : Due to pollen allergy, I want to avoid a wing next to the garden.

Request by Y : I want to live as far from the washrooms as possible, since I am very sensitive to smell.

Request by Z : I believe in Vaastu and so want to stay in the South-west wing.

The shaded room are already occupied. WR is washroom.

(1)

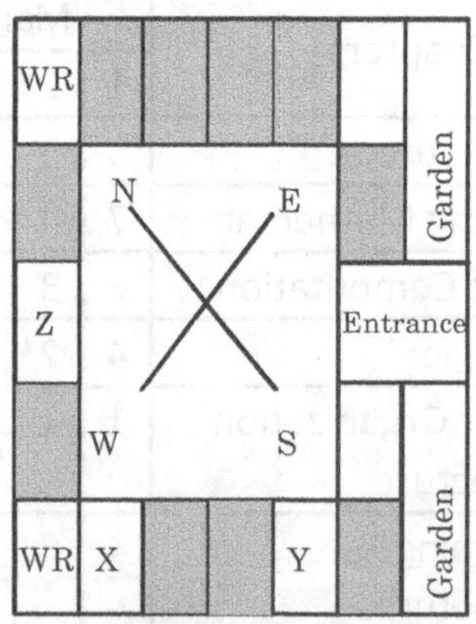

(2)

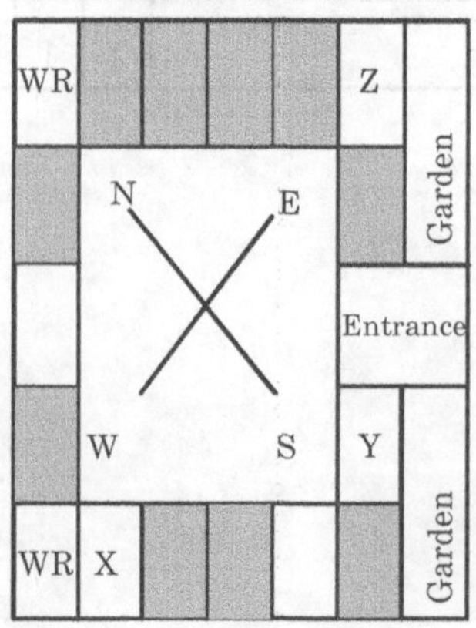

(3)

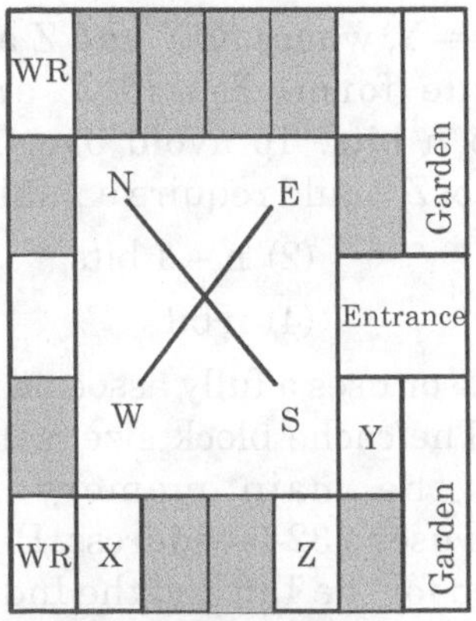

(4)

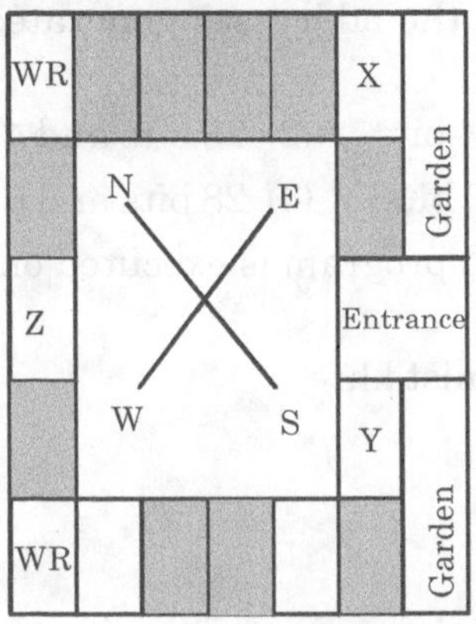

9. The police arrested four criminals – P, Q, R and S. The criminals knew each other. They made the following statements :

P says "Q committed the crime."

Q says "S committed the crime."

R says "I did not do it."

S says "What Q said about me is false."

Assume only one of the arrested four committed the crime and only one of the statements made above is true. Who committed the crime?

(1) R (2) P

(3) Q (4) S

10. "A recent High Court judgement has sought to dispel the idea of begging as a disease — which leads to its stigmatization and criminalization — and to regard it as a symptom. The underlying disease is the failure of the state to protect citizens who fall through the social security net."

Which one of the following statements can be inferred from the given passage?

(1) Begging is an offence that has to be dealt with firmly

(2) Beggars are lazy people who beg because they are unwilling to work

(3) Beggars are created because of the lack of social welfare schemes

(4) Beggings has to be banned because it adversely affects the welfare of the state

COMPUTER SCIENCE AND INFORMATION TECHNOLOGY

1. Which of the following protocol pairs can be used to send and retrieve e-mails (in that order)?

(1) IMAP, SMTP (2) IMAP, POP3

(3) SMTP, POP3 (4) SMTP, MIME

2. Consider the following C program :

```
#include <studio.h>
int main ( ) {
    int arr [ ] = {1, 2, 3, 4, 5, 6, 7, 8, 9, 0, 1, 2, 5},
    *ip=arr +4;
    print f("%d\n", ip[1]);
    return 0;
}
```

The number that will be displayed on execution of the program is ________.

3. Which one of the following kinds of derivation is used by LR parsers?

(1) Rightmost in reverse

(2) Rightmost

(3) Leftmost in reverse

(4) Leftmost

4. If L is a regular language over $\Sigma = \{a, b\}$, which one of the following language is NOT regular?

(1) $L \cdot L^R = \{xy \mid x \in L, y^R \in L\}$

(2) $\{ww^R \mid \omega \in L\}$

(3) Suffix (L) = $\{y \in \Sigma^* \mid \exists x \in \Sigma^* \text{ such that } xy \in L\}$

(4) Prefix (L) = $\{x \in \Sigma^* \mid \exists y \in \Sigma^* \text{ such that } xy \in L\}$

5. Consider three concurrent processes P1, P2 and P3 as shown below, which access a shared variable D that has been initialized to 100.

P1	P2	P3
⋮	⋮	⋮
⋮	⋮	⋮
D = D + 20	D = D – 50	D = D + 10
⋮	⋮	⋮
⋮	⋮	⋮

The processes are executed on a uniprocessor system running a time-shared operating system. If the minimum and maximum possible values of D after the three processes have completed execution are X and Y respectively, then the value of Y – X is ________.

6. An array of 25 distinct elements is to be sorted using quicksort. Assume that the pivot element is chosen uniformly at random. The probability that the pivot element gets placed in the worst possible location in the first round of partitioning (rounded off to 2 decimal places) is ________.

7. Which one of the following statement is NOT correct about the B+ tree data structure used for creating an index of a relational database table?

(1) B+ Tree is a height-balanced tree

(2) Non-leaf nodes have pointers to data records

(3) Each leaf node has a pointer to the next leaf node

(4) Key values in each node are kept in sorted order

8. Consider the grammar given below:

$S \rightarrow Aa$

$A \rightarrow BD$

$B \rightarrow b \mid \epsilon$

$D \rightarrow d \mid \epsilon$

Let a, b, d, and $ be indexed as follows:

a	b	d	$
3	2	1	0

Compute the FOLLOW set of the non-terminal B and write the index values for the symbols in the FOLLOW set in the descendign order. (For example, if the FOLLOW set is {a, b, d, $}, then the answer should be 3210)

9. The chip select logic for a certain DRAM chip in a memory system design is shown below. Assume that the memory system has 16 address lines denoted by A_{15} to A_0. What is the range of addresses (in hexadecimal) of the memory system that can get enabled by the chip select (CS) signal?

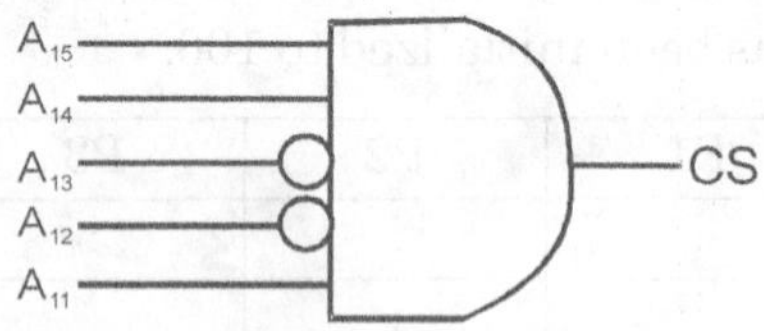

(1) CA00 to CAFF

(2) C800 to CFFF

(3) DA00 to DFFF

(4) C800 to C8FF

10. Which one of the following is NOT a valid identity?

(1) $x \oplus y = x + y$, if $xy = 0$

(1) $x \oplus y = (xy + x'y')'$

(3) $(x + y) \oplus z = x \oplus (y + z)$

(4) $(x \oplus y) \oplus z = x \oplus (y \oplus z)$

11. Consider Z = X – Y, where X, Y and Z are all in sign-magnitude form. X and Y are each represented in n bits. To avoid overflow, the representation of Z would require a minimum of:

(1) n + 2 bits (2) n + 1 bits

(3) n – 1 bits (4) n bits

12. A certain processor uses a fully associative cache of size 16 kB. The cache block size is 16 bytes. Assume that the main memory is byte addressable and uses a 32-bit address. How many bits are required for the Tag and the Index fields respectively in the addresses generated by the processor?

(1) 24 bits and 4 bits (2) 28 bits and 4 bits

(3) 24 bits and 0 bits (4) 28 bits and 0 bits

13. The following C program is executed on a Unix/ Linux system:

```
#include <unistd.h>
int main()
{
int i;
for (i = 0; i < 10; i ++)
  if (i%2 == 0) fork();
return 0;
}
```

The total number of child processes created is ________.

14. Compute $\lim_{x \to 3} \frac{x^4 - 81}{2x^2 - 5x - 3}$

(1) 53/12

(2) 1

(3) Limit does not exist

(4) 108/7

15. Let X be a square matrix. Consider the following two statements on X.

I. X is invertible

II. Determinant of X is non-zero

Which one of the following is TRUE?

(1) I and II are equivalent statements.

(2) I implies II; II does not imply I.

(3) I does not imply II; II does not imply I.

(4) II implies I; I does not imply II.

16. Consider the following C program:

```
#include <stdio.h>
intjumble(int x, int y){
    x = 2*x + y;
    return x;
```

```
}
int main(){
    int x = 2, y = 5;
    y = jumble (y, x);
    x = jumble(y, x);
    printf("%d /n", x);
    return 0;
}
```

The value printed by the program is _______.

17. Let U = {1, 2, ..., n}. Let A = {(x, X | x ∈ X, X ⊆ U }. Consider the following two statements on | A |.

I. $|A| = n2^{n-1}$

II. $|A| = \sum_{k=1}^{n} k\binom{n}{k}$

Which of the above statements is/are TRUE?

(1) Neither I nor II (2) Only I

(3) Only II (4) Both I and II

18. Let G be an undirected complete graph on n vertices, where n > 2. Then, the number of different Hamiltonian cycles in G is equal to

(1) n! (2) $\frac{(n-1)!}{2}$

(3) 1 (4) (n – 1)!

19. Consider the following two statements about database transaction schedules:

I. Strict two-phase locking protocol generates conflict serializable schedules that are also recoverable.

II. Timestamp-ordering concurrency control protocol with Thomas' Write Rule can generate view serializable schedules that are not conflict serializable.

Which of the above statements is/are TRUE?

(1) Both I and II

(2) II only

(3) I only

(4) Neither I nor II

20. The value of 3^{51} mod 5 is _______.

21. For Σ = {a, b}, let us consider the regular language $L = \{x \mid x = a^{2+3k} \text{ or } x = b^{10+12k}, k \geq 0\}$. Which one of the following can be a pumping length (the constant guaranteed by the pumping lemma) for L?

(1) 9 (2) 5

(3) 3 (4) 24

22. Consider a sequence of 14 elements: A = [–5, –10, 6, 3, –1, –2, 13, 4, –9, –1, 4, 12, –3, 0]. The subsequence sum $S(i, j) = \sum_{k=i}^{j} A[k]$. Determine the maximum of S(i, j), where $0 \leq i \leq j < 14$. (Divide and conquer approach may be used.)

23. Let G be an arbitrary group. Consider the following relations on G:

R_1: ∀ a, b ∈ G, a R_1 b if and only if ∃ g ∈ G such that $a = g^{-1}bg$

R_2: ∀ a, b ∈ G, aR_2b if and only if $a = b^{-1}$

Which of the above is/are equivalence relation/ relations?

(1) Neither R_1 nor R_2

(2) R_2 only

(3) R_1 only

(4) R_1 and R_2

24. Two numbers are chosen independently and uniformly at random from the set {1, 2,..., 13}. The probability (rounded off to 3 decimal places) that their 4-bit (unsigned) binary representations have the same most significant bit is _____.

25. In 16-bit 2's complement representation, the decimal number –28 is:

(1) 1111 1111 1110 0100

(2) 1111 1111 0001 1100

(3) 1000 0000 1110 0100

(4) 0000 0000 1110 0100

26. Consider the following statements:

I. The smallest element in a max-heap is always at a leaf node

II. The second largest element in a max-heap is always a child of the root node

III. A max-heap can be constructed from a binary search tree in Θ(n) time

IV. A binary search tree can be constructed from a max-heap in Θ(n) time

Which of the above statements are true?

(1) I, II and III (2) II, III and IV

(3) I, III and IV (4) I, II and IV

27. Consider the following C program

```
#include <stdio.h>
int main()(
float sum = 0.0, j = 1.0, i = 2.0;
while (i/j > 0.0625){
j = j + j;
sum = sum + i/j;
printf("%f\n", sum);
```

```
}
return 0;
}
```

The number of times the variable sum will be printed, when the above program is executed is _______.

28. Consider the following sets:

S1. Set of all recursively enumerable languages over the alphabet {0, 1}

S2. Set of all syntactically valid C programs

S3. Set of all languages over the alphabet {0, 1}

S4. Set of all non-regular languages over the alphabet {0, 1}

Which of the above sets are uncountable?

(1) S2 and S3 (2) S1 and S2

(3) S1 and S4 (4) S3 and s4

29. Consider three 4-variable functions f_1, f_2 and f_3, which are expressed in sum of-minterms as

$f_1 = \Sigma(0, 2, 5, 8, 14)$,

$f_2 = \Sigma(2, 3, 6, 8, 14, 15)$,

$f_3 = \Sigma(2, 7, 11, 14)$

For the following circuit with one AND gate and one XOR gate, the output function f can be expressed as:

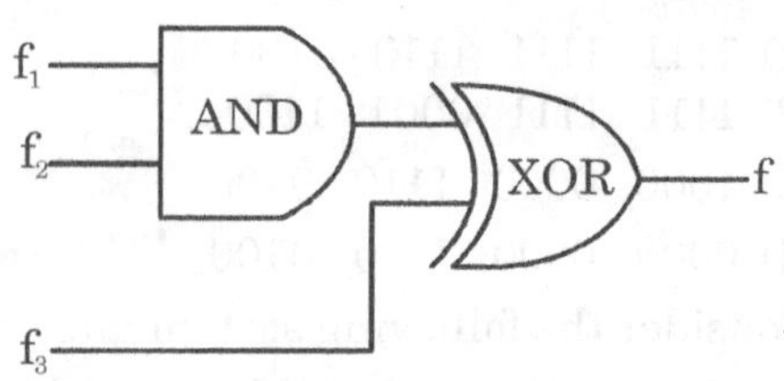

(1) $\Sigma(2, 14)$

(2) $\Sigma(0, 2, 3, 5, 6, 7, 8, 11, 14, 15)$

(3) $\Sigma(2, 7, 8, 11, 14)$

(4) $\Sigma(7, 8, 11)$

30. Let G be any connected weighted undirected graph.

I. G has a unique minimum spanning tree, if no two edges of G have the same weight.

II. G has a unique minimum spanning tree, if, for every cut of G, there is a unique minimum-weight edge crossing the cut.

Which of the above two statements is/are TRUE?

(1) Both I and II (2) I only

(3) Neither I nor II (4) II only

31. Consider the following C program

```
#include <stdio.h>
int main()
{
int a[] = {2, 4, 6, 8, 10};
int i, sum = 0, *b = a + 4;
for (i = 0; i < 5; i ++)
sum = sum + (*b – i) – *(b – i);
printf("%d/n", sum);
return 0;
}
```

The output of the above C program is _____.

32. Consider the following four processes with arrival times (in milliseconds) and their length of CPU bursts (in milliseconds) as shown below:

Process	P1	P2	P3	P4
Arrival time	0	1	3	4
CPU burst time	3	1	3	Z

These processes are run on a single processor using preemptive Shortest Remaining Time First scheduling algorithm. If the average waiting time of the processes is 1 milliseconds, then value of Z is _____.

33. Assume that in a certain computer, the virtual addresses are 64 bits long and the physical addresses are 48 bits long. The memory is word addressible. The page size is 8kB and the word size is 4 bytes. The Translation Look-aside Buffer (TLB) in theaddress translation path has 128 valid entries. At most how many distinct virtual addresses can be translated without any TLB miss?

(1) 8×2^{20} (2) 256×2^{10}

(3) 4×2^{20} (4) 16×2^{10}

34. Let the set of functional dependencies F = {QR → S, R → P, S → Q} hold on a relation schema X = (PQRS). X is not a BCNF. Suppose X is decomposed into two schemas Y and Z, where Y = (PR) and Z = (QRS).

Consider the two statements given below.

I. Both Y and Z are in BCNF

II. Decomposition of X into Y and Z is dependency preserving and lossless

Which of the above statements is/are correct?

(1) Both I and II (2) II only

(3) Neither I nor II (4) I only

35. There are n unsorted arrays: $A_1, A_2, ..., A_n$. Assume that n is odd. Each of $A_1, A_2, ..., A_n$ contains n distinct elements. There are no common elements between any two arrays. The worst-case time complexity of computing the median of the medians of $A_1, A_2, ..., A_n$ is

(1) $O(n^2)$ (2) $\Omega(n^2 \log n)$

(3) $O(n \log n)$ (4) $O(n)$

36. Consider the augmented grammar given below:

$S' \to S$

$S \to \langle L \rangle \mid id$

$L \to L, S \mid S$

Let I_0 = CLOSURE ({[$S' \to \bullet S$]}). The number of items in the set GOTO(I_0, ⟨) is: ______.

37. Let Σ be the set of all bijections from {1, ..., 5} to {1, ..., 5}, where id denotes the identity function, i.e. id(j) = j, $\forall$ j. Let $\circ$ denote composition on functions. For a string $x = x_1x_2....x_n \in \Sigma^n, n \geq 0$,

let $\pi(x) = x_1 \circ x_2 \circ ... \circ x_n$.

Consider the language $L = \{\in \Sigma^* \mid \pi(x) = id\}$. The minimum number of states in any DFA accepting L is ______.

38. Let T be a full binary tree with 8 leaves. (A full binary tree has every level full.) Suppose two leaves a and b of T are chosen uniformly and independently at random. The expected value of the distance between a and b in T(i.e., the number of edges in the unique path between a and b) is (rounded off to 2 decimal places)

39. The index node (inode) of a Unix-like file system has 12 direct, one single-indirect and one double -indirect pointers. The disk block size is 4 kB, and the disk block address is 32-bits long. The maximum possible file size is (rounded off to 1 decimal place)______ GB

40. Consider the following grammar and the semantic actions to support the inherited type declaration attributes. Let $X_1, X_2, X_3, X_4, X_5,$ and X_6 be the placeholders for the non-terminals D, T, L or L_1 in the following table:

Production rule	Semantic action
$D \to TL$	X_1.type = X_2.type
$T \to int$	T.type = int
$T \to float$	T.type = float
$L \to L_1, id$	X_3.type = X_4.type add Type(id.entry, X_5.type)
$L \to id$	add Type(id.entry, X_6.type)

Which one of the following are the appropriate choices for X_1, X_2, X_3 and X_4?

(1) $X_1 = T, X_2 = L, X_3 = L_1, X_4 = T$

(2) $X_1 = T, X_2 = L, X_3 = T, X_4 = L_1$

(3) $X_1 = L, X_2 = L, X_3 = L_1, X_4 = T$

(4) $X_1 = L, X_2 = T, X_3 = L_1, X_4 = L$

41. Suppose Y is distributed uniformly in the open interval (1, 6). The probability that the polynomial $3x^2 + 6xY + 3Y + 6$ has only real roots is (rounded off to 1 decimal place)______.

42. Consider the following relations P(X, Y, Z), Q(X, Y, T) and R(Y, V).

P

X	Y	Z
X1	Y1	Z1
X1	Y1	Z2
X2	Y2	Z2
X2	Y4	Z4

Q

X	Y	T
X2	Y1	2
X1	Y2	5
X1	Y1	6
X3	Y3	1

R

Y	V
Y1	V1
Y3	V2
Y2	V3
Y2	V2

How many tuples will be returned by the following relational algebra query?

$$\prod_x(\sigma_{P.Y=R.Y \wedge R.V=V2})(P \times R) - \prod_x(\sigma_{Q.Y=R.Y \wedge Q.T>2})(Q \times R)$$

43. A relational database contains two tables Student and Performance as shown below:

Student

Roll_no.	Student_name
1	Amit
2	Priya
3	Vinit
4	Rohan
5	Smita

Performance

Roll_no	Subject_code	Marks
1	A	86
1	B	95
1	C	90
2	A	89
2	C	92
3	C	80

The primary key of the Student table is Roll_no. For the Performance table, the columns Roll_no. and Subject_code together form the primary key. Consider the SQL query given below:

SELECT S. Student name, sum(P. Marks)

FROM Student S, Performance P

WHERE P. Marks > 84

GROUP BY S. Student_name;

The number of rows returned by the above SQL query is ______.

44. Consider the following snapshot of a system running n concurrent processes. Process i is holding Xi instances of a resource R. $1 \leq i \leq n$. Assume that all instances of R are currently in use Further, for all i, process i can place a request for at most Yi additional instances of R while holding the Xi instances it already has. Of the n processes, there are exactly two processes p and q such, that $Y_p = Y_q = 0$. Which one of the following conditions guarantees that no other process apart from p and q can complete execution?

1. $Min(X_p, X_q) \geq Min\{Y_k \mid 1 \leq k \leq n, k \neq p, 1 \neq q\}$
2. $X_p + X_q < Min\{Y_k \mid 1 \leq k \leq n, k \neq p, k \neq q\}$
3. $Min(X_p, X_q) \leq Max\{Y_k \mid 1 \leq k \leq n, k \neq p, k \neq q\}$
4. $X_p + X_q < Max\{Y_k \mid 1 \leq k \leq n, k \neq p, k \neq q\}$

45. Consider three machine M, N, and P with IP addresses 100.10.5.2, 100.10.5.5, and 100.10.5.6 respectively. The subnet mask is set to 255.255.255.252 for all the three machines. Which one of the following is true?

1. M, N, and P belong to three different subnets
2. M, N, and P all belong to the same subnet
3. Only N and P belong to the same subnet
4. Only M and N belong to the same subnet

46. Consider the following C program:

```
#include <stdio,h>
int r () {
    static int num = 7;
    return nun --;
}
int main() {
    for (r(); r(); r())
        printf("%d",r());
    return 0;
}
```

Which one of the following values will be displayed on execution of the programs?

1. 41
2. 52
3. 630
4 63

47. Consider the following C function.

```
void convert(int n){
        if (n<0)
            printf ("%d", n);
        else {
            convert(n/2);
            printf ("%d",n%2);
        }
}
```

Which one of the following will happen when the function convert is positive integer n as argument?

1. It will print the binary representation of n in the reverse order and terminate
2. It will print the binary representation of n but will not terminate
3. It will not print anything and will not terminate
4. It will print the binary representation of n and terminate

48. Consider the following matrix:

$$R = \begin{bmatrix} 1 & 2 & 4 & 8 \\ 1 & 3 & 9 & 27 \\ 1 & 4 & 16 & 64 \\ 1 & 5 & 25 & 125 \end{bmatrix}$$

The absolute value of the product of Eigen values of R is ______.

49. Which one of the following languages over $\Sigma = \{a, b\}$ is NOT context-free?

1. $\{wa^n w^R b^n \mid w \in \{a,b\}^*, n \geq 0\}$
2. $\{a^n b^i \mid i \in \{n, 3n, 5n\}, n \geq 0\}$
3. $\{ww^R \mid w \in \{a, b\}^*\}$
4. $\{wa^n b^n w^R \mid w \in \{a, b\}^*, n \geq 0\}$

50. Consider that 15 machines need to be connected in a LAN using 8-port Ethernet switches. Assume that these switches do not have any separate uplink points. The minimum number of switches needed is___________.

51. In an RSA cryptosystem, the value of the public modulus parameter n is 3007. If it is also known that $\varphi(n) = 2880$, where $\varphi()$ denotes Euler's Totient Function, then the prime factor of n which is greater than 50 is_______________.

52. Suppose that in an IP-over-Ethernet network, a machine X wishes to find the MAC address of another machine Y in its subnet. Which one of the following techniques can be used for this?

1. X sends an ARP request packet to the local gateway's IP address which then finds the MAC address of Y and sends to X
2. X sends an ARP request packet with broadcast IP address in its local subnet
3. X sends an ARP request packet to the local gateway's MAC address which then finds the MAC address of Y and sends to X
4. X sends an ARP request packet with broadcast MAC address in its local subnet

53. A certain processor deploys a single-level cache. The cache block size is 8 words and the word size is 4 bytes. The memory system uses a 60-MHz clock. To service a cache miss, the memory controller first takes 1 cycle to accept the starting address of the block, it then takes 3 cycles to fetch all the eight words of the block, and finally transmits the words of the requested block at the rate of 1 word per cycle. The maximum bandwidth for the memory system when the program running on the processor issues a series of read operations is ___________ $\times 10^6$ bytes/sec.

54. What is the minimum number of 2-input NOR gates required to implement a 4-variable function expressed in sum-of-minterms form as $f = \sum(0, 2, 5, 7, 8, 10, 13, 15)$? Assume that all the inputs and their complements are available. Answer ___________.

55. Consider the first order predicate formula φ :

$\forall x\ [(\forall z\ z \mid x \Rightarrow ((z = x) \vee (z = 1)))$

$\Rightarrow \exists w\ (w > x) \wedge (\forall z\ z \mid w \Rightarrow (w = z) \vee (z = 1)))]$

Here 'a/b' denotes that 'a divides b', where a and b are integers. Consider the following sets:

S1. {1,2,3, ⋯ 100}

S2. Set of all positive integers

S3. Set of all integers

Which of the above sets satisfy φ ?

1. S2 and S3
2. S1 and S2
3. S1 and S3
4. S1, S2 and S3

ANSWERS

General Aptitude (GA)

1. (*b*) **2.** (*c*) **3.** (*b*) **4.** (*a*) **5.** (*c*) **6.** (*b*) **7.** (*d*) **8.** (*c*) **9.** (*a*) **10.** (*c*)

Computer Science and Information Technology

1. (*c*)	**2.** 6	**3.** (*b*)	**4.** (*b*)	**5.** 80	**6.** 0.08	**7.** (*b*)
8. 31	**9.** (*b*)	**10.** (*d*)	**11.** (*b*)	**12.** (*d*)	**13.** 31	**14.** (*d*)
15. (*a*)	**16.** 26	**17.** (*d*)	**18.** (*b*)	**19.** (*a*)	**20.** 2	**21.** (*d*)
22. 29	**23.** (*c*)	**24.** 0.503	**25.** (*a*)	**26.** (*a*)	**27.** 5	**28.** (*d*)
29. (*d*)	**30.** (*a*)	**31.** 10	**32.** 2	**33.** (*b*)	**34.** (*b*)	**35.** (*a*)
36. 5	**37.** 120	**38.** 4.85	**39.** 4.0	**40.** (*d*)	**41.** 0.8	**42.** 1
43. 5	**44.** (*b*)	**45.** (*c*)	**46.** (*b*)	**47.** (*a*)	**48.** 12	**49.** (*a*)
50. 3	**51.** 97	**52.** (*d*)	**53.** 160	**54.** 3	**55.** (*a*)	

EXPLANATIONS

GENERAL APTITUDE

1. Let share of each student be Rs. x

   Now, cost of gift = 10 × x

   According to question

   $$x = 8(x + 150)$$
   $$x = 600$$
   $$\therefore \quad \text{cost of gift} = 10 \times 600 = (6000)$$

2. Court is a place where a judge works.

   Similarly, school is a place where a teacher works.

3. Fulcrum is any thing that plays a central or an essential role in an activity, event, or situation.

   Hence among the given options, 'revolves' is the most appropriate.

4. Speed of 1st car = 50 km/hr

   Speed of 2nd car = 60 km/hr

   Since, both cars A and B are moving in same direction, the relative speed = (60 – 50) = 10 km/hr

   Distance to be covered = 20 km

   $$\therefore \text{ Time} = \frac{\text{Distance}}{\text{Speed}} = \frac{20}{10} = 2 \text{ hrs}$$

5. 'Breaks down' means to divide something such as a total amount into separate parts.

6. Percentage of Administrators

   $$= \left[\frac{\text{Administrators}}{\text{Total number of people}} \times 100\right]\%$$
   $$= \left[\frac{50}{160} \times 100\right]\% = 31.25\%$$

7. According to question, following venn diagram is formed

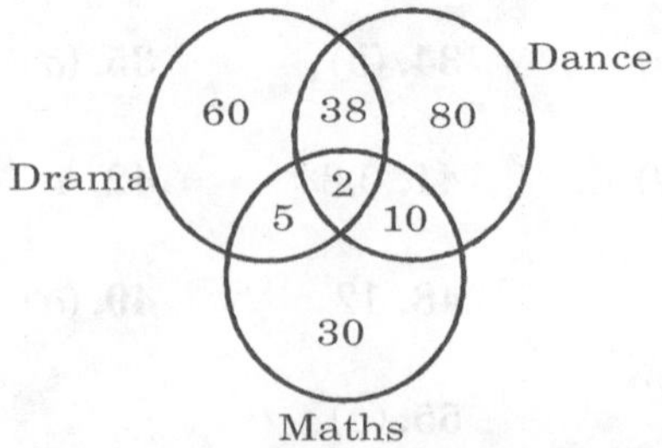

Total number of students = 60 + 80 + 30 + 38 + 5 + 10 + 2 = 225

$$25\% = 225$$

If $$25\% = 225$$

$$\therefore \quad 100\% = \frac{225}{25} \times 100 = 900$$

9. Suffix C as criminal, NC as not criminal.

Case I :

Criminals	P	Q	R	S
Assumption	T	F	F	F
Result	Q_C	S_{NC}	R_C	S_C

Q and R are criminal in the result is impossible because only one person committed the crime.

Case II :

Criminals	P	Q	R	S
Assumption	F	F	T	F
Result	Q_{NC}	S_{NC}	R_{NC}	S_C

S_{NC} and S_C in the result which is contradiction. [S committed crime and same time not committed crime which is contradiction]

Case III :

Criminals	P	Q	R	S
Assumption	F	T	F	F
Result	Q_{NC}	S_C	R_C	S_C

S and R are criminal in the result is impossible because only one person committed the crime.

Case IV :

Criminals	P	Q	R	S
Assumption	F	F	F	T
Result	Q_{NC}	S_{NC}	R_C	S_{NC}

R is criminal in the result.

Hence this case satisfies only one person committed the crime.

So option (a) is correct.

10. The passage states that the underlying disease behind begging is the failure of the state to protect citizens who fall through the social security net. Only option (b) can be inferred from this.

COMPUTER SCIENCE AND INFORMATION TECHNOLOGY

1. SMTP is push protocol and is used to send email and while POP3 is pull protocol and is used to retrieve email.

3. LR parser is a bottom up parser and so it uses right most derivation in reverse order.

   ∴ option (b) is the correct.

4. • Suffix (L) and Prefix(L) are also regular by closure property.

- If L is regular, $L \cdot L^R$ is also regular by closure property.

However option(d) $\{ww^R \mid w \in L\}$ need not be regular since if L is an infinite regular language, then $\{ww^R \mid w \in L\}$ will not only be infinite, but also non-regular.

7. • Below is the structure of B^+ tree non leaf node.

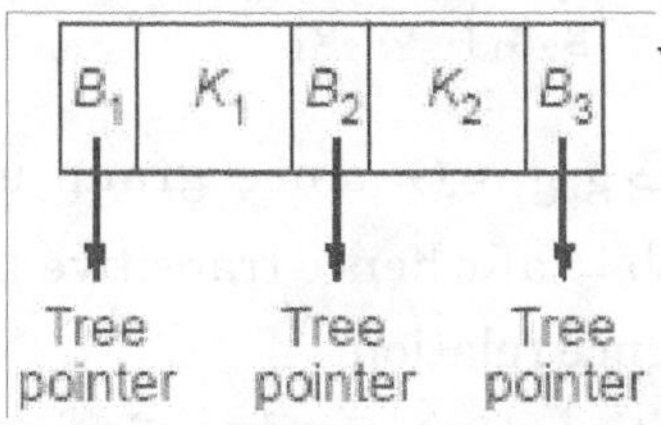

where K_1 and K_2 are keys

- B^+ tree non leaf node consists of only keys and tree pointers (node pointers).
- B^+ tree non leaf node have pointer to data records is false statement.

8. $S \rightarrow Aa$

$A \rightarrow BD$

$B \rightarrow b \mid \epsilon$

$D \rightarrow d \mid \epsilon$

Follow (B) = {d, a}

Hence index value in descending order is 31.

9. 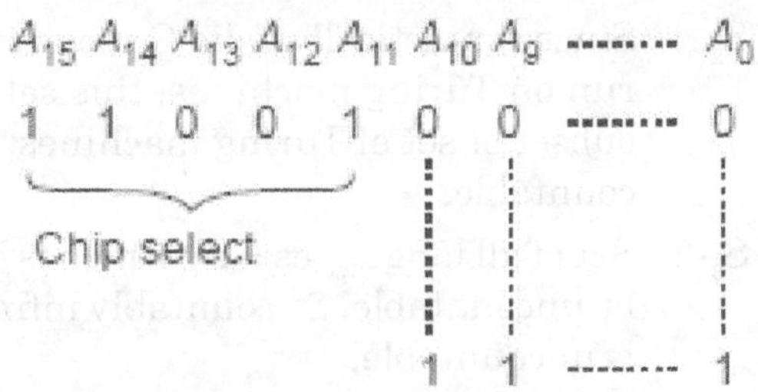

[C800 to CFFF]

10. (a) $(x \oplus y) \oplus z = x \oplus (y \oplus z)$

Associativity is true on Ex-OR operator so it valid.

(b) $x \oplus y = (x+y)(\overline{x}+\overline{y})$

$= (x+y)\overline{xy} = (x+y)\overline{0}$

$= (x + y)$, so it is valid.

(c) $x \oplus y = (xy + x'y')' = (x \odot y)'$

$= x \oplus y$, it is valid.

(d) $(x+y) \oplus z = \overline{(x+y)} \cdot z + (x+y)\overline{z}$

$= \underset{1}{\overline{x}\,\overline{y}z} + \underset{4,6}{x\overline{Z}} + \underset{2,6}{y\overline{Z}} = \sum m(1, 2, 4, 6)$

$x \oplus (y+z) = \overline{x}(y+z) + x\overline{(y+z)}$

$= \underset{2,3}{\overline{x}y} + \underset{1,3}{\overline{x}z} + \underset{4}{x\overline{y}\,\overline{z}} = \sum m(1, 2, 3, 4)$

$(x+y) \oplus z \neq x \oplus (y+z)$

Hence it is invalid.

11. For example:

Let,

$$\left.\begin{array}{l} X = +6, n = 4 \\ Y = -5, n = 4 \end{array}\right\} \Rightarrow (X - Y) = +11$$

So Z = 11 which required 5 bits which is (n + 1) bits

12. Cache memory size = 16 kB

Block size = 16 B

Main memory address = 32 bit

$$\text{Number of lines (N)} = \frac{16K}{16}$$

$$\Rightarrow \frac{2^{14}}{2^4} = 2^{10}$$

Fully associative cache memory (N-way)

$$\therefore \text{ number of sets (S)} = \frac{N}{\text{P-way}}$$

$$\therefore \frac{2^{10}}{2^{10}} = 1$$

32 bit

∴ Address format :

TAG	WO
28 bit	$\log_2 16 = 4$bit

∴ TAG = 28 bit

Index = 0 bit

14. $\lim_{x \to 3} \frac{x^4 - 81}{2x^2 - 5x - 3} \left(\frac{0}{0} \text{form}\right)$

Now applying L' Hospital rule we get

$$= \lim_{x \to 3} \frac{4x^3}{4x - 5} = \frac{108}{7}$$

17. $A = \{(x, X), x \in X \text{ and } X \subseteq U\}$

The number of k element subsets of a set U with n elements $= {}^nC_k$.

The number of possible ordered pairs (x, X) where $x \in X$ is $k \cdot {}^nC_k$ $1 \le k \le n$ 1 to n.

So total number of ordered pairs in A is given

$$= |A| = \sum_{k=1}^{n} k \cdot {}^nC_k = \sum_{k=1}^{n} k \cdot \binom{n}{k}$$

So II is correct.

But by the combinational identity

$$\sum_{k=1}^{n} k\cdot\binom{n}{k} = n\cdot 2^{n-1}$$

So I is also correct.

So both I and II are correct.

18. In a complete graph we can traverse the n vertices in any order and return to the starting vertex and form a Hamiltonian cycle. The number of such cycles required is n!

While for is circular rotations ignored. Since for example K_4 with vertices {1, 2, 3, 4}, the cycle 1-2-3-4 is same as 2-3-4-1 is same as 3-4-1-2 etc. we now get only (n – 1)! distinct Hamiltonian cycles. Further, the cycle 1-2-3-4 and 1-4-3-2 are also same (clockwise and anticlockwise).

$\therefore$ we get $\frac{(n-1)!}{2}$ distinct Hamiltonian cycles

19. I. Strict 2PL guaranteed conflict serializable because of 2PL condition and also strict recoverable.

II. Thomas Write time stamp ordering ensures serializable. Thomas write rule time stamp ordering allowed to execute schedule which is view equal serial schedule based on time stamp ordering.

20. By Fermat's theorem

$3^{(5-1)} \bmod 5 = 1$

$\therefore\ 3^4 \bmod 5 = 1$

Now $3^{51} \bmod 5 = (3^4)^{12}.3^3 \bmod 5 = 3^3 \bmod 5 = 2$

21. $L = \{a^{2+3k} \text{ or } b^{10+12k}\}$ for $k \geq 0$

$= a^2(a^3)^* \text{ or } b^{10}(b^{12})^*$

$= \{a^2, a^5, a^7, ..., b^{10}, b^{22}, b^{34}....\}$

The smallest string which can be pumped is a^5

$$a^5 = \underset{x}{a^2}\ \underset{y}{(a^3)}\ \underset{z}{\in}$$

So minimum pumping length = 5

23. $R_1 : \forall\ a, b \in G, a R_1 b$ if and only if $\exists g \in G$ such that $a = g^{-1} bg$

Reflexive: $a = g^{-1}$

ag can be satisfied by putting g = e, identity "e" always exists in a group.

So reflexive

Symmetric: $aRb \Rightarrow a = g^{-1} bg$ for some g

$\Rightarrow b = gag^{-1} = (g^{-1})^{-1} ag^{-1}$

g^{-1} always exists for every $g \in G$.

So symmetric

Transitive: aRb and bRc $\Rightarrow a = g_1^{-1} bg_1$ and $b = g_2^{-1} cg_2$ for some $g_1 g_2 \in G$.

Now $a = g_1^{-1} g_2^{-1} cg_2 g_1 = (g_2 g_1)^{-1} cg_2 g_1$

$g_1 \in G$ and $g_2 \in G \Rightarrow g_2 g_1 \in G$ since group is closed so aRb and aRb $\Rightarrow$ aRc hence transitive

Clearly R_1 is equivalence relation.

R_2 is not equivalence it need not even be reflexive, since $aR_2 a \Rightarrow a = a^{-1}\ \forall$ a which not be true in a group.

R_1 is equivalence relation is the correct answer.

25. '28' in binary code is written as

+28 $\Rightarrow$ 0000 0000 0001 1100

Now, (2's complement form)

–28 $\Rightarrow$ 1111 1111 1110 0100

28. S_1 : Infinite as it hence it is countable corresponds with set of turing machines.

S_2 : Since syntactically valid C programs surely run on Turing machines, this set is also a subset of set of Turing machines, which is countable.

S_3 : Set of all languages = 2^{Σ^*} which is known to be uncountable. Σ^* countably infinite $\Rightarrow 2^{\Sigma^*}$ is uncountable.

S_4 : Set of all non-regular languages includes set $L_{NOT\ RE}$ which is uncountable infinite and hence is uncountable

So, S_3 and S_4 are uncountable.

29. $f_1.f_2 = \Sigma(2, 8, 14)$

$f_1 = f_3 \oplus (f_1.f_2)$

$= \Sigma(7, 8, 11)$

30. If no two edges of G have same weight surely G will have unique spanning tree is true. So I is true

And if, for every cut of G, there is a unique minimum weight edge crossing the cut then G will have unique spanning tree is also true. So II is true

So both I and II are true.

Option (d) is correct.

32. Assume Z = 2

	Arrival time	CPU burst time	Completion time	Waiting time
P_1	0	3	4	1
P_2	1	1	2	0
P_3	3	3	9	3
P_4	4	Z = 2	6	0

$$\text{Average waiting time} = \frac{1+0+3+0}{4} = \frac{4}{4} = 1 \text{ ms}$$

Hence, Z = 2

33. 1 word = 4 bytes

Page size = 8 kB = 2^{13} B

$$\text{Now, Number of words in 1 page} = \frac{2^{13}}{2^2} = 2^{11}$$

TLB can hold 128 valid entries so, at most 128×2^{11} memory address can be addressed

$128 \times 2^{11} = 128 \times 2 \times 2^{10} = 256 \times 2^{10}$

So option (d) is correct.

34. X(PQRS) {QR → S, R → P, S → Q} decomposed into

Y(PR)	Z(QRS)
{R → P}	{QR → S, S → Q}
Candidate key: R	Candidate key: QR, RS
Relation Y in BCNF	Relation Z in 3NF but not BCNF

Common attribute between Y and Z relations is R which is key for relation Y. So that given decomposition is lossless join decomposition.

R → P in Y

$\left.\begin{matrix} QR \rightarrow S \\ S \rightarrow Q \end{matrix}\right\}$ are in Z

and dependency preserving decomposition.

36.

S′ → .S S → .<L> S → .id	—<→	S → <.L> L → .L, S L → .S S → .<L> S → .id

Hence total number of items in the set GOTO (I_0, ⟨) is 5.

37. The DFA for accepting L will have 5! = 120 states, since we need one state for every possible permutation function on 5 elements. The starting state will be "id" state, name as $\begin{pmatrix}12345\\12345\end{pmatrix}$ and from there n! arrows will go the n! states each named with a distinct permutation of the set {1, 2, 3, 4, 5}. Since composition of permutation function is closed every arrow has to go to some permutation and hence some state.

Since the language only has those strings where π(x) = id only the starting ("id" state) will be the final state. Sample machine with only 2 states is shown below

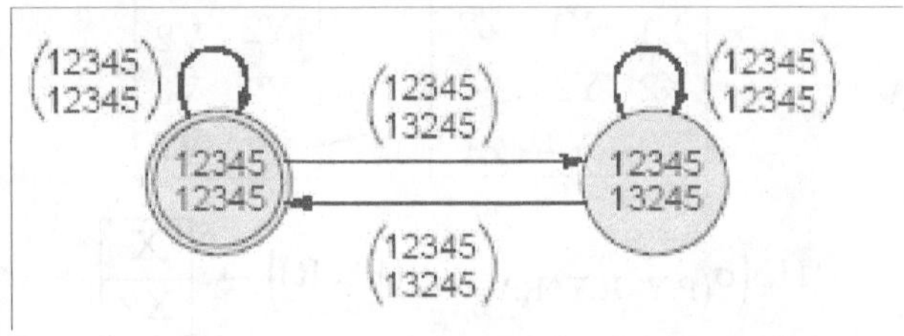

38. Two nodes can be selected in $^8C_2$ = 28 ways

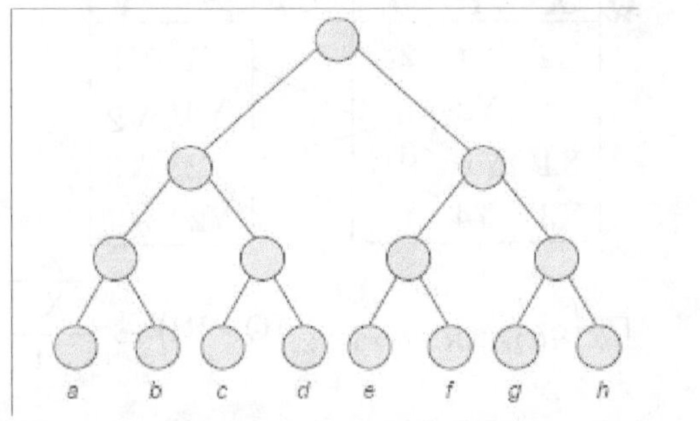

Where X is length between two nodes selected

X	2	4	6
P(x)	$\frac{4}{28}$	$\frac{8}{28}$	$\frac{16}{28}$

Expected length between a and b is given by

$$E[X] = 2\left(\frac{4}{28}\right) + 4\left(\frac{8}{28}\right) + 6\left(\frac{16}{28}\right)$$

$$= \frac{8+32+96}{28} = \frac{136}{28} = 4.857$$

41. Polynomial $3x^2 + 6xY + 3Y + 6$ has only real roots

$\therefore\ b^2 - 4ax \geq 0$

$(6Y)^2 - 4(3)(3Y+6) \geq 0$

$Y^2 - Y + 2 \geq 0$

$Y \in (-\infty, -1] \cap [2, \infty)$

$\Rightarrow Y \in [2, 6)$

Now y is uniformly distributed in (1, 6)

Probability distribution function

$$f(Y) = \frac{1}{5} \qquad 1 < y < 6$$

$$\therefore\ p(2 \leq y < 6) = \int_2^6 f(Y)dy$$

$$\frac{1}{5}[Y]_2^6 = \frac{1}{5}(6-2) = \frac{4}{5} = 0.8$$

42.

P

X	Y	Z
X1	Y1	Z1
X1	Y1	Z2
X2	Y2	Z2
X2	Y4	Z4

R

Y	V
Y1	V1
Y2	V2
Y2	V3
Y2	V2

$\Pi_X\left(\sigma_{(P.Y=R.Y \wedge R.V=V2)}(P \times R)\right) \Rightarrow$

X
X2

... (I)

Q

X	Y	Z
X2	Y1	2
X1	Y2	5
X1	Y1	6
X3	Y4	1

R

Y	V
Y1	V1
Y3	V2
Y2	V3
Y2	V2

$\Pi_X\left(\sigma_{(Q.Y=R.Y \wedge Q.T>2)}(Q \times R)\right) \Rightarrow$

X
X1

... (II)

I – II $\Rightarrow$

X
X2

one record in result.

43.

Student	
Roll_no.	**Student_name**
1	Amit
2	Priya
3	Vinit
4	Rohan
5	Smita

Performance		
Roll_no.	**Student_code**	**Marks**
1	A	86
1	B	95
1	C	90
2	A	89
2	C	92
3	C	80

Hence total S rows is returned by above SOL

45.

	100.10.5.2	2	00000010
M→	255.255.255.252	252	11111100
	194.56.10.0	0	00000000
	100.10.5.5	2	00000101
N→	255.255.255.252	252	11111100
	194.56.10.4	4	00000100
	100.10.5.6	6	00000110
P→	255.255.255.252	252	11111100
	194.56.10.4	4	00000100

N and P belongs to same subnet.

47. SDT for inserting type information in the symbol table

D → TL {L.idtype = T.stype}

T → int {T.stype = int}

T → float {T.stype = float}

L → L_1, id {L_1.itype = L.itype}

addtype(id.entry, L.itype)

L → id addtype (id.entry, L.itype)

Replace these attribute information in the given SDT.

So option (a) is the correct answer.

48. Product of eigen values is same as the determinant of a matrix.

$$\begin{vmatrix} 1 & 2 & 2^2 & 2^3 \\ 1 & 3 & 3^2 & 3^3 \\ 1 & 4 & 4^2 & 4^3 \\ 1 & 5 & 5^2 & 5^3 \end{vmatrix} = \begin{vmatrix} 1 & 2 & 2^2 & 2^3 \\ 0 & 3-2 & 3^2-2^2 & 3^3-2^3 \\ 0 & 4-2 & 4^2-2^2 & 4^3-2^3 \\ 0 & 5-2 & 5^2-2^2 & 5^3-2^3 \end{vmatrix}$$

$$= (3-2)(4-2)(5-2)\begin{vmatrix} 1 & 5 & 19 \\ 1 & 6 & 28 \\ 1 & 7 & 39 \end{vmatrix}$$

$$= 1.2.3\begin{vmatrix} 1 & 5 & 19 \\ 0 & 1 & 9 \\ 0 & 2 & 20 \end{vmatrix}$$

$$= 1 \times 2 \times 3 \times 2 = 12$$

So the product of eigen value is 12.

49. (a) $\{wa^nb^nw^R \mid w \in \{a,b\}^*, n \geq 0\}$ is a CFL, since we can first push w, then a's, b's pop with a's and w^R pops with the w. So PDA can accept the language.

(b) $\{ww^R \mid w \in \{a,b\}^*\}$ is a CFL

(c) $\{wa^nw^Rb^n \mid w \in \{a,b\}^*, n \geq 0\}$ is a not CFL because after pushing w, we need to push a's into stack which will stop the w from being matched with w^R. If we don't push a's after w, than later we cannot match with b^n. So this language is not acceptable by a PDA and hence not a CFL.

(d) $\{a^nb^i \mid i \in \{n, 3n, 5n\}, n \geq 0\}$

$= a^nb^n \cup a^nb^{3n} \cup a^nb^{5n}$ is CFL since each of the three parts is a CFL and closure under union guarantees that result also is a CFL.

50. 3 switches of ethernet are required to connect 15 computers.

51. $n = p \times q = 3007$

$\phi(n) = (p-1)(q-1) = 2880$

Using RSA algorithm, $n = 31 \times 97$ in which 97 is prime factor which is greater than 50.

53. Total time to transfer a cache block = 1 + 3 + 8 = 12 cycles

8 W______ 12 cycles

8 × 4 bytes ______ 12 cycles

? B ______ 1 sec

$$= \frac{32B}{12 \times \left(\frac{1}{60} + 10^{-6}\right) \text{sec}}$$

$= 160 \times 10^6$ bytes/sec

54. $f = \Sigma_m(0, 2, 5, 7, 8, 10, 13, 15)$

$f = \Pi_M(1, 3, 4, 6, 9, 11, 12, 14)$

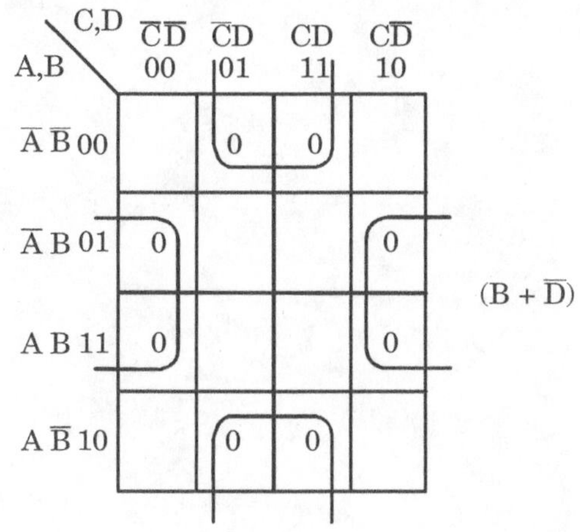

$$f = (\overline{B} + D)(B + \overline{D})$$

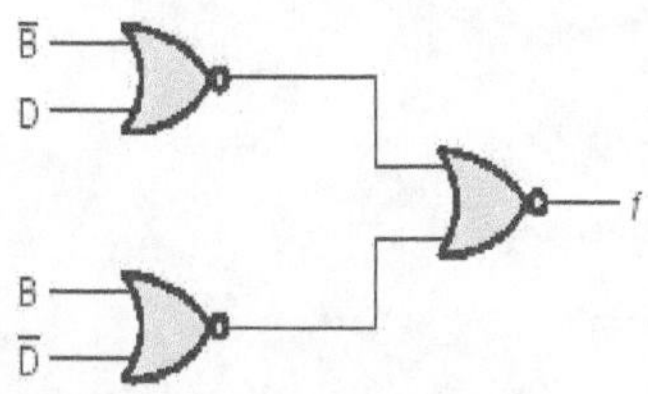

So 3 NOR gates is required to implement above function.

SOLVED PAPER - 2020

INSTRUCTIONS

1. Total of 65 questions carrying 100 marks, out of which 10 questions carrying a total of 15 marks are in General Aptitude (GA)
2. The Engineering Mathematics will carry around **15% of the total marks,** the General Aptitude section will carry **15% of the total marks** and the **remaining 70% of the total marks.**
3. **Types of Questions**
   (*a*) **Multiple Choice Questions (MCQ)** carrying 1 or 2 marks each in all papers and sections. These questions are objective in nature, and each will have a choice of four options, out of which the candidate has to mark the correct answer(s).
   (*b*) **Numerical Answer Questions** of 1 or 2 marks each in all papers and sections. For these questions the answer is a real number, to be entered by the candidate using the virtual keypad. No choices will be shown for these type of questions.
4. For **1-mark** multiple-choice questions, **1/3 marks** will be deducted for a wrong answer. Likewise, for **2-marks** multiple-choice questions, 2/3 marks will be deducted for a wrong answer. There is no negative marking for numerical answer type questions.

Chapter-Wise Analysis

#	Chapters	Marks		
		1	2	Total
1	General Aptitude	5	5	15
2	Engineering Mathematics	3	8	19
3	Theory of Computation	1	1	3
4	Digital Logic	2	2	4
5	Computer Organization & Architecture	4	5	14
6	Programming & Data Structures	3	3	9
7	Algorithm	2	2	6

#	Chapters	Marks		
		1	2	Total
8	Compiler Design	4	2	8
9	Operating System	2	4	10
10	Data Bases	2	3	8
11	Computer Networks	2	1	4
12	* Software Engineering	0	0	0
13	* Web Technology	0	0	0

GENERAL APTITUDE (GA)

Q. 1 to Q. 5 : Carry One Mark Each.

1. Raman is confident of speaking English ________ six months as he has been practising regularly ________the last three weeks.

(a) during, for (b) for, since
(c) for, in (d) within, for

2. His knowledge of the subject was excellent but his classroom performance was ________.

(a) extremely poor (b) good
(c) desirable (d) praiseworthy

3. Select the word that fits the analogy:

Cook : Cook :: Fly : ________

(a) Flyer (b) Flying
(c) Flew (d) Flighter

4. The dawn of the 21st century witnessed the melting glaciers oscillating between giving too much and too little to billions of people who depend on them for fresh water. The UN climate report estimates that without deep cuts to man-made emissions, at least 30% of the northern hemisphere's surface permafrost could melt by the end of the century. Given this situation of imminent global exodus of billions of people displaced by rising seas, nation-states need to rethink their carbon footprint for political concerns, if not for environmental ones.

Which one of the following statements can be inferred from the given passage?

(a) Nation-states do not have environmental concerns.
(b) Nation-states are responsible for providing fresh water to billions of people.
(c) Billions of people are responsible for man-made emissions.
(d) Billions of people are affected by melting glaciers.

5. There are multiple routes to reach from node 1 to node 2, as shown in the network.

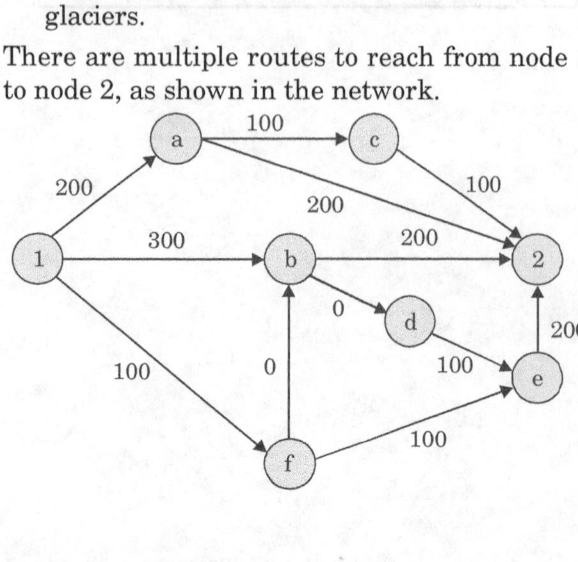

The cost of travel on an edge between two nodes is given in rupees. Nodes 'a', 'b', 'c', 'd', 'e' and 'f' are toll booths. The toll price at toll booths marked 'a' and 'e' is Rs. 200 and is Rs. 100 for the other toll booths. Which is the cheapest route from node 1 to node 2?

(a) 1-a-c-2 (b) 1-f-b-2
(c) 1-b-2 (d) 1-f-e-2

Q. 6 to Q. 10 : Carry Two Marks Each.

6. Goods and Services Tax (GST) is an indirect tax introduced in India in 2017 that is imposed on the supply of goods and services, and it subsumes all indirect taxes except few. It is a destination-based tax imposed on goods and services used, and it is not imposed at the point of origin from where goods come. GST also has a few components specific to state governments, central government and Union Territories (UTs).

Which one of the following statements can be inferred from the given passage?

(a) GST is imposed on the production of goods and services.
(b) GST includes all indirect taxes.
(c) GST does not have a component specific to UT.
(d) GST is imposed at the point of usage of goods and services.

7. If P = 3, R = 27, T = 243, then Q + S = ________.

(a) 40 (b) 80
(c) 90 (d) 110

8. The figure below shows an annular ring with outer and inner radii as b and a, respectively. The annular space has been painted in the form of blue colour circles touching the outer and inner periphery of annular space. If maximum n number of circles can be painted, then the unpainted area available in annular space is _____.

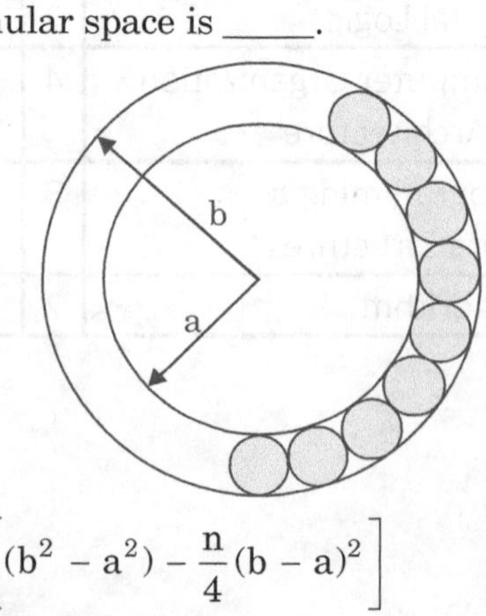

(a) $\pi\left[(b^2 - a^2) - \frac{n}{4}(b - a)^2\right]$

(b) $\pi\left[(b^2 - a^2) - n(b - a)^2\right]$

(c) $\pi\left[(b^2 - a^2) + \frac{n}{4}(b - a)^2\right]$

(d) $\pi\left[(b^2 - a^2) + n(b - a)^2\right]$

9. Two straight lines are drawn perpendicular to each other in X-Y plane. If α and β are the acute angles the straight lines make with the X-axis, then $\alpha + \beta$ is ______.

(a) 60° (b) 90°

(c) 120° (d) 180°

10. The total revenue of a company during 2014-2018 is shown in the bar graph. If the total expenditure of the company in each year is 500 million rupees, then the aggregate profit or loss (in percentage) on the total expenditure of the company during 2014-2018 is ______.

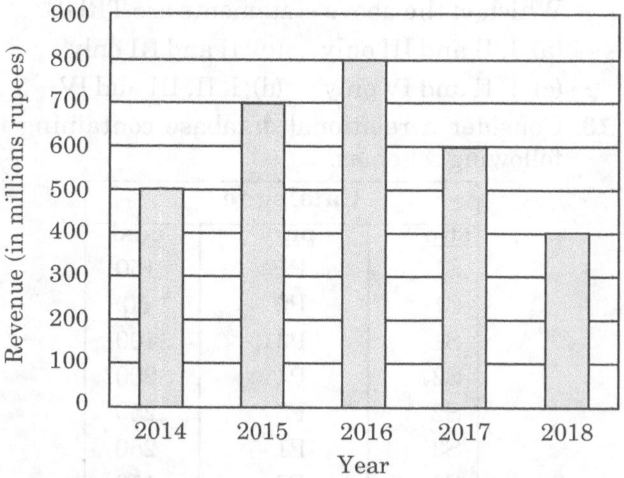

(a) 16.67% profit (b) 16.67% loss

(c) 20% profit (d) 20% loss

COMPUTER SCIENCE & IT

Q. 1 to Q. 25 : Carry One Mark Each.

1. Consider the functions:

I. e^{-x}

II. $x^2 - \sin x$

III. $\sqrt{x^3 + 1}$

Which of the above functions is/are increasing everywhere in [0, 1]?

(a) III only (b) II only

(c) II and III only (d) l and III only

2. For parameters a and b, both of which are $\omega(1)$, $T(n) = T(n^{1/a}) + 1$, and $T(b) = 1$. Then T (n) is

(a) $\Theta(\log_a \log_b n)$ (b) $\Theta(\log_{ab} n)$

(c) $\Theta(\log_b \log_a n)$ (d) $\Theta(\log_2 \log_2 n)$

3. Consider the following statements:

I. Daisy chaining is used to assign priorities in attending interrupts.

II. When a device raises a vectored interrupt, the CPU does polling to identify the source of interrupt.

III. In polling, the CPU periodically checks the status bits to know if any device needs its attention.

IV. During DMA, both the CPU and DMA controller can be bus masters at the same time.

Which of the above statements is/are TRUE?

(a) I and II only

(b) I and IV only

(c) I and III only

(d) III only

4. Consider the following data path diagram.

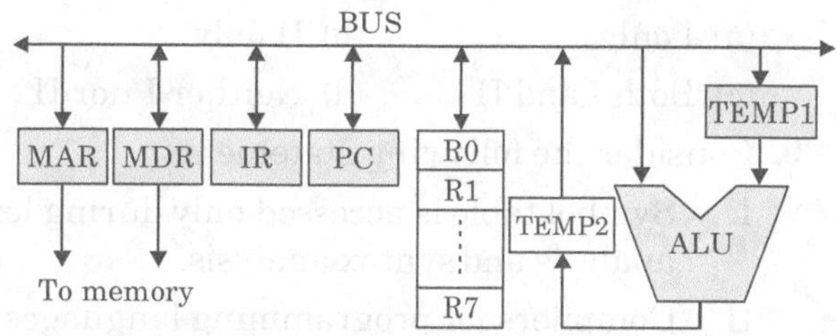

Consider an instruction: R0 ← R1 + R2. The following steps are used to execute it over the given data path. Assume that PC is incremented appropriately. The subscripts r and w indicate read and write operations, respectively.

1. $R2_r$, $TEMP1_r$, ALU_{add}, $TEMP2_w$
2. $R1_r$, $TEMP1_w$
3. PC_r, MAR_w, MEM_r
4. $TEMP2_r$, $R0_w$
5. MDR_r, IR_w

Which one of the following is the correct order of execution of the above steps?

(a) 2, 1, 4, 5, 3 (b) 1, 2, 4, 3, 5

(c) 3, 5, 2, 1, 4 (d) 3, 5, 1, 2, 4

5. The preorder traversal of a binary search tree is 15, 10, 12, 11, 20, 18, 16, 19.

Which one of the following is the postorder traversal of the tree?

(a) 10, 11, 12, 15, 16, 18, 19, 20

(b) 11, 12, 10, 16, 19, 18, 20, 15

(c) 20, 19, 18, 16, 15, 12, 11, 10

(d) 19, 16, 18, 20, 11, 12, 10, 15

6. What is the worst case time complexity of inserting n^2 elements into an AVL-tree with n elements initially?

(a) $\Theta(n^4)$ (b) $\Theta(n^2)$

(c) $\Theta(n^2 \log n)$ (d) $\Theta(n^3)$

7. Which one of the following regular expressions represents the set of all binary strings with an odd number of 1's?

(a) ((0 + 1)* 1(0 + 1)*1)*10*

(b) (0*10*10*)*0*1

(c) 10* (0*10*10*)*

(d) (0*10*10*)*10*

8. Consider the following statements.

I. If $L_1 \cup L_2$ is regular, then both L_1 and L_2 must be regular.

II. The class of regular languages is closed under infinite union.

Which of the above statements is/are TRUE?

(a) I only (b) II only

(c) Both I and II (d) Neither I nor II

9. Consider the following statements.

I. Symbol table is accessed only during lexical analysis and syntax analysis.

II. Compilers for programming languages that support recursion necessarily need heap storage for memory allocation in the run-time environment.

III. Errors violating the condition '*any variable must be declared before its use*' are detected during syntax analysis.

Which of the above statements is/are TRUE?

(a) I only (b) I and III only

(c) II only (d) None of I, II and III

10. Consider the language $L = \{a^n \mid n \geq 0\} \cup \{a^nb^n \mid n \geq 0\}$ and the following statements.

I. L is deterministic context-free.

II. L is context-free but not deterministic context-free.

III. L is not LL(k)for any k.

Which of the above statements is/are TRUE?

(a) I only (b) II only

(c) I and III only (d) III only

11. Consider allocation of memory to a new process. Assume that none of the existing holes in the memory will exactly fit the process's memory requirement. Hence, a new hole of smaller size will be created if allocation is made in any of the existing holes. Which one of the following statements is TRUE?

(a) The hole created by first fit is always larger than the hole created by next fit.

(b) The hole created by worst fit is always larger than the hole created by first fit.

(c) The hole created by best fit is never larger than the hole created by first fit.

(d) The hole created by next fit is never larger than the hole created by best fit.

12. Consider the following statements about process state transitions for a system using preemptive scheduling.

I. A running process can move to ready state.

II. A ready process can move to running state.

III. A blocked process can move to running state.

IV. A blocked process can move to ready state.

Which of the above statements are TRUE?

(a) I, II and III only (b) II and III only

(c) I, II and IV only (d) I, II, III and IV

13. Consider a relational database containing the following schemas.

Catalogue

<u>sno</u>	<u>pno</u>	cost
S1	P1	150
S1	P2	50
S1	P3	100
S2	P4	200
S2	P5	250
S3	P1	250
S3	P2	150
S3	P5	300
S3	P4	250

Suppliers

<u>sno</u>	sname	location
S1	M/s Royal furniture	Delhi
S1	M/s Balaji furniture	Bangalore
S3	M/s Premium furniture	Chennai

Parts

<u>pno</u>	sname	part_spec
P1	Table	Wood
P2	Chair	Wood
P3	Table	Steel
P4	Almirah	Steel
P5	Almirah	Wood

The primary key of each table is indicated by underlining the constituent fields.

```
SELECT   s.sno, s.sname
FROM     Suppliers s,   Catalogue c
WHERE    s.no = c.sno AND
         cost> (SELECT AVG (cost)
                FROM Catalogue
                WHERE pno = `P4´
                GROUP BY pno);
```

The number of rows returned by the above SQL query is

(a) 4 (b) 5

(c) 0 (d) 2

14. Which one of the following is used to represent the supporting many-one relationships of a weak entity set in an entity-relationship diagram?

(a) Diamonds with double/bold border

(b) Rectangles with double/bold border

(c) Ovals with double/bold border

(d) Ovals that contain underlined identifiers

15. Consider the following statements about the functionality of an IP based router.

I. A router does not modify the IP packets during forwarding.

II. It is not necessary for a router to implement any routing protocol.

III. A router should reassemble IP fragments if the MTU of the outgoing link is larger than the size of the incoming IP packet.

Which of the above statements is/are TRUE?

(a) I and II only (b) I only

(c) II and III only (d) II only

16. What is the worst case time complexity of inserting n elements into an empty linked list, if the linked list needs to be maintained in sorted order?

(a) $\Theta(n)$ (b) $\Theta(n \log n)$

(c) $\Theta(n^2)$ (d) $\Theta(1)$

17. Let R be the set of all binary relations on the set {1,2,3}. Suppose a relation is chosen from R at random. The probability that the chosen relation is reflexive(round off to 3 decimal places) is _____.

18. Let G be a group of 35 elements. Then the largest possible size of a subgroup of G other than G itself is _______.

19. A multiplexer is placed between a group of 32 registers and an accumulator to regulate data movement such that at any given point in time the content of only one register will move to the accumulator, The minimum number of select lines needed for the multiplexer is ________.

20. If there are m input lines and n output lines for a decoder that is used to uniquely address a byte addressable 1 KB RAM, then the minimum value of m + n is ________.

21. A direct mapped cache memory of 1 MB has a block size of 256 bytes. The cache has an access time of 3 ns and a hit rate of 94%. During a cache miss, it takes 20 ns to bring the first word of a block from the main memory, while each subsequent word takes 5 ns. The word size is 64 bits. The average memory access time in ns (round off to 1 decimal place) is ________.

22. Consider the following C program:

```
#include <stdio.h>
int main( )  {
    int a[4][5] ={{1, 2, 3, 4, 5},
                  {6, 7, 8, 9, 10},
                  {11, 12, 13, 14, 15},
                  {16, 17, 18, 19, 20}};
printf("%d\n",*(*(a+**a+2)+3));
return(0);
}
```

The output of the program is ________.

23. Consider a double hashing scheme in which the primary hash function is $h_1(k) = k \bmod 23$ and the secondary hash function is $h_2(k) = 1 + (k \bmod 19)$. Assume that the table size is 23. Then the address returned by probe 1 in the probe sequence (assume that the probe sequence begins at probe 0) for key value k = 90 is ______.

24. Consider the following grammar.

$S \to aSB \mid d$

$B \to b$

The number of reduction steps taken by a bottom-up parser while accepting the string aaadbbb is _______.

25. Assume that you have made a request for a web page through your web browser to a web server. Initially the browser cache is empty. Further, the browser is configured to send HTTP requests in non-persistent mode. The web page contains text and five very small images. The minimum number of TCP connections required to display the web page completely in your browser is ________.

Q. 26 to Q. 55 : Carry Two Marks Each.

26. Which of the following languages are undecidable? Note that $\langle M \rangle$ indicates encoding of the Turing machine M.

$L_1 = \{\langle M \rangle \mid L(M) = \phi\}$

$L_2 = \{\langle M \rangle w, q\rangle \mid$ M on input w reaches state q in exactly 100 steps}

$L_3 = \{\langle M \rangle \mid$ L(M) is not recursive)

$L_4 = \{\langle M \rangle \mid$ L(M) contains at least 21 members}

(a) L_1, L_3 and L_4 only

(b) L_1 and L_3 only

(c) L_2 and L_3 only

(d) L_1, L_3 and L_4 only

27. Let A and B be two n × n matrices over real numbers. Let rank(M) and det(M) denote the rank and determinant of a matrix M, respectively. Consider the following statements:

I. rank (AB) = rank(A) rank(B)

II. det(AB) = det(A) det(B)

III. rank(A + B) ≤ rank(A) + rank(B)

IV. det(A + B) ≤ det(A) + det(B)

Which of the above statements are TRUE?

(a) I and II only (b) I and IV only

(c) II and III only (d) III and IV only

28. Consider the Boolean function z(a, b, c).

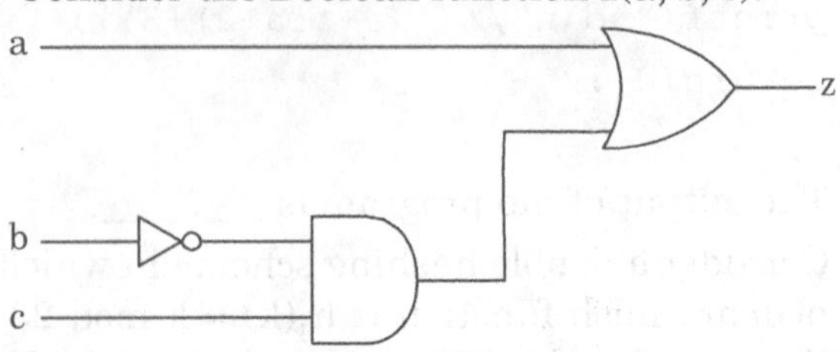

Which one of the following minterm lists represents the circuit given above?

(a) $z = \Sigma(0, 1, 3, 7)$ (b) $z = \Sigma(1, 4, 5, 6, 7)$

(c) $z = \Sigma(2, 4, 5, 6, 7)$ (d) $z = \Sigma(2, 3, 5)$

29. Consider three registers R1, R2, and R3 that store numbers in IEEE-754 single precision floating point format. Assume that R1 and R2 contain the values(in hexadecimal notation) 0x42200000 and 0xC1200000, respectively.

If $R3 = \frac{R1}{R2}$, what is the value stored in R3?

(a) 0x40800000 (b) 0xC0800000

(c) 0x83400000 (d) 0xC8500000

30. A computer system with a word length of 32 bits has a 16 MB byte-addressable main memory and a 64 KB, 4-way set associative cache memory with a block size of 256 bytes. Consider the following four physical addresses represented in hexadecimal notation.

A1 = 0×42C8A4, A2 = 0×546888, A3 = 0×6A289C, A4 = 0×5E4880

Which one of the following is TRUE?

(a) A1 and A4 are mapped to different cache sets.

(b) A2 and A3 are mapped to the same cache set.

(c) A3 and A4 are mapped to the same cache set.

(d) A1 and A3 are mapped to the same cache set.

31. Let G = (V, E) be a weighted undirected graph and let T be a Minimum Spanning Tree (MST) of G maintained using adjacency lists. Suppose a new weighted edge $(u, v) \in V \times V$ is added to G. The worst case time complexity of determining if T is still an MST of the resultant graph is

(a) $\Theta(|E| + |V|)$ (b) $\Theta(|E|\ |V|)$

(c) $\Theta(|E| \log |V|)$ (d) $\Theta(|V|)$

32. Consider the following languages.

$L_1 = \{w\,x\,yx \mid w, x, y \in (0 + 1)^+\}$

$L_2 = \{xy \mid x, y \in (a + b)^*, |x| = |y|, x \neq y\}$

Which one of the following is TRUE?

(a) L_1 is regular and L_2 is context-free.

(b) L_1 is context-free but not regular and L_2 is context-free.

(c) Neither L_1 nor L_2 is context-free.

(d) L_1 is context-free but L_2 is not context-free.

33. Consider the productions $A \to PQ$ and $A \to XY$. Each of the five non-terminals A, P, Q, X and Y has two attributes: s is a synthesized attribute, and *i* is an inherited attribute. Consider the following rules.

Rule 1: P.i = A.i + 2, Q.i = P.i + A.i and A.s = P.s + Q.s

Rule 2: X.i = A.i + Y.s and Y.i = X.s + A.i

Which one of the following is TRUE?

(a) Both Rule 1 and Rule 2 are L-attributed.

(b) Only Rule 1 is L-attributed.

(c) Only Rule 2 is L-attributed.

(d) Neither Rule 1 nor Rule 2 is L-attributed.

34. Each of a set of n processes executes the following code using two semaphores a and b initialized to 1 and 0, respectively. Assume that count is a shared variable initialized to 0 and not used in CODE SECTION P.

CODE SECTION P

```
wait(a); count=count+1;
if (count==n) signal(b);
signal(a); wait(b); signal(b);
```

CODE SECTION Q

What does the code achieve?

(a) It ensures that no process executes CODE SECTION Q before every process has finished CODE SECTION P.

(b) It ensures that at most two processes are in CODE SECTION Q at any time.

(c) It ensures that all processes execute CODE SECTION P mutually exclusively.

(d) It ensures that at most n – 1 processes are in CODE SECTION P at any time.

35. Consider the following five disk access requests of the form (request id, cylinder number) that are present in the disk scheduler queue at a given time.

(P, 155), (Q, 85), (R, 110), (S, 30), (T, 115)

Assume the head is positioned at cylinder 100. The scheduler follows Shortest Seek Time First scheduling to service the requests.

Which one of the following statements is FALSE?

(a) T is serviced before P.

(b) Q is serviced after S, but before T.

(c) The head reverses its direction of movement between servicing of Q and P.

(d) R is serviced before P.

36. Consider a relational table R that is in 3NF, but not in BCNF. Which one of the following statements is TRUE?

(a) R has a non-trivial functional dependency $X \rightarrow A$, where X is not a superkey and A is a prime attribute.

(b) R has a non-trivial functional dependency $X \rightarrow A$, where X is not a superkey and A is a non-prime attribute and X is not a proper subset of any key.

(c) R has a non-trivial functional dependency $X \rightarrow A$, where X is not a superkey and A is a non-prime attribute and X is a proper subset of some key.

(d) A cell in R holds a set instead of an atomic value.

37. Consider a schedule of transactions T_1 and T_2:

T_1	RA			RC		WD		WD	Commit	
T_2		RB	WB		RD		WC			Commit

Here, RX stands for "Read(X)" and WX stands for "Write(X)"". Which one of the following schedules is conflict equivalent to the above schedule?

(a)

T_1				RA	RC	WD	WB		Commit	
T_2	RB	WB	RD					WC		Commit

(b)

T_1	RA	RC	WD	WB					Commit	
T_2					RB	WB	RD	WC		Commit

(c)

T_1	RA	RC	WD				WB		Commit	
T_2				RB	WB	RD		WC		Commit

(d)

T_1					RA	RC	WD	WB	Commit	
T_2	RB	WB	RD	WC						Commit

38. An organization requires a range of IP addresses to assign one to each of its 1500 computers. The organization has approached an Internet Service Provider (ISP) for this task. The ISP uses ClDR and serves the requests from the available IP address space 202.61.0.0/17. The ISP wants to assign an address space to the organization which will minimize the number of routing entries in the ISP's router using route aggregation.

Which of the following address spaces are potential candidates from which the ISP can allot any one to the organization?

I. 202.61.84.0/21 II. 202.61.104.0/21

III. 202.61.64.0/21 IV. 202.61.144.0/21

(a) I and II only (b) II and III only

(c) III and IV only (d) I and IV only

39. Which one of the following predicate formulae is NOT logically valid?

Note that W is a predicate formula without any free occurrence of x.

(a) $\forall x(p(x) \vee W) \equiv \forall x\, p(x) \vee W$

(b) $\exists x(p(x) \wedge W) \equiv \exists x\, p(x) \wedge W$

(c) $\forall x(p(x) \rightarrow W) \equiv \forall x\, p(x) \rightarrow W$

(d) $\exists x(p(x) \rightarrow W) \equiv \forall x\, p(x) \rightarrow W$

40. Let $G = (V, E)$ be a directed, weighted graph with weight function $w : E \rightarrow R$. For some function $f : V \rightarrow R$, for each edge$(u, v) \in E$, define $w'(u, v)$ as $w(u, v) + f(u) - f(v)$. Which one of the options completes the following sentence so that it is TRUE?

"The shortest paths in G under w are shortest paths under w′ too, ________".

(a) for every $f : V \rightarrow R$

(b) if and only if $\forall u \in V$, $f(u)$ is positive

(c) if and only if $\forall u \in V$, $f(u)$ is negative

(d) if and only if $f(u)$ is the distance from s to u in the graph obtained by adding a new vertex s to G and edges of zero weight from s to every vertex of G

41. In a balanced binary search tree with n elements, what is the worst case time complexity of reporting all elements in range [a, b]? Assume that the number of reported elements is k.

(a) $\Theta(\log n)$ (b) $\Theta(\log n + k)$

(c) $\Theta(k \log n)$ (d) $\Theta(n \log k)$

42. The number of permutations of the characters in LILAC so that no character appears in its original position, if the two L's are in distinguishable, is ________.

43. Consider a non-pipelined processor operating at 2.5 GHz. It takes 5 clock cycles to complete an instruction. You are going to make a 5-stage pipeline out of this processor. Overheads associated with pipelining force you to operate the pipelined processor at 2 GHz. In a given program, assume that 30% are memory instructions. 60% are ALU instructions and the rest are branch instructions. 5% of the memory instructions cause stalls of 50 clock cycles each due to cache misses and 50% of the branch instructions cause stalls of 2 cycles each. Assume that there are no stalls associated with the execution of ALU instructions. For this program, the speedup achieved by the pipelined processor over the non-pipelined processor (round off to 2 decimal places) is ________.

44. A processor has 64 registers and uses 16-bit instruction format. It has two types of instructions: I-type and R-type. Each I-type instruction contains an opcode, a register name, and a 4-bit immediate value. Each R-type instruction contains an opcode and two register names. If there are 8 distinct I-type opcodes, then the maximum number of distinct R-type opcodes is ________.

45. For n > 2, let $a \in \{0,1\}^n$ be a non-zero vector. Suppose that x is chosen uniformly at random from $\{0, 1\}^n$. Then, the probability that $\sum_{i=1}^{n} a_i x_i$ is an odd number is ________.

46. Consider the following C functions:

```
int fun1 (int n) {
   static int i = 0;
   if (n > 0) {
      ++i;
      fun1 (n - 1);
   }
   return (i);
}
int fun2 (int n) {
   static int i = 0;
   if (n > 0) {
      i = i + (fun1(n);
      fun2 (n-1);
   }
   return (i);
}
```

The return value of fun2 (5) is ________.

47. Consider the array representation of a binary min-heap containing 1023 elements. The minimum number of comparisons required to find the maximum in the heap is ________.

48. Consider the following C functions:

```
int tob (int b, int* arr) {
   int i;
   for (i=0, b>0; i++) {
   if (b%2)  arr [i] = 1;
   else      arr[i]=0;
   b=b/2;
   }
   return (i);
}
int pp(int a, int b) {
   int arr[20];
   int i, tot=1, ex, len;
   ex=a;
   len=tob (b,arr);
   for(i=0; i<len; i++) {
      if (arr[i]==1)
       tot=tot * ex;
      ex = ex * ex;
   }
   return (tot);
}
```

The value returned by pp (3,4) is ________.

49. Consider a graph G = (V, E), where V = $\{v_1, v_2, ..., v_{100}\}$, E = $\{(v_i, v_j) \mid 1 \le i < j \le 100\}$, and weight of the edge (v_i, v_j) is $|i - j|$. The weight of minimum spanning tree of G is ________.

50. Consider the following set of processes, assumed to have arrived at time 0. Consider the CPU scheduling algorithms Shortest Job First (SJF) and Round Robin (RR). For RR, assume that the processes are scheduled in the order P_1, P_2, P_3, P_4.

Processes	P_1	P_2	P_3	P_4
Burst time (in ms)	8	7	2	4

If the time quantum for RR is 4 ms, then the absolute value of the difference between the average turnaround times (in ms) of SJF and RR (round off to 2 decimal places) is ________.

51. Consider the following language.

L = $\{x \in \{a, b\}^* \mid$ number of a's in x is divisible by 2 but not divisible by 3$\}$

The minimum number of states in a DFA that accepts L is ________.

52. Graph G is obtained by adding vertex s to $K_{3,4}$ and making s adjacent to every vertex of $K_{3,4}$. The minimum number of colours required to edge-colour G is ________.

53. Consider a paging system that uses 1-level page table residing in main memory and a TLB for address translation. Each main memory access takes 100 ns and TLB lookup takes 20 ns. Each page transfer to/from the disk takes 5000 ns. Assume that the TLB hit ratio is 95%, page fault rate is 10%. Assume that for 20% of the total page faults, a dirty page has to be written back to disk before the required page is read in from disk. TLB update time is negligible. The average memory access time in ns (round off to 1 decimal places) is ________.

54. Consider a database implemented using B+ tree for file indexing and installed on a disk drive with block size of 4 KB. The size of search key is 12 bytes and the size of tree/disk pointer is 8 bytes. Assume that the database has one million records. Also assume that no node of the B+ tree and no records are present initially in main memory. Consider that each record fits into one disk block. The minimum number of disk accesses required to retrieve any record in the database is _______.

55. Consider a TCP connection between a client and a server with the following specifications: the round trip time is 6 ms, the size of the receiver advertised window is 50 KB, slowstart threshold at the client is 32 KB, and the maximum segment size is 2 KB. The connection is established at time t = 0. Assume that there are no timeouts and errors during transmission. Then the size of the congestion window (in KB) at time t + 60 ms after all acknowledgments are processed is _______.

ANSWERS

General Aptitude (GA)

1. (d)	**2.** (a)	**3.** (a)	**4.** (d)	**5.** (b)	**6.** (d)	**7.** (c)	**8.** (a)
9. (b)	**10.** (c)						

Computer Science & IT

1. (a)	**2.** (a)	**3.** (c)	**4.** (c)	**5.** (b)	**6.** (c)	**7.** (d)	**8.** (d)
9. (d)	**10.** (c)	**11.** (c)	**12.** (c)	**13.** (a)	**14.** (a)	**15.** (d)	**16.** (c)
17. (0.125)	**18.** (7)	**19.** (5)	**20.** (1034)	**21.** (13.5)	**22.** (19)	**23.** (13)	**24.** (7)
25. (6)	**26.** (a)	**27.** (c)	**28.** (b)	**29.** (b)	**30.** (b)	**31.** (d)	**32.** (a)
33. (b)	**34.** (a)	**35.** (b)	**36.** (a)	**37.** (a)	**38.** (b)	**39.** (c)	**40.** (a)
41. (b)	**42.** (12)	**43.** (2.15to2.18)	**44.** (14)	**45.** (0.5)	**46.** (55)	**47.** (511)	**48.** (81)
49. (99)	**50.** (5.25)	**51.** (6)	**52.** (7)	**53.** (154.5 to 155.5)		**54.** (4)	**55.** (44)

EXPLANATIONS

GENERAL APTITUDE

1. "Within" Preposition that is used to express something that occurs inside a particular period of time.
Here, because Sentance is in 'present perfect continuous tense' "For is" used when we talk about a period of time.
2. Here, we have to note that the confunction used is 'but'. 'But' is used for introducing an idea which contrasts with the statement that has been already said.
3. (i) Flyer : Relation is Verb : Noun
(ii) One who cooks is a cook, and one who flies any aircraft is a flyer.
5. • Cost of 1-a-C-2 : 200 + 200 + 100 + 100 + 100 = 700
• Cost of 1-f-e-2 : 100 + 100 + 100 + 200 + 200 = 700
• Cost of 1-b-2 : 300 + 100 + 200 = 600
• Cost of 1-f-b-2 : 100 + 100 + 100 +200 = 500
Hence, 1-f-b-2 is having minimum cost.
6. According to given passage GST is imposed on the usage or supply of goods and services hence, option (d) is correct.
7. As given that
$P = 3^1, Q = 9 = 3^2, R = 27 = 3^3, S = 81 = 3^4,$
$T = 243 = 3^5$
Hence, Q + S = 9 + 81 = 90.
8. Unpainted area = Area of annular ring – Area of n blue color circles
Area of annular ring = $\pi b^2 - \pi a^2$
i.e. $\pi(b^2 - a^2)$
$$\text{Area of 1 blue circle} = \pi\left(\frac{b-a}{2}\right)^2$$
$$\text{Hence, area of n blue circles} = n\pi\left(\frac{b-a}{2}\right)^2$$
$$\Rightarrow \text{Unpainted area} = \pi\left[(b^2 - a^2) - \frac{\pi}{4}(b-a)^2\right]$$
9. Since, α and β are acute angles hence it will form the interior angles of straight lines $\alpha + \beta = 180° - 90° = 90°$
10. As given that,
Total expenditure = 2500 million
Total revenue = 3000 million
Total profit = 3000 – 2500 = 500
$$\text{So,} \quad \text{profit \%} = \frac{500}{2500} \times 100 = 20\%$$

COMPUTER SCIENCE & IT

1. If, $f(x) = \sqrt{x^3 + 1}$
$$f'(x) = \frac{1}{\sqrt{x^3 + 1}} \cdot 3x^2 \geq 0$$
Here, for all points in [0, 1]
$\therefore$ Therefore, it is increasing function.
4. The correct order is as fallowing steps:
Step 1: Send the address to memory via MAR.
Step 2: Read the opcode into R from the memory via MBR.
Step 3: Send the first operand to Temp 1(ALU).
Step 4: Read the second operand directly from the R2 and process the data in ALU and store the result into TEMP2.
Step 5: Store the result into R0.
5. **Inorder:** 10, 11, 12, (15), 16, 18, 19, 20
LST RST
Preorder: (15), 10, 12, 11, 20, 18, 16, 19
1st root
→ The BST, we can make usign preorder and inorder.

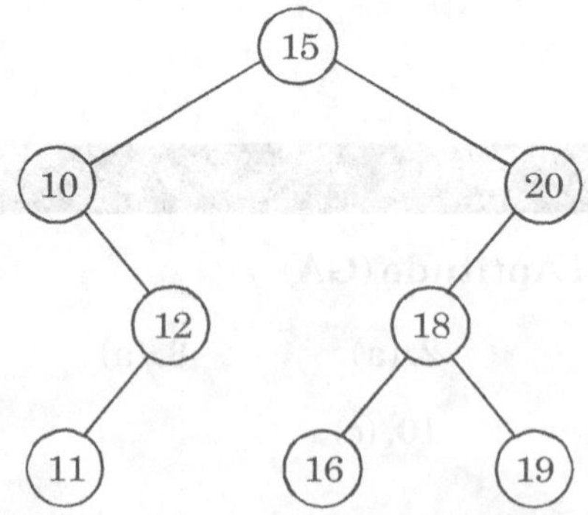

So, postorder : 11, 12, 10, 16, 19, 18, 20, 15
6. AVL with n element : [height balanced [–1, 0, + 1] BST]
log n level due to balanced BST.
(i) Every insertion of element:
log n: Find place to insert.
long n: If properly no satisfied do rotation.
(ii) n^2 element insertion :
For 1 element $\equiv$ 2 log n
So, for (upper bound function) n^2 element $\equiv$ $\theta(\log(n)^{n2})$ $\theta(n^2 \log n)$

7. Try to find counter example to show expression incomplete.

(a) is incorrect because it force to end "10".

(b) is incorrect because it forces the string to start with "1" and hence cannot generate a string like "01", which has odd number of ones.

(c) is same as (0 + 1)* 10* which will generate some wrong string like "110" which has even number of 1's. It is a superset and hence not correct.

(d) is same as (0* 1 0* 1 0*)* 1 0* which is most suitable answer for the given problem according to given options.

8. If $L_1 U L_2$ is Regular, then L_1 and L_2 are also regular languages: false, since $\{a^nb^n\} \cup \{a^nb^n\} = \Sigma^*$ which is regular, but $\{a^nb^n\}$ not regular.

Infinite union of regular languages are also regular: false, since may infinite language can be broken into invidual strings which will be infinite union of finite languages. So if regular is closed under infinite union, then all infinite language will become regular, which is untrue. Hence, II is also false.

9. Symbal table can be accessed only in Lexical analysis and syntex analys is.

None of the given statements are correct.

10. $L = \{a^n | ^n \geq 0\} \cup R\ a^nb^n \mid n \geq 0\}$

L = {ε, a, aa, aaa, b, bb, ab, aabb ....}

$L = \{a^nb^n \mid n \geq 0\}$ is a well known DCFL.

$\{a^n\ b^n \mid n \geq 0\}$ is a well known regular language.

So, L = DCFL ∪ Regular = DCFL by closure properly.

DCFL is the strongest correct answer.

11. The hole created by best fit is never larger than the hole created by first fit.

Best fit always allocates the request that provided minimum hole sizes. Thus, best fit will never produce hales that are greater than the holes created by first fit.

12. From the process state diagram, we can see that there cannot be a transition from the waiting/blocked state to the running state. Hence, statement I, II and IV are correct.

13. SELECT S.sno, S. sname

From Supplier S, catalog C

WHERE S. sno = C.sno AND

cost > (SELECT AVG (cost)

FROM Catalog

WHERE pno = 'P4' GroupBy pno);

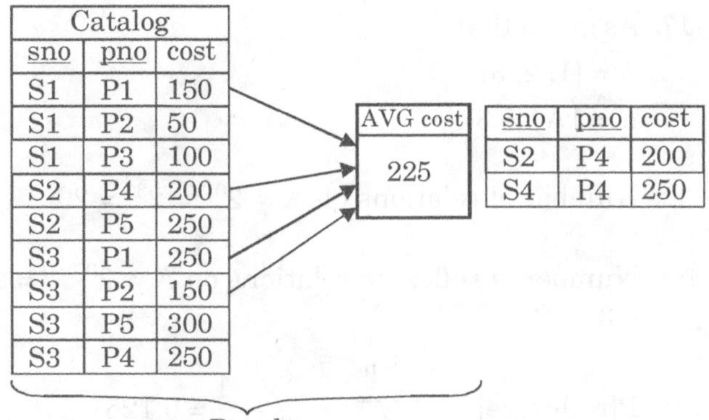

Results

sno	sname
S1	RF
S2	BF
S3	PF
S2	PF

$$\left[\because \text{Avg cost} = \left[\frac{200+250}{2}\right]\right] = 225$$

Here, the outer query will return S_{no} and S_{name} of supliers having cost > 225. So the total number of tuples returned by the query is 4.

14.

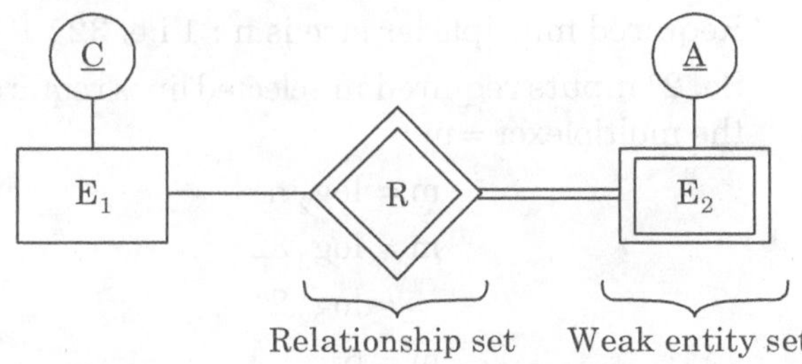

In this the identification relationship represented by a Diamond shape with double line bold borders

15. I. A router modifies the IP packets during forwarding because TTL is changing.

II. A router can also be used in LAN network routers are configured with routing algorithms so, it does not require routing protocol at that time.

III. Packet fragmentation is done if packet size is more than MTU.

16. Insert element at the beginning of empty linked list, take Θ (1)

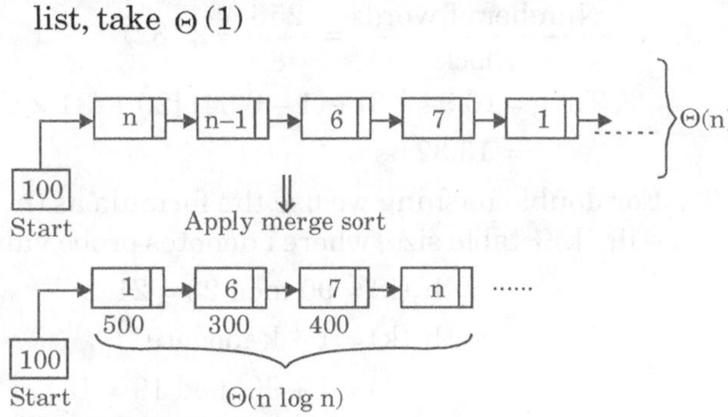

$\Rightarrow \Theta(n\log n) + \Theta(n)$

$= \Theta(n\log n)$

17. As given that,

A = {1, 2, 3}

n = |A| = 3

Number of relations on A = $2^{n^2} = 2^{3^2} = 29$

Number of reflexive relations on A = $2^{n^2-n} = 2^{3^2} - 3 = 2^6$

$$P[\text{reflexive}] = \frac{2^{n^2-n}}{2^{n^2}} = \frac{2^6}{2^9} = \frac{1}{8} = 0.125$$

18. The order of a subgroup always divides the order of groups.

Size of group = O(G) = 35

Let H be subgroup of G

∴ O(H) | O(G)

Possible orders of H are 1,5,7,35

So, size of largest possible proper subgroup of G other than G itself would be = 7.

19. Number of registers = n = 32

Required multiplexer size is n : 1 i.e. 32 : 1

So, 2^n inputs required m selected lines required to the multiplexer = m

$$\therefore \quad m = \log_2 n$$
$$m = \log_2 32$$
$$= \log_2 2^5$$
$$m = 5$$

20. We need 10 input lines and 1024 outputs lines to map 1 KB RAM.

For this we need 10×2^{10} decoder.

Here, M = 10 and N = 2^{10} = 1024

Therefore, M + N = 1034

21. As given that

Hit ratio = 94%

Word length or size = 64 bit = 8B

Block size = 256 B

$$\therefore \frac{\text{Number of words}}{\text{Block}} = \frac{256}{8} = 2^5(32)$$

Tavg = (0.94 × 3) + (1 – 0.94) [20 + (31 × 5)]

= 13.32 ns

23. For double hashing we use the formula as (h_1(k) + ih_2(k)% table size, where i denotes probe value.

$$h_1(k) = 90 \bmod 23 = 21$$
$$h_2(k) = 1 + k \bmod 19$$
$$= 1 + 90 \bmod 19 = 15$$

For probe 1 the value of i = 1 so, (21 + 15) mod 23 = 13

24. S → aSB

→ aaSBB [S → aSB]

→ aaaSBBB [S → aSB]

→ aaadBBB [S → d]

→ aaabBB [B → b]

→ aaadbbB [B → b]

→ aaadbbb [B → b]

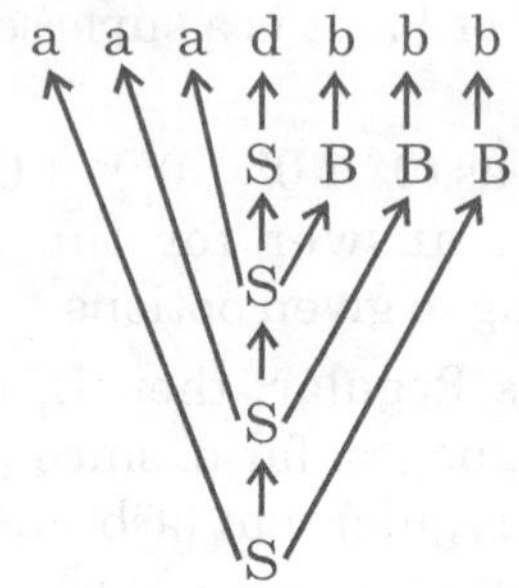

So, Total number of steps/reductions in the derivation is: 7 required.

25. In non persistent HTTP for every objects there is a TCP connection required. So, 1 TCP connection for text and 5 TCP connections for images required.

1 Text + 5 images = 6 objects

So total 6 connections are required.

26. (i) L_1 = {<M > | M is a TM with L(M) = φ } is emptiness problem of TM, which is undecidable, by Rice's theorem since it is a non-trival problem.

(ii) L_2 = {<M, w, q > | M on input-w reaches state q in exactly 100 steps} Decidable after 100 steps. It is non-recursive and non-trivbal problem, since some TM can accept non-recursive language and some may not, so by Rice's theorem it is undecidable.

(iii) L_3 = {M>/M is not recursive} Rice's theorem applied and hence L_3 is undecidable.

(iv) L_4 = {M>/M contains at least, 21 members} Membership problems with UTM we can check it M accept string by 100 steps. So L_4 decidable L_1, L_2 and L_3 are undecidable.

27. (i) When two (3 × 3) non-singular matrices each having rank is 3. Then the product of these two non-singular matrices also has rank (A.B) = 3.

(ii) The properties of the determinant |AB| = |A| · |B|

Statement 2 and 3 are correct statements.

28. The given functions:

$$\therefore \quad z(a,b,c) = a + \bar{b}c$$

K-map of the output z is

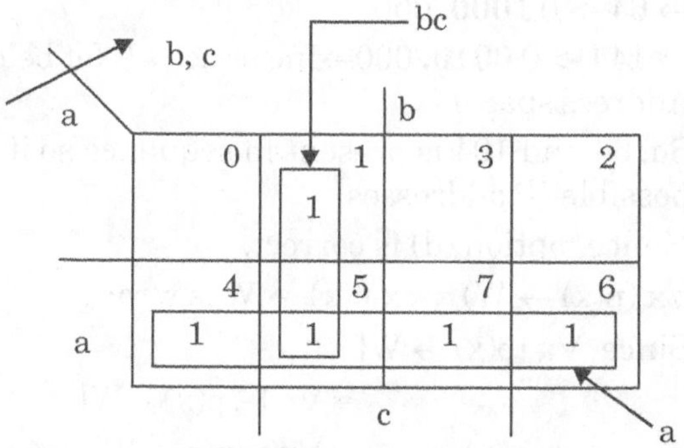

$\therefore \quad z(a, b, c) = \Sigma m(1, 4, 5, 6, 7)$

Therefore, the minterm $\sum(1, 4, 5, 6, 7)$ represents the function Z = a + b'c

29. R1 : 0×42200000

R2 : 0×C1200000

32 bit format

	S	BE	M
R1 :	0	100000100	010000.........

32 bit format

	S	BE	M
R21 :	0	10000010	010000.........

Step 1: Subtract the exponents i.e. divisor exponent from the divided exponent.

```
     2
  10000100          AE :   111111
                           00000010
  10000010        Bias :   01111111  (+ 127)
AE : 00000010       AE :   10000001
```

Step 2: Divide the mantissa i.e.

R1 M : 1.010...

R2 M : 1.010... (Divide)

Result : 1

Step 3: Sign (opposite sign division result sing is –ve)

32 bit formate

R3 :	1	100000001	000000......

C 0 8 00000

30. As given that,

Word length = 32 bit, MM size = 16 MB

Physical address = 24 bit, CM size = 64 KB

4-way set associative

Block size = 256 Blocks

Cache size or number of lines (N)

$$= \frac{64\text{ K}}{256} \Rightarrow \frac{2^{16}}{2^{8}} = 2^{8}$$

= 256 Blocks

4-way set associative cache:

$$\text{Number of sets index (S)} = \frac{N}{\text{P-way}} \Rightarrow \frac{2^8}{4} = 2^6$$

= 64 = 6 bits

Address format:

TAG	No. of set	Word offset
10	6	8
10 bit	$\log_2 2^6$	$\log_2 2^8$

← 24 bit →

A1 : $(42C8A4)_H$

4211	001000	A4

Set offset = 8th set

A2 : $(546888)_H$

5401	001000	88

Set offset = 40th set

A3 : $(6A289C)_H$

6A00	001000	9C

Set offset

A2 and A3 are in same set

A4 : $(5E4880)_H$

5E01	001000	80

Set offset

A1 and A4 are in same set = 8th set

Hence, option (b) is correct choice.

32. L1 is regular and L2 is CFL.

In L1 putting x as 0 and 1 we get a subset

$$w0y0 + w1y1 = (0 + 1)^+ 0 (0 + 1)^+ 0 + (0 + 1)^+ 1(0 + 1)^+ 1$$

Now by putting x as 00, 01, 10, 11 we can show that above minimal regular expression covers all such things and hence above expression is not a subset but is equal to given language.

$S \rightarrow AB/BA$

$A \rightarrow XAX \mid 0$

$B \rightarrow XBX \mid 1$

$X \rightarrow 0/1$

Since we wrote regular expression for L1, it is regular.

33. Rule 1 : $P \cdot i = A \cdot i + 2, Q \cdot i = P \cdot i + A \cdot i$

$As = P \cdot s + Q \cdot s$

It is L-attributed by definition.

Rule 2 : It is not L-attributed because this expression $(X \cdot i = X \cdot i + Y \cdot s)$ and $(Y \cdot i = X \cdot S + A) \cdot i$ fails to satisfy the definition of L-attributed.

34. All the processes running the given code will remain block due to wait(b) until the value of count becomes n.

When the value of count will become equals to n, value of b changes to 1 which will subsequently allow a process to go into section Q.

So, no process can go to section Q until all the process executes code section P.

36. R(A, B, C, D, E)

key : ABC, BCD

FD : $\underbrace{BC}_{x} \rightarrow \underbrace{D}_{A}$:

Thus, for a non-trivial dependency X-> A

'x' should not super key and 'A' is prime attribute in order to satisfy 3NF and not BCNF.

37.

T_1	T_2
$r_1(A)$	
	$r_2(B)$
	$w_2(B)$
$r_1(C)$	
	$r_2(D)$
$w_1(D)$	
	$w_2(c)$
$w_1(B)$	
Commit	
	Commit

$\Longrightarrow$ conflict equal

T_1	T_2
	$r_2(B)$
	$w_2(B)$
	$r_2(D)$
$r_1(A)$	
$r_1(C)$	
$w_1(D)$	
$w_1(B)$	
	$w_2(c)$
Commit	
	Commit

Conflicting operations are:

$R_1(C) \rightarrow W_2(C)$, $R_2(B) \rightarrow W_1(B)$, $W_2(B) \rightarrow W_1(B)$, $R_2(D) \rightarrow W_1(D)$

Now, check, all the given options then we get option (b) had equivalent conflicting.

38. /17 ⇒ 11111111 11111111
10000000 00000000
⇒ 255.255.128.0

$1500 \simeq 2048 = 2^{11} = 2^3 \times 2^8$

$= 2^{32-21} = 2^{11} = /21$

/17 ⇒ 202.61.0.0/17

00000000.00000000
00000111.11111111 } (0.0 – 7.255)

0.0 ⇒ 00001000.00000000
00001111.11111111 } (8.0 – 15.255)

00010000.00000000
00010111.11111111 } (16.0 – 23.255)

Sequence is 0, 8, 16, 24, 32, 40, 48, 56, 64, 72, 80, 96, 104, 112, 120.

By Analyze the third octet:

Total of 17 net bits, 4 subnet bits, 11 host bits

→ 84 -> 0 **1010** 100 →Incorrect ↓ (host bit contains 1)

→ 104 -> 0 **1101** 000

→ 64 -> 0 **1000,** 000

→ 144 -> 0 **0010,** 000→Incorrect ↓ (Not belong to Address space)

So, 64 and 104 is present in sequence so it is the possible IP addresses.

Hence, option (d) is correct.

39. $\forall x\, (p(x) \rightarrow W) \equiv \forall x\, p(x) \rightarrow W$ is wrong

Since, $\forall x\, [p(x) \rightarrow W]$

$\equiv \forall x\, [\neg\, p(x) \vee W]$

$\equiv \forall x(\neg\, p(x) \vee W$

$\equiv \neg\, (\exists x\, p(x)) \vee W$

$\forall x\, [\, p(x) \rightarrow W] \equiv \exists x\, p(x) = \rightarrow W$

Hence, LHS and RHS are not equivalent.

So, If is not valid.

40. As given that:

$w(u, v) = (u, v)$ edge weight

$w(u,v) = w(u, v) + \underbrace{f(u) - f(v)}_{0}$

$= w(u, v)$

Hence, option (a) correct.

41.

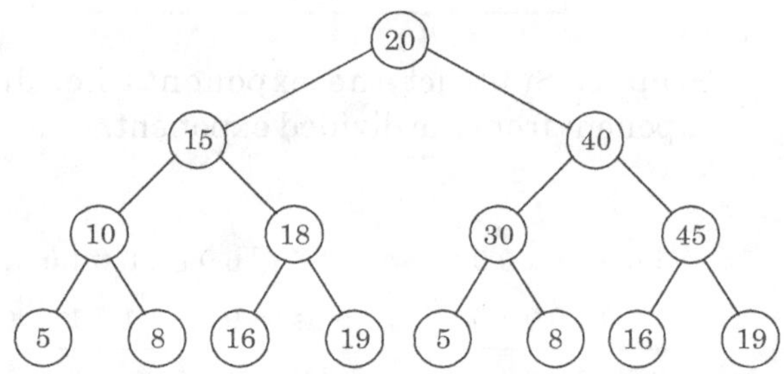

We need first find the indices of (a) & (b).

Let a = 16, b = 42

16 : Find the '16' element in the BST = O(log n)

42 : Find the '42' element in the BST = O(log n)

[16, 42]: Inorder sorted element between 16 to 42

[16, 18, 19, 20, 25, 30, 35, 40, 42] ⇒ requires O(k) time for k element. As 'K' can significantly larger than log n.

Hence, total time: ≡ O(log n + k)

42. Number of derangement

Since both L's are indistinguishable.

First L's can be arranged remaining 3 positions in $^3C_2$ ways.

[i.e., = _ L _ L _ or _ L _ L _ or _ L _ _ L]

For each of these cases remaining 3 letters can be deranged in 2 × 2! ways = 4 ways

[i.e., _ L _ L _ C can lake only 1 or 3 positions 2 → ways. For each of this IA can be arranged in remaining 2 positions in 2 ways].

Number of derangements = ${}^3C_2 \times 2 \times 2! = 12$

They are:

CLILA, ILCLA, ALCIL, CLAIL, ILACL, ALICL, CAILL, ACILL, ICALL, IACLL, ALCLI, CLALI.

43. Non-pipeline:

Clock frequency = 2.5 GHz

$$\text{Cycle time} = \frac{1}{2.5\,\text{GHz}} = 0.4\ \text{ns}$$

$$\text{CPI} = 5$$

So, time for the non-pipelined processor

$$ET_{\text{non-pipe}} = \text{CPI} \times \text{Cycle time}$$
$$= 5 \times 0.4\ \text{ns} = 2\ \text{ns}$$

Pipeline:

Clock frequency = 2.5 GHz

$$\text{Cycle time} = \frac{1}{2\,\text{GHz}} = 0.5\ \text{ns}$$

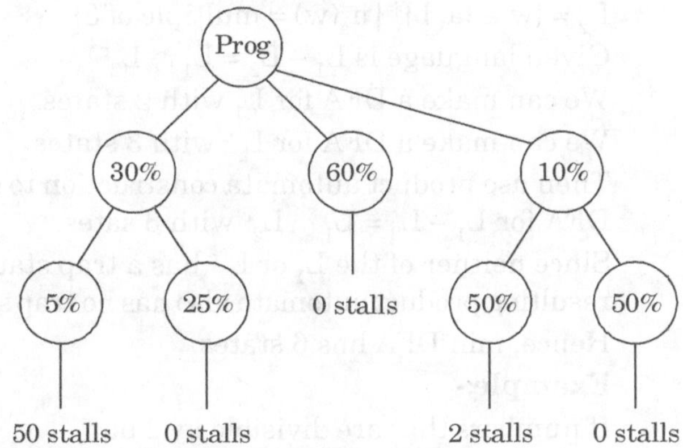

Number of stalls cycle/instruction

$= 0.3(0.05 \times 50) + 0.1(0.5 \times 2)$

$= 0.75 + 0.1 = 0.85$

Time for pipelined processor is:

$ET_{\text{pipe}} = (1 + \text{Number of stalls/instruction}) \times \text{Cycle time}$

$= (1 + 0.85) \times 0.5\ \text{ns} = 0.925\ \text{ns}$

$$\text{Speed up: (S)} = \frac{ET_{\text{non-pipe}}}{ET_{\text{pipe}}}$$

$$= \frac{2}{0.925}$$

$= 2.16$

44. As given that, 16 bit instruction and 64 registers

I-type:

It contans opcode Register name 4-bit immediate data.

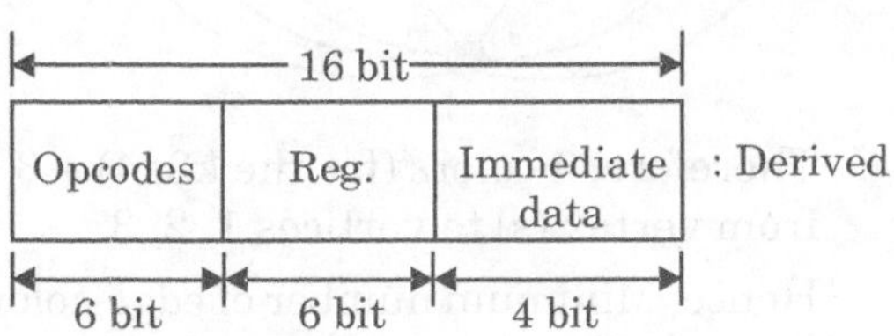

R-type: It contains opcode, Register name 1, Register name 2.

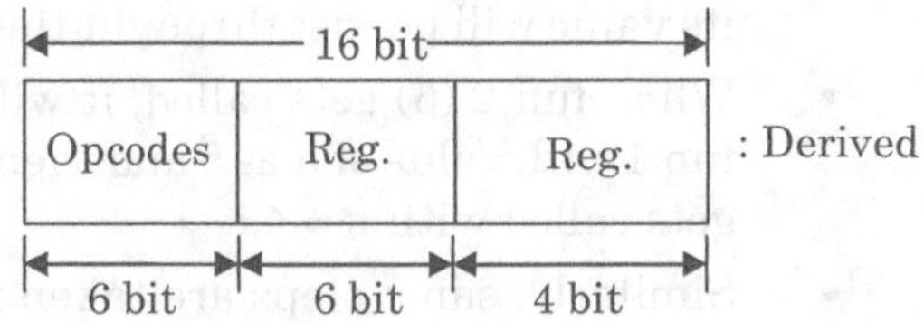

1. Primitive instruction

R-type:

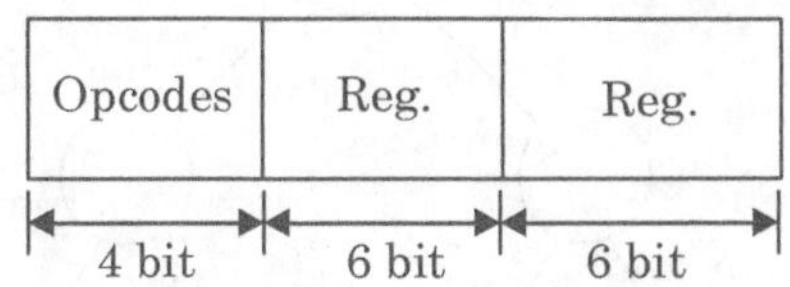

2. Number of operation possible = $2^4 = 16$

3. Number of tree opcodes = (16 – R)

Assume x is number of R-type instruction existed.

4. Number of I-type instruction possible = $(16 - R) \times 2^2$

$$8 = 64 - 4R$$
$$4R = 64 - 8 = 56$$
$$R = \frac{56}{4} \Rightarrow 14$$

Hence, possible R-type instructore are 14.

45. $a = \begin{bmatrix} a_1 \\ a_2 \\ \vdots \\ a_n \end{bmatrix}, x = \begin{bmatrix} x_1 \\ x_2 \\ \vdots \\ x_n \end{bmatrix}$

Fixed non-zero

$a_i = 0$ or 1

$x_i = 0$ or 1

$\sum_{i=1}^{n} a_i x_i$ as an odd and even number that value lies between 0 to n.

Total number cases = 2n

$a_i x_i$	0	1	2	……	n
fav	${}^nC_0$	${}^nC_1$	${}^nC_2$	……	${}^nC_n$

$$P\left[\sum_{i=1}^{n} a_i x_i \text{ is odd}\right] = \frac{{}^nC_1 + {}^nC_3}{2^n}$$

$$= \frac{2^{n-1}}{2^n} = \frac{1}{2}$$

$= 0.5$

Hence, the over all the probability (that the result is odd) = 0.5.

46. According to the given program:

- Variable i is static in both the functions thus its value will persist throught the program.
- When fun 2 (5) gets called, it will first call fun 1 with value of n as 5 and then fun 2 will gets called with n = 4.
- Similarly, same steps are taken for all the upcoming values of n.

47.

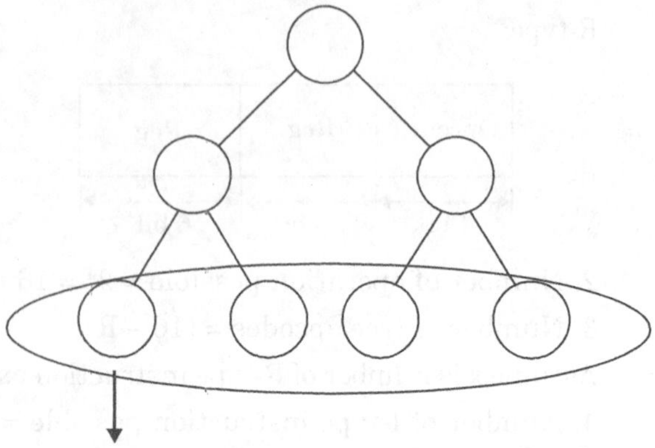

Maximum element can only be found at leaf level nodes

Number of element = $\left\lceil \frac{1023}{2} \right\rceil$ = 512

To get the maximum value of these leaf nodes we requires 511 comparisons.

48. After executing the given C program integer 81 is returned.

49. Consider small instance of 4-vertices

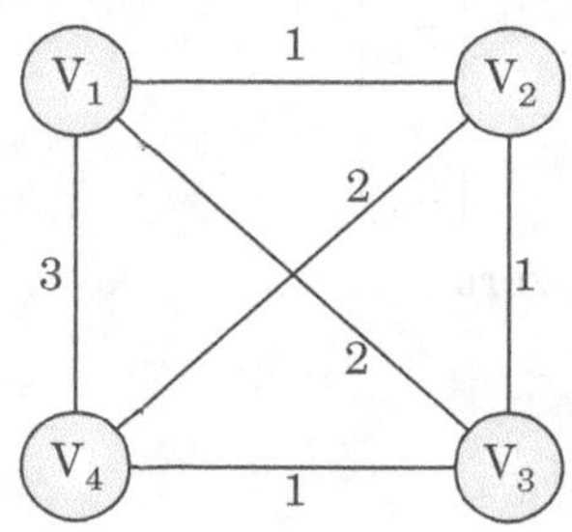

Clearly,

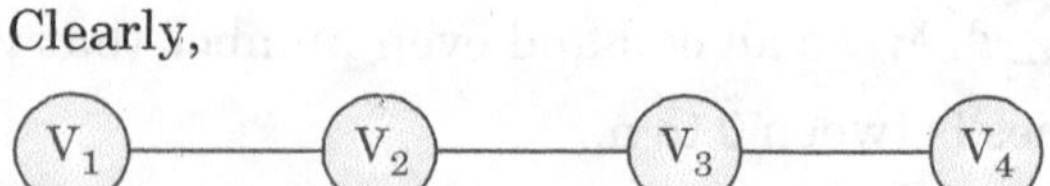

would be a MST with cost 3.

The number of edges of the MST is |V| – 1, in case of the given question |V| = 100, now the cost for this is = |V| – 1 = 99.

Hence, for 100 vertices, 99 will the weight of minumum spanning tree.

50. STF:

P_3	P_4	P_2	P_1

0 2 6 13 21

So, Turn Around Time (TAT) = (21 – 0) + (13 – 0) + (2 – 0) + (6 – 0)

Average TAT = $\frac{42}{4}$ = 10.5

RR:

P_1	P_2	P_3	P_4	P_1	P_2

0 4 8 10 14 18 21

Turn Arount Time (TAT)

= (18 – 0) + (21 – 0) + (10 – 0) + (14 – 0)

= 18 + 21 + 10 + 14 = 63

Average TAT = $\frac{63}{4}$ = 15.75

Hence, Absolute difference

= | SJE (TAT) – RR(TAT) |

= | 10.5 – 15.75 |

= 5.25 units

51. $L = \{w \in \{a, b\}^* \mid n_a(w) = \text{multiple of 2 but not 3}\}$

Let $L_1 = \{w \in \{a, b\}^* \mid n_a(w) = \text{multiple of 2}\}$

$L_2 = \{w \in \{a, b\}^* \mid n_a(w) = \text{multiple of 3}\}$

Given language is $L_1 - L_2 = L_1 \cap L_2^c$

We can make a DFA for L_1 with 2 states.

We can make a DFA for L_2^c with 3 states.

Then use product automata construction to get a DFA for $L_1 - L_2 = L_1 \cap L_2^c$ with 6 sates.

Since neither of the L_1 or L_2^c has a trap state, so resulting product automata also has no trap state.

Hence, min DFA has 6 states.

Example:-

If numbers that are divisible by 2 but not by 3 = {2, 4, 8, 10, 14, 16, ...}

= {aaa, aaaa, aaaaaaaa, ...}

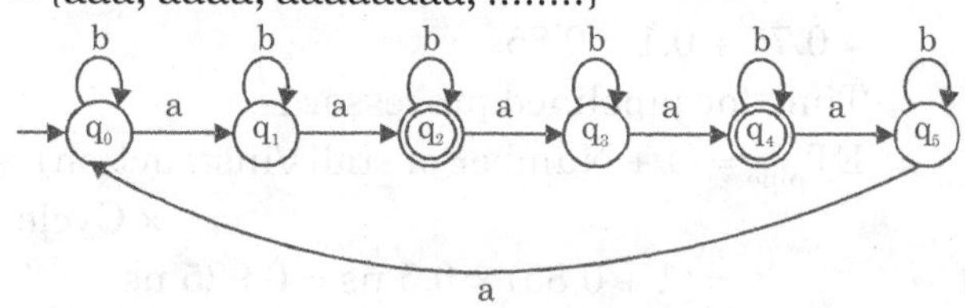

52.

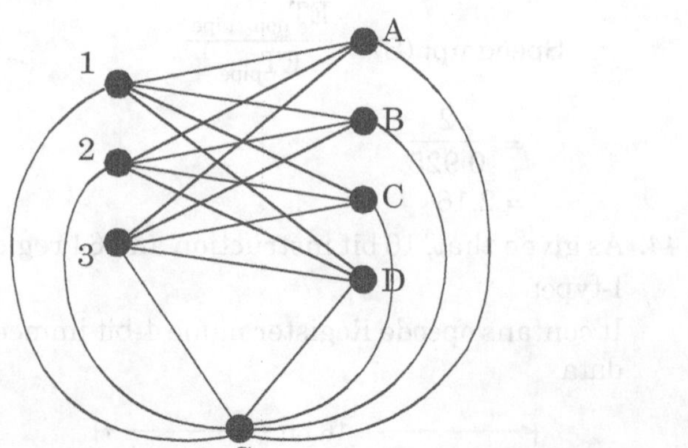

Therefore, 4 colors (for the k3, 4) + 3 new colors from vertex (s) to vertices 1, 2, 3.

Hence, Minimum number of edge-colors required = 3 + 4 = 7.

53. EMAT = 0.95 × (20 + 100) 0.05 × (20 + 0.10 × (0.80 × 5000 + 0.20 × 10000))

(TLB hit ratio, TLB time, MMAT, TLB miss, TLB time, Pare fault rate, Not a dirty page fault rate, PFST, Dirty page fault rate, PFST 2 times)

= 725 ns

54. As given that,

Block size = 4 KB

Search key = 12 bytes

Tree pointer = 8 bytes

DB records 1 million = 1000000

As we know that,

B+ tree index each record fits into one block

⇒ Keys given to find levels of B+ tree : Bulk loading B + tree design we can use

⇒ Order or B tree nodes $P \times B_p + (P - 1)$ keys $\leq$ Block size

$P \times 8 + (P - 1)\, 12 \leq 4096$

$20P \leq 4108$

$$P = \left\lfloor \frac{4108}{20} \right\rfloor = 205$$

⇒ Minimum levels and index : Max fill factor of each node.

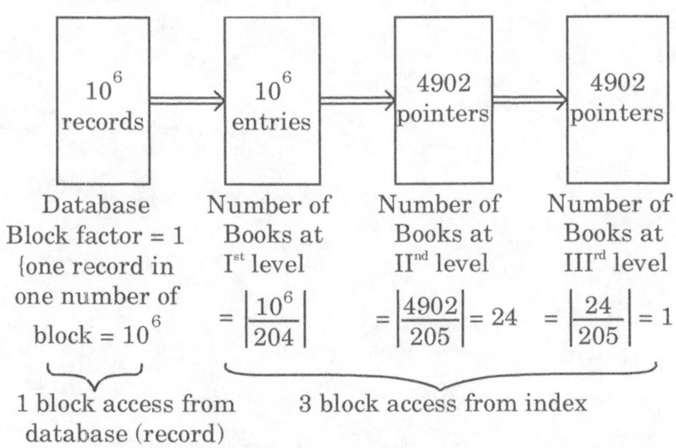

Thus, the total block access for a search is 3 + 1

So, Minimum 4 block access required to access record.

55. At time t = 0 there are not timeouts

Threshold = 32 KB

MSS = 2 KB

So,

	(Window size) time(t)
(1) First transmission :	2KB → 6ms
(2) Second transmission :	2KB → 6ms
(3) Third transmission :	2KB → 6ms
(4) Fourth transmission :	2KB → 6ms
(5) Fifth transmission :	2KB → 6ms
(6) Six transmission :	2KB → 6ms
(7) Seventh transmission :	2KB → 6ms
(8) Eighth transmission :	2KB → 6ms
(9) Nineth transmission :	2KB → 6ms
(10)Tenth transmission :	2KB → 6ms

After 10 ms completion, total time = 6 × 10 = 60 ms

At 11th transmission time t + 60, then window size = 44

SOLVED PAPER - 2021
SET 1

INSTRUCTIONS

1. Total of 65 questions carrying 100 marks, out of which 10 questions carrying a total of 15 marks are in General Aptitude (GA)
2. The Engineering Mathematics will carry around **15% of the total marks,** the General Aptitude section will carry **15% of the total marks** and the **remaining 70% of the total marks.**
3. **Types of Questions**
   (*a*) **Multiple Choice Questions (MCQ)** carrying 1 or 2 marks each in all papers and sections. These questions are objective in nature, and each will have a choice of four options, out of which the candidate has to mark the correct answer(s).
   (*b*) **Numerical Answer Questions** of 1 or 2 marks each in all papers and sections. For these questions the answer is a real number, to be entered by the candidate using the virtual keypad. No choices will be shown for these type of questions.
   (*c*) **Multiple Select Questions (MSQ)** carrying 1 or 2 marks each in all the papers and sections. These questions are objective in nature, and each will have choice of four answers, out of which ONE or MORE than ONE choice(s) is / are correct.
4. For **1-mark** multiple-choice questions, **1/3 marks** will be deducted for a wrong answer. Likewise, for **2-marks** multiple-choice questions, **2/3** marks will be deducted for a wrong answer. There is no negative marking for numerical answer type questions & multiple selection questions.

Chapter-Wise Analysis

#	Chapters	Marks		
		1	2	Total
1	General Aptitude	5	5	15
2	Engineering Mathematics	5	6	17
3	Theory of Computation	2	3	8
4	Digital Logic	1	2	5
5	Computer Organization and Architecture	2	2	6
6	Programming & Data Structures	2	3	8
7	Algorithm	4	4	12

#	Chapters	Marks		
		1	2	Total
8	Compiler Design	2	3	8
9	Operating System	3	1	5
10	Databases	2	3	8
11	Computer Networks	2	3	8
12	Software Engineering	0	0	0
13	Web Technology	0	0	0

GENERAL APTITUDE (GA)

Q. 1 to Q. 5 : Carry One Mark Each.

1. The ratio of boys to girls in a class is 7 to 3.
Among the options below, an acceptable value for the total number of students in the class is :

(a) 21 (b) 37
(c) 50 (d) 73

2. A polygon is convex if, for every pair of points, P and Q belonging to the polygon, the line segment PQ lies completely inside or on the polygon.
Which one of the following is NOT a convex polygon ?

(a)  (b) 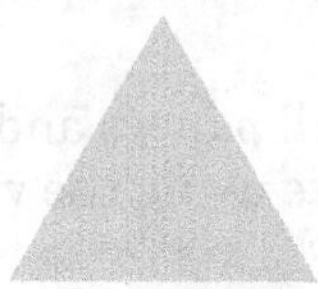

(c)  (d) 

3. Consider the following sentences :

(i) Everybody in the class is prepared for the exam.

(ii) Babu invited Danish to his home because he enjoys playing chess.

Which of the following is the CORRECT observation about the above two sentences ?

(a) (i) is grammatically correct and (ii) is unambiguous
(b) (i) is grammatically incorrect and (ii) is unambiguous
(c) (i) is grammatically correct and (ii) is ambiguous
(d) (i) is grammatically incorrect and (ii) is ambiguous

4. 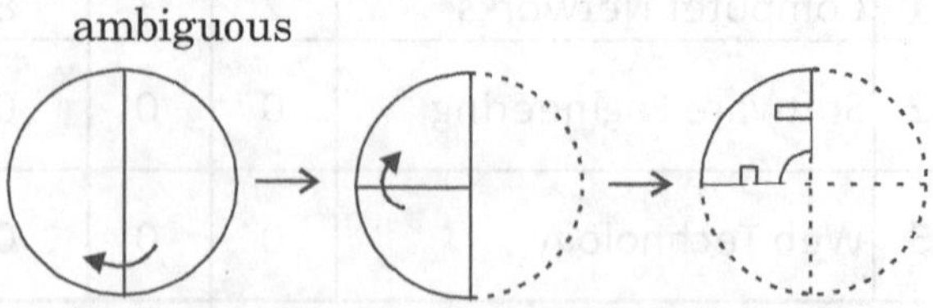

A circular sheet of paper is folded along the lines in the directions shown. The paper, after being punched in the final folded state as shown and unfolded in the reverse order of folding, will look like ______.

(a) 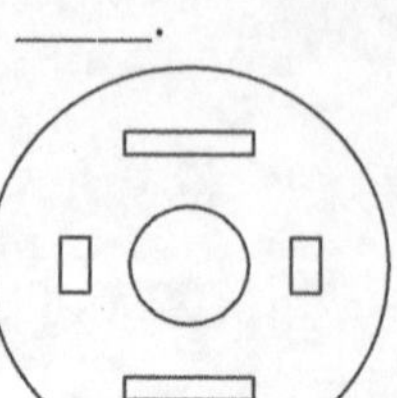 (b) 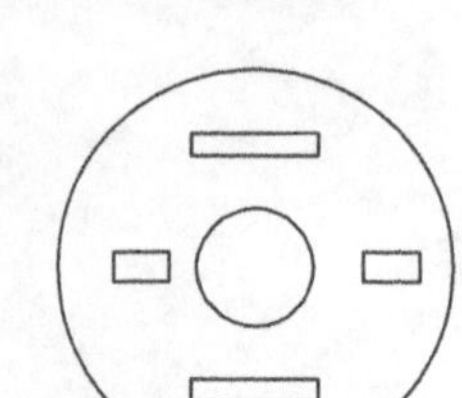

(c) 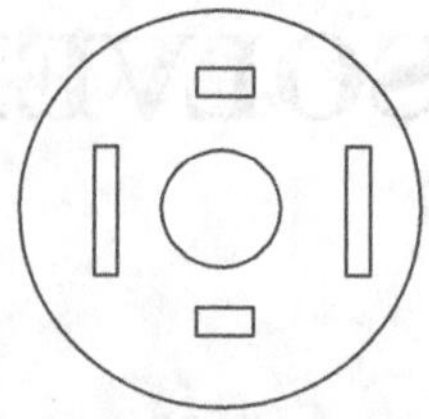 (d) 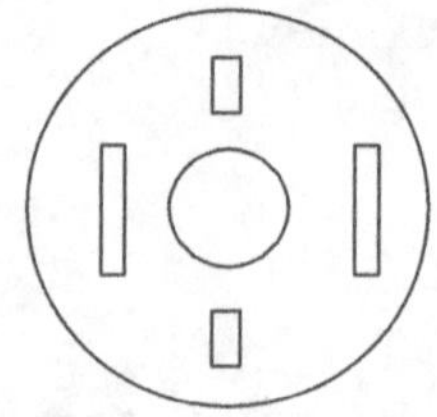

5. ____ is to *surgery* as *writer* is to ______.
Which one of the following options maintains a similar logical relation in the above sentence ?

(a) Plan, outline (b) Hospital, library
(c) Doctor, book (d) Medicine, grammar

Q. 6 to Q. 10 : Carry Two Marks Each

6. We have 2 rectangular sheets of paper, M and N, of dimensions 6 cm × 1 cm each. Sheet M is rolled to form an open cylinder by bringing the short edges of the sheet together. Sheet N is cut into equal square patches an assembled to form the largest possible closed cube. Assuming the ends of the cylinder are closed, the ratio of the volume of the cylinder to that of the cube is ______.

(a) $\frac{\pi}{2}$ (b) $\frac{3}{\pi}$

(c) $\frac{9}{\pi}$ (d) 3π

7.

Items	Cost (₹)	Profit %	Marked Price (₹)
P	5,400	--	5,860
Q	---	25	10,000

Details of prices of two items P and Q are presented in the above table. The ratio of cost of item P to cost of item Q is 3:4. Discount is calculated as the difference between the marked price and the selling price. The profit percentage is calculated as the ratio of the difference between selling price and cost, to the cost

$$\left(\text{Profit \%} = \frac{\text{Selling price} - \text{Cost}}{\text{Cost}} \times 100\right).$$

The discount on item Q, as a percentage of its marked price, is _____.

(a) 25 (b) 12.5
(c) 10 (d) 5

8. There are five bags each containing identical sets of ten distinct chocolates. One chocolate is picked form each bag.
The probability that at least two chocolates are identical is ________.

(a) 0.3024 (b) 0.4235
(c) 0.6976 (d) 0.8125

9. Given below are two statements 1 and 2, and two conclusions I and II.

Statement 1 : All bacteria are microorganisms.

Statement 2 : All pathogens are microorganisms.

Conclusion I : Some pathogens are bacteria.

Conclusion II : All pathogens are not bacteria.

Based on the above statements and conclusions, which one of the following option is logically CORRECT ?

(a) Only conclusion I is correct

(b) Only conclusion II is correct

(c) Either conclusion I or II is correct.

(d) Neither conclusion I nor II is correct.

10. Some people suggest anti-obesity measures (AOM) such as displaying calorie information in restaurant menus. Such measures sidestep addressing the core problems that cause obesity: poverty and income inequality.

Which one of the following statements summarizes the passage ?

(a) The proposed AOM addresses the core problems that cause obesity.

(b) If obesity reduces, poverty will naturally reduce, sine obesity causes poverty.

(c) AOM are addressing the core problems and are likely to succeed.

(d) AOM are addressing the problem superficially.

COMPUTER SCIENCE & INFORMATION

Q. 1 to Q. 10 : Carry One Mark Each.

1. Suppose that L_1 is a regular language and L_2 is a context-free language. Which one of the following languages is NOT necessarily context-free ?

(a) $L_1 \cap L_2$ (b) $L_1 . L_2$

(c) $L_1 - L_2$ (d) $L_1 \cup L_2$

2. Let P be an array containing n integers. Let t be the lowest upper bound on the number of comparisons of the array elements, required to find the minimum and maximum values in an arbitrary array of n elements. Which one of the following choices is correct ?

(a) $t > 2n - 2$

(b) $t > 3\left\lceil \frac{n}{2} \right\rceil$ and $t \le 2n - 2$

(c) $t > n$ and $t \le 3\left\lceil \frac{n}{2} \right\rceil$

(d) $t > \lceil \log_2(n) \rceil$ and $t \le n$

3. Consider the following three functions.

$$f_1 = 10^n \quad f_2 = n^{\log n} \quad f_3 = n^{\sqrt{n}}$$

Which one of the following options arranges the functions in the increasing order of asymptotic growth rate ?

(a) f_3, f_2, f_1 (b) f_2, f_1, f_3

(c) f_1, f_2, f_3 (d) f_2, f_3, f_1

4. Consider the following statements.

S_1 : The sequence of procedure calls corresponds to a preorder traversal of the activation tree.

S_2 : The sequence of procedure returns corresponds to a postorder traversal of the activation tree.

Which one of the following options is correct ?

(a) S_1 is true and S_2 is false

(b) S_1 is false and S_2 is true

(c) S_1 is true and S_2 is true

(d) S_1 is false and S_2 is false

5. Consider the following statements.

S_1 : Every SLR (1) grammar is unambiguous but there are certain unambiguous grammars that are not SLR(1).

S_1 : For any context-free grammar, there is a parser that takes at most $O(n^3)$ time to parse a string of length n.

Which one of the following options is correct ?

(a) S_1 is true and S_2 is false

(b) S_1 is false and S_2 is true

(c) S_1 is true and S_2 is true

(d) S_1 is false and S_2 is false

6. Let the representation of a number in base 3 be 210. What is the hexadecimal representation of the number ?

(a) 15 (b) 21

(c) D2 (d) 528

7. Let p and q be two propositions. Consider the following two formulae in propositional logic.

$$S_1 : (\neg p \wedge (p \vee q)) \rightarrow q$$

$$S_2 : q \rightarrow (\neg p \wedge (p \vee q))$$

Which one of the following choices is correct ?

(a) Btoh S_1 and S_2 are tautologies

(b) S_1 is a tautology but S_2 is not a tautology.

(c) S_1 is not a tautology but S_2 is a tautology.

(d) Neither S_1 nor S_2 is a tautology.

8. Consider the following two statements.

S_1 : Destination MAC address of an ARP reply is a broadcast address.

S_2 : Destination MAC address of an ARP request is a broadcast address.

Which one of the following choices is correct ?

(a) Btoh S_1 and S_2 are true.

(b) S_1 is true and S_2 is false.

(c) S_1 is false and S_2 is true.

(d) Btoh S_1 and S_2 are false.

9. Consider the following array.

23	32	45	69	72	73	89	97

Which algorithm out of the following options uses the least number of comparisons (among the array elements) to sort the above array in ascending order ?

(a) Selection sort

(b) Mergesort

(c) Insertion sort

(d) Quicksort using the last element as pivot

10. A binary search tree T contains n distinct elements. What is the time complexity of picking an element in T that is smaller than the maximum element in T ?

(a) $\Theta(n \log n)$ (b) $\Theta(n)$

(c) $\Theta(\log n)$ (d) $\Theta(1)$

Q. 11 to Q. 15 : Carry One Mark Each.

11. In the context of operating systems, which of the following statements is/are correct with respect to paging ?

(a) Paging helps solve the issue of external fragmentation.

(b) Page size has no impact on internal fragmentation.

(c) Paging incurs memory overheads.

(d) Multi-level paging is necessary to support pages of different sizes.

12. Let $\langle M \rangle$ denote an encoding of an automaton M. Suppose that $\Sigma = \{0, 1\}$. Which of the following languages is/are NOT recursive ?

(a) $L = \{\langle M \rangle \mid M \text{ is a DFA such that } L(M) = \theta\}$

(b) $L = \{\langle M \rangle \mid M \text{ is a DFA such that } L(M) = \Sigma^*\}$

(c) $L = \{\langle M \rangle \mid M \text{ is a PDA such that } L(M) = \theta\}$

(d) $L = \{\langle M \rangle \mid M \text{ is a PDA such that } L(M) = \Sigma^*\}$

13. Suppose a database system crashes again while recovering from a previous crash. Assume checkpointing is not done by the database either during the transactions or during recovery.

Which of the following statements is/are correct?

(a) The same undo and redo list will be used while recovering again.

(b) The system cannot recover any further.

(c) All the transactions that are already undone and redone will not be recovered again.

(d) The database will become inconsistent.

14. Which of the following standard C library functions will always invoke a system call when executed from a single-threaded process in a UNIX/ Linux operating system ?

(a) exit (b) malloc

(c) sleep (d) strlen

15. Consider a linear list based directory implementation in a file system. Each directory is a list of nodes, where each node contains the file name along with the file metadata, such as the list of pointers to the data blocks. Consider a given directory foo.

Which of the following operations will necessarily require a full scan of foo for successful completion ?

(a) Creation of a new file in foo

(b) Deletion of an existing file from foo

(c) Renaming of an existing file in foo

(d) Opening of an existing file in foo

Q. 16 to Q. 25 : Carry One Mark Each.

16. In an undirected connected planar graph G, there are eight vertices and five faces. The number of edges in G is ______.

17. Consider the following undirected graph with edge weights as shown :

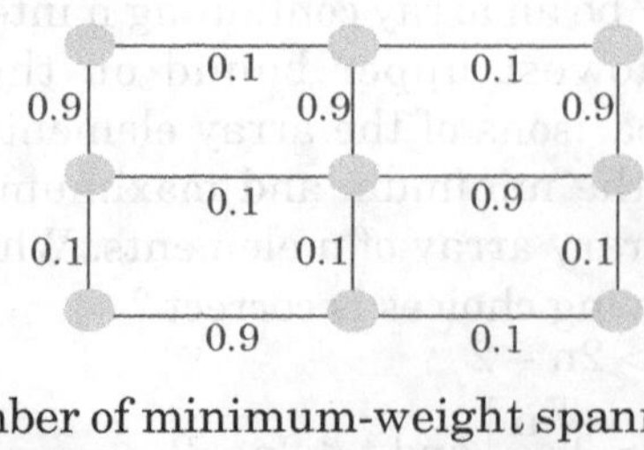

The number of minimum-weight spanning trees of the graph is ______ .

18. The lifetime of a component of a certain type is a random variable whose probability density function is exponentially distributed with parameter 2. For a randomly picked component of this type, the probability that its lifetime exceeds the expected lifetime (rounded to 2 decimal places) is ______ .

19. There are 6 jobs with distinct difficulty levels, and 3 computers with distinct processing speeds. Each job is assigned to a computer such that :

- The fastest computer gets the toughest job and the slowest computer gets the easiest job.

- Every computer gets at least one job.

The number of ways in which this can be done is ______ .

20. Consider the following expression.

$$\lim_{x \to -3} \frac{\sqrt{2x+22}-4}{x+3}$$

The value of the above expression (rounded to 2 decimal places) is ________ .

21. Consider the following sequence of operations on an empty stack.

push (54); push (52); pop (); push (55); push (62); s = pop ();

Consider the following sequence of operations on an empty queue.

enqueue (21); enqueue (24); dequeue (); enqueue (28); enqueue (32); q = dequeue () ;

The value of s + q is ________ .

22. Consider a computer system with a byte-addressable primary memory of size 2^{32} bytes. Assume the computer system has a direct-mapped cache of size 32 KB (1 KB = 2^{10} bytes), and each cache block is of size 64 bytes.

The size of the tag field is ________ bits.

23. A relation r(A, B) in a relational database has 1200 tuples. The attribute A has integer values ranging from 6 to 20, and the attribute B has integer values ranging from 1 to 20. Assume that the attributes A and B are independently distributed.

The estimated number of tuples in the output of $\sigma_{(A>10) \vee (B=18)}(r)$ is ________ .

24. Consider the following representation of a number in IEEE 754 single-precision floating point format with a bias of 127.

S : 1 E : 10000001 F : 11110000000000000000000

Here S, E and F denote the sign, exponent and fraction components of the floating point representation.

The decimal value corresponding to the above representation (rounded to 2 decimal places) is ________ .

25. Three processes arrive at time zero with CPU bursts of 16, 20 and 10 milliseconds. If the scheduler has prior knowledge about the length of the CPU bursts, the minimum achievable average waiting time for these three processes in a non-preemptive scheduler (rounded to nearest integer) is __________ milliseconds.

Q. 26 to Q. 39 : Carry Two Mark Each.

26. Consider the following grammar (that admits a series of declarations, followed by expressions) and the associated syntax directed translation (SDT) actions, given as pseudo-code :

$P \rightarrow D^* E^*$

$D \rightarrow$ int ID {record that ID.lexeme is of type int}

$D \rightarrow$ bool ID {record that ID.lexeme is of type bool}

$E \rightarrow E_1 + E_2$ {check that E_1.type = E_2.type = int;set E.type := int}

$E \rightarrow !E_1$ {check that E_1.type = bool; set E.type : = bool}

$E \rightarrow$ ID {set E.type := int}

With respect to the above grammar, which one of the following choices is correct ?

(a) The actions can be used to correctly type-check any syntactically correct program.

(b) The actions can be used to type-check syntactically correct integer variable declarations and integer expressions.

(c) The actions can be used to type-check syntactically correct boolean variable declarations and boolean expressions.

(d) The actions will lead to an infinite loop.

27. The following relation records the age of 500 employees of a company, where empNo (indicating the employee number) is the key :

empAge(<u>empNo</u>, age)

Consider the following relational algebra expression :

Π_{empNo} (empAge $\bowtie_{(age > age1)} \rho_{empNo1,\, age1}$ (empAge))

What does the above expression generate ?

(a) Employee numbers of only those employees whose age is the maximum.

(b) Employee number of only those employees whose age is more than the age of exactly one other employee.

(c) Employee numbers of all employees whose age is not the minimum.

(d) Employee numbers of all employees whose age is the minimum.

28. Consider a 3-bit counter, designed using T flip-flops, as shown below :

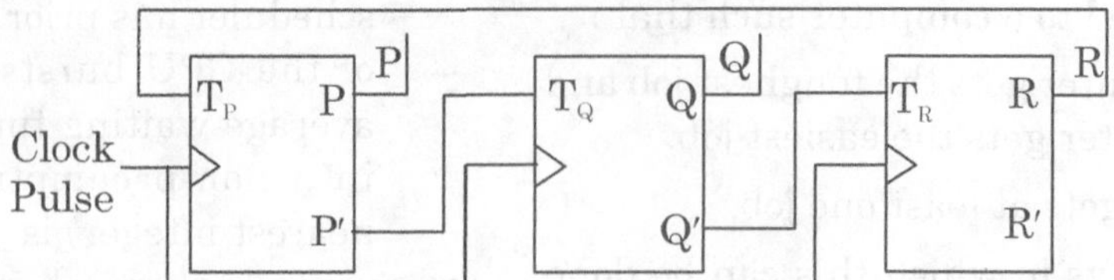

Assuming the initial state of the counter given by PQR as 000, what are the next three states ?

(a) 011, 101, 000 (b) 001, 010, 111

(c) 011, 101, 111 (d) 001, 010, 000

29. Assume that a 12-bit Hamming codeword consisting of 8-bit data and 4 check bits is $d_8d_7d_6d_5c_8d_4d_4d_3d_2c_4d_1c_2c_1$, where the data bits and the check bits are given in the following tables :

Data bits							
d_8	d_7	d_6	d_5	d_4	d_3	d_2	d_1
1	1	0	x	0	1	0	1

Check bits			
c_8	c_4	c_2	c_1
y	0	1	0

Which one of the following choices gives the correct values of x and y ?

(a) x is 0 and y is 0. (b) x is 0 and y is 1.

(c) x is 1 and y is 0. (d) x is 1 and y is 1.

30. Consider the following recurrence relation.

$$T(n) = \begin{cases} T\left(\frac{n}{2}\right) + T\left(\frac{2n}{5}\right) + 7n & \text{if } n > 0 \\ 1 & \text{if } n = 0 \end{cases}$$

Which one of the following options is correct ?

(a) $T(n) = \Theta(n^{5/2})$

(b) $T(n) = \Theta(n \log n)$

(c) $T(n) = \Theta(n)$

(d) $T(n) = \Theta\left((\log n)^{\frac{5}{2}}\right)$

31. Consider the following context-free grammar where the set of terminals is {a, b, c, d, f}.

$S \rightarrow da\,T \mid Rf$

$T \rightarrow aS \mid ba\,T \mid \in$

$R \rightarrow ca\,T\,R \mid \in$

The following is a partially-filled LL(1) parsing table.

	a	b	c	d	f	$
S			①	S → d a T	②	
T	T → a S	T → b a T	③		T → ∈	④
R			R → c a TR		R → ∈	

Which one of the following choices represents the correct combination for the numbered cells in the parsing table ("blank" denotes that the corresponding cell is empty) ?

(a) ① S → Rf ② S → Rf ③ T → ∈ ④ T → ∈

(b) ① blank ② S → Rf ③ T → ∈ ④ T → ∈

(c) ① S → Rf ② blank ③ blank ④ T → ∈

(d) ① blank ② S → Rf ③ blank ④ blank

32. Let $r_i(z)$ and $w_i(z)$ denote read and write operations respectively on a data item z by a transaction T_i. Consider the following two schedules.

$S_1 : r_1(x)\,r_1(y)\,r_2(x)\,r_2(y)\,w_1(y)\,w_1(x)$

$S_2 : r_1(x)\,r_2(x)\,r_2(y)\,w_2(y)\,r_1(y)\,w_1(x)$

Which one of the following options is correct ?

(a) S_1 is conflict serializable, and S_2 is not conflict serializable.

(b) S_1 is not conflict serializable, and S_2 is conflict serializable.

(c) Both S_1 and S_2 are conflict serializable.

(d) Neither S_1 nor S_2 is conflict serializable

33. Consider the relation R(P, Q, S, T, X, Y, Z, W) with the following functional dependencies.

PQ → X; P → YX; Q → Y; Y → ZW

Consider the decomposition of the relation R in to the constituent relations according to the following two decomposition schemes.

D_1 : R = [(P, Q, S, T); (P, T, X); (Q, Y); (Y, Z, W)]

D_2 : R = [(P, Q, S); (T, X); (Q, Y); (Y, Z, W)]

Which one of the following options is correct ?

(a) D_1 is a lossless decomposition, but D_2 is a lossy decomposition.

(b) D_1 is a lossy decomposition, but D_2 is a lossless decomposition.

(c) Both D_1 and D_2 are lossless decompositions.

(d) Both D_1 and D_2 are lossy decompositions.

34. Let G be a group of order 6, and H be a subgroup of G such that $1 < |H| < 6$. Which one of the following options is correct ?

(a) Both G and H are always cyclic.

(b) G may not be cyclic, but H is always cyclic.

(c) G is always cyclic, but H may not be cyclic.

(d) Both G and H may not be cyclic.

35. Consider the two statements.

S_1 : There exist random variables X and Y such that $(\mathbb{E}[(X-\mathbb{E}(X))(Y-\mathbb{E}(Y))])^2 > \text{Var}[X]\,\text{Var}[Y]$

S_2 : For all random variables X and Y, $\text{Cov}[X, Y] = \mathbb{E}[\,|X-\mathbb{E}[X]|\,|Y-\mathbb{E}[Y]|\,]$

Which one of the following choices is correct ?

(a) Both S_1 and S_2 are true.

(b) S_1 is true, but S_2 is false.

(c) S_1 is false, but S_2 is true.

(d) Both S_1 and S_2 are false.

36. Let G = (V, E) be an undirected unweighted connected graph. The diameter of G is defined as :

$$\text{diam}(G) = \max_{u,v \in V} \{\text{the length of shortest path between } u \text{ and } v\}$$

Let M be the adjacency matrix of G.

Define graph G_2 on the same set of vertices with adjacency matrix N, where

$$N_{ij} = \begin{cases} 1 & \text{if } M_{ij} > 0 \text{ or } P_{ij} > 0, \text{ where } P = M^2 \\ 0 & \text{otherwise} \end{cases}$$

Which one of the following statements is true ?

(a) $\text{diam}(G_2) \le \left\lceil \text{diam}\frac{(G)}{2} \right\rceil$

(b) $\left\lceil \text{diam}\frac{(G)}{2} \right\rceil < \text{diam}(G_2) < \text{diam}(G)$

(c) $\text{diam}(G_2) = \text{diam}(G)$

(d) $\text{diam}(G) < \text{diam}(G_2) \le 2\,\text{diam}(G)$

37. Consider the following ANSI C program.

```
#include <stdio.h>
int main ()
{
    int i, j, count;
    count = 0;
    i = 0;
    for (j = -3; j <= 3; j++) }
    {
        if ((j >= 0) && (i++))
        count = count + j;
    }
    count = count + i;
    printf("%d", count);
    return 0;
}
```

Which one of the following options is correct ?

(a) The program will not compile successfully

(b) The program will compile successfully and output 10 when executed.

(c) The program will compile successfully and output 8 when executed.

(d) The program will compile successfully and output 13 when executed.

38. Consider the following language.

$L = \{w \in \{0, 1\}^* \mid w \text{ ends with the substring } 011\}$

Which one of the following deterministic finite automata accepts L ?

(a) 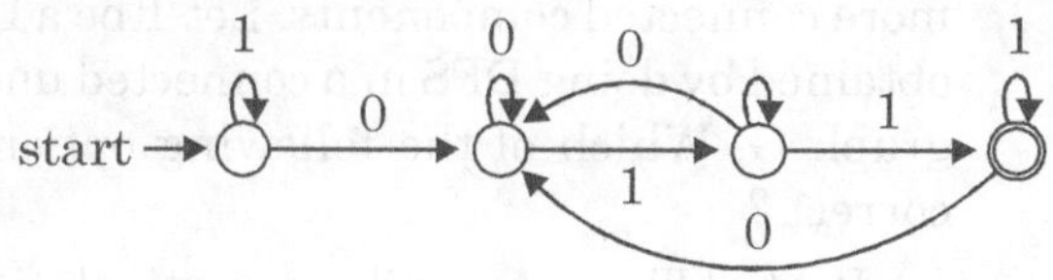

(b) 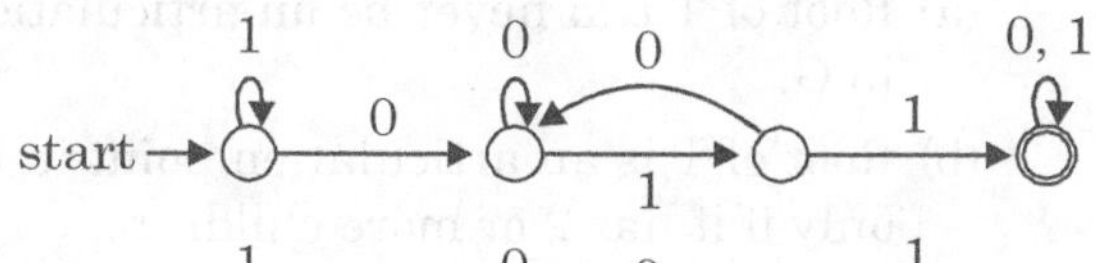

(c) 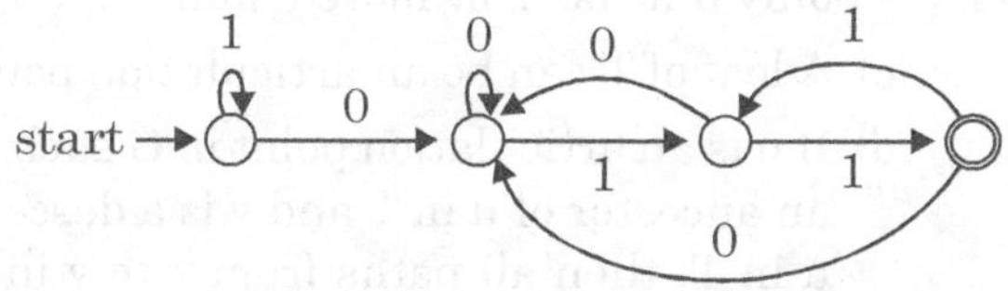

(d) 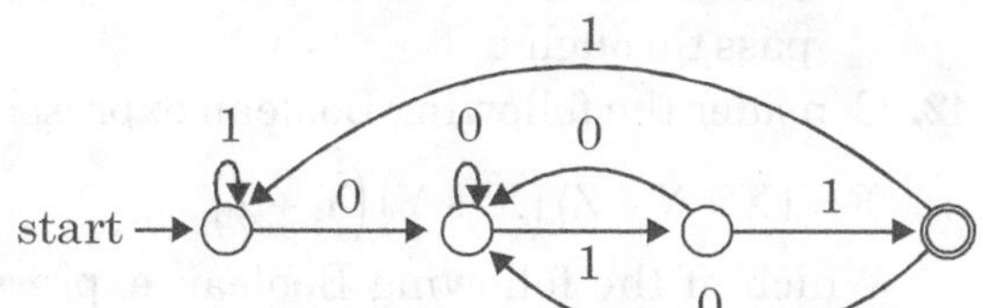

39. For a Turing machine M, ⟨M⟩ denotes an encoding of M. Consider the following two languages.

L_1 = {⟨M⟩ | M takes more than 2021 steps on all inputs}

L_2 = {⟨M⟩ | M takes more than 2021 steps on some input}

Which one of the following options is correct ?

(a) Both L_1 and L_2 are decidable.

(b) L_1 is decidable and L_2 is undecidable.

(c) L_1 is undecidable and L_2 is decidable.

(d) Both L_1 and L_2 are undecidable.

Q. 40 to Q. 47 : Carry Two Mark Each.

40. Define R_n to be the maximum amount earned by cutting a rod of length n meters into one or more pieces of integer length and selling them. For $i > 0$, let p[i] denote the selling price of a rod whose length is i meters. Consider the array of prices :

p[1] = 1, p[2] = 5, p[3] = 8, p[4] = 9, p[5] = 10, p[6] = 17, p[7] = 18

Which of the following statements is/are correct about R_7?

(a) $R_7 = 18$

(b) $R_7 = 19$

(c) R_7 is achieved by three different solutions.

(d) R_7 cannot be achieved by a solution consisting of three pieces.

41. An articulation point in a connected graph is a vertex such that removing the vertex and its incident edges disconnects the graph into two or more connected components. Let T be a DFS tree obtained by doing DFS in a connected undirected graph G. Which of the following options is/are correct ?

(a) Root of T can never be an articulation point in G.

(b) Root of T is an articulation point in G if and only if it has 2 or more children.

(c) A leaf of T can be an articulation point in G.

(d) If u is an articulation point in G such that x is an ancestor of u in T and y is a descendent of u in T, then all paths from x to y in G must pass through u.

42. Consider the following Boolean expression.

$$F = (X + Y + Z)(\overline{X} + Y)(\overline{Y} + Z)$$

Which of the following Boolean expressions is/are equivalent to $\overline{F}$ (complement of F) ?

(a) $(\overline{X} + \overline{Y} + \overline{Z})(X + \overline{Y})(Y + \overline{Z})$

(b) $X\overline{Y} + \overline{Z}$

(c) $(X + \overline{Z})(\overline{Y} + \overline{Z})$

(d) $X\overline{Y} + Y\overline{Z} + \overline{X}\overline{Y}\overline{Z}$

43. A relation R is said to be circular if aRb and bRc together imply cRa. Which of the following options is/are correct ?

(a) If a relation S is reflexive and symmetric, then S is an equivalence relation.

(b) If a relation S is circular and symmetric, then S is an equivalence relation.

(c) If a relation S is reflexive and circular, then S is an equivalence relation.

(d) If a relation S is transitive and circular, then S is an equivalence relation.

44. A TCP server application is programmed to listen on port number P on host S . A TCP client is connected to the TCP server over the network.

Consider that while the TCP connection was active, the server machine S crashed and rebooted. Assume that the client does not use the TCP keepalive timer.

Which of the following behaviors is/are possible ?

(a) If the client was waiting to receive a packet, it may wait indefinitely.

(b) The TCP server application on S can listen on P after reboot.

(c) If the client sends a packet after the server reboot, it will receive a RST segment.

(d) If the client sends a packet after the server reboot, it will receive a FIN segment.

45. Consider two hosts P and Q connected through a router R. The maximum transfer unit (MTU) value of the link between P and R is 1500 bytes, and between R and Q is 820 bytes.

A TCP segment of size 1400 bytes was transferred from P to Q through R, with IP identification value as 0x1234. Assume that the IP header size is 20 bytes. Further, the packet is allowed to be fragmented, i.e., Don't Fragment (DF) flag in the IP header is not set by P.

Which of the following statements is/are correct ?

(a) Two fragments are created at R and the IP datagram size carrying the second fragment is 620 bytes.

(b) If the second fragment is lost, R will resend the fragment with the IP identification value 0x1234

(c) If the second fragment is lost, P is required to resend the whole TCP segment.

(d) TCP destination port can be determined by analysing only the second fragment.

46. Consider the following pseudocode, where S is a semaphore initialized to 5 in line#2 and counter is a shared variable initialized to 0 in line#1. Assume that the increment operation in line#7 is not atomic.

```
1. int counter = 0;
2. Semaphore S = init (5);
3. void parop (void)
4. {
5.        wait (S) ;
6.        wait (S) ;
7.        counter++;
8.        signal (S) ;
9.        signal (S) ;
10. }
```

If five threads execute the function parop concurrently, which of the following program behavior(s) is/are possible ?

(a) The value of counter is 5 after all the threads successfully complete the execution of parop.

(b) The value of counter is 1 after all the threads successfully complete the execution of parop.

(c) The value of counter is 0 after all the threads successfully complete the execution of parop.

(d) There is a deadlock involving all the threads.

47. Consider a dynamic hashing approach for 4-bit integer keys :

1. There is a main hash table of size 4.
2. The 2 least significant bits of a key is used to index into the main hash table.
3. Initially, the main hash table entries are empty.
4. Thereafter, when more keys are hashed into it, to resolve collisions, the set of all keys corresponding to a main hash table entry is organized as a binary tree that grows on demand.
5. First, the 3rd least significant bit is used to divide the keys into left and right subtrees.
6. To resolve more collisions, each node of the binary tree is further sub-divided into left and right subtrees based on the 4th least significant bit.
7. A split is done only if it is needed, i.e., only when there is a collision.

Consider the following state of the hash table.

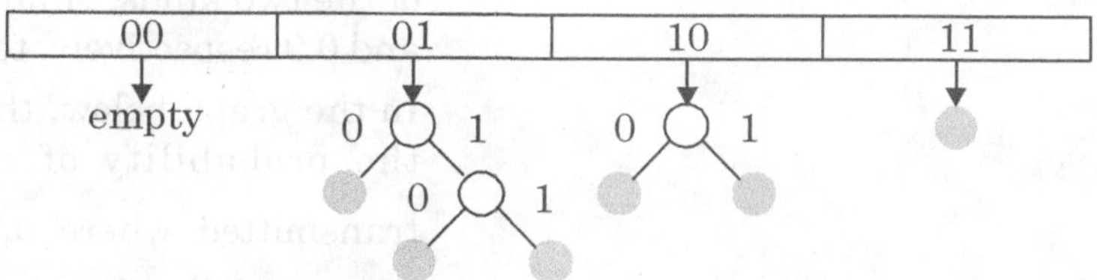

Which of the following sequences of key insertions can cause the above state of the hash table (assume the keys are in decimal notation) ?

(a) 5, 9, 4, 13, 10, 7

(b) 9, 5, 10, 6, 7, 1

(c) 10, 9, 6, 7, 5, 13

(d) 9, 5, 13, 6, 10, 14

Q. 48 to Q. 55 : Carry Two Mark Each.

48. Consider the following ANSI C function :

```
int SimpleFunction(int Y[ ], int n, int x)
{ int total = Y [0], loopIndex;
for (loopIndex = 1; loopIndex <= n – 1; loopIndex++)
total = x * total + Y[loopIndex];
return total;
}
```

Let Z be an array of 10 elements with Z[i] = 1, for all i such that $0 \le i \le 9$. The value returned by SimpleFunction (Z, 10, 2) is ________ .

49. Consider the sliding window flow-control protocol operating between a sender and a receiver over a full-duplex error-free link. Assume the following :

- The time taken for processing the data frame by the receiver is negligible.
- The time taken for processing the acknowledgement frame by the sender is negligible.
- The sender has infinite number of frames available for transmission.

- The size of the data frame is 2,000 bits and the size of the acknowledgement frame is 10 bits.
- The link data rate in each direction is 1 Mbps (= 10^6 bits per second).
- One way propagation delay of the link is 100 milliseconds.

The minimum value of the sender's window size in terms of the number of frames, (rounded to the nearest integer) needed to achieve a link utilization of 50% is ________ .

50. Consider the following C code segment :

a = b + c;
e = a + 1;
d = b + c;
f = d + 1;
g = e + f;

In a compiler, this code segment is represented internally as a directed acyclic graph (DAG). The number of nodes in the DAG is ________ .

51. In a pushdown automaton $P = (Q, \Sigma, \Gamma, \delta, q_0, F)$, a transition of the form,

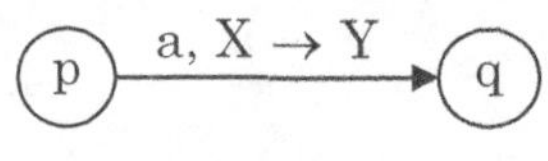

where $p, q \in Q$, $a \in \Sigma \cup \{\epsilon\}$, and $X, Y \in \Gamma \cup \{\epsilon\}$, represents $(q, Y) \in \delta(p, a, X)$.

Consider the following pushdown automaton over the input alphabet $\Sigma = \{a, b\}$ and stack alphabet $\Gamma = \{\#, A\}$.

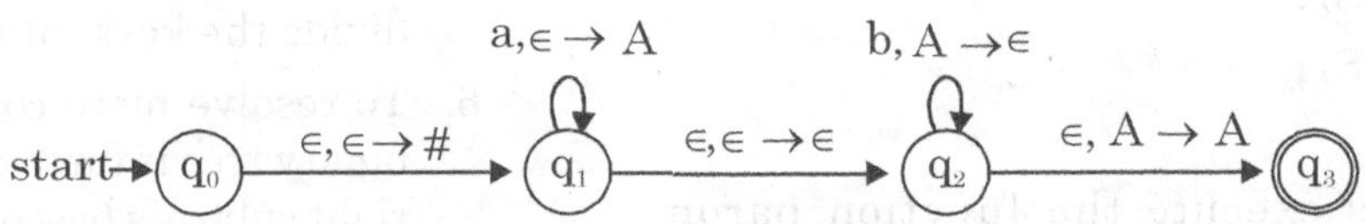

The number of strings of length 100 accepted by the above pushdown automaton is ________ .

52. Consider the following matrix.

$$\begin{pmatrix} 0 & 1 & 1 & 1 \\ 1 & 0 & 1 & 1 \\ 1 & 1 & 0 & 1 \\ 1 & 1 & 1 & 0 \end{pmatrix}$$

The largest eigenvalue of the above matrix is ________ .

53. A five-stage pipeline has stage delays of 150, 120, 150, 160 and 140 nanoseconds. The registers that are used between the pipeline stages have a delay of 5 nanoseconds each.

The total time to execute 100 independent instructions on this pipeline, assuming there are no pipeline stalls, is ________ nanoseconds.

54. A sender (S) transmits a signal, which can be one of the two kinds; H and L with probabilities 0.1 and 0.9 respectively, to a receiver (R).

In the graph below, the weight of edge (u, v) is the probability of receiving v, when u is transmitted, where $u, v \in \{H, L\}$. For example, the probability that the received signal is L given the transmitted signal was H, is 0.7.

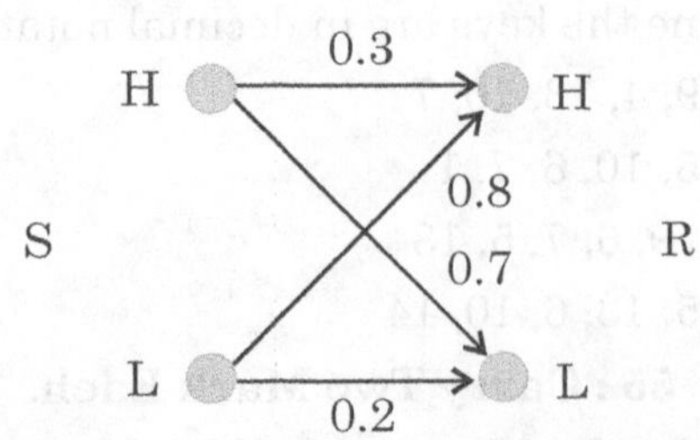

If the received signal is H, the probability that the transmitted signal was H (rounded to 2 decimal places) is ________ .

55. Consider the following instruction sequence where registers R1, R2 and R3 are general purpose and MEMORY[X] denotes the content at the memory location X.

Instruction	Semantics	Instruction Size (bytes)
MOV R1, (5000)	R1 ← MEMORY[5000]	4
MOV R2, (R3)	R2 ← MEMORY[R3]	4
ADD R2, R1	R2 ← R1+R2	2
MOV (R3), R2	MEMORY[R3] ← R2	4
INC R3	R3 ← R3+1	2
DEC R1	R1 ← R1-1	2
BNZ 1004	Branch if not zero to the given absolute address	2
HALT	Stop	1

Assume that the content of the memory location 5000 is 10, and the content of the register R3 is 3000. The content of each of the memory locations from 3000 to 3010 is 50. The instruction sequence starts from the memory location 1000. All the numbers are in decimal format. Assume that the memory is byte addressable. After the execution of the program, the content of memory location 3010 is _______ .

ANSWERS

General Aptitude (GA)

1. (c)	**2.** (a)	**3.** (c)	**4.** (a)	**5.** (c)	**6.** (c)
7. (c)	**8.** (c)	**9.** (d)	**10.** (d)		

Computer Science and Informatin Technology

1. (c)	**2.** (c)	**3.** (d)	**4.** (c)	**5.** (c)	**6.** (a)
7. (b)	**8.** (c)	**9.** (c)	**10.** (d)	**11.** (a; c)	**12.** (d)
13. (a)	**14.** (a; b; c)	**15.** (a; c)	**16.** (11 to 11)	**17.** (3 to 3)	
18.(0.35 to 0.39)	**19.** (65 to 65)	**20.** (0.25 to 0.25)	**21.** (86 to 86)	**22.** (17 to 17)	**23.** (820 to 820)
24. (-7.75 to -7.75)	**25.** (12 to 12)	**26.** (b)	**27.** (c)	**28.** (a)	**29.** (a)
30. (c)	**31.** (a)	**32.** (b)	**33.** (a)	**34.** (b)	**35.** (d)
36. (a)	**37.** (b)	**38.** (d)	**39.** (a)	**40.** (a; c)	**41.** (b)
42. (b; c; d)	**43.** (c)	**44.** (a; b; c)	**45.** (a; c)	**46.** (a; b; d)	**47.** (c)
48. (1023 to 1023)	**49.** (50 to 52)	**50.** (6 to 6)	**51.** (50 to 50)	**52.** (3 to 3)	
53. (17160 to 17160)	**54.** (0.04 to 0.04)	**55.** (50 to 50)			

EXPLANATIONS

GENERAL APTITUDE

1. Let us consider the number of boys = B
And total number of students = S
So, we have

$$\frac{B}{(S-B)} = \frac{7}{3}$$

$$B = \frac{7S}{10}$$

Thus, S must be multiple of 10. Hence, answer is 50.

2. If we choose two points P, Q such that P is the top-left corner and Q is the bottom left corner then the line joining P, Q will not lie on the polygon. Hence, option (a) is the correct answer.

3. Every body is prepared means they are ready for the exam, the second sentence does not clearly state whether babu will play with Danish or not.

Babu loves playing chess the does not means danish knows how to play chess. So statement

(i) is grammatically correct and

(ii) is ambiguous.

Statement (ii) is ambiguous because we do not know who enjoys playing chees, Babu or Danish.

So, statement (i) is grammatically correct.

Hence, option (c) is the correct answer.

4. Unforhed in reverse order of folding, it's look like option (a)

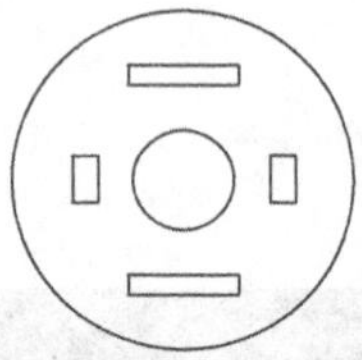

5. A doctor performs surgery just as a writer writes a book. It is the relation of person and skill.

6.

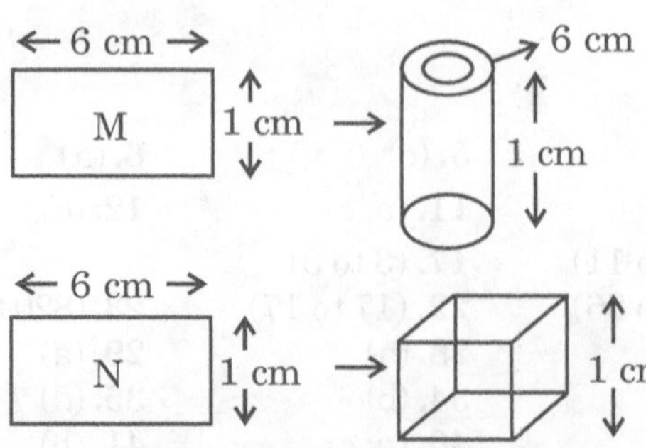

The circumference of lower circle $2\pi r = 6$

$$\Rightarrow r = \frac{3}{\pi}$$

Volume of a cylinder $= \pi r^2 h = \pi \times \frac{3}{\pi} \times \frac{3}{\pi} \times 1 = \frac{9}{\pi}$

Volume of a cube = $(1)^3$

So, request ratio

$$= \frac{\left(\frac{9}{\pi}\right)}{1} = \frac{9}{\pi}$$

Hence, option (c) is the correct answer.

7. As given that

$CP_p = 5400$

$MP_P = 5860$

Cost of $Q(CP_q) = \left(\frac{4}{3}\right) * CP_p = 7200$

Let, selling price (S.P) of Q = S

$$25 = \left(SP_q - 7200\right) * \frac{100}{7200}$$

$SP_q = 9000$

Discount on Q = $MP_q - SP_q = 10000 - 9000 = 1000$

$$\text{Discount\%} = \frac{1000}{10000} \times 100 = 10\%$$

Discount on SPq i.e. 1000 is 10% of marked price (MP_q) of Q i.e. 10, 000.

So, answer is 10%.

Hence, option (c) is the correct answer.

8. P (exactly 1 =) Probability that all the picked chocolates are different:

$$= \frac{(10 * 9 * 8 * 7 * 6)}{10^5} = 0.3024$$

Probability that at least two of the picked chocolates are identical:

$\Rightarrow$ 1 – (Probability that all the picked chocolates are different)

$\Rightarrow 1 - 0.3024 = 0.6976$

9.

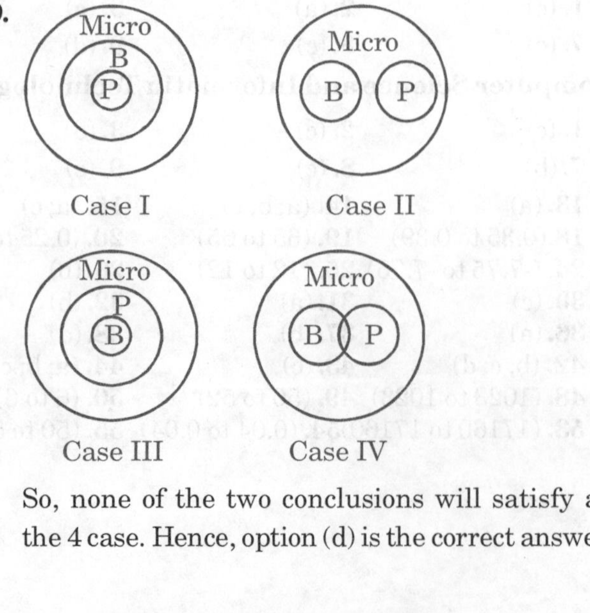

So, none of the two conclusions will satisfy all the 4 case. Hence, option (d) is the correct answer.

10. Superficially is the deciding key word which means apparently or seemingly.

As AOM are not addressing the core problems, they are superficial.

Superficial means shallow, cursory mean lacking in depth or solidity. Superficial implies a concern only with surface aspects or obvious features. A superficial analysis of the problem shallow is more generally derogatory in implying lack of depth in knowledge, reasoning, emotions, or character. Hence, option (d) is the correct answer.

COMPUTER SCIENCE AND INFORMATION

1. As given that

L1 is a regular language

L2 is a context free language

then $L_1 \leq L_2$

$\Rightarrow L_1 \cap L_2$ is a C.F

$\Rightarrow L_1 \cup L_2$ is a C.F

$\Rightarrow L_1, L_2$ is a C.F

But, $L_1 - L_2 = L_1 \cap \overline{L_2}$ is not C.F

Because Context free language is not closed under complement so, $\overline{L2}$ may be non-Context free language. So, $L_1 \cap L_2$ and $L_1 - L_2$ are not Context free language.

Hence, option (c) is the correct answer.

2. To find the Maximum and Minimum Elements in an array simultaneously, Ceil(n/2) - 2 comparisons are necessary and sufficient in the worst case to find both the maximum and minimum of n numbers.

So, $t = \text{Ceil}\left(\frac{n}{2}\right) - 2$

Now by applying divide & conquer method, so the number of comparision element are $\left[\frac{3n}{2} - 2\right]$

Hence, option (c) is correct.

3. As given that $f_1 = 10^n$, $f_2 = n^{\log n}$

$f_3 = n^{\sqrt{n}}$

By taking log of all

$f_1 = n\log 10 = n.c$

$f_2 = \log n \log n = (\log n)^2$

$f_3 = \sqrt{n} \log n \left(\because \sqrt{n} > \log n\right)$

f_1 is exponential function, so grows fastest. And between f_2, f_3 ; f_3 grows faster than f_2.

Hence, the increasing order is $f_1 < f_2 < f_3$.

4. We can make the following observations about these procedure calls.

(i) If an activation of p calls q, then that activation of p terminates no earlier than the activation of q.

(ii) The order of activations (procedure calls) corresponds to a preorder traversal of the call tree.

(iii) The order of de-activations (procedure returns) corresponds to postorder traversal of the call tree.

(iv) If execution is currently in an activation corresponding to a node N of the activation tree, then the activations that are currently live are those corresponding to N and its ancestors in the tree.

(v) These live activations were called in the order given by the root-to-N path in the tree, and the returns will occur in the reverse order.

The use of a run-time stack is enabled by several useful relationships between the activation tree and the behavior of the program:

- The sequence of procedure calls corresponds to a preorder traversal of the activation tree.
- The sequence of returns corresponds to a postorder traversal of the activation tree.
- Suppose that control lies within a particular activation of some procedure, corresponding to a node N of the activation tree. Then the activations that are currently open (live) are those that correspond to node N and its ancestors. The order in which these activations were called is the order in which they appear along the path to N , starting at the root, and they will return in the reverse of that order.

Hence, both statement are true.

5. As we know that Every SLR (1) grammar is unambigous but every unambiguous grammar need not be SLR (1). And for any CFG, there is a parsor that takes almost $O(n^3)$ time to parse a string of length 'n'.

According to question,

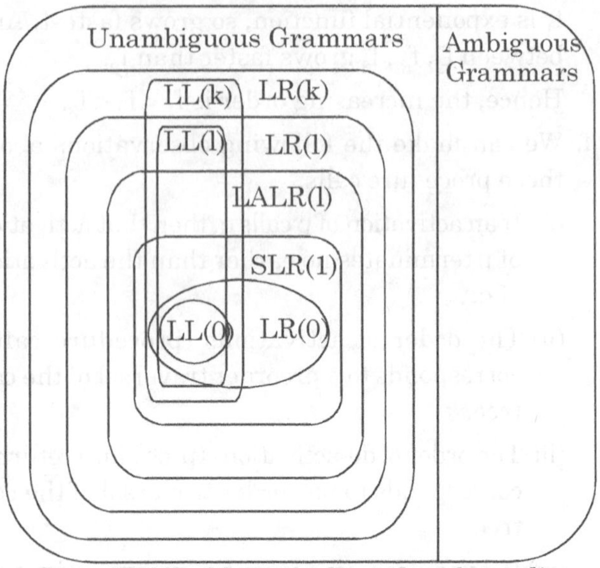

S1 is TRUE; If you look at the above diagram only unambiguous grammar are parsed by SLR and outside of SLR there are many grammar not parable by SLR.

S2 is also TRUE, The complexity of brute-force-search parsing with backtracking is $O(n^3)$ because, after each of the n words is accepted, the whole O(n) process may have to be done over from the beginning.

Hence, option (c) is the correct answer.

6. As given that $(210)_3 = (N)_{16}$,

$(210)_3 = [(2 \times 3^2) + (1 \times 3^1) + (0 \times 3^0) = (21)_{10} = (15)_{16}]$

So, $(210)_3 = (15)_{16}$ i.e., N = 15

Hence, option (a) is the correct answer.

7. As given that,

S1, S2 are implication statements

S1 : $(p' \wedge (p \vee q)) \rightarrow q$

When y = q is false, then $(p' \wedge (p \vee q))$ cannot become true, so S1 is tautology.

S2 : $q \rightarrow (p' \wedge (p \vee q))$

When x = q is true, still $(p' \wedge (p \vee q))$ can become false, so, S2 is not a tautology.

Hence, option (b) is the correct answer.

8. Address Resolution Protocol:

If a machine talks to another machine in the same network, it requires its physical or MAC address. But,since the application has given the destination's IP address it requires some mechanism to bind the IP address with its MAC address.This is done through Address Resolution protocol (ARP).IP address of the destination node is broadcast and the destination node informs the source of its MAC address.

(i) Assume broadcast nature of LAN

(ii) Broadcast IP address of the destination

(iii) Destination replies it with its MAC address.

(iv) Source maintains a cache of IP and MAC address bindings

There are four types of arp messages that may be sent by the arp protocol. These are identified by four values in the "operation" field of an arp message. The types of message are:

- ARP-Request (Broadcast, source IP address of the requester). So ARP-Request is broad costing.
- ARP-Reply (Unicast to requester, the target). So, ARP reply is unicasting.

Hence, option (c) is the correct answer.

9. The given array is already sorted in ascending order.

So, for already sorted array we can used these sort techniques:

(i) Selection sort :

No matter how the data is arranged there would always be comparisons and swaps made and so the time complexity for best, average and worst case is : O(n^2).

In first pass, we need n–1 comparisons (Or n comparisons, depending on the implementation) In second pass, we need n–2 comparisons (Or n–1 comparisons, depending on the implementation) and so on.

So, The number of comparisons required by a selection sort of n items can be computed by the formula :

$$(n-1) + (n-2) + \dots + 1 = (n)\frac{(n-1)}{2}$$

or

Number of selection sort comparisons

$$= (n+1)\frac{(n)}{2}$$

Basically, number of comparisons are Θ(n^2) in all cases.

(ii) Insertions Sort :

When elements are sorted, there are no swaps and the correct position of the element in the sorted list is the current index itself. The time complexity is : O(n). Insertion sort takes least Number of comparisons = n – 1

Comparisons in total : 1 + 1 + ... + 1

$= n - 1 \in \Theta(n)$.

(iii) Merge Sort :

We are dividing the list into two no matter if the list is sorted or no. But if the array is sorted, while merging the list there are no swaps merging results into an array itself. Thus, the best, average and worst case time complexity is : O(nlogn).

Number of comparisons, in all cases, will be O(nlogn).

(iv) Quick Sort :

The best case is when the elements are in a sorted manner. The best and average case time complexity is : O(nlogn).

Number of comparisons, in best case, will be O(nlogn).

Since, for a number which is to be inserted in the already sorted array, only one comparison will be required.

So, answer will be insertion sort.

Hence, option (d) is correct answer.

10. If our data structure contains n distinct elements then :

Example:

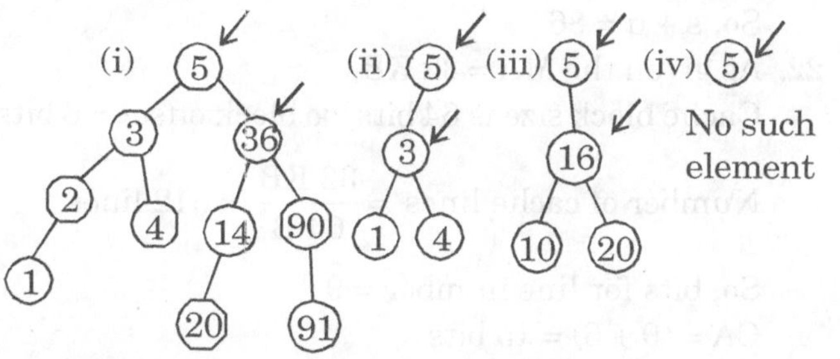

5 < max element 3 < max element5 < max element

In all the standard data structures. If we want to pick/find an element which is Not maximum (smaller than maximum) then time complexity will be $\Theta(1)$ because we only need to compare any two elements. Take any two elements that you can access in constant time, compare them and return smaller of those two elements.

In any case, we can find one element that is less in just 2 seeks = $\Theta(1)$.

Hence, option (d) is the correct answer.

11. Paging: does not suffer from external fragmentation and help to solve the issue of external fragmentation. And Paging suffers from internal fragmentation.

Page tables are memory overheads,

So, option (c) is also correct.

Hence, option (a) &)c) are correct answer.

12. (a) is L = { M | M is a DFA such that L(M) is Σ^* } is a trivial problem for DFA and DECIDABLE and **Recursive.**

(b) is **DECIDABLE** and **Recursive**; The language accepted we can check for usefulness of start symbol. If the start symbol is useful then L(G) non empty otherwise L(G) is empty

(c) is **UNDECIDABLE** and **NOT Recursive**; we can't check whether L(G) = Σ^* or not but rather we can check complemented of L(G) is $\varnothing$. Since context free language are not closed under complement operation $\overline{L(G)}$ may be language accepted by Turing Machine and we can't check emptiness for Turing machine.

Option (d) is **DECIDABLE** and **recursive**; emptiness of the finite state machine can be checked by reachability of the final state from initial state in transition graph. If the final state is reachable then non empty otherwise empty.

Hence, option (d) is the correct answer.

13. In order to recover the database even on multiple crashes the same undo and redo lift will used. Hence, option (a) is the correct ansser.

14. Types of library functions:

Library functions can be of two types :

Functions which do not call any system call.

Functions that make a system call.

There are library functions that do not make any system call. For example, the string manipulation functions like strlen() etc fall under this category. Also, there are library functions that further make system calls, for example the fopen() function which a standard library function but internally uses the open() system call.

The function call malloc() is a library function call that further uses the brk() or sbrk() system call for memory allocation.

The correct answer is a, b & c.

As exit , malloc, sleep invoke system calls but strlen does not.

15. While creating new file we have to check whether same name file exist or not , so we always need full scan for this

Renaming a file:

While renaming a file we have to check whether file with same name as newly named file exist or not , so we always need full scan for this.

Deletion, Opening of an existing file:

For deleting file, file can be present at any node (best case if present as first node, worst if present at last). So, we don't always need to full scan list. Similarly, for Opening a file. So, option (a) & (c) would require to traverse the directly foofully. The other two operation does not required.

16. Let V be the number of vertices, E is the number of edges and F is the number of faces in planer (G). Now, By Euler formula for connected planar graph,

$f = e - v + 2$

So, e = 11

17.

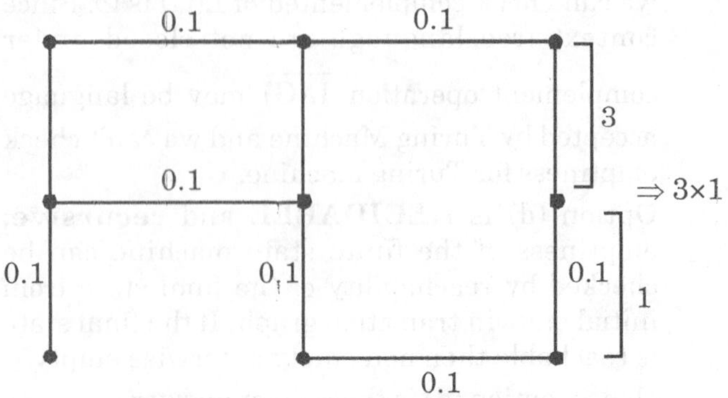

Apply Kruskal's algorithm. All the edges with weights 0.1 will be in the MST. Now we need to pick one edge out of three parallel edge with weight of 0.9, one can be taken in $^3c_1$ ways. Hence, 3 MST are possible.

18. Let X be exponential random variable denote lifetime of a component.

$$\Rightarrow f(x) = \begin{cases} \theta e^{-\theta x}, & x \geq 0 \\ 0 & \text{otherwise} \end{cases}$$

and θ = 2 is parameter

$$\Rightarrow E(x), \text{mean} = \frac{1}{\theta} = 0.5 \text{ is expected life time}$$

$$\therefore \text{ Required probability is } P(X > 0.5) = \int_{0.5}^{\infty} f(x)\,dx$$

$$= 2\left(\frac{e^{-2x}}{-2}\right)_{a-5}^{\infty} = \left(-e^{-\infty}\right) - \left(-e^{-2} \times \left(\frac{1}{2}\right)\right)$$

$= (0 + e^{-1})$

$$= \frac{1}{e} \approx 0.37$$

19. Let us consider jobs be J1 to J6, where J1 is toughest. Let computers be C1, C2, C3 where C1 is the fastest.

So, J1 goes to C1, J6 goes to C3.

Now remaining 4 jobs can go to any computer, But computer C2 must get at least one job.

So, Total Cases when Remaining 4 jobs can go to any computer = 3^4

And Cases when computer C2 is Not assigned any job = 2^4

So, Cases when every computer gets at least one job = 81 – 16 = 65

20. As given expression : $\lim\limits_{x \to -3} \dfrac{\sqrt{2x+22} - 4}{x+3}$ is $\dfrac{0}{0}$ form

$$\lim_{x \to -3} \frac{2 \times \dfrac{1}{2\sqrt{2x+22}} - 0}{1+0}$$

$$\left(\text{Using L – Hospital's rule and } \frac{d}{dx}\left(\sqrt{x}\right) = \frac{1}{2\sqrt{x}}\right)$$

$$= \frac{1}{\sqrt{2(-3) + 22^2}} = \frac{1}{\sqrt{16}} = \frac{1}{4} = 0.25$$

21. Stack is LIFO,

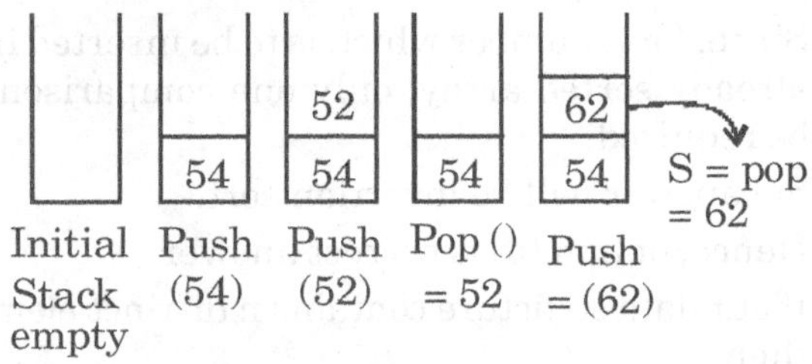

Hence, s = 62

Similarly, Queue is FIFO, so, q = 24

So, s + q = 86

22. As given the MA = 32 KB

Cache block size is 64 bits, so block offset = 6 bits

$$\text{Number of cache lines} = \frac{32 \text{ KB}}{64 \text{ B}} = 512 \text{ lines}$$

So, bits for line number = 9

CA = (9 + 6) = 15 bits

Hence, tag bits = (MA – CA) = (32 – 15) = 17 bits

23. There are 10 distinct integer (A > 10) out of 15. There are distinct integer (B = 18) out of 20

$$\text{Now, probability } (A > 10) = \frac{10}{15}$$

$$\text{Probability } (B = 18) = \frac{1}{20}$$

So, probability (A > 10 and B = 18)

$$= \left[\frac{10}{15} \times \frac{1}{20}\right] = \frac{1}{30}$$

Now, probability (A > 10 or B = 18)

= Probability (A > B) + Probability (B = 18) – Probability (A > 10 and B = 18)

$$= \frac{10}{15} + \frac{1}{20} - \frac{1}{30} = \frac{41}{60}$$

$$\text{Hence, estimated number of tuples} = \frac{41}{60} \times 1200$$

= 820 tuples.

24. As given that IEEE 754 format with bias 127

S = 1 $\Rightarrow$ Number is negative

E =10000001 $\Rightarrow 2^7 + 2^6 = 128 + 1 = 129$

F =1111

Biased exponent: 129

Exponent: Biased exponent – 127 = 129 – 127 = 2

Now, Binary number:

$= -1.1111 \times 2^2$

$= -(111.11)_2$

$= -[(1 \times 2^2) + (1 \times 2^1) + (1 \times 2^0) + (1 \times 2^{-1}) + (1 \times 2^{-2}]$

$= [4 + 2 + 1 + 0.5 + 0.25] = -7.75$

25. Minimum waiting time will be given by SJF algo. So, execution order will be P3,P1, P2. Waiting times of P1,P2,P3 respectively will be 10, 26,0.

Gantt chart:

CPU	P_3	P_1	P_2

0 10 26 46

Waiting time (P_1) = 10

Waiting time (P_2) = 26

Waiting time (P_3) = 0

So, Avg waiting time $= \frac{36}{3} = 12$

Hence, average waiting time = 12 ms.

26. The given grammar does type checking and also it syntactically checks integer expressions.

So, the grammar deriving variables but not booleam variables. So, options a, c and d are ruled out.

27. Rename operation is used here inside the given query which is Renaming the attributes in intermediate result.

So, In the given query, We have two snapshots of the table empAge :

Another is empAge(emp No1, age 1)

Now, we are performing Conditional Join operation on both snapshots, where condition is "age > age1".

Note that the conditional join operation "logically" works as follows :

First it will do Cross product of both snapshots, then it will select those records/tuples which satisfy the condition "age > age1".

So, the inner query will give us a intermediate result which has the following schema, let me call it M :

M (empNo, age empNo1, age1)

And in the above intermediate result M, we have those tuples where "age" value is greater than "age1" value.

So, we have those employee numbers "empNo" whose age is greater than "some" employee.

Also, we have those employee numbers "empNo1" whose age is less than "some" employee.

Finally, we are applying Projection operation on the M which will project the attribute "empNo".

So, we have those employee number "empNo" whose age is greater than "some" employee.

Emp No	Age
1	20
2	19
3	18

The quary return on:

Emp No
1
2

So, the query returns employee number of all employers whose age is not the minimum.

Hence, option (c) is the correct answer.

28. As the given counter circuit we need to obtain the counting states for 3 clock cycles.

Present state			Flip flops inputs (R) ($\bar{P}$) ($\bar{Q}$)			Next state		
P	Q	R	T_P	T_Q	T_R	P^+	Q^+	R^+
0	0	0	0	1	1	0	1	1
0	0	1	1	1	1	1	1	0
0	1	0	0	1	0	0	0	0
0	1	1	1	1	0	1	0	1
1	0	0	0	0	1	0	0	1
1	0	1	1	0	1	0	0	0
1	1	0	0	0	0	1	1	0
1	1	1	1	0	0	0	1	1

By referring the given circuit flip flop input expression are written. Using Flip flop input (T) and present states, and state table of TFI next state are obtained.

So, for T flip flop $\Rightarrow$

T	$Q_n + 1$
0	Q_n
1	Q_n

Clock	T_P	T_Q	T_R	P^+	Q^+	R^+
0	–	–	–	0	0	0
1	0	1	1	0	1	1
2	1	1	0	1	0	1
3	1	0	1	0	0	0

So the next three state are obtained.

Hence, the counting pattern is:

000 → 011 → 101 → 000 → 011 → 101

Hence, option (a) is the correct answer.

29.

D_{12}	D_{11}	D_{10}	D_9	D_8	D_7	D_6	D_5	D_4	D_3	P_2	P_1
1	1	0	x	y	0	1	0	0	1	1	0

$P_1 = 0 + 1 + 0 + 0 + x + 1$; x = 0(even)

$P_2 = 1 + 1 + 1 + 0 + 0 + 1 =$ (even)

$P_4 = 0 + 0 + 1 + 0 + 1 =$ (even)

$P_8 = y + x + 0 + 1 + 1 = 0$

So, x = 0 and y = 0.

Hence, option (a) is the correct answer.

30. As given recurrence relation:

$$T(n) = T\left(\frac{n}{2}\right) + T\left(\frac{2n}{5}\right) + 7n$$

With recursion tree approach the cost at every level is proportional to n.

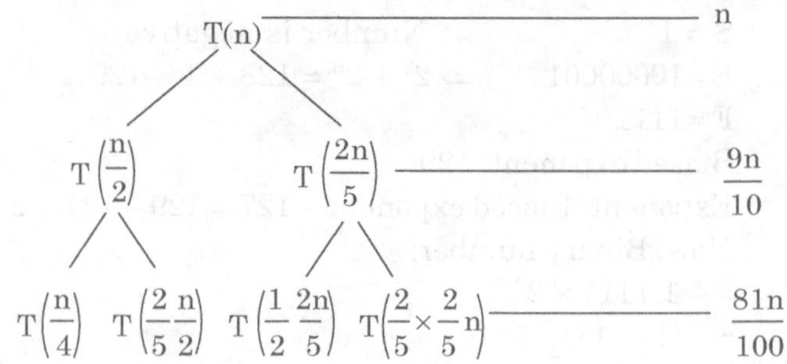

$$n + \frac{9}{10}n + \left(\frac{9}{10}\right)^2 n + \ldots \log n \text{ times}$$

$$n\left[1 + \frac{9}{10} + \left(\frac{9}{10}\right)^2 + \ldots \log n \text{ times}\right]$$

$= \Theta(n)$

Hence, option (c) is the correct ansser.

31. According to the question:

	a	b	c	d	f	$
S			$S \to Rf$	$S \to daT$	$S \to Rf$	
T	$T \to as$	$T \to baT$	$T \to \varepsilon$		$T \to \varepsilon$	$T \to \varepsilon$
R			$R \to caTR$		$R \to \varepsilon$	

Calculation of blank space 1 and 2

$S \to Rf$ will be the entry

Hear this entry will go to first of R which is {c,ε}

In c column we will put the entry$S \to Rf$ and for epsilon we will consider the next symbol which is f

For the black space 3 and 4

$T \to \varepsilon$

We will consider follow (T) which is follow(S) which is $

Follow(T) will be also first(R) which is c

And if R derives ε then we will also consider Follow of R which is f.

Hence, option (a) is the correct answer.

32. Precedence graph of S_1:

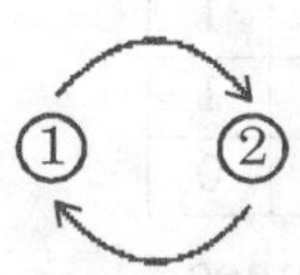

Precedence graph of S_2:

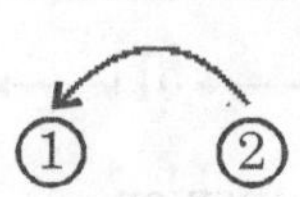

S1 is Not conflict serializable because :

Due to r1(y) ---> w2(y), we get edge from T1 to T2 in precedence graph of S1.

Due to r2(x) ---> w1(x), we get edge from T2 to T1 in precedence graph of S1.

So, we have cycle in precedence graph, hence, not conflict serializable.

S2 is conflict serializable because we only have edge from T2 to T1 in the precedence graph of S2.

Hence, option (b) is the correct answer.

33. Decomposition D1: R_3 (Q,Y) and R_4 (Y,W,Z) have common attribute Y which is key in R_4 (Y,W,Z), so we can merge them in lossless manner. Now (Q,Y,W,Z) and R_1(P,Q,S,T) have Q in common which is key in (Q,Y,W,Z). Then (Q,Y,W,Z,P,S,T) and R_2(P,T,X) have P,T in common which is key in R_2(P,T,X)

So, D1 is lossless.

Decompasition D_2:

R_1 (PQS), R_2 (TX), R_3(QY), R_4 (YZW)

$(R_1 \text{ join } R_3 \text{ join } R_4) \cap R_2 = \phi$

So, D2 is lossy because (T,X) has nothing common in above relations.

Hence, option (a) is the correct answer.

34. For any element g in any group G, one can form the subgroup of all integer powers (g) = {g^k | k ∈ Z}, called the cyclic subgroup of g.

The order of g is the number of elements in (g); that is, the order of an element is equal to the order of its cyclic subgroup.

A cyclic group is a group which is equal to one of its cyclic subgroups: G = (g) for some element g, called a generator.

(Lagrange's theorem) Let G be a finite group and $H \subset G$ a subgroup of G. Then $|H|$ divides $|G|$.

As we know that

If G is a finite group with $|G|$ prime, then G is cyclic.

For, authentication:

Let us consider $p = |G|$. Since $p \geq 2$, there is an element $g \in G$ with $g \neq e$. Consider the subgroup $\langle g \rangle \subset G$ generated by g. We have $|\langle g \rangle| \geq 2$ since both $e, g \in \langle g \rangle$. So by Lagrange's theorem $|\langle g \rangle| = p$. Thus $\langle g \rangle = G$, and so, by definition, G is cyclic as claimed.

Classification of Groups of Order $n \leq 3$:

n = 1 : The trivial group <e> is the only group with 1 element.

n = 2, 3 : These orders are prime, so Lagrange implies that any such group is cyclic.

Given that G has order 6, and H is subgroup of G so, H has order either 1 or 2 or 3 or 6 But it is given that $1 < |H| < 6$, So, order of H could be either 2 or 3, so H is cyclic.

So, a group G of order 6 may or may not be cyclic.

Hence, option (b) is the correct answer.

35. By the definition, cov(X,Y)

= E[(X – E(X)) (Y – E(Y)]

But CoV (x, y) = E[| X– E(X) | | Y – E[Y] |]

$\therefore S_2$ is false.

As, We know that, $r = \dfrac{\text{cov}(X,Y)}{\sigma_X \sigma_Y}$ is correlation coefficient and $0 < r^2 < 1$

$\left(\text{cov}(X,Y)\right)^2 < \sigma_X^2 \sigma_Y^2$

$\Rightarrow (E[X - E(X)]) . (Y - E(Y))^2 < \text{Var}(X)\,\text{Var}(Y)$

$\Rightarrow S_1$ is false.

Hence, both statements are false.

36. If M is adjacency matrix of G then When we $M^2 + M$, we get G2 in which all the edges of G are already there, additionally we have edges between those vertices of G which have a path of length less than or equal to 2 between them. So, Diam(G2) will be half the diam(G). Hence, option (a) is correct answer.

37. The program will compile successfully.

When j goes from –3 to –1, then "i++" and "count = count + j" statements do not execute.

When j = 0, count = 0, i = 1.

When j = 1, count = 1, i = 2.

When j = 2, count = 3, i = 3.

When j = 3, count = 6, i = 4.

Then for loop terminates, and count = count + i, So, count = 10.

Hence, option (b) is the correct answer.

38.

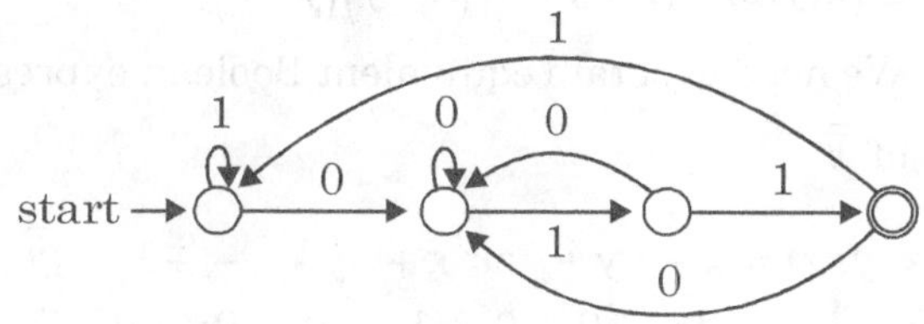

Ending pattern required n+1 states where n is length of the string, in this case 3 and at least on input goes out of the final state.

Here input 1 from the final state goes to initial state which remember all 1's

And input 0 goes to second state which remember last alphabet as 0. And other than option (d) are Accepting 01111. Hence, option (d) is correct.

39. L2 is decidable. Run M runs for 2021 steps on each input x of length upto 2021. If M halts before or in exactly 2021 steps on all such inputs then reject M, else accept.

L1 is also decidable. Run M runs for 2021 steps on each input x of length upto 2021. Check if M runs for more than 2021 steps on each input x of length upto 481. If so accept, else reject. Hence, option (a) is the correct answer.

40. R7 = 18 is maximum.

We can achieve it by three ways :

Way 1 : Take P[7]

Way 2 : Take P[6] , P[1]

Way 3 : Take P[3], P[2], P[2]

Hence, option (a) & (c) are the correct answer.

41. Articulation points can be identified in a single DFS.

The root of the dfs tree is an articulation point iff it has more than one child. If there are two children, there cannot be an edge from one subtree to the other, because non-tree edges are back edges and can only go to an ancestor.

The root of the DFS tree is an articulation if it two or more children. So option (b) is true.

Any other internal vertex v in the DFS tree, if it has a subtree rooted at a child of v that does NOT have an edge which climbs 'higher' than v, then v is an articulation point.

Leaf is never an articulation point.

Non-leaf, non-root node u is an articulation point if and only if no non-tree edge goes above u from a sub-tree below some child of u.

Option (a) is false because consider a graph G, a---b----c, and start DFS from b. b is root of DFS, but b is also articulation point in G.

Hence, option (a) & (c) are the correct answer.

42. As given that,

$$F(x,y,z) = (x+y+z)(\bar{x}+y)(\bar{y}+z)$$

We need to obtain equivalent Boolean expression of $\overline{F}$

F(x, y, z) = x +	y +	z	$\bar{x}$ +	y +	–	+ – +	$\bar{y}$	+z
0	0	0	1	0	0	0	1	0
			1	0	1	1	1	0

$$F(x, y, z) = \pi m(0, 2, 4, 5, 6) = \Sigma m(1, 3, 7)$$

$$\overline{F}(x, y, z) = \pi(1, 3, 7) = \Sigma m(0, 2, 4, 5, 6)$$

Option (a)

$$\overline{F} = (\bar{x}+\bar{y}+\bar{z})(x+\bar{y})(y+\bar{z})$$

$$= \pi(1,2,3,5,7) = \Sigma m(0,4,6)$$

$$= (\bar{x}+\bar{y}+\bar{z})\ (x+\bar{y}\ -)(-+y+\bar{z})$$

$\bar{x}$	$\bar{y}$	$\bar{z}$	x	$\bar{y}$	–	–	y	$\bar{z}$
1	1	1	0	1	0	0	0	1
			0	1	1	1	0	1

So option (a) is not equivalent to $\overline{F}$

$$\overline{F} = x\bar{y} + \bar{z} = \Sigma m(0, 2, 4, 5, 6) = \pi(1, 3, 7)$$

x	$\bar{y}$	–	+	–	–	$\bar{z}$
1	0	0		0	0	0
1	0	1		0	1	0
				1	0	0
				1	1	0

So option (b) is equivalent to $\overline{F}$.

Option (c)

$$\overline{F} = (x+\bar{z})(\bar{y}+\bar{z}) = \pi(1, 3, 7) = \Sigma m(0, 2, 4, 5, 6)$$

x +	–	+ $\bar{z}$	–	+y	+ $\bar{z}$
0	0	1	0	1	1
0	1	1	1	1	1

So option (c) is also equivalent to $\overline{F}$

Option (d)

$$\overline{F} = x\bar{y} + y\bar{z} + \bar{x}\bar{y}\bar{z} = \Sigma m(0, 2, 4, 5, 6) = \pi m(2, 3, 7)$$

= 100 101 000

= 101 110

So option (d) is also equivalent to $\overline{F}$

Alternative method:

$$\overline{F} = \bar{y}(\overline{xz} + x) + y\bar{z}$$

$$= \bar{y}[(\bar{x}+x)](x+\bar{z}) + y\bar{z}$$

$$= \bar{y}(x+\bar{z}) + y\bar{z}$$

$$= x\bar{y} + \bar{y}\bar{z} + y\bar{z}$$

$$= x\bar{y} + \bar{z}$$

Option (b) is matching.

$$x\bar{y} + \bar{z}$$

$$= (x+\bar{z}) + (\bar{y}+\bar{z})$$

Using distributing propertys

So, option (c) is matching

$$F = (x+y+z)(\bar{x}+y)(\bar{y}+z)$$

$$\overline{F} = \overline{(x+y+z)(\bar{x}+y)(\bar{y}+z)}$$

$$= \overline{(x+y+z)} + \overline{(\bar{x}+y)} + \overline{(\bar{y}+z)}$$

$$= \bar{x}\bar{y}\bar{z} + x\bar{y} + y\bar{z}$$

So, option (d) is matching.

Hence, option (b), (c), (d) represent equivalent expression of $\overline{F}$.

43. Option (a) is false. For counter example, take a set A = {1,2,3}, define relation R on A as follows: R = { (1,1), (2,2),(3,3), (1,2),(2,1), (1,3),(3,1) }, R is symmetric and reflexive but not transitive so not equivalence relation.

Option (b) is false. For counter example, take a set A = {1,2,3}, define relation R on A as follows: R = { (1,1) }, R is symmetric and circular but not equivalence relation.

Option (d) is false. For counter example, take a set A = {1,2,3}, define relation R on A as follows: R = { (1,1) }, R is transitive and circular but not equivalence relation.

If R is reflexive and circular then it is symmetric: Assume xRy. Since R is reflexive, we have yRy. Since R is circular, so, xRy, yRy imply yRx, so, R is symmetric.

If R is reflexive and circular then it is transitive because assume xRy, yRz. Since R is circular, so, zRx, and since R is symmetric so xRz so R is transitive.

Hence, option (c) is correct answer.

44. After server reboots, it does not have any information of previous connection, so, client may have to wait indefinitely as client does not have keep alive timer. Also, as a general rule, reset (RST) must be sent whenever a segment arrives which apparently is not intended for the current connection.

Since, the previous connection got terminated now server can again listen on P.

Hence, option (a), (b) & (c) are the correct answer.

45. If the second fragment is lost P is required to resend the whole TCP segment. The second fragment size at R is 1400 – 800 + 20 (header size) = 620 bytes

Hence, option (a) & (c) are the correct answer.

46. Deadlock is possible if all the processes execute Line#5, then in Line#6, all processes will get into deadlock.

Counter = 5 is possible if all processes execute the given program in serial manner, one after other.

Counter = 1 is possible if process P1 reads counter value, but not changes it, and all other processes execute complete program one after another in serial manner, then at last P1 makes counter = 1.

Counter = 0 is Not possible after successful execution of all 5 processes.

Hence, option (a), (b) & (d) are the correct answer.

47. Option (a) is false because key 4 is 0100 so it will go in the slot 00, which should be empty according to the given diagram.

Option (b) is false because key 5,9,1 will go in the slot 01, but 1,9 will go on the left side, and 5 on right side, so, false.

Option (d) is false because key 14,6,10 will go in the slot 10, which should have only two keys according to the given diagram.

Hence, option (c) is the correct answer.

48. x = 2 ; every element of array Z is 1.

So, In every iteration of for loop, we are making

Total = 2*total + 1

So, in ith iteration, total will become

So, the series: 3, 7, 15, 31, 63, 127, 255, 511, 1023.

$a_n = (2 \times a_{n-1} + 1)$.

Hence, after last iteration i.e. 9th iteration, total = 1023.

49. As given that. Efficiency = 50% = $\frac{1}{2}$

Propagation delay (T_P) = 100 m sec.

As we know that,

$$T_t \text{ (Packet)} = \frac{L}{B.W}$$

$$\frac{2000}{10^6 \text{ bps}} = 2 \times 10^{-3} \text{sec} = 2 \text{ millisecond}$$

$$T_t \text{ (ACK)} = \frac{L}{R.W}$$

$$\frac{10 \text{ bits}}{10^6 \text{ bps}} = 10^{-5} \text{ sec} = 10^{-2} \text{ millisecond}$$

= 0.01 milli sec

Total time = T_t (Packet) + T_P + T_t (ACK)

= 2 + 100 + 0.01

= 102.01 milli sec.

We also know that

$$\text{Efficiency} = \frac{\text{useful time}}{\text{Total time}}$$

$$\frac{1}{2} = \frac{n \times T_t}{\text{Total time}}$$

$$2 \times n \times 1 = 1 \times 102.01$$

$$n = \frac{102.01}{2}$$

$$\boxed{n = 51.005}$$

Hence, for minimum we have to take ceil, so size of the window is 51.

50. According to the question:

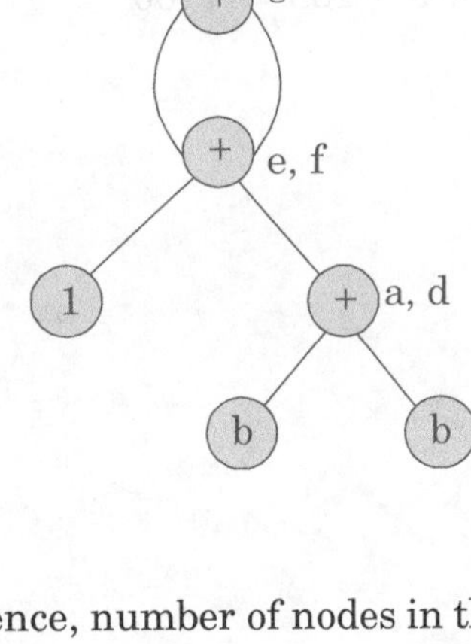

Hence, number of nodes in the DAG is 6 nodes.

51. The give PDA accepts language $\{ a^n b^m \mid n > m \}$

Now, number of strings in this language whose length is <= 100 :

When #b = 0, then #a = 100 ; So, one such string.

When #b = 1, then #a = 99 ; So, one such string.

When #b = 2, then #a = 98 ; So, one such string.

And so on...

When #b = 49, then #a = 51 ; So, one such string.

So, total 50 strings.

52. Characteristic equation is

$|A - \lambda I| = 0$

So,

$$\begin{vmatrix} -\lambda & 1 & 1 & 1 \\ 1 & -\lambda & 1 & 1 \\ 1 & 1 & -\lambda & 1 \\ 1 & 1 & 1 & -\lambda \end{vmatrix} = 0$$

$$\left[\because \begin{vmatrix} x & y & y & y \\ y & x & y & y \\ y & y & x & y \\ y & y & y & x \end{vmatrix} = (x + 3y)(x - y)^3 \right]$$

$\Rightarrow (-\lambda + 3)(-\lambda - 1)^3 = 0$

$\Rightarrow = -1, -1, -1, 3$ are the eigen values of A

So, Largest eigen value is 3

53. Let Tp denote cycle duration of the pipeline processor

Tp = max(stage delay)+Buffering Overhead

Tp = max(150, 120, 150, 160, 140)+ 5

Tp = 165 Nano seconds

Time required to execute N instruction

= (K + (n – 1))Tp

n = 100

K = 5

Hence, N = (5 + 99)*165 = 17160

54. $$P\left(\frac{TH}{RH}\right) = \frac{P\left(\frac{RH}{TH}\right) * P(TH)}{\left(P\left(\frac{RH}{TH}\right) * P(TH) + P\left(\frac{RH}{TL}\right) * P(TL)\right)}$$

where,

P (TH) = Probability that the transmitted signal is H

P (RH) = Probability that the received signal is H

P (TL) = Probability that the transmitted signal is L

$$= \frac{0.3 * 0.1}{(0.3 * 0.1 + 0.8 * 0.9)}$$

$$= \frac{0.03}{(0.03 + 0.72)}$$

$$= \frac{0.03}{0.75} = 0.04$$

55. In line # 1, we are assigning value 10 to R1.

So, R1 will go from 10 to 0. But the program from line#2 to line#7 will only execute 10 times, when R1 is going from 10 to 1. When R1 becomes 0, we come out of this loop and Halt.

The given program will modify the values of Memory location from 3000 to 3009 only. So, Memory location 3010 will have value 50, unchanged, at the end.

M[3000] = 60

M[3001] = 59

M[3002] = 58

⋮

M[3009] = 51

M[3010] = 50

Hence, the correct of memory location 3010 is 50.

SOLVED PAPER - 2021
SET 2

INSTRUCTIONS

1. Total of 65 questions carrying 100 marks, out of which 10 questions carrying a total of 15 marks are in General Aptitude (GA)
2. The Engineering Mathematics will carry around **15% of the total marks,** the General Aptitude section will carry **15% of the total marks** and the **remaining 70% of the total marks.**
3. **Types of Questions**
   (*a*) **Multiple Choice Questions (MCQ)** carrying 1 or 2 marks each in all papers and sections. These questions are objective in nature, and each will have a choice of four options, out of which the candidate has to mark the correct answer(s).
   (*b*) **Numerical Answer Questions** of 1 or 2 marks each in all papers and sections. For these questions the answer is a real number, to be entered by the candidate using the virtual keypad. No choices will be shown for these type of questions.
   (*c*) **Multiple Select Questions (MSQ)** carrying 1 or 2 marks each in all the papers and sections. These questions are objective in nature, and each will have choice of four answers, out of which ONE or MORE than ONE choice(s) is / are correct.
4. For **1-mark** multiple-choice questions, **1/3 marks** will be deducted for a wrong answer. Likewise, for **2-marks** multiple-choice questions, **2/3** marks will be deducted for a wrong answer. There is no negative marking for numerical answer type questions & multiple selection questions.

Chapter-Wise Analysis

#	Chapters	Marks		
		1	2	Total
1	General Aptitude	5	5	15
2	Engineering Mathematics	5	7	19
3	Theory of Computation	3	4	11
4	Digital Logic	2	1	4
5	Computer Organization and Architecture	2	3	8
6	Programming & Data Structures	3	1	5
7	Algorithm	1	2	5

#	Chapters	Marks		
		1	2	Total
8	Compiler Design	1	3	7
9	Operating System	1	4	9
10	Databases	3	3	9
11	Computer Networks	4	2	8
12	Software Engineering	0	0	0
13	Web Technology	0	0	0

GENERAL APTITUDE (GA)

Q. 1 to Q. 5 : Carry One Mark Each.

1. Gauri said that she can play the keyboard ____ her sister.

(a) as well as (b) as better as
(c) as nicest as (d) as worse as

2.

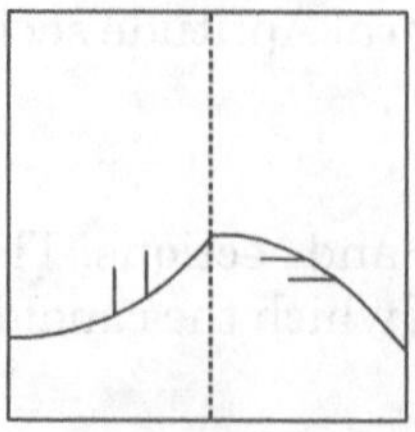

As transparent square sheet shown above is folded along the dotted line. The folded sheet will look like ____.

(a) 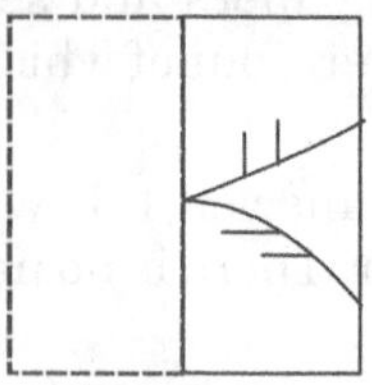

(b) 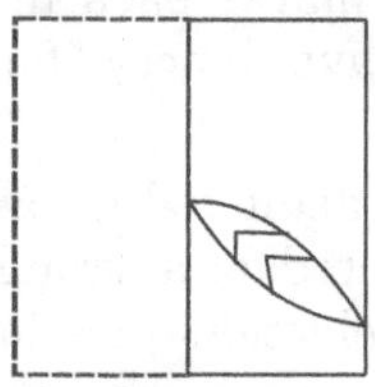

(c) 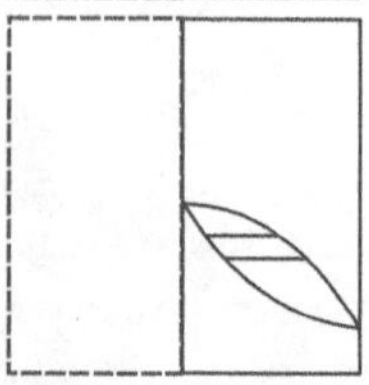

(d) 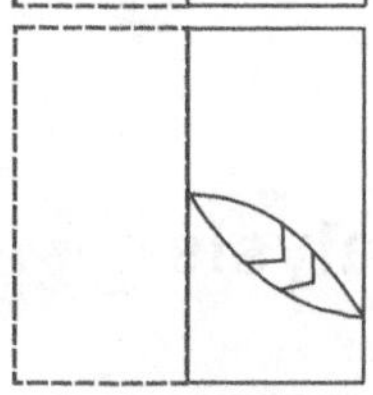

3. If θ is the angle, in degrees, between the longest diagonal of the cube and any one of the edges of the cube, then, cos θ =

(a) $\frac{1}{2}$ (b) $\frac{1}{\sqrt{3}}$

(c) $\frac{1}{\sqrt{2}}$ (d) $\frac{\sqrt{3}}{2}$

4. If $\left(x-\frac{1}{2}\right)^2-\left(x-\frac{3}{2}\right)^2 = x+2$, then the value of x is :

(a) 2 (b) 4
(c) 6 (d) 8

5. Pen : Write :: Knife : ____.

Which one of the following options maintains a similar logical relation in the above ?

(a) Vegetables (b) Sharp
(c) Cut (d) Blunt

Q. 6 to Q. 10 : Carry Two Marks Each.

6. Listening to music during exercise improve exercise performance and reduces discomfort. Scientists researched whether listening to music while studying can help students learn better and the results were inconclusive. Students who needed external stimulation for studying fared worse while students who did not need any external stimulation benefited from music.

Which one of the following statements is the CORRECT inference of the above passage ?

(a) Listening to music has no effect on learning and a positive effect on physical exercise.
(b) Listening to music has a clear positive effect both on physical exercise and on learning.
(c) Listening to music has a clear positive effect on physical exercise. Music has a positive effect on learning only in some students.
(d) Listening to music has a clear positive effect on learning in all students. Music has a positive effect only in some students who exercise.

7.

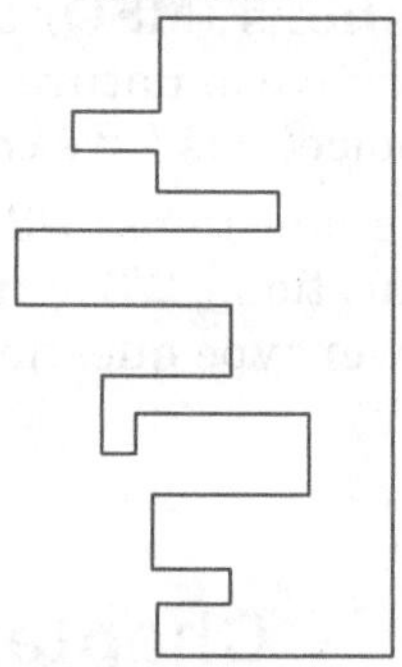

A jigsaw puzzle has 2 pieces. One of the pieces is shown above. Which one of the given options for the missing piece when assembled will form a rectangle ? The piece can be moved, rotated or flipped to assemble with the above piece.

(a) 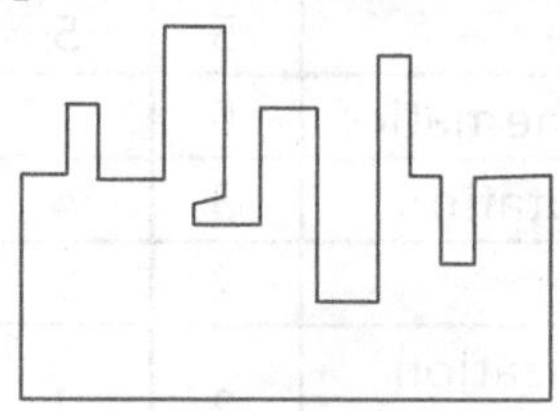

(b) 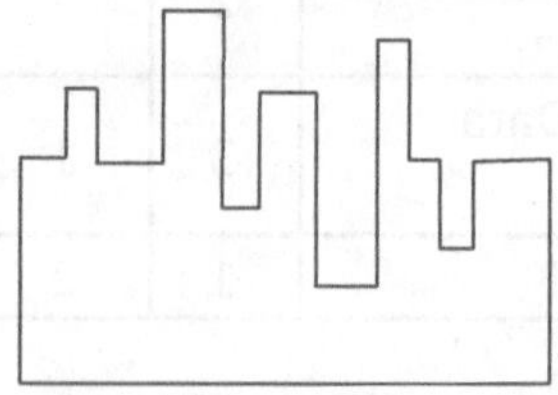

(c) 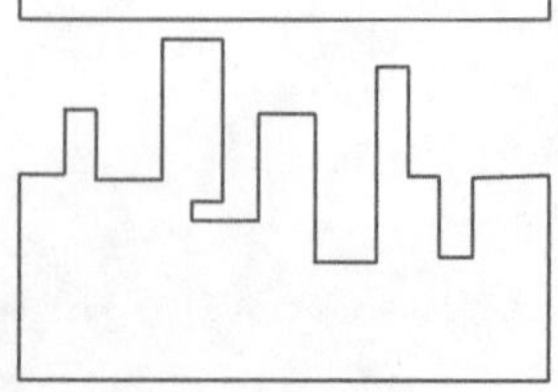

(d) 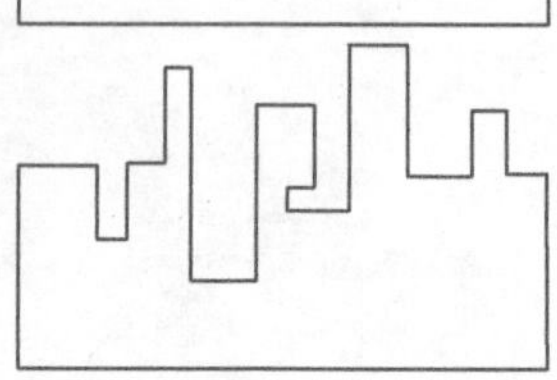

8. The number of students in three classes is in the ratio 3 : 13 : 6. If 18 students are added to each class, the ratio changes to 15 : 35 : 21.

The total number of students in all the three classes in the beginning was :

(a) 22 (b) 66 (c) 88 (d) 110

9.

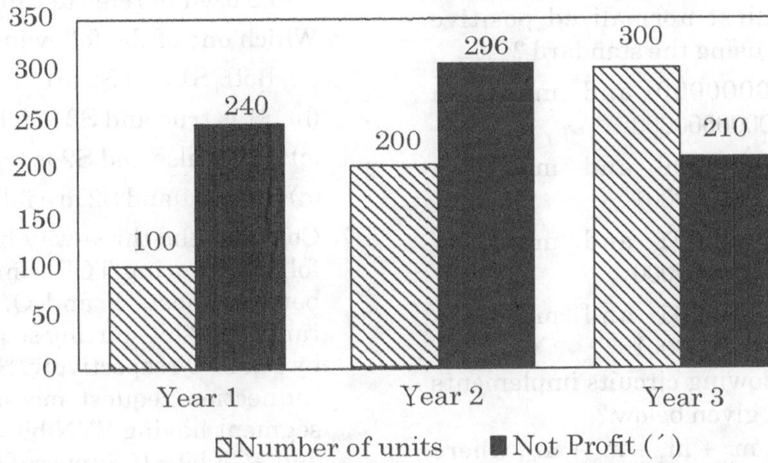

The number of units of a product sold in three different years and the respective net profits are presented in the figure above. The cost/unit in Year 3 was ´1, which was half the cost/unit in Year 2. The cost/unit in Year 3 was one-third of the cost/unit in Year 1. Taxes were paid on the selling price at 10%, 13% and 15% respectively for the three years. Net profit is calculated as the difference between the selling price and the sum of cost and taxes paid in that year.

The ratio of the selling price in Year 2 to the selling price in Year 3 is ____.

(a) 4 : 3 (b) 1 : 1 (c) 3 : 4 (d) 1 : 2

10. Six students P, Q, R, S, T and U, with distinct heights, compare their heights and make the following observations.

Observation I: S is taller than R.

Observation II: Q is the shortest of all.

Observation III: U is taller than only one student.

Observation IV: T is taller than S but is not the tallest.

The number of students that are taller than R is the same as the number of students shorter than ____.

(a) T (b) R

(c) S (d) P

COMPUTER SCIENCE AND INFORMATION

Q. 1 to Q. 10 : Carry One Mark Each.

1. Let G be a connected undirected weighted graph. Consider the following two statements.

S_1 : There exists a minimum weight edge in G which is present in every minimum spanning tree of G.

S_2 : If every edge in G has distinct weight, then G has a unique minimum spanning tree.

Which one of the following options is correct ?

(a) Both S_1 and S_2 are true.

(b) S_1 is true and S_2 is false.

(c) S_1 is false and S_2 is true.

(d) Both S_1 and S_2 are false.

2. Let H be a binary min-heap consisting of n elements implemented as an array. What is the worst case time complexity of an optimal algorithm to find the maximum element is H ?

(a) $\Theta(1)$ (b) $\Theta(\log n)$

(c) $\Theta(n)$ (d) $\Theta(n \log n)$

3. Consider the following ANSI C program :

```
int main () {
    Integer x ;
    return 0 ;
}
```

Which one of the following phases in a seven-phase C compiler will throw an error ?

(a) Lexical analyzer

(b) Syntax analyzer

(c) Semantic analyzer

(d) Machine dependent optimizer

4. The format of the single-precision floating-point representation of a real number as per the IEEE 754 standard is as follows :

sign	exponent	mantissa

Which one of the following choices is correct with respect to the smallest normalized positive number represented using the standard ?

(a) exponent = 00000000 and mantissa = 00000000000000000000000

(b) exponent = 00000000 and mantissa = 00000000000000000000001

(c) exponent = 00000001 and mantissa = 00000000000000000000000

(d) exponent = 00000001 and mantissa = 00000000000000000000001

5. Which one of the following circuits implements the Boolean function given below ?

$f(x, y, z) = m_0 + m_1 + m_3 + m_4 + m_5 + m_6$, where m_i is the ith minterm,

(a)

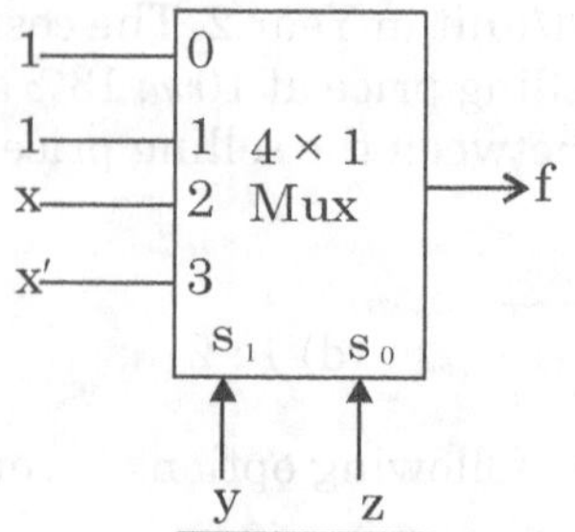

(b)

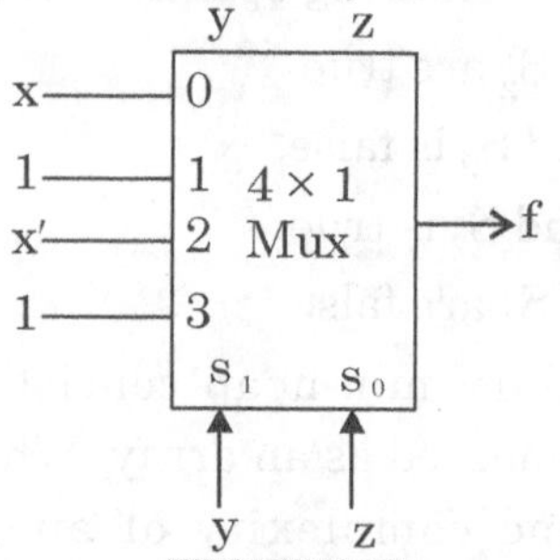

(c)

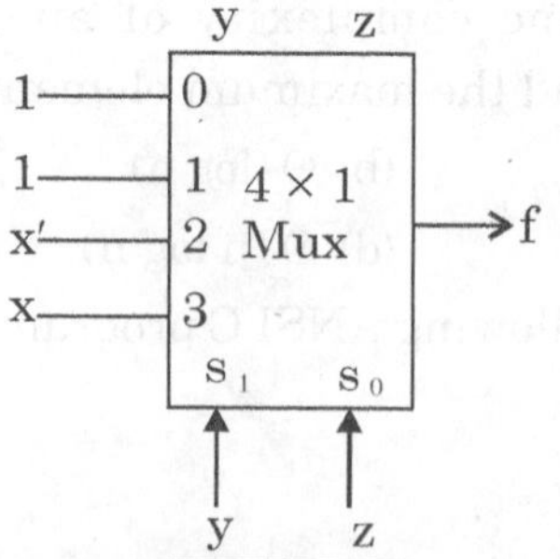

(d)

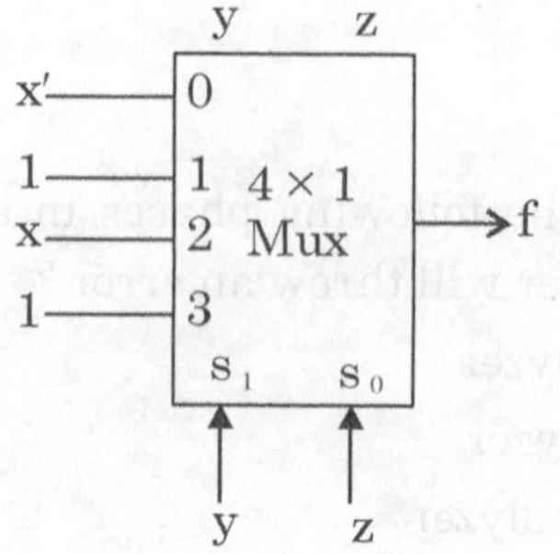

6. Consider the following statements S1 and S2 about the relational data model :

S1: A relation scheme can have at most one foreign key.

S2 : A foreign key in a relation scheme R cannot be used to refer to tuples of R.

Which one of the following choices is correct ?

(a) Both S1 and S2 are true.

(b) S1 is true and S2 is false.

(c) S1 is false and S2 is true.

(d) Both S1 and S2 are false.

7. Consider the three-way handshake mechanism followed during TCP connection establishment between hosts P and Q. Let X and Y be two random 32-bit starting sequence numbers chosen by P and Q respectively. Suppose P sends a TCP connection request message to Q with a TCP segment having SYN bit = 1, SEQ number = X, and ACK bit = 0. Suppose Q accepts the connection request. Which one of the following choices represents the information present in the TCP segment header that is sent by Q to P ?

(a) SYN bit = 1, SEQ number = X + 1, ACK bit = 0, ACK number = Y, FIN bit = 0

(b) SYN bit = 0, SEQ number = X + 1, ACK bit = 0, ACK number = Y, FIN bit = 1

(c) SYN bit = 1, SEQ number = Y, ACK bit = 1, ACK number = X + 1, FIN bit = 0

(d) SYN bit = 1, SEQ number = Y, ACK bit = 1, ACK number = X, FIN bit = 0

8. What is the worst-case number of arithmetic operations performed by recursive binary search on a sorted array of size n ?

(a) $\Theta(\sqrt{n})$ (b) $\Theta(\log_2(n))$

(c) $\Theta(n^2)$ (d) $\Theta(n)$

9. Let $L \subseteq \{0, 1\}^*$ be an arbitrary regular language accepted by a minimal DFA with k states. Which one of the following languages must necessarily be accepted by a minimal DFA with k states ?

(a) $L - \{01\}$ (b) $L \cup \{01\}$

(c) $\{0, 1\}^* - L$ (d) $L . L$

10. Consider the following ANSI C program.

```
# include <stdio . h>
int main () {
    int arr [4] [5] ;
    int i, j ;
    for (i = 0 ; i < 4 ; i++) {
        for (j = 0 ; j<5 ; j++) {
            arr [i] [j] = 10*i + j ;
```

```
        }
    }
    printf ("%D", * (arr [1] + 9) ) ;
    return 0;
}
```

What is the output of the above program ?

(a) 14 (b) 20

(c) 24 (d) 30

Q. 11 to Q. 15 : Carry one Mark Each.

11. Consider the following sets, where $n \geq 2$:

S_1 : Set of all $n \times n$ matrices with entries from the set {a, b, c}

S_2 : Set of all functions from the set $\{0, 1, 2,..., n^2 - 1\}$ to the set {0, 1, 2}

Which of the following choice(s) is/are correct ?

(a) There does not exist a bijection from S_1 to S_2.

(b) There exists a surjection from S_1 to S_2.

(c) There exists a bijection from S_1 to S_2.

(d) There does not exist an injection from S_1 to S_2.

12. Let L1 be a regular language and L2 be a context-free language. Which of the following languages is/are context-free ?

(a) $L_1 \cap \overline{L_2}$

(b) $\overline{\overline{L_1} \cup \overline{L_2}}$

(c) $L_1 \cup \left(L_2 \cup \overline{L_2}\right)$

(d) $\left(L_1 \cap L_2\right) \cup \left(\overline{L_1} \cap L_2\right)$

13. In the context of compilers, which of the following is/are NOT an intermediate representation of the source program ?

(a) Three address code

(b) Abstract Syntax Tree (AST)

(c) Control Flow Graph (CFG)

(d) Symbol table

14. Which of the following statement (s) is/are correct in the context of CPU scheduling ?

(a) Turnaround time includes waiting time.

(b) The goal is to only maximize CPU utilization and minimize throughput.

(c) Round-robin policy can be used even when the CPU time required by each of the processes is not known apriori.

(d) Implementing preemptive scheduling needs hardware support.

15. Choose the correct choice(s) regarding the following propositional logic assertion S :

$S : ((P \wedge Q) \rightarrow R) \rightarrow ((P \wedge Q) \rightarrow (Q \rightarrow R))$

(a) S is neither a tautology nor a contradiction.

(b) S is a tautology.

(c) S is a contradiction.

(d) The antecedent of S is logically equivalent to the consequent of S.

16. Consider a complete binary tree with 7 nodes. Let A denote the set of first 3 elements obtained by performing Breadth-First Search (BFS) starting from the root. Let B denote the set of first 3 elements obtained by performing Depth-First Search (DFS) starting from the root. The Value of $|A - B|$ is ____.

17. Consider the following deterministic finite automaton (DFA).

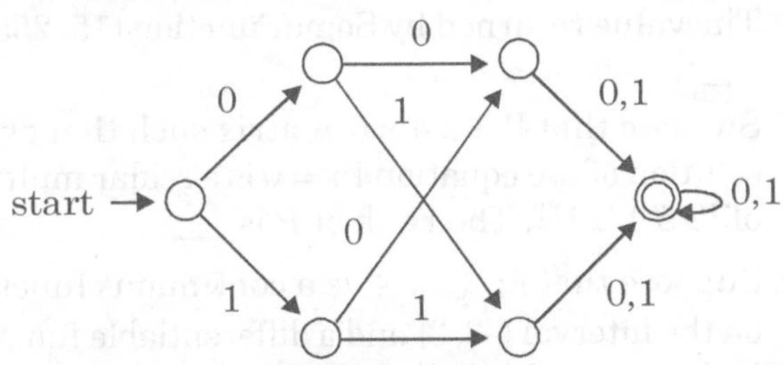

The number of strings of length 8 accepted by the above automaton is ____.

18. If x and y are two decimal digits and $(0.1101)_2 = (0.8\,xy5)_{10}$, the decimal value of x + y is ____.

19. Consider a set-associative cache of size 2KB (1KB $= 2^{10}$ bytes) with cache block size of 64 bytes. Assume that the cache is byte-addressable and a 32-bit address is used for accessing the cache. If the width of the tag field is 22 bits, the associativity of the cache is ____.

20. Consider a computer system with DMA support. The DMA module is transferring one 8-bit character in one CPU cycle from a device to memory through cycle stealing at regular intervals. Consider a 2 MHz processor. If 0.5% processor cycles are used for DMA, the data transfer rate of the device is ____ bits per second.

21. A data file consisting of 1,50,000 student-records is stored on a hard disk with block size of 4096 bytes. The data file is sorted on the primary key RollNo. The size of a record pointer for this disk is 7 bytes. Each student-record has a candidate key attribute called ANum of size 12 bytes. Suppose an index file with records consisting of two fields, ANum value and the record pointer to the corresponding student record, is built and stored on the same disk. Assume that the records of data file and index file are not split across disk blocks. The number of blocks in the index file is ____.

22. For a given biased coin, the probability that the outcome of a toss is a head is 0.4. This coin is tossed 1,000 times. Let X denote the random variable whose value is the number of times that head appeared in these 1,000 tosses. The standard deviation of X (rounded to 2 decimal places) is ____.

23. Consider the following ANSI C function :

```
int SomeFunction (int x, int y)
{
    if ( (x ==1) | | (y == 1) ) return 1 ;
    if (x ==y) return x ;
    if (x > y) return SomeFunction (x – y, y) ;
    if (y > x) return Some Function (x, y – x) ;
}
```

The value returned by SomeFunction (15, 255) is ____.

24. Suppose that P is a 4 × 5 matrix such that every solution of the equation Px = 0 is a scalar multiple of $[2\ 5\ 4\ 3\ 1]^T$. The rank of P is ____.

25. Suppose that $f : \mathbb{R} \rightarrow \mathbb{R}$ is a continuous function on the interval [–3, 3] and a differentiable function is the interval (–3, 3) such that for every x in the interval, $f'(x) \le 2$. If $f(-3) = 7$, then $f(3)$ is at most ____.

Q. 26 to Q. 39 : Carry two Marks Each.

26. Consider the string abbccddeee. Each letter in the string must be assigned a binary code satisfying the following properties :

1. For any two letters, the code assigned to one letter must not be a prefix of the code assigned to the other letter.
2. For any two letters of the same frequency, the letter which occurs earlier in the dictionary order is assigned a code whose length is at most the length of the code assigned to the other letter.

A mont the set of all binary code assignments which satisfy the above two properties, what is the minimum length of the encoded string ?

(a) 21 (b) 23

(c) 25 (d) 30

27. Assume a two-level inclusive cache hierarchy, L1 and L2, where L2 is the larger of the two. Consider the following statements.

S_1 : Read misses in a write through L1 cache do not result in writebacks of dirty lines to the L2.

S_2 : Write allocate policy must be used in conjunction with write through caches and no-write allocate policy is used with writeback caches.

Which of the following statements is correct ?

(a) S_1 is true and S_2 is false

(b) S_1 is false and S_2 is true

(c) S_1 is true and S_2 is true

(d) S_1 is false and S_2 is false

28. Suppose we want to design a synchronous circuit that processes a string of 0's and 1's. Given a string, it produces another string by replacing the first 1 in any subsequence of consecutive 1's by a 0. Consider the following example.

Input sequence : 00100011000011100

Output sequence : 00000001000001100

A Mealy Machine is a state machine where both the next state and the output are functions of the present state and the current input.

The above mentioned circuit can be designed as a two-state Mealy machine. The states in the Mealy machine can be represented using Boolean values 0 and 1. We denote the current state, the next state, the next incoming bit, and the output bit of the Mealy machine by the variables *s*, *t*, *b* and *y* respectively. Assume the initial state of the Mealy machine is 0.

What are the Boolean expressions corresponding to t and y in terms of s and b ?

(a) $t = s + b$

$y = sb$

(b) $t = b$

$y = sb$

(c) $t = b$

$y = s\bar{b}$

(d) $t = s + b$

$y = s\bar{b}$

29. In an examination, a student can choose the order in which two questions (QuesA and QuesB) must be attempted.

- If the first question is answered wrong, the student gets zero marks.
- If the first question is answered correctly and the second question is not answered correctly, the student gets the marks only for the first question.
- If both the questions are answered correctly, the student gets the sum of the marks of the two questions.

The following table shows the probability of

correctly answering a question and the marks of the question respectively.

Question	Probability of answering correctly	Marks
QuesA	0.8	10
QuesB	0.5	20

Assuming that the student always wants to maximize her expected marks in the examination, in which order should she attempt the questions and what is the expected marks for that order (assume that the questions are independent)?

(a) First QuesA and then QuesB. Expected marks 14.

(b) First QuesB and then QuesA. Expected marks 14.

(c) First QuesB and then QuesA. Expected marks 22.

(d) First QuesA and then QuesB. Expected marks 16.

30. Consider the following ANSI C code segment :

```
z = x + 3 + y->f1 + y->f2;
for (i = 0; i < 200; i = i + 2) {
  if (z > i) {
    p = p + x + 3;
    q = q + y->f1;
  } else {
    p = p + y->f2;
    q = q + x + 3;
  }
}
```

Assume that the variable y points to a struct (allocated on the heap) containing two fields f1 and f2, and the local variables x, y, z, p, q, and i are allotted registers. Common sub-expression elimination (CSE) optimization is applied on the code. The number of addition and dereference operations (of the form y–> f1 or y–> f2) in the optimized code, respectively, are :

(a) 403 and 102
(b) 203 and 2
(c) 303 and 102
(d) 303 and 2

31. The relation scheme given below is used to store information about the employees of a company, where empId is the key and deptId indicates the department to which the employee is assigned. Each employee is assigned to exactly one department.

emp (<u>empId</u>, name, gender, salary, deptId)

Consider the following SQL query :

```
select deptId, count (*)
from emp
where gender = "female" and salary > (select avg
(salary) from emp) group by deptId ;
```

The above query gives, for each department in the company, the number of female employees whose salary is greater than the average salary of

(a) employees in the department.

(b) employees in the company.

(c) female employees in the department.

(d) female employees in the company.

32. Let S be the following schedule of operations of three transactions T_1, T_2 and T_3 in a relational database system :

$R_2(Y)$, $R_1(X)$, $R_3(Z)$, $R_1(Y)$, $W_1(X)$, $R_2(Z)$, $W_2(Y)$, $R_3(X)$, $W_3(Z)$,

Consider the statements P and Q below :

P : S is conflict-serializable.

Q : If T_3 commits before T_1 finishes, then S is recoverable.

Which one of the following choices is correct ?

(a) Both P and Q are true.

(b) P is true and Q is false.

(c) P is false and Q is true.

(d) Both P and Q are false.

33. A bag has r red balls and b black balls. All balls are identical except for their colours. In a trial, a ball is randomly drawn from the bag, its colour is noted and the ball is placed back into the bag along with another ball of the same colour. Note that the number of balls in the bag will increase by one, after the trial. A sequence of four such trials is conducted. Which one of the following choices gives the probability of drawing a red ball in the fourth trial ?

(a) $\frac{r}{r+b}$

(b) $\frac{r}{r+b+3}$

(c) $\frac{r+3}{r+b+3}$

(d) $\left(\frac{r}{r+b}\right)\left(\frac{r+1}{r+b+1}\right)\left(\frac{r+2}{r+b+2}\right)\left(\frac{r+3}{r+b+3}\right)$

34. Consider the cyclic redundancy check (CRC) based error detecting scheme having the generator polynomial $X^3 + X + 1$. Suppose the message $m_4m_3m_2m_1m_0 = 11000$ is to be transmitted. Check bits $c_2c_1c_0$ are appended at the end of the message by the transmitter using the above CRC scheme. The transmitted bit string is denoted by $m_4m_3m_2m_1m_0c_2c_1c_0$. The value of the checkbit sequence $c_2c_1c_0$ is

(a) 101 (b) 110

(c) 100 (d) 111

35. Consider the following ANSI C program :

```
#include <stdio.h>
#include <stdlib.h>
struct Node{
        int value;
        struct Node *next;};
int main () {
    struct Node *boxE, *head, *boxN; int index
    = 0;
    boxE = head = (struct Node *) malloc (sizeof
    (struct Node)) ;
    head->value = index ;
    for (index = 1; index <= 3; index++) {
        boxN = (struct Node *) malloc (sizeof (struct
        Node)) ;
        boxE–>next = boxN;
        boxN–>value = index;
        boxE = box; N; }
    for (index = 0; index <= 3; index++) {
        printf ("Value at index %d is %d\n", index,
        head–> value) ;
        head = head–>next ;
        printf ("Value at index %d is %d\n", index
        + 1, head–>value) ; } }
```

Which one of the statements below is correct about the program ?

(a) Upon execution, the program creates a linked-list of five nodes.

(b) Upon execution, the program goes into an infinite loop.

(c) It has a missing return which will be reported as an error by the compiler.

(d) It dereferences an uninitialized pointer that may result in a run-time error.

36. Consider the following two statements about regular languages :

S1 : Every infinite regular language contains an undecidable language as a subset.

S2 : Every finite language is regular.

Which one of the following choices is correct ?

(a) Only S_1 is true.

(b) Only S_2 is true.

(c) Both S_1 and S_2 are true.

(d) Neither S_1 nor S_2 is true.

37. For two n-dimensional real vectors P and Q, the operation s(P, Q) is defined as follows :

$$s(P,Q)=\sum_{i=1}^{n}(P[i].Q[i])$$

Let $\mathcal{L}$ be a set of 10-dimensional non-zero real vectors such that for every pair of distinct vectors P, Q $\in \mathcal{L}$, s(P, Q) = 0. What is the maximum cardinality possible for the set $\mathcal{L}$?

(a) 9 (b) 10

(c) 11 (d) 100

38. For a statement S in a program, in the context of liveness analysis, the following sets are defined :

USE (S) : the set of variables used in S

IN (S) : the set of variables that are live at the entry of S

OUT (S) : the set of variables that are live at the exit of S

Consider a basic block that consists of two statements, S_1 followed by S_2. Which one of the following statements is correct ?

(a) OUT (S_1) = IN (S_2)

(b) OUT (S_1) = IN (S_1) $\cup$ USE (S_1)

(c) OUT (S_1) = IN (S_2) $\cup$ OUT (S_2)

(d) OUT (S_1) = USE (S_1) $\cup$ IN (S_2)

39. For constants $a \geq 1$ and $b > 1$, consider the following recurrence defined on the non-negative integers :

$$T(n) = a.T\left(\frac{n}{b}\right) + f(n)$$

Which one of the following options is correct about the recurrence T(n) ?

(a) If f(n) is $n \log_2(n)$, then T(n) is $\Theta(n \log_2(n))$.

(b) If f(n) is $\frac{n}{\log_2(n)}$, then T(n) is $\Theta(\log_2(n))$.

(c) If f(n) is $O\left(n^{\log_b(a)-\epsilon}\right)$ for some $\epsilon > 0$, then T(n) is $\Theta\left(n^{\log_b(a)}\right)$.

(d) If f(n) is $\Theta\left(n^{\log_b(a)}\right)$, then T(n) is $\Theta\left(n^{\log_b(a)}\right)$.

40. Suppose the following functional dependencies hold on a relation U with attributes P, Q, R, S, and T :

$P \to QR$

$RS \to T$

Which of the following functional dependencies can be inferred from the above functional dependencies ?

(a) $PS \to T$ (b) $R \to T$
(c) $P \to R$ (d) $PS \to Q$

41. For a string w, we define w^R to be the reverse of w. For example, if w = 01101 then w^R = 10110. Which of the following languages is/are context-free ?

(a) $\{wxw^Rx^R \mid w, x \in \{0, 1\}^*\}$
(b) $\{ww^Rxx^R \mid w, x \in \{0, 1\}^*\}$
(c) $\{wxw^R \mid w, x \in \{0, 1\}^*\}$
(d) $\{wxx^Rw^R \mid w, x \in \{0, 1\}^*\}$

42. Consider the following multi-threaded code segment (in a mix of C and pseudo-code), invoked by two processes P1 and P2, and each of the processes spawns two threads T1 and T2 :

```
int x = 0;  //  global
Lock L1;  //  global
main () {
    create a thread to execute foo (); // Thread T1
    create a thread to execute foo (); // Thread T2
    wait for the two threads to finish execution;
    print (x); }
foo ()  {
    int y = 0;
    Acquire L1;
    x = x + 1;
    y = y + 1;
    Release L1;
    print (y) ; }
```

Which of the following statement (s) is/are correct?

(a) Both P1 and P2 will print the value of x as 2.
(b) At least one of P1 and P2 will print the value of x as 4.
(c) At least one of the threads will print the value of y as 2.
(d) Both T1 and T2, in both the processes, will print the value of y as 1.

43. Consider a computer system with multiple shared resource types, with one instance per resource type. Each instance can be owned by only one process at a time. Owning and freeing of resources are done by holding a global lock (L). The following scheme is used to own a resource instance :

```
function OWNRESOURCE (Resource R)
    Acquire lock L // a global lock
    if R is available then
        Acquire R
        Release lock L
    else
        if R is owned by another process P then
            Terminate P, after releasing all resources
            owned by P
            Acquire R
            Restart P
            Release lock L
        end if
    end if
end function
```

Which of the following choice(s) about the above scheme is/are correct ?

(a) The scheme ensures that deadlocks will not occur.
(b) The scheme may lead to live-lock.
(c) The scheme may lead to starvation.
(d) The scheme violates the mutual exclusion property.

44. If the numerical value of a 2-byte unsigned integer on a little endian computer is 255 more than that on a big endian computer, which of the following choices represent (s) the unsigned integer on a little endian computer?

(a) 0x6665 (b) 0x0001
(c) 0x4243 (d) 0x0100

45. Consider a computer network using the distance vector algorithm in its network layer. The partial topology of the network is as shown below.

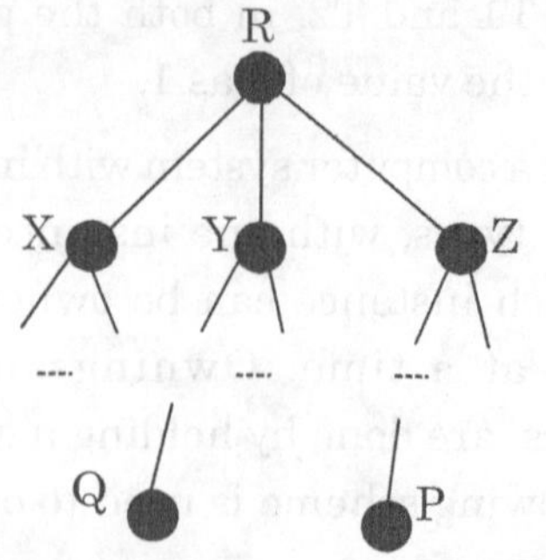

The objective is to find the shortest-cost path from the router R to routers P and Q. Assume that R does not initially know the shortest routes to P and Q. Assume that R has three neighbouring routers denoted as X, Y, and Z. During one iteration, R measures its distance to its neighbours X, Y, and Z ans 3, 2, and 5, respectively. Router R gets routing vectors from its neighbours that indicate that the distance to router P from routers X, Y, and Z are 7, 6, and 5, respectively. The routing vector also indicates that the distance to router Q from routers X, Y, and Z are 4, 6, and 8, respectively. Which of the following statement(s) is /are correct with respect to the new routing table of R, after updation during this iteration ?

(a) The distance from R to P will be stored as 10.

(b) The distance from R to Q will be stored as 7.

(c) The next hop router for a packet from R to P is Y.

(d) The next hop router for a packet from R to Q is Z.

46. Consider the following directed graph :

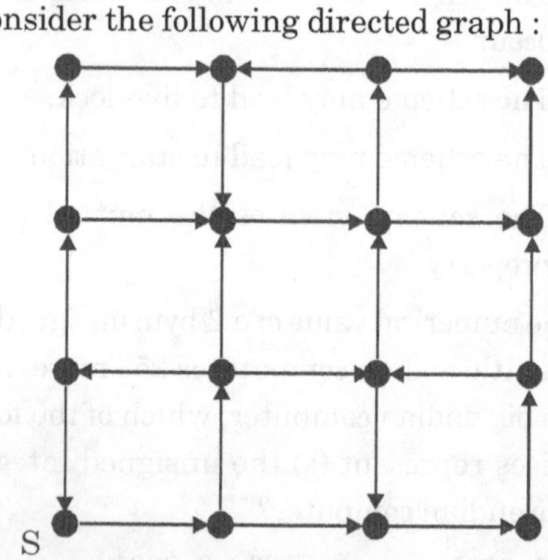

Which of the following is/are correct about the graph ?

(a) The graph does not have a topological order.

(b) A depth-first traversal starting at vertex S classifies three directed edges as back edges.

(c) The graph does not have a strongly connected component.

(d) For each pair of vertices u and v, there is a directed path from u to v.

47. Which of the following regular expressions represent(s) the set of all binary numbers that are divisible by three ? Assume that the string ∈ is divisible by three.

(a) (0 + 1(01*0)*1)*

(b) (0 + 11 + 10 (1 + 00)*01)*

(c) (0*(1(01*0)*1)*)*

(d) (0 + 11 + 11 (1 + 00)*00)*

48. Consider a three-level page table to translate a 39-bit virtual address to a physical address as shown below.

< – – – – 39 – bit virtual address – – – – >

Level1 offset	Level 2 offset	Level3 offset	Page offset
9 bits	9 bits	9 bits	12 bits

The page size is 4KB (1KB = 2^{10} bytes) and page table entry size at every level is 8 bytes. A process P is currently using 2GB (1GB = 2^{30} bytes) virtual memory which is mapped to 2GB of physical memory. The minimum amount of memory required for the page table of P across all levels is _____ KB.

49. Consider the following ANSI C program.

```
#include <stdio.h>
int foo (int x, int y, int q)
{
    if ((x <= 0) && (y <= 0))
        return q;
    if (x <= 0)
        return foo (x, y–q, q);
    if (y <= 0)
        return foo (x–q, y, q);
    return foo (x, y–q, q) + foo (x–q, y, q);
}
int main ()
```

```
{
    int r = foo (15, 15, 10);
    printf ("%d", r);
    return 0;
}
```

The output of the program upon execution is ____.

50. Let S be a set consisting of 10 elements. The number of tuples of the form (A, B) such that A and B are subsets of S, and $A \subseteq B$ is ____.

51. Consider the following augmented grammar with {#, @, <, >, a, b, c} as the set of terminals.

$S' \rightarrow S$

$S \rightarrow S \# cS$

$S \rightarrow S S$

$S \rightarrow S @$

$S \rightarrow < S >$

$S \rightarrow a$

$S \rightarrow b$

$S \rightarrow c$

Let I_0 = CLOSURE ({$S' \rightarrow \bullet S$}). The number of items in the set GOTO (GOTO (I_0, <), <) is ____.

52. Consider a Boolean function f(w, x, y, z) such that

f (w, 0, 0, z) = 1

f(1, x, 1, z) = x + z

f(w, 1, y, z) = wz + y

The number of literals in the minimal sum-of-products expression of f is ____.

53. Consider a pipelined processor with 5 stages, Instruction Fetch (IF), Instruction Decode (ID), Execute (EX), Memory Access (MEM), and Write Back (WB). Each stage of the pipeline, except the Ex stage, takes one cycle. Assume that the ID stage merely decodes the instruction and the register read is performed in the EX stage. The EX stage takes one cycle for ADD instruction and two cycles for MUL instruction. Ignore pipeline register latencies.

Consider the following sequence of 8 instructions:

ADD, MUL, ADD, MUL, ADD, MUL, ADD, MUL

Assume that every MUL instruction is data-dependent on the ADD instruction just before it and every ADD instruction (except the first ADD) is data-dependent on the MUL instruction just before it. The Speedup is defined as follows:

$$\text{Speedup} = \frac{\text{Execution time without operand forwarding}}{\text{Execution time with operand forwarding}}$$

The *Speedup* achieved in executing the given instruction sequence on the pipelined processor (rounded to 2 decimal places) is ____.

54. Consider a network using pure ALOHA medium access control protocol, where each frame is of length 1,000 bits. The channel transmission rate is 1 Mbps (= 10^6 bits per second). The aggregate number of transmissions across all the nodes (including new frame transmissions and retransmitted frames due to collisions) is modelled as a Poisson process with a rate of 1,000 frames per second. Throughput is defined as the average number of frames successfully transmitted per second. The throughput of the network (rounded to the nearest integer) is ____.

55. In a directed acyclic graph with a source vertex s, the quality-score of a directed path is defined to be the product of the weights of the edges on the path. Further, for a vertex v other than s, the quality-score of v is defined to be the maximum among the quality-scores of all the paths from s to v. The quality-score of s is assumed to be 1.

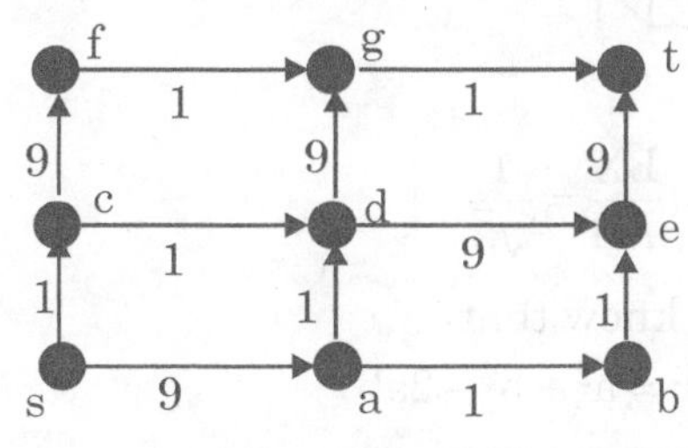

The sum of the quality-scores of all the vertices in the graph shown above is ____.

ANSWERS

General Aptitude (GA)

1. (a)	**2.** (b)	**3.** (b)	**4.** (b)	**5.** (c)	**6.** (c)
7. (a)	**8.** (c)	**9.** (a)	**10.** (c)		

Computer Science and Information Technology

1. (c)	**2.** (c)	**3.** (c)	**4.** (c)	**5.** (a)	**6.** (d)
7. (c)	**8.** (b)	**9.** (c)	**10.** (c)	**11.** (b, c)	**12.** (b, c, d)
13. (d)	**14.** (a, c, d)	**15.** (b, d)	**16.** (1 to 1)	**17.** (256 to 256)	**18.** (3 to 3)
19. (2 to 2)	**20.** (80000 to 80000)		**21.** (698 to 698)	**22.** (15.00 to 16.00)	
23. (15 to 15)	**24.** (4 to 4)	**25.** (19 to 19)	**26.** (b)	**27.** (a)	**28.** (b)
29. (d)	**30.** (d)				
31. (b)	**32.** (b)	**33.** (a)	**34.** (c)	**35.** (d)	**36.** (c)
37. (b)	**38.** (a)	**39.** (c)	**40.** (a, c, d)	**41.** (b, c, d)	**42.** (a, d)
43. (a, b, c)	**44.** (a, d)	**45.** (b, c)	**46.** (a, b)	**47.** (a, b, c)	
48. (4108 to 4108)	**49.** (60 to 60)	**50.** (59049 to 59049)		**51.** (8 to 8)	**52.** (6 to 6)
53. (1.87 to 1.88)	**54.** (130 to 140)	**55.** (929 to 929)			

EXPLANATIONS

GENERAL APTITUDE (GA)

1. 'As well as' is used in positive degree.

2. The folded sheet is look like option (b).

3.

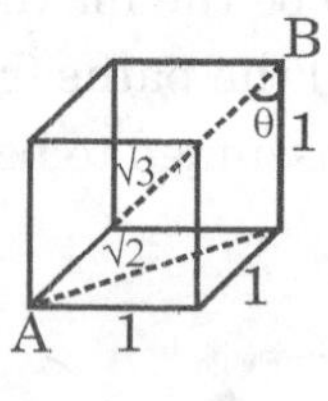

$$\cos\theta = \frac{BX}{AB} = \frac{1}{\sqrt{3}}$$

4. As we know that

$(a - b)^2 = a^2 + b^2 - 2ab$

As given expression

$$\left(x - \frac{1}{2}\right)^2 - \left(x - \frac{3}{2}\right)^2 = (x + 2)$$

So,

$$\Rightarrow \left[x^2 + \left(\frac{1}{2}\right)^2 - 2(x)\left(\frac{1}{2}\right)\right] - \left[x^2 + \left(\frac{9}{4}\right) - 2(x).\left(\frac{3}{2}\right)\right]$$

$= [x + 2]$

$$\Rightarrow \left[x^2 + \frac{1}{4} - x - x^2 - \frac{9}{4} + 3x\right] = [x + 2]$$

$\Rightarrow [-2 + 2x] = [x + 2]$

$x = 4$

5. Pen is to write just as knife is to cut.

6. Listening to music improves exercise performance and reduces discomfort. Music as positive effort only on few students during learning.

7. When the piece can be moved, rotated or flipped to assemble with the given piece is option (a)

8. The total number of students in three classes in the beginning.

Let us consider:

$3a + 13a + 6a = 22a = n$

after addition of 18 student total number of students.

$15b + 35b + 21b = 71b$

$3a + 18 + 13a + 18 + 6a + 18 = 22a + 54$

$22a + 54 = 71b$

$n + 54 = 71b$

$n = 71b - 54$

Let $(b = 2)$

So, $n = 71 \times 2 - 54$

$= 88$

9. Let us consider, the selling price in year '2' be 'x'.

$\therefore$ Net profit = Selling price – (Cost + Taxes)

$296 = x - (400 + 0.13x)$

$296 = 0.87x - 400$

$$x = \frac{696}{0.87} = 800$$

So, selling price in year '2' = Rs.800

In year 3, total cost = 300 × 1 = Rs.300

Taxes paid = 0.15% of selling price.

Now, let us consider, the selling price in year 3 be 'y'

$\therefore 210 = y - (300 + 0.15y)$

$\Rightarrow 210 = (0.85y - 300)$

$$y = \frac{510}{0.85} = 600$$

∴ Selling price in year '3' = 600

So, $\frac{x}{y} = \frac{800}{600} = \frac{4}{3}$.

10. I: S > R

II: Q < P, R, S, T, U

From III & IV observation

P > T > S > R > U > Q

The number of students that are taller than 'R' is same as the number of students shorter than S.

COMPUTER SCIENCE AND INFORMATION

1. Statement 1 is false, take complete graph on three vertices with all the edge weights being same. Statement 2 it is true by basic property of graph with distinct edge weights.

2. The maximum element can be present anywhere in leaf level of the min heap, so, we need to have $\frac{n}{2}$ comparisons because we have $\frac{n}{2}$ leaf nodes in min heap of n elements. So, correct minimum-heap to maximum-heap with Healify method at complexity of Θ (n). Hence, answer is Θ (n).

3. Integer X; is not matching the syntex of 'C' program because Integer is not a keyword in C language but a valid identifier. This error will be caught in syntax analysis phase.

4. For the smallest positive normalized number

Biased exponent will be equal to 000000001, since 00000000 is reserved for the special purpose.

And normalized mantissa can 1.

Here option (c) & (d) are used for implicant number representation but in these, option (c) is used to represent the smallest positive number.

$$\underbrace{000\ 0000000000000000000000}_{\text{23 zeros}}$$

Hence, correct answer is option (c).

5. Method 1:

As given that $f(x, y, z) = (m_0 + m_1 + m_3 + m_4 + m_5 + m_6)$

A multiplexer based circuit to be implement of where $f(x, y, z) = \Sigma m(0, 1, 3, 4, 5, 6)$, need to select the correct design.

Option (a):

$f = \bar{y}\bar{z} + \bar{y}z + xy\bar{z} + \bar{x}yz$

$= \Sigma m\ (0, 1, 3, 4, 5, 6)$

= (000, 100) (001, 101) (110) (011)

m_0, m_4 m_1, m_5 m_6 m_3

So option (a) is correct.

Option (b):

$f = \bar{y}\bar{z}x + \bar{y}z + y\bar{z}\bar{x} + yz$

$= \Sigma m\ (1, 2, 3, 4, 5, 7)$

$= x\bar{y}\bar{z} + \bar{y}z + \bar{x}y\bar{z} + yz$

$= x\bar{y}\bar{z} + -\bar{y}z + \bar{x}y\bar{z} + -yz$

(100) (001, 101) (010) (011, 111)

m_4 m_1, m_5 m_2 m_3, m_7

So option (b) is not correct.

Option (c):

$f = \bar{y}\bar{z} + \bar{y}z + \bar{x}y\bar{z} + xyz$

$= \Sigma m\ (0, 1, 2, 4, 5, 7)$

= (000, 100) (001, 101) (010) (111)

m_0, m_4 m_1, m_5 m_2 m_7

So option (c) is not correct.

Option (d):

$f = \bar{x}\bar{y}\bar{z} + \bar{y}z + \bar{y}z + yz$

$= \Sigma m\ (0, 1, 3, 5, 6, 7)$

$= \bar{x}\bar{y}\bar{z} + -\bar{y}z + xy\bar{z} + -yz$

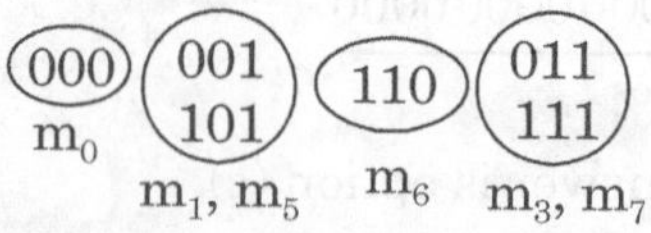

So option (d) is not correct.

Method 2:

If y, z are in select lines x should be data line

	I_0	I_1	I_2	I_3
$\overline{x}$	(0)	(1)	2	(3)
x	(4)	(5)	(6)	7
	1	1	x	$\overline{x}$

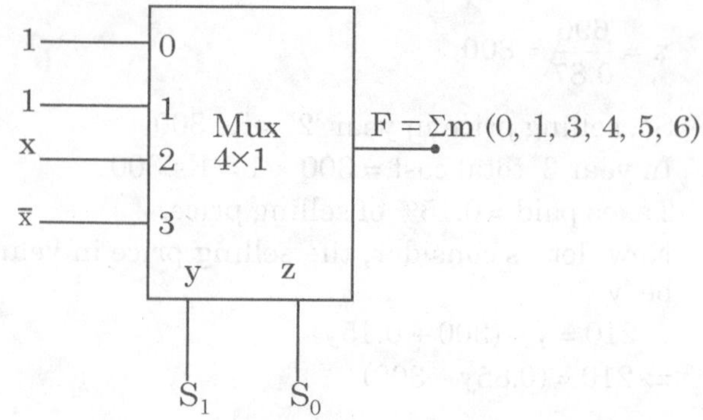

Hence option (a) is correct answer.

6. Foreign key is the Set of fields in one relation that is used to 'reference'. a tuple in another (or same) relation. S_1: A relation schema can have more than one foreign key. S_2: A foreign key in a relation can 'reference'. a tuple in same relation. Hence, both statements are false.

7. According to the question:

TCP (Transport Connection Establishment)

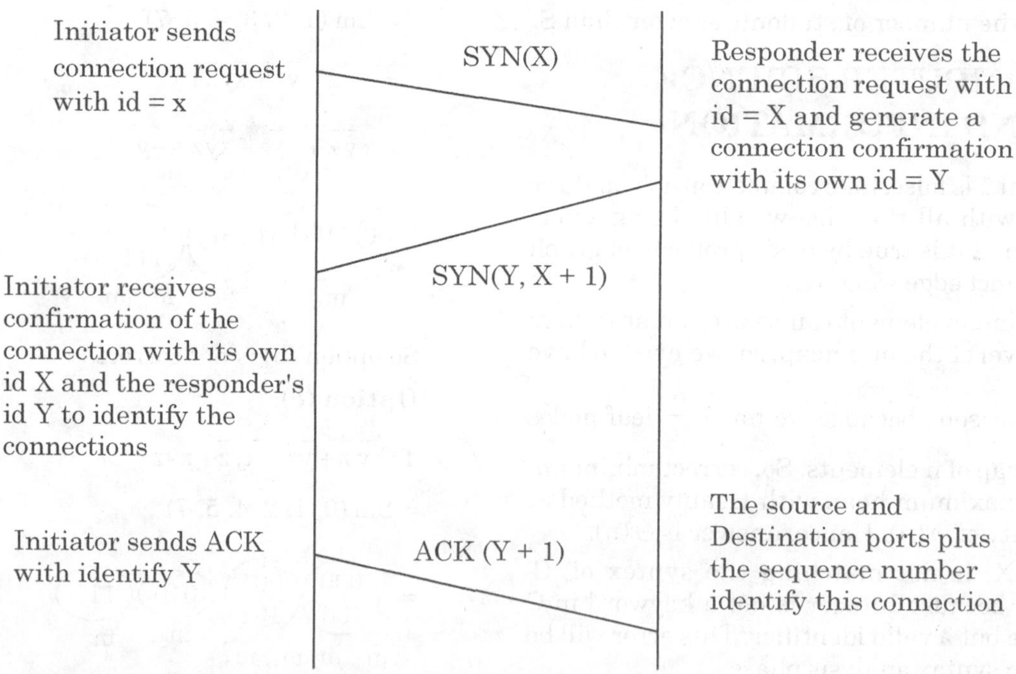

Hence, option (c) is the correct answer.

8. In worst case it will take θ(logn) time (when element is not present in the array). So, time complexity of Binary search on a sorted input of size 'n' is Θ (logn).

9. The Regular language (accepted by DFA) is closed under complementation and L and $\overline{L}$ have same number of state in minimal DFA.

So, $L \subseteq (0 + 1)^*$ is the language accepted by MDFA with K states than compliment of L is $(0 + 1)^* - L$ is also accepted by MDFA with K states.

10. Int a[4][5]

[*(a+1)+9]

it means skip one row and then skip 9 elements

So, the resultant output of the above program will be 24.

11. There exist a bijection from S1 to S2 as $|S1| = |S2| = 3^{n^2}$ And because bijection injection surjection will also exist from S_1 to S_2.

12. By taking each options:

(a) $L1 \cap \overline{L2}$

We know that Context free language is not closed under complement hence $\overline{L2}$ may be the non-Context free language.

$L1 \cap \overline{L2}$ may be a **non-context free language.**

(b) $\left(\overline{\overline{L1} \cup \overline{L2}}\right) = L1 \cap L2$ is Intersection if Regular and context free and Outer set in Chomsky is preferred hence context free.

(c) $L1 \cup \left(L2 \cup \overline{L2}\right)$ here $\left(L2 \cup \overline{L2}\right)$ is Σ^* hence Regular. The union with regular language will make this as regular language hence context free

(d) $(L1 \cap L2) \cap \left(\overline{L1} \cup L2\right)$, In this $(L1 \cap L2)$ is context free and $\left(\overline{L1} \cup L2\right)$ is also context free (L1 is regular and its complement will be also regular).

The intersection of these two language may **not context free**, since Context free language are not closed under intersection operation.

13. Three major categories of Intermediate representation called structural, linear and hybrid.

Structural Intermediate representation or Graphical IR (parse tree, abstract syntax trees, AST DAG. . .)

Linear Intermediate representation or postfix expression: (i.e. , non graphical) and three Address Code (TAC) instructions of the form "result=op1operator op2"

Hybrid Intermediate representation or Static single assignment (SSA) form: each variable is assigned once.

14. (a) Turnaround time includes waiting time : True Turnaround time = waiting time + burst time

(c) Round-robin policy can be used even when the CPU time required by each of the processes is not known apriori. : True, SJF needs the CPU time required by each of the processes to be known apriori

(d) Implementing preemptive scheduling needs hardware support : true

15. The antecedent of S is $(P \wedge Q) \rightarrow R$. Which can be written as P' V Q' + R

The consequent of S is $(P \wedge Q) \rightarrow (Q \rightarrow R)$ Which can be written as P' V Q' + Q' + R which is

$P' \vee Q' + R$

Antecedent and consequent, both are equivalent. Hence, option (b & d) are correct answer.

16. According to the question consider a complete binary tree with 7 nodes:

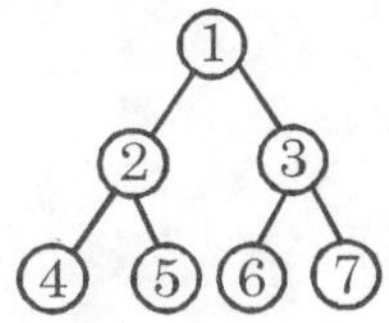

If the given CBT has root node 1, its children 2,3, and children of 2 are 4,5 then BFS will visit from root {1,2,3}, A = 3 as first three nodes, and DFS will visit from root {1,2,4}, B = 4 so, cardinality of the set $|A - B| = 1$

17. The regular expression for the given DFA is $= (0(0 + 1)(0 + 1) + 1(0 + 1)(0 + 1))(0 + 1)^*$

It can be written as:

$= (0 + 1)(0 + 1)(0 + 1)(0 + 1)^*$

Which can be defined as all string over {0, 1} of length greater than 3

As per the given condition in the string length it should be exactly 8.

We can write the expression for length 8 string as:

$\Rightarrow (0 + 1)(0 + 1)(0 + 1)(0 + 1)(0 + 1)(0 + 1)(0 + 1)(0 + 1) = [0 + 1]^8$

So, all possible combination

For length 8, all $2^8 = 256$ string will be accepted.

18. As given that $(0.1101)_2 = (0.8\,xy5)_{10}$, we need to obtain decimal value of x + y.

$(0.1101)_2 = (1 \times 2^{-1}) + (1 \times 2^{-2}) + (0 \times 2^{-3}) + (1 \times 2^{-4})$

$= \frac{1}{2} + \frac{1}{4} + 0 + \frac{1}{16}$

$= \frac{13}{16}$

$= 0.8125$

$\Rightarrow (0.110)_2 = (0.8125)_0 = (0.8\,xyz)_{10}$

Now, By comparison x = 1, y = 2.

Hence x + y = 3.

19. The block size is given as 64 (2^6) Bytes Byte offset will consists of 6 bits

The number of blocks are in the cache is

$\frac{2KB}{2^6} = \frac{2^{11}B}{2^6 B} = 2^5$

If the set is 2^K way set Associative then number of sets

$= \frac{2^5}{2^k} = 2^{5-k}$

The number of bits required for the byte index us 5-k

Since main memory is addressed by 32 bits

← 32bits →

22	5 – k	6
Tag	Set offset	byte offset

22 + 5 – k + 6 = 32

K = 1

Hence, the associativity of the cach is = 2k = 2^1 = 2

20. In One sec number type of data transfer is cycle steel i.e. one 8 bit characters one request of cycle generated by the CPU is 2×10^6 Since 0.5% cycles are used By DMA The number of cycle used by the DMA is

$= 2 \times 10^6 \times \frac{0.5}{100}$

$= 2 \times 10^6 \times \frac{1}{200}$

$= 10^4$

In 1 cycle 8 bits transferred

∴ 10^4 cycles ------- $10^4 \times 8$

= 80000 bits

21. As given that,

Number of index records = 1,50,000

Size of index record = 12 + 7 = 19

Block factor = $\left\lfloor \frac{4096}{19} \right\rfloor = 215$

Number of index blocks

$= \left\lceil \frac{1,50,000}{215} \right\rceil = 698$ blocks

22. As given that

n = 1000 (very large)

Let p = P_r (getting a head in any toss) = 0.4

⇒ p is not very small

⇒ q = 1 – p = 0.6

Let us consider X be a random variable denote number of times that head appears in 1000 tosses.

⇒ X is a Binomial distribution

∴ Standard deviation

$\sigma = \sqrt{npq} = \sqrt{1000 \times 0.4 \times 0.6} = \sqrt{240} \approx 15.49$

23. /*

fun (15, 255)

⇒ fun (15, 240)

⇒ fun (15, 225)

⇒ fun (15, 210)

.

.

.

⇒ fun (15, 15)

⇒ 15

*/

24. As given that P is a 4 × 5 matrix. PX = 0 is homogeneous system, where X (is solution) is a scalar multiple of $[2\ 5\ 4\ 3\ 1]^T$

⇒ PX = 0 has infinitely many solutions and all solutions are of the form λ.X, where λ is scalar

⇒ number linearly independent solutions is 1

⇒ n – r = 1, where n is number of unknowns and r is rank of P.

5 – r = 1 = r = 4

Hence, Rank of P is 4

25. As given that,

f(x) is continuous in [–3, 3].

f(x) is differentiable in [–3, 3]

By Lagrange's mean value theorem,

$f'(x) = \frac{f(3) - f(-3)}{3 - (-3)}$ where x ∈ (–3, 3)

$f'(x) = \frac{f(3) - 7}{6}$

More over $f'(x) \le 2$

$f'(x) \le 2, x \in (-3, 3)$

$\therefore \frac{f(3) - 7}{6} \le 2 \Rightarrow f(3) \le 19$

Hence, f(3) is atmost 19

26. Using Huffman encoding, minimum length of encoded string:

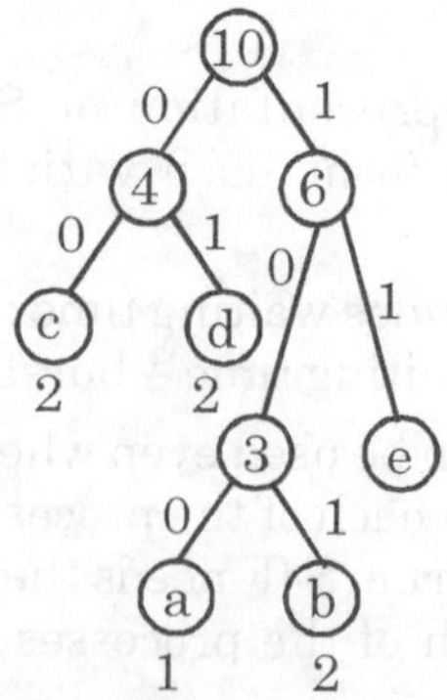

abbccddeee

100 101 101 000 000 101 111 11

= Sum of frequency count using Guffman coding

= 1 × 3 + 2 × 3 + 2 × 2 + 2 × 2 + 3 × 2

= 3 + 6 + 4 + 4 + 6 = 23

27. S1 is False, in write through policy both cache and main memory updated simultaneously hence there is no Dirty lines will be present in the cache.
S2 is false, A write-back cache is more complex to implement, since it needs to track which of its locations have been written over, and mark them as dirty for later writing to the backing store. The data in these locations are written back to the backing store only when they are evicted from the cache, an effect referred to as a lazy write. For this reason, a read miss in a write-back cache (which requires a block to be replaced by another) will often require two memory accesses to service: one to write the replaced data from the cache back to the store, and then one to retrieve the needed data.
Other policies may also trigger data write-back. The client may make many changes to data in the cache, and then explicitly notify the cache to write back the data.
Since no data is returned to the requester on write operations, a decision needs to be made on write misses, whether or not data would be loaded into the cache. This is defined by these two approaches:
Write allocate (also called fetch on write): data at the missed-write location is loaded to cache, followed by a write-hit operation. In this approach, write misses are similar to read misses.
No-write allocate (also called write-no-allocate or write around): data at the missed-write location is not loaded to cache, and is written directly to the backing store. In this approach, data is loaded into the cache on read misses only.
Both write-through and write-back policies can use either of these write-miss policies, but usually they are paired in this way:
A write-back cache uses write allocate, hoping for subsequent writes (or even reads) to the same location, which is now cached.
A write-through cache uses no-write allocate. Here, subsequent writes have no advantage, since they still need to be written directly to the backing store.
Hence, option (a) is the correct answer.

28.

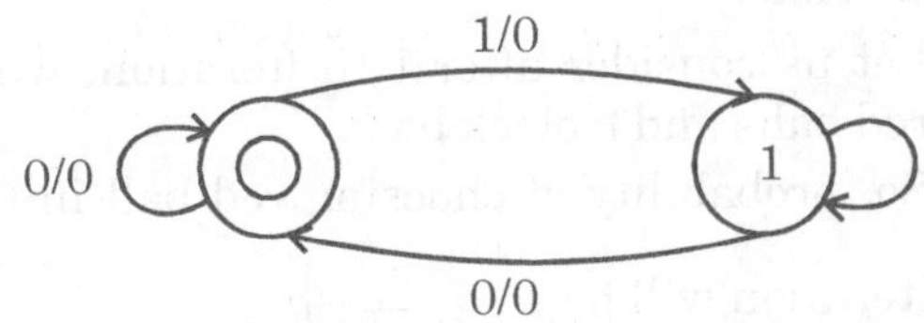

PS	Next state t	Output y
S	b = 0	b = 1
0	0,0	1,0
1	0,0	1,1

t = Sb + Sb = b, y = Sb

29. Let us consider
M = marks obtained by students.
Case(i) Student answer and question A followed by question B.

M	0	10	30
P(M)	0.2	0.8×0.5	0.8×0.5

$E(M) = (10 \times 0.8 \times 0.5 + 30 \times 0.8 \times 0.5)$
$= (4 + 12) = 16$
Case (ii) Student answer question B followed by question A

M	0	20	30
P(M)	8.5	0.5×0.2	0.8×0.5

E(M) = (2 + 12) = 14.

30. The Optimization code will be

Code	
t_1 = x+3 ; (1 add)	1 Addition
t_2 = y–> f_1;	1 de reference
t_3 = y–> f_2	1 de reference
z = t_1 + t_2 + t_3;	2 Addition
for (i = 0; 1 < 200; (i = i + 2) {	100 Addition
if (z > i) { p = p + t_1; q = q + t_2; }	Either if or else part will be execute,
	If Part has 2 addition
else { p = p + t_3; q = q + t_1; } }	Else part has 2 addition
	∴ In loop the number of additions = 100 × 2 = 200 addition.
Total	303 Addition and 2 references

31. The above query gives, for each department in the company, the number of female employees whose salary is greater than the average salary of all employees in the company.

32. As there is no cycle in precedence graph so, S is conflict serializable.

If T3 commits after T1 then only recoverability is possible.

33. Let us consider after i_th iteration, we have r red balls and b black balls.

So, probability of choosing red ball in (i + 1)th iteration will be $= \left[\frac{r}{(b+b)}\right]$

So, probability of choosing red ball in (i + 2)th iteration will be :

(note that, in (i + 1)th iteration, we could either pick black or red ball.)

$$\left[\frac{r}{(r+b)}\right]\left[\frac{(r+1)}{(r+b+1)}\right]+\left[\frac{b}{(r+b)}\right]\left[\frac{(r)}{(r+b+1)}\right]$$

$$=\left[\frac{r}{(r+b)}\right]$$

So, in the beginning we have r red balls, and b green balls.

Hence in every iteration, the probability of choosing a red ball will be $\left[\frac{r}{(r+b)}\right]$

34. By doing the simple CRC based calculation where the general or polynomial is 1011

$x^3 + x + 1 = 1011$

```
1011 | 11000000
       1011
       ----
        1110
        1011
        ----
         1010
         1011
         ----
          100
```

35. It will result in run time error because it dereferences an uninitialized pointer in the loop when index value is 3.

Hence, option (d) is correct answer.

36. S1 is TRUE, With the particular focus on regular languages, the intended solution might have been something like using the pumping lemma to find x,y,z such that xy^nz is in your language for every n, and then consider the subset $\{xy^nz \mid n \in A\}$, where A is your favorite undecidable set of natural numbers.

S2 is also TRUE, Any finite language is regular.

Hence, option (c) is the correct answer.

37. s(P,Q) represents Dot product of two vectors.

The dot product of a = < 1, 3, –2 > and b = < –2, 4, –1 > is

$\vec{a}.\vec{b} = 1(-2) + 3(4) + (-2)(-1) = 12$

Two vectors are orthogonal if the angle between them is 90 degrees.

The dot product of two vectors is zero when they are perpendicular/orthogonal, as we are dealing with 10 dimensional vectors the maximum number of mutually-perpendicular vectors can be 10.

Hence, option (b) is the correct answer.

38. The set of variables that are live at the exit of S_1 is the set of variables that are live at the entry of 'S'; where 'S' is all successors for S_1.

The variable live at the end or out of the block S1 will be IN for the next Block S2.

39. Master Theorem

The Master Theorem applies to recurrences of the following form:

$$T(m) = aT\left(\frac{n}{b}\right) + f(n)$$

Where $a \geq 1$ and $b > 1$ are constant and f(n) is an asymptotically positive function.

There are 3 cases:

(i) If $f(n) = O\left(n^{\log_b a-\epsilon}\right)$ for some constant $\epsilon > 0$, then $T(n) = \Theta\left(n^{\log_b a}\right)$.

(ii) If $f(n) = \Theta\left(n^{\log_b a}\log^k n\right)$ with $1k \geq 0$, then $T(n) = \Theta\left(n^{\log_b a}\log^{k+1} n\right)$

(iii) If $f(n) = \Omega\left(n^{\log_b a+\epsilon}\right)$ with $\epsilon > 0$, f(n) satisfier the regularity condition, then $T(n) = \Theta(f(n))$.

Regularity condition: $af\left(\frac{n}{b}\right) \leq cf(n)$ for some constant $c < 1$ and all sufficiently large n.

Hence, option (c) is the correct answer.

40. According to the question,

$(P)^+ = \{P, Q, R\}$

$(PS)^+ = \{P, QR, S, T\}$

$(R)^+ = \{R\}$

$\therefore R \rightarrow T$ is not possible

Hence, options (a), (c) & (d) are correct answer.

41. (i) $\{wxw^Rx^R \mid w, x \in \{0, 1\}^*\}$ is context sensitive language

(ii) $\{wxw^Rxx^R \mid w, x \in \{0, 1\}^*\}$ is **context free language**, Single stack can be used for pushing w and popping wR. Then we can push x and pop xR.

(iii) $\{wxw^R \mid w, x \in \{0, 1\}^*\}$ is regular language hence **context free**. The regular expression is (0+1)*

(iv) $\{wxw^Rw^R \mid w, x \in \{0, 1\}^*\}$ is **context free**, We can push w as well as x and pop x^R and w^R.

42. 'y' is a local variable 'x' is a global variable incrementing the value of x & y are under lock control. So the final value of both will be 2 respectively but printing of y is done individually by both the threads whenever x is printed by after the termination of both.

43. When R is owned by another process P then we can Terminate P, after releasing all resources owned by P.

So, consider a scenario where process R is free, P acquires lock, acquires R, releases lock, now process Q comes, acquires lock, since R is not available, so, Q Terminates P, after releasing all resources owned by P, then acquires R, restart P, release lock. So, now assume P comes and takes R away from Q. So, this continuous scenario can happen again and again. Thus live lock is possible, so starvation is possible.

Deadlock is not possible, because no one is waiting. Process is terminating and restarting.

Mutual exclusion is satisfied because at one time, at most one process can own a resource.

Hence, option (a), (b) & (c) are correct answer.

44. Take 0×6665:

0×6665 is the representating integer on a little endian computer, so it means that the original number must have been 0×6566. Similarly take 0×d00.

		0 × 100	0 × 101	0 × 102	0 × 103		
		01	23	45	67		

Big Endian

		0 × 100	0 × 101	0 × 102	0 × 103		
		67	45	23	01		

Little Endian

Suppose the number is 1 (A good guess)

In two byte unsigned representation

0000 0000 (Byte–0) 0000 0001 (Byte–1)

This representation is big endian representation.

The little-endian representation is

0000 0001 (Byte–1) 0000 0000 (Byte–0),

equivalent to the numeric value 256 And which is 255 higher than bigger than little endian representation.

In hexadecimal representation

0000 (0) 0001 (1) 0000 (0) 0000 (0)

45. Here, the path chosen to Q would be from X and distance is 7 so, the distance from R to Q is 7 via X. And, the path chosen to P would be from Y and distance is 8, so the distance from R to P is 8 via Y.

46. Because the graph is direction & when DFS is performed from 'S' three back edges will result.

Since the graph does not have a source vertex. So topological order is not possible. Hence, statement (a) is true and with these respect statement (b) is also true. Remaining options (c) & (d) can be varified to be false.

47. The DFA accepting all binary number divisible by 3 is given by

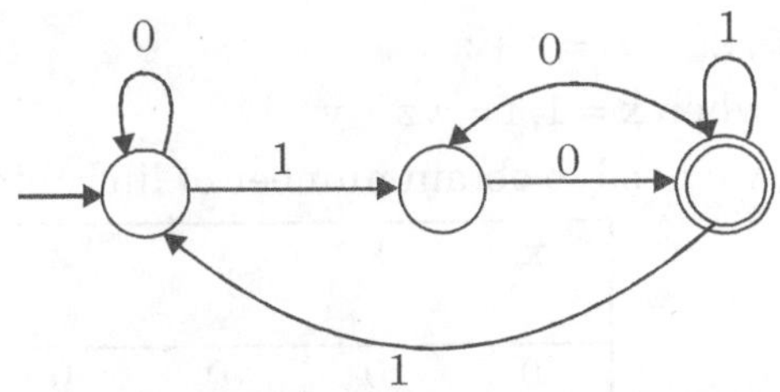

The regular expression for the above DFA (direct method, considering two loops)

(0 + 1 (01*0)*1)*, which goes with option 3

We know that (a + b)* can also equal to (a*b*)*

So, (0+1(01*0)*1)* = (0*(1(01*0)*1)*)*

Hence, 1, 2 and 3 are correct.

Option (4) will generate string 11100 = 57 not divisible by 3 and also it can not generate string 1001 = 9.

48. As in the question minimum memory is asked so we will consider 1 page at each level with 2 entries. Total number of page table = 210 + 2 + 1 = 1027 per table. So page table size at one level = 2^9 * 8.

Total page table size = 1027 × 29 × 8 byte

= 4108 kb

49. Reason:

foo (15, 15, 10):

= foo(15, 5, 10) + foo(5, 15, 10)

= 30 + 30 = 60

foo(15, 15, 10):

= foo(15, –5, 10) + foo(5, 5, 10)

= 30

foo(15, –5, 10):

= foo(5, –5, 10) + foo(–5, –5, 10)

= 10

foo(5, 5, 10)

= foo(5, –5, 10) + foo(–5, 5, 10)

= 10 + 10 = 20

Hence, the output of the program is 60.

50. If we make a pair (A, B) such that A has k elements in it then B for we have $2^{(10-k)}$ possible choices.

So answer will be

$\Rightarrow 2^{10}$ (when A is empty set) + ${}^{10}C_1 \times 2^9$ (when $|A| = 1$) + ${}^{10}C_2 \times 2^8$(when $|A| = 2$) + ...soon.

$= (1 + 2)^{10} = 59049$

51. Goto $(I_0, <) = I_1$

and Goto$(I_1, <) = I_1$

Therefore Goto

(Goto $(I_0, <), <) = I1$

and I_1 contains 8 items.

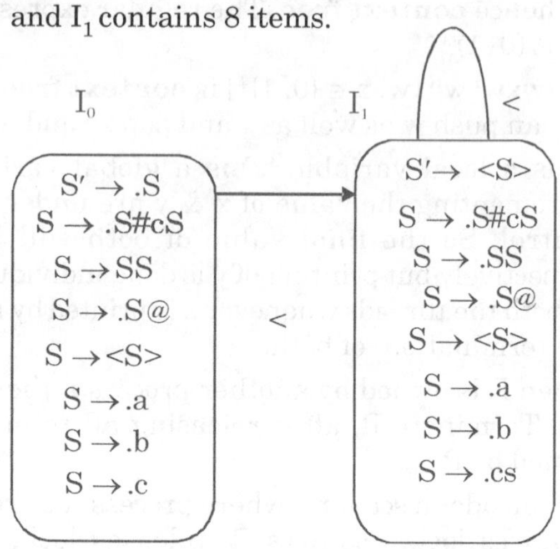

52. As given that for a function f (w, x, y, z)

f (w, 0, 0, z) = 1

$\Rightarrow$ i.e., when x = 0, y = 0, f = 1

f (w, x, 1, z) = x + z

$\Rightarrow$ when x = 1, f = wz + y

So, we need to obtain number of literal in minimum SOP of f.

x	x	y	z	x = 0, y = 0, f = 1	w = 1, y = 1, f = x + z	x = 1 f = wz + y	Overall f
0	0	0	0	1			1
0	0	0	1				
0	0	1	0				
0	0	1	1			0	0
0	1	0	1			0	1
0	1	1	0			1	1
0	1	1	1			1	1
0	1	1	1			0	1
1	0	0	0	1		0	1
1	0	0	1	1		0	1
1	0	1	0		0	0	0
1	0	1	1		1	0	1
1	1	0	0			0	0
1	1	0	1			1	1
1	1	1	0		1	1	1
1	1	1	1		1	1	1

Now information for w, x, y, z = 00010 and 0011, so f is taken don't care for unit combination f (w, x, yz) = Σm (0, 1, 6, 7, 8, 9, 11, 13, 14, 15) + d(2, 3)

By using k-map

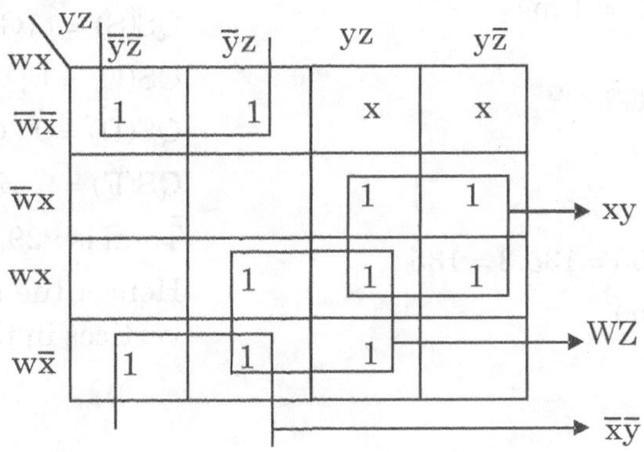

So $f = \bar{x}\bar{y} + xy + wz$ (minimized SOP expression) ear term of f containing 2 literal, so total 6 literal in expression of f.

53. Execution time without operand forwarding

ADD
MUL
ADD
MUL
ADD
MUL
ADD
MUL
ADD

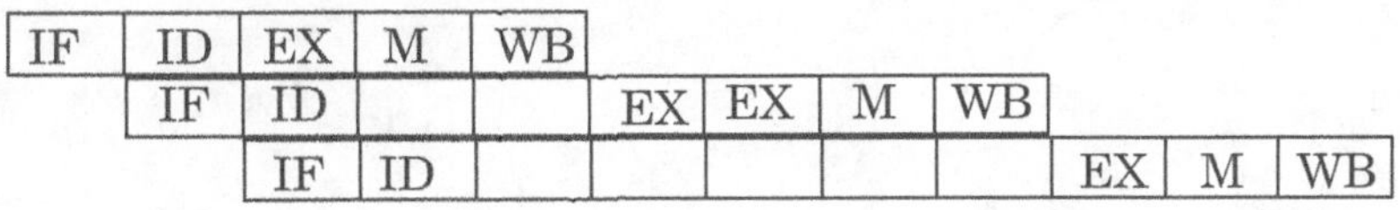

The First add instruction completes at 5 cycles, second dependent instruction will start execution phase after Write back (Register Read happens at Execute stage)

Instruction	Completion cycle No.
ADD	5
MUL	8
ADD	12
MUL	16
ADD	19
MUL	23
ADD	26
SUB	30

With Operand forwarding

ADD
MUL
ADD
MUL
ADD
MUL
ADD
MUL
ADD

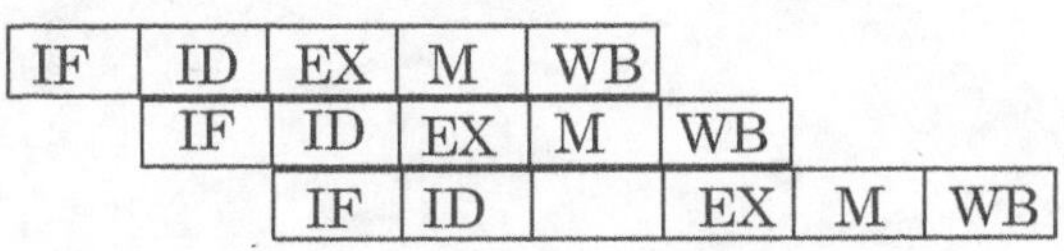

With operand forwarding every Multiplication instruction will come out in offset of 2 but ADD instruction will come out in 1 cycle offset

Instruction	Completion cycle No.
ADD	5
MUL	7
ADD	8
MUL	10
ADD	11
MUL	13
ADD	14
SUB	16

Speed up

$$= \frac{\text{Execution time without operand forwarding}}{\text{Execution time with operand forwarding}}$$

$$= \frac{30}{16} = 1.875$$

Hence, speed up achieved in executing the given instruction sequence on the pipelined processor is 1.875.

54. Transmission time $= \frac{1000}{10^6} = 1$ ms

Efficiency of pure aloha = G^*e^{-2G}

Here G =1,

Efficiency = $1^*2.718^{-2^*1} = 0.1353$

Throughput = 1000 * 0.1353 = 135.3 = 135

(rounded to nearest integer)

55. Quality scores of the vertices are as follows :

QS(S) = 1 (Given)

QS(C) = 1 ; QS(A) = 9

QS(D) = 9 ; QS(B) = 9 ; QS(E) = 9*9 = 81

QS(F) = 9 ; QS(G) = 81 ; QS(T) = 81*9 = 729

Total is 929.

Hence, the sum of the quality scores of all the vertices in the graph is 929.